DILLAVOU AND HOWARD'S

Principles of
BUSINESS LAW

Ninth Edition

ROBERT N. CORLEY
Professor of Business Law
and Business Administration
University of Illinois

WILLIAM J. ROBERT
Professor of Business Law
University of Oregon

Prentice-Hall, Inc., Englewood Cliffs, New Jersey

Dillavou and Howard's
Principles of Business Law
Ninth Edition

Robert N. Corley

William J. Robert

Previously published under the title of
Principles of Business Law

© 1971, 1967, 1964, 1962, 1957, 1952, 1948, 1940
by Prentice-Hall, Inc., Englewood Cliffs, N.J.

All rights reserved.
No part of this book may be
reproduced in any form or by an means
without permission in writing
from the publisher.

Printed in the United States of America

13-214361-5

Library of Congress Catalog Card No. 71 - 152341

Current Printing (last digit)
10 9 8 7 6 5

PRENTICE-HALL INTERNATIONAL, INC., *London*
PRENTICE-HALL OF AUSTRALIA, PTY. LTD., *Sydney*
PRENTICE-HALL OF CANADA, LTD., *Toronto*
PRENTICE-HALL OF INDIA PRIVATE LIMITED, *New Delhi*
PRENTICE-HALL OF JAPAN, INC., *Tokyo*

Preface

This edition is designed to keep step with developments in the broad field of commercial law during the 1970's. It is a decade in which a closer look is being taken at the obligations of business toward society, with special emphasis upon consumer protection. Many of the cases contained in the text reflect the attitudes of the courts with regard to these obligations, and there are references to new statutory provisions such as are involved in consumer protection.

Since the Uniform Commercial Code has now been adopted in all states except Louisiana, few references are made to the laws that have been repealed by the Code. Some references are found in the cases that refer to prior law, in order to explain the Code. Such cases also illustrate the need for interpretation of statutes and the significant role of the court in applying statutes to facts. The lack of uniformity in the Uniform Commercial Code is explained, and the processes of legal reasoning are well illustrated by the cases that discuss Code problems.

Historical background is believed to be important to the understanding of modern law. For this reason, a number of pages are devoted to the history of the law of contracts, negotiable instruments, and general background of the Code.

While organization of the book is similar to that of the previous edition, there is more emphasis on the environmental aspects of law. This emphasis is consistent with trends in the field. It also recognizes the difference in the educational needs of lawyers and of businessmen. We have attempted to meet the needs of businessmen in the years ahead by stressing those aspects of law that are essential to the decision-making process. We believe the material will make a valuable contribution to the education of tomorrow's business leaders, who must be familiar with the legal aspects of business problems.

Present users, nevertheless, will be pleased to note that this edition continues the basic format maintained by the authors in previous editions. The combination text-case method of presentation is used, selecting cases, as far as possible, that are free from complicated procedural questions but that introduce the student to current problems and procedures confronting business.

Excerpts from the Uniform Commercial Code are copyrighted by and reprinted with the permission of the American Law Institute and the National Conference of Commissioners on Uniform State Laws.

Material from the Restatement of the Law, Second, Torts and the Restatement of the Law of Contracts copyrighted by and is reprinted with the permission of the American Law Institute.

The authors continue to be indebted more than we can say to Essel R. Dillavou and to Charles G. Howard for their inspiration, guidance, counseling, and assistance in our efforts to maintain the standards and quality of their book. To the extent we are successful, the credit is theirs. To the extent we fail, the fault is ours. We hope that the tradition of excellence has been maintained.

We are also indebted to many current and past users of the text for helpful suggestions. These suggestions have been of substantial assistance to the authors in the preparation of this edition, and in helping to produce a text which they feel is an unusually effective teaching tool. We appreciate the assistance of Professor William Brabham, University of Idaho, and Professor Donald Radman, The Cleveland State University, who read the manuscript and offered their suggestions.

Robert N. Corley
William J. Robert

Contents

BOOK THREE: THE UNIFORM COMMERCIAL CODE

29: Bank Deposits and Collections, 562

30: Secured Transactions: Security Interest, 578

31: Secured Transactions: Priorities, Default, and Remedies, 604

BOOK FOUR: CREDITORS' RIGHTS

32: The Debtor-Creditor Relationship, 623

33: Suretyship, 638

BOOK ONE

Law, Its Functions
and
Procedures

Law
and Legal Theory

1-1. Introduction to Law. The subject matter of this text is business law. Before undertaking a study of the law as it relates to business, it is helpful to examine the nature of law, its sources, and its role in our society. Also, if the business-related portion of the subject is to be understood, it is essential that certain terms be defined and classifications be established in advance. Thus, the first six chapters of this text will be devoted to a study of law, its functions and procedures.

Each of us from day to day uses such terms as "law," "legal," and "illegal." Moreover, such phrases as "due process of law," "law and order," and the "rule of law" have become an integral part of our vocabulary despite the complexities of the concepts they represent. The fact that such words and phrases are widely used does not mean that they are understood or even that they have a definite meaning, for in fact they do not. It is not possible to give the word "law" any one meaning or to accurately define it. The word has many meanings depending on the context in which it is used, and it also expresses a variety of concepts. The same is true of the words "legal" and "illegal." The adjective "illegal" may for instance be used to describe a forward pass in football, or it may be used to describe a contract which violates some statute. "Law" has been used in a narrow sense as a noun synonomous with "statute," as well as broadly to describe the general subject matter. It has also been used for rules of physics and other sciences, such as Newton's law, Boyle's law. It should always be remembered that when "law" is used in this text its meaning is derived from the context in which it is used.

Law in its broad context expresses a variety of concepts and has been defined as those rules and regulations established by government and applied to people in order for civilization to exist. Law and legal theory, however, are far too complex for such a simple definition to suffice; thus other definitions must be examined if the connotations of the word "law" are to be effectively understood. It is well to note that all of the definitions discussed herein are significant and should be borne in mind throughout the study of this subject.

The subject of law is as old as man himself. Our study of it, however, need go back no further than 1215 at Runnymede with the promise by King John to his barons that, "No free man shall be taken or imprisoned or disseized or exiled or in any way destroyed, nor will we go upon him, nor send upon him, except by the lawful judgment of his peers or (*per legem terrae*) by the law of the land." This promise in the Magna Charta recognized that it was the law that would determine man's basic rights and protect them in relation to the sovereign and also that royal power should be exercised subject to the law. In effect, law was defined as the means of limiting royal power or governmental action.

Many legal scholars have defined law in relation to the sovereign. For example, Blackstone, the great legal scholar of the eighteenth century, defined law as "that rule of action which is prescribed by some superior and which the inferior is bound to obey." This concept of law as a command from a superior to an inferior is operative in many areas of democracy. For example, the income tax law commands that taxes shall be paid to the sovereign, and is in the nature of an order by the government of the United States (the superior) enacted by the people's representatives to all people (the inferior).

Law has also been defined as the product of the legal system. For example, Justice Oliver Wendell Holmes in the case of *American Banana Co.* v. *United Fruit Co.* (U.S. Supreme Court, 1909) said, "Law is a statement of the circumstances in which the public force will be brought to bear through courts." In this definition, Holmes is using the word "law" in its broad sense and is taking cognizance of the fact that in our society, all issues and disputes—political, social, religious, economic, or otherwise—ultimately become legal issues to be resolved by courts. Law, according to this definition, is simply what the courts determine it to be as an expression of the public will.

Law has also been defined as a scheme of social control. This definition acknowledges the role of law in governing and regulating a civilized society. Implied in this definition is the dynamic role of law as an instrument of social, political, and economic change. The law is both an instrument of change and a result of change. It is often difficult to determine whether the law brings about changes in society or whether changes in society bring about a change in the law. In our legal system both are true. The law—responding to the goals, desires, needs, and aspirations of society—is in a constant state of change. In some areas, it changes more rapidly than does the attitude of a majority of society. In these areas, the law and our legal system provide leadership in bringing about desirable changes. In some areas, most of society is ahead of the law in moving in new directions; other institutions then assume leadership, with the law cast in the role of follower. In either case, the legal system is an integral part of any change in society.

The definition of law as a scheme of social control recognizes that law exists for the protection of social interests, both those between government and individual and those between individuals. In a sense, law as a means of social control influences people in their actions because the control sought may be obtained by state action if necessary. For example, President Eisenhower used federal troops to enforce a court order integrating schools in Little Rock,

Arkansas. The law as a scheme of social control and as an instrument of change ordered the integration. People were expected to abide by the order as a valid influence on their conduct and lives, and failure to do so brought the power of government to bear to ensure compliance. Fortunately in our society the instances in which people willfully refuse to follow court orders are very few, and it is generally recognized that the losing party to a lawsuit will follow the mandate of the law without the necessity of governmental force being applied. One of the cornerstones of our democratic society is our commitment to abide by rules of law and legal decisions.

Law has also been defined as the body of principles, standards, and rules which the courts apply in the decision of controversies brought before them. By this definition, law consists of three elements: (1) formulated legislation including constitutions, statutes, and treaties; (2) case law or the common law created by judicial decision and followed by the courts; and (3) the system of legal concepts, procedures, and techniques which form the basis of the judicial action of courts. This definition considers law in terms of its sources and gives recognition to the difference between substantive law and procedural law; the latter is simply the law which provides methods and techniques for resolving the actual substantive issue in dispute.

1-2. Schools of Legal Thought. Throughout history, legal scholars have written about the nature and origin of law, its purposes, and the factors that influence its development. Legal philosophers have generally acknowledged that logic, history, custom, religion, and social utility are among the major influences and forces that shape and direct the law. But there has been disagreement as to the relative importance of these forces, and the influence of each has varied throughout history. Legal philosophers and the theories they have expounded may be grouped into five general categories or schools of legal thought—the historical, the analytical, the natural, the sociological, and the realist.

a. Historical. " . . . all law is originally formed in the manner in which in ordinary, but not quite correct, language, customary law is said to have been formed, i.e., that it is first developed by custom and popular faith, next by jurisprudence, everywhere therefore by internal silently operating powers, not by the arbitrary will of a lawgiver." (Savigny, Friedman, *Legal Theory,* 136, 1953)

Here the scholar in his definition has given weight to the evolutionary process of ideas and contends that as customs and practices gain popular acceptance and approval, they become formalized into rules of conduct. The historical aspect has been emphasized and made important. From primitive times community living has required order. Hence, as society developed, there evolved customary and traditional rules of conduct. Law was found in these rules and evolved from them. Custom results from repeated approved usage, and when such usage by common adoption and acquiescence justifies each member of society in assuming that every other member of society will conform thereto, a rule of conduct has been formulated. When such a rule is adopted by a court as controlling in a particular case or is enacted into legislation, law has been made. Cardozo, in his book *The Paradoxes of Legal Science,* describes this concept as follows:

When changes of manners or business have brought it about that a rule of law which corresponded to previously existing norms or standards of behavior corresponds no longer to the present norms or standards but on the contrary departs from them, then those same forces or tendencies of development that brought the law into adaptation to the old norms and standards are effective, without legislation, but by the inherent energies of the judicial processes, to restore the equilibrium. My illustrations have been drawn from changing forms of business . . . Manners and customs (if we may not label them as law itself) are at least a source of law. The judge, so far as freedom of choice is given to him, tends to a result that attaches legal obligations to the folkways, the norms or standards of behavior exemplified in the life about him.

Such has been the history of commercial paper, partnerships, sales, and many other areas of commercial law. Case law developed in line with common business practice or custom and the case law ultimately became codified. Book Three, dealing with the Uniform Commercial Code, contains a brief history of commercial law, which illustrates the influence of custom and business practice on the law.

b. Analytical.   "Law emanates from the sovereign not from its creatures. The sum total of all those rules of human conduct for which there is a state sanction. . . . Law in its essence is made up of those rules of human conduct which are made mandatory by the state upon all its citizens and without which social order and well-being could not exist." (Justice Stone)

Analytical jurisprudence relates to the study and examination of law in terms of its logical structure. The definition above, which is almost identical to Blackstone's, gives weight to the need for certainty and to a system of positive rules logically deduced from fundamental principles dictated by a sovereign state, with power to command. Law is a rule laid down by a superior power, to guide and regulate those under the power. The state as the lawgiver hands down the law and as sovereign is bound by no overriding superior divine law or principle. Thus, law is a system of principles or rules in the nature of commands. Such commands may be the orders of a monarch or of a totalitarian authority, or they may be the legislative enactments, administrative orders, or judicial pronouncements of a democratic state.

c. Natural.   Law is "a rule of conduct arising out of the natural relations of human beings established by the Creator, existing prior to any positive precept, discovered by right, reason and the rational intelligence of man." (Kent)

This definition gives significance to the idea that man by nature seeks an ideal of absolute right and justice as a higher law by which to measure all other rules of conduct.

Law, when set against a background of divine principles, becomes a rule of reason, pronounced by reasonable men for the benefit of mankind and the establishment of the good community. Man as a reasonable being is able to distinguish between good and evil. Above him there exists law resting on reason and divine authority, which validates man-made law. Thus, when the state by legislation or by judicial process lays down rules of conduct that are unfair, unreasonable, or inimicable to the common good, they are in violation of natural and divine law.

Blackstone, notwithstanding his definition of law in terms of a command from a sovereign, in his *Commentaries,* says, "This law of nature being coeval with mankind and dictated by God himself, is of course superior in obligation to any other. It is binding all over the globe in all countries and at all times; no human laws are of any validity if contrary to this. . . . "

Natural law, nurtured by the church, softened the rigid common law of England; became the basis of equity; and, finding its way to America is expressed in the Declaration of Independence in the words "certain unalienable Rights, . . . Life, Liberty and the pursuit of Happiness." Professor Friedman, in *Legal Theory,* observed:

> Natural law thinking in the United States undoubtedly inspired the fathers of the Constitution and it has dominated the Supreme Court more than any other law court in the world. Such thinking has not prevented the court from vacillating from the unconditional comdemnation of legislative regulation of social and economic conditions to its almost unrestricted recognition, from the recognition of almost unrestricted freedom of speech and assembly to virtual outlawing of a political party, and, on the other hand, from the toleration of the most blatant discrimination against Negroes to the strong protection given in recent judgments. Yet the American Constitution gives as near an approach to the unconditional embodiment of natural rights as can be imagined.

d. Sociological. "Law is an experimental process in which the logical factor is only one of many leading to a certain conclusion. . . . Law is a means to an end. . . . The Law is both a result of social forces and an instrument of social control." (W. Friedman)

By this definition the writer seeks to find and describe law by what it does, its method, its purpose, and how it functions in balancing conflicting social interests. Many aspects of society are emphasized and made important. In order to find how the law is made, and how it functions, investigations into many areas of society are required. Economic theories, political, religious, and social considerations are factors in formulating the law. Under the pressure of conflicting interests, legislators and courts make law. Thus, law, when enacted by legislatures or pronounced by courts, is in the end the result of finding an equilibrium between conflicting interests.

Law is not only generalization deduced from a set of facts, a recognized tradition, a prescribed formula for determining natural justice, but it also consists of rules for social control growing out of the experiences of mankind. Current social mores, political ideologies, international situations and conditions, and economic and business interests are all elements to be investigated and evaluated in making the law and in determining how it operates.

e. Realist. "The life of the law has not been logic; it has been experience." (Justice O.W. Holmes) In this statement and in his definition of law as a prediction of what courts will decide, Justice Holmes follows the realist school of legal thought. This school stresses the empirical and pragmatic aspects of the law. Yet, one of its hallmarks is the recognition that law is actually unpredictable and uncertain.

A development of twentieth-century American jurisprudence, the realist school of legal thought is primarily concerned with facts. Realists prefer scientific analysis to theoretical reasoning. They distrust formulas and traditional, simple rules of law. To them, the law must develop to conform with social needs. These needs can only be determined by the facts; technical legal analysis is not enough. Realists also acknowledge that different rules of law have various degrees of relevant significance and that courts cannot treat all legal principles as equals.

The uncertainty of the law to a realist is the result of several premises which are basic to his philosophy. First of all, realists recognize that much of our law is judicially created. Since society is constantly changing, the law must change along with it to meet its needs and goals. In this regard, the realist philosophy is similar to the philosophy of the sociological school of legal thought. Law that is judge-made and changing is not susceptible to easy prediction. There is less possibility of accurately predicting what courts will do than the other schools of legal thought would lead one to believe.

Secondly, the realist gives recognition to the fact that there are two variables contributing to uncertainty in the law. The first is the law itself. Since the law may change, any prediction of what a court will do always has a probability of accuracy factor less than one. The second variable is the facts of the case. This latter variable is probably most important because no two people will view the evidence in the same way or draw the same inferences from it. Since a reviewing court may view the facts differently from the trial court or a trial judge may view them differently from a jury, a substantial amount of uncertainty is inherent in all litigation.

It is sometimes said that realists are concerned with what the law is—not with what it ought to be. This statement is misleading because the realist uses facts to determine the law and realizes that the product, law, is frequently made and not found. In determining what the law is, realists use scientific methods to measure social desires and to make the choice between conflicting values. In the 1970s a realist would use computers, symbolic logic, and behaviorial analysis in determining what the law is. If necessary, realists are willing to group facts in new or different categories so that the law will best serve society. To them, law is a means to a social end—not the end itself. And both the means and the end are subject to constant review and change.

These schools of legal thought illustrate the difficulty of defining law and the many factors which influence each definition. In studying legislation, judicial opinions, and other legal materials, an understanding of what jurisprudential theory motivated the writer is of great assistance in determining what idea an author wishes to convey, the intention of a legislature, and why and how a judge reached his decision.

1-3. The Role of Law—An Ordered Society.   In the preceding section, law was discussed from the standpoint of its origin; but to speak of the origin, or source of law, does not tell what law is. In order to determine what it is, we shall consider "The Law" from two points of view. First, law may be considered as the rules enacted or declared by a sovereign or its agencies to be used as a means to regulate and control man in his relation to man. Second, we may consider that "The Law" is not the rules, but an ordered society, the result which follows from the operation of "the rules."

Thus "The Law" under the first point of view is that great mass of rules found in constitutions, judicial decisions, legislative enactments, city ordinances, and administrative orders which regulate and control man. Laws are nothing more than the rules promulgated by government as a means to an ordered society.

It is obvious that there are other rules which operate as a means of social control—moral and social rules, religious beliefs, family relations, community mores, custom, etc. Chambers of Commerce, fraternities, unions, churches, trade associations, country clubs, athletic clubs, gangs, and all groups that organize for a definite purpose become entities and regulate their members by rules. Such organizations have their own legislative assemblies, however crude, which make bylaws and rules, establish official positions, and give officers power not only to regulate and control their members but also to influence others who are not members. These cohesive and coercive rules that maintain and control the entity and its members are not rules of law. The sanction that enforces penalties for breach of the rules is within the unit itself. Fines, expulsion, and other disciplinary actions exercised by the entity are not a matter for the state. If, however, such enforcement of the entity's rules violates contract relations between the members, or the disciplinary action breaches state criminal law, then legal sanctions must be imposed—the state will enforce rules which are "The Law." It is not enough to use the term "Law" simply to mean rules for the regulation of man.

Under the second point of view "The Law" is something more. In a broad and significant sense, "The Law" is a result; it is an established way of thinking and acting which is produced by the rules. It is "Ordered Society." "The Law" is collective conduct which ends in a result—an adjusted ordered social condition. It is a community of peace and well-being. It is "an alternative to chaos." It is the essential element of civilization.

"The Law" is all-pervading; it is an atmosphere or climate. It overlays and operates in all areas of society. It is always present. For example, it is the orderly behavior of others which contributes to the undisturbed possession of one's home and allows movement from place to place without fear of injury.

If, however, there is noncompliance with the rules of law, sanctions will be imposed. Such sanctions are essential if the goals of society are to be achieved. Where noncompliance occurs, the detailed rules concerning specific conduct —rules of law—come into play. In a traffic accident, for example, not only will speed rules and other motor vehicle regulatory rules be involved, but many other legal rules—concerning ownership, due care, negligence, agency, insurance, and so forth—also have relevance. The goal sought is traffic safety and order; it is obtained by compliance with the rules.

In order to distinguish between "The Law" as social order and the detailed rules which produce the social order, an illustration from our national pastime, baseball, may be helpful. In order to produce a desired result—the game— predetermined rules which make for a controlled activity are essential. These are the "rules of the game." But the rules, however important, are not the most significant element. The most significant feature is the game. The game, the totality of all thoughts, rules, and prescribed activity, is a regulated spectacle. Spectators do not carry rule books; umpires do. The spectators are concerned with a performance; they go to see the game—not to check whether the pitcher's mound is so many feet from home plate. The game is a living, progressive, regulated spectacle, the conduct of which may be relied upon and predicted. The spectator can expect with certainty that during the game the left fielder will not throw the ball over the fence, the hitting batter will not run to third base, nor the pitcher throw the ball into the grandstands. Such conduct would not produce a ball game, but only chaos.

Thus, a ball game in its totality is a controlled and ordered activity, operating under baseball rules. On a greater scale, our social order is "The Law" operating under rules. The important difference is the sanctions imposed for the breach of the rules. There is no appeal from a decision of a baseball umpire to a state court. However, the baseball game is conducted within the orbit of legal order. If a player or spectator commits assault and battery upon the umpire, not only baseball rules but legal rules are violated.

Business relations are broad and comprehensive. To be effective, such relations must comply with rules, and operate in an ordered society. Business has to do with supplying human wants. People must be fed, clothed, housed, transported, entertained, secured, and supplied with a multiplicity of goods and services.

Only in an ordered society can business function. Controls that make an ordered society and are enforced by government are *legal* controls. As stated above, there are many nonlegal controls and sanctions arising out of organized group action, as well as ethical considerations, that influence the climate within which business operates, but it is the legal rules that constitute the far greater portion of the environment in which business operates. In making a business decision, the law will always be a factor. The proper decision is more likely to follow if the businessman has some idea of the implications of the law applicable to the problem. Judgment resting on a previous study of law, its history, and its evolution is more likely to produce a correct decision than one made without this background. It is true that one cannot know all the rules; yet one can know some of them and their purpose. Keeping in mind the end result—an ordered society—it will be our purpose in this text to present and discuss specific rules of law as they are applicable to commercial transactions and controversies which arise out of contractual relations, the creation and operation of unincorporated and incorporated institutions, the marketing of goods and services, the extension of credit, agency, labor-management relations, and other business conduct.

1-4. Law and Ethics.   Decisions by individuals as to whether or not they should do any particular act may be divided into three categories. Some decisions involve matters over which a person is said to have a free choice. For example, a decision by a high school graduate whether or not to seek a college education involves essentially a free choice. Actually no choice is completely free because there are always pressures, such as financial ability, and factors that affect decisions. All freedoms, including the freedom of choice to do a legal act, are limited and are not absolute freedoms.

Other decisions involve acts that are within the dominion of the law, and the doing of the act is illegal. "Illegal," as used here does not refer strictly to the criminal law, but encompasses all acts for which the law would impose a sanction. Such decisions necessarily involve the weighing of the legal consequences which will follow if the act is committed. Society uses law to govern conduct, and a major function of the law is to apprise people of the consequences that will flow from conduct.

The third category involves decisions which are concerned with acts that are not illegal but over which the actor feels that he does not have a free choice, either because of the internal force usually referred to as conscience or because of social pressure from others. A decision not to do such an act is actually obedience to the unenforceable. Such obedience is based on the ethical and moral values of the person making the decision, and of others. It involves such human traits as manners, courtesy, honesty, self-restraint, bravery, tolerance, fairness, and a sense of values. This category of decision is quite broad and may involve an infinite variety of subjects. Moreover, many acts which, in the first instance, would fall into this category ultimately become illegal acts because of the influence of ethics and morality on the law as was discussed in the section on the natural school of legal thought. For example, segregated schools were considered immoral by many before they were declared illegal.

Obedience to the law and obedience to the unenforceable are interrelated and complementary to each other. They are the hallmarks of a great people. The former is an absolute necessity if anarchy and chaos are to be avoided, and the latter is an integral part of a democratic society that seeks to guarantee the blessings of liberty to all. The extent to which an individual, a business, or a nation is obedient to the guides to human conduct that are unenforceable is the measure of his or its greatness.

Many difficult decisions having ethical connotations confront business today. For example, should business hire unqualified employees who are members of disadvantaged groups? It may be argued that it is preferable for an unqualified employee to work and take home a paycheck rather than do nothing and receive a welfare check. In other words, does business have a moral obligation to assist in breaking the welfare cycle by hiring the unqualified and training them? It should be noted that a similar issue exists in higher education. Should universities have double admission and grading standards in order to assist disadvantaged students?

Another issue which is essentially ethical involves the extension of credit by businesses to doubtful risks. Should a business sell a product on credit to persons who cannot actually afford it? To what extent should a businessman be his brother's keeper? This question is involved in many business decisions.

Acts may be moral, immoral, legal, illegal, or any combination thereof. Legality and morality will depend on the subject matter, the time and place of the act, and the person making the moral judgment. For example, at one time employing child labor was regarded by many as neither immoral nor illegal. However, as such conduct took on strong moral implications and met with public disapproval, it likewise became illegal. The sale of fireworks offers a striking example of what formerly was considered both moral and legal but is now illegal, although not considered immoral by many. Some consider gambling immoral, yet all aspects of gambling are not illegal, though other aspects may be both immoral and illegal. The manufacture and sale of intoxicating liquor is another illustration of conduct that has at different times been moral and legal, immoral and illegal, illegal and moral, and to some individuals immoral although legal. Another illustration of how changing moral standards affect legal standards is found in the law of the sale of goods. In early, less complex society, trading and sales transactions were face-to-face affairs. The seller and buyer, standing before one another with equal bargaining capacity, dickered over the specific article before them. The law developed the doctrine of *caveat emptor,* "let the buyer beware." And sales made because of extravagant statements or trickery were considered accomplishments rather than vices.

In today's complex technology with its great productive capacity accompanied by extensive advertising and mass marketing and distributing systems, the uninformed buyer-consumer does not stand in an equal bargaining position with trained sellers and producers. Most buyer-consumers cannot be expected, even upon inspection, to understand the quality, character, construction, or operational capacity of complicated merchandise. This is especially true of such items as television sets and automobiles. Neither can buyer-consumers possibly have full understanding of the content and quality of drugs, cosmetics, and other synthetic materials. By the very nature of things, equal bargaining power is impossible. Consumers, no longer equal with sellers, are vulnerable to all types of deceptive merchandising practices: price manipulation, false advertising, extravagant statements, undisclosed interest rates and financing charges, and extreme advertising and promotional schemes. Consequently, legal duties founded on moral sanctions are being imposed upon manufacturers, processors, distributors, and sellers under the doctrine of *caveat venditor,* "let the seller beware." The old doctrine of *caveat emptor* is passing from the scene.

1-5. Law and Justice.   Ethics and values tend to influence the law. As they do, it may be observed that the law tends toward social justice. It is obvious that "law" and "justice" are not synonymous. The law is created by agents of society, but each person has his own view of whether justice is present. What is right or wrong from the standpoint of justice may differ widely from person to person. For example, should the death penalty be imposed for murder? Does the death penalty accomplish justice?

Society may have laws that are not just; thus, law can exist without achieving justice. Without laws, society could theoretically have a system of justice in which each case was decided simply by asking, What would be a just result? But such a system would lead to injustice because of the differing views of what is just and what is justice in any given case. Our system is said to be one of laws and not of men. This principle means that disputes are resolved by the law and not by any man, even if he happens to be a judge. The role of a man in our system is to apply the law to resolve the dispute, though he may personally disagree with the law. To this extent, we are law oriented rather than justice oriented.

Of course our laws *strive* for justice. That is the goal, but the system being operated by men is imperfect, and complete justice by anyone's view is probably not attainable. Today there is much discussion of social justice. Social justice describes the *goal* of law, and it tends to be synonymous with legal justice. The question remains, however, whose view of social justice is to prevail? Reasonable men have entirely different views as to what is justice in any situation. For this reason, it has been concluded that it is better to have a system of laws that seek justice than simply to have a system of justice which is not predicated on a substantial body of substantive law.

CHAPTER 1
REVIEW QUESTIONS AND PROBLEMS

1. Name and discuss the school of legal thought reflected in each of the following judicial statements:

   a. "If a debtor obtains a discharge under an insolvent act, a subsequent promise to pay the debt is regarded as a new contract, supported by the pre-existing moral obligation, as a consideration for the new promise." (Justice Harns, *Carshore* v. *Huyck,* 6 Barb. 583 N.Y., 1849)

   b. "We must weigh the purpose to be served, the desire to be gratified, the excuse for the deviation from the letter, the cruelty of enforced adherence." (Justice Cardozo, *Jacob & Youngs* v. *Kent,* 230 N.Y. 239, 129 N.E. 889, 1921)

   c. "There must be power in the states and the nation to remould through experience our economic practices and institutions to meet changing social and economic needs. I cannot believe that the framers of the Fourteenth Amendment, or the States which ratified it, intended to deprive us of the power to correct the evils of technological unemployment and excess productive capacity which have attended the progress of useful arts." (Justice Brandeis dissenting in *New State Ice Co.* v. *Liebman,* 285 U.S. 262, 276, 1932)

   d. "The principle embodied in this exception was established by the old custom of merchants, which 'before the end of the thirteenth century was already conceived as a body of rules which stood apart from common law.' . . . at that stage these rules were applied merely as the general custom of commercial transactions . . . but later became a part of the common law." Leventritt, Referee, *Brown et al.* v. *Perera,* 176 N.Y. Supp. 215, 219, 1918)

   e. "The word 'law' imports a general rule of conduct with appropriate means for its enforcement declared by some authority possessing sovereign power over the subject; it implies command and not treaty." (Opinion of the Justices, 262 Mass. 603, 160 N.E. 439, 440, 1928)

   f. "General propositions do not decide concrete cases. The decision will depend on a judgment or intuition more subtle than any articulate major premise." (Justice Holmes dissenting in *Lochner* v. *New York,* 198 U.S. 45, 1905)

2. Distinguish between rules of law and "The Law" as an institution.
3. Compare law and ethics.
4. Compare law and justice.

The Subject Matter of Law

1-6. Classifications of Law. In the attempt to classify the law into different categories, it is not possible to achieve complete accuracy in outlining the various areas because so many are overlapping and interrelated. One of the basic differentiations is *substantive law* as opposed to *adjective,* or *procedural law.* Substantive law is the substance of the law—the rules and principles that are applied by the courts in resolving conflicts. It has been defined as that part of the law which creates, defines, and limits rights as contrasted with that branch of the law which establishes the procedures whereby such rights are enforced and protected.

For example, rights which a person has in land are determined by the substantive rules of the law of property. If his rights in the land are invaded, the procedural law would prescribe the method for obtaining redress for such invasion.

Adjective law provides the legal machinery whereby substantive rules are given effect. Included in this category are procedures for instituting legal action and determining the issues to be decided at the trial of a case. The conduct of a trial, the appeal to a higher court, and the enforcement of judgments and decrees issued by the court are also part of adjective or procedural law. The material in Chapter 5 treats of these legal procedures in more detail.

Law is also frequently classified into areas of *public* and *private* law. Public law includes those bodies of law that affect the public generally as contrasted with the areas of the law that are concerned with the relationship between individuals.

Public law may be divided into three general categories: (1) *Constitutional law,* which concerns itself with the rights, powers, and duties of federal and state governments under the U.S. Constitution and the constitutions of the various states; (2) *Administrative law,* which is concerned with the multitude of administrative agencies such as the Interstate Commerce Commission, the Federal Trade Commission, and the National Labor Relations Board; and (3) *Criminal law,* which consists of statutes and general maxims that forbid certain conduct as being detrimental to the welfare of the state and provides punishment therefor. Constitutional law will be discussed as one of the sources of law in Chapter 3. Administrative law and criminal law will be discussed in the sections that follow.

Private law is that body of law which pertains to the relationships between individuals in an organized society. Private law encompasses the subjects of contracts, torts, and property. Each of these subjects includes several bodies of law. For example, the law of contracts may be subdivided into the subjects of sales, commercial paper, agency, and business organizations. The major portion of this text covers these subjects, which constitute the body of law usually referred to as business law.

The law of torts is the primary source of litigation in this country and is also a part of the total body of law in such areas as agency and sales. It is concerned with wrongful acts against a person or his property and is predicated upon the premise that in a civilized society, people who injure other persons or their property must compensate them for their loss.

The law of property may be thought of as a branch of the law of contracts, but in many ways our concept of private property, as is discussed more fully in Chapter 49, contains much more than the contract characteristics. Property is the basic ingredient in our economic system, and the subject matter may be subdivided into several areas such as wills, trusts, estates in land, personal property, bailments, and many more.

Any attempt at classification of subject matter, particularly in the private law, is difficult because the law is indeed, a "seamless web." For example, assume that an agent or servant acting on behalf of his employer commits a tort. The law of agency, although a subdivision of the law of contracts, must of necessity contain a body of law to resolve the issues of tort liability of the employer and employee. Likewise, assume that a person is injured by a product he has purchased. The law of sales, even though a part of the law of contracts, contains several aspects that could best be labeled a branch of the law of torts. Therefore it is apparent that even the general classifications of contract and tort are not accurate in describing the subject matter of various bodies of law.

ADMINISTRATIVE LAW

1-7. Administrative Agencies. In a complex industrial society, social and economic problems are so numerous that courts and legislative bodies cannot possibly deal with all of them. Legislation must be general in character and cannot possibly cover all the problems and situations that may arise in connection with the problem or evil the law seeks to control or correct. There must be a method of filling in the gaps in legislation and for adding meat to the bones of legislative policy. Not only are there too many problems for traditional methods of solution, but interrelationships and conflicting social goals as well as advances in technology require constant changes. Administrative agencies are necessary in order to lighten the burdens which otherwise must be borne by the executive branch, legislative bodies, and courts. The multitude of administrative agencies performing governmental functions today encompasses almost every aspect of business operation and, indeed, almost every aspect of our daily lives. These agencies provide flexibility in the law and adaptability to changing conditions.

The direct day-to-day legal impact on business of the many local, state, and federal administrative agencies is far greater than the impact of the courts and legislative bodies. Administrative agencies create and enforce the greater bulk of the laws which make up the legal environment of business.

The functions of administrative bodies generally are described as (1) rule making, (2) adjudicating, (3) prosecuting, (4) advising, (5) supervising, and (6) investigating. These functions are not the concern of all administrative agencies to the same degree. Some agencies are primarily adjudicating bodies, such as the industrial commissions which rule on workmen's compensation claims. Others, such as the Federal Power Commission, are concerned primarily with a special industry, and still others, such as the Federal Trade Commission, with a particular phase of business. Others are primarily supervisory, such as the Securities and Exchange Commission, which supervises the issue and sale of investment securities. Most agencies perform all the foregoing functions to some degree in carrying out their responsibilities.

In addition to traditional executive functions, the administrative process involves performance of both legislative and judicial functions. Some agencies are best described as quasi-legislative and others are best described as quasi-judicial.

1-8. Legislative Functions.   The legislative function in the administrative process is to make rules. The rule-making function is based on the authority delegated to the agency by the legislature. A delegation of legislative authority is valid only if limitations are imposed on the exercise of the power and if standards are prescribed by which a court can determine whether these limitations have been exceeded. Thus, in cases involving the legislative function of an administrative agency, there are two fundamental issues. First, is the delegation of the rule-making function valid? Second, has the agency exceeded its authority?

In deciding the first question, the court will examine the standards contained in the grant of authority to see if they are sufficiently definite or, as Justice Cardozo said, "The delegated power of legislation (must be) canalized within banks that keep it from overflowing." The modern trend of cases is to approve very broad delegations of authority to these agencies. For example, a delegation to make such rules, regulations, and decisions as the public interest, convenience, and necessity may require has been held to be a valid standard. Also, directions to be "fair and equitable" constitute a sufficient standard. Today, delegations of legislative authority are quite broadly stated and business must recognize that it is very doubtful if any rule of an administrative agency can be successfully challenged on the first issue.

The second issue is another matter, however. There are many examples of administrative agencies exceeding their authority. For example, draft boards that reclassified protestors against the war in Vietnam were held to have exceeded their authority. Such issues are present when an agency greatly expands its area of interest and activity. For example, the Federal Communica-

but most attorneys will seek to maintain it as long as possible because of the financial importance of such litigation to the legal profession.

Tort liability is sometimes imposed without fault. This is usually referred to as *strict liability* and is imposed in situations where harm is caused by dangerous or trespassing animals, blasting operations, or fire. Also, there is a trend in the law to impose strict liability upon manufacturers where persons are injured because of defects in manufactured products, such as automobiles and appliances. This will be discussed in detail in Chapter 22.

Tort liability may also be predicated upon the unreasonable use by a person of his own property. Any improper or indecent activity that causes harm to another's person, to his property, or to the public generally is tortious. Such conduct is usually described as a *nuisance*. Nuisances may be either private or public. A private nuisance is one that disturbs only the interest of some private individual, whereas the public nuisance disturbs or interferes with the public in general. The legal theory supporting tort liability in these areas is that an owner of property, although conducting a lawful business thereon, is subject to reasonable limitations and must use his property so as not to unreasonably interfere with the health and comfort of his neighbors, or with their right to the enjoyment of their property. Liability may be imposed on business for nuisances even in the absence of negligence. For example, slaughter houses, stables, chemical works, refineries, and tanneries, because of their offensive odors, may interfere with the peaceful enjoyment of property of adjacent landowners. Also, garages, filling stations, rock crushers, and lighted golf courses may be nuisances because of noise or lights; factories and smelters by reason of the escape of noxious gases. In addition to tort liability, the remedy of an injunction is used to abate a nuisance. There is a growing body of law creating liability for pollution of air and water, a problem fraught with economic, social, and political implications as well as legal ones.

The determination of the existence of a nuisance in any case requires a balancing of the equities since society requires that these business activities be conducted somewhere. No rule may be defined to govern these cases since each must be decided on its own facts.

Some fundamental aspects of the tort of *trespass* need to be considered since this tort is a common one and affects both real and personal property. A trespass to personal property—goods and the like, as distinguished from land and buildings—is the unlawful interference by one person with the control and possession of the goods of another. One is entitled to have exclusive possession and control of his personal property and may recover for any physical harm to his goods by reason of the wrongful conduct of another. Closely allied to trespass is the tort of *conversion*. Conversion is the wrongful disposition and detention of goods of one person by another.

The one in exclusive possession of land is entitled to enjoy the use of the land free from interference of others, either by direct interference or by indirect interference through instrumentalities placed upon the land. Entry upon the land of another is a trespass even though the one who enters is under the mistaken belief that he is the owner by purchase, or has a right, license, or privilege to enter thereon.

1-12. Business Torts.   Each person in the conduct of a business has a duty not to injure others. Breach of this duty will entitle the person wronged to damages just as if an assault or a negligence act had been committed. This duty may be violated by conduct that constitutes unfair competition, by acts of disparagement, by inducing a breach of contract, and by infringing on trademarks and trade names.

Unfair Competition.   As a general rule, freedom of contract has been the cornerstone of our economic system. Freedom of contract, as in the case of all freedoms, is not absolute, however; it is subject to many statutory limitations. For example, the Sherman Antitrust Act as amended and the Federal Trade Commission Act declare many contracts and business practices to be illegal. These laws prohibit contracts in restraint of trade, attempts to monopolize, and unfair methods of competition. A party that is damaged as a result of a violation of the antitrust laws is not limited to simply recovering his damages. He is entitled to treble damages plus court costs and attorney's fees. This treble-damage provision is designed to punish the wrongdoer and to deter violations of the law and not simply in order to make the party which was wronged whole.

The special business torts discussed below also constitute unfair methods of competition.

Disparagement.   One who disparages or belittles the goods of another may be enjoined from doing so, and in certain instances may be compelled to pay damages to the injured party. This tort is based on the law of libel and slander. There appear to be four distinct elements of disparagement which must be proven in a tort action.

1. An express or implied misstatement of fact—as distinguished from words of comparison which indicate merely an opinion. Such expressions as "good" or "bad," "better" or "best" are in effect opinions.

2. The statement must concern the injured party's goods.

3. The statement must be made for the deliberate purpose of injuring the other party.

4. The injured party must allege and show special—as distinct from general —damages. That is, he must be able to prove loss of specific sales as a result of the statements.

A showing of the first two elements will entitle one to an equitable injunction against a repetition of such statements.

Inducing breach of contract.   To induce one person to breach his contract with another is to commit a tort.[5] The effect is the same even though the one who induced the breach did so in order to sell his own goods or services.

Mere passive presentation of the merits of one's products which has the net result of causing one to breach a contract and to purchase the goods of another is not actionable. It is only where one is active in persuading another to violate one agreement in order to be free to make another that a tort is committed.

[5] Herron v. State Farm Mut. Ins. Co., page 30

Appropriation of competitor's trade values.   Another facet of the security afforded to one's legally protected business interests is that of preserving his rights to somewhat abstract business values.

Wrappers and trade dress used to make merchandise more attractive and convenient to display do not of themselves have an exclusive trade value. No one has an exclusive right to the use of color combinations and package methods. Wrappers and color designs to be protected must be so distinctive as to entitle them to registration under the copyright or trademark law. However, if a distinctive wrapper or color design accompanying a distinctive name has by usage acquired a secondary meaning by becoming so identified with the goods that it distinguishes them from others and identifies the origin of the goods, the owner has an exclusive right to their use, and others may be enjoined from the use of the wrapper as an act of unfair competition.

Technically a trademark is supposed to be some mark or stamp imprinted upon the product, whereas a name does not have to be attached to the product. So far as the legal rights of the owner are involved, there is practically no difference between the two.

The first user of a trademark or name has a right to its exclusive use. The second user of such a mark or name, or of one which is deceptively similar, may be enjoined from its further use. Just how similar the mark, name, or trade dress must appear before relief will be granted presents an interesting problem. In general, it can be said that, whenever the casual observer, as distinct from the careful buyer, tends to be misled into purchasing the wrong article, an injunction is available to the injured party.

A name or mark which is descriptive of the nature of the article sold may not be exclusively appropriated by any one concern. Such terms as "Always Closed" for revolving doors and "Rubberoid" for roofing fall in the descriptive class and may be used by anyone. However, if the words used are so fanciful and remote from a description of the subject matter, such as "floating power" for engine mountings and "stronghold" for ribbed nails, it is appropriate for trademark use.

Geographical or place-names indicating a specific origin cannot be technical trademarks. Such words are in the public domain. Every manufacturer or producer has a right to indicate upon his product or article where it is produced. The same is true in the case of proper names. Every individual has a right to make use of his name in connection with his business. Any goodwill or favorable reputation that attaches to it should not be denied to him. Consequently, one generally cannot exclusively appropriate another's proper name.

The three rules indicated above are subject to one well-recognized exception. If a descriptive, geographical, or proper name has been used so long as to become identified with a certain product, thus having a secondary meaning, the first user will be protected in its use on the principles of unfair competition. Newcomers in the field who desire to use a descriptive term, a geographical location of their plant, or their names in identifying their products will have to qualify the use in such a manner as to avoid possible injury to the first user's goodwill. The latest cases indicate that such names cannot be identified as the name of the product by the second user, but that the maker's name or location may be placed on the product in some inconspicuous manner. Thus, it is clear that no one by the name of Ford could manufacture an automobile and call it Ford, although the name Ford could undoubtedly be used by the manufacturer in his business.

A trademark or name is protected only against infringement on articles of the same class. A first user cannot enjoin a second user from use of a mark or name on an article of an entirely different character. Three tests have been applied by the courts in determining whether articles are of the same class.

1. Are the articles so similar that one can be substituted for the other, as cocoa or chocolate?

2. Are the articles allied products, or are they used together, such as automobiles and automobile tires?

3. An association of ideas test: Does one article call the other to mind? Are they usually associated together in retail establishments? Hats and shoes offer an illustration of this group.

Through the adoption of these tests the courts attempt to prevent the confusion of goods by consumers, attempt to make possible the expansion of a line to include new articles similar in nature, and attempt to protect the goodwill of a business concern from the assault of a predatory competitor or one attempting to profit from the efforts of another.

A second user who makes an improper use of a trademark, name, or wrapper can always be enjoined from using it in the future. In addition, if the user is an intentional wrongdoer—if he intentionally profits from the use of another's goodwill—the injured party may recover damages or the profits of the wrongdoer. In some courts, including the federal courts, the first user may recover both profits and damages. It should be borne in mind, however, that damages or profits can be recovered only in case of intentional wrongdoing. If the second user copies the mark or name exactly or so nearly as to indicate bad faith, damages or profits are recoverable. If the second user has no knowledge of the first user's name or mark, an injunction is the only remedy available in most of the states.

The user of a trademark that is used in interstate commerce may have it registered with the federal government. If a trademark or name is registered, a presumption immediately arises that the party registering the mark or name is the first user. This presumption can be rebutted by another's proof of prior use. The first user is protected regardless of registration. However, if it has been registered and used for a period of five years without protest on the part of another user, it then becomes conclusively presumed that the registered user was the first in point of time to make use of the mark. The marks are registered for use with the specific types of merchandise indicated in the application for registration. Descriptive and geographical names that have been used in business for at least one year may receive a limited amount of protection by registering the name with the government. Registration continues for a period of twenty years unless the user or his assignee has abandoned the use of the mark or it has been canceled. Procedure is also made available for having the registration renewed for an additional twenty years.

Information about one's trade, customers, processes, or manufacture is confidential in nature. If a competitor can discover this information fairly through research, study, or observation, he may use it freely in the absence of a patent or a copyright. However, if he obtains such information by bribery of an employee of the first concern or by engaging an employee of the first concern with the understanding that he will use this information, the second party may be enjoined from making use of it.

In this connection it should be emphasized that an idea once exposed to the public may thereafter be used by anyone. The forward march of civilization is dependent upon the freedom with which new ideas are adopted. A book or magazine article containing new ideas may be copyrighted, but the ideas set forth therein may be used by anyone so long as the language used is not published by another. One who unfolds to an interested party a plan for financing his product or for merging several industries may discover later that the interested party has made use of these ideas without compensating the originator of them. To forestall such a possibility, the originator of the idea should, before explaining his idea, obtain a promise of payment in case his plan is adopted.

THE SUBJECT MATTER OF LAW CASES

Grossman v. Baumgartner
218 N.E.2d 259 (N.Y.) 1966

The New York City Board of Health was authorized by the City Charter "to add to and to alter, amend or repeal any part of the Health Code." The Board adopted a regulation prohibiting tattooing. Plaintiff, whose business was being declared illegal by the rule of the Board filed suit contending that the regulation was arbitrary, capricious and unreasonable and a taking of his property without due process of law and therefore unconstitutional.

FULD, J. . . . A statute—or an administrative regulation which is legislative in nature—will be upheld as valid if it has a rational basis, that is, if it is not unreasonable, arbitrary or capricious. In the case before us, there is no warrant for the charge that the Board of Health acted arbitrarily or capriciously or that the regulation under attack was unreasonable. A review of the evidence given by the defendants' witnesses thoroughly demonstrates the compelling medical necessity for section 181.15 of the Health Code. Not only was a connection shown between tattooing and hepatitis but the proof convincingly established that rigorous regulation would be ineffective. The police power is exceedingly broad, and the courts will not substitute their judgment of a public health problem for that of eminently qualified physicians in the field of public health. As the Supreme Court has expressed it, "The judicial function is exhausted with the discovery that the relation between means and end is not wholly vain and fanciful, an illusory pretense." In its wisdom, the board in the case before us decided that the prohibition of lay tattooing was essential for the protection of the public health, and, as stated above, it may not be said that that determination was unreasonable or without justification. It follows, therefore, that the legislation is valid, and this is so notwithstanding that it will occasion the discontinuance of an existing business.

Affirmed.

Massiah v. United States

84 S.Ct. 1199 (1964)

The defendant was charged and convicted of violating the federal narcotics laws. While free on bail he had a conversation with another person (Colson) who was charged with the same offense. Unknown to the defendant, Colson had agreed to help the prosecution and had placed a radio transmitter in the car in which they held their conversation. The prosecution used the defendant's incriminating statements against him at the trial. Defendant contended that his rights under the Fourth, Fifth, and Sixth Amendments to the United States Constitution were violated.

STEWART, J. . . . Any secret interrogation of the defendant, from and after the finding of the indictment, without the protection afforded by the presence of counsel, contravenes the basic dictates of fairness in the conduct of criminal causes and the fundamental rights of persons charged with crime. . . .

This view no more than reflects a constitutional principle . . . that . . . during perhaps the most critical period of the proceedings . . . that is to say, from the time of their arraignment until the beginning of their trial, when consultation, thoroughgoing investigation and preparation [are] vitally important, the defendants . . . [are] as much entitled to such aid [of counsel] during that period as at the trial itself. . . .

We hold that the petitioner was denied the basic protections of that guarantee when there was used against him at his trial evidence of his own incriminating words, which federal agents had deliberately elicited from him after he had been indicted and in the absence of his counsel. . . .

Reversed.

Mr. Justice White, with whom Mr. Justice Clark and Mr. Justice Harlan join, dissenting.

The current incidence of serious violations of the law represents not only an appalling waste of the potentially happy and useful lives of those who engage in such conduct but also an overhanging, dangerous threat to those unidentified and innocent people who will be the victims of crime today and tomorrow. This is a festering problem for which no adequate cures have yet been devised. . . .

But dissatisfaction with preventive programs aimed at eliminating crime and profound dispute about whether we should punish, deter, rehabilitate or cure cannot excuse concealing one of our most menacing problems until the millennium has arrived. In my view, a civilized society must maintain its capacity to discover transgressions of the law and to identify those who flout it. This much is necessary even to know the scope of the problem, much less to formulate intelligent counter measures. It will just not do to sweep these disagreeable matters under the rug or to pretend they are not there at all.

It is therefore a rather portentous occasion when a constitutional rule is established barring the use of evidence which is relevant, reliable and highly probative of the issue which the trial court has before it—whether the accused committed the act with which he is charged. Without the evidence, the quest for truth may be seriously impeded and in many cases the trial court, although aware of proof showing defendant's guilt, must nevertheless release him be-

cause the crucial evidence is deemed inadmissible. This result is entirely justified in some circumstances because exclusion serves other policies of overriding
importance, as where evidence seized in an illegal search is excluded, not
because of the quality of the proof, but to secure meaningful enforcement of
the Fourth Amendment. But this only emphasizes that the soundest of reasons
is necessary to warrant the exclusion of evidence otherwise admissible and the
creation of another area of privileged testimony. With all due deference, I am
not at all convinced that the additional barriers to the pursuit of truth which
the Court today erects rest on anything like the solid foundations which
decisions of this gravity should require. . . .

Whatever the content or scope of the rule may prove to be, I am unable to
see how this case presents an unconstitutional inference with Massiah's right
to counsel. Massiah was not prevented from consulting with counsel as often
as he wished. No meetings with counsel were disturbed or spied upon. Preparation for trial was in no way obstructed. It is only a sterile syllogism—an
unsound one, besides—to say that because Massiah had a right to counsel's
aid before and during the trial, his out-of-court conversations and admissions
must be excluded if obtained without counsel's consent or presence. The right
to counsel has never meant as much before, and its extension in this case
requires some further explanation, so far unarticulated by the Court.

Since the new rule would exclude all admissions made to the police, no
matter how voluntary and reliable, the requirement of counsel's presence or
approval would seem to rest upon the probability that counsel would foreclose
any admissions at all. This is nothing more than a thinly disguised constitutional policy of minimizing or entirely prohibiting the use in evidence of
voluntary out-of-court admissions and confessions made by the accused. Carried as far as blind logic may compel some to go, the notion that statements
from the mouth of the defendant should not be used in evidence would have
a severe and unfortunate impact upon the great bulk of criminal cases.

Viewed in this light, the Court's newly fashioned exclusionary principle goes
far beyond the constitutional privilege against self-incrimination, which neither requires nor suggests the barring of voluntary pretrial admissions. The
Fifth Amendment states that no person "shall be compelled in any criminal
case to be a witness against himself. . . . " The defendant may thus not be
compelled to testify at his trial, but he may if he wishes. Likewise, he may not
be compelled or coerced into saying anything before trial; but until today he
could if he wished to, and if he did, it could be used against him. Whether as
a matter of self-incrimination or of due process, the proscription is against
compulsion—coerced incrimination. Under the prior law, announced in count-
less cases in this Court, the defendant's pretrial statements were admissible
evidence if voluntarily made; inadmissible if not the product of his free will.
Hardly any constitutional area has been more carefully patrolled by this Court,
and until now the Court has expressly rejected the argument that admissions
are to be deemed involuntary if made outside the presence of counsel.

The Court presents no facts, no objective evidence, no reasons to warrant
scrapping the voluntary-involuntary test for admissibility in this area. Without
such evidence I would retain it in its present form. . . .

Applying the new exclusionary rule is peculiarly inappropriate in this case.
At the time of the conversation in question, petitioner was not in custody but

free on bail. He was not questioned in what anyone could call an atmosphere of official coercion. What he said was said to his partner in crime who had also been indicted. There was no suggestion or any possibility of coercion. What petitioner did not know was that Colson had decided to report the conversation to the police. Had there been no prior arrangements between Colson and the police, had Colson simply gone to the police after the conversation had occurred, his testimony relating Massiah's statements would be readily admissible at the trial, as would a recording which he might have made of the conversation. In such event, it would simply be said that Massiah risked talking to a friend who decided to disclose what he knew of Massiah's criminal activities. But if, as occurred here, Colson had been cooperating with the police prior to his meeting with Massiah, both his evidence and the recorded conversation are somehow transformed into inadmissible evidence despite the fact that the hazard to Massiah remains precisely the same—the defection of a confederate in crime.

Reporting criminal behavior is expected or even demanded of the ordinary citizen. Friends may be subpoenaed to testify about friends, relatives about relatives and partners about partners. I therefore question the soundness of insulating Massiah from the apostasy of his partner in crime and of furnishing constitutional sanctions for the strict secrecy and discipline of criminal organizations. Neither the ordinary citizen nor the confessed criminal should be discouraged from reporting what he knows to the authorities and from lending his aid to secure evidence of crime. Certainly after this case the Colsons will be few and far between; and the Massiahs can breathe much easier, secure in the knowledge that the Constitution furnishes an important measure of protection against faithless compatriots, guarantees sporting treatment for sporting peddlers of narcotics.

Meanwhile, of course, the public will again be the loser and law enforcement presented with another serious dilemma. . . .

Undoubtedly, the evidence excluded in this case would not have been available but for the conduct of Colson in cooperation with Agent Murphy, but is it this kind of conduct which should be forbidden to those charged with law enforcement? It is one thing to establish safeguards against procedures fraught with the potentiality of coercion and to outlaw "easy but self-defeating ways in which brutality is substituted for brains as an instrument of crime detection." But here there was no substitution of brutality for brains, no inherent danger of police coercion justifying the prophylactic effect of another exclusionary rule. Massiah was not being interrogated in a police station, was not surrounded by numerous officers or questioned in relays, and was not forbidden access to others. Law enforcement may have the elements of a contest about it, but it is not a game. Massiah and those like him receive ample protection from the long line of precedents in this Court holding that confessions may not be introduced unless they are voluntary. In making these determinations the courts must consider the absence of counsel as one of several factors by which voluntariness is to be judged.

This is a wiser rule than the automatic rule announced by the Court, which requires courts and juries to disregard voluntary admissions which they might well find to be the best possible evidence in discharging their responsibility of ascertaining truth.

Fergerstrom v. Hawaiian Ocean View Estates

441 P.2d 141 (Hawaii) 1968

LEVINSON, J. This case comes to us on interlocutory appeal from an order denying the defendant's motion for summary judgment. The plaintiffs' complaint alleges that they, husband and wife, purchased a parcel of land from the defendant, a corporation, for the construction of a house. The defendant's employees took pictures of one of the plaintiffs and of the house at various stages of construction. The defendant used the photographs and the plaintiffs' name in sales brochures, in advertisements in publications, and in television commercials. The complaint alleged that the defendant's acts constituted an actionable invasion of their right of privacy. Count I alleged:

The use of said photographs and the names of the plaintiffs as aforesaid was without the prior knowledge and consent of plaintiffs and constitutes multiple continuing and multifarious violations of plaintiffs' right of privacy, by reason of which plaintiffs have been held up to public exposure and ridicule, their right of privacy has been invaded by a continuous stream of defendant's "sales prospects" coming on to plaintiffs' property, using plaintiffs' facilities and generally bothering plaintiffs in their said home, causing humiliation, annoyance and embarrassment to plaintiffs to their damage in the sum of $25,000.

. . . The defendant moved for summary judgment on the grounds that there is no common-law action for invasion of privacy and that the legislature has not provided for such an action.

The defendant contends that since the ancient common law did not afford a remedy for invasion of privacy, and there is no case in Hawaii recognizing such a right, only the legislature can provide for such a cause of action. The magnitude of the error in the defendant's position approaches Brobdingnagian proportions. To accept it would constitute more than accepting a limited view of the essence of the common law. It would be no less than an absolute annihilation of the common law system. . . .

A case decided, 4 to 3, by the New York Court of Appeals best articulates the arguments against judicial recognition of an action for invasion of privacy, *Roberson* v. *Rochester Folding Box Co.,* 171 N.Y. 538. The majority opinion presents five basic arguments. First, there was no precedent in the ancient English common law. Second, the injury was of a purely mental character. Third, a "vast amount of litigation" would be encouraged. Fourth, the distinction which would have to be drawn between public and private characters could not be effectively drawn. Fifth, it might unduly restrict free speech and press. However persuasive these arguments may have been in 1902, they amount to little more than straws in the wind today.

On the issue of lack of precedent, there is a substantial question whether the common law provided no basis for recognizing a right of privacy. In any event, the absence of precedent is a feeble argument. The common-law system would have withered centuries ago had it lacked the ability to expand and adapt to the social, economic, and political changes inherent in a vibrant human society.

"[T]he genius of the common law, upon which our jurisprudence is based, is its capacity for orderly growth." Indeed, tort law as we know it today bears little, if any, resemblance to tort law in its early development, when a writ held the key to entry into the room of justice. This court recognized the relatively new tort of intentional infliction of emotional distress although there was no more precedent in the ancient common law for that tort than for the protection of the right of privacy.

As for the argument that the injury is purely mental in character, even if it were true it would not be persuasive. . . .

The argument that recognizing the tort will result in a vast amount of litigation has accompanied virtually every innovation in the law. Assuming that it is true, that fact is unpersuasive unless the litigation largely will be spurious and harassing. Undoubtedly, when a court recognizes a new cause of action, there will be many cases based on it. Many will be soundly based and the plaintiffs in those cases will have their rights vindicated. In other cases, plaintiffs will abuse the law for some unworthy end, but the possibility of abuse cannot obscure the need to provide an appropriate remedy.

As to the need to distinguish between public and private figures, the difficulty of drawing a line is no bar to the recognition of a cause of action. But such a distinction is irrelevant in this case since the defendant has appropriated the plaintiffs' name and personality for its own benefit in advertising. Even were the defendant able to establish at trial that the plaintiffs were public figures, that would not be a defense to this cause of action. Furthermore, distinguishing between private and public figures is not as difficult a task as the defendant suggests.

Finally, the recognition of a right not to have one's name and picture used without his permission as part of an advertising campaign does not involve a restriction on free speech and press. The only communications the defendant made in which it used the plaintiffs' name and pictures were for the purpose of selling its product. Whatever limitations on other aspects of the right of privacy may have to be recognized because of the need to protect the First Amendment freedoms we hold so precious, the infringement alleged in this case does not raise the issue.

We hold that the plaintiffs' complaint states a cause of action for invasion of the right of privacy. We go no further than to indicate that protection is available for appropriation of name or picture for commercial purposes. We do not now decide whether other aspects commonly included under a general right of privacy will receive similar protection. These issues remain to be decided in subsequent cases raising them, preferably after a trial on the merits.

Affirmed.

Herron v. State Farm Mut. Ins. Co.

363 P.2d 310 (Cal.) 1961

GIBSON, J. Plaintiffs, attorneys at law brought this action against Mr. and Mrs. Donald Halverson for breach of contract and against State Farm Mutual Insurance Company and its agent, Anthony Caruso, for intentional interference with contractual relations. The Halversons were not served, and a demurrer of State Farm and Caruso (who will be referred to as defendants) was sustained without leave to amend. Plaintiffs have appealed from the ensuing judgment.

The following is a summary of plaintiffs' allegations: The Halversons entered into a contingent fee contract with plaintiffs concerning claims reasonably worth $60,000 for personal injuries sustained in an automobile accident caused by the negligence of a person insured by State Farm. Plaintiffs were to advance all expenses necessary for the preparation of the case and for court costs and were to receive one-third of the amount of the recovery remaining after deduction of the costs. No settlement was to be made without the consent of plaintiffs and the Halversons, and in the event there was no recovery plaintiffs were to receive nothing for their services or for costs advanced. Plaintiffs notified defendants of the agreement immediately after its execution, and they proceeded to hire private investigators, photographers, and a draftsman, make an investigation, and incur expenses in the amount of $1,250. Defendants, by telling the Halversons that they did not need an attorney and that a satisfactory settlement would be made, induced them to breach the contingent fee contract and to discharge plaintiffs and deprive them of the benefits of the contract and the expenses incurred for investigation and preparation. Defendants assisted the Halversons in preparing letters which informed plaintiffs of their dismissal. The conduct of defendants was maliciously designed to injure plaintiffs' rights and lawful business, and it violated the rules of the National Conference Committee on Adjusters of which State Farm or its agents are members. The rules provide, in part, that an insurance company will not deal directly with any claimant represented by an attorney without the consent of the attorney and will not advise the claimant to refrain from seeking legal advice or retaining counsel to protect his interest. As a result of the conduct of defendants, plaintiffs suffered the loss of the expenses incurred in investigation and preparation and did not receive their one-third contingent fee.

Plaintiffs prayed for judgment against defendants for $20,000 or one-third of the judgment or settlement recovered by the Halversons, whichever is the lesser, and, in addition, for $25,000 punitive damages.

An action will lie for the intentional interference by a third person with a contractual relationship either by unlawful means or by means otherwise lawful when there is a lack of sufficient justification. . . . There is no valid reason why this rule should not be applied to an attorney's contingent fee contract. Such an agreement is a legal and valid contract entitled to the protection of the law, and an attorney who is wrongfully discharged is generally entitled to the same amount of compensation as if he had completed the contemplated services. . . . While a client is permitted to discharge his attorney without cause, this is allowed not because the attorney's interest in performing his services and obtaining his fee is unworthy of protection but because of the importance of the client's interest in the successful prosecution of his cause of action. . . . An attorney's interest in his contingent fee agreement is greater than that of a party to a contract terminable at will, as to which it has been held that an intentional and unjustifiable interference is actionable. . . .

Whether an intentional interference by a third party is justifiable depends upon a balancing of the importance, social and private, of the objective advanced by the interference against the importance of the interest interfered with, considering all circumstances including the nature of the actor's conduct and the relationship between the parties. . . . Justification is an affirmative defense and may not be considered as supporting the trial court's action in sustaining a demurrer unless it appears on the face of the complaint. . . . The only allegation relied upon by defendants as showing justification is that State Farm had issued an automobile public liability insurance policy to the person whose negligence caused the injuries to the Halversons. In our opinion this allegation does not establish justification.

The conduct of an insurance company in inducing an injured person to repudiate his contract with an attorney may be detrimental not only to the interests of the attorney but also to the interests of the client since, as we have seen, the client, in addition to being deprived of the aid and advice of his attorney, may also be liable for the full contract fee. Defendants argue that the policy of the law is to encourage settlement, that an insurance company has a legal duty to effect a settlement of a claim against its insured in an appropriate case . . . and that furtherance of the actor's own economic interests will justify an intentional interference with a contractual relationship in some circumstances where his interests are threatened by the contract. However, these considerations standing alone cannot justify inducing the Halversons to repudiate the contract to deprive plaintiffs of its benefits. So far as appears from the complaint, no cause for the dismissal of plaintiffs existed, no efforts were made to negotiate with them, and there is no indication that State Farm could not have protected its interests and obtained a satisfactory settlement without interfering with the contract.

The judgment is reversed with directions to overrule the demurrer.

CHAPTER 2
REVIEW QUESTIONS AND PROBLEMS

1. What is the difference between substantive law and procedural law?
2. List three categories of the public law.
3. State *X* enacts an open occupancy law which requires owners of real estate to sell their property to any ready, willing, and able buyer regardless of race, creed, or color. Is this law a part of the public law or the private law? Explain.
4. Name the three general categories of crimes and distinguish them from each other.
5. Give reasons for the large number of governmental administrative agencies.
6. What are some of the objections of lawyers to administrative agencies exercising judicial powers?
7. Why has the Supreme Court been criticized recently for its decisions in the criminal law area?
8. Under what circumstances may a court reverse the decision of an administrative agency?
9. List five intentional torts.

10. What are some of the reasons for abandoning the "fault system" in automobile accident cases?
11. What are the elements of the tort of disparagement?

Sources of Law

1-13. Introduction. As discussed in Chapter 1, it is difficult to define law with accuracy or to identify with particularity all of its sources. The various schools of legal thought at best only provide insight to the forces, ideas, and influences which give direction to the law. While people in early times thought that law came from supernatural sources, we now recognize that law is man-made for man, though it is perhaps influenced by concepts and forces beyond man himself.

The desire of man for knowledge and for certainty in his affairs has been evidenced in the constant trend toward reducing law to a written form. During the entire recorded history of civilization, man has reduced "law" to writing through the use of legislative bodies. Legislative bodies have provided us with constitutions, statutes, ordinances, codes, and treaties, all of which may be grouped under the source heading "Written Law." Insofar as treaties are concerned, our Constitution provides that treaties are negotiated by the executive branch of the federal government, but they become effective only when ratified by the Senate. A treaty is the supreme law of the land, and any state law which conflicts with a treaty or which interferes with foreign relations is unconstitutional.[1] The federal government is the only governmental body with power over the external affairs of the country.

Another source of law is the reported decisions of the courts. This judge-made law is found in the written opinions of courts that support and explain their decisions. These opinions at the level of reviewing courts (the levels of courts will be discussed in Chapter 4) are bound into volumes so that lawyers may study them and derive the rules of law which form the basis of the decisions. This case law, known as the *common law,* is predicated upon a reliance on precedent. It will be discussed more fully later in this chapter.

[1] Zschernig v. Miller, page 48

The term "common law" is also used to distinguish between the English system of law and the systems of law developed in other European countries. The European form of law, usually referred to as the civil law or Roman law, has its basis in the legal system of the Roman Empire. The civil law system is primarily predicated upon a written codification or compilation of all of the law. This system does not allow much room for the creation of law by judges as they decide cases. The civil law operates predominantly on the basis of statutes, while the common law emphasizes law created by courts in deciding controversies.

In the United States common law has been the predominant influence. Since most of the colonists were of English origin, they naturally were controlled by the laws and customs of their mother country. But in Louisiana, and to some extent Texas and California, the civil law has influenced the legal systems, because these states were founded by French and Spanish peoples. It must not be overlooked, however, that much of the law in every state of the United States is statutory, and statutes are becoming increasingly important. Case law, or common law, remains an important source of law because of the extreme difficulty in reducing all law to writing in advance of an issue being raised.

A third source of law was previously discussed in Chapter 2 under the classification of administrative law. Administrative agencies operating at all levels of government make "law" by promulgating rules and regulations as well as by adjudicating matters within their jurisdiction.

In summary, our law comes from written laws, such as constitutions, statutes, ordinances, and treaties; from case law, which is judge-made by judicial decision; and from the rules and decisions of administrative agencies.

WRITTEN LAW

1-14. Constitutions.   The Constitution of the United States and the constitutions of the various states are the fundamental written law in this country. Article VI of the Constitution of the United States provides: "This Constitution and the laws of the United States which shall be made in pursuance thereof, and all treaties made, or which shall be made under the authority of the United States, shall be the supreme law of the land; and the judges in every state shall be bound thereby, anything in the Constitution or laws of any state to the contrary notwithstanding." All state laws must conform to, or be in harmony with the federal Constitution as well as with the constitution of the state.

The federal Constitution is a grant of power by the states to the federal government whereas the constitutions of the various states basically limit the powers of state government. In other words, the federal government possesses those powers *granted* to it by the states, and state governments possess reserved powers, all powers not taken away in the state constitution or specifically denied to them by the United States Constitution. The state constitution is the fundamental written law of the state. Legislative enactments by state legislatures, by cities and towns, and by other smaller governmental units must conform to these constitutions and find in them their authority, either expressed or implied.

There are two very important legal doctrines based on constitutional provisions which are discussed in the section that follows.

1-15. Separation of Powers and Judicial Review.   Both the state and federal Constitutions provide for a scheme of government consisting of three branches —the legislative, the executive, and the judicial. A doctrine usually referred to as the doctrine of separation of powers, ascribes to each branch a separate function and a check and balance on the functions of the other branches. The doctrine of separation of powers infers that each separate branch will not perform the function of the other and that each branch has limited powers. The system of checks and balances may be briefly summarized as follows: The Senate retains the power to approve key executive and judicial appointments. The legislative branch exercises control through its power to appropriate funds. In addition, Congress can limit or expand the authority of the executive branch or the jurisdiction of the judicial branch in most cases. The executive has the power to veto legislation and to appoint judges (in some states the judiciary is elected). The judiciary has the power to review actions of the executive and to review laws passed by the legislative branch to determine if such laws are constitutional. This power of judicial review is discussed more fully later in this section.

The separation of powers concept has contributed toward stable government. Justice Frankfurter, in a special concurring opinion in *Youngstown Sheet and Tube Co.* v. *Sawyer* (343 U.S. 579), had occasion to discuss this doctrine. He stated:

> A constitutional democracy like ours is perhaps the most difficult of man's social arrangements to manage successfully. Our scheme of society is more dependent than any other form of government on knowledge and wisdom and self-discipline for the achievement of its aims. For our democracy implies the reign of reason on the most extensive scale. The Founders of this Nation were not imbued with the modern cynicism that the only thing that history teaches is that it teaches nothing. They acted on the conviction that the experience of man sheds a good deal of light on his nature. It sheds a good deal of light not merely on the need for effective power, if a society is to be at once cohesive and civilized, but also on the need for limitations on the power of governors over the governed.
>
> To that end they rested the structure of our central government on the system of checks and balances. For them the doctrine of separation of powers was not mere theory; it was a felt necessity. Not so long ago it was fashionable to find our system of checks and balances obstructive to effective government. It was easy to ridicule that system as outmoded—too easy. The experience through which the world has passed in our own day has made vivid the realization that the Framers of our Constitution were not inexperienced doctrinaires. These long-headed statesmen had no illusion that our people enjoyed biological or psychological or sociological immunities from the hazards of concentrated power. . . . The accretion of dangerous power does not come in a day. It does come, however slowly, from the generative force of unchecked disregard of the restrictions that fence in even the most disinterested assertion of authority.
>
> Marshall's admonition that "it is a *constitution* we are expounding" is especially relevant when the Court is required to give legal sanctions to an underlying principle of the Constitution—that of separation of powers. "The great ordinances of the Constitution do not establish and divide fields of black and white." (Holmes, J.)
>
> . . . The judiciary may, as this case proves, have to intervene in determining

where authority lies as between the democratic forces in our scheme of government. But in doing so we should be wary and humble. Such is the teaching of this Court's role in the history of the country. . . .

A scheme of government like ours no doubt at times feels the lack of power to act with complete, all-embracing, swiftly moving authority. No doubt a government with distributed authority subject to being challenged in the courts of law, at least long enough to consider and adjudicate the challenge, labors under restrictions from which other governments are free. It has not been our tradition to envy such governments. In any event our government was designed to have such restrictions. The price was deemed not too high in view of the safeguards which these restrictions afford. I know no more impressive words on this subject than those of Mr. Justice Brandeis: "The doctrine of the separation of powers was adopted by the Convention of 1787, not to promote efficiency but to preclude the exercise of arbitrary power. The purpose was, not to avoid friction, but, by means of the inevitable friction incident to the distribution of the governmental powers among three departments, to save the people from autocracy." *(Myers* v. *United States,* 272 U.S. 52, 240, 293)

The doctrine of judicial review is the heart of the concept of separation of powers. This doctrine and the doctrine of supremacy of the Constitution were established at an early date in our country's history in the celebrated case of *Marbury* v. *Madison.* In this case, Chief Justice Marshall literally created for the court a power which the founding fathers had refused to include in the Constitution. This was the power of the judiciary to review the actions of the branches of government and to set them aside as null and void if in violation of the Constitution. In creating this power to declare laws unconstitutional, Chief Justice Marshall stated: "Certainly, all those who have framed written constitutions contemplated them as forming the fundamental and paramount law of the nation, and consequently, the theory of every such government must be that an act of the legislature, repugnant to the constitution, is void. This theory is essentially attached to a written constitution and is, consequently, to be considered by this court, as one of the fundamental principles of our society." Justice Marshall then decided that courts have the power to review the action of the legislative and executive branches of government to determine if they are constitutional. This doctrine of judicial review has, to some extent, made the courts the overseer of government, even though Justice Frankfurter questioned this authority. The great power of the judiciary can be seen in the following language in *Marbury* v. *Madison:*

It is, emphatically, the province and duty of the judicial department to say what the law is. Those who apply the rule to particular cases must of necessity expound and interpret that rule. If two laws conflict with each other, the courts must decide on the operation of each. So, if a law be in opposition to the constitution . . . the court must determine which of these conflicting rules governs the case: this is of the very essence of judicial duty.

1-16. Interpretation of Statutes.   The power of courts over legislation is not limited to the doctrine of judicial review. Courts also interpret legislation by resolving ambiguities and filling in the gaps in the statutes. There would be no need to interpret a statute which was direct, clear, and precise. However, most legislation is by its very nature general, and courts are faced with the problem of finding the meaning of general statutes as applied to specific facts. Interpretation is designed to find the intent of the legislature.

One technique of statutory interpretation is to examine the legislative history of an act to determine the purpose of the legislation, or the evil it was designed to correct. Legislative history does not always give a clear meaning to a statute because many of the questions of interpretation which confront courts were never even visualized by the legislature. The real problem often is to determine what the legislature *would have* intended, had it considered the question. There are several generally accepted rules of statutory interpretation which are used by judges in construing legislative intent. Some of the more frequently used rules are

1. Statutes which are consistent with one another, and which relate to the same subject matter, are *in pari materia* and should be construed together, and effect be given to them all, although they may contain no reference to one another and were passed at different times.

2. Criminal statutes[2] and taxing laws should be strictly or narrowly construed so that doubts as to the applicability of the law will be resolved in favor of the accused or the taxpayer as the case may be.

3. Unless contrary intent appears, statutory words are uniformly presumed to be used in their ordinary and usual sense, and with the meaning commonly attributed to them.

4. A thing may be within the letter of the statute and yet not within the statute because not within its spirit nor within the intention of the makers.

5. Statutes in derogation of the common law are to be strictly or narrowly construed so that their application is limited.

6. Remedial statutes (those creating a judicial remedy on behalf of one person at the expense of another) are to be liberally construed in order that the statute will be effective in correcting the condition sought to be remedied.

7. Where a general word in a statute follows particular and specific words of the same nature as itself, it takes its meaning from them, and is presumed to be restricted to the same genus as those words. For example, the words "and any other immoral or illegal purpose" would be defined and take their meaning from whatever specific words preceded them. This rule is called *ejusdem generis.*

8. Popular words are to be construed in the popular sense and technical words in the technical sense, but if a word has both popular and technical meaning, its meaning will be determined from the context in which it is used.

9. The meaning of a doubtful word may be ascertained by reference to the meaning of words with which it is associated. (This rule is sometimes referred to as *noscitur a sociis;* it is similar to the rule of *in pari materia* but is applied to sentences and sections of a single statute.)

Many of the above rules conflict with one another, and courts frequently use the rule which justifies its selected interpretation.

[2] Director of Division of Milk Control v. Haseotes, page 49

Such other matters as the objectives of the legislation as stated in preambles and debates, statements by executives in requesting legislation, prior judicial decisions involving the same subject matter, and the title of the act are used as extrinsic aids in judicial interpretations.

In the final analysis, it is what the court says that a statute means that determines its effect.

1-17. Uniform State Laws.   Since there are fifty states, each with its own constitution, statutes, and body of case law developed by its court system, there are bound to be very substantial differences in the law among the various states. It is important to note that ours is a federal system wherein each state has a substantial degree of autonomy; thus it can be said that there are really fifty-one legal systems—a system for each of the states plus the federal legal structure. In many legal situations it does not matter that legal principles are not uniform throughout the country. This is true when the parties to a dispute are citizens of the same state; then the controversy is strictly an *intrastate* one as opposed to one having *interstate* implications. But when citizens of different states are involved (for example, where a buyer in one state contracts with a seller in another), many difficult questions can arise from the lack of uniformity in the law. For instance, does the law of the buyer's state control, or does that of the seller's state? It is true that a body of law called "conflict of laws" has developed, which relates to the choice of laws in such a situation. But certainly trade between citizens of different states has been impeded and made more difficult because the laws of commerce are not uniform. Conflict of laws is discussed in Section 1-21.

Two solutions to the problem are possible: (1) federal legislation governing business law (but this would only apply to interstate transactions and would result in there being two conflicting laws—one applicable to interstate contracts and another to intrastate contracts); and (2) adoption by the legislatures of all the states of the same laws concerning at least certain phases of business transactions. The latter procedure has actually been attempted by creation of a legislative drafting group known as the National Conference of Commissioners on Uniform State Laws. This group is made up of commissioners appointed by the governors of the states, and has for its purpose: "(1) The promotion of the uniformity in state laws on all subjects where uniformity is deemed desirable and practicable; (2) to draft model acts on (a) subjects suitable for interstate compacts, and (b) subjects in which uniformity will make more effective the exercise of state powers and promote interstate cooperation; and (3) to promote uniformity of judicial decisions throughout the United States."

When approved by the National Conference, proposed uniform acts are recommended to the state legislatures for adoption.

The first uniform state law, the Uniform Negotiable Instruments Law (NIL), was promulgated in 1896. Since then over 100 uniform laws concerning such subjects as partnerships, sale of goods, conditional sales, warehouse receipts, bills of lading, stock transfers, and many others have been promulgated and presented to the various state legislatures. The response from the state legislatures has varied. Very few of the uniform laws have been adopted by all of the states. Some states have adopted the uniform law in principle but have changed some of the provisions to meet local needs or to satisfy strong lobbying groups so that the result has often been "nonuniform uniform state laws."

The most significant development for business in the field of uniform state legislation has been the Uniform Commercial Code. This Code was prepared in cooperation with the American Law Institute for the stated purpose of collecting in one body the law that "deals with all the phases which may ordinarily arise in the handling of a commercial transaction from start to finish. . . . The concept of the Code is to treat a commercial transaction as a single subject of the law notwithstanding its many facets."

The field of commercial law is not the only area of new uniform statutes. Many states are adopting revised criminal codes which contain modern procedures and concepts. In addition, the past few years have seen dynamic changes in both state and federal statutes setting forth civil procedures and revising court systems. The future will undoubtedly bring many further developments to improve the administration of justice. The trend, despite some objection, is to cover more areas of the law with statutes and to rely less on precedent in judicial decisions, or common law, as a source of law.

1-18. Other Forms of "Written Law."   In the fifth century the Roman Emperor Justinian compiled the law of Rome into a written code so that all could know the law. Since that time legal scholars have been writing summaries of the law on various subjects, and in modern times legal publishing companies have been feverishly attempting to keep up with our ever-changing law. These written compilations are not written law in the sense that a statute is written law, but they are nevertheless an important "source of law" for one seeking to determine what the law is on any given question.

These works on law take various forms. Some are texts on particular subjects. For example, Professor Corbin prepared several volumes on contract law, as did Professor Williston. These volumes, in addition to summarizing the state of the law, provide references to cases and other authorities for the rules of law set forth. Many of these texts are so widely accepted as authoritative that courts will refer to them in their decisions. Some of the cases in Book Two on contracts will refer to Professor Corbin's and Professor Williston's works on contracts.

Other treatises are in the form of general encyclopedias of the law. They purport to cover all areas and provide both statutory and case citations in support of the legal principles set forth. Examples of these are *American Jurisprudence* and *Corpus Juris Secundum.*

The American Law Institute, which assisted in preparing the Uniform Commericial Code, has made a very valuable contribution to the field of written law. It has published texts, known as Restatements of the Law, in various subject areas such as contracts, torts, agency, or property. Each Restatement covers only one area and not only sets forth what the law is but, in many cases, what it should be in the opinion of legal scholars. Restatements of the Law are frequently used by courts as the basis for a decision. (You will note references to various Restatements in the cases included in this text.) When a Restatement is used as authority, the law is tending toward justice and the desirable result, at least insofar as the American Law Institute and its judges, lawyers, and scholars are concerned.

CASE LAW

1-19. *Stare Decisis.* Notwithstanding the trend toward reducing law to statutory form, a substantial portion of our law finds its source in decided cases. This case law, or common law, is based on the concept of precedent and the doctrine of *stare decisis,* which means "to stand by decisions and not to disturb what is settled." The doctrine of *stare decisis* must be contrasted with the concept of *res adjudicata,* or *res judicata,* which means that the "thing has been decided." *Res adjudicata* applies when, between the parties themselves, the matter is closed at the conclusion of the lawsuit.[3] *Stare decisis* means that when a court of competent jurisdiction has decided a controversy and has, in a written opinion, set forth the rule or principle which formed the basis for its decision, that rule or principle will be followed by the court in deciding subsequent cases. Likewise, subordinate courts in the same jurisdiction will be bound by the rule of law set forth in the decision. *Stare decisis,* then, affects persons who are not parties to the lawsuit, while *res ajudicata* only applies to the parties.

Stare decisis provides both certainty and predictability to the law. It is also expedient. Through reliance upon precedent established in prior cases, the common law has resolved many legal issues and brought stability into many areas of the law, such as the law of contracts. The doctrine of *stare decisis* provides a system wherein a businessman may act in a certain way with confidence that his action will have a certain legal effect. People can rely on prior decisions and, knowing the legal significance of their action, act accordingly. There is reasonable certainty as to the results of conduct. Courts usually hesitate to renounce precedent and generally assume that if a principle or rule of law announced in a former judicial decision is unfair or contrary to public policy, it will be changed by legislation. Precedent has more force on trial courts than on courts of review; the latter have the power to make precedent in the first instance.

The common-law system as used in the United States has several inherent difficulties. First of all, the unbelievably large volume of judicial decisions, each possibly creating precedent, places "the law" beyond the comprehension of lawyers let alone laymen. Large law firms employ lawyers whose sole task is to search the case reports for "the law" to be used in lawsuits and in advising their clients. Legal research involves the examination of cases in hundreds of volumes. Since the total body of ruling case law is beyond the grasp of lawyers, it is obvious that laymen who are supposed to know the law and govern their conduct accordingly do not know the law and cannot always follow it, even with the advice of legal counsel.

Another major problem involving case law arises because conflicting precedents are frequently presented by the parties to an action. One of the major tasks of the courts in such cases is to determine which precedent is applicable to the case at bar and which precedent is correct. In addition, even today, many questions of law arise on which there has been no prior decision or in areas where the only authority is by implication. In such situations, the judicial

[3] Mettee v. Boone, page 50

process is "legislative" in character and involves the creation of law, not merely its discovery.

It should also be noted that there is a distinction between precedent and mere dicta. As authority for future cases, a judicial decision is coextensive only with the facts upon which it is founded and the rules of law upon which the decision is actually predicated. Frequently courts make comments on matters not necessary to the decision reached. Such expressions, called "dicta," lack the force of an adjudication and, strictly speaking, are not precedent which the court will be required to follow within the rule of *stare decisis.* However, dicta or implication in prior cases may be followed if sound and just, and dicta which have been repeated frequently are often given the force of precedent.

Finally, our system of each state having its own body of case law creates serious legal problems in matters that have legal implications in more than one state. This problem will be discussed in more detail in Section 1-21 under the heading "Conflict of Laws."

1-20. Rejection of *Stare Decisis.* However, the doctrine of *stare decisis* has not been applied in such a fashion as to render the law rigid and inflexible. If a court, and especially a reviewing court, should find that the prior decision was "palpably wrong," it may overrule it and decline to follow the rule enunciated by that case. By the same token, if the court should find that a rule of law established by a prior decision is no longer sound because of changing conditions, it may not consider the rule to be a binding precedent. The strength and genius of the common law is that no decision is *stare decisis* when it has lost its usefulness or the reasons for it no longer exist. The doctrine does not require courts to multiply their errors by using former mistakes as authority and support for new errors. Thus, just as legislatures change the law by new legislation, so also do courts change the law, from time to time, by reversing former precedents. Judges are subject to social forces and changing circumstances just as are legislatures. The personnel of courts change, and each new generation of judges deems it a responsibility to reexamine precedents and to adapt them to the world of the times.

It should be noted, also, that in many cases a precedent created by a decision will not be a popular one and may be "out of step" with the times. The effect of the decision as a precedent can be nullified by the passage of a statute providing for a different result than that reached by the court as to future cases involving the same general issue.

Stare decisis may not be ignored by mere whim or caprice. It must be followed rather rigidly in the daily affairs of men. In the whole area of private law, uniformity and continuity are necessary. It is obvious that the same rules of tort and contract law must be applied in the afternoon as in the morning. *Stare decisis* must serve to take the capricious element out of law and to give stability to a society and to business.

However, in the area of public law, and especially constitutional law, the doctrine is frequently ignored. The Supreme Court recognizes that "it is a constitution which we are expounding, not the gloss which previous courts may have put on it." Justice Douglas, speaking before the Association of the Bar of the City of New York at the Eighth Annual Benjamin N. Cardozo Lectures, expressed this concept when he said:

A judge looking at a constitutional decision may have compulsions to revere past history and accept what was once written. But he remembers above all else that it is the Constitution which he swore to support and defend, not the gloss which his predecessors may have put on it. So he comes to formulate his own views, rejecting some earlier ones as false and embracing others. He cannot do otherwise unless he lets men long dead and unaware of the problems of the age in which he lives do his thinking for him.

This reexamination of precedent in constitutional law is a personal matter for each judge who comes along. When only one new judge is appointed during a short period, the unsettling effect in constitutional law may not be great. But when a majority of a Court is suddenly reconstituted, there is likely to be substantial unsettlement. There will be unsettlement until the new judges have taken their positions on constitutional doctrine. During that time—which may extend a decade or more—constitutional law will be in flux. That is the necessary consequence of our system and to my mind a healthy one. The alternative is to let the Constitution freeze in the pattern which one generation gave it. But the Constitution was designed for the vicissitudes of time. It must never become a code which carries the overtones of one period that may be hostile to another.

So far as constitutional law is concerned *stare decisis* must give way before the dynamic component of history. Once it does, the cycle starts again. Today's new and startling decision quickly becomes a coveted anchorage for new vested interests. The former proponents of change acquire an acute conservatism in their new *status quo*. It will then take an oncoming group from a new generation to catch the broader vision which may require an undoing of the work of our present and their past. . . .

From age to age the problem of constitutional adjudication is the same. It is to keep the power of government unrestrained by the social or economic theories that one set of judges may entertain. It is to keep one age unfettered by the fears or limited vision of another. There is in that connection one tenet of faith which has crystallized more and more as a result of our long experience as a nation. It is this: If the social and economic problems of state and nation can be kept under political management of the people, there is likely to be long-run stability. It is when a judiciary with life tenure seeks to write its social and economic creed into the Charter that instability is created. For then the nation lacks the adaptability to master the sudden storms of an era. It must be remembered that the process of constitutional amendment is a long and slow one.

That philosophy is reflected in what Thomas Jefferson wrote about the Constitution, "Some men look at constitutions with sanctimonious reverence, and deem them like the ark of the covenant, too sacred to be touched. They ascribe to the men of the preceding age a wisdom more than human, and suppose what they did to be beyond amendment. I knew that age well; I belonged to it, and labored with it. It deserved well of its country. It was very like the present, but without the experience of the present; and forty years of experience in government is worth a century of book-reading; and this they would say themselves, were they to rise from the dead."

Jefferson's words are *a fortiori* germane to the fashioning of constitutional law and to the lesser lawmaking in which the judiciary necessarily indulges.

Because we have adopted the English common-law system, it is significant to us that the House of Lords, Britain's court of last resort, announced a few years ago that it was abandoning "the binding force of precedent" in some circumstances in order to make English law more modern and flexible. The impact of the action, however, was lessened somewhat by virtue of the fact that, while the House of Lords exempted itself from the legal principles of previous similar cases, the rule of precedent is still binding on Britain's other courts. In discussing precedent, a member of the House of Lords is reported to have said:

> the use of precedent is an indispensable foundation upon which to decide what is the law and its application to individual cases . . . their lordships nevertheless recognize that too rigid adherence to precedent may lead to injustice in a particular case and unduly restrict the proper development of the law.
>
> They propose, therefore, to modify their present practice and, while treating former decisions of this house as normally binding, to depart from a previous decision when it appears right to do so. . . .

He also said that modernization was a major aim, especially in cases where the Lords must "consider that the earlier decision was influenced by the existence of conditions which no longer prevail, and that in modern conditions the law ought to be different." Thus, rigid adherence to precedent is no longer deemed necessary nor desirable in both the founding and adopting country.

1-21. Conflict of Laws.   Certain basic facts about our legal system must be recognized. First of all, statutes and precedents, in all legal areas, vary from state to state. For example, in most states the plaintiff in an automobile accident case must be completely free of fault in order to recover judgment, but in some states the doctrine of comparative negligence is used so that a plaintiff found to be 20 percent at fault could recover 80 percent of his injuries. Secondly, the doctrine of *stare decisis* does not require that one state recognize the precedent or rules of law of other states. Each state is free to decide for itself questions concerning its common law and interpretation of its own constitution and statutes. (However, courts will often follow decisions of other states if they are found to be sound. They are considered persuasive authority. This is particularly true in cases involving the construction of statutes such as the uniform acts, where each state has adopted the same statute.) Thirdly, many legal issues arise out of acts or transactions that have contact with more than one state. For example, a contract may be executed in one state, performed in another, and the parties may live in still others; or an automobile accident may occur in one state involving citizens of different states.

These three basic facts raise the following fundamental question: Which state's *substantive* laws are applicable in a multiple state case where the law in one of the states differs from the law in the other? (The court in which the case is tried uses its own rules of procedure.)

The body of law known as conflict of laws answers this question. It provides the court or forum with the applicable substantive law in the multistate transaction or occurrence. For example, the law applicable to a tort is generally said to be the law of the state of place of injury. Thus, a court sitting in state X would follow its own rules of procedure, but it would use the tort law of state Y if the injury occured in Y. There are several rules which are used by courts on issues involving the law of contracts.[4] These include the law of the state where the contract was made; the law of the place of performance; and the "grouping of contacts" or "center of gravity" theory, which uses the law of the state with the most substantial contact with the contract.

[4] Sperry Rand Corporation v. Industrial Supply Corporation, page 51

It is not the purpose of this text to teach conflict of laws, but the student should be aware that such a body of law exists and should recognize those situations in which conflict of law principles will be used. The trend toward uniform statutes and codes has tended to decrease these conflicts, but many of them still exist. So long as we have a federal system and fifty separate state bodies of substantive law, the area of conflicts of law will continue to be of substantial importance in the application of the doctrine of *stare decisis.*

Our dual system of federal and state courts creates a unique problem in "conflicts." The federal courts use their own body of procedural law and their own body of substantive law on questions arising under the federal Constitution, codes, statutes, or treaties. Decisions of the United States Supreme Court on questions involving the U.S. Constitution, treaties, federal statutes, and matters of interstate commerce are binding on state courts. Federal courts also have jurisdiction of cases involving citizens of different states under the Constitution, even though no federal question is at issue. The jurisdiction of federal courts is discussed more fully in Chapter 4, Section 1-27, but it must be noted here that there is no body of federal common law and that in suits based on diversity of citizenship, to determine the rights and duties of the parties, federal courts use the substantive law, including conflict of laws principles, of the state in which they are sitting. As in all cases, the federal courts do use their own rules of procedure, however. Thus, just as the state courts are bound by federal precedent in cases involving federal law and federally protected rights, so also are federal courts bound by state precedent in others.

One further aspect of the scope of precedent must be noted. Article IV, Section 1 of the United States Constitution provides: "Full Faith and Credit shall be given in each State to the Public Acts, Records, and judicial Proceedings of every other State. . . . " This does not mean that the precedent in one state is binding in other states, but only that the final decisions or judgments rendered in any given state by a court with jurisdiction shall be enforced as between the original parties in other states. "Full Faith and Credit" is applicable to the result of a specific decision as it affects the rights of the parties, and not to the reasons or principles upon which it was based.

1-22. The Nature of the Judicial Process.   In this chapter we have examined the great powers of the judiciary in our society which result from the doctrine of judicial review, from the role of courts in interpreting and applying statutes, and from the very nature of the concept of *stare decisis.* We now turn to an examination of the processes by which these powers are exercised. Recognizing that a court may declare a law unconstitutional, when and why will it do so? Why does a court announce one rule of law or follow one precedent rather than another? What type of reasoning is used by courts? What factors influence the courts in their decisions? Of course, no absolute answers can be given to these questions, but a consideration of them is essential to an understanding of the legal process and is, accordingly, the subject of this section.

The judicial system has a rather obvious priority of sources. Constitutions prevail over statutes, and statutes prevail over case law. Precedent would prevail over dicta and dicta would usually be persuasive over mere argument. However, it should be acknowledged that, in spite of our almost two hundred years as a nation, there are many legal issues that are not directly covered by a statute or case precedent. Litigation is frequently brought to challenge the validity of a statute or to seek to change a precedent that does exist. Frequently the decided cases are in conflict, or the case involves issues of conflicting social policies.

Thus, the law is not a system of known rules. When many legal issues are presented to a court, the law applicable to those issues is made and not merely found by the court in some statute or case. In the sense that the law is made and not found, the role of the courts is legislative in character. When the applicable law is not known or clearly established, the court must examine the rationale, or *ratio decidendi,* of existing statutes and cases and then extend or contract this *"ratio"* in deciding the case before it.

In describing *The Nature of the Judicial Process,*[5] Justice Cardozo indicated that there are four forces which influence judges in the application of the *ratio decidendi.* These are logic, history, custom, and utility. The use of logic or analogy has been evident in our common-law system and is ordinarily considered to be the chief method employed by courts. Using logic satisfies our desire for certainty and predictability in the law. History and custom have past. . . . major role in the development of business law. Throughout this text, there will be references to the historical development of various concepts and statutes; it should be noted that statutory changes in the law frequently come about because of the customary practices of businessmen. It is interesting to *speculate,* for example, whether checks not containing a signature might someday be legal.

The fourth element, "utility," refers to the elements of justice, morals, and social welfare. This factor, which Cardozo called the method of sociology, has become the major influence in many areas of the law in recent years. As public policy considerations have played an ever-increasing role in the development of our law, utility can be recognized as the dominant influence in such areas as civil rights, reapportionment, and antitrust actions.

The forces discussed by Cardozo can also be seen in the various kinds of reasoning used by courts in determining a rule of law or its applicability. For example, a court may base its determination upon the literal meaning of words appearing in the rule, upon the purpose of the rule, upon similarities between the facts of the case to be decided and the facts of decided cases, or upon considerations of social policy. Thus, reasoning may be literal, purposive, precedent-oriented, or policy-oriented. Adherents of the different schools of jurisprudence discussed in Chapter 1 may be identified in terms of which of these approaches to judicial decision they emphasize or prefer. Thus, members of the historical school would emphasize precedent-oriented analysis. Some analytical legal scholars would emphasize the literal approach. Adherents of sociological and natural law jurisprudence would prefer the purposive and policy-oriented approaches.

Few principles are more firmly established in Anglo-American law than the principle of *stare decisis.* Accordingly, many judicial decisions are precedent oriented, and in nearly every case, lawyers and judges expend considerable time and energy analyzing and discussing similarities and differences between the facts of decided cases and the facts of the case to be decided.

[5] New Haven, Conn.: Yale University Press, 1921.

The great mass of cases are decided within the confines of *stare decisis.* Yet there is a steady evolution, for it is not quite true that there is nothing new under the sun; rarely is a case identical with the one that went before. Courts have a creative job to do when they find that a rule has lost its touch with reality and should be abandoned or reformulated to meet new conditions and new moral values. And in those cases where there is no *stare decisis* to cast its light or shadow, the court must hammer out new rules that will respect whatever values of the past have survived the tests of reason and experience and anticipate what contemporary values will best meet the tests. The task is not easy—human relations are infinitely complex, and subtlety and depth of spirit must enter into their regluation. Often legal problems elude final solution and courts then can do more than find what Cardozo called the least erroneous answer to insoluble problems. (Traynor, Judge, 2 Univ. of Ill. *Law Forum* 232, 1956)

Policy considerations influence the decision of many cases. Such considerations often influence a court to apply or refuse to apply an existing rule, and are usually of paramount significance in those relatively infrequent cases in which a court is called upon to resolve problems not heretofore adjudicated by that court. Policy-oriented reasoning may be illustrated as follows: *P* claimed damages for harm to an eye due allegedly to *D*'s negligent failure to place safety guards over a grindstone. Immediately after the harm to *P* occurred, *D* placed safety guards over the grindstone. At the trial, *P* sought to introduce evidence of *D*'s action for the purpose of showing that *D* had, by placing the guards over the grindstone, admitted that he had been careless. *D* objected to the admission of this evidence, but the court overruled his objection, and the jury rendered a verdict for *P.* On appeal, the appellate court decided that admission of this type of evidence was error. The court stated that there was a strong policy to encourage employers to establish and maintain optimum safety conditions at all times. The admission of the proffered evidence would frustrate this policy because an employer would, after an accident, hesitate to improve safety conditions for fear that this might be used against him in a lawsuit by the injured employee.

The literal, the purposive, the precedent-oriented, and the policy-oriented approaches to determining the application of legal rules may each influence the decision of a particular case. Sometimes these approaches point in different directions, and a choice between conflicting policies is often required. For example, cases in which one party claims that another has infringed a trademark usually pose a conflict between the policy of protecting an established property right and the policy of fostering competition. The illustrations could be multiplied by citing numerous cases in which the courts carefully weigh all factors in determining which approach is to be decisive.

Occasionally, a case arises presenting issues that have been decided differently by different courts. The court must then choose between conflicting precedents. This choice is frequently made primarily on the basis of an evaluation of the policy considerations supporting each precedent. Often, courts also consider other factors, such as the standing of the tribunals which decided the conflicting precedents.

When reading assigned cases, the student should attempt to analyze the court's reasoning in terms of the discussion in this section. The student will thereby enhance his comprehension of the cases and also improve his own reasoning powers.

SOURCES OF LAW CASES

Zschernig v. Miller
88 S.Ct. 664 (1968)

The Oregon law of descent and distribution prohibited nonresident aliens from inheriting property unless Oregon residents were allowed to inherit property by the government of the foreign country in which the heir resided and unless this reciprocal right of inheritance included a provision prohibiting confiscation of inherited property by the foreign government. Failure of an heir to meet these conditions would result in the property passing, or escheating, to the State of Oregon. A citizen of Oregon who owned both real and personal property in that state died without leaving a will. His next of kin and only heirs resided in East Germany. The Oregon courts held that the heirs were not entitled to inherit the property because of their failure to prove that it would not be confiscated by Communist East Germany.

DOUGLAS, J. . . . [W]e conclude that the history and operation of this Oregon statute make clear that [it] is an intrusion by the State into the field of foreign affairs which the Constitution entrusts to the President and the Congress.

. . . State courts, of course, must frequently read, construe, and apply laws of foreign nations. It has never been seriously suggested that state courts are precluded from performing that function, although there is a possibility, albeit remote, that any holding may disturb a foreign nation—whether the matter involves commercial cases, tort cases, or some other type of controversy. . . . It now appears that in this reciprocity area under inheritance statutes, the probate courts of various States have launched inquiries into the type of governments that obtain in a particular foreign nation—whether aliens under their law have enforceable rights, whether the so-called "rights" are merely dispensations turning upon the whim or caprice of government officials, whether the representation of consuls, ambassadors, and other representatives of foreign nations are credible or made in good faith, whether there is in the actual administration in the particular foreign system of law any element of confiscation.

. . . As we read the decisions . . . , we find that they radiate some of the attitudes of the "cold war," where the search is for the "democracy quotient" of a foreign regime as opposed to the Marxist theory. The Oregon statute introduces the concept of "confiscation," which is of course opposed to the Just Compensation Clause of the Fifth Amendment. And this has led into minute inquiries concerning the actual administration of foreign law, into the credibility of foreign diplomatic statements, and into speculation whether the fact that some received delivery of funds should "not preclude wonderment as to how many may have been denied 'the right to receive' . . . . "

As one reads the Oregon decisions, it seems that foreign policy attitudes, the freezing or thawing of the "cold war" and the like are the real desiderata. Yet they of course are matters for the Federal Government, not for local probate courts. . . . [The Oregon court has] held that not only must the foreign law give inheritance rights to Americans, but the political body making the law must have "membership in the family of nations," because the purpose of the Oregon provision was to serve as "an inducement to foreign nations to so frame the inheritance laws of their respective countries in a manner which would insure to Oregonians the same opportunities to inherit and take personal property abroad that they enjoy in the State of Oregon." . . .

In short, it would seem that Oregon judges . . . seek to ascertain whether "rights" protected by foreign law are the same "rights" that citizens of Oregon enjoy. If, . . . the alleged foreign "right" may be vindicated only through Communist-controlled state agencies, then there is no "right" of the type require[d]. . . .

It seems inescapable that the type of probate law that Oregon enforces affects international relations in a persistent and subtle way. The practice of state courts in withholding remittances to legatees residing in Communist countries or in preventing them from assigning them is notorious. The several States, of course, have traditionally regulated the descent and distribution of estates. But those regulations must give way if they impair the effective exercise of the Nation's foreign policy. Where those laws conflict with a treaty, they must bow to the superior federal policy. "Experience has shown that international controversies of the gravest moment, sometimes even leading to war, may arise from real or imagined wrongs to another's subjects inflicted, or permitted, by a government." Certainly a State could not deny admission to a traveler from East Germany nor bar its citizens from going there. If there are to be such restraints, they must be provided by the Federal Government. The present Oregon law is not as gross an intrusion in the federal domain as those others might be. Yet, as we have said, it has a direct impact upon foreign relations and may well adversely affect the power of the central government to deal with those problems.

The Oregon law does, indeed, illustrate the dangers which are involved if each State, speaking through its probate courts, is permitted to establish its own foreign policy.

Reversed.

Director of Division of Milk Control v. Haseotes

220 N.E.2d 910 (Mass.) 1966

Plaintiff, the Director of the Division of Milk Control, brought suit to enjoin the defendants from giving away milk. A statute prohibited the sale of milk at a price less than the cost of the milk. Cost was defined to include both direct and indirect costs, including physical handling. The defendant contended that the law was not applicable because the milk was given away as part of a promotion campaign.

REARDON, J. . . . The defendants are in the business of selling milk and other dairy products and grocery items in retail stores which they own and operate under the name "Cumberland Farms" throughout the Commonwealth and in other New England States. In May, 1964, and May, 1965, Cumberland Farms held "seventh and eighth anniversary celebrations," at which times they had "a 'contest' or 'drawing' at each of their stores, where any person could fill out a 'contest entry form' (without making any purchase)." At the conclusion of the ten day contests, one name was drawn from among the contestants at each of the stores and "lucky winners" thereafter received a half gallon of milk every other day for a year. Four hundred quarts of milk a day were thus given away by the Cumberland Farms stores. Approximately 2,300,000 quarts of milk are sold to the consuming public daily in Massachusetts. . . .

The plaintiff contends that the activities of the defendants described above are prohibited by the statute in that the legislative history discloses "that all milk sold or offered or exposed for sale, or any service rendered in connection with milk, was under the regulation and control of the [milk control] Board or the Commission," and that since the act prohibits the sale of milk below cost it must necessarily follow that it likewise prohibits the giving away of milk.

As the trial judge pointed out, the statute which is the basis of the petition is a criminal statute and as such is to be strictly construed. . . . The statute prohibits the "sale" or rendering of "any service in connection with the sale or distribution of milk, at a price less than the cost of such milk or service. . . ." It does not expressly prohibit any person from giving away milk. Since the statute is criminal in nature, it "is not to be enlarged to comprehend matters beyond its plain import."

This construction limiting § 14(d) to the "sale" of milk is consistent with the purpose of statutes such as the milk control law which seek to prevent unbridled competition from destroying the wholesale price structure on which the farmer depends for his livelihood and the community for an assured supply of milk. It has not been shown that this promotional sales scheme is violative of the legislative intent to protect the farmer and the public. The judge took the view that the Legislature, foreseeing the problems inherent in any attempt to forbid the giving away of milk, carefully limited the scope of § 14(d) to the "sale" of milk, or services rendered in conjunction therewith, for a price less than cost.

We are in agreement with his conclusion. The defendants have employed a competitive device which is not clearly barred by the statute. It may be that an abuse of this device or others similar to it may at some point conflict with the provisions of the milk control act. Such abuse may be dealt with at the appropriate time. In the circumstances above set forth the order must be

Decree affirmed.

Mettee v. Boone

247 A.2d 390 (Md.) 1968

Mettee, a property owner, brought suit against a contractor to recover damages for breach of contract. The contract was for construction of a house, and the suit arose because the water pipes installed by the defendant leaked. The contract was signed September 3, 1959. The leaks occurred in October, 1965, and suit was brought May 17, 1967. The Court held that the statute of limitations had run out and entered a judgment for the defendant. Six weeks later plaintiff filed another suit on the same facts, but alleging negligence in the construction of the house as well as a breach of warranty. Defendant claimed that the suit was barred by the doctrine of *res judicata*.

MCWILLIAMS, J. . . . In *Alvey* v. *Alvey,* 225 Md. 386, 389-390, 171 A.2d 92, 93-94 (1961), Judge Marbury, for the Court, said:

> Here the appellant seeks to litigate an issue which he could have litigated in the first case. . . . [E]nlightened hindsight must give way to a higher principle based on the protection and security of rights, and the preservation of the repose of society.

> .   .   .

> The appellant uses the same facts as in the first case but only seeks different conclusions. . . .

Judge Marbury concluded his opinion with a quotation from *Henderson* v. *Henderson,* 3 Hare 115, which is peculiarly applicable to the case at bar and which is worth repeating:

> In trying this question, I believe I state the rule of the Court correctly that where a given matter becomes the subject of litigation in, and of adjudication by, a Court of competent jurisdiction, the Court requires the parties to bring forward their whole case, and will not, except under special circumstances, permit the same parties to open the same subject of litigation in respect of a matter which might have been brought forward as a part of the subject in contest, but which was not brought forward only because they have from negligence, inadvertence, or even accident, omitted a part of their case. The plea of *res judicata* applies, except in special cases, not only to the points upon which the Court was required by the parties to form an opinion and pronounce a judgment, but to every point which properly belong to the subject of litigation, and which the parties, exercising reasonable diligence might have brought forward at the time.

Just as the embittered French Legionnaire who described a camel as a horse designed by a committee knew perfectly well that it was still a camel, Mettee should have known that the same facts, having once been used, without success, in pursuit of one conclusion, cannot, under another label, still be used to obtain a different conclusion. We see no reason for disturbing the judgments entered by Judge Weant.

Affirmed.

Sperry Rand Corporation v. Industrial Supply Corporation

337 F.2d 363 (1964)

The Industrial Supply Corporation sued Sperry Rand Corporation to cancel a contract whereby it had agreed to purchase a certain business record system and to recover damage for breach of an implied warranty concerning the system. Sperry Rand is a Delaware corporation, with its principal place of business in New York. The plaintiff is a Florida corporation, with its principal place of business in Florida. The contract involved in the litigation was signed in New York. The action was brought in a federal district court, with jurisdiction based on diversity of citizenship.

JONES, J. . . . Our first concern is to decide what law governs. . . . We are in accord with the view of the district court that the law of Florida, as the law of the forum, determines the applicable conflicts of law rules. The district court

stated that "under Florida law the interpretation of the contract of sale between the parties and the applicable law of sales is determined by the law of
the place" of contracting, that is, by the law of the State of New York. The
Supreme Court has stated, as the general conflicts rule pertaining to contracts,
that matters bearing upon the execution, interpretation and validity of a contract are determined by the law of the place where it is made; matters connected with its performance are regulated by the law prevailing at the place
of performance; and matters respecting the remedy depend upon the law of the
place where the suit is brought. This statement of principle has been approved
by Florida courts.

These rules, however, are not decisive of the conflicts question here presented. An implied warranty, the basis for the relief here granted, is an incident
of the sale. It arises apart from and independent of the contract of sale from
the nature of the transaction and the situation of the parties. While the implied
warranty arises independently, nevertheless, as a warranty, it is a contractual
right. Although there may be an express contractual disclaimer of any implied
warranty, and a warranty is not to be implied where inconsistent with a valid
contractual provision, we think our tenet of conflict of laws must be that which
governs sales, rather than the general rules applicable in contract situations.
Professor Ehrenzweig has said:

> The scope of the parties' obligations at the time of the alleged breach or discharge
> may be affected by events subsequent to the conclusion of the contract. Conflicts
> questions have perhaps arisen most frequently concerning damages for alleged
> breaches of implied warranties. To treat such warranties as a part of the parties'
> original obligations, is a fiction perhaps innocuous for the domestic law of contracts.
> But it would be most unfortunate to give reality to this fiction in the law of conflict
> of laws by subjecting to the 'law of the contract' the question whether a seller is
> liable for defective goods by virtue of an implied warranty of fitness. (Ehrenzweig
> on *Conflict of Laws*, 497, § 187)

The only decision of a Florida court which has come to our attention involving
a question as to the law applicable in an action on an implied warranty is
Farris & Co. v. *William Schluderberg, etc. Co.*, 141 Fla. 462. A Florida
vendor agreed by a contract executed in Maryland to sell and deliver in
Maryland meat to be shipped from Florida. The place of contracting and the
place of performance were the same. The court held that the contract was "a
Maryland one, governed by the law of that State." There is no indication
whether the court regarded the law of the place of contracting or the law of
the place of performance as providing the substantive rules for decision. In
Pennsylvania the law of the place of performance would govern. Such is also
the rule of Delaware. The same doctrine is said to apply in Ohio. In New York
the newly developed center of gravity theory would be applicable.

The modern text writers seem to favor the application of the law of the situs
of the property at the time of the sale. The Reporter for the American Law
Institute proposes to adopt new language covering contracts to sell interests
in chattels and injects a new term, the place where the seller is "to surrender"
the chattel, which would fix the governing law unless the center of gravity
doctrine requires another law to be applied. However, no change is proposed
in the rule that questions arising from a sale, as distinguished from a contract

to sell, are to be governed by the law of the situs. In *Florida Jurisprudence* it is said, "It is stated generally that every state has the right to regulate the transfer of property within its limits and that the law of the situs in general controls the transfer of personalty."

But whether the applicable substantive law is that of the situs, the place of performance or the center of gravity is immaterial, as the law of Florida would be selected by any of these conflict of laws principles. The district court was of the opinion that the law of New York, the law of the place of contracting, controlled. The court followed the conflicts rule for ascertaining the substantive law in determining validity of and in construing contracts generally. We think the district court was in error in its choice of the applicable law, but it does not, of course, follow that its judgment was wrong.

The Court then went on to discuss the Florida law and concluded that by using Florida law the result would be the same and affirmed the decision.

CHAPTER 3
REVIEW QUESTIONS AND PROBLEMS

1. The term "common law" is used to describe two different concepts. Discuss these concepts.
2. What is the status of a treaty in our judicial system?
3. What is the basic distinction between the approach of the federal Constitution and the approach of the various state constitutions?
4. What is the significance of the doctrine of separation of powers?
5. Did the Constitution make the judiciary the overseer of our government? Explain.
6. Why do we have rules of statutory construction?
7. List five rules of statutory construction.
8. Insofar as business is concerned, what is the most significant uniform law?
9. What is the difference in meaning between *stare decisis* and *res judicata?*
10. What are some of the defects in our common-law system?
11. Contrast the application of the doctrine of *stare decisis* in the public area of the law with that in the private area.
12. What is the function of the body of law known as conflict of laws?
13. What is meant by the term "Full Faith and Credit? "
14. What are the four forces which Cardozo said shaped the law?

The Judicial
System

1-23. The Function of Courts. It is essential for the functioning of an ordered society that institutions for resolving conflicts be established and maintained. Our system of government has selected courts for this purpose. The word "court" is derived from the word *cors* of Latin origin, meaning an open space near the king's palace, where disputants came to have their differences adjudicated either by the king himself or his representatives.

Courts settle controversies between persons, and between persons and the state. The court is the judge and the judge is the court. The terms are used interchangeably. In civilized communities controversies are settled by the orderly process of adjudication rather than by the use of force.

The rule of law applied by the court to the facts, as found by the jury or court, produces a decision which settles the controversy. While there are obviously other agencies of government which resolve controversies, it is peculiar to our system that for final decision all controversies must ultimately end up in court.

Organized society has other decision-making institutions besides courts. The democratic process permits decision-making procedures through the ballot box, executive orders, and legislation. The following are illustrations of economic, political, and social issues for which the solutions are usually made by the legislative and executive processes rather than the judicial: What shall be the policy of the United States toward China and Vietnam? What kind of tax laws shall be adopted? Shall Town *B* issue bonds to build a new City Hall? What is the responsibility of government for public welfare, schools, transportation, safety of automobiles, pollution of water and air, water, power, price regulation, safety, labor, housing, civil liberties, and a host of other social problems?

Such issues are general or universal and may be either transitory or continuous. Whether they get solved does not necessarily threaten the existence or impede the continued activity of society. For example, Town *B* will continue even though it does not immediately acquire a new City Hall. An immediate answer is not an absolute necessity. Such problems are the concern of all the people, though they may be of more concern to one individual than to another. What answers shall be given to such questions is primarily the responsibility of the representatives of the people by the legislative process.

If a conflict between individuals or between an individual and the state arises and continues to the injury of a person or his property, a particular personal controversy is present. If the injured person or state seeks relief through the court, the court is required to make a decision. A decision *must* be made. The court may give the plaintiff relief or it may not—in either case a decision has been made.

Whether Town *B* shall have a new City Hall is an important question, but not an urgent one. But if a citizen alleges the election by which the decision to build the City Hall was improperly conducted and by proper procedure presents the question to the court, a judicial problem is presented which requires an immediate answer. If the election was not held in compliance with the election statutes, the decision to have a new City Hall is illegal and void. To impose taxes upon the plaintiff's property by an unlawful election would be taking his property without due process of law. The question of whether a valid election has been held becomes a particular personal problem. It is a justiciable issue for the court. If the court decides the election was unlawfully conducted, the authority to tax and build the City Hall is not granted, thus a particular personal problem has been solved. The court by a predetermined judicial process conducted in compliance with procedural rules has adjudicated the issue of the legality of the election. A specific question has been answered. The judgment of the court has resolved the question. The result— the judgment has references to the past. What was done by way of the election has gone for naught. This finality of a solution is different from a solution made by the legislative process. Passing an ordinance authorizing the proper officers to issue bonds and build the City Hall pertains to affirmative action in the future. Legislation is law making which is universal in its application and a guide to the future, while adjudication is the interpretation and application of law, retrospective in character, which determines a particular issue.

A dramatic illustration of a general social situation which has raised particular personal problems is in the area of civil rights. Discrimination by reason of race has been a general social problem for years. When a particular citizen alleges he has been denied his constitutional rights, either by local law or illegal conduct by others, and for relief presents his cause to the court, a particular issue is raised which the court must decide. A favorable decision, although particular for the plaintiff, redounds to the benefit of all other persons in a similar situation. Past conduct has been determined to be illegal, and past and present rights are restored.

A distinction between issues, controversies, and problems that are general, and for solution have relevance to the executive and legislative branches of the government, and those that are personal and particular and are issues for the courts, are not always as clearly defined as those illustrated above. For example, Congress may pass special appropriations giving relief to particular individuals or groups; or, special legislation may be enacted endowing a particular person with special privileges such as honorary citizenship, or an alien with the right of residence . A court, in adjudicating a bankrupt business, by decree may enter an order which not only affects the particular parties to the litigation but the future of a large number of other persons, his creditors. Likewise, the adjudication of constitutional questions, such as the legality of the use of free textbooks for children in private schools, although limited in its particular application to the parties to the action will nevertheless be an authoritative guide for all school officials.

1-24. Courts and Change.   Many people have the mistaken notion that the law is a set of known rules applied by a judge. To them the problem is simple. If the judge does not know the law on a particular subject, he need only look it up in one of hundreds of books in his library. This is definitely not so, especially in the area of constitutional law. Law in all areas is frequently made and not found. It is also changed from time to time to meet changing conditions as was discussed in Chapter 3. Thus courts are an instrument of social, political, and economic change. The law changes as it is applied to new cases. It may expand or contract its application or take off in a new direction, but it is seldom static. Whole new legal principles that change society may also be created by courts.

Courts at different times play different roles in bringing about changes in our society. Some judges and courts adopt what is usually described as the philosophy of "judicial restraint." This philosophy admonishes courts to change only those rules of law which they must change and to decide only those matters which they must decide. According to this view, change for the most part should be left to the political processes and to the legislative and executive branches which are responsive to the political process. Justice Franfurter in *Youngstown Sheet and Tube Co.* v. *Sawyer* (343 U.S. 579) summarized this philosophy when he said:

> The Framers [of the Constitution], however, did not make the judiciary the overseer of our government. They were familiar with the revisory functions entrusted to judges in a few of the states and refused to lodge such powers in this Court. Judicial power can be exercised only as to matters that were the traditional concern of the courts at Westminister, and only if they arise in ways that to the expert feel of lawyers constitute "Cases" or "Controversies." Even as to questions that were the staple of judicial business it is not for the courts to pass upon them unless they are indispensably involved in a conventional litigation—and then, only to the extent that they are so involved. Rigorous adherence to the narrow scope of the judicial function is especially demanded in controversies that arouse appeals to the Constitution. The attitude with which this Court must approach its duty when confronted with such issues is precisely the opposite of that normally manifested by the general public. So-called constitutional questions seem to exercise a mesmeric influence over the popular mind. This eagerness to settle—preferably forever—a specific problem on the basis of the broadest possible constitutional pronouncements may not unfairly be called one of our minor national traits. . . .
>
> The pole-star for constitutional adjudications is John Marshall's greatest judicial utterance that "it is a *constitution* we are expounding." That requires both a spacious view in applying an instrument of government "made for an undefined and expanding future" and as narrow a delimitation of the constitutional issues as the

circumstances permit. Not the least characteristic of great statesmanship which the Framers manifested was the extent to which they did not attempt to bind the future. It is no less incumbent upon this Court to avoid putting fetters upon the future by needless pronouncements today.

The other philosophy of many courts and judges has been often referred to as the "activist" philosophy. According to activist judges, the political processes and the other branches of government may either fail to bring about necessary changes in society or may do so too slowly. They view the law and the courts as being leaders of social, political and economic change. To them, the Constitution must be interpreted in the light of the times and our experience as a people and not merely by what was said. Some scholars have called this belief that the Constitution is a relative document, the sociological approach to constitutional decisions. According to the activist view, the law is not as concerned with what the Founding Fathers intended when they wrote the Constitution as with what they would have intended had they known of contemporary problems. This view of the court's role as an instrument of social change and of the Constitution as a relative document was graphically illustrated in the school desegration case of *Brown* v. *Board of Education,* 347 U.S. 497 (1954) in which Chief Justice Warren said in part while discussing the meaning of the Fourteenth Amendment to the United States Constitution:

> In approaching this problem, we cannot turn the clock back to 1868 when the Amendment was adopted, or even to 1896 when *Plessy* v. *Ferguson* was written. We must consider public education in the light of its full development and its present place in American life throughout the Nation. Only in this way can it be determined if segregation in public schools deprives these plaintiffs of the equal protection of the laws.
>
> Today, education is perhaps the most important function of state and local governments. Compulsory school attendance laws and the great expenditures for education both demonstrate our recognition of the importance of education to our democratic society. It is required in the performance of our most basic public responsibilities, even service in the armed forces. It is the very foundation of good citizenship. Today it is a principal instrument in awakening the child to cultural values, in preparing him for later professional training, and in helping him to adjust normally to his environment. In these days, it is doubtful that any child may reasonably be expected to succeed in life if he is denied the opportunity of an education. Such an opportunity, where the state has undertaken to provide it, is a right which must be made available to all on equal terms.
>
> We come then to the question presented: Does segregation of children in public schools solely on the basis of race, even though the physical facilities and other "tangible" factors may be equal, deprive the children of the minority group of equal educational opportunities? We believe that it does.

Thus in a single decision, the court was able to change the course of history and alter our social life.

Throughout our history, the Supreme Court has at least to some degree followed the activist theory. Some Supreme Courts have been more activist than others. The era of the Warren court from 1954 to 1969 was generally known for its activist majority, while the Supreme Courts of the early thirties were generally labeled as conservative or judicial restraint oriented. The extent to which the Court is an instrument of change will vary from time to time depending upon the makeup of the Court. However, the Court will always be an instrument of change to some degree.

1-25. State Court Systems.   The judicial system of the United States is a dual system consisting of state courts and federal courts. The courts of the states, although not subject to uniform classification, may be grouped as follows: supreme courts, intermediate courts of appeal (in the more populous states) and trial courts. Some trial courts have general jurisdiction while others have a limited jurisdiction. For example, a justice of the peace has power to hear civil and criminal cases only if the amount in controversy does not exceed a certain sum or the penalty for the crime is restricted.

Law suits are instituted in one of the trial courts. Even a court of general jurisdiction has geographical limitations. In many states the trial court of general jurisdiction is called a circuit court because in early times a single judge sitting as a court traveled the circuit from one county to another. In other states it is called the Superior Court or the District Court. Each area has a trial court of general jurisdiction.

Each state also has courts of limited jurisdiction. They may be limited as to subject matter, amount in controversy, or as to the area in which the parties live. For example, courts with jurisdiction limited to a city are often called municipal courts.

Courts may also be named according to the subject matter with which they deal. Probate courts deal with wills and the estates of deceased persons; family courts, with divorces, family relations, juveniles, and dependent children; criminal and police courts with violators of state laws and municipal ordinances; and traffic courts with traffic violations. For an accurate classification of the courts of any state, the statutes of that state should be examined. The chart on page 59 illustrates the jurisdiction and organization of reviewing and trial courts in a typical state.

1-26. The Federal Court System.   The courts of the United States are created by Congress under the authority of the Constitution, and their jurisdiction is limited by the grant of power given to the federal government by the states by the Constitution. They are thus courts of limited jurisdiction as will be discussed more fully later. The Constitution creates the Supreme Court and authorizes such inferior courts as the Congress may from time to time ordain and establish. Congress pursuant to this authority has created eleven United States courts of appeal, the United States district courts (at least one in each state), and others such as the Court of Customs and Patent Appeals, the Court of Claims, and the Tax Court which handle special subject matter as indicated by the name of the court. The chart on page 60 illustrates the federal court system.

The district courts are the trial courts of the federal judicial system. They have original jurisdiction, exclusive of the courts of the states, over all federal crimes, i.e., all offenses against the laws of the United States. The accused is entitled to a trial by a jury in the state and district where the crime was committed. The same facts may constitute a crime against both state and federal authority. For example, robbery of a bank is a crime against both sovereigns. The robber may be tried by both the federal and state courts.

A TYPICAL
STATE JUDICIAL SYSTEM

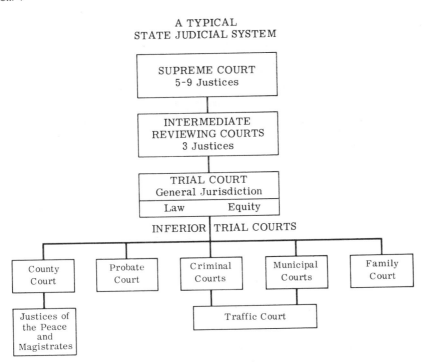

In civil actions the district courts have jurisdiction only when the matter in controversy exceeds the sum or value of $10,000, exclusive of costs and interest, and is based on either diversity of citizenship or a federal question. Diversity of citizenship exists in suits between (1) citizens of different states, (2) a citizen of a state and a citizen of a foreign country, and (3) a state and citizens of another state. The plaintiff or all plaintiffs, if more than one, must be citizens of a different state than any one of the defendants for diversity of citizenship to exist. Diversity of citizenship does not prevent the plaintiff from bringing his suit in a state court, but if the defendant is a citizen of another state, the defendant has the right to have the case removed to a federal court. A defendant, by having the case removed to the federal court, has an opportunity of having a jury selected from a larger area than the county where the cause arose, thus hopefully avoiding the possibility of jurors prejudicial to the plaintiff.

For the purpose of suit in a federal court, a corporation is considered a "citizen" of the state where it is incorporated and of the state in which it has its principal place of business. As a result, there is no federal jurisdiction in many cases in which one of the parties is a corporation. If any one of the parties on the other side of the case is a citizen either of the state in which the corporation is chartered or is doing its principal business, there is no diversity of citizenship and thus no federal jurisdiction.

Federal jurisdiction based on a federal question also exists if the controversy involves more than $10,000 and if the lawsuit arises out of rights granted by the Constitution, laws, or treaties of the United States. The district courts also have jurisdiction of cases arising under the Constitution or federal laws and

FEDERAL COURT SYSTEM

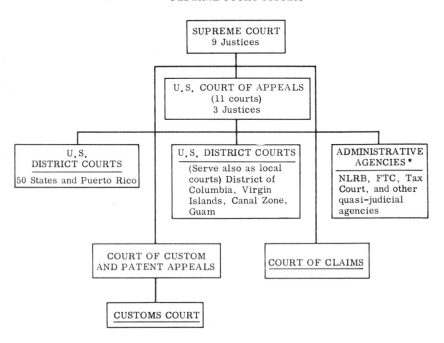

* The federal administrative agencies are not officially part of the Federal Court System but are included in this chart because their rulings can be appealed to a federal court.

treaties that involve personal rights without reference to the money value of the controversy. For example, the amount of the controversy is not a jurisdictional question when the suit is brought by the United States or an officer thereof and arises under the Constitution or federal laws and treaties. The civil actions relating to personal rights may involve bankruptcy; setting aside orders of administrative boards—like the Interstate Commerce Commission; matters relating to patents, copyrights, trademarks, taxes, elections, restraint of trade, of federal lands, commerce, and the rights of freedom of speech, press, and religion; the liberty of the individual protected by the Fifth Amendment; also those rights secured to individual citizens by the Fourteenth Amendment. In addition, by statute the district courts now have original jurisdiction to try tort cases involving damages to citizens caused by officers or agents of the federal government, and the power to issue writs of habeas corpus and to grant injunctions in a variety of cases. In cases where injunctions are sought, three judges must hear the case.

Direct appeals from the decisions of the district courts to the United States Supreme Court may be made in several situations, such as: (1) in criminal cases when the decision of the lower court is based upon the invalidity or construction of a statute upon which the indictment or information was founded; (2) when the lower court has held an Act of Congress unconstitutional, and when an agency of the government is a party; (3) when the lower court consisting of three judges has either granted or denied after notice an interlocutory or permanent injunction. However, in most cases, an appeal is taken from a U. S. district court to the court of appeals.

The intermediate courts of appeal from the United States district courts are called the United States Courts of Appeals. In 1891, because of the heavy burden placed upon the United States Supreme Court, Congress established the courts of appeals. The federal judicial districts are divided into eleven circuits, and a court of appeals has been established for each circuit. These courts are not trial courts and are limited to appellate jurisdiction. After a case has been decided by a district court, a dissatisfied party may appeal to the Court of Appeals of the circuit in which the district courts lies.

In most cases the decisions of the courts of appeals are final. The jurisdiction of the court is determined by Congress and it may be changed from time to time. Cases in the courts of appeals may be reviewed by the Supreme Court by a writ of certiorari granted upon a petition of any party to any civil or criminal case before or after a judgment or decree in the courts of appeals. The writ of certiorari to review a judgment of the courts of appeals is within the discretion of the Supreme Court. The writ will be issued when necessary to secure uniformity of decision or to bring cases of grave public concern to the court of last resort for decision.

Court of appeals decisions may also be reviewed by the Supreme Court in cases in which a state statute has been held unconstitutional and a federal question is presented. In addition, the courts of appeals may by certification seek instructions from the Supreme Court on any question of law in any civil or criminal case.

The United States district courts and the courts of appeals cannot review, retry, or correct the judicial errors charged against a state court. Final judgments or decrees rendered by the highest court of a state are reviewed only by the Supreme Court of the United States. State cases appealed to the United States Supreme Court must concern the validity of a treaty or statute of the United States or must present a question involving the validity of a state statute on the grounds that the statute is repugnant to the Constitution, treaties, or laws of the United States and that the state decision is in favor of the statute's validity. When a case involves the constitutionality of a state statute or treaty, or when a citizen's rights, privileges, or immunities under the constitution or laws are impaired, the case may be brought to the United States Supreme Court by writ of certiorari. In all other cases the decision of the highest state court is not subject to review.

1-27. Law and Equity. The trial courts in the United States have been frequently divided into two parts—a court of law and a court of equity or chancery. The term "equity" is peculiar to Anglo-American law. Courts of equity arose because of the failure of the law courts to give adequate and proper remedies. In early English law the courts could not give remedies for injuries received unless the king's original writs covered the particular remedy sought. Consequently, the proceedings at law were so limited that it was often impossible to obtain justice in the king's courts.

In order that justice might be done, the person seeking a remedy sought redress from the king in person. Since the appeal was to the king's conscience, he referred such matters to his spiritual adviser, the chancellor. Such an individual was usually a church official, and in giving a remedy he usually favored the ecclesiastical law and the civil law.

By such method there developed a new system of procedure and new rules. Actions involving these rules were said to be brought in "chancery" or in "equity," in contradistinction to suit "at law" in the king's courts. Courts of equity were courts of conscience and recognized many rights which were not recognized by common law courts. For example, trusts in lands were recognized; rescission was allowed on contracts created through fraud; injunction and specific performance were developed.

In a few states, courts of equity are separate and distinct from courts of law. In most states the equity and law courts are organized under a single judge who has two dockets—one in law, the other in equity. Whether the case is in equity or in law is determined by the remedy desired. Modern Civil Practice Acts have abolished the common law names heretofore used to distinguish different forms of actions at law and in equity, but pleadings usually must denote whether the action is legal or equitable because as a general rule there is no right to a jury trial of an equitable action. The constitutional guarantee to a trial by jury applies only to actions at law. By statute in some states, a jury may hear the evidence in equity cases, but the determination of the jury in these cases is usually advisory only and is not binding on the court. The judge passes upon questions of both law and fact, and he may decide the case upon the pleadings without the introduction of oral testimony. If the facts are voluminous and complicated, the judge often refers the case to another person, called a master, to take the testimony. This is the usual procedure when a complicated accounting is required. The master hears the evidence and reports back to the judge his conclusions of fact and law. Sometimes the master's duty is confined only to the hearing and reporting of testimony.

Courts of equity use maxims instead of strict rules of law. There are no *legal* rights in equity, for the decision is based on moral rights and natural justice.

Some of the typical maxims of equity are:

1. "Equity will not suffer a right to exist without a remedy."
2. "Equity regards as done that which ought to be done."
3. "Where there is equal equity, the law must prevail."
4. "He who comes into equity must do so with clean hands."
5. "He who seeks equity must do equity."
6. "Equity aids the vigilant."
7. "Equality is equity."

These maxims serve as guides to the chancellor to use in exercising his discretion. For example, the clean hands doctrine (no. 4) prohibits a party who is guilty of misconduct in the matter in litigation from receiving the aid of the court.

The decision of the court in equity is called a decree. A judgment in a court of law is measured in damages, whereas a decree of a court of equity is said to be *in personam,* that is, it is directed to the defendant, who is to do or not to do some specific thing.

Decrees are either final or interlocutory. A decree is final when it disposes of the issues in the case, reserving no question to be decided in the future. A decree quieting title to real estate, granting a divorce, or ordering specific performance is usually final. A decree is interlocutory when it reserves some question to be determined in the future. A decree granting a temporary injunction, appointing a receiver, and ordering property to be delivered to such a receiver would be interlocutory.

Failure upon the part of the defendant to obey a decree of a court of equity is contempt of court because the decree is *in personam*. Any person in contempt of court may be placed in jail or fined by order of the court.

Equity jurisprudence plays an ever-increasing role in our legal system. The movement toward social justice requires more reliance on the equitable maxims and less reliance on rigid rules of law. This also contributes to the further decay of the doctrine of *stare decisis*.

1-28. The Jurisdiction of Courts.   Jurisdiction means the power given to a court by the constitution or the legislature to adjudicate concerning the subject and parties, to determine the cause, to render a judgment, and to carry such judgment into effect. For example, "probate courts" have the original jurisdiction of all probate matters, namely, the settlement of estates of deceased persons by administration and the probate of wills, the appointment of guardians and conservators, etc.

Jurisdiction which is original is frequently also exclusive. This means that no other court has the *power* to hear such cases. For example, the Supreme Court of the United States has original and exclusive jurisdiction in all controversies between two or more states, all proceedings against ambassadors, public ministers, consuls, and domestics of foreign states, all controversies between the United States and a state, and all actions by a state against citizens of another state or country.

Jurisdiction has two aspects, jurisdiction over the subject matter and jurisdiction over the person. Jurisdiction over the subject matter means that the lawsuit is of the type which the court has the power to hear, and the actual subject matter of the cases comes within the limits of the court. For example, a probate court would not have jurisdiction to determine questions of law involving a civil suit for damages, and a circuit court in one county would have no jurisdiction to determine title to the land lying within the boundaries of another county. Courts may also be limited by the amounts of money involved as noted in the federal jurisdictional amount of $10,000.

Jurisdiction over the person refers to jurisdiction over the parties—the plaintiff and defendant. Jurisdiction over the plaintiff is obtained by the filing of the lawsuit. A plaintiff voluntarily submits to the jurisdiction of the court when he files his complaint.

Jurisdiction over the defendant is accomplished by the service of a summons that issues out of the court in which the case is to be tried. It is delivered to a sheriff or other person to be served upon the defendant. Jurisdiction over a defendant in some cases is obtained by publishing a notice in a newspaper. This latter is possible in a limited number of cases involving status such as a suit for divorce or cases involving real estate in which the "thing" involved is of sufficient importance that notice by publication is deemed sufficient to actually notify the defendant. Publication may also be accompanied by proper attachment proceedings, in which case service by publication brings under the court's jurisdiction all attached property of a nonresident which lies within the territorial limits of the court, so that such attached property is liable for the judgment debt and may be used to satisfy the judgment. Most cases, however, require the actual service of a summons on the defendant in order to give him notice of the suit.

Historically, the jurisdiction of courts to enter judgment against a person required actual personal service of the summons on the defendant in the state in which the suit was brought. This was necessary in order to give the defendant notice of the suit and an opportunity to defend. Since the jurisdiction of courts is limited to geographical areas such as a state or a county, power to issue and serve summons beyond the borders of the state or county did not exist. To extend judicial jurisdiction across a state boundary for the purpose of acquiring jurisdiction over the person of a nonresident was a denial of due process of law. To remove a person from his own state or county to another state or county for trial imposed undue burdens on the defendant and denied him of his right to fair play and a fair trial.

Such limitation of jurisdiction is no longer tenable. Personal jurisdiction over nonresidents has been expanding because modern transportation and communication facilities have minimized the inconveniences to a nonresident defendant who must defend himself in courts beyond his domicile. There is no longer any logical reason to deny to a local citizen a remedy in local courts for an injury caused by a nonresident. Under the old law nonresident motorists, for example, were not subject to suit in the state where the accident occurred unless they were served with summons while in the state or unless they owned property in the state which could be attached, as previously explained. In most cases the injured person was left without a remedy, unless he could afford to bring action in the motorist's home state. To correct the situation most states have passed statutes which generally provide that a nonresident by using the state highways has automatically appointed a designated state official, usually the secretary of state, as his agent to accept service of process for any actions arising out of an injury caused by the operation of his automobile on the state highways.

These nonresident motorist statutes opened the door for adoption of other statutes called "long-arm" statutes, which further extend the jurisdiction of courts over nonresidents, whether they are individuals or corporations. The nonresident motorist statutes are limited to actions to recover for injuries arising out of automobile accidents; however, more recent statutes extend the jurisdiction to cover situations in which a tort injury has been caused by a nonresident "doing business" in the state or owning property, either personal or real property, situated in the state. Thus a nonresident individual or corporation may be subject to suit for injuries if either has certain "minimal contacts" within the state, so long as the maintenance of the suit does not offend "traditional notions of fair play and substantial justice."[1]

What "minimal contacts" and activities are necessary to bring the "corporate presence" into a state is a fact question depending upon each particular case. Whatever the basis for the action may be, either in contract or tort, the

[1] Foye v. Consolidated Baling Machine Company, 65

court can acquire jurisdiction over the defendant, if these minimal contacts are present.

1-29. Venue. As previously discussed, the term "jurisdiction" defines the power of the court to hear and adjudicate the case. Jurisdiction includes the court's power to inquire into the facts, apply the law to the facts, make a decision, and declare and enforce a judgment. Venue relates to and defines the particular territorial area within the state, county, or district in which the civil case or civil prosecution should be brought and tried. Matters of venue are determined by statute. Venue statutes usually provide that actions concerning interests in land must be commenced and tried in the county or district in which the land is located. Actions for the recovery of penalties imposed by statute against public officers must be commenced and tried in the county or district where the cause of action arose. Suits for divorce must be commenced and tried in the county in which one of the parties resides. All other suits or actions must be commenced and tried in the county in which the defendants or one of them resides or may be found at the commencement of the action. In the alternative, the action may be commenced in the county in which the transaction took place or where the wrong was committed. For example, a tort action may be commenced and tried either in the county or district where the tort was committed or where the defendant resides or may be found. If the defendants are nonresidents, and assuming that proper service can be made upon them under a "long-arm" statute, the suit may be commenced and tried in any county the plaintiff designates in his complaint.

The judge may change the place of trial at the request of either party when it appears from an affidavit of either party that the action was not commenced in the right county. A change may also be requested on the ground that the judge has an interest in the suit or is related to any parties to the action or has manifested a prejudice so that he cannot be expected to conduct a fair and impartial trial. A change of venue may be requested when the inhabitants of the county manifest a prejudice that makes a fair trial doubtful. The convenience of witnesses and the parties may also justify a change of venue.

THE JUDICIAL SYSTEM CASE

Foye v. Consolidated Baling Machine Company
229 A.2d 196 (Maine) 1967

WEBBER, J. This case requires an interpretation of . . . , our so-called "long-arm" statute. . . . As applicable to the facts of the instant case the statute subjects a nonresident "to the jurisdiction of the courts of this State as to any cause of action arising from . . . *B.* The commission of a tortious act within the State *resulting in physical injury to person or property."* This statute was borrowed with only slight change from the Illinois "long-arm" statute. The change referred to is found in the addition of the italicized words, "resulting in physical injury to person or property," not found in the Illinois statute. "In *Nelson* v. *Miller* (1957) 11 Ill., 2d 378, the Illinois Supreme Court said that the Illinois long-arm statute upon which the Maine act was based reflected 'a conscious purpose to assert jurisdiction over nonresident defendants to the extent permitted by the due process clause.' ... We are satisfied ... that the Legislature intended to fashion a "long-arm" statute of maximum permissible reach "to the extent permitted by the due process clause."

In the case before us the complaint charged the nonresident defendant as manufacturer and vendor of a dangerous and defective paper press. It charged defendant with knowledge of defects and failure to warn. Plaintiff was alleged to have been injured as a result of these defects while operating the machine in Maine. Service was made on defendant in New York. Defendant appeared specially and filed motion to dismiss on jurisdictional grounds. An affidavit filed in support of the motion showed that defendant was vendor but not manufacturer of the paper press, that it purchased the machine from the manufacturer and sold it to a Massachusetts company and that upon the order and request of the purchaser the defendant shipped the machine directly to the plaintiff's employer in Maine. ... It is not disputed that defendant maintained no office or employees within this State, transacted no other business here, and jurisdiction must rest if at all, on this single transaction.

In our view a vendor who by direct shipment places a dangerous instrumentality in the hands of a citizen of this State where it can and subsequently does cause injury thereby commits a "tortious act" within this State, at least within the broad interpretation which we have said should be given to the "long-arm" statute. In discussing the New Hampshire "long-arm " statute which has also been interpreted as "exerting jurisdiction over foreign corporations up to the constitutional limit," Kenison, C. J. said:

" ... If a defendant, whether an individual or foreign corporation, negligently shoots a bullet from state X into state Y, or while engaged in blasting operations in state X causes a stone to be hurled into state Y causing damage, we do not seriously question the right of the injured person to seek redress in state Y and exercise judicial jurisdiction over the defendant in state Y. ... 'While no one recently seems to have stood in one state and fired a gun at a human target across the state line, currently we do find jurisdiction over nonresidents in civil damage cases based on such out-of-state activities as sending dangerous or defective products into the state and broadcasting defamatory statements received within the state. ... ' " This dictum suggests to us the concept of what we may term the continuing act. For jurisdictional purposes from the time the dangerous instrumentality set in motion by the defendant enters the State and while it proceeds within the State to the point of injurious contact with the plaintiff, the defendant may property be deemed to be "acting" within the State. ...

We go no farther than the facts of this case. We treat the defendant who makes the intentional direct shipment of the dangerous and injury-producing product to the consumer as "acting" within the forum state. We conclude that the papers in this case sufficiently allege that the defendant committed a "tortious act within this State. ... "

The defendant here contends that if the statute be so construed, the subjection of the defendant to the jurisdiction of the Maine courts under the circumstances of this case would constitute a deprivation of due process of law. We cannot agree. The modern rule was first announced in *International Shoe Co.* v. *State of Washington, Etc.* (1945) 326 U.S. 310, wherein the Supreme Court said: "But now that the capias ad respondendum has given way to personal service of summons or other form of notice, due process requires only that in order to subject a defendant to a judgment in personam, if he be not present within the territory of the forum, he have certain minimum contacts with it such that the maintenance of the suit does not offend 'traditional notions of fair play and substantial justice.' " In *McGee* v. *International Life Insurance Co.* (1957) 355 U.S. 220, the court held that a *single transaction* could under appropriate circumstances satisfy the "minimum contacts" requirement. . . . Mr. Justice Black, speaking for a unanimous court in *McGee,* said: "Looking back over this long history of litigation a trend is clearly discernible toward expanding the permissible scope of state jurisdiction over foreign corporations and other nonresidents. In part this is attributable to the fundamental transformation of our national economy over the years. Today many commercial transactions touch two or more States and may involve parties separated by the full continent. With this increasing nationalization of commerce has come a great increase in the amount of business conducted by mail across state lines. At the same time modern transportation and communication have made it much less burdensome for a party sued to defend himself in a State where he engages in economic activity."

We are satisfied that, giving consideration to the nature of defendant's alleged activity in this State and the relative convenience and protection of the parties if Maine be the forum for trial, maintenance of the suit in this State will not offend "traditional notions of fair play and substantial justice."

Remanded to Superior Court for further proceedings not inconsistent with this opinion.

CHAPTER 4
REVIEW QUESTIONS AND PROBLEMS

1. Compare the philosophies of "judicial restraint" and "judicial activism."
2. Prepare a chart of the judicial system of your state.
3. What is the jurisdictional amount in the federal courts?
4. *D* Company is incorporated in Delaware with its principal place of business in Illinois. *P,* a citizen of Illinois, sues *D* Company for $20,000 in the Federal District Court for injuries received in using a product manufactured by *D. D* moves to dismiss on the grounds of lack of federal jurisdiction. What result? Why?
5. Is there a jurisdictional amount on all federal question cases? In any federal question cases? Explain.
6. What is meant by the term "jurisdiction"?
7. Why did courts of equity develop?
8. Name five equitable maxims.
9. What is a "long-arm" statute?
10. What is the "minimal contacts" theory?
11. What is the distinction between venue and jurisdiction?
12. If *X,* a citizen of Illinois, sues *Y,* a citizen of Indiana, and *Z,* a citizen of Illinois, does a federal court have jurisdiction if the subject matter of the suit is not a federal question?

13.   *X,* a citizen of Alabama sues *Y,* a citizen of Mississippi, in the Alabama State Court for $7500. Jurisdiction is obtained by service of process in Mississippi. Can *Y* have the case removed to the federal courts?

14.   *X* and *Y* are discussing a matter and disagree on the legality of proposed action. *X* suggests that a suit be filed to determine the legality of the proposed conduct. Will a court settle their dispute?

15.   Is the Supreme Court of the United States a court of general jurisdiction? Explain.

chapter 5

The Lawsuit

1-30. The Need for Adjective Law. As previously noted, there are two kinds of law: substantive law and procedural or adjective law. Substantive law defines the rights and duties of citizens—it is the result of legislative action or judicial action. It defines the legal relations between citizens and between the citizen and the state. Procedural, or adjective, law specifies the method, means, and way the substantive law is made, enforced, and administered by legislators, administrators, judges, and citizens. Legislative procedure consists of the rules of order by which legislation is made. For example, "a majority vote of the assembly is required for the passage of a bill." Administrative procedures prescribe the rules of order by which administrative boards such as the Federal Trade Commission and the National Labor Relations Board shall function.

Judicial procedure is concerned with the rules by which a lawsuit is conducted. One common method of classifying judicial procedure is to divide it into two parts—criminal and civil. Criminal procedure prescribes the rules of law for the apprehension, prosecution, and fixing of punishment of persons who have violated the criminal law. Civil procedure prescribes the rules by which parties to civil lawsuits use the courts to settle their disputed claims. Procedure is the legal mechanism by which a substantive law question is presented to the courts for decision. For example, it is the method by which an aggrieved person, who claims to have suffered injury to his property or person, is able to proceed against the person who committed the alleged wrong for damages. Likewise, it is the method by which one against whom a contract has been breached is able to proceed to obtain redress.

Procedural rules prescribe the methods by which courts apply substantive law to resolve conflicts. Substantive rights have no value unless there are procedures that provide a means for enforcing them.

By a procedure known as pleading, the parties define the issues that are in dispute. In every case, there are three basic questions to be answered: (1) What are the facts? (2) What evidence is relevant to prove the facts? and (3) What rules of law apply to the facts? It is the function of the jury to answer the first question; the court furnishes the answer to the second; and the court provides the answer to the third by instructing the jury as to the law to be applied to the facts as found by the jury.

An orderly method for settling disputes by an impartial third party is the prime function of any legal system. As a substitute for force, judicial procedure has been found the most effective method for resolving disputes.

1-31. Pleadings.   A pleading is a legal document prepared by a lawyer and filed with the court which sets forth the position and contentions of a party. The purpose of pleadings in civil actions is to define the issues of the lawsuit. This is accomplished by each party making allegations of fact and the other party either admitting the allegations or denying them. The procedure is as follows: The plaintiff files with the clerk of the court a pleading usually called a *complaint.* In some types of cases this initial pleading is called a *declaration* or a *petition.* The clerk then issues a summons which, together with a copy of the complaint, is served on the defendant by leaving it with the defendant personally or, in some states, by leaving it with some member of his family of at least a specified age. When a summons is left with a member of the family, a copy is also mailed to the defendant. The summons notifies him of the date by which he is required to either file a pleading in answer to the allegations of the complaint, or to file some other pleading attacking the complaint.

If the defendant has no legal basis to attack the sufficiency of the complaint, he may simply file an entry of appearance, or he may file an answer either admitting or denying each material allegation of the complaint. This answer will put in issue all allegations of the complaint which are denied. A simple entry of appearance is an admission of the truth of all of the allegations of the complaint.

In addition to the admissions and denials, an answer may contain affirmative defenses, which if proved will defeat the plaintiff's claim. The answer may also contain causes of action the defendant has against the plaintiff, called *counterclaims.* Upon receipt of the defendant's answer, the plaintiff will, unless the applicable rules of procedure do not so require, file a reply that specifically admits or denies each new allegation in the defendant's answer. These new allegations are those found in the affirmative defense and counterclaims. Thus the allegations of each party are admitted or denied in the pleadings. Allegations of fact by either party that are denied by the other become the issues to be decided at the trial.

The first pleading (complaint), in order to be legally sufficient, must allege facts sufficient to set forth a right of action or right to legal relief in the plaintiff. The defendant's attorney, after studying the complaint, may (instead of answering) choose one of several different ways to challenge its legal sufficiency. For example, by motion to the court, the defendant may object to the complaint, pointing out specifically its defects. The defendant, through such motion, admits for purposes of argument all of the facts alleged in the complaint. His position is that those facts are not legally sufficient to give the plaintiff a cause of action. Such motion, called a *demurrer* at common law, raises questions of law, not questions of fact. If the court finds that the complaint does set forth facts sufficient to give the plaintiff a cause of action, it will deny the motion. The defendant will then be granted leave to answer the complaint; should he fail to do so within the time limit set by the court, a judgment by default will be entered for the plaintiff. If the court finds, however, that the complaint fails to state facts sufficient to give the plaintiff a cause of action against the defendant, the court will allow the motion, dismiss the suit, and grant leave to the plaintiff to file an amended complaint. The plaintiff will thus be given an opportunity to restate his facts so that he may be able to set forth a cause of action. If he fails to do so, the order of dismissal becomes final.

In addition to a motion to dismiss for failure to state a cause of action, a defendant may also move to dismiss the suit for reasons which as a matter of law would prevent the plaintiff from winning his suit. Such matters as a discharge in bankruptcy, lack of jurisdiction of the court to hear the suit, or expiration of the time limit during which the defendant is subject to suit may be raised by such a motion. These are matters of a technical nature which raise questions of law for the court's decision.

Most states and the federal courts have procedures known as "motions for summary judgment" or "motions for judgment on the pleadings," by which either party may submit the case for final decision without a trial. In hearings on these motions, the court examines all papers on file in the case, including affidavits that may have been filed with the motion or in opposition to it, to see if a genuine material issue of fact remains. If there is no such question of fact, the court will then decide the legal question raised by the facts and find for one party or the other.

If a defendant subject to the jurisdiction of the court fails to file an answer either originally or after his motions have been overruled, he is in default and a court of law may enter a default judgment against him. A court of equity would enter a similar order known as a decree *pro confesso.*

1-32. Pretrial Stage.   During the pleading stage and in the interval before the trial, the law provides for procedures called *discovery* procedures which are designed to take the "sporting aspect" out of litigation and to ensure that the results of lawsuits are based on the merits of the controversy and less on the ability, skill, or cunning of counsel. Without these procedures an attorney with no case on the facts or law might win a lawsuit through surprise—by keeping silent about a fact or by concealing his true case until the trial. Lawsuits should not be based on the skill or lack thereof of counsel, but on the relative merits of the controversy. Discovery practice is designed to ensure that each side is fully aware of all the facts involved in the case and of the contentions of the parties, prior to trial. Another of its avowed purposes is to encourage settlement of suits and to avoid actual trial.

Discovery practices include the taking of the deposition of other parties and witnesses, the serving of written questions to be answered under oath by the opposite party,[1] compulsory physical examinations in personal injury cases by doctors chosen by the other party, orders requiring the production of

[1] West Pico Furniture Company v. Superior Court, page 85

statements, exhibits, documents, maps, photographs, etc., and the serving by one party on the other of demands to admit facts under oath. Some court procedures even allow the discovery of the amount of insurance coverage possessed by the defendant in a personal injury case. The Federal Rules of Civil Procedure illustrate the trend and scope of discovery procedures. They allow discovery of

> any matter, not privileged, which is relevant to the subject matter involved in the pending action, whether it relates to the claim or defense of the examining party or to the claim or defense of any other party, including the existence, description, nature, custody, condition and location of any books, documents, or other tangible things and the identity and location of persons having knowledge of relevant facts. It is not ground for objection that the testimony will be inadmissible at the trial if the testimony sought appears reasonably calculated to lead to the discovery of admissible evidence. . . .

Just prior to the trial a pretrial conference between the lawyers and the judge will be held in states with modern rules of procedure. At this conference, the pleadings, results of the discovery process, and probable evidence are reviewed in an attempt to settle the suit. The issues may be further narrowed and the judge may even give his prediction of the outcome in order to encourage settlement. It is significant that a very substantial number of all lawsuits which are filed are settled sometime prior to trial. Discovery procedures contribute significantly to these settlements.

1-33. The Trial.   Not every case can be settled even under modern procedures. Some must go to trial on the issues of fact raised by the pleadings which remain after the pretrial conference. If the only issues are questions of law, the court will decide the case without a trial by a ruling on one of the motions previously mentioned. If the case is at law and either party has demanded a jury trial, the cause will be set for trial and a jury empaneled. If the case is in equity or if no jury demand has been made, it will be set down for trial before the court or possibly a Master in Chancery. For purposes of discussion the following assumes trial before a jury.

The first step of the trial is to select the jury. Prior to the calling of the case, the clerk of the court will have summoned potential jurors known as the *venire.* They will be selected at random from lists of eligible citizens, and twelve of them will be called into the jury box for the conduct of *voir dire* examination. (Section 1-38 explains this process in greater detail.) *Voir dire* examination is a method by which the court and the attorneys for each party examine the jurors as to their qualifications to be fair and impartial. Each side in the lawsuit may challenge or excuse a juror for cause, e.g., for bias, prejudice, or relation to one of the parties. In addition, each side will be given a certain number of challenges known as "peremptory challenges" for which no cause need be given. Each side is given an opportunity to question the prospective jurors and either to accept them or reject them until his challenges are exhausted. The prospective jurors are sworn to give truthful answers to the questions on *voir dire.* The process continues until the full jury is selected.

After selecting the jurors, the attorneys make opening statements. An opening statement is not evidence, but is only used to familiarize the jury with the essential facts in the case which each side expects to prove in order that the jury may understand the overall picture of the case and the relevancy of each piece of evidence as presented. After the opening statements, the plaintiff presents his evidence.

Evidence is presented in open court by means of examination of witnesses and the production of documents and other exhibits. The party calling a witness questions him to establish the facts about the case. As a general rule, a party calling a witness is not permitted to ask "leading questions," questions in which the desired answer is indicated by the form of the question. After the party calling the witness has completed his direct examination, the other party is given the opportunity to cross-examine the witness. Matters inquired into on cross-examination are limited to those matters which were raised on direct examination. After cross-examination, the party calling the witness again has the opportunity of examining the witness, and this examination is called redirect examination. It is limited to the scope of those matters covered on cross-examination and is used to clarify matters raised on cross-examination. After redirect examination, the opposing party is allowed re–cross-examination, with the corresponding limitation as to scope of the questions. Witnesses may be asked to identify exhibits. Expert witnesses may be asked to give their opinion, within certain limitations, about the case, and sometimes experts are allowed to answer hypothetical questions.

In the conduct of a trial, the rules of evidence govern the admissibility of testimony and exhibits and establish which facts may be presented to the jury and which facts may not. Each rule of evidence is based on some policy consideration and the desire to give each party an opportunity to present his evidence and contentions without unduly taking advantage of the other party. Rules of evidence were not created to serve as a stumbling block to meritorious litigants or to create unwarranted roadblocks to justice. On the contrary, the rules of evidence were created and should be applied to ensure fair play and to aid in the goal of having controversies determined on their merits.

To illustrate the policy considerations which form the basis of the rules of evidence, an examination of the rules relating to privileged communications is helpful.

The policy behind the Fifth Amendment's privilege against self-incrimination is obvious. There are other communications, such as between husband and wife, doctor and patient, clergy and penitent, and attorney and client, which are also considered privileged by the law in order that these communications can be made without fear of their subsequent use against the parties involved. Fair play requires that an attorney not be required to testify as to matters told him in confidence by his client. The preservation of the home requires that a spouse not be required to testify against the other spouse regarding confidential communications. The existence of insurance coverage for a party is privileged because of the impact that knowledge of the existence of insurance would have on a jury. Jurors might award damages or increase the amount simply because of the ability of an insurance company to pay. By the rules of fair play, privileged matters should not be admitted into evidence. Similar policy considerations support all rules of evidence. Each rule is designed to assist in the search for truth.

A basic rule of evidence is that a party cannot introduce evidence unless it is competent and relevant to the issues raised by the pleadings. A connection between the pleadings and trial stage of the lawsuit is also present in certain motions made during the trial. For example, after the plaintiff has presented his evidence, the defendant will often make a motion for a directed verdict. This motion asks the court to rule as a matter of law that the plaintiff has failed to establish a right against the defendant and that judgment should be given to the latter. The court can only direct a verdict if the evidence taken in the light most favorable to the party resisting the motion establishes as a matter of law that the moving party is entitled to a verdict. The defendant argues that the plaintiff has failed to prove each allegation of his complaint. Just as a plaintiff must *allege* certain facts or have his complaint dismissed by motion to dismiss, he must have some *proof* of each essential allegation, or lose his case on a motion for a directed verdict. If he has some proof of each allegation, the motion will be overruled.

In cases tried without a jury, either party may move for a finding in his favor. Such a motion will be allowed during the course of the trial if the result is not in doubt. The judge in ruling on such motions weights the evidence, but he may end the trial only if there is no room for a fair difference of opinion as to the result.

If the defendant's motion for directed verdict is overruled, the defendant then presents his evidence. It should be noted that a party calling a witness vouches for his credibility and is not allowed to impeach or attempt to discredit a witness whom he has called. After the defendant has presented all his evidence, the plaintiff may bring in rebuttal evidence. When neither party has any additional evidence, the attorneys and the judge retire for a conference to consider the instructions of law to be given the jury.

The purpose of the jury instructions is to acquaint the jury with the law applicable to the case. Since the function of the jury is to find the facts, and the function of the court is to determine the applicable law, there must be a method to bring them together in an orderly manner that will result in a decision. At the conference, each attorney submits to the court the instructions he feels should be given to the jury. The court examines these instructions and confers with the attorneys. The court then decides which instructions will be given to the jury. A typical jury instruction in a case in which a minor is seeking to recover money paid by him in purchase of an item is as follows: The court instructs the jury that contracts of minors may be avoided by the minor upon return of so much of the consideration received by the minor as he has left, providing the consideration is not a "necessary." If you find from the evidence that the plaintiff was a minor, that the consideration received by him was not a necessary, and that he has returned so much of what he received as he has left, then your verdict will be for the minor, plaintiff.

In this instruction, the court is in effect saying that the plaintiff must prove that he was a minor, that the contract does not involve necessaries and that he has returned all of what he received that he had left. Thus the law of minors is applied to the facts, and the jury is instructed as to the result to be returned if they find certain facts.

After the conference on jury instructions, the attorneys argue the case to the jury. The party with the burden of proof, usually the plaintiff, is given an opportunity to open the argument and to close it. The defendant's attorney is only allowed to argue after the plaintiff's argument and is only allowed to argue once. After the arguments are completed, the court reads the instructions to the jury.

In the federal courts and in some state courts, the judge while giving instructions may comment on the evidence. He may indicate the importance of certain portions of evidence, the inferences that might be drawn therefrom, point out the conflicts, and indicate what statements are more likely to be true than others and state why. The court, however, is dutybound to make clear to the jury that it is not obligated to follow his evaluation of the evidence and that it is its duty to determine the facts of the case. The jury then retires to deliberate upon its verdict.

There are two kinds of verdicts—general and special. A general verdict is one in which the jury makes a complete finding and single conclusion on all issues presented to it. First it finds the facts, as proven by the evidence, then applies the law as instructed by the court and returns a verdict in one conclusion that settles the case. Such verdict is reported as follows: "We the jury find the issues for the plaintiff (or defendant, as the case may be) and assess his damages at One Thousand Dollars." The jury does not make separate findings of fact, or report what law is applied.

In a special verdict the jury only makes findings of fact. It is the duty of the court to apply the law to the facts as found by the jury. A special verdict is not a decision of the case; it resolves only the questions of fact. Since the jury finds only the facts, it receives no instructions from the court as to the law. The duty of applying the law to the fact is left to the court. The circumstances under which a general or a special verdict may be used are controlled by statute.

Upon reaching a verdict the jury returns from the jury room, announces its verdict, and judgment is entered. Judgments are either *in rem* or *in personam*. A judgment *in rem* is an adjudication entered against a thing—property, real or personal. The judgment is a determination of the status of the subject matter. Thus a judgment of forfeiture of goods for the violation of a revenue law is a judgment *in rem*. Although a judgment *in rem* is limited to the subject matter, it nevertheless affects the rights and duties of persons. For example, while a decree dissolving a marriage seriously affects persons, it is nevertheless a judgment *in rem* because it affects a "status," the marriage relation. A judgment *in rem* is binding not only on the persons previously concerned with the status or thing but on all other persons.

A judgment against a particular person is a judgment *in personam*. It is limited in its application to such person only, whereas a judgment *in rem* is conclusive on all persons.

After judgment is entered, the losing party starts the procedure of posttrial motions, which raise questions of law concerning the conduct of the lawsuit. These motions seek such relief as a new trial or a judgment notwithstanding the verdict of the jury. A motion seeking a new trial may be granted if the judge feels that the verdict of the jury is contrary to the manifest weight of the evidence. The court may enter a judgment opposite to that of the verdict of the jury if the judge finds that the verdict is, as a matter of law, erroneous. To reach such a conclusion, the court must find that reasonable men viewing the evidence could not reach the verdict returned. For example, a verdict for the plaintiff may be based on sympathy instead of evidence.

From the ruling on the posttrial motion, the losing party may appeal. It should be noted that lawsuits usually end by a ruling on a motion, either before trial, during the trial, or after the trial. Motions raise questions of law which are decided by the court. The right to appeal, which is discussed in the next section, is absolute if perfected within the prescribed time.

1-34. Appeals. A dissatisfied party, plaintiff or defendant, has a right to appeal the decision of the trial court to a higher court, provided that he proceeds promptly and in the proper manner. It should be noted that the cases collected and abstracted in this text are with a few exceptions decisions of a reviewing court. Whether he is plaintiff or defendant, the person who appeals is called the appellant and the opposite party is called the appellee, or respondent. The appellant is often named first in the title of the case on appeal, although in the trial court he may have been the defendant. Therefore care must be used in reading reported cases in order to properly identify each party as a plaintiff or defendant.

Appellate procedures are not uniform among the states and the appellant must comply with the appropriate statute and rules of the particular court. Appeals are usually perfected by the appellant giving "notice of appeal" to the trial court and opposing parties. Statutes provide that appeals must be taken within a certain number of days from the entry of the judgment, such as thirty, sixty, or ninety days, and these limitations refer to the time of giving the "notice of appeal." The filing of the notice of appeal and its entry upon the journal of the court where the trial was held give the appellate court jurisdiction of the case. After the appellate court has acquired jurisdiction, it may dismiss the appeal upon its own motion or that of the respondent if there are any statutory omissions in perfecting the appeal.

Most states require that within at least ten days after giving notice of appeal the appellant must file an appeal bond which, in effect, guarantees that the appellant will pay costs that may be charged against him on the appeal. This is to protect the respondent so that he may collect his costs if the appellant loses on appeal.

The statutes usually require that within a specified time after the appeal is perfected, the appellant shall file with the clerk of the appellate court what is known as a *transcript.* The transcript consists of a copy of the judgment, decree, or order appealed from, the notice of appeal, the proof of service upon the respondent, the appeal bond, the pertinent portions of the stenographic transcript of the evidence, and such other papers as are required by the rules of the court. The record also includes all depositions and other papers filed with the clerk in the lower court. The respondent, or appellee, receives a copy of the evidence, and if he feels that additional parts of the record are pertinent, he may file an additional transcript.

Some states require, in addition, the filing of a bill of exceptions. A bill of exceptions is a written instrument in which are set out the objections or exceptions made and taken by the attorneys during the trial to the decisions, rulings, and instructions of the trial judge. The rulings excepted to are stated with an enumeration of as much evidence as is necessary to explain the exceptions. Sometimes the bill of exceptions may include all of the testimony, including the exhibits offered, received, or rejected, and the instructions to the jury, given or refused. In these states, the bill of exceptions must be agreed to by the parties, "settled" or "allowed," signed by the trial judge, and filed with the clerk of the trial court. When this is done, it becomes a part of the record of the case.

The transcript alone is not enough to present the case to the appellate court. The appellant must prepare and file a "brief" which contains a statement of the case, a list of the assignment of errors upon which the appellant has based his appeal, his legal authorities and argument.

A statement of the legal points and authorities relied upon for reversal and the appellant's arguments in written form which are set forth in the "brief" are illustrated by the following:

a. The court, upon the examination of witness X, erred in failing to sustain the objection to the admission of testimony in response to the following questions: (Here in the brief are set forth the questions, the objections, the answers given, and so forth.)

b. The court erred in denying a motion for a nonsuit or directed verdict. (Here are set out the exact motion and the court's ruling.)

c. The court erred in giving or in failing to give the following instructions: (Here are set out the instructions, the objections made, and so forth.)

d. The court erred in its decision because the statute under which the action was brought is unconstitutional. (Here are set out the statute and the reasons for its unconstitutionality.)

The next division of the brief sets out the points and authorities relied upon by the appellant relating to the particular assignments of error. In this section the attorney also presents the particular propositions he seeks to establish. Statutes, previously decided cases, and other legal authorities will be cited for the propositions proposed.

The brief contains the arguments on both fact and law by which the attorney attempts to show how the court below committed the errors alleged.

The appellee (respondent) files a brief of like character setting out his side of the case with points, authorities, and arguments. By such procedure the case on the issues raised gets to the appellate court for decision.

The appellate court upon receipt of the appeal will place it on the calendar for hearing. The attorneys will be notified of the time and will be given an opportunity for oral argument. After the oral argument there is deliberation by members of the court and an opinion will be written stating the law involved and giving the court's reasons for its decision. The court by its decision may affirm or reverse the court below, or the court may send the case back for a new trial. At the end of each published opinion found in the reports, there will appear in a few words the result of the court's decision. Such words may be "affirmed," "reversed," "reversed and remanded," and so forth, as the case requires.

1-35. Enforcement of Judgments and Decrees.   A decision of a court becomes final when the time provided for a review of the decision has expired. In cases in the trial court, it is the expiration of the time for appeal. In cases in a reviewing court, it is the expiration of the time to request a rehearing or to request a further review of the case. After the decision has become final, judicial action may be required to enforce the decision. In most cases, the losing party will voluntarily comply with the decision and satisfy the judgment or otherwise do what the decree requires, but the assistance of the court is sometimes required to enforce the final decision of the court.

If a judgment for dollar damages is not paid, the judgment creditor may apply for a *writ of execution.* This writ directs the sheriff to seize personal property of the judgment debtor and to sell enough thereof to satisfy the judgment and to cover the costs and expenses of the sale. The writ authorizes the sheriff to seize both tangible and intangible personal property, such as bank accounts. If the judgment debtor's personal property seized and sold by the sheriff does not produce sufficient funds to pay the judgment, the writ of execution is returned to the court with a statement of the extent to which the judgment is unsatisfied. If an execution is returned unsatisfied in whole or in part, the judgment becomes a lien on any real estate owned by the debtor within the jurisdiction of the court which issued the writ of execution. A judgment creditor with a judicial lien on real estate of a judgment debtor is entitled to have the real estate sold at a judicial sale and to have the net proceeds of the sale applied on the judgment. A judgment creditor with an unsatisfied writ of execution not only has a lien on real property owned by the judgment debtor at the time the judgment becomes final, he also has a judicial lien on any real property acquired by the judgment debtor during the life of the judgment. The life of a judgment is prescribed by statute. The time period is usually several years and there are provisions for renewal of the judgment. A judgment debtor cannot convey clear title to real estate as long as the judicial lien is unsatisfied.

A judgment creditor is entitled to more than one writ of execution. He may ask for such writs from the court as long as the judgment remains unsatisfied. The writ of execution is not the only method of enforcing a judgment but it is almost always used to ensure that there will be a judicial lien on any real estate owned by the judgment debtor.

Another important method used by judgment creditors to collect a judgment is known as *garnishment.* A judgment creditor can "garnish" the wages of the judgment debtor, or his bank account, or any other obligation owing to him from a third party. In the process of garnishment, the person owing the money to the judgment debtor—the employer, bank of deposit, third party —will be directed to pay the money into court rather than to the judgment debtor, and such money will be applied against the judgment debt.

In connection with writs of execution and garnishment proceedings, it is extremely significant that the laws of the various states have statutory provisions that exempt certain property from writs of execution and garnishment. The state laws limit the amount of wages that can be garnished and usually provide for both real property and personal property exemptions. For example, most states provide for a homestead exemption and also exempt necessary household items, clothing, and the tools used by a person in his trade, as well as a certain amount of other personal property. These exemptions are discussed more fully in Chapter 32, Section 4-6.

In recent years, many states have adopted a procedure, known as a *citation proceeding,* which greatly assists the creditor in collecting a judgment. The citation procedure is commenced by the service of a "citation" on the judgment debtor to appear in court at a stated time for the purpose of examination under oath about his financial affairs. It also prohibits the judgment debtor from making any transfer of property until after the examination in court. At the hearing, the judgment creditor or his attorney questions the judgment debtor about his income, property, and affairs. Any nonexempt property that is discovered during the questioning may be ordered sold by the judge, with the proceeds applied to the judgment. The court may also order that weekly or monthly payments be made by the judgment debtor. Such payments must not violate the laws relating to garnishment. In those states that have adopted the citation proceeding, the difficulties in collecting a judgment have been substantially reduced.

One important method of collecting a judgment is also relevant to the procedures that may be used to commence a lawsuit. This procedure with these dual purposes is known as *attachment.* Attachment is a method of acquiring *in rem* jurisdiction of a nonresident defendant who is not subject to the service of process. The court may "attach" property of the nonresident defendant and in so doing, the court acquires jurisdiction over the defendant to the extent of the value of the property attached. Attachment as a means of obtaining *in rem* jurisdiction is used in cases involving the status of a person, such as divorce, or the status of property, such as in eminent domain proceedings.

Attachment as a method of ensuring collection of a judgment is used by a plaintiff who fears that the defendant will dispose of his property before the court is able to enter a final decision. The plaintiff has property of the defendant seized pending the outcome of the lawsuit.

Attachment and the procedures controlling its use are governed by statutes that vary among the states. The attaching plaintiff-creditor must put up a bond with the court for the protection of the defendant, and the statutes provide methods whereby the attachment may be vacated by the defendant. If the plaintiff receives a judgment against the defendant, the attached property will be sold to satisfy the judgment.

THE LAWSUIT CAST

1-36. The Judge. "Judges ought to be more learned than witty, more reverent than plausible, more advised than confident. Above all things, integrity is their portion and proper virtue." (Bacon)

The judge, by virtue of his office, is in his personal conduct under duties to the state, its people, the litigants, the law, the witness, and the jury. He must remember that the court is for the litigants, not the litigants for the court. He must observe and apply constitutional limitations and guarantees. A judge should be temperate, attentive, patient, impartial, studious, diligent, industrious, and prompt in ascertaining the facts and applying the law. He should organize his court with a view to the prompt and convenient dispatch of its business. He should be courteous, civil, and considerate of jurors, witnesses and others in attendance upon the court, but should criticize and correct unprofessional conduct of attorneys. He should appoint all court personnel with a view solely to their character and fitness and not act in a controversy in which he or a near relative has an interest. He should not be swayed by public clamor or consideration of personal popularity nor be apprehensive of unjust criticism. He should not improperly interfere in the conduct of a trial except to prevent waste of time and to clarify obscurity. He should be mindful of the general law and administer justice with due regard for the integrity of the legal system. He should not compel a person brought before him to submit to humiliating acts or discipline of his own making. He should abstain from making personal investments in enterprises that are apt to be involved in litigation in the court and should not participate in partisan politics or contribute to party funds. He should not, and in many states by law cannot, engage in the private practice of law. He should not accept gifts or favors from litigants or lawyers whose interests are likely to be submitted to him for judgment. He should conduct the court proceedings so as to reflect the importance of ascertaining the truth.

Such are the virtues required of the trial judge, who renders his decisions at a level which deals directly with the people. It is in the trial courts where the law is made alive and its words are given meaning. Trial judges see and deal intimately with persons in conflict. Whatever provocations may disturb him personally, the judge is burdened with the task of upholding the dignity of the courts and maintaining respect for the law. Since he represents the only contact that most people have with the law, it is apparent that the effective function of the law must depend largely upon the character and training of the trial judge.

1-37. The Justice.   Members of reviewing courts are usually called *justices* to distinguish them from trial court judges. The roles of the justice and the judge are substantially different. For example, the trial judge has direct contact with the litigation and the litigants, whereas the justice rarely has any contact with litigants. In many cases he does not even have direct contact with the attorneys because when oral argument is not requested, the case is submitted for review solely in writing in the form of briefs and records of proceedings as was discussed in Section 1-34. Oral argument is presented in most cases, however.

Justices must do much more than simply decide a case—they are required to give the reasons for their decision in written form so that anyone who desires to do so may examine it and comment on its merits. Each decision will become precedent to some degree and will become a part of our body of law. Thus, the legal opinion of the justice, unlike that of the trial judge whose decision has direct effect only upon the litigants, affects society as a whole. The justice in deciding the case before him must consider not only the result between the parties involved but the total effect of his decision on the law. In this sense, his role is that of a "legislator."

Because of this difference in roles, the personal qualities required for a justice are somewhat different from those for a trial judge. The duties of a justice bring him into the area of legal scholarship. He is required to be articulate in presenting his ideas in writing and to use the written word as the primary source of his decision. Whereas the trial judge, being a part of the trial arena, observes the witnesses and essentially uses knowledge gained from his participation for his decision, the justice spends hours studying the briefs, the record of proceedings, as well as the law, before preparing and handing down his decisions.

1-38. The Jury. In Anglo-American law, the right of trial by jury, particularly in criminal cases, is traced to the famous Magna Charta issued by King John of England in 1215, wherein it is stated:

> . . . that no freeman shall be taken or imprisoned or disseised or outlawed or exiled . . . without the judgment of his peers or by the law of the land. . . .

In early English legal history the juror was a witness, that is, he was called to tell what he knew, not to listen to others testify. The word "jury" comes from the French word *jure* which means "sworn." The jury gradually developed into an institution to determine facts. The function of the jury today is to ascertain the facts just as the function of the court is to ascertain the law.

A juror must come to a trial with an open mind; otherwise his previous knowledge might prejudice him in evaluating the testimony presented at the trial. The jury system as brought to the colonies from England was adopted as a matter of right in the Constitution of the United States. The Sixth and Seventh Amendments to the United States Constitution guarantee the right of trial by jury in both criminal and civil cases; in addition, the Fifth Amendment provides for indictment by a grand jury for capital offenses and infamous crimes. In civil cases the right to trial by jury is preserved in suits at common law when the amount in controversy exceeds twenty dollars. State constitutions have like provisions guaranteeing the right of trial by jury in state courts.

The persons who are selected to serve on trial juries are drawn at random from lists of qualified voters in the county or city where the trial court sits. Most states by statute have listed certain occupations and professions such as doctors, dentists, pharmacists, embalmers, policemen, firemen, lawyers, and newspapermen who are exempt from jury duty. When a case is called for trial, those selected as noted above will appear as the jury panel and unless excused by the judge for personal reasons will be available to serve as jurors. Twelve persons will be selected by drawing, and *voir dire* examination will be conducted to select the jury in a particular case. Serving on the jury is an important civic duty. It is one significant way in which a citizen can take part in his government and participate in the administration of justice.

For many years the jury system has been subject to criticism. It is contended that most jurors are not qualified to distinguish fact from fiction, that they are easily influenced by public opinion, vote their prejudices, and are too easily emotionally moved by persuasive trial lawyers. Admitting the frailties of men, the average American still believes in the "right to be tried by a jury of his peers" in criminal cases. Safeguarded by the rules of trial procedure, it is felt by most members of the bench and bar that the jury system is as fair and effective a method of ascertaining the truth and giving an accused "his day in court" as has been devised.

In most states the decision of the jury except in particular situations prescribed by constitution or statute must be unanimous. It is expected that in most cases the jury's verdict "will be a total assertion." It is asserted that the truth is more nearly to be found and justice rendered if the jury acts only on one common conscience, on what is almost immediately obvious, not on what is elaborated by a little group. It operates in "the native way of deciding an issue," that is, "to discuss it until there is unanimity of opinion or until the opposition feels it is no longer worthwhile to argue its point of view." Statutes and constitutions provide the number of jurors who must concur for a verdict. In some states the concurrence of only three-fourths of the jurors is required in civil cases.

A jury is not permitted to take notes as a general rule and is not permitted to give reasons for its decision. Actually, it would be almost impossible for the jury to agree as to the reasons for its verdict. A jury may agree as to the result, but disagree on some of the facts, and different jurors may have different ideas on the significance of various items of testimony.

1-39. The Lawyer.   English law not only gave us the common law, it gave us the profession of attorney at law. Attorneys at law are also known as lawyers, solicitors, or counselors at law. The term, attorney at law, is used to distinguish the lawyer from an agent known as an attorney in fact. This latter person is simply authorized by a power of attorney to perform some stated duty on behalf of a principal, whereas an attorney at law is a person qualified in character and by training to serve as an officer of courts in representing and advising people in regard to the law.

The direct ancestors of the common-law lawyers were persons hired as "champions" in trial by battle in early English "litigation." In criminal actions a defendant was required to establish his innocence by defeating the plaintiff or his champion. In civil actions the bout was waged by champions, not by the parties themselves, because under the law at that time if either party to the case were killed, the suit would end and no judgment could be taken.

"Trials" of this sort were later abolished in England, and trial by jury was substituted. However, the idea of a "contest" survived, so that today a trial is in a sense a contest between the lawyers, as advocates for their clients, like champions in olden times. The court acts as referee, within an adversary system so conducted as to fairly persuade a jury toward a just result. In early England, after William the Conqueror, land law and pleadings became so complex that there developed of necessity a class of legal advisers increasingly experienced and competent.

While a Utopian society could in theory avoid the need for lawyers, any complex society cannot, in reality, do without them—they are essential in all countries if order is to be maintained.

The practice of law is one of the most important, if not *the* most important, occupation in our society. It is that profession that gives order to society. Law has been described as the difference between an alley fight and a debate. Lawyers are engaged in giving meaning to such terms as "individual liberty" and "due process" of law. Without lawyers, these concepts would be mere abstractions.

The practice of law may be divided into several categories, or types of practice. Some types of practice may be described as trial practice, and trial lawyers as a group are subdivided into plaintiffs counsel and defense counsel because of the different aspects of these activities. Office practice is another type and is concerned with such matters as preparing documents, advising businesses, settling estates, etc. Many office practice lawyers never participate in a lawsuit but leave the trial arena to the specialist in trial work. Large law firms have lawyers practicing in all areas, but small law firms or sole practitioners often refer matters out of their area of expertise to other lawyers. Of course, the general practitioner, especially in the smaller community, will handle practically every matter that is brought to his office. The term "house counsel" is used to describe another large group of attorneys. House counsel is employed by business to assist in the internal operations of the business by preventing and solving legal problems. Unsolved problems that result in litigation are usually referred to outside counsel for trial. Lawyers can also be categorized geographically. For example, the country lawyer practices in the smaller community and usually handles the whole gamut of the practice of law. He is a generalist rather than a specialist and plays a role in all aspects of his community. The city lawyer will tend to specialize, and this is especially true in the larger firms where each member has an area of specialization.

Whatever the area or location of a lawyer's practice, he will be engaged in certain activities that are of primary significance to society. First of all, he is an adviser. A lawyer's product is advice—advice on an infinite variety of subjects. Much of the advice requested and given is not strictly legal but may involve such matters as business decisions or family affairs. Of course, most of his advice will be connected with the law.

Secondly, every lawyer is an advocate for his client. The office lawyer negotiating a contract is an advocate just as is the trial lawyer. His advocacy is directed at other attorneys and their clients rather than to judges and juries. Thirdly, every lawyer is a negotiator of compromise. He seeks to avoid litigation and to find a mutually satisfactory alternative to the expense and difficulties of litigation. These three roles, adviser, advocate, and negotiator provide insight into the background required for the practice of law.

Hundreds of thousands of words have been written about the personal qualities required for the practice of law. It is generally conceded that a lawyer must be cultured in the sense that he appreciates the historical relevance of our fundamental freedoms and the role of law in our society. He must be keenly aware of the world in which he lives, what is right about it and what is wrong, so that he can fulfill his role as an instrument of change. He must be compassionate and sensitive to human problems and weaknesses because the practice of law is a very personal matter.

Lawyers must be courageous and willing to represent unpopular causes because the right to counsel exists as a necessity. He must be willing not only to defend such causes, but to defend the system which requires such representation. He must stand up for the system when it is unpopular to do so.

A lawyer must be a good loser. It has often been said that the only lawyer who has not lost a case is the lawyer who has not tried one. Carl Sandburg has reminded us that it was Stephen A. Douglas, the loser in the bitter fight for the presidency, who held Lincoln's hat during the inaugural ceremony. Lawyers must remember that the clients and not the lawyers are the litigants.

Lawyers are also policy makers in our society. In this role the lawyer contributes to public order not only by participating personally in the legislative and judicial functions of government, but also when he is a legal consultant to decision makers both in business and government.

A lawyer's duties are diverse, in that his responsibilities are by the very nature of the profession fourfold. His first duty is to the state as a licensed official and a citizen. Secondly, he is an officer of the court, and an aid in the administration of justice; thirdly, he is a trustee and fiduciary for his client; and fourthly, he is obligated to deal honestly and fairly with other lawyers and the public in maintaining the honesty and integrity of the profession.

It is not always easy to keep these obligations in proper balance. The lawyer must not give his sole attention to one of these obligations and neglect the others. In his zeal to assist his client he cannot be dishonest to the court. The court assisted by the lawyer is the public instrument for the administration of justice. Justice cannot be done if the court's decisions rest upon false proof and misquoted law. To be dishonest to the court is not only to be dishonest to the client but also to the state and to his fellow lawyers.

A lawyer's conduct is governed by the Canons of Legal Ethics which touch upon every aspect of a lawyer's duty: his duty to the court, his client, the public, the jury, the profession, as well as his professional conduct in relation to such matters as advertising, unjustifiable litigation, fees, witnesses, and the unauthorized practice of the law. The problem of unauthorized practice of law arises in the services performed by many business specialists, that is, when such specialists—accountants, bankers, insurance brokers, real estate agents, and stockbrokers—give advice of a legal nature. The lawyers's product is legal advice; it is illegal to practice law without a license. The business specialist should recognize that the practice of law is an activity affecting the public interest and that it is limited to those persons duly licensed to practice. Licenses to practice law are issued by the highest court of the jurisdiction involved, and the regulation of lawyers is solely a judicial function because of the doctrine of separation of powers.

What activities of business men constitute the practice of law? It is obvious that appearance in court on behalf of another person is the practice of law. Although a party may represent himself in court, only attorneys can represent others. The giving of legal advice out of court and the preparation of legal documents have also been held to constitute the practice of law. Such holdings do not resolve the issues, however, because the question remains: When is advice legal advice? This question is of utmost significance to accountants engaged in tax work, to real estate dealers, to bankers working in the area of wills, trusts, and estates, and to other business specialists.[2] Unfortunately, the line of demarcation between legal business services and unauthorized practice of law is not very clear at this time. One fact is clear, however, there are services that business specialists cannot render because they involve the practice of law. In most states, these services include preparing real estate contracts, drafting wills, trusts, or estate plans, and assisting in complicated tax matters requiring research. Hopefully, the area of permissible conduct by business specialists will be clarified in the near future.

Our system of law may be described as an adversary system. By tradition and definition, the courtroom is a place of strife. The modern lawsuit is a substitute for the ancient physical combat; the lawyer today is in a sense a "combatant" for his client. Instead of using physical force, a lawyer today

---

[2] The Florida Bar v. Keehley, page 87

represents his client in litigation by the use of words. Through pleadings, persuasion, psychology, and argument, he represents his client in a forum called a court room.

Contesting lawyers as partisan advocates, operating within the rules of procedure and evidence, and supervised by the court, make possible the exploration of every aspect of the case. A single arbiter acting as judge, advocate, and jury would by the very nature of the method used find himself prematurely reaching a fixed opinion. Such preconceived judgments will not prevail under the adversary system. The narrowing of issues by the rules of procedure, preparation, and presentation of the case to the jury by partisan advocates; examination and cross-examination of the witnesses; argument by counsel; and the control, supervision, and instruction by the judge make premature conclusions impossible. During the process of a trial, the court and jury has the benefit of seeing both sides of the issue, clearly defined, and they are able to arrive at a just conclusion. Settling private contentions by a public adversary system, manipulated by intelligent advocates, operating under an orderly process supervised by a neutral third party—the judge—is believed to be one of the most important institutions of American democracy.

However, there are many critics of the adversary process. That such a system is best able to find the truth and render justice has been questioned. It is argued by many that the adversary system permits lawyers to overreach witnesses, mislead the jury, use rules of evidence to cover up facts rather than disclose the truth, and that it makes it possible for a clever, experienced lawyer to dominate the proceedings to such an extent that the other less experienced party has "not had his day in court."

While these objections may be valid in some cases, it nevertheless must be recognized that the adversary system is the best method yet devised to search for truth. Lawyers are an indispensable part of this search.

THE LAWSUIT CASES

West Pico Furniture Company v. Superior Court
364 P.2d 295 (Cal.) 1961

Petitioner in this cause sued Pacific Finance Loans, hereafter referred to as Pacific, to have certain transactions declared to be usurious. Petitioner filed written interrogatories on Pacific. Pacific answered some of the interrogatories and filed objections to others. The court sustained the objections to some of the interrogatories and this action was commenced by the petitioner against the court to order the court to set aside its decision sustaining the objections.

PETERS, J. . . . Interrogatory No. 4 requests the names and addresses of all employees who participated in the various transactions between the parties, together with the duties performed by each, and the period of time during which each such employee participated. . . .

It is apparent that the information requested in this interrogatory is "reasonably calculated to lead to the discovery of admissible evidence." (Subd. (b) of § 2016.) From a list of the names of Pacific's employees who handled the transactions, together with some indication of dates and duties, petitioner will be placed in a position so that it can select one or more such employees for the purpose of taking depositions. . . .

Pacific's contention that the interrogatory calls for its opinions and conclusions is unsound. Obviously the names and duties of one's own employees, and the dates on which they performed specific duties, is not a matter of opinion. . . .

Moreover, even if it be conceded that the question does call for an opinion and conclusion, that fact, *of itself,* is not a proper objection to an interrogatory. . . .

The last objection of Pacific to interrogatory No. 4 is that it is burdensome and oppressive. In support of that objection Pacific filed, in the trial court, the declaration of the manager of its commercial operations and administration department, alleging that the information requested could only be obtained by a search of the records of 78 of its branch offices. Other specific requirements were also set forth, but no estimate was made of the total man-hours required to accomplish the task. Certainly that declaration indicated some burden would be imposed on Pacific to answer the interrogatory, but the extent thereof was not specifically set forth. But the declaration did not indicate any evidence of oppression. Oppression must not be equated with burden. The objection based upon burden must be sustained by evidence showing the quantum of work required, while to support an objection of oppression there must be some showing either of an intent to create an unreasonable burden or that the ultimate effect of the burden is incommensurate with the result sought. Certainly, in the instant case, . . . the trial court, in its discretion, could properly hold that interrogatory No. 4 was burdensome. . . . But, under the pertinent code sections burden, alone, is not a ground for objection. . . .

The objection of burden is valid only when that burden is demonstrated to result in injustice. Hence, the trial court is not empowered to sustain an objection in toto, when the same is predicated upon burden, unless such is the only method of rendering substantial justice. From the facts presented here, it is clear that total rejection of the interrogatory indicates a failure by the trial court to recognize the discretionary power to grant in part and deny in part, and to balance the equities, including costs, that is to balance the purpose and need for the information as against the burden which production entails. . . .

The order of the respondent court, insofar as it applies to interrogatory No. 4, should be set aside to permit a review at the trial level for the purpose of determining whether or not justice requires that the objection be sustained in toto or in part, or be denied in toto, or be denied with limitations as to the manner of bearing the burden and the party who should bear it.

Interrogatories Nos. 6a to 6g, inclusive, . . . are what, for the lack of a better phrase, can be described as "shotgun" questions. The form is such that requires the reader to spend extra unnecessary time and effort in order to ascertain that he has not overlooked the impact of references back to preceding subinterrogatories. This type of interrogatory should be avoided, and the trial court possesses the power to regulate them. But, such form alone cannot be made the sole basis for sustaining an objection in toto to the requested interrogatory. Rather, it is a fact to be considered by the trial court in arriving at the exercise of its discretion. Rather than deny the interrogatory in toto, the trial court, in a proper case, of which this may be one, should require it to be rephrased. . . .

There is another reason why the objection now under consideration may not be sustained. The objection overlooks the provisions of subdivision (c) of section 2030. That section provides, in part:

> Where the answer to any interrogatory may be derived or ascertained from the business records of the party to whom such interrogatory is addressed or from an examination, audit or inspection of such business records . . . it shall be a sufficient answer to such interrogatory to specify the records from which the answer may be derived or ascertained and to afford to the party by whom the interrogatory was proposed reasonable opportunity to examine. . . .

Under this section, if Pacific did not desire to answer interrogatory No. 6, and each of its subdivisions, in full, it had the opportunity to place the burden of obtaining that information on the petitioner by simply specifying the documents in which the information is contained, and affording petitioner an opportunity to examine them. It failed to avail itself of this procedure. It is, therefore, in no position to object to the interrogatories on the ground that they call for the inspection of documents.

Let a peremptory writ of mandate issue requiring respondent court to vacate its order sustaining the objections to the specified interrogatories, and directing it to reconsider those objections, and to make its order in reference thereto in accordance with the views expressed herein.

The Florida Bar v. Keehley

190 So.2d 173 (Fla.) 1966

PER CURIAM. The cause is before us on petition of The Florida Bar charging respondent with the unauthorized practice of law. . . .

The Florida Bar filed its petition charging the respondent, L. James Keehley, with the unauthorized practice of law in the formation of corporations and otherwise. The respondent replied, admitting that he had formed two corporations and performed certain acts as a business broker and business consultant, but asserted that it is not compulsory that an attorney prepare certificates of incorporation and denied that he was guilty of the unauthorized practice of law. . . .

The matter was submitted to the Referee upon the pleadings, depositions, exhibits, stipulation of the parties, and arguments of counsel for both parties. The essential facts are undisputed and the issues of law are uncomplicated.

Respondent is not a lawyer and has not held himself out to be a lawyer. Before coming to Florida, he had for many years been engaged by the United States of America in performing services which entailed familiarity with contract documents and business procedures. Since coming to Florida about five years ago, he has been engaged in business as a business broker and business consultant.

In 1962, he inquired of the Secretary of State and was informed that "it is not compulsory that an attorney prepare certificates of incorporation." About the same time he researched questions of law pertaining to joint tenancies. During the same year he prepared articles of incorporation for business associates or prospective business associates and himself in Southern Technical (or Southern Tech) Electronics School, Inc., which were submitted to a member of The Florida Bar for approval before they were utilized by the incorporators. Armed with this experience, he formed two corporations in Florida during the year 1965. . . . In submitting the articles of incorporation which he had prepared, respondent in each instance wrote to the Secretary of State that "the writer will assure a corporate meeting is held to approve the by-laws and otherwise finalize the organization of the company as required by Florida Statutes." The amounts which each incorporator agreed to subscribe ranged from $500.00 to $2,450.00. Stock certificates were issued to the subscribers and their respective spouses in each corporation "as joint tenants with right of survivorship." None of the incorporators realized that, by signing the articles of incorporation, they had committed themselves to subscribe to the stipulated amounts and none of them had made the agreed investments in the corporations, nor were they aware of the gift, gift tax and other implications of taking title to the stock certificates as joint tenants.

Respondent was not aware, prior to the complaint resulting in these unauthorized practice of law proceedings, of the decision in *The Florida Bar* v. *Town,* 174 So.2d 395 [sic], in which this Court last year decided that the preparation of corporate charters and related documents constitute the practice of law. However, respondent points out that in the *Town* case the respondent had charged a fee for his services, whereas the respondent in the present case made no charge for forming the two corporations, and further that these two corporations were formed for friends and family, with an interest or prospective interest on the part of respondent himself in both ventures. It is the referee's conclusion that neither the absence of compensation, nor the close personal relationship between the respondent and the persons for whom the services were rendered, nor his present or prospective future interest in the transaction, legalizes his formation of these corporations, and his services which undoubtedly constitute the practice of law in connection with these corporations. It is equally inimical, dangerous and contrary to the welfare of the public to permit untrained and unqualified persons, who have not been admitted to The Florida Bar, to perform such services for individuals who desire to incorporate and to operate as corporations under the Florida law, whether a fee is charged, whether the parties are closely related, or whether the untrained person is one of the interested parties.

In his capacity as a business consultant and business broker, or as an associate of a business broker operating in Tampa, Florida, respondent admittedly has prepared listing agreements, agreements of sale in the form of deposit receipts, bills of sale, general affidavits and other documents, usually by filling in the blanks upon printed forms and tailoring each of these forms to the circumstances of the individual transaction. These services were performed at the request or under the direction of the broker and in some, but not all, instances were reviewed by members of The Florida Bar representing sellers or buyers or both. Respondent states that in doing so he relied upon the office procedures which he encountered when he became associated with a business broker in Tampa, and also he urges that real estate brokers prepare comparable documents.

While there may be real estate brokers who are violating this Court's decisions in *Keyes Co.* v. *Dade County Bar Ass'n.,* 46 So.2d 605, and *Cooperman* v. *West Coast Title Company,* 75 So.2d 818, it is clear from both of those decisions that real estate brokers may prepare listing agreements and deposit receipts or other forms of agreement first bringing the buyer and seller together; they may not as brokers complete conveyancing forms such as deeds, mortgages, notes, assignments and satisfaction of mortgages or other documents required to consummate the contract. The preparation of bulk sales affidavits, as well as other acts in compliances [sic] with the bulk sales law, are beyond the province of the broker. Business brokers and their associates and employees are similarly prohibited from preparing any documents in connection with the sale of businesses other than listing agreements and deposit receipts or other initial contracts bringing the buyers and sellers together. If respondent is aware of instances of the unauthorized practice of law by real estate brokers, salesmen and employees, he should bring them to the attention of the proper authorities, but he cannot rely upon them as effecting any change in the applicable law.

.   .   .

It is therefore, the order of this Court that:

1. Respondent be enjoined from forming corporations, including the preparation of charters, by-laws, resolutions, stock certificates, and other documents incidental to the contractual rights of the corporation, its incorporators, and stockholders, and from advising others in respect thereto.

2. Respondent be enjoined from advising others on the legal effect of joint tenancies or other types of ownership.

3. Respondent be enjoined from preparing any documents for others in connection with the purchase and sale of businesses with the exception of listings and deposit receipts or other initial agreements bringing buyers and sellers of businesses together.

It is so ordered.

CHAPTER 5
REVIEW QUESTIONS AND PROBLEMS

1. What is the first step in a suit at law?
2. Upon whom may a summons be served?
3. What is meant by a judgment by default or a decree *pro confesso*?
4. What function do the pleadings serve?
5. Who is an appellant? An appellee?
6. What are the purposes of a pretrial conference?
7. Name four discovery procedures?
8. Distinguish between a verdict and a judgment.
9. What is *voir dire* examination and what is its purpose?

10. What are instructions for the jury? Why are they necessary? Who finds the facts and who pronounces the law?
11. Give the qualifications for a judge. Considering these qualifications, how should judges be chosen—by appointment or by election? Discuss.
12. What is a writ of execution?
13. What is a motion for directed verdict? What is its function?
14. What are the uses of a writ of attachment?
15. Contrast the duties of a trial judge with those of a justice of a reviewing court.
16. When may a person give legal advice?
17. List four business specialists some of whose activities may constitute the unauthorized practice of law.

chapter 6

Nonjudicial
Methods for
Resolving Conflicts

1-40. Introduction. In our society, there are a variety of methods which can be used to resolve conflicts and disputes. The most common is by a compromise or settlement agreement between the parties to the dispute. Conflicts and disputes which are not settled by agreement between the parties may be resolved by litigation. A third important method for resolving conflicts and disputes is known as *arbitration*. Arbitration is the submission of a controversy to a nonjudicial body for a binding decision. The legal principles applicable to compromise agreements and arbitration will be discussed in this chapter.

1-41. Compromises and Settlements. Most disputes are resolved by the parties involved, without resort to lawyers or courts for assistance. Only a small fraction of the disputes in our society end up in court or even in a lawyer's office. There are a multitude of reasons why compromise is so prevalent a technique for settling disputes. Some of the reasons may be described as personal and others as economic.

The desire to compromise is part of human nature and may be considered to be almost a matter of instinct. Many persons have a fundamental dislike for trouble and a fear of "going to court." The moral and ethical values of a majority of society encourage compromise and settlement. The opinion of persons other than the parties to the dispute is often influential and is a motivating force in many compromises. Thus, both internal and external forces exist which encourage people to settle their differences amicably.

Compromise and settlement of disputes is also encouraged by the economics of many situations. Lawsuits are expensive to both parties. As a general rule, each party must pay his own attorney's fees, and the losing party must pay the court costs. As a matter of practical economics, the winning party in a lawsuit is a loser to the extent of the fees he must pay his attorney.

At least two additional facts of economic life encourage business to settle disputes. First, business must be concerned with its public image and the goodwill of its customers. While the motto "the customer is always right" is not universally applicable today, the influence of the philosophy it represents cannot be underestimated. Second, juries are frequently sympathetic to individuals who have suits against large corporations or defendants who are covered by insurance. Close questions of liability, as well as the size of verdicts, are more often than not resolved against business concerns because of their presumed ability to pay. As a result, business seeks to settle disputes rather than submit them to a jury for decision.

The duty of lawyers to seek compromise and to achieve it where possible is not usually understood by laymen. In providing services to his client, a lawyer will devote a substantial amount of his time, energy, and talent to seeking a compromise solution of the dispute which involves the client. Attempts at compromise will be made before resort to the courts in most cases. Of all the disputes that are the subject of legal advice, the great majority are settled without resort to litigation. Of those that do result in litigation, the great majority are settled without benefit of a final judicial decision. Literally, the attempt of the lawyers to resolve the dispute never ends. It occurs before suit, before and during the trial, after verdict, during appeal and even after appeal. As long as there is a controversy, it is the function of lawyers to attempt to resolve it.

Lawyers on both sides of a controversy seek compromise for a variety of reasons. A lawyer may view his client's case as weak, either on the law or the facts. The amount involved, the necessity for a speedy decision, the nature of the contest, the uncertainty of a legal remedy, the unfavorable publicity, and the expense entailed are some other reasons for avoiding a court trial. Each attorney must evaluate the cause of his client and seek a satisfactory—though not necessarily the most desirable—settlement of the controversy. The settlement of disputes is perhaps the most significant contribution of lawyers to our society.

The compromise of disputes involves certain legal principles of the law of contracts and especially a concept known as *accord and satisfaction.* An accord is an agreement to accept a substituted performance. A satisfaction is the performance of an accord. In and of itself, an accord will not avoid litigation; satisfaction, or performance of the accord, is also required. If the accord is broken, resort to the courts is necessary to enforce the promise to give or receive substituted performance. This subject will be discussed further in the chapters of Book Two on consideration and discharge of contracts.

ARBITRATION

1-42. Introduction.   Arbitration is a procedure whereby a controversy is submitted for a final and binding decision to a person or persons other than the judicial tribunals provided by ordinary process of law. Arbitration usually results from agreement of the parties in dispute, but in some cases it is required by statute. For example, in most states, the decision of the administrative agency in a workmen's compensation dispute between an employer and employee is made by an arbitrator.

There are several advantages to using arbitration as a substitute for litigation. For one thing, it is much quicker and far less expensive. An issue can be submitted to arbitration and decided in less time than it takes to complete the pleading phase of a lawsuit. Then too, arbitration creates less hostility than does litigation, and it allows the parties to continue their business relationship while the dispute is being decided. Finally, under the arbitration process, complex issues can be submitted to an expert for decision. For example, if an issue arises concerning construction of a building, by using arbitration, it can be submitted to an architect for decision. Besides lawyers, other specialists frequently serve as arbitrators; physicians decide issues relating to physical disabilities, certified public accountants on those regarding the book value of stock, and engineers decide issues relating to industrial production. Of course, a substantial amount of arbitration is also conducted by the academic community, especially in the area of labor relations.

The process of arbitration must be distinguished from *mediation.* Arbitration provides a binding decision. In mediation, the third party assists the parties in seeking a compromise, but the mediator lacks authority to impose a binding solution. The purpose of mediation is to supply unbiased input into the negotiations and to encourage conciliation. The purpose of arbitration is the final solution of the dispute.

Ordinarily arbitration is similar to a judicial proceeding. The rules to be followed are either prescribed by statute or agreed upon in the arbitration agreement. The usual arbitration procedure is as follows: The parties to the dispute are given notice of the time and place of the hearing; a hearing at which testimony is received is held; the arbitrator or arbitrators deliberate and render a decision. There are no formal pleadings or motions, and the strict rules of evidence used in trials frequently are not followed. Most often the decision is given without the reasons for it. All in all, the procedure is quite informal. In deciding whether a dispute should be submitted to arbitration, it is necessary to weight the disadvantages caused by this informality against the advantages of the arbitration process.

1-43. Terminology. Two terms, "submission" and "award," have special significance in the law of arbitration. The term "submission" is used to describe the act of referring an issue or issues to the arbitration process. The submitted issues may be factual, legal, or both; they may include questions concerning the interpretation of the arbitration agreement.

Submission may occur under two circumstances. First, the parties may enter into an agreement to arbitrate an existing dispute. The arbitration agreement serves as the "submission" in this case. Second, the parties may contractually agree to submit all issues that *may* arise to arbitration, or they may agree that either party *may* demand arbitration of any issue that arises. Submission to arbitration under the second circumstance occurs when a demand to arbitrate is served on the other party. This may take the form of a notice that a matter is being referred to the arbitrator agreed upon by the parties or a demand that the matter be referred to arbitration. Merely informing the other party that a controversy exists is not an act of submission or a demand for arbitration.[1]

The term "award" describes the decision of the arbitrator. An award is binding on all issues submitted and may be judicially enforced. The award itself is not subject to judicial review on the merits of the decision. There are, however, many issues concerning arbitration which may be litigated. For example, courts may consider the validity of the arbitration contract and attempts to repudiate it. Courts may decide if the arbitrator has exceeded his authority or if a particular issue is subject to the terms of the arbitration agreement.

1-44. Common-Law Arbitration.   Arbitration was recognized by the common law, and it has been the subject of legislation in many states and by the federal government. Arbitration at common law was not a matter of right but was based on an agreement to arbitrate. The agreement to arbitrate was revocable until the time of the final award, because it required continued consent of the parties. Thus, a party who felt that the proceeding was not going favorably would frequently withdraw by repudiating the agreement. When this occurred, the other party could sue for breach of contract, but any recovery was limited to the expenses incurred to date in the proceedings. A distinction existed at common law between an agreement to arbitrate an existing dispute and an agreement to submit future disputes to arbitration. In the latter case, the agreement was unenforceable, and a party who refused to arbitrate when a dispute arose had no liability.

At common law, a party was bound by the award of the arbitrator. The award was enforceable in court by an action brought for that purpose. Since litigation to enforce the award was necessary, many of the advantages of arbitration over litigation did not exist.

1-45. Types of Arbitration Statutes.   The various states have taken four distinct approaches to arbitration. A few have not enacted arbitration legislation. In these states the principles of the common law are applicable. An agreement to arbitrate is revocable, but a final award is enforceable. Other states have enacted statutes which cover only the method of enforcing awards. These states have taken advantage of the cost savings and time reduction aspects of arbitration by eliminating the necessity for a suit on an award. In these states, an agreement to arbitrate is revocable, but there is a quick and inexpensive method for enforcing the award, if rendered.

The majority of states fall into a third category. They have enacted comprehensive arbitration statutes which cover all aspects of submission, the award, and its enforcement. They also recognize common-law arbitration. In these states, an arbitration agreement is revocable if common-law arbitration is being used but is not revocable if the statutory method is being used. If a question arises as to which method the parties are using, this matter is resolved by reference to the statute. If all of the statutory requirements are met in the submission agreement, the arbitration agreement is irrevocable. If any of the statutory requirements for a submission are not met, the arbitration is subject to the common-law principles and the agreement to arbitrate is revocable.

---

[1] Electronics Corp. of America v. Canter Const. Co., page 97

The fourth and final approach to arbitration which has been followed by some states in their legislation is to make the statutory method exclusive. In these states, the statutory requirements for submission must be met, and all proceedings must comply with the statue. Failure to comply with any portion of the statute renders the agreement and the award, if any, a nullity. Statutory compliance makes the agreement irrevocable and the award enforceable.

1-46. General Aspects of Arbitration Statutes.   Arbitration statutes may authorize voluntary arbitration, or they may provide for compulsory arbitration. Statutes authorizing voluntary arbitration have all been held to be constitutional because a party has the right to waive a trial by jury and access to the court system. However, many statutes imposing compulsory arbitration have been declared unconstitutional as a denial of due process of law and a violation of the right to trial by jury. Where the right of judicial review exists, compulsory arbitration statues have been held to be constitutional. But any compulsory arbitration statute is subject to challenge on the above-mentioned constitutional grounds, and it should be noted that legal scholars differ as to the constitutionality of compulsory arbitration statutes that are being proposed in the field of labor-management relations.

The Commissioners on Uniform State Laws have prepared a Uniform Arbitration Act. As of this writing, this Act has been adopted by only nine states, but it is being favorably considered by others. There is also a Federal Arbitration Act, which covers businesses engaged in maritime and interstate commerce. Both of these statutes authorize voluntary arbitration.

Most statutes authorizing voluntary arbitration require a written agreement to arbitrate. Written agreements are required as a corollary of the provision that makes the agreement to arbitrate irrevocable. It should be remembered, however, that in many states, failure to follow the statute is not completely fatal because common-law arbitration is a concurrent method of proceeding.

Most statutes also contain provisions requiring submission within a stated time after the dispute arises—usually six months.[2] These provisions are consistent with the goal of arbitration to obtain a quick resolution of disputes. These statutes recognize too that arbitration contracts can be rescinded on the same grounds as any other contract. For example, fraud, mutual mistake, or lack of capacity would be grounds for voiding arbitration contracts. Revocation by operation of law is provided for also. Such revocation occurs on the death, bankruptcy, or insanity of a party, and by destruction of the subject matter of the agreement.

1-47. Judicial Procedures in Arbitration.   One purpose of arbitration is to avoid the time and expense of litigation. Judicial action may be necessary, however, if either party refuses to submit the dispute to arbitration or refuses to carry out the terms of the award. Statutes usually contemplate the following as the procedures to be followed when a party to an arbitration contract refuses to submit the dispute to arbitration as agreed:

1. The aggrieved party may petition the court for an order directing that the arbitration be carried out according to the terms of the agreement. Upon

[2] See Electronics Corp. of America v. Canter Const. Co., page 98

hearing, if the court finds that making the contract to arbitrate or submission to arbitrate is not an issue, the court directs the parties to proceed to arbitrate according to the terms of the agreement.

2. If, however, there is disagreement as to the making of the contract or submission, the court will try that issue, either with or without a jury. If it is found that no contract was made, the petition is dismissed. If it is found that a contract to arbitrate or to submit was made, and there was a default, the court will issue an order directing the parties to proceed with arbitration according to the contract.

If the parties do submit the issues to arbitration as agreed or if arbitration is conducted pursuant to a court order, certain judicial proceedings may be necessary in order to enforce the award. These procedures as prescribed by most statutes are

1. After the award is made, it is filed with the clerk of the court. After twenty days, if no exceptions are filed, it becomes a judgment upon which a writ of execution may issue in the same manner as if a judgment had been entered in a civil action.

2. A dissatisfied party may file exceptions to the award for such reasons as (1) the award covered matters beyond the issues submitted, (2) the arbitrators failed to follow the statutory requirements, and (3) fraud or corruption permeated the decision. The court does *not* review the *merits* of the decision.

3. Appeals from the judgment may be taken as in any legal action, and such appeals cannot be denied by contractual provisions.

4. If it appears that the award should be vacated, the court may refer it back to the arbitrators, with instructions for correction and rehearing.

Other important judicial aspects of arbitration proceedings are

1. As a general rule, a court cannot remove an arbitrator for bias or interest in the subject matter of the dispute.[3]

2. If a party makes an appearance before the arbitrators and does not raise objection to the proceedings, he has thereby ratified the terms of the arbitration contract and the submission. He cannot later challenge the validity of the proceedings.

3. Repudiation of a contract that contains an arbitration clause does not invalidate the arbitration clause therein. The issues arising out of the repudiation of the contract, such as the liability for breach of contract, will still be decided by arbitration rather than by judicial proceedings.

1-48. Conclusion. Arbitration, as a "substitute for the courts in settling controversies" is a very useful arrangement and one rapidly growing in importance to business. Commercial arbitration clauses are being added to many business contracts, and compulsory arbitration statutes are being considered at least a partial solution to such problems as strikes by public employees and strikes in industries directly affecting the public interest, such as transporta-

[3] Astoria Medical Group v. Health Ins. Plan of Gr. N.Y., page 98

tion. The American Arbitration Association will furnish experienced arbitrators for parties in a dispute; many standard contract clauses provide for submission to this group. Arbitration costs are deductible business expenses, and this speedy, inexpensive solution to conflicts should be carefully considered by business and legal counsel in all possible areas of dispute.

NONJUDICIAL METHODS FOR RESOLVING CONFLICTS CASES

Electronics Corp. of America v. Canter Const. Co.

178 N.E.2d 1 (Mass.) 1961

Plaintiff (Electronics) filed a petition for acceptance and confirmation of an arbitration award and for judgment thereon. On June 20, 1956, the parties had agreed to submit "all disputes, claims or questions pertaining to the interpretation of this contract or the performance by either party" to arbitration. On January 22, 1958, Electronics gave notice to Canter of alleged defects in Canter's performance, especially leakage in the walls. On June 18, 1959, Electronics demanded arbitration. On March 31 and April 1, 1960, the demand was heard by the arbitrators. In May, 1960, the arbitrators awarded Electronics $6,045. Canter contended at the arbitration proceeding that the submission to arbitration was not timely and was in violation of the statute on arbitration which required submission within six months. The same defense was asserted to the petition filed with the lower court. The lower court confirmed the award of the arbitrators.

CUTTER, J. . . . We think that, in a case like this where an agreement for arbitration of future controversies is contained in a contract, "submission" . . . refers to the completion by the party demanding arbitration of the action necessarily to be performed by that party, in accordance with the arbitration clause in his contract, to bring about arbitration. Indeed, as is pointed out in Kellor, *Arbitration in Action,* pp. 67-68, where, "in a primary contract," there is a clause providing for the "arbitration of a *future* undisclosed dispute," then a "party to such a contract and clause may demand arbitration in the same manner as under a submission." He points out that such a clause is "enforceable . . . as a submission," and that when "such a clause is used, no additional . . . submission is required." If a party to such a clause upon demand can have arbitration, regardless of the current wishes of other parties, then, in substance, the demand serves the same function that is performed by a submission in the case of agreements to arbitrate preexisting controversies. In a case like this, the demand really constitutes the submission. . . .

This contract merely provided that a matter "shall be submitted . . . in accordance with provisions . . . of the American Arbitration Association." The record does not establish what those provisions were, beyond stating that they did not require that a "demand . . . be filed by stipulation or agreement or within any specified time." The demand for arbitration filed with the American Arbitration Association on June 18, 1959, contained both (a) a demand for arbitration, and (b) a statement of Electronics' claims. The record reveals no evidence which required the trial judge to find that any further action by Electronics was necessary to initiate the arbitration proceeding. The trial judge would have been warranted in treating the demand of June 18, 1959, as a submission. . . .

. . . Although the language . . . ("within six months . . . after due notice by any party . . . claiming the arbitration of any controversy") is confusing, we think that its most reasonable meaning is that the notice which starts the six-months' period running is a notice of a claim for arbitration and not a notice of a controversy. It would be hard to determine when a complaint in process of negotiation becomes a controversy because the parties cannot agree on a settlement. A claim for arbitration is an identifiable event.

. . . No evidence suggests that there was any earlier demand for arbitration than that of June 18, 1959. Since we hold that this demand constituted both a "notice claiming arbitration" and a submission, the submission was within six months of (because simultaneous with) the demand.

Our conclusions are consistent with the general purpose of the 1925 legislation to facilitate arbitration proceedings. They are also consistent with the present tendency to interpret and apply arbitration statutes, agreements, and procedures broadly. . . .

Although a considerable period elapsed between January 22, 1958, and the demand for arbitration of June 18, 1959, there is no suggestion that either the demand for arbitration or the court petition to enforce the award was filed after the expiration of any applicable statute of limitations. . . .

Exceptions overruled.

Astoria Medical Group v. Health Ins. Plan of Gr. N.Y.

182 N.E.2d 85 (N.Y.) 1962

FULD, J. The intensely practical question presented by this appeal revolves about the attempt of one party to a typical tripartite arbitration agreement to have the court intervene, before an award has been made, and disqualify the arbitrator designated by the other party because of his asserted personal interest and partiality.

The appellant Health Insurance Plan . . . is engaged in writing policies of insurance which provide complete medical care. And, to assure such care to its policyholders, HIP enters into contracts with a number of partnerships of physicians, called Medical Groups, whereby they agree to furnish the necessary medical services. In identical contracts made by HIP with those Medical Groups which are the respondents herein, it was agreed that each of them would be paid a fixed sum, or "capitation," for each insured person receiving the services of the particular Group. In addition to such "capitation," HIP agreed to pay each Group an additional sum—termed "supplemental capitation"—in an amount depending upon criteria and standards which were to be established in the future.

The contract further recited that, if the parties were unable to agree upon such criteria by a specified date, "the unresolved issues [were] to go to arbitration" in accordance with the arbitration clause of the contract. This provided, in part, that "One arbitrator shall be appointed by HIP and another by the GROUP, who jointly shall appoint a third arbitrator" and that, if the third arbitrator could not be agreed upon, either party was to request the American

Arbitration Association to select him. The decision of two of the three arbitrators was to be final and binding upon both parties.

When the parties failed to agree on the essential criteria for "supplemental capitation," the Medical Groups demanded arbitration and appointed an attorney, Samuel Seligsohn, Esq., as their arbitrator, HIP, in turn, designated, as its arbitrator, Dr. George Baehr, a physician with a long and distinguished career in medicine. The Groups objected to the designation of Dr. Baehr. Noting that he was one of the incorporators of HIP and its president from 1950 to 1957 and that he is, currently, a member of its board of directors and one of its paid consultants, they moved for an order (1) disqualifying him on the ground of personal interest, bias and partiality arising out of his relationship with HIP and (2) requiring HIP "to designate an impartial arbitrator." The justice of Special Term granted the motion and the Appellate Division affirmed by a divided court, granting leave to appeal to us on certified questions. . . .

Although we recognize that a strong argument may be advanced, in reliance upon our statute, to support the appellant HIP's contention that the court lacks authority to intervene until after the arbitrators have made an award, we are persuaded that, in an appropriate case, the courts have inherent power to disqualify an arbitrator before an award has been rendered. . . . However, the present is not such a case.

Arbitration is essentially a creature of contract, a contract in which the parties themselves charter a private tribunal for the resolution of their disputes. The law does no more than lend its sanction to the agreement of the parties, the court's role being limited to the enforcement of the terms of the contract. . . .

It is indisputable, as a general proposition, that the parties to an arbitration contract are completely free to agree upon the identity of the arbitrators and the manner in which they are to be chosen. Indeed, our statute so provides, declaring as it does that, "If, in the contract for arbitration . . . provision be made for a method of naming or appointing an arbitrator or arbitrators . . . such method shall be followed" (Civ.Prac.Act, § 1452). And, in interpreting the provision, this court has expressed the view that "The spirit of the arbitration law being the fuller effectuation of contractual rights, the method for selecting arbitrators and the composition of the arbitral tribunal have been left to the contract of the parties."

In order to determine, therefore, whether HIP's choice of Dr. Baehr was permissible or impermissible, we look to the agreement between the parties. It provides, as we have seen, that "One arbitrator shall be appointed by HIP and another by the GROUP, who jointly shall appoint a third arbitrator."

This type of tripartite arbitration provision, requiring each side to name its own arbitrator and such party-designated arbitrators to agree upon a third neutral arbitrator, is one which has been widely used in both labor and commercial arbitration. Arising out of the repeated use of the tripartite arbitral board, there has grown a common acceptance of the fact that the party-designated arbitrators are not and cannot be "neutral," at least in the sense that the third arbitrator or a judge is. And, as might be expected, the literature is replete with references both to arbitrators who are "neutrals" and those who are "partial," "partisan" or "interested" and to arbitration boards composed entirely of "neutrals" and those contrastingly denominated "tripartite in their membership."

In short, usage and experience indicate that, in the type of tripartite arbitration envisaged by the contract before us, each party's arbitrator "is not individually expected to be neutral."

In fact, the very reason each of the parties contracts for the choice of his own arbitrator is to make certain that his "side" will, in a sense, be represented on the tribunal. And, it was with that thought in mind that this court held the choice of an arbitrator to be a "valuable" contractual right not lightly to be disregarded.

Turning to the case before us, there can be no doubt that, when HIP and the Medical Groups agreed upon the use of a tripartite tribunal, they must be taken to have contracted with reference to established practice and usage in the field of arbitration. In the light of accepted practice, which sanctions and contemplates two non-neutral arbitrators on a tripartite board, the parties must be deemed to have intended that each was to be free to appoint any arbitrator desired, however close his relationship to it or to the dispute. Moreover, this conclusion is reinforced by the fact that the provision relating to arbitration contains no word of limitation on the identity, status or qualifications of the arbitrators; had the parties intended that their appointees be completely impartial or disinterested, they could have readily so provided.

It is hardly necessary to observe that we enforce the tripartite arbitration clause before us because it is the one chosen by the parties, not because we favor it or regard it as ideal or even desirable. . . . If they choose to have their disputes resolved by a body consisting of two partisan arbitrators, and a third neutral arbitrator, that is their affair. We may not rewrite their contract.

Nor do we perceive any public policy which condemns or forbids this arrangement. On the contrary, this court many years ago recognized that, although every arbitrator must act fairly and impartially in arriving at a decision and making an award, "a known interest does not disqualify, and the parties may not complain merely because the arbitrators named were known to be chosen with a view to a particular relationship to their nominator or to the subject matter of the controversy." In point of fact, even in cases where the contract expressly designated a *single* arbitrator who was employed by one of the parties or intimately connected with him, the courts have refused to disqualify the arbitrator on the ground of either interest or partiality.

.   .   .

Our decision that an arbitrator may not be disqualified solely because of a relationship to his nominator or to the subject matter of the controversy does not, however, mean that he may be deaf to the testimony or blind to the evidence presented. Partisan he may be, but not dishonest. Like all arbitrators, the arbitrator selected by a party must (unless the requirement is waived) take the prescribed oath that he will "faithfully and fairly . . . hear and examine the matters in controversy and . . . make a just award according to the best of [his] understanding." And, if either one of the party-appointed arbitrators fails to act in accordance with such oath, the award may be attacked on the ground that it is the product of "evident partiality or corruption." Such an attack, however, must be based on something overt, some misconduct on the part of an arbitrator, and not simply on his interest in the subject matter of the controversy or his relationship to the party who selected him.

It may well be that there is greater danger that party-designated arbitrators will overstep the bounds of propriety than will those who are disinterested neutrals. But this risk, quite apart from being one to which the parties submitted, is thought by many to be more than offset by certain benefits gained from use of the tripartite board. One such benefit is that arbitrators selected by the parties are, generally speaking, experts on the subject in controversy and bring to their task a wealth of specialized knowledge. As one commentator has indicated, "the expert guidance" furnished by "partisan" arbitrators "can be of assistance to the neutral member, who is not in a position to appreciate the problem and the fine points of its setting." Consequently, to disqualify an arbitrator because of his relationship to, or association with, his nominator would be to withhold from the arbitration board a source of the specialized knowledge which contributes to the unique value of the arbitration process. Moreover, any personal advantage to be derived from the power to select as arbitrator anyone he wishes is available to each party and, experience tells us, is ordinarily availed of by both.

In brief, it is our view that, since both parties, by agreeing upon tripartite arbitration, have necessarily accepted the idea of "partisan" appointees, neither may object to the other's designation of someone associated with his interest or related to him.

The order appealed from should be reversed and the petitioner's motion denied, with costs in all courts.

CHAPTER 6
REVIEW QUESTIONS AND PROBLEMS

1. What is the difference between arbitration and mediation?
2. Name four situations in which business may want to include an arbitration provision in a contract.
3. *X* Co., by contract with *Y* labor union, agreed to submit disputes to arbitration. As a result of being permanently disabled, an employee was paid workmen's compensation under a settlement contract. *X* Co. refused to permit the employee to return under a contract provision that allowed it to do so. The union objected and demanded arbitration. The company refused, contending that there was nothing to arbitrate since the contract terms were not in dispute and the employee admitted his disability. Must the company submit the dispute to arbitration?
4. What are the advantages of arbitration over a judicial decision?
5. What are the three methods for resolving conflicts in our society?
6. List three reasons why lawyers encourage business to settle controversies out of court.
7. Define submission and award.

8. What is the principal distinction between common-law arbitration and statutory arbitration?
9. To what businesses is the Federal Arbitration Act applicable?
10. What remedy is available to a party to an arbitration agreement if the arbitrator exceeds his authority?
11. What is meant by the term "tripartite arbitration"?

BOOK TWO

Contracts

Introduction
to Contracts

2-1. Nature and Importance of the Contractual Relationship. The law of contracts is concerned with the creation, transfer, and disposition of property rights through promises. Property in this sense refers not only to physical items, but also to a "bundle of rights" which the law will enforce and protect in connection with such items. The "bundle of rights" concept is discussed in Chapter 49. A contract is a promise or a set of promises for the breach of which the law gives a remedy or the performance of which the law recognizes as a duty. In other words, a contract is based upon legally enforceable promises.

The law of contracts is the oldest branch of the law relating to business or to commercial transactions. In one form or another it has existed from the beginning of organized society. Just as the safety of person and of property depends upon the rules of criminal law, so the security and stability of the business world are dependent upon the law of contracts. It is the legal mechanism by which the free enterprise system has developed and been enabled to operate. It is the tool by which promises are made and expectations created to the end that there will be a continuous flow of goods and services to meet man's economic needs.

To a very high degree our whole philosophy of personal liberty, with its concept of private property—the right to acquire and to dispose of property freely and to operate private business enterprises—has as one of its main structural supports the law of contracts. In order for a contract to serve as an instrument to create wealth and enhance the economic good, freedom to contract, accompanied by legal machinery for the enforcement of contracts is essential.

When they enter into a contract, the parties, by mutual assent, either expressed or implied, "fix their own terms and set bounds upon their liabilities." Thus, it may be said that in a very real sense, the parties freely create for themselves their own law, leaving it only to the state to set up the machinery for the interpretation of the contract and the enforcement of the promises.

Although the parties to a contract fix their own terms and set bounds upon their liabilities, they are subject to limitations. To create a valid contract, the expression of "the terms" of the contract must be in compliance with rules of law. Many factors enter into the determination of whether or not a promise is in compliance with the rules of law. What is the status of the person who made the promise? What is the status of the person to whom it was made? How was the promise expressed? Was it intended to be the final expression of agreement between the parties? Was the promise made orally or was it in writing? Does the exchange of promises or the promise given in return for expected performance result in a contract, that is, are the necessary contractual requirements and elements present: consideration, legal capacity of the parties, a legal purpose in light of the rules of law and of sound public policy?

This latter requirement recognizes that in our society parties do not possess *absolute* freedom of contract. For example, the public interest demands that parties not be allowed to enter into contracts unduly limiting competition or resulting in unreasonable restraint of trade. In addition, inequality of bargaining power between the parties often requires action by legislative, judicial, and administrative bodies to control the terms and provisions of contracts. Moreover, there is a growing body of law about the obligation of businesses affected with the public interest to *enter into* contracts. The courts are frequently called upon to answer the question: Must the defendant contract with the plaintiff ? [1]

"Freedom of contract" is a relative term and has different meanings, depending upon the context in which it is used. It is as difficult to define as "justice," "equality," "due process," and "morality." Freedom of contract as a part of our legal and economic systems will be discussed in the various portions of this Book on Contracts. Although it is a branch of the private sector of the law, the law of contracts has many aspects that make it a part of the public law. Indeed, one trend in the law today is to consider that more and more contracts are sufficiently connected with the public interest to warrant more and more governmental participation in setting their terms.

Since the law of contracts furnishes the foundation for other branches of commercial law, a study of the general rules applicable to contract law logically comes first in the study of business law. The special rules of law pertaining to agency, sales, commercial paper, corporations, partnerships, and secured transactions are all based upon general principles of contract law. These special areas are discussed in the books that follow this one.

2-2. Environment of Contract Law.   The materials in Book One are of special importance to the subject of contracts. For example, the law of contracts reflects the application of both equitable and legal concepts, includes a combination of common law and statutory law, contains significant problems of statutory interpretation, and illustrates the influence of social forces on the law. Law does not exist in a "vacuum;" therefore, it is helpful to study this subject from the aspect of its historical background, its present state and the manner in which present trends augur significant changes and developments.

[1] Bloss d.b.a. Eastown Theaters v. Federated Publications, Inc., page 116

Developments in recent years have produced many advances in the social aspects of the law of contracts.

The social and environmental elements of contract law are of great interest and concern to the business community not only for the purpose of efficient legal operation and maximization of profits, but also from the standpoint of the obligations of business to society. There are many indications that a substantial segment of the business community recognizes that obligations do exist with regard to racial problems, ecological problems, consumer problems, and utilization of technological advances for the public good. To better understand and appreciate contract law as it is today and trends for the future, a brief survey of some aspects of the historical development of contracts will serve to set the stage.

2-3. Some Historical Aspects. Until about a century ago a person who wished to bring legal action against another could do so only if the facts of his case would fit into certain patterns evidenced by "forms of action." At first only a few forms of action were available. These forms of action were represented by "writs"—outlines of the various types of redressable wrongs. These writs were collected in a register, and a plaintiff would attempt to select a writ into which the facts of his claim would fit. If there was no writ for his particular type of case, he was without remedy. In civil cases the writs were either in contract or in tort.

Prior to the sixteenth century there were only two forms of action in contract. One of these, the action of *covenant,* allowed an action to be brought for failure to perform a promise, but only if the promise was under seal. The seal was a waxen impression affixed to a document bearing the symbol of the person obligated to perform. Promises not under seal, even though in writing, did not fall within the writ of covenant, and no remedy at law was available for their breach. The basis for the action was not the promise but rather the seal affixed to the writing.

The other ancient form of contractual action was *debt.* This form of action enabled a plaintiff to recover a definite sum of money owed to him by the defendant, which sum the defendant had promised to pay. It was not necessary that the promise to pay be under seal. The remedy was a restricted one—it was not available if the obligation was to do anything other than pay a "sum certain" in money.

Covenant and debt had this in common—the promises that could be enforced were not being enforced *as such.* In covenant, the formality of the seal was the important factor. In debt, it was the idea that the defendant had something that belonged to the plaintiff and that he should be ordered to return it.

For centuries these were the only legal remedies available for the breach of a contractual promise. Later, a remedy was made available for breach of a promise in cases in which one of the parties had performed his part of the bargain. The next step in the development of contract law was the gradual recognition that many promises, as such, should be enforced even though the person to whom the promise was made had not yet rendered any performance. At this point in legal history the law of contracts truly began to provide the tools for commercial transactions, and a period of development and refinement which continues to this day was made possible.

Since the common law did not purport to recognize the enforceability of *all* promises, there had to be some test by which promises could be analyzed to determine which were and which were not enforceable. To provide a reasonable test is a continuing modern problem, for the quest continues for further clarification as to what the requirement should be and, indeed, if there should be any technical requirement at all for a promise to be enforceable.

The one which evolved and which is still recognized is the requirement that *consideration* be present as a requisite of an enforceable promise. A later chapter is devoted to consideration, but it should be here noted that this requirement is in the law of contracts because of the viability of the concept that there must be a *quid pro quo*—something given to a promisor—in order to render his promise enforceable. The concept of consideration as an essential element in making a promise enforceable is unique to the common law in the Anglo-American culture.

Lack or failure of consideration is only one of many grounds that may make a promise unenforceable. There is a distinction between the *requirements* for a contract, of which consideration is of basic importance, and those elements which preclude the *enforceability* of an agreement. Thus, an agreement may be unenforceable (even though consideration is present) because it was made for an illegal purpose or its purpose was otherwise contrary to public policy —a matter of great importance in the 1970s. Also, contracts that lack certain required formalities will not be enforced by the courts.

The chapters that follow will show how the law of contracts has adjusted to needs of business and society. Note that some of these changes have been brought about by legislation, whereas many others are products of the courts. The most significant legislation affecting the law of contracts today is the Uniform Commercial Code, referred to hereafter as the Code. The Code has been adopted by forty-nine states, the District of Columbia, and the Virgin Islands. Louisiana, presumably because of its civil law heritage, has not adopted the entire Code, but has adopted Article 2—Sales. Article 2 of the Code will be covered in Book Three, and it is suggested that Chapter 17 be studied at this time. As the materials in contracts are discussed in the pages to follow, there will be frequent references to Code provisions. It must be remembered at all times that the Code provisions discussed in this Book on Contracts are only applicable to contracts for the sale of goods. Its provisions are not applicable to contracts involving the sale of real property, to contracts of personal service, or to contracts involving intangible personal property. For these contracts, the common law provides the legal principles. This means that the rules and principles of contract law have been adjusted, changed, and modified by statute to meet the needs of transactions in goods. A major part of all contracts involve goods. In this discussion some of the significant changes wrought by the Code are mentioned, and others are discussed in Book Three, Introduction to the Uniform Commercial Code.

2-4. Classification of Contracts.   For certain purposes it is desirable to classify contracts according to the characteristics which they possess. They may be classified as follows:

1. Valid, voidable, or unenforceable.[2]
2. Executed or executory.
3. Bilateral or unilateral.
4. Express or implied (in fact or in law).

An *executed* contract is one that has been fully carried out by the contracting parties. An *executory* contract is one that is yet to be performed. An agreement may be executed on the part of one party and executory on the part of the other. For example, a contract for the purchase of a suit of clothes on credit, followed by the delivery of the suit, is executed on the part of the merchant and executory on the part of the purchaser.

Contracts ordinarily result from an offer made by one party to another and accepted by the latter. A *bilateral* contract involves two promises, one made by each of the parties to the agreement. To illustrate: *A* offers to sell to *B* certain merchandise at an established price. *B*, after receiving the offer, communicates his acceptance to *A* by promising to buy the merchandise and to pay the price set forth in the offer. After the promises are exchanged, it becomes the legal duty of each party to carry out the terms of the agreement. Most contracts are bilateral in character.

A *unilateral* contract consists of a promise for an *act*. The acceptance by the offeree is the performance of the act requested rather than the promise to perform it. The Restatement of Contracts in defining a unilateral contract and in differentiating it from a bilateral contract states:

> A unilateral contract is one in which no promisor receives a promise as consideration for his promise. A bilateral contract is one in which there are mutual promises between two parties to the contract; each party being both a promisor and a promisee.

An order for merchandise sent by a retailer to a manufacturer, asking for prompt shipment of the goods ordered, illustrates a unilateral offer. The buyer requests and desires shipment, rather than a promise to ship. Until the goods are shipped, the retailer is at liberty to withdraw his offer. The problems inherent in this rule of law, especially to the seller, are obvious. Accordingly, the Uniform Commercial Code provides that the manufacturer can accept (and thereby bind the retailer) either by shipping the merchandise or by *promising* to ship.

A contract may result from an oral or written agreement in which event it is said to be an *express* contract. On the other hand, a contract may be entirely implied from conduct and acts of the parties, the acts being such that a contract may be inferred from them. This is called a contract *implied in fact*. In other instances, the contract may be, and often is, partially expressed and partially implied. Thus, if a person delivers his TV set to a repairman to be repaired, he impliedly agrees to pay the repairman a reasonable fee for his services and materials.

A contract may be implied in fact whenever one person, without protest, knowingly accepts a benefit at the expense of another under circumstances that negate the intent to make a gift. The person who accepts the benefit impliedly

---

[2] To be discussed in detail in chapters that follow.

promises to pay the fair value of the benefit that he receives. However, no implied promise to pay arises when the person who receives a benefit is unaware that such a benefit is being conferred. It is the acceptance of benefits at a time when it is possible to reject them that raises the implied promise to pay for them. To illustrate: *A,* by mistake, and during the absence of *B,* made certain repairs on *B's* residence, having mistaken it for *C's* residence. Upon his return, *B* was under no duty to pay for the repairs, although he of necessity made use of them in connection with his occupancy of the property. The use of the house created no implied promise to pay for the repairs, since *B* had never had the opportunity to reject them. However, if *B* had been present and had watched the repairs being made, his silence might well obligate him to pay the reasonable value of the improvement.

In accord with recent governmental attempts to protect consumers, actions by administrative agencies and others have been and are directed at changing the law relating to implied-in-fact contracts. For example, the Federal Trade Commission, as part of its responsibility to prevent unfair and deceptive practices by business, has proposed a regulation that in effect nullifies the existing law of implied-in-fact contracts in certain cases. This regulation provides that if a business mails goods to a consumer who has not ordered them, the consumer need not pay for them or return them. This regulation is designed to eliminate the practice of mail-order businesses sending out unsolicited goods requesting the consumer to either pay for them or return them. This regulation is presumably not applicable to cases where goods are mailed by mistake. This federal protection of consumers is another indication of the trend away from strict application of contract law to consumer transactions.

2-5. Quasi Contract.   A contract implied in fact must be distinguished from a contract implied in law, generally known as *quasi contract.*[3] An implied-in-fact contract is a true contract, created by inference from facts and circumstances which show the assent and intention of the parties. Quasi contract is not a contract in the technical sense; it is a remedy used by courts to do justice and to avoid unjust enrichment. Quasi contract imposes a duty upon a party and considers the duty as arising from a contract. It is a legal fiction dictated by reason, justice, and equity to prevent fraud, wrongdoing, or the unjust enrichment of one person at the expense of another. The law in effect infers a promise by a party to do what in equity and good conscience he ought to do, even though he does not in actuality want or intend to do it. To be entitled to the remedy of quasi contract, the plaintiff must prove that a benefit has been conferred on the defendant, that the defendant has accepted and retained the benefit, and that the circumstances are such that to allow the defendant to keep the benefits without paying for them would be inequitable.[4] A typical case might involve the receipt of money which was paid to the recipient by mistake. The person improperly receiving the money would have a duty to return it, and since no actual contract existed, the law would imply one.

Quasi contract, as a remedy, is used in a variety of situations when one person, unofficiously and without fault or misconduct, confers a benefit upon

[3] Gulberg v. Greenfield, page 117
[4] Circle v. O'Harra, page 118

another, for which the latter in equity and good conscience ought to pay.[5] Additional situations are those in which property is wrongfully appropriated or converted; money or property is obtained by trespass, fraud, or duress; or necessities of life are furnished a person who is under legal disability. In each of these situations no contract exists, but the quasi contract remedy is given because one person would be unjustly enriched if he were not required to pay for the benefits received.

2-6. Elements of a Contract.   As noted at the beginning of this chapter, a contract is defined in terms of promises. The Restatement defines a "promise" as an undertaking "however expressed, either that something shall happen, or that something shall not happen, in the future." The basic elements of a contract are:

1. The *Agreement* which consists of an *offer* by one party and its *acceptance* by the other.
2. *Consideration,* which is the price paid by each party to the other or what each party receives and gives up in the Agreement.
3. *Competent parties* which means that the parties must possess legal capacity to contract (be of legal age and sane).
4. A *legal purpose* consistent with law and sound policy.

These elements will be considered in detail in the chapters which follow. The legal procedures used in contract litigation are discussed in the sections which follow.

2-7. Judicial Remedies for Breach of Contract.   The breach of a contract or the threat thereof defeats the expectations of the parties and may even have consequences that affect persons other than the contracting parties. There is a natural desire to quickly and expeditiously resolve the problems arising from the breach. Three primary methods are used to obtain a resolution: negotiation and compromise, arbitration, and legal action. The third method is one of last resort and is used less frequently than the first. Most differences which arise over breaches of contract are settled by the parties without litigation.

However, many contract cases do reach the courts, and remedies are provided for the purpose of compensating the injured party for his loss and otherwise giving him relief. The threat of court action often has a salutary effect on a person who has either breached or threatened to breach a contract and often produces cooperation in effecting an out-of-court settlement.

Three basic remedies are afforded for breach of contract: dollar damages, specific performance, and rescission. In general, these remedies are exclusive, and a party is required to elect one to the exclusion of others. The Code, however, is much more flexible in the matter of remedies and allows an "aggrieved party," a person entitled to resort to a remedy, the privilege of recovering damages *in addition* to one of the other remedies. In other respects, also, the Code greatly expands the remedies and provides flexibility in

[5] Anderson v. Copeland, page 119

their application. Under the Code the remedies are to be liberally administered to the end that the aggrieved party may be put in as good a position as if the other party had fully performed.

Money damages are recoverable in a court of law; specific performance and rescission are equitable remedies. While damages are always recoverable for a loss sustained as the result of a breach, the equitable remedies are not so readily available and will be allowed less often and usually only if the remedy at law by way of damages is not an adequate one under the circumstances of the case. The equity court will order specific performance of a contract—that the party who has breached actually do what he had agreed to do under the contract. For example, in a contract to sell land, the court will order that the seller execute a deed to the buyer. Rescission—disaffirmance of a contract and a return of the parties to the status quo, or position each occupied prior to entering into the contract—is afforded where a transaction has been induced by fraud or misrepresentation. Rescission will also be granted to a minor in order that he may exercise his privilege of withdrawing from a contract.

A party who discovers facts which warrant rescission of a contract has a duty to act promptly and, if he elects to rescind, to notify the other party within reasonable time so that rescission may be accomplished at a time when parties may still be restored, as nearly as possible, to their original positions.[6] The party who seeks rescission must return what he has received in substantially as good a condition as when he received it. Since this remedy is an equitable one, it is subject to the usual maxims of courts of equity.

DAMAGES

2-8. Theory of Damages.   The purpose and the theory of damages is to make the injured party whole or to place him, as nearly as a payment of money can, in the same position he would have occupied had the breach of contract not occurred. The fundamental idea is to give just compensation for the losses which flowed from the breach. The theory is that a party should be compensated for the damages that arise naturally from the breach and were within the contemplation of the parties at the time of making the contract as those that might arise in the event of a breach. The injured party is not entitled to a profit from the breach of the contract; his recovery is limited to an amount that will place him in the same position in which he would have been had the contract been carried out. Unusual and unexpected damages resulting from peculiar facts unknown to either party at the time the agreement was entered into are generally not recoverable.

The question as to the amount of damages is usually one of fact for the jury. While a jury may not speculate or guess as to the amount of damage, the fact that the amount is not capable of exact computation will not prevent a recovery. Justice and public policy require that a wrongdoer bear the risk of uncertainty which his wrong may have created. A reasonable basis of computation for recovery is used, but damages which are uncertain, contingent, remote, or speculative cannot be used. Loss of profits may be included as an element of

---

[6] Galati v. Potamkin Chevrolet Co., page 121.

recoverable damages if they can be computed with reasonable certainty from tangible and competent evidence.

The plaintiff is not entitled to recover the amount which he expends for attorney's fees, unless the contract so provides or special legislation permits it. Litigation is expensive, and the party who wins the law suit is still "out of pocket," since the legal expenses will usually reduce the net recovery substantially. Court costs, however, which include witness fees and filing costs, are usually assessed against the losing party.

2-9. Special Types of Damages.   Several terms are used to describe special types of damages. "Nominal damages" are awarded if no measurable actual loss is established. A small and inconsequential sum, usually one dollar, is awarded to the plaintiff to show that a technical breach had occurred.

The term "liquidated damages" or "liquidated damage clause" is used to describe the situation in which the parties provide in their contract for the amount of damages to be awarded in the event of a breach. These provisions will be enforced unless the court considers the stipulation to be a penalty for failure to perform, rather than compensation for damages. Should the court find the term to have been inserted primarily to force actual performance and not to compensate for probable injury, it will not be enforced. In order to be upheld as liquidated damages and not as a penalty, the amount of recovery agreed upon must bear a reasonable relation to the probable damage to be sustained by the breach.[7] Recovery is allowed for the amount agreed upon by the parties, although the damages actually suffered may vary somewhat from those agreed upon in the contract.[8]

The Code specifically provides that a contract clause which calls for unreasonably large liquidated damages is void. To be valid under the Code, a liquidated-damages clause must be reasonable in light of the anticipated or actual harm caused by the breach, the difficulties of proof of loss, and the inconvenience or nonfeasibility of otherwise obtaining an adequate remedy. Another form of liquidation of damages is the forfeiture of goods when a buyer defaults after paying part of the price or making a deposit as security. The Code provides that, absent a liquidated-damages clause, a buyer who defaults is entitled to recover back from the seller, any amount (1) by which his payments exceed 20 percent of the price, or (2) $500, whichever is smaller. Thus, if the buyer had made a deposit of $500 on the purchase of appliances for a price of $1,500, he would after his breach and return of the goods be entitled to recover $200 from the seller. If the sale contract contained a liquidated-damages clause, such a buyer would be entitled to recover the excess of the amount by which his deposit exceeds the amount provided for in such clause. Thus, a buyer who has made a part payment will not be unduly penalized by his breach, and the seller will not receive a windfall. It is restricted to relatively small purchases and is another consumer-oriented provision of the Code.

The term "punitive" or "exemplary" damages refers to damages awarded to one party in order to punish the other for his conduct. While it is not the purpose of a civil proceeding to punish a party, punitive damages are allowed in cases of intentional torts such as fraud or libel. These damages are imposed

[7] Security Safety Corp. v. Kuznicki, page 122
[8] Knutton v. Cofield, page 123

in the interest of society to deter the commission of these acts. Punitive damages may be awarded only when there are also actual damages. Punitive damages are seldom allowed in contract cases.

2-10. Rules Concerning Damages.   The injured party is dutybound to mitigate the damages. It is his duty to take reasonable steps to reduce the actual loss to a minimum. He cannot add to his loss or permit the damages to be enhanced when it is reasonably within his power to prevent such occurrence. For example, an employee who has been wrongfully discharged cannot sit idly by and expect to draw his pay. A duty is imposed upon him to seek other work of the same general character in the same community. Another rule makes a distinction between a willful as opposed to an unintentional breach. Contracts that are willfully and substantially breached after part performance has taken place may or may not confer some benefit on the nonbreaching party. Furthermore, even if a benefit has been conferred, it may be of such character that the nonbreaching party cannot surrender it to the other. For example, in construction contracts and contracts of similar nature, in which the benefit received from partial performance cannot be returned, the person entitled to performance is not required to pay for the benefit conferred upon him if the party conferring it is guilty of a substantial and willful breach. The party who has refused to complete the job is penalized because of his failure to perform.

A different result obtains when the breach is unintentional—resulting from a mistake or a misunderstanding. In this situation, the party may be required to pay for the net benefit which he has received on a theory of quasi contract. The court may award damages in the amount necessary to complete the performance, in which event the defaulting party is automatically credited for his partial performance.

In those contracts where partial performance confers benefits of such a nature that they can be returned, the recipient must either return the benefits or pay for their reasonable value.

The Code provision relating to the obligations of buyers and sellers when there has been a breach after part of the goods has been delivered provides that the buyer may, on notifying the seller of his intention to do so, deduct the damages suffered because of the seller's breach from the price due under the contract.

2-11. Specific Performance.   The legal remedy of dollar damages or the equitable remedy of rescission may not be adequate to provide a proper remedy to a party injured by a breach of contract. The only adequate remedy may be to require the party in breach to perform the contract.

Specific performance is granted in cases when the chancellor or judge in the exercise of his discretion determines that dollar damages would not be an adequate remedy.[9] Dollar damages are considered inadequate and specific performance the proper remedy when the subject matter of the contract is unique. Since each parcel of real estate differs from every other parcel of real estate, all land is unique, and courts of equity will therefore specifically enforce contracts to sell real estate. Examples of unique personal property are antiques, racehorses, heirlooms, and the stock of a closely held corporation. The latter

[9] Hogan v. Norfleet, page 124

is unique because each share of stock has significance in the power to control the corporation. The Code takes a liberal viewpoint and allows specific performance in contracts for the sale of goods when commercial needs and considerations make it equitable to do so.

Contracts that involve personal services or relationships will not be specifically enforced—the only remedy in such cases is money damages. Thus courts will not usually order specific performance of employment contracts.[10]

2-12. Construction and Interpretation of Contracts. Just as it is necessary for the courts to interpret legislative enactments and constitutions, they are often called upon to construe or interpret contracts which are drafted by the parties in their attempt to "fix their own terms and set bounds upon their liabilities." The basic purpose of construing or interpreting a contract is to determine the intent of the parties.[11] If the language is clear and unambiguous, construction or interpretation is not required, and the intent expressed in the agreement will be followed. When the language of a contract is ambiguous or obscure, courts apply certain established rules of construction in order to ascertain the supposed intent of the parties. However, these rules will not be used to make a new contract for the parties or to rewrite the old one, even if the contract is inequitable or harsh. They are applied by the court merely to resolve doubts and ambiguities within the framework of the agreement.

The general standard of interpretation is to use that meaning which the contract language would have to a reasonably intelligent person who is familiar with the circumstances in which the language was used. Thus, language is judged objectively, rather than subjectively, and is given a reasonable meaning. What one party says he meant or thought he was saying or writing is immaterial, since words are given effect in accordance with their meaning to a reasonable man in the circumstances of the parties. In determining the intention of the parties, it is the expressed intention which controls, and this will be given effect unless it conflicts with some rule of law, good morals, or public policy.

The language is judged with reference to the subject matter of the contract, its nature, objects and purposes. Language is usually given its ordinary meaning, but technical words are given their technical meaning. Words with an established legal meaning are given that legal meaning. The law of the place where the contract was made may be considered a part of the contract. Isolated words or clauses are not considered, but instead the contract is considered as a whole to ascertain the intent of the parties. If one party has prepared the agreement, an ambiguity in the contract language will be construed against him since he had the chance to eliminate the ambiguity. As an aid to the court in determining the intention of the parties, business custom, usage, and prior dealings between the parties are considered, and the Code makes special provision for this.

One might inquire as to the extent to which courts are actually called upon to interpret contracts, especially contracts involving merchants. It is stated in a comment to the Code: "The parties themselves know best what they have meant by their words of agreement and their action under that agreement is

[10] Felch v. Findlay College, page 126
[11] Henry v. Lind, page 127

the best indication of what that meaning was." (U.C.C. 2-208, comment) While the parties "know best," it is still a fact that they frequently use ambiguous language in describing what they intend, or they fail to take into account many potential areas of dispute or potential problems. Hence the Code provision relating to "practical construction" takes on added significance: It provides:

> (1) Where the contract for sale involves repeated occasions for performance by either party with knowledge of the nature of the performance and opportunity for objection to it by the other, any course of performance accepted or acquiesced in without objection shall be relevant to determine the meaning of the agreement.
> (2) The express terms of the agreement and any such course of performance, as well as any course of dealing and usage of trade, shall be construed whenever reasonable as consistent with each other; but when such construction is unreasonable, express terms shall control course of performance and course of performance shall control both course of dealing and usage of trade. . . . (U.C.C. 2-208)

It should be noted that the foregoing section does not encompass a single occasion of conduct, and the number of repetitive performances required would necessarily vary with differing circumstances.

INTRODUCTION TO CONTRACTS CASES

Bloss d.b.a. Eastown Theaters v. Federated Publications, Inc.
145 N.W.2d 800 (Mich.) 1966

The plaintiff, a theater owner, brought this action against the defendant newspaper publisher in an attempt to compel the latter to accept his advertisements. The advertisements were for adult motion pictures and defendant had refused them because of their prurient content. The plaintiff in his complaint asked for (1) mandatory injunction which would require the defendant to accept such advertising and (2) damages resulting from the prior refusal to accept such advertisements. The lower court entered a summary judgment for the defendant on the ground that the defendant was free to contract with whomever it saw fit, and the plaintiff appealed.

HOLBROOK, J. . . . Plaintiff asserted in his oral argument on hearing of the summary judgment motion that a newspaper is affected with a public interest and that his complaint contains allegations of fact that require such a determination as a matter of law or at least raise a question of fact to be determined on the merits. . . .

The trial court made a finding that it could not under the existing law determine that the publishing of a newspaper is affected with a public interest, and therefore granted the motion for summary judgment and dismissed Plaintiff's complaint. . . .

We do not find nor has there been cited any Michigan case in point. We therefore, in order to ascertain the prevailing law pertaining to the subject, turn for enlightenment to 87 A.L.R. 979: . . .

> With the exception of one case, it has been uniformly held in the few cases which have considered the question that the business of publishing a newspaper is a strictly

private enterprise, as distinguished from a business affected with a public interest, and that its publisher is under no legal obligation to sell advertising to all who may apply for it.

.   .   .

The weight of authority is that the publishing of a newspaper is a strictly private enterprise, and the publishers thereof are free to contract and deal or refuse to contract and deal with whom they please. And at any rate, it is for the Legislature, and not for the courts, to declare that a business has become impressed with a public use. . . .

The First Amendment to the Federal Constitution declares and safeguards the sanctity of freedom of the press. Our founding fathers recognized that well-informed citizens are essential for the preservation of democratic institutions, and toward this end, an independent press is indispensable. The public interest, therefore, insofar as it affects the operation of a newspaper, demands that the press shall remain independent, unfettered by governmental regulation regardless of whether that regulation stems from legislative enactments or judicial decisions. There may come a time when the highest courts in our land may modify or alter the established common-law rules applicable to newspapers, or reasonable and constitutional regulations applied by statute. Until that time, we subscribe to and are bound by the prevailing authority, that a newspaper is strictly a private enterprise. Therefore plaintiff's contention that defendant newspaper is in a business that is affected with a public interest must fall. . . .

The circuit court properly granted the motion for summary judgment dismissing the plaintiff's complaint.

Gulberg v. Greenfield

146 N.W.2d 298 (Iowa) 1966

The defendants contracted with a builder, Clouse, to construct a house. Clouse sublet the plumbing, heating, and eave trough construction to the plaintiff. Clouse had financial difficulties and did not complete the house. He later filed for bankruptcy. The plaintiff was not paid by Clouse and while he could have filed a lien against the property for his services and materials, he failed to do so until after the time allowed by law to file. He sought to hold defendants liable on three theories: a contract implied in fact; a quasi contract; an express contract. The lower court gave judgment for the plaintiff and defendants appealed.

GARFIELD, J. . . . We think the principal question this appeal presents is whether a subcontractor who fails to file his mechanic's lien and bring action to enforce it within the times required, may recover a personal judgment against the owners, secured by an equitable lien against the property, on a theory of implied contract or unjust enrichment. We hold this may not be done under the record we have here. . . .

A contract is express when the parties show their assent in words. A contract is implied in fact, commonly called an implied contract, when the parties show their assent by acts. A quasi contract or contract implied in law rests upon the equitable principle that one shall not be permitted to unjustly enrich himself at the expense of another or to receive property or benefits without making compensation therefor.

We have held many times that one who pleads an express oral contract cannot ordinarily recover upon an implied contract or *quantum meruit.* . . .

17 C.J.S. Contracts § 4c, page 564 (1963), accurately states the law applicable to plaintiff's right to recover from defendants on the theory of implied contract: "Thus, where one at the request of the owner performs work and labor in constructing or repairing, without an express agreement for compensation, the law implies a promise on the part of the owner to make a reasonable compensation therefor, and it has been held that where one stands by in silence and sees work done in the improvement of his premises, of which he accepts the benefit, a promise to pay therefor may be implied."

"Where, however, the contractor sublets his contract, the law will not imply any agreement on the part of the owner to compensate the subcontractor for the work and labor performed by him; the implied obligation of the owner to make compensation to one who performs work and labor in the improvement of his property is taken away by the special contract between the contractor and the subcontractor." . . .

The precise scope of the doctrine of unjust enrichment need not be discussed. As indicated . . . "restitution" and "unjust enrichment" are modern designations for the older terms of quasi contracts or contracts implied in law.

If our conclusion is sound that plaintiff was a subcontractor under Clouse and furnished the material and labor in performance of his subcontract, any benefits plaintiff conferred upon defendants do not justify recovery from them. Plaintiff's predicament stems from Clouse's failure to pay him as agreed. Plaintiff was entitled to the benefits of the mechanic's lien law but failed to avail himself thereof. Defendants paid Clouse all that was owing him under the principal contract and in all have paid out considerably more, in completing the house and satisfying mechanic's liens that were timely filed, than the contract called for.

Restatement, Restitution, section 110, states: "A person who has conferred a benefit upon another as the performance of a contract with a third person is not entitled to restitution from the other merely because of the failure of performance by the third person."

Our reversal of the judgment against defendants for the amount of plaintiff's account of course carries with it the provision of the decree that plaintiff has a lien against the property for the amount of the judgment. . . .

Circle v. O'Harra

235 N.E.2d 252 (Ohio) 1968

DUFFEY, J. . . . This is an appeal from a judgment of the Common Pleas Court of Franklin County in favor of plaintiff-appellee for $1,401.

Plaintiff-appellee is a licensed surveyor and civil engineer. Defendent-appellant was the owner of a tract of some 100 acres of land. Defendant-appellant contracted to sell 30 acres to one Ralph Holley at $2,000 per acre. Holley was to subdivide and develop the land and pay the purchase price as lots were sold.

Holley contracted with the plaintiff-appellee to survey and prepare a plat of the property. This was discussed by Holley and plaintiff-appellee with defendant-appellant. After the platting work was done, the plats were presented to defendant-appellant for his signature as owner. After the plats were filed, defendant-appellant deeded the lots to Holley, taking promissory notes in exchange. Holley subsequently defaulted on both his obligation to plaintiff-appellee and those to defendant-appellant. However, Holley did deed back to defendant-appellant all lots still remaining in his, Holley's, name.

Upon reviewing the record, the court cannot find sufficient evidence to support an actual contract between plaintiff-appellee and defendant-appellant, i.e., one based upon mutual assent, evidenced by explicit agreement or implied from the facts. Counsel for plaintiff-appellee has not relied upon such a theory. The case is briefed solely upon a theory of recovery based on quasi contract for unjust enrichment.

There is no doubt that Holley's ability to pay defendant-appellant was assisted by the performance of plaintiff-appellee's services to Holley, since Holley intended to and did use the proceeds from lots to pay defendant-appellant. We fail to see how the fact that plaintiff-appellee contracted and performed services for Holley conferred any unjust benefit on defendant-appellant. In essence, Holley had a contract to purchase property from O'-Harra. Holley then contracted with plaintiff-appellee, Circle, to perform services which operated to enhance the value of the property, and the services were completed before performance of the contract of purchase was completed. That exact situation typifies those that gave rise to the constitutional provision for and statutory implementation of the so-called "mechanic's lien." However, plaintiff-appellee did not attempt to perfect a lien and probably could not qualify under the law. . . . We see no basis to create a judicial mechanic's lien in favor of a person in plaintiff-appellee's position.

There is no doubt that when Holley deeded the unsold lots back to defendant-appellant, plaintiff-appellee's services and the materials and services of other unsecured creditors who did business with Holley had increased the value of the land, i.e., it was subdivided and partially developed.

The transfer was clearly for an antecedent debt. It may have been a preference under the bankruptcy law. It may have been a transfer in fraud of creditors. However, the evidence does not establish either. Further, we reject a mere preference or possible preference as an unjust enrichment giving rise to recovery in quasi contract. To do so would move that most valuable judicial remedial tool deeply into the field of insolvency statutes. It is not apparent that such a judicial development in creditor rights is either feasible or desirable.

The judgment of the Common Pleas Court will be reversed. An entry granting judgment for defendant-appellant may be submitted.

Judgment reversed.

Anderson v. Copeland

378 P.2d 1006 (Okla.) 1963

PER CURIAM. This is an appeal from the District Court of Cotton County. The parties will be referred to in this Court as they appeared in the court below.

Plaintiff, Jack Copeland, doing business as Copeland Equipment Company, brought this action against defendant, Walter Anderson, to recover for the rental value of a tractor owned by plaintiff which was in defendant's possession for approximately two weeks.

The facts giving rise to this claim were for the most part undisputed. Defendant orally agreed to purchase a used tractor from plaintiff for the sum of $475.00. For eleven days thereafter defendant attempted to borrow money to cover the purchase price but was unable to, and so advised plaintiff. Plaintiff asked defendant to return the tractor, which was done within a few days. The only dispute appears to be in that defendant says the sale was conditioned on defendant's ability to borrow money to pay for it, while plaintiff says the sale was final and without conditions. In any event, both parties agree that the sale contract was rescinded when plaintiff asked that the tractor be returned.

The case was tried to a jury which returned a verdict for plaintiff in the amount of $50.00. Defendant's motion for new trial was overruled and he appeals.

It appears from the facts that the parties, instead of attempting to enforce such rights as they may have had under the sale contract, rescinded it. The parties were then in the same position as before the agreement was made, except that defendant had had the use of plaintiff's tractor without paying for it. Under those circumstances the law would imply a contract for defendant would be unjustly enriched.

In the first paragraph of the syllabus in *Piggee* v. *Mercy Hospital,* (199 Okl., 411, 186 P.2d 817), we held:

> Contracts implied by law, or more properly quasi or constructive contracts, are a class of obligations which are imposed or created by law without regard to the assent of the party bound, on the ground that they are dictated by reason and justice, and may be enforced by an action *ex contractu.*

Defendant contends that there cannot exist at the same time an express contract and an implied contract between the same parties covering the same subject matter. This statement of law is not applicable in the instant case for the reason that the subject matter of the express contract was a sale, whereas the subject matter of the contract implied in law was a rental. The case of *Berry* v. *Barbour* (Okl., 279 P.2d 355) is somewhat similar. In that case a contractor was employed to make improvements and repairs of the owner's building. During the owner's absence in Europe, the roof of the building was partially destroyed by fire without the fault of the contractor who made necessary repairs of the fire damage, without knowledge of the owner. We held that a quasi contract arose obligating the owner to reimburse the contractor for the reasonable cost of material and labor furnished.

Defendant further contends that the trial court's instructions to the jury were erroneous. The instruction requested by defendant, however, covered contracts implied in fact. Such instruction was not applicable. In *First Nat. Bank of Okmulgee* v. *Matlock* (99 Okl., 150, 226 P.328, 36 A.L.R. 1088) we distinguished between contracts implied in fact and contracts implied in law. In the former the intention of the parties is ascertained and enforced. We believe that the instructions to the jury in the instant case sufficiently covered

the law to be applied to the facts. There was ample evidence in the case to support the verdict of the jury and the trial court's judgment rendered thereon.
   Affirmed.

Galati v. Potamkin Chevrolet Co.

181 A.2d 900 (Pa.) 1962

Plaintiff, an automobile purchaser, brought suit in equity against the seller to rescind an installment sales contract for an automobile. Plaintiff alleged that defendant filled in the blanks on the contract in an amount of $427.42 more than agreed upon. Plaintiff, who discovered the excess charge on August 1, 1957, made a payment on August 18, 1957 and monthly thereafter through the August 1958 installment which was paid October 10, 1958. On May 17, 1958 plaintiff had a discussion with the salesmen where he was told that no adjustment would be made. On November 10, 1958 the auto was repossessed for nonpayment of the September 1958 installment. On August 7, 1959 plaintiff sued to rescind the contract. The trial court found for the plaintiff despite defendant's contention that plaintiff had lost his right to rescind because of the delay, and defendant appealed.

FLOOD, J. When a party discovers facts which warrant rescission of his contract, it is his duty to act promptly, and, if he elects to rescind, to notify the other party within a reasonable time so that the rescission may be accomplished at a time when the parties may still be restored, as nearly as possible, to their original positions. In the present case prompt restoration of the parties to their original positions would have permitted the defendant to reacquire possession of the vehicle, and would have prevented plaintiff's using the vehicle rent-free for a period of from five to fifteen months. The grafting of new equities upon a transaction by the passage of time is one of the reasons why the right of rescission must be asserted within a reasonable time after the discovery of the fraud.

A buyer is not entitled to a return of the price unless promptly after knowledge of the breach he returns or offers to return what he has received in substantially as good condition as when it was transferred to him. (Restatement, Contracts, § 349(1)). None of the exceptions to this rule, contained in § 349(2), are applicable here: Illustration 2 to § 349(1) reads:

> *A* sells an automobile to *B* for cash. After driving it for a few hundred miles, *B* learns of such a substantial breach of warranty by *A* as justifies rescission; and he at once tenders the return of the machine and demands his money back, the tender being conditioned on repayment. The slight use of the machine by *B* did not substantially affect its physical condition, although it considerably reduced its market value. *B* can get judgment for restitution of the price paid. Had *B* continued to make use of the machine after knowledge of the breach, he could not get judgment for his money back.

In *Ajamian* v. *Schlanger* (20 N.J.Super. 246, 89 A.2d 702 (App. Div. 1952)), the relevant facts of which are similar to those in the instant case, the plaintiff sought rescission on the ground of fraud. In ruling that he had forfeited his right to rescind, the court stated (Id. at page 249, 89 A.2d at page 704):

A party entitled to rescission on the ground of fraud may either avoid the transaction or confirm it; he cannot do both; and once he elects, he must abide by his decision. When he has discovered the fraud, or has been informed of facts and circumstances from which such knowledge would be imputed to him, he must thereupon act with diligence and without delay if he desires to rescind; and the transaction will be deemed ratified if he does any material act which assumes the transaction is valid. His continued dealing with the property purchased, after knowledge of the fraud, as if the contract were subsisting and binding, is evidence of an election to treat the contract as valid; so, also, is the payment of purchase money after such knowledge. . . . Since this plaintiff, with full knowledge of the alleged fraud, continued for more than six months to deal with the property as his own, and made the monthly payments on the purchase price, his actions afford plenary evidence of an election to abide by the contract; and once made, this election is irrevocable.

Certainly it was up to the plaintiff here to rescind within a reasonable time after May 17, 1958 when he learned that his dispute with the defendant could not amicably be resolved. Far from doing so, the plaintiff retained the automobile, continued to make payments on it and continued to use it for a period of more than five months. Whatever the effect was of plaintiff's conduct before, his conduct subsequent to May 17, 1958 constituted a binding election to affirm his transaction with the defendant, barring rescission. Therefore, the plaintiff's recovery, if any, must be limited to the difference between the amount which he would have been obligated to pay if the contract had been completed properly and the amount due under the instrument as filled in by the defendant, a sum in the neighborhood of $400.

The decree of the court below is reversed and the record is remanded for further proceedings consistent with this opinion.

Security Safety Corp. v. Kuznicki

213 N.E.2d 866 (Mass.) 1966

The defendant contracted with the plaintiff for the installation of a fire detection system. The contract provided that defendant agreed to pay 33 1/3 percent of the contract price in the event of cancellation. The defendant canceled the contract on the morning of the day after he had signed it. The plaintiff brought action for damages and was given a judgment of $1. The plaintiff appealed.

WILLKINS, J. . . . The case was submitted on agreed facts. The contract was signed the evening of March 25, 1964. The defendants made a deposit of $1 and agreed to pay the balance in "cash Sept. 15th." About nine o'clock on the morning following the signing of the contract the defendants canceled "before the plaintiff did anything in respect to the work it was to perform." "No evidence was agreed upon or offered as to the actual damage suffered by the plaintiff."

There was no error. . . . For aught that appears, the damages in event of breach were not going to be difficult of ascertainment. Time was lacking for an opportunity for the plaintiff to incur much expense of performance. The stipulated sum is unreasonably and grossly disproportionate to the real damages from the breach. In these circumstances, the aggrieved party will be

awarded no more than his actual damage. . . . Of actual damage there was no
evidence.

Order dismissing report affirmed.

Knutton v. Cofield

160 S.E.2d 29. (N.C.) 1968

The plaintiff, operator of a music company and the defendant, a restaurant
owner, entered into a contract whereby a coin-operated phonograph was installed in the restaurant. The two parties were to share the receipts. The
contract contained a liquidated-damage clause that if the defendant discontinued the use of the phonograph the plaintiff would be entitled to recover from
defendant the sum which he would have received for the balance of the term
of the contract. The defendant disconnected the phonograph and installed one
from another company. Plaintiff brought action and recovered judgment in the
lower court. Defendant appealed.

HUSKINS, J. . . . Finally, defendant contends that plaintiff seeks to recover
a penalty erroneously denominated in the contract as liquidated damages.
"Liquidated damages may be collected; a penalty will not be enforced."

"The phrase 'liquidated damages' means a sum stipulated and agreed upon
by the parties, at the time of entering into a contract, as being payable as
compensation for injuries in the event of a breach. . . . [A] stipulated sum
which is determined to be liquidated damages rather than a penalty is enforceable."

"*Liquidated damages* are a sum which a party to a contract agrees to pay
or a deposit which he agrees to forfeit, if he breaks some promise, and which,
having been arrived at by a good-faith effort to estimate in advance the actual
damage which would probably ensue from the breach, are legally recoverable
or retainable. . . . if the breach occurs. A *penalty* is a sum which a party
similarly agrees to pay or forfeit . . . but which is fixed, not as a pre-estimate
of probable actual damages, but as a *punishment,* the threat of which is
designed to prevent the breach, or as *security* . . . to insure that the person
injured shall collect his actual damages."

. . . Whether a stipulated sum will be treated as a penalty or as liquidated
damages may ordinarily be determined by applying one or more aspects of the
following rule: "[A] stipulated sum is for liquidated damages only (1) where
the damages which the parties might reasonably anticipate are difficult to
ascertain because of their indefiniteness or uncertainty and (2) where the
amount stipulated is either a reasonable estimate of the damages which would
probably be caused by a breach *or* is reasonably proportionate to the damages
which have actually been caused by the breach." This rule was generally
followed in *Bradshaw* v. *Millikin,* 173 N.C. 432, 92 S.E. 161, where the Court
stated:

> In deciding whether the sum fixed by the contract as the measure of a recovery,
> if there is a breach, should be regarded as a penalty or as liquidated damages, the
> court will look at the nature of the contract, and its words, and try to ascertain the
> intentions of the parties; and also will consider that the parties, being informed as
> to the facts and circumstances, are better able than any one else to determine what

would be a fair and reasonable compensation for a breach; but the courts have been greatly influenced by the fact that in almost all the cases the damages are uncertain and very difficult to estimate.

While early opinions tended to regard stipulations in contracts purporting to fix sums to be paid in the event of breach as penalties rather than as liquidated damages, and courts were slow to enforce stipulated sums, "it is doubtful that there is any longer sufficient authority to support a rule that the courts tend to regard such provisions as penalties. In fact, some courts have given expression to the opposite rule and have said that the modern tendency is to look upon stipulated sums with candor, if not with favor.""Ordinarily, even a court of equity will not relieve against a stipulation for liquidated damages." 22 Am. Jur.2d Damages § 211.

Applying the foregoing principles of law to the contract before us, we are of the opinion that the terms of the agreement are within the principles under which such contracts are held to be valid and that the sum to be paid upon breach should be considered as liquidated damages and not as a penalty. The formula for ascertaining the amount of damages, contained in Clause F of the contract, affords a mathematical method of making certain that which otherwise is very uncertain. Furthermore, the result of such calculation is a reasonable estimate of the damages which would probably be caused by a breach as it appeared to the parties at the time the contract was made. In addition, absent Clause F there is no standard by which a jury could fix with any degree of certainty the amount of damages sustained by plaintiff by reason of the breach. "Where the damages resulting from a breach of contract cannot be measured by any definite pecuniary standard, as by market value or the like, but are wholly uncertain, the law favors a liquidation of the damages by the parties themselves; and where they stipulate for a reasonable amount, the agreement will be enforced."Hale on Damages p. 133.

In light of these principles, defendant's exceptions and assignments of error are overruled. There is evidence to support the findings of fact and the authorities cited support the conclusions of law.

Appellant concludes his brief by saying: "Admittedly, there was a breach of the written agreement alleged by the plaintiff; but the damages awarded to the plaintiff in this case, if upheld, would not only compensate him for any loss suffered by the breach, but would enrich him to such an extent that he would reasonably hope that all of his contracts similar to the one in question would be broken." Even so, it is the general rule that the amount stipulated in a contract as liquidated damages for a breach thereof, if regarded by the court as liquidated damages and not as a penalty, may be recovered in the event of a breach even though no actual damages are suffered. . . .

Affirmed.

Hogan v. Norfleet

113 S.2d 437 (Fla. App.) 1959

MOODY, J. Appellant, plaintiff below, brought a suit for specific performance after exercising his option to purchase a franchised bottled gas business. The appellee, defendant below, filed a motion to dismiss and, upon hearing, the court dismissed the complaint, or in the alternative, granted plaintiff leave to file a suit on the law side of the court. To this order plaintiff filed interlocutory appeal.

Defendant is the owner of Norfleet Gas and Appliance, a bottled gas business based on a franchise covering a particular territory. The complaint alleges that in October, 1951, defendant induced the plaintiff to enter his business stating that he needed help in his business and planned to retire; that if the plaintiff would work for him the defendant would sell his business to the plaintiff and that in furtherance thereof, in December 1952, the parties signed a written option setting forth price and terms under which the plaintiff could purchase said business if such option were exercised. The complaint further alleges plaintiff exercised his option in October, 1957, but that the defendant has failed and refused to transfer said business to the plaintiff; that said business is prosperous; that it is the type of business and franchise which cannot be obtained in the open market; that the plaintiff fully performed his part of the agreement, and, that defendant should be required to convey all of the assets of said business including the franchise and privileges of such business.

The sole point argued on appeal and the only point covered in this opinion is whether or not specific performance should be granted for the sale of the business as set forth in the complaint. The general rule is that, although the remedy of specific performance is available to enforce contracts for the sale of realty, specific performance of contracts relating to personal property will not be enforced for the reason that ordinarily compensation for breach of contract may be had by way of an action at law for damages. Such an action would be regarded as fully adequate.

The apparent reluctance of equity to grant specific performance of [a] contract relating to personalty does not arise from any less regard for contracts involving contracts for personalty than for those involving realty, but is simply a corollary of the principle upon which equity acts in decreeing specific performance, namely, the inadequacy of the remedy at law for damages. . . .

Our Florida courts have held that specific performance of a contract is a matter of equitable cognizance as applied both to real and personal property, and where, in the case of personal property, it is of a peculiar character and value, specific performance will be granted. . . .

In the case now before us, it appears that contract of sale involves a going business including good will and an operating franchise covering a particular territory. Obviously, such a franchise would not be available in the open market and its value would be very difficult, if not impossible, to ascertain. The value of good will or of a going business is an intangible asset of an indefinite, speculative or uncertain value. The contract executed in 1952 provides the method of determining the purchase price. However, the measure of damages in an action at law would entail the determination of the *present* value of such business which involves elements of going business value, good will and prospective profits. Certainly these are matters which cannot be readily ascertainable or fixed and could not conform with the rule in a law action that any recoverable damages must be susceptible to reasonable ascertainment.

For the reasons stated the decree is reversed and the cause is remanded for further appropriate proceedings.

Felch v. Findlay College
200 N.E.2d 353 (Ohio) 1963

Plaintiff, a faculty member of Findlay College, contended that he had been discharged without compliance with the required hearing procedures. He brought suit asking that "defendant be enjoined from carrying into effect the dismissal" and that the college be ordered to retain him on the faculty. The lower court ruled in favor of the defendant and plaintiff appealed.

GUERNSEY, J. . . . In essence and in legal effect plaintiff seeks by injunction the specific performance of an employment contract. There are no Ohio statutes which purport to entitle plaintiff to the relief prayed for, and plaintiff's rights must be determined by general equitable principles.

The first and primary issue before this court is as to the remedy which plaintiff seeks and to determine this issue we will assume, without deciding, that a binding contract has existed between the plaintiff and defendant purporting to give plaintiff continuing employment status with a covenant by the defendant that plaintiff should not be dismissed for cause without a hearing conducted at the place, time, and in the manner provided by such convenant, and we will further assume, without deciding, that the defendant has breached this contract of employment by dismissing plaintiff without compliance with the hearing provisions of said covenant.

In *Masseta* v. *National Bronze & Aluminum Foundry Co.,* 159 Ohio St. 306, 112 N.E.2d 15, the Supreme Court held that "[a] court of equity will not, by means of mandatory injunction, decree specific performance of a labor contract existing between an employer and its employees so as to require the employer to continue any such employee in its service or to rehire such employee if discharged," and in Judge Middleton's opinion, . . . it was stated, . . . "It has long been settled law that a court of equity will not decree specific performance of a contract for personal services. This court has recognized this principle of law whenever occasion arose. . . . "

In 81 C.J.S. Specific Performance § 82, p. 591, the rule is stated as follows:

"In general, specific performance does not lie to enforce a provision in a contract for the performance of personal services requiring special knowledge, ability, experience, or the exercise of judgment, skill, taste, discretion, labor, tact, energy, or integrity, *particularly where the performance of such services would be continuous over a long period of time."* This rule is based on the fact that mischief likely to result from an enforced continuance of the relationship incident to the service after it has become personally obnoxious to one of the parties is so great that the interests of society require that the remedy be denied, and on the fact that the enforcement of a decree requiring the performance of such a contract would impose too great a burden on the courts. . . .

For these reasons it is the opinion and judgement of this court that the remedy of specific performance, either in itself or by means of the injunctive process, is not available to the plaintiff to enforce the provisions of the employment contract which he claims to exist between himself and defendant private college.

Judgment affirmed.

Henry v. Lind

455 P.2d 927 (Wash.) 1969

HALE, J. . . . This case seems to prove the old saying that actions speak louder than words. Although the parties drew their own contract and now disagree as to its meaning, they did act on it and we look to their conduct to ascertain their intentions.

Harvey and Lavine Henry sold their small advertising business and their home to the defendants, Reuben and Mary Lind, husband and wife, on a written agreement prepared by Mr. Henry. The typewritten contract said in part that Lavine Henry would retain a $275 per month salary from Firland Magazine (published by Pep Publishing Co.) during the 4-year term of the contract.

For about a year after the parties had signed this agreement, Mrs. Henry received the salary and then was advised that Firland Magazine would discontinue its payments to her and would pay the Linds instead. She thereupon brought this action to recover the $275 per month for the remainder of the 4-year contract term, and now appeals the judgment of the trial court in favor of the defendants. . . .

The agreement appears to us to be unclear and ambiguous and, therefore, not susceptible of a literal construction. We are unable from the following language to determine precisely what the parties intended: "The salary received by Lavine Henry from the Firland Magazine of $275.00 per month is to be retained by her, also 5 percent of the gross sales of all advertising are to be paid to Lavine Henry each month." To ascertain its meaning then, it must be read in *pari materia* with the whole contract and in light of all of the circumstances surrounding it, and, if it remains unclear, resort must be had to extrinsic interpretative aids, including the conduct of the parties under it. . . .

To ascertain the parties' intentions, the contract must be read as a whole. Taken as a whole, the agreement, we think, remains unclear and ambiguous and leaves the intention of the parties in doubt. Thus, we think that the conduct of the parties in pursuance of the contract provides in this case the best clue to their intentions. If a contract is ambiguous in meaning, the practical construction put upon it by the parties thereto is of great weight. Or, expressed another way when the language is indefinite or of doubtful construction, the practical interpretation of the parties themselves is entitled to great, if not controlling influence. Here, the language was both indefinite and of doubtful meaning, and the parties themselves interpreted it. . . .

For 11 or 12 months after the signing of the agreement for the purchase of the business, during which time the buyers were in managerial control of the business, Mrs. Henry received the check from Pep Publishing Company and a 5 percent commission on the gross advertising revenue without argument, protest, or disagreement from the Linds. This period represented about 25 percent of the total 4-year term of the contract. We think that the parties by their conduct put the ambiguity to rest.

We adhere to the rule that, where a contract is unclear and ambiguous, the interpretation placed upon it by the parties to it is entitled to great weight and may, in some cases, be of controlling influence.

Accordingly, the judgment is reversed with instructions to grant plaintiff judgment in accordance with the views set forth herein.

CHAPTER 7
REVIEW QUESTIONS AND PROBLEMS

1. *A* had a basement in his home suitable for living quarters. He allowed *B* to occupy the basement, and *B* remodeled it. *B* lived in it for five years without paying rent. *A* then informed *B* that he would have to pay rent. *B* claimed that he was entitled to recover from *A* the cost of the remodeling. Is *B* entitled to recover from *A?*

2. *A,* a manufacturer of dentures, entered into a three-year contract with *B* for the purchase of Duralium, a metal alloy. *A* agreed to use Duralium exclusively during the period. After one year *B* canceled the contract, and *A* then used another alloy, Zenium. *A* brought action for breach of contract against *B* and introduced evidence of his profits before termination to establish his damages. *B* offered evidence as to *A's* profits after he substituted Zenium. The court excluded this evidence. Was the court's ruling correct?

3. *A* sent a letter to *B* requesting that *B* ship merchandise to him as soon as possible. In his reply, *B* stated that he would ship the merchandise the following week. Is there a contract between *A* and *B?*

4. *A* applied for insurance on his automobile and made a down payment on the premium. The receipt stated that coverage would not be effective until the policy was issued. Other factors, however, indicated immediate coverage. How will the contract between *A* and the insurance company be interpreted?

5. *A,* a restaurant owner, entered into a contract with *B* for the installation of a jukebox. The income from the jukebox was to be divided equally. The contract provided that *A* would pay *B* $780 damages if he discontinued the use of *B's* jukebox. Would such a clause be valid?

6. *P,* a country club, sued *D* a former member, for the balance of *D's* yearly dues. *D* had paid the dues until the date of his withdrawal, but the membership application provided that withdrawing members had to pay the entire year's dues even if someone else took over for him. *D* alleges that the agreement is unenforceable as a penalty and in the alternative that he is entitled to offer proof in mitigation of damages. What result?

7. *A,* a gas furnace manufacturer, wished to display his furnace at the convention of the American Gas Association. He engaged the *B* Transport Company to ship the furnace and specified the date the furnace had to arrive at the convention site. *B* failed to deliver all of the parts and as a result *A* was not able to display his furnace. *A* seeks to recover damages from *B* including the cost of renting display space at the convention. Should he succeed?

8. *P* sued *D,* a contractor, for breach of a contract to build a house. If built in accordance with the plans and specifications, the house would have

been worth $20,000. As completed, it was worth $10,000 and $5,000 of labor and materials would be required to complete work and eliminate defects. How much is *P* entitled to collect?

9. *X,* a college faculty member, had a contract of continuing employment with *Y* college. *Y* college dismissed *X* and he sued for specific performance of the contract contending that his services were unique. What result?

10. *A* agreed to sell 1,000 shares of the *XYZ* Company, a closely held corporation to *B. A* then refused to carry out the agreement and *B* sued for specific performance. What result?

chapter 8

The Agreement – Offer and Acceptance

FORMATION OF OFFERS

2-13. The Offer. The first requirement of a valid, enforceable contract is an *agreement* between the parties. The agreement is usually created by one party, the offeror, making an offer and the other party, the offeree, accepting it. Offer and acceptance have been described as the acts by which the parties have a "meeting of minds" or establish a "manifestation of mutual assent."[1] According to the Restatement "An offer is a promise which is in its terms conditional upon an act, forbearance or return promise being given in exchange for the promise or its performance." In the case of a unilateral contract, the offeror's promise is conditional upon an act or a forbearance by the offeree; in an offer for a bilateral contract, upon the offeree's giving a return promise. Basically, the *offer* is a communication of what the offeror is willing to do for a stated price or consideration to be furnished by the offeree.

Not all communications that invite future business transactions are worded so as to constitute offers. Many are of a preliminary character, being transmitted primarily for the purpose of inducing the person to whom they are addressed to respond with an offer. Within this class of communications fall most catalogs, circulars, advertisements, estimates, proposals in which major terms are not included, and oral statements of general terms where it is understood that the detailed terms will be reduced to writing and signed before the agreement is to be binding. Such communications may, however, constitute offers, and in a growing number of cases advertisements are considered to be

[1] McLaughlin v. Stevens, page 143

130

offers.[2] Legislation in most states provides that advertising must be truthful and honest—that a merchant must provide in reasonable amounts the merchandise he advertises as being a "special" or reduced in price.

The main reason that proposals of the kind indicated do not qualify as offers is that the parties making them do not intend to enter into a binding agreement on the basis of the terms expressed. The parties to whom the proposals are directed are expected to realize this. The party making the statement, as the other party should reasonably understand, does not intend that any legal consequences necessarily flow from his action, sometimes because major terms are lacking and sometimes because of the circumstances under which the statements are made.

Many transactions involve lengthy negotiations between the parties and often an exchange of numerous letters and proposals, as well as conversations. It is frequently difficult to establish the point at which the parties have concluded the negotiation stage and have actually entered into a binding contract. The key question in such situations is whether a definite offer has been made or whether the proposals were simply part of continuing negotiations.[3] The courts must examine the facts of each case and apply the basic contract rules concerning the requirements of an offer to the facts as found. An offer must be definite, and the proposal must be made under such circumstances that the person receiving it has reason to believe that the other party is willing to deal on the terms indicated.[4]

One of the reasons for the requirement of definiteness is that courts may have to determine at a later date whether or not the performance is in compliance with the terms. Consequently, if the terms are vague or impossible to measure with some precision, or if major terms are absent, no contract results. Time for performance and the price to be paid are important elements of a contract and would normally be specified and not left open. However, their absence will not preclude enforcement of the contract if the court is satisfied that the parties intended to be bound by contract. Absent a time clause, the court will imply a "reasonable time" for performance; if no price is specified, the court may assume that a "reasonable price" was intended. However, if neither party has yet performed, i.e., the contract is executory as to both parties, an agreement in which the price is not specified will normally not be enforced.

The Uniform Commercial Code recognizes that parties often do not include all the terms of the contract in their negotiations or even in their contract. It provides that even though one or more terms are left open, a contract for the sale of goods does not fail for indefiniteness if the parties have intended to make a contract and if there is a reasonably certain basis for giving an appropriate remedy. It further provides that an agreement which is otherwise sufficiently definite to be a contract is not made invalid by the fact that it leaves some of the particulars of performance to be determined by one of the parties. Specification of such particulars must be made in good faith and within limits set by commercial reasonableness. Unless otherwise agreed, specifications as

[2] Lefkowitz v. Great Minneapolis Surplus Store, page 144
[3] Neece v. Dohren, page 146
[4] McGinn v. American Bank Stationery Co., page 147

to the assortment of the goods are at the buyer's option, and those relating to method and mode of shipment are at the seller's option.

2-14. Communication of the Offer.   An offer is not effective until it has been communicated to the offeree by the offeror. For example, an offer to remain open ten days, mailed on March 1 and received on March 3, would remain open until March 12, or ten days from receipt. But the offeror could have stipulated that the offer would remain open for ten days from the date of the offer, March 1. An offer can be effectively communicated only by the offeror or his duly authorized agent. If the offeree learns of the offeror's intention to make an offer from some outside source, no offer results. To be effective, the offer must be communicated through the medium or channel selected by the offeror.

An offer to the public may be made through the newspapers or the posting of notices, but as far as a particular individual is concerned, it is not effective until he learns that the offer has been made. This may be illustrated by a case in which a person apprehended a fugitive without knowing that a reward had been posted for his capture. His claim of the reward was denied because he had not acted in reliance upon the posted offer.

An offer is effective even though it is delayed in reaching the offeree. Since the delay normally results from the negligence of the offeror or his chosen means of communication, he should bear the loss resulting from the delay. However, if the delay is apparent to the offeree, his acceptance will be good only if it is communicated to the offeror within a reasonable time after the offer would normally have been received.

The unexpressed desire to enter into an agreement can never constitute an offer. Thus the writing of a letter embodying a definite proposition does not create an offer unless the letter is mailed.

2-15. Construction of Offers.   Courts have often stated that unless there is a "meeting of the minds" of the parties on the subject matter and terms of the agreement, no contract is created. In order to determine whether the minds have met, both the offer and the acceptance must be analyzed. The person making the offer may have had in mind something quite different from that of the person who accepted it.

A classic example of the rule that an uncertain or ambiguous manifestation of intent by either party may preclude formation of a contract is the illustration used in paragraph 71 of the Restatement of Contracts:

> A offers B to sell goods shipped from Bombay ex steamer "Peerless." B expresses assent to the proposition. There are, however, two steamers of the name "Peerless." It may be supposed, firstly, that A knows or has reason to know this fact, and that B neither knows nor has reason to know it; secondly, conversely, that B knows or has reason to know it and that A does not; thirdly, that both know or have reason to know of the ambiguity; or, fourthly, that neither of them knows or has reason to know it at the time when the communications between them take place. In the case first supposed there is a contract for the goods from the steamer which B has in mind. In the second case there is a contract for the goods from the steamer which A has in mind. In the third and fourth cases there is no contract unless A and B in fact intend the same steamer. In that event there is a contract for goods from that steamer.

The rule that the minds of the parties must be in accord is limited in one important respect; namely, that the intention of the parties is to be determined by their individual conduct—what each leads the other reasonably to believe —rather than by their innermost thoughts, which can be known only to themselves. It is the objective manifestation of intent rather than the subjective that controls. Thus, the courts hold the minds of the parties to have met when a written agreement is signed. Each person possessing legal capacity to contract who signs a written document with the idea of entering into a contract is presumed to know the contents thereof. Since the act of signing manifests a person's intention to be bound by the terms contained in the writing, he is in no position at a later date to contend effectively that he did not mean to enter into the particular agreement. All contracts should therefore be read carefully before they are signed.

Offers clearly made in jest or under the strain or stress of great excitement are usually not enforced, since one is not reasonably justified in relying on them. Whether an offer is made in jest can be determined by applying the objective standard previously discussed.

OFFERS IN SPECIAL SITUATIONS

2-16. Auctions and Advertisements for Bids.   When articles are sold at public auction, the offer is said to be made by the bidder and accepted by the seller at the drop of the auctioneer's hammer. Because of this rule, the seller can withdraw his article from sale at any time during the auction. The purchaser may withdraw his bid at any time before the auctioneer has concluded the sale. The seller may, by statements in circulars relating to the sale or by statements made on the part of the auctioneer, prescribe the conditions under which the contract is to be concluded. Thus, an auction advertised "without reserve" means that the property will be sold to the highest bidder—the seller has surrendered his right to withdraw an article put up for sale. "Reserve" relates to the privilege of withdrawing an article, which an auction seller would otherwise have. In any case, the bidder has the right to retract his bid anytime before the fall of the auctioneer's hammer and the withdrawal of a bid does not have the effect of reviving any prior bid.

Unless it is otherwise announced before the sale, the seller has no right to bid at his own sale. For him to bid or have an agent do so would amount to fraud, the potential buyers having the right to presume that the sale is held in good faith. If an auctioneer knowingly accepts a bid on the seller's behalf, or if the seller makes or procures such a bid without giving notice of such bidding, the buyer has the alternatives of avoiding the sale or taking the goods for the amount of the last good faith bid before his.

The Code has a separate section relating to sale of goods by auction. It codifies the principles discussed above but specifies in detail how certain special problems are to be handled. For example: "Where a bid is made while the hammer is falling in acceptance of a prior bid, the auctioneer may in his discretion reopen the bidding or declare the goods sold under the bid on which the hammer was falling." (U.C.C. 2-328) If the auctioneer knowingly receives a bid on the seller's behalf, "and notice has not been given that liberty for such bidding is reserved, the buyer may at his option avoid the sale or take the goods at the price of the last good faith bid prior to the completion of the sale." (U.C.C. 2-328)

A related matter is that of bids which are solicited for a particular service or other purpose. When one advertises that bids will be received for construction work, it is held that the person calling for bids makes no offer, but that the party who submits a bid is the offeror.[5] The one calling for the bids may reject any or all of them, and in the absence of some statute, the bidder is free at any time to withdraw his bid until it has been accepted. The same is true of public construction. Since the statutes of most states only provide that public work must be let to the lowest responsible bidder, courts have held that all bids may be rejected.

2-17. Tickets. Tickets purchased for entrance into places of amusement or as evidence of a contract for transportation often contain matter in small print that attempts to limit or define the rights of the holder. Some conflict exists relative to the effectiveness of these restrictions, but it is generally held that they become a part of an offer and are accepted by the holder if he is aware of the printed matter even though he does not read it. There are some cases, such as those involving steamship tickets, in which the purchaser is presumed to know about the printed matter even though his attention is not called to it at the time the ticket is delivered on the theory that the ticket purports on its face to be a contract.

If a ticket is received merely as evidence of ownership and is to be presented later as a means of identification, the provisions are ineffective, unless the recipient is aware of the contractual aspects or his attention is specifically directed to them at the time the ticket is accepted.[6] Thus, tickets given at checkrooms or repair shops are usually received as a means of identifying the article to be returned rather than as setting forth the terms of the contract.

It should be noted that printed material often found on the back of contract forms and occasionally on letterheads, unless embodied in the contract by reference thereto, is not generally considered part of any contract set forth on such a form or letterhead.

2-18. Credit Cards. The widespread use of credit cards and charge-a-plates has resulted in much litigation about the liability of a card holder for unauthorized purchases. Many of the cases indicate the sympathy of the courts for the unfortunate person whose card has been lost or stolen; others impose liability upon the basis of strict contractual principles. The nature and variety of the cards and the numerous forms used in applying for credit cards largely account for the apparent lack of consistency in the cases.

Frequently the card will contain the terms of the contract on its reverse side. If the language used specifies that the holder will be responsible for any purchases made prior to reporting its loss to the company, the holder will be liable for unauthorized purchases. Likewise, the application for the card may state the holder's liability. On the other hand, it has been held that if there was no contractual agreement regarding liability, the owner of the card would not

[5] O. C. Kinney, Inc. v. Paul Hardeman, Inc., page 148
[6] Kergald v. Armstrong Transfer Exp. Co., page 149

be liable.[7] As a general proposition the holder of a card which has been lost or stolen will not be responsible for unauthorized purchases, unless (1) the contract specifically provides for liability or (2) he has been careless in his handling of the card. If the issuer of the card has been careless in handling the account, the holder may be relieved of liability in spite of his own negligence.[8]

It seems clear from the cases that the holder of a credit card should give prompt notice of its loss or theft, even though his obligation to do so is not specified in any contract. Some courts have treated credit cards and devices as negotiable instruments, and under this view, a store would be protected in honoring purchases by a thief or the finder of a card.

2-19. Options and Firm Offers.   An option is a *contract* based upon some consideration whereby the offeror binds himself to hold an offer open for an agreed period of time. It provides the holder of the option the right to accept the continuing offer within a specified time. Quite often the offeree pays or promises to pay in order to have the offer remain open. The consideration need not be money—it may be any other thing of value. The significant fact is that the offer has been transformed into a contract of option because of consideration supplied by the offeree. The offer becomes irrevocable for the period of the option.

Frequently an option is part of another contract. A lease may contain a clause that gives to the tenant the right to purchase the property within a given period at a stated price, or a sale of merchandise may include a provision that obligates the seller to supply an additional amount at the same price if ordered by the purchaser within a specified time. Such options are enforceable, since the initial promise to pay rent serves as consideration for both the lease and the right to buy, and the original purchase price of goods serves as consideration for the goods purchased and the option to buy additional goods.

The Code contains a provision which creates a limited option, without the requirement of consideration. If a merchant states in an offer that the offer will remain open for a stated period, such an offer is called a firm offer, and in such case, the merchant may not withdraw the offer during the stated period, provided it does not exceed three months, or for a reasonable length of time not exceeding three months, if no period is stated. The firm offer must be a signed, written offer, and in the event the offer is set forth on a form supplied by the offeree, it must be separately signed by the offeror in addition to his signature as a party to the contract. The offeree in a firm offer can rely upon the continuing legal obligation of the offeror and can make other commitments on the strength of it.

DURATION OF OFFER

2-20. Introduction.   An offer that has been properly communicated continues until it lapses or expires, is revoked by the offeror, is rejected by the offeree, or becomes illegal or impossible by operation of law. Also, an offer ceases to be an offer and is merged into the contract when it is accepted by the offeree.

---

[7] Thomas v. Central Charge Service, page 150
[8] Allied Stores of New York v. Funderburke, page 151

An offer does not remain open indefinitely, even though the offeror fails to withdraw it. If the offer stipulates the period during which it is to continue, it automatically lapses or expires at the end of that period. An attempted acceptance after that date can amount to no more than a new offer being made to the original offeror by the offeree of the original offer. An offer that provides for no time limit remains open for a reasonable time—a reasonable time being such period as a reasonable person might conclude was intended. Whether an offer has lapsed because of the passage of time is usually a question of fact for the jury after it has given proper weight to all related circumstances, one of which is the nature of the property. For example, an offer involving property, the price of which is constantly fluctuating, remains open a relatively short time in comparison with property, the price of which is more stable. Other factors that should be considered are the circumstances under which the offer is made, the relation of the parties, and the means used in transmitting the offer. For example, an offer made orally usually lapses when the conversation ends unless the offeror clearly indicates that the proposal may be considered further by the offeree.

2-21. Revocation.   Except for options and firm offers by merchants under the Code, an offeror may revoke an offer at any time before it has been accepted. This is true even though the offeror has promised to hold his offer open for a definite period.[9] As long as it is a mere offer and not an option, the offer can be legally withdrawn, even though morally or ethically such action may seem unjustified.

A few recent decisions, however, have held that it is too late to withdraw an offer after the offeree, in reliance on it, has substantially changed his position, particularly if the offeror promised to hold it open for a certain period. This situation is illustrated by the case of general contractors who submit bids for improvements in reliance upon bids made to them by subcontractors or suppliers of material.[10] This doctrine, commonly referred to as the doctrine of promissory estoppel, is discussed in detail in the next chapter. *Promissory estoppel* is in effect a substitute for consideration, and when applied it is legally sufficient to create a binding obligation to keep an offer open.

As was previously noted in the discussion of options and firm offers, the Code reaches somewhat the same result in connection with firm offers by merchants, as does the theory of promissory estoppel in contracts in general. Under the Code, however, the firm offer does not require a material change of position by the offeree in order to have binding effect.

The revocation of an offer becomes effective only when it has been communicated to the offeree. The mere sending of a notice of revocation is insufficient. It must be received by the offeree or have reached a destination where it would have been available to him. But communication of a revocation is effective when actually received regardless of how or by whom it is conveyed. If the offeree obtains knowledge from any source of the offeror's conduct clearly showing an intent by the latter to revoke, the offer is terminated. The reason for the rule that direct notice of revocation is not required is that it

---

[9] Seelye v. Broad, page 153
[10] Drennan v. Star Paving Company, page 154

would be unjust to let the offeree knowingly take advantage of the offeror's position. To illustrate: An offeree who learns from some reliable source that an industrial site offered to him for sale has been sold by the offeror to a third party cannot thereafter accept the offer and seek to recover damages for breach of a contract to sell. The offer is considered to be revoked as soon as the offeree learns of the sale, regardless of the source of his information.

An offer made to the public presents a special problem to an offeror who desires to revoke such an offer. It would be impossible to give personal notice of revocation to all persons who may have learned of the offer. Accordingly, the offeror is allowed to withdraw his offer by giving the same general publicity to the revocation that he gave to the offer. A public offer made through the newspapers in a certain locality may be withdrawn through the same medium. While it is thus possible that persons who were made aware of the offer may not actually be aware of its withdrawal, the result is justified on the premise that the offeror is still the master of his offer and that he has taken reasonable means to give notice of revocation.

2-22. Rejection. Rejection by the offeree causes an offer to terminate. A rejection has this effect, even though the offeror had promised to keep the offer open for a specified time. After his rejection, the offeree cannot change his mind and accept the offer. An attempt to do so will, at best, amount to a new offer made by him, which must be accepted by the original offeror in order to create a contract. For example, if *B* has paid *S* for a ten-day option to purchase property at a given price, but on the seventh day tells *S* that he does not want it, *S* is immediately free to sell to another buyer.

An attempted acceptance which departs from the terms of the offer is a rejection of the offer and is in effect a counteroffer, since it implies that the terms set forth in the offer are not acceptable. Under the Code, however, it is provided that in some circumstances a variance between the offer and the acceptance will not prevent the formation of a contract for the sale of goods.

It is often difficult to determine whether a communication by an offeree is a rejection or merely an expression of a desire to negotiate further on the terms of the agreement. Thus it is possible to suggest a counterproposal in such a way as to make it clear that the offer is still being considered—is not being rejected—but that the offeree wishes a reaction by the offeror to the suggested changes. Also, the offeree may, in his acceptance, set forth terms not included in the offer, but the terms may be those which would be implied as ones normally included in such an agreement. The inclusion of such terms will not prevent formation of a contract.[11] A request for further information by an offeree who indicates that he still has the offer under consideration will not constitute a rejection of the offer.

Rejection of an offer is not effective in terminating it until the rejection has been received by the offeror or his agent or is available to him at his usual place of business. Consequently, a rejection which has been sent may be withdrawn at any time prior to delivery to the offeror. Such action does not bar a later acceptance.

2-23. Operation of Law. There are several events that will terminate an offer

[11] Department of Public Works v. Halls, page 156

as a matter of law. Notice of the happening of these events need not be given or communicated to the offeree, as the offer ends instantaneously upon the happening of the event. Such events include the death or insanity of either party or the destruction of the subject matter of the offer. The happening of one of these events eliminates one of the requisites for a contract, thereby destroying the effectiveness of the acceptance of the offer to create a contract. Another event is the promulgation by a law-making body of a statute or ordinance making illegal the performance of any contract that would result from acceptance of the offer.

There is a distinct difference between the termination of an offer and the termination of a contract. It should be emphasized that death, for example, terminates an offer but not a contract. As a general rule, death does not excuse performance of contracts, although it would in contracts for personal service. To illustrate the effect of the death of one of the parties to an offer: assume that Adams offers to sell to Barnes a certain electronic computer for $15,000 and that after Adams's death, Barnes, without knowledge of his decease, mails his acceptance to Adams and immediately enters into a contract to resell the computer to Curtis for $17,000. The estate of Adams has no duty to deliver the machine, even though Curtis may have a claim against Barnes for breach of contract if the latter fails to deliver the computer to Curtis. Had Barnes's acceptance become effective before Adams's death, the executor of Adams's estate would have been obligated to deliver the computer.

ACCEPTANCE

2-24. Definition.   A contract consists of an offer by one party and its acceptance by the person or persons to whom it is made. Figuratively speaking, an offer hangs like a suspended question, and the acceptance should be a positive answer to that question. The offeror says, "I will sell you this article for $200. Will you buy it? " A contract results when the offeree-acceptor answers in the affirmative. An *acceptance* is an indication by the offeree of his willingness to be bound by the terms of the offer. Acceptance may, if the offer permits, take the form of an act (unilateral offer), an oral return promise communicated to the offeror (bilateral offer), or the signing and delivery of a written instrument. The latter method is the most common in transactions of considerable importance and in those that are more formal. If a written contract is the agreed method of consummating the transaction, the contract is formed only when it has been signed by both parties and has been delivered. However, delivery of the contract may be conditional upon the happening of some event; then unless the event occurs, no contract exists.

2-25. Acceptance of a Unilateral Offer.   As indicated previously, contracts are either unilateral or bilateral, depending upon whether the offer must be accepted by an act on the part of the offeree or whether a promise to perform will create the contractual relation. Most contracts are bilateral in nature, and when offers are ambiguous in regard to whether they are unilateral or bilateral, the courts tend to construe them as bilateral. However, many contracts are unilateral in form. In such cases the offeror does not require—in fact, does not desire—a promise or assurance of performance, but before he is obligated by contract, he insists on substantial completion of the act requested.

Since a unilateral offer is not accepted until completion of the requested act, many courts have held that the offeror is at liberty to withdraw his offer at any point prior to the time the offeree renders substantial performance. If only partial performance has occurred prior to withdrawal and if it has benefited the offeror, on a theory of a quasi contract, he must pay for the benefit conferred, but by the prevailing view, he is not obligated to permit the offeree to complete his performance. If substantial completion of performance has occurred before the attempted withdrawal, the offeror has lost his right to withdraw.

The rule with regard to revocation of an offer for a unilateral contract is stated in the Restatement as follows:

> If an offer for a unilateral contract is made, and part of the consideration requested is given or tendered by the offeree in response thereto, the offeror is bound by a contract, the duty of immediate performance of which is conditional on the full consideration being given or tendered within the time stated in the offer, or, if no time is stated therein, within a reasonable time.

Thus the main offer of a unilateral contract would include, by implication, a subsidiary promise that if part of the requested performance is given, the offeror will not revoke his offer. The consideration for this subsidiary promise is the part performance by the offeree. It is the *part performance* by the offeree that gives rise to the obligation of the offeror to keep his offer open. The offeree may incur expense in *preparation* for performance, but this is not part performance and does not affect the offeror's right to revoke.

Frequently an offer contemplates a series of independent contracts by separate acceptances. For example, *A* is the owner of ten identical cottages at a beach resort. He offers to pay *B* $200 for each cottage that he paints. After *B* paints five of them, *A* gives notice of revocation. A contract is formed each time a cottage is painted, but the revocation prevents formation of any contracts thereafter. Thus, there may be a revocation so as to terminate the power to create future contracts though one or more of the proposed contracts have already been formed by the offeree's acceptance.

Another example of the foregoing is the contract of continuous guaranty, which is discussed in Book Four, Chapter 33, Section 4-9. It arises when one person agrees with another that if the latter will extend credit to a third party over a period of time, the former will pay should the third party fail to do so. This continuing offer of guaranty can be revoked at any time by proper notice, and the guarantor will be relieved of liability for debts incurred thereafter.

The distinction between bilateral and unilateral contracts with respect to revocation of offers may be illustrated by two fairly typical situations. In the first, a hardware merchant, who is approached by a salesman of a manufacturer, signs a purchase order for certain goods, the order being subject to approval by the manufacturer's home office. The merchant who signed the purchase order has made an offer to the manufacturer for a bilateral contract. The manufacturer accepts the offer by sending notice of his approval to the merchant. After this is done, both parties are bound, and neither can thereafter revoke. On the other hand, if a merchant needs several items of merchandise right away and mails a letter to a certain concern asking for immediate ship-ment of the articles listed, his offer would be unilateral at common law. It could be accepted by the act of shipment, even though the buyer had no actual knowledge of the acceptance. The buyer, however, could withdraw his offer at any time before the seller's delivery to the carrier, even though the seller might have incurred expense in anticipation of delivery by way of procuring, assembling, or packing the goods for shipment.

Under the Code, such an offer may be treated either as a unilateral offer and accepted by shipment, or it may be treated as a bilateral offer and accepted by a promise to ship. The seller is thus afforded an opportunity to bind the bargain prior to the time of shipment if he wants to do so. The Code provides that "an order or other offer to buy goods for prompt or current shipment shall be construed as inviting acceptance *either* by a prompt promise to ship or by a prompt or current shipment of . . . goods. . . . " (U.C.C. 2-206(1)(b)) If the seller ships goods which do not conform to the order, he may notify the buyer that the shipment is not an acceptance but is only offered as an accommodation to the buyer. This is, in effect, a counteroffer which the buyer may accept or reject, and the seller may not be charged with having breached the contract because of the nonconformity.

2-26. Acceptance of a Bilateral Offer.   An offer for a bilateral contract is accepted by a promise from the offeree returned in response to the promise of the offeror. The offeree's promise is to perform as stipulated in the offer. The promise of the offeree (acceptance) must be communicated to the offeror or his agent and may consist of any conduct on the part of the offeree which clearly evinces an intention to be bound by the conditions prescribed in the offer. In construing the language of a purported acceptance, the usual rules of construction, including the principle that ambiguous language is construed against the person using it, are applied.[12] The acceptance may take the form of a signature to a written agreement or of a nod of the head. No formal procedure is *generally* required by the law of contract. If the offer is made to a group of persons in the aggregate, the acceptance is not complete until each member of the group has indicated his acceptance. Until all have responded, the offeror is at liberty to withdraw his offer.

Where it is understood that the agreement will be set forth in a written instrument, the acceptance is effective only when the document has been signed and delivered, unless it was clearly the intention of the parties that the earlier verbal agreement be binding and that the writing act merely as a memorandum or evidence of their oral contract.

2-27. Silence as Assent.   As a general rule, the offeror cannot force the offeree to speak. In most cases, therefore, mere silence by the offeree does not amount to acceptance, even though the offeror in his offer may have stated that a failure to reply would constitute an acceptance. However, a previous course of dealing between the parties or the receipt of goods by the offeree under certain circumstances could impose a duty on the offeree to speak in order to

[12] Hill's Inc. v. William B. Kessler, Inc., page 158

avoid a contractual relationship.[13] The Restatement provides that silence on the part of the offeree can operate as an acceptance:

> Where because of previous dealings or otherwise, the offeree has given the offeror reason to understand that the silence or inaction is intended by the offeree as a manifestation of assent, and the offeror does so understand.

Silence *of itself* never constitutes an acceptance, but silence with intent to accept may do so. For example, the receipt of a renewal fire insurance policy retained by the insured with intent to keep and pay for it constitutes acceptance of the offer to insure for the new period. Mailing out the renewal policy constituted the offer to insure, and the retention of the policy was the acceptance if the offeree intended to avail himself of the insurance protection. The Restatement provides that silence may be an acceptance:

> Where the offeror has stated or given the offeree reason to understand that assent may be manifested by silence or inaction, and the offeree in remaining silent and inactive intends to accept the offer.

Obviously the requisite intent will often be difficult to determine.

A related acceptance problem is illustrated by the Code provision that a buyer has accepted *goods* when he fails to make an effective rejection or does any act inconsistent with the seller's ownership. However, failure to reject will not be construed as an acceptance unless the buyer has had a reasonable opportunity to examine the goods.

2-28. Acceptance by Offeree.   Only the person to whom the offer is made can accept the offer. Offers to the public may be accepted by any member of the public who is aware of the offer. An offeree cannot assign the offer to a third party. Option contracts, however, although a form of offer, are usually assignable and may be accepted by the assignee.

If goods are ordered from a firm that has discontinued business and the goods are shipped by its successor, the offeree-purchaser is under no duty to accept the goods. If he does accept them knowing that they were shipped by the successor, then by implication he agrees to pay the new concern for the goods at the contract price. If he does not know of the change of ownership when he accepts the goods, he is not liable for the contract price—his only liability is in quasi contract for the reasonable value of the goods.

2-29. Acceptance Must Follow Offer.   As a general proposition of contract law, to be effective an acceptance must conform exactly to the terms of the offer. If the acceptance contains new terms or conditions or if it otherwise deviates from the terms of the offer, it is a counteroffer and constitutes a rejection of the offer, unless the offeree explicitly states that it is not to be considered a rejection. Provisions in an offer relating to time, place, or manner of acceptance must be strictly complied with by the offeree. If there is any deviation from these terms, the purported acceptance will be construed a counteroffer and, therefore, a rejection of the offer.

---

[13] Hendrickson v. International Harvester Co. of America page 159

The drafters of the Code reexamined the application of the so-called "mirror image rule," which required exact compliance between offer and acceptance, and they decided that some relaxing of the rule was desirable in transactions involving the sale of goods, especially when a transaction was between "merchants." Accordingly, the Code provides that a communication may operate as an acceptance, even though it states terms additional to or different from those set forth in the offer. The additional or different terms are construed merely as *proposals* that may be approved or disapproved by the other party, but *between merchants* these terms may actually become part of the contract.[14]   Circumstances under which such terms are incorporated into agreements between merchants are discussed in Book Three, Chapter 18, Section 3-6.

The problem of variance between an offer and an acceptance frequently arises because of the widespread use of standard printed forms by merchants. Such forms are used in accepting offers as well as in making them. Quite naturally, the offer form and the acceptance form will differ in some respects, but businessmen nevertheless expect that their exchange of forms will result in a binding contract. Code provisions allow this justifiable expectation to be realized, but within well-defined limits.

2-30. Time of Taking Effect.   A bilateral offer is accepted only upon *communication* of the acceptance to the offeror. A conflict has long existed in the law as to whether or not the acceptance is effective to create a contract at the moment the communication is deposited in the mail, or whether its effectiveness is delayed until the offeror actually receives it. It will be recalled that other communications associated with contracts—revocations of offers and rejections of offers—do not have legal effect until they are received. In early English law, the case of *Adams* v. *Lindsell* established the "deposited acceptance rule"—that an acceptance was effective when deposited in the offeror's channel of communication or the one indicated by him to be used by the offeree. If none was indicated, the acceptance was effective when deposited with the post or mails. This rule has been challenged on the ground that there could not actually be a meeting of the minds upon deposit of the acceptance because the offeror would not know that it had been deposited. In recent years, postal rules have authorized withdrawal of letters, and this change has been the basis of further attacks on the "deposited acceptance rule." Notwithstanding the strength of these arguments, most courts still adhere to the rule of *Adams* v. *Lindsell,* and as a general rule an acceptance is considered effective when deposited in the offeror's channel of communication or in the mail if no other channel is indicated.[15] If the offeree uses a different means of communication, the acceptance is not effective until received by the offeror. A rule has been adopted by the Restatement of Contracts which provides: "An acceptance may be transmitted by any means which the offeror has authorized the offeree to use and, if so transmitted, is operative and completes the contract as soon as put out of the offeree's possession, *without regard to whether it ever reaches the offeror,* unless the offer otherwise provides." (Emphasis supplied.)

[14] Roto-Lith, Ltd. v. F. P. Bartlett & Co., page 159 .
[15] Morrison v. Thoelke, page 161

The Code has adopted and expanded the deposited acceptance rule and provides that, unless otherwise unambiguously indicated by the terms of the offer, "an offer to make a contract shall be construed as inviting acceptance *in any manner* and *by any medium* reasonable in the circumstances." (U.C.C. 2-206(1)(a))

The deposited acceptance rule has the effect of placing on the offeror any possible loss resulting from a failure on the part of the communicating agency to deliver the acceptance. Although a letter of acceptance is lost in the mails, a contract may exist. The offeror, in such cases, is dutybound to perform, even though he may have entered into other contracts as a result of his failure to receive a reply. He can avoid this result only by stating in his offer that the acceptance shall be ineffective until it is actually received by him.

OFFER AND ACCEPTANCE CASES

McLaughlin v. Stevens
296 F. Supp. 610 (1969)

Plaintiffs sued the defendant for a "finder's fee" of $300,000 allegedly due on the sale of stock of a retail outlet and broadcasting company. The defendant had entered into a contract to purchase the stock, but the sale was enjoined by the Supreme Court of Rhode Island. Plaintiffs alleged that an agreement was reached with the defendant's agent, Wood, to pay the plaintiffs a commission in the event the stock was sold to the defendant. Defendant contended that there was no contract to pay a finder's fee.

PETTINE, J.... It goes without saying that a manifestation of mutual assent by the parties to an informal contract is essential to the formation of that contract. Moreover, the manifestation of mutual assent almost invariably takes the form of an offer or proposal by one party accepted by the other party or parties. And an offer is a promise which is in its terms conditional upon an act, forbearance or return promise being given in exchange for the promise or its performance. If, then, a contract was created by the January or February oral exchanges between Wood, as agent for Stevens, and the plaintiffs, an offer must be delineated. The plaintiffs point to the following language of the plaintiff McLaughlin's deposition:

> If I don't get paid by the Outlet Company, then I was entitled to a finder's fee. I said 'By whom?' He (Wood) said, 'By the buyer.'

It is difficult, in the first instance, to see the promissory made (sic) of the alleged offeror's language. But it is even more difficult to see what act, forbearance, or return promise was being sought by the alleged offeror. The words quoted simply leave too much to the process of implication. Hence, not only do they raise a grave question with respect to the existence of the offer but also they invite consideration of whether they satisfy the rule that an offer must be so definite in its terms, or require such definite terms in the acceptance, that the promises and performances to be rendered by each party are reasonably certain. On the basis of the deposition of the plaintiffs it is entirely unclear what the plaintiffs were to do, whether, how and in what amounts they were to be paid, and whether there were any conditions to their receipt of payment. Finally, there are indications in the deposition of the plaintiffs that these oral communications were mere preliminary negotiations, and that the defendant wanted a written statement from the plaintiffs setting out the terms and condition of the agreement. While the court thinks that each of these objections is a sufficient barrier in and of itself to the plaintiffs' claims as to the creation of an oral contract, certainly all of them taken together present an insuperable obstacle to the plaintiffs. Accordingly, on the basis of undisputed facts, and drawing all inferences favorable to the non-movant plaintiffs, the court concludes that, as a matter of law, no oral contract was created. . . .

Defendant's motion for summary judgment granted.

Lefkowitz v. Great Minneapolis Surplus Store

86 N.W.2d 689 (Minn.) 1957

The defendant published the following advertisement in a Minneapolis newspaper.

Saturday 9 A.M.

2 Brand New Pastel

Mink ´3-Skin Scarfs

Selling for $89.50

Out they go

Saturday. Each. . . . $1.00

1 Black Lapin Stole

Beautiful,

worth $139.50. . . . $1.00

First Come

First Served

Plaintiff was the first person to go to the appropriate counter in defendant's store on the Saturday following publication of the ad. He demanded the stole and indicated his willingness to pay the sale price of $1. The defendant refused to sell the merchandise to the plaintiff and stated that by a "house rule" the offer was intended for women only. The plaintiff brought action and was given judgment in the amount of $138.50—the value as stated in the ad less the $1 quoted purchase price. Defendant appealed.

MURPHY, J. . . . The defendant contends that a newspaper advertisement offering items of merchandise for sale at a named price is a "unilateral offer" which may be withdrawn without notice. He relies upon authorities which hold that, where an advertiser publishes in a newspaper that he has a certain quantity or quality of goods which he wants to dispose of at certain prices and on certain terms, such advertisements are not offers which become contracts as soon as any person to whose notice they may come signifies his acceptance by notifying the other that he will take a certain quantity of them. Such advertisements have been construed as an invitation for an offer of sale on the terms stated, which offer, when received, may be accepted or rejected and which therefore does not become a contract of sale until accepted by the seller; and until a contract has been so made, the seller may modify or revoke such prices or terms. (Cases cited.) . . .

The defendant relies principally on *Craft* v. *Elder & Johnston Co., supra.* In that case, the court discussed the legal effect of an advertisement offering for sale, as a one-day special, an electric sewing machine at a named price. The view was expressed that the advertisement was "not an offer made to any specific person but was made to the public generally. Thereby it would be properly designated as a unilateral offer and not being supported by any consideration could be withdrawn at will and without notice." It is true that such an offer may be withdrawn before acceptance. Since all offers are by their nature unilateral because they are necessarily made by one party or on one side in the negotiation of a contract, the distinction made in that decision between a unilateral offer and a unilateral contract is not clear. On the facts before us we are concerned with whether the advertisement constituted an offer, and, if so, whether the plaintiff's conduct constituted an acceptance.

There are numerous authorities which hold that a particular advertisement in a newspaper or circular letter relating to a sale of articles may be construed by the court as constituting an offer, acceptance of which would complete a contract. (Cases cited.)

The test of whether a binding obligation may originate in advertisements addressed to the general public is "whether the facts show that some performance was promised in positive terms in return for something requested." 1 Williston, *Contracts,* (Rev. ed.), § 27.

The authorities above cited emphasize that, where the offer is clear, definite, and explicit, and leaves nothing open for negotiation, it constitutes an offer, acceptance of which will complete the contract. The most recent case on the subject is *Johnson* v. *Capital City Ford Co.,* in which the court pointed out that a newspaper advertisement relating to the purchase and sale of automobiles may constitute an offer, acceptance of which will consummate a contract and create an obligation in the offeror to perform according to the terms of the published offer.

Whether in any individual instance a newspaper advertisement is an offer rather than an invitation to make an offer depends on the legal intention of the parties and the surrounding circumstances. We are of the view on the facts before us that the offer by the defendant of the sale of the Lapin fur was clear, definite, and explicit, and left nothing open for negotiation. The plaintiff having successfully managed to be the first one to appear at the seller's place of business to be served, as requested by the advertisement, and having offered the stated purchase price of the article, he was entitled to performance on the part of the defendant. We think the trial court was correct in holding that there was in the conduct of the parties a sufficient mutuality of obligation to constitute a contract of sale.

The defendant contends that the offer was modified by a "house rule" to the effect that only women were qualified to receive the bargains advertised. The advertisement contained no such restriction. This objection may be disposed of briefly by stating that, while an advertiser has the right at any time before acceptance to modify his offer, he does not have the right, after acceptance, to impose new or arbitrary conditions not contained in the published offer.

Judgment affirmed for plaintiff.

Neece v. Dohren

219 N.E.2d 137 (Ill.) 1966

CRAVEN, J. The plaintiff, by this action, sought specific performance of an alleged contract for the sale of real estate or as alternative relief damages for breach of the contract. . . . Judgment was entered for the defendant and this appeal is from that judgment. . . .

. . . The defendant was the owner of a 195-acre farm. In January of 1965 the parties discussed the sale of the farm by telephone at a price of $500.00 an acre. This telephone conversation was by long-distance phone, the plaintiff in Illinois and the defendant in California. Subsequent to this conversation and allegedly pursuant thereto, the plaintiff sent to the defendant a written offer for the purchase of the farm. On January 18, 1965, the defendant wrote the plaintiff a letter in which the sale of the farm was discussed in considerable detail, as was the sale of certain crops then in storage and the tax consequences of the sale. The letter concluded the discussion by inquiring of the plaintiff:

> How does this sound to you?
> Let me hear your decision as soon as possible because if you don't buy it, I will put it in the hands of Alex McWilliams.

The complaint then alleges that on January 24, 1965, the plaintiff telephoned an acceptance of the terms as set forth in the letter, followed on January 30 by a check to the defendant in the amount of $2,500.00 as an alleged down payment. On February 8 the defendant returned the check and by his letter of transmittal the defendant stated that he had been waiting for a letter, as well as a contract to evaluate, and since these items had not arrived he had reconsidered his position and was cancelling further progress on the projected sale. Thereafter the plaintiff, through his attorney, sent the defendant two checks totalling $10,500.00 and a proposed contract, signed by the plaintiff, describing the premises and making provisions for the payment of the purchase price and the usual provisions relevant to a contract for the purchase of land. The checks and contract were returned by the defendant to the plaintiff, and again by the letter of transmittal, the defendant stated:

> . . . I thought that we had agreed on terms and you promised to have a contract sent. I waited for many days for this contract and it never arrived. On January 30, 1965—many days after our tentative agreement—Mr. Dunn sent a check for $2,500 and again promised that a contract would follow. None came.
> . . . I returned the check and cancelled out any further dealings. . . .

The complaint alleges that thereafter the defendant entered into a contract with a third party to sell the premises at a price substantially higher than that involved in the negotiation between these parties. . . .

It is the essence of the plaintiff's contention that the initial phone call constituted an offer by him to buy and that the defendant's first letter was a counteroffer, which counteroffer was accepted by the plaintiff in the manner intended, thereby establishing as between the parties an enforceable contract. . . .

It is our conclusion that these pleadings establish only negotiations that did not ripen into an agreement between the parties. The letter of the defendant of January 18 is not a counteroffer, but rather one step in the negotiation process. It is further clear that the actions of the plaintiff subsequent to that letter were clearly inconsistent with the present contention that the letter and the telephone acceptance constituted a binding agreement. The fact that in January the parties were engaged in a process of continuing negotiation is apparent by examining plaintiff's exhibit C in which, over a month after the alleged agreement, he caused the terms and conditions of a proposed contract to be reduced to writing and mailed the same to the defendant together with two checks representing a down payment. In the case of *Whitelaw* v. *Brady* in discussing offers and acceptances, the Court said:

> ... 'It is a necessary requirement in the nature of things that an agreement in order to be binding must be sufficiently definite to enable a court to give it an exact meaning. If an offer contemplates an acceptance by merely an affirmative answer, the offer itself must contain all the terms necessary for the required definiteness. An offer may, however, contain a choice of terms submitted to the offeree from which he is to make a selection in his acceptance. Such an offer is necessarily indefinite but, if accepted in the way contemplated, the ultimate agreement of the parties is made definite by the acceptance. A lack of definiteness in an agreement may concern the time of performance, the price to be paid, work to be done, property to be transferred, or miscellaneous stipulations in the agreement.'

The reasoning of the Court in *Whitelaw* is determinative of the issues here. That which is here sought to be enforced as an agreement between the parties is but one step in a negotiating process wherein the proposals and counterproposals, each to the other, resulted in a narrowing of the differences between the parties on certain matters, leaving always specifics yet to be determined.

The circuit court of Livingston County, therefore, properly entered judgment for the defendant in this case, and that judgment is affirmed.

Affirmed.

McGinn v. American Bank Stationery Co.

195 A.2d (Md.) 1963

SYBERT, J. The plaintiff below appeals from a decree granting a motion for a summary judgment in favor of the defendants. The appellant [McGinn, the plaintiff] had filed an equity suit against the appellees, American Bank Stationery Company and its president, J. Wilford Sheridan, to enforce an alleged contract to sell 100 shares of the corporation's treasury stock at $50.00 per share.

Appellant claims that a contract arose in the following manner. In June 1960 the board of directors of the corporation passed a resolution authorizing the sale of stock "to such persons as may be selected by the President." At a subsequent meeting of all the salesmen of the corporation, including the appellant, a company official stated that treasury stock was being made available for sale to them, and that if they desired to purchase some, they should make a written request to the president. The salesmen were informed that if the requests exceeded the number of shares which the company intended to sell, then the stock would be prorated on the basis of the amount requested.

The appellant subsequently wrote the appellee Sheridan stating that he would like to buy 100 shares at $50.00 each. At a later conference with Sheridan, according to the appellant's own testimony, Sheridan did not indicate whether the corporation would sell "100 shares or any amount." Thereafter the appellant was told that 100 shares would not be made available to him, apparently because of the large number of subscriptions, but that he could buy a lesser amount if he so desired. He never requested fewer shares. Later the appellant asked Sheridan when he could expect to get the stock and was told that the corporation did not need money at that time but that the appellant would be informed when it did. No note or memorandum of the alleged contract was ever signed. Appellant never tendered payment in any amount because, to use his own words, "how could I, not knowing how much stock I was going to get or when? " The appellees' principal defense was that the evidence disclosed no contract.

We think the summary judgment was properly granted. The pleadings and the testimony of the appellant show that there was no genuine dispute as to any material fact and that the appellees were entitled to judgment as a matter of law. In order to create a valid contract there must be both an offer and an acceptance. The appellant contends that the statement made at the meeting of the salesmen, that stock would be made available for sale to them, was an offer and his written request for 100 shares was an acceptance thereof. However, we agree with the Chancellor that the statements made at the meeting constituted only an invitation to submit offers, and that the appellant's response requesting 100 shares was merely an offer to buy, which was never accepted. There was never any meeting of minds as to the number of shares to be sold to the appellant. "A contract, to be final, must extend to all the terms which the parties intend to introduce, and material terms cannot be left for future settlement. Until actual completion of the bargain either party is at liberty to withdraw his consent and put an end to the negotiations." *(Peoples Drug Stores* v. *Fenton Realty Corp.).* No contract having arisen between the parties, the appellees' motion for summary judgment was properly granted.
    Affirmed.

O. C. Kinney, Inc. v. Paul Hardeman, Inc.

379 P.2d 628 (Colo.) 1963

Plaintiff was low bidder on a certain job related to construction of an Air Force base. Defendant, the prime contractor, had solicited bids; he did not award the contract to the plaintiff but gave it to another contractor as part of a two-site bid, and this suit for damages resulted. The trial court granted a summary judgment for the defendants.

SUTTON, J. . . . In the instant case the record discloses no meeting of the minds to create an express contract nor can one be implied from proof of custom and usage or from the circumstances shown here. A bid is normally considered only as an offer until such time as it is accepted. Mere notification or knowledge that one's bid is low cannot of itself create a contract between the parties.

Even if defendant's uncommunicated desire to have bids submitted could be relied upon by plaintiff, it is obvious that, at best, it was merely an invitation to bid and not an operative offer. Plaintiff's bid itself constituted the offer and it would take defendant's acceptance to complete a contract.

Plaintiff's assertion that here there was no provision in the specifications reserving the right to defendant to reject any and all bids makes no difference, for it has been held that an owner is under no obligation to accept any bid. Of course, the express terms and conditions of a call for bids might alter that rule, but we are not faced with that situation here.

The depositions here also show that even if plaintiff's dollar amount had been acceptable to defendant, other material provisions of a written contract, including conditions and bonding terms, would have had to be agreed upon. The bid submitted by plaintiff in this case was not capable of being acted upon without reference to these matters so could not be considered complete in any event.

Plaintiff's theory that it was a trade custom for low bids to be automatically accepted is not helpful to plaintiff. The applicable rule, correctly applied by the trial court, is that evidence of a trade custom, where such in fact exists, is admissible only to show the terms with reference to which parties in a trade are presumed to agree in a contract actually entered into, and is not admissible where no contract has been first shown to exist.

We find no merit in any of plaintiff's grounds urged as error.

The judgment is affirmed.

Kergald v. Armstrong Transfer Exp. Co.

113 N.E.2d 53 (Mass.) 1953

LUMUS, J. This is an action of contract, begun by writ dated August 26, 1949, in which the plaintiff sues for the loss of her trunk and its contents. The defendant is an intrastate common carrier. There was evidence that the plaintiff arrived with her trunk at the South Station in Boston late in an evening in May, 1949, and went to the defendant's office there. She was not asked the value of her trunk, but was given a small pasteboard check by the defendant which was not read to her and which she did not read, but put in her purse. The trunk was to be delivered at her home in Boston. The defendant failed to deliver her trunk, and admitted that it had been lost. The small check had on one side the order number and the words "Read contract on reverse side," and on the other the words, "The holder of this check agrees that the value of the baggage checked does not exceed $100 unless a greater value has been declared at time of checking and additional payment made therefor . . . "

The judge instructed the jury, over the exception of the defendant, that the plaintiff is bound by that limitation if she had knowledge of it when she took the check, and otherwise is not. The jury returned a verdict for the plaintiff for $1,700, and the defendant brought the case here.

Where what is given to a plaintiff purports on its face to set forth the terms of a contract, the plaintiff, whether he reads it or not, by accepting it assents to its terms, and is bound by any limitation of liability therein contained, in the absence of fraud. . . .

On the other hand, whereas in this case what is received is apparently a means of identification of the property bailed, rather than a complete contract, the bailor is not bound by a limitation upon the liability of the bailee unless it is actually known to the bailor. (Cases cited.)

The cases in this Commonwealth so clearly show the law applicable to the facts of this case that we need not discuss decisions elsewhere. But we may say that our conclusions are supported by well-reasoned cases in New York as well as other jurisdictions.

Judgment for plaintiff affirmed.

Thomas v. Central Charge Service

212 A.2d 533 (D.C.) 1965

CAYTON, J. This appeal concerns the liability of a credit card holder for purchases made with the card after it had been lost or stolen. The suit was brought by Central Charge Service, Inc., a retail credit organization which claimed to be the owner of accounts receivable assigned to it by certain merchants.

At trial plaintiff offered evidence that a charge account had been opened by defendant Thomas and charge plates issued to him and his wife; that between March 27 and April 13, 1964, purchases in excess of $500 were made on Thomas' account; that the sales checks representing these purchases bore the imprint of Thomas' charge plate; that a week after the last of the purchases Central Charge sent Thomas a telegram notifying him of the unusual activity in the account; and that on the day thereafter Thomas went to the Central Charge Office and denied that he had made or authorized any of the purchases.

During his own testimony, Thomas again denied having made or authorized the purchases in question. He testified that he had received the charge plate but had not signed it on the back, as was required for validation; that he had made only one small purchase at a drugstore with the card still unsigned, and after that had looked for the card, could not locate it and assumed that it had been lost; and that he did not notify Central Charge or any of its member merchants of the card's disappearance.

We must first consider the nature of the contractual relation between Central Charge and the customer Thomas. The only writing on which it was based is a credit application which merely contained the names of Thomas and his wife, their addresses, and the name of his employer. The signature space was not filled in and the application contained no contractual language of any kind and no reference to any duty or obligation on the part of the customer with reference to the use of the charge plate; indeed, a charge card or plate was not even mentioned. Assuming that Central Charge did actually acquire these accounts by assignment—which was not proved—and assuming that as a result of the unsigned credit application Thomas agreed to accept and use a charge plate for himself and his wife, it by no means follows that he bound himself to pay for unauthorized purchases made by someone else. Whatever contract existed between these parties was completely devoid of any reference to that contingency. Not having bound himself by direct agreement, it follows that Thomas' responsibility for the unauthorized purchases could arise, if at all, only by implication.

We do not think, however, that a promise to pay for unauthorized purchases, restricted even to purchases made prior to notifying the company of the card's disappearance, can fairly be implied from the described relationship between these parties. At most, it may be said by implication that Thomas agreed to exercise due care in the use of his card. And while he perhaps failed in that agreement, it is plain that such failure is insufficient to support this action.

Nor is there here any sound or valid basis for invoking the rule, apparently relied on below, that as between two innocent parties the one who made the loss possible should bear it. In cases based on similar facts that approach has been rejected. We reject it here. Whatever the rule should be when a customer expressly binds himself by contract to promptly report a lost or stolen credit card, we are satisfied that on the facts of this case the card holder should not be held liable.

Reversed.

Allied Stores of New York v. Funderburke

277 N.Y.S.2d 8 (1967)

Defendant's credit card, issued by the plaintiff, was stolen without her knowledge immediately before her departure on a trip. She did not discover the loss until her return two weeks later. In the meantime, 237 purchases totaling over $2,300 had been charged to her account. There was a $200 limit on the defendant's line of credit. Plaintiff brought action to recover the amount of the account, relying on the defendant's application for credit in which she agreed "To pay for all purchases made by any person presenting the identification plate which Seller will send me, until Seller receives my notice by certified mail that same has been lost or stolen." This card meets the requirements of section 512 of the General Business Law which provides: "A provision to impose liability on an obligor for . . . use of a credit card after its loss or theft is effective only if it is conspicuously written or printed in a size at least equal to 8-point bold type either on a card, or on a writing accompanying the card when issued or on the obligor's application for the card, and then only until written notice of the loss or theft is given to the issuer. . . . "

BIRNS, J. . . . These sections of the General Business Law impose limitations of liability on the credit card obligor for use of lost or stolen credit cards where notice of such theft or loss is transmitted to the issuer. Liability may be imposed only where such notice is not given as required. With prophetic vision it was anticipated: "A serious ambiguity arises, however, with respect to the effect of this provision on any common law liability which might arise in the absence of any contractual provision whatever."

It has been held that credit card provisions under which the holder assumes liability for all purchases made, even by unauthorized users, are enforceable.

But under the credit agreement here, . . . although the plaintiff issuer assumes all the risk of loss or theft after receipt of notice of such facts, the agreement does not expressly provide that the holder assumes all risk occasioned by loss or theft of the credit card where the credit card holder is unaware of such facts and thus is unable to give the required notice.

In this case purchases were made with the defendant's credit card but the defendant was unaware of its loss or theft. Obviously until notified by the plaintiff, as will be seen hereafter, of the purchases made in her name, the defendant was unable to give the notice required by statute and her agreement. Thus the statute as well as the agreement does not precisely meet the problem raised and each "leaves unclear its effect on liability not imposed by any 'provision' in the contract." . . .

Plaintiff contends that lack of negligence or knowledge that the card was lost has no relevance to the issue of liability. . . .

The fact that the credit card was being used without authorization as a result of loss or theft, standing alone, cannot be equated with a finding that defendant failed to exercise reasonable care.

Since the legislation in issue is not specifically directed to the facts herein, recourse must be made to the common law for the principles which determine responsibility.

For centuries the law of torts has been founded on the principle that there can be no liability without fault.

In the few cases which have considered similar problems arising from the use of credit cards or credit devices, the determination of liability fluctuated slightly from an equitable rule that as between innocent parties he who makes the loss possible should bear the consequences to the rule that in the absence of an express contract each party owes the other a duty of due care, the card holder in using the card and the issuer merchant in honoring it. It has also been held that in the absence of an express contract each party owes the other a duty of due care.

It is to be noted that the relationship between the plaintiff and the defendant in this case is a modest two-party arrangement entitling the user to credit at the plaintiff's store and no other. It is unlike the "omnipotent credit card . . . used to procure U-drive automobiles, airline tickets, luxurious hotel suites, food and drink, multifarious items of men's wear, a silver mink stole for a newly acquired girl friend, and a puppy dog" for the sole user, where a credit card is characterized as "like an Aladdin's lamp and you didn't even have to rub it." It is the use of this latter card, with broad, diversified application and which involves three or more parties—issuers, holders, users, independent retailers and thieves—which has caused courts to fashion the rule that the holder of a credit card is responsible, even in the absence of an express contractual provision, for all unauthorized purchases except if he can establish negligence on the part of the retailer responding to the presentation of the credit card.

A parallel situation under the tripartite relationship may be seen in *Texaco, Inc.* v. *Goldstein,* where the holder of the lost credit card containing liability limitation provisions similar to the case at bar failed promptly to notify the plaintiff of his loss. The trial court, Wahl, J., held the credit card was a binding contract the provisions of which were assumed by defendant, and the defendant was liable for purchases made at numerous Texaco stations in various states. Implicit in this decision is not merely a finding that the defendant failed to exercise due care with respect to the card but that the various retail stations had no reason to question the presentation of the card by its larcenous holder.

The answer to the question whether in this case plaintiff's business conduct contributed to its loss is much simpler. Two hundred thirty-seven sales slips bearing forged signatures were permitted to accumulate in a thirty-day period. Under the data-processing procedures then in use in plaintiff's store, if the customer's account balance exceeded $200 a "spill-out" was to occur, indicating purchases over and above the limit provided by the credit agreement. Plaintiff argues that it was unable to minimize defendant's liability until it sorted and collected all outstanding sales slips and processed them through its data-processing equipment. Only then did suspicions arise that something was amiss and it summoned its customer, whom it now sues.

While it may be imperative in this age of modernization for mercantile establishments to embrace, compress and sort information from differing departments through the use of electronic data-processing equipment, it is manifestly unfair to shift the burdens of its inadequacies or failures to the innocent consumer whose status, in this modern day, remains unchanged. It is immaterial whether the defendant is the sole customer or is one of one and a half million customers to whom credit cards have been issued by plaintiff.

To pursue the plaintiff's position to an absurd end were the rule that espoused by plaintiff, depending upon how quickly plaintiff discovered suspicious sales a customer could, without negligence on his part, be chargeable through the use of plaintiff's credit card for items totaling $10,000 or $100,000 as well as the $2,460 sought here.

While a vendor granting credit status to a customer assumes the risk that it may not be paid for goods, it issues credit in order to enlarge its reservoir of prospective sales. However, there is a concurrent duty owing from the vendor to the customer that it will not permit this credit status of the customer to be abused. *Thus I must conclude that under common law principles of tort law applicable plaintiff has established no right to a recovery. . . .*

Seelye v. Broad
139 N.W.2d 126 (Mich.) 1966

MC GREGOR, J. Warren O. Seelye, Jr., the plaintiff herein, had obtained an exclusive listing agreement from the defendants, Mr. and Mrs. Eli Broad, for the sale of certain real estate owned by the defendants. After expiration of the agreement on May 8, 1962, the plaintiff continued his efforts to find a purchaser for the property. On the morning of May 10, 1962, plaintiff submitted the written offer of Jack Peltz to purchase the property for $65,000.00. This offer was rejected by defendants. Later the same day, defendant Eli Broad prepared an offer to sell for $70,000.00 on a standard offer-to-purchase form, signed the same in the place marked for seller's acceptance, and inserted the provision that the offer would be open for one day. Plaintiff took this instrument and returned it the same afternoon, signed by the prospective purchaser Peltz, but with the sales price changed to $69,000.00 and a provision inserted requiring the defendants to pay the cost of connecting the sewer to the house. Defendants took the offer under advisement and informed plaintiff that they would let him know by 5:00 p.m.

When plaintiff went to defendants' office, about 10:00 a.m. on May 11, 1962, they told him they had sold the property to another party. Plaintiff then secured acceptance of defendant's original offer. At about 10:30 a.m., on May 11th (within the one-day period for which the defendants' offer to sell was to remain open), plaintiff presented the defendants with the instrument of offer signed by Jack Peltz, stating the price at $70,000.00 and omitting the provision requiring the defendants to pay for the sewer connection. Defendants sold the property to a party unknown to plaintiff for the sum of $60,000.00. . . .

In spite of the fact that the written offer purported on its face to be irrevocable for one day, defendant retained the power to terminate at any time the offer of unilateral contract to the plaintiff, since the record fails to show any consideration for irrevocability. The principle stated in *Night Commander Lighting Company* v. *Brown* applies here, even though that case was concerned with the contract for the sale of goods:

> It is elemental that an order such as this, though it contained the words 'not subject to countermand,' may be countermanded at any time before acceptance. Until so accepted, it is simply an offer to purchase, and in no way creates a binding agreement. (Authorities cited.)

The trial judge found that the defendants, acting in good faith, legally revoked their offer to sell by informing the plaintiff of the sale to the other party. The agreed statement of facts sustains this conclusion. The actual purchaser was not obtained by the plaintiff. This is not a case in which the seller revoked the broker's listing in order to avoid the payment of commissions and then sold to a purchaser obtained by the efforts of the broker. A revocation in such circumstances is not effective to deprive broker of his commission.

Since the plaintiff failed to obtain a ready purchaser before his authority to sell the property was revoked, he is not entitled to a commission.

The judgment of the trial court is affirmed and costs are awarded to appellees.

Drennan v. Star Paving Company

333 P.2d 757 (Cal.) 1958

Drennan, the plaintiff, was a general contractor and in preparation for submitting a bid on a school job requested the defendant to submit a bid for certain paving which was involved. The defendant offered to do the work for $7,131.60, and the plaintiff used this subcontractor's offer in making his bid. The contract was awarded to plaintiff, but as he approached the defendant, he was notified that it could not perform as it had made an error in its calculations. The plaintiff got another to do the work at a cost of $10,948.60 and sought to recover this difference from the defendant. The lower court gave judgment for plaintiff in the amount of $3,817.00.

TRAYNOR, J. . . . There is no evidence that defendant offered to make its bid irrevocable in exchange for plaintiff's use of its figures in computing his bid. Nor is there evidence that would warrant interpreting plaintiff's use of defendant's bid as the acceptance thereof, binding plaintiff, on condition he received the main contract, to award the subcontract to defendant. In sum, there was neither an option supported by consideration nor a bilateral contract binding on both parties.

Plaintiff contends, however, that he relied to his detriment on defendant's offer and that defendant must therefore answer in damages for its refusal to perform. Thus the question is squarely presented: Did plaintiff's reliance make defendant's offer irrevocable?

Section 90 of the Restatement of Contracts states: "A promise which the promisor should reasonably expect to induce action or forbearance of a definite and substantial character on the part of the promisee and which does induce such action or forbearance is binding if injustice can be avoided only by enforcement of the promise." . . .

Defendant's offer constituted a promise to perform on such conditions as were stated expressly or by implication therein or annexed thereto by operation of law. (See 1 Williston, *Contracts* [3rd ed.], § 24a, p. 56, § 61, p. 196.) Defendant had reason to expect that if its bid proved the lowest it would be used by plaintiff. It induced "action. . . . of a definite and substantial character on the part of the promisee."

Had defendant's bid expressly stated or clearly implied that it was revocable at any time before acceptance we would treat it accordingly. It was silent on revocation, however, and we must therefore determine whether there are conditions to the right of revocation imposed by law or reasonably inferable in fact. In the analogous problem of an offer for a unilateral contract, the theory is now obsolete that the offer is revocable at any time before complete performance. Thus section 45 of the Restatement of Contracts provides: "If an offer for a unilateral contract is made, and part of the consideration requested in the offer is given or tendered by the offeree in response thereto, the offeror is bound by a contract, the duty of immediate performance of which is conditional on the full consideration being given or tendered within the time stated in the offer, or, if no time is stated therein, within a reasonable time." In explanation, comment *b* states that the "main offer includes as a subsidiary promise, necessarily implied, that if part of the requested performance is given, the offeror will not revoke his offer, and that if tender is made it will be accepted. Part performance or tender may thus furnish consideration for the subsidiary promise. Moreover, merely acting in justifiable reliance on an offer may in some cases serve as sufficient reason for making a promise binding (see § 90)."

Whether implied in fact or law, the subsidiary promise serves to preclude the injustice that would result if the offer could be revoked after the offeree had acted in detrimental reliance thereon. Reasonable reliance resulting in a foreseeable prejudicial change in position affords a compelling basis also for implying a subsidiary promise not to revoke an offer for a bilateral contract.

The absence of consideration is not fatal to the enforcement of such a promise. It is true that in the case of unilateral contracts the Restatement finds consideration for the implied subsidiary promise in the part performance of the bargained-for exchange, but its reference to section 90 makes clear that consideration for such a promise is not always necessary. The very purpose of section 90 is to make a promise binding even though there was no consideration "in the sense of something that is bargained for and given in exchange." (See 1 Corbin, *Contracts* 634 et seq.) Reasonable reliance serves to hold the offeror in lieu of the consideration ordinarily required to make the offer binding. . . .

When plaintiff used defendant's offer in computing his own bid, he bound himself to perform in reliance on defendant's terms. Though defendant did not bargain for this use of its bid neither did defendant make it idly, indifferent to whether it would be used or not. On the contrary it is reasonable to suppose that defendant submitted its bid to obtain the subcontract. It was bound to realize the substantial possibility that its bid would be the lowest, and that it would be included by plaintiff in his bid. It was to its own interest that the contractor be awarded the general contract; the lower the subcontract bid, the lower the general contractor's bid was likely to be and the greater its chance of acceptance and hence the greater defendant's chance of getting the paving subcontract. Defendant had reason not only to expect plaintiff to rely on its bid but to want him to. Clearly defendant had a stake in plaintiff's reliance on its bid. Given this interest and the fact that plaintiff is bound by his own bid, it is only fair that plaintiff should have at least an opportunity to accept defendant's bid after the general contract has been awarded to him.

It bears noting that a general contractor is not free to delay acceptance after he has been awarded the general contract in the hope of getting a better price. Nor can he reopen bargaining with the subcontractor and at the same time claim a continuing right to accept the original offer. (See *R. J. Daum Const. Co.* v. *Child,* Utah, 247 P.2d 817, 823) In the present case plaintiff promptly informed defendant that plaintiff was being awarded the job and that the subcontract was being awarded to defendant. . . .

Judgment for plaintiff affirmed.

Department of Public Works v. Halls
210 N.E.2d 226 (Ill.) 1965

SMITH, J. While the pleadings and the number of parties would seem to indicate numerous complexities, only one question is presented for review and it can be simply stated: Was an option to purchase real estate properly exercised? It reads:

> AND, IT IS HEREBY FURTHER AGREED by and between said parties, that lessee shall have the right and option to purchase said above described premises for the sum of TWENTY-FIVE THOUSAND DOLLARS ($25,000.00), at any time during the term of this lease.

Lessee decided to purchase the premises and notified lessor as follows:

> YOU ARE HEREBY NOTIFIED that I have elected to exercise the option to purchase the real estate described in that certain lease dated the 23rd day of June, A.D. 1955 by and between Vera A. Garowski as lessor and the undersigned Charles Jordan, as lessee, the real estate being more particularly described as follows: (Describing same) the said lease providing that the option could be exercised at any time during the term of the lease, which was a period of ten (10) years from the 1st day of July, 1955, at the purchase price of Twenty-five Thousand ($25,000.00) Dollars.
> The abstract should be submitted to my attorney, Charles R. Young, 500 McMullen Building, Danville, Illinois, for examination, and the purchase price will be available upon the furnishing of a merchantable abstract of title and warranty deed.

For a proper exercise, lessee must accept in toto the conditions contained in the option and he cannot add new ones of his own. Lessor [defendant] says he did, indeed, add new ones—that she furnish a merchantable abstract of title and warranty deed—and hence she need not perform. With this the trial court agreed, and lessee appeals.

An option is defined as a right acquired by contract to accept or reject a present offer within the time limited. If an optionee does signify his acceptance of an offer within the time limited and upon the terms stated, the obligations become mutual and are capable of enforcement at the instance of either party. Nothing is said expressly in this option as to the character of the deed, or for that matter *any* deed, nor is there any allusion apropos of a merchantable abstract of title. Should lessee, in exercising this option, have signified his acceptance and delivered $25,000.00 to lessor and let it go at that? What if after lessee had done just that but fee simple title had not been immediately put in him, could he have changed his mind? Or what if after a conveyance of some sort, lessee had discovered that his title was something less than fee simple, could he have backed away, or would lessor be given a reasonable time to remedy the defect? By these few questions, and we could posit many more, we are suggesting, what we all know, that all agreements, options included, have implied promises or conditions, even including those that purport to cover every conceivable situation, and indeed, say so. As Chief Judge Cardozo remarked in *Wood* v. *Lucy, Lady Duff-Gordon,* (222 N.Y. 88, 118 N.E. 214 (1917)):

> The law has outgrown its primitive stage of formalism when the precise word was the sovereign talisman, and every slip was fatal. It takes a broader view today. A promise may be lacking, and yet the whole writing may be "instinct with an obligation," imperfectly expressed.

It is true, of course, that lessor did not promise in so many words that she would give a deed or furnish merchantable abstract of title, but we think that such, or their equivalents, can fairly be implied. To put legal, as opposed to equitable title, in lessee, requires some type of legal conveyance. The fact that lessee happened to request a warranty deed, in our opinion, does not provide lessor with a convenient loophole to avoid her promise. We are not saying that lessor need furnish a warranty deed as such—only that she find some legal vehicle to get the job done. It is an implied promise or condition. So too, with regard to furnishing a merchantable abstract of title. Her promise was to put fee simple title in lessee and she can give him such assurance in any reasonable way she can find. She is not bound, however, to do it this way, but she must do it. It is also an implied condition or promise. Lessee's so-called "counter-conditions," are in reality only suggested ways and means by which his purchase of the premises can be appropriately effected by lessor. They are not iron-bound and double riveted pre-conditions that must be met by lessor. By the same token, assuming performance by lessor by some other way, their lack would not prevent her from enforcing payment by lessee.

. . .

We think lessee properly exercised the option and we view lessor's stance as strained. The option reads that the lessee can purchase the premises. We cannot agree that lessee in any way added new conditions to the option by suggesting to lessor appropriate avenues to that end.

... We think the option reasonably implies some sort of conveyance and some sort of evidence of ownership; that such was within the reasonable contemplation of the parties; and that the type of deed and the evidence of ownership related to suggested means to a performance of the contract to sell and not to a conditional acceptance of the option.

Accordingly, the order appealed from is reversed and the cause remanded with directions to enter judgment for the lessees and for such further orders not inconsistent with this opinion.

Reversed and remanded with directions.

Hill's, Inc. v. William B. Kessler, Inc.

246 P.2d 1099 (Wash.) 1952

Action by Hill's, Inc., against William B. Kessler, Inc., for breach of contract. The Superior Court rendered judgment for the plaintiff, and defendant appealed.

MALLERY, J. The plaintiff, Hill's, Inc., ordered thirty-four men's suits from the defendant, using a printed form supplied by defendant through its salesman.

The printed form provided that the order would not become a binding contract until it had been accepted by an authorized officer of the defendant at its office in Hammonton, New Jersey.

The defendant's salesman procured the order on May 16, 1950, and on May 23, 1950, the defendant by form letter, advised the plaintiff that "You may be assured of our very best attention to this order." What occurred next is shown by the trial court's finding of fact:

> ... but notwithstanding, on or about July 18, 1950, defendant intentionally and deliberately, at the instigation of a large store selling defendant's clothing in the downtown Seattle area, wrongfully cancelled said order and breached its agreement with plaintiff to deliver said suits as ordered, or at all. That at the time defendant cancelled said order and breached its agreement, the period for placing orders for delivery of fall suits had passed, and it was impossible for plaintiff to thereafter procure comparable suits from any other source to meet its fall trade....

Thereupon, plaintiff brought this action for loss of profits in the amount of a 66-2/3 per cent markup aggregating $815.83. From a judgment in favor of the plaintiff, the defendant appeals.

The defendant contends that its letter of May 23, 1950, in which it said "You may be assured of our very best attention to this order," was not an acceptance of the plaintiff's order.

In *Bauman* v. *McManus* the court said:

> ... The promise that the order shall receive prompt and *careful* attention seems to imply something more than that the manufacturers will quickly and cautiously investigate the advisability of accepting it. The care they might expend in that direction—in looking up defendants' financial standing, for instance—is not presumably a matter in which anyone but themselves would be greatly interested. The engagement to use care seems more naturally to relate to the manner of filling the order than to the settling of a doubt whether to fill it at all. The expression of thanks for the favor has some tendency in the same direction. We incline strongly to the

opinion that the letter standing by itself was as effectual to close a contract as though in set phrase it had said that the goods would be shipped; that to permit any other construction to be placed upon it would be to countenance the studied use of equivocal expressions, with a set purpose, if an advantage may thereby be derived, to keep the word of promise to the ear and break it to the hope.

Judgment is affirmed for plaintiff.

Hendrickson v. International Harvester Co. of America

135 Atl. 702 (Vt.) 1927

Action was brought by Peter Hendrickson against the International Harvester Company of America to recover damages on account of the defendant's failure to deliver to him a broadcast seeder. The defendant's agent took the order for the machine, which order was retained by the defendant an unreasonable time. Until this controversy arose, defendant had not indicated that it either accepted or rejected the offer of the plaintiff to buy the seeder mentioned.

POWERS, J. . . . The order was subject to approval. . . . The fact that the defendant kept the order without approving it or notifying the plaintiff of its disapproval would amount to an acceptance.

True it is that it takes two to make a bargain, and that silence gives consent . . . only when there is a duty to speak. And true it is that it is frequently said that one is ordinarily under no obligation to do or say anything concerning a proposition which he does not choose to accept; yet we think that, when one sends out an agent to solicit orders for his goods, authorizing such agents to take such orders subject to his (the principal's) approval, fair dealing and the exigencies of modern business require us to hold that he shall signify to the customer within a reasonable time from the receipt of the order his rejection of it, or suffer the consequences of having his silence operate as an approval.

Judgment for plaintiff.

Roto-Lith, Ltd. v. F. P. Bartlett & Co.

297 F.2d 497 (1962)

ALDRICH, J. Plaintiff-appellant Roto-Lith, Ltd., is a New York corporation engaged *inter alia* in manufacturing, or "converting," cellophane bags for packaging vegetables. Defendant-appellee is a Massachusetts corporation which makes emulsion for use as a cellophane adhesive. This is a field of some difficulty, and various emulsions are employed, depending upon the intended purpose of the bags. In May and October 1959 plaintiff purchased emulsion from the defendant. Subsequently bags produced with this emulsion failed to adhere, and this action was instituted in the district court for the District of Massachusetts. At the conclusion of the evidence the court directed a verdict for the defendant. This appeal followed. . . .

On October 23, 1959, plaintiff, in New York, mailed a written order to defendant in Massachusetts for a drum of "N-132-C" emulsion, stating "End use: wet pack spinach bags." Defendant on October 26 prepared simultaneously an acknowledgment and an invoice. The printed forms were exactly the same, except that one was headed "Acknowledgment" and the other "Invoice," and the former contemplated insertion of the proposed, and the latter of the actual, shipment date. Defendant testified that in accordance with its regular practice the acknowledgment was prepared and mailed the same day. The plaintiff's principal liability witness testified that he did not know whether this acknowledgment "was received, or what happened to it." On this state of the evidence there is an unrebutted presumption of receipt. The goods were shipped to New York on October 27. On the evidence it must be found that the acknowledgment was received at least no later than the goods. The invoice was received presumably a day or two after the goods.

The acknowledgment and the invoice bore in conspicuous type on their face the following legend, "All goods sold without warranties, express or implied, and subject to the terms on reverse side." In somewhat smaller, but still conspicuous, type there were printed on the back certain terms of sale, of which the following are relevant:

> 1. Due to the variable conditions under which these goods may be transported, stored, handled, or used, Seller hereby expressly excludes any and all warranties, guaranties, or representations whatsoever. Buyer assumes risk for results obtained from use of these goods, whether used alone or in combination with other products. Seller's liability hereunder shall be limited to the replacement of any goods that materially differ from the Seller's sample order on the basis of which the order for such goods was made.
>
> 7. This acknowledgment contains all of the terms of this purchase and sale. No one except a duly authorized officer of Seller may execute or modify contracts. Payment may be made only at the offices of the Seller. *If these terms are not acceptable, Buyer must so notify Seller at once.*

It is conceded that plaintiff did not protest defendant's attempt so to limit its liability, and in due course paid for the emulsion and used it. It is also conceded that adequate notice was given of breach of warranty, if there were warranties. The only issue which we will consider is whether all warranties were excluded by defendant's acknowledgment.

The first question is what law the Massachusetts court would look to in order to determine the terms of the contract. Under Massachusetts law this is the place where the last material act occurs. Under the Uniform Commercial Code (Mass. Gen. Laws Ann. (1958) ch. 106, § 2-206) mailing the acknowledgment would clearly have completed the contract in Massachusetts by acceptance had the acknowledgment not sought to introduce new terms. Section 2-207 provides:

> (1) A definite and seasonable expression of acceptance or a written confirmation which is sent within a reasonable time operates as an acceptance even though it states terms additional to or different from those offered or agreed upon, unless acceptance is expressly made conditional on assent to the additional or different terms.
>
> (2) The additional terms are to be construed as proposals for addition to the contract. Between merchants such terms become part of the contract unless:
>
>   (a) the offer expressly limits acceptance to the terms of the offer;
>
>   (b) they materially alter it; or
>
>   (c) notification of objection to them has already been given or is given within a reasonable time after notice of them is received.

Plaintiff exaggerates the freedom which this section affords an offeror to ignore a reply from an offeree that does not in terms coincide with the original offer. According to plaintiff, defendant's condition that there should be no warranties constituted a proposal which "materially altered" the agreement. As to this we concur. (See Uniform Commercial Code comment to this section, Mass. Gen. Laws Ann., *supra,* paragraph 4) Plaintiff goes on to say that by virtue of the statute the acknowledgment effected a completed agreement without this condition, and that as a further proposal the condition never became part of the agreement because plaintiff did not express assent. We agree that section 2-207 changed the existing law, but not to this extent. Its purpose was to modify the strict principle that a response not precisely in accordance with the offer was a rejection and a counteroffer. Now, within stated limits, a response that does not in all respects correspond with the offer constitutes an acceptance of the offer, and a counteroffer only as to the differences. If plaintiff's contention is correct that a reply to an offer stating additional conditions unilaterally burdensome upon the offeror is a binding acceptance of the original offer plus simply a proposal for the additional conditions, the statute would lead to an absurdity. Obviously no offeror will subsequently assent to such conditions.

The statute is not too happily drafted. Perhaps it would be wiser in all cases for an offeree to say in so many words, "I will not accept your offer until you assent to the following: . . . " But businessmen cannot be expected to act by rubric. It would be unrealistic to suppose that when an offeree replies setting out conditions that would be burdensome only to the offeror he intended to make an unconditional acceptance of the original offer, leaving it simply to the offeror's good nature whether he would assume the additional restrictions. To give the statute a practical construction we must hold that a response which states a condition materially altering the obligation solely to the disadvantage of the offeror is an "acceptance . . . expressly . . . conditional on assent to the additional . . . terms."

Plaintiff accepted the goods with knowledge of the conditions specified in the acknowledgment. It became bound. . . .

Morrison v. Thoelke

155 So.2d 889 (Fla.) 1963

The defendants (Morrison) made an offer to buy real property owned by the plaintiffs (Thoelke). They executed a contract for sale and purchase and mailed it to the plaintiffs for their acceptance and signature. The latter signed the contract and mailed it to the defendants. Before it was received by the defendants, the plaintiffs repudiated the contract by telephone. Nonetheless, when the defendants received the contract they recorded it, thereby establishing their interest in the property as a matter of public record. Claiming that no contract existed, the plaintiffs brought this suit to "quiet title" to the property—to remove the defendant's claim of an interest in it from the record. The defendants counterclaimed, seeking specific performance of the contract. The lower court entered a summary decree for the plaintiffs, and the defendants appealed.

ALLEN, J. . . . Turning to the principal point raised in this appeal, we are confronted with a question apparently of first impression in this jurisdiction. The question is whether a contract is complete and binding when a letter of acceptance is mailed, thus barring repudiation prior to delivery to the offeror, or when the letter of acceptance is received, thus permitting repudiation prior to receipt. Appellants, of course, argue that posting the acceptance creates the contract; appellees contend that only receipt of the acceptance bars repudiation. . . .

The appellant, in arguing that the lower court erred in giving effect to the repudiation of the mailed acceptance, contends that this case is controlled by the general rule that insofar as the mail is an acceptable medium of communication, a contract is complete and binding upon posting of the letter of acceptance.

Appellees, on the other hand, argue that the right to recall mail makes the Post Office Department the agent of the sender, and that such right coupled with communication of a renunciation prior to receipt of the acceptance voids the acceptance. In short, appellees argue that acceptance is complete only upon receipt of the mailed acceptance. . . .

The rule that a contract is complete upon deposit of the acceptance in the mails, hereinbefore referred to as "deposited acceptance rule" and also known as the "rule in *Adams* v. *Lindsell*," had its origin, insofar as the common law is concerned, in *Adams* v. *Lindsell,* (1 Barn. & Ald. 681,106 Eng.Rep. 250 (K.B. 1818). . . .

In support of the rule proponents urge its sanction in tradition and practice. They argue that in the average case the offeree receives an offer and, depositing an acceptance in the post, begins and should be allowed to begin reliance on the contract. They point out that the offeror has, after all, communicated his assent to the terms by extending the offer and has himself chosen the medium of communication. Depreciating the alleged risk to the offeror, proponents argue that having made an offer by post the offeror is seldom injured by a slight delay in knowing it was accepted, whereas the offeree, under any other rule, would have to await both the transmission of the acceptance and notification of its receipt before being able to rely on the contract he unequivocally accepted. Finally, proponents point out that the offeror can always expressly condition the contract on his receipt of an acceptance and, should he fail to do so, the law should not afford him this advantage.

Opponents of the rule argue as forcefully that all of the disadvantages of delay or loss in communication which would potentially harm the offeree are equally harmful to the offeror. Why, they ask, should the offeror be bound by an acceptance of which he has no knowledge? Arguing specific cases, opponents of the rule point to the inequity of forbidding the offeror to withdraw his offer after the acceptance was posted but before he had any knowledge that the offer was accepted; they argue that to forbid the offeree to withdraw his acceptance, as in the instant case, scant hours after it was posted but days before the offeror knew of it, is unjust and indefensible. Too, the opponents argue, the offeree can always prevent the revocation of an offer by providing consideration, by buying an option.

In short, both advocates and critics muster persuasive argument. As . . . indicated, there must be a choice made, and such choice may, by the nature of things, seem unjust in some cases. Weighing the arguments with reference not to specific cases but toward a rule of general application and recognizing the general and traditional acceptance of the rule as well as the modern changes in effective long-distance communication, it would seem that the balance tips, whether heavily or near imperceptibly, to continued adherence to the "Rule in *Adams* v. *Lindsell*." This rule, although not entirely compatible with ordered, consistent and sometime artificial principles of contract advanced by some theorists, is, in our view, in accord with the practical considerations and essential concepts of contract law. See Llewellyn, "Our Case Law of Contracts; Offer and Acceptance," II, 48 *Yale L. J.* 779,795 (1939). Outmoded precedents may, on occasion, be discarded and the function of justice should not be the perpetuation of error, but, by the same token, traditional rules and concepts should not be abandoned save on compelling ground.

In choosing to align this jurisdiction with those adhering to the deposited acceptance rule, we adopt a view contrary to that of the very able judge below, contrary to the decisions of other respected courts and possibly contrary to the decision which might have been reached had this case been heard in a sister court in this State. However, we are constrained by factors hereinbefore discussed to hold that an acceptance is effective upon mailing and not upon receipt. Necessarily this decision is limited in any prospective application to circumstances involving the mails and does not purport to determine the rule possibly applicable to cases involving other modern methods of communication.

In the instant case, an unqualified offer was accepted and the acceptance made manifest. Later, the offerees sought to repudiate their initial assent. Had there been a delay in their determination to repudiate permitting the letter to be delivered to appellant, no question as to the invalidity of the repudiation would have been entertained. As it were, the repudiation antedated receipt of the letter. However, adopting the view that the acceptance was effective when the letter of acceptance was deposited in the mails, the repudiation was equally invalid and cannot alone, support the summary decree for appellees.

The summary decree is reversed and the cause remanded for further proceedings.

CHAPTER 8
REVIEW QUESTIONS AND PROBLEMS

1. *A* was the manager of a building owned by *B*. *B* sold the building to *C*. *A* had a conversation with *X*, *C*'s agent, and offered to continue on the same terms that he had with *B*. *X* said that any arrangement would have to be made with *C*. Six weeks later *C* appointed a new manager. Does *A* have any claim against *C*, assuming that *C* did not respond to his offer?

2. *A* offered to sell stock to *B* by letter dated August 13. The offer stated, "It is a condition of this offer that it be accepted in writing within five

days from this date." *B* mailed an acceptance on August 18, which was received by *A* on August 20. The trial judge ruled that there was no contract. Was this ruling proper?

3. *A,* who operated a hardware store, placed an order for fifty power saws with *B,* a manufacturer. The order form supplied by *B*'s salesman stated that the order would not become a contract until accepted by the home office. Thereafter *A* received a letter from *B* acknowledging receipt of the order and promising prompt attention. *B* then wrote to *A,* expressing regret that it could not fill his order. *A* then sued *B* for damages in the amount of the profit he would have made on the fifty power saws. Should *A* succeed?

4. *A* placed an advertisement in the *B* newspaper for a special sale of fur scarfs at a price of $15. When the advertisement appeared, it stated a price of $5. During the period of the sale *A* sold forty-eight furs at a price of $5. He now seeks to recover $480 from the newspaper. Should he succeed?

5. *A* and *B* had been drinking in a bar. During their conversation the subject of *A*'s farm came up and *B* said, "I bet you wouldn't take $50,000 cash for that farm." *A* replied that he would and *B* asked if he would put it in writing. *A* then wrote a statement to that effect. *B* seeks to enforce the agreement; *A* contends that it was all a joke. Would a court grant specific performance to *B*?

6. *A* advertised that he would sell his estate at public auction "without reserve." Bids were made, *B* finally bidding $41,000. At this point *A* ordered the auctioneer to stop the sale, saying that he would not accept anything less than $100,000. *B* seeks to obtain a decree that *A* sell him the property for $41,000. Should he succeed?

7. *A,* as vendor, and *B,* as purchaser, had been negotiating for the sale and purchase of land. *B* executed a contract and mailed it to *A. A* signed it and placed it in the mail. Before *B* received it, *A* telephoned *B* that he would not sell; *B* should disregard the contract. Thereafter *B* received the contract in the mail. *B* contends that *A* is bound by the contract. Is *B* correct?

8. *X* submitted a bid for certain brick work to *C,* who used it as a basis for a general contract bid on a certain job. *C*'s bid was accepted, and he notified *X* that he had been successful and would have a form contract ready soon. When the form arrived, it contained two or three new terms and *X* refused to sign or to perform. Is *X* liable to *C*?

9. *O* parked his car in a parking lot, paid 35 cents, and received a ticket which stated that the operator of the lot was not liable for contents. *O* did not notice the ticket provision; the car was stolen but was later found without contents. Has *O* a good cause of action against the operator?

10. *O* offered in writing to lease property to *T* for three years at a monthly rental of $700. *T* accepted in writing with three minor modifications to the offer and mailed his check of $700 for the first month's rent. *O* cashed the check, and *T* moved in at considerable expense. *O* now contends the contract is unenforceable because of the changed terms. What result?

9

Consideration

2-31. Introduction. In the development of the common law of contracts it was not regarded as either necessary or desirable that *all* promises be enforced. Even today many promises are not legally enforceable. Historically, our courts have refused to impose sanctions upon a promisor who failed to keep his promise unless the promise was made in a solemn and formal way or unless the promisee would suffer some legally recognized detriment as the result of the failure to perform. The seal provided the necessary formality, and consideration developed as the test for determining which informal promises would be enforced.

Most states have altered the effect of a person adding a seal to his signature; the presence of a seal creates only a *presumption* of consideration. Other states have provided that adding a seal is ineffective to create a binding contract if the promise is unsupported by consideration. The Code adopts the latter view.

Consideration has been defined as the price bargained for and paid for a promise. It usually takes the form of some benefit to the promisor or a detriment to the promisee. Benefit as used in this context is not limited to tangible benefits, but means that the promisor has, in return for his promise, acquired some legal right to which he otherwise would not have been entitled.[1] Detriment means that the promisee has forborne some legal right which he otherwise would have been entitled to exercise. Consideration has also been defined as the surrender or promise to surrender a legal right at the request of another. More succinct definitions are: "consideration is what each party to a bargain gives to the other"; "consideration is the price paid for a promise." By all definitions, the performance or the promise to perform an act or the surrender or promise to surrender a right as requested by the promisor supplies the consideration to make the promise enforceable. Without this

---

[1] Stelmack et al. v. Glen Alden Coal Co., page 176

"benefit" or "detriment," the promisor might be morally obligated to carry out his promise, but the law would consider it to be *nudum pactum* and legally unenforceable.

The Restatement of the Law of Contracts provides that consideration for a promise is:

(a) an act other than a promise, or
(b) a forbearance, or
(c) the creation, modification or destruction of a legal relation, or
(d) a return promise, bargained for and given in exchange for the promise.

It is convenient to start from this basic proposition that consideration is required for a valid contract and then to examine in detail some of the exceptions and some of the substitutes for consideration.

It has already been noted that in some states a seal creates a presumption of consideration, and that a firm offer (option contract) is valid under the Code without consideration. The doctrine of promissory estoppel was mentioned in Section 2-21 in connection with revocation of offers. This equitable doctrine also allows enforcement of a promise in the absence of actual consideration when the promise is such that the promisor should reasonably expect the promisee to take some substantial action or forbearance in reliance on the promise, and the promisee does materially change his position in reliance on the promise to such an extent that injustice can be avoided only by enforcing the promise.[2] The doctrine of promissory estoppel has many ramifications and its application may result in the enforcement of promises that would otherwise be unenforceable because of lack of consideration.

The requirement of consideration is often a barrier to enforcement of promises, and application of the estoppel doctrine provides only a limited means of enforcing promises that fail to pass the test of consideration. In a sense, consideration is an anachronism which has endured over the centuries, and its usefulness has been the subject of judicial and legislative scrutiny in light of modern commercial needs and practices. Some states have legislation that provides that any agreement entered into in writing is enforceable without further requirement. The Code has certainly made substantial inroads on the consideration element of a contract, especially with regard to authorizing alteration or modification of contracts without requiring consideration to support the changes. The trend of the law is toward recognition of contracts and enforceability of promises on one theory or another and to circumvent technical consideration requirements. Nevertheless, consideration is very much a part of the framework of modern contract law and even under the Code it is a viable element.

2-32. Adequacy of Consideration.   It is not the function of law to make value or economic judgments concerning contracts voluntarily entered into by the parties.[3] As a general rule, courts do not attempt to weight the consideration received by each party to determine if it is fair in light of that which the party gave. It is sufficient in law if a party receives something of legal value for which he bargained. The law is only concerned with the existence of consideration,

[2] Feinberg v. Pfeiffer Company, page 178
[3] Osborne v. Locke Steel Chain Company, page 179

not with its value. It does not inquire into the question of whether the bargain was a good one or a bad one for either party. In the usual case, any inadequacy is for the person to judge at the time the contract is created and not for determination by the courts at the time of enforcement. In the absence of fraud, oppression, undue influence, or statutory limitation, a party may make any contract he pleases; the fact that it is onerous or improvident is immaterial.

However, in contracts that call for the exchange of money between the parties, the adequacy of the consideration will be scrutinized. A promise to pay $1,000 in one year in return for an immediate $10 loan would not only be usurious, and therefore illegal, but would also be unenforceable because of inadequacy of consideration. Money has a fixed value and there is therefore no basis for holding that the payment of $10 is sufficient consideration to support the promise to pay $1,000. Although it could be argued that the borrower may have needed the $10 so badly that it was worth it for him to promise to pay the larger sum, such has not been an acceptable argument to the courts. It is one thing to indulge in the presumption that the parties have provided for a reasonable relationship between the detriment to the promisee and the benefit to the promisor in ordinary contracts, but the basis for the presumption fails when money alone is involved on both sides. Note, however, that if something in addition to money is provided by the promisee, adequacy of consideration is no longer in issue. Thus, for example, if *A* pays $10 to *B* and in addition promises to attend a political meeting in return for *B's* promise to pay him $1,000, the promise would be supported by consideration. The "grubstake" arrangement provides another variation on the theme of adequacy of consideration. If a person gives a prospector $100 to enable him to search for a uranium deposit in return for the latter's promise to pay $10,000 if he "strikes it rich," the promise would be enforceable even though it involves money on both sides. Here again there is a contingent element—something in addition to money—and the courts would not inquire as to whether or not the prospector made an economically sound arrangement.

It is to be noted that contemporary case law and legislation provide increasing protection to consumers and others who have entered into contracts that are unfair and overreaching. In many situations relief will be afforded even though the technical requirement of consideration has been satisfied. The Uniform Consumer Credit Code adopted in a few states, the federal Truth-in-Lending Act, and the Uniform Commercial Code are examples of legislation in this field. The Uniform Commercial Code provides that a court may refuse to enforce "unconscionable" contracts for the sale of goods. Under the Code the court may pass directly upon the one-sidedness or oppressiveness of a contract, or a contract clause, without the necessity of manipulating existing rules in order to reach a just result. It is interesting to note that some courts were able to reach somewhat the same result under the law as it existed prior to the Code. The avowed purpose of the Code is to make it possible for the courts to police explicitly against contracts they find to be "unconscionable" —a term that has been the subject of interpretation in a large number of cases under the Code.

A promise to make a gift is unenforceable. The fact that the recipient of a proposed gift must take certain steps to place himself in a position to receive it cannot be substituted for the required consideration. If, however, the promisee of the gift is requested to act in a certain manner, and the action is considered to be the price paid for the promise, the taking of such action as is requested will serve as consideration. It is often difficult to determine whether the promisee's conduct acted as consideration or merely as a move to meet the conditions for a gift. For example, a promise by an uncle to give a family heirloom to a nephew does not become enforceable simply because the nephew goes to visit the uncle to pick up the item. However, it could be contended that consideration was present if the nephew could show that he made a long trip for the purpose of taking delivery of the heirloom and because the uncle had promised the item on the premise that he pay him a visit. It should be noted here that once the promisor has delivered the gift, he cannot set it aside because of the lack of consideration. Once a gift has been completed, the property involved belongs to the donee.

Frequently, in an effort to clothe an agreement with an appearance of consideration or to technically "bind a bargain," it is stipulated that a nominal consideration has been given or will be given in return for a promise. Generally, this effort will not be successful unless it can be proved that the nominal consideration was "bargained for" and that it was actually to be furnished.[4] Thus, a substantial promise may be given in return for "one dollar in hand paid and other good and valuable consideration," when there never had been any intention to actually pay the dollar. In this situation no consideration would be present, unless, in fact, some other consideration was actually provided; and the promise would not be enforceable if the person who made the promise chose to assert the defense of lack of consideration. The general rule, therefore, is that a mere recital of consideration may be questioned in an action to enforce the alleged contract. A recital of consideration will stand up in the absence of evidence to contradict the recital, and of course, $1 actually bargained for and paid may be good consideration. Just as a court may examine a contract to determine the presence of consideration, even though consideration is recited, it may also receive evidence of the presence or absence of consideration when the agreement is silent on this score.

2-33. Forbearance.   Consideration, which usually takes the form of a promise or an action may take the opposite form, forbearance from acting or a promise to forebear.[5] The law considers the waiver of a right or the forbearance to exercise a right to be sufficient consideration for a contract. The right that is waived or not exercised may be one that exists either at law or in equity. It may even be a waiver of a right that one has against someone other than the promisor who bargains for such waiver. A common form of forbearance is a promise not to bring a law suit, generally referred to as a release or a covenant not to sue. Such forbearance is good consideration, regardless of the validity of the claim which is surrendered, provided there is a reasonable and sincere belief in its validity. Giving up the right to litigate is something of value and a legal detriment even though it is ultimately discovered that the claim was worthless. However, if the claim is frivolous or vexatious, or if the claimant knows it is not well founded, forbearance to sue would not be good consideration.

---

[4] Allen v. Allen, page 182
[5] Grombach v. Oerlikon Tool & Arms Corp. of America, page 183

There are numerous other examples of forbearances that may constitute consideration. For instance, the relinquishment of alleged rights in an estate or of the right to enforce a lien will support a return promise. An agreement by the seller of a business not to compete with a person who has bought a business from him is another example of a forbearance. Mutual promises to forbear are sufficient to support each other.

SPECIAL CONCEPTS

2-34. Existing Obligations.   Given the proposition that a promisor must receive something of value in return for his promise, the corollary is that if he gets nothing more than he was entitled to without making the promise, he has not obtained any benefit and there is no consideration for the promise. It is not a question of whether there was adequate consideration, but rather whether there was any consideration at all to support his promise. Applying the detriment-benefit test, the promisor has not received any benefit, and the promisee has suffered no legal detriment. The latter is only doing what he would have been required to do in any event.

The problem of existing obligations has arisen in various circumstances. A common situation is one in which one party to a contract refuses to continue performance unless and until the terms of the contract are modified. The other party may, in order to assure continued performance, assent to the demands and agree to terms that are more onerous than those provided in the agreement. He may promise to pay more than the contract price or to accept less in the way of performance. Generally, a promise to pay more than the agreed price is not enforceable. The exceptions to this general rule are discussed in the following sections.

Usually, an owner who promises a contractor an additional sum to complete a job already under contract is not legally bound to pay the additional sum. If, however, the promisee-contractor agrees to do anything other than, or different from, that which the original contract required, consideration is provided. The contractor who agrees to complete his work at an earlier date or in a different manner may recover on a promise of the owner to pay an additional amount. It would also be possible for the parties to cancel the original contract and enter into an entirely new agreement, one that included the new amount.

Also, a promise to perform a statutory duty does not support a return promise. Thus, a promise to pay a public official a sum of money in return for his promise to perform the duties of his office would not only be of questionable legality, but would also be without consideration.

Some conflict exists in those cases in which a *third party* promises added compensation to one of the two contracting parties, if such party will perform his obligations under the contract. The majority of the courts hold that a promise made by a third party to pay money to one of the parties if he will perform an existing contractual obligation offers no consideration. Some recent judicial decisions appear to favor the promisee when the third-party promisor stands to gain by the performance. However, in most states a promise by a third party to a contractor to pay an additional sum upon the latter's completion of a certain construction job is unenforceable even though the contractor can prove he fulfilled his contract only because of the promise of the additional sum. Here also, if the contractor is requested to do anything new or different, the promise becomes binding because of the new consideration.

The Code has a different rule with regard to modification of the terms of a contract for the sale of goods. No consideration is required either to modify such a contract or to rescind it. However, the parties must act in good faith in doing so, and the exercise of bad faith in order to escape the duty to perform under the original terms is not permitted. The "extortion" of a modification without a legitimate reason therefore is ineffective, since it violates the good faith requirement. To safeguard against false allegations that oral modifications have been made, it is permissible to include in the contract a provision that modifications are not effective unless they are set forth in a signed writing. Except as between merchants such a requirement on a form supplied by the merchant must be separately signed by the other party. Accordingly, a consumer in addition to signing the contract must also sign the restrictive provision to assure that he is aware of the limitation—otherwise it is not effective as to him. This is apparently designed to protect the unwary consumer against reliance upon statements made to him that certain provisions of the contract do not apply to him or that others are subject to oral change. He is forewarned not to rely upon anything but the printed word, and it is expected that the double signing will bring the message to his attention.

The changing attitude toward the law is reflected in the abolition of some of the consideration requirements in the Code. The strict requirements of contract law are yielding to moral and ethical considerations and to the needs and practices of business. The Code allows necessary and desirable modifications of sales contracts without regard to the technicalities that hamper such adjustments under traditional contract law. The safeguards against improper and unfair use of this freedom are found in the requirements of good faith and the "observance of reasonable commercial standards of fair dealing in the trade." There is recognition of the fact that changes and adjustments in sales contracts are daily occurrences and that the parties do not cancel their old contract and execute an entirely new one each time a change or modification is required.

The problems of contract modifications are difficult to resolve under traditional contract law with its requirement of consideration. The courts, in their efforts to achieve a just result, have sought to find from the facts of cases submitted to them the underlying reasons for the modifications of the terms and to determine whether there was a justification for the changes. If the changes were justified, a court may conclude either that the required consideration was present or that under the circumstances none was required.[6] A finding that no such justification existed could lead to a finding that no consideration was present. Thus, under traditional legal principles a court may reach the same result as the Code but in an indirect fashion. This approach is well illustrated by the cases in which the parties agree to a modification of contract terms because of a change in circumstances or conditions between the time when the contract was executed and performance was completed.

---

[6] Graham v. Jonnel Enterprises, Inc., page 184 .

2-35. Unforeseen Difficulties. The parties to a contract often make provisions for contingencies which may arise during the course of performance. They are well advised to exercise this foresight. However, they frequently do not make any provisions at all, or make some that do not encompass all of the difficulties which may render performance by either party more burdensome than anticipated. In the absence of an appropriate contract clause three questions are raised when unanticipated difficulties arise during the course of performance: (1) Was the difficulty unforeseen? (2) Will the party whose performance is rendered more difficult be required to complete performance without any adjustment in compensation? (3) Will a promise to pay an additional sum because of the difficulty be enforceable?

The problem is posed in the famous case of *Linz* v. *Shuck* (Md. 1907) in these terms:

> When two parties make a contract, based on supposed facts which they afterwards ascertain to be incorrect, and which would not have been entered into by the one party if he had known the actual conditions which the contract required him to meet, not only courts of justice but all right-thinking people must believe the fair course for the other party to the contract to pursue is either to relieve the contractor of going on with his contract or to pay him additional compensation. If the difficulties be unforeseen, and such as neither party contemplated, or could have from the appearance of the thing to be dealt with anticipated, it would be an extremely harsh rule of law to hold that there was no legal way of binding the owner of property to fulfill a promise made by him to pay the contractor such additional sum as such unforeseen difficulties cost him. But we do not understand the authorities to sustain such a rule. On the contrary, they hold that the parties can rescind the original contract, and then enter into a new one, by which a larger consideration for the same work and materials that were to be done and furnished under the first contract can be validly agreed upon.

A promise to pay additional compensation for the completion of a contract is deemed binding by some courts where *unforeseen* difficulties are encountered after the original agreement is executed and the promise to pay more is made in consideration of this fact.[7] The result is most often justified on the theory that, in effect, the parties rescinded the old agreement because of new circumstances and formed a new one. However, it is prudent for the promisee either to furnish some new consideration or to have the old agreement formally rescinded and a new one executed. Unforeseen difficulties are those that occur seldom and are extraordinary in nature. Price changes, strikes, inclement weather, and shortage of material occur frequently and are not considered to fall in this category. However, it must be emphasized that when unforeseen difficulties do arise, the promisor is obligated to perform at the original contract price unless the other party is willing to modify the contract.

The Code has provisions relating to the problem of unforeseen difficulties in connection with contracts for the sale of goods. First, a promise to pay an additional sum is enforceable without consideration—the unforeseen difficulty would clearly involve a "good-faith" adjustment. Second, a seller may be excused from liability for a delay in delivery or nondelivery of goods " . . . if

---

[7] Pittsburgh Testing Lab. v. Farnsworth & Chambers Co., Inc., page 185

performance as agreed upon has been made impracticable by the occurrence of a contingency the nonoccurrence of which was a basic assumption on which the contract was made. . . . " (U.C.C. 2-615(1))

2-36. Discharge of Debts and Claims.

Courts are not generally concerned with the adequacy of consideration, but if the consideration on each side involves money—money given to satisfy a money debt—the consideration must be equal on both sides. Because of this rule, an agreement between a debtor and his creditor to have a liquidated (fixed in amount) debt discharged upon the payment of a sum less than the amount agreed to be owing is unenforceable. In most states, the unpaid portion is collectable even though the lesser sum has been paid.[8] The payment of the lesser sum is the performance of an existing obligation and cannot serve as consideration for a release of the balance. If there is evidence that the creditor made a gift of the balance to the debtor, no recovery of such balance may be had by the creditor. A receipt given to the debtor by the creditor, which states that the payment is in full satisfaction of the account, is in many states regarded as an indication that a gift was intended. Furthermore, where the debt is evidenced by a note, the cancellation and return of the note upon receipt of part payment discharges the full debt. Just as a promise to pay an additional sum for the completion of an existing contract is enforceable if the promisee does something other than, or in addition to, the required performance, a debtor may obtain a discharge of the debt by paying a lesser sum than the amount owing if he gives the creditor something in addition to the money. The settlement at the lower figure will then be binding on the creditor.

Since the value of consideration is ordinarily unimportant, the added consideration may take any form. For example, payment in advance of the due date, payment at a place other than that agreed upon, surrender of the privilege of bankruptcy, and the giving of a *secured* note for less than the face of the debt have all been found sufficient to discharge a larger amount than that paid. The mere giving of a note for a lesser sum than the entire debt will not release the debtor of his duty to pay the balance. The note is merely a promise to pay, and consequently the mere promise to pay less than is due will not discharge the debt. A promise to forbear from prosecuting a claim is sufficient consideration to support a promise to pay for a release, and the compromise of a claim results in a binding settlement. In each case, the parties are surrendering their rights to litigate the dispute. When one party has a claim against another party and the amount due is disputed, unliquidated (uncertain in amount), a compromise settlement at a figure between the amount claimed or demanded and the amount admitted to be owing is binding on the parties.[9] It does not matter whether the claim is one arising from a dispute which is contractual in nature, such as one involving damaged merchandise, or is tortious in character such as one arising from an automobile accident. The compromise figure operates as a contract to discharge the claim. Such a settlement contract is known legally as an *accord and satisfaction.* The dispute as to the amount owed by the debtor must be in good faith or the rules for liquidated debts are applicable,

[8] Monroe v. Bixby, page 187
[9] Nardine v. Kraft Cheese Co., page 187

and the creditor could pursue the debtor for the difference, his agreement to settle for a lesser amount notwithstanding.

It is important to remember the distinction between the settlement of a claim which is liquidated, i.e., the amount due is certain and the debtor admits that he owes the amount claimed, and one which is unliquidated or disputed as to the amount owed.

An additional method of satisfying a debt by payment of a lesser sum than the amount claimed or admitted is a "composition of creditors." This is a procedure whereby a person's creditors agree to accept a certain sum of money and/or property in full and complete settlement of the debtor's obligations to them. The creditors prorate the debtor's assets, which are made available to them, and agree with each other and the debtor to accept a percentage of their claims in full satisfaction. The composition is a type of insolvency proceedings enabling a person in debt to satisfy his debts by making most, if not all, of his assets available for distribution to his creditors. Of course, this raises a legal question as to the consideration to support the acceptance of a lesser sum in full satisfaction than the amount admittedly due. The consideration for which each of the assenting creditors bargains may be any one of the following: (1) the promise of each of the other creditors to forego a portion of his claim; (2) the action of the debtor in securing the acquiescense of the other creditors; (3) forbearance or a promise to forbear by the debtor to pay the assenting creditors more than the stipulated proportion. Thus the law encourages mutual agreements between a debtor and his creditors to the extent of precluding the participating creditors from thereafter collecting the difference between their pro rata share and the amount of the debt.

2-37. Moral Obligation and Past Consideration.   A mere moral obligation or duty unconnected with any legal obligation is not consideration to support a promise made by a person who feels so obligated.[10] The law will not enforce an obligation resting only on ethical or moral principles; it requires the presence of a legal benefit or detriment to create enforceable contracts. The doctrine of promissory estoppel, however, may render enforceable a promise that appears to be based only on moral consideration. For example, X promises his church $1,000 to be used to construct a new church. The church, in reliance on X's promise and on promises and pledges by others, undertakes the construction project. X's promise may be binding because he induced the church to materially change its position in reliance on his promise. However, if his $1,000 pledge were to be used to discharge an existing mortgage, the promise would likely be unenforceable for lack of consideration. The church did not change its position in reliance on the promise.

Past consideration is insufficient to support a present promise. The consideration must consist of some present surrender of a legal right. Some act that has taken place in the past will not suffice. Hence, an express warranty concerning property sold, when made after the sale has taken place, is unenforceable,[11] nor is a promise to pay for a gift previously received. Many businesses do recognize and live up to subsequent warranties and recognize such warran-

---

[10] Pascali v. Hempstead, page 189
[11] James v. Jacobsen, page 189

ties as a matter of good business practice and ethics, but they may not be compelled to do so.

The past consideration rule does not apply, for example, to those cases in which one person requests another to perform some work for him without definitely specifying the compensation to be paid, and after the work is completed, the parties agree upon a certain sum to be paid for the work. Although it would appear that the work done in the past furnishes the consideration to support the promise made later to pay a definite sum, such is not really the case. As soon as the work is completed, the party performing it is entitled to reasonable compensation. His later surrender of this right is consideration for a promise to pay a definite sum. The surrender of the right to receive a reasonable wage is the consideration for the new contract.

In addition to promissory estoppel, there are a few other seeming exceptions to the rules of law concerning moral and past consideration. For example, a new promise to pay a debt that has been discharged in bankruptcy is enforceable without any added consideration. The promise to pay must be clearly expressed. Acknowledgment of the debt or part payment does not import a promise to pay the creditor. Most states by statute require the new promise to be in writing, and provide that the promise may be to pay only a part of the debt or to pay it only when certain conditions are satisfied. Many states have a similar provision for a promise to pay a debt outlawed by the statute of limitations.

A creditor who has given a voluntary and binding release of part of a debt may not enforce a later promise by his debtor to pay the balance. If the release of the unpaid portion is considered in the nature of a gift, the rule relating to a promise to pay for a gift previously received renders such a promise unenforceable.

2-38. Mutuality of Consideration.   Difficult problems in the law of consideration arise in the area of mutuality of consideration or illusory promises. As a general rule, mutual promises furnish a sufficient consideration to support a valid enforceable contract. However, each of these mutual promises must be valuable, certain, and not impossible of performance or they will not suffice as consideration. As a general proposition, if one party is not bound by his promise, neither is bound. A promise is valuable only if it meets the benefit-detriment test previously discussed. The requirement that a promise be definite and certain involves the same issues as mentioned in the chapter entitled "Offer and Acceptance." A promise which cannot possibly be accomplished is not a binding promise and does not constitute consideration. However, a promise which has even a remote possibility of being performed may be binding and will be consideration for the other promise.

The requirement of mutuality of consideration presents particular problems in unilateral contracts. The promisor-offeror is at liberty to withdraw his offer at any time prior to the requested conduct by the offeree; but he loses his power to revoke after the offeree has performed or tendered performance of a part of what was requested. Thus, the offeror is in a sense bound, whereas the offeree can theoretically either continue performance to completion or abandon the project. The beginning of performance does not constitute an acceptance, but it does bar the offeror's power of revocation. The Code provides that the beginning of performance can be effective as a bar to revocation only if the offeree gives *notice* within a reasonable time that he accepts the offer. Should the offeror not receive such notice of acceptance within a reasonable time, he can treat the offer as having been rejected and thus terminate his responsibility. Of course, he also has the option to treat the offer as having been accepted if the offeree does complete performance in response to it.

The foregoing is an excellent example of a compromise adjustment in contract law to meet the needs of business. The long-standing common-law rule that the beginning of performance of a unilateral contract may bar the revocation of the offer continues to be the rule, but the notice requirement substantially limits the *time* afforded to the offeree in which to decide whether (1) he will complete performance or (2) that he will stop performance and prevent a contract from being formed. In this connection note again that the Code provides that "an order or other (unilateral) offer to buy goods for prompt or current shipment shall be construed as inviting acceptance *either* by a prompt *promise* to ship or by prompt or current *shipment. . . .* " (U.C.C. 2-206(1)) [Emphasis supplied.]

The law requires mutuality of consideration, not mutuality of obligation, although many cases indicate that these are two separate requirements. As was previously noted, the law is not concerned with the adequacy of the consideration, only with its actual existence. To determine if mutuality of consideration is present or if the purported promise is illusory, a careful examination of the language of the contract is required. For example, an agreement that gives to one of the parties the right to cancel the contract at any time prior to the time for performance is not binding and is illusory.[12] However, if the right to cancel is not absolute, but is conditioned upon whether some event happens or does not happen, the contract is such that neither party may avoid it unless the condition occurs and it is not illusory. Mutuality does not require that a contract be definite in all details or that there be reciprocity or a special promise for each obligation.[13] Neither does it require mutuality of remedies between the parties.

Many promises that appear to assure something of value, but when fully understood, do not embody such an assurance, are illusory promises because real mutuality is lacking.[14] Consider the following agreement: *B,* a trucker, promises to purchase from *S* all he *wants* of *S*'s gasoline at 20 cents a gallon plus taxes, and *S* promises to sell all that *B wants* at that price. Careful analysis of this agreement makes it clear that *B* has not *agreed to buy* any gasoline. He has promised to purchase only in case he wants it, which is equivalent to no promise at all. Since *B* has thus given *S* no consideration for his promise, *B*'s promise being illusory, *S* is at liberty to withdraw, and his withdrawal becomes effective as soon as notice thereof reaches *B*. Until withdrawn by *S,* the agreement stands as a continuing offer on his part, and any order received prior to revocation must be filled at the quoted price.

In the above case, if *B* had agreed to buy his gasoline *needs* or *requirements* from *S* for a period of one year, the agreement would have been binding. Whenever the buyer is reasonably certain to have needs or require-

---

[12] Cooper v. Jensen, page 190
[13] Graphic Arts Finish. v. Boston Redevelopment Authority, page 191
[14] Streich v. General Motors Corp., page 192

ments, an agreement to purchase all of one's needs or requirements will support the promise to supply them even though the amount to be needed is uncertain. Past experience will, in a general way, aid the seller in estimating the amount required.

The Code provides that a term in a contract that measures the quantity by the output of the seller or by the requirements of the buyer means such actual output or requirements as may occur in good faith. In addition, no quantity unreasonably disproportionate to any stated estimate, or in the absence of a stated estimate, to any normal or otherwise comparable prior output or requirement may be tendered or demanded. In other words, under the Code, quantity must bear a reasonable relationship to estimates given or to past outputs or requirements.

As a general proposition of contract law, if a party who has given an illusory promise actually performs the promise, the other party is bound to perform also. Lack of mutuality is not a defense to an executed contract; it becomes binding upon the promisor after performance by the promisee.

CONSIDERATION CASES

Stelmack et al. v. Glen Alden Coal Co.

14 A.2d 127 (Pa.) 1940

Plaintiffs brought suit against defendant to recover the cost of repairs to their building which was damaged as a result of mining operations of the defendant. Plaintiffs purchased the surface rights subject to a reservation and condition in a prior deed in the chain of title by which defendant had disclaimed any liability for damage to the surface caused by mining and the parties agreed that defendant had no liability except by reason of certain promises made in 1927. Defendant by a duly authorized agent made an oral agreement that if plaintiffs would permit the coal company's employees to enter upon their land and prop up their building to prevent its collapse, or to minimize any damages which might occur, the company would make all repairs necessary to restore the property to its original condition.

Plaintiffs permitted the ties and supports to be erected about their building which rendered it "unsightly" and resulted in some loss of rents, although it is not contended that the work was performed negligently. As the operations continued during the period from 1928 to 1935, it became necessary, according to plaintiffs, to reconstruct the building, due to the further subsidence of the surface. From time to time the defendant made repairs to the property, but later refused to restore it to its previous condition.

The lower court excluded all evidence of the oral agreement, upon the ground that plaintiffs had failed to show that it was supported by a consideration, and directed a verdict in favor of the defendant. From the order of the court *in banc* refusing a new trial, and entering judgment for the defendant, plaintiffs appeal.

BARNES, J. . . . Plaintiffs contend that (1) there was consideration for the oral agreement because of the detriment suffered by them in permitting the defendant to enter upon their land and place props and ties about their building; (2) the promise to repair was supported by a "moral consideration"; and (3) they are entitled to recover under the doctrine of promissory estoppel.

That consideration is an essential element of an enforceable contract is one of our fundamental legal concepts, and there are but few exceptions to the rule. "Consideration is defined as a benefit to the party promising, or a loss or detriment to the party to whom the promise is made." The terms "benefit" and "detriment" are used in a technical sense in the definition, and have no necessary reference to material advantage or disadvantage to the parties.

It is not enough, however, that the promisee has suffered a legal detriment at the request of the promisor. The detriment incurred must be the "quid pro quo," or the "price" of the promise, and the inducement for which it was made. "Consideration must actually be bargained for as the exchange for the promise." (Restatement, *Contracts,* Section 75, Comment (b)); . . . If the promisor merely intends to make a gift to the promisee upon the performance of a condition, the promise is gratuitous and the satisfaction of the condition is not consideration for a contract. . . .

In the present case it clearly appears that the defendant's offer to repair the plaintiffs' building was entirely gratuitous. The permission to enter upon the land and erect props and ties was sought by defendant merely for the purpose of conferring a benefit upon plaintiffs as a voluntary act, and not as the price or consideration of its alleged promise to restore the building to its original condition. The placing of supports about the structure was of no conceivable advantage to the defendant, for, as we have seen, it had no liability whatever "for any injury or damage that may be caused or done to the said surface or right of soil, or to the buildings or improvements" under the provisions of the deeds in plaintiffs' chain of title. The interest of plaintiffs alone was served by the defendant's efforts to prevent the collapse of the structure and to minimize the damages resulting from the mining operations. As this was done at the expense of the defendant, and solely for the protection of the plaintiffs, we are unable to see how it could have constituted a consideration for the defendant's promise, and have converted a purely gratuitous undertaking into a binding contract.

Here there was no preexisting legal or equitable obligation which could serve as the foundation of a moral obligation. The plaintiffs and their predecessors in title were fully compensated, as expressly stated in the original deed, for any loss which might result from the withdrawal of surface support by the owner of the mining rights. The possibility of damage was reflected in the reduced purchase price paid for the property. Plaintiffs accepted the deed with full knowledge of the reservations and waiver of damages, and with the express stipulation that defendant should have no liability whatsoever for a subsidence of the land.

Nor can plaintiffs' final contention that the defendant should be estopped from repudiating its promise be sustained. The doctrine of promissory estoppel, upon which they rely, may be invoked only in those cases where all the elements of a true estoppel are present, for if it is loosely applied, any promise, regardless of the complete absence of consideration, would be enforceable. The principle involved is defined in the Restatement, *Contracts,* Section 90, in the following terms:

A promise which the promisor should reasonably expect to induce action or forbearance of a definite and substantial character on the part of the promisee and which does induce such action or forbearance is binding if injustice can be avoided only by enforcement of the promise. . . .

Here no action was taken by plaintiffs in reliance upon the defendant's promise which resulted in disadvantage to them. They did not alter their position adversely or substantially. They have suffered no injustice in being deprived of a gratuitous benefit to which they have no legal or equitable right. We are satisfied there is nothing in the present record to bring this case within any recognized exception to the well-established principle of contract law, that a promise unsupported by consideration is *nudum pactum,* and unenforceable.

The judgement of the court below is affirmed.

Feinberg v. Pfeiffer Company

322 S.W.2d 163 (Mo.) 1959

Plaintiff, a former employee of the defendant, brought suit on an alleged contract whereby defendant agreed to pay the plaintiff $200 per month for life upon her retirement. Plaintiff had been employed by defendant for 37 years when the Board of Directors at an annual meeting passed a resolution increasing her salary and affording her the privilege of retiring at any time she may elect to do so at $200 per month. Eighteen months later plaintiff retired and commenced to receive her pension. Approximately seven years later and after a change in management, the defendant attempted to reduce the pension to $100 per month and considered the payment to be a mere gift. The trial court awarded judgment for the plaintiff and the defendant appealed.

DOERNER, Commissioner. . . . We come, then, to the basic issue in the case. . . . whether plaintiff has proved that she has a right to recover from defendant based upon a legally binding contractual obligation to pay her $200 per month for life.

It is defendant's contention, in essence, that the resolution adopted by its Board of Directors was a mere promise to make a gift, and that no contract resulted either thereby, or when plaintiff retired, because there was no consideration given or paid by the plaintiff. It urges that a promise to make a gift is not binding unless supported by a legal consideration; that the only apparent consideration for the adoption of the foregoing resolution was the "many years of long and faithful service" expressed therein; and that past services are not a valid consideration for a promise. Defendant argues further that there is nothing in the resolution which made its effectiveness conditional upon plaintiff's continued employment, that she was not under contract to work for any length of time but was free to quit whenever she wished, and that she had no contractual right to her position and could have been discharged at any time.

Plaintiff concedes that a promise based upon past services would be without consideration, but contends that her change of position, i.e., her retirement, and the abandonment by her of her opportunity to continue in gainful employment, made in reliance on defendant's promise to pay her $200 per month for life. . . . We must agree with plaintiff. By the terms of the resolution defendant promised to pay plaintiff the sum of $200 a month upon her retirement.

Consideration for a promise has been defined in the Restatement of the Law of Contracts, Section 75, as:

(1)   Consideration for a promise is
   (a)   an act other than a promise, or
   (b)   a forbearance, or
   (c)   the creation, modification or destruction of a legal relation, or
   (d)   a return promise, bargained for and given in exchange for the promise.

As the parties agree, the consideration sufficient to support a contract may be either a benefit to the promisor or a loss or detriment to the promisee. . . .

Section 90 of the Restatement of the Law of Contracts states that: "A promise which the promisor should reasonably expect to induce action or forbearance of a definite and substantial character on the part of the promisee and which does induce such action or forbearance is binding if injustice can be avoided only by enforcement of the promise." This doctrine has been described as that of "promissory estoppel." . . .

Was there such an act on the part of the plaintiff, in reliance upon the promise contained in the resolution, as will estop the defendant, and therefore create an enforceable contract under the doctrine of promissory estoppel? We think there was. . . .

The fact of the matter is that plaintiff's subsequent illness was not the "action or forbearance" which was induced by the promise contained in the resolution. As the trial court correctly decided, such action on plaintiff's part was her retirement from a lucrative position in reliance upon defendant's promise to pay her an annuity or pension. In a very similar case, *Ricketts* v. *Schothorn,* (57 Neb. 51, 77 N.W. 365, 367, 42 L.R.A. 794), the Supreme Court of Nebraska said:

> . . . According to the undisputed proof, as shown by the record before us, the plaintiff was a working girl, holding a position in which she earned a salary of $10 per week. Her grandfather, desiring to put her in a position of independence, gave her the note accompanying it with the remark that his other grandchildren did not work, and that she would not be obliged to work any longer. In effect, he suggested that she might abandon her employment, and rely in the future upon the bounty which he promised. He doubtless desired that she should give up her occupation, but, whether he did or not, it is entirely certain that he contemplated such action on her part as a reasonable and probable consequence of his gift. Having intentionally influenced the plaintiff to alter her position for the worse on the faith of the note being paid when due, it would be grossly inequitable to permit the maker, or his executor, to resist payment on the ground that the promise was given without consideration.

The Commissioner therefore recommends, for the reasons stated, that the judgment be affirmed.

PER CURIAM. *The foregoing opinion by* DOERNER, C., *is adopted as the opinion of the court. The judgment is, accordingly, affirmed.*

Osborne v. Locke Steel Chain Company

218 A.2d 526 (Conn.) 1966

COTTER, J. This action was brought by the plaintiff to recover damages for breach of contract, alleged to have been caused by the defendant's refusal to make payments to him under a written agreement entered into between the parties under date of November 4, 1960.

The terms of this agreement provided that the defendant pay the plaintiff $20,000 during the year ending September 30, 1961, and thereafter, $15,000 a year for the remainder of the plaintiff's life. The plaintiff agreed to hold himself available for consultation and advice with the company and its officers and not to engage in or be employed by any business enterprise, directly or indirectly, which is engaged in any line of business in competition with the company within the states of Connecticut, New York, Pennsylvania, Ohio, Indiana, Illinois, Michigan, California, or Washington, or in any of the areas abroad in which the company does business. The defendant made payments in accordance with the terms of the agreement for approximately two and one-half years, following which, after the plaintiff refused to consent to a modification of the agreement, the defendant discontinued further payments. The plaintiff then initiated the present action to recover payments due under the agreement. The defendant, by way of special defenses, alleged that the agreement was invalid and unenforceable, claiming in effect (1) inadequate consideration because the contract was based on past services, (2) it was manifestly unfair to the defendant, (3) it was procured through undue influence, (4) it was a lifetime employment contract not authorized or ratified by the shareholders, and (5) the board of directors had no authority to enter into it. The issues were tried to the court, which concluded that the agreement was legally unenforceable. Judgment was rendered for the defendant, and the plaintiff took the present appeal.

The facts necessary to a disposition of the question involved are undisputed. The plaintiff was employed by the defendant from 1912 until November of 1961, progressively holding the positions of order clerk, traffic manager, salesman, sales manager, president, and chairman of the board. He was president of the company from 1941 to 1958 and a member of the board of directors from 1941 until 1961. From 1958 until his retirement in November, 1961, he served as chairman of the board of directors.

The agreement in suit was approved by the board of directors at a special meeting held in November 1961. . . .

After its approval by the board, the agreement was signed by the plaintiff and by the company acting through its president. Regular payments were made to the plaintiff until April, 1963, at which time the company repudiated the agreement and discontinued payments.

The trial court concluded that there was no consideration for the agreement on the part of the plaintiff and that the directors did not have authority to enter into the agreement. . . .

We first pass to the question of consideration. The doctrine of consideration is of course fundamental in the law of contracts, the general rule being that in the absence of consideration an executory promise is unenforceable. In defining the elements of the rule, we have stated that consideration consists of "a benefit to the party promising, or a loss or detriment to the party to whom the promise is made."

The recited consideration in the present case consists of the plaintiff's promise to hold himself available for consultation with the defendant in connection with the defendant's business and to avoid serving any enterprise in competition with the defendant within a designated area. In essence, what the defendant bargained for, as contained in the terms of the written agreement, was the exclusive right to the plaintiff's knowledge and experience in his chosen field for the remainder of his life.

Absent other infirmities, "bargains . . . moved upon calculated considerations, and, whether provident or improvident, are entitled nevertheless to the sanctions of the law." The defendant cannot now be heard to claim, for its own benefit, that the actual undertaking of the parties was other than that which appears in their written agreement. Even though it might prefer to have the court decide the plain effect of this agreement to be contrary to the expressed intention set forth in the contract between the parties, it is not within the power of the court to make a new or different contract.

Under the facts of this case, the recited consideration constituted a benefit to the defendant, as well as a detriment to the plaintiff, and was therefore sufficient consideration. . . . An exclusive right to the counseling of the plaintiff, who had had almost fifty years of experience in the defendant's business, including some twenty years in positions of ultimate responsibility, and whose capacities are unchallenged, cannot reasonably be held to be valueless. Exactly what value might be placed on such a right is of course irrelevant to this issue. The doctrine of consideration does not require or imply an equal exchange between the contracting parties. "That which is bargained for by the promisor and given in exchange for the promise by the promisee is not made insufficient as a consideration by the fact that its value in the market is not equal to that which is promised. Consideration in fact bargained for is not required to be adequate in the sense of equality in value." The general rule is that, in the absence of fraud or other unconscionable circumstances, a contract will not be rendered unenforceable at the behest of one of the contracting parties merely because of an inadequacy of consideration. . . . The courts do not unmake bargains unwisely made. The contractual obligation of the defendant in the present case, whether wise or unwise, was supported by consideration, in the form of the plaintiff's promises to give advice and not to compete with the defendant, and that obligation cannot now be avoided on this ground.

One additional aspect of the issue of consideration needs discussion. The defendant has claimed that the agreement was motivated by a desire to compensate the plaintiff during his retirement years for his past services to the company. Judging from certain language in the preamble to the agreement referring to the company's custom of paying pensions to its retired personnel, this was undoubtedly true in part. The general rule is that past services will not constitute a sufficient consideration for an executory promise of compensation for those services. It is well established, however, that if two considerations are given for a promise, only one of which is legally sufficient, the promise is nonetheless enforceable. Since the agreement contained promises by the plaintiff which we have held to constitute sufficient consideration, the fact that there was additional consideration, not legally sufficient to support the agreement, cannot excuse the defendant from performance. . . .

On review of the issues presented, therefore, we hold that the agreement was supported by consideration, was fair to the defendant and was a proper exercise of corporate powers by the board of directors.

Allen v. Allen

133 A.2d 116 (D.C.) 1957

HOOD, J. In 1898 by deed of conveyance from an aunt, appellees, who are brother and sister, became tenants in common of certain improved real estate. The conveyance was subject to the condition that appellees provide their father and mother a comfortable home on the premises for as long as they lived, unless the mother became the wife of another husband. By 1938 the father had died and the family consisted of appellees, their mother, and three brothers who were born after the 1898 conveyance. In that year appellees at the request of the mother, entered into a written agreement with her whereby "in consideration of the sum of One ($1.00) Dollar to them paid by Julia A. Allen (the mother), the receipt whereof is hereby acknowledged," they promised and agreed that in the event of the sale of the property during their lifetime, they would divide the proceeds equally among themselves and their three brothers.

The mother died in 1951 and in 1953 appellees sold the property for $15,000. These suits were then brought by one of the three brothers, one suit being on his own behalf and the other as administrator of a deceased brother's estate, each claiming one-fifth share of the $15,000. The original 1938 agreement had either been lost or misplaced, but a copy thereof was received in evidence. While the agreement recited that appellees and the mother "have hereunto set their hands and seals," the copy did not disclose anything purporting to be a seal after the signatures of the parties.

The trial court found that the agreement was a simple contract not under seal, and ruled that the consideration of one dollar was "grossly inadequate" to support the contract. Judgment was entered for appellees and these appeals followed.

.   .   .

Appellant next argues that it was error for the trial court to question the adequacy of the consideration recited in the agreement. In ruling that the consideration was grossly inadequate, the trial court relied on our case of *Sloan* v. *Sloan* (D.C. Mun.App., 66 A.2d 799), wherein we held that, although generally a court will not inquire as to the adequacy of the consideration, where there is an agreement to exchange unequal sums of money and the sums are grossly disproportionate, the agreement will not receive the sanction of the courts. . . .

The testimony was that the one dollar mentioned in the agreement as consideration was never paid by the mother to appellees and they received no consideration whatever for signing, that they signed in order to please their mother, and that one of appellees even paid the lawyer's fee of $10 for preparing the agreement. We think it is plain from this testimony, and implicit in the trial court's reference to the "stated payment of One ($1.00) Dollar" as the only consideration, that the one dollar not only was not paid but was never intended to be paid.

As stated in the Sloan case, adequacy of consideration is not required; and if one dollar is intended as the consideration and paid and accepted as such, it is sufficient consideration. However, a stated consideration which is a mere pretense and not a reality is not sufficient; because if in fact no consideration was intended and none given, recital of a consideration cannot make the promise enforceable. . . .

The recital in the agreement of a consideration and acknowledgment of payment thereof was evidence that such consideration was agreed upon by the parties and that payment was actually made; but such evidence was not conclusive. Recital of consideration in an unsealed instrument may be contradicted by parol evidence. On the evidence here the court found no actual but only a stated consideration. We conclude, therefore, that the promise of the appellees was without consideration and unenforceable.

Affirmed.

Grombach v. Oerlikon Tool and Arms Corp. of America
276 F.2d 155 (1960)

The plaintiff and defendant had a written contract by which the plaintiff would serve as a public relations representative for the defendant. The employer had the right to cancel the contract by giving written notice of cancellation before May 1, 1953. The period of performance extended for several years in the event of no cancellation by that date. On April 27, 1953 the employee agreed to an extension of the cancellation option to June 30, 1953. On June 24, 1953 the employer exercised the option and cancelled the contract. Plaintiff-employee sues the defendant-employer contending among other things that the period of cancellation had expired because the extension of the cancellation option was invalid due to lack of consideration.

BARKSDALE, J. . . . Nor can we agree with plaintiff's belated contention that this agreement to extend the time within which the contract of February 10, 1953, might be canceled, was invalid because not supported by a valuable consideration. As set out in paragraph VI(a) of the contract, Buehrle had the right to cancel the contract by giving written notice before May 1, 1953. By cable, on April 27, 1953, Grombach agreed to an extension of the cancellation option to June 30, 1953. The crux of the situation is that Buehrle requested, and Grombach agreed to, the extension of the time in which the option to cancel might be exercised, within the period during which, according to the terms of the written contract, Buehrle had the unquestioned option to cancel. Buehrle's forbearance to cancel at a time when he, by the terms of the contract, had the undoubted right to do so, constituted consideration for the extension of time.

> The waiver of a right or forbearance to exercise the same is a sufficient consideration for a contract, whether the right be legal or equitable, or exists against the promisor or a third person, provided it is not utterly groundless. (17 C.J.S. *Contracts* 103, p. 456)

In the case of *Millikan* v. *Simmons* (244 N.C. 195, 93 S.E.2d 59), it was held that an agreement to extend an option for the purchase of real estate made before the expiration of the original option, was valid, the agreement to forego the right to close the transaction at once, constituting sufficient consideration to support the agreement to extend the option.

See also *Brown* v. *Taylor* (174 N.C. 423, 93 S.E. 982, 984, L.R.A.1918B, 293), where the principle is stated as follows:

There is a consideration if the promisee in return for the promise, does anything legal which he is not bound to do, or refrains from doing anything which he has the [legal] right to do, whether there is any actual loss or detriment to him or actual benefit to the promissor or not. . . .

Affirmed.

Graham v. Jonnel Enterprises, Inc.

257 A.2d 256 (Pa.) 1969

O'BRIEN, J. Appellants, Jonnel Enterprises, Inc. [Jonnel] and Arenze, Inc., are the general contractor and owner of the real estate, respectively, which were involved in the construction of a dormitory to house students of Clarion State College. Both corporations are controlled by Elmer Jonnett, who was their agent. Appellees, John F. Graham and Roy C. Long, are electrical contractors.

On May 6, 1966, appellees and Jonnel entered into a written agreement by which appellees, in return for $70,544.66 were to perform electrical work and supply materials for the dormitory at Clarion State. According to appellees, they were under the impression that the May 6 agreement obligated them to perform the electrical work on only one building or only one wing of a building, and they had no knowledge of any second wing. They discovered the second wing only after three or four days' work, and informed Elmer Jonnett at that time that they would not wire both wings for $70,544.66. They further testified that a new contract was agreed upon orally and prepared. Under the new contract, appellees were to wire both wings and were to be paid only $65,000, but they were relieved of the obligation to supply entrances and a heating system. Appellees testified that Jonnett approved the prepared contract and stated that he would take it to Pittsburgh and have it signed. It was never signed.

Acting on Jonnett's alleged agreement with regard to the second contract, appellees resumed work. Payment was to be made in eight 90 percent progress payments. Seven were made in accordance with the terms of the second contract, but appellants failed to pay the last 90 percent progress payment. Appellees then brought suit for the last 90 percent progress payment, the 10 percent retained by appellants, and some extra work allegedly agreed to by appellants, the entire amount sought totalling $15,629.88. Appellants in their answer averred that the written contract of May 6 was operative and that appellees had breached it causing them damages of more than $20,000.00. Further, appellants counterclaimed for an amount "in excess of $10,000."

The jury returned a verdict in favor of appellees in the amount they sought, $15,629.88. . . .

Appellants' main contention on this appeal is that the jury was improperly permitted to find an amendment to the written contract, because no consideration could have existed for such an amendment. Reliance is placed on our recent decision in *Nicolella* v. *Palmer,* 432 Pa. 502, 248 A.2d 20 (1968), in which we discussed an alleged oral amendment calling for additional compensation to the plaintiff: "The only possible consideration would be appellant's agreement to proceed with the work. Yet appellant was already obligated to do so. The general rule is stated in 17 C.J.S. Contracts § 112a: 'The promise

of a person to carry out a subsisting contract with the promisee or the performance of such contractual duty is clearly no consideration, as he is doing no
more than he was already obliged to do, and hence has sustained no detriment,
nor has the other party to the contract obtained any benefit. Thus, a promise
to pay additional compensation for the performance by the promisee of a
contract which the promisee is already under obligation to the promisor to
perform is without consideration, and this rule has been applied to building
and construction contracts.' "

However, that case is clearly distinguishable from the instant one. Without
even passing on the various possible sources of consideration cited by the court
below, such as the compromise of a disputed claim, we note that the amendment here called for appellees to receive *less* money than they would have
received under the written contract. Appellants respond that appellees would
receive only about $5,000.00 less while performing about $26,000.00 less work.
Yet the function of a court is merely to determine whether consideration
existed, not to examine into the adequacy of that consideration. Appellees
suffered a detriment in contracting for some $5,000.00 less under the amend-
ment, and thus consideration surely existed.

The judgment is affirmed.

Pittsburgh Testing Lab. v. Farnsworth & Chambers Co., Inc.

251 F.2d 77 (1958)

MURRAH, J. This is an appeal from a judgment of the District Court
invalidating, for lack of consideration, an oral contract to pay additional
compensation for services rendered in connection with the performance of an
antecedent written contract. Jurisdiction is based upon diversity of citizenship
and requisite amount in controversy.

According to the unchallenged findings of the trial court, the appellant,
Pittsburgh Testing Laboratory, entered into a written subcontract with the
appellee, Farnsworth & Chambers, Inc., under the terms of which the Testing
Company agreed to do all of the testing and inspection of materials required
under a master contract between Farnsworth and the Douglas Aircraft Corporation for the construction of concrete ramps and runways at Tulsa, Oklahoma. The consideration for the performance of the service was $24,450, to
be paid in seven monthly installments, less 10 percent retainage until completion of the contract. In the preliminary negotiations, Farnsworth estimated
that the job would be completed in seven months, or October 15, 1952, on the
basis of a ten-hour day, sixty-hour work week, and that the Testing Company's
work would be concluded about November 1. While these representations
undoubtedly formed the basis for Pittsburgh's proposal and for the lump-sum
compensation in the contract, there was no guarantee of a completion date or
hour work week. Before the end of the seven-months period, and in September
1952, it became manifest that the contract would not be completed within the
estimated time, due principally to the necessity of moving 1,200,000 tons of
dirt or material instead of the estimated 600,000 tons. A controversy thereupon arose between the parties as to Pittsburgh's obligation under the written
contract and Farnsworth's liability for overtime compensation to Pittsburgh's
personnel for work in excess of the sixty-hour week. Pittsburgh was told by

Farnsworth's representatives that if it would continue to perform its services, it would be compensated. When, however, no payments were made in December 1952, Pittsburgh refused to proceed unless a new contract was entered into providing payment for the remaining work at the rate of $3,492.85 per month from November 1 until the completion of the work, plus time and one-half for all man-hours worked over sixty hours per week. On December 20, the parties entered into an oral contract to that effect and Pittsburgh continued to perform the same service and to submit invoices for the monthly compensation, and separate invoices for overtime pay in excess of the sixty hours per week. Although Farnsworth did not remit for the invoices or reply to Pittsburgh's persistent statements, it made no protest or objection to either the statements for the stipulated additional compensation or the separate statements for the overtime. After the work was completed in the Spring of 1953, and Pittsburgh had been paid the balance of the retainage under the original contract, Farnsworth finally repudiated the oral agreement and this suit followed.

The trial court specifically found that at the time of making the oral contract to pay additional compensation, plus overtime, a bona fide dispute existed between the parties concerning their respective obligations under the written contract. The trial court also specifically found, however, that the Testing Company performed no services pursuant to the oral contract which it was not already bound to do by the terms of the written contract. Based on these findings, the trial court finally concluded that the oral contract was unenforceable for want of consideration, and that Farnsworth was not estopped to defend on that basis.

It is the general rule, followed in Oklahoma where this contract was made and performed, that a promise to pay additional compensation for the doing of that which the promisee is already legally bound to do or perform, is insufficient consideration for a valid and enforceable contract. . . .

Another more widely accepted exception might properly be called the "unforeseeable difficulties exception," under which the courts have recognized the equities of a promise for additional compensation based upon extraordinary and unforeseeable difficulties in the performance of the subsisting contract. In these circumstances, the courts generally sustain the consideration for the new promise, based upon standards of honesty and fair dealing and affording adequate protection against unjust or coercive exactions. . . .

As far as we can determine, Oklahoma courts have not had occasion to embrace or reject what seems to us a salutary exception to the rule. But, there can be no doubt that the oral contract was made in the face of unforeseen and substantial difficulties—circumstances which were not within the contemplation of the parties when the original contract was made, and which were recognized when the subsequent oral contract was entered into. The performance of the contract took more than twice as long as the parties estimated. Pittsburgh's primary cost was expensive skilled labor, and the consideration for the contract was necessarily based upon the estimated time required for performance. We should be content to sustain the contract on the assumption that the Oklahoma courts would recognize and apply the so-called unforeseen difficulties exception in a case like ours. But the contract need not rest upon that ground alone. There can be no doubt that an agreement which compromises a bona fide dispute concerning duties and obligations under a subsisting contract, is supported by valid consideration and is enforceable. . . . The trial court's specific finding in that regard is amply supported by the evidence, and we hold the contract valid and enforceable.

The judgment is accordingly reversed.

Monroe v. Bixby
47 N.W.2d 643 (Mich.) 1951

The plaintiff entered into a contract to sell real estate to the defendant for $4,000, payable in monthly installments. Defendant claimed that three years later the plaintiff agreed to reduce the price to $2,500. When the defendant had paid $2,500 she refused to pay more and demanded a deed to the property. The plaintiff claimed that the agreement to accept a lesser amount was without consideration and brought this suit to foreclose on the contract. The lower court ruled for the defendant and plaintiff appealed.

BOYLES, J. . . . Assuming that defendant's position was supported by the proofs, and that the plaintiff had agreed to accept less than the full amount of the purchase price, such an agreement must be considered as unenforceable for lack of consideration. Plaintiff's claim of . . . [the] balance of the purchase price and interest, was a liquidated demand, and any agreement to accept less than the full amount could not be considered as a compromise and settlement of an unliquidated or doubtful claim.

Under the law in this state there is no doubt that a payment of less than the full amount of a past-due liquidated and undisputed debt, although accepted and receipted for as in full satisfaction, is only to be treated as a partial payment, and does not estop the creditor from suing for and recovering the balance. . . .

We have many times held that part payment of a past-due, liquidated and undisputed claim, even though accepted in full satisfaction thereof, does not operate to discharge the debt, but constitutes a payment *pro tanto* only. . . .

We conclude that the claimed "agreement" to accept less than the amount due for principal and interest on the contract, being without consideration, was void. That being true, there is no occasion to consider the claim that it also was void because of the statute of frauds.

Judgment for plaintiff.

Nardine v. Kraft Cheese Co.
52 N.E.2d 634 (Ind.) 1944

FLANAGAN, J. For several years prior to August 24, 1941, the appellant, Lattie Nardine, a resident of Vincennes, Indiana, had operated a grocery in Lexington, Kentucky, under the name of Standard Market. During that time she had been an open account customer of appellee. In July 1941 she purchased from appellee 515-3/4 pounds of longhorn cheese. After a short time a dispute developed as to this cheese. Appellant said it was spoiled when received and that appellee should take it back. Appellee said that appellant spoiled it trying to force-cure it and therefore it could not be returned. This dispute continued until after appellant closed her business on August 24, 1941.

Thereafter letters were exchanged between the parties concerning settlement of appellant's account, whereby it developed that there were other differences as to items in the account. About October 1, 1941, appellee's Lexington manager went to Vincennes to discuss the account with appellant but they were unable to agree as to the amount appellant owed. The dispute concerning the shipment of longhorn cheese above referred to was continued at that conference.

On October 30, 1941, appellant wrote appellee the following letter:

> Enclosed please find check in the amount of One Hundred Forty Six Dollars and one cent ($146.01) which according to our records pays my account in full.
>
> You will notice that I have taken a 10 cents per lb. deduction on the 515-3/4 lb. bad longhorn cheese, that I received from you. We are still at quite a loss on this cheese, as we really had to sacrifice it to get rid of it.
>
> In regard to the balance on your statement of overcharges and deductions, I wish to advise that I find it impossible to check upon this as they are so old. I feel that if the deductions were not in order, that I should have been notified at the time they were taken from the checks. As you told me, these were left over from before the time you took over this account.
>
> We are sorry to have had to make the above deductions, but I really feel that it is a just one. It has been a pleasure to do business with the Kraft Cheese Company at Lexington, and I want to thank you for all past favors.
>
> With best regards to you, I remain,

Enclosed with the letter was a check for $146.01, marked, "This pays my account in full to date." After receiving the letter and check appellee mailed the check to the Vincennes bank on which it was drawn for certification. The bank certified the check and returned it to appellee who still retains it.

Thereafter appellee brought this action against appellant seeking to recover on account for the balance it claimed due after deducting the sum of $146.01. Appellant answered among other things that there had been an accord and satisfaction. Trial resulted in judgment for appellee in the sum of $87.88 and this appeal followed. The sufficiency of the evidence is properly challenged.

When the holder of a check has it certified by the bank on which it is drawn, the drawer is discharged and the debt becomes that of the bank. ... If it was tendered in full payment of a claim which was unliquidated or concerning which a bona fide dispute existed, the acceptance of the check discharged the debt. ...

Appellee says that there was no dispute because the trial court found that the longhorn cheese which appellant claims was spoiled when it arrived was in fact spoiled by appellant in trying to force-cure it. The trial court could, and undoubtedly did, find that appellant spoiled the cheese. But in determining whether there was an accord and satisfaction we are not concerned with the question as to who was right and who was wrong in an existing dispute. We are concerned only with the question as to whether a good-faith dispute existed at the time the check was tendered in full payment. The evidence on this question by both parties was all to the effect that such a dispute did exist.

It is true as appellee contends that the question of accord and satisfaction is ordinarily a question of fact, but where the controlling facts requisite to show accord and satisfaction are undisputed the question becomes one of law. ...

Our conclusion is that the facts in this case show an accord and satisfaction of the claim sued upon.

Judgment for defendant Nardine.

Pascali v. Hempstead

73 A.2d 201 (N.J.) 1950

EASTWOOD, J. Defendant appeals from a judgment entered in favor of plaintiff by the Bergen County District Court, sitting without a jury, in the sum of $125.01. The court found for the plaintiff in the sum of $143.51 and in favor of the defendant for $18.50 on his counterclaim. Plaintiff has not filed a brief nor did he appear at the argument.

In the first count of plaintiff's complaint, he alleges negligence on the part of defendant in the performance of certain work on his automobile, a 1941 Plymouth sedan, causing damage thereto; in his second count, he alleges that defendant admitted that said work was negligently performed and promised to pay the cost of repairs. Defendant's answer denied the plaintiff's allegations.

Defendant conducts what is generally known as a "gas service station" and does not undertake expert mechanical motor vehicle repairs. Plaintiff entrusted his vehicle to defendant for the sole purpose of having its spark plugs cleaned and adjusted. This is the only work that was done on the car. When plaintiff returned for his car, he discovered that it would not start. Although defendant installed a new battery, the motor could not be started until employees of the defendant rocked the vehicle and "unjammed" the starter; a "rattling noise" was then heard in the engine. Subsequently, the vehicle was towed to Decker Brothers garage where it was repaired. . . .

. . . Plaintiff testified that the defendant promised to pay the cost of the repairs and deduct same from the wages of the employee allegedly responsible for the damage. It is now well settled that a mere moral obligation or conscientious duty arising wholly from ethical motives or a mere conscientious duty unconnected with any legal obligation, perfect or imperfect, or with the receipt of benefit by the promisor of a material or pecuniary nature will not furnish a consideration for an executory promise. (12 Am.Jur., *Contracts,* Sec. 97, p. 590.) "A moral obligation which has at no time been a legal duty will not, according to the great weight of authority, afford a consideration for a promise." (13 C. J., *Contracts,* 219(10), p. 358) . . . In view of the fact that defendant was not liable to plaintiff, the promise to pay was unenforceable.

The judgment of the trial court in favor of the plaintiff is reversed and the judgment in favor of the defendant on his counterclaim in the sum of $18.50, representing the price of the battery, is affirmed.

James v. Jacobsen

91 S.E.2d 527 (Ga.) 1956

Jacobsen brought an action against James, defendant, to recover for alleged breach of warranty to the effect that the property purchased was free of termites. The warranty was given after the contract of sale had been signed.

GARDNER, J. The record reveals that this is an action ex contractu and not ex delicto. This leads us to consider first whether or not the instrument regarding termite infestation was a legal and binding contract with sufficient consideration to vary the terms of the original contract of sale and contract of purchase. It is our understanding of the law that where the vendor of realty stipulates the terms upon which the property is offered for sale and such offer is accepted by a proposed purchaser, such contract between them is executed within the terms of the agreement. The contract of sale set up certain specifications, all of which were fulfilled by the vendor and the purchaser within the specified time. Before the consummation of the sale there was executed an instrument in which the seller guaranteed to the purchaser, in writing, that the premises in question were free of termite infestation and free of damage due to any previous termite infestation. . . .

The original contract was based on legal consideration and was valid and enforceable. The original contract of sale here, as the record reveals, was executed on January 14, 1955 and the express warranty with regard to termites was given by the defendant on February 10, 1955. The sale had not taken place and no delivery of the property had been made and the parties had not yet done what the original contract obligated them to do. (See *Woodruff* v. *Graddy & Sons,* 91 Ga. 333, 17 S.E. 264) Where, as here, the termite instrument is relied upon as a part of the original contract of sale, there are decisions to the effect that such a reliance is not tenable but is *nudum pactum.* . . .

Judgment for defendant.

Cooper v. Jensen
448 S.W.2d 308 (Mo.) 1969

The Jensens entered into a contract with John R. McCall who was then 84 years old which provided that they would care for him in their home. The contract provided that upon his death the Jensens would receive $20,000. It also provided:

> Either party may cancel this contract at any time they desire, however, in the event the first party cancels this contract, then first party shall be obligated to pay for the time he has been in the home of second parties, at the rate of Eighty Dollars ($80.00) per month.

McCall stayed with the Jensens for several months, then went to the hospital for treatment and upon his release did not return to their home but spent his remaining years in the Odd Fellows' Home. The Jensens filed a claim against the estate for $20,000. The probate court allowed the claim but upon appeal by the executor it was disallowed. The Jensens appealed.

SHANGLER, J. . . . Our courts have held that the essential elements of a contract are (1) parties competent to contract, (2) a subject matter, (3) legal consideration, (4) mutuality of agreement, and (5) mutuality of obligation. By those criteria, the instrument of May 28, 1963 was not an enforceable agreement because it was lacking in consideration and so, devoid of mutuality of obligation. That is to say, neither party came under any duty to the other, as neither made a binding promise to the other. It provided that *"(e)ither party may cancel this contract at any time they desire. . . . "* Therefore, Jensens' promise to furnish Mr. McCall with a home and the other specified services for as long as he lived and to receive from him $5 per month for doing so, *unless he or they canceled the arrangement,* was merely illusory, because its performance or nonperformance rested unconditionally with the pleasure or future will of the Jensens. Mr. McCall retained a similar unlimited option to perform or not perform his promise to bequeath so that his, also, was a promise in form only, and equally illusory. Nothing that either party promised was exempt from their respective power to cancel. Each had it always in his power to keep his promise and yet to escape performance of anything detrimental to himself or beneficial to the promisee. Neither of these apparent promises is enforceable against the one(s) making it, nor is either operative as a consideration for a return promise. Therefore, the agreement of May 23, 1963, when signed, was not an enforceable bilateral contract and remained unenforceable to the extent that it remained executory. To the extent that a party-promisee performed under it, however, the consideration theretofore lacking was supplied, and to that extent, the party-promisor was bound. Despite any partial performance, however, the respective parties, as promisors, were not bound by those promises made, but not yet acted upon by the other, because of the continuing lack of consideration for them. As to the future, each retained the power to cancel the agreement. . . .

The judgment is affirmed.

Graphic Arts Finish., Inc. v. Boston Redevelopment Authority

225 N.E.2d 793 (Mass.) 1970

SPALDING, J. This case comes here on the plaintiff's appeal from an order sustaining a demurrer to its second amended declaration. The case involves an alleged agreement by the Boston Redevelopment Authority (BRA) to pay the expenses of relocating a business displaced by the Government Center Urban Renewal Project. . . .

We summarize the allegations of the first count as follows. On October 25, 1961, BRA, acting under its power of eminent domain, took the buildings known as 42-52 Chardon Street and 41-43 Pitt Street, Boston. The buildings were owned by Greenbaum Realty, Inc., a Massachusetts corporation. The plaintiff's business was located at these premises. The stockholders of the plaintiff and Greenbaum Realty, Inc. are identical. The plaintiff's president, after several conferences subsequent to the taking with the defendant's agents and employees, reached an agreement whereby the plaintiff would receive its "total certified actual moving expenses" on an installment basis in return for performance of certain promises. The plaintiff promised (1) to depart the premises peacefully and expeditiously, without requiring the defendant to resort to legal action; (2) to relocate its business elsewhere and not liquidate; and (3) to induce Greenbaum, the landlord, to consider wiring, plumbing, and other property as the plaintiff's personal property, so that Greenbaum would not claim greater damages from the defendant. The plaintiff alleges performance of these promises, and compliance with all the administrative requirements and conditions set forth by the defendant as a prerequisite for payment. The plaintiff's moving expenses amounted to approximately $130,000 of which it failed to receive $54,069.11.

The sufficiency in law of count 1 depends on whether the plaintiff's alleged promises constitute valid consideration for the defendant's promise to pay moving expenses. . . .

The essentials of consideration are summarized in Williston, Contracts (3d ed.) § 102A: "[Legal detriment] means giving up something which immediately prior thereto the promisee was privileged to retain, or doing or refraining from doing something which he was then privileged not to do, or not to refrain from doing. Benefit correspondingly must mean the receiving as the exchange for his promise of some performance or forbearance which the promisor was not previously entitled to receive." The plaintiff's promise to relocate its business and not liquidate clearly is the "doing something which . . . [it] was then privileged not to do." The defendant, however, argues first that this promise could not be consideration because it involved no detriment to the plaintiff. Staying in business, it argues, is merely following one's business interests, and thus incurs no detriment. It is apparent, however, that for the plaintiff to stay in business, it would cost about $130,000, the cost of relocating. It would appear that the defendant's promise was an inducement for the plaintiff to stay in business, a course of action which the plaintiff, for financial reasons, might not otherwise have taken. In fact, according to the allegations, the plaintiff advanced, as part of the moving arrangements, a considerable sum of money with the expectation of being repaid. Staying in business, without receiving the promised reimbursement, would thus constitute a detriment to the plaintiff.

The defendant's second argument is that the plaintiff's promise was illusory in that it specified no definite time period during which the plaintiff would remain in business and hence was not valid consideration. It is true that a promise that binds one to do nothing at all is illusory and cannot be consideration. *Gill* v. *Richmond Co-op. Assn. Inc.,* 309 Mass. 73, 79-80, 34 N.E.2d 509 (plaintiffs' promise to buy such milk as they might order). But here the plaintiff has bound itself to do something, namely, to relocate and open its business elsewhere. If, after having done so, the plaintiff decided to liquidate, it cannot be said that the original promise was entirely lacking in consideration. The law does not concern itself with the adequacy of consideration; it is enough if it is valuable. . . . The plaintiff's promise is to be distinguished from a promise to relocate if it so desired, which clearly would be illusory. . . .

Order sustaining demurrer reversed.

Streich v. General Motors Corp.
126 N.E.2d 389 (Ill.) 1955

The plaintiff, Streich, as seller sues for breach of what he contends is a contract to supply the defendant with its requirements for certain air magnet valves from September 1, 1948 to August 31, 1949. This would have been approximately 1,600 units based on previous requirements. The so-called contract consisted of a purchase order reading as follows:

> This Purchase Order is issued to cover shipments of this part, to be received by us from September 1, 1948, to August 31, 1949, as released and scheduled on our 48 'Purchase Order release and Shipping Schedule.'

It described the valves and set a price of $13.50 each, and on the reverse side the order said it constituted the final agreement between buyer and seller. It called itself a contract, but said, "Deliveries are to be made both in quantities and at times specified in schedules furnished by Buyer."

The defendant contended there was no contract since no goods had been ordered, although the plaintiff spent considerable sums of money for machinery and tooling in preparation for production.

MC CORMICK, J. . . . There is no question but that under the law a contract properly entered into whereby the buyer agrees to buy all its requirements of a commodity for a certain period, and the seller agrees to sell the same as ordered, is a valid and enforceable contract and is not void for uncertainty and want of mutuality. . . . The contract in the instant case is not such a contract. Purchase Order No. 11925 states that it is issued to cover "shipments of this part, to be received by us from Sept. 1, 1948 to August 31, 1949 as released and scheduled on our series 48 'Purchase Order release and Shipping Schedule' No. 478412 attached and all subsequent Purchase Order releases." . . . Reading and construing the two documents together, notwithstanding the detailed provisions contained on the reverse side of the purchase order, the result is an agreement on the part of the seller to sell a certain identified valve at a certain fixed price in such quantities as the buyer may designate, when and if it issues a purchase order for the same. The word "release" as used throughout these documents is treated by both parties as equivalent to "order."

In *Corbin on Contracts,* Vol. 1, § 157, the author says:

> In what purports to be a bilateral contract, one party sometimes promises to supply another, on specified terms with all the goods or services that the other may order from time to time within a stated period. A mere statement by the other party that he assents to this, or "accepts" it, is not a promise to order any goods or to pay anything. There is no consideration of any sort for the seller's promise; and he is not bound by it. This remains true, even though the parties think that a contract has been made and expressly label their agreement a "contract." In cases like this, there may be no good reason for implying any kind of promise by the offeree. Indeed, the proposal and promise of the seller has the form of an invitation for orders; and the mode of making an operative acceptance is to send in an order for a specific amount. By such an order, if there has been no previous notice of revocation, a contract is consummated and becomes binding on both parties. The standing offer is one of those that empowers the offeree to accept more than once and to create a series of separate obligations. The sending in of one order and the filling of it by the seller do not make the offer irrevocable as to additional amounts if the parties have not so agreed.

(See also *Williston on Contracts,* Rev. Ed., Vol. 1.104A)

Here, the buyer proffers purchase order 11925, with its twenty-five or more clauses, to the seller for acceptance. In the instrument it makes no promise to do anything. On the surface it appears to be an attempt to initiate a valid bilateral contract. The seller accepts, and as by a flash of legerdemain the positions of the buyer and the seller shift. The buyer now becomes the promisee and the seller the promisor. The promise of the seller to furnish identified items at a stated price is merely an offer and cannot become a contract until the buyer issues a release or order for a designated number of items. Until this action is taken the buyer has made no promise to do anything, and either party may withdraw. The promise is illusory, and the chimerical contract vanishes. "An agreement to sell to another such of the seller's goods, wares, and merchandise as the other might from time to time desire to purchase is lacking in mutuality because it does not bind the buyer to purchase any of the goods of the seller, as such matter is left wholly at the option or pleasure of the buyer. . . . "

The agreement in question is an adaptation of what was termed an "open end contract," which was used extensively by the federal government during the late war. However, it was used only in cases where the commodities dealt with were staples and either in the possession of or easily accessible to the seller. In this case the use of the contract is shifted and extended to cover commodities which must be manufactured before they are available for sale. According to the admitted statements in the complaint, special tools had to be manufactured in order to produce the item herein involved. The seller here, misled by the many and detailed provisions contained in purchase order No. 11925 and ordinarily applicable to an enforceable bilateral contract, undoubtedly, as he alleged in his complaint, did go to considerable expense in providing tools and machines, only to find that by the accepted agreement the buyer had promised to do absolutely nothing. A statement of expectation creates no duty. Courts are not clothed with the power to make contracts for parties, nor can they, under the guise of interpretation, supply provisions actually lacking or impose obligations not actually assumed. . . .

The agreement contained in purchase order No. 11925 was artfully prepared. It contains, in print so fine as to be scarcely legible, more than twenty-three clauses, most of which are applicable to bilateral contracts. It has all the indicia of a binding and enforceable contract, but it was not a binding and enforceable contract because the promise was defective. Behind the glittering facade is a void. This agreement was made in the higher echelons of business, overshadowed by the aura of business ethics. To say the least, the agreement was deceptive. In a more subterranean atmosphere and between persons of lower ethical standards it might, without any strain of the language, be denominated by a less deterged appellation.

Nevertheless, as the law is today, on the pleadings in the instant case, the trial court could no nothing but sustain the motion to dismiss the complaint. The judgment of the Circuit Court is affirmed.

Judgment for defendant affirmed.

CHAPTER 9
REVIEW QUESTIONS AND PROBLEMS

1. *A* constructed a building for *B* and presented a final bill in the amount of $500. *B* questioned the amount and sent a check for $200 marked "paid in full." *A* crossed out the words "paid in full" and cashed the check. Thereafter he sent a bill for $300. Is *B* required to pay?
2. *A* pledged $1,000 to a charitable organization whose purpose was to

help needy people. The charity borrowed money on the strength of this and other pledges. *A* died and the charity presented a claim against his estate. Should the claim be allowed?

3. *A*, a real estate broker, was engaged to sell property for *B*. *C* made an offer for the property and signed an agreement that he would not withdraw the offer during a specified period. However, he did withdraw the offer, and *A* brought an action against him. Should *A* collect from *C*?

4. *A* owned a mine in Alaska. He told *B* that if he would give him $50 so that he could go to Alaska he would pay him $10,000 if the mine produced gold. The mine produced a half million dollars in gold. Is *B* entitled to $10,000?

5. *A* paid 25 cents in return for an option to purchase real estate from *B* for $100,000. *B* sought to revoke the option. Can *B* revoke the option?

6. *A* lost a valuable bracelet and advertised, offering a liberal reward. *B* had found the bracelet and was holding it until the owner could be located. He read the advertisement and claimed the reward. Is he entitled to it?

7. *A* is a designer of women's clothing and apparel. She also places her indorsement on such articles made by others and receives substantial remuneration for doing so. *A* entered into a contract with *B* who was given the exclusive right to handle all of her products and indorsements in return for which he would pay her one-half of all profits and revenues. *A* thereafter entered into transactions on her own and *B* sued her for damages. *A* contended that there was not a binding contract, since *B* was not obligated under the terms of the contract to assert efforts to sell her products or indorsements. Is *A*'s contention correct?

8. *A*, a plumbing contractor, entered into a contract with *B*, a builder, to furnish plumbing installations for nineteen houses. Payment was to be made in stages as the work progressed. The progress payments were not made, and *A* halted work. *C*, a title company, promised that *A* would be paid in full if he would complete the job. Is *C*'s promise enforceable?

9. *A* had a written contract to manage *P*'s hotel for two years at $18,000 a year. At the end of three months *A* received a better offer, whereupon *P* in writing agreed to pay *A* an additional $5,000 if *A* remained the full two-year period. At the end of two years, is *P* liable for the $5,000 if *A* remained and did an excellent job during the period?

10. *X* purchased a used automobile from *Y* on credit, the original debt being $1,000. *X* discovered that the car had a cracked valve and demanded that *Y* correct it. When *Y* refused to do so, *X* sent *Y* a check for $750 marked paid in full of account. Should *Y* cash the check?

Capacity of Parties

2-39. In General.   Many legal problems and social problems related thereto arise from the legal disability to contract of such parties as minors and insane persons. A person so intoxicated as to lack understanding that he is entering into a contract is also said to lack the legal capacity to contract. Rules for lack of capacity to contract arose early in the law, and originally, in addition to those parties previously noted, affected married women too. Married women were only relieved of their burden of contractual incapacity by statute during the present century. At present the law still reflects attitudes of the past with regard to the treatment of contractual obligations and rights of infants, although there is some evidence of recognition of a need for change here also.

Most of this chapter deals with minors, whom the law frequently refers to as *infants.* Tort as well as contractual issues will be discussed. In most states an infant, or minor reaches majority (not to be confused with maturity) at the age of twenty-one. But a great variety of statutory provisions exist among the states; therefore, the statutes and cases of each state must be examined to determine the status of a minor in any given jurisdiction. In some states, for example, a female person attains her majority at the age of eighteen.

There are numerous statutes prescribing a minimum age for various purposes. The minimum age for contracting may be substantially different than the minimum age for (1) holding public office, (2) voting, (3) purchasing alcoholic beverages, (4) making a will, (5) imposing tort liability, (6) imposing criminal liability, and (7) serving in the armed forces. Serious social implications result from this variety of statute-imposed age minimums. For example, should not a person who is old enough to defend his country, be old enough to vote? Why should a sixteen-year-old have tort and criminal liability but not contractual liability? These and other questions are gradually causing our legislative bodies to reconsider our laws respecting age, and the minimums are being lowered in many areas. One notable exception is that in some states the minimum age for purchasing alcoholic beverages, has been raised recently from eighteen to twenty-one.

2-40. Minor's Contracts—General Principles. Contracts of minors fall within the classification of voidable contracts. (The general topic of voidable contracts is the subject of the next chapter.) A *voidable contract* is one that may be disaffirmed, or avoided, by use of the equitable remedy of rescission, which is designed to restore the parties to their original position.

As a matter of public policy for the protection of those who lack capacity to contract, such persons are allowed to avoid their contractual obligation. But this power to disaffirm a contract is a mixed blessing. It is offset by the fact that adults often refuse to sell goods to minors or otherwise deal with them.

In the right of minors to disaffirm contracts there are economic and social implications. For example, is the purchasing power of minors so significant that business can afford to take the risk of occasional rescissions by them? Is the legal protection of disaffirmance really necessary? Is this legal protection actually present in contracts involving relatively small amounts of money? A partial answer to these questions may be found in the growing popularity of young adult charge accounts.

The courts do not agree as to the extent of the protection afforded a minor, but all concur in his right to disaffirm or avoid a contract. All recognize that the law grants minors this power in order to promote justice and to protect minors from their presumed immaturity, lack of judgment and experience, limited will power, and imprudence.[1] An adult deals with a minor at his own peril because, although there are a few statutory exceptions, the right of a minor to disaffirm a contract is practically absolute. An important point should be recognized at the outset: A contract between an infant and an adult is voidable only by the infant; the adult finds his obligation enforceable unless the infant desires to disaffirm.

The right to disaffirm exists irrespective of the fairness or favorability of the contract and whether or not the adult knew he was dealing with a minor. It even extends to contracts involving two minors.[2] It should be noted, however, that legislation in many states has in a limited way altered the right of minors to avoid their contracts. For example, many states provide that a contract with a college or university is binding. Some statutes take away the minor's right to avoid after he marries, and a few give the courts the right to approve freedom of contract upon a minor's showing of maturity. These and other exceptions to the general rule are found in some states, but in most the rule allows the minor the right to avoid any contract made during his minority.

A minor's participation in certain business transactions creates difficult questions of conflicting policy. For example, an eighteen-year-old minor appoints his father to serve as his agent. Should the minor be allowed to disaffirm contracts entered into in his name by his father as his agent? The traditional view has been that the appointment of an agent by an infant is absolutely void and that contracts entered into by such an agent do not bind the infant in any way. But the tendency of the courts at present seems to be to place contracts of this nature in the same category as any other contract of the minor, thus

[1] Harvey v. Hadfield, page 204
[2] Hurwitz v. Barr, page 205

requiring that in order to escape liability, he disaffirm contracts made on his behalf by his agent.

Another difficult problem arises when an infant joins a partnership. The current view is that, regardless of the terms of the agreement, he may withdraw from the partnership at any time and avoid liability in damages to his partners resulting from his untimely withdrawal. The capital which he has invested in the firm is nevertheless subject to firm debts. To the extent of the capital he has invested, he cannot avoid payment of firm creditors on the ground of infancy.

2-41. Requirements and Right to Disaffirm.   As long as an infant does not disaffirm his contract, he is bound by its terms. He cannot refuse to carry out his part of the bargain and at the same time require the adult party to perform. If he decides to disaffirm, he must satisfy certain conditions in order to accomplish this. There have been many conflicting court decisions as to what an infant must do as a condition of obtaining a return of any consideration with which he has parted.

It is clear that an infant can disaffirm any purely executory contract, and he may do so either by directly informing the adult party or by doing any act that clearly indicates an intent to disaffirm. Of course, such disaffirmance relieves the adult party from his duty to perform. The adult party, however, cannot unilaterally disaffirm; he may be required by the infant to perform unless and until the latter disaffirms.

If the contract has been fully or partially executed, the infant has the right to avoid it and obtain a return of his consideration. If the infant is in possession of a consideration that has passed to him, he must return it to the other party. He cannot disaffirm the contract and at the same time retain the benefits. If the minor has the consideration received by him but now in a different form —for example, if he has traded it for something else—he is bound to return whatever consideration he has, as a prerequisite to disaffirmance. A minor's right to disaffirm is based upon equitable principles—if he seeks equity, he must "do equity." Likewise, any burdens imposed by the contract upon the infant must be met by him until such time as he may decide to disaffirm. Actually, the overwhelming majority of minors live up to their contracts; comparatively few ever seek to assert their infancy as a means of avoiding a contract.

The courts of the various states are somewhat in conflict as to the judicial treatment of those situations in which an infant has spent or squandered money he received under a contract or in which he either cannot return property he purchased or has damaged such property or allowed it to deteriorate. The majority of the states hold that the infant may disaffirm the contract and demand the return of the consideration with which he has parted, even though he is unable to return that which he received. Hence, in many states, an infant may purchase an automobile, and after driving it for a year or two, rescind his contract and demand the full amount which he paid for it, or after having an accident that demolishes the car, he may follow the same procedure. A few of the courts, however, hold that if the contract is advantageous to the infant and if the adult has been fair in every respect, the contract cannot be disaffirmed unless the infant returns the consideration he received. These courts also take into account the depreciation of the property while in the possession of the infant.[3]

An infant may have the appearance of an adult; he may be conducting a business in the role of an adult; or he may otherwise seem to be of age. Under these circumstances, an adult who contracts with the infant may be completely misled by appearances. However, the law is well established that this does not affect the minor's privileges either at law or in equity. In some states, however, by statute, if a minor engages in business as an adult, he cannot disaffirm if the other party reasonably believes him to be capable of contracting.

A similar situation is that in which a minor is guilty of actual misrepresentation of his age. The majority view is that if an action is brought against the minor, he may even in this circumstance assert his privilege as an infant with all the ordinary consequences of this status. This, too, has been changed in some states by statute. However, if the infant seeks to rescind the contract, it is generally held that he cannot avoid a transaction in which he has made such misrepresentation, *unless* he can restore any consideration which he has received. However, a substantial number of states allow rescission without restoration of the consideration when it is impossible to restore it. Another feature of the misrepresentation situation is that the adult party may acquire the right to disaffirm the contract; a contract induced by fraud is always voidable. Does this mean that an infant is liable for the tort of fraud and deceit? Some courts say that he is not, while a number of others say that he is. As will be noted later in this chapter, as a general rule, an infant is liable for all torts or civil wrongs committed by him. Should this rule be altered when the injurious consequences of his tort affect contractual rights? In answering this question some courts say that the primary objective is to protect minors and that to hold them liable in tort would have the indirect affect of imposing contractual liability upon them.[4] Other courts in imposing tort liability say that holding him liable in tort does not have this effect.[5]

These states regard the common law as "a growing institution, keeping pace with social and economic conditions," and believe that the purpose of the rule relating to contracts of minors "is to shield minors against their own folly and inexperience, and against unscrupulous persons." The rule, however, is not designed to give "old" minors "a sword with which to wreak injury upon unsuspecting adults." The necessity to protect "adults against depredations by minors who knowingly employ fraudulent methods, outweighs the interest of such minors," and, therefore, adults should have available for their protection the remedies not based on contract.

Of course, a minor may make a variety of other false statements in connection with business transactions. For example, he may falsely assert that he has title to an article he is selling. He may make warranties about the quality of the article that he knows are not in keeping with its true condition. Warranties of title and quality are contractual in nature, but they also have a tort "flavor" because of the misrepresentation element. With regard to the liability of an infant who knowingly misrepresents facts, there is division among the courts. One line of decisions holds that the tort element is paramount even in an action

[3] Haydocy Pontiac Inc. v. Lee, page 206
[4] Lesnick et al v. Pratt, page 207
[5] Byers v. Lemay Bank & Trust Co., page 208

for breach of a contractual warranty and that the defense of infancy will not avail. Another holds that an infant warrantor cannot be held liable under any circumstances. Some courts draw a distinction between cases in which the misrepresentation by the minor relates to his age and those in which it relates to warranty.

2-42. Actions by and Against Infants.   Although an infant has rights under contract law and may in some situations be held accountable under such law, he cannot personally bring an action in court. Any action on his behalf must be brought by a "next friend." The concept of next friend is derived from early English law; it allows such person to sue for the infant if his guardian is unwilling to bring such action or is in some way disqualified from doing so.

If an infant is sued, his guardian is under duty to appear and defend the action, if he has no guardian the court will appoint one. A guardian appointed by the court to act for and on the behalf of the infant for the purposes of a particular suit or action is called a "guardian *ad litem*." This requirement that a suit or action must be brought by or defended by a guardian is in keeping with the philosophy of the law which is predicated upon a minor's inability to "hold his own" in cases where his adversaries are adults.

2-43. Third-Party Rights.   If an infant sells goods to an adult, the latter obtains only a voidable title to the goods: The infant can disaffirm and recover possession from the adult buyer. At common law, even a good faith purchaser of property *formerly* belonging to an infant cannot retain the property if the infant elects to rescind. This rule has been changed under the Uniform Commercial Code, which provides that a person with voidable title has "power to transfer a good title to a good faith purchaser for value." (U.C.C. 2-403) The common-law rule, however, is still applicable to sales of real property by an infant. For example, if a minor sells his farm to *Y,* who in turn sells it to *Z,* the minor may disaffirm against *Z* and obtain his farm back. This is not unfair, since the minor's name appeared in the chain of title.

2-44. Time of Disaffirmance.   The general rule is that a minor may avoid both executed and executory contracts at any time during his infancy and for a reasonable period of time after he attains his majority. The rationale of the privilege to disaffirm *after* reaching twenty-one is that the former infant should have a reasonable time in which to evaluate and reflect upon the purchase, sale, or other transaction made during his minority to determine whether or not it was a prudent act.

If a contract entered into by an infant is still executory when he reaches twenty-one, then he can either (1) notify the adult of his disaffirmance, (2) refuse to perform it, or (3) plead his prior status as an infant if he is sued for breach of contract. The same result would obtain, of course, if the infant wished to disaffirm while still a minor.

As to executed contracts, an infant may avoid any relating to *personal property* before he is of age; but a deed to *real property* cannot be disaffirmed during his minority. The infant can however, enter on the land and take the profits until he reaches majority, at which time he has the legal capacity to affirm or disaffirm the deed. Conceivably, the infant who had entered into possession could still affirm the deed after he becomes twenty-one. This is but one of many legal principles in which different rules are applied to real property and to personal property. It should again be noted that the Uniform Commercial Code applies only to personal property.

The lack of uniformity in the law relating to infants is especially noticeable with respect to the time within which a person may disaffirm a contract after reaching his majority. Most states adhere to one of the following:

1. The infant must disaffirm contracts for sales of goods and conveyances of land within a reasonable time after he reaches his majority.

2. A conveyance of land by an infant may be disaffirmed by an infant within any period short of the statute of limitations—as long as ten years in many states.

3. By statute some states provide that an infant is bound on *all* his contracts unless he disaffirms them within a reasonable time after he attains his majority.

This leaves open the perplexing question of what is a "reasonable time." There is no rule of thumb or guideline other than the usual one that "what constitutes a reasonable time depends on the nature of the property involved and the surrounding circumstances." Obviously, a judge or jury has wide latitude in making this determination.

2-45. Ratification.   "Ratification" is a word which has wide application to many fields of law. It is a variation of the verb "ratify," which means to approve and sanction, to make valid, to confirm, to give sanction to. It applies to the approval of a voidable transaction by one who previously had the right to relieve himself from its obligations. Basically, as applied to contracts entered into by infants, it means the conduct of a person, after he becomes twenty-one, which indicates his approval of or satisfaction with a contract which he entered into as an infant. If ratification has taken place, the right to disaffirm no longer exists.

A few states provide by statute that no action shall be maintained on any contract made by an infant, unless he has ratified it in writing after he attained his majority. In general, an executed contract is ratified by a person who entered into it as a minor when he retains the consideration received for an unreasonable time after he reaches majority.[6] Ratification also results from acceptance of the benefits incidental to ownership, such as rents, dividends, or interest; a sale of the property received; or after he becomes of age, from any other act which clearly indicates his satisfaction with the bargain made during his minority. In general, a contract that is wholly executory is disaffirmed by continued silence or inaction after majority is reached. Some of the states hold that ratification is not effective unless the minor knows of his right to disaffirm at the time of the alleged act of ratification, but inaction for an unreasonable length of time will constitute a ratification of an executed contract, irrespective of knowledge of the right to disaffirm. In no state is ratification possible until the minor reaches his majority, since action prior to that date could always be avoided.

2-46. Liability for Necessaries.   The ability of an infant to find adults who

[6] Camp v. Bank of Bentonville, page 209

are willing to contract with him—to sell goods to him, etc.—is obviously impaired because of the legal right of the infant to avoid his transactions. People are justifiably disinclined to contract with minors, and it is not always convenient or possible to find an adult willing to assume responsibility for the infant's contracts. If the infant could be held liable for goods or services furnished to him and if he could not assert his lack of capacity as a basis for avoiding his obligations, this reluctance would largely disappear.

For these and other reasons the law has developed the concept that certain transactions are clearly for the benefit of an infant and hence are binding upon him. *Necessaries* furnished to an infant fall within this rule. The infant is not liable in *contract* for necessaries, but he is liable in *quasi contract.* The fact that his liability is quasi-contractual has two significant features: (1) he is not liable for the contract price of necessaries furnished to him, but rather for the reasonable value of the necessaries, and (2) he is not liable on executory contracts but only for necessaries actually furnished to him.

What are necessaries? In general, the term includes whatever is needed for an infant's subsistence as measured by his age, state, condition in life, etc.[7] Food and lodging, medical services, education, and clothing are the general classifications of necessaries. While the courts sometimes use the words interchangeably, there is a distinction between "necessaries" and "necessities" to the extent that the latter implies a minimum required to survive.

In determining whether a given item is a necessary, one must consider the needs of the minor, and it is possible for a contract to involve an item ordinarily a basic need but which in a particular case may be more of a luxury. For example, if an infant already possesses four suits and his station in life does not demand more, or if he is adequately supplied with clothes by a parent or guardian, another suit cannot be considered a necessary, although, as a general rule, clothing falls within the list of necessaries.

As more and more infants are getting married, the scope of necessaries is gradually being broadened by the courts. Frequently they have held that an automobile was not a necessary, but there are situations in which a court might rule to the contrary—an automobile used by a minor to earn his living may be so held.

Modern legal concepts have, by decision and statute, broadened some areas of contractual liability for minors. For example, most states have statutes which provide that life insurance contracts entered into by infants and contracts with universities for room and board are binding obligations. However, the general rule still exists that minors are not liable for business contracts. Therefore, adults dealing with minors should do so only through a properly authorized guardian.

2-47. The Parent's Liability for Infant's Contract.   Many persons labor under a misapprehension concerning the parent's liability for the contracts of an infant. The parent is liable on a contract made by a minor only when the minor is acting as the duly authorized agent of the parent or when the parent becomes a party to the contract. It should also be noted that the parent has a duty to support his minor children, and having failed in this duty, he is responsible for any necessaries furnished the infant by third parties. For example, a parent is

---

[7] Gastonia Personnel Corp. v. Rogers, page 210

responsible for medical care given to a minor child. Also the parent is entitled to any compensation which an infant earns, unless the parent has in some manner surrendered this right. Payment to the infant does not discharge this duty owed to his parent, unless the parent has authorized the payment or has left the minor to support himself. (This is very important in the settlement of tort claims for loss of income during minority. Any release must come from the parent.) The "liberation" of a minor is known as emancipation, and the minor, having assumed the obligation to support himself, is entitled to the compensation earned by his services.

2-48. Infant's Torts. In general, an infant is liable for his own torts. Several factors are taken into account in determining an infant's tort liability—his age, the nature of the tort involved, and whether the tort is intentional. At common law and in many states, a child under the age of seven is conclusively presumed to be incapable of negligence, and from ages seven to ten, a child is presumed to be incapable, but the presumption may be rebutted. If the child is older than ten, he is treated as any other person in so far as his torts are concerned. Some states use the age fourteen instead of ten for these rules. In some situations, as when driving a motor vehicle or engaging in an adult activity such as a game of golf, an infant has been held to the same standard of care as an adult is.

Another area of substantial misunderstanding of the law is concerned with the parent's liability for the torts of his children. As a general rule, a parent is not responsible for such torts.[8] He is liable if the child is acting as an agent of the parent or if the parent is himself at fault. For example, the parent is responsible for his child's torts if they are committed at his direction or in his presence when the child should have been controlled. In addition, some states have adopted the "family-purpose" doctrine, which provides that when an automobile is maintained by a parent for the pleasure and convenience of his family, a member of the family including an infant who uses it for his own pleasure or convenience is considered the owner's agent, and the owner is responsible for his negligence.

2-49. Other Persons Lacking Capacity. According to the view of most courts, contracts made by insane persons, are voidable much the same as those of infants. There is a tendency to go a step further and hold that, provided the contract is reasonable and no advantage has been taken of the disabled party's condition, an insane person cannot disaffirm unless he can return the consideration received. Appointment of a conservator for an insane person vests the conservator with full control over the property of his charge. For this reason, any contracts made by a lunatic after such an appointment are absolutely void and not merely voidable.

If a person becomes so intoxicated as to be incapable of understanding the effects of his action, he is thereby incapacitated, and his contracts are voidable. They differ from those of the infant and the insane person in that these contracts cannot be disaffirmed against a third party who has subsequently in good faith purchased the property which was sold by such an intoxicated person. Drunkards, like infants, are liable in quasi contract for necessaries.

[8] Stephans v. Stewart, page 211

CAPACITY OF PARTIES CASES

Harvey v. Hadfield

372 P.2d 985 (Utah) 1962

CROCKETT, J. Plaintiff, a minor, sues by his guardian *ad litem* to recover $1,000 he had advanced defendant under a proposed contract to buy a house-trailer. From adverse judgment he appeals.

Plaintiff, a student attending college at Logan, turned 19 years of age on the 13th day of October, 1959. A few days after his birthday he quit school and got a job. In the latter part of October he went to the defendant's lot and selected a trailer he liked. He told the defendant of the above facts, of his plans to be married, and of his desire to buy the trailer. The defendant advised him that he would have to get his father's signature to get financing through the defendant.

Plaintiff responded that he thought he could arrange financing and that he could raise a thousand dollars as a down payment. He paid $500 on November 6 and another $500 on November 13 and applied for financing at the bank. The bank finally refused to accept his application for a loan because of his minority and because his father would not sign with him.

After plaintiff's plans failed to materialize, he asked the defendant to return his money. Defendant refused but finally did agree to a statement which the plaintiff typed up and which both signed. It released the trailer in question for sale and granted plaintiff $1,000 (plus interest) credit on a trailer of his choice the next spring. About February 1, 1960, plaintiff's attorney sent a letter to the defendant disaffirming the contract and demanding the return of his money. Upon refusal, this suit was commenced.

Since time immemorial courts have quite generally recognized the justice and propriety of refusing to enforce contracts against minors, except for necessities. It is fair to assume that because of their immaturity they may lack the judgment, experience, and will power which they should have to bind themselves to what may turn out to be burdensome and long-lasting obligations. Consequently, courts are properly solicitous of their rights and afford them protection from being taken advantage of by designing persons, and from their own imprudent acts, by allowing them to disaffirm contracts entered into during minority which upon more mature reflection they conclude are undesirable. We agree that justice requires that minors have such protection. It is the responsibility of our courts to so safeguard their rights until they have attained their majority and thus presumably have the maturity of judgment necessary to deal with opposing parties on equal terms so that it is fair and equitable to bind them by their acts. Accordingly, adults dealing with minors must be deemed to do so in an awareness of the privilege the law affords the minor of disaffirming his contracts. The rule relating to disaffirmance is codified in our law, Sec. 15-2-2, U.C.A.1953:

> A minor is bound not only for reasonable value of necessaries but also by his contracts, unless he disaffirms them before or within a reasonable time after he attains his majority and restores to the other party all money or property received by him by virtue of said contracts and remaining within his control at any time after attaining his majority.

Defendant advances the following propositions which he claims exclude this case from the general rule allowing a minor to disaffirm:

... That even if the contract be disaffirmed, he is entitled to an offset of the actual damages he has sustained from loss of sale of the trailer from the $1,000.

... Defendant urges that from the fact that the plaintiff was "on his own," living away from home, working, and contemplating marriage, he could reasonably regard him as "engaged in business as an adult" and that he was therefore capable of entering into a binding contract. The defendant's position is not sound. ...

Our statute cannot be construed to support the defendant's contention that the disaffirming minor must compensate him for damages he may have incurred. Sec. 15-2-2, U.C.A.1953, hereinabove quoted, requires only that the minor restore "to the other party all money or property received by him by virtue of said contracts and remaining within his control at any time after attaining his majority." The trailer was left in the possession of the defendant. That fulfills the requirement of the statute.

The plaintiff minor having disaffirmed the contract is entitled to the return of his money. *The judgment is reversed. Costs to Plaintiff (appellant).*

Hurwitz v. Barr
193 A.2d 360 (D.C.) 1963

QUINN, J. Appellee, an infant, purchased a motor scooter for $240 from appellant, also an infant. Approximately one week later, appellee sought to rescind the contract on the ground that the motor scooter was defective. Appellee tendered back to appellant the scooter, but appellant refused to return the purchase price. Thereafter suit was brought and judgment entered for appellee ordering the return of the purchase price upon tender to appellant of the scooter. This appeal followed.

The question presented is whether the general rule that the contracts of an infant are voidable at his option applies to an executed contract between two infants. Appellant contends the rule is inapplicable. We disagree.

The law renders an infant's contracts unenforceable to protect infants from improvident bargains and injustice. It seeks to restore the infant to his position prior to contracting. We feel these rules are equally applicable when both parties to the contract are infants. To hold otherwise would convert the privilege of infancy, which the law intends as a shield to protect the infant, into a sword to be used to the possible injury of others. Indeed, appellant is apparently trying to use the privilege of infancy to enforce the contract because it is appellee who made the improvident bargain. While appellant as an infant has the option of affirming the contract, this option cannot nullify any rights or privileges which appellee, also an infant, is capable of asserting. Hence appellant cannot destroy appellee's right to rescind, and the contract was therefore voidable by appellee.

Appellant also contends that there is no evidence that he is still in possession of the consideration and is capable of restoring it to appellee. He cites two cases in which the courts refused to rescind a contract between two infants because the defendant had spent the money before the plaintiff sought to avoid the contract.

[W]here in an executed contract the consideration can be restored, in whole or in part, equity will treat the infant as a trustee for the other party and require restoration, on the ground that the infant is in possession of property which, in good conscience, he will not be permitted to retain when he has elected to disaffirm. The record before us is devoid of any indication that appellant cannot return the purchase price upon tender by appellee of the scooter. The judgment is therefore *affirmed.*

Haydocy Pontiac Inc. v. Lee

250 N.E.2d 898 (Ohio) 1969

Plaintiff sold a car to the defendant, a minor who represented that she was 21 years of age. She gave a note for the balance of the purchase price. The defendant gave possession of the car to another person, and neither plaintiff nor defendant has been able to regain possession. Plaintiff brought action to recover on the note. The trial court gave judgment for the defendant, and the plaintiff appealed.

STRAUSBAUGH, J. . . . At a time when we see young persons between 18 and 21 years of age demanding and assuming more responsibilities in their daily lives; when we see such persons emancipated, married, and raising families; when we see such persons charged with the responsibility for committing crimes; when we see such persons being sued in tort claims for acts of negligence; when we see such persons subject to military service; when we see such persons engaged in business and acting in almost all other respects as an adult, it seems timely to re-examine the case law pertaining to contractual rights and responsibilities of infants to see if the law as pronounced and applied by the courts should be redefined.

To allow infants to avoid a transaction without being required to restore the consideration received where the infant has used or otherwise disposed of it causes hardship on the other party. We hold that where the consideration received by the infant cannot be returned upon disaffirmance of the contract because it has been disposed of, the infant must account for the value of it, not in excess of the purchase price, where the other party is free from any fraud or bad faith and where the contract has been induced by a false representation of the age of the infant. Under this factual situation the infant is estopped from pleading infancy as a defense where the contract has been induced by a false representation that the infant was of age.

The necessity of returning the consideration as a prerequisite to obtaining equitable relief is still clearer where the infant misrepresents age and perpetrated an actual fraud on the other party. The disaffirmance of an infant's contract is to be determined by equitable principles, whether sought in a proceeding in equity or a case at law.

The common law has bestowed upon the infant the privilege of disaffirming his contracts in conservation of his rights and interests. Where the infant, 20 years of age, through falsehood and deceit, enters into a contract with another who enters therein in honesty and good faith and, thereafter, the infant seeks to disaffirm the contract without tendering back the consideration, no right or interest of the infant exists which needs protection. The privilege given the infant thereupon becomes a weapon of injustice.

The judgment is reversed and the cause is remanded in accordance with this opinion.

Judgment reversed.

Lesnick et al. v. Pratt

78 A.2d 487 (Vt.) 1951

CLEARY, J. . . . This is an action of tort for fraud and deceit involving the sale of an automobile to the plaintiff by the defendant (Pratt). The defendant pleaded infancy. Trial was by the court with judgment for the plaintiffs. Both parties excepted.

The findings of fact show that at the time of the sale on January 20, 1949, the defendant falsely and fraudulently represented that the automobile was fully paid for and was free of liens and encumbrances and on September 13, 1949, the plaintiffs were obliged to pay the balance owing on a conditional sale contract which the defendant had signed when he purchased the automobile on January 10, 1949. The defendant was born on July 29, 1928, so when he bought the automobile and when he sold it to the plaintiffs he was a minor.

Thus it is clear that the cause of action arises out of a contract and, as this court said in *West* v. *Moore* (14 Vt. 447, 450): "It is for us to declare the law as we find it." In that case, which was trespass on the case for false warranty in the sale of a horse, this Court held: "Though an infant is liable for positive wrongs, and constructive torts, or frauds, yet, to charge him, the fraudulent act must be wholly tortious. If the matter arises from contract, though the transaction is infected with fraud, it cannot be turned into a tort to charge the infant by a change in the form of action."

In *Gilson* v. *Spear* (38 Vt. 311), another case for deceit, or fraudulent concealment of unsoundness in the sale of a horse, and a plea of infancy, where both the English and American cases on the subject are collected and discussed, this Court held 38 Vt. at page 315: "We think that the fair result of the American as well as of the English cases is that an infant is liable in an action *ex delicto* for an actual and wilful fraud only in cases in which the form of action does not suppose that a contract has existed; but that where the gravamen of the fraud consists in a transaction which really originated in contract the plea of infancy is a good defense. For simple deceit on a contract of sale or exchange, there is no cause of action unless some damage or injury results from it, and proof of damage could not be made without referring to and proving the contract. An action on the case for deceit on a sale is an affirmance by the plaintiff of the contract of sale, and the liability of the defendant in such an action could not be established without taking notice of and proving the contract." That case then repeats and adopts the principle as stated in *West* v. *Moore, supra.* . . .

We are governed by the law we have quoted. If modern youth has become so sophisticated that he no longer needs protection from his contracts or public opinion demands that the long recognized rule be changed, it can be done by statute. We are constrained to hold that the plea of infancy in the present case was a full defense. Therefore, it is unnecessary to consider other questions raised by the exceptions.

Judgment reversed and judgment for the defendant to recover his costs.

Byers v. Lemay Bank & Trust Company

282 S.W.2d 512 (Mo.) 1955

Plaintiff, a minor, borrowed from defendant bank and gave the bank his notes in the amount of the loans. He represented that he was 23 years of age. The notes were not paid, and the bank applied money from the plaintiff's account in the bank in partial satisfaction of the debt. The plaintiff brought action to recover the amount which had been applied against the indebtedness, alleging that he desired to invoke his rights and immunities as a minor. In its answer the bank charged that plaintiff fraudulently represented that he was 23 years of age and that the bank was deceived and entrapped thereby. The bank filed a counterclaim for the amount of the unpaid notes. The lower court ruled against the plaintiff on his claim to recover the amount applied by the bank and in favor of the bank on its counterclaim. The minor appealed.

BOHLING, J. . . . Protecting those lacking in experience and of immature mind from designing adults developed in the common law of feudal England. The purpose is to shield minors against their own folly and inexperience and against unscrupulous persons, but not to give minors a sword with which to wreak injury upon unsuspecting adults. With the advancement of civilization, the spread of education, and modern industrial conditions minors attain a high state of sophistication. Many earn their own livelihood and are more wordly-wise than their parents. Plaintiff's father testified plaintiff never came to him for fatherly advice. The common law is said to be a growing institution, keeping pace with social and economic conditions. The protection of adults against depredations by minors knowingly employing fraudulent methods outweighs the interests of such minors, and adults should have available the remedies not founded on contract for their protection. Every case involving a contract to which a minor is a party should not necessarily be forced into the Procrustean bed of the rule that allows a minor to escape responsibility for his other acts upon exercising the privilege of rescinding his contract at his will. Plaintiff was not a toddler, or a teen-ager, but an "old" infant, cunning enough to conceive and perpetrate a fraud upon experienced adults.

Different results have been reached in different jurisdictions and in some instances within the same jurisdiction on the responsibility of a minor who, as an inducement for an adult to contract with him, misrepresents that he is of age and deceived the adult by his false statement to the adult's resulting injury. Some jurisdictions tend to uncompromisingly permit minors to rescind their contracts. A number of jurisdictions hold that the minor is not estopped by misrepresentations as to his age in actions at law and a lesser number where the suit is in equity; but other jurisdictions hold estoppel is available in an action at law and a greater number apply estoppel where the suit is in equity. An apparently increasing number of jurisdictions hold the infant liable in tort for inducing the contract by misrepresentations that he is of age. . . .

... Liability *ex delicto* and liability *ex contractu* are based on different principles and involve different measures of recovery. If an infant is liable for his torts generally, the better reasoned decisions hold he is liable for his deceit in misrepresenting his age. His deceit induces the contract. It does not involve the subject matter of the contract. The recovery is the damage resulting to the defrauded person and not the contract consideration. He is not held liable on the contract in form or substance.

Plaintiff argues that he was only asked his age, and that since defendant did not ask him to show his service card, or ask him where he was born, or ask him for his birth certificate, defendant did not exercise reasonable diligence and may not successfully assert it was misled by plaintiff's statement. We do not agree. The misrepresentation is the vital fact. All the elements of a deceit are present. Plaintiff stated his age was 23. Plaintiff knew this was untrue. Plaintiff made the statement with the intent that defendant act upon it. Defendant acted upon the statement in the manner contemplated by plaintiff. Defendant suffered actual damage by reason of plaintiff's misrepresentation as to his age, and the damage was the natural and probable consequences of plaintiff's fraud.

The effect of plaintiff's claim is to rescind his contract and recover the money defendant applied to the discharge of his obligation. We hold the trial court correctly ruled against plaintiff's claim.

Defendant's counterclaims are suits on the two notes executed by plaintiff while a minor, and the judgment, which includes interest and attorney fees, is a judgment on said notes. Defendant's counterclaims are not in tort. Section 431.060, *supra,* provides that, in the circumstances here of record, "no action shall be maintained whereby to charge any person upon any debt contracted during infancy." . . .

. . . On its presentation, defendant is not entitled to hold the judgment on its counterclaims.

The judgment for defendant on plaintiff's claim is affirmed, but the judgment against plaintiff on defendant's counterclaims is reversed and the cause as to said counterclaims remanded for such action as defendant may properly take.

Camp v. Bank of Bentonville
323 S.W.2d 556 (Ark.) 1959

MC FADDIN, J. Jerry Lee Camp appeals from a decree of the Chancery Court which found that Camp, now of lawful age, had ratified a debt which he made while a minor. The question is whether Camp's acts under the circumstances here shown were sufficient to support the decree holding that there had been ratification.

On January 9, 1957, Camp executed his note to A. V. Bright, doing business as "Bright's Used Cars," for $3,000 [probably for the truck], payable $125 per month until paid in full. The note was secured by a chattel mortgage covering: (a) one 1952 2-ton Chevrolet truck; (b) one 1954 Plymouth sedan; (c) miscellaneous stock of automotive parts valued at $500; and (d) eleven cows and increase. Bright immediately and unconditionally transferred the note and mortgage to the appellee, Bank of Bentonville (hereinafter called "Bank"). The payments made to the Bank on the note were:

Date	Amount	Nature of Payment
2/25/57	$ 50.00	Cash.
3/20/57	100.00	Cash.
4/20/57	800.00	Proceeds of sale of Plymouth car.
5/ 1/57	47.52	Return of insurance premium cancelled when Plymouth car was sold.
7/ 1/57	51.00	Probably cash.
11/ 8/57	102.00	To be discussed later in this opinion.
12/ 9/57	100.00	To be discussed later in this opinion.
12/13/57	56.00	To be discussed later in this opinion.

When Camp defaulted, the Bank filed suit for judgment and foreclosure of the mortgage. Camp's defense was: that he was not 21 years of age until August 19, 1957; that the three payments credited on the note thereafter (i.e., November 8th, December 9th, and December 13th) were not sufficient to constitute ratification; and that he now disaffirmed the entire transaction. The said three payments came about in this manner: each was made to the Bank by A. V. Bright from money due by him to Camp, and each payment was made with Camp's implied consent. The $100 on December 9, 1957, was part of the proceeds of the sale of a car. The payments of November 8th and December 13th were for money that Bright owed Camp for work. Camp was doing considerable hauling of some kind for Bright, and Bright, with Camp's implied consent, made the two payments on the dates mentioned.

The Chancery Court held that Camp, after reaching full age, had ratified the note and mortgage; and under all the facts and circumstances here existing, we cannot say that the Chancery Court was in error. . . .

From our own cases, and from all of the foregoing (cases in other states), we are not willing to hold that payment after reaching full age is, in itself, sufficient to constitute ratification as a matter of law: rather, we think the better rule is, to examine each case on its own facts and determine whether payment, along with all the other facts and circumstances, constitutes ratification. We have done that in the case at bar. There is no claim of any kind that Bright ever imposed on Camp when the note and mortgage were executed on January 9, 1957. Camp was working for Bright all along; and thought he was of full age, as he considered eighteen to be the lawful age. It was not until after this suit was filed and he had consulted an attorney that he ever had any idea of disaffirmance of any part of the trade. This is the case of a man who was doing his own work, carrying on his own business, making trades in which there is no claim that he was imposed on, and who, after reaching twenty-one, continued to make payments on the obligation, with no thought of disaffirming the transaction. Under all these facts and circumstances, we reach the conclusion that Camp, after reaching full age, ratified the particular transaction here involved.

Affirmed.

Gastonia Personnel Corp. v. Rogers

168 S.E.2d 31 (N.C.) 1969

Plaintiff is a professional employment agency. The nineteen-year-old defendant went to the plaintiff to seek aid in finding work. He agreed to pay a fee if a job were found for him. Defendant obtained a job, and according to the agency's schedule, the fee was $295. Plaintiff brought suit for this amount. The trial court entered a judgment dismissing the plaintiff's action. Plaintiff appealed.

MORRIS, J. This appeal presents but one question. That is, whether the employment of the services of a professional employment agency may be considered a "necessary" expense so that an infant is obligated to pay for them?

The general rule is that a minor may disaffirm a contract made by him. The exception to this rule is that a minor is obligated to pay for necessaries.

What are necessaries?

> In *Freeman* v. *Bridger,* Pearson, J., speaking to the subject: "Lord Coke says, 'It is agreed by all the books, that an infant may bind himself to pay for his necessary meat, drink, apparel, physic and *other* necessaries.' These last words embrace boarding; for shelter is as necessary as food and clothing. They have also been extended so as to embrace schooling, and nursing (as well as physic) while sick. In regard to the quality of the clothes and the kind of food, etc., a restriction is added, that it must appear that the articles were suitable to the infant's degree and estate."

In North Carolina the question of whether a particular item or service is a necessity is a mixed question of law and fact. Whether the article or service is within one of the classes for which he is liable is a question of law. Whether the item or service was in fact necessary and of reasonable price is a question for the jury.

We do not think that the services of a professional employment agency may be considered "necessary" so that a minor may not disaffirm a contract for such services. It makes no difference that the defendant has profited by the efforts of the plaintiff. He is still free to disaffirm the contract. The plaintiff's services were advantageous to the defendant, and clearly he was in need of a job when they were rendered; however, it does not appear that they were necessary for him to earn a livelihood. The judgment below is *affirmed.*

Stephans v. Stewart

165 S.E.2d 572 (Ga.) 1968

This action was brought by the parents of a sixteen-year-old boy who was killed by a motorboat while swimming. The boat, operated by a thirteen-year-old girl, was owned by the girl's father, the defendant in the suit. The lower court entered judgment for the plaintiff, and the defendant appealed.

WHITMAN, J. At common law a parent incurred no liability for the tort of a child from the mere relation of parent and child. Liability could be based, however, on the ordinary principles of liability of a principal for the acts of his agent, or of a master for his servant. . . .

Thus: "A father is not liable for a tort of his minor child, with which he was in no way connected, which he did not ratify, and from which he did not derive any benefit."

Also, consistent with common law principles, a parent may be held liable for an injury caused directly by his minor child where the parent's own original negligence or contributing negligence has made the child's act possible. For example, an action will lie for negligently permitting a child to have access to a dangerous weapon.

Also, if a parent *knows* his child is irresponsible, incompetent, or unqualified regarding certain activities, *and knowingly permits* the child to engage in such activities, this may constitute such negligence on the part of the parent as will support a recovery. . . .

In such cases, predicated on the parent's negligence, the ordinary elements of all negligence cases must be shown, including, of course, the requirement that the parent should have foreseen or anticipated that some injury would likely result from the negligence.

There was an allegation in the complaint that the defendant's minor daughter was inexperienced and incompetent to have control of the boat. . . . However, this allegation was not supported by *any* competent evidence on the trial. There was general testimony that an older person "with the same experience" would have better judgment in boat operation. But the evidence was that the daughter had been trained and was competent in boat operation.

There was absolutely no evidence that would support a finding that the daughter was carrying out any of her defendant-father's business, or was acting at the time under his command, or that defendant received any benefit from her action, or that he ratified her action, which would support a recovery under the theory of *respondeat superior.*

But the case was submitted to the jury on the theory that any negligence found against the daughter was imputable by law to the defendant.

The question for determination is whether the minor child's negligence in these circumstances could be imputed to the father. [T]he negligence of the daughter could be imputed to the father if the daughter committed the tort at his command or while acting within the scope of her authority as his agent or servant. There is an analogous situation in which the requirement that agency be found is simplified or perhaps dispensed with, i.e., in cases where the head of a family who owns an automobile may be held liable for the negligent acts of family members in the use of the automobile. This is the "family-purpose" doctrine. "The doctrine as applied in Georgia is that where one furnishes an automobile to members of his family for pleasure or convenience, etc., he is liable for injuries inflicted by the machine while it is being negligently operated by a member of the family for a purpose for which it was furnished, on the theory that the furnishing and using of the car for such purposes is the business of the husband, and the one operating it is the agent or servant of the owner in the course of his business." The doctrine is an extension of the principles of agency and *respondeat superior* brought about by the problems which the automobile brought to society. No decision of the courts of this state has been brought to our attention wherein the family-purpose doctrine has been extended beyond its application to automobiles. In *Calhoun* v. *Pair,* the court declared that a father who furnishes a bicycle to his minor son (14 years old) for the purpose of going to and from school would not be liable for injuries to another caused by the son's negligence in the use of the bicycle. In *Felcyn* v. *Gamble,* the family-purpose doctrine was held to have no application to motorboats. The same result obtained in *Grindstaff* v. *Watts,* relating to a motorboat, and in *Meinhardt* v. *Vaughn,* relating to a motorcycle. We agree with the court's observation in *Grindstaff* v. *Watts, supra,* that any extension of the doctrine should be left to legislation. Indeed, such legislation was enacted by the last session of the Georgia Legislature and it provides:

The owner of a watercraft shall be liable for any tort caused by the operation of such watercraft in the same manner and to the same degree as is the owner of an automobile liable for torts caused by its operation. (Ga.L.1968,pp. 1416, 1417.)

This Act was approved April 12, 1968. However, this statute altered a substantive right between parties, is not retroactive, and can have no relation to the events in the present case which occurred on July 5, 1963.

There being no basis in the law or the evidence for the imposition of liability on the defendant for the negligence of his daughter in the operation of the motorboat, it was error to deny the defendant's motion for a directed verdict. It is not necessary to pass upon the additional enumerations of error.

Judgment reversed.

CHAPTER 10
REVIEW QUESTIONS AND PROBLEMS

1. *A,* a small child, climbed into *B*'s truck which was parked on a hill. He released the brake; the truck rolled down the hill and was damaged. *B* seeks to hold *A*'s parents liable for the damages. Should he succeed?
2. While *A* was a minor, he entered into an employment contract with *B* and agreed that he would not compete with *B* if he left his employment. *A* is now of legal age, and *B* is seeking an injunction to restrain him from competing. Should the injunction be granted?
3. *A,* a minor, was married and had one child. He entered into an install-ment contract to buy furniture from *B.* After making several payments, he defaulted and the furniture was repossessed. *A* seeks to recover the payments he had made. Should he succeed?
4. *A,* a minor, bought a car from *B* and paid for it in full. Shortly thereafter *A* demanded his money back and offered to return the car. *B* refused to return the money, and *A* filed suit to recover the purchase price. While awaiting trial of the case *A* turned twenty-one and continued in possession of the car. Is *A* entitled to recover his money?
5. *A,* a minor, wished to enter into a contract with *B. B* refused to contract with him unless he could obtain a responsible adult to also be a party to the contract. *C* assumed this responsibility. Thereafter *A* disaffirmed the contract. Can *B* hold *C* liable?
6. *A,* a minor, entered into a contract with a motion picture studio to serve as an actress. The contract was for seven years, and after *A* became twenty-one she attempted to disaffirm and work for another studio. Would there be any reason for refusing to allow disaffirmance?
7. *M,* a minor, purchased and paid $93 on a diamond engagement ring, *J* being the seller. The engagement was later terminated, but the girl refused to return the ring to *M. M,* nevertheless, seeks to avoid his contract with *J* and to recover the down payment. Is he entitled to do so?

8. A minor purchased a car by giving his age as twenty-three. After making one payment in addition to the down payment, he defaulted, and the seller repossessed. May the minor rescind and recover the payments made?

9. *M*, a minor, contracted to buy a truck from the *A* Company for his transfer business, paying for it in thirty-six installments. He became of age on March 1 and on March 2 paid his sixth installment. On March 10, *M* seeks to avoid the contract by offering to return the truck. May he do so?

10. Driving the family car to a high school social event, *X*, a minor, negligently injures *Y*. *Y* sues *X*'s parents for the tort. What result?

Reality of Assent

2-50. Introduction. The preceding chapter was concerned with the rights and liabilities of persons who lack capacity to contract, especially the right of minors to disaffirm or avoid contracts. There are several additional reasons or situations in which one party or the other may avoid or disaffirm a contract. In addition to lack of capacity, the other grounds for avoiding contracts are fraud, or misrepresentation, bilateral mistake, and lack of free will of one of the parties. These matters are discussed in this chapter.

FRAUD

2-51. Definition. The word "fraud" has a variety of meanings, including criminal acts. As used in the law of contracts, however, it means a mistake as to a material fact that has been wrongfully induced by the other party to a contract in order that it will be acted upon by the innocent party. In order to establish a fraudulent misrepresentation, the following elements must be proved and established to the satisfaction of the trier of fact:

1. The statement was made with the *intent* to deceive.
2. The misrepresentation was of a *material* existing fact.
3. The plaintiff was justified in relying on the statement.
4. The plaintiff was injured (in the legal sense) by the false statement.

Obviously, this is a formidable undertaking by a plaintiff who feels that he has been wronged. Each of the elements must be established by adequate proof, and the failure to prove any one of the requirements is fatal to recovery.[1]

The usual result of any misrepresentation of a material fact in a contractual

[1] Broberg v. Mann, page 222

setting is to cause the "representee" to take action he would not otherwise have taken. For this reason such person suffers the same loss whether the false statements were made innocently or in bad faith. Accordingly, the law affords the remedy of rescission for the victim of an innocent misrepresentation, although such misrepresentation is not fraudulent, but the remedy of a tort action of deceit is not afforded to the victim of innocent misrepresentation. It is, of course, easier to establish a basis for recovery predicated upon an innocent, though false, statement, since proof of intent to mislead is not required. The other requirements, however, are the same.

2-52. Intention to Mislead.   The intent to mislead—the factor which distinguishes an innocent misrepresentation from a fraudulent one—is often referred to by courts and writers as *scienter.*[2] This Latin word means "knowingly." *Scienter* has broad implications, which extend far beyond the confines of a false statement made with actual intent to deceive. For example, *scienter* is found when there has been a concealment of a material fact or a nondisclosure of such a fact. Moreover, a statement which is partially or even literally true may be fraudulent in law if it was made in order to create a substantially false impression. Intention to mislead may also be established by showing that a statement was made with such reckless disregard as to whether it is true or false that intention to mislead may be inferred.

2-53. Misstatement of Fact.   An actual or implied false representation of a *matter of fact* relating to the present or to the past and which is material to the transaction is the gist of fraud. False statements of opinion, of conditions to exist in the future, or of matters promissory in nature will not, even if the other elements are present, constitute fraud. Obviously every failure to perform a promise is not fraudulent, but failure to perform the promise justifies a suit for breach of contract. However, if the promisor never intended to carry out his promise at the time he made it, he misstated his intention and a fact (the party's actual intention) has been misstated.[3] This misstatement of fact must be material or significant to the extent that it has a moving influence upon the contracting party, but it need not be the sole inducing cause for entering into the contract.

False statements as to matters of opinion, such as a representation as to value of property, are not factual and are not considered actionable. Whether a particular statement is one of fact or opinion is a matter for the jury to resolve. However, if there is a confidential or fiduciary relationship between the parties, the ordinary doctrine of "puffing" does not apply and a statement of opinion may be the basis of fraud action. For example, if a partner sells property to the firm of which he is a member, a false statement of opinion by the selling partner as to the value of the property will supply the misstatement of fact element. Each partner is a fiduciary toward his fellow partners and the firm and must give honest opinions.

The misstatement may be oral and may in fact be true in part. A half-truth, or partial truth, which has the net effect of misleading may form the basis of fraud just as if it were entirely false. The untruth may be the result of a series

[2] Whipp v. Iverson, page 223
[3] Bresler Ice Cream Co. v. Millionaire's Club, Inc., page 224

of statements, the net result of which is to mislead. Although each statement taken alone may be true, there is fraud if all of them taken together tend to mislead the party to whom they are made. A partial truth in response to a request for information becomes an untruth whenever it creates a false impression and is designed to do so.

An intentional misrepresentation of existing local or state law affords no basis for rescission, since the law is presumably a matter of common knowledge, open and available to all who desire to explore its mysteries. A misstatement as to the law of another state or nation, however, is one of fact and may be used as a basis for redress.

As was previously noted, a misrepresentation may be made by conduct as well as by language. Any physical act which has for its ultimate object the concealment of the true facts relating to the property involved in a contract is, in effect, a misstatement. One who turns back the speedometer on a car, fills a motor with heavy grease to keep it from knocking, or paints over an apparent defect—in each case concealing an important fact—asserts an untruth as effectively as if he were speaking. Such conduct, if it misleads the other party, amounts to fraud and makes rescission or an action for damages possible.

2-54. Silence as Fraud.   In the absence of a fiduciary relationship—one of trust and confidence such as exists between principal and agent or guardian and ward—neither party to an agreement is under any duty to inform the other of special facts and circumstances that might vitally affect the value of the subject matter under consideration. In general, parties to a contract deal "at arm's length," and silence, of and by itself, does not constitute fraud. To this rule two exceptions exist: One is that it is the duty of the vendor of property who knows of a latent defect—one that is not apparent upon inspection—to inform the purchaser of the defect. Also, a person who has misstated an important fact on some previous occasion is obligated to correct the statement when negotiations are renewed or as soon as he learns about his misstatement.

The gist of these exceptions is that one of the parties has the erroneous impression that certain things are true, whereas the other party is aware that they are not true and also knows of the misunderstanding. It therefore becomes his duty to disclose the truth.[4] And unless he does so, most courts would hold that fraud exists. This does not mean that a potential seller or buyer has to disclose all the factors about the value of property he is selling or buying. It is only when he knows that the other party to the agreement is harboring a misunderstanding on some vital matter that the duty to speak arises.

2-55. Justifiable Reliance.   Before a false statement of fact can be considered fraudulent, the party to whom it has been made must reasonably believe it to be true, must act thereon to his damage, and in so acting must rely on the truth of the statement. If he investigates and the falsity is revealed, no action can be brought for fraud. The cases are somewhat in conflict as to the need to investigate. Some courts have indicated that if all the information is readily available for ascertaining the truth of statements, blind reliance upon the misrepresentation is not justified. In such a case, the party is said to be

---

[4] Andolsun v. Berlitz Schools of Languages of America, page 225

negligent in not taking advantage of the facilities available for confirming the statement.

Thus, if a party inspects property or has an opportunity to do so, he is not misled if a reasonable investigation would have revealed untruths with regard to its condition. On the other hand, some courts have stated that one who by misrepresentation has induced another to act to the other's prejudice cannot impute negligence to the other merely because of his reliance on the misrepresentation.[5] He cannot be heard to say, "You should not have believed me." Nor can he relieve himself of liability for misrepresentations in advance by a disclaimer. Courts generally agree that reliance is justified when substantial effort or expense is required to determine the true facts.

2-56. Injury or Damage.   In order to prevail, the party relying upon the misstatement must offer proof of resulting damage. Normally such damage is proved by evidence which indicates that the property which is the subject of the contract would have been more valuable provided the statements had been true. Injury results when the party is not in as good a position as he would have been had the statements been true. Where fraud is established, a party may rescind all related existing contracts with the other party, as fraud is said to vitiate all contracts between parties.

2-57. Remedies.   Fraud gives to the injured party a choice of two basic remedies—an action for damages or a suit for rescission. In addition, if the contract is executory, the injured party may plead fraud as a defense in the event that action to enforce is brought against him. If the contract has been executed, he may rescind and demand a return of the consideration furnished by him. In order to do this he must offer to restore the consideration he has received. In the alternative, he may bring action to recover the dollar damages he has suffered by reason of the fraud.

Rescission is permitted only in case the defrauded party acts with reasonable promptness after he learns of the falsity of the representation. Undue delay on his part effects a waiver of his right to rescind, thus limiting the defrauded party to an action for recovery of damages. A victim of fraud loses his right to rescind if, after having acquired knowledge of the fraud, he indicates an intention to affirm, or if he exercises dominion over property which he would have to surrender in order to rescind the contract.

It should be noted that the only remedy for unintentional misrepresentation is rescission. Since the gist of the action for damages is *scienter* and this element is not present in simple misrepresentation, the action at law for dollar damages is unavailable.

A third party, one not a party to the contract, may also be liable for fraudulent misrepresentations. If such a third party makes false statements which he could reasonably expect to be relied upon, he can be held liable to the contracting party who relies thereon to his detriment.

[5] Walsh v. Edwards, page 226

MISTAKE

2-58. In General.   The Restatement of Contracts provides: "In the Restatement of this subject, mistake means a state of mind that is not in accord with the facts." The focus is on the effect of a mistake as related to the contract and the negotiation of contracts. What is the effect of a mistake made by one or both of the parties? There are a variety of mistakes, and they may occur at various stages of a transaction; they may involve errors in arithmetic, in execution of the contract, and in setting forth the terms of the contract, either orally or in writing, to name but a few. The mistake may be bilateral; both parties are mistaken. Or it may be unilateral; only one party is laboring under mistake.

In order that a mistake by one or both of the parties may warrant relief to either of them, the mistake must be a material one. The relief afforded by virtue of the mistake will depend upon a number of factors, including the point of time at which the mistake is discovered; the extent to which performance has already progressed; the extent to which one or the other of the parties has changed his position in reliance upon the contract before the mistake was discovered; and the extent to which the parties can be restored to the *status quo ante.*

In contract law the basic remedy for mistake is rescission. The general rule is that one who has made a mistake and wishes to rescind can do so only if he can substantially return the other party to the *status quo.* No relief will be afforded if the other party has changed his position in reliance on the contract to the extent that he cannot be restored to his former position. For example, *S,* by mistake, enters into a surety agreement with *C* whereby he agrees to guarantee repayment of loans which *C* may make to *P* for up to $10,000. Assume that the mistake was an error in *P*'s financial statement. Obviously, the problem will be different if *C,* on the strength of *S*'s guarantee has already lent money to *P* before the mistake is discovered. Also, it will be different if only $5,000 rather than the full $10,000 has been lent before the mistake was discovered and called to the attention of *C.*

2-59. Bilateral Mistake.   The word "bilateral" as used in this context means two-sided. Both parties to the contract have made an assumption which is false. While relief is generally restricted to "mutual mistakes," it would be inaccurate to state that mutuality is an absolute requirement. It is often difficult to classify mistakes as either mutual mistakes or unilateral mistakes, although it is convenient to do so, and the courts sometimes seem to say arbitrarily that no relief can be afforded for the unilateral mistakes. The famous Peerless case discussed in Chapter 8 illustrates the problem. Each party correctly stated the vessel he meant; the mistake was not in the name of the vessel but that each thought the other meant the same vessel as he. There is no absolute rule of thumb which determines the remedy to be afforded when a mistake is discovered, nor to determine whether it is mutual or unilateral. However, the facts of most disputes indicate the nature of the mistake quite clearly, and as a broad principle, it can be stated that a unilateral mistake is at the expense of the party who makes it, while relief will be afforded if it is mutual. Exceptions to this are discussed in the next section.

A bilateral mistake exists when parties enter into a contract on a mistaken assumption regarding a material fact.[6]   This mutual assumption, called *mutual mistake of fact,* arises in two situations, in one the minds of the parties fail to meet so that no contract results. In the other situation the mistake merely makes the agreement more onerous for one of the contracting parties, and therefore renders it voidable at his option.

Typical of the first type are those cases in which, unknown to either party, the subject matter of the contract has been destroyed prior to the date of the agreement; and also cases in which the language used in the contract is clearly subject to two interpretations, and each party construes it differently. In either case, no contract results since there was no valid offer and acceptance or meeting of the minds. (See Chapter 8.) The second type is illustrated by the sale of floor covering for a certain room at a lump-sum figure on the assumption by both parties that only a certain number of square feet are involved. If the area is greater than both parties thought to be true, the contract is voidable at the instance of the party who would suffer a loss because of the mistake.

In the transaction of business, it is customary in many situations to dispose of property about which the contracting parties willingly admit that all of the facts are not known. In such instances, the property is sold without regard to its quality or characteristics. Such agreements may not be rescinded if it later appears that the property has characteristics which neither of the parties had reason to suspect, or if it otherwise differs from their expectations. Under such conditions, the property forms the subject matter of the agreement, regardless of its nature. Thus, *A* sells *B* a farm, and shortly thereafter a valuable deposit of ore is discovered on it. The agreement could not be rescinded by the seller on the ground of mutual mistake.

2-60. Unilateral Mistake.   As previously stated, a contract entered into because of some mistake or error on the part of only one of the contracting parties usually affords no basis for relief to such party. The majority of such mistakes result from carelessness or lack of diligence on the part of the mistaken party, and should not, therefore, affect the rights of the other party.

This rule is subject to one well-recognized exception. Where a mistake has been made in the calculation or transmission of the figures which form the basis of a contract, and prior to acceptance, such mistake is clearly apparent to the offeree who thereupon accepts the mistaken offer, the contract may be avoided by the offeror. Hence, a contractor who arrives at or transmits his estimates for a bid on construction work using the wrong figure may be relieved of his contract if the error was so great as to be obvious and therefore apparent to the offeree before the latter's acceptance.[7]   In such a case, the courts refuse to allow one party knowingly to take advantage of another's mistake.

2-61. Reformation of Written Contracts.   In most instances a written contract is preceded by negotiations between the parties who agree orally upon

[6] MacKay v. McIntosh, page 227
[7] Rushlight Auto Sprinkler Co. v. City of Portland, page 228

the clauses and terms to be set forth in the final written contract. This is certainly the case when the parties contemplate a written statement signed by both as necessary to the final consummation of the agreement, i.e., the oral agreement was not itself to have binding effect. Of course, the parties could intend otherwise. They could regard the oral agreement as binding without any writing, or they could regard the writing as simply a subsequent memorial of their oral agreement.

In any event, a question is presented: Can oral evidence be admitted in court to show that a written agreement does not comport with the terms orally agreed upon? Also, can a written agreement be modified by such oral evidence? These questions present a basic problem of the sanctity of a writing—a subject to be discussed in Chapter 13. It will be noted that parol (oral) evidence is admissible in some cases to show that a written contract is not an enforceable obligation. A special situation in which oral evidence is allowed to establish a mutual mistake is that in which an error has been made in reducing the oral agreement to a written contract. Frequently, the draftsman or typist may have made an error which was not discovered prior to the signing of the contract, and the party benefiting from the error seeks to hold the other party to the agreement as written. Courts of equity provide a remedy known as *reformation* for such situations.[8] Reformation is only available where there is clear and positive proof of the drafting error. Courts frequently justify this remedy on the basis that the contract is not being changed—that the written evidence is only being corrected. This problem can be prevented by a careful reading of contracts before execution. It should be noted that the court will not make a new agreement for the parties under the guise of reforming a contract.

LACK OF FREE WILL

2-62. Duress and Undue Influence.   Equity allows a party to rescind an agreement that was not entered into voluntarily. The lack of free will may take the form of duress or undue influence. A person who has obtained property under such circumstances should not in good conscience be allowed to keep it. A person may lose his free will because of duress—some threat to his person, his family or property—or it may result from a more subtle pressure whereby one person overpowers the will of another by use of moral, social, or domestic force as contrasted with physical or economic force. Cases of undue influence frequently arise in situations involving the elderly. In those cases where free will is lacking, some courts hold that the minds of the parties did not meet. At early common law, duress would not be present where a courageous man would have possessed a free will in spite of a threat, but modern courts do not require this standard of courage or firmness as a prerequisite for the equitable remedy. If the pressure applied in fact affected the individual involved to the extent that the contract was not voluntary, there is duress. If a person has a free choice, there is no duress, even though some pressure may have been exerted upon him.

Broberg v. Mann

213 N.E.2d 89 (Ill.) 1965

The plaintiff purchased a tract of land from the defendant in the belief that

---

[8] Nash v. Kornblum, page 230

it contained twenty-six acres. In fact it contained only eighteen. The complaint alleged that the defendant "well knew that the land described in the said deed of conveyance to the plaintiff and his wife was not in quantity the twenty-six acres of land as bargained for and paid for by plaintiff, and that the defendant by trick and device of substituting a new description by metes and bounds on the day that the deal was closed in the office of defendant's attorney and by fraudulently and falsely secreting and failing to inform the plaintiff or his attorney of the fact that the land described in the substituted description was not in fact and did not describe land in quantity of approximately twenty-six acres."

The defendant contended that the basis of the plaintiff's complaint was an action for fraud and deceit and that the elements necessary to establish fraud and deceit had not been proven. The trial court ruled for the plaintiff, and the defendant appealed.

DAVIS, J. . . . Comprehensively stated, a misrepresentation to be the basis of a charge of fraud, either in a suit at law or in equity, must contain the following elements:

(1)   It must be a statement of material fact, as opposed to opinion;
(2)   it must be untrue;
(3)   the party making the statement must know or believe it to be untrue;
(4)   the person to whom the statement is made must believe and rely on it, and have a right to do so;
(5)   it must have been made for the purpose of inducing the other party to act; and
(6)   the reliance by the person to whom the statement is made must lead to his injury.

It is essential to the establishment of fraud that the person charged must either have knowledge of the falsity of his statement and, hence, an intent to deceive the other party or must make the false representations in culpable ignorance of their truth or falsity. The state of mind and intent of the party charged with fraud is fraudulent if it "includes anything calculated to deceive."

The presence or absence of the requisite knowledge and intent to establish fraud may be determined from the evidence and the circumstances surrounding the transaction. . . .

Under the circumstances . . . we find that the plaintiff has failed to establish either that he had a right to rely upon defendant's representations as to acreage, or that the defendant had knowledge of the falsity of his representations or intended to deceive the plaintiff.

The defendant's explanations of the manner in which he arrived at the acreage computations are credible, and constitute evidence that he neither had knowledge of the falsity of his representations as to acreage, nor were his statements made in culpable ignorance of the truth. His representations were inaccurate, but not fraudulent. His actions were not "calculated" to deceive the plaintiff. The defendant possessed no superior knowledge of the acreage involved. He furnished to the plaintiff and his attorney, a survey, which, if examined along with the preliminary report of title and the proposed deed, would have clearly indicated that plaintiff was not receiving 26.18 acres. . . .

Under the circumstances of this case, we cannot hold that the evidence of fraud was clear and convincing and that the conduct of the defendant amounted to fraud. Therefore, the decision of the trial Court was against the manifest weight of the evidence and the law. Accordingly, the judgment is reversed and judgment is entered here for the defendant.

Judgment reversed.

Whipp v. Iverson

168 N.W.2d 201 (Wis.) 1969

Plaintiff entered into a contract to purchase the Iverson Motor Company from the defendant. The latter allegedly represented that the sale included the Oldsmobile agency and franchise. Subsequently, the Oldsmobile Division of General Motors refused to transfer the franchise to the plaintiff, who thereupon returned possession of the business to the defendant and demanded the return of his down payment and the amount of capital invested in the business. The defendant filed a demurrer to the complaint, contending that no cause of action was stated since there was no allegation of intentional misrepresentation. The trial court overruled the demurrer, and the defendant appealed from that ruling. The following opinion therefore relates only to the question as to whether or not the complaint sets forth an actionable wrong.

HALLOWS, J. . . . . Rescission of a contract in equity may be grounded on misrepresentations not intentionally made for the purpose of defrauding or inducing a person to act to his detriment for the speaker's economic benefit.

At law in the action for deceit the basis of responsibility for misrepresentation was intention, generally called *scienter* or the intent to deceive. This elusive state of mind may be proved by proof the speaker believes his statement to be false or the representation is made without any belief as to its truth. . . .

. . . Certainly what is grounds for damages in deceit is grounds for rescission, but rescission is not restricted to deceit. Before the recognition of strict responsibility for misrepresentation at law, equity recognized that an honest misrepresentation was a ground for rescission.

It is not necessary for rescission of a contract "that the party making a misrepresentation should have known that it was false." Recovery is allowed even though misrepresentation is innocently made because "It would be unjust to allow one who has made false representations, even innocently, to retain the fruits of a bargain induced by such representations." This statement of law is adopted by the Restatement of Contracts, s. 476, which states "Where a party is induced to enter into a transaction with another party that he was under no duty to enter into by means of the latter's fraud or material misrepresentation, the transaction is voidable as against the latter and all who stand in no better position, subject to certain qualifications." A misrepresentation may be innocent, negligent, or known to be false (Restatement, 2 *Contracts,* p. 890, s. 470, Comment a,) and if innocently made is voidable. (s. 476(2)).

In *McKearn* v. *Lerman Tire Service, Ltd.,* we stated rescission could be had for a misrepresentation either knowingly or inadvertently made which was a substantial breach of the contract. Thus grounds for rescission may be at least those facts which would give rise to an action for damages for deceit or for strict responsibility. We do not decide whether rescission can be grounded upon negligence.

Under modern liberality of pleading and the fusion of law in equity, a demurrer must be overruled if the complaint states facts which entitle the plaintiff to any relief. We think an express allegation of *scienter* is not required for rescission which is asked for in this complaint. The defendants are alleged to have known or ought to have known the Oldsmobile franchise could not be sold as part of the business. Iverson was the owner of the franchise he was purporting to sell and should know whether he could or could not sell the franchise. There is no question of Iverson's economic interest in the sale and his lack of intent to deceive is not material to the cause of action. We think therefore a cause of action is stated for rescission on the strict responsibility theory if not on the ground of deceit.

Order affirmed.

Bresler Ice Cream Co. v. Millionaire's Club, Inc.

218 N.E.2d 891 (Ill.) 1966

The plaintiff ice cream company brought action for damages for breach of a requirements contract. The complaint alleged (1) that on August 21, 1963, defendant entered into a contract whereby it agreed to purchase all of its requirements of ice cream and ice cream products from the plaintiff for a period of three years; (2) that on January 2, 1964, defendant discontinued the purchase of its requirements of ice cream in breach of the contract; and (3) that plaintiff is entitled to liquidated damages under the contract. In its answer, defendant admitted the existence of the contract but alleged that it was unenforceable and that plaintiff fraudulently induced the defendant to enter into the contract, in that plaintiff loaned money to the defendant on or about the date of the agreement and falsely and fraudulently represented that it intended to keep the loan open and credit thereunder available for the duration of the contract; that plaintiff knew the representation to be false at the time it was made and intended that defendant act thereupon; and that defendant relied upon that representation, but the loan was called and paid, to its detriment, within one month after the date of the requirements contract. The plaintiff was given a judgement on the pleadings, and the defendant appealed.

DRUCKER, J. . . . Fraud in the inducement renders a contract voidable at the option of the injured party. Any false representation of a material fact made with the knowledge of its falsity and intent that it shall be acted upon, and which is acted upon to the injury of the other contracting party, constitutes such fraud. Defendant's verified answer shows that the contract and the loan agreement were so inextricably bound together as to be but parts of a single transaction, and properly sets forth the allegation that defendant was fraudulently induced to enter into the requirements contract by plaintiff's false representation that the loan would remain open for the duration of the three years.

. . . Since defendant's answer properly sets forth the legal defense of fraud in the inducement, the judgment of the trial court is reversed and the cause remanded with directions to overrule the plaintiff's motion for judgment on the pleadings and to take such other action as is appropriate to resolve the issues presented by the pleadings.

Reversed.

Andolsun v. Berlitz Schools of Languages of America.

196 A.2d 926 (D.C.) 1964

Defendant, a language school, had a contract with the United States Army to supply interpreter-translators to the Army Special Warfare School at Fort Bragg, North Carolina. Plaintiff, an alien who had been employed by the United States Information Agency for twelve years, applied to defendant in May, 1962, for a position as an interpreter-translator. During his interview the plaintiff inquired if his being an alien would affect his being able to hold the job, and defendant's interviewer replied No, stating that there was no question of the defendant's employing aliens for the job with the Army. On May 15, 1962, defendant gave the plaintiff a one-year contract to commence June 1, 1962. He began work on June 1 but was discharged early in July because he was an alien. He brought this action against the defendant for loss of earnings, alleging that by the defendant's misrepresentations, he had been induced to leave his former employment and enter into the one-year contract, which he expected would actually be in the nature of permanent employment. The lower court found for the defendant and the plaintiff appealed.

HOOD, J. . . . The trial court found that at the time of entry into the contract defendant told plaintiff that there was no question of its right to hire aliens; and that plaintiff's employment was terminated for the reason that he was an alien; but the court concluded that there was no misrepresentation of material facts which defendant knew to be untrue and made for the purpose of inducing plaintiff to enter into the contract, and the court denied any recovery.

The conclusion of the trial court that defendant made no misrepresentation appears to be based on its finding that at the time of employment of plaintiff the defendant was not prohibited from hiring aliens for the performance of its contract with the Army. This finding is technically correct, as is evidenced by the fact that plaintiff was accepted by the Army and worked for approximately six weeks. But on the very same day that plaintiff signed his contract (May 15, 1962) defendant's Director in a memorandum to the Army wrote: "Confirming our conversation of last week we will make every effort to recruit U.S. Citizens as Interpreter-Translators and in case we are unable to do so in 100 percent of the cases, we will replace all non-citizens by U.S. Citizens within the one year between June 1st 1962 and May 30th 1963."

Thus it is plain that there was a question about an alien retaining his position and this question arose prior to plaintiff's signing his contract. On the day that plaintiff was signing a one-year contract defendant was assuring the Army of its efforts to employ U.S. citizens only and promising that all aliens would be replaced within the year that plaintiff was engaged to work. Defendant's Director admitted that plaintiff was told nothing about this.

Defendant knew plaintiff was hesitant about leaving a position he had held for twelve years and taking a new position if his alien status might prevent him from retaining the new position. Since plaintiff had made this known, defendant was under a duty to make a full disclosure. Concealment or suppression of a material fact is as fraudulent as a positive direct misrepresentation.

We hold that the uncontroverted evidence established that defendant misrepresented the position offered plaintiff and that plaintiff is entitled to judgment for the damages resulting from such misrepresentations. . . .

With respect to plaintiff's damages, such must be confined to those within the one-year employment period called for by the contract. He was employed for one year and at the end of that period either he or defendant could have refused to renew the contract for any reason.

The judgment is reversed with instructions to enter judgment for plaintiff for loss of earnings sustained in the one-year period.

Reversed with instructions.

Walsh v. Edwards

197 A.2d 424 (Md.) 1964

Plaintiffs brought an action for fraud and deceit against the defendants who had sold them a home. During an inspection of the property and at the time of closing the contract, plaintiffs expressed concern about a creek at the rear of the property. The defendant stated, "It would come over its banks in heavy rain, but it never came near the house." Actually the creek had overflowed several times in the past, and each time water had entered the house. After the purchase the creek overflowed causing extensive damage to the house. The plaintiffs brought action to recover damages. The lower court gave judgment to the plaintiff, and the defendant appealed.

HORNEY, J. . . . The purchaser testified that when he inquired, prior to signing the contract of purchase, as to the likelihood of the creek overflowing during a storm, the seller replied that "it would come over its banks in heavy rain, but it never came near the house." That there had been a discussion concerning the creek was corroborated by the saleswoman. But the seller testified that the purchaser had not mentioned the creek to her and denied that she had made any representation with regard to it. She contends that even if she had made the statement attributed to her by the purchaser, it was not such as to represent that the property as an entirety had never been flooded and damaged.

We think that when the statement attributed to the seller by the purchaser and other parts of the evidence produced at the trial are considered together, there was enough evidence of misrepresentation to justify submission of the case to the jury and, if believed, to warrant finding a verdict for the plaintiffs.

Ordinarily, of course, the seller of real property is not legally obliged to disclose to a prospective purchaser the objectionable or undesirable conditions or features of the property offered for sale, and mere silence or nondisclosure of material facts by the seller would not constitute actionable fraud. But where, as here, the seller, in addition to not disclosing the facts, made an active misstatement of fact, or only a partial or fragmentary statement of fact, which misled the purchaser to his injury, the legal situation of the seller was reversed and there was imposed on her a duty to disclose all that she knew as to the probability of the creek overflowing. . . . Under the circumstances in this case, the failure to disclose the facts constituted actionable fraud.

The appellant further contends that the purchasers failed to prove by admissible evidence that they had relied on the representation made by the seller, but such is not the case. During the course of the examination of Nathen Edwards, he was asked whether he relied on the representation made by the seller, and he replied that he did. When he was asked on the next question whether he would have purchased the property if the representation had not been made, the witness answered that "we would not have purchased the house."

In the instant case there was proof that the representation was false, that its falsity was known to the seller, that it was made for the purpose of deceiving the purchasers, that the purchasers relied on the misrepresentation and would not have purchased the property had the misrepresentation not been made, and that the purchasers actually suffered damage as a direct result of the fraudulent misrepresentation. That is all that was required in this case. . . .

Judgment Affirmed.

MacKay v. McIntosh

153 S.E.2d 800 (N.C.) 1967

Plaintiff entered into a contract to sell land to the defendant. Both parties thought the property was zoned for business, and the defendant's sole interest in the property was for use by her for a retail store. In fact the property was not so zoned. Plaintiff seeks to compel the defendant to purchase the property. The court ruled that the contract was rescinded, and the plaintiff appealed.

BOBBITT, J. . . . Plaintiff contends an oral agreement in conflict with the writing should be disregarded. This contention is based on a misconception of defendant's position.

"The parol evidence rule presupposes the existence of a legally effective written instrument. It does not in any way preclude a showing of facts which would render the writing inoperative or unenforceable. Thus it may be proved that . . . there was such mistake as to prevent the formation of a contract or make it subject to reformation or rescission." (Stansbury, N.C. *Evidence,* Second Edition), § 257. "[P]arol evidence is admissible to show a mutual mistake as to the existence of the subject matter of an agreement which prevents the formation of a contract."

Defendant does not seek to contradict the writing or to enforce a parol agreement. She contends that, since both Mrs. Cooper and defendant negotiated and acted in the honest but mistaken belief the subject property was in fact zoned for business, no contract, either written or oral, resulted; and that, there being no agreement, she is not obligated to purchase property which cannot be used for a retail store.

"The formation of a binding contract may be affected by a mistake. Thus, a contract may be avoided on the ground of mutual mistake of fact where the mistake is common to both parties and by reason of it each has done what neither intended. Furthermore a defense may be asserted when there is a mutual mistake of the parties as to the subject matter, the price, or the terms, going to show the want of a consensus *ad idem.* Generally speaking, however, in order to affect the binding force of a contract, the mistake must be of an existing or past fact which is material; it must be as to a fact which enters into and forms the basis of the contract, or in other words it must be of the essence of the agreement, the *sine qua non,* or, as is sometimes said, the efficient cause of the agreement, and must be such that it animates and controls the conduct of the parties."

In our opinion, and we so hold, whether the subject property was within the boundaries of an area zoned for business is a factual matter; and, under the evidence, the mutual mistake as to this fact related to the essence of the agreement.

The conclusion reached is that the evidence fully supports Judge Hasty's findings and judgment. For the reasons stated, the judgment of the court below is affirmed.

Affirmed.

Rushlight Auto Sprinkler Co. v. City of Portland
219 P.2d 732 (Or.) 1950

The plaintiff, in submitting its bid to the defendant City of Portland for a certain sewage and disposal project, hurriedly submitted a bid of $429,444.20 and issued its certified check of $21,472.21 to be retained by the city in event plaintiff failed to enter into a contract after notice that his bid had been accepted. When the bids were opened, it was discovered that the next lowest bid was $671,600. All were quite concerned because plaintiff's bid was exceedingly low and plaintiff discovered that it had omitted an item for steel of $99,225.68. Plaintiff requested that its bid be withdrawn, but it was accepted, and the certified check was cashed when plaintiff refused to proceed with the work, the contract being let to another. Plaintiff seeks to recover the amount of the check. The lower court gave judgment for the plaintiff, and the defendant appealed.

ROSSMAN, J. . . . As we said, the City concedes the mistake concerning the steel item which the plaintiff's officers, to their manifest embarrassment, described. The plaintiff prays that its mistake be deemed excusable; the City insists that the error was a culpable one. . . .

So far as we can ascertain, the plaintiff's bid was compiled by an adequate staff of estimators. No one challenged the competence of the estimators nor questioned the methods they pursued. The record shows that one of the estimators, after having calculated the amount of earth that would have to be moved in one phase of the construction work, called upon a member of the City Board of Engineers for the purpose of comparing his estimate with that made by the board. He found that the two were virtually the same. That fact and an occasional other one mentioned in the record tend to show that the estimators were careful. . . .

We believe that it is manifest from the evidence that the difference between the plaintiff's bid and the next higher was so large that all of those concerned with the undertaking were rendered uneasy. The plaintiff's officers at once returned to their work sheets, fearing that they must have committed a mistake. The City Engineer, according to his own words, found the variation so great that it "scared us to death." A member of the Board of Engineers, who seemingly expressed himself in wary words, described the plaintiff's bid as "a very low" one and termed the difference between it and the City's estimate "a very decided difference." The bid aroused suspicion in all minds. We think that the difference apprised the City that a mistake had probably occurred.

It is true, as already indicated, that the steel item accounts for only $99,-225.68 or 41 percent of the total disparity of $242,155.80 between the plaintiff's and the next higher bid. Therefore, it alone did not provoke the misgivings. The $99,225.68 was a substantial part of the total difference. The variation between the second and third high bids was only $2,232.06. The difference between the second and the fourth high bids was $13,291.50. The material fact is that the omission of the steel was a substantial factor in reducing the bid to such a low amount that the city officials surmised that it was too good to be true. . . .

From Williston on *Contracts* (rev. ed.), § 1573, the following is taken:

> In two classes of cases, mistake of one party only to a contract undoubtedly justifies affirmative relief as distinguished from a mere denial to enforce the contract specifically against him;
> (1) Where the mistake is known to the other party to the transaction. . . .

Section 503, Restatement of the Law, *Contracts,* says: "A mistake of only one party that forms the basis on which he enters into a transaction does not of itself render the transaction voidable; . . . "

The Reporters' Notes to that section cites many illustrative decisions and some treatises. From the notes, we take the following: "Where one party knows or has reason to know that the other party has made a basic mistake (see Comment *c*) restitution is granted. This situation has frequently arisen where there has been an error in the price given. In this case rescission is ordinarily allowed. . . . "

We believe that in this State an offer and an acceptance are deemed to effect a meeting of the minds, even though the offeror made a material mistake in compiling his offer, provided the acceptor was not aware of the mistake and had no reason to suspect it. But if the offeree knew of the mistake, and if it was basic, or if the circumstances were such that he, as a reasonable man, should have inferred that a basic mistake was made, a meeting of the minds does not occur. The circumstances which should arouse the suspicions of the fairminded offeree are many, as stated in § 94 of Williston on *Contracts* (rev. ed.): " . . . And the same principle is applicable in any case where the offeree should know that the terms of the offer are unintended or misunderstood by the offeror. The offeree will not be permitted to snap up an offer that is too good to be true; no contract based on such an offer can then be enforced by the acceptor. . . . "

It is unnecessary to state once more that the proof in cases of this kind must possess a high degree of cogency. The bidder must prove, not only that he made a material mistake, but also that the offeree was aware of it. In this case, the facts which we have mentioned are unchallenged.

It is our belief that although the plaintiff alone made the mistake, the City was aware of it. When it accepted the plaintiff's bid, with knowledge of the mistake, it sought to take an unconscionable advantage of an inadvertent error. Equity is always prepared to grant relief from such situations.

The decree of the Circuit Court is affirmed.

Nash v. Kornblum

186 N.E.2d 551 (N.Y.) 1962

The plaintiff, a fence builder, entered into a contract to fence an area surrounding the defendant's tennis courts. An estimate of cost was submitted to the defendant, who accepted it. In the estimate the length of the area to be fenced was improperly stated. And the error was not discovered until after the fence was installed. The plaintiff brought suit to have the agreement reformed to coincide with the actual measurements. He contended that the mistake was an inadvertent error on the part of his secretary and that it did not represent the agreement previous to its reduction to writing. The lower court dismissed the complaint, and the plaintiff appealed.

FOSTER, J. . . . The sole issue before us is whether reformation should have been granted. In *Ross* v. *Food Specialties* (6 N.Y.2d 336, 341, 189 N.Y.S.2d 857, 859, 860, 160 N.E.2d 618, 620, 621) this court stated: "We have consistently and repeatedly held that before a reformation can be granted the plaintiff '*must establish his right to such relief by clear, positive and convincing evidence*. Reformation may not be granted upon a probability nor even upon a mere preponderance of evidence, but only upon a certainty of error' nor may the plaintiff 'secure reformation merely upon a showing that he or his attorney made a mistake.' In the absence of fraud, the mistake shown 'must be one made by both parties to the agreement so that the intentions of neither are expressed in it.' " [Emphasis in original.]

. . . "Reformation is not designed for the purpose of remaking the contract agreed upon but, rather, solely for the purpose of stating correctly a mutual mistake shared by both parties to the contract; in other words, it provides an equitable remedy for use when it clearly and convincingly appears that the contract, as written, does not embody the true agreement as mutually intended."However, in *Hart* v. *Blabey* (287 N.Y. 257, 262, 39 N.E.2d 230, 232), this court invoked the equitable doctrine of reformation on the following basis: " 'Where there is no mistake about the agreement, and the only mistake alleged is in the reduction of that agreement to writing, such mistake of the scrivener, or of either party, no matter how it occurred, may be corrected.'*Born* v. *Schrenkeisen* (110 N.Y. 55, 59, 17 N.E. 339, 341) 'In such a case equity will conform the written instrument to the parol agreement which it was intended to embody.' " (*Pitcher* v. *Hennessey,* 48 N.Y. 415, 423).

It clearly and convincingly appears from the record here that this is a case of a mistake on the part of the plaintiff's agent in typing the erroneous linear ground measurement, which plaintiff did not discover before submission to the defendant, and the latter with knowledge of the mistake, trying to take advantage of the error. The writing itself did not represent the understanding of either party as to the area to be fenced which had been agreed upon previous to the writing, and thus did not embody the true agreement, as mutually intended, relating to the area.

This is not a case where the plaintiff unilaterally and mistakenly estimated the linear feet and defendant, without a duty to speak and absent fraud, agreed to the proposal. Should these circumstances have been present in the contract's reduction to writing, there would be no scrivener's mistake or mutual mistake of fact, the agreement would be the intended one by the parties, and equity would not "reform" the executed contract. This set of circumstances is not presented here by the record. . . .

The situation presented clearly calls for relief, and the only practicable method of achieving such a result is by the equitable remedy of reformation. The Trial Judge, dismissed the complaint with the finding that the proof failed to show fraud on the part of the defendant. In our view of the case it was unnecessary for the plaintiff to establish fraud on the part of the defendant. Perhaps reformation could have been predicated upon a unilateral mistake on one side and deceptive conduct on the other side which tended to obscure the true agreement. However, the situation presented as a result of the scrivener's error was closely akin, if not precisely, to a mutual mistake of fact, and as such was sufficient to call for the application of the equitable doctrine of reformation. Therefore, the judgment should be reversed and the case remitted to Special Term for proceedings not inconsistent with this opinion.

Judgment reversed. . . .

CHAPTER 11
REVIEW QUESTIONS AND PROBLEMS

1. *A* responded to a newspaper advertisement for three acres of land. A deed was executed which recited that it was a 1.5 acre tract, and this same description was set forth in the mortgage which *A* executed. When *A* moved onto the property, he became aware that it did not contain three acres. *A* then brought an action for fraud and deceit. Should he obtain a judgment?

2. *A* sold land to the Ohio Turnpike Commission with the understanding that he would have ingress and egress from his property adjoining the road. By mistake this provision was not included in the deed signed by *A*. Thereafter *C* purchased *A*'s property and brought suit to have the deed reformed to show ingress and egress rights. Should the deed be reformed?

3. *A* was a tenant of *B* under a lease. The leased premises were being remodeled, and it was agreed that the rent would be reduced until the remodeling was completed. *B* told *A* that unless he paid the full amount during this period *B* would cancel the lease and evict him. Under this compulsion *A* paid the full rent. He now seeks to recover the overpayment. Should he succeed?

4. *A* was in need of ten tons of steel. He telephoned *B* and by mistake ordered fifty tons. Later he sought to avoid the contract because of the mistake. Should he succeed?

5. *A* purchased a duplex from *B. B* had built the duplex two years previously. *A* moved into one side of the duplex and discovered that large cracks had appeared in the walls. Tests showed that the cracks were caused by a defective fill of the soil. *A* was not aware that the ground had been filled. Does *A* have any cause of action against *B*?

6. *A* purchased a diamond ring from *B,* a jeweler, for $700. *B* warranted the value of the ring and that it would have a trade-in value of that amount. *A* later sought to trade the ring for another, and he was not able to get a trade-in of more than $350 from other jewelers. He seeks to recover $350 from *B.* Should he succeed?

7. *A* entered into a contract to purchase a motel from *B.* During the negotiations *B* told *A* that the motel took in a gross of $2,500 every month, and he offered his books for *A*'s inspection. Actually the gross was much less than this; the books reflected this fact. *A* now seeks to rescind the contract on the basis of the misrepresentation. Should he succeed?

8. *S* sold goods on credit to *B,* the latter being asked to indicate how he stood financially. He said he had $3,000 in his business assets but neglected to say he had liabilities of $2,100. *S* seeks to avoid the contract and recover the goods sold. Has he a right to do so?

9. *P* purchased a house from *D.* The contract contained a recital that *P* had inspected the house and accepted it in its current condition. There were several serious defects which an inspection would not reveal. If *D* knew of these defects, is he guilty of fraud?

10. *P,* when buying land from *D,* was told by *D*'s agent that the land was capable of producing an income of $2,300 per year. If it is not, is *P* entitled to rescind?

Illegality

2-63. In General. An additional requirement for a valid contract is that it have a lawful purpose or object. Contracts that do not have a lawful object are illegal and therefore unenforceable. In one sense, such contracts can be designated as void, but that connotation is misleading—in reality, the contract is simply *unenforceable.* The status of an illegal contract is such that in general a court will not entertain litigation involving it—it will not aid either party. This means that if the illegal contract is executory, neither party may enforce performance by the other, and if it is executed, the court will not give remedy by way of rescission—it will not allow recovery of what was given in performance.

The application of the general rule presents a good example of the role of law and its concern for societal needs. In an illegal contract situation the court literally "leaves the parties where it finds them." It necessarily follows that (1) a party to an illegal contract cannot recover damages for breach of such contract; (2) if one party has performed he cannot, generally, recover either the value of his performance or any property or goods transferred to the other. Thus, one wrongdoer is enriched at the expense of the other wrongdoer, but the courts will not intercede to rectify this. What social good is advanced by this "hands-off" attitude? The courts in their judgment have felt that such an attitude will serve as a deterrent from entering into illegal bargains. The rule is an ancient one and was well expressed by the eminent English jurist, Lord Mansfield, in 1775, when he wrote: "If from the plaintiff's own statement or otherwise the cause of action appears to arise *ex turpi causa* (out of illegal or immoral consideration) or the transgression of a positive law of this country, there the court says he has no right to be assisted. It is upon that ground the court goes; not for the sake of the defendant, but because they will not lend their aid to the plaintiff."

There are many examples of the application of this principle even today. Many of these involve suits for money claimed due for services rendered. If the service that is rendered requires a license before it can legally be given, the party receiving the benefit of the service can successfully refuse to pay for the service on the ground the contract is illegal because the plaintiff has no license.[1] Most professional services such as those rendered by a doctor, lawyer, pharmacist, accountant, engineer, or real estate broker require a license in each state in which services are rendered. Many cases hold that a professional person licensed in one state cannot perform services in another state and if he does so, he cannot collect for the services.

The practice of law by unauthorized persons is a significant problem. A person who practices law without a license is not only denied the right to a fee but is also subject to criminal prosecution in many states and such activity may also be enjoined. Since the practice of law primarily entails the giving of advice, difficult questions are presented when advice is given by business specialists such as certified public accountants, insurance brokers, bankers, and real estate brokers. Although the line between permissible and impermissible activities of these business specialists is often difficult to draw, it is clear that some of the activities and services that may be performed by the various business specialists do constitute the unauthorized practice of law. For example, the handling of a complicated tax case by an accountant has been held to constitute unauthorized practice of law, and the preparation of a real estate contract of sale by a real estate broker is illegal in most states. Business specialists should be aware that the giving of legal advice and the preparing of legal documents by one not licensed to practice law is illegal.

There are three basic exceptions to the rule which precludes the granting of any relief to a party to an illegal contract. First, if a person falls under the category of those for whose protection the contract was made illegal, he may obtain restitution of what he has paid or parted with or may even obtain enforcement. For example, both federal and state statutes require that a corporation follow certain procedures before securities (stocks and bonds) may be offered for sale to the public. It is illegal to sell such securities without having complied with the legal requirements. Nevertheless, a purchaser would be allowed to enforce bonds against the corporation.

A second exception applies when a person is induced by fraud or duress to enter into an illegal agreement. In such cases, the courts do not regard the defrauded or coerced party as being an actual participant in the wrong, and will, therefore, allow restitution of what he has rendered by way of performance. It has been suggested that the same result would obtain if the party were induced by strong economic pressure to enter into an illegal agreement.

Thirdly, there is an interesting legal doctrine called *locus poenitentiae* which, as applied to illegal contracts, provides the remedy of restitution to one who has become a party to such a contract. Literally, the phrase means "a place for repentance; by extension, an opportunity for changing one's mind." As applied to an illegal contract, it means that within very strict limits, a person who repents before actually having performed any illegal part of the contract may rescind it and obtain restitution of his part performance. Thus,

[1] Markus & Nocka v. Julian Goodrich Architects, Inc., page 241.

wagers are illegal transactions except under certain circumstances. Suppose that *A* and *B* wager on the outcome of an election, and each places $100 with *C,* the stakeholder, who agrees to turn $200 over to the winner. Prior to the election either *A* or *B* could recover his $100 from *C* by legal action, since the execution of the illegal agreement would not yet have occurred. Actually, the loser could obtain a judgment against *C* if he gives notice of his demand prior to the time that the stake has been turned over to the winner. Once the stake has been turned over, however, *locus poenitentiae* no longer allows remedy.

In this decade, the social implications of contracts are of especial significance. A part of this picture is the conflict between freedom of contract and protection of the public.

As has been stressed, the law does not grant complete freedom of contract, and if a contract or a provision thereof is specifically prohibited by statute, contravenes the rule of the common law, or is contrary to public policy, courts will declare it illegal. A contract provision is contrary to public policy if it is injurious to the interests of the public, contravenes some established interest of society, violates the policy or purpose of some statute, or tends to interfere with the public health, safety, morals, or general welfare. While all agreements are subject to the paramount power of the sovereign and to the judicial power to declare contracts illegal, contracts are not to be lightly set aside on the grounds of public policy, and doubts will usually be resolved in favor of legality. The term "public policy" is vague and variable and changes as our social, economic, and political climates change. As society becomes more complex, courts turn more and more to statutory enactments in search of current public policy. A court's own concept of right and wrong as well as its total philosophy will frequently come into play in answering complex questions of public policy. Cases involving public policy are often in conflict with each other and what is sound public policy is always questionable. Care should be taken to ascertain the reason behind each rule and each result and any indicated trends in the law should be noted.

Illegality may take the form of illegal consideration or illegal performance. The purpose of the parties to a contract usually indicates the presence of illegality, and illegality is measured by what is intended rather than by what is accomplished. Legal contracts are not rendered illegal by illegal acts of performance if legal performance is possible or was intended.

2-64. Freedom of Contract and the Public Interest. The law early declared that absolute freedom of contract existed in a barter situation because of the equal bargaining position of the parties. Each party could agree to the offered exchange or could reject it and the law would not interfere. At the other extreme are the contracts with public utilities in which there is no equality of bargaining power between the parties because of the existence of a virtual monopoly. The law therefore denies freedom of contract to utilities in return for the monopoly power and government regulates all contractual provisions including rates. The need for this regulation is readily apparent. For example: imagine the problem if bargaining over the price of water were possible.

The difficulty today is that most contracts do not fall within these two extremes. There are many contracts which are entered into between parties

with unequal bargaining power. When the subject matter of the contracts
involves items of everyday necessity, courts frequently hold that one of the
parties is a quasi-public institution and that such institutions are not entitled
to complete freedom of contract because freedom of contract is not in the
public interest. Thus, all contracts or parts of the contracts of such institutions
may be held illegal whenever the quasi-public institution has taken advantage
of its superior bargaining power, and drawn a contract, or included a provision
in a contract which in the eyes of the court excessively favors the quasi-public
institution to the detriment of the other party and the public. A typical
example is an exculpatory clause in which one party seeks to disclaim liability
for his own negligence. Such contracts are discussed in the next section. There
are numerous other situations in which the public interest or public policy
determines the legality of a private agreement or a part thereof. This is true
in cases when to allow the contract provision to stand would have a harmful
effect on the public generally. Many areas of heretofore private law of contract
are becoming or have become, at least in part, affected with the public interest
in recent years, thus reducing freedom of private contract.

2-65. Exculpatory Clauses.   An exculpatory clause is a provision of a contract
which relieves a party of liability for his own negligence. These disclaimers of
liability are not favored by the law, are strictly construed against the party
relying on them, and are frequently declared to be illegal by courts as contrary
to public policy.[2] Some states have by statute declared these clauses in certain
types of contracts such as leases to be illegal and void.

The judicial decisions which declare such contracts to be illegal usually
involve cases in which the disclaiming party owes a duty to the public or cases
in which the duty owed is private but involves the public interest. The public
interest is involved in cases of private contract when the subject matter of the
contract is an everyday necessity and there is inequality of bargaining power
between the parties. For example, a parking lot might seek to avoid its liability
for damages to cars caused by its negligence, but such contract would be illegal
because parking is an everyday necessity and there is inequality of bargaining
power between car owners and parking lot operators. As a duty owed to the
public, the law provides that a public carrier such as a railroad may not
disclaim its liability for damages to freight resulting from its negligence.

2-66. Contracts in Restraint of Trade.   There are several aspects to agreements which unreasonably restrain trade—there are several ways in which
trade may be restrained. Public policy prohibits any agreement which unreasonably restrains a person from exercising his trade, business, or profession.
Again, the conflict between the protective influence of public policy and the
right to freedom of contract comes into play.

Historically, it was considered at an early date in England that it was
inherently wrong to restrain a person's right to exercise his trade or calling.
Therefore, any agreement whereby a person agreed to refrain from exercising
his usual calling was illegal and unenforceable as being per se in violation of
public policy. A famous case decided in 1414 (the Dyer's Case) firmly established this rule which was followed by the courts for three centuries. It was

[2] Hunter v. American Rentals Inc., page 242

not until 1711 that the precedent was called into question and a more liberal rule was established. The later case enunciated the modern principle that restraints are legal if they are reasonable and if they are designed to give needed protection to the party in whose favor the restraint operates. The ideal of freedom of contract prevailed over the protective concept of the earlier decision.

The other type of restraint of trade contract is that in which agreements are entered into to establish monopolies through price-fixing, division of territories, limitations on production, and the like. While the common law prohibits such combinations in restraint of trade as being injurious to the public which prospers on free and open competition, the bulk of the law is found in federal and state statutes.

The federal government in the United States by statute on several occasions has attempted to ensure a competitive economic system. These statutes, beginning with the Sherman Antitrust Act in 1890 are discussed in Chapter 48.

2-67. Agreements Not to Compete.   Contracts in partial restraint of trade are valid if such restraint has reference to and is ancillary to the sale of property, the creation or sale of a business interest or a profession, or to the discontinuance of employment, and if such restraint is reasonably necessary for the protection of the purchaser, the remaining member of the business, or the employer. Such agreements will be enforced in a court of equity, provided that they are (1) reasonable in point of time, (2) reasonable in the area of restraint, (3) necessary to protect good will, (4) do not place an undue burden on the covenantor and (5) do not violate the public interest. Each agreement will be examined by the court, without a jury, from the standpoint of reasonableness to both parties and to the general public. The court in making the examination will have to examine the agreement in light of the nature of the business. Such factors as uniqueness of product, patents, trade secrets, type of service, employee's contact with customers, and other goodwill factors are significant.[3] It is difficult to determine which factors will influence any particular court to decide what is or what is not in the public interest; but certainly in the employment situation whether or not the employee will become a burden on society and whether or not the public is being deprived of his skill, etc., will usually be considered. If the restriction exceeds what is reasonably necessary, a few courts will reform the contract so as to make the restrictions reasonable, but most courts hold that the entire limiting clause is illegal, thus leaving the person to be benefited by the restriction without protection.[4] It must be recognized that the law will look with more favor on these contracts if they involve the sale of a business interest than it will in the case of such a provision included in an employment contract. In fact, an agreement not to compete may even be presumed in the case of a sale of business and its goodwill, and the seller must not thereafter directly or by circular solicit business from his old customers, although he may advertise generally. The reason courts are more likely to hold the agreements between a buyer and seller or partners valid as contrasted with employer-employee contracts is that in these situations there is more equality of bargaining power than in the case of the employer and

[3] Terminal Vegetable Co., Inc. v. Beck, page 243
[4] McCook Window Co. v. Hardwood Door Corporation, page 246

employee. A seller or a former partner could readily refuse to sign an agreement not to compete, whereas an employee seeking a job might feel obliged to sign almost anything in order to gain employment. The law generally sympathizes with persons whose bargaining power is not equal to that of the other party and is inclined to provide relief for them.[5] In addition, it is evident that there is a goodwill factor involved in the sale of almost any going business and that goodwill as an asset deserves protection; whereas in employee-employer situations it is less evident that the employee is able to create goodwill or take it with him upon termination of his employment. A few states have by statute or by their constitutions declared agreements to restrict an employee's right to seek other employment to be illegal as a matter of public policy.

What course of action should the employer follow in those instances in which an employee who had signed a restrictive covenant does nevertheless either compete directly or go to work for a competitor? The employer not desiring the publicity and the inconvenience of a lawsuit, may refrain from taking action in the hope that the former employee's new activities will not adversely affect his business. He may ultimately find that the employee's competition is creating an adverse effect and at that time decide to institute suit or action against his former employee. If suit is instituted to enjoin the employee from this competitive activity, the employee may contend that by failing to raise the issue promptly when the breach occurred, the employer has waived his rights. The point may be a good one since an employer should not allow his former employee to expend money or otherwise materially alter his position by establishing a business or going to work for another firm and then seek to prevent his action by attempting to enforce the contract. The doctrines of estoppel and waiver can thus frequently be used by an employee to prevent the use in equity of the contract rights to which the employer would otherwise have been entitled. Equity does not favor a party who "sleeps on his rights" and the failure to promptly seek enforcement of the agreement may very well preclude its enforcement.

A situation comparable to that of the employee's agreement not to compete is that of a restrictive provision in a contract for the sale or lease of property. The owner of land may wish to prevent the use of this land for any purpose that would be competitive with his own business. Suppose that *A* owns an entire block, one-half of which is occupied by his appliance store. He may lease the other half of the property to *B* with a stipulation that *B* will not operate an appliance store on the land. As long as the vendor or lessor does not desire to have competition on property that he controls, he may avoid such competition by contract. Since other property in the community may be used for competitive purposes, the agreement is binding, although it does to some extent restrain trade. There is this caveat, however, that if the restriction is a part of a scheme to create a monopoly, the contract may be unenforceable as an illegal restraint on trade.

2-68. Usury.   State statutes limit the amount of interest that may be charged upon borrowed money or for the extension of the maturity of a debt. Any

---

[5] *Vander Werf v. Zunica Realty Co.,* page 247

contract by which the lender is to receive more than the maximum interest allowed by the statute is illegal. In most states the lender is denied the right to collect any interest in such cases, although one state denied collection of even the principal when the interest rate was usurious. A few states permit recovery of interest at the legal rate. The law against usury is generally not violated by collection of the legal maximum interest in advance or by adding a service fee that is no larger than reasonably necessary to cover the incidental costs of making the loan—inspection, legal, and recording fees. It is also allowable for a seller to add a finance or carrying charge on long-term credit transactions in addition to the maximum interest rate. Many of these exceptions are created by statute. Other statutes allow special lenders such as pawnshops, small loan companies or credit unions to charge in excess of the otherwise legal limit. In fact, the exceptions to the maximum interest rate in most states far exceed the situations in which the general rule is applicable. The laws relating to usury were designed to protect debtors from excessive interest; this goal has been thwarted by these exceptions so that only modest protection is actually available.

The purchase of a note at a discount greater than the maximum interest is not usurious, unless the maker of the note is the person who is discounting it. Thus if *A*, who is in need of funds, sells to *B* a $500 note payable in 6 months to himself for $100, the sale is not usurious, although the gain to *B* could be very large. A note is considered the same as any other personal property and may be sold for whatever it will bring upon the market. Some courts, however, hold that if the seller of the note indorses the negotiable paper and thus remains personally liable on it, a discount greater than the legal rate of interest is usurious. This is particularly true if the paper is considered worthless except for the indorsement. In such a case the sale of the paper is regarded as actually being a loan for the period the note has yet to run.

As long as one lends the money of others, he may charge a commission in addition to the maximum rate. A commission may not be legally charged when one is lending his own funds, even though he has to borrow the money with which to make the loan and expects to sell the paper shortly thereafter.

The whole question of credit charges and loans has been of concern to both federal and state governments. The federal Truth-in-Lending Act and the Uniform Commercial Credit Code require disclosures for the benefit and protection of consumers. Several devices have been used to charge excessively high interest rates and these have come under scrutiny by the courts. One of these is to have a different "credit" price than a "cash" price.[6] Another is to charge extra interest for delinquent payments. The add-on interest factor and the collection of the obligation in installments also raise questions as to whether usury is involved.

Another device that has been used to the detriment of the consumer is the "sales referral plan." This involves a statement made by the seller to the buyer that if he gives him a list of prospects, he will receive a commission to be applied against the amount he owes the seller. Such a scheme has been held

[6] Lloyd v. Gutgsell, page 249

by some courts to be illegal either as a lottery or because the agreement lacks mutuality.[7]

Interest rates have increased substantially over the past few years. The prime interest rate now exceeds the maximum rate allowed by many states. This presents a problem that must be resolved either by judicial action or by legislation. One facet of the problem is that federal laws supersede state laws with regard to federally guaranteed loans such as FHA mortgage loans. As a result interest on such loans can exceed the maximum allowed by the states.

2-69. Unconscionable Bargains.   As a general proposition, a court of equity will not enforce a contract if its provisions are so harsh, severe, and unfair that the party resisting performance would be unduly oppressed.[8] An unconscionable bargain or contract has been defined as " . . . one which no man in his senses, not under delusion, would make, on the one hand, and which no fair and honest man would accept, on the other." The Code has a special provision in Article 2—Sales—which provides:

> (1) If the court as a matter of law finds the contract or any clause of the contract to have been unconscionable at the time it was made, the court may refuse to enforce the contract; or it may enforce the remainder of the contract without the unconscionable clause; or it may so limit the application of any unconscionable clause as to avoid any unconscionable result.
>
> (2) When it is claimed or appears to the court that the contract or any clause thereof may be unconscionable, the parties shall be afforded a reasonable opportunity to present evidence as to its commercial setting, purpose and effect to aid the court in making the determination. (U.C.C. 2-302)

The Code does not define the term "unconscionable" but the official comments to the above section states:

> The basic test is whether, in the light of the general commercial background and the commercial needs of the particular trade or case, the clauses involved are so one-sided as to be unconscionable under the circumstances existing at the time of the making of the contract. The principle is one of the prevention of oppression and unfair surprise . . . and not of disturbance of allocation of risks because of superior bargaining power. (Official Comment, U.C.C. 2-302)

The Code provision on unconscionability has had influence in transactions not covered by the Code. It is evident that the concept is in keeping with the tenor of the times—protection of consumers from overreaching sellers.[9]

2-70. Other Illegal Agreements.   There is an endless variety of other contracts that may be against public policy. Examples are wagering agreements; contracts to affect the administration of justice, such as to conceal evidence or suppress a criminal investigation; and contracts to influence legislative or executive action or to interfere with or injure public service. Such contracts are frequently declared illegal by statute or held to be illegal as being contrary to

---

[7] Sherwood & Roberts-Yakima, Inc. v. Leach, page 250
[8] Campbell Soup Co. v. Wentz, page 252
[9] Williams v. Walker-Thomas Furniture Co., page 254

public policy.[10] Of course, lobbying is legal as long as it does not amount to bribery or undue influence.

Contracts quite similar to those involving the relation of an individual to his government are those which involve the relation of an employee to his employer. Any attempt by contract to persuade an employee to violate his duty to his employer is illegal.

ILLEGALITY CASES

Markus & Nocka v. Julian Goodrich Architects, Inc.

250 A.2d 739 (Vt.) 1969

BARNEY, J. . . . The defendant was the principal architect on a project involving an addition to the DeGoesbriand Hospital in Burlington, Vermont. The hospital directed the defendant to engage the services of the plaintiff firm as consulting architects. The plaintiff is a Massachusetts architectural firm specializing in hospital design. The arrangement was accomplished and evidenced in an exchange of letters between the parties. The project with which the plaintiff was connected involved the development of an outpatient department, emergency department, laboratory and x-ray departments. The duties of the plaintiff included a study of the medical needs to be incorporated into the addition, inspection of the premises, consultation with hospital staff, preparation of construction and equipment estimates, detail drawings of specialized rooms, participation in revision of preliminary sketches, and provision of specifications for cost and bid purposes. The plaintiff's staff made numerous trips to Burlington, consulting with hospital personnel and medical staff, and prepared plans and detailed drawings. As the matter finally wound up, the design recommendations of the plaintiff were not accepted by the hospital staff, and the new expansion was finally put out to bid and constructed on the basis of plans and working drawings of the defendant. The compensation of the plaintiff was to be 1 percent of construction cost plus travel expenses, and this 1 percent figure was the basis of the judgment in favor of the plaintiff awarded below.

It is unquestioned that these activities were carried on in connection with construction to be undertaken within Vermont. The facts show that the plans and sketches were developed on the basis of information obtained from visits to the Vermont site and consultation with the Vermont hospital personnel. Indeed, the acts evidencing performance under the contract, sufficient at law or not, have no other relevance than to this Vermont project on its Vermont site. Thus they are within the ambit of the Vermont architectural registration statute. . . .

Architectural contracts entered into in violation of such registration statutes are held to be illegal, and the provisions for payment of commissions under them are unenforceable. The underlying policy is one of protecting the citizens of the state from untrained, unqualified, and unauthorized practitioners. It has been applied to many professions and special occupations for similar protective purposes. . . .

[10] Troutman v. Southern Railway Co., page 256

26 V.S.A. § 121 specifically mentions consultation as one of the activities proscribed for one not registered. This is not to say that any kind of consultation between architects of different states can be contractually valid only with registration. It does mean that when the nonresident architect presumes to consult, advise, and service, in some direct measure, a Vermont client relative to Vermont construction, he is putting himself within the scope of the Vermont architectural registration law. Nothing in that law suggests that the services must be somehow repetitive to be prohibited. No basis for excusing this plaintiff from its express provisions appears here. . . .

Judgment reversed and judgment for the defendants to recover their costs.

Hunter v. American Rentals, Inc.

371 P.2d 131 (Kan.) 1962

This was a tort action of negligence for damages brought by Everett L. Hunter, plaintiff (appellee), against American Rentals, Inc., defendant (appellant). Plaintiff rented a trailer and hitch from defendant. Defendant's agents attached the trailer and hitch to plaintiff's car and advised plaintiff that the trailer was ready for travel. Plaintiff paid the rental charges and while driving the car, the trailer hitch broke, leaving the trailer and automobile attached only by the safety chain. This chain had been attached by the defendant's agent in such a manner that it permitted the trailer to start moving from one side of the highway to the other. This caused plaintiff's car to overturn, and plaintiff received personal injuries and damaged the automobile.

By its answer defendant sought to avoid liability, contending that the plaintiff entered into a written rental agreement which contained the following clause absolving the defendant of any liability:

> The renter hereby absolved the AMERICAN RENTALS of any responsibility or obligation in the event of accident, regardless of causes or consequence, and that any costs, claims, court or attorney's fees, or liability resulting from the use of described equipment will be indemnified by the renter regardless against whom the claimant or claimants institute action. . . .
>
> AMERICAN RENTALS makes no warranty of fitness or usage, express or implied. The undersigned received said property in its present condition and waives all claims present and future against AMERICAN RENTALS including those resulting from defects, latent or apparent.

Plaintiff contended that the above provisions were void as being contrary to public policy. The trial court held that the contract terms did not constitute a valid defense and held for the plaintiff. The defendant appeals.

WERTZ, J. . . . Contracts for exemption for liability from negligence are not favored by the law. They are strictly construed against the party relying on them. The rule is unqualifiedly laid down by many decisions that one cannot avoid liability for negligence by contract. The rule against such contracts is frequently limited to the principle that parties cannot stipulate for the protection against liability for negligence in the performance of a legal duty or a duty of public service, or where the public interest is involved or a public duty owed, or when the duty owed is a private one where public interest requires the performance thereof. There is no doubt that the rule that forbids a person to protect himself by agreement against damages resulting from his own negligence applies where the agreement protects him against the consequences of a breach of some duty imposed by law. It is, of course, clear that a person cannot, by agreement, relieve himself from a duty which he owed to the public, independent of the agreement. An analysis of the decisions indicates that even under the view that a person may, under some circumstances, contract against the performance of such duties, he cannot do so where the interest of the public requires the performance thereof.

. . . The defendant, being engaged in the business of renting trailers to the general public, including trailer hitches and other attendant equipment necessary to connect the rented trailers to the automobiles, owed a duty, not only to the plaintiff but also to the general public, to see that the trailer hitch was properly installed and the trailer properly attached thereto in order that the same might be safely driven on the highway for the purpose and use for which it was intended; and defendant, by contract, could not relieve itself from its negligent acts of failing to make those safe connections and installations. The contract on the part of the defendant to relieve itself from such negligent liability is against the public policy of this state and void.

An agreement is against public policy if it is injurious to the interests of the public, contravenes some established interest of society, violates some public statute, or tends to interfere with the public welfare or safety.

For the reasons stated, this court is of the opinion that the contract pleaded, being in contravention of the statute and the public policy of this state, is void and unenforceable and constitutes no defense to plaintiff's cause of action.

Affirmed.

Terminal Vegetable Co., Inc., v. Beck

196 N.E.2d 109 (Ohio) 1964

SKEEL, J. This appeal comes to this court on questions of law from a judgment entered for defendants on defendants' demurrer by the Court of Common Pleas of Cuyahoga County. The action is one for money damages for breach of plaintiff's rights under a contract whereby the plaintiff purchased the wholesale vegetable business of the defendants, Russell H. and Anna L. Beck, for the wrongful interference with plaintiff in the conduct of the business purchased.

The petition alleges that in December of 1959, plaintiff purchased from the defendants, Anna L. Beck and Russell H. Beck, under the terms of a written agreement, the Becks' wholesale vegetable business which they (the Becks) were then operating. It further alleges that as an inducement to persuade the plaintiff to enter into the purchase of said going business, the Becks promised that if the plaintiff would agree to employ Russell H. Beck during the summer of 1960 that he (Russell H. Beck) would retire from the wholesale produce business. It is alleged that except for such assurances, the plaintiff would not have entered into the purchase agreement.

In 1961, it is alleged Russell H. Beck made a demand to the plaintiff that it reemploy him for the summer (of 1961), the demand including the threat that if said employment was not agreed to on Beck's terms, he would accept employment from the defendant, The Cleveland Growers Market, whose place of business was next door to the plaintiff's business address. (The Cleveland Growers Market is a competitor, transacting like business with that of the plaintiff.) It is further alleged that upon plaintiff's refusal to reemploy Beck on the terms he demanded, the defendant, Russell H. Beck, in violation of his obligations under the sale, entered into employment with the defendant, The Cleveland Growers Market, the latter being fully informed of the fact that Beck, in entering its employ for the year 1961, was violating his obligations to the plaintiff. It is alleged that for the benefit of his new employer, who was fully advised of plaintiff's rights to the goodwill of Beck's former business for its benefit, Russell H. Beck solicited his former customers, informing them that he was to be affiliated with defendant, The Cleveland Growers Market, thereby attempting to induce the customers with whom he once had done business when operating the business he sold to plaintiff, and, as a consequence, a great many of plaintiff's customers transferred their business to Russell H. Beck and his new employer, The Cleveland Growers Market, to plaintiff's damage.

The defendants Beck demurred to plaintiff's amended petition, stating as the grounds for the demurrer that the petition did not state a cause of action. It needs no citation of authority to declare that the demurrer admits for the purposes of the demurrer all of the well-pleaded allegations of the petition. By giving the allegations their most favorable interpretation in favor of the pleader, it must be concluded that the sale of the "business" must have included the "goodwill" it had generated under the management of the Becks. The sale was of the business as a going concern.

The inducement to enter into the contract, as pleaded, was made on behalf of the present owners, for their benefit. It was not an employment contract. We are not, therefore, concerned with the law dealing with restrictive covenants as a part of employment agreements. Nor is the question here presented, as argued in the briefs, one concerning a restrictive covenant not to compete with plaintiff after the sale of a business. No such claim is pleaded. The legal claim presented is whether or not the defendant, Russell H. Beck, and his new employer, may attempt to destroy or purposely minimize the value of the goodwill of a business which he has sold, by aggressive competition within a time necessarily needed by the plaintiff to obtain the benefits of the goodwill purchased under the assurances pleaded. There is no time alleged within which the defendants Beck agreed (by his promise to retire) not to interfere with the goodwill of the business sold. It must be concluded that a reasonable time within which to possess the advantages of the commercial relationship between the plaintiff and the former customers of the defendants Beck must pass before Beck can seek, without violating plaintiff's rights in the goodwill purchased, to do business with his former customers.

The meaning of the term "goodwill" is clearly set out in *Black's Law Dictionary* and is, in part, as follows:

> . . . The advantage or benefit which is acquired by an establishment, beyond the mere value of the capital, stocks, funds, or property employed therein, in consequence of the general public patronage and encouragement which it receives from the constant or habitual customers, on account of its local position. . . .

In the case of *Snyder Manufacturing Co.* v. *Snyder* (54 Ohio St. 86, on page 91, 43 N.E. 325, on page 326, 31 L.R.A. 657), the court in defining "goodwill" states:

> Without attempting an accurate or exhaustive definition of the good will of a business, it may be said that it practically consists of that favorable reputation it has established creating a disposition or inclination of persons to extend their patronage to the business on that account; and, as the business is always associated with the name under which it is conducted, the name becomes a part, and often an important part of its good will.

Also, in the case of *Lima Tel. & Tel.* v. *Public Utilities Comm. of Ohio* (98 Ohio St. 110, 120 N.E. 330), the court said that the goodwill value of any business enterprise is the value that results from the probability that old customers will continue to trade with the established concern.

It must be concluded that the goodwill transferred to a buyer is a property right that must be respected by the seller for a sufficient time to permit the buyer to make the business customers his own. In the case of *Suburban Ice Mfg. & Cold Storage Co.* v. *Mulvihill* (21 Ohio App. 438, 153 N.E. 204), the court said in the third paragraph of the syllabus:

> 3. Seller of ice business, including good will, cannot impair good will by soliciting business of old customers before buyer has time to make them his own.

And in the case of *Soeder* v. *Soeder,* (82 Ohio App. 71, 77 N.E.2d 474), the court said in the fourth paragraph of the syllabus:

> 4. While the vendor of a business with goodwill included in the sale cannot impair the goodwill by directly soliciting the old customers of the business before the buyer has had time to make them his own, nevertheless, a period of three years must be considered a sufficient time to attach goodwill to the buyer and make it his own.

The time which must be allowed a purchaser to make the customers of the purchased business "his own" is a question of fact for the determination of the jury or the court in the event a jury is waived on the allegations set out in the petition. Certainly to accept employment by a competitor who joins with him in active solicitation of his former customers that he had developed when he owned the business sold to the plaintiff, thus diminishing the value of the goodwill of such business, requires the defendant to show as a defense that sufficient time had elapsed under the surrounding circumstance for the plaintiff to make the customers his own unless the time elapsing between the sale and defendants subsequent acts can be said as a matter of law to be sufficient to protect the plaintiff to the extent necessary in the enjoyment of that which he purchased. The facts coming within "the circumstances to be considered" —in addition to the sale of a going business—is the fact that the defendant, Russell H. Beck, continued as an employee of plaintiff during the summer of 1960, striving to maintain the goodwill of plaintiff's business and then attempted to destroy it by accepting employment with plaintiff's next door competitor in 1961 by soliciting the same customers for his new employer.

The judgment of the trial court is, therefore, reversed as contrary to law and the cause is remanded to the trial court with instructions to overrule the demurrer and for further proceedings according to law.

McCook Window Co. v. Hardwood Door Corporation
202 N.E.2d 36 (Ill.) 1964

The defendant, seller, entered into an agreement that a corporation owned by him would not engage in wholesale manufacturing or selling of window frames within a 150-mile radius of plaintiff-buyer's plant so long as the buyer would be engaged in that business. The defendant did engage in manufacturing and plaintiff brought action. The lower court ordered that an injunction issue to enforce the agreement, and defendant appealed.

FRIEND, J. . . . The enforceability of a restraint ancillary to the sale of a business or property depends on the reasonableness of the restraint as to time and as to the extent of the territory; neither one is conclusive but both are important factors in the determination of the reasonableness of the restraint. Since the duration of the restraint is only one factor in deciding whether a restraint is reasonable, the provision for an indefinite duration of the restraint is not, by and of itself, sufficient to render the agreement unenforceable. In *Pelc* v. *Kulentis,* 257 Ill.App. 213, 218 (1930), the court said:

> It is to be noted that in each of the cases cited, the contract there in litigation contained a restriction unlimited as to time. While no opinion of a court of review in this State has turned upon the precise question, the general rule is that where a contract by which a person covenants not to engage in or carry on a particular business is limited as to territory and is reasonable and proper in other respects, the fact that the duration of the restriction is unlimited will not render the contract invalid, and this was true even according to the early rule. . . .

On the other hand, if the uncertain duration of the restraint is unreasonable under the circumstances of the particular case, the restraint will not be upheld. Stated differently, the rule is that the restraint, in order to be enforceable, must be limited to a reasonable time and to a reasonable territorial area, the reasonableness of the restraint being judged by the circumstances of the particular case.

The concept of reasonableness can be divided into three elements: the restraint as to time and as to territory must be necessary in its full extent for the protection of the purchaser, but must at the same time not be oppressive on the seller, and must not be injurious to the interests of the general public.

First, in order that the restraint be reasonable for the purchaser, it must protect him in the enjoyment and possession of the good will of the property transferred to him, but the protection lasts only as long as the good will transferred lasts and can cover only that territory to which the good will extends . . . and to which it might be reasonably expected to extend during the existence of the restraint. . . .

The good will of the business is primarily characterized by a personal relationship and specifically by the customer contacts which the former owner of the business was able to develop. This purchaser's need for protection exists so long as and covers as much territory as is necessary to prevent the seller from drawing away customers and suppliers from the purchaser if the seller were to re-enter the same business in the restricted territory. . . .

Protection against the potential loss of these assets is the true test to be applied in determining the necessary duration and territorial extent of the restraint.

Second, the restraint as to the seller, in order to be reasonable, must not be unduly harsh or oppressive. The duration and territorial extent of the restraint are unreasonable if they impose on the seller a hardship much greater, relatively speaking, than the ensuing advantage to the purchaser. Since the seller, in determining the sale price of a business, usually includes therein the value of its good will, which value is enhanced by the agreement not to compete, the showing of a hardship must be substantial.

Third, the restraint must be reasonable as to the general public.

In the case at bar paragraph 7 provides for a restraint that covers a 150-mile radius of plaintiff's plant in McCook, Illinois, for an indefinite duration—as long as plaintiff is engaged in the same business in the same area. Applying the foregoing principles to the case at bar, we believe that in the present circumstances paragraph 7 does not provide for a reasonable time and territorial limitation. The unreasonableness in this case stems from the fact that the restraints are greater than necessary for the protection of plaintiff, the purchaser of the stock. There is no showing that the restraints are reasonably related to the protection of plaintiff in the enjoyment and possession of the good will of the business transferred to it; no showing that the restraints provided for are necessary to prevent defendants from drawing away customers and suppliers from plaintiff if defendants were to resume the same business; no showing that plaintiff had customers as far away as 150 miles from its plant; no showing that if defendants resumed the wholesale manufacturing of exterior window frames at any time while plaintiff is engaged in the same business in the same area plaintiff would suffer more than if a stranger began to compete. We hold, therefore, that paragraph 7 of the agreement is void as an unreasonable restraint on trade. . . .

Decree affirmed in part and reversed in part with directions.

Vander Werf v. Zunica Realty Co.
208 N.E.2d 74 (Ill.) 1965

This was an action for a declaratory judgment to determine the plaintiff's (employee) rights under a restrictive covenant in an employment contract. He was employed by Zunica as a real estate salesman. The covenant provided:

> . . . in consideration for one dollar ($1.00) in hand paid, receipt of which is hereby acknowledged, and the further consideration of receiving aid, assistance, and certain commissions, to be determined from time to time, also access to certain confidential files and information belonging to said party of the first part and his associates, does hereby contract and agree, that upon the discontinuance of his position of salesman or of any other position in the organization of Zunica Realty Company that he may hold from time to time, he will not engage in the Real Estate Business Or Any Department Thereof Within two (2) years after leaving the employ of said party of the first part at any point within five miles of the present offices of Zunica Realty Company, at 824 E. Sibley Blvd., Dolton, Illinois, 27 West 159th St., Harvey, Illinois and 14322 Indiana Ave., Riverdale, Illinois. It is understood

that this agreement is to remain in force regardless of the reason for which the position of salesman is terminated.

The defendant cross-complained for an injunction which the lower court granted. Plaintiff appealed.

KLUCZYNSKI, J. . . . Defendant contends that it has a right to be protected from competition by a former employee when such protection is reasonably limited as to time and place, even though its business is not unique or special. It is conceded that the area and time limitations involved here are not unreasonable. However, the test is whether the agreement, under the circumstances of the particular case, is reasonably necessary for the protection of the employer's business. It is unenforceable when its purpose is the prevention of competition rather than the protection of the employer's business against competition by methods commonly regarded as improper and unfair.

Generally, how much protection is needed by an employer depends upon the legitimate interests for which he may claim protection. Legitimate interests is only another term to describe those "special circumstances" which render an employee's restraint necessary, but protection against ordinary competition itself is not sufficient. The authorities indicate that the "special circumstances" which have been controlling and important in determining the reasonableness of the restraint imposed generally involve elements of trade secrets and unfair dealings.

Wherever the courts have held that the employee did acquire trade secrets or confidential information, the restrictive covenant has been held reasonable.

In the *Solar Textiles* case a manufacturer of grille cloth was refused an injunction prohibiting a former salesman from selling grille cloth for a competitor. We there stated at pages 442-443 of 46 Ill.App.2d 436, 196 N.E.2d at page 723:

> The latest cases in Illinois do not deviate from the rule requiring the existence of some secrets of the trade or profession which the employer can legitimately prevent his former employee from divulging or using in competition with him. [Citing cases]. In *Brunner & Lay, Inc.* v. *Chapin*, 29 Ill. App.2d 161, 172 N.E.2d 652 (1961), the court held, in a similar situation to the one at bar, that it was an unreasonable protection for an employer, who was engaging in the manufacture and sale of pneumatic tool accessories, to prevent his employee, a sales manager, from taking a similar position with one of its competitors and soliciting its customers. The court, 29 Ill.App.2d at pages 165-166, 172 N.E.2d at page 654, enunciated the test as to whether an injunction could properly issue to restrain an employee from competing with his former employer, saying: "In all cases such as this, one has to ask one's self what are the interests of the employer that are to be protected, and against what is he entitled to have them protected. He is undoubtedly entitled to have his interest in trade secrets protected, such as secret processes of manufacture which may be of vast value. And that protection may be secured by restraining the employee from divulging these secrets or putting them to his own use. He is also entitled not to have his old customers, by solicitation or such other means, *enticed away from him.* [Italics ours]. But freedom from all competition per se apart from both these things, however lucrative it might be to him, he is not entitled to be protected against. He must be prepared to encounter that even at the hands of a former employee. . . . "

In the instant case defendant does not seriously contend that trade secrets, customer lists, or confidential information are involved. There is no allegation of irreparable harm in its counterclaim, and there was no evidence offered by it to show that plaintiff was soliciting or enticing its customers, or that plaintiff has taken real estate listings with him. In fact, defendant objected to questions put to plaintiff in an attempt to elicit testimony as to the manner in which plaintiff was obtaining his leads. There was, in addition, no showing by defendant that its methods of doing business were original or unique, and there was certainly no affirmative showing that plaintiff used defendant's listings or that he had solicited its former customers who, in the real estate trade, are usually transient, and not repeaters.

The drastic method of injunctive relief will not lie to deprive a man of his right to work where no irreparable harm is being done, and where enforcement of the restrictive covenant is unnecessary to protect the legitimate business interests of his employer. The protection sought by defendant in the instant case does not meet the standard of reasonableness, but on the contrary, the restrictive covenant has the effect of preventing competition per se and depriving plaintiff of following his trade and earning a livelihood. We hold the restrictive covenant unenforceable for the reasons herein given and that the lower court erred in dismissing plaintiff's complaint and issuing the injunction. The judgment is therefore reversed.

Reversed.

Lloyd v. Gutgsell

124 N.W.2d 198 (Neb.) 1963

The plaintiffs purchased a trailer from defendant on an installment contract. The "time price" was computed by applying a certain schedule of rates to the cash price. The question was whether the resulting figure was interest. The plaintiffs claimed usury and sought to cancel the conditional sale contract and the note they had given. The lower court ruled for plaintiffs and defendant appealed.

SPENCER, J. . . . It is apparent on the face of exhibit No. 1 (conditional sale contract) that we have a finance transaction, and that usurious interest is being exacted. As we said in *General Motors Acceptance Corp.* v. *Mackrill,* 175 Neb. 631, 122 N.W.2d 742, regardless of the term used, if the result is a charge for the loan of money or for the forbearance of a debt, the result is interest.

Defendant argues that this transaction was an installment sale and that the usury rules are not applicable to installment sales. With this broad statement we must disagree. We have repeatedly said that in considering whether such a transaction is a time sale made in good faith or a loan, the court will look through the form and examine the substance. Here exhibit No. 1 clearly discloses the nature of the transaction, and we find it to be a scheme or artifice to avoid the effect of the usury statute. Unless this is true, usury could be avoided in every case by placing the transaction in the mere form of a time sale contract. Our law is well settled that if a purported time sale is in fact a loan, and the loan is in violation of the Installment Loan Act, the penalties of the act apply to it.

There seems to be an impression that if a cash price is quoted and the buyer is unable to pay cash, it is then possible to apply a certain schedule of rates or charges to the cash price in order to determine the time sale price, the difference being denominated a time price differential. It is possible to do so if the resulting charge does not exceed 9 percent simple interest. If it does, we have a usurious transaction. Where a time sale price is determined by applying a certain schedule of rates or charges to the cash price, the resulting product is interest. This is merely a sale for a cash price, with the difference between the money the buyer has and what he needs being financed. When we look through the form, can we come to any other conclusion but the one that the difference between the price and what the buyer finally pays is the cost of carrying the balance of the cash price? To put it another way, the charge is for the forbearance to collect the full cash price, or for the use of money. A rose is still a rose though we may label it a violet. This charge, regardless of its label, is interest. See *General Motors Acceptance Corp.* v. *Mackrill, supra.* A transaction handled in this manner is essentially a loan to finance the balance of the cash purchase price, and if payable in installments must meet the requirements of the law covering finance transactions.

We specifically pointed to this conclusion when we said in *State ex rel. Beck* v. *Associates Discount Corp.* 168 Neb. 298, 96 N.W.2d 55: "It is not a time sale if a car dealer, in selling a car, actually agrees with the buyer that he will finance (take care of) the balance of the cash purchase price agreed upon and does so, either directly or through others, even though he obtains the schedule of payments and the total amount thereof from a rate chart furnished by a finance company or obtains that information from a finance company by calling its office and then fully informs the buyer of the amount he will be required to pay and the terms thereof. Such a transaction would be a loan to finance the balance of the cash purchase price and if payable in installments must meet the requirements of the statutes relating thereto. And the fact that the buyer knew the terms and provisions of such loan at the time it was made and voluntarily entered into it would not have the effect of waiving the illegality of any provision thereof, if such provision was actually in violation of any of the inhibitory provisions of the installment loan statutes, for the purpose of the Legislature in enacting such laws was, as a matter of public policy under its police powers, to regulate the lenders of money on installment loans as a protection to those of the general public who find it necessary to borrow money on that basis."

Affirmed as modified.

Sherwood & Roberts-Yakima, Inc. v. Leach

409 P.2d 160 (Wash.) 1966

Lifetone Electronics, Inc., sold radio intercoms and fire alarm systems. Defendants purchased a system on a conditional sale contract with the assurance that it would not cost them anything as they would receive a "commission" on sales made to persons whose names were given to the salesman by the plaintiffs. Defendants signed a contract, and the contract was assigned to plaintiff who brought this action to collect. The trial court rendered summary judgment for defendants and plaintiff appealed.

LANGENBACH, J. . . . Respondents took a chance on whether they could get something for nothing. This chance permeates the entire scheme of referral selling. This court holds that the referral selling scheme is a lottery.

Since the referral selling agreement is contrary to the terms and policy of RCW 9.59.010, it is illegal and unenforceable, and when an instrument is intimately connected with an illegal one, the former becomes tainted with that illegality and is likewise unenforceable.

Here, the referral agreement and the conditional sale contract were all part of one transaction. The Lifetone salesman represented to respondents that the conditional sale contract obligation would easily be paid from "commissions earned" from the referral selling agreement, and Mr. Leach so intended to pay the conditional sale contract. It is clear respondents would have a good defense against Lifetone. It also appears that they have a good defense against appellant. The appellant, as assignee of a conditional sale contract, takes the contract subject to all defenses.

Appellant, however, argues that it is entitled to maintain this action on either of two grounds: (1) it was not in *pari delicto* with respondents, or (2) it can establish its case without relying on an illegal transaction.

A person who is not in *pari delicto* can maintain an action based on an illegal contract. Appellant bases its argument on the facts that it was not a party to the transaction; it did not have knowledge of any agreement between respondents and Lifetone until after the agreements were made; and respondents have the equipment.

The fact that respondents have the equipment is not material. In an action to recover on an illegal contract, this court leaves the parties where it finds them whether or not the situation is unequal as to the parties. The facts, that appellant was not a party to the transaction and that it did not have knowledge of any agreement between Lifetone and respondents until after the agreements were made, are material. However, they must be considered with all the undisputed facts and circumstances.

At the outset, it should be noted that, in order for Lifetone successfully to employ its referral selling scheme, a finance company participation is required; that is, Lifetone must get its money before discontinuing sales. Accordingly, before Lifetone made any sales, it contacted appellant and explained the selling scheme. Appellant agreed to finance the contracts. In fact, Lifetone and respondents agreed at the time of contracting that the conditional sale contract would be assigned to appellant. It is hard to see that appellant is not in *pari delicto* with respondents; it was knowingly an integral part of the referral selling scheme. This fact substantially outweighs any innocence that may be otherwise evidenced by the facts that appellant was not a formal party to the sale contract and that appellant did not have knowledge of this particular transaction at the time of contracting.

Appellant, understanding the referral selling scheme, required respondents to agree that the obligation to appellant would be paid notwithstanding whether any commissions were paid under the referral selling agreement. This is the basis of appellant's next argument, that it can establish its case without relying on the illegal transaction because either there was independent consideration or respondents are estopped.

> An agreement will be enforced, even if it is incidentally or indirectly connected with an illegal transaction, provided it is supported by an independent consideration, or if plaintiff will not require the aid of the illegal transaction to make out his case. . . .

Respondents' promise to pay appellant the conditional sale contract notwithstanding the payment of any commissions was not supported by consideration. It was a mere naked promise. The conditional sale contract and the referral selling agreement had been executed prior to this time and the personal property and equipment therein described had already been received and installed in respondents' home.

Appellant's argument of estoppel or waiver is without legal basis.

> The nonenforcement of illegal contracts is a matter of common public interest, and a party to such contract cannot waive his right to set up the defense of illegality in an action thereon by the other party. . . . Validity cannot be given to an illegal contract through any principle of estoppel. . . .

The judgment is affirmed.

Campbell Soup Co. v. Wentz
172 F.2d 80 (1949)

Goodrich, C. J. These are appeals from judgments of the District Court denying equitable relief to the buyer under a contract for the sale of carrots. The defendants . . . are the contract sellers. . . .

The transactions which raise the issues may be briefly summarized. On June 21, 1947, Campbell Soup Company (Campbell), a New Jersey corporation, entered into a written contract with George B. Wentz and Harry T. Wentz, who are Pennsylvania farmers, for delivery by the Wentzes to Campbell of all the Chantenay red-cored carrots to be grown on fifteen acres of the Wentz farm during the 1947 season. Where the contract was entered into does not appear. The contract provides, however, for delivery of the carrots at the Campbell plant in Camden, New Jersey. The prices specified in the contract ranged from $23 to $30 per ton according to the time of delivery. The contract price for January, 1948 was $30 a ton.

The Wentzes harvested approximately 100 tons of carrots from the fifteen acres covered by the contract. Early in January, 1948, they told a Campbell representative that they would not deliver their carrots at the contract price. The market price at that time was at least $90 per ton, and Chantenay red-cored carrots were virtually unobtainable. The Wentzes then sold approximately 62 tons of their carrots to the defendant Lojeski, a neighboring farmer. Lojeski resold about 58 tons on the open market, approximately half to Campbell and the balance to other purchasers.

On January 9, 1948, Campbell, suspecting that Lojeski was selling it "contract carrots," refused to purchase any more, and instituted these suits against the Wentz brothers and Lojeski to enjoin further sale of the contract carrots to others, and to compel specific performance of the contract. The trial court denied equitable relief. We agree with the result reached, but on a different ground from that relied upon by the District Court.

. . . A party may have specific performance of a contract for the sale of chattels if the legal remedy is inadequate. Inadequacy of the legal remedy is necessarily a matter to be determined by an examination of the facts in each particular instance.

We think that on the question of adequacy of the legal remedy the case is one appropriate for specific performance. . . . We think if this were all that was involved in the case specific performance should have been granted.

The reason that we shall affirm instead of reversing with an order for specific performance is found in the contract itself. We think it is too hard a bargain and too one-sided an agreement to entitle the plaintiff to relief in a court of conscience. For each individual grower the agreement is made by filling in names and quantity and price on a printed form furnished by the buyer. This form has quite obviously been drawn by skillful draftsmen with the buyer's interests in mind.

Paragraph 2 provides for the manner of delivery. Carrots are to have their stalks cut off and be in clean sanitary bags or other containers approved by Campbell. This paragraph concludes with a statement that Campbell's determination of conformance with specifications shall be conclusive.

The defendants attack this provision as unconscionable. We do not think that it is, standing by itself. We think that the provision is comparable to the promise to perform to the satisfaction of another and that Campbell would be held liable if it refused carrots which did in fact conform to the specifications.

The next paragraph allows Campbell to refuse carrots in excess of twelve tons to the acre. The next contains a covenant by the grower that he will not sell carrots to anyone else except the carrots rejected by Campbell nor will he permit anyone else to grow carrots on his land. Paragraph 10 provides liquidated damages to the extent of $50 per acre for any breach by the grower. There is no provision for liquidated or any other damages for breach of contract by Campbell.

The provision of the contract which we think is the hardest is paragraph 9, set out in the margin. It will be noted that Campbell is excused from accepting carrots under certain circumstances. But even under such circumstances the grower, while he cannot say Campbell is liable for failure to take the carrots, is not permitted to sell them elsewhere unless Campbell agrees. This is the kind of provision which the late Francis H. Bohlen would call "carrying a good joke too far." What the grower may do with his product under the circumstances set out is not clear. He has covenanted not to store it anywhere except on his own farm and also not to sell to anybody else.

We are not suggesting that the contract is illegal. Nor are we suggesting any excuse for the grower in this case who has deliberately broken an agreement entered into with Campbell. We do think, however, that a party who has offered and succeeded in getting an agreement as tough as this one is, should not come to a chancellor and ask court help in the enforcement of its terms. That equity does not enforce unconscionable bargains is too well established to require elaborate citation.

The plaintiff argues that the provisions of the contract are separable. We agree that they are, but do not think that decisions separating out certain provisions from illegal contracts are in point here. As already said, we do not suggest that this contract is illegal. All we say is that the sum total of its provisions drives too hard a bargain for a court of conscience to assist. . . .

The judgments will be affirmed.

Williams v. Walker-Thomas Furniture Company

350 F.2d 445 (1965)

Plaintiff, Walker-Thomas Furniture Company operated a retail furniture store in the District of Columbia. During the period from 1957 to 1962 the defendant purchased a number of household items from Walker-Thomas, for which payment was to be made in installments. The terms of each purchase were contained in a printed form contract which set forth the value of the purchased item and purported to lease the item to defendant for a stipulated monthly rent payment. The title would remain in Walker-Thomas until the total of all the monthly payments made equaled the stated value of the item, at which time purchaser could take title. In the event of a default in the payment of any monthly installment, Walker-Thomas could repossess the item.

The contract further provided that

> the amount of each periodical installment payment to be made by (purchaser) to the Company under this present lease shall be inclusive of and not in addition to the amount of each installment payment to be made by (purchaser) under such prior leases, bills or accounts; *and all payments now and hereafter made by (purchaser) shall be credited pro rata on all outstanding leases, bills and accounts due the Company by (purchaser) at the time each such payment is made.*

The effect of this provision was to keep a balance due on every item purchased until the balance due on all items, whenever purchased, was liquidated. As a result, the debt incurred at the time of purchase of each item was secured by the right to repossess all the items previously purchased by the same purchaser, and each new item purchased automatically became subject to a security interest arising out of the previous dealings.

On April 17, 1962, Williams bought a stereo set of stated value of $514.95. She defaulted shortly thereafter, and plaintiff sought to replevy all the items purchased since December, 1957. (At the time of this purchase her account showed a balance of $164 still owing from her prior purchases. The total of all the purchases made over the years in question came to $1,800. The total payments amounted to $1,400.) The Court of General Sessions granted judgment for plaintiff. The District of Columbia Court of Appeals affirmed, and an appeal was taken to the Court of Appeals.

WRIGHT, J. . . . Appellant's principal contention, rejected by both the trial and the appellate courts below, is that these contracts, or at least some of them, are unconscionable and, hence, not enforceable. In its opinion . . . the District of Columbia Court of Appeals explained its rejection of this contention as follows:

> Appellant's second argument presents a more serious question. The record reveals that prior to the last purchase appellant had reduced the balance in her account

to $164. The last purchase, a stereo set, raised the balance due to $678. Significantly, at the time of this and the preceding purchases, appellee was aware of appellant's financial position. The reverse side of the stereo contract listed the name of appellant's social worker and her $218 monthly stipend from the government. Nevertheless, with full knowledge that appellant had to feed, clothe and support both herself and seven children on this amount, appellee sold her a $514 stereo set.

We cannot condemn too strongly appellee's conduct. It raises serious questions of sharp practice and irresponsible business dealings. A review of the legislation in the District of Columbia affecting retail sales and the pertinent decisions of the highest court in this jurisdiction disclose, however, no ground upon which this court can declare the contracts in question contrary to public policy. . . .

We do not agree that the court lacked the power to refuse enforcement to contracts found to be unconscionable. In other jurisdictions, it has been held as a matter of common law that unconscionable contracts are not enforceable. While no decision of this court so holding has been found, the notion that an unconscionable bargain should not be given full enforcement is by no means novel. In *Scott* v. *United States* . . . the Supreme Court stated:

> . . . If a contract be unreasonable and unconscionable, but not void for fraud, a court of law will give to the party who sues for its breach damages, not according to its letter, but only such as he is equitably entitled to. . . .

Since we have never adopted or rejected such a rule, the question here presented is actually one of first impression.

Congress has recently enacted the Uniform Commercial Code, which specifically provides that the court may refuse to enforce a contract which it finds to be unconscionable at the time it was made. (28 D.C. Code 2-302). . . . The enactment of this section, which occurred subsequent to the contracts here in suit, does not mean that the common law of the District of Columbia was otherwise at the time of enactment, nor does it preclude the court from adopting a similar rule in the exercise of its powers to develop the common law for the District of Columbia. In fact, in view of the absence of prior authority on the point, we consider the congressional adoption of 2-302 persuasive authority for following the rationale of the cases from which the section is explicitly derived. (See Comment, 2-302, Uniform Commercial Code (1962). Compare Note, 45 Va.L.Rev. 583, 590 (1959), where it is predicted that the rule of 2-302 will be followed by analogy in cases which involve contracts not specifically covered by the section.) Accordingly; we hold that where the element of unconscionability is present at the time a contract is made, the contract should not be enforced.

Unconscionability has generally been recognized to include an absence of meaningful choice on the part of one of the parties together with contract terms which are unreasonably favorable to the other party. Whether a meaningful choice is present in a particular case can only be determined by consideration of all the circumstances surrounding the transaction. In many cases the meaningfulness of the choice is negated by a gross inequality of bargaining power. The manner in which the contract was entered is also relevant to this consideration. Did each party to the contract, considering his obvious education or lack of it, have a reasonable opportunity to understand the terms of the contract, or were the important terms hidden in a maze of fine print and minimized by deceptive sales practices? Ordinarily, one who signs an agreement without full knowledge of its terms might be held to assume the risk that he has entered a one-sided bargain. But when a party of little bargaining power, and hence little real choice, signs a commercially unreasonable contract with little or no knowledge of its terms, it is hardly likely that his consent, or even an objective manifestation of his consent, was ever given to all the terms. In such a case the usual rule that the terms of the agreement are not to be questioned should be abandoned and the court should consider whether the terms of the contract are so unfair that enforcement should be withheld.

In determining reasonableness or fairness, the primary concern must be with the terms of the contract considered in light of the circumstances existing when the contract was made. The test is not simple, nor can it be mechanically applied. The terms are to be considered "in the light of the general commercial background and the commercial needs of the particular trade or case." (Comment, Uniform Commercial Code 2-307.) Corbin suggests the test as being whether the terms are "so extreme as to appear unconscionable according to the mores and business practices of the time and place. . . . " We think this formulation correctly states the test to be applied in those cases where no meaningful choice was exercised upon entering the contract.

Because the trial court and the appellate court did not feel that enforcement could be refused, no findings were made on the possible unconscionability of the contracts in these cases. Since the record is not sufficient for our deciding the issue as a matter of law, the cases must be remanded to the trial court for further proceedings.

So ordered.

Troutman v. Southern Railway Co.

296 F. Supp. 963. (1968)

Plaintiff brought action against defendant railway for services in expediting action by the Interstate Commerce Commission on application to purchase another railway and for his services in procuring abandonment of the I.C.C. order on reduction in grain rates. Defendant railway moved for a summary judgment which was denied.

EDENFIELD, J. . . . . The right of plaintiff to claim compensation for services rendered in the "grain rate case" presents a more complex question.

In this regard it may be noted that the practice of seeking personal and political favors from kings and public officials is a sport as old as government itself—and, within certain limits, there appears to be nothing wrong with it. It is sanctioned by history, and in one instance is virtually invited by the last clause of the First Amendment to the Federal Constitution. It has built railroads and launched fleets. In Spain it is reputed to have made financially possible the discovery of this continent. In England, Spain and France, to some degree and in one way or another, it led to the founding of every colony in the New World. But in one respect, personal or political influence is like virtue; it must not be sold. And if it is sold, or even contracted for, the courts may not and will not enforce the bargain.

This much is clear. But what is political influence? To simply furnish facts or law or even theories to an official to be considered on their merits is clearly not prohibited. To seek action based on facts so furnished may or may not be. To seek favors irrespective of the facts clearly is. In this area, the line between what is permissible and what is not is frequently dim. Often a decision has to be based on inference alone, and the question is usually one of fact. Numerous authorities might be cited, but since the court has decided that on this point the motion for summary judgment must be denied in any event, only a few will suffice.

Thus, in stating the existence of such a public policy, the Supreme Court of the United States . . . has said:

> Agreements upon pecuniary considerations, or the promise of them, to influence the conduct of officers charged with duties affecting the public interest, or with duties of a fiduciary capacity to private parties, are against the policy of the State to secure fidelity in the discharge of all such duties and are void. . . .

The Georgia authorities . . . hold, in substance, that contracts to influence government officials are not void merely upon an appearance before the official to make arguments upon the merits of a question, and that only the elements of "personal influence" and "sinister means" will void the contract and deny it enforcement. . . .

Finally, see *Old Dominion Transportation Co.* v. *Hamilton,* 146 Va. 594, 131 S.E. 850, 857, 46 A.L.R. 186, where the Court said:

> . . . [E]ven if the jury believed from the evidence that either personal or political influence was exerted by the plaintiff, but merely to secure a hearing from the city authorities, and an opportunity to present the matter in issue upon its merits, and that when such opportunity was secured the case was presented upon its merits and upon its merits alone, then in that event the jury should have been told that the plaintiff was entitled to a judgment.

Here, the conduct of plaintiff might very well support a strong inference that plaintiff was seeking to influence the President to influence his brother to take an action favorable to plaintiff's client. A jury may draw such an inference, but on summary judgment this court cannot do so. On summary judgment, inferences are for juries, not for the court.

Under the facts, many questions remain unanswered. Unquestionably, the plaintiff presented memorandums of fact and law to the President. Did he present the matter solely on its merits, or did he ask the President, for some other reason, to intercede with his brother, who was Attorney General? Or did he do both? What was he employed to do? All of these questions will have to be submitted to a jury under proper instructions. See the instruction recommended by the Virginia Court of Appeals in *Old Dominion Trans. Co.* v. *Hamilton, supra.*

As to this aspect of the case, the motion for summary judgment is denied.

CHAPTER 12
REVIEW QUESTIONS AND PROBLEMS

1. *A* sold his grocery store to *B* and agreed not to compete with him directly or indirectly for a specified time. *A* then began the construction

of a shopping center building nearby with the intention to lease space in it for a grocery store. Does *A's* action constitute a violation of the agreement?

2. *A* lost $9,000 in a card game with *B.* He brought action against *B* to recover this amount and asserted that *B* had used a "marked deck." Should *A* recover?

3. *A,* landlord, brought an action to evict *B,* tenant, from a rented house for nonpayment of rent. *B* contended that *A* could not bring action because the premises were uninhabitable in violation of Housing Code regulations. Is *B's* contention correct?

4. *A* was employed by *B* under a contract that provided that he would not compete upon termination of employment and that he should pay *B* $5,000 as liquidated damages if he violated the covenant. Would the court enforce this agreement?

5. *A* had been employed by *B* under a contract that provided that he would not enter into a competitive business for two years after termination of employment and that he would not contact any of *B's* customers. *A* requested the court for a determination of his rights under the contract. What determination would a court be likely to make?

6. The ABC Lumber Company prepared plans and specifications for a building to be erected by *B. B* refused to pay for the architectural services performed by ABC Lumber Company, and the company brought an action to recover for its services. Should ABC Lumber Company succeed?

7. *A* went to XYZ Loan Service Company to arrange for a $25 loan. The company informed *A* that there would be a $13 charge for arranging the loan. The money was actually loaned by a company in which the XYZ Company had a substantial interest. Is *A* liable for $38?

8. *A* developed a self-service drive-in food establishment system and granted franchises throughout the country. *B* obtained a franchise and agreed that he would not set up any competing business but would limit himself to the franchised operation. *B* established another eating place very similar to the one franchised. *A* seeks to enjoin *B* from operating the competitive drive-in. Should he succeed?

9. *X* Council of the Boy Scouts of America admitted boys to its summer camp program only if the boys and their parents signed an agreement releasing the camp of all liability for injury even though camp officials were careless. *F* was injured and brought suit. Is the exculpatory clause illegal?

10. Three doctors formed a medical clinic. As a part of the agreement forming the clinic each doctor agreed that if he left the clinic, he would not practice medicine for five years in the county in which the clinic operates. *X* left the clinic and the others sought to enforce the agreement. *X* contended that the agreement was illegal as contrary to public policy, since there was a shortage of doctors in the county. What result?

Form of the Agreement

2-71. Introduction. As a general rule, contracts may be oral or written or may result from conduct of the parties. Except for the statutory exceptions many of which are discussed in this chapter, an oral contract is just as valid and enforceable as a written contract. However, there are obvious advantages to written contracts over oral contracts. For example, it is much easier to establish the existence and terms of a written contract, since the contract is its own proof of terms. The terms of oral agreements must be established by testimony, and the testimony is often conflicting. Moreover, as a general rule the terms of a written contract cannot be varied by oral evidence. This rule, known as the parol evidence rule, is discussed in the next section.

By statute it is required that some contracts be evidenced by a writing before they are legally enforceable. These provisions, which are usually contained in legislation known as the statute of frauds and perjuries, are based on the recognition that there is a need for written evidence of the existence of certain types of contracts because of their susceptibility to fraudulent proofs and perjured testimony. The various types of contracts covered by the statute of frauds will be discussed later in this chapter.

A few states also have statutes which require that certain types of contracts be executed with special formality. These statutes require a seal on contracts involving land and may require that the signatures of the parties be acknowledged before a notary public. Some statutes, such as those relating to wage assignments by an employee, require that a contract of assignment be on a sheet of paper which is separate from other contracts to which the assignment is related. The purpose of this type of statute is to protect a wage earner against a blanket assignment of his wages without his being fully aware of the import of his action.

The statute of frauds is the basic legislation dealing with the requirement of a writing, but there are a variety of other statutes requiring that special types of agreements be evidenced by a writing. These vary substantially from one state to another. Some of the more significant statutes require a writing in the case of negotiable instruments and indorsements thereof, insurance contracts, listing agreements with real estate brokers, and promises to pay debts which have been discharged in bankruptcy. Such contracts have been singled out for the same reasons that have caused enactment of the statute of frauds—to remove the possibility of perjured testimony which could establish a nonexistent contract and to produce certainty where that element is of special importance.

Another aspect relating to the form of the agreement involves the situation in which an informal agreement is reached with the understanding that the parties will subsequently execute and sign a formal instrument. This raises the question of whether the informal agreement is binding until the document is prepared and signed. The mere fact that a subsequent formal writing was contemplated does not prevent the informal agreement from being enforceable.[1] The parties, however, could stipulate that a signed writing would be a condition to enforceability.

2-72. The Parol Evidence Rule. The parol evidence rule prevents the introduction of oral testimony to alter or vary the terms of a written agreement. Thus, a party to a contract or other witness may not introduce testimony about oral statements of the parties prior to or contemporaneous with the written agreement if such statements are in conflict with the written agreement. The written contract is the only evidence of the agreement, since all matters which were agreed upon prior to its execution are presumed to have been incorporated or integrated in the written agreement. All negotiations and oral understandings are said to have merged in the agreement.

Applications of the parol evidence rule are predicated on this concept of merger and on general principles of equity. There are, however, exceptions to the rule, which allow the introduction of oral testimony for certain purposes. For example, parol evidence is admissible to establish modifications agreed upon subsequent to the execution of the written agreement and also to establish cancellation of the contract by mutual agreement. If the contract is one of those within the purview of the statute of frauds, in most states, any modification or cancellation must be in writing.

Several other exceptions to the parol evidence rule exist; these find their basis in equity, good conscience, and common sense. Evidence of fraudulent misrepresentation, lack of delivery of an instrument when delivery is required to give it effect, and errors in drafting or reducing the contract to writing are admissible under various exceptions to the rule. Also, oral evidence is allowed to clarify the terms of an ambiguous contract.

Sellers of items such as appliances, mobile homes, and automobiles often include in their contracts a provision which limits any warranties or servicing to that provided by the manufacturer. Such a provision is designed to exclude any claims by the customers that special promises or warranties have been

---

[1] H. B. Zachry Company v. O'Brien, page 267

made to them. The courts have held that written disclaimers further buttress the parol evidence rule in excluding the evidence of oral warranties.[2]

The Uniform Commercial Code contains provisions relating to the parol evidence rule in cases involving construction or interpretation of an agreement for the sale of goods. The Code recognizes that terms of an agreement may be explained or supplemented by a prior course of dealing between buyer and seller, by usage of trade, or by the course of performance. Thus, in the latter situation, if a contract of sale involves repeated occasions of performance by either party with knowledge of the nature of the performance and opportunity for objection to it by the other, any course of performance of the agreement accepted or acquiesced in, without objection by the other party is relevant in determining the meaning of the agreement. If there is an inconsistency, express terms will prevail over an interpretation based on the course of performance, and the course of performance will prevail over an interpretation predicated upon either the course of dealing or the usage of trade. In addition, the Code allows the admission of oral evidence of consistent additional terms unless the court finds the writing to have been intended as a complete and exclusive statement of the terms of the agreement.

While application of the parol evidence rule is a problem for judges and lawyers, businessmen should recognize the importance of the protection afforded them in connection with their written agreements by this rule.

THE STATUTE OF FRAUDS

2-73. Historical Development.   In 1677 An Act for Prevention of Frauds and Perjuries was enacted in England. This Statute was designed to prevent fraud by excluding from consideration by the courts legal actions on certain contracts unless there was written evidence of the agreement signed by the defendant or his duly authorized agent. The object of this Statute was stated to be: "the prevention of many fraudulent practices, which are commonly endeavored to be upheld by perjury and subornation of perjury." While the title "Statute of Frauds" has been perpetuated, "Statutes which Require Written Contracts or Other Satisfactory Evidence of Their Existence" might be more descriptive.

The need for these statutes arose out of the peculiar rules of evidence used by English courts during the seventeenth century. A party was not allowed to testify in his own behalf, and lawsuits were frequently tried with either professional witnesses or with testimony of friends of the parties. Perjury was commonplace, and in the law of contracts it soon became apparent that defendants were at a distinct disadvantage because of the difficulty of proving a negative —that no contract in fact had been made. For example, suppose that A sued B and alleged that B orally agreed to sell certain land for £100. C testified that he heard B agree to the sale. Would it help B any to have D testify that D didn't hear B enter into the agreement? Obviously not. This difficulty was overcome by requiring written evidence that a contract actually had been entered into in contracts of substantial importance. Since the purpose of the

---

[2] Hathaway v. Ray's Motor Sales, page 268

statute was to prevent fraud and the use of perjured testimony, it became known as the statute of frauds and perjuries.

The seventeenth-century parliament singled out those contracts in which there appeared to be the greatest danger of false testimony and those transactions which were regarded as the most important in that day and place. Obviously, a legislative body preparing such statutes today would likely approach the problem quite differently. But the modern statutes are basically the same as the originals except for substantial modernization under the Uniform Commercial Code.

The seventeenth-century Statute had many sections, only two of which relate directly to contracts. The seventeenth section of the original Statute related to those for the sale of goods. And Section 4 of the original Statute provided, in effect, that the following were not actionable unless evidenced by a written memorandum or note thereof, signed by the party to be charged: (1) contracts to be liable for another person's debts; (2) contracts involving real property and (3) agreements that cannot be performed within one year from the date of making. Of lesser significance were agreements made upon the consideration of marriage and special promises by the personal representative of a deceased to pay claims against the estate of the deceased out of such representative's own estate.

All states have enacted a statute of frauds in essentially the same format as the early English Statute. Although the rules of evidence which created the need for the Statute have long since been changed to allow parties to contracts to testify, the statute of frauds has remained essentially intact. Today, Section 4 of the statute may be used as a defense, even though there is no factual dispute as to the existence of the contract or to its terms. A contract that requires a writing may come into existence at the time of the oral agreement, but it is not enforceable until written evidence of the agreement is available. The agreement is valid in every respect except for the lack of proper evidence of its existence. The statute creates an immunity from suit for the breach of oral contracts if such contracts are encompassed by its provisions.

The Code retains the statute of frauds concepts of Section 17 but drastically limits their application, thus taking a major step toward modernization of this old English Statute. A substantial argument, however, could be made for repeal of the statute of frauds in light of present-day trial techniques, such as discovery procedures. The sections which follow discuss the modern version of the classes of contracts covered by the statute of frauds.

2-74. Promise to Answer for the Debt of Another.   To be within the provisons of the statute, a promise to answer for the "debt, default, or miscarriage" of another must be a *secondary* promise. If it is a primary promise it is not within the statute and is enforceable even though oral.[3] For example, *P* wishes to purchase goods on credit from *C* but does not have a financial standing satisfactory to *C. S,* a friend of *P,* promises *C* that if he will sell on credit to *P,* he *(S)* will pay if *P* fails to do so. On the strength of this promise *C* sells to *P* on credit. Must the promise made by *S* to *C* be in writing in order to be enforceable? Yes, the promise comes within the statute, since it is a promise to be responsible for the debt of another. Note that on these facts the primary

---

[3] Finch v. Kirkwood, page 269

liability is on *P;* the liability of *S* is *secondary*—to pay only in the event that *P* fails to do so. Suppose that the hypothetical facts are changed so that *S* says to *C,* "Sell and deliver goods to *P,* and I will pay for them." In this situation *S* is assuming primary liability, and it would appear that *C* is not extending credit to *P.* Hence, the oral promise by *S* is binding upon him, and the statute of frauds is no defense. Many variations in the fact patterns can arise, but in general the common question is whether or not the promissor (*S* in this case) is assuming sole and direct responsibility or whether his obligation is collateral to that of the principal debtor.

An agreement that has for its object the substitution of one debtor for another does not fall within the statute, and no writing is required. Thus, if *A* says to *Y,* "If you will release *B* from his liability to you, I will pay the same," and *Y* consents, although made orally, the agreement is binding because it is a primary promise of *A* and is not secondary to *B's* promise.

When a third party agrees to become responsible for the default or debt of another because of some pecuniary advantage he may gain from the transaction, no writing is required. Thus, an oral guaranty by a *del credere* agent— a consignee who sells consigned goods on credit, but who guarantees to the consignor that the buyers will pay for the goods purchased—is enforceable. Since the agent obtains a commission for selling the merchandise, his pecuniary interest in the consignment disposes of the necessity of a writing, and if the purchaser fails to pay, the consignor may collect from the consignee on the oral guaranty.

2-75. Contracts Involving Real Property.   Contracts involving interests in land have always been considered important by the law; therefore, it is logical that such contracts are covered by the statute of frauds. The statute requires a writing for a contract creating or transferring any interest in land. In addition to contracts involving a sale of an entire interest, the statute is applicable to contracts involving interests for a person's lifetime, called life estate; to mortgages; to easements; and to leases for a period in excess of one year.

The section of the statute under consideration requires a writing in contracts for real property—land and those things affixed thereto. What is the status of such things as standing timber, buildings upon the land, minerals, growing crops, and the like? Is an oral contract to sell timber or to sell a building that is to be moved to another site enforceable? The general rule is that these items are real property if the title to them is to pass to the buyer before the timber is cut or the building is removed; they are personal property if title to them passes subsequently. The Code provides that a contract for the sale of timber, minerals, and the like or for a structure or its materials to be removed from realty is a contract for the sale of goods if they are to be severed by the seller. If the buyer is to sever them, the contract affects and involves land and is subject to the real estate provisions of the statute of frauds. The Code also provides that a contract for the sale apart from the land of growing crops or things other than timber or minerals attached to realty and capable of severance without material harm to the land is a contract for the sale of goods, whether the subject matter is to be severed by the buyer or by the seller, even though it forms part of the realty at the time of contracting, and the parties can by identification effect a present sale before severance.

The rule that oral contracts involving real estate are not enforceable is a harsh one, and the strict application of it may result in inequities. What, for example, should the result be if one of the parties to an oral land contract has substantially changed his position in reliance upon the contract; what if he has paid part of the purchase price? Does part performance of the oral contract negate the writing requirement? It would seem that if adequate and convincing proof of the contract is available, such evidence could take the place of the required writing. The party who has rendered part performance in an oral land contract and is confronted with refusal to transfer by the seller, who asserts the statute of frauds as a defense, has two potential remedies: (1) to obtain restitution of money paid or the value of his performance if it is nonmonetary, or (2) specific performance of the oral contract. Courts allow a buyer to recover payments made on the purchase price when the seller refuses to perform. The same is true if the buyer's performance is a payment in property or services —he can recover the property or value thereof, or the value of his services.

Despite the statute of frauds, a court of equity will grant specific performance to a purchaser if there has been a substantial part performance by him which stemmed from reliance on the oral contract, provided the legal remedy of restitution of the value of his part performance is so inadequate that justice could only be served by requiring specific performance.

What conduct on the buyer's part constitutes "substantial performance," and when is the legal remedy of restitution not an adequate remedy? [4] These two questions are so closely interwoven that to answer one is to answer the other. It is clear that the transaction is taken out of the statute if the buyer has taken possession, paid all or part of the price, and made valuable improvements. However, a lesser part performance will also take the contract out of the statute. If the buyer takes possession and pays part of the price, there is good evidence of a contract, and if he also pays taxes and mortgage payments, specific performance is warranted. Payment of the price, standing alone, is not a basis for specific performance. If the buyer enters into possession and makes valuable improvements, there is sufficient part performance to make the contract enforceable. There is a difference of opinion as to whether improvements without possession would qualify, but the trend is in the direction of granting specific performance on that factor alone.

2-76. Contracts Not to be Performed Within One Year.   A promise is within the statute if by its terms, it cannot be carried out within one year from the time it is made. The period is measured from the time the oral contract is entered into to the time when the promised performance is to be completed. [5] Thus, oral agreements to hire a person for two years, to form and carry on a partnership for ten years, or to grant a three-year extension on the maturity of a debt would not be enforceable.

The decisive factor in determining whether a long-term contract comes within the statute is whether performance is *possible* within a year from the date of making the contract. [6] Even though it is most unlikely or improbable that performance could be rendered within one year, the statute does not apply

[4] Brunette v. Vulcan Materials Co., page 270.

[5] Eisenbeck v. Buttgen, page 270.

[6] Haveg Corporation v. Guyer, page 272.

if there is even a remote possibility that it could. Thus, a promise to pay $10,000 "when cars are no longer polluting the air" would be enforceable though given orally. There is a split of authority on the question of enforceability of an oral contract which extends for a period of more than a year but which contains a provision allowing cancellation by one or both parties within a year. Some courts hold that such an oral contract is not enforceable, while the majority hold that such a contract is not within the statute because there is possibility of discharge within one year.

A question arises when one party to a bilateral contract has performed completely in less than a year, but the other party's performance is not capable of being completed within a year. Does the complete performance by one take the contract out of the statute? The majority rule is that it does; a minority of the courts require full performance on both sides. It must be borne in mind that an *executory* oral contract is not enforceable unless both parties can perform within a year.

2-77. Nature of the Writing.   The statute of frauds does not require a formal written document signed by both parties. All that is required is a note or memorandum concerning the transaction. It must be signed by the party sought to be bound by the agreement (the defendant). The memorandum need contain only the basic terms of the contract. However, a memorandum of sale of real property must state the terms of the contract with such certainty that the essentials of the contract can be determined from the memorandum itself without the necessity of referring to other sources.[7]

Under the statute one party may be bound by an agreement although the other party is not. Only the party who resists performance need sign. Such a result is predicated on the theory that the agreement is legal in all respects, but proper evidence of such an agreement is lacking, and this is furnished when the person sought to be charged with the contract has signed a writing. The moving party is simply seeking to enforce the contract whose formal existence the other denies. Any kind of note or memorandum that describes the property involved, that sets forth the major terms, and that indicates the parties to the agreement is sufficient. If one memorandum is incomplete, but it is clear that two or more writings relate to the same subject matter, they may be joined to supply the necessary memorandum. This is true only if it is clear that the writings relate to the same agreement. If, prior to the time when the defense is asserted, the party sought to be held signs any writing sufficient to satisfy the statute, he furnishes the necessary evidence.

As to the signature, it may be quite informal and need not necessarily be placed at the close of the document. It may be in the body of the writing or elsewhere so long as it identifies the writing with the signature of the person sought to be held.

THE CODE

2-78. Contracts for the Sale of Goods. The Code contains statute of frauds provisions. The provision applicable to goods provides that, as a general rule, a contract for the sale of goods for the price of $500 or more is not enforceable unless there is some writing sufficient to indicate that a contract for sale has

---

[7] Marsico v. Kessler, page 273

been made.[8] The writing must be signed by the defendant or his authorized agent or broker.

The writing need not contain all material terms of the contract, and errors in stating a term will not affect the fact that the statute of frauds is not a defense. The writing need not indicate which party is the buyer or which is the seller or include the price or time of payment. The only term which must appear is the quantity term, which need not be accurately stated. However, a contract is not enforceable beyond the quantity stated in the writing. Since the requirement is that it be signed by the party to be charged, it need not be signed by a plaintiff who is seeking to enforce it.

The Code provisions relating to goods contain several exceptions to the rule requiring a writing if the contract involves over $500. One exception is an innovation with regard to the type of writing which is required. This exception is limited to transactions between "merchants," and it arises from the business practice of negotiating contracts by oral communication, such as on the telephone. A merchant who contracts orally with another merchant can unilaterally satisfy the requirement by sending a writing to the other confirming the contract. This confirmation is sufficient against the party receiving it, unless written notice of objection to its contents is given within ten days after it is received. In order to be valid, the confirmation must be sufficient to bind the sender.

Other exceptions are based on partial performance of the contract for the sale of goods. An oral contract is enforceable with respect to goods (1) for which payment has been made or (2) which have been received and accepted. Either of these conditions constitutes an "unambiguous overt admission" by both parties that a contract actually exists. Thus, there is no need for a writing to establish this fact. The effect of this part performance is limited to the payment actually made or the goods actually received, i.e., the existence of a contract for the total alleged amount or price is *not* established.

Another substitute for a writing under the Code also relates to conduct which in and of itself clearly indicates that a contract has been entered into. If (1) the goods are to be specially manufactured for the buyer (e.g., according to the buyer's specifications) and are not suitable for sale to others, (2) the seller has either made a substantial beginning of their manufacturing or commitments for their procurement, and (3) the circumstances reasonably indicate that the goods are for the buyer, the contract is enforceable without a writing. This simply means, however, that the statute of frauds has been satisfied—the seller still must establish and prove the terms of the contract.

The final substitute for a writing is predicated upon the fact that the required writing is a formality; a contract may very well exist, but no action can be taken unless and until the necessary proof of its existence is forthcoming —the contract is simply unenforceable pending such proof. The proof may become available at a later date, and its effect will be retroactive. If the party who is resisting the contract admits its existence in the proper circumstances and surroundings, such admission will substitute for a writing. Thus, the Code provides that an oral contract is enforceable " . . . if the party against whom enforcement is sought admits in his pleading, testimony or otherwise *in court*

---

[8] Acuri v. Weiss, page 274

that a contract for sale was made, but the contract is not enforceable under this provision beyond the quantity of goods admitted. . . . " (U.C.C. 2-201(3)(b)) This provision is particularly significant in light of modern judicial procedures such as discovery practices. Under the statute of frauds other than the Code, a party may admit the existence of a contract in court and still rely upon the statute as a defense. If the contract involves goods, however, he will lose his defense.

Since the statute is applicable only to sales where the price is $500 or more, it must be determined whether a transaction involves more than that amount. In determining whether the value of property is such as to cause it to fall within the statute, it often becomes necessary to decide how many contracts have been entered into. Thus, *A* orders from *B* $400 worth of one item to be delivered at once and $200 of another item to be delivered ten weeks later. Either item considered alone is worth less than $500; both items total over $500. If the parties intended only one contract, the statute of frauds is applicable; however, if two contracts were entered into, no writing is required. The intention of the parties in these cases is gleaned from such factors as the time and the place of the agreement, the nature of the articles involved, and other surrounding circumstances.

2-79. Contracts for the Sale of Personal Property Other than Goods. The Code has four statute of frauds provisions, one of which relates to sales of goods as discussed in the prior section. The other provisions relate (1) to contracts for the sale of securities, (2) to security agreements in secured transactions, and (3) to contracts for the sale of personal property of a type which does not fit into any of the other categories. Typical of the latter are the sale of bilateral contracts, royalty rights, and other rights of an intangible character. Under this "catchall" provision, a contract for the sale of such property is not enforceable "beyond five thousand dollars in amount or value of remedy unless there is some writing which indicates that a contract for sale has been made between the parties at a defined or stated price, reasonably identifies the subject matter, and is signed by the party against whom enforcement is sought or by his authorized agent." (U.C.C. 1-206)

2-80. Contracts Involving More than One Section of the Statute of Frauds.
One agreement may involve more than one provision of the statute of frauds. A contract for the sale of personal property might not be possible of full performance within a year. If the contract is unenforceable under any provision of the statute of frauds, it is entirely unenforceable. The fact that one provision of the statute of frauds is satisfied will not make it enforceable if some other provision is not satisfied. For example, a written confirmation between merchants will satisfy the Code requirement, but it would not satisfy the requirement of a writing for a contract of long duration. This problem also arises when part performance satisfies one provision but not another.

FORM OF THE AGREEMENT CASES

H. B. Zachry Company v. O'Brien
378 F.2d 423 (1967)

The plaintiffs, a partnership, brought action against the defendant for breach of a construction subcontract. A memorandum had been prepared by the defendant's project manager which set forth the items which would be handled by the plaintiffs as subcontractors, this had also been signed by the defendant's project manager, Bryan. The memorandum contained an addendum signed by one of the plaintiff-partners, Gore, which read: "I agree to the above conditions as the basis for a formal subcontract." The defendant's contention was that the memorandum was not binding and that a formal contract was contemplated. The court gave a summary judgment to the plaintiffs, and the defendant appealed.

HICKEY, J. . . . The addendum attached to the memorandum must be viewed in the light of the facts established surrounding its execution. Gore testified by deposition that when he learned from the Army Engineers, for whom the project was being built, that appellant was considering a subcontract, he visited with Bryan. All the plans and specifications, the contract prices and complete information of the job were willingly given to Gore. At a subsequent date, Bryan called Gore and discussed with him his reaction to the information given at this meeting. Gore told him they were interested in the job and Bryan then prepared the memorandum and transmitted it to Gore. The testimony of Gore together with the supporting instruments considered by the court evidence a mutual manifestation of assent on the part of appellant and appellees.

"The document [memorandum] was only a memorial of the completed oral agreement and did not affect its validity." *R. H. Lindsay Co.* v. *Greager* (204 F.2d 129, 131 (10 Cir. 1953)).

The Kansas Supreme Court has said: "The general rule is well stated in a comprehensive note at 165 A.L.R. 757. There it is stated: 'The mere intention to reduce an oral or informal agreement to writing, or to a more formal writing, is not of itself sufficient to show that the parties intended that until such formal writing was executed the parol or informal contract should be without binding force.' . . . " In *Willey* v. *Goulding,* (99 Kan. 323, 161 P. 611, 612), in considering an analogous situation we said: "The fact that the parties may have contemplated the subsequent execution of a formal instrument as evidence of their agreement does not necessarily imply that they had not already bound themselves to a definite and enforceable contract whose terms could be changed only by mutual consent."

Affirmed.

Hathaway v. Ray's Motor Sales
247 A.2d 512 (Vt.) 1968

Plaintiffs purchased a mobile home from the defendant. The purchase agreement contained a provision disclaiming any warranty other than that of the manufacturer. The plaintiffs experienced difficulties with the mobile home and contended the defendant had promised that if they had any problems with it, the defendant "would take care of them." The plaintiffs brought action for damages and were awarded judgment. The defendant appealed.

SHANGRAW, J. . . . It is the claim of the defendant that the parol evidence rule, on the facts present, precluded the introduction of evidence tending to establish an express oral warranty. The admission of this testimony over objection was crucial and failed to come within any of the exceptions to the parol evidence rule. . . . It is a well-established general rule that when contracting parties embody their agreement of sale in writing, evidence of a prior or contemporaneous oral agreement is not admissible to vary or contradict the written agreement. This is the well-recognized rule in Vermont.

The facts do not present an exception to the parol evidence rule. This rule applies to a written contract of sale and oral testimony is inadmissible to add to or contradict the written provisions. The above quoted evidence upon which plaintiff relies directly contradicts the written disclaimer set forth in Defendant's Ex. A. and violates the parol evidence's rule. Error appears. . . .

Judgment reversed, and cause remanded.

Finch v. Kirkwood

194 A.2d 292 (Md.) 1963

The plaintiff had been selling food and other supplies on credit to a corporation conducting a restaurant business in an apartment house. The corporation was in arrears in paying its bills, and the plaintiff got in touch with the defendant about the matter. In a telephone conversation, the defendant agreed to assume responsibility for supplies delivered to the restaurant. The plaintiff brought action to recover from the defendant the amount due for supplies so delivered, and the defendant asserted the Statute of Frauds as a defense. The trial court ruled for the plaintiff, and the defendant appealed.

PER CURIAM. . . . According to testimony of the plaintiff, he telephoned the defendant in May, 1961, about the account, and the defendant agreed to assume responsibility for supplies delivered to the restaurant. Thereafter the vast majority of the invoices (some 175 in number) carried the name "Mr. Finch," Mr. Finch being the defendant. Some of the invoices (about 22 in number) carried the name of the restaurant, but not of the defendant. None of these invoices carried the corporate name of the corporation said by the defendant to have been the customer. There are also two credit bills or memoranda in the record for supplies returned or charged in error. These, like the minority of the invoices, do not name the defendant and are in a name identifying the restaurant by the name of the apartment house in which it was located, but do not carry the name of the corporation operating the restaurant.

In addition to the plaintiff's testimony as to the above telephone conversation and the evidence as to the overwhelming majority of the invoices issued thereafter, the evidence shows that the defendant had taken over the direction of the restaurant business and that he had a substantial financial interest in it and a business purpose of his own for entering into the alleged agreement.

We think that the evidence was sufficient to warrant the finding of the trial court, sitting without a jury, that credit was extended to the defendant, and hence that he cannot successfully invoke the provisions of the Statute of Frauds relating to oral agreements to answer for the debt of another. . . .

Affirmed.

Brunette v. Vulcan Materials Co.

256 N.E.2d 44 (Ill.) 1970

Plaintiffs purchased a tract of land from the defendants and procured an oral agreement that they would have first priority for the purchase of an adjoining tract. Subsequently, the parties entered into negotiations for the other tract and exchanged correspondence concerning it. The plaintiffs alleged that the correspondence constituted a contract, and that in any event, their part performance satisfied the requirement of the statute of frauds. The defendants contended that no contract existed and that the statute of frauds was a defense to the plaintiff's suit for specific performance. The lower court dismissed the plaintiff's suit and the plaintiff appealed.

SCHWARTZ, J. . . . Plaintiffs finally contend that they have alleged sufficient partial performance to remove this transaction from the operation of the Statute of Frauds. There are three requisites for the application of the doctrine of partial performance: (1) the performance must be in reasonable reliance on the contract, (2) the remedy of restitution must be inadequate, and (3) the performance must be one which in some degree evidences the existence of a contract and is not readily explainable on any other ground. In support of their contention plaintiffs aver that during the year 1965 they ordered a survey of the land at a cost of $135; that they expended time and effort in obtaining a reduction of real estate taxes on the tract; that Vulcan knowingly allowed them to assume possession of the property and to repair structures and store materials thereon and that they grazed animals (two goats used for advertising purposes) on the land.

To successfully invoke the doctrine of partial performance it is essential that the facts alleged be strongly evidential of a contract. The partial performance must itself play a part in the proof. *Corbin on Contracts,* Vol. 2 § 430, (1950). That plaintiffs' actions are insufficient in this regard is manifest from their own statements. In a letter dated September 11, 1967 they say, "[we]are interested in purchasing the property *remaining* in your hands . . . ." [Emphasis added.] By way of explaining plaintiffs' use of the property during this period in the absence of a contract we note the following statement made by plaintiffs in a letter to defendants dated October 4, 1967: "From the day of our first contact with your company to the present our relations with your people have been most cordial, ranging from our use of neighboring property through installation of glass in your buildings and equipment . . . ." Whether that was merely neighborly indulgence on the part of defendants in the expectation that some agreement might ultimately be concluded is not material. The fact remains that there was as yet no underlying agreement between the parties as to the sale of the property. Accordingly the doctrine of partial performance is not available and the Statute of Frauds applies.

The judgment of the Circuit Court is affirmed.

Judgment affirmed.

Eisenbeck v. Buttgen

450 S.W.2d 696 (Tex.) 1970

Plaintiff went to work for the defendant under an oral agreement which he alleged provided for a stipulated salary plus a percentage of the gross receipts of the defendant's business. The defendant claimed that the contract was unenforceable under the statute of frauds and refused to pay the additional amount. The lower court ruled for the plaintiff, and the defendant appealed.

WILLIAMS, J. . . . Contending that the oral contract was incapable of being performed within one year following the date of its inception, appellant insists that the same is void and unenforceable by virtue of the statute of frauds. The essence of appellant's argument is that the oral contract was made between the parties about the middle of February, 1966, or two weeks prior to appellee's going to work for appellant on February 28, 1966, and that the percentage of gross sales or "bonus" was to be paid "annually" which meant that such payment would not have been payable prior to February 28, 1967, a date one year and two weeks from the date of the agreement.

Art. 3995, Sec. 5, *Vernon's Ann.Civ.St. of Texas,* commonly referred to as our statute of frauds, provides that no action shall be brought upon an oral agreement which is not to be performed within the space of one year from the making thereof. We cannot agree with appellant that the facts apparent in this record bring the case within the provisions of this statute. The facts are undisputed that the contract between the parties was oral and consummated about the middle of February, 1966; that appellee actually went to work for appellant about February 28, 1966; that appellee was to receive a salary paid in semi-monthly installments plus a percentage of the gross receipts. While appellee testified that such "bonus" was to be paid annually, he also said that such payment was to be made at Christmastime of the year. Appellant did not contradict this testimony. The "bonus" which would have been due at or near the end of the year 1966 was discussed by the parties but not paid by appellant to appellee. The contract contained no agreement concerning duration of employment so that it could have been terminated at any time by either party.

To invoke the prohibition of the statute of frauds it must appear that the agreement could not, by its terms or by the nature of the required performance, have been performed within one year. (26 Tex. Jur.2d, § 32, pp. 192-193). "If completion or termination of performance within a year is a possibility and is consistent with the provisions of an agreement, the fact that the entire performance within that period is not required, or expected, will not bring an agreement within the statute."(26 *Tex.Jur.*2d, § 33, p. 195). Where no time is fixed by the parties for the performance of their agreement, and there is nothing in the agreement itself to show that it cannot be performed within a year according to its tenor and the understanding of the parties, the agreement is not within the statute under consideration. (49 *Am.Jur.,* p. 388).

Our Supreme Court in *Bratcher* v. *Dozier* (162 Tex. 319, 346 S.W.2d 795 (1961)) said:

> We think that the question of whether this contract comes within the statute of frauds is a question of law, and that there were no issues to be submitted to the jury on the question of duration. The agreement in question is a simple contract of employment for an indefinite period of time. Generally, where no period of performance is stated in such contracts the statute is inapplicable.

We hold that appellant has not demonstrated that the contract could not have been performed within one year from its inception and therefore the statute of frauds is no bar to appellee's recovery. . . .

Affirmed.

Haveg Corporation v. Guyer

211 A.2d 910 (Del.) 1965

This is an action by the seller for breach of five alleged oral contracts. The plaintiff, Guyer, agreed to furnish all the requirements for cutting and sewing certain nylon phenolic tape used by the defendant corporation in its business. It was agreed that the contracts were exclusive and were not to terminate until the defendant had no further requirement for the services involved. The defendant defended by, among other things, stating that the alleged contracts violated the statute of frauds. The defendant moved for a summary judgment, and when the trial court denied the motion, it appealed.

HERRMANN, J. The question for decision in this facet of the case is whether a contract contemplating continued performance for an indefinite period of time comes within the Statute of Frauds.

The majority rule is that an oral promise of a long-extended performance, which the agreement provides shall come to an end upon the happening of a certain condition, is not within the Statute of Frauds if the condition is one that may happen in one year. There is a minority rule to the contrary.

The Superior Court applied the majority rule and held that, since the defendant's requirements for the services to be rendered under the alleged contracts may have actually and finally terminated within a year, the Statute of Frauds does not apply.

We agree with the Superior Court's conclusion on this point. It has been the law in Delaware for many years that the Statute of Frauds does not apply to a contract which may, by any possibility, be performed within a year. In *Devalinger* v. *Maxwell* (4 Pennewill 185, 54 A. 684, 686 (1903)), this court approved the following statement of the rule:

> . . . the statute (of frauds) does not extend to an agreement which may by any possibility be performed within a year, in accordance with the understanding and intention of the parties at the time when the agreement was entered into. And if the specific time of performance be not determined upon at the time of the making of the contract, yet, if by any possibility it may be performed within a year, the statute does not apply, and such an agreement need not be in writing. And likewise when the performance of the agreement rests upon a contingency which may happen within a year.

And in *Duchatkiewicz* v. *Golumbuski* (12 Del. Ch. 253, 111 A. 430 (1920)), the Chancellor stated:

> In this state the law is settled authoritatively that if any agreement by any possibility may, under the contract, be performed within one year it is valid notwithstanding the statute (of frauds); or rather, unless it appear that the contract could not possibly be performed within one year from the making thereof, its enforcement is not prohibited by the statute. . . .

We approve and adhere to the rule as thus stated and restated.

Since the defendants were unable to show that the alleged contracts could not possibly be performed within a year, we affirm the conclusion of the Superior Court that the alleged agreements are not within the Statute of Frauds.

It follows that the order denying the defendants' motion for summary judgment is affirmed insofar as it is based upon the ruling that the alleged contracts are not within the Statute of Frauds; and insofar as the appeal attempts to present the other issues discussed herein, it is dismissed.

Marsico v. Kessler

178 A.2d 155 (Conn.) 1962

SHEA, J. The plaintiff brought this action for specific performance and damages because of the refusal of the defendants to carry out an alleged agreement to sell certain real property to him. In their answer, by way of special defense, the defendants asserted that the agreement did not satisfy the requirements of the Statute of Frauds. Judgment was rendered for the defendants, and the plaintiff has appealed.

The facts are not in dispute. The parties signed a written agreement whereby the defendants were to sell and the plaintiff was to buy real estate situated in Stamford. The agreement recites a price of $30,000, payable $500 in "Cash herewith" and $25,000 in "Cash on signing superseding contract or on delivery of deed if superseding contract is not signed." The agreement makes no reference to the difference of $4,500 between the cash payments of $25,500 and the $30,000 stated to be the price for the property.

The pertinent portion of our Statute of Frauds reads as follows: "No civil action shall be maintained . . . upon any agreement for the sale of real estate or any interest in or concerning it . . . unless such agreement, or some memorandum thereof, is made in writing and signed by the party to be charged therewith or his agent." (General Statutes, § 52-550).

"The requirements of a memorandum of sale to satisfy the Statute of Frauds in this state (Gen.St.1918, § 6130) [are] too well established to require extended consideration. It must state the contract between the parties with such certainty that the essentials of the contract can be determined from the memorandum itself without the aid of parol proof, either by direct statement or by reference therein to some other writing or thing certain; and these essentials must at least consist of the subject of the sale, the terms of it and the parties to it, so as to furnish evidence of a complete agreement."

The plaintiff claims that the failure to specify in the agreement the manner of payment of the $4,500 balance on the purchase price does not render the agreement unenforceable and that the law presumes that payment is to be made in cash. This argument is based upon the assumption that the total price was $30,000, but, even if we assume that it was, a presumption that the balance is to be paid in cash prevails only where no method of payment has, in fact, been agreed upon by the parties. The presumption rests upon the failure to agree rather than upon a failure to state what was agreed. It has no application here, since the sum payable in cash is definitely specified.

The plaintiff also contends that he is entitled to relief because the defendants cannot be harmed, for the reason that he is willing to pay in cash the maximum price mentioned in the agreement. This argument overlooks the requirement that the terms of the agreement must be stated with reasonable certainty. Failure to comply with this requirement makes the agreement unenforceable.

There is no error.

Acuri v. Weiss

184 A.2d 24 (Pa.) 1962

Plaintiff sued to recover $500 deposit made on tentative purchase of a restaurant business. Plaintiff had given the defendant a check with the following notation on left side of check: "Tentative deposit on tentative purchase of 1415 City Line Ave., Phila. Restaurant, Fixtures, Equipment, Goodwill." An inventory was subsequently prepared by defendant's attorney and accountant to which the terms of the contract were added and the agreement was sent to plaintiff. Plaintiff then refused to complete the transaction and sued for his deposit. Defendant contended that the contract of sale was enforceable and plaintiff relied upon the statute of frauds to establish that the agreement was unenforceable. The jury returned a verdict for the defendant and plaintiff appealed.

WATKINS, J. . . . Appellant's (plaintiff) first question: "Does the Statute of Frauds of the Uniform Commercial Code, 1953, . . . render the defense to the claim insufficient as a matter of law? " . . . The pertinent portions of the section are:

> (1) Except as otherwise provided in this section a contract for the sale of goods for the price of $500 or more is not enforceable by way of action or defense unless there is some writing sufficient to indicate that a contract for sale has been made between the parties and signed by the party against whom enforcement is sought or by his authorized agent or broker. A writing is not insufficient because it omits or incorrectly states a term agreed upon but the contract is not enforceable under this paragraph beyond the quantity of goods shown in such writing. . . .
>
> (3) A contract which does not satisfy the requirements of subsection (1) but which is valid in other respects is enforceable
>
> (a) if the goods are to be specially manufactured for the buyer and are not suitable for sale to others in the ordinary course of the seller's business and the seller, before notice of repudiation is received and under circumstances which reasonably indicate that the goods are for the buyer, has made either a substantial beginning of their manufacture or commitments for their procurement; or
>
> (b) if the party against whom enforcement is sought admits in his pleading or otherwise in court that a contract for sale was made; or
>
> (c) with respect to goods for which payment has been made and accepted or which have been received and accepted. . . .

The writing upon which the appellee relies to satisfy the requirement of the statute is the check with the marginal notation. We cannot escape the clear meaning of the key words in this notation, "Tentative deposit on tentative purchase." The word tentative is not an uncommon word in the English language and has been defined thusly: "Of the nature of an attempt, experiment, or hypothesis to which one is not finally committed." Antonyms being:

definite, final, conclusive. In fact, when Weiss read the notation the warning flag immediately went up, and when he inquired as to their purpose he was told that was just until the formal papers were made up. This writing does not satisfy the requirement of the statute.

Since this is the first appellate decision touching upon this question we feel some comment is needed. The purpose of the Uniform Commercial Code, which was written in terms of current commercial practices, was to meet the contemporary needs of a fast-moving commercial society. It changed and simplified much of the law which it has supplanted but it also sets forth many safeguards against sharp commercial practices. This section we feel is one such safeguard. While it does not require a writing which embodies all the essential terms of a contract, and even goes so far as to permit omission of the price, it does require some writing which indicates *that a contract for sale has been made.* [Emphasis writer's.]

... *Judgment reversed and judgment notwithstanding the verdict entered for appellant.*

CHAPTER 13
REVIEW QUESTIONS AND PROBLEMS

1. *A,* a magazine company, owed a large sum to *B,* a printing company. *B* refused to do further printing unless it could be assured of payment. *C,* a director of *A,* agreed to lend *A* $150,000 and informed *B* orally of this arrangement. *B* printed the next issue of the magazine. *C* did not make the loan to *A,* and *B* brought action against *C. C* asserted the statute of frauds as a defense. What result?

2. *A* signed an order form to purchase a new car from the B Auto Company for $2,500. B Company did not sign the form. *A* made a $25 down payment. Later the B Company told *A* that a mistake had been made and that the price would be $2,675. *A* sued the B Company which defended on the ground that it had not signed the form. What result?

3. *A* ordered plastic materials from *B,* a supplier, by telephone. This was followed by a purchase order enclosed with a letter stating it was being sent in accordance with the telephone conversation. Thereafter, *B* refused to deliver the material and contended that the statute of frauds had not been satisfied. What result?

4. *A,* a beverage company, orally promised *B* that he would be the exclusive wholesale distributor for *B* in a certain county as long as *A* continued to do business within an area which included that county. *A* sought to avoid this promise on the ground that it was oral. What result?

5. *A* entered into an oral contract to purchase land from *B.* In reliance upon the oral contract *A* passed up an opportunity to purchase other land which would have been suitable for his needs. *B* refused to sell the property to *A,* and *A* sought to enforce the oral contract. What result?

6. On June 15, 1965, *G* orally promised *H* that he, *G,* would work for *H* as an architect until January 1, 1970, or until the project was completed. On January 1, 1967, *G* resigned his position and refused to finish the project. *H* sues *G* for breach of contract. What result? (Assume that *G* uses the statute of frauds as a defense.)

7. *X* and *Y* entered into a written contract which provided that *Y* would be paid $10,000 per year for his services. Prior to the execution of the agreement *X* had told *Y* that his salary would be $12,000. In a suit by *Y* for the remaining $2,000, will the court allow *Y* to testify concerning *X*'s oral statement?

8. *P* contracted to do certain construction work for *G,* the written contract providing that no additional work was to be done unless agreed to in writing. Later *G* made several oral requests for added work at specified rates, but after the work was completed, he refused to pay because the requests were not in writing. Is *P* permitted to recover?

9. *A* made an oral contract with *B* whereby *A* was to convey certain real estate to *B* for the price of $6,000. In reliance upon the oral agreement, *B* hauled certain fertilizer to the farm, piped water to the feed lots, and made cement platforms for feeding livestock. Under these conditions was the oral agreement enforceable?

10. *X* orally sold his house to *Y*. *Y* made a down payment, sold his old residence, moved to the house and made substantial improvements thereon. Is *X*'s contract enforceable?

chapter 14

Rights of Third Parties

2-81. Introduction. The discussion to this point has primarily dealt with the law of contracts as applied to the two contracting parties. This chapter deals with the rights and duties of third parties—those who did not participate in negotiating and creating the contract. At early common law no recognition was given to the rights of any parties other than those "privy" to the contract.

Two basic situations are encompassed in this discussion. First, the *assignment* of a contract—a party to a contract transfers to a third party his rights under the contract. Second, the *third-party beneficiary* contract, in which one party contracts with another party for the purpose of conferring a benefit upon a third party—one who is not a party to the contract. In each situation, the primary question is the enforceability of the contract by the third person.

ASSIGNMENTS

2-82. Basic Concepts. Prior to the seventeenth century, the assignment of a contract right was not legally possible, because of the prevailing attitude that a contract right was simply too personal to be subject to transfer to a person who was not a party to the contract. Although over the years this prohibition has been gradually relaxed, it has not been eliminated completely. This relaxation was largely due to the demands of the business community.

The terminology of the law as applied to assignments is important. A bilateral contract creates *rights* for each party and imposes on each corresponding *duties*. With respect to the duties each is an obligor (has an obligation to perform); likewise as to rights, each is an obligee (entitled to receive the performance of the other). Either party may desire to transfer to another his rights or both his rights and his duties. A party *assigns* his rights and *delegates* his duties. The term "assignment" may mean a transfer of one's rights under a contract, or it may mean a transfer of both his rights and his duties.

The transferor is called the *assignor,* and the one receiving the transfer is called the *assignee.*

The Code contains provisions that generally approve assignment of rights and delegation of duties by buyers and sellers of goods. The duties of either party may be delegated *unless* the parties have agreed otherwise or the non-delegating party has " . . . a substantial interest in having his original promisor perform or control the acts required by the contract."(U.C.C. 2-210(1))

Under the Code an assignment of "the contract" or of "all my rights under the contract" or an assignment in similar general terms is an assignment of rights, and, unless the language or the circumstances (as in an assignment for security) indicate the contrary, it is also a delegation of performance of the duties of the assignor. Its acceptance by the assignee constitutes a promise by him to perform those duties. This promise is enforceable by either the assignor or the other party to the original contract.

If an obligor delegates his duties as well as assigns his rights, he is not thereby relieved of his liability for proper performance if the assignee fails to perform. He continues to be responsible because one cannot avoid his obligations under a contract by delegating to someone else the responsibility to perform.

2-83. Requisites of Assignment.   No particular formality is essential to an assignment. Consideration, although usually present, is not required. However, an assignment without consideration, a gratuitous assignment, where the right assigned has not been realized, e.g., through the collection of money, may in most states be rescinded by the assignor upon notice of such rescission to the debtor or obligor.

As a general proposition, an assignment may be either oral or written, although it is, of course, desirable to have a written assignment. Some statutes require a writing in certain assignment situations; therefore it is advisable to check the statutes of each state to determine which assignments must be in writing to be enforceable.

Any contract, including the rights arising therefrom, may be assigned provided both parties to the agreement are willing. What, however, is the effect of an assignment where the other (nonassigning) party to the original contract refuses to respect the assignment and insists upon performance by the original party? In the section that follows the particular legal principles that are helpful in determining which rights and contracts may not be assigned over the objection of the other party are set forth.

2-84. Approval Necessary for Assignment.   Of the several classes of contracts that may not be transferred without the consent of the other party, the most important are contracts involving personal rights or personal duties. A personal right or duty is one in which personal trust and confidence is involved or one in which the skill, knowledge, or experience of one of the parties is important. In such cases, the personal acts and qualities of one or both of the parties form a material and integral part of the contract. For example, a lease contract where the rent is a percent of sales, is based on the ability of the lessee and would be unassignable without the consent of the lessor. Likewise, an exclusive agency contract would be unassignable.[1] The Code provides that rights cannot be assigned where the assignment would materially change the duty of the other party, or increase materially the burden or risk imposed on him by his contract, or impair materially his chance of obtaining return performance.

Some duties that might appear to be personal in nature are not considered so by the courts. For example, a building contractor may delegate responsibility for certain portions of the structure. If the construction is to be done according to agreed specifications, the entire agreement to build is assignable. It is presumed that all contractors are able to follow specifications, and since the duties are mechanical in nature, the owner is bound to permit the assignee to build the entire structure. It must be kept in mind that the assignee contractor must substantially complete the building according to the plans and specifications or he will not be entitled to payment and that the assignor continues liable in event of default by the assignee.

Another example of a contract that is unassignable is one in which an assignment would place an additional burden or risk upon a party—one not contemplated at the time he made the agreement. Such appears to be true of an assignment of the right to purchase merchandise on credit. Most states hold that one who has agreed to purchase goods on credit and has been given the right to do so, may not assign his right to purchase the goods to a third party (assignee) since the latter's credit may not be as good as that of the original contracting party—the assignor.

This reasoning is questionable because the seller could hold both the assignor and the assignee responsible. However, the inconvenience to the seller in connection with collecting has influenced most courts to this result. However, in contracts where the seller has security for payment such as retention of title to the goods, a mortgage on the goods, or a security interest in the goods, the seller has such substantial protection that the courts have held that the right to purchase on credit is assignable.

Some contracts contain a provision that they are not assignable. Under the Code, such a clause is generally construed to bar only a delegation of duties. However, most states strictly enforce such a provision. A few states hold an assignment of such a contract to be valid, although the other party is allowed to recover damages for a breach of this provision.

The Code specifies that a prohibition against assignment of a contract does not prevent the assignment of a claim for damages for breach of a contract nor does it prevent assignment of the right to receive money payments which are due or to become due under the contract.

2-85. Claims for Money. All claims for money, due or to become due under existing contracts, may be assigned. For example, employees frequently assign a portion of their wages to a creditor when obtaining credit or to satisfy an obligation. There is a trend in the law toward greatly reducing or eliminating the use of wage assignments. For example, the Uniform Consumer Credit Code adopted in a few states imposes severe restrictions upon assignments of earnings by employees. A seller cannot take an assignment of earnings for payment of a debt arising out of a consumer credit sale, and a lender is not allowed to

[1] Wetherell Bros. Co. v. United States Steel Co., page 284

take an assignment of earnings for payment of a debt arising out of a consumer loan. The Consumer Credit Code is a part of the trend toward greater consumer protection. Limitations upon garnishment of wages is another facet of the attempt to preserve earnings and wages and to insulate these to some extent from the reach of creditors. This is discussed more fully in Chapter 32.

An assignment is more than a mere authorization or request to the employer or other debtor to pay the assignee rather than the assignor. In a true assignment, the obligor-debtor *must* pay the assignee—payment to the assignor does not discharge the obligation to the assignee, who now in effect owns the right to payment.

What is the liability of the assignor in case the assignee is unable to collect from the debtor-obligor? If the assignee takes the assignment merely as *security* for a debt owing from the assignor to the assignee, it is clear that, if the assigned claim is not collected, the assignor will still have to pay the debt which he owes to the assignee. On the other hand, if the assignee has purchased a claim against a third party from the assignor, he would generally have no recourse against the assignor upon default by the debtor-obligor. However, if the claim is *invalid* for some reason or if the claim is sold expressly "with recourse," the assignor would be required to reimburse the assignee. The mere inability of the debtor-obligor to pay or his unwillingness to do so does not give the assignee recourse against the assignor—the assignment is "without recourse" unless otherwise specified.

In any event, the assignor *warrants* that the claim he assigns is a valid legal claim which the debtor-obligor is legally obligated to pay and that there are no valid defenses to the assigned claim. If this warranty is breached, i.e., if there are valid defenses or the claim is otherwise invalid, the assignee has recourse against the assignor if the obligor's refusal to pay is based upon these grounds. The assignor would then have to return to the assignee the amount the latter had paid for the claim.

2-86. Rights of the Assignee.   Unless the contract assigned provides otherwise, the assignee receives the identical rights of the assignor. Since the rights of the assignee are neither better nor worse than those of the assignor, any defense which the third party (obligor) has against the assignor is available against the assignee.[2] For example, part payment, fraud, duress, or incapacity can be used as a defense by the third party (obligor) if an action is brought against him by the assignee, just as the same defense could have been asserted against the assignor had he been the plaintiff. A common expression defining the status of the assignee is that he "stands in the shoes" of the assignor. In consumer sales contracts the seller frequently inserts a provision to the effect that "if the seller assigns the contract to a finance company or bank, the buyer agrees that he will not assert against such assignee any defenses that he has against the seller-assignor." This, of course, places the assignee in a favored position and makes contracts with such clauses quite marketable. This practice is subject to some restrictions, and recent cases cast doubt upon its legal effectiveness. At any rate, a buyer may, in spite of such clause assert "real defenses"—those of a substantial nature—against the assignee. Included

[2] Hudson Supply & Equipment Company v. Home Factors Corp., page 286

among real defenses are infancy, illegality, forgery, extreme duress, and the like.

The Code does not take a position on the controversial question whether a buyer of *consumer goods* may effectively waive defenses by a contractual clause like that presented above. In some states such waivers have been invalidated by statute; in other states judicial decisions have either rendered them illegal as against public policy or have cast severe doubt upon their enforceability. The Code partially leaves the development of this phase of the law to the courts but generally does provide that such clauses are effective to protect the assignee " . . . subject to any statute or decision which establishes a different rule for buyers or lessees of consumer goods" (U.C.C. 9-206(1)) provided, however, that the assignee " . . . takes his assignment for value, in good faith, and without notice of any claim or defense." (U.C.C. 9-206(1)) Real defenses, of course, may always be asserted.

2-87. Duties of Assignee and Assignor. If an "entire contract" has been assigned, i.e., duties have been delegated to the assignee as well as the assignment of the rights, a failure by the assignee to render the required performance gives rise to a cause of action in favor of the third party (obligee). In a majority of the states the disappointed obligee can elect to sue *either* the assignor or the assignee, provided the assignee has agreed, either expressly or by implication, to assume the burdens as well as the benefits of the contract. The assignor is always liable because he cannot relieve himself of contractual obligations by simply delegating them to an assignee. The *mere assignment* of a contract which calls for the performance of affirmative duties by the assignor, with nothing more, does not impose those duties upon the assignee,[3] although there is a decided trend in such cases to hold that an assignment of an entire contract carries an implied assumption of the liabilities. It is only when the assignee undertakes and agrees to perform the duties as a condition precedent to enforcement of the rights, or has assumed the obligation to perform as part of the contract of assignment, that he has liability for failure to perform. To illustrate: If a tenant assigns a lease, the assignee is not liable for future rents if he vacates the property prior to expiration of the period of the lease, unless he expressly assumes the burdens of the lease at the time of the assignment. He is obligated simply to pay the rent for the period of his actual occupancy. To the extent that an assignee accepts the benefits of a contract, he becomes obligated to perform the duties that are related to such benefits.

The foregoing rules are modified somewhat by the Code. As noted, an assignment of a contract does obligate the assignee to perform the duties. Although the assignor remains liable, the obligee may feel insecure as to the ability of the assignee to perform the delegated duties. The obligee may demand that the assignor furnish him with adequate assurance that the assignee will in fact render proper performance.

2-88. Notice. Immediately after the assignment, the assignee should notify the third party, obligor or debtor, of his newly acquired right. This notification is essential for two reasons:

---

[3] Chatham Pharmaceuticals, Inc. v. Angier Chemical Co., Inc., et al., page 286

1. In the absence of any notice of the assignment, the third party is at liberty to perform—pay the debt or do whatever else the contract demands—for the original contracting party, the assignor. In fact, he would have no knowledge of the right of anyone else to require performance or payment. Thus, the right of the assignee to demand performance can be defeated by his failure to give this notice. The assignor who receives performance under such circumstances becomes a trustee of funds or property received from the obligor, and can be compelled to turn them over to the assignee. As soon as notice of the assignment is given to him, the third party *must perform* for the assignee, and his payment or performance to the assignor would not relieve him of his obligation to the assignee.

2. The notice of assignment is also for the protection of innocent third parties. The assignor has the *power,* although not the *right,* to make a second assignment of the same subject matter. If notice of the assignment has been given to the obligor, it has much the same effect as the recording of a mortgage. It furnishes protection for a party who may later consider taking an assignment of the same right. A person considering an assignment should, therefore, always confirm that the right has not previously been assigned by communicating with the debtor. If the debtor has not been notified of a previous assignment, and if the assignee is aware of none, the latter can, in many states, feel free to take the assignment. He should immediately give notice to the debtor. In other words, the first assignee to give notice to the debtor, provided such assignee has no knowledge of a prior assignment, will prevail over a prior assignee in most states.[4]

In some other states, it is held that the first party to receive an assignment has a prior claim, regardless of which one gave notice first. In this, the courts act on the theory that the assignor has parted with all of his interest by virtue of the original assignment and has nothing left to transfer to the second assignee. In all states, however, the party who is injured by reason of the second assignment has a cause of action against the assignor to recover the damages he has sustained—the assignor has committed a wrongful and dishonest act by making a double assignment.

CONTRACTS FOR BENEFIT OF THIRD PARTIES

2-89. Nature of Such Contracts.   Contracts are often made for the express purpose of benefiting some third party. The most typical example of such an agreement is the contract for life insurance in which the beneficiary is someone other than the insured. The insured has made a contract with the life insurance company for the purpose of conferring a benefit upon a third party, namely the beneficiary named on the policy.

There are two types of third-party beneficiaries: "donee beneficiaries" and "creditor beneficiaries." Both are entitled to enforce a contract made in their behalf—the promisee has provided that the performance shall go to the beneficiary rather than to himself.

If the promise was purchased by the promisee in order to make a gift to the

---

[4] Boulevard National Bank of Miami v. Air Metals Industry, page 287

third party, such party is a donee-beneficiary. The life insurance situation is illustrative of this.

If the promisee has contracted for a promise to pay a debt which he owes to a third party, such third party is a creditor-beneficiary—the debtor has arranged to pay the debt by purchasing the promise of the other contracting party to satisfy his obligation. The promisee obtains a benefit because his obligation to the creditor will presumably be satisfied. To illustrate: *A* operates a department store. He sells his business together with furniture, fixtures, and inventory to *B* who, as part of the bargain, agrees to pay all of *A*'s business debts. *A*'s purpose for making this contract was to have his debts paid and he obtained *B*'s promise to pay them in order to confer a benefit on his creditors. *A*'s creditors are creditor-beneficiaries and can enforce their claims directly against *B*. To the extent that *B* does not pay them, the creditors have recourse against *A*. The situation closely resembles an assignment in this respect.

An interesting problem is raised by virtue of the fact that a creditor-beneficiary can bring direct action on the obligor's promise to the promisee-debtor. Upon failure of the obligor to pay the promisee's creditors he has breached two obligations—one to the promisee and one to the promisee's creditor. The failure to pay could result in substantial damages to the promisee who paid for the promise. The obligor could thus be subjected to two lawsuits. The solution has been to allow both the promisee and the creditor-beneficiary to sue, but a recovery by either of them is a bar to recovery by the other.

2-90. Legal Requirements.   A third-party beneficiary is not entitled to enforce a contract unless he can establish that the parties actually intended to make the contract for his benefit. The intent to benefit the third party must appear from the terms of the contract, but such intent is easily inferred in creditor-beneficiary situations. The third party need not be named as an individual in the contract if he can show that he is a member of a group for whose benefit the contract was made.[5] The fact that the actual contracting party could also sue to enforce the agreement will not bar a suit by the beneficiary if he was intended to directly benefit from the contract.

If the benefit to the third party is only incidental, the beneficiary cannot sue. Thus, an orphanage lost a suit which was based on an agreement between several merchants to close their places of business on Sunday with a provision that each one that remained open was to pay one hundred dollars to the orphanage. The court stated that the contract was entered into primarily to benefit the contracting parties, and the orphanage was only indirectly to be a beneficiary. Contracts of guaranty which assure the owner of property that contractors performing construction contracts for him will properly complete the project and pay all bills have been held in many states to benefit the materialmen and laborers. A few states have held otherwise, indicating their belief that the agreement was made primarily to protect the owner.

In most states, a contract made for the express purpose of benefiting a third party may not be rescinded without the consent of the beneficiary after its terms have been accepted by the beneficiary. The latter has a vested interest in the agreement from the moment it is made and accepted. For example, an

---

[5] Pacific N.W. Bell Telephone Co. v. DeLong Corp., page 290

insurance company has no right to change the named beneficiary in a life insurance policy without the consent of the beneficiary, unless the contract gives the insured the right to make this change. Until the third-party benefici- ary has either accepted or acted upon provisions of a contract for his benefit, the parties to the contract may abrogate the provisions for the third party's benefit and divest him of the benefits that would otherwise have accrued to him under contract. Minors, however, are presumed to accept a favorable contract upon its execution and such contract may not be changed so as to deprive the minor of its benefits.

One who seeks to take advantage of a contract made for his benefit takes it subject to all legal defenses arising out of contract. Thus, if the obligee has not performed or satisfied the conditions precedent to the other party's obliga- tion, the third party would be denied recovery.

RIGHTS OF THIRD PARTIES CASES

Wetherell Bros. Co. v. United States Steel Co.

105 F. Supp. 81 (1952)

Wetherell Bros. Co., a Massachusetts corporation, had held a contract since 1930 with the defendant whereby it had the exclusive right in the New England states to sell cold, rolled steel strips on a 5 percent commission and stainless steel products on a 7 percent commission. The contract was to run indefinitely except as it might be terminated by two years' notice. On March 1, 1950, the Massachusetts corporation liquidated and ceased to function, but sold some assets to Penn Seaboard Iron Co., a Pennsylvania corporation, and so far as possible sought to assign to the latter their right to represent United States Steel Co. in New England. The Pennsylvania corporation changed its name to Wetherell Bros. Co., but refrained from giving notice of the assignment to the defendant. Learning of the new arrangement, however, the defendant notified the parties of the immediate termination of the sales relationship. Plaintiff, the Pennsylvania corporation, brings suit for breach of contract.

MC CARTHY, J. . . . The plaintiff seeks to hold the defendant liable be- cause of its action in terminating the contract between it (defendant) and Wetherell-Massachusetts. Since admittedly no contract was ever entered into between the plaintiff and the defendant, the question of law is whether the duties of Wetherell-Massachusetts under the contract could be effectively assigned to plaintiff without the consent of the defendant. The conclusion is inescapable: the assignment to the plaintiff of the duties of Wetherell-Massa- chusetts under its sales agency contract without the consent of the defendant was ineffective for the purpose of substituting the plaintiff for the "assignor" corporation with whom the defendant contracted.

This was a contract for a sales agency within a particular geographical area, an exclusive agency in that only the principal could compete with Wetherell- Massachusetts in obtaining customers for the defendant's products.

"In a contract for a sales agency the personal performance of the agent is practically always a condition precedent to the duty of the principal and employer. The performance of the agent's duty cannot be delegated to a substitute. The assignee of the agent's right must fail, therefore, in his attempt to enforce it if he merely tenders a substituted performance." IV Corbin, Contracts (1951) § 865 p. 444.

... "The claim has been made also that it is only in a technical sense that these two companies could be called distinct entities. They had the same capital stock and practically the same stockholders, officers, and agents; the Maine company had taken over all the assets and assumed all the liabilities of the other, and was carrying on the same business, at the same stand, in the same manner, and under the same management. The master has found that for practical purposes the two companies were the same. Accordingly, the plaintiff claims that an agreement with the one is the same as an agreement with the other, that the defendant's ignorance of their separate identity was immaterial, that the agreement may be treated as made with either company indifferently, was capable of enforcement by either or at least by the Maine company, and is valid in the hands and for the benefit of the plaintiff. But we cannot assent to this reasoning. These are two distinct corporations, created by the laws of two different states. The powers of each corporation are limited and controlled by the statutes of the state which created it, and it is scarcely conceivable that the statutes of the two states are the same or that the franchises and powers of the two corporations are identical. But if this were so, it would remain true that they are the creation of two different governments, the offspring of different parents, and not only distinct legal entities, but having separate and distinct existences. ... " 97 N.E. 780, 782.

The contract in this case is one requiring a relationship of particular trust and confidence, and such a contract cannot be assigned effectively without the consent of the other party to the contract. The grant of an exclusive agency to sell one's goods presupposes a reliance upon and confidence in the agent by the principal, even though the agent be what is frequently called a large "impersonal" corporation. It is apparent that the principal in this case must have relied upon the "legal equation" represented by the corporation which it chose as its sole sales representative in a large area; otherwise, the surrender of the right to grant additional agencies is illogical.

The plaintiff has argued that the fact that the assignment is made from one corporation to another alters the rule of nonassignability of the agent's duties under the contract. ...

"The plaintiff was not only technically but substantially a different entity from its predecessor. It is true that in dealing with corporations a party cannot rely on what may be termed the human equation in the company. The personnel of the stockholders and officers of the company may entirely change. But though there is no personal or human equation in the management of a corporation, there is a legal equation which may be of the utmost importance to parties contracting with it. In dealing with natural persons in matters of trust and confidence, personal character is or may be a dominant factor. In similar transactions with a corporation, a substitute for personal character is the charter rights of the corporation, the limits placed on its power, especially to incur debt, the statutory liability of its officers and stockholders. These are matters of great importance when, as at present, many states and territories seem to have entered into the keenest competition in granting charters; each seeking to outbid the other by offering to directors and stockholders the greatest immunity from liability at the lowest cash price. . . . "73 N.E. 48, 51-52.

Judgment must be entered for the defendant.

Hudson Supply & Equipment Company v. Home Factors Corp.

210 A.2d 837 (D.C.) 1965

The plaintiff, Home Factors Corp., was the assignee of two accounts receivable for brick sold to the defendant by the Eastern Brick & Tile Co., Inc. The accounts were not paid and the plaintiff brought action. The defendant admitted that it had purchased the tile on open account but claimed that Eastern was indebted to it for an amount in excess of the assigned account receivable. The defendant thus claimed that it was entitled to set-off against the assigned claims the amount which Eastern owed to the defendant on the basis of other transactions. The trial court gave judgment to the plaintiff for the full amount of its claim. The defendant appealed.

HOOD, J. Home Factors Corp., to which Eastern Brick & Tile Co., Inc. had assigned two accounts receivable for brick sold and delivered to Hudson Supply & Equipment Company, brought this action against Hudson for the amount due under the accounts, namely, $1,034.25.

Hudson's defense was that Eastern was indebted to it in an amount in excess of that sued for, and that it was entitled to a set-off for the full amount claimed.

At trial Hudson offered testimony that at the time of the assignment of the two accounts by Eastern to Home Factors, Hudson had claims of over $2,200 against Eastern growing out of other purchases.

The trial court ruled that there was a proper assignment from Eastern to Home Factors and that Home Factors was entitled to judgment for the full amount of its claim. However, the trial court stated "that the evidence indicated that the problem was between Hudson and Eastern and that defendant Hudson was entitled to credits of $229.22 and $172.31 from Eastern and in addition had other claims for credits against Eastern—all of which indicated that Eastern and Hudson should litigate separately the issues between them."

The general rule here and elsewhere is that the assignee of a chose in action takes it subject to all defenses, including set-offs, existing at the time of the assignment. Since it is undisputed in this case that the asserted claims of Hudson existed at the time of the assignment, it is apparent that the trial court misconceived the law relating to assignments. When it was found that Hudson was entitled to certain credits, those credits should have been set off against the claim of Home Factors; and Hudson's "other claims for credits against Eastern" should have been determined, and, if established, should also have been set off against Home Factors' claim.

Reversed with instructions to grant a new trial.

Chatham Pharmaceuticals, Inc. v. Angier Chemical Co., Inc., et al.

196 N.E.2d 852 (Mass.) 1964

SPIEGEL, J. This is a bill to establish the amount due from the defendant corporation Angier and to reach and apply the alleged obligations of the noncorporate defendants (the assignees) "to assume the obligations and liabilities" of the defendant corporation. A final decree was entered favorable to the plaintiff Chatham from which only the assignees appealed . . .

The trial judge made a report of material facts, which we summarize. On September 1, 1957, the plaintiff and the defendant Angier Chemical Co., Inc. (Angier), entered into an agreement. Under the terms of this agreement, the plaintiff was granted an exclusive license "to manufacture, use and sell the product, use or process covered by United States Letters Patent No. 2,688,-585." The plaintiff agreed to pay royalties to Angier and to purchase Angier's then existing inventory of the licensed product, and Angier agreed that "if the license granted should be terminated or surrendered . . . it would buy back from the . . . plaintiff, at the same cost, any part of said inventory then remaining in the possession of the . . . plaintiff." Pursuant to this agreement, the plaintiff purchased Angier's inventory. On February 24, 1958, Angier assigned "all its right, title and interest in said agreement" to the assignees, who accepted the assignment. On January 18, 1960, the plaintiff terminated the agreement, but Angier has refused to repurchase said remaining inventory.

The assignees contend *inter alia* that the 1958 assignment was an assignment of rights only and not of obligations and that they are not obligated to perform any of Angier's duties under the licensing agreement. Although there is a paucity of cases in point, it is the law of this Commonwealth that "an assignment of what is due, or is to become due, under a contract is not an assignment of both the duty of performing the contract and receiving payment therefor." . . .

Where, however, "the contract, as a whole, is assigned, there is no separation between the benefits and burdens." See Restatement: Contracts, §164, which treats the assignment of a whole contract, still partly executory, "in the absence of circumstances showing a contrary intention, as an assignment of the assignor's rights under the contract and a delegation of the performance of the assignor's duties." In the present case, whether the assignees impliedly promised to perform the assignor's duties thereunder is a question of interpretation of the assignment, read in the context of the circumstances.

There is nothing in the ambiguous instrument of assignment to indicate that Angier intended the assignees to assume any obligations under the agreement. There is no express assumption by the assignees of obligations under the licensing agreement. It appears to be undisputed that the assignees were Angier's shareholders and that Angier was heavily indebted to them. . . . There remained few duties to be performed by Angier under the licensing agreement. In these circumstances, it is particularly dubious that the assignees also assumed duties. The use of the words "right, title and interest" does not necessarily show that the assignment was intended to include obligations. . . .

We are constrained to hold that construing the instruments in the light of those circumstances which are essentially undisputed, the assignees did not assume the obligations under the agreement. . . .

Accordingly, the final decree is to be modified by dismissing the bill as against the assignees with costs of appeal, and as so modified is affirmed.

So ordered.

Boulevard Nat. Bank of Miami v. Air Metals Industry

176 So. 2d 94 (Fla.) 1965

Plaintiff bank sued several defendants including a contractor (Tompkins-Beckwith) on a construction project which had a subcontract with Air Metals

Industries, Inc., also a defendant. On January 3, 1962, Air Metals procured performance bonds and as security for said bonds assigned to the bonding company (American Fire) "all monthly, final or other estimates and retained percentages; pertaining to or arising out of or in connection with any contracts performed or being performed or to be performed, such assignment to be in full force and effect as of the date hereof, in the event of default in the performance of—any contract as to which the surety has issued, or shall issue, any surety bonds or undertakings."

On November 26, 1962, the bank lent money to Air Metals and to secure the loans Air Metals purported to assign to the bank certain accounts receivable it had with the contractor which arose out of subcontracts being done for that contractor.

In June 1963, Air Metals defaulted on contracts covered by the performance bonds and on July 1, 1963, the bonding company notified the contractor of its assignment. On August 12, 1963, the bank notified the contractor of its assignment. On October 9, 1963, the contractor paid all funds due to the bonding company and the bank filed suit. The trial court found for the defendants because the notice of the bonding company preceded the notice by the bank. The district court of appeal affirmed.

WILLIS, J. . . . The "question" is whether the law of Florida requires recognition of the so-called "English" rule or "American" rule of priority between assignees of successive assignments of an account receivable or other similar chose in action. Stated in its simplest form, the American rule would give priority to the assignee first in point of time of assignment, while the English rule would give preference to the assignment of which the debtor was first given notice. Both rules presuppose the absence of any estoppel or other special equities in favor of or against either assignee. The English rule giving priority to the assignee first giving notice to the debtor is specifically qualified as applying "unless he takes a later assignment with notice of a previous one or without a valuable consideration." The American rule giving the first assignee in point of time the preference is applicable only when the equities are equal between the contending assignees, and if a subsequent assignee has a stronger equity than an earlier one, he would prevail.

In the case here there are no special equities and no rights, such as subrogation, which would arise outside of the assignments.

.   .   .

The American rule for which petitioner contends is based upon the reasoning that an account or other chose in action may be assigned at will by the owner; that notice to the debtor is not essential to complete the assignment; and that when such assignment is made the property rights become vested in the assignee so that the assignor no longer has any interest in the account or chose which he may subsequently assign to another.

The English rule (holds) that in the case of a chose in action an assignee must do everything toward having possession which the subject admits and must do that which is tantamount to obtaining possession by placing every person who has an equitable or legal interest in the matter under an obligation to treat it as the assignee's property. It was stated:

For this purpose you must give notice to the legal holder of the fund; in the case of a debt, for instance, notice tantamount to possession. If you omit to the debtor is, for many purposes, to give that notice [*sic*] you are guilty of the same degree and species of neglect as he who leaves a personal chattel, to which he has acquired a title, in the actual possession, and, under the absolute control, of another person.

It is undoubted that the creditor of an account receivable or other similar chose in action arising out of contract may assign it to another so that the assignee may sue on it in his own name and make recovery. Formal requisites of such an assignment are not prescribed by statute and it may be accomplished by parol, by instrument in writing, or other mode, such as delivery of evidences of the debt, as may demonstrate an intent to transfer and an acceptance of it. . . .

It seems to be generally agreed that notice to a debtor of an assignment is necessary to impose on the debtor the duty of payment to the assignee, and that if before receiving such notice he pays the debt to the assignor, or to a subsequent assignee, he will be discharged from the debt. To regard the debtor as a total nonparticipant in the assignment by the creditor of his interests to another is to deny the obvious. An account receivable is only the right to receive payment of a debt which ultimately must be done by the act of the debtor. For the assignee to acquire the right to stand in the shoes of the assigning creditor he must acquire some "delivery" or "possession" of the debt constituting a means of clearly establishing his right to collect. The very nature of an account receivable renders "delivery" and "possession" matters very different and more difficult than in the case of tangible personalty and negotiable instruments which are readily capable of physical handling and holding. However, the very principles which render a sale of personal property with possession remaining in the vendor unexplained fraudulent and void as to creditors applies with equal urgency to choses in action which are the subject of assignment. It would seem to follow that the mere private dealing between the creditor and his assignee unaccompanied by any manifestations discernible to others having or considering the acquiring of an interest in the account would not meet the requirement of delivery and acceptance of possession which is essential to the consummation of the assignment. Proper notice to the debtor of the assignment is a manifestation of such delivery. It fixes the accountability of the debtor to the assignee instead of the assignor and enables all involved to deal more safely.

We do not hold that notice to the debtor is the only method of effecting a delivery of possession of the account so as to put subsequent interests on notice of a prior assignment. The English rule itself does not apply to those who have notice of an earlier assignment. The American rule is not in harmony with the concepts expressed. It seems to be based largely upon the doctrine of *caveat emptor* which has a proper field of operation, but has many exceptions based on equitable considerations. It also seems to regard the commercial transfers of accounts as being the exclusive concern of the owner and assignee and that the assignee has no responsibility for the acts of the assignor with whom he leaves all of the indicia of ownership of the account. This view does not find support in the statute or decisional law of this State. . . .

After examining the authorities we conclude . . . that "as between successive assignments of the same right the assignee first giving notice prevails." . . .

.   .   .

We concur in the decision of the district court of appeal in this case.

Pacific N.W. Bell Telephone Co. v. DeLong Corp.
425 P.2d 498 (Oreg.) 1967

While defendant DeLong was building a bridge across the Columbia River its employees cut plaintiff's telephone cable that ran under the river. The contract between DeLong and the Oregon Highway Commission imposed liability for damage to others including telephone, telegraph, and power lines. Plaintiff brought an action for damages as a third-party beneficiary. Judgment was rendered for plaintiff and defendant appealed.

SLOAN, J. . . . It is plaintiff's theory that these requirements of the contract subjected DeLong to a contractual liability for the damage to the cable, that DeLong breached the contract and that the contract entitled plaintiff to bring this action for the breach. We agree.

The evident purpose of the conditions in the contract is to make the contractor directly responsible for damage to property, in this instance, which results from highway construction. It does not appear that these provisions were intended to indemnify the highway commission nor to limit the liability to negligent conduct. The highway commission is justified, for obvious reasons, in relieving a property owner, whose property is damaged by highway construction, of the burden of finding a negligent actor who caused the damage. It is also evident that the contract was intended to make the contractor directly liable to a damaged third person.

The authorities sustain our decision. . . . *LaMourea* v. *Rhude,* 1940, 209 Minn. 53, 58, 295 N.W. 304, 307, includes a review of the authorities on the present question to the date of that decision. The Minnesota court concluded that the weight of authority and "the entire weight of all inherent factors of the problem speak for recovery" by the third party. The court explained its decision in this language:

> We affirm plaintiff's right to sue as a beneficiary of the contract. An opposite holding would defeat obligation where obligation is not only intended but also expressed and paid for. Implicit in such holding would be the indefensible hypothesis that, although a party to a contract may stipulate for such benefits to himself as he wants and the other party will allow, yet the two of them by the same process and for the same consideration cannot secure similar benefit to a stranger. In the contractual promise for the benefit of one not a party, there is nothing illegal or contrary to public policy. The promise is within the right of one party to exact and the other to make. No reasonable ground can be suggested for its not being enforceable according to its expressed intent.

DeLong says that *Waterway Terminals* v. *P. S. Lord,* 1965, 242 Or. 1, 406 P.2d 556, rejects this theory. The Waterway Terminals' opinion expressly stated that the contract there involved gave no indication of an intent to benefit anyone but the parties to the contract. In the instant case the contract expressly extended its benefit to plaintiff. . . .

Affirmed.

CHAPTER 14
REVIEW QUESTIONS AND PROBLEMS

1. *A*, an automobile dealer, sold a car to *B* and promised to obtain "full coverage" insurance for him. Subsequently, *B* had a collision with *C*, and it was discovered that *A* had not obtained liability insurance. *C* brought an action against *A* to recover for property damage and personal injuries. The court gave a judgment in favor of *C*. What was the basis for the court's decision?

2. *A*, the owner of a building, was obligated to furnish heat to an adjoining building owned by *B*. *A* sold his property to *C* who assumed *A*'s obligation to furnish heat. Can *B* force *C* to furnish heat to his building?

3. *A*, an employer, had entered into a contract that contained a clause relieving him of liability in certain situations. *B*, an employee of *A*, while acting in the course of his employment was charged with liability for an act that was within his employer's protective clause. Can *B* have the benefit of his employer's protective clause?

4. *A*, an employee of ABC Company, was injured when the elevator he was operating fell. ABC Company had a contract with *C* Elevator Company whereby *C* was to inspect and service the elevator on a regular basis. *A* contended that *C* had not properly inspected the elevator and that its omission to do so caused the accident. Was *A* entitled to the benefits of the contract between ABC Company and *C* Company?

5. *A* sold sponges to *B* on open account and then assigned the account receivable to *C*. *B* rejected the sponges because they were not of proper quality. *C* seeks to collect from *B*. Should he succeed?

6. After careful investigation of his financial position, *A*, the owner of an office building, agreed to lease the building to *B*. *B* then assigned the contract to *C* who prepared a lease for the signature of *A*. *A* refused to sign the lease and *C* sought specific performance. Was *A* justified in refusing to sign?

7. *X*, a contractor, assigned his claim for work being done to *Y*, a bonding company. *Y* did not notify the obligor. *X* later assigned his claim to *Z* who did notify the obligor. To whom should the obligor make payment?

8. *X* leased his drugstore to *Y* for five years at a monthly rental of $1,000. The rent was to be paid to the City Hospital. Later *X* and *Y* agreed to reduce the rent to $500 in return for *Y*'s installing new fixtures. City Hospital objects to the rent reduction and sues *Y* for the balance of the rent. What result? Could *X* cancel the hospital's rights and direct that the rent be paid to him?

9. *P* employed *A* to work, the latter agreeing to a reasonable restraint from competing when employment terminated. *P* sold his business to

T, and assigned the contract. *A* quit and began to compete immediately in the area. Has *T* a good cause of action against *A,* who urged such a contract could not be assigned?

10. *A* contracts with *B* to build a house for *B. A* assigns the contract to *C,* who substantially performs the contract but commits several minor breaches. From whom can *B* collect?

chapter 15

Performance of Contracts

2-91. Introduction.   The focus of this chapter is on the problems which arise during the period of the performance of a contract. Such problems come up in a variety of ways. One of the parties may refuse to perform or may perform in an unsatisfactory manner; he may not render complete performance; he may be unable to perform because of circumstances beyond his control; or he may contend that because of changed conditions he should be excused from performing. Questions arise as to the order of performance—who must perform first in a bilateral contract? Usually, a default or breach of a contract will occur at or after the time when performance was due, but as will be noted, a contract can be breached prior to the date for performance.

It is inevitable that some contracts will be breached, either because of inability to render the required performance or because it may not appear to be profitable or expedient to perform. Fluctuations in the market, for example, will often cause a party to have "second thoughts" about completing a purchase of goods when their market price has dropped sharply in the interim between entering into the contract and performing it. Fortunately, the overwhelming majority of contracts entered into are executed by both parties; comparatively few give rise to a dispute, and only a small fraction of these are the subject of litigation.

In most instances it can be readily determined whether or not a breach has occurred, but there are some in which the breach is not so apparent. An example of this is a lease in which the rent is a fixed sum plus a percentage of the gross profits. Can the tenant simply abandon the premises and fulfill his obligation by paying only the fixed sum? It has been ruled that there is an implied condition that the tenant would continue to operate his store.[1]

Often a breach of a contract occurs through no fault of the parties, and the

[1] Simhawk Corp. v. Egler, page 309

law recognizes that there are instances in which a failure to perform will be excused, as for example, when performance becomes a literal impossibility. This problem is discussed in the concluding sections of this chapter.

When there has been a default or breach of a contract, there are three basic remedies for an aggrieved party. The primary remedy is money damages awarded by a court of law to compensate for the loss sustained. The equitable remedies are rescission and specific performance. The materials in this chapter relate primarily to rescission and money damages and the determination of the circumstances under which a party may rescind or refuse to perform because of the other party's breach.

Money damages—the usual remedy—will be afforded to an aggrieved party even though the loss sustained is not significant; nominal damages may be awarded for minor breaches. The equitable remedy of rescission, on the other hand, is reserved for situations in which the breach is a substantial one and involves an important aspect of the contract. The basic question presented is, What breaches justify rescission of a contract? To illustrate: *A* agrees to construct a building for *B* for $100,000 and to have it completed on June 1, 1972. *A* is ten days late in finishing the building. The breach being of minor importance, *B* must accept the building and pay the contract price less any damages sustained because of the delay. However, if the breach had been a failure to provide a proper foundation for the building, this would certainly be of major importance and would justify rescission.

CONDITIONS

2-92. In General.   Those terms of a contract the breach of which justifies rescission are called *conditions.* Conditions may be either *precedent, concurrent, or subsequent.* This chapter will deal mainly with the first two; it should be explained, however, that a condition subsequent is an event the occurrence of which takes away rights which would otherwise exist; it may extinguish a duty to make compensation for breach of contract after the breach has occurred. An insurance policy which takes away the right to recover for a fire loss unless the insured gives notice of the loss within a stated period has included within it a condition subsequent. Failure to give notice within the prescribed time relieves the company from its obligation to pay for the loss.

In the context of this chapter, the word "condition" means basically an act or event which must take place before a promisor is obligated to render performance. The condition may be one which is under the promisor's control, or it may be an event over which he has no control. The condition may be an *express condition,* specifically provided for in the contract, or it may be a *constructive, or implied* condition. Substantial performance required by one party to a contract is a constructive condition to the duty of performance on the other. And a failure to provide substantial performance will discharge the other party from his duty of performance.

2-93. Conditions Precedent.   A contract may expressly provide that one party must perform before he obtains a right to performance by the other party. The other party's performance is a *condition precedent*—a prerequisite to his duty to perform. Since one party must perform before the other is under a duty to do so, it follows that the failure of the first party to perform permits the other to refuse to perform and to cancel the contract or sue for damages.

Not all of the terms which impose a duty of performance on a person are of sufficient importance to constitute conditions precedent. As a general rule, if a provision is relatively insignificant, its performance is not required before recovery may be obtained from the second party. In such cases, the party who was to receive performance merely deducts the damages caused by the breach before performing on his part. Judging whether the breach of a particular provision is so material as to justify rescission often presents a problem. If damage caused by the breach can be readily measured in money, or if the nature of the contract has not been so altered as to defeat the justifiable expectations of the party entitled to performance, the clause breached is generally not considered a condition precedent.[2]

The condition may be an express condition, specifically provided for in the contract; or it may be an implied or constructive condition.

2-94. Express Conditions. An express condition is one which is included in a contract and is designated as a condition which must be strictly performed before the other party's duty to perform arises. The effect of express condition clauses is to compel the other party to perform properly and on time. The penalty for failure to properly perform such a condition may be the loss of the right to receive payment or to otherwise obtain the return performance. The parties may stipulate that something is important—a condition precedent— even though it would not ordinarily be considered so. In such a case, failure to perform exactly as specified affords ground for rescission, unless the court construes the clause to be a penalty provision and therefore unenforceable.

Thus a contract may provide that "time is of the essence." This means that performance on or before the date specified is a condition precedent to the duty of the other party to pay or to perform.

It is common in building contracts to provide that the duty of the owner to make the final payment on completion of the building is conditional upon the builder's securing an architect's certificate. This is certification by the owner's architect that the construction is satisfactory and in accordance with the plans and specifications. Quite naturally, the architect's evaluation of the building contains a subjective element; he may refuse to grant a certificate on the basis of rather minor deviations or substitutions of materials, etc. Thus the condition is to a large degree outside the control of both parties and within the exclusive control of a third party, the architect. Obviously, the builder is in a serious dilemma if the certificate is arbitrarily withheld; in order to obtain payment, the only avenue open to him is to have the condition excused. Of course, the architect must exercise honest judgment, and proof that he did not act in good faith will dispense with the condition. If it can be shown that he refused the certificate arbitrarily and refused to explain why, if he failed to make a reasonably thorough inspection of the building, or otherwise acted in bad faith, the builder can recover the price without producing the architect's certificate.

In most states if the architect has refused to give a certificate because of his honest, though mistaken, belief that the building substantially deviated from

---

[2] Nolan v. Williamson Music, Inc., page 310

the specifications, the condition is not excused. While it might appear reasonable to allow a court to substitute its judgment as to whether or not there was substantial compliance in this situation, thereby excusing the builder from the requirement, such has not usually been the ruling. The courts feel that to substitute their judgment or that of the jury for that of the architect is not proper or in keeping with the intent of the parties. However, in at least one state the unreasonable refusal to certify, even though honest and in good faith, will not prevent recovery by the builder. The basis of this rule is that to do otherwise would impose upon the builder a serious forfeiture. The majority rule is harsh, but the minority rule, in effect, eliminates the express condition. It is another example of a legal dilemma, and it can be readily seen that further expansion of the minority rule could wreak havoc in the law respecting conditions. Fortunately, the minority rule has been strictly limited to certifications of the sort described above.

A related situation is that in which a contract expressly conditions the duty to pay the price upon the promisor's "satisfaction" with the promisee's performance; the duty to accept and pay for goods furnished or services rendered depends on the recipient's satisfaction. In contracts with this provision, the burden is upon the promisee to establish—and prove in court if necessary—that the condition has been met.

This raises the question as to what is meant by the term "to the satisfaction of the promisor." Here again, there is a subjective element involved, for it could mean *literally,* in which event the personal, though mistaken, judgment of the promisor would prevent recovery. In any event, however, he would be required to act in good faith and evidence an honest dissatisfaction. If the contract involves painting a portrait for example, the satisfaction is almost entirely subjective.

Generally in contracts the requirement is held to be satisfied if the performance is such that it would satisfy the promisor as a "reasonable man." Thus, in contracts which do not involve personal taste or judgment, the condition is fulfilled if a reasonable person would judge the performance satisfactory. But where the personal element is present, courts have interpreted the satisfaction provision literally. The eminent Judge Learned Hand, for example, stated in an opinion:

> . . . The contract of employment provided that appellant [plaintiff] should render "satisfactory services," for which he was to receive the sum of $250 per week. It contained no provision in any manner limiting the appellee [defendant] in the exercise of his judgment as to what should be deemed "satisfactory services." The appellant did not undertake to render services which should satisfy a court or jury, but undertook to satisfy the taste, fancy, interest and judgment of appellee. It was the appellee who was to be satisfied, and if dissatisfied he had the right to discharge the appellant at any time for any reason, of which he was the sole judge.

2-95. Constructive or Implied Conditions.   Probably the most common problems of conditions precedent arise when parties have simply entered into a contract and have not mentioned anything about conditions. The contract describes the duties and performance required of each, and for all that appears in the contract, the performance of each party is quite independent from that of the other. Often one party has promised to render a certain service or deliver certain goods, and the other has promised to pay a certain sum for such goods or services. In such a contract, the question is presented: Will the law *imply* that the performance by one party is a condition precedent to the duty of the other party to render his performance? Will the latter be required to perform in spite of the other's breach, obtaining relief by deducting the damages caused by the other's breach? If under the contract one party is to perform first in time, that performance is construed to be a condition precedent.

A condition precedent must be distinguished from a promise. One party may promise to do something in order that the other party may proceed with his own performance. Failure to keep this promise does not amount to a failure of a condition precedent. For example, if *A* contracts to build a building for *B,* and *B* promises to obtain a building permit, *B*'s failure to obtain the permit will not relieve him from liability under the contract.[3]

There are many ramifications to the law of constructive conditions; many questions are presented when the basic principle is applied to the great variety of fact patterns. What *degree* of performance is required before the other party is obligated to perform on his part? Is it significant that the failure to render complete performance was willfull, as opposed to a good faith effort which simply fell short of the mark? The general rule is that the conditions must be substantially performed; that substantial performance will not, however, suffice if the party willfully or in bad faith renders something short of complete performance.

Since substantial performance is the basic test for satisfaction of the constructive condition, it becomes necessary to measure the performance. The general principle is that a failure to render full and complete performance will amount to a breach of a constructive condition only if the failure was so significant and important that the other party is deprived of what he bargained for. Stated differently, if the breach is immaterial, there has been substantial performance; if the breach is material, a party is relieved of his obligation to perform.[4] Of course, whether a breach is material or immaterial, damages are recoverable.

To illustrate, assume that *R,* a retail grocer, contracts to buy from *S* 10,000 pounds of Ole's oleo at 35 cents a pound. *R* is to pay for the margarine within thirty days and *S* is send a salesman to display and assist in selling the oleo. If *S* fails to send a salesman and the margarine does not sell, must *R* pay for it or may he return it and rescind the contract? In other words, was the provision for sending a salesman a condition precedent to *R*'s duty to pay? Whether the provision is an important one would doubtless depend in part on whether *R* had previously sold oleo and upon whether Ole's brand was new to the trade. If the brand is a new one and needs special promotion, and if *R* is a somewhat inexperienced grocer, it seems likely that the breach would be substantial enough to justify rescission. On the other hand, it would not be substantial in more usual situations.

Several general principles can be derived from the numerous cases concerning materiality of a breach.

[3] Bergman v. Parker, page 311
[4] Surety Development Corporation v. Grevas, page 312

A failure to perform on a specified date will not usually be treated as a material breach, especially if there is some justification for the delay. Delays in payment of money or completion of building contracts are regarded as less significant than delays in shipment of goods. Nor is exact compliance with time provisions always required in contracts for the sale of real property.[5] A provision establishing the time for performance of a contract that involves primarily the expenditure of labor and materials or the production of a commodity of little value to anyone other than the contracting party is normally not considered of major significance. Thus, the failure of a contractor to complete a house by the date set in the contract would not justify rescission by the owner, although he could deduct from the contract price such damages as resulted from the delay.

In a contract for the sale of marketable goods, a clause calling for performance within a certain time is usually held to be a condition precedent to the extent that rather strict compliance is required. In contracts whereby retailers purchase goods that are normally bought and sold in the market, performance by the seller on the date specified is considered quite important. Sales promotion campaigns and provisions for the normal needs of customers are built around delivery dates. To replace merchandise not received promptly, other sources must be tapped. Failure to comply with the time provisions of such contracts usually justifies the buyer in rejecting an offer to perform at a later date. Eventually, an extended delay becomes material in the performance of any contract, and ultimately it justifies rescission. Also, if partial performance has not taken place, a relatively short delay may justify rescission; whereas if performance is under way and time is not of the essence, a delay of some time may be required before rescission is justified. If the contract does not provide a specific date for performance, it is implied that performance will take place within a reasonable time—the length of time being dependent upon the nature of the commodity involved and the surrounding circumstances. In those contracts in which time for performance normally is deemed not to be a condition precedent, by adding a clause that "time is of the essence in this agreement," it can be made so.

Many decisions indicate that a willfull breach—one made in bad faith—will more likely be considered material than will one which lacks this element.

The quantitative element of a breach will often determine materiality. For example, *A* contracted with *B* for the purchase of an electric generator capable of producing 2,500 kilowatts of electricity. If *B* delivers and installs equipment which turns out only 2,400 kilowatts, it might be contended that there has been substantial performance. On the other hand, if it generated only 1,250 kilowatts, *B* would be justified in refusing to accept and pay for it.

If a breach occurs after a party has partly performed, the courts are less likely to consider the breach material than would be the case if the breach had occurred prior to any performance. The reason for this is that the person who has partly performed stands to forfeit the value of such performance if his deviation is deemed material.

The foregoing principles are not conclusive. In any given case, a plaintiff

[5] Carsek Corp. v. Stephen Schifter, Inc., page 314

may have almost completely performed, yet the defendant may be substantially deprived of what he bargained for.

2-96. Concurrent Conditions.   Many contracts are so drawn that the parties thereto are to act simultaneously as to certain matters. An agreement that calls for a conveyance by *A* of a certain farm upon payment of $60,000 by *B* is illustrative of such a situation. The deed is to be delivered at the time payment is made. Those terms of a contract that require both parties to the agreement to perform contemporaneously are designated *concurrent conditions.* Under the terms of such an agreement, neither party is placed in default until the other has offered to perform. Such offer on his part is called a tender, and actual performance is unnecessary to place the other party in default. For this reason *B* could not successfully sue *A* for failure to deliver the deed until he had offered to make the payment required. Actual payment is not required unless *A* offers to deliver the deed; tender of payment is sufficient.

2-97. Tender.   A *tender* in the law of contracts is an offer to perform—to carry out a promise to do something or to pay something. It is also an attempt to perform by one who is "ready, willing and able" to perform. The tender is especially significant in those bilateral contracts in which both parties are required to perform contemporaneously. The reciprocal performances are constructive conditions concurrent. Under the terms of such contract, neither party is placed in default until the other has *offered* to perform. Such offer on his part is a tender, and actual performance is unnecessary to place the other party in default. Thus, actual payment is not required unless the other party proffers performance, e.g., a deed; tender of payment is sufficient.

Simultaneous performance may be required not only if the contract specifies the same date for the performance by each party but also if no time is fixed for either performance, or if the time for performance is specified for only one party.

Not only is the concept of tender applied to concurrent condition situations but also to contract performance in general. As noted, the tender may be either an offer to pay or an offer to perform. Suppose that *B* and *S* enter into a contract for the sale of goods; that *S,* the seller, proffers the proper goods at the proper time and place to *B,* the buyer; and that *B* refuses to accept the goods. *B*'s refusal of the tender discharges *S*'s obligation, and he can proceed to bring action against *B* for damages. Also, should *B* subsequently seek to enforce the contract, *S*'s tender would be a defense.

The results are somewhat different if the tender is an offer to pay money which is due to a creditor. Frequently, one party will tender the money due the other party, and the payment will not be accepted for any number of reasons. Usually, either there is a dispute as to the amount owing, or a party may feel that his legal rights will be affected by accepting payment. A tender obviously does not pay or discharge the debt. It does, however, have three important legal effects: (1) it extinguishes any security interest such as a mortgage or pledge that secures the debt, (2) it stops interest from accruing thereafter, and (3) in case the creditor later brings suit recovering no more than the amount tendered, he must pay the court costs.

A valid tender consists of an unconditional offer to pay, at the proper time, in legal tender, the amount to the creditor or his agent. A tender before the maturity of an obligation is not a proper tender, and the creditor is under no duty to accept it as would be the case if the obligation was interest bearing. Tender of payment in something other than legal tender—such as a check— is good unless the creditor refuses it because it is not legal tender. If he refuses it for some other reason, a proper tender has been made.

There are two aspects to tender under the Uniform Commercial Code. Unless otherwise agreed, *tender of payment* by the buyer is a condition to the seller's duty to tender and complete any delivery. Such tender may be made by any means or in any manner current in the ordinary course of business, unless the seller demands payment in legal tender and gives a reasonable extension of time to procure it. Thus payment by check is quite customary, but such payment is conditional—it is defeated if the check is dishonored. The Code also provides for the manner of a seller's *tender of delivery.* Basically, the requirement is that the seller put and hold conforming goods at the buyer's disposition and that he give the buyer reasonable notification that the goods are available for him.

2-98. Anticipatory Repudiation.   A breach of a contract usually occurs when a party fails to perform at the time agreed upon. However, a party may announce his intention not to perform prior to the time of the agreed perform- ance. This is called an anticipatory breach, or repudiation, and may be treated by the other party as a present and complete breach. He may proceed to bring an action at once to recover damages or for other appropriate relief.

There are limitations upon the application of the doctrine. One is that it does not apply to promises to pay money on or before a specified date. For example, if a promissory note matures on June 1, 1975, a statement by the maker in 1972 that he will not pay it when the maturity date arrives, would not give rise to a present cause of action by the holder. Also, in order that the right of immediate action for breach can arise, the repudiation must be *posi- tive* and *unequivocal.*[6] *Such repudiation need not be expressed in words; conduct evidencing it will suffice.* If *A* contracts on June 1, 1972, to sell his store building and to give occupancy to *B* on July 1, 1973, but sells the store to *X* and gives occupancy to him on October 1, 1972, he has clearly repudiated —he has made impossible his own performance. On the other hand, if *S* who is under a contract to deliver 10,000 TV sets to *B* on July 1, 1973, announces on January 1, 1973, that a threatened strike casts doubt upon his ability to perform, this would not be a positive and unequivocal repudiation.

When an anticipatory breach occurs, the party entitled to performance has a choice of several remedies. It is important that he make the right choice, and this is often difficult to do. He can sue at once and recover damages for the breach, but as a condition to recovery, he must be able to establish his own readiness and ability to perform. Secondly, he may elect to seek restitution, a remedy which is available to both anticipatory and present breaches. Restitu- tion comes from the latin *restitutio* meaning to "restore." If there is a breach after the nonbreaching party has rendered a part of his performance, he is entitled to be restored to his original position—to recover that with which he has parted. If this remedy is elected, the repudiation would be treated as a

[6] Diamos v. Hirsch, page 315

mutual rescission. Also, the aggrieved party can cease to perform his part of the contract and await performance by the repudiating party.

The practical aspects of business will often dictate the remedy to be used. For example: *M* is a manufacturer of mobile homes. He purchases components from many different sources and assembles the trailers in his plant. The XYZ Manufacturing Company is under contract to deliver 1,000 spring and axle units at the rate of 100 per week, commencing on June 1, 1973. Prior to any deliveries XYZ announces that it will not fill the orders. What should *M* do? To wait until the delivery date before taking any action would not only disrupt the assembly line, but would be an enhancement, or increase, of his damages. One solution would be to arrange for purchase of the axles from some other source and bring action later for damages resulting from the breach. The Code provides that after a breach including anticipatory repudiation, the buyer may "cover" by making in good faith and without unreasonable delay any reasonable purchase of or contract to purchase goods in substitution for those due from the seller. The buyer may recover from the seller as damages the difference between the cost of cover and the contract price together with any incidental or consequential damages, less expenses saved in consequence of the seller's breach. Failure of the buyer to effect cover does not bar him from recovery damages for nondelivery. However, in the latter event, damages will be limited to those which could not have been obviated by proper cover. It should be noted that the test of proper cover is good faith. It is immaterial that the method of cover used was not the cheapest or most effective.

As a general proposition of contract law, a party may retract his repudiation, provided he does so prior to any material change of position by the other party in reliance upon it. The retraction would simply be a notice that he will perform the contract after all. The Code allows a retraction of anticipatory repudiation until the repudiating party's next performance is due, unless the aggrieved party has since the repudiation canceled or materially changed his position or otherwise indicated that he considers the repudiation final. Retraction may be by any method which clearly indicates to the aggrieved party that the repudiating party intends to perform, but it must include any assurance justifiably demanded. Retraction reinstates the repudiating party's rights under the contract, with due excuse and allowance to the aggrieved party for any delay occasioned by the repudiation.

Thus, the repudiating party's right to reinstate the contract depends upon what action has been taken by the aggrieved party. Naturally, the repudiation would in and of itself cause some concern to the aggrieved party as to whether he could rely upon performance by the repudiator. For this reason, the Code provides that a condition to an effective retraction is that the repudiating party give "adequate assurance" that he will, in fact, render the required performance.

The Code contains provisions with regard to anticipatory repudiation in addition to cover. These provide that when either party repudiates the contract with respect to a performance not yet due, the loss of which will substantially impair the value of the contract to the other, the aggrieved party may (*a*) for a commercially reasonable time await performance by the repudiating party; (*b*) resort to any remedy for breach, even though he has notified the repudiating party that he would await the latter's performance and has urged retraction; and (*c*) in either case, suspend his own performance or proceed on the seller's right to identify goods to the contract notwithstanding breach, or to salvage unfinished goods.

2-99. Divisibility—Installment Contracts.   While many contracts require a single performance by each party and are completely performed at one point of time, others require or permit performance by one or both parties in installments over a period of time. The rights and obligations of parties during the period when the contract is being performed frequently depend upon whether the contract is "entire" or "divisible." A contract is said to be divisible if performance by each party is divided into two or more parts *and* performance of each part by one party is the agreed exchange for the corresponding part by the other party. It is to be noted that a contract is not divisible simply by virtue of the fact that it is to be performed in installments.

The parties may specify whether a contract is divisible or entire. Thus a contract may contain a clause stipulating that each delivery is a separate contract, or other language may be used to show the intention of the parties that their agreement is to be treated as if it were a series of contracts.

Where performance of a contract may take place in portions rather than all at one time, several questions arise: (1) Is the contract divisible on both sides so that the second party is under a duty to perform in part after the first party performs an installment? (2) Does a material breach of any installment justify a rescission of the balance of the agreement? (3) If one party is in default, may he nevertheless recover for the performance rendered prior to default?

The concept of divisibility is applicable to a variety of contracts including employment contracts, construction contracts, and sales contracts. As a general proposition employment contracts are interpreted to be divisible, but construction contracts are usually deemed to be entire. The divisibility of contracts for the sale of goods under the Code is the subject of several provisions discussed later in this section.

If *A* employs *B* to serve as a financial consultant for one year at a salary of $2,000 per month, *B* would be entitled to $2,000 after one month's service. *B* would not have to complete a year's service as a condition to payment. If he wrongfully resigned after working for one month, he would nevertheless be entitled to his salary. *A* could, of course, sue *B* for damages for breach of contract, and if sued by *B* for his salary *A* could counterclaim for damages.

If *C* contracts with *D* to build an additional bedroom on *D*'s house for $5,000, the contract might provide for payments to be made by *D* as the work progresses: $500 upon execution of the contract: $1,000 upon completion of the rough carpentry; $1,000 when the electrical wiring is done; $1,000 upon completion of the plumbing; and $1,500 when the room is completed. If *C* abandoned the work after completing the rough carpentry, he would not be able to recover for that portion of the work. The breach would be one of the entire contract, and no recovery would be allowed for the partial performance.

There have been numerous cases involving the question of whether or not a contract is divisible. No general test can be derived from these cases, and the parties seldom provide specifically for this in their contract. The courts are called upon to determine in any given case whether the parties intended that (1) each would accept the part performance of the other in return for his own without regard to subsequent events or (2) the division of the contract into parts was only for the purpose of providing periodic payments which would apply toward the amount due upon completion of the entire contract. In any event, as noted previously, the party who breaches is liable for damages resulting from his breach.

Under the Code, unless the parties have otherwise agreed, a sales contract is entire—all of the goods called for by the contract must be tendered in a single delivery, and payment in full is due upon such tender. If the contract permits installment deliveries, the seller can demand a proportionate share of the price for each delivery as it is made, provided the price can be apportioned, as is the case when the goods are sold for a certain price per item. If there is a substantial default on an installment, such as when the goods tendered or delivered do not conform to the contract, the buyer may reject the installment. When an installment breach indicates that the seller will not satisfactorily perform the balance of the contract or that he is unreliable, the buyer can rescind the entire contract. Should the buyer accept a nonconforming installment without giving notice of cancellation or demanding that the seller deliver goods that do conform, he may not use the breach as a basis for rescission. Thus in a divisible contract the buyer may waive a breach and demand full performance, or he may rescind the contract if there is a substantial breach of an installment—one which materially impairs the value of the entire contract.

EXCUSES FOR NONPERFORMANCE

2-100. In General.   Even though the contract is silent on the point, a party may be relieved from performing a contract including conditions precedent, or his liability for breach of contract may be eliminated if he is legally excused from performance of the contract. As noted previously, performance by one party is excused when the other party has failed to perform a condition precedent or when a defense, such as fraud or lack of capacity is present. In addition there is no liability for breach of contract when (1) one party has waived performance by indicating that he does not intend to hold the other party to the terms of the contract, (2) one party has prevented the other party from carrying out the agreement, (3) performance of the contract has been frustrated, or (4) the contract has become impossible of performance, as contrasted with performance merely becoming more burdensome for one of the parties.

In addition, the Code allows substituted performance when the agreed carrier or other facilities have become unavailable, the agreed manner of delivery becomes commercially impracticable, or when the agreed means or manner of payment fails because of some governmental regulation. In such cases, a reasonable substitute or equivalent method of performance will discharge the contract. The Code also gives a seller an excuse if performance has become impracticable by the failure of presupposed conditions. If a seller cannot make delivery because of "unforeseen supervening circumstances not within the contemplation of the parties at the time of contracting," (U.C.C. 2-615 Official Comment) he will be relieved of his obligation.

2-101. Waiver.   A *waiver* been defined as the passing by of an occasion to enforce a legal right, whereby the legal right is lost. As applied to contract law it means (1) a promise to forgo the benefit of a condition to the promisor's duty or (2) an election to continue under a contract after the other party has breached. The essence of waiver is conduct that indicates an intention not to enforce certain provisions of the agreement. The waiver may be made either before or after a breach. If it is made before, it constitutes an assurance that performance of the condition will not be insisted upon. If a building contract provides for completion on a certain date and the owner grants an extension of six months, he has waived his right to insist upon completion at the earlier date. The waiver may be retracted unless it is supported by consideration or the promisee has made a substantial change of position in reliance upon it. The Code provides that a party who has made a waiver affecting an executory provision of a contract may retract it upon giving reasonable notice that he will require strict performance of any term waived, "unless the retraction would be unjust in view of a material change of position in reliance on the waiver." (U.C.C. 2-209(5))

A party against whom a condition has been breached has two general courses of action. He can terminate the contract and sue for damages, or he can continue his performance and accept the nonconforming performance. In the latter event, he waives the breach and cannot later assert it as a basis for his own refusal to proceed. He does, however, still have the right to recover damages for the breach. Under the Code the retention or acceptance of defective goods may constitute a waiver. A buyer who fails to particularize defects in goods may in fact be waiving his objections based on these defects.

2-102. Prevention.   It is obvious that a person may not recover for nonperformance of a contract if he is responsible for the nonperformance. If a party creates a situation which makes it impossible for the other party to perform, the other party is excused. It is an implied condition of every contract that neither party will prevent performance by the other.

Prevention often occurs when, by his conduct, one party stops or hinders the occurrence or fulfillment of a condition in the contract. Whenever one party's cooperation is necessary to the agreed performance of the other, but is not forthcoming, the Code provides that the other party is excused for any resulting delay in his own performance and may proceed to perform in any reasonable manner.

2-103. Impossibility of Performance In General.   Actual impossibility of performance is a valid excuse for breach of contract and releases a party from his duty to perform. Impossibility is to be distinguished from "additional hardship." As a general rule, in the absence of an appropriate contract provision, circumstances which impose additional hardship on one party do not constitute an excuse for breach of contract.[7] Therefore, many contracts provide that manufacturers, suppliers, or builders shall be relieved from performance in case of fire, strikes, difficulty in obtaining raw materials, or other incidents over which they have no control. To be effective, however, it is generally held that such provisions must be included in the body of the agreement.

[7] Luria Engineering Co. v. Aetna Cas. & Surety Co., page 317

It is often difficult to draw the line between additional hardship and impossibility. The modern trend is to be somewhat more lenient in finding impossibility to exist. The liberalizing trend has been developed on the basic premise that if a problem develops which a promisor had no reason to anticipate and for the presence of which he is not at fault, then the promisor in equity and good conscience ought to be discharged.

There are many situations in which a real impossibility may exist, and the effects of the impossibility may be quite varied. As was noted in Section 2-94, an architect's certificate may be a condition precedent to payment. If the architect becomes insane or dies, there is an impossibility which excuses the condition, and the builder can recover without it.

The law relating to impossibility of performance has an interesting history. At an early date the common-law rule was that impossibility was not an excuse for nonperformance. The common-law judges felt that the chance that performance might become impossible was a risk borne by a contracting party and that he should, therefore, be prepared to respond in damages. This concept has been altered, and now true impossibility—that resulting from factors of an unforeseeable character—is a defense to an action for damages for breach of contract. The prevailing view is that if a promisor's performance becomes objectively impossible, his duty to perform is excused, provided the impossibility was not his own fault. In effect, the courts attach an implied condition to contracts that performance must be rendered only if it is possible to do so.

To have the effect of releasing a party from his duty to perform, the impossibility must render performance "physically and objectively impossible." If objective impossibility is present, the discharge is mutual; i.e., the promisor is discharged, and the promisee is also discharged from his corresponding obligation. Many cases state that in order to constitute impossibility there must be a fortuitous or unavoidable occurrence which was not reasonably foreseeable.[8] In addition such occurrence must not be caused by the promisor or by developments which he could have prevented, avoided, or remedied by corrective measures. For this reason, the failure of a third party, such as a supplier, to make proper delivery does not create impossibility. Impossibility will not be allowed as a defense when the obstacle was created by the promisor or was within his power to eliminate.

In some cases the ability to perform is the essence of the contract, it having been contemplated at the time of the agreement that the performance may or may not be possible. A promisor who knowingly accepts the risk of performance under such circumstances is in no position to ask for relief when it is later determined that he will be unable to perform.

Assume that *A* contracts to sell and deliver 500 bales of cotton from a certain plantation, delivery from any other source not being permitted by the contract terms. *A* actually raises only 200 bales of cotton, and seeks to be released from his duty to deliver the balance. Naturally, if his inability to deliver has developed because he failed to plant a sufficient acreage or was careless in his planting, cultivation, or harvesting of the crop, *A* should not be relieved of his duty to deliver. However, if he planted enough to have produced 800 bales under normal conditions, but the weather or other factors

[8] Trans-State Investments, Inc. v. Deive, page 318

were such as to decrease the yield materially below that normally grown, failure to perform would be excused. In such a case, *A* is obligated to deliver the 200 bales at the contract price, provided the buyer desires such partial performance. Had the parties, at the time of making the contract, taken into account such contingencies, and *A* had nevertheless promised performance, impossibility could not be effectively urged by him as a defense. It is because people seldom take such factors into consideration when making a contract that relief is provided when impossibility develops.

Another facet of impossibility of performance is illustrated by those cases in which one of the parties, by his conduct, is responsible for the impossibility. In such situations, the party so responsible will not be permitted to rely upon impossibility as a basis for relieving himself of the obligation to perform.[9]

2-104. Impossibility of Performance—Specific Cases.   There are four basic situations in which impossibility of performance is frequently offered as an excuse for nonperformance. In the first of these performance becomes illegal because of the enactment of some law, or because of some act on the part of the government. Illustrative of this are instances in which a manufacturer is prevented from making delivery of merchandise because the armed forces make a superior demand for it. Governmental action, however, may merely make an agreement more burdensome than was anticipated; then it does not afford a basis for relief.

The second situation is the death or incapacitating illness of one of the contracting parties. This is not deemed to be a form of impossibility, unless the nature of the contract is such as to demand the personal services of the disabled or deceased person. Ordinary contracts of production, processing, and sale of property are unaffected by the death or illness of one or both of the parties. In the event of death, it is assumed that the contract will be carried out by the estate of the deceased. However, if a contract is one for personal services or is of such a character as to clearly imply that the continued services of the contracting party are essential to performance, death or illness will excuse nonperformance. If an artist contracts to paint a portrait or an architect agrees to draw plans and specifications for a building, the death or illness of the artist or architect concerned renders performance impossible. The nature of their service is such as to demand their personal attention. In contracts for personal services, illness excuses a laborer for his inability to perform, but it does not bar the employer from terminating the contract of employment, provided the employee's absence constitutes a material breach. In contracts for personal services, the death of the employer also terminates the relation. In such a case, the estate of the employer is not liable to the employee in damages for prematurely terminating the contract.

Many agreements involve certain subject matter, the continued existence of which is essential to the completion of the contract. The third rule is that destruction of any subject matter that is essential to the completion of the contract will operate to relieve the parties from the obligations assumed by their agreement. Another somewhat analogous situation arises where property that one of the parties expected to use in his performance is destroyed. If a factory from which the owner expected to deliver certain shoes is destroyed

---

[9] Hansen v. Johnston, page 318

by fire, performance is not excused, inasmuch as performance is still possible, although an undue hardship may result. The shoes needed to fill the order can be obtained from another source. Had the contract stipulated that the shoes were to be delivered from this particular factory, however, its destruction would have operated to excuse a failure to perform. Stated in other language, the destruction of the source from which one of the parties *expects* to make performance does not relieve him. He is still under duty to obtain the property from some other source. A destruction of the source from which a party has *agreed* to make delivery will excuse him, for he is not at liberty to use any other source. As was previously noted, there has been a liberal trend based on the theory of implied conditions, which holds that where both parties *understood* that delivery was to be made from a certain source, even though it was not expressly so agreed, destruction of the source of supply will relieve the obligor from performing.

The last form of impossibility arises when there is an essential element lacking. It has never been satisfactorily defined, but apparently, when some element or property which the parties assumed existed or would exist is in fact lacking, the agreement may be rescinded. This is said to be a form of impossibility at the time of making the contract, and courts have always tended to consider the contract null and void in such cases. Mere additional burden or hardship is not sufficient to relieve the party from the duties imposed by the agreement. It must be definitely proved that performance is substantially impossible because of the missing element. For example, *A* contracts to build an office building at a certain location. Because of the nature of the soil, it is utterly impossible to build the type of building provided for in the agreement; the agreement must therefore be terminated. The missing element is the proper condition of the soil. In other words, from the very beginning, the contract terms could not possibly have been complied with, and in such cases the courts are prone to release the contracting party.

2-105. Right to Recover for Part Performance—Impossibility.   Often impossibility of performance becomes apparent only after the agreement has been partially performed. One coat of paint, for instance, is placed upon a house before the house is destroyed. In such cases, is the loss of the work already completed to fall upon the one doing the work or upon the party who was to have the benefit of the labor? Most states permit the person who has partially performed to recover the value of the benefit the other party would have received had impossibility not arisen. This is simply another way of saying that the recipient of the work must pay for all labor and material expended up to the date of impossibility, provided the labor and material had attached to the property of the one for whom the work was being done. However, there are many states which do not allow any recovery.[10]

Care should be taken in such cases, however, to differentiate between impossibility and mere additional burden. The destruction of a partially completed building does not make recovery for the work done impossible. By starting construction anew, performance is still possible, although the cost will be greater than was anticipated. In the latter case, the additional cost must be borne by the contractor.

[10] Hipskind Heating & Plumbing Co. v. General Industries, page 320

2-106. Frustration. Frequently, an event occurs which does not create actual impossibility but does prevent the achievement of the object or purpose of the contract. In such cases, the courts may find an implied condition that certain developments will excuse performance. Frustration has the effect of excusing nonperformance and arises whenever there is an intervening event or change of circumstances which is so fundamental as to be entirely beyond that which was contemplated by the parties. Frustration is not impossibility, but it is more than mere hardship. It is an excuse created by law to eliminate liability when a fortuitous occurrence has defeated the reasonable expectations of the parties.

An interesting fact situation was presented in an early twentieth-century English case which gave rise to the frustration doctrine. The defendant had rented an apartment in London in order to use the balcony to watch the coronation procession. The King became ill, and the coronation was canceled. The court held that the purpose of the contract had been frustrated, and the defendant was relieved of his duty to pay.

In some cases parties have sought to terminate contracts upon the basis of the economic unfeasability of remaining in business. Often theories of frustration combined with impossibility are urged.[11]

2-107. Commercial Impracticability. The Code makes provision for several situations in which the promised performance in connection with the sale of goods becomes impracticable. It is important to note that there is a difference between "impossibility" and "impracticability." The latter may be compared with frustration. In the event that it should become "commercially impracticable" to make *delivery* of the goods in the manner agreed upon, the seller must tender a "commercially reasonable" substitute, if such is available, and the buyer must accept it. This concept of a substituted performance when that agreed upon fails without fault of either party also extends to *payment* difficulties, within the limitations of the following section:

> If the agreed means or manner of payment fails because of domestic or foreign governmental regulation, the seller may withhold or stop delivery unless the buyer provides a means or manner of payment which is commercially a substantial equivalent. If delivery has already been taken, payment by the means or in the manner provided by the regulation discharges the buyer's obligation unless the regulation is discriminatory, oppressive or predatory. (U.C.C. 2-614(2))

In addition the Code has rejected the strict requirements of the law of impossibility in other respects. It provides that a seller who is unable to deliver the goods, in whole or in part, as required under the contract is not in breach if his inability to perform as agreed " . . . has been made impracticable by the occurrence of a contingency, the nonoccurrence of which was a basic assumption on which the contract was made. . . . " (U.C.C. 2-615(a))

If the seller is able to furnish a part of the goods—the contingency affects only a part of his capacity to perform—he is required to: " . . . allocate production and deliveries among his customers but may at his option include regular customers not then under contract as well as his own requirements for further

---

[11] 407 East 61st Garage, Inc. v. Savoy Fifth Ave. Corp., page 320

manufacture. He may so allocate in any manner which is fair and reasonable." (U.C.C. 2-615(b))

The Code requires that the seller "notify the buyer seasonably that there will be delay or non-delivery and, when allocation is required . . . , [he must notify the buyer] of the estimated quota thus made available to the buyer." (U.C.C. 2-615(c)) Upon receiving this notice of a material or indefinite delay or an allocation justified under the Code, the buyer "may by written notification to the seller as to any delivery concerned, and where the prospective deficiency substantially impairs the value of the whole contract . . . (a) then also as to the whole, terminate the contract and thereby discharge any unexecuted portion of the contract; or (b) modify the contract by agreeing to take his available quota in substitution. (2) If after receipt of such notification from the seller the buyer fails so to modify the contract within a reasonable time (not exceeding thirty days), the contract lapses with respect to any deliveries affected." (U.C.C. 2-616)

2-108. Government Contracts. There are in practice many differences between contracts in which the government is a party and those in which the parties are private citizens. The United States Supreme Court in 1875 in the case of *Cooke* v. *United States* stated that when the federal government "comes down from its position of sovereignty and enters the domain of commerce, it submits itself to the same laws that govern individuals there." But it has been suggested that this is more true in theory than in practice. The Federal government has established unique tribunals for resolving disputes stemming from the performance of its contracts.

PERFORMANCE OF CONTRACTS CASES

Simhawk Corp. v. Egler
202 N.E.2d 49 (Ill.) 1964

In 1953 the defendant, Egler, entered into a written lease for retail store premises. The lease provided for a minimum rental of $250.00 per month and contained a provision for percentage rental:

> Tenant shall pay a total rental of five percent (5%) of the gross sales less credits and allowances for returned merchandise on his first seventy-five (75) thousand dollars ($75,000.00) of sales annually, four percent (4%) on his next twenty-five thousand dollars ($25,000.00) of net sales annually, and (2-1/2%) two and one-half percent on the excess of his net sales over one hundred thousand dollars ($100,-000.00) annually. Net sales is hereby defined to mean gross sales less allowances and credits for returned merchandise.

The lease also contained the following provision: "Tenant agrees that he will use the premises only for the purpose of a shoe store engaged in the sale at retail of children's shoes and footwear."

In 1962 the defendant moved his retail shoe business to a new location and after October 1 did not sell any shoes in the plaintiff's store space. Thereafter he sent to the plaintiff a check for $250.00 each month, and the checks were returned. Subsequently plaintiff brought legal action asking that the court declare the rights of the parties under the lease. The trial court ruled that the defendant must pay more than the minimum rental. The defendant appealed. CARROLL, J. . . . Defendant contends on this appeal that the written lease is complete in itself; that it contained no provision requiring the continued use of the leased premises by the lessee; that the trial court in reaching its decision implied a covenant of continued operation of defendant's business in the premises; and that the basis upon which such covenant was implied was the lease provision for a percentage rental.

That the lease in question contained an express provision requiring the continued use of the premises as a retail shoe store would appear to be beyond dispute. The language used is clear and unambiguous and when the lease is examined as a whole the purpose served by such covenant becomes apparent. In addition to the minimum rent of $250.00 per month the lease required defendant to pay percentage rental based on gross shoe sales from the store operating in plaintiff's building. If as defendant contends the lease did not require him to conduct a retail shoe store in the rented premises during the term of the lease, then computation of the percentage rental which defendant agreed to pay could not be made. The construction which defendant urges would nullify an essential part of the rental provisions of the lease and would relieve the defendant of any obligation to pay more than the minimum rental. It is abundantly clear from the record that such was not the intention of the parties. . . .

. . . We are in accord with defendant's statement that the written lease is complete in itself. This being true, we are required to give meaning and effect to each clause thereof. The parties saw fit to include therein a provision that defendant in addition to the minimum rental would pay a percentage of the gross sale of shoes made in the shoe store conducted on plaintiff's premises. The source of the percentage rental was the shoe store and to insure its continued operation the lease specified that the defendant would use the premises only for such purpose. With the intention of the parties thus clearly expressed by the language of the lease, the trial court had no occasion to imply a covenant of continued operation. . . .

For the reasons herein indicated, the judgment of the Circuit Court of Winnebago County is affirmed.

Affirmed.

Nolan v. Williamson Music, Inc.

300 F. Supp. 1311 (1969)

The plaintiff, composer of a musical composition "Tumbling Tumbleweed," sought to rescind his publishing agreement with the defendant. Plaintiff alleged that the defendant had failed to properly account for all royalties and that other breaches of the agreement had occurred.

EDELSTEIN, J. . . . The question to be resolved at this juncture is whether these breaches, when considered together, provide a sufficient basis for rescission.

It is accepted law that not every breach of a contract will justify rescission. Rather, rescission can be permitted only when the complaining party has suffered breaches of so material and substantial a nature that they affect the very essence of the contract and serve to defeat the object of the parties. . . .

Cases which have considered the problem of rescission in situations analagous to the one presented by the case at bar have granted rescission only after finding the equivalent of a total failure in the performance of the contract. In *Raftery* v. *World Film Corp.,* the plaintiff temporarily turned over to the defendant prints from which movies were to be made and then distributed. The contract provided that the defendant was to render weekly accounts of the earnings on the movies and to pay the plaintiff fifty percent thereof. The prints were to be returned at the expiration of the contract term. The court found that the defendant never paid plaintiff the full amount due, deliberately maintained a set of fictitious records, deliberately rendered false accountings, refused to permit inspection of the records as was required by the contract, and failed to return the prints to the plaintiff. Based on all of these factors rescission was granted. . . .

Rescission is not justified in this case. The fact [is] that fraud has not been established. . . . Although defendant has been guilty of divers breaches, these breaches involve a failure to comply fully with the contractual provisions for payment of royalties in various categories, and as to these breaches, it is clear to the court that plaintiff may be rendered whole by an award of monetary damages. Moreover, there seems little danger that Nolan will be deprived of his royalties in the future. This is not a case in which defendant has repudiated his obligation to pay royalties, nor is this a case in which plaintiff's song has not been exploited fully in the past or threatened with not being exploited fully in the future.

Thus, plaintiff is not entitled to rescission.

Bergman v. Parker

216 A.2d 581 (D.C.) 1966

The plaintiff, a partnership, entered into a contract to construct an apartment for the defendant. The defendant submitted plans for the building to the contractor. The contract provided that the defendant would obtain building permits and that work would commence when the permits were issued. The defendant decided to abandon the project when it found that the District of Columbia would not issue a building permit without certain changes and amplifications of the plans. The defendant refused to allow the plaintiff to commence work, and the latter brought action for breach of contract. The lower court awarded a judgment for damages, based upon the plaintiff's loss of profits. The defendant appealed.

MYERS, J. . . . Appellant first complains that the trial judge erred in finding that a valid contract was executed by him with the partnership for the erection of the building. He bottoms his argument upon the theory that their agreement was to take effect only upon the issuance of the building permits. He asserts that until this occurred, he was not obligated under the contract.

Appellant confuses a condition precedent with a promise. A condition precedent is a fact, other than the passage of time, which must exist before the duty of immediate performance of a promise can arise, whereas a promise is an express or implied declaration which raises a duty to perform and subjects the promisor to liability for damages for failure to do so.

In the instant case the only limitation was that appellees were not to begin work until the building permits were obtained, which did not in any way affect the meeting of the minds of the parties. The intentions of parties to a contract must be determined not only from the terms of the written agreement but also from the actions of the parties in relation thereto. The evidence produced at trial established that appellant intended to enter into a contract for the construction of a low-cost apartment and submitted to appellees five sets of plans which formed the foundation for the ultimate contract price. Building permits were never issued because appellant failed to supply the detailed specifications. In our opinion the provision in the contract that construction would commence when the building permits were issued was not tantamount to a condition precedent which had to be performed before appellant was to be bound by his contract.

Appellant next claims it was error not to find that the contract was impossible of performance in view of his inability to obtain building permits. The record does not support this contention. It is true that when the performance of an agreement is rendered impossible due to circumstances beyond the control of the parties, the party failing to perform is exonerated. Such impossibility is not limited to absolute or legal impossibility and includes impracticability due to extreme or unreasonable difficulty. However, it must be a real impossibility and not a mere inconvenience or unexpected difficulty. Moreover, the burden rests upon the party asserting this defense to prove it. The record demonstrates that appellant did not meet this burden. There is no question that building permits could have been issued after modification of existing plans, either in the form of additional specifications or actual changes in the plans. Fault for failure to obtain the permits must rest upon appellant. The trial judge correctly found that the contract was not impossible of performance. . . .

Affirmed.

Surety Development Corporation v. Grevas

192 N.E.2d 145 (Ill.) 1963

SMITH, J. When is a house a home? In our context a house is a home when it can be lived in. But when is that: When substantially completed or completely completed? We posit the question, because the answer is decisive.

Plaintiff sells prefabricated houses. Defendants selected one of their models, styled "Royal Countess, elevation 940." A contract was signed. The cost was $16,385.00; completion date September 27, 1961. Around 4:00 P.M. on that date defendants refused to accept the house asserting non-completion. Plaintiff then sued for the balance due and defendants counter-claimed for their down payment. Both alleged performance by them and non-performance by the other. The issue is therefore relatively simple: Who performed and who didn't? The facts are more elusive—plaintiff at times says one thing, defendants another. We narrate them briefly.

On the morning of the twenty-seventh, "Royal Countess, elevation 940" was far from being a house, let alone a home. Racing the clock, plaintiff initiated a crash program. When defendants arrived on the scene at 4:00, at plaintiff's behest for final inspection, the crash program was still crashing— workmen were all over the place, slapping on siding, laying the floors, bulldozing the yard, hooking up the utilities, and so on. Defendant's tour was not a success, to put it mildly. Instead of a home, they found, to their dismay, a hive buzzing with activity. They did not tarry, in spite of the foreman's assurances that all would be right by 5:30. Nor did they come back. They should have. Believe it or not, the foreman was right. The job *was* substantially completed by 5:30, with only a service walk, some grading and blacktopping left undone.

The trial court found that the house had been substantially completed and concluded that there had been, therefore, substantial compliance with the contract and with this we agree. But because the house was not completely completed, it found that there had not been *complete* compliance. With this, too, we agree, but such finding is beside the point. Substantial—not complete —compliance in a construction contract is all that is required. By 5:30, there had been just that, in other words, substantial performance of the contract. Plaintiff's contretemps in having inspection set for 4:00 o'clock was hardly the way to make friends and influence people, but such happenstance is of no moment in determining whether or not there had been substantial compliance, unless such can be said to indicate bad faith. We do not think that it does. What it indicates is bad timing, not bad faith.

That substantial performance or compliance is the key needs no extensive citation. In *Bloomington Hotel Company* v. *Garthwait,* (227 Ill. 613, 81 N.E. 714), it was said:

> Literal compliance with the provisions of a contract is not essential to a recovery. It will be sufficient if there has been an honest and faithful performance of the contract in its material and substantial parts, and no willful departure from or omission of the essential points of the contract.

In 12 Ill. Law & Practice Contracts, (§ 402, p. 547), it is said:

> In building contracts a literal compliance with the provisions of the particular contract, and the plans, specifications and drawings, is not necessary to a recovery by the contractor. It is sufficient that there is a substantial performance in good faith or that there is an honest and faithful performance of the contract in its material and substantial parts, with no willful departure from, or omission of, the essential points of the contract.

No substantial sum was required to complete the items left undone. Nor were they of so essential a character that defendants could not have been ensconced in their new home that night if they had so desired. We have thus answered our question: A house is ready to be lived in, to become a home, when it has been substantially completed.

Defendants make one further point. By motion they assert that plaintiff waived its right of appeal by having paid the judgment on the counter-claim. The court conditioned such payment upon a reconveyance by defendants of title to the premises which they had held so that a mortgage could be obtained. Their argument is that this constituted an acceptance by plaintiff of the benefits of the adverse judgment, if such a thing is possible. No waiver occurred. The appeal is not rendered moot by payment, conditioned though it was on reconveyance. Plaintiff's choice was either to pay or to seek a stay. The judgment is therefore appealable regardless of their choice and so long as they made it in time. This they did.

The issue of damages was never reached except on the counter-claim. Since the court should have found for plaintiff and against defendants, there must be a determination apropos thereof. Accordingly, the judgment below is reversed and remanded with directions to enter judgment for plaintiff on their complaint and against defendants on their counter-claim and thereafter to determine plaintiff's damages.

Reversed and remanded with directions.

Carsek Corp. v. Stephen Schifter, Inc.

246 A.2d 365 (Pa.) 1968

The plaintiff (Carsek) entered into a contract to purchase a 57-acre tract from the defendant for the purpose of constructing a housing development thereon. The agreement of sale provided for a price of $200,000—$25,000 in cash on or before settlement and the balance of $175,000 to be paid in four years time, secured by a purchase-money mortgage. The agreement (Paragraph Seven) stipulated that the buyer would have prepared by the Registered Engineer a statement of the costs to install streets, sidewalks, sewers, etc. and that the seller would absorb the costs in excess of $160,000. The plaintiff was forty-five days late in submitting the statement of costs, and the defendant refused to give any credit. The lower court ruled that the plaintiff was not entitled to any relief. Plaintiff appealed.

O'BRIEN, J. . . . The Chancellor held that Paragraph Seven of the agreement of sale . . . required that the cost estimates be submitted prior to settlement, and that, having failed to submit the estimates prior to settlement, plaintiff was not entitled to any relief. We disagree.

In the first place, we cannot agree with the Chancellor that time was of the essence of this contract. "It is a well-established general principle in equity that time is not ordinarily regarded as of the essence in contracts for the sale of real property unless it is so stipulated by the express terms thereof, or it is necessarily to be so implied."

. . . When it is so easy to insert the commonly-used phrase "time to be of the essence" when that is the desired result, we are loathe to ascribe that result to any other language.

Nor do the circumstances necessarily imply that time is of the essence. On the contrary, they provide a strong indication that time was not to be of the essence. One of those circumstances is the type of performance required. Appellee relies heavily on the language of the agreement providing that the credit for the estimates above $160,000 should be deducted from the consideration being paid by buyer at settlement as indicating that time must be of the essence. Although we have found no Pennsylvania cases directly in point, at least one jurisdiction has decided this precise issue and held that a requirement that a credit be given against a designated payment does not make time of the essence. . . .

Furthermore, appellant's delay really resulted in no harm to appellee. The Chancellor stated that time was of the essence "because, otherwise, final settlement would have been held and defendant still would have been uncertain as to the net consideration it would ultimately receive for its property" Yet this hardly constitutes harm cognizable by a court of equity. Neither party had the right to rescind the contract regardless of what the estimates totalled. When appellee made the agreement, it left itself open to an uncertain purchase price. A month or two more of uncertainty is scarcely the harm required in order that it be inferred that time is necessarily of the essence. Moreover, the delay resulted in no loss whatsoever of cash in hand, since appellee took a four-year purchase-money mortgage. . . .

Whereas appellee suffered virtually no harm from a slightly delayed performance, it would work a tremendous forfeiture to deny appellant the relief sought. This Court has always sought to avoid forfeitures, and has interpreted contracts in such a way as to effectuate that purpose. Particularly is this so where there has been part performance. The Restatement of Contracts, § 276 provides in part, as follows: "In determining the materiality of delay in performance, the following rules are applicable: . . . (c) If delay of one party in rendering a promised performance occurs before any part of his promise has been rendered, less delay discharges the duty of the other party than where there has been part performance of that promise." Here, appellant clearly performed part of its obligation under Paragraph Seven by submitting the cost estimates for Section One. To hold that it forfeited some $45,000 by submitting the remainder approximately forty-five days late would be unconscionable. Time was not stated to be of the essence of this contract, and the circumstances afford absolutely no basis for considering a forty-five day breach to be so material as to discharge appellee from any duty under Paragraph Seven.

.   .   .

The decree is reversed and remanded for proceedings consistent with this opinion, costs to be borne by appellee.

Diamos v. Hirsch

372 P.2d 76 (Ariz.) 1962

Plaintiff commenced suit to recover damages sustained as a result of an alleged breach of contract by anticipatory repudiation. Defendants filed a counterclaim alleging the breach was by the plaintiff. The trial court found for the defendants.

On November 20, 1956, plaintiff and defendants entered into an agreement the terms of which provided that plaintiff would construct a building on land owned by him and lease it to defendants for ten years. The rent clause of the agreement set forth a mathematical formula, the purpose of which was to establish the total amount of payment for the ten-year period. There was a mistake in the written provision which both parties acknowledged. Defendants were to give plaintiff a letter setting out the correct rent but instead gave plaintiff an addendum to the contract, which in addition to the rent provision contained four additional items to which the plaintiff refused to agree. The addendum was not signed, and all further discussions were by the attorneys. Plaintiff offered to carry out the original contract with the rent as corrected in the unsigned addendum. When defendants did not answer, plaintiff commenced suit for expenses incurred by reason or defendants' alleged breach of the agreement. Defendants filed a counterclaim alleging that plaintiff had breached the agreement by failing to construct the building. Thereafter plaintiff filed an amended complaint alleging that on or about January 28, 1957, defendants repudiated the agreement and refused to perform any of the conditions therein.

STRUCKMEYER, J. . . . Plaintiff's first assignment of error directs our attention to the question of whether the trial court erred in directing a verdict against plaintiff on his claim of repudiation. . . .

Plaintiff in his amended complaint alleged that defendants repudiated the agreement on January 28, 1957, when defendant Hirsch met with plaintiff and submitted the addendum. Plaintiff further contends . . . that in any event the letter written by defendant's attorney on February 13, 1957, constituted a repudiation of the agreement.

We have recognized that an action may be maintained for breach of contract based upon the anticipatory repudiation by one of the parties to the contract. It is well established that in order to constitute an anticipatory breach of contract there must be a positive and unequivocal manifestation on the part of the party allegedly repudiating that he will not render the promised performance when the time fixed for it in the contract arrives. And as succinctly pointed out in § 319 of the Restatement of the Law of Contracts, the effect of a repudiation is nullified:

> (a) Where statements constituting such a repudiation are withdrawn by information to that effect given by the repudiator to the injured party before he has brought an action on the breach or has otherwise materially changed his position in reliance on them.

At the conclusion of plaintiff's case the trial judge upon defendants' motion for a directed verdict reviewed the evidence and concluded that there was insufficient evidence to support plaintiff's contention that there had been a repudiation and that if defendants had repudiated, the repudiation had been nullified thereafter.

We have examined the evidence and are of the opinion that the trial court did not err in granting defendants' motion. George Nick Diamos, son of plaintiff, was present at the January 28th conference and testified (plaintiff did not testify) that Hirsch implied that he wanted plaintiff to sign the addendum or defendants would not perform. However, this witness, the only witness who testified on behalf of plaintiff on this point, admitted on cross-examination and on re-direct examination that he couldn't recall what Hirsch said in this respect and further admitted that Hirsch never made a positive statement that defendants would not perform unless plaintiff agreed to the addendum. Viewing this evidence in the light most favorable to plaintiff, it is clear that it falls far short of the requisite proof that in order to constitute a breach by anticipatory repudiation there must be a positive and unequivocal refusal to perform.

Plaintiff's further contention that defendants' letter of February 13, 1957, repudiated the agreement is equally without merit. This letter merely clarified defendant's position and expressed their willingness to have plaintiff proceed to erect the building since defendants considered the terms of the agreement as signed binding upon the parties. Nowhere in this letter is there contained any statement which could reasonably be construed to be a positive and unequivocal repudiation of the agreement. In view of our conclusion it is unnecessary to determine whether defendants subsequently nullified the claimed repudiation. . . .

For the foregoing reasons the judgment of the court below is affirmed.

Luria Engineering Co. v. Aetna Cas. & Surety Co.

213 A.2d 151 (Pa.) 1965

A general contract to construct a school building was awarded to the plaintiff, who had subcontracts with a number of firms including General Roofing Company, one of the defendants. Aetna, the other defendant, is a bonding company which executed a performance bond on behalf of General Roofing. Work on the school ceased for a period of time as a result of a labor dispute stemming from the fact that one of the subcontractors employed nonunion labor. General Roofing wrote to the plaintiff that the delay had prejudiced it and asked to be released from the contract. Plaintiff refused and gave notice that unless General Roofing commenced work within forty-eight hours, it would engage another contractor. Plaintiff brought suit to recover the difference between the contract price agreed to by General Roofing and the price paid to the subsequent roofing contractor. Judgment was awarded to the plaintiff, and the defendant appealed.

JACOBS, J. . . . We believe the present rule in Pennsylvania to be that acts of a third party making performance impossible or causing a delay resulting in substantial increase in expense to the contracting party do not excuse failure to perform if such acts were foreseeable because it was the duty of the contracting party to provide for that situation in his contract. . . .

In today's union-conscious society, in a job involving the construction of a building of some magnitude, a labor dispute or strike is certainly foreseeable. Especially is this true where, as in our situation, there were at least five different contractors, one of whom employed nonunion labor. Furthermore the parties themselves foresaw the possibility of a strike and provided in Section 8 of the contract for a manner of dealing with claims resulting from "any *damage* which may be caused by strike, fire, flood . . . " [Emphasis added.] The only relevance of this section of the contract is that here the parties indicated that the possibility of a strike was foreseeable, but they failed to provide that a strike or a delay caused by strike should excuse performance.

Our holding is not inconsistent with the Restatement of the Law of Contracts. Appellants argue that under Section 462 of the Restatement, General Roofing's duty to perform was discharged on the basis that the labor dispute created a temporary impossibility which imposed a substantial burden on General Roofing. The argument fails because the alleged "temporary impossibility" here was a "supervening impossibility" within the meaning of Section 457 of the Restatement and is qualified by Section 457. Under Section 457, the duty of the promisor is discharged if he "had no reason to anticipate" the occurrence making performance impossible. Since we have determined that a labor dispute was foreseeable, General Roofing was not discharged of its duty to perform.

Judgment affirmed.

Trans-State Investments, Inc. v. Deive

262 A.2d 119 (D.C.) 1970

The plaintiff operates a physical fitness and recreation program. Defendant signed up for the program, which entitled him to use the numerous facilities such as swimming pool, steam room, and massage equipment. He contracted to pay the membership fee in twenty-four monthly installments. However, he did not use the facilities because several months after the contract date he was advised by his physician that a lung condition made it inadvisable to do so, nor did he pay any of the installments. The lower court ruled for the defendant in an action by the plaintiff to require payment. The plaintiff appealed.

KELLY, J. . . . A contract cannot be rescinded for mistake or impossibility of performance if the inability to perform was foreseeable to or caused by the promisor and unknown to the promisee at the time the contract was made. Moreover, by promising to pay the membership fee whether the facilities were used or not, Deive assumed the risk of any unforeseeable inability to perform.

Because appellee was not represented by counsel below and has made no argument on appeal, we have examined the record with particular care. However, even giving credence to his unsupported, hearsay testimony that a doctor told him that the use of Holiday's facilities would be dangerous to his health, we see no reason why Deive cannot be deemed to have breached the contract. Although he stated in his answer below that Holiday took advantage of his difficulty with the English language, he admitted that an interpreter-friend was with him when he signed the contract and explained the contract terms to him in his native tongue. He also admitted that he understood the contract provision containing the unconditional promise to pay the membership fee and that it was specifically explained to him at the time he signed the contract. Further, he stated that he operated his own business establishment and was familiar with business practices in the District of Columbia.

We hold the trial court erred in entering judgment for appellee.

Hansen v. Johnston

249 N.E.2d 133 (Ill.) 1969

Plaintiff Hansen was principal stockholder in a ski lodge and resort. The corporation was having financial difficulties and needed operating capital. Hansen pledged his stock in the corporation to secure a debt of $280,000, which defendant Johnston (the other shareholder) had advanced to the corporation. The corporation's total obligation to Johnston was $485,000. Hansen and Johnston were unable to agree on management and decided to abandon their joint operation. They entered into an agreement whereby Johnston agreed to pay Hansen $30,000 for Hansen's stock payable as follows:

(a) If Kenneth Johnston secures financing in the sum of $350,000.00, he will pay the $30,000.00 to Kenneth J. Hansen when the loan proceeds of $350,000.00 are disbursed.

(b) If Kenneth Johnston is unable to secure financing in the sum of $350,000.00, then the $30,000.00 will be paid after all corporate debts due as of this date are repaid. It is agreed between the parties that in this instance the $30,000.00 will be paid from corporate profits. Hansen was given the right to assist the corporation in securing the $350,000.00 loan.

Johnston had been given a corporate note secured by a deed of trust in the amount of $485,000 representing the money owed by the corporation to him. The defendant, Johnston, after entering into the agreement with plaintiff recorded the deed of trust, thus indicating that the corporation's property was encumbered in that amount. With the encumbrance a matter of record there was no possibility of obtaining a mortgage loan. Plaintiff sued for $30,000. Defendant contended that the sum was not due, as the conditions of (a) and (b) had not been met. Plaintiff was given a judgment. The defendant appealed.

SEIDENFELD, J. . . . The principal issue is whether the recording of the $485,000.00 trust deed made the agreement impossible to perform. Defendant argues that it was only sound business practice to secure himself for advances made to the corporation and that in any event the trust deed should be considered legally subordinate to the agreement, and, if not, we should consider that he expressed a willingness to subordinate the trust deed in a post-trial motion.

It is clear that when performance of an agreement is rendered impossible by the willful acts of one of the contracting parties, the agreement to pay becomes absolute.

And it seems apparent here that, unless the trust deed was subordinated to the agreement, the recording of the instrument (which included some debts contemplated to be repaid from the $350,000.00 financing mentioned in the agreement) would render the securing of the expressed financing, or a sale of the property, practically impossible.

.   .   .

Johnston, however, argues that even assuming the trust deed made a loan impossible that there are other contingencies still available, sale or profits, which are not impossible. He refers to the quotation in the Restatement of Contracts, Section 469: "Impossibility of performing one or more but less than all of a number of performances promised in the alternative in a contract discharges neither the duty of the promisor if by the terms of the contract he had the privilege of choice, nor the duty of the promisee if he had that privilege, but merely destroys or limits the possibility of choice. . . . "

It should be noted that the alternatives are truly under the control of Johnston whereas the securing of the finances by Hansen is the only condition which would be clearly under Hansen's control.

The quotation in the Restatement of Contracts, *supra,* does not apply to the facts of this particular case. . . . Section 469 refers to cases where one of two or more alternatives to completing a contract becomes impossible due to some circumstances not within the control of the parties. A duty is imposed by law upon a party not to interfere at all with the completion of the agreement by the opposite party. . . .

We hold that the trial judge properly found that defendant by his own acts made it impossible for plaintiff to retain any real ability to secure the benefits of the contract, thereby making the liability absolute.

We therefore affirm.

Hipskind Heating & Plumb. Co. v. General Industries

204 N.E.2d 339 (Ind.) 1965

ARTERBURN, J. This case is before us on petition to transfer from the Appellate Court. . . .

In this case a building in the process of repairs by the installation of a sprinkler system was destroyed by fire. The destruction of a building which is the subject of the contract for repairs excuses the performance of the remainder of the contract as to each party. The majority rule is that an event unforeseen which creates an impossibility of performance by reason of the destruction of the subject matter of the contract will excuse the performance thereof by each of the parties.

However, that is not the exact question here. The question here is: may a contractor who was originally obligated to perform a contract with reference to repairs on a building which has been destroyed by fire recover for partial work done not on the expressed contract but on *quantum meruit*? The authority on the latter question is divided in this country.

However, in Indiana it seems under the authority of *Krause* v. *Board, etc.* (1904, 162 Ind. 278, 70 N.E.2d 264, 65 L.R.A. 111), this Court has said that it leaves both parties as it finds them in a case such as this and that neither can recover from the other if each is "equally blameless and irresponsible for the accident by which the property is destroyed."

Petition to transfer is denied.

407 East 61st Garage, Inc. v. Savoy Fifth Ave. Corp.

244 N.E.2d 37 (N.Y.) 1968

BREITEL, J. . . . Plaintiff garage seeks damages for defendant Savoy's alleged breach, by termination, of a contract between the parties, resulting from Savoy's discontinuance of its operation of the Savoy Hilton Hotel. Under a written agreement the garage had undertaken to furnish garage services for a period of five years to guests of the Savoy Hilton and to pay Savoy 10 percent of its gross transient storage charges to the hotel guests. Savoy ageed to use all reasonable efforts to provide the garage with exclusive opportunity for storage of the motor vehicles of the hotel guests.

The issue is whether the closing of the hotel prior to the expiration of the contract period, due to the asserted financial inability of Savoy to remain in the hotel business, subjects it to continued liability under the contract. The Supreme Court, characterizing the agreement as a requirements contract, held that, absent an express contract provision requiring Savoy to remain in the hotel business, and absent allegations of bad faith, Savoy is not liable for anticipatory breach of contract.

It is concluded that, by ceasing operation of its hotel, Savoy is not excused, as a matter of law, from obligations under its agreement with the garage, and that there is, at least, an issue of fact as to implied conditions in the agreement. . . .

The agreement does not explicitly obligate Savoy to remain in the hotel business during the contract term or, put another way, to fulfill its obligations for the term even if it should wish to cease operation of a hotel. On the other hand, the only provision concerning termination allows Savoy to terminate the contract should the garage default in the performance of any condition, including the provision of adequate service, and then fail to cure the default within 30 days after receiving written notice. It was provided further that all duties of each of the parties were to be performed "during the term" of the contract. . . .

Under familiar rules a promise that a party will continue to remain in business may be implied in fact as part of an agreement for the rendition of services to a business.

Such a promise to remain in business will be implied particularly where the promisee has undertaken certain burdens or obligations in expectation of and reliance upon the promisor's continued activity. Here, the garage may have undertaken certain additional continuing responsibilities, such as the obtaining of adequate insurance and perhaps even the signing of employment contracts and agreements for the purchase of supplies for the lifetime of the contract. . . .

At the very least, therefore an issue of fact is presented whether the agreement did import an implied promise by Savoy to fulfill its obligations for an entire five-year period.

Assuming such an implication, Savoy might, nevertheless, assert the hotel's financial situation as a legal excuse for its failure to continue operation of the hotel. It does point out that it was economically impossible (or rather extremely burdensome) for it to remain in the hotel business. Thus, it may be argued that the basic purpose of the contract to insure that guests of the hotel would receive adequate garage services, was rendered impossible of performance, or, perhaps, was frustrated, when the hotel was no longer in a financial position to cater to guests. Phrased in these terms, the issue is sometimes regarded as a matter of excuse from performance, apart from the contract, rather than being treated as an implied condition for performance derived from the contractual arrangements between the parties.

Generally, however, the excuse of impossibility of performance is limited to the destruction of the means of performance by an act of God, *vis major,* or by law. . . . Thus, where impossibility or difficulty of performance is occasioned only by financial difficulty or economic hardship, even to the extent of insolvency or bankruptcy, performance of a contract is not excused. . . . Notably, in this case, Savoy does not even assert that bankruptcy or insolvency was a likely consequence of continuing operation of the hotel. Further, in view of its admittedly comtemporaneous financial difficulties, Savoy could and should have insisted that the agreement provide for the anticipated contingency of economic hardship (cf. Restatement, Contracts, § 457). In sum, performance by Savoy was at all times possible, although unprofitable, since the hotel could simply have remained in business, and the legal excuse of impossibility of performance would not be available to it.

Cases involving frustration of the purpose of the contract are inapposite. Here, the purpose of providing garage services to hotel guests was frustrated only when Savoy itself made a business decision to close the hotel, and did not result from unanticipated circumstances. . . . Moreover, rather than relying on a circumstance that was unanticipated, Savoy itself argues that its financial stringency was always known.

In short, the applicable rules do not permit a party to abrogate a contract, unilaterally, merely upon a showing that it would be financially disadvantageous to perform it; were the rules otherwise, they would place in jeopardy all commercial contracts. If, in fact, the agreement expresses or implies a promise that the hotel would remain liable for the contract term, that promise should be honored, regardless of financial hardship.

Concededly, it would not have made sense for Savoy to stay in the hotel business solely to avoid liability for breach of its contract with the garage. Such lack of business reason does not nullify the liability for damages, whatever effect it may have on a right to specific performance. However, if the patronage at the hotel had declined, proof of that situation, although perhaps not justifying termination of the garage's contract right, may have a significant bearing on the measure of damages sustained by the garage through loss of future profits. . . .

Judgment for defendant reversed.

CHAPTER 15
REVIEW QUESTIONS AND PROBLEMS

1. *A* contracted to install carpeting in an apartment building being constructed by *B.* On July 1, the date set for performance, *B* called *A* and informed him that the contract was terminated because *A* had not performed on time. *B* then contracted with *C* to do the work. *C* was not able to start work until September because the apartment was not finished until that time. *A* sued *B* for breach of contract. Should *A* prevail?

2. Dr. *A* was employed as chief of pediatrics in the D hospital. His appointment was to continue as long as he rendered satisfactory service in carrying out the hospital's program. He was discharged and brought an action for damages, contending that he could only be discharged for just cause and that none had been shown. Should he receive damages for breach of contract?

3. *A,* a clothing manufacturer, entered into a contract to sell ladies' coats to *B,* a retailer. The contract called for shipment on August 15. *A* did not ship the goods until September 28, and they did not arrive until October 12. Upon arrival *B* refused to accept or pay for them. *A* sued for the purchase price. What result?

4. *A,* a furniture manufacturer, ordered 1,000 drawer bottoms from *B.* They were manufactured in accordance with the specifications of *A. A* refused to accept the bottoms on the ground that his furniture factory had in the meantime burned to the ground. *B* brought action on the contract. Should he succeed?

5. The ABC Shipping Company had a contract with the United States to

ship wheat to the Middle East. Before shipment was made the Suez Canal was closed, and *A* had to take a longer route. Is *A* entitled to extra payment?

6. *A* entered into a contract with *B* to build a building. There was an error in the written agreement and *A* prepared an additional clause for signature, which not only corrected the error but added further conditions. Was *A*'s conduct an anticipatory repudiation?

7. The CDE Company installed and leased to *E* at his restaurant a burglar alarm system for five years at a certain rental. The CDE Company was to maintain and repair said system as needed. The state condemned *E*'s property for public use. CDE sued for rental falling due thereafter, and *E* claimed impossibility as a defense. What result?

8. XYZ Company agreed to repair the refrigeration system on *M*'s ship and to test it for effectiveness at a cost of $4,700. The work was done, but before XYZ could test it, *M* took the ship on a trip. *M* claims to have suffered damages because the work was not effective. In spite of this, the court allowed recovery by XYZ Company. What defense did XYZ Company have against *M*'s claim of poor workmanship?

9. *O* leased property to *T* for five years; the latter expected to use it in the sale of automobiles. War intervened, automobiles were not available, and *T* desires to be released from his contract. Is the contract binding?

10. *X* leased premises to *Y* at a rental of $250 per month plus a percentage of profits. *Y* ceased operations but continued to pay the $250 per month. *X* sued *Y* for the percentage of anticipated profits. What result?

chapter 16

Discharge of
Contracts

2-109. Introduction. The rights and duties created by a contract continue in force until the contract is discharged. The usual and intended method of discharge is the complete performance by both parties of their obligations under the agreement. When this has been accomplished the parties are automatically discharged—the contract is completely executed. There are, however, many other ways in which a discharge may be brought about.

In previous chapters we discussed discharge predicated upon impossibility of performance, mutual mistake, and commercial frustration. It was noted also that the happening of a condition subsequent could result in a termination of rights and duties under a contract. In the former instances the law provides for a discharge because the intended performance by either or both parties is in some way not in keeping with the situation as it existed or was believed to exist when the parties entered into their agreement.

It is always possible for the parties to an agreement to rescind the contract. As long as the contract is executory on both sides, both parties are free to agree that it is discharged. However, if there has been a part performance by one party, his agreement to discharge is not enforceable unless it is supported by consideration. The requirement of consideration also applies to agreements to modify a contract when the new terms are less desirable to one of the parties than the former ones. Under the Code, however, an agreement to rescind a contract needs no consideration to be binding and the same applies to modification of contract terms.

If the contract is in writing, the surrender and cancellation of the contract *may* result in the discharge of the obligor to whom the surrender is made. While this seems quite obvious and manifests a clear intent on the obligee's part to release and discharge the obligor, general contract law principles often dictate a different result. The contract is *not* necessarily discharged, absent agreement based upon consideration, unless the writing is itself the legal obligation. A distinction is thus made between a writing that is merely the *evidence* of the obligation and one that *is* the obligation. There is no particular sanctity in the law to the physical evidence of an ordinary contract, and the destruction of this evidence does not destroy the contract. However, certain written contracts are for a variety of reasons regarded as something more than evidence. For example, a negotiable instrument such as a promissory note is in this category, and the surrender of it to the drawer or its cancellation by the holder works a discharge. The surrender or cancellation of a nonnegotiable instrument would not of itself discharge it.

In addition to the foregoing methods, a contract and the obligations under it may be discharged by the passage of time under statutes of limitation. Also, a discharge in bankruptcy will relieve a debtor of his obligation to pay his creditors. The legal doctrine of *novation* provides for the substitution of one obligor for another and the discharge of the one who is replaced. The legal concept of *accord and satisfaction* allows discharge of a contract by a performance different from that agreed upon in the agreement. Each of these methods of discharge are discussed in subsequent sections.

2-110. Payment, Generally. The obligation of one party to a contract will be to pay the other for goods sold, services rendered, and the like. Payment may be in currency or more likely by delivery of a negotiable instrument such as a check or a note. The payment may be made in settlement of a claim for breach of contract by the payer. For example, *A* may have sold goods under warranty to *B;* if the goods are defective, *B* would have a claim for damages against *A*. The payment by *A* in settlement of *B's* claim would discharge *A's* obligation for his breach. The problems involved in the settlement of accounts when the amount due is in dispute and the acceptance in full settlement of a claim of a lesser sum than the amount due were discussed in Chapter 9.

There are three especially significant questions about payment that affect the matter of discharge: What constitutes payment? What is good evidence that payment has been made and that the obligation has been discharged? When a debtor has several obligations to a creditor, how will a payment be applied?

Certainly, the transfer of money constitutes payment, but this is not necessarily the case when the payment is by a negotiable instrument such as a check or a promissory note. The instrument may be one executed by the debtor in favor of the creditor, or it may be one in which the debtor is the party entitled to payment which he transfers to the creditor in payment. For example, *A,* a debtor, is the payee of a note made by *X* in the sum of $1,000, payable in six months. *A* could endorse the note to *B,* a creditor, in payment of an obligation.

Generally, payment by delivery of a negotiable instrument drawn or endorsed by the debtor to the creditor is a conditional payment and not an absolute discharge of the obligation. If the instrument is paid at maturity, the debt is discharged; if it is not so paid, the debt then exists as it did prior to the conditional payment. In the latter situation, the creditor can either bring an action to recover on the defaulted instrument or pursue his rights under the original agreement.[1] The important point is that a payment by negotiable instrument furnishes only a conditional discharge. However, the parties may agree that such payment *is* an absolute discharge, in which event, if the instrument is not paid at maturity, the only recourse of the creditor is to bring action on the instrument—the original contract is discharged. A similar situation exists when accounts receivable are assigned by a debtor to his creditor. Accounts receivable are not negotiable but can be transferred by assignment. An assignment of accounts is also a conditional payment—if the accounts are not collected, the debtor is still obligated to pay his indebtedness. If the parties intend that the receipt of negotiable instruments or accounts receivable be treated as a discharge of the obligation, they may so specify.

As to what constitutes acceptable evidence of payment and discharge, a receipt given by the creditor will usually suffice. Such receipt should clearly indicate the amount paid and specify the transaction to which it relates. However, the creditor may be able to rebut the receipt by evidence that it was in error or that it was given under mistake. A canceled check is also evidence of payment, but the evidence is more conclusive when the purpose for which it is given is stated on the check. The drawer of a check may specify on the instrument that the payee by endorsing or cashing it acknowledges full satisfaction of an obligation of the drawer.

Where a debtor owes several obligations to one creditor or has a running account with him that consists of several items, he may specify how any payment is to be applied. The creditor who receives such payment is obligated to follow the debtor's instructions. In the absence of any instructions, the creditor may apply the payment against any one of several obligations that are due, or he may credit a portion of the payment against each of several obligations. The creditor may apply a payment against a claim that has been outlawed, but this will not cause the outlawed claim to revive as to the balance. If the source of a payment is someone other than the debtor and this fact is known to the creditor, the payment must be applied in such a manner as to protect the third party who makes the payment. Hence, if a surety who has guaranteed that a particular obligation will be paid by the debtor, supplies the money for the payment, and the creditor knows it, he is bound to apply the payment on the obligation for which the surety was secondarily liable. Finally, if the creditor fails to make a particular application prior to the time the issue is raised, the payment will be applied against the debtor's obligations in the order of their maturity. However, where the creditor holds both secured and unsecured obligations, the courts are inclined to apply it on an unsecured obligation which has matured.[2] Similarly, if both principal and interest are due, the court considers the interest to be paid first, any balance being credited on the principal.

2-111. Accord and Satisfaction.   An accord consists of an agreement between contracting parties whereby one of them is to do something different by way of performance than that called for by the contract. This accord is *satisfied* when the substituted performance is completed. The cashing of a check marked "paid in full" when it is tendered to settle a disputed claim is an accord

---

[1] Central Stove Co. v. John Ruggiero, Inc., page 328
[2] Miller Brewing Company v. Gregg, page 329

and satisfaction.[3] Both accord and satisfaction must take place before the old obligation is discharged, unless it is expressly stated that it is being substituted for the old obligation. Otherwise, the new agreement of itself does not terminate the old agreement. To illustrate: *A* purchased a used car from *B* and agreed to pay him $600 within sixty days. *A* failed to pay *B* at the end of the period and agreed to paint *B's* building in full payment of the debt. At any time before *A* commences to perform, *B* may recover upon the original contract. The painting of the building constitutes the satisfaction of the accord, and thus discharges the original contract.

2-112. Novation.   *Novation* is an agreement whereby an original party to a contract is replaced by a new party. In order for the substitution to be effective, it must be agreed to by all of the parties. The remaining contracting party must agree to accept the new party and at the same time consent to release the withdrawing party.[4] The latter must consent to withdraw and to permit the new party to take his place. The new party must agree to assume the burdens and duties of the retiring party based on consideration received by him. If all of these essentials are present, the withdrawing party is discharged from the agreement. To illustrate: *A* purchases an automobile from *B,* making a small down payment and agreeing to pay the balance of $400 within six months. Finding times somewhat hard, *A* sells the car to *C,* who agrees to pay the balance to *B.* Both parties notify *B* of this arrangement. As yet no novation is completed because *B* has not agreed to release *A* and to look only to *C* for payment. If *B* releases *A,* then *A* is discharged from any duty arising under the original agreement, and a novation is created. A mere assignment and delegation of duties does not create a novation.

2-113. Statute of Limitations.   The statute of limitations prescribes a time limit within which suit must be started after a cause of action arises. An action for breach of any contract for sale of personal property under the Code must be commenced within four years. The Code further provides that the parties in their agreement may reduce the period of limitation to not less than one year but may not extend it. Contracts that are not controlled by the Code are covered by a variety of limitation periods, the most common being six years. Some states distinguish between oral and written contracts, making the period longer for the latter. The purpose of a statute of limitations is to prevent actions from being brought long after evidence is lost or important witnesses have died. A contract action must be brought within the prescribed period after the obligation matures or after the cause of action arises.

Any voluntary[5] part payment made on a money obligation tolls the statute, starting it to run anew. Similarly, any voluntary part payment, new promise, or clear acknowledgment of the indebtedness made after the claim has been outlawed reinstates the obligation, and the statute commences to run again.[6] No new consideration is required to support the reinstatement promise. If the old obligation has been outlawed, a new promise may be either partial or conditional. Since there is no *duty* to pay the debt, the debtor may

---

[3] Burgamy v. Davis, page 330
[4] Strunk Chain Saws, Inc. v. Williams, page 331
[5] Nilsson et al. v. Kielman et al., page 333
[6] Whale Harbor Spa, Inc. v. Wood, page 333

attach such conditions to his new promise as he sees fit or may promise to pay only part of the debt. A few states require the new promise or acknowledgment to be in writing. The Code does not alter the law on tolling of the statute of limitations.

The period during which a debtor removes himself from the state or the period during which the debtor or creditor is incapacitated by minority or insanity is usually totally or partially eliminated from the period prescribed by statute. In other words, the debtor's absence from the state extends the period within which an action may be brought against him, and a minor usually has a short time in which to bring action after he reaches his majority, although the full period set by statute has expired earlier.

2-114. Bankruptcy and Composition of Creditors.   Congress by statute has provided procedures which if followed will cause debts to be discharged. The discharge is in the nature of a defense which may be pleaded in the event suit is brought on the claim. The discharge may be waived and the debt may be revived by a new promise to pay.[7]

A discharge in bankruptcy may result from the debtor voluntarily petitioning the court that his debts be discharged, or may result from a petition filed by his creditors called involuntary bankruptcy. There are numerous rules of law concerning these petitions and other matters such as debts which are not discharged, recoverable preferences, and priority of claims. These matters are discussed in Chapter 48.

A composition of creditors (see Section 2-36) is an agreement by the creditors to accept less than full payment in return for the discharge of the debt. This usually occurs when the debtor is insolvent and the creditors wish to avoid further losses and expenses which would be involved in formal bankruptcy proceedings. A part of the consideration for such contracts is the promise by each creditor not to file a petition in involuntary bankruptcy and a promise by the debtor not to file voluntary bankruptcy. The assets of the debtor are prorated among the creditors and they accept their allocated amount in full discharge of the debtor.

DISCHARGE OF CONTRACTS CASES

Central Stove Co. v. John Ruggiero, Inc.

268 N.Y.S.2d 172 (N.Y) 1966

TOMSON, J. . . . The plaintiff seeks to recover for work, labor, and services. The defendant contends that, although the value of the work done was as claimed by the plaintiff, a payment of $2,250 was made by negotiating to the plaintiff a promissory note of a third party in that sum. The defendant's endorsement was "without recourse."

The testimony was sharply conflicting as to the conversation at the time the note was given. The defendant urges that his version of the discussion and the restrictive endorsement, though not conclusive, should result in the inference that there was an agreement between the parties to accept the note as an unconditional payment. . . .

---

[7] Domestic Loan, Inc. v. Peregoy, page 334

The Uniform Commercial Code, Sec. 3-802, entitled "Effect of Instrument of Obligation for Which It Is Given" reads:

(1) *Unless otherwise agreed* where an instrument is taken for an underlying obligation . . . (b) in any other case the obligation is suspended *pro tanto* until the instrument is due or if it is payable on demand until its presentment. *If the instrument is dishonored action may be maintained on either the instrument or the obligation; discharge of the underlying obligor on the instrument also discharges him on the obligation.* . . . [Emphasis Supplied]

See also 43 New York Jur., "Payment," section 42 et seq. where it is stated at page 487:

Prior to the Uniform Commercial Code the intention of the parties ordinarily prevailed in determining whether the delivery and acceptance of a negotiable instrument drawn by the debtor or by a third person was to be treated as payment in themselves, or as payment conditional on the honoring of the paper by the drawee. But in the absence of a demonstrated intention the general rule was that the acceptance of a commercial paper by a creditor for an antecedent debt did not constitute an absolute payment. . . .

Of some interest is *Herold* v. *Fleming,* 17 Misc. 581, 582, 40 N.Y.S. 690, 691 (Appellate Term First Department) where the court below refused to charge as requested "that the taking of the note of a third person, endorsed 'without recourse,' constitutes a payment, and that the writing must control any oral statements made at the time." The Appellate Court said, (p. 582, 40 N.Y.S. p. 691) "The vice of the proposed charge was that it eliminated the element of an agreement as a constituent of the fact of payment."

On the evidence here it cannot be said, despite the endorsement "without recourse," that the defendant met the burden imposed upon it to prove that it was the intention of the parties to treat the note as absolute rather than conditional payment.

The defendant's indebtedness was not therefore discharged by the delivery of the note; the defendant's obligation was merely suspended *pro tanto* until the instrument became due on September 18, 1964, at which time the plaintiff had the election of maintaining an action either on the instrument or on the obligation.

Accordingly, judgment is directed to be entered in favor of the plaintiff for the relief demanded in the complaint, together with costs, disbursements and interest from September 18, 1964.

Miller Brewing Company v. Gregg

389 F.2d 878 (1968)

The defendant, Gregg, had guaranteed payments to plaintiff of sums owing by Surf Beverage Corporation, a corporation of which he was the president. The question was presented as to whether payments made by the corporation would be applied on the old account made before the date of guaranty or against current obligations. The court did not give a requested instruction to the jury that it should determine the intention of the parties in this regard. A judgment was entered for the plaintiff and defendant appealed.

COMBS, J. . . . Gregg had the burden, however, of showing either by express agreement or by the attending circumstances that the parties intended that payments made after the date of the guaranty would be applied first against current withdrawals. In the absence of such a showing by Gregg, Miller had the right to apply the payments against the old account. The general rule is stated in 57 A.L.R.2d 855, 859 (1958):

> In the event it becomes the duty of a court to make application of a voluntary payment the intention of the parties as determined from all the circumstances will be followed irrespective of the rights of a surety or guarantor, but if no intention can be inferred or implied, generally in jurisdictions in which the common law is followed the interests of the creditor are preferred, and the payment will be applied to a debt other than that for which the surety is liable. . . .

The Wisconsin courts, to which, by the terms of the guaranty agreement, we look for guidance in construction, follow the general rule. . . .

The question of what the parties intended as to application of payments made by Surf, that is whether they were to be applied on the old account or against current withdrawals, was properly a question for the jury and that issue should have been submitted under proper instructions. For the purpose of showing the intention of the parties Gregg had the right, of course, to insist on the production of the original records of the account. Since timely objection was taken by Gregg to the court's failure to instruct on the question of the parties intention with regard to application of payments, the judgment must be reversed and the case remanded for a new trial.

Reversed and remanded for proceedings consistent with this opinion.

Burgamy v. Davis

313 S.W.2d 365 (Tex.) 1958

RENFRO, J. Appellant Burgamy, as plaintiff, sued appellee Davis for the sum of $328.73 and foreclosure of a mechanic's and materialmen's lien. Defendant pleaded accord and satisfaction. Trial, without a jury, resulted in judgment for defendant.

Findings of fact and conclusions of law were filed by the trial court.

The court found: Appellant and appellee entered into an oral contract by the terms of which appellant was to furnish material and labor, on a cost plus basis, for plumbing modifications in a house owned by appellee. Prior to completion of the contract, appellant made demand on appellee for the sum of $328.73, which appellee paid on March 19, 1957. About the 22nd of March, appellant completed the job and made demand for an additional $537.45. About the first of April, a dispute in good faith arose between appellant and appellee as to the amount due appellant. Thereafter, while the dispute still existed, appellee delivered a check in the sum of $208.73 to appellant, with the words, "Payment of account in full," written on the check. The check was intended to be in full payment of the disputed claim. Appellant accepted and received the amount of the check.

. . . The dispute had not been settled when appellee sent the check of April first. Appellant admitted that, without communication with appellee, he marked out the words, "Payment of account in full," and wrote on the check the words, "Paid on account," endorsed the check and deposited it to his account. . . .

Sufficient consideration for accord may inhere in or arise out of a dispute as to liability upon a liquidated claim. This presupposes that denial of liability, in whole or in part, is not merely factitious or *mala fides.*

The test is not whether the debtor was correct in his contention, in that he really had a legal or equitable defense to the claim in whole or in part, but consists in the fact that he in good faith urged or asserted a defense which he really believed was substantial.

If the one who is sought to be held liable in good faith urges a defense which he believes to be substantial, and which he claims will defeat the demand in whole or in part, and in good faith raises a controversy and dispute as to his liability, a settlement and compromise of the demand, based upon such contention, will not be disturbed. Existence of a dispute of that character affords a good consideration for the new agreement of accord.

In *Firestone Tire & Rubber Co.* v. *White,* (Tex. Civ. App. 274 S.W.2d 452, 454), the court recognizes the rule "where a claim is unliquidated or disputed, the cashing of a check marked 'in full payment' is a binding accord and satisfaction and extinguishes the claim. . . . The cashing of the check is held to constitute an acceptance even though the words 'in full payment' are erased by the creditor before he cashes the check."

It is well settled that when an account is made the subject of bona fide dispute between the parties as to its correctness, and the debtor tenders his check to the creditor upon condition that it be accepted in full payment, the creditor must either refuse to receive the check or accept the same burdened by its attached condition. If he accepts the check and cashes the same, he impliedly agrees to the condition, although he may expressly notify the debtor that he is not accepting the same with the condition, but is only applying the same as a partial payment on account.

When appellant, knowing appellee was disputing in good faith the amount of the claim, received the check marked "Payment of account in full," he was given the option either to accept the check as full payment or to return the check to appellee, unaccepted, and hold appellee for his full claim. He chose to accept and deposit the check to his account. Under the findings of the trial court, there was a valid accord and satisfaction.

The judgment of the trial court is affirmed.

Affirmed.

Strunk Chain Saws, Inc. v. Williams

111 So.2d 195 (La.) 1959

This is an action against defendant, Williams, to collect $500, the balance of an account. The defendant asserts novation as a defense. The plaintiff had difficulty collecting a $2,430.72 account from defendant for merchandise sold when a partnership, S & F Repair Service, offered to take defendant's assets and assume the obligation, payable in monthly installments. It paid $500 on account and gave its notes for the balance, defendant's name not appearing on the notes. S & F became insolvent, leaving $500 of the amount unpaid, and plaintiff seeks to recover of the defendant. The lower court gave judgment for defendant, implying that the taking of another's note indicated a release of the original party.

GLADNEY, J. . . . The only defense urged herein is a plea of novation, in which it is contended defendant's obligation was extinguished by plaintiff's substitution of a new obligation for the original debt, and a new debtor for the defendant. The plea was sustained by the trial judge.

Novation is defined and explained in the following articles of the LSA-Civil Code:

> Art. 2185 Novation is a contract, consisting of two stipulations; one to extinguish an existing obligation, the other to substitute a new one in its place.
>
> Art. 2189 Novation takes place in three ways:
>
> 1. When a debtor contracts a new debt to his creditor, which new debt is substituted to the old one, which is extinguished.
>
> 2. When a new debtor is substituted to the old one, who is discharged by the creditor.
>
> 3. When by the effect of a new engagement, a new creditor is substituted to the old one, with regard to whom the debtor is discharged.
>
> Art. 2192 The delegation, by which a debtor gives to the creditor another debtor who obliges himself towards such creditor, does not operate a novation, unless the creditor has expressly declared that he intends to discharge his debtor who has made the delegation.

Counsel for appellant earnestly insists novation does not take place by the substitution of one debtor for another unless there is an express declaration by the creditor to discharge the debtor who has made the delegation. The evidence as presented, it must be admitted, does not show that by oral or written expression plaintiff stipulated the release of the defendant from his original obligation. But we are of the opinion our jurisprudence has accorded a more liberal construction to the above-quoted articles and a debtor may be discharged where the intent of the creditor to novate is clearly indicated. . . .

We deem it unnecessary to attempt a review of the jurisprudence relating to the application of Articles 2189, and 2192, LSA-C.C. This has been excellently done in an article entitled "The Requisites and Effects of Novation: A Comparative Survey," written by Walter L. Nixon, Jr., *Tulane Law Review,* Volume 25, page 100. The author therein, page 113, concluded:

> Despite the fact that Article 2192 of the Louisiana Civil Code provides that express intention on the part of the creditor is requisite to novation by the substitution of a new debtor for the old one, the Louisiana jurisprudence indicates that acts tantamount [sic] to an express declaration will suffice. . . .

As observed above, our courts have not adhered to the strict construction contended for by appellant but have ruled a release or discharge can be evidenced by acts of a creditor clearly disclosing an intent to no longer look to the original debtor for payment.

For the reasons herein assigned, the judgment from which appealed is affirmed at appellant's cost.

Nilsson et al. v. Kielman et al.

17 N.W.2d 918 (S. Dak.) 1945

Action by M. T. Nilsson and E. P. Nilsson against Ethel E. Kielman and L. T. Nilsson on a note. The note matured in 1926 and the statute of limitations had run against it unless certain payments indorsed thereon had extended the life of the note. One payment resulted from the sale of certain property pledged as security and a second payment was the result of the collection of a note which had been assigned as collateral. Ethel E. Kielman made no payments and the security for the note had been given plaintiff many years before the money was realized and the credit given on the note.

ROBERTS, J. . . . It appears from the provisions of SDC33.0213 that an acknowledgment or promise to be effectual to interrupt the running of the statute of limitations must be in writing and signed by the party to be charged, but this requirement does not alter or take away the effect of a part payment. It is the settled law of this state that a part payment to be effectual to interrupt the running of the statute must have been made voluntarily and must have been made and accepted under circumstances consistent with an intent to pay the balance. . . . Payments made by a joint debtor bind only the person making the payments and do not operate to interrupt the running of the statute as to the other debtors not participating or acquiescing in the payments. . . . The principle on which part payment operates to take a debt without the statute is that the debtor by the payment intends to acknowledge the continued existence of the debt.

The agreement with reference to the amount of credit on January 19, 1940, constitutes neither a new promise in writing nor a part payment as of that date. It is the fact of voluntary payment made by the debtor, and not entry of credit, that interrupts the running of the statute. Nor did the collection of the account amounting to $74.40 give new life to the debt. Plaintiffs were authorized to collect the accounts and apply the proceeds to payment of the debt, but this did not have the same effect as if made personally by the defendants. There is no vital distinction between such a case and one where money received by the payee of a note from collateral security such as notes and mortgages of third parties pledged by the maker is credited on the principal note. Such payment does not interrupt the running of the statute. . . . The underlying reason for the doctrine is that a creditor is not an agent of the debtor to such an extent as to make an act done by him in the name of the debtor operate as a new promise to himself without which element the payment cannot operate to interrupt the statute.

Judgment for defendant affirmed.

Whale Harbor Spa, Inc. v. Wood

266 F.2d 953 (1959)

JONES, J. The appellant, Whale Harbor Spa, Inc., is a Florida corporation. Its stock was owned in equal shares by Dorothy W. Wood and Al B. Luckey.

The corporation was managed by Luckey. The Luckey and Wood families had been close friends over a period of many years. Between May 1, 1946, and October 14, 1948, Mrs. Wood made six open loans aggregating $24,750 to the corporation. These loans were not evidenced by promissory notes or other written obligation. On July 10, 1950, Mrs. Wood loaned the corporation $5,000 upon its demand note. On April 7, 1947, the corporation paid Mrs. Wood $3,000 on account. The amount of the advances unpaid remains at $26,750. The indebtedness was set up on the corporation's books and was carried as a liability of the corporation to Mrs. Wood. On July 10, 1950, the corporation, by an endorsement on a letter from Mrs. Wood's agent, acknowledged the existence of the indebtedness and the amount of it. From at least as early as November, 1952, and at intervals of never more than six months, the bookkeeper of the corporation, at the direction of Luckey, sent to Mrs. Wood or her agent profit and loss statements and balance sheets of the corporation. The balance sheets showed an indebtedness to Mrs. Wood of $26,750. After the death of both Mrs. Wood and Luckey, the executor of Mrs. Wood brought suit against the corporation for the amount of the unpaid advances. The corporation did not deny that the loans had been made nor did it contend that payment had been made. Its sole defense is that the indebtedness is barred by the Florida statute of limitations. The plaintiff, as executor of Mrs. Wood's estate, contended that the balance sheets were written acknowledgements of the debt sufficient to toll the statute, and further contended that the corporation was equitably estopped to plead the statute of limitations. The court, after a trial without a jury, determined that no part of the debt was barred by the statute of limitations and entered judgment against the corporation. It has appealed.

It is not questioned that the period of limitation has run and that the statute of limitations is a bar to recovery unless the statute has been tolled or the corporation is estopped to assert it. The Florida statute requires that "Every acknowledgment of or promise to pay a debt barred by the statute of limitations, must be in writing and signed by the party to be charged." (F.S.A. § 95.04.) This statute does not apply to promises made before the expiration of the period of limitations, and verbal promises made before the cause of action had run will take the cause of action out from the operation of the statute. . . . Where there is a distinct acknowledgment in writing of the debt, a promise to pay it will be inferred. . . .

The precedents of the decided cases point to a rule, which we think is sound in principle, that the requirement of an acknowledgment of an indebtedness which will interrupt the running of the statute of limitations is met by a balance sheet of a corporate debtor where the obligations in question are listed as liabilities of the corporation.

No error is shown in the judgment of the district court for the appellee. That judgment is affirmed.

Domestic Loan, Inc. v. Peregoy

184 N.E.2d 457 (Ohio) 1962

Plaintiff obtained a judgment for $509.94 against defendant on a promissory note. Defandant then filed a petition in voluntary bankruptcy and was adjudged a bankrupt. Plaintiff and defendant then entered into a "Revivor Agreement" by the terms of which the defendant agreed to pay the plaintiff $250.00 at the rate of $15 per month. The defendant failed to make these payments and plaintiff seeks to enforce the original judgment as revised by the agreement. The trial court held for the defendant.

KOVACHY, J. . . . The appellant claims that under this agreement defendant appellee revived the judgment against him even though it was listed as a dischargeable debt in the bankruptcy proceeding and authorized it to execute on the same upon default of the terms contained in the "Revivor Agreement."

The defendant appellee contends that the "Revivor Agreement" constituted a new promise which superseded the judgment and gave the plaintiff a new remedy—a right of action for defaulted payments, and that it must sue anew on such cause of action.

The law with respect to a discharge of a debt or a judgment in bankruptcy is well-settled. The debt or judgment is not paid, satisfied, extinguished or canceled. The bankrupt is merely afforded the privilege to interpose the discharge as a defense against the enforcement of the debt or judgment. And, since the matter is personal with the bankrupt, he has the choice of either interposing such defense to an action on the debt or judgment or of waiving the same, as he sees fit.

Remington on Bankruptcy, Vol. 8, page 133, "Revival of Discharged Debts" states the following in Section 3288:

> A discharge in bankruptcy although it is a "release" of liability on provable debts generally, is a defense against the liability rather than an annihilation of it and as a defense it can be waived. The obligation or liability still has vitality. . . . The moral obligation is still there and it can be adequate consideration for a new promise to pay.

The Supreme Court, in a case decided in 1851, held that *a new promise* to pay a debt discharged in bankruptcy was adequate consideration to sustain a cause of action on the *old debt* for the reason that the bar to a recovery of a debt discharged in bankruptcy is "strictly a personal privilege" and is waived by a subsequent promise.

The syllabus of *Turner* v. *Chrisman,* (Admr. of Moore, 20 Ohio 332, 333), reads:

> A new promise is, in law, available to sustain a recovery upon an old contract, against a plea of bankruptcy.
> The "bar" arising from the bankruptcy is strictly a personal privilege and is "waived" by the subsequent promise.
> When the "bar" is "waived" by a new promise to pay an old debt, it is competent to declare on the old liability without suing on the new promise.

. . . The "Revivor Agreement" entered into recites in plain language that the defendant revives his liability to Domestic Loan, Inc., *in the partial sum of $250.00,* that such revivor covers the obligation of a note and chattel mortgage executed October 21, 1959, that it applies to all claims, warrants of attorney and/or judgments which Domestic Loan, Inc. may hold or have against the defendant by virtue of the above described note and chattel mortgage, and that Domestic Loan, Inc. *shall be authorized to proceed against* *him upon said judgments* in the event of his failure to comply with the terms contained in the agreement.

It seems to us, therefore, that the defendant in the use of such clear and unmistakable language revived his obligation to the plaintiff in the sum of $250.00 and at the same time authorized the plaintiff in case he (the defendant) defaulted on his new promise, to execute on the judgment standing against him in the Cleveland Municipal Court. The default was with respect to monthly payments beginning February 17, 1961.

We accordingly hold that the plaintiff had the right to institute proceedings in aid of execution on the existing judgment and to enforce such payments and that it is entitled to recover a total sum not exceeding $250.00 from the date of his adjudication in bankruptcy which occurred on January 5, 1961.

CHAPTER 16
REVIEW QUESTIONS AND PROBLEMS

1. *A* and *B* entered into a compromise settlement of a dispute. Thereafter *B* contended that his investigation showed that there was no validity to *A*'s contentions regarding the dispute. Is *B* required to perform his part of the settlement?

2. *A* sold property to *B* on a contract. The price was $30,000 and *B* made a down payment of $100. *B* was unable to pay the balance of $29,900 and *A* brought suit for specific performance. *B* contended that he should be discharged because his business had declined and he did not have nor could he borrow the money. Is this a good defense?

3. *A* borrowed money from the B Loan Company and was then adjudicated a bankrupt. *A* then entered into a written agreement to pay the loan company. He did not pay and B Loan Company would like to garnish his wages. May it do so?

4. *A* leased an airplane to *B*. The airplane was defective and *B* threatened to rescind the agreement. He refrained from doing so on the basis of *A*'s promise to make repairs to the airplane. *A* failed to make the repair and *B* now seeks to rescind. May he do so?

5. *A* had made a number of purchases from *B*. *A* made a payment on account to *B,* and a question arose as to how *B* might apply this payment to the various accounts. How should this question be resolved?

6. Doctor *A* operated on *B* for a gallbladder condition in 1958. In 1966 an X ray revealed that surgical clamps had been left in *B*'s body during the operation. Does the statute of limitations prevent *B* from bringing an action against the doctor for negligence?

7. *L* & *B,* a partnership, sued *W* for services rendered, and *W* urged accord and satisfaction as a defense. *W* claimed the bill to be excessive and mailed a check for a lesser amount marked "in full of account." *L* & *B* drew a line through the statement and cashed the check. Was this an accord and satisfaction?

8. *A* sold a printing machine to *B* on the installment plan. *B* sold the machine to *C,* who agreed to pay the balance of the purchase price. Both parties notified *A* of the arrangement. *C* failed to make the payments, and *A* now seeks to hold *B*. May he do so?

9. *B,* a buyer, and *S,* a seller, had a dispute over a sales contract. A settlement agreement was signed which provided that the seller's promised performance will complete and cancel the remaining contract. Did the settlement agreement discharge the original contract?

10. *P* sent *D* a letter which stated that a statement of account was enclosed. *D* replied that the statement had not been enclosed but this was immaterial since *D* would not pay the amount claimed due to a dispute. *P* then sent the statement to which *D* replied by sending a partial payment marked "paid in full." *P* cashed the check and sued for the balance. What result?

BOOK THREE

The Uniform
Commercial Code

Introduction
to the Uniform
Commercial Code

3-1. History of "Commercial Law."   The rules and principles of commercial law are of ancient origin. Throughout the centuries merchants engaged in trade and commerce have recognized many customs and usages which regulate and control their conduct and their relationships with one another. Gradually over the years a body of law developed based upon the practices of merchants— the *lex mercatores,* or law merchant. The disputes between merchants were resolved by application of recognized principles derived from custom and usage in special courts established by the merchants themselves. The greater part of commercial activity in England was conducted at great fairs to which all merchants came, both foreign and local, to display their wares. At each of these fairs a court sat to adjust differences between buyers and sellers. The very nature of the situation demanded speedy and permanent termination of the disputes. These special mercantile courts were called "The Courts of Pie-poudres" (*pieds poudres*—"dusty feet"), so called because justice was administered as the dust still fell from the litigants' feet. These courts were later created by statute and continued as separate bodies until about 1756. Through royal prerogative the king's court, by this time jealous of the administration of justice by others, gradually won its way and absorbed the merchants' court. However, in deciding commercial cases, the king's court continued to apply the law merchant. When determining suits between merchants, or when a merchant was a party to the suit, before the court would recognize the law merchant, the party pleading such custom and usage was under duty to show himself to be a merchant. This rule prevailed until about one hundred years ago. The absorption of these merchants' courts by the king's courts wove the law merchant into and made it a part of the common law. The practice of permitting the proof of custom and usage of the merchants in the common-law courts made possible the development of separate rules which became established rules of law. The union of these mercantile customs with the legal system already in operation resulted in the formation and further development of the law merchant by judicial action. Cases decided in the common-law courts created precedents, and for many years the law relating to the sale of goods and other areas of the law merchant was found largely in the reports of judicial decisions. In these judicial decisions previous usage and custom were interpreted and applied according to the prevailing and established usage of the particular community. This situation led to varying interpretations and a consequent lack of uniformity. In order to find the law, it was necessary to examine many decisions. The result of such search was often futile, owing to the conflicts and contradictions of important rules. Consequently, in England, in 1893, Parliament enacted what is known as the Sale of Goods Act. The Act completely codified the law as found in the decisions and harmonized the existing rules in as complete and comprehensive a manner as possible. Thus, in England the law relating to the sale of goods was governed by a body of rules and principles which were in a large measure extracted from the cases involving sales problems. In the United States a very similar effort at codification resulted in the promulgation in 1906 of the Uniform Sales Act, patterned very closely upon its English counterpart. The same situation in the field of negotiable instruments led to the earlier enactment in England of the Bills of Exchange Act in 1882.

In 1895, in the United States, under the leadership of the American Bar Association and the American Bankers Association, a commission was appointed for the purpose of revising and codifying the law merchant in the United States. This committee, taking the English Bills of Exchange Act as a model, derived with modifications, the Uniform Negotiable Instruments Law (NIL). This Act was completed in 1896, and was submitted to the legislatures of the various states with recommendation for adoption. The Act was adopted by every state, with some changes being made in states seeking to make the Act more suitable for their purposes.

Over the ensuing years other uniform laws were promulgated in other areas of commercial law and were adopted by varying numbers of states. These laws related to warehouse receipts, bills of lading, transfers of corporate securities, and devices for utilizing personal property as security for the financing and sale of goods.

Notwithstanding these uniform laws, the rules of law pertaining to business transactions varied from state to state. Variances were created by judicial decisions in areas not covered by statute and by judicial decisions interpreting statutes differently from state to state. In addition, many of the states changed provisions of the Uniform Statutes so that they were not truly uniform.

As more and more business transactions were conducted on a nationwide basis with buyers and sellers from all parts of the country dealing with each other, the search for uniformity gained momentum. The wide variations were causing problems for businessmen and were creating a business climate which was uncertain and in which the legal effects of any given act were not entirely predictable.

One solution to the problem of uncertainty in the legal climate of business was to provide a modern code of laws relating to all aspects of the business or commercial transaction, in keeping with modern business practices and technology, which would be uniform throughout the country. As a result, the

Commissioners on Uniform State Laws and the American Law Institute with the assistance of legal scholars, lawyers and judges, businessmen and bankers prepared the Uniform Commercial Code.

The Code was promulgated by the National Conference of Commissioners on Uniform State Laws and the American Law Institute with the endorsement . of the American Bar Association in 1951, following several years of painstaking effort and constant review and revision. It was a massive project and involved not only a revision of the law as found in statutes and cases, a weighing of alternative provisions, a consideration of commercial utility in keeping with commercial practices, but also an integration of all of the articles and sections so that the resulting codification would be internally sound and a unified whole.

The Code was made available for presentment to the legislatures of the then forty-eight states. At first the Code did not gain legislative acceptance. The first state to adopt it was Pennsylvania in 1953. During the next few years there were few adoptions, but when some of the commercially important states adopted the Code, many other states rapidly followed suit, primarily in the 1960s. Now all fifty states except one, Louisiana, have adopted the Code and it would appear that general uniformity in the law of commercial transactions has now been almost accomplished.

However, complete uniformity is lacking in that (1) the legislatures of some of the states have altered certain sections of the Code in line with local economic and financial factors; (2) the Code provides certain alternative sections wherein the legislatures make a choice as to the alternative best suited to the state; (3) the Code purposely has left certain areas open to further development by the courts and has left room for continued expansion as new methods of doing business and new media of communication come into use; (4) some areas were deemed better suited to local regulation in keeping with social problems and other conditions which can best be handled at the individual state level; (5) it is possible that the courts in interpreting the various sections of the Code and applying them to factual situations may reach somewhat varying conclusions. This is especially true of some sections which courts have critized as being ambiguous. In the case of *Roto-Lith, Ltd.* v. *F. P. Bartlett & Co.* on page 159 the court commented that: "The Statute was not too happily drafted."

The continually expanding use of electronic data-processing equipment may require a reappraisal of some Code sections and amendments thereof in the near future. Certainly, problems have arisen and will arise that may be difficult to resolve under the existing Code provisions. This is especially true of the Articles on Commercial Paper, Bank Deposits and Collections, and Investment Securities. For example, Articles 3 and 4 of the Code, which deal primarily with the check, will surely become obsolete because we may soon be living in a "checkless" society. It is estimated that approximately 250 computer centers located throughout the country could handle the process of settlement and deposit accounting. Through the use of a data communications network, the computers at such centers could electronically transfer funds from payer to payee's accounts.

At the present time most banks make extensive use of EDP (electronic data processing) in conjunction with MICR (magnetic ink character recognition) in handling the collection and handling of checks. Banks currently using EDP hold the great bulk of all commercial bank deposits. The absolute need for some better method of handling and expediting the transfer of funds from payer to payee accounts is illustrated by the enormous volume of checks written each year—well over 20 billion.

The impact of this tremendous and increasing number of checks written (called by bankers the "paper tiger") is magnified by the fact that an average check must pass through two and one-third banks and be handled up to twenty times before being returned to the check writer.

In view of the legal problems resulting from the use of EDP and MICR, the National Automation Conferences have sought suitable amendments to Article 4—Bank Deposits and Collections—of the Uniform Commercial Code. One example of the problems that arise is that of mistakes made in MICR encoding of the amount of a check.

As more and more cases interpret and apply the Code, it will tend to be less uniform, but more fixed and certain on a state-by-state basis. In the final analysis, the Code will mean what the courts say it means.

3-2. Purposes of the Code. The purposes of the Code are to simplify, clarify, and modernize the law governing commercial transactions; to permit the continued expansion of commercial practices through custom, usage, and agreement of the parties; and to make uniform the law among the various jurisdictions.

While the Code provides definite rules which govern commercial transactions, the parties may, by mutual agreement, provide for a different result, except that the obligations of good faith, diligence, reasonableness, and care prescribed by the Code may not be successfully disclaimed. However, the parties may by agreement determine the *standards* by which the performance of such obligations is to be measured if such standards are not manifestly unreasonable. Thus, the parties to a transaction can, within limits, tailor their agreement to suit their needs. The Code supplies the rules and principles that will apply if the parties have not otherwise agreed.

In order to accomplish the aforesaid purposes, the concept of the Code is that a "commercial transaction" is a single subject of the law, notwithstanding its many legal relations. In the Official Comment to the Code it is stated:

> . . . "Commercial transactions" is a single subject of the law. . . . A single transaction may very well involve a contract for sale, followed by a sale, the giving of a check or draft for a part of the purchase price, and the acceptance of some form of security for the balance. The check or draft may be negotiated and will ultimately pass through one or more banks for collection. If the goods are shipped or stored, the subject matter of the sale may be covered by a bill of lading or warehouse receipt or both. Or, it may be that the entire transaction was made pursuant to a letter of credit either domestic or foreign.
>
> Obviously, every phase of commerce involved is but a part of one transaction, namely the sale of and payment for goods.

Thus the Code, to effectuate its purpose, purports to deal with all the phases that may ordinarily arise in the handling of a commercial transaction, from start to finish. Although each Article is restricted to a specialized area, it is recognized that in certain situations more than one Article could be applicable.

The Code makes provision for such overlapping. The component parts of the Code are briefly discussed in the next section.

3-3. Scope of the Code.   It is important to note that the Code is restricted to transactions involving various aspects of the sale, financing, and security in respect to *personal property*—tangible and intangible. It relates only tangentially to *real property*—land and interests in land—in a few isolated circumstances. It does not cover contracts other than those mentioned.

The Code has had a great influence upon the growth and development of the law in many areas outside of those to which the Code has specific application. Many of its basic principles and concepts have been utilized and applied to situations which do not strictly come within the purview of the Code because of the rationale behind them. For example, Code law has been applied to determine whether a franchise was properly terminated.[1]

The Code contains ten Articles, of which eight deal with specific aspects of commercial transactions in detail, one contains General Provisions applicable to the whole body of Code law, and one designates statutes which are repealed by the Code. The content of these Articles is discussed generally in material which follows in this chapter and in detail in the ensuing chapters.

General provisions. Article 1—General Provisions—sets forth certain rules which are applicable in general to all of the other Articles, including rules of construction and interpretation. Separate definitions of generally applicable terms and a *general* "Statute of Frauds" are also included in Article 1.

While the Code contains rules which provide for most situations likely to arise in a commercial transaction, Article 1 provides that

> the principles of law and equity, including the law merchant and the law relative to capacity to contract, principal and agent, estoppel, fraud, misrepresentation, duress, coercion, mistake, and bankruptcy . . . supplement its provisions. (U.C.C. 1-103)

Thus, general rules of law with respect to an infant's right to disaffirm a contract are applicable under the Code unless there is a special Code provision relating to this matter. The Code does provide that an infant can disaffirm liability on a negotiable instrument and that an infant cannot recover goods he has sold if the goods have been transferred to a subsequent good-faith purchaser. However, there are many other ways in which the capacity to contract is involved and the Code is supplemented by the general law on the subject.

Sales. Article 2—Sales—is restricted to transactions involving the sale of "goods," which are defined generally as "movable" physical property. This definition excludes intangible items of property such as contract claims and also excludes contracts for sale of investment securities—stocks and bonds. In many instances the sale of goods is the underlying transaction which brings into play the other articles relating to protection of the seller by means of security for the sale, financing, and the like. Article 2 replaced the Uniform Sales Act.

---

[1] *Division of Triple T Service, Inc. v Mobil Oil Corp.*, page 348

Commercial paper. Article 3—Commercial Paper—is limited to instruments which satisfy the formal requirements of negotiability as set forth in the Article—drafts, checks, certificates of deposit, and notes. These instruments are generally short-term credit paper designed to be utilized as a part of a transaction such as a sale of goods and not intended for purposes of investment. Article 3 does *not* apply to money, documents of title, or investment securities. In its application to drafts, checks, certificates of deposit, and notes, it supersedes the Uniform Negotiable Instruments Law.

Bank deposits and collections. Article 4—Bank Deposits and Collections—is related to Article 3 and sets forth the rules for the negotiable instruments specified in Article 3 as they pass through banking channels in the collection process. Article 4 also prescribes the relationship between a bank and its customer in such matters as overdrafts, stop-payment orders, duties with respect to forgeries, and the like. Article 4 is not limited to transactions involving checks or other "commercial paper" but also covers collections of bonds and like instruments handled by banks. Article 4 is in general a codification of the well-recognized and defined patterns of banking operations.

Letters of credit. Article 5—Letters of Credit—covers a device which has long been used in international trade to facilitate sales of goods between remote buyers and sellers.[2] It is expected that it will now be used more extensively in domestic transactions. Basically, a letter of credit is an engagement whereby one party, usually a bank, agrees in advance with a prospective buyer of goods to honor a draft (order to pay) drawn upon it by a seller of goods upon compliance with certain conditions. The seller must present to the bank bills of lading and other documents that represent and relate to the goods sold. The letter of credit furnishes a financing device which substitutes the financial responsibility of a bank vis-a-vis the seller of goods for that of a buyer of goods. The main commercial function of the letter of credit is to facilitate sales of goods and to afford proper protection to all parties concerned. The buyer is protected because the bank with which he has made the arrangements for the letter of credit will not honor drafts drawn against it by the seller except upon the latter's presentation of documents which provide that the goods are available to the buyer. The seller is protected because the bank has obligated itself to honor drafts drawn by him for payment for the goods. It is important to note that banks dealing with letters of credit are primarily concerned with *documents* and not with enforcing the underlying sales contract. Thus, if the documents are in order, the bank will pay the seller without regard to the condition of the goods which have been bought and sold.

A letter of credit is typically used when a person wishes to purchase goods from a seller with whom he has not previously established his credit. Such person will make arrangements with a bank whereby the latter agrees to honor drafts drawn upon it by a prospective seller of goods. The letter of credit constitutes the bank's promise, and the bank will ordinarily require the potential buyer to post collateral sufficient to protect the bank. The buyer will now contract with the seller for the purchase of goods, and the seller on the strength of the letter of credit will ship the goods. He will send the bill of lading and

[2] Banco Espanol de Credito v. State Street Bank & Trust Co., page 350

other documents along with a draft for payment of the goods to the bank which issued the letter of credit or to an "advising bank," which acts on behalf of the issuing bank. The bank will examine these documents and if they are in good order will pay or accept the draft and surrender the documents to the buyer so that he can obtain the goods from the carrier. The buyer will then in most cases sell the goods in the course of his business and pay the bank. If the bank has merely *accepted* the draft which is payable at a later date, the buyer will reimburse the bank prior to its having paid any money. In such case the bank is truly "lending its credit" to the buyer.

The terminology of Article 5 can be simply described: The buyer (customer of the bank) makes an arrangement with his bank (issuer) whereby the bank agrees to honor drafts drawn upon the bank by the seller (beneficiary) in payment for goods sold to the buyer, when the seller presents proof that he has in fact complied with the documentary terms of his agreement with the buyer.

Article 5 deals with the duty of the bank to honor drafts drawn under the terms of the letter of credit and all of the aspects of the letter of credit transactions; the formal requirements of a letter of credit; the relations between issuer and customer, issuer and beneficiary, and customer and beneficiary; and the rights and duties of other parties who participate as intermediaries, including banks other than the issuing bank. In general, the beneficiary or a nonissuing bank which relies upon the letter of credit will be protected. The Article is new in the field of codification—letters of credit were not previously covered by uniform legislation. It is predicated to a large extent on the "Uniform Customs and Practice for Commercial Documentary Credits," of the International Chamber of Commerce and applies many of these customs and practices to domestic transactions.

Bulk transfers. Article 6—Bulk Transfers—relates to sales or transfers "in bulk and not in the ordinary course of the transferor's business, of a major part of the materials, supplies, merchandise or other inventory of an enterprise subject to this Article." Typically, a sale of an entire retail store would be a "bulk transfer." The Article, which replaces a variety of divergent state statutes, provides protection for unsecured creditors of the seller against the possibility that he might "sell out" and not make provision to pay his creditors.

Documents of title. Article 7 deals with commodity paper—paper which may be negotiable and which represents goods or commodities in storage or transportation. Such paper is to be distinguished from "commercial paper" which represents an obligation to pay *money*—a document of title enables the holder to obtain *goods.* Both have the characteristic of *negotiability* and holders of either have a degree of protection not available to holders of nonnegotiable instruments. This Article replaces the Uniform Warehouse Receipts Act and the Uniform Bills of Lading Act.

Investment securities. Article 8 also relates to instruments which have negotiable characteristics and deals with the transfer of securities and the protection afforded to the transferee. Such instruments as stock certificates and corporate bonds are within the purview of this Article, which is a sort of negotiable instruments law dealing with securities. The instruments are, however, usually long-term rather than short-term credit instruments, and are intended not as a medium of exchange but as a medium of investment. The Article replaces the Uniform Stock Transfer Act.

Secured transactions. Article 9 applies to any transaction which is intended to create *a security interest* in personal property—goods, documents, instruments, accounts receivable, and other items. A retailer may sell an article and retain an interest in the article as security for the payment of the purchase price; he may borrow money against his inventory; he may borrow against the security of his accounts receivable, or against notes payable to him. There are a great variety of security arrangements. The above are but a few examples. The Article also covers the outright *sale* of accounts receivable and certain other intangibles. It replaces the Uniform Trust Receipts Act and the Uniform Conditional Sales Act and many other security devices, including the chattel (personal property) mortgage.

INTRODUCTION TO THE UNIFORM COMMERCIAL CODE CASES

Division of Triple T Service, Inc. v. Mobil Oil Corp.
304 N.Y.S.2d 191 (1969)

The plaintiff had operated a service station for a number of years under a franchise and lease from the defendant. The contract provided for termination upon ninety days' notice. The defendant gave such notice and plaintiff contends that the termination was not justified. He argued that under the Uniform Commercial Code the defendant's action was arbitrary and not in good faith —that it was an attempt to seize the goodwill that had been created by the plaintiff during a five-year period. The plaintiff sought an injunction against the termination and the defendant moved for dismissal.

GAGLIARDI, J. . . . The ultimate question raised herein is whether franchisors or distributors with tremendous bargaining power can terminate agreements with franchisees pursuant to their contract but without cause? . . .

Plaintiff contends that the Uniform Commercial Code requires defendant to exercise "good faith" in terminating his agreements and that the clause permitting defendant to terminate without cause is unconscionable. Defendant, for its part, does not question the applicability of the aforementioned statute but argues that it in no way affects its rights under the contract. At first blush one might assume that the Uniform Commercial Code does not reach franchise or distributorship agreements. . . . However, the courts have not been reluctant to enlarge the type of commercial transactions clearly encompassed within the spirit and intendment of the statute (see . . . *Vitex Manufacturing Corp.* v. *Caribtex Corp.,* 3 Cir., 377 F.2d 795, holding damage remedies provided for in the Uniform Commercial Code available in a non-Code case. . . .) Furthermore, in *Hertz Commercial Leas. Corp.* v. *Transportation Cr. Cl. H.,* 59 Misc.2d 226, 298 N.Y.S.2d 392, the court held that the Uniform Commercial Code governed the rights of parties to an equipment leasing contract. The court there noted (at 395):

> In view of the great volume of commercial transactions which are entered into

by the device of a lease, rather than a sale, it would be anomalous if this large body of commercial transactions were subject to different rules of law than other commercial transactions which tend to the identical economic result.

That reasoning would appear to be of persuasive force here since franchising presently accounts for at least 20 percent of all retail business equaling $80 billion in annual sales (115 *Congressional Record,* April 25, 1969). That the retail dealer contract is not so alien in everyday commercial transactions and therefore falls within the purview of the Uniform Commercial Code seems clear (see *Sinkoff Bev. Co.* v. *Joseph Schlitz Brewing Co.,* 51 Misc.2d 446, 273 N.Y.S.2d 364, holding beer distributorship contract within terms of the Code; *Mastrian* v. *William Freihofer Baking Co.,* 45 Pa.Dist. & Co.R.2d 237, 5 UCC Rep.Serv 988, holding "sales distributorship arrangement" within purview of the Code). The Code is designed to "provide its own machinery for expansion of commercial practices" and is intended for the courts to develop the law "in light of unforeseen and new circumstances and practices" within reason (Uniform Commercial Code, § 1-102 [2] [a], Official Comment 1). However, the Code provisions governing sales are limited in scope to "transactions in goods" (Uniform Commercial Code § 2-102) and by no mean application of judicial sophistry can the lease of real property be deemed to fall within its intendment (*Newton* v. *Allen,* 220 Ga. 681, 141 S.E.2d 417; 17 A.L.R.3d 1010, 1029, Anno., "Uniform Commercial Code—Sales"). Consequently, if plaintiff be entitled to an injunction at all, such relief may only be directed against the termination of his retail dealer contract. . . .

While the Code generally provides that sales contracts carry the obligations of good faith, diligence, reasonableness and care (Uniform Commercial Code § 1-102 [3]), this is a codification of pre-Code case law which was also codified in the predecessor statute and merely relates to the honesty imposed upon the parties during the *term* of the contract. . . . Consequently, unless the termination clause be deemed unconscionable there is no implicit requirement that it be exercised other than as provided for in the contract. . . .

The Code provides that "when it is claimed" that a clause may be unconscionable the court "shall" afford the parties an opportunity to present evidence (Uniform Commercial Code § 2-302 [2]). It has been held that once the court accepts the possibility of unconscionability the hearing called for is mandatory. . . . However, the Court is of the opinion that that part of the termination clause reviewed here is not unconscionable *per se* since the basic test is whether under the circumstances existing at the time of the making of the contract and "in the light of the general commercial background and the commercial needs of the particular trade or case, the clauses involved are so one-sided" as to oppress or unfairly surprise a party. . . . The test does not reach the question of allocation of risks because of superior bargaining power and, in any event, neither party claims lack of mutual benefits inuring from the reciprocal covenants. Moreover, while recent cases concerning warranty disclaimers . . . and exorbitant financing charges . . . appear to have adopted a broader test . . . , the factual consideration peculiar to those cases have not emerged herein and plaintiff claims neither surprise nor oppression. . . . Furthermore, the Court of Appeals had occasion recently to observe that there is nothing inherently wrong in having a termination clause such as the one at bar in a franchise agreement . . . and the Code itself does not prohibit termination clauses on reasonable notice. . . . Additionally, the Federal Congress has gone on record that ninety days' notice is more than ample to permit a franchisee to adequately wind up his affairs; also see Uniform Commercial Code § 2-309, Official Comment 8, which speaks of "a substitute arrangement."

Defendant's motion granted.

Banco Espanol de Credito v. State Street Bank & Trust Co.

385 F.2d 230 (1968)

Lawrence, an American importer, wished to import clothing from Spain. In order to expedite the purchases in Spain he obtained two letters of credit from the defendant bank, issuer. The letters of credit named the plaintiff, the Spanish bank, as "advising bank." The exporters (sellers) were named as the beneficiaries. The letters stipulated that the drafts drawn under the credits be accompanied by an inspection certificate certifying that "the goods are in conformity with the order." The certificate issued stated substantially the same thing—that the samples taken were found conforming, but did not use the exact wording specified. The Spanish bank deemed the inspection certificate to be proper and took the drafts for value from the exporters. The defendant bank refused to honor the drafts. The lower court ruled for the defendant and the plaintiff appealed.

COFFIN, J. . . . We note, at the outset, that an issuing bank's duty to honor a demand for payment is, to some extent, determined by statute. The Uniform Commercial Code . . . § 5-114(1) provides, in relevant part, that "An issuer must honor a draft or demand for payment which complies with the terms of the relevant credit regardless of whether the goods or documents conform to the underlying contract for sale or other contract between the customer and the beneficiary." This Code provision, however, simply codifies long-standing decisional law and does not assist us here in determining whether the inspection certificate submitted by Supervigilancia complied with the terms of the credit.

We take as a starting point the substantial body of case law which establishes and supports the general rule that documents submitted incident to a letter of credit are to be strictly construed. This is because international financial transactions rest upon the accuracy of documents rather than on the condition of the goods they represent. But we note some leaven in the loaf of strict construction. Not only does *haec verba* not control absolutely, . . . but some courts now cast their eyes on a wider scene than a single document. We are mindful, also, of the admonition of several legal scholars that the integrity of international transactions (i.e., rigid adherence to material matters) must somehow strike a balance with the requirement of their fluidity (i.e., a reasonable flexibility as to ancillary matters) if the objective of increased dealings to the mutual satisfaction of all interested parties is to be enhanced. . . . Finally, we recognize that this is not a litigation about the nomenclature of goods. Consequently, we are not measurably helped by such cases as those cited in the margin which turn on discrepancies between the actual term of invoices or bills of lading and requirements of a letter of credit.

What we face here is a matter of procedure which can, in the first instance, be structured by the purchasing party. How may a buyer in the international marketplace be assured before payment that his purchase as delivered is of the quality agreed upon by the parties? As buyers become more concerned about quality, this issue is likely to become more important. That there are so few cases or comments addressed to the issue of reasonable precautions to assure quality is indicative of the relatively novel status of the problem, at least so far as courts have dealt with it. We are mindful of the testimony in this case that an official of appellee, a busy bank, engaged in passing upon the issuance of 1,500 to 2,000 letters of credit a year for several decades, has encountered in this case his first experience with a letter of credit calling for a certificate of conformity to the order.

What are the realities of such a requirement on the part of the buyer? It is not enough that he receive the quantity of goods he ordered, nor that he receive goods capable of standard measure or grade. He must also, in such a case as this, receive them cut, tailored, sewn according to a style he has in mind. He must therefore rely on a sample he has seen and liked. Being in a distant part of the globe, the buyer must usually elect one of two alternatives. He may be present during the inspection process to verify the sample or he may select, with his seller's acquiescence, a person or firm in whom he has confidence to represent him. Unless he elects to be present, he is acting on faith—faith that the representative is capable and honest, and faith that the representative has the right samples or criteria to serve as a standard. Even if he mails an approved sample direct to the representative, he must rely on the integrity of the mails.

This act of faith—or its converse, the risk that merchandise will not turn out as hoped—is that of the buyer. As one contemporary student has written,

> ... there is one risk against which protection is required and which is less easy to guard against. That is the risk that the goods shipped may not comply with the terms of the sales contract as to quality. This is a risk which normally the buyer will have to bear ... but ... [he] can guard against the risk by requiring in his letter of request to the bankers that, in addition to the usual shipping documents, the vendor shall deliver a certificate of quality showing the goods to be as specified in the contract, signed by some reasonable person at the place of shipment. The only risk then left to the buyer is that the person nominated to give the certificate may fail in his duty. But an entire absence of risk would mean an absence of business." (A. G. Davis, *The Law Relating to Commercial Letters of Credit*, 3d ed., London, Sir Isaac Pitman & Sons Ltd., 1963, p. 19.)

These observations go to the heart of this case. For the buyer here—Lawrence—was striving to assure the delivery of quality goods. To be sure, it deliberately postponed the problem when it caused the letters of credit to be issued without resolving the question of the inspecting agent. Then it naively sought to have the sellers accept one of its own representatives. It had long since sewn the seeds of dispute by sending to the sellers both "stock sheets" which were really orders and "orders" which were merely preliminary papers. When it finally reached agreement with the seller as to an inspecting agency, it neglected to specify precisely how it would conduct the inspection operation, leaving only the bland instruction that the goods must conform to orders. And, so far as the inspecting agency was concerned, the orders merely referred to samples that might very well have been inspected in Spain at some past time.

Consequently when faced on the eve of the shipping deadline both with a barrage of contradictory telegrams from the buyer and with samples which the sellers under oath stated "corresponded" with samples approved earlier by the buyer's representative in Barcelona, Supervigilancia had to act to the dissatisfaction of one of the parties to the basic contract. That it took the word, under oath, of the seller as to the appropriateness of the sample is no more than any inspector must ordinarily do. Unless the buyer is physically present (and Lawrence presumably could have arranged this during the frenetic two-week period of cable traffic), the inspector must take someone's word that he is judging by the proper samples. . . .

Webster's Dictionary (3d Int'l ed.) gives such meanings of "correspond" as "in agreement," "conformity," "equivalent," "match," "equal." In the context and considering the language difficulty, we think these meanings apply more than the looser ones like "analogous," "parallel," or "similar." In effect, Lawrence in this case, by providing as a referent to the letter of credit requirement of conformity to orders merely the early cryptic description on the stock sheets ("Coats . . . to be as samples inspected in Spain"), procured no more reliable assurance of authenticity than the credit termination clause in *Fair Pavilions, Inc.* v. *First Nat'l City Bank,* 24 A.D.2d 109, 264 N.Y.S.2d 255 (1965), which was to be triggered " . . . if our Travelers Letter of Credit Department receives . . . from an officer (or one describing himself therein as an officer) of [bank's customer] an affidavit that one or more . . . events . . . has occurred." . . .

To hold otherwise—that a buyer could frustrate an international transaction on the eve of fulfillment by a challenge to authenticity of sample—would make vulnerable many such arrangements where third parties are vested by buyers with inspection responsibilities but where, apart from their own competence and integrity, there is no ironclad guarantee of the sample itself.

As for the argument that Supervigilancia's finding that the goods conform "to the conditions estipulated on the Order-Stock-sheets" is a meaningful variance from the terms of the letters of credit, we confess to semantic myopia. "The conditions" mean, as we read the certificates, all the conditions, hence the order itself. As for the dual use by the agency of the words "Order-Stock-sheets," we have already indicated both the nature and cause of the confusion and conclude that Supervigilancia acted solomonically in borrowing the substance of the stock sheets and the label of the "orders." We do not see how it could have done otherwise.

The remaining contention that "under reserves" has some mysterious meaning which infects the entire certificate is not borne out by the inapposite cases cited to us and is directly refuted by the limiting language immediately following—"not as far as the goods are concerned." Further reading of the document indicates clearly that the phrase was directed to the underlying dispute between buyer and seller, which could not be the concern of the advising bank.

We hold, therefore, that the inspection certificate in this case conformed in all significant respects to the requirements of the letter of credit.

Reversed and remanded.

CHAPTER 17
REVIEW QUESTIONS AND PROBLEMS

1. The comment to the U.C.C. in describing the preparation of the Code states that frequent consultations were had with "practicing lawyers, hard-headed businessmen and operating bankers who contributed generously of their time and knowledge. . . . " What insight does this give as to the nature of the Code?

2. In view of the years of intensive study which went into the preparation of the Code, is it to be anticipated that it will be revised in the near future?

3. Does the Code relate to all contracts and activities involving business-legal relationships?

4. *A* and *B* have entered into a contract for the sale of "goods." Article 2 of the Code deals with such a contract. What other articles of the Code might have a bearing on this transaction?

5. What is the function of a bank in a transaction involving a letter of credit? What must a seller of goods furnish to the bank in order to obtain the benefit of the letter of credit?

6. *A* is arranging to sell his hardware store to *B.* The sale is to include all the assets of the business. What problem might this sale present to creditors of *A*? What provisions of the Code would be particularly applicable to this transaction?

7. A merchant, *A,* wishes to sell goods to *B* but desires to protect himself against the possibility of *B's* default in payment and the exposure of the goods to claims of other creditors of *B.* How may he accomplish this result?

8. Merchant *A* is in need of "working capital," as he has engaged in many credit sales and has numerous outstanding accounts receivable. His present inventory is substantial, but he wishes to expand it. Advise *A* as to how he might arrange for the needed money and inventory.

9. *A* is the holder of a negotiable promissory note. He wishes to borrow money from *B* and pledge the note as security. Can this be accomplished? What articles of the Code would govern this transaction?

10. *A* sold a car to *B* on an installment contract and retained a security interest in the car. *B* later took the car to *X* for repairs. *B* was unable either to pay for the repairs or to continue his installment payment to *A.* How would the rights of *A* and *X* in the car be determined?

chapter 18

The Sales Contract

3-4. Introduction. The sales provisions of the Code are applicable to transactions in "goods" as that term is defined in the Code and particularly to "contracts for sale" of goods. They are not applicable to sales of other types of property, personal service contracts, or to a transaction in goods which may appear to be a sale but which is intended only as a security transaction. This latter subject is covered by a separate article in the Code and is discussed in Chapters 30 and 31. Article 2—Sales is essentially a complete codification of the law of the sale of goods.

The Sales Article is premised upon certain fundamental concepts which relate to many phases of the contract for the sale of goods and which condition many of the rights, duties, and obligations of the parties. Many of these concepts are expressed in various definitions. These basic definitions not only explain a number of the Code provisions but also illustrate the philosophy of the law in its approach to the sale of goods. The following are definitions of some of the more significant terms used in the law of sales.

 1. Seller and buyer. A *seller* is a person who either sells or contracts to sell goods, and a *buyer* is a person who either buys or contracts to buy goods.

 2. Sale. A *sale* consists in the passing of title to goods from the seller to the buyer for a price. The seller is obligated to transfer and deliver or tender delivery, and the buyer is obligated to accept and pay in accordance with the contract. In general, the parties to a contract for sale can agree upon any terms and conditions which are mutually acceptable.

 3. Goods. The term "goods" encompasses all things which are movable,[1] i.e., items of personal property (chattels) which are of a tangible, physical nature. The definition excludes investment securities, such as stocks

---

[1] Foster v. Colorado Radio Corporation, page 364

and bonds, and things in action, such as negotiable instruments. The limitation of coverage to *goods* necessarily excludes sales of real property. However, the sale of timber, minerals, or a building which is to be removed from the land is a sale of goods if these things are to be severed by the seller. Growing crops are also included within the definition of goods, whether they are to be removed by the buyer or the seller.[2] This is in recognition of the fact that such crops are frequently sold prior to harvesting.

    4. Merchant.   A merchant is "a person who deals in goods of the kind or otherwise by his occupation holds himself out as having knowledge or skill peculiar to the practices or goods involved in the transaction. . . . "[3] (U.C.C. 2-104(1)) This designation is of great importance and is recognition of a professional status for businessmen, justifying the application of different standards to their conduct than to "nonprofessionals." In a sense it is a modern application of the special treatment afforded merchants in the early development of the law merchant.

    5. Good faith.   "Good faith" means honesty in fact in the conduct or transaction. In the case of a merchant, "good faith" also includes the observance of reasonable commercial standards of fair dealing in the trade. The Code premises its rules of law on the parties' acting in good faith; failure to do so will take away rights that would otherwise be enforced or will relieve duties that would otherwise be imposed.

    6. Future goods.   Future goods are goods which are not in existence at the time of the agreement or which have not been "identified," or designated as the specific goods which will be utilized in the transaction. Future goods may be the subject of a "contract to sell" goods at a future time, but they obviously may not be the subject of a "present sale," which is a sale accomplished by the making of a contract.

    7. Contract for sale.   This term encompasses both a present sale and a contract to sell goods at a future time. In general, the rights of the buyer and seller are the same whether the transaction is a present sale or a contract to sell, but there are some specific Code provisions in which the distinction is significant.

3-5. A Comparison of General Contract Principles and Code Principles.   As was discussed in Book Two on contracts, the drafters of the Code recognized that many of the principles of general contract law were not desirable in contracts for the sale of goods. Rules and principles of contract law which produced a desirable result in a transaction for the sale or construction of a building or in a contract between an employer and an employee would not necessarily produce a good result in a contract for the purchase and sale of goods. Accordingly, many contract rules have been changed or modified by the Code in order to achieve a commercially desirable result. Most of the changes are based on common business practice and the customary way of doing business.

    Various changes in the law of contracts for the sale of goods were discussed in the chapters on contracts. Some of these will be discussed further in subsequent sections. The chart immediately following contains a summary of these

[2] United States v. Greenwich Mill & Elevator Company, page 365
[3] Cook Grains, Inc. v. Paul Fallis, page 366

differences and also references to the text section which discusses them, as well as the Code provision which made the change.

Any of the foregoing differences between the Code and general contract principles which are not understood should be reviewed at this time. The subject of variance between offer and acceptance will be discussed in the next section.

3-6. Variance between Offer and Acceptance. At common law a variance between the acceptance and the offer caused the acceptance to be considered a counteroffer and a rejection. Frequently, this requirement that the acceptance exactly match the terms of the offer has not produced a commercially desirable result. The normal expectation of businessmen that a contract was in fact formed by the exchange of offer and acceptance was often frustrated because of this technicality.

The Code attempts to resolve the problem by providing that a variance is not necessarily fatal to the formation of a contract. This is in keeping with the objective of recognizing the existence of a contract when it is apparent that a contract was intended. The Code provides that a definite expression of acceptance or a written confirmation operates as an acceptance, even though it states terms additional to or different from those offered or agreed upon, *unless* acceptance is made conditional upon agreement to the additional or different terms. This means that the additional terms do not prevent the formation of a contract, unless they are expressed in the form of a counterproposal. The terms in question will otherwise be treated simply as proposals.

However, when the contract is *between merchants,* such terms become part of the contract unless "(a) the offer expressly limits acceptance to the terms of the offer; (b) they materially alter it; or (c) notification of objection to them has already been given or is given within a reasonable time after notice of them is received." (U.C.C. 2-207(2))

It will be noted that this section of the Code relates to two similar situations: (1) where an acceptance states terms additional to or different from those offered, and (2) where a written confirmation of an informal or oral agreement sets forth terms additional to or different from those agreed upon during the negotiations which led to the agreement. The parties may have reached an agreement either orally or by informal exchange of correspondence. Thereafter one or both of them in order to "firm up" the agreement will ordinarily send a formal acknowledgment setting forth the terms agreed upon. In these confirmatory memoranda, terms which were not discussed may be added. The Code takes the position that in either of the above situations " . . . a proposed deal which in commercial understanding has in fact been closed is recognized as a contract." (U.C.C. 2-207 Official Comment) Moreover,

> conduct by both parties which recognizes the existence of a contract is sufficient to establish a contract for sale although the writings of the parties do not otherwise establish a contract. In such case the terms of the particular contract consist of those terms on which the writings of the parties agree, together with any supplementary terms incorporated under any other provisions of this Act.[4] (U.C.C. 2-207(3))

[4] Construction Aggregates Corp. v. Hewitt-Robins Inc., page 367

Special Rules for Contracts of Sale of Goods

Rule	Code Section	Contracts Section and Page
Offer and Acceptance		
1. Unilateral offers may be accepted either by a promise to ship or by shipment.	2-206 (1) (b)	Sec. 2-25, P. 135
2. Firm written offers by *merchants* for three months or less are irrevocable.	2-205	Sec. 2-19, P. 130
3. All terms need not be included in negotiations in order for a contract to result.	2-204	Sec. 2-13, P. 126
4. Particulars of performance may be left open.	2-311 (1)	Sec. 2-13, P. 126
5. Failure to reject may constitute an acceptance.	2-206 (1) (b)	Sec. 2-27, P. 136
6. Variance in terms between offer and acceptance may not be a rejection and may be an acceptance.	2-207	Sec. 2-29, P. 137
7. An acceptance may be made by any reasonable means of communication and is effective when deposited.	2-206 (1) (a)	Sec. 2-30, P. 138
8. Acceptance by performance requires notice within a reasonable time, or the offer may be treated as lapsed.	2-206 (2)	Sec. 2-25, P. 135
9. To have a contract, the price need not be included.	2-305	Sec. 2-13, P. 126
Consideration		
1. Consideration is not required to support a modification of a contract for the sale of goods.	2-209 (1)	Sec. 2-31, P. 162
2. Adding a seal is of no effect.	2-203	Sec. 2-31, P. 161
Capacity		
1. A minor may not disaffirm against an innocent third party.	2-403	Sec. 2-43, P. 196
Reality of Assent		
1. Rescission is not a bar to a suit for dollar damages.	2-721	Sec. 2-7, P. 106
Illegality		
1. Unconscionable bargains will not be enforced.	2-302	Sec. 2-69, P. 236
Form of the Agreement		
1. Statute of Frauds:	2-201	Sec. 2-78, P. 262
a. $500 price for goods.		
b. Written confirmation between merchants.		
c. Memorandum need not include all terms of agreement.		
d. Payment, acceptance, and receipt limited to quantity specified in writing.		

Rule	Code Section	Contracts Section and Page
e. Specially manufactured goods.		
f. Admission pleadings or court proceedings that a contract for sale was made.		

Rights of Third Parties
1.   An assignment of the "the contract" or of "rights under the contract" includes a delegation of duties.

	2-210 (4)	Sec. 2-82, P. 274

Performance of Contracts
1.   Tender of payment is a condition precedent (rather than a condition concurrent) to a tender of delivery.

	2-511	Sec. 2-97, P. 296

2.   Anticipatory breach may not be withdrawn if the other party gives notice that it is final.

	2-610 , 2-611	Sec. 2-98, P. 297

3.   Rules on divisible contracts.

	2-307 , 2-612	Sec. 2-99, P. 299

4.   Impracticability of performance in certain cases is an excuse for nonperformance.

	2-614	Sec. 2-107, P. 304

5.   Claims and rights may be waived without consideration.

	1-107	Sec. 2-101, P. 300

Discharge
1.   The statute of limitations is four years, but parties can reduce by mutual agreement to not less than one year.

	2-275	Sec. 2-113, P. 323

Because of the practice of the business community to use "forms" in the conduct of business problems of variance are common. Printed forms are widely used in making offers, and the same is true of acceptances. It is to be expected that the printed forms used by each of the parties will differ in many respects, due in part to the fact that each seeks to use forms that are advantageous to him. Therefore, while there will usually be agreement as to the basic terms of the contract, there is likely to be conflict in the "fine print" on the forms.

To illustrate the problem of variance in offer and acceptance, and the Code solution, assume the following: Merchant *A* sends to Merchant *B* an offer to sell him 1,000 boxes of select Anjou pears at $10 per box, F.O.B. Medford, Oregon (*A*'s place of business). *B* replies by wire: "Accept your offer to sell 1,000 boxes of select Anjou pears at $10 per box, F.O.B. Champaign, Illinois. Boxes to be made of wood, and pears individually wrapped." There are two matters to consider here. First, the terms of delivery were changed. Under the Code provisions, a contract has been formed, and *A*'s provision on delivery (Medford, Oregon) prevails. *A* had effectively objected to *B*'s proposal, since *A* had stated the terms of delivery in the offer. The law considers the statement of a term as an objection to a change in that term. Second, there were new or additional terms concerning the boxes and wrapping added in the acceptance. As to these additional terms, they would be included *unless* either (1) *A* objects to these additional terms within a reasonable time, or (2) the additional terms are found to "materially alter" the contract. If *A* does seasonably object to the additional terms or if a court finds that they constituted a material alteration, they are not included.

It is to be noted that either party could easily have protected himself against the contingencies posed by this example. *A,* the offeror, could have expressly stipulated in his offer that acceptance was limited to the terms of the offer, or he could have seasonably communicated to *B* his refusal to include the additional terms. *B,* the offeree, could have stated in his acceptance that it was to be effective only if *A* agreed to ship F.O.B. Champaign, Illinois, and to pack in wooden boxes, with each pear separately wrapped. In this event his acceptance would constitute a *counteroffer.*

In the example offeror and offeree are merchants; if merchants were not involved on both sides, the additional terms would not become a part of the contract unless mutually agreeable. They would simply be proposals for additions to the contract which *A* could accept or reject.

As previously noted, variances also arise as a result of the use of written confirmations of informal or oral agreements. Written confirmations are used to satisfy the statute of frauds, and their use is considered sound business practice. In some transactions, only one party may confirm the agreement, but in most cases, both parties are likely to confirm in order to ensure that each has complete records. In such cases, the confirmations frequently cross in the mail. Confirmation may be on a form prepared for that purpose. If so, the "battle of the forms" may be on again because of the likelihood that the forms used by the parties may have conflicting standard provisions. In addition, a confirmation may add terms not mentioned in the oral negotiations. The Code seeks the same result (1) when a variance arises because of conflicting confirmations, (2) when it arises as a result of new terms in the confirmations, and (3) when the variance arises by virtue of a conflict between the acceptance and the offer. If the parties are not merchants, the new terms in the confirmation or confirmations are not included in the agreement but are construed as proposals for addition to the contract. If the confirmation or confirmations are sent between merchants, the new terms become part of the agreement unless they materially alter the agreement or the other party has previously objected or does object to them within a reasonable time. A merchant who receives a confirmation should promptly object to any new term or changed terms that are unsatisfactory.

The problem of variances caused by conflicting confirmations is further complicated when a party who has sent a confirmation commences performance immediately after sending it. For example, assume that: Merchant *A* and Merchant *B* have entered into an oral agreement for the sale and purchase of goods for a price of $10,000 and have agreed that the sale shall be without warranties. Merchant *A,* the seller, sends a written confirmation on a form which specifies "no warranties as per the agreement" and immediately ships the goods to *B.* Thereafter, *A* receives *B's* confirmation form which provides for both express and implied warranties of the seller. *B* receives the goods and does not reject them. It is clear that if the goods had not been shipped, the sale would be without warranties because *A* had objected to warranties and had communicated his objection to *B.* However, as a result of *A's* act of shipping the goods and *B's* act of accepting them, the parties have recognized the existence of a contract. The contract includes those terms on which the writings of the parties agree and such other terms as the court finds were included in the oral agreement. Proof of the terms of the oral agreement involves an application of the parol evidence rule. The provisions of the parol evidence rule will not prevent the use of oral evidence to prove the actual oral agreement where the confirmations are in conflict. Evidence which explains or supplements the written agreement is also admissible. See Section 3-10.

3-7. The Terms of the Contract in General.   The parties to a contract for sale are privileged to specify in detail the terms of their agreement relating to the price to be paid, the quantity of goods involved, the details of delivery of the goods, the time for performance, the time for payment, any provisions for inspection of the goods by the buyer, and provisions for the protection for the seller. Often, however, the parties do not specify all of these terms; accordingly, the Code sets forth rules which are applicable to interpret the contract in the absence of such specific terms.

   The price term.   The price term of the contract can be left open, with the price to be fixed by later agreement of the parties, or some agreed market standard or other standard may be designated for fixing the price. For example, a dairy farmer might enter into a contract to sell milk to a dairy company; the contract could provide that the price will be based on the butterfat content of the milk, to be determined later by appropriate tests, and also on the average market price of milk for the particular month involved. It may even be agreed that the buyer or the seller shall fix the price, in which event he is obligated to exercise good faith in doing so. If the contract is silent on price, or if for some reason the price is not set in accordance with the method agreed upon, it will be determined as a reasonable price at the time of delivery. Thus, if it appears that it is their intention to do so, parties can bind themselves even though the price is not settled. Obviously, the absence of any definite price term might indicate that no contract exists, but such is not necessarily the case. The parties always have the privilege of stipulating expressly either (1) that even though the price is not settled, they intend to be bound or (2) that they do not intend to be bound until the price is fixed.

   The quantity term.   The Code also allows flexibility in the quantity term of the contract. There may be an agreement to purchase the entire output of the seller, or the quantity may be specified as all that is required by the buyer. Limitations are imposed in order to ensure fair dealing between the parties where the quantity is specified in this manner. In their agreement the parties may express an estimate as to the quantity involved, and no quantity which is unreasonably disproportionate to the estimate will be enforced. If the parties have not agreed upon an estimate, a quantity which is in keeping with normal or other comparable prior output or requirements is implied.[5]

   The buyer and the seller may enter into an "exclusive dealing contract," whereby either (1) the seller may agree to sell his product only to the buyer within a specified territory and not to any of the latter's competitors, or (2) the buyer may agree that he will exclusively purchase all of his requirements from the seller. In either event, the Code requires that each party act in good faith. The seller must refrain from supplying any other dealer within the

[5] Mass. Gas & Electric Supply Corp. v. V.M. Corp., page 368

exclusive territory and must use his best efforts to supply the buyer's requirements. The buyer must use "reasonable effort and due diligence" in the expansion of the market and the promotion of the product. The legality of exclusive dealings arrangements is decided under appropriate state or federal antitrust laws.

The delivery term. Absent any contract provision, the place for delivery is the seller's place of business or, if he has none, his residence, unless the goods are known to both parties to be at some other place, in which event that place is the place for their delivery.

Goods are frequently in the possession of a bailee such as a warehouseman. In this event, in order to make delivery, the seller is obligated to either (1) tender a negotiable document of title (warehouse receipt) representing the goods or (2) procure acknowledgment by the bailee (warehouseman) that the buyer is entitled to the goods. In recognition of actual commercial practices, instruments such as delivery orders may be given to the buyer in satisfaction of the seller's delivery obligation unless the buyer objects.

If the goods are stored in a public warehouse and a negotiable warehouse receipt has been issued, this establishes ownership in the seller. The receipt may be negotiated to the buyer of the goods in order to transfer ownership of the goods to him. The buyer can take delivery of the goods from the warehouse by surrendering the indorsed warehouse receipt to the warehouseman.

The seller is required to tender the goods in a single delivery rather than in installments over a period of time, and the buyer's obligation to pay is not due until such a tender is made. In some situations the seller may not be able to deliver all of the goods at once or the buyer may not be able to receive the entire quantity at one time, in which event more than a single delivery is allowed. The time within which the goods are to be delivered is a reasonable time if the parties have not otherwise specified. The buyer's obligation to pay for the goods arises at the time he is to receive the goods, and this is true even though the place of shipment is the place of delivery. The delivery terms of the contract for sale are particularly important, since they determine to a large extent which of the parties has the risk of loss during shipment, as well as which of them is obligated to pay the costs of shipping.

The term "delivery" signifies a transfer of possession of the goods from the seller to the buyer. The obligation of the seller is to *transfer* and *deliver* and that of the buyer is to *accept* and *pay* in accordance with the contract. A seller makes delivery when he physically transfers into the possession of the buyer the actual goods which conform to the requirements of the contract. However, in keeping with the possessory aspect of delivery, a seller satisfies the requirement that he "transfer and deliver" when he "tenders delivery." Tender as a general concept was discussed in Section 2-97 of this text and will be discussed again in later chapters treating commercial paper.

In the context of a contract for the sale of goods, a proper tender of delivery requires the seller to make available conforming goods at the buyer's disposition and to give the buyer any notification reasonably necessary to take delivery. The particulars as to time, place, and manner of tender are to be determined on the basis of their agreement as supplemented by the Code provisions of Article 2. It is to be noted that each of the parties is required to act "reasonably"; (1) the seller's tender must be at a reasonable hour, and he must keep the goods available for a reasonable time to enable the buyer to take possession, and (2) unless there is an agreement to the contrary, the buyer must furnish facilities suited to his receiving the goods.

The time term. The Code provides that where it has not been agreed upon by the parties, the time for shipment or delivery or any other action under a contract shall be a *reasonable* time. What a reasonable time is depends upon what constitutes acceptable commercial conduct under all of the circumstances. There are several guidelines with regard to determining this —the obligation of good faith; the nature, purpose, and circumstances of the action to be taken; and reasonable commercial standards of fair dealing in the trade. There is a subjective element to the determination of reasonableness, and it is apparent that fairness is required.

It should be noted that a definite time for performance may be found to exist, even though the contract did not express it. Such definite time may be implied from a usage of the trade or course of dealing or performance or from the circumstances of the contract. Thus, in a given type of business, it may be customary to ship goods within seven days of receipt of an order.

Payment is due at the time and place where the buyer is to receive the goods. *Receipt of goods* means taking physical possession of them. The buyer thus has a chance to inspect the goods before paying for them. In order to make possible a preliminary inspection by the buyer, the seller does not have to surrender possession of the goods. Of course, the parties may agree on the time of payment and on inspection rights, and would ordinarily be well advised to do so. When the shipment is C.O.D., the buyer is not entitled to inspect the goods before payment of the price.

The term "seasonably" is used throughout the Code. An action is taken seasonably when it is taken at or within the agreed time or if no time is agreed, at or within a reasonable time.

The parties may enter into a contract which calls for successive performances, such as 1,000 barrels of flour per week, but does not state the duration of the contract. The contract will be valid for a reasonable time, but unless otherwise agreed, either party can terminate it any time. Notification of termination is required in such a "going contract" relationship to enable the other party to make a reasonable substitute arrangement. The parties may agree that notification is not required, but this would not be enforced if it would produce an unconscionable result.

3-8. Special Terms. As a matter of convenience, a number of terms are commonly used in contracts for the sale of goods; this removes the necessity for the parties to spell out in detail the duties of each. Several mercantile abbreviations are frequently employed, and the Code specifies the meaning and import of each. "F.O.B." (Free on Board) is the most commonly used. F.O.B. the place of shipment means that the seller is obligated to place the goods in the possession of a carrier so that they may be shipped to the buyer. The seller's obligation ends when he has made the necessary arrangements with the carrier. Thus, "F.O.B. Eugene, Oregon," where Eugene, Oregon, is the seller's place of business is a *shipment contract.* "F.O.B. Champaign, Illinois," where Champaign is the place where the buyer is to receive the goods, is a *destination contract.* The seller must provide transportation to that place at his own risk and expense; he is responsible for seeing to it that the goods are made available to the buyer at the designated place.

If the term of the contract is also "F.O.B. vessel, car, or other vehicle," in addition, the seller must at his own expense and risk load the goods on board. Another delivery term, "F.A.S. vessel" (Free alongside) at a named port requires the seller at his own expense and risk to deliver the goods alongside the vessel in the manner usual in the port, or on a dock designated and provided by the buyer. "C.I.F." means that the price includes, in a lump sum, the cost of the goods and of the insurance and freight to the named destination. The seller's obligation is to load the goods, to make provision for payment of the freight, and also to obtain an insurance policy in favor of the buyer. If the seller has properly performed all his obligations with respect to the goods, risk of subsequent loss or damage to the goods passes to the buyer upon shipment. Generally the C.I.F. term means that the parties will deal in terms of the documents which represent the goods; the seller performs his obligation by tendering to the buyer the proper documents, including a negotiable bill of lading and an invoice of the goods. The buyer is required to make payment against the tender of the required documents.

The contract may provide that the price will not be definitely arrived at until arrival of the goods. Another term in common usage is "no arrival, no sale." Under this, the seller is relieved of liability for *nondelivery* if the goods are destroyed or lost as a result of the hazards of transportation. "No arrival, no sale" is used in connection with overseas contracts; it leaves the risk of loss on the seller but exempts him from liability to the buyer for damages resulting from nondelivery.

In many cases it is known to both buyer and seller that in the transaction the seller is reselling goods which he has bought from someone else and that the goods are to be shipped by the person from whom the seller has bought. Under these circumstances since the seller is not under obligation to make the shipment himself, he is entitled to a clause which exempts him from payment of damages for nondelivery if the goods do not arrive or if the goods which actually do arrive are not in conformity with the contract. This may be accomplished by using the term "no arrival, no sale."

3-9. Sale on Approval: Sale or Return. The arrangement made between the buyer and the seller may be such that the buyer has the privilege of returning the goods that have been delivered to him. If the goods are delivered primarily for use, as in the case of a consumer purchase, the transaction is designated a "sale on approval"; whereas if the goods are delivered primarily for resale, it is called "sale or return." The distinction is an important one because goods held on approval are not subject to the claims of the buyer's creditors until the buyer has indicated his acceptance of the goods; goods held on "sale or return," however, are subject to the claims of the buyer's creditors while such goods are in his possession. A delivery of goods on consignment, such as a transaction in which a manufacturer or a wholesaler delivers goods to a retailer who has the privilege of returning any unsold goods, is a "sale or return." The goods in possession of the buyer-consignee are subject to the claims of the buyer's creditors, unless the seller makes it known that he has an interest in the goods or complies with the filing provisions of Article 9 dealing with secured transactions.

A characteristic of the sale on approval is that risk of loss does not pass to the buyer until he accepts the goods. Failure to seasonably notify the seller of his decision to return the goods will be treated as an acceptance. After notification of election to return, the seller must pay the expenses of the return and bear the risk, but if the buyer is a merchant, he must follow any reasonable instructions given him by the seller with reference to the return of the goods. In contrast, under a sale or return, the return of the goods is at the buyer's risk and expense.

3-10. Parol Evidence. When is a contract for sale subject to contradiction, explanation, or supplementation in the event of a dispute between the parties as to its terms? If it appears that the writing was intended to be the final expression of the agreement between the parties, its terms may not be contradicted by oral evidence.[6] However, the writing may be explained or supplemented by showing that in past dealings between the parties certain ground rules had been established, or that a usage of the trade was to be considered part of the agreement, although not expressed. In substance, the rules are designed to ascertain the true understanding of the parties as to the agreement and to place the agreement in its proper perspective. The assumption is that prior dealings between the parties and the usages of the trade were taken for granted when the contract was worded. Often a contract for sale involves repetitive performance by both parties over a period of time. The course of performance is indicative of the meaning which the parties by practical construction have given to their agreement and is relevant to its interpretation.[7]

THE SALES CONTRACT CASES

Foster v. Colorado Radio Corporation

381 F.2d 222 (1967)

MURRAH, J. Colorado Radio Corporation brings this diversity suit for damages resulting from Mrs. Foster's alleged breach of promise to purchase certain of the assets of a New Mexico radio station. On trial to the court Colorado Radio prevailed, and Mrs. Foster appeals raising questions concerning breach and the proper measure of damages, if any. We affirm with modification. . . .

The trial court concluded that "The contract . . . did not fall within the Uniform Commercial Code." The apparent basis for this conclusion, and the reasoning which Colorado here offers in support of it, is that the subject matter of this contract is not "goods" and therefore this sale contract was not governed by Article 2 of the Code. We agree that the evidence is clearly sufficient to support a finding that the license, good will, real estate, studios and transmission equipment were not movables and hence not "goods."

It is conceded by Colorado Radio, however, that the remaining assets sold under the contract, i.e., office equipment and furnishings, were movables. As

---

[6] Whirlpool Corp. v. Regis Leasing Corp., page 369
[7] Associated Hardware Supply Co. v. Big Wheel Distributing Co., page 371

to these "goods" Colorado Radio argues that their sale was incidental to the contract's main purpose of transferring the station as a going concern, and therefore . . . the Code should not apply to their sale. We cannot agree. We find nothing in the pertinent Code provisions or comments to indicate that it is not to apply to all sales of goods. Instead we think that the clear language of Sec. 50A-2-102 to the effect that "Unless the context otherwise requires, this article applies to transactions in goods . . . ," makes Article 2 and specifically Sec. 50A-2-706(3) applicable to the sale of these goods. The *Epstein* case is, we think, distinguishable on its facts. It involved the sale of beauty services, during the course of which a product was applied to the purchaser of the service. The question was whether the use of the beauty product constituted a sale of goods so as to bring the action within the warranty sections of the Code. The court held that there was no sale of goods on the theory that the predominant feature of the transaction was the sale of the service. But, in our case there was no sale of a service but instead the sale of a group of assets, some of which are non-goods but others of which concededly are statutory goods. The principle of the *Epstein* case is thus inapplicable. Nor do we think that because the primary purpose of the parties was to transfer the station as a going concern, the Code should not apply to the goods that were sold as part of the deal. It happens in this case that the uncontradicted testimony is to the effect that the value of the goods constituted some five to ten per cent of the contract price. It is quite conceivable, however, that a business could be sold in which all the assets aside from good will would be goods. Nonapplication of the Code to the sale of goods in such a case, and in our case, is we think, plainly contrary to the intention of the drafters.

But, what we have said does not require a reversal *in toto.* We see no reason not to view the Foster contract in two parts as effecting the sale of goods and non-goods. As to the former, since no notice of resale was given, the remedy provided by 50A-2-706 may not be utilized. And since the parties stipulated that contract price less resale price was to be the measure of damages, if any, the breach of promise to purchase the goods is unremediable. As to the non-goods notice of intent to resell was not mandatory; there is no contention that the resale price was not reasonable . . . and the stipulated remedy may be properly utilized. Taking the undisputed testimony most favorably to Mrs. Foster, i.e., that the value of the goods was ten per cent of the value of all the assets sold, it is reasonable to assume that ten per cent of the damage award represented damages for the refusal to purchase the goods. Accordingly the award shall be reduced ten per cent from $15,750 to $14,175, and affirmed since the remaining contentions on damages are resolved against Mrs. Foster. . . .

Affirmed.

United States v. Greenwich Mill & Elevator Company

291 F.Supp. 609 (1968)

The plaintiff, Farmers' Home Administration, loaned $2,000 to a farmer, Butler, and, in return, received and perfected a security interest in his crops. Thereafter, the defendant, Greenwich Mills, sold supplies to Butler and received payment by harvesting part of his soybean crop. The plaintiff sought to recover the value of the harvested crop. The defendant claimed that it could set-off the amount of the value of the crop against the amount Butler owed it.

YOUNG, J. . . . Before the question of the claimed set-off can be determined it is necessary to determine whether the Administration has a security interest in the soybeans in the possession of the defendant. It is clear that the Administration is subject to the law of Ohio, which in this case is Article IX of the Uniform Commercial Code. The security interest of the Administration attached as soon as the crop was planted.

. . . The interest of the agency was perfected by filing.

. . . The question then becomes whether the transaction between the Butlers and Greenwich Mills was a sale, and if so, whether the security interest of the Administration continued through this sale and was attached to the soybeans in the hands of the defendant.

A sale is defined as the passing of title from the seller to the buyer for a price.

. . . A contract for the disposition of growing crops to be severed from the land is a contract for the sale of goods, and thus a sale within the terms of the Uniform Commercial Code.

. . . The definitions used in Article II of the Uniform Commercial Code determine whether the transaction is a sale. Both parties agree that the transaction is a sale. . . .

Where a sale is authorized by the security agreement, the buyer takes free of the security interest. Otherwise the security interest continues in the original collateral and in the identifiable proceeds, the latter only being perfected for ten days before a new filing is necessary. . . .

A buyer in the ordinary course also takes free from a security interest by purchase of the goods unless he knows that the sale is in violation of the security agreement, or unless he is a buyer purchasing farm products from a person engaged in farming operations. Defendant is not a buyer in the ordinary course since it took in satisfaction of an antecedent indebtedness. . . .

Set-off not allowed.

Cook Grains, Inc., v. Paul Fallis

395 S.W.2d 555 (Ark.) 1965

The plaintiff, a grain dealer, brought action against the defendant, a farmer, for breach of a contract to sell soybeans. The parties had been negotiating for the sale of 5,000 bushels, and there was conflicting testimony as to whether or not an agreement had been reached. The grain company had sent a proposed written contract to the defendant and had stipulated that it would be bound if the defendant signed it. The defendant neither signed nor returned the contract. The plaintiff contended that the defendant's failure to indicate disapproval resulted in a contract, while defendant claimed that no obligation was imposed on him because the statute of frauds had not been satisfied. The trial court entered a judgment for the farmer-seller-defendant, and the plaintiff appealed.

ROBINSON, J. The appellant grain company concedes that ordinarily the alleged cause of action would be barred by the statute of frauds, but contends that here the alleged sale is taken out of the statute of frauds by the Uniform Commercial Code. Ark. Stat. Ann. Sec. 85-2-201 (1961 Addendum) is relied on.

Formal requirements—Statute of Frauds.—(1) Except as otherwise provided in this section a contract for the sale of goods for the price of $500 or more is not enforceable by way of action or defense unless there is some writing sufficient to indicate that a contract for sale has been made between the parties and signed by the party against whom enforcement is sought or by his authorized agent or broker. A writing is not insufficient because it omits or incorrectly states a term agreed upon but the contract is not enforceable under this paragraph beyond the quantity of goods shown in such writing.

(2) Between merchants if within a reasonable time a writing in confirmation of the contract and sufficient against the sender is received and the party receiving it has reason to know its contents, it satisfies the requirements of subsection (1) against such party unless written notice of objection to its contents is given within ten (10) days after it is received. . . .

Thus, it will be seen that under the statute, if appellee (farmer) is a merchant he would be liable on the alleged contract because he did not, within ten days, give written notice that he rejected it.

The solution of the case turns on the point of whether the appellee Fallis is a "merchant" within the meaning of the statute. Ark. Stat. Ann. Sec. 85-2-104 (1961 Addendum) provides:

"Merchant" means a person who deals in goods of the kind or otherwise by his occupation holds himself out as having knowledge or skill peculiar to the practices or goods involved in the transaction or to whom such knowledge or skill may be attributed by his employment of an agent or broker or other intermediary who by his occupation holds himself out as having such knowledge or skill. . . .

There is not a scintilla of evidence in the record, or proffered as evidence that appellee is a dealer in goods of the kind or by his occupation holds himself out as having knowledge or a skill peculiar to the practices or goods involved in the transaction, and no such knowledge or skill can be attributed to him.

The evidence in this case is that appellee is a farmer and nothing else. He farms about 550 acres and there is no showing that he has any other occupation. . . .

If the General Assembly had intended that in the circumstances of this case a farmer should be considered a merchant and therefore liable on an alleged contract to sell his commodities, which he did not sign, no doubt clear and explicit language would have been used in the statute to that effect. There is nothing whatever in the statute indicating that the word "merchant" should apply to a farmer when he is acting in the capacity of a farmer, and he comes within that category when he is merely trying to sell the commodities he has raised. . . .

Judgment affirmed.

Construction Aggregates Corp. v. Hewitt-Robins Inc.

404 F.2d 505 (1968)

The plaintiff, CAC, had negotiated with the defendant for the latter to design a conveyor system. Negotiations involved an offer by the plaintiff and a counterproposal by the defendant. The plaintiff requested only a change in the payment proposal and did not raise any question as to the other changes, one of which was a warranty provision more limited than that of the offer. The plaintiff brought action for breach of warranty. The lower court ruled in favor of the defendant, and the plaintiff appealed.

CUMMINGS, J. . . . When H-R's Melrose Park office received CAC's purchase order, CAC was told that the order would not be accepted until one of H-R's corporate officers approved all the conditions and agreements. On July 20, 1962, H-R wrote CAC about the purchase order and advised that acceptance was "predicated on the following clarifications, additions or modifications to the order." including the substitute warranty clause. . . . Since H-R's acceptance was "expressly made conditional on assent to the additional or different terms" contained in its July 20th letter, the exception in the last clause of Section 2-207(1) of the Uniform Commercial Code was clearly applicable. Hence the district court was justified in permitting the jury to treat that letter as a counter-offer.

Section 2-207(3) recognizes that the subsequent conduct of the parties can establish a contract for sale. Since CAC's July 3 purchase order and H-R's July 20 counter-offer did not in themselves create a contract. Section 2-207(3) would operate to create one because the subsequent performance by both parties constituted "conduct by both parties which recognizes the existence of a contract." Such a contract by operation of law would consist only of "those terms on which the writings of the parties agree, together with any supplementary terms incorporated under other provisions of this Act." There having been no agreement on the warranty terms, the implied warranties provided in Sections 2-314 and 2-315 would then ordinarily become applicable. . . .

Here, however, there is no occasion to create a contract by operation of law in default of further actions by the negotating parties, for CAC can be said to have accepted the terms of H-R's counter-offer. CAC sought a change only in the payment terms of the counter-offer, raising no objection to H-R's other modifications of the original purchase order. H-R granted CAC's requested change in a letter of July 31 and could reasonably have assumed that CAC's single objection was an acquiescence in the remaining terms of the counter-offer. CAC did not object to this implication in H-R's July 31st letter reference to the terms of its counter-offer and therefore CAC could appropriately be held to the terms of the July 20th letter. . . .

Affirmed.

Mass. Gas & Electric Supply Corp. v. V.M. Corp.
387 F.2d 605 (1967)

The plaintiff, a distributor of appliances, had a contract with the defendant, an appliance manufacturer, under which the defendant was to supply plaintiff's needs for a stated period. The contract provided for termination on 30 days' notice. Upon learning that the defendant intended to terminate the plaintiff placed an order on June 28 for 892 appliances, almost nine times the usual 100-unit order. Plaintiff had been ordering for 30 days' needs—this order would supply him for over six months. The defendant refused to fill the order and canceled the contract on July 3. The lower court entered judgment for the defendant, and the plaintiff appealed.

ALDRICH, J. . . . At the trial without jury it appeared that plaintiff's normal inventory was about 100 units, and that 892 units was its estimated need for the full balance of the year. The court found, *inter alia.*

> Clearly the June 28 order was for merchandise far in excess of what plaintiff could hope to sell by August 3. . . . Furthermore, there was no evidence that up to August 3 plaintiff had actually lost any prospective sale because of defendant's failure to deliver any of the products ordered on June 28.

The court entered judgment for the defendant and plaintiff appeals.

A number of paragraphs in the agreement collectively establish the atmosphere of the arrangement and one, particularly when read in this atmosphere, dictates the correctness of the court's result. The agreement was a distributorship and not a mere sales agreement, and it was the disclosed intention that when plaintiff ceased to be a distributor it should, at least shortly cease to carry defendant's goods. Thus in paragraph 5 it was provided that defendant would supply plaintiff with goods "for resale by it during said term." Paragraph 8 restricted defendant's obligation to such deliveries as would be needed by plaintiff "to maintain a reasonable inventory for its current sales." Paragraph 15 permitted defendant to reject all orders received after it had sent a 30-day cancellation notice, or within 30 days of the calendar termination date, and to stop delivering at termination.

In the light of the above it might well be that defendant would have been required to fill an order, made on June 28, to maintain a reasonable inventory through the coming month. We could not construe defendant's obligation to be any greater than this. Moreover, when we consider a further paragraph, plaintiff is in difficulties even here. Under paragraph 14 of the agreement, at the option of the defendant exercised at any time within 30 days after termination, plaintiff was obliged to return, at essentially the price paid, plus freight, all goods purchased from the defendant and then unsold. Had the defendant filled the June 28 order in its entirely, in the light of the above-quoted findings which are fully supported in the record, the clear purport of which is that no part of these goods would have been sold, the defendant could have required the return of the entire order. . . . Plaintiff's order was not a good faith attempt to accomplish this, see U.C.C. §§ 1-203, 2-103(1) (b), 2-306, but an effort to nullify the termination clause. And when defendant offered to take plaintiff's possible termination difficulties into consideration and fill a part of the June 28 order, plaintiff took the position, to quote the language of the district court, that it "wanted the whole order or nothing." Of these alternatives the court gave it nothing. We agree.

Affirmed.

Whirlpool Corp. v. Regis Leasing Corp.

288 N.Y.S.2d 337 (N.Y.) 1968

BASTOW, J. This appeal from an order denying plaintiff's motion for summary judgment presents anew the question as to whether parol evidence that defendant proposes to introduce upon a trial is consistent with and not contradictory of a written instrument for the purchase of merchandise or on the other hand is inadmissible because inconsistent with the writing, or if consistent therewith is such that if agreed upon would have been included in the document.

It appears that certain individuals—not parties to this action—proposed to form a corporation (Credelco) to operate a laundry and dry cleaning plant. They negotiated with plaintiff for the purchase of the necessary equipment. The negotiations collapsed because of the lack of adequate financing. Thereafter, the Credelco group turned to defendant—a corporation apparently engaged in the long-term leasing of equipment and personal property.

On March 17, 1965, defendant issued to plaintiff an order in writing signed by its controller for the purchase of certain described equipment with instructions to ship the same to Credelco at a stated address in New Jersey. The writing discloses that the list price of the personalty was $31,140. Credited thereto was a discount ($1,557) and the sum of $3,115 representing the amount previously paid to plaintiff by the Credelco group.

The purchase order (on defendant's printed form) provided that "Seller agrees to furnish the above items in accordance with the conditions and terms" therein stated. These provided, among other things, that "Modifications hereof shall be made only in accordance with the written approval of both parties" and "No verbal modifications hereof shall be effective." A further condition was that "Discount and payment periods will start from the date of receipt of the material and/or equipment by the Buyer."

The substance of the proposed defense is that prior to issuance of the purchase order the parties orally agreed to the further condition that plaintiff would "supervise installation, fully check out all the equipment, provide operational training to the Credelco group and have [it] notify [defendant] that the [plant] was fully equipped, installed and operational" before defendant would be obligated to pay plaintiff.

In *Meadow Brook National Bank* v. *Bzura,* (20 A.D.2d 287, 289, 246 N.Y.S.2d 787, 789), this court wrote that "While generally an integrated written agreement may be shown not to have taken effect because of an oral condition precedent, this being an exception to the parol evidence rule, the exception does not apply where the oral condition precedent would contradict the express terms of the writing." The opinion further quoted this language from *Hicks* v. *Bush* (10 N.Y.2d 488, 491, 225 N.Y.S.2d 34, 36, 180 N.E.2d 425, 427): "The applicable law is clear, the relevant principles settled. Parol testimony is admissible to prove a condition precedent to the legal effectiveness of a written agreement . . . if the condition does not contradict the express terms of such written agreement. . . . A certain disparity is inevitable, of course, whenever a written promise is, by oral agreement of the parties, made conditional upon an event not expressed in the writing. Quite obviously, though, the parol evidence rule does not bar proof of every orally established condition precedent, but only of those which in a real sense contradict the terms of the written agreement. . . . Upon the present appeal, our problem is to determine whether there is such a contradiction."

This legal principle has been incorporated into the statute (Uniform Commercial Code, Sec. 2-202) relating to the sale of goods. In *Hunt Foods & Industries, Inc.,* v. *Doliner* (26 A.D.2d 41, 43, 270 N.Y.S.2d 937, 940), this court stated with precision the applicable test: "In a sense any oral provision which would prevent the ripening of the obligations of a writing is inconsistent with the writing. But that obviously is not the sense in which the word is used. . . . To be inconsistent the term must contradict or negate a term of the writing. A term or condition which has a lesser effect is provable."

Judged by this test the proposed oral proof would contradict the provision of the writing that the discount and payment periods should start from the date of the receipt of the equipment by defendant. In so concluding attention should be directed to the further language of the purchase order [prepared by defendant] that no verbal modifications should be effective; that modifications should be made "only in accordance with the written approval of both parties" and that "Time of delivery is of the essence of this contract."

Moreover, "an inspection of this contract shows a full and complete agreement, setting forth in detail the obligations of each party. On reading it one would conclude that the reciprocal obligations of the parties were fully detailed." If perchance, therefore, the oral proof could be found to be consistent with the terms of the instrument within the meaning of paragraph (b) of Section 2-202 of Uniform Commercial Code, it would be objectionable in the light of the official Comment of the drafters of the Code. They wrote that "If the additional terms are such that, if agreed upon, they would certainly have been included in the document in the view of the court, then evidence of their alleged making must be kept from the trier of fact."

It taxes credulity to believe that defendant having prepared the writing with considerable precision would not have included therein the all-important provisions that plaintiff was to supervise installation of the equipment, provide for training of personnel and thereafter notify defendant that it had an operable plant. The incredibility of these assertions is demonstrated by proof supplied by defendant. The real reasons for noninstallation of the equipment were that construction of the building to be used had not been completed and the Credelco group and the constructors of the building were "experiencing such financial difficulties as to render the completion of [the equipment installation] impossible at present."

There is no merit to defendant's contention that the writing is unenforceable because it was not signed by plaintiff. The statute requires only the signature of the party against whom enforcement is sought. (Uniform Commercial Code, Sec. 2-201). We have examined the other contentions advanced by respondent and find them to be without substance or merit.

The order denying plaintiff's motion for summary judgment should be reversed on the law and summary judgment granted to plaintiff with interest from March 17, 1965, with costs and disbursements.

Associated Hardware Supply Co. v. Big Wheel Distributing Co.

236 F.Supp. 879 (1965)

DUMBAULD, J. Plaintiff creditor [Associated Hardware Supply Co.] seeks to recover $40,185.62 as the balance of an open unpaid account for merchandise sold and delivered, together with interest.

Defendant debtor [Big Wheel Distributing Co.] pleaded fraud and counterclaimed, alleging overpayment, and failure of plaintiff to furnish certain promotional assistance in merchandising the goods for profitable resale.

After extensive *discovery proceedings,* plaintiff on November 5, 1964 filed a motion to dismiss the counterclaim, for judgment on the pleadings and for summary judgment for the amount of the debt and interest. . . .

When the voluminous verbiage with which this case has been surrounded is penetrated and disentangled, the issue is seen to be one of price. Defendant contends that the goods were to be sold at cost plus 10 percent, whereas plaintiff billed them at dealers' catalogue price (representing a 20 percent mark-up) less 11 percent. Defendant's counterclaim is based upon a recomputation at defendant's assumed price of all past transactions between the parties, and much of defendant's voluminous discovery aims to determine plaintiff's costs, which enter into the price as defendant would compute it. Defendant's allegations of fraud and misrepresentation are based on the lack of identity, allegedly asserted by plaintiff, between prices computed under plaintiff's method and defendant's method.

What was the contract between the parties, as shown by the undisputed facts in the record?

Plaintiff in a letter of February 9, 1962 (Ex. A. to Complaint) made an offer, subject to a volume of $5,000 per week at catalogue price less 11 percent discount. Defendant being a new corporate operation, personal liability of Mr. Irving Molever was insisted upon in the letter, together with a request for acknowledgement and signature. Apparently Molever did not sign the letter, but considered himself personally liable and later secured a release from such liability after defendant established a satisfactory payment history.

However, dealings between the parties went ahead. Defendant ordered, received, retained, and paid for a large volume of merchandise, billed at catalogue price less 11 percent discount.

As calculated in plaintiff's brief, defendant's purchases from February 1962 through May 1964 aggregated $860,000. This figure apparently includes the unpaid amount of $40,185.62, to collect which the present suit was bought. Over $800,000 of merchandise was thus bought and paid for under billings computed under plaintiff's method.

What effect did these dealings of the parties have upon their legal rights, in the light of the Uniform Commercial Code?

We conclude as a matter of law, after consideration of numerous provisions of the Code, that there was a contract between the parties, and that the price was governed by plaintiff's formula.

The alleged misrepresentation or fraud on plaintiff's part we are unable to consider as anything more than normal commercial "puffing" which could not have misled an astute trader such as defendant's negotiator, Mr. Molever. We conclude that defendant simply later decided that its bargain was not a good one and decided not to pay because the agreed price was too high.

Obviously, to say that cost plus 10 percent is the same as catalogue price less 11 percent is to indulge in approximation, and the mathematical relationships were as obvious to defendant as to plaintiff. We compute the price on defendant's theory as 1.1 times plaintiff's costs, whereas under plaintiff's system the price would be 1.068 times plaintiff's costs. Whether these are to be treated as substantially identical is obviously a matter of commercial judgment or opinion, and a contract duly negotiated on an assumption that the two methods are to be considered as equivalent can not be set aside for "fraud."

Turning to the Code provisions involved, we begin with 12A P.S. 1-103 that "Unless displaced by the particular provisions of this Act, the principles of law and equity, including . . . the law relative to . . . fraud, misrepresentation, duress, coercion, mistake . . . or other validating or invalidating cause shall supplement its provisions." This section merely invites us to look to more specific provisions of the Code to determine whether a contract arose between the parties, and what its terms were.

Section 1-201(3) defines "Agreement" as "the bargain in fact as found in the language of the parties or in course of dealings or usage of trade or course of performance or by implication from other circumstances."

Section 1-201(11) defines "Contract" as "the total obligation in law which results from parties' agreement as affected by this Act and any other applicable rules of law."

Section 1-205(1) says: "A course of dealing is a sequence of previous conduct between the parties to a particular transaction which is in fact fairly to be regarded as establishing a common basis of understanding for interpreting their words and conduct."

Section 1-205(3) provides: "The parties to a contract are bound by any course of dealing between them."

Section 1-205(4)(a) declares that "Unless contrary to a mandatory rule of this Act: (a) A course of dealing . . . gives particular meaning to and supplements or qualifies terms of the agreement."

Section 2-104(1) and (3) defines "merchants" and "between merchants," and we consider both parties to this litigation as knowledgeable merchants. . . .

Section 2(202(a) provides that a writing "may be explained or supplemented . . . by course of dealing."

Section 2-204(1) says: "A contract for sale of goods may be made in any manner sufficient to show agreement."

Section 2-204(2) provides that "Contract by both parties which recognizes the existence of a contract is sufficient to establish a contract for sale even though the moment of its making cannot be determined."

Section 2-204(3) provides: "Even though one or more terms are left open a contract for sale does not fail for indefiniteness if the parties have intended to make a contract and there is a reasonably certain basis for giving an appropriate remedy."

Section 2-206(1) says: "Unless the contrary is unambiguously indicated by the language or circumstances (a) an offer to make a contract shall be construed as inviting acceptance in any manner and by any medium reasonable in the circumstances."

Section 2-206(3) provides that "The beginning of a requested performance can be a reasonable mode of acceptance."

Section 2-208 provides: "Where the contract for sale involves repeated occasions for performance by either party with knowledge of the nature of the performance and opportunity for objection by the other, any course of performance accepted without objection shall be relevant to determine the meaning of the agreement or to show a waiver or modification of any term inconsistent with such course of performance."

Review of the foregoing Code provisions shows that the Code attaches great weight to the course of dealing of the parties, even in the absence of a written agreement with respect to every term of the contract. Weighing in the light of the Code the conduct of the parties here, it seems clear that the mode of calculating price set forth in plaintiff's letter of February 9, 1962, although not accepted formally by signature of a copy, was adhered to by both parties during an extensive course of dealing, during which defendant received, accepted, and paid for over $800,000 worth of merchandise. This course of dealing must be held applicable and governing with respect to the remaining merchandise which has been received and accepted but not paid for. Judgment should be rendered for plaintiff for the amount due.

There is no genuine dispute of fact with regard to any legally relevant circumstance.

The disputed facts concerning which defendant by discovery and other-wise seeks to inquire extensively relate to matters which are not pertinent, *since the law gives effect to the contract recognized by the parties in their course of dealings, regardless of other provisions which the parties might have adopted during their negotiations if they had seen fit to do so.*

It is ordered, adjudged and finally determined that plaintiff's motion to dismiss defendant's counterclaim be and the same hereby is granted, and that said counterclaim be and the same hereby is dismissed, and that judgment be and it hereby is entered in favor of plaintiff, Associated Hardware Supply Co., a corporation, and against defendant, The Big Wheel Distributing Company, a corporation, in the amount of $40,-185.62, together with interest and costs.

CHAPTER 18
REVIEW QUESTIONS AND PROBLEMS

1. *A,* a fruit grower, entered into a contract to sell fruit to *B,* a food processor. The contract did not contain a specified price. Is the contract enforceable?

2. *A* and *B* reached an oral agreement with regard to the sale of fabrics by *A* to *B. A* thereafter mailed a printed form of confirmation to *B* and requested that he sign and return it. *B* did not do so. Does the mailing of the confirmation form have any significance?

3. *A* entered into an oral contract with *B* to manufacture specially designed sliding doors for installation in a building under construction. *B* refused to accept the doors, and *A* brought suit. *B* contends that the contract was not enforceable. Is *A* entitled to recover?

4. *A* obtained a blood transfusion at B Hospital. In spite of due care on the part of the hospital, the blood was not suitable, and *A*'s condition worsened. Can *A* recover damages from the hospital?

5. *A* delivered several barrels of olives to *B.* The arrangement was that *B* would pay for each barrel as it was used. *B* became bankrupt and had in his possession ten barrels, which the trustee in bankruptcy took over. Can *A* recover the barrels of olives from the trustee?

6. *A* contracted to purchase cattle and farm machinery from *B,* and *B*

executed a bill of sale. During litigation over the transaction, *B* offered evidence that at the time of the sale *A* had agreed to execute a note and security agreement. Is this evidence admissible?

7. *A* made an oral promise to *B* that if *B* would assist *A* in the development of a new type of detergent, *A* would give *B* the exclusive right to sell the detergent. Is this agreement enforceable?

8. *A* entered into a contract to lease equipment to *B*. *B* contended that one of the machines broke down and that *A* did not repair it. He also contended that *A* breached certain warranties. Does this transaction come within the Uniform Commercial Code?

9. *A* delivered record racks and phonograph records to *B,* a music store owner, on consignment. Can *B's* creditors reach these items? Can *A* protect himself from the claims of *B's* creditors?

10 *A,* in Omaha, ordered a carload of lumber from *B* in Portland. The terms were C.I.F. Omaha. *B* shipped the lumber and forwarded the bill of lading and other documents to *A*. *A* contends that he does not have to pay until the lumber is unloaded in Omaha. Is this correct?

Title and
Risk of Loss

3-11. Introduction.   The concept of *title to goods* is somewhat nebulous, but it is generally equated with ownership. The Code has deemphasized the importance of title because of the abstract and intangible nature of this concept. Therefore, it should be kept in mind that title to goods or the location of title at any given time is not usually a controlling factor in determining the rights of parties to goods.[1] And unless there is a reference to title in a Code provision, the rights, obligations, and remedies of the seller, the buyer, purchasers, or other third parties are determined without regard to title. This is in direct contrast to pre-Code law in which title location resolved many important questions such as risk of loss, remedies, and the like.

The title to goods cannot be completely ignored, however. Passage of title is important in connection with statutes relating to taxation and regulation. The incidence of taxes and the application of rules and regulations are frequently determined by title. Title is likewise important in many statutes such as the Bankruptcy Act. The concept and location of title are also significant in some aspects of a sales transaction. Title, in fact, is basic to the sales transaction, since by definition, a sale involves the passing of title from the seller to the buyer.

3-12. Passage of Title.   The parties can, with few restrictions, determine by their contract the manner in which title to goods passes from the seller to the buyer. They can specify any conditions which must be fulfilled in order for this to happen. However, since the parties to a contract for a sale seldom indicate any intention regarding title or its passage and usually do not even consciously consider the title concept as such, the Code sets forth specific provisions about the rights and duties of the buyer and seller on such issues as risk of loss,

---

[1] William F. Wilke, Inc. v. Cummins Diesel Engines, Inc., page 385

remedies, and the like. It does not, however, base these matters on where title may be at any point of time.

The basic rule is that title cannot pass until the goods have been identified to the contract. Identification requires that the seller specify the particular goods involved in the transaction. Title passes when the seller "commits himself" insofar as the specific goods are concerned. This occurs when the seller completes his performance with respect to the physical delivery of the goods. In a shipment contract where he is to send the goods to the buyer but is not required to deliver them at the destination, title passes at the time and place of shipment. On the other hand, if the contract requires that he deliver at the destination, title will not pass until the seller has tendered the goods to the buyer at that point.

It may be that the contract does not involve the transportation of the goods. For example, the goods may be stored in a warehouse, and the buyer will obtain the goods from that place. Commonly, the seller will deliver a document of title, such as a warehouse receipt, which represents the goods, and evidences the right of the holder to them. In this event, title passes at the time and place where the documents are delivered. If the goods that are the subject of the contract were identified at the time the parties entered into the contract and no further action by the seller is required, title passes at the time and place of contracting. For example, the parties may agree upon the specific goods sold and provide that the buyer take possession at the seller's plant or other place of business.

If the buyer rejects the goods when tendered to him, title will be revested in the seller. Upon the buyer's refusal to receive or retain the goods, the title automatically returns to the seller, whether the buyer was justified in his action or not. The same result obtains if the buyer has accepted the goods but subsequently revokes his acceptance for a justifiable reason.[2]

As a means of assurance that the price will be paid before the buyer can obtain title to the goods, a seller may ship or deliver goods to the buyer and reserve title in himself. Under the Code such a reservation of title does not prevent title from passing to the buyer. It is limited to the reservation of a security interest in the goods. In order to give protection to the seller, the security interest must be perfected under the provisions of Article 9. Accordingly, a seller who simply reserves a security interest will not have availed himself of protection against the claims of third parties.

3-13. Identification. Identification means the process by which the particular goods to which the contract refers are designated and specified.[3] For example, *A* may contract with *B* to purchase 100 mahogany desks of a certain style. *B* may have several hundred of these desks in his warehouse. Identification takes place when *A* or *B* specify the particular 100 desks which will be sold to *A*. There could not, of course, be a present identification of future goods —those not yet in existence or not owned by the seller.

Identification can be made at any time and in any manner "explicitly agreed to" by the parties. However, the parties usually do not make provision for identification, in which event the Code rules determine when it has occurred.

---

[2] Tennessee-Virginia Construction Co. v. Willingham, page 387
[3] In re Colonial Distributing Co., page 388

Identification takes place when the contract is made if the goods are existing and identified. As to future goods, the seller provides identification when he ships the goods or marks them as the goods to which the contract refers. The requirement is that the seller make an appropriate designation of the specific goods. There are special provisions for agricultural items—crops and animals —because of their nature. When there is a sale of a crop to be grown, identification occurs when the crop is planted. If the sale is of the unborn young of animals, identification takes place when they are conceived. The sale of a crop of wool would be included within this framework of identification.

3-14. Special Property, Insurable Interest.   The buyer acquires two rights when identification takes place. He obtains an "insurable interest" in the identified goods and also a "special property" in them. This means that the buyer is permitted to carry insurance upon the goods, as he has a sufficient interest in them to justify doing so. The seller retains an insurable interest in the goods so long as he has title or a security interest in them. Thus, after identification, each party may have an insurable interest in the goods, and title may be in the seller with a "special property" in the buyer. If the seller becomes insolvent while he is still in possession of the goods after all or part of the price has been paid, a buyer who has a special property is in a favored position. He can recover the goods from the seller if the seller becomes insolvent within ten days after receipt of the first installment on their price. This may prove a very valuable right to a buyer who might otherwise suffer a substantial loss. Were he not able to claim the goods, they would be subject to the claims of the creditors of the insolvent seller.

Also, a person with a special property is entitled to bring suit against a third party whose actions interfere with his rights in the identified goods. Even though he does not have title, his special property gives him standing in court to recover damages resulting from the improper conduct of a third person.[4]

3-15. Creditors' Rights.   While the buyer's rights in identified goods are generally superior to those of unsecured creditors of the seller, an identification or sale may be set aside by the seller's creditors, and they can reach the goods if they can prove that the seller's retention of possession of the goods was fraudulent as to them. By retaining possession of identified goods, the seller may have created the impression that he still owned them. Creditors may have loaned money to him or otherwise extended him credit upon his apparent assets. The matter of fraud is governed by state law, but the Code provides that retention of possession in good faith by a merchant-seller for a commercially reasonable time after identification or sale is not fraudulent.

Identification or delivery made not in the course of trade but rather to satisfy a preexisting debt will not impair the rights of creditors of the seller, if such action is fraudulent or a voidable preference under the Bankruptcy Act as to them.

3-16. Good Faith Purchasers.   There are various situations in which a merchant or other person may have in his possession goods which do not belong to him. A question arises as to the rights of a purchaser from such person as against the rightful owner. A person who has a voidable title to goods—e.g.,

---

[4] Draper v. Minneapolis Moline, Inc., 389

he obtained the goods by fraud or paid for them with a check which was later dishonored—can transfer a good title to a good faith purchaser for value, thereby cutting off the rights of the party who was deceived.[5] The same applies if the transferor obtained the goods under an agreement that it was a "cash sale" and that title would not pass until the price was paid.

If goods are placed with a merchant on consignment, a purchaser in the ordinary course of business will be protected and will obtain a "good" title to the goods. This is quite fair, since the very purpose of having goods in inventory is to turn them into cash by sale.

The Code provisions are designed to protect persons who buy in ordinary course out of inventory.

3-17. Risk of Loss.   The Code sets forth a number of rules for determining which party to a sales contract must bear the risk of loss or damage to goods during the period of the performance of the contract. The approach is contractual rather than title oriented. Two basic situations are encompassed: (1) where no breach of contract is involved and (2) where one of the parties is in breach.

If the contract has been breached, the loss will be borne by the party who has breached. Thus, if the seller has tendered or delivered goods which are "nonconforming" and which the buyer has a right to reject, the seller bears the risk of loss for such goods. He remains responsible until such time as he rectifies the nonconformity or the buyer accepts the goods notwithstanding their defects. In this regard, it should be noted that the seller is ordinarily given the right to effect a "cure," which means an opportunity to perform in the agreed-upon fashion. This may involve a repair of the goods or the furnishing of goods which properly conform to the contract. The buyer also has the privilege of revoking his acceptance of the goods under proper circumstances, and if he does do so for good cause, the risk is that of the seller to the extent that the buyer's insurance does not cover the loss. In this situation the seller has the benefit of any insurance carried by the buyer—the party most likely to carry insurance.

The loss may occur while the goods are in the seller's control before the risk of loss has passed to the buyer. If the buyer repudiates the sale at a time when the seller has identified proper goods to the contract, the seller can impose the risk of loss upon the buyer for a reasonable time, to the extent that the seller's insurance does not cover the loss. The foregoing rules implement the basic concept of the Code that the burden should be that of the party who has failed to perform as required by contract.

There are a number of factors which enter into a determination of who must bear the risk of loss when neither party has breached. Three distinct situations may be present. First of all, the contract may call for shipment of the goods. Second, the goods may be the subject of a bailment, and third, the contract may be silent on shipment and no bailment exists.

Shipment.   Where the contract between buyer and seller provides for shipment by carrier, the risk of loss passes to the buyer when the goods are delivered to the carrier if it is a shipment contract (F.O.B. shipping point); if it is destination contract (F.O.B. destination), risk of loss does not pass to the buyer until the goods arrive at the destination and are made available to

[5] Hollis v. Chamberlin, page 390

him so that he can take delivery. A shipment contract is one which requires only that the seller make the necessary arrangements for transport, while a destination contract imposes upon the seller the obligation to deliver at a destination. At this point, the mercantile shipping terms discussed in Section 3-8 have further significance. Thus, for example, F.O.B. the place of destination is a destination contract; C.I.F. contracts are shipment contracts. The use of defined terms and abbreviations, such as C.I.F. and F.A.S. precludes problems as to the point at which risk of loss passes. When the parties do not use these symbols or otherwise make provision for risk of loss, it will be necessary to determine whether a contract does or does not require the seller to deliver at a destination. The presumption is that a contract is one of shipment not destination, and that the buyer should bear the risk of loss until arrival, unless the seller has either specifically agreed to do so or the circumstances indicate such an obligation.[6]

Bailment.   Often the goods will be in the possession of a bailee such as a warehouse, and the arrangement is for the buyer to take delivery at the warehouse. If the goods are represented by a negotiable document of title, a warehouse receipt for instance, when the seller tenders such document to the buyer, the risk of loss passes to the buyer. Likewise, risk passes to the buyer upon acknowledgment by the bailee that the buyer is entitled to the goods. In this situation, it is proper that the buyer assume the risk, as the seller has done all that could be expected to make the goods available to the buyer, who controls the goods at this point. It should be noted that if a nonnegotiable document of title is proffered to the buyer, risk of loss does not pass until the buyer has had a reasonable time to present the document to the bailee. A refusal by the bailee to honor the document defeats the tender, and the risk of loss remains with the seller. This points up one of the distinctions between a negotiable and a nonnegotiable document of title.

Other Cases.   In all cases other than shipment and bailment as mentioned above, the passage of risk to the buyer depends upon the status of the seller. If the seller is a merchant, risk of loss will not pass to the buyer until he *receives* the goods, which means takes physical possession of them. A nonmerchant seller transfers the risk by *tendering* the goods. A tender of delivery requires that the seller make conforming goods available to the buyer and give him reasonable notice so that he may take delivery. The risk remains with the merchant-seller even though the buyer has paid for the goods in full and has been notified that the goods are at his disposal. Continuation of the risk in this case is justified on the basis that the merchant would be likely to carry insurance on goods within his control, while a buyer would not likely do so until he had actually received the goods.

The foregoing rules are subject to any reasonable agreement between the parties with reference to the allocation of risk of loss.

DOCUMENTS OF TITLE

3-18. General Concepts: Definitions.   A document of title is defined as any "document which in the regular course of business or financing is treated as

---

[6] Ninth Street East, Ltd. v. Harrison, page 391

adequately evidencing that the person in possession of it is entitled to receive, hold and dispose of the document *and the goods it covers.*" (U.C.C. 1-201(15)) Such a document must indicate that it was issued by a bailee or directed to a bailee and that it covers goods in the bailee's possession. The term includes bills of lading and warehouse receipts, which are the most commonly used documents, as well as certain other documents.

Documents of title are covered by Article 7 of the Code and are frequently referred to in other Articles. However, there are numerous statutes, both state and federal, which regulate the business of carriers and warehousemen. The Federal Bills of Lading Act, for example, controls bills of lading covering foreign exports and interstate shipments of goods. The Code does not displace such statutes, and basically, Article 7 deals only with rights related to documents of title and not to the regulation of the services rendered by carriers or warehousemen.

Documents of title are discussed at this point in the text because of the close relationship of such documents to sales transactions and particularly to title and risk of loss. It should be noted, however, that these documents are also significant to other transactions, particularly secured transactions—Article 9 of the Code.

These documents play an important role in modern commerce and facilitate the shipment and storage of merchandise; they also serve to integrate these functions with various aspects of sales and financing transactions. The use of such documents dates back many centuries; it was recognized at an early date that a written instrument could represent goods and stand in their place and stead. Thus, when goods were stored with a warehouseman or delivered to a carrier for shipment and a receipt was issued, the receipt could be treated as a token of the goods shipped or stored. In a sense the piece of paper represented the goods and could be transferred, sold, or pledged as representative of the goods described therein.

Documents of title can serve a dual function. They may serve as a receipt for goods stored or shipped, and they may also be representative of the goods. In the latter capacity they are most useful in financing commercial transactions. In addition, the document is the contract for storage or shipment, as the case may be.

A warehouse receipt is defined as "a receipt issued by a person engaged in the business of storing goods for hire." (1-201(45)) A *bill of lading* "means a document evidencing the receipt of goods for shipment issued by a person engaged in the business of transporting or forwarding goods, and includes an airbill." (1-201(6)) *An airbill* is the air-freight equivalent of the bill of lading issued by surface transporters. Another commonly used document is a *delivery order.* This is an order directed to a carrier or warehouseman that he deliver goods as instructed.

The drafters of the Code defined the term "document of title" broadly so that new types of documents may be included as they develop and are used in commercial transactions. It is suggested that modern technology will, in all likelihood, necessitate quite different forms and documents to serve the needs now filled by warehouse receipts and bills of lading. Computerization and the widespread use of the teletype make evident the need for documents which can keep pace with modern technology.

A number of important definitions in Article 7 describe the various parties who are involved in transactions with documents of title. A *bailee* is the person who acknowledges that he has possession of the goods and who contracts to deliver them. This would include the carrier and the warehouseman. An *issuer* is a bailee who prepares the document of title. A *consignor* is the person named in a bill of lading as the person from whom the goods have been received for shipment. A *consignee* is the person named in a bill of lading as the one to whom delivery is to be made.

Documents of title may be negotiable or nonnegotiable. The concept of negotiability is discussed in Chapter 23 in connection with negotiable instruments—commercial paper. The basic philosophy of the concept is to render certain written instruments capable of free movement in commerce. In order to accomplish this, such instruments must be readily transferable, acceptable by merchants, and must afford substantial security and protection to the holder. Between documents of title as negotiable instruments and commercial paper, there are similarities but also substantial differences. Commercial paper is payable in money; it is in a sense a substitute for money and symbolic of money. Documents of title are symbols of goods.

The holder of a negotiable document is in a much more favorable position than one who holds a nonnegotiable one; his rights may be much greater than those of the person who transferred the negotiable document to him. Among other things, the holder of a negotiable document obtains the direct obligation of the issuer to hold or deliver the goods free from most defenses and claims. In essence, the holder is so well protected that he can almost regard the document as the equivalent of the goods it represents.

3-19. Negotiation and Transfer.   A warehouse receipt, bill of lading, or other document is negotiable if by its terms the goods are to be delivered to the bearer or to the "order of" a named person. A document not containing these "words of negotiability" is not negotiable. Thus, a bill of lading which states that goods are consigned to John Doe would not be negotiable.

Both negotiable and nonnegotiable documents can be transferred, but the method of transfer is different. A nonnegotiable document can be "assigned"; then the assignee acquires only the rights of the assignor and is subject to all defenses which are available against the assignor. The assignee is burdened with all defects in the assignor's title. *Negotiation*—the process whereby negotiable documents are transferred—places the transferee in a much more favorable position. If there is "due negotiation," the transferee is free from the defects of the transferor's title and the claims of third persons. His rights are superior and he enjoys a favored position as transferee-holder of a negotiable document.

There are two methods of negotiating a document of title depending upon whether it is an "order" document or a "bearer" document. The former is negotiated by indorsement and delivery; the latter by delivery alone. An indorsement consists of the transferor's (indorser's) signature on the document. The indorser's signature without more is called a "blank indorsement," and with such the document can be further negotiated by delivery alone. The same result obtains if the indorsement includes the clause, "Deliver to Bearer." However, if the indorsement is special—the indorsee's name is specified—for further negotiation, indorsement of the special indorsee would be required. Thus, an indorsement by John Doe "Deliver to Richard Roe," would require further indorsement by Roe if he wished to negotiate the document. If the instrument specifies on its face that it "runs to bearer," no indorsement is required for negotiation. It is therefore possible for an unauthorized person to negotiate a bearer document—one that specifies on its face that it runs to bearer or one which is indorsed in blank. It must be noted that the last indorsement is controlling; if it is special, further indorsement is required; if blank, it can be further negotiated by delivery.

In order for the holder of a negotiable document of title to have the preferred status mentioned above, there must have been a due negotiation, which means not only any necessary indorsement and/or delivery but also that the holder must satisfy certain requirements. He must have purchased the document in good faith, without notice of a defense against or claim to it on the part of any person. He must have paid value for it, and the negotiation must have been in the regular course of business or financing. One to whom a document is negotiated in satisfaction or payment of a prior debt has not paid value.

If there has been due negotiation, the holder acquires title to the document, title to the goods, and the "direct obligation of the issuer" (carrier or warehouseman) to hold or deliver the goods according to the terms of the document and free from any defense or claim of the issuer other than those afforded him by Article 7. The holder's rights cannot be defeated by any stoppage of the goods or surrender of them by the bailee. His rights are not impaired "even though the negotiation or any prior negotiation constituted a breach of duty or even though any person has been deprived of possession of the document by misrepresentation, fraud, accident, mistake, duress, loss, theft or conversion; or even though a previous sale or other transfer of the goods or document has been made to a third person." (U.C.C. 7-502(2)) The foregoing is premised upon a rightful bailment of the goods in the first instance. A thief or unauthorized person cannot pass title to stolen or misappropriated property by delivering it to a public warehouse and then negotiating the warehouse receipt which he receives therefor. In such a situation the owner of the goods would prevail against the holder of the document of title.

The position of a transferee of a nonnegotiable document, or of a negotiable one which has not been duly negotiated, is that of an assignee. His rights are subject to being defeated by certain creditors of the transferor, by a purchaser of the goods from the transferor, or by the bailee who has dealt in good faith with the transferor. Likewise, his rights may be defeated by a stoppage of delivery. It is to be noted that the transferee of a negotiable document in order form to whom the document was transferred without indorsement has a specifically enforceable right to such indorsement.

3-20. Liability of Indorser or Transferor.   The indorser or transferor of a document of title makes three warranties to his immediate purchaser.

1. He warrants that the document is genuine. One who purchases a forged document of title may, upon discovery of the forgery, recover from the person who sold it to him.

2. He warrants that he has no knowledge of any facts which would impair its validity or worth.

3. He warrants that his sale of the document is rightful and fully effective with respect to the title to the document and the goods it represents. However, unless he has also sold the goods, he does not make any additional warranties as to the goods. If he is also the seller of the goods, he makes other warranties (see Chapter 22.) The indorser of a document of title does not warrant performance by the bailee.

His warranties are satisfied when the purchaser obtains a good right against the warehouseman or carrier. If the bailee has misappropriated the goods or refuses to surrender them, the holder of the document has, as his only recourse, an action against the bailee who issued the document.

If a bank or other person has been authorized to deliver a document of title, acting as an agent for this purpose, the delivery of the document creates no warranty by the agent as to the document itself. Thus, no liability would be assumed by any such agent if the document were not genuine.

3-21. Obligations of Bailee.   A public warehouse which issues a negotiable receipt is not at liberty to surrender the goods to the original bailor unless he surrenders the receipt for cancellation. The receipt represents the goods and must be surrendered before the goods may be obtained. A warehouse that surrenders goods without the return of the receipt may be called upon for the goods by someone who has purchased the document. The goods should be delivered only to the person who possesses the receipt, and then only if the receipt has been properly indorsed when such indorsement is required. Much of the foregoing applies also to common carriers and any other organizations that issue negotiable documents of title.

It should be noted, however, that the bailee can refuse to deliver the goods called for by the document until payment of his just charges has been made. Applicable law may prohibit delivery without payment.

A bailee is responsible for documents which have been issued when no goods are delivered. Thus, an agent of a bailee who fraudulently issues a negotiable document of title without receiving any goods makes it possible for an innocent purchaser of the receipt to hold the warehouseman according to the terms.

If a receipt was complete when issued but was later altered without authority, the warehouse's liability is determined by the original terms of the document. If a receipt was issued with blanks, a good faith purchaser of the completed receipt may recover from the warehouse that issued the incomplete receipt.

A warehouse receipt, even though it has been properly negotiated, will, in one situation, be inferior to the rights of a buyer of the goods represented by the receipt. The Code provides that when a buyer in the ordinary course of business buys fungible goods from a warehouseman who is also engaged in the business of buying and selling such fungible goods, he takes the goods free of any claim under the receipt. A typical case might involve the purchase of grain from an elevator. The holder of a receipt for grain stored would have no claim to grain purchased by a person from the owner of the elevator if the latter became insolvent and unable to deliver to the receipt holder.

It will be recalled that this concept is consistent with the result in a previously discussed similar situation involving the sale of goods that have been entrusted to him for some other purpose, by a merchant who deals in such goods.

A warehouseman is liable for damages for loss of or injury to goods caused by his negligence—his failure to exercise such care in regard to them as a reasonably careful man would exercise under like circumstances. He may limit his responsibility in damages to a certain amount, but in return for an increased storage rate, he must increase the limit at the bailor's request. A similar liability is imposed on carriers. A carrier may insert in a bill of lading a statement to the effect that the goods were loaded by the shipper. A commonly used term "shipper's weight, load and count," is used to relieve the issuer from liability for damages caused by improper loading. But there is a division among the courts as to the carrier's obligation to check the loading before proceeding to transport the goods.[7]

TITLE AND RISK OF LOSS CASES

William F. Wilke, Inc. v. Cummins Diesel Engines, Inc.

250 A.2d 886 (Md.) 1969

The plaintiff, Wilke, required a diesel generator in connection with a government construction job on which he was a subcontractor. He ordered the machine from Cummins; the latter delivered it to the site, but did not put it in operable condition. Wilke paid the purchase price less a small sum which was withheld for "start up and field tests." The following spring it was discovered that the machine had frozen during the winter and was badly damaged. Cummins took the machine into its shop and repaired it but refused to redeliver it to Wilke until he paid the repair bill. Wilke sought to replevy the generator, but the court ruled against him on the ground that he had "title" to it at the time of the freezing and was therefore responsible for the repair costs. Wilke appealed.

SINGLEY, J. . . . One of the more startling differences between the U.C.C. and the Sales Act is the U.C.C.'s adoption of a flexible contractual approach instead of following the more rigid concept of title to which the Sales Act adhered.

The Official Comment to U.C.C. § 2-101, the first section in the Subtitle on Sales, puts it this way:

> The arrangement of the present Sub-title is in terms of contract for sale and the various steps of its performance. The legal consequences are stated as following directly from the contract and action taken under it without resorting to the idea of when property or title passed or was to pass as being the determining factor. *The purpose is to avoid making practical issues between practical men turn upon the location of an intangible something, the passing of which no man*

[7] D. H. Overmyer Co. v. Nelson-Brantly Glass Co., page 393

can prove by evidence and to substitute for such abstractions proof of words and actions of a tangible character. [Emphasis added.]

Hawkland, *A Transactional Guide to the Uniform Commercial Code* (1964), goes somewhat further:

> Under the U.C.C. the location of title is relatively unimportant, because the Code rejects the "lump-concept approach" of the common law and U. S. A. [Uniform Sales Act]. . . .
> The U.C.C. has adopted the policy of "narrow-issue" thinking. A number of specific rules govern the rights and duties of the buyer and seller, and often these provisions are not predicated upon ownership considerations. *Under the U.C.C., the analysis of a sales problem does not start with a location of title, but with an analysis of the problem in terms of narrow issues and an ascertainment of whether or not the U.C.C. contains specific provisions dealing with these issues. If it does, those rules govern the transaction, and title will play no part in its solution.* If it does not, the title concept may still be employed. [Emphasis added]. (Hawkland, *supra*, § 1.2401 at 143).

If we analyze the problem before us in terms of what Dean Hawkland calls the "narrow issues" and then ascertain how these are dealt with by the U.C.C., we come unerringly to the conclusion that, in the absence of a delivery of conforming goods, the risk of damage remained with Cummins, the seller, notwithstanding the delivery of the generator to the job site, the receipt of payment from Wilke, and some eight months' delay in start-up.

U.C.C. § 2-401 follows the contractual approach in providing that title cannot pass prior to the identification of the goods to the contract; that it will pass "in any manner and on any conditions explicitly agreed on by the parties"; and in the absence of explicit agreement, that it will pass "at the time and place at which the seller completes his performance with reference to the physical delivery of the goods. . . . " This is described in the Official Comment as the "step by step" performance of the contract. Hawkland, *supra,* § 1.3202 at 184 adds a cautionary note:

> The seller does not fully perform his contract merely by getting *goods* to the right place at the right time, and thereafter making them available to the buyer. He must get "conforming" goods to the right place at the right time and properly tender them.

The narrow issue here is, whether Cummins made a "delivery" of goods which conformed to the contract. . . .

U.C.C. § 2-106(2) provides that "Goods or conduct including any part of a performance are 'conforming' or conform to the contract when they are in accordance with the obligations under the contract." Non-conformity cannot be viewed as a question of the quantity and quality of goods alone, but of the performance of the totality of the seller's contractual undertaking. Section 2-510(1) reads, "Where a tender or delivery of goods so fails to conform to the contract as to give a right of rejection the risk of their loss remains on the seller until cure or acceptance" and the Official Comment notes, "Under subsection (1) [of § 2-510] the seller by his individual action cannot shift the risk of loss to the buyer unless his action conforms with all the conditions resting on him under the contract."

Under the facts of this case, we have no difficulty in holding that the delivery of the generator to the job site, while identifying the goods to the contract, did not amount to a delivery of goods or the performance of obligations conforming to the contract. It could not constitute such a delivery and performance until the generator had been installed, started up, and field tests completed to the satisfaction of the government. Until then, risk of loss remained with Cummins regardless of where title may have stood. . . .

Judgment reversed.

Tennessee-Virginia Construction Co. v. Willingham

160 S.E.2d 444 (Ga.) 1968

Plaintiff Willingham sold a tractor to the defendant construction company. Thereafter the defendant returned the tractor on the grounds that it was "unsatisfactory." Plaintiff claimed that the defendant was obligated to pay for the tractor, and in a proceeding to collect the amount due, had it "attached" by the sheriff. At the time of the attachment, the tractor was in the plaintiff's possession. The attachment would be invalid, and the court would be without jurisdiction, unless the defendant had title to the tractor at the time of the attachment. The lower court ruled that the defendant had title, and the defendant appealed.

WHITMAN, J. . . . With regard to ownership of the Allis Chalmers tractor at the time of the levy, Tennessee takes the position in its brief that it had the right under the Uniform Commercial Code to inspect the machine and reject it within a reasonable time after delivery and that it did so, . . .

We are concerned here with who had title to the machine. Code Ann. § 109A-2-401 states in Subsection (2) that: "Unless otherwise explicitly agreed title passes to the buyer at the time and place at which the seller completes his performance with reference to the physical delivery of the goods. . . . "

But Subsection (4) provides that: "A rejection or other refusal by the buyer to receive or retain the goods, whether or not justified, or a justified revocation of acceptance revests title to the goods in the seller. . . . "

The court is of the view that Subsection (4) has relation to an election a buyer may make *at the time* the goods are presented to him for delivery. If the buyer *at that time* rejects or refuses to receive them (in delivery) or to retain them (for some purpose such as conducting a conformity inspection), whether justified or not, then title revests in the seller and the seller is relegated to the various remedies provided in the Commercial Code. Or even if the buyer has accepted delivery or conditionally received the goods for some purpose he may thereafter revoke his acceptance and revest title in the seller *provided* his revocation is "*justified*."

In the present case, there was no rejection or refusal to receive or retain the machine when it was delivered. The evidence was that Tennessee did nothing *at the time of delivery* which could be construed as revesting title to the machine in Willingham, rather it received and retained the machine for two or three months. One receives goods when he takes physical possession of them. (Code Ann. § 109A-2-103 (c))

However, as discussed above, a buyer may, even after he has accepted, revest title in the seller by revoking his acceptance *provided* his revocation is *justified.* The question of whether a revocation of acceptance is justified will ordinarily be a question of fact. In the present case, the burden was upon Tennessee to justify its revocation. The only evidence presented in this regard by Tennessee was that the machine was "unsatisfactory."

The trial court sitting without a jury heard this evidence and ruled against Tennessee, finding in effect that Tennessee's revocation of acceptance was not justified and had not operated to revest title in Willingham. "Unsatisfactory" can refer to anything from color to performance. The net effect of the evidence and the trial court's finding was that Tennessee had title to the machine and that the contention in the traverse and plea to the jurisdiction that Tennessee did not own the property levied on was without merit. We agree with the trial court. . . .

Affirmed.

In re Colonial Distributing Company

291 F.Supp. 154 (1968)

FOSTER, Special Master . . . This matter arises out of a common business practice in the marketing of alcoholic beverages. To enjoy a quantity discount price, retailers enter into an arrangement with distributors to purchase larger amounts of wines and liquors than they can conveniently store in their shops, paying the entire purchase price at the time of the agreement, with the wholesaler to hold possession of a part of the order until notice of delivery from the retailer. Claimants and the Bankrupt, Colonial Distributing Company, were operating under such a "bill and hold" arrangement. Upon learning of Bankrupt's financial difficulties, Claimants seized a portion of undelivered wines and liquors called for in the arrangements and after bankruptcy adjudication filed claims against the estate for the value of the remainder. . . .

The essence of the Trustee's contention is that the "bill and hold" agreement in January of 1967 created a creditor-debtor relation between the Bankrupt and Claimants. That is, when Claimants paid the full purchase price and received partial delivery of the goods they become mere creditors of the bankrupt for the value of the liquors held for future delivery. Thus when the goods were delivered to claimants on February 28 and March 1, 1967 through Claim and Delivery proceedings, this was in payment of the debt created earlier when the purchase price had been paid under the terms of the agreement. If the Trustee's major premise of the creditor-debtor relation is correct, there is no doubt of the syllogistic conclusion that the transfer of possession was a preference under Section 60 of the Bankruptcy Act. . . .

Claimants contend, however, that title to the liquors passed to them at the time of the "bill and hold" agreements and payment of the purchase price, with possession deferred until a later time. Under this premise, the claim and delivery proceedings whereby they acquired possession of such wines and liquors as could be found in Bankrupt's warehouse, was merely a reclamation of their property held by the Bankrupt. Thus the essential elements of a Section 60 preference of "a transfer of property of a debtor" and "for or on account of an antecedent debt" are absent.

This brings us to the essence of the conflict in this matter testing the conflicting major premises of the parties: whether title to all of the liquors called for in the "bill and hold" agreements passed to claimants at the time of entering into the agreements?

    . . . [W]here the contract calls for the sale of goods from a larger stock, title does not pass to the buyer until the portion contracted to be sold is separated and set apart for the buyer by an actual choice of a specific article or specific goods to be supplied in the performance of the contract. . . .

    Claimants contend that there was an appropriation of the goods to the contract by the fact that following the agreements Bankrupt reported the transactions as sales and paid taxes thereon to the South Carolina Tax Commission. . . . Had the Bankrupt not actually owned the liquors at the time of the agreement (which was true in an indeterminate amount), Claimants would not seriously assert that by these acts of reporting, title would have passed to non-existing goods. The requirement of appropriation or identification of goods to the contract applies equally to unascertained goods to be sold from a larger lot and non-existent or future goods. The minimal requirement for the passage of title that the goods sold must be separated out of the larger mass and identified to the contract was not met by description of the filed reports. . . .

    We return then to the governing rule in this dispute that title does not pass to unascertained goods until they have been appropriated or identified to the contract which dictates the result that at the time Claimants took possession of the wines and liquors they were creditors and not owners of the goods. . . .

    . . . The additional factual bases for the Trustee's position that the parties understood that the purchase price would be refunded for any liquors not delivered when requested by Claimants does, however, further support the position that the goods were not ascertained at the time of contracting and thus title could not pass until they had been identified to the contract.

CONCLUSIONS

    Title to goods transferred to Claimants was in the Bankrupt and such transfer meets all of the elements of a voidable preference under Section 60 of the Bankruptcy Act. This establishes the basis for the Trustee's objection to the allowance of Claimants' claims under Section 57(g) of the Bankruptcy Act pending a return of the goods and invokes the summary jurisdiction of the Bankruptcy Court to order such a return of the goods to the Trustee.

Draper v. Minneapolis Moline, Inc.
241 N.E.2d 342 (Ill.) 1968

    The plaintiff entered into a contract to purchase a tractor and plow from a dealer. His old equipment was traded in as part payment. The dealer did not have the items in stock and ordered them from the defendant. They were delivered under an agreement in which the defendant retained a security interest. Plaintiff refused to take delivery until certain additional equipment was installed. At this point because of the financial condition of the dealer, the defendant repossessed all of the inventory including the tractor and plow which had been sold to plaintiff. The plaintiff was deprived of the use of the plow for his spring planting and brought action for damages. Judgment was awarded the plaintiff, and the defendant appealed.

CULBERTSON, J. . . . The authority for plaintiff's action is found in Section 2-722 of Article 2 of the Uniform Commercial Code, (hereinafter referred to as the Code,) which, in substance, gives to one having a special property interest in goods a right of action against a third party who "so deals with goods which have been identified to a contract for sale as to cause actionable injury to a party to that contract." The quoted language, we believe, intends that a third party would be liable for conversion, physical damage to the goods, or interference with the rights of a buyer in the goods. Section 2-103(1) (a) of Article 2 states that in such Article: " 'Buyer' means a person who buys *or contracts to buy goods*," and it is thereafter provided in Section 2-501(1) in pertinent part:

> The buyer obtains a special property and an insurable interest in goods by identification of existing goods as goods to which the contract refers *even though the goods so identified are non-conforming* and he has an option to return or reject them. Such identification can be made at any time and in any manner explicitly agreed to by the parties. In the absence of explicit agreement identification occurs . . .
> (b) if the contract is for the sale of future goods . . . , when goods are shipped, marked or otherwise designated by the seller as goods to which the contract refers. . . .

While defendant makes a mild argument that the tractor did not conform to the contract because the extras had not been installed when it was pointed out by the dealer, we think it manifest from the evidence that there was a complete and sufficient identification of the tractor to the contract within the purview of Section 2-501(1). It is apparent, too, that defendant's conduct made it impossible for the dealer to deliver the tractor to plaintiff, and that defendant so dealt with the goods as to interfere with plaintiff's special property interest. And, without more, it could be said that plaintiff has standing to maintain an action for damages as authorized by Section 2-722. However, there next arises the question of whether plaintiff obtained his special property interest, and its attendant rights, free and clear of defendant's security interest. . . .

. . . The very intent of the commercial papers involved was that the tractor could be sold to a buyer, free and clear of the security interest of the seller's creditor. Accordingly, we hold that plaintiff obtained his special property interest in the tractor free and clear of defendant's security interest, and that such security interest is no bar to the action for damages given to plaintiff by Section 2-722. . . .

Affirmed.

Hollis v. Chamberlin

419 S.W.2d 116 (Ark.) 1967

The plaintiff, Chamberlin, a Missouri dealer, sold a camper unit to one Crowder and received a check in full payment. Crowder sold the camper, which had a retail value of $1,757.44, the following day to the defendant, Hollis, in Arkansas for $500. The check which Crowder gave Chamberlin was dishonored, and Chamberlin brought action to recover the camper from Hollis. The lower court gave judgment to the plaintiff, and the defendant appealed.

JONES, J. . . . The parties seem to agree that this transaction is controlled by the Uniform Commercial Code . . . and that Crowder obtained a voidable title by the delivery of the camper in exchange for the worthless check.

The appellant has cited the correct section of the Uniform Commercial Code applicable to this case.

> A purchaser of goods acquires all title which his transferor had or had power to transfer except that a purchaser of a limited interest acquires rights only to the extent of the interest purchased. A person with voidable title has power to transfer a good title to a good faith purchaser for value. When goods have been delivered under a transaction of purchase the purchaser has such power even though . . . (b) The delivery was in exchange for a check which is later dishonored.

Under the above statute, this case presented a fact question to the trial court as to whether or not appellant was "a good faith purchaser for value," and in this court on review, the question is whether or not there was any substantial evidence to support the trial court in finding that the appellant "was not an innocent purchaser for value." We accept the terms "good faith purchaser for value" and "innocent purchaser for value," as being synonymous as used in this case, and we conclude that there was substantial evidence to support the trial court's finding on this point. . . .

Crowder advised appellants that he wanted to sell the camper because it did not properly fit on his truck and interfered with the safe and proper driving of the truck. "They said: 'Our truck will not haul the camper'." Appellant did not know Crowder nor any of the other three people with him when he purchased the camper unit from Crowder, but he did know that the camper unit looked new and was worth at least $1,000.00. Appellant knew that the unit was "purportedly" transported from Springfield, Missouri, when he purchased it, yet the camper unit did not fit the truck it was on, it was not tied down on the pickup and no explanation was made, and apparently no questions were asked, as to why it was not tied down. Crowder had no bill of sale, or other evidence of title from appellee, and apparently appellant asked no questions concerning Crowder's title. He did, however, require and receive a bill of sale *from* Crowder. . . .

The trial court was sitting as a jury in this case and there was substantial evidence to support the finding that appellant was not a good faith purchaser of the camper unit for value.

The judgment of the trial court is affirmed.

Ninth Street East, Ltd. v. Harrison

259 A.2d 772 (Conn.) 1968

LEVINE, J. This is an action to recover the purchase price of merchandise sold to defendant by plaintiff. Plaintiff is a manufacturer of men's clothing, with a principal place of business in Los Angeles, California. Defendant is the owner and operator of a men's clothing store, located in Westport, Connecticut, known as "The Rage."

Pursuant to orders received by plaintiff in Los Angeles on November 28, 1966, defendant ordered a variety of clothing items from plaintiff. On November 30, 1966, plaintiff delivered the merchandise in Los Angeles to a common carrier known as Denver-Chicago Trucking Company, Inc., hereinafter called Denver, and received a bill of lading from the trucker. Simultaneously, plaintiff mailed defendant four invoices, all dated November 30, 1966, covering the clothing, in the total sum of $2,216. All the invoices bore the notations that the shipment was made "F.O.B. Los Angeles" and "Via Denver-Chicago." Further, all four invoices contained the printed phrase, "Goods Shipped at Purchaser's Risk." Denver's bill of lading disclosed that the shipment was made "collect," to wit, that defendant was obligated to pay the freight charges from Los Angeles to Westport. Denver subsequently transferred the shipment to a connecting carrier known as Old Colony Transportation Company, of South Dartmouth, Massachusetts, hereinafter called Old Colony, for ultimate delivery at defendant's store in Westport. The delivery was attempted by Old Colony at defendant's store on or about December 12, 1966. A woman in charge of the store, identified as defendant's wife, requested the Old Colony truck driver to deliver the merchandise inside the door of defendant's store. The truck driver refused to do so. The dispute not having been resolved, Old Colony retained possession of the eight cartons comprising the shipment, and the truck thereupon departed from the store premises.

Defendant sent a letter, dated December 12, 1966, and received by plaintiff in Los Angeles on December 20, 1966, reporting the refusal of the truck driver to make the delivery inside defendant's store. This was the first notice to plaintiff of the nondelivery. The letter alleged that defendant needed the merchandise immediately for the holidays but that defendant nevertheless insisted that the merchandise must be delivered inside his store, as a condition of his acceptance. Plaintiff tried to reach defendant by phone, but without success. Similarly, its numerous attempts to locate the shipment were fruitless. Plaintiff filed a claim against Denver for the lost merchandise, but up to the date of trial had not been reimbursed, in whole or in part, by the carrier. Defendant never recovered possession of the merchandise at any time following the original refusal.

The sole special defense pleaded was, "The Plaintiff refused to deliver the merchandise into the Defendant's place of business." Therefore defendant claimed that he is not liable for the subsequent loss or disappearance of the shipment, or the purchase price thereof, and that the risk of loss remained with plaintiff.

The basic problem is to determine the terms and conditions of the agreement of the parties as to transportation, and the risks and hazards incident thereto. The court finds that the parties had originally agreed that the merchandise would be shipped by common carrier F.O.B. Los Angeles, as the place of shipment, and that the defendant would pay the freight charges between the two points. The notations on the invoices, and the bill of lading, previously described, make this clear. The use of the phrase "F.O.B.," meaning free on board, made this portion of the agreement not only a price term covering defendant's obligation to pay freight charges between Los Angeles and Westport but also a controlling factor as to risk of loss of the merchandise upon delivery to Denver and subsequently to Old Colony as the carriers. . . .

Title to the goods, and the right to possession, passed to defendant at Los Angeles, the F.O.B. point. . . . Upon delivery to the common carrier at the F.O.B. point, the goods thereafter were at defendant's sole risk. . . .

[T]he court, [280 F. Supp. 550] in commenting on § 42a-2-319, stated: "Thus, an F.O.B. term must be read to indicate the point at which delivery is to be made unless there is specific agreement otherwise and therefore it will normally determine risk of loss."

It is highly significant that all the invoices sent to defendant contained the explicit notation "Goods Shipped at Purchaser's Risk." This was, initially, a unilateral statement by plaintiff. The validity of this phrase, as expressing the understanding of both parties, was, however, never actually challenged by defendant, at the trial or in his brief. The contents of the invoices therefore confirm the statutory allocation of risk of loss on F.O.B. shipments. . . .

The law erects a presumption in favor of construing the agreement as a "shipment" contract, as opposed to a "destination" contract. Under the presumption of a "shipment" contract, plaintiff's liability for loss or damage terminated upon delivery to the carrier at the F.O.B. point, to wit, Los Angeles. The court finds that no persuasive evidence was offered to overcome the force of the statutory presumption in the instant case. Thus, as § 42a-2-509(1) indicates, "[w]here the contract requires or authorizes the seller to ship the goods by carrier (a) if it does not require him to deliver them at a particular destination, the risk of loss passes to the buyer when the goods are duly delivered to the carrier." Accordingly, at the F.O.B. point, when the risk of loss shifted, Denver and Old Colony, as carriers, became the agents or bailees of defendant. The risk of subsequent loss or delay rested on defendant, and not plaintiff. A disagreement arose between defendant's wife and the truck driver, resulting in nondelivery of the merchandise, retention thereof by the carrier, and, finally, disappearance of the shipment. The ensuing dispute was fundamentally a matter for resolution between defendant and the carriers, as his agents. Nothing in the outcome of that dispute could defeat or impair plaintiff's recovery against defendant.

.   .   .

The issues are found for plaintiff. Judgment may therefore enter for plaintiff to recover of defendant the sum of $2,216, plus taxable costs.

D. H. Overmyer Co. v. Nelson-Brantly Glass Co.

168 S.E.2d 176 (Ga.) 1969

The glass company filed a claim against both D. H. Overmyer Co. (seller and shipper) and Alabama/Georgia Express (carrier) for damages to plate glass which was being shipped to the plaintiff. The complaint alleged that the defendants were negligent in failing to pack the glass properly and in transporting it without determining whether it was properly packed. The loading and packing was done by the shipper's employees. The trial court directed a verdict for the plaintiff against the shipper but released the carrier from liability. The shipper appealed.

QUILLIAN, J. . . . The bill of lading stated that "Shipper load and consignee unload." Plaintiff's counsel contends under the terms of the bill of lading

the carrier is relieved from liability because of the provision of Code Ann. §
109A-7-301(4) which states: "The issuer may by inserting in the bill the words
'shipper's weight, load and count' or other words of like purport indicate that
the goods were loaded by the shipper; and if such statement be true the issuer
shall not be liable for damages caused by the improper loading. But their
omission does not imply liability for such damages."

The actual effect of the "shipper's weight, load and count" bill of lading
is a state of confusion. There is an extensive discussion of the conflict which
exists in both the state and federal courts contained in the opinion of *Hershel
Radio Co.* v. *Pa. R.R. Co.* (344 Mich. 75, 80, 73 N.W.2d 319, 321), which
reads: "However, it is plaintiff's contention that despite its own negligence and
the 'Shipper's Load and Count' designation the carrier may be, and in this case
is, liable if it knew of or had the means of knowing of the improper loading
of the car. . . . There is support for the rule as advanced by plaintiffs.

"The Federal courts are in seeming disagreement as to what is the correct
and proper rule. In short, some say the railroad is liable if it knew or could
have found out, some say it is not liable even if it knew, and some say it is not
liable unless it actually knew, whether discoverable or not, about the shipper's
fault in loading. There has been expressed no readily discernible 'majority' or
'better' rule and to say that there has is to ignore some cases and emphasize
others, all equally pertinent."

We feel the sounder view is to give effect to the plain unambiguous language
of the statute. That is, where the evidence establishes that the damage was the
direct result of improper loading the "shipper's weight, load and count" bill
of lading shall operate as a complete defense for the carrier as to such damage.

There being evidence that the improper packing was the cause of the damage and none which would have authorized a finding that the glass breakage
was the result of the carrier's negligent transportation thereof, the trial judge's
direction of the verdict was not error.

Affirmed.

CHAPTER 19
REVIEW QUESTIONS AND PROBLEMS

1. The A Auto Company sold a car to the B Auto Company. It was
    subsequently discovered that the car had been stolen and the serial
    number was altered. The true owner demands that the car be returned
    to him, and the B Auto Company claims the right to retain it. Who is
    entitled to the car?

2. *A* sold and delivered a car to *B,* along with the papers of ownership.
    B paid for the car by check and, in turn, sold the car to *C. B*'s check
    was dishonored, and *A* seeks to recover the car from *C.* Should he
    succeed?

3. *A* purchased an automobile from *B,* who delivered to him a certificate
    of title apparently in good order. Actually, the vehicle had been stolen.
    The deception was made possible through a false application for the title

made by *B.* The owner of the car now seeks to recover possession of it from *A.* Should he succeed?

4. *A* in California sold goods to *B* in New York. *A* loaded the goods into a boxcar. He did not pack the goods properly, and they were damaged in transit. Can *B* recover damages from the railroad?

5. *A,* a Connecticut merchant, ordered goods from a supplier in California, *B.* The shipment was made "F.O.B. Los Angeles," and *B* delivered the goods to the carrier in Los Angeles. Subsequently, the goods were lost. Which party suffers the loss?

6. *A,* an Austrian manufacturer, sold paper to *B* in New York. X Shipping Company issued a negotiable bill of lading naming *A's* collecting agent, a New York bank, as consignee. The paper, however, was delivered directly to *B,* who did not pay the purchase price. Does *A* have any claim against the X Company?

7. *A* Publishing Company delivered comic books to *B* wholesale. *B* in turn delivered them to retailers. The retailers returned unsold books to *B* who tore off the covers and returned the covers to *A. B* was supposed to destroy the books, but instead he sold them to a wastepaper dealer, who, in turn, sold them to *X,* a dealer in secondhand books and magazines. *A* contends that the wastepaper dealer did not have the right to sell the magazines to *X.* Is *A* correct?

8. *A* of Eugene, Oregon, entered into a contract to purchase magnesium flares from *B,* whose plant is in Elgin, Illinois. The contract calls for delivery F.O.B. Eugene. While the flares were enroute, a bolt of lightning struck the car, and the flares were destroyed. Who must bear the loss?

9. *A* sold goods to *B.* At the time of the sale the goods were in storage at *X* warehouse. *X* had given *A* a negotiable warehouse receipt. *A* indorsed the warehouse receipt to *B.* Before *B* removed the goods from the warehouse, a creditor of *A* notified *B* that he had a judgment against *A* and was about to seize the goods in storage. What is *B's* position?

10. *A* ordered 500 tables from *B. B* crated the tables, awaiting shipping instruction from *A. B* wishes to know if he should carry insurance on these tables. Advise him.

Performance
of the Contract

3-22. Introduction.   Each party to a contract for sale of goods is obligated to perform in the manner prescribed by the contract and in accordance with provisions of the Code. The parties have considerable leeway in making their own rules as to what each is required to do, and the Code to a large degree "fills the gap" as to those aspects of performance not specified by the parties. But because both the buyer and the seller expect that each will perform properly they often fail to make provisions for various contingencies that can interfere with the successful completion of the transaction.

The seller is obligated to deliver or tender delivery of goods that measure up to the requirements of the contract and to do so at the proper time and at the proper place. The buyer is obligated to accept the goods and pay for them. However, many events or circumstances may stand in the way of a complete performance of the contract.

Some unexpected event may occur rendering performance by one of the parties impossible or impractical. One of the parties may repudiate the contract, i.e., state in advance that he does not intend to perform. The seller may tender goods that do not meet the specifications of the contract, do not arrive on time, or are defective. The buyer may unjustifiably or capriciously reject goods tendered by the seller or may refuse to pay the price of the goods. Either the buyer or the seller may become insolvent during the course of the transaction. The Code covers all of these eventualities and provides appropriate remedies for both the seller and the buyer. Remedies are discussed in the next chapter.

Both parties are required to act in "good faith" in their dealings with each other. As noted previously, in the case of merchants, this means honesty in fact and observance of reasonable commercial standards of fair dealing in the trade.

3-23. Obligations of the Parties. The contract for sale of goods imposes obligations on both the buyer and seller. Basically, the seller is obligated to transfer and deliver or tender delivery, and the buyer is obligated to accept and pay in accordance with the contract. In general, the parties can agree upon any terms and conditions relating to performance that are mutually acceptable. There are, of course, some limitations and these are set forth in the Code.

A very significant limitation is found in the concept of unconscionability. If the court as a matter of law finds the contract or any clause in the contract to have been unconscionable at the time it was made, the court may refuse to enforce the contract. In the alternative, the court may simply not enforce the unconscionable clause or it may temper the effect of such a clause. The significance of this provision is that a court may strike unfair and overreaching clauses in a contract for sale of goods if it feels that the clauses involved are so one-sided as to be improper when tested in the light of the general commercial background and the commercial needs of the particular trade or case. [1]

As mentioned previously, the obligations of the seller include furnishing the proper goods at the proper time and place. The goods and other performance of the seller must "conform" to the contract. The Code provides that "Goods or conduct including any part of a performance are 'conforming' or conform to the contract when they are in accordance with the obligations under the contract." (U.C.C. 2-106(2))

The seller is required to tender delivery as a condition to the buyer's duty to accept the goods and pay for them. Thus, the seller has performed when he has made the goods available to the buyer. The buyer in turn must render his performance, which means to accept the goods and pay for them. These obligations are discussed in detail in the following sections.

3-24. Delivery. Some aspects of the seller's obligation with respect to delivery have been discussed in the previous chapters. The Code speaks in terms of *tender* of delivery, which means that the seller must "put and hold conforming goods at the buyer's disposition and give the buyer any notification reasonably necessary to enable him to take delivery." (U.C.C. 2-503(1)) The tender of the goods must be made in a reasonable fashion so that the buyer can make the necessary arrangements to take possession of them. The buyer is obligated to furnish facilities that are reasonably suited to the receipt of the goods. Thus, the seller and the buyer must cooperate in effecting a delivery and receipt of the goods.[2] The Code imposes a general obligation of cooperation between the parties.

The seller is required to tender all of the goods in a single delivery and payment is due only upon such tender. However, the parties may agree otherwise, and in appropriate circumstances either party has the right to make or demand an installment delivery. It may not be commercially feasible to deliver or receive the goods in a single lot. For example, *A* is obligated to ship ten carloads of lumber. If only four freight cars are available at the time, a single-lot delivery would be excused. The parties may provide for an "install-

---

[1] Toker d.b.a. Budget Associates v. Perl, page 401
[2] Aetna Insurance Co. v. Maryland Cast Stone Co., Inc., page 402

ment contract," which requires or authorizes the delivery of goods in separate lots to be separately accepted.

In a shipment contract the seller is required to make all of the necessary arrangements with the carrier and put the goods in the carrier's possession. In addition, he must furnish to the buyer any documents which are required to obtain the goods from the carrier at destination and he must promptly notify the buyer of the shipment.

3-25. Payment and Tender. The price can be made payable in money or in goods or otherwise. The buyer is not required to make payment, absent an agreement to the contrary, until the goods have been tendered to him. In an installment contract he must make payment as each installment is tendered to him. The seller's tender of the goods entitles him to payment from the buyer according to the terms of the contract. Thus, a tender of payment and a tender of the goods are concurrent conditions. Actually, the tender of payment requirement applies mainly to noncommercial sales and to ordinary sales at retail. Most commercial contracts carry credit terms.

Tender of payment is sufficient "when made by any means or in any manner current in the ordinary course of business." (U.C.C. 2-511(2)) The seller has the right, however, to demand payment in legal tender. If he so demands, he must give the buyer any extension of time reasonably necessary to procure it. In any given situation it might be difficult to obtain a large sum in currency on short notice.

If payment is made by check, such payment is conditional upon the check being honored. If it is dishonored, payment has not been made and the seller can rely upon his remedies for breach of the contract. The seller has the choice of either bringing action on the check or on the obligation to pay.

The contract may require payment before the buyer has had an opportunity to inspect the goods. In such a case, the buyer may not refuse to pay on account of a nonconformity of the goods unless the nonconformity is obvious without inspection. The buyer is thus required to "pay first and litigate later."

3-26. Inspection. The parties may provide in their contract for inspection of the goods by the buyer prior to payment or acceptance. In the absence of a provision the Code provides that the buyer has a right before payment or acceptance to inspect the goods at any reasonable time and place and in any reasonable manner. The place for the inspection would be determined largely by the nature of the contract. If the seller is to send the goods to the buyer, the inspection could be postponed until after arrival of the goods.

There are two situations in which payment must be made prior to inspection. One of these is a C.O.D. delivery, and the other when payment is to be made against documents of title as discussed in Chapter 19.

The buyer must pay the expenses of inspection, but he can recover his expenses from the seller if the inspection reveals that the goods are nonconforming and the buyer accordingly rejects them.

It should be noted that when the buyer is required to make payment prior to inspection, such payment does not impair his right to pursue remedies if subsequent inspection reveals defects.

3-27. Cure. If upon inspecting the goods the buyer finds that they do not conform to the contract, he may reject them. Although the buyer has the right to reject goods tendered by the seller if they do not meet the specifications of the contract, he must act fairly in doing so. If the rejection is for a relatively minor deviation from the contract requirements, the seller must be given an opportunity to correct the defective performance. This is called *cure*.[3] He may accomplish this by notifying the buyer of his intention to cure and then tendering proper or conforming goods if the time for performance has not expired. If the time for performance has expired, as for example, when the buyer makes a last-minute rejection, the seller, if he had reasonable grounds to believe that the goods would be acceptable in spite of the nonconformity, will be granted further time to substitute goods which are in accordance with the contract. The main purpose of this rule allowing cure is to protect the seller from being forced into a breach by a surprise rejection at the last moment by the buyer. The seller, in order to take advantage of this privilege, must notify the buyer of his intention to cure.

The provision for cure by the seller does not detract from his obligation to render a performance which conforms to the contract.[4] The seller is obligated to tender and the buyer is entitled to receive the goods as specified in the contract. If the goods are not conforming, the buyer may reject them—such nonconformity constitutes a breach of the contract by the seller.

3-28. Excuses of Performance.   Both parties may be relieved of their obligations under a contract for sale if the goods suffer casualty—are damaged, destroyed, or have deteriorated, without fault of either party, prior to delivery. Avoidance of the contract will result if (1) the casualty occurs prior to the time when the risk of loss passes to the buyer, and (2) the goods have been "identified to the contract." If the loss is only partial, the buyer can either treat the contract as avoided or accept the remaining goods with due adjustment of the contract price to allow for the deficiency. The avoidance principle applies whether the goods were already destroyed at the time of contracting without the parties' knowledge or whether they were destroyed subsequently but before risk of loss passed to the buyer. The protection afforded to the seller is quite limited since he may still be under an obligation to perform if the contract did not require for its performance specific goods identified when the contract was made.

The seller is excused from timely delivery of goods where supervening circumstances not within the contemplation of the parties at the time of contracting have made his performance impracticable. Thus, if an unforeseen event occurs that adversely affects the ability of the seller to perform, he may be relieved of the normal consequences resulting from a late delivery, a partial delivery, or nondelivery. The seller is excused only if (1) the nonoccurrence of the contingency was a basic assumption upon which the contract was made, and (2) its occurrence made the agreed performance commercially impracticable. The Code does not elaborate on these matters, but it seems clear that increased costs and a rise or collapse of the market are basic business risks which would not in themselves justify a seller's failure to perform.[5] On the other hand, if it were understood that a particular source would supply the seller with the goods to be used in fulfillment of the contract, and, due to

---

[3] Bartus v. Riccardi, page 403
[4] Graulich Caterer, Inc. v. Hans Holterbosch, Inc., page 405
[5] United States v. Wegematic Corp., page 408

casualty, the supplier could not furnish such goods, then the seller would be relieved. If the seller's capacity to perform is only partially curtailed, he is obligated to allocate the available goods among his customers in a fair and reasonable manner. The seller must give proper notice to the buyer that there will be a delay or nondelivery, and when, in the case of partial curtailment, allocation is required, he must furnish the buyer an estimate of the quota available to the buyer. The buyer, upon receiving such notification, may terminate the contract as to any delivery concerned, or he may agree to modify the contract and take his available quota.

3-29. Anticipatory Repudiation.   Either a buyer or a seller may in advance of the date when final performance is due indicate by word or action that he will not continue with his performance. The aggrieved party who has been informed of such repudiation may (1) treat the contract as having been breached and resort to any remedy for breach, or (2) await performance by the repudiating party for a commercially reasonable time, and (3) in either case suspend his own performance. The repudiating party can retract his repudiation and reinstate his rights under the contract unless the aggrieved party has indicated that he considers the repudiation final as by canceling or by materially changing his position on the basis of the repudiation.

3-30. Adequate Assurance.   A problem analogous to anticipatory repudiation is one in which circumstances arise which give either party cause for concern as to whether or not the other will *actually render* the performance due. It is not enough to give either party—buyer or seller—a right to sue and collect damages for the ultimate breach. There is need for some protection to be afforded to the party whose reasonable expectation that he will receive due performance is jeopardized. The Code grants such protection by providing that the contract for sale imposes an obligation on each party that the other's expectation of receiving due performance will not be impaired. A party who has reasonable grounds for insecurity as to the other's performance can demand in writing that the other offer convincing proof that he will in fact perform. Having made such demand, he may then suspend his own performance until he receives such assurance. If none is forthcoming within a reasonable time, not to exceed thirty days, he may treat the contract as repudiated. Two factual problems are presented: What are reasonable grounds for insecurity and what constitutes an adequate assurance of performance? The Code does not particularize but does provide that as between merchants commercial standards shall be applied to answer these questions.

3-31. Delegation of Performance.   The Code provides that a party may "perform his duty through a delegate unless otherwise agree or unless the other party has a substantial interest in having his original promisor perform or control the acts required by the contract." (U.C.C. 2-210(1)) Accordingly, a seller can ordinarily delegate to someone else the duty to perform the seller's obligations under the contract. This would occur when no substantial reason exists why the delegated performance would be less satisfactory than the personal performance. It should be noted that delegation does not relieve the original party from his duty to perform nor does it relieve him from liability if his delegate does not perform or does not properly perform.[6]

When there is an assignment of "the contract" or "all my rights under the contract" this will be regarded as including an assumption by the assignee of the duty to perform. Such assignee becomes responsible to both the assignor and the other party to the contract.

The other party may treat any assignment which delegates performance as creating reasonable grounds for uncertainty as to whether he will receive proper performance. He can demand adequate assurances from the assignee. The assignor will not be relieved of his liability if the other party follows this course of action.

PERFORMANCE OF CONTRACT CASES

Toker d.b.a. Budget Associates v. Perl
247 A.2d 701 (N.J.) 1968

The defendants entered into an installment sales contract with People's Foods, Inc., for a food purchase plan. They signed the contract without realizing that they were obligating themselves to purchase a freezer as well as the food. The contract was assigned by People's Foods to the plaintiff. Plaintiff in turn assigned to a bank with recourse. Defendants refused to make the installment payments and plaintiff brought this action to recover the balance due.

TRIARSI, J. . . . At trial defendants presented an expert witness who testified that the freezer delivered by People's Foods had a maximum value of $300. The installment contract signed by defendants provided for a purchase price of $799.95, sales tax of $24, group creditor life insurance of $16.93 and a credit service charge or time-price differential of $252.08. The total price of the freezer was $1,092.96, to be paid in 36 monthly installments of $30.36.

It has been stipulated that plaintiffs are subject to any defenses defendants may allege against their assignor, People's Foods.

Defendants allege fraud in the procurement of the contract by the agent of People's Foods, and also that the contract is unconscionable under N.J.S. 12A:2-302, N.J.S.A.

It is beyond contention in this State that a knowing misrepresentation by one party as to the contents of a contract amounts to fraud. Such a contract may be voided on the theory that the defrauded party never agreed to the terms of the contract. . . .

In the present case it is the opinion of this court that People's Foods defrauded defendants when it procured their signatures on the freezer contract. Their agent led defendants to believe that the freezer was included in the price for the food plan. Nowhere in the record is there any evidence that defendants ever knew they were signing an installment contract for a freezer.

Plaintiffs, however, contend that the failure of defendants to read what they were signing contributed to their own misfortune. It is therefore plaintiffs'

[6] Noblett v. General Electric Credit Corp., page 409

contention that defendants should be estopped from alleging fraud because of their own negligence.

This court does not disagree with plaintiffs' statement of the law. It agrees with it. . . . However, this court is constrained to apply the doctrine of the late Mr. Justice Frankfurter in *United States* v. *Bethlehem Steel Corp.,* 315 U.S. 289, 62 S.Ct. 581, 86 L.Ed. 855 (1942). . . .

> . . . [T]he courts will not permit themselves to be used as instruments of inequality and injustice. Does any principle in our law have more universal application than the doctrine that courts will not enforce transactions in which the relative positions of the parties are such that one has unconscionably taken advantage of the necessities of the other?

If this court were to hold that defendants were negligent and therefore estopped from alleging fraud, it would permit itself to be used as an instrumentality of "inequality and injustice."

The facts in *Westfield Investment Co.* v. *Fellers,* 74 N.J.Super. 575, 181 A.2d 809 (Law Div.1962), are remarkably similar to the facts of the case at bar. There, too, defendants signed a conditional sales contract for a freezer in the belief that they were signing a food plan contract. And there also the court felt that plaintiffs' actions were fraudulent.

It is also the opinion of this court that the exorbitant price of the freezer makes this contract unconscionable and therefore unenforceable. N.J.S. 12A:2-302, N.J.S.A. provides:

> (1) If the court as a matter of law finds the contract or any clause of the contract to have been unconscionable at the time it was made the court may refuse to enforce the contract, or it may enforce the remainder of the contract without the unconscionable clause, or it may so limit the application of any unconscionable clause as to avoid any unconscionable result.

Although the courts of this State have never been asked to apply this section of the Uniform Commercial Code to the price term of a contract, our sister state of New York has recently held that "excessively high prices may constitute unconscionable contractual provisions within the meaning of section 2-302 of the Uniform Commercial Code." . . .

The conscience of this court is shocked by the price imposed upon these defendants for the freezer. The testimony in court valued the freezer at no more than $300. The price charged was in excess of 2 1/2 times the maximum value. The time-price differential alone almost equaled the value of the freezer. In the light of these facts, this court is constrained to hold the price in this contract unconscionable.

It is therefore the opinion of this court that the contract is unenforceable because it was procured by fraud and is unconscionable.

Aetna Insurance Co. v. Maryland Cast Stone Co., Inc.

253 A. 2d 872 (Md.) 1969

The plaintiff stone company brought action to recover on a surety bond issued by defendant to the owner of an apartment building. Plaintiff had a subcontract to furnish precast concrete balconies for the building. The balconies were prepared but the general contractor would not accept delivery. The surety company contended that plaintiff could not recover payment because the stone had never been delivered to the contractor. The lower court ruled in favor of the plaintiff and defendant appealed.

SINGLEY, J. . . . There remains the . . . question raised by Aetna: Must Maryland Cast Stone prove delivery to Gilbert in order to recover on the bond? It must be remembered that Maryland Cast Stone is claiming under a contract which protected suppliers of material "used or reasonably required for use" and not under our mechanic's lien statute . . . which allows a lien "for materials furnished for or about the [building]."

Aetna would have us analogize the situation to the mechanic's lien cases, which hold that, for materials to be "furnished," they must have been delivered. . . . We think that the resolution of the question is found in the Uniform Commercial Code . . . § 2-503 Manner of seller's tender of delivery.

> (1) Tender of delivery requires that the seller put and hold conforming goods at the buyer's disposition and give the buyer any notification reasonably necessary to enable him to take delivery. The manner, time and place for tender are determined by the agreement and this subtitle, and in particular
>> (a) Tender must be at a reasonable hour, and if it is of goods they must be kept available for the period reasonably necessary to enable the buyer to take possession; but
>> (b) Unless otherwise agreed the buyer must furnish facilities reasonably suited to the receipt of the goods.
>
> .   .   .
>
> (3) Where the seller is required to deliver at a particular destination tender requires that he comply with subsection (1). . . .
> § 2-507 Effect of seller's tender; delivery on condition.
> (1) Tender of delivery is a condition to the buyer's duty to accept the goods and, unless otherwise agreed, to his duty to pay for them. Tender entitles the seller to acceptance of the goods and to payment according to the contract.

Maryland Cast Stone was in Rockville; the Park Heights project, in Baltimore. The contract for precast concrete balconies, sills, copings and Miami Brick Stone at an aggregate cost of $25,539 provided: "Prices are furnished and delivered only." . . . Prices are F.O.B. trucks, job site," "*Terms:* —Net 10th Prox." It will be recalled that "Maryland Cast Stone timely manufactured the ordered materials and requested delivery instructions for Gilbert. These were never received and the materials were never delivered" nor, under the facts before us, did they have to be delivered. The materials, which were specially fabricated, were, under the language of the bond, "reasonably required for use in the performance of the contract." Under the circumstances of the case, Maryland Cast Stone's tender of goods which conformed to the contract was the equivalent of delivery and fixed Gilbert's duty to pay for them. . . .

Order affirmed; costs to be paid by appellant.

Bartus v. Riccardi

284 N.Y.S.2d 222 (N.Y.) 1967

HYMES, J. The plaintiff is a franchised representative of Acousticon, a manufacturer of hearing aids. On January 15, 1966, the defendant signed a contract to purchase a Model A-660 Acousticon hearing aid from the plaintiff. The defendant specified Model A-660 because he had been tested at a hearing aid clinic and had been informed that the best hearing aid for his condition was this Acousticon model. An ear mold was fitted to the defendant and the plaintiff ordered Model A-660 from Acousticon.

On February 2, 1966, in response to a call from the plaintiff the defendant went to the plaintiff's office for his hearing aid. At that time he was informed that Model A-660 had been modified and improved, and that it was now called Model A-665. This newer model had been delivered by Acousticon for the defendant's use. The defendant denies that he understood this was a different model number. The hearing aid was fitted to the defendant. The defendant complained about the noise, but was assured by the plaintiff that he would get used to it.

The defendant tried out the new hearing aid for the next few days for a total use of fifteen hours. He went back to the hearing clinic, where he was informed that the hearing aid was not the model that he had been advised to buy. On February 8, 1966, he returned to the plaintiff's office complaining that the hearing aid gave him a headache, and that it was not the model he had ordered. He returned the hearing aid to the plaintiff, for which he received a receipt. At that time the plaintiff offered to get Model A-660 for the defendant. The defendant neither consented to nor refused the offer. No mention was made by either party about canceling the contract, and the receipt given by the plaintiff contained no notation or indication that the plaintiff considered the contract canceled or rescinded.

The plaintiff immediately informed Acousticon of the defendant's complaint. By letter dated February 14, 1966, Acousticon writing directly to the defendant, informed him that Model A-665 was an improved version of Model A-660, and that they would either replace the model that had been delivered to him or would obtain Model A-660 for him. He was asked to advise the plaintiff immediately of his decision so that they could effect a prompt exchange. After receiving this letter the defendant decided that he did not want any hearing aid from the plaintiff, and he refused to accept the tender of a replacement, whether it be Model A-665 or A-660. . . .

The question before the court is whether or not the plaintiff, having delivered a model which admittedly is not in exact conformity with the contract, can nevertheless recover in view of his subsequent tender of the model that did meet the terms of the contract.

The defendant contends that since there was an improper delivery of goods, the buyer has the right to reject the same under Sections 2-601 and 2-602(2)(c) of the Uniform Commercial Code. He further contends that even if the defendant had accepted delivery he may, under Section 2-608(1) (b) of the U.C.C., revoke his acceptance of the goods because "his acceptance was reasonably induced . . . by the seller's assurances." He also relies on Section 2-711, claiming that he may recover not only the down payment but also consequential damages.

The defendant, however, has neglected to take into account Section 2-508 of the Uniform Commercial Code which has added a new dimension to the concept of strict performance. This section permits a seller to cure a nonconforming delivery under certain circumstances. Sub-paragraph (1) . . . permits a seller to cure a nonconforming delivery *before the expiration of the contract time* by notifying the buyer of his intention to so cure and by making a delivery within the contract period. . . .

However, the U.C.C. in sub-paragraph (2) of Section 2-508 goes further and extends *beyond the contract time* the right of the seller to cure a defective performance. Under this provision, even where the contract period has expired and the buyer has rejected a nonconforming tender or has revoked an acceptance, the seller may "substitute a conforming tender" if he had "reasonable grounds to believe" that the nonconforming tender would be accepted, and "if he seasonably notifies the buyer" of his intention "to substitute a conforming tender."

This in effect extends the contract period beyond the date set forth in the contract itself unless the buyer requires strict performance by including such a clause in the contract.

"The section (2-508(2) U.C.C.) rejects the time-honored and perhaps time-worn notion that the proper way to assure effective results in commercial transactions is to require strict performance. Under the Code a buyer who insists upon such strict performance must rely on a special term in his agreement or the fact that the seller knows as a commercial matter that strict performance is required."

This section seeks to avoid injustice to the seller by reason of a surprise rejection by the buyer.

An additional burden, therefore, is placed upon the buyer by this section. "As a result a buyer may learn that even though he rejected or revoked his acceptance within the terms of Sections 2-601 and 2-711, he still may have to allow the seller additional time to meet the terms of the contract by substituting delivery of conforming goods." [Bender's U.C.C. Service—Sales and Bulk Transfers—Vol. 3, Section 14-02(1)(a)(ii).]

Has the plaintiff in this case complied with the conditions of Section 2-508?

The model delivered to the defendant was a newer and improved version of the model than was actually ordered. Of course, the defendant is entitled to receive the model that he ordered even though it may be an older type. But under the circumstances the plaintiff had reasonable grounds to believe that the newer model would be accepted by the defendant.

The plaintiff acted within a reasonable time to notify the defendant of his tender of a conforming model. (Section 1-204 U.C.C.) The defendant had not purchased another hearing aid elsewhere. His position had not been altered by reason of the original nonconforming tender.

The plaintiff made a proper subsequent conforming tender pursuant to Section 2-508(2) of the Uniform Commercial Code.

Judgment is granted to plaintiff.

Graulich Caterer Inc. v. Hans Holterbosch, Inc.

243 A.2d 253 (N.J.) 1968

The plaintiff entered into a contract to supply food to the defendant's restaurant at the New York World's Fair. The food in the first delivery was faulty and the plaintiff agreed to correct it. The second delivery was also faulty and defendant canceled the contract. Plaintiff brought action for expenses and lost profits as a result of buyer's cancellation of the contract. The lower court ruled for defendant and the plaintiff appealed.

FOLEY, J. . . . Giving due regard to the original trier's opportunity to observe the demeanor and to judge the credibility of the witnesses, we find as a matter of fact that the deliveries of April 23 and 25, 1964 did not conform to the samples originally presented and approved. Since warranties of sample and description are characterized as "express warranties," the "whole of the goods shall conform to the sample or model." The "goods" to "conform" to the sample or model must be in "in accordance with the obligations under the contract"; here, to comply with the standards established by the March 17 taste-test of the samples. Any distinguishing language would be controlled by the sample as presented on March 17. Additionally, the implied warranty of fitness for purpose attaches to contracts of this type, where, as here, they are not specifically excluded. A breach of these warranties triggers a buyer's rights following seller's breach as catalogued in N.J.S. 12A:2-711, N.J.S.A. These remedies include, but are not limited to, cancellation . . . "if the breach goes to the whole of the contract."

N.J.S. 12A:2-612, N.J.S.A. discloses the rights of the parties to installment contracts:

> (1) An "installment contract" is one which requires or authorizes the delivery of goods in separate lots to be separately accepted, even though the contract contains a clause "each delivery is a separate contract" or its equivalent.
>
> (2) The buyer may reject any installment which is nonconforming if the non-conformity substantially impairs the value of that installment and cannot be cured or if the non-conformity is a defect in the required documents; but if the non-conformity does not fall within subsection (3) and the seller gives adequate assurance of its cure the buyer must accept that installment.
>
> (3) Whenever non-conformity or default with respect to one or more installments substantially impairs the value of the whole contract there is a breach of the whole. But the aggrieved party reinstates the contract if he accepts a non-conforming installment without seasonably notifying of cancellation or if he brings an action with respect only to past installments or demands performance as to future installments.

Here, Holterbosch had the right to reject any installment that was nonconforming, provided that the nonconformity substantially impaired the value of that installment and could not be cured. . . . "Cure," permits the seller to cure a defective tender through repair, replacement or price allowance if he reasonably notifies the buyer of his curative intention and, in effecting the cure, makes a timely conforming delivery.

The effect of the installment contract section, N.J.S. 12A:2-612(2), N.J.S.A., is to extend the time for cure past the contract delivery date for that nonconforming installment, provided the nonconformity does not "substantially [impair] the value of that installment" and can be cured. We find that Holterbosch was justified in rejecting Graulich's tender of the April 23 initial installment since the nonconformity of the tendered goods with the accepted sample was incurable, and thus substantially impaired the value of that installment.

Replacing considerations of anticipatory repudiation and the material injury with the test of substantial impairment, N.J.S. 12A:2-612, N.J.S.A. adopts a more restrictive seller-oriented approach favoring "the continuance of the contract in the absence of an overt cancellation. . . . To allow an aggrieved party to cancel an installment contract, N.J.S. 12A:2-612(3), N.J.S.A. requires (1) the breach be of the whole contract which occurs when the nonconformity of "one or more installments substantially impairs the value of the whole contract"; and (2) that seasonable notification of cancellation has been given if the buyer has accepted a nonconforming installment.

What amounts to substantial impairment presents a question of fact. Analyzing this factual question, the New Jersey commentators counsel that the test as to whether the nonconformity in any given installment justifies canceling the entire contract depends on whether the nonconformity substantially impairs the value of the whole contract, and not on whether it indicates an intent or likelihood that the future deliveries also will be defective. Continuing, the Comment relates the intent underlying a breach to insecurity and those sections of the Code providing buyer with adequate assurance of performance, § 2-609, and anticipatory repudiation, § 2-610. More practical in its treatment of "substantial impairment," the official Comment states that "substantial impairment of the value of an installment can turn not only on the quality of the goods but also on such factors as time, quantity, assortment and the like. It must be judged in terms of the normal or specifically known purposes of the contract."

At the Lowenbrau Pavilion on April 23, 1964 plaintiff Graulich, timely noticed of the nonconforming initial tender, gave assurance that future tenders would be cured to match the original samples. Unequivocally committed to the microwave kitchen method, defendant lent plaintiff three members from its staff in aid of this adjustment. Since plaintiff was given the opportunity to cure, there is no need to touch upon the substantiality of the initial nonconforming installment.

The second installment tender was as unsatisfactory as the first. The meat was dry, the gravy "gooey" and the complaints abundant. After the nonconforming second delivery it became apparent that eleventh-hour efforts attempting to rework and adjust the platters failed. Translating this into legal parlance, there was a nonconforming tender of the initial installment on a contract for the sale of goods; upon tender the buyer Holterbosch notified the seller Graulich of the nonconformity and unacceptable nature of the platters tendered; the failure of the cure assured by plaintiff, seller, was evidenced by a subsequently defective nonconforming delivery. The second unacceptable delivery and the failure of plaintiff's additional curative efforts left defendant in a position for one week without food. Time was critical. Plaintiff knew that platters of maximum quality were required on a daily installment basis. Because of defendant's immediate need for quality food and plaintiff's failure to cure, we find that the nonconformity of the second delivery, projected upon the circumstances of this case, "substantially impair[ed] the value of the whole contract [and resulted in] a breach of the whole." If the breach goes to the whole contract the buyer may cancel the whole contract. . . . Accordingly, we find that Holterbosch was justified in canceling the installment agreement signed on April 1, 1964. . . .

Judgment in favor of defendant for the reasons herein stated. Costs to defendant.

United States v. Wegematic Corp.

360 F. 2d 674 (1966)

The defendant entered into a contract with the Federal Reserve Board to furnish an electronic digital computer system with delivery to be made on June 30, 1957. After several delays defendant announced that because of engineering difficulties it would not be able to deliver the computer and asked that the contract be canceled without damages. The plaintiff proceeded to obtain a computer from IBM and brought an action for damages. The lower court awarded damages and defendant appealed.

FRIENDLY, J. . . . The principal point of the defense, which is the sole ground of this appeal, is that delivery was made impossible by "basic engineering difficulties" whose correction would have taken between one and two years and would have cost a million to a million and a half dollars, with success likely but not certain. Although the record does not give an entirely clear notion what the difficulties were, two experts suggested that they may have stemmed from the magnetic cores, used instead of transistors to achieve a solid-state machine, which did not have sufficient uniformity at this stage of their development. Defendant contends that under federal law, which both parties concede to govern, . . . the "practical impossibility" of completing the contract excused its defaults in performance. . . .

We find persuasive the defendant's suggestion of looking to the Uniform Commercial Code as a source for the "federal" law of sales. . . .

Section 2-615 of the U.C.C., entitled "Excuse by failure of presupposed conditions," provides that:

> Except so far as a seller may have assumed a greater obligation . . . delay in delivery or non-delivery . . . is not a breach of his duty under a contract for sale if performance as agreed has been made impracticable by the occurrence of a contingency the non-occurrence of which was a basic assumption on which the contract was made. . . .

The latter part of the test seems a somewhat complicated way of putting Professor Corbin's question of how much risk the promisor assumed. We see no basis for thinking that when an electronics system is promoted by its manufacturer as a revolutionary breakthrough, the risk of the revolution's occurrence falls on the purchaser; the reasonable supposition is that it has already occurred or, at least, that the manufacturer is assuring the purchaser that it will be found to have when the machine is assembled. As Judge Graven said: "The Board in its invitation for bids did not request invitations to conduct a development program for it. The Board requested invitations from manufacturers for the furnishing of a computer machine." Acceptance of defendant's argument would mean that though a purchaser makes his choice because of the attractiveness of a manufacturer's representation and will be bound by it, the manufacturer is free to express what are merely aspirations and gamble on mere probabilities of fulfillment without any risk of liability. In fields of developing technology, the manufacturer would thus enjoy a wide degree of latitude with respect to performance while holding an option to compel the buyer to pay if the gamble should pan out. . . .

We do not think this the common understanding—above all as to a contract where the manufacturer expressly agreed to liquidated damages for delay and authorized the purchaser to resort to other sources in the event of non-delivery. . . .

If a manufacturer wishes to be relieved of the risk that what looks good on paper may not prove so good in hardware, the appropriate exculpatory language is well known and often used.

Beyond this the evidence of true impracticability was far from compelling. . . . While the unanticipated need for expending $1,000,000 or $1,500,000 on redesign might have made such a venture unattractive, as defendant's management evidently decided, the sums are thus not so clearly prohibitive as it would have them appear. What seemingly did become impossible was on-time performance; the issue whether if defendant had offered prompt rectification of the design, the Government could have refused to give it a chance and still recover not merely damages for delay but also the higher cost of replacement equipment, is not before us.

Affirmed.

Noblett v. General Electric Credit Corp.

400 F.2d 442 (1968)

Noblett operated a bowling alley, the equipment for which was under a bowling equipment rental lease from Bowl-Mor Company. Bowl-Mor assigned the lease to General Electric Credit Corporation. The rental agreement provided that the lessor could assign the lease and that the assignee would not be liable for any of the lessor's obligations. Noblett alleged that the equipment was faulty. The plaintiff, assignee, brought action to recover the balance due under the lease. The question presented was whether Noblett could assert his defenses against the assignee. The lower court ruled for plaintiff-assignee and defendant appealed.

CHRISTENSEN, J. . . . An assignment in general terms under the Uniform Commercial Code, and, hence, under the present Massachusetts law, is an assignment of rights, and unless the language or the circumstances indicate the contrary, it is also a delegation of performance of the duties of the assignor and its acceptance by the assignee, constituting a promise by him to perform those duties. The promise is enforceable by either the assignor or the other party to the original contract. In general, whether there is a delegation of duties as well as rights in and of itself does not affect defenses available to the other original contracting party. If there is a delegation of obligations, failure of consideration remains a defense, and the same is true even though there is no delegation of obligation to the assignee in the absence of waiver; the assignee stands in the shoes of the assignor as far as the right to recover is concerned in either event. Moreover, if there is a delegation of obligation to the assignee, this in and of itself does not relieve the assignor from the obligation of performance. If the assignor is required to respond to the other contracting party after duties have been delegated by the assignor, the assignee may be rendered liable to the assignor, which is a reason why a nondelegation agreement may be important to the assignee in the absence of a waiver of defenses.

The point of these general principles is that defenses are available against the assignee in the absence of a waiver, not because of the delegation or nondelegation of duties but because the assignee in either event must claim under the original contract and is subject to the defenses allowed thereby. The fact that the lease recited that the lessee should continue to be bound to his contracted obligations despite any assignment does not suggest in context that he agreed to waive defenses any more than the agreement that responsibilities of the assignor were not to be deemed delegated had anything to do with the waiver of defenses. The intent and meaning of the lease in this respect is made all the more clear by Bowl-Mor's assignment to the credit corporation which simply provides on the point that "Assignee shall have no obligations of lessor under said lease."

Whether responsibilities of the assignor were or were not delegated pursuant to § 2-210(4), or as a matter of general law, the rule continued operative that failure of consideration could be raised as a defense either against the assignee or the assignor in the absence of a waiver as authorized by the other provision of the Code. There was no such waiver. To enlarge the agreement concerning the nondelegation of obligation into such a waiver would be not only unwarranted but unfair. When appellant consented to the nondelegation to the assignee of obligations of the assignor under the lease, whether viewed from the standpoint of one learned in the law and capable of appreciating these distinctions, or as one only generally aware of the meaning of language, he reasonably could have assumed that the purpose was what it purported to be and was not to preclude his defenses should he not receive the consideration for which he bargained. We are of the opinion that as a matter of law there was no waiver of defenses. . . .

Reversed.

CHAPTER 20
REVIEW QUESTIONS AND PROBLEMS

1. *A* purchased goods from *B* on an installment contract and then assigned his rights in such goods to *C. C* did not pay the balance due under the contract to *B,* and *B* seeks to hold *A* liable. Should he succeed?

2. *A* ordered a hearing aid from B Company. B Company delivered a newer model than the one ordered, and *A* refused to accept it. Does *B* have the right to tender the model ordered?

3. *A* entered into a contract to manufacture goods for *B* who required them for use in a construction project. *A* requested delivery instructions, but *B* did not furnish them, and as a result the goods were never delivered. Is *A* entitled to recover the price of the goods?

4. *A* purchased a color television set from *B,* a dealer. When it was installed, the color was not clear and *B* who came to *A's* home said that

it would be necessary to take it to his shop to repair it. *A* refused to allow this and demanded that the set be replaced immediately by another new one. Is *A* entitled to this?

5. A salesman for A Company sold *B* a home freezer for $900. The purchase price totaled $1,200 when other charges were included. At a time when *B* had paid $600 the company claimed a balance still due of $800. The retail value of the freezer is $300. Is *B* entitled to any relief?

6. *A* entered into a contract to purchase fruit from *B.* Several months prior to the delivery date *A* announced that he would not take the fruit. *B* did not attempt to resell the apples until after the delivery date specified in the contract. Is *B* entitled to recover damages from *A* ?

7. *A* had contracted to purchase a boat from *B.* He tendered a check in payment, but *B* refused to accept it. Was *B* justified in refusing the check?

8. *A* contracted to deliver to *B's* factory 520 bushels of No. 1 tomatoes by June 25. On June 15, *A* delivered the tomatoes but it was discovered that 200 bushels were damaged by frost. *A* told *B* that he would replace them, but *B* stated that he would refuse to accept them. If *A* replaces the damaged tomatoes, must *B* accept them?

9. *A* contracted to buy 5,000 bushels of corn from *B.* Just before harvest a hailstorm destroyed the crop. Is *B* relieved from the obligation of the contract?

10. *A,* a clothing manufacturer, contracted to buy 500 gross of fancy buttons from *B* for delivery on July 25. On June 1, *B* notified *A* that because of a shortage of mother-of-pearl he would not deliver the buttons on the date specified. *A* promptly made arrangements to satisfy his button requirements from *X.* Shortly thereafter *B* stated that he would make delivery. Advise *A* as to his rights in this situation.

Rights, Remedies, and Obligations

3-32. Introduction. In the event that a contract of sale is breached or one of the parties becomes insolvent, there are a number of remedies available to the aggrieved party, whether he be the buyer or seller. The breach or insolvency may occur at any point in time between the making of the contract and full performance by both parties. Therefore, in selecting and applying the proper remedy, all of the circumstances surrounding the breach or insolvency must be considered. This chapter discusses these remedies and the situations in which they may be used.

BUYER'S RIGHTS AND OBLIGATIONS

3-33. In General. The remedies available to an aggrieved buyer are intertwined with his conduct in connection with the goods. He may have accepted the goods (not to be confused with acceptance of an offer); rejected them; or having accepted them, thereafter revoked his acceptance. It is therefore appropriate to discuss these concepts as a part of the subject of remedies.

3-34. Rejection. If the goods or the tender of delivery fail to conform to the contract, the buyer has the right to reject them. [1] Several options are available to him. He may reject the whole, or he may accept either the whole or any commercial unit or units and reject the rest. A commercial unit is one that is generally regarded as a single whole for purposes of sale, and that would be impaired in value if divided. Thus, the buyer could accept those portions of the goods that would be satisfactory to him as long as he did not thereby break up a unit. The buyer, whether he accepts the whole or any unit, does not impair his right of recourse against the seller. Provided he notifies the seller of the

[1] Zabriskie Chevrolet, Inc. v. Smith, page 424

breach within a reasonable time, he may still pursue his remedy for damages for breach of contract. Frequently, the contract will authorize or require delivery in stated lots or in installments to be separately accepted. The buyer's right to reject a nonconforming installment is restricted in two ways: the nonconformity (1) must substantially impair the value of that installment and (2) must be one that could not be cured by the seller. The buyer can treat the defective performance of the installment as a breach of the whole contract only if it can be said to substantially impair the value of the whole contract.

In order to avoid acceptance, the buyer is required to take some action within a reasonable time after the goods are tendered or delivered to him. This is true even though the goods tendered or delivered do not come close to conforming to the contract. If the buyer rejects, he must seasonably notify the seller of this fact, and his failing to do so would render the rejection ineffective. The buyer can withdraw his rejection by a later acceptance if the seller has indicated that he is keeping the tender open. However, if the seller has changed his position upon the basis of the rejection, the buyer would be liable in damages if he thereafter exercised ownership of the goods.

A buyer who rejects the goods after taking physical possession of them is required to hold the goods with reasonable care, at the seller's disposition, for a time sufficient for the seller to remove them. If the buyer has paid all or part of the purchase price prior to his rejection, he has a security interest in the goods to that extent, and he may resell the goods to satisfy this claim. The security interest also includes expenses incurred in connection with such items as transportation and care and custody of the goods. Of course, the right to resell exists only if the rejection was rightful in all respects.

The merchant-buyer has a greater obligation with regard to goods he has rightfully rejected and which are in his possession. Subject to any security interest which the buyer may have in the goods, e.g., because of part payment or payment of shipping costs, a merchant-buyer is under a duty to follow any reasonable instructions from the seller with respect to what is to be done with the rejected goods. This duty arises if the seller does not have an agent or place of business at the market of rejection. If the seller does not furnish instructions as to the disposition of the rejected goods, the merchant-buyer must make reasonable efforts to sell them for the seller's account if they are perishable or if they threaten to decline in value speedily. The seller's instructions, however, need not be followed unless they are reasonable. They are not reasonable if the seller does not, upon the buyer's demand, agree to guarantee that expenses incurred in following the instructions will be paid by the seller. When the buyer resells the goods, he is entitled to reimbursement for his expenses in caring for the goods and selling them. Such expenses may be deducted from the proceeds if the seller does not pay them. For selling the goods, the reselling buyer is entitled to a commission on the basis of what is usual in the trade; otherwise, he will receive a reasonable sum not to exceed 10 percent of the gross proceeds.

If the seller does not give any instructions to the buyer within a reasonable time after notice of rejection, and if the goods are not perishable, the buyer has three options. He may store the rejected goods for the seller's account; he may reship them to the seller; or he may resell them for the seller's account. This provision enables the buyer to act with dispatch and safety when he faces the problem of what to do with rejected goods in the absence of instructions from the seller. His rights are predicated, of course, upon actual nonconformity of the goods *and* proper notice of rejection to the seller.

The requirement of notice of rejection is very important. Without such notice the rejection is ineffective. Accordingly, the Code sets forth particular rules with regard to this notice. These are designed to allow a simple procedure for the buyer and also provide for the protection of the seller. The notice of rejection may be simply to the effect that the goods are not conforming, without particular specification of the defects relied upon by the buyer. If, however, the defect could have been cured by the seller had he been given notice, then the failure to particularize will take away from the buyer the right to rely upon that defect as a breach justifying a rejection. On the assumption that particularization of defects is more important to a merchant-seller, special rules govern the notice that is required in transactions between merchants. Therefore, the merchant-seller is entitled to require that he be furnished a full and final written statement of all the defects, and if the statement is not forthcoming, the buyer may not rely upon such defects to justify his rejection or to establish that a breach has occurred.

3-35. Acceptance.   The buyer has *accepted* goods: (1) if after a reasonable opportunity to inspect them, he indicates to the seller that the goods are conforming or that he will take or retain them in spite of their nonconformity; (2) if he has failed to make an effective rejection of the goods; or (3) if he does any act inconsistent with the seller's ownership.[2]

The acceptance of the goods has several important effects insofar as the rights and duties of the buyer and seller are concerned. From the seller's point of view, it entitles him to receive the price of the goods. If the acceptance is partial, he becomes entitled to a pro rata portion based on the contract rate. As to the buyer, it means that he has lost his right to thereafter reject the goods. Thus acceptance establishes the framework within which the parties must operate thereafter.

The buyer may still revoke his acceptance under proper circumstances. In many instances, the buyer will have accepted nonconforming goods because either (1) the defects were not immediately discoverable, or (2) the buyer reasonably assumed that the seller would cure by substituting goods which did conform. In either of these events the buyer has the privilege of "revoking his acceptance" by notifying the seller of this fact. Such revocation must take place within a reasonable time after the buyer has discovered, or should have discovered, the reason for revocation. If a buyer revokes his acceptance, he is then placed in the same position with reference to the goods as if he had rejected them in the first instance.

Notice of nonconformity must be given to the seller within a reasonable time after the buyer has discovered it or should have discovered it. His failure to do so will bar him from any remedy. The buyer is required to inform the seller that he claims a breach has occurred.

The buyer who has accepted nonconforming goods may still within limits revoke the acceptance or, by giving proper notice, recover damages. It should be noted that the buyer and the seller may provide in their contract that the buyer's acceptance bars any remedies. Also, the continued use of the goods by

[2] Park County Implement Co. v. Craig, page 426

the buyer over a considerable period of time would indicate his satisfaction, even though the goods were nonconforming.

BUYER'S REMEDIES

3-36. In General. An aggrieved buyer's remedies depend on a variety of factors. He has a choice of remedies and a special remedy in the event of the seller's insolvency at a time when the seller is in possession of the goods which are the subject of the contract for sale. It will be noted that the buyer's remedies are in general the equivalent of those provided for the aggrieved seller.

The wrongful conduct of the seller which gives rise to the application of the remedies includes a failure to make delivery, repudiation of the contract, and a tender or delivery of nonconforming goods. Note, however, the right of the seller in some instances to cure a nonconforming tender.[3]

The Code provides that when the *seller* fails to make delivery or repudiates or the *buyer* rightfully rejects the goods or revokes his acceptance of them, then with respect to any goods involved, and with respect to the whole, if the breach goes to the whole contract, the buyer may cancel it. Cancellation means putting the contract to an end by reason of breach. It does not cut off the canceling party's remedies which arise by reason of the breach. Whether the aggrieved buyer cancels or not, he may recover any part of the price that he has paid, and he also has the right either to cover—obtain the goods from some other source—or to recover damages for nondelivery. In some situations the buyer may bring suit for specific performance or an action to recover the goods specified in the contract.

As noted previously, the buyer who rightfully rejects or justifiably revokes his acceptance has a security interest in goods in his possession or control for payments made and expenses incurred in connection with the goods.

The remedies of the buyer may be classified as those which permit the recovery of money damages and those which permit reaching the goods. The nature of the buyer's remedies will depend upon whether he (1) has rejected or has revoked his acceptance or (2) has finally accepted the goods.

3-37. Cover—Damages. The buyer who has not received the goods he bargained for may cover—arrange to purchase the goods he needed from some other source in substitution for those due from the seller. This is a practical remedy, as the buyer must often proceed without delay in order to obtain goods needed by him for his own use or for resale to others. The only limitation is that he must act reasonably and in good faith in arranging for the cover. He may recover from the seller the difference between what he paid for the substitute goods and the contract price. In addition, he may recover any incidental or consequential damages sustained. *Incidental damages* are defined as those which are reasonably incurred in connection with handling rejected goods, and "commercially reasonable charges, expenses or commissions in connection with effecting cover and any other reasonable expense incident to the delay or other breach." (U.C.C. 2-715(1)) *Consequential* damages include "any loss resulting from general or particular requirements and

---

[3] Zabriskie Chevrolet v. Smith, *supra*, page 424

needs of which the seller at the time of contracting had reason to know and which could not reasonably be prevented by cover or otherwise." (U.C.C. 2-715(2)) The buyer is thus obligated to keep his damages at a minimum by making an appropriate cover insofar as his right to any consequential damages is concerned.

The cover remedy has the advantage of providing certainty as to the amount of the buyer's damages. The difference between the contract price and the price paid by the buyer for substitute goods can be readily determined. While the buyer must act reasonably and in good faith, he need not prove that he obtained the goods at the cheapest price available.

3-38. Damages for Nondelivery or Repudiation.   The aggrieved buyer who did not receive any goods from the seller or who received nonconforming goods is not *required* to cover; instead, he may bring an action for damages. The measure of damages for nondelivery or repudiation is the difference between the *market price at the time when the buyer learned of the breach* and the contract price. The buyer is also entitled to any incidental or consequential damages that he has suffered.

The aggrieved buyer's damages are, in effect, determined on the basis of the difference between what the goods would have cost had the buyer elected to cover and the contract price. The market price would be that prevailing at the place at which the buyer would have attempted to cover. The Code has provisions for situations in which it is difficult to determine what the prevailing price may be.

3-39. Damages—Accepted Goods.   As noted, a buyer who has accepted goods may in certain circumstances revoke his acceptance and thereby place himself in the same position as if he had rejected the goods in the first instance. He could then exercise the remedies described in the preceding sections. The Code provides a remedy for the buyer who has accepted nonconforming goods and who does not have the power to revoke his acceptance. In order to avail himself of the right to damages, the buyer must have seasonably notified the seller of the breach.

The Code provides that the buyer may "recover as damages for any nonconformity of tender the loss resulting in the ordinary course of events from the seller's breach as determined in any manner which is reasonable." (U.C.C. 2-714(1)) The buyer can deduct the damages from the amount which is still due in payment for the goods.

Nonconformity includes any breach of warranty with regard to the goods. Accordingly, if the goods were not as warranted, the buyer can recover damages measured by the difference between the actual value of the goods and the value they would have had if they had been as warranted. Also included in the damages are personal injuries or property damage proximately caused by the breach of warranty.

3-40. Right to Goods.   Under proper circumstances the buyer has rights in and to the goods. The Code makes available the remedy of specific performance when the goods are unique and also where other circumstances make it equitable that the seller render the required performance. It would appear that in order to invoke this remedy the buyer must have been unable to cover. While the Code does not define "unique," it is fair to assume that it would encompass output and requirement contracts in which the goods are not readily or practically available from other sources. The choice of specific performance as a remedy is not exclusive, in that a court may also award damages or other relief.

Another remedy is that of replevin, the right to obtain the goods which are identified to the contract. This remedy is available only if the buyer is unable to cover.

A related remedy which also reaches the goods in the hands of the seller is the buyer's right to recover them if the seller becomes insolvent. The right arises only if (1) the buyer has a "special property" in the goods and (2) the seller becomes insolvent within ten days after he received the first installment payment from the buyer. Absent such factors, the buyer is relegated to the position of a general creditor of the seller. It is apparent that if the buyer can recover the goods, he is in a much better position than he would be as a general creditor, particularly if he had paid a substantial amount of the purchase price. In order to exercise this remedy the buyer must make and keep good a tender of any unpaid portion of the price.

3-41. Deduction of Damages. The Code provides that the aggrieved buyer may deduct the damages resulting from any breach of contract from any part of the price still due under the same contract. The buyer is thus enabled to determine, in conformity with the principles established by the Code, what his damages are, and he may withhold this amount when he pays the seller. He is required to give notice to the seller of his intention to deduct. Where the buyer's damages are established by the cover price, the amount would be clear-cut. In other instances the seller might question the amount of the deduction, and this dispute would have to be resolved between the parties.

It is to be noted that the damages may be deducted only as against the price due under the *same* contract. Accordingly, a buyer could not deduct damages for goods under one contract from the price due under other contracts from the same seller.

SELLER'S REMEDIES

3-42. In General. The remedies for an aggrieved seller allow him in some instances to retain or reclaim the goods and in others to recover damages or the price of the goods. One remedy is available when the seller becomes aware of the fact that the buyer is insolvent, and thus doubt is cast upon his ability to pay for the goods. Basically, the remedy is in this instance to reach the goods.

Other remedies arise because of the improper conduct of the buyer. When the buyer fails to live up to the terms of the contract and thereby disappoints the seller's expectation that he will accept the goods and pay for them, the aggrieved seller usually has the choice of several courses of action or remedies. He will therefore select that course of action which produces the best result for him. The wrongful conduct of the buyer, which brings the seller's remedies into play, may consist of any of the following:

1. The buyer wrongfully rejects goods tendered by the seller.

2. The buyer having accepted the goods thereafter wrongfully revokes his prior acceptance of them.

3. The buyer fails to make a payment which was specified as due on or before delivery of the goods.

4. The buyer repudiates the contract—announces before the time he is to receive the goods that he will not live up to his obligations as a buyer.

5. The buyer fails to pay the price as it becomes due.

The Code enumerates the remedies available to the seller who is aggrieved because of this wrongful conduct. They are to

1. Withhold delivery.
2. Stop delivery of the goods by the bailee.
3. Identify the goods to the contract if this has not been done prior to the breach.
4. Resell the goods and recover damages.
5. Recover damages for nonacceptance.
6. Recover the price of the goods.
7. Cancel the contract.

It will thus be noted that there is a remedy which is suited to the reasonable needs of the seller in a variety of circumstances. The remedies are cumulative, and the exercise of one does not necessarily bar the others. Which of these remedies would be available to a seller in any given case will depend upon the nature of the buyer's breach and the nature, condition, and location of the goods involved.

3-43. Insolvency.   Upon discovery of the insolvency of the buyer to whom he has sold goods on credit, the seller will be best protected if he can reclaim the goods from such buyer. A person is insolvent "who either has ceased to pay his debts in the ordinary course of business or cannot pay his debts as they become due or is insolvent within the meaning of the federal bankruptcy law." (U.C.C. 1-201(23))

Obviously, a claim against an insolvent person is of doubtful value, and the Code accordingly makes provision for some relief to a seller who has dealings with such a person. Upon discovering that the buyer is insolvent, the seller may refuse to make any further deliveries except for cash, and he may demand that payment be made for all goods theretofore delivered under the contract. If goods are enroute to the buyer, they may be stopped in transit and recovered from the carrier. If they are in a warehouse or other place of storage awaiting delivery to the buyer, the seller may stop delivery by the bailee. Thus, the seller can protect his interests by retaining or reclaiming the goods prior to the time they come into the possession of the insolvent buyer.

This right to reclaim the goods has been extended by the Code to include situations in which the goods have come into the buyer's possession. If the buyer has received goods on credit while he is insolvent, the seller can reclaim the goods by making a demand for them within ten days after their receipt by the buyer. He must act within the ten-day period in order to exercise this right.[4] By receiving the goods the buyer has, in effect, made a representation that he is solvent and able to pay for them. If the buyer has made a written misrepresentation of solvency within the three-month period before the goods were delivered to him, and the seller has justifiably relied on the writing, the period during which the seller can reclaim the goods from the insolvent buyer is extended. To extend the time period, all of the usual elements of misrepresentation are required.

The importance to a seller of the privilege of reclaiming goods or stopping them in transit should be stressed. If the insolvent buyer is adjudicated a bankrupt, the goods will become a part of the bankrupt estate and will be sold by the trustee in bankruptcy for the benefit of *all* the creditors of the buyer. If the seller is able to reclaim the goods, his loss will be kept to a minimum, but by the same token, he will be deprived of any claim against the insolvent person for damages.

If the buyer within the ten-day or three-month period has sold the goods to an innocent purchaser, such purchaser will be protected against the claim of the creditor that the goods be surrendered.

3-44. Withhold or Stop Delivery. The right to stop goods in transit or in the hands of a bailee, or to withhold delivery is not restricted to the insolvency situation. Where the buyer has wrongfully rejected a tender of goods, revoked his acceptance, failed to make a payment due on or before delivery, or repudiated with respect to either a part of the goods or the whole contract, the seller can also use this remedy. His right extends to any goods directly affected by the breach, and if the breach is of the whole contract, then also to the whole undelivered balance. If the contract is an installment contract and the breach with respect to one or more installments substantially impairs the value of the whole contract, it will be treated as a breach of the whole.

The right to withhold or stop delivery on the basis of failure to make a payment due also extends to the dishonor of a check given in payment.

In order to exercise his right to stop delivery by a carrier, the seller must give proper and timely notice to such carrier so that there is reasonable time to follow the instructions given. Once the goods have been received by the buyer or the bailee has acknowledged that he holds the goods for the buyer, the right of stoppage is at an end. Except in the case of insolvency as previously noted, the seller cannot reclaim the goods after they are in the buyer's possession.

The right to stop delivery is here restricted to carload, truckload, planeload, or larger shipments. This restriction is designed to ease the burden on carriers which could develop if the right to stop for reasons other than insolvency applied to all small shipments. The seller who is shipping to a buyer of doubtful credit can always send the goods C.O.D. and thus preclude the necessity for stopping in transit. Of course, the seller must exercise care in availing himself of this remedy, as improper stoppage is a breach by the seller and would subject him to an action for damages by the buyer.

Certainly the right to withhold or stop delivery is a valuable tool to the seller, since once the goods are in the buyer's possession, the likelihood of a

---

[4] Stumbo v. Paul B. Hult Lumber Co., page 427

successful outcome is often quite remote, and it may be necessary to litigate in order to resolve the differences between buyer and seller.

3-45. Resale.   The seller who has reclaimed goods, withheld them, or is otherwise in possession of goods at the time of the buyer's breach or repudiation has the right to resell the goods. If part of the goods have been delivered, he can resell the undelivered portion. In this way the seller can quickly realize at least a part of the amount due from the buyer; he also has a claim against the buyer for the difference between the resale price and the price which the buyer had agreed to pay. To the extent that the seller suffered additional damages, he is also entitled to recover these. The resale remedy thus affords a very practical method and course of action for the seller who has possession of goods which were intended for a breaching buyer.

The right to resell is a very broad one, and the Code makes the mechanics of the process simple yet fair. The resale may be either private or public (auction sale). It must be identified as one relating to the broken contract. Where the resale is private, the seller must give the buyer reasonable notification of his intention to resell. If the resale is public, the seller must give the buyer reasonable notice of the time and place so that he can bid or can obtain the attendance of other bidders. With goods that are perishable or threaten to speedily decline in value, the notice is not required. The seller is permitted to buy at a public sale. The rules set forth in the Code regarding resale are easily complied with and are designed to assure fairness. The prime requirement is that the sale be conducted in a commercially reasonable manner.

It is to be noted that the resale could conceivably bring a higher price than that provided for in the contract. Then the seller is not accountable to the buyer for any profit.

3-46. Damages for Nonacceptance or Repudiation.   In many situations resale would not be an appropriate or satisfactory remedy. The seller may elect to bring an action for damages if the buyer refuses to accept the goods or repudiates the contract. The measure of damages is the difference between the market price at the time and place for tender and the unpaid contract price, plus incidental damages. The seller, of course, retains ownership of the goods. If the market price is for some reason difficult to ascertain, the Code provides reasonable leeway in receiving evidence of prices current in other comparable markets or at other times comparable to the one in question.

In some situations this measure of damages would not be adequate to restore the seller to as good a position as would have been accomplished by performance by the buyer. Under such circumstances the measure of damages is the profit which the seller would have made from full performance by the buyer. In computing profit, the reasonable overhead of the seller may be taken into account.

This remedy recognizes that a seller may have suffered a loss, even though he may ultimately resell for the same amount that he would have received from the buyer. He has lost a sale, and the profit on the sale should be a factor taken into account. Thus, a dealer in office furniture may have entered into a contract for the sale of a number of desks, chairs, and filing cabinets at a price of $15,000. He has a warehouse which contains hundreds of each item and maintains at all times a large inventory. If the buyer were to refuse to accept the items contracted for or were to repudiate the contract, the seller could, and would of course ultimately, sell these items to other parties, but the fact remains that as a result of the breach, the seller has lost the profit which he would have made had the buyer properly performed. The remedy would generally include all standard-priced goods.

3-47. Recovery of the Price.   When the buyer fails to pay the price as it becomes due, the seller may sue for the contract price of the goods if (1) the goods were accepted by the buyer; (2) the goods were lost or damaged within a commercially reasonable time after the risk of loss passed to the buyer; or (3) the goods were identified to the contract and the seller was unable to sell them at a reasonable price, or the circumstances indicated that the effort to do so would be unavailing. Thus an action for the price is generally limited to those situations in which the buyer has accepted the goods, the goods were destroyed after risk of loss passed to the buyer, or the resale remedy is not practicable. In other cases the damage remedy would be used.

If the seller sues for the price, the goods involved are, of course, held by the seller on behalf of the buyer; they become in effect the buyer's goods. After the seller obtains a judgment against the buyer, the seller may still resell the goods at any time prior to collection of the judgment, but he must apply the proceeds toward satisfaction of the judgment. Payment of the balance due on the judgment entitles the buyer to any goods not resold.

The seller may be unsuccessful in his suit for the price, as when the court rules that he has not sustained the burden of proof with regard to the impracticability of resale. But in the same action the court may award damages for nonacceptance to the seller who is unsuccessful in his suit for the price.

3-48. Identify Goods to the Contract.   This remedy is ancillary to those discussed in the previous section. The aggrieved seller who had not at the time he learned of the breach or repudiation identified the goods to the contract may proceed to do so. Having done so, he may then pursue his remedy of resale or an action for the price if resale is not practicable. The aggrieved seller, however, may identify goods to the contract regardless of their resalability. If the goods are unfinished, the seller may treat these as the subject of resale if he can establish that the unfinished goods were intended for the particular contract.

In addition, the seller can complete the manufacture of unfinished goods and identify these to the contract or resell the goods for scrap or salvage value. This judgment on the part of the seller as to the action he will take with regard to unfinished goods pertains to the doctrine of mitigation of damages. He is to decide on the basis of "reasonable commercial judgment for the purposes of avoiding loss and of effective realization. . . . " (U.C.C. 2-704(2)) Presumably, an important factor would be the extent to which the manufacture had been completed at the time the seller learned of the breach. Another factor would be the resalability of the goods if the manufacture were completed.

Thus, the seller, by virtue of the foregoing, is able to utilize his other remedies in much the same fashion as if the goods had been completed and identified at the time he learned of the breach.

3-49. Seller's Incidental Damages.   In addition to his recovery of the price or damages, the aggrieved seller is entitled to incidental damages. The purpose is to allow reimbursement to the aggrieved seller for expenses reasonably incurred and damages incurred as the result of the buyer's breach.[5] For example, in addition to the usual damages for the breach, the seller who stopped goods in transit would be entitled to recover the expenses of stopping the goods and obtaining their return to his place of business. These incidental damages round out the reimbursement of the aggrieved seller.

MISCELLANEOUS MATTERS AFFECTING THE SALE OF GOODS

3-50. Liquidation of Damages.   The damages for breach by either the buyer or the seller may be liquidated, i.e., provided for in advance by their agreement. However, such liquidated damages must be reasonable in light of several factors: (1) the anticipated or actual harm caused by the breach, (2) the difficulties of proof of loss, and (3) the inconvenience or nonfeasibility of otherwise obtaining an adequate remedy. As in general contract law, a term fixing unreasonably large liquidated damages is void as a penalty.

In keeping with the trend to avoid penalties for breaches of contract and to prevent a windfall for sellers, the Code provides for restitution to the buyer of a part of the payments made to the seller prior to his breach in certain cases. Where the seller justifiably withholds delivery of goods to the buyer because of the latter's breach, e.g., he has defaulted in his payments, the seller is not permitted to retain all of the payments made by the buyer. He must return to the buyer that amount which is in excess of the liquidated damages term of the contract. If there is no provision for liquidated damages, he must return 20 percent of the "value of the total performance for which the buyer is obligated under the contract or $500, whichever is smaller." (U.C.C. 2-718(2)(b)) The seller, however, is entitled to set off against this amount any damages which he can establish against the buyer. Thus the seller might be able to establish incidental damages resulting from the buyer's breach and could deduct this from the amount which he would otherwise have to return to the buyer.[6]

The provision relating to restitution applies to amounts deposited by the buyer as security for his performance as well as to down payments or part payments.

3-51. Modification and Limitation.   Related to the preceding section are contractual provisions by which the parties have limited or modified the remedies for breach. By agreement, the parties can provide for remedies in addition to those set forth by the Code. Likewise they can replace Code remedies with those they have designed. The measure of damages provided by the Code may be limited or altered. For example, the agreement may limit the buyer's remedies to return of the goods and repayment of the price or to replacement of goods or parts.

The parties may limit or exclude consequential damages, and such limitations and exclusions will be enforced if they are not unconscionable. It is

[5] Keystone Diesel Engine Co. v. Irwin, page 428
[6] Procter & Gamble D. Co. v. Lawrence Amer. F.W. Corp. et al., page 429

interesting to note that under the Code a limitation of consequential damages for injury to the *person* in the case of *consumer goods* is prima facie unconscionable, but limitations where the loss is commercial are not. This will be discussed in detail in the next chapter dealing with warranties and product liability.

The Code leaves the parties free to shape their own remedies to their specific needs and requirements, but it does require that there be a certain minimum of adequate remedies and that the contract not be unconscionable.[7]

3-52. Suits Against Third Parties. In the event that some third party so deals with goods as to cause a loss to the buyer or the seller, a question arises as to who may bring suit against such third party. The problem would present itself where the goods have been identified to the contract. For example, *A* has contracted to sell a machine to *B,* and *C* negligently damages the machine while it is still on *A's* property. The Code provides that the right of action against the third party, *C,* is in either party who has *title* to or a *security interest* or a *special property* or an *insurable interest* in the goods.[8] The loss could be of any sort and would not be limited to destruction or wrongful use of the property. However, if it is either of these, the party who bore the risk of loss under the contract for sale is also a proper party plaintiff. The basic idea behind the provision is to allow the real party in interest to bring the action. Obviously, both the buyer and the seller could have an interest in a proceeding against the third party. This would be especially true during the period between identification and final acceptance. In this event, the parties could agree upon who would bring action, and any recovery would be for the benefit of both.

3-53. Clarification Provisions. It must be remembered that the Code was drafted with the purpose of overcoming certain drawbacks in prior case law which interfered with desirable commercial practices. Under pre-Code law there was a lack of clarity as to the meaning of certain terms such as "cancellation" and "rescission" as applied to a contract. Also, there was a general concept that rescission precluded any right to recover damages for a breach. The Code defines "cancellation" in such a way as to make it clear that the party who cancels retains any remedy for breach of the contract. "Termination" occurs when either party puts an end to a contract otherwise than for its breach. Here also, while the termination discharges all obligations which are still executory on both sides, any right based on a prior breach or a prior performance survives.

In order to bring all of this into proper perspective and to safeguard a person holding a right of action from any unintentional loss of his rights because of his carelessly or ill-advisedly using terms like "rescission" or "cancellation," the Code provides: "Unless the contrary intention clearly appears, expressions of 'cancellation' or 'rescission' of the contract or the like shall not be construed as a renunciation or discharge of any claim in damages for an antecedent breach." (U.C.C. 2-720) To illustrate, a person might be willing to cancel a contract for the sale and purchase of a machine which did not function

[7] Wilson Trading Corp. v. David Ferguson, Ltd., page 430
[8] National Compressor Corp. v. Carrow, page 432

properly, but he would not thereby forego his right to damages to the extent that the malfunction had interfered with his operation and his ability to service his customers.

3-54. Statute of Limitations.   Statutes of limitations were discussed in Chapter 16. Basically such statutes provide that a person who has a legal cause of action against another must bring his suit within a limited period of time; otherwise it will be barred or outlawed.

The Code provides that an action for breach of a contract for sale must be brought within four years after it accrued. The parties, however, may shorten this period to not less than one year. They cannot, however, extend it beyond four years.

The Code resolves the question, When does a cause of action *accrue*? The rules are

1. A cause of action accrues when the breach occurs, regardless of the aggrieved party's lack of knowledge of the breach.
2. A breach of warranty with respect to goods occurs when tender of delivery of the goods is made to the buyer.
3. If the warranty is expressly related to *future performance* of the goods, the cause of action does not accrue until the breach is discovered or should have been discovered.

It will be noted that this section takes sales contracts out of the general laws limiting the time for commencing contractual actions. The four-year period includes actions for personal injuries based on the theory of breach of warranty as well as breach of contract actions. The four-year period was selected because this is the normal commercial record-keeping period. State law relating to the tolling of the statute of limitations continues to be controlling under the Code.

RIGHTS, REMEDIES, AND OBLIGATIONS CASES

Zabriskie Chevrolet, Inc. v. Smith
240 A.2d 195 (N.J.) 1968

DOAN, J. This action arises out of the sale by plaintiff to defendant of a new 1966 Chevrolet automobile. Within a short distance after leaving the showroom the vehicle became almost completely inoperable by reason of mechanical failure. Defendant the same day notified plaintiff that he cancelled the sale and simultaneously stopped payment on the check he had tendered in payment of the balance of the purchase price. Plaintiff sues on the check and the purchase order for the balance of the purchase price plus incidental damages and defendant counterclaims for the return of his deposit and incidental damages. . . .

. . . [T]he . . . issue presented is whether defendant properly rejected under the Code. That he cancelled the sale and rejected the vehicle almost concomitantly with the discovery of the failure of his bargain is clear from the evidence. N.J.S. 12A:2-601, N.J.S.A. delineates the buyer's rights following nonconforming delivery and reads as follows:

. . . if the goods or the tender of delivery *fail in any respect to conform* to the contract, the buyer may

    (a) reject the whole; . . . " [Italics added.]

Section 12A:2-602 indicates that one can reject after taking possession. Possession, therefore, does not mean acceptance and the corresponding loss of the right of rejection. . . . "Rejection of goods must be within a reasonable time after their delivery or tender. It is ineffective unless the buyer seasonably notifies the seller." . . .

N.J.S. 12A:2-106, N.J.S.A. defines conforming goods as follows:

(2) Goods or conduct including any part of a performance are "conforming" or conform to the contract when they are in accordance with the obligations under the contract.

The Uniform Commercial Code Comment to that section states:

2. Subsection (2): It is in general intended to continue the policy of requiring *exact performance* by the seller of his obligations as a condition to his right to require acceptance. However, the seller is in part safeguarded against surprise as a result of sudden technicality on the buyer's part by the provisions on seller's cure of improper tender or delivery. . . .

In the present case we are not dealing with a situation such as was present in *Adams* v. *Tramontin Motor Sales* (42 N.J.Super. 313, (App.Div.1956)). In that case, brought for breach of implied warranty of merchantability, the court held that minor defects, such as adjustment of the motor, tightening of loose elements, fixing of locks and dome light, and a correction of rumbling noise, were not remarkable defects, and therefore there was no breach. Here the breach was substantial. The new car was practically inoperable and endowed with a defective transmission. This was a "remarkable defect" and justified rejection by the buyer. . . . [P]laintiff urges that under the Code, it had a right to cure the nonconforming delivery. N.J.S. 12A:2-508, N.J.S.A. states:

(1) Where any tender or delivery by the seller is rejected because non-conforming, and the *time for performance has not yet expired,* the seller may seasonably notify the buyer of his intention to cure and may then within the contract time make a conforming delivery.

(2) Where the buyer rejects a non-conforming tender which the *seller had reasonable grounds to believe would be acceptable* with or without money allowance the seller may if he seasonably notifies the buyer have a further reasonable time to substitute a conforming tender. [Italics added]. . . .

The Uniform Commercial Code Comment to 12A:2-508 reads:

2. Subsection (2) seeks to avoid injustice to the seller by reason of a surprise rejection by the buyer. However, the seller is not protected unless he had "reasonable grounds to believe" that the tender would be acceptable.

It is clear that in the instant case there was no "forced breach" on the part of the buyer, for he almost immediately began to negotiate for another automobile. The inquiry is as to what is intended by "cure," as used in the Code. This statute makes no attempt to define or specify what a "cure" shall consist of. It would appear, then, that each case must be controlled by its own facts. The "cure" intended under the cited section of the Code does not, in the court's opinion, contemplate the tender of a new vehicle with a substituted transmission, not from the factory and of unknown lineage from another vehicle in plaintiff's possession. It was not the intention of the Legislature that the right to "cure" is a limitless one to be controlled only by the will of the seller. A "cure" which endeavors by substitution to tender a chattel not within the agreement or contemplation of the parties is invalid.

For a majority of people the purchase of a new car is a major investment, rationalized by the peace of mind that flows from its dependability and safety. Once their faith is shaken, the vehicle loses not only its real value in their eyes, but becomes an instrument whose integrity is substantially impaired and whose operation is fraught with apprehension. The attempted cure in the present case was ineffective.

Accordingly, judgment is rendered on the main case in favor of defendant. On the counterclaim judgment is rendered in favor of defendant and against plaintiff....

Park County Implement Co. v. Craig

397 P.2d 800 (Wyo.) 1964

PARKER, J. Plaintiff sued defendants for the amount due on a purchase of a truck chassis and cab.... [T]he court entered a summary judgment for defendants, from which judgment this appeal is taken.

On February 16, 1962, defendants ordered a 1962 International A-162 chassis and cab from plaintiff, which advised that one was not on hand but should be in the area. Three days later defendants were informed that such a vehicle was at the International Harvester Company in Billings, Montana, whereupon defendant Holler drove to Billings and there received the vehicle from that company, asking the International employee from whom the vehicle was received for a statement of origin, title certificate, or some evidence of title. The employee responded that the company did not have the same. The agreed selling price was approximately $3,150 delivered in Cody, Wyoming, or approximately $3,115 if defendants took delivery of the truck at Billings. ... [D]efendants brought the vehicle to Cody, put it in their shop, and were installing a hoist and dump bed when a fire occurred March 1, destroying the chassis and cab. Defendants said [that since they did not have a title, they had no liability]. ...

[T]he transaction in this case was within the Uniform Commercial Code-Sales. The buyers accepted the goods under the provisions of 34-2-606(1)(c), ... "Acceptance of goods occurs when the buyer does any act inconsistent with the seller's ownership," when they began installing a hoist and dump bed on the vehicle. At that time the buyer became liable under the provisions of 34-2-607(1), "The buyer must pay at the contract rate for any goods accepted." ...

Under the admitted facts the defendants accepted the goods at an agreed price. The summary judgment granted to defendants was in error; the motion of plaintiff for summary judgment should have been granted. The cause is reversed with instructions to enter judgment for plaintiff.

   Reversed.

Stumbo v. Paul B. Hult Lumber Co.

444 P.2d 564 (Oreg.) 1968

The plaintiffs had sold and delivered logs to Keystone Lumber Company. The lumber company suffered a fire which destroyed the mill, and the insurance proceeds were not sufficient to cover its obligations. The plaintiffs, who had not been paid, proceeded to remove logs from Keystone's storage area and sold them to Hult, who processed them into lumber. The proceeds of this sale are now in question. The holder of a security interest in the logs, claims them, as do the plaintiffs. The lawsuit was for a declaratory judgment as to the rights of the various parties. The lower court ruled for the plaintiff, and the defendant appeals.

   O'CONNELL, J. . . . The Code provides that a seller of goods may, under certain circumstances, recover goods delivered to the buyer. Thus ORS 72.-7020(2) permits a reclamation of goods from a buyer who received the goods while insolvent. However, reclamation under this section is conditioned upon a demand made within ten days after the receipt of the goods by the buyer. No such demand was made in the present case.

   A seller also may have the right to recover goods from a buyer under ORS 72.5070(2), which provides as follows:

> (2) Where payment is due and demanded on the delivery to the buyer of goods or documents of title, his right as against the seller to retain or dispose of them is conditional upon his making the payment due.

However, plaintiffs acquired no interest in the logs under the foregoing section for the reason that payment was neither "due" nor "demanded" on the delivery of the logs. . . .

   Plaintiffs contend that their removal of the logs constituted a reclamation of goods under ORS 72.7050(1). That section provides as follows:

> (1) The seller may stop delivery of goods in the possession of a carrier or other bailee when he discovers the buyer to be insolvent as provided in ORS 72.7020 and may stop delivery of carload, truckload, planeload or large shipments of express or freight when the buyer repudiates or fails to make a payment due before delivery or if for any other reason the seller has a right to withhold or reclaim the goods.

This section is applicable only when goods are in the process of delivery and before the buyer has acquired possession. It cannot be understood as providing an independent right of recovery of goods in the possession of a buyer. The language "or if for any other reason the seller has a right to withhold or reclaim goods" clearly is intended to indicate only that a seller may stop the delivery of goods in transit or in the possession of a bailee where the conditions of withholding or recovering goods from the buyer himself are otherwise satisfied. In the present case all of the logs had been delivered to Keystone's millpond before plaintiffs attempted to reclaim them. . . .

   Consequently, we conclude that plaintiffs had no right to recover the logs from Keystone and were no more than unsecured general creditors without any interest in particular assets of Keystone, including the logs taken from Keystone's millpond. The security interest of M D M was clearly superior to the claim of such a creditor. . . .

Reversed and remanded.

Keystone Diesel Engine Co. v. Irwin

191 A.2d 376 (Pa.) 1963

The plaintiff, Keystone Diesel, sold a diesel engine to the defendant who operates tractor-trailers as a contract carrier. The engine was installed in one of the defendant's tractors. It did not function properly, and the plaintiff made repairs and modifications at its own expense. Subsequent repairs were required, and the plaintiff billed the defendant for these in the amount of $623.08. Defendant contended that he should not have to pay. Plaintiff brought suit for the amount of the repairs, and the defendant counterclaimed for $5,150 for loss of the use of the tractor for twenty-seven days as the result of breakdowns. The lower court struck the counterclaim. Defendant appealed.

EAGEN, J. . . . Where a contract is breached without legal justification, the injured party is entitled to recover (absent contrary provisions in the contract) whatever damages he suffered, provided (1) they were such as would naturally and ordinarily follow from the breach; (2) they were reasonably foreseeable and within the contemplation of the parties at the time they made the contract; (3) they can be proved with reasonable certainty.

There is no doubt that in a contract of this nature a breach causing malfunction of the engine would produce a halt in productive capacity and some damage could flow therefrom. Moreover, there would be no difficulty in measuring these damages with reasonable accuracy. The real issue to be determined is whether the damages sought for loss of profit were within the contemplation of the parties to the contract here in dispute.

The Uniform Commercial Code provisions which are appropriate in the instant case read as follows:

> The measure of damages for breach of warranty is the difference at the time and the place of acceptance between the value of the goods accepted and the value they would have had if they had been as warranted, unless *special circumstances* show proximate damages of a different amount.
>
> In a proper case any incidental and consequential damages under the next section may also be recovered.
>
> Consequential damages *resulting from the seller's breach* include (a) any loss resulting from general or particular requirements and needs of which the seller at the time of contracting had reason to know and which could not reasonably be prevented by cover or otherwise.

"Special circumstances" entitling the buyer to damages in excess of the difference between the values as warranted and the value as accepted exist where the buyer has communicated to the seller at the time of entering into the contract sufficient facts to make it apparent that the damages subsequently claimed were within the reasonable contemplation of the parties. The language in *Globe Refining Co.* v. *Landa Cotton Oil Co.* (190 U.S. 540, at 545, (1903), 23 S.Ct. 754 at 756, 47 L.Ed. 1171) gives the rationale of the foregoing rule as follows: "[O]ne of two contracting parties ought not to be allowed to obtain an advantage which he has not paid for . . . . If [a liability for the full profits that might be made by machinery which the defendant was transporting . . .] had been presented to the mind of the ship owner at the time of making the contract, as the basis upon which he was contracting, he would at once have rejected it. . . . The knowledge must be brought home to the party sought to be charged, under such circumstances that he must know that the person he contracts with reasonably believes that he accepts the contract with the special condition attached to it."

In the case at bar, no facts are alleged that would put the plaintiff on guard to the fact that the defendant would hold the plaintiff responsible for any loss of profit arising from the inability to use the engine in question. Following the defendant's theory to its logical conclusion, whenever a motor vehicle is sold for use in a profit motivated enterprise and the seller warrants that the vehicle will function properly, the seller will be liable in damages for a breach of warranty to the extent of profits lost on completely unrelated business contracts, where those profits are lost due to the vehicle malfunctioning.

In *Macchia* v. *Megow* (355 Pa. 565, 569, 50 A.2d 314, 316 (1947), the rule was stated, "Parties, when they enter into contracts, may well be presumed to contemplate the ordinary and natural incidents and consequences of performance or non-performance; but they are not supposed to know the conditions of each other's affairs, nor to take into consideration any existing or contemplated transactions, not communicated nor known, with other persons. Few persons would enter into contracts of any considerable extent as to subject-matter or time if they should thereby incidentally assume the responsibility of carrying out, or be held legally affected by, other arrangements over which they have no control and the existence of which are [*sic*] unknown to them." (Sutherland on Damages, 4th ed. vol. 1, p. 182, § 47) Anticipated profits are not recoverable unless within the contemplation of the parties when the contract was made. Clearly, the claim for loss of profits in the instant case was not within the contemplation of the parties to this contract.

The order of the court below is affirmed.

Procter & Gamble D. Co. v. Lawrence Amer. F.W. Corp. et al.

213 N.E.2d 873 (Ohio) 1965

The plaintiff was the holder of warehouse receipts for oil stored in the warehouse. When the receipts were presented, it was discovered that the oil was not in the tanks. There was no explanation for the missing oil. The oil had been sold to Allied Crude Vegetable Oil Refining Corporation, and that company had paid part of the purchase price. Allied had defaulted on its contract to purchase, and one of the questions in the case was the right of Allied to recover part of the purchase price it had paid.

VAN VOORHIS, J. . . . It was firmly settled in New York and in New Jersey that one who has failed to perform his part of an executory contract of sale may not recover the purchase money he has paid thereon. It was so held also in most of the rest of the United States. This has been changed by the Uniform Commercial Code. . . . These sections destroy the old rule that the buyer forfeits his down payment by breaching the contract, by providing that where the seller justifiably withholds delivery of goods because of the buyer's breach, the buyer is entitled to restitution of any amount by which the sum of his payments exceeds reasonable liquidated damages specified in the agreement, or "in the absence of such terms, twenty per cent of the value of the total performance for which the buyer is obligated under the contract or $500, whichever is smaller."

That does not necessarily mean, however, that plaintiff would be entitled to retain as against Allied only $500 of the $217,279.66 which was Allied's part payment on these contracts. The Uniform Commercial Code allows the seller actual damages where liquidated damages have not been stipulated . . . . They include (§ 2-708) damages measured by "the difference between the market price at the time and place for tender and the unpaid contract price" together with any incidental damages provided by section 2-710, plus whatever amount may be necessary "to put the seller in as good a position as performance would have done."

Manifestly, if Allied defaulted on these contracts, plaintiff was entitled to retain as against Allied so much of the $217,279.66 part payment as would be necessary to offset its damages due to a falling market plus incidental damages, such as extra transportation, storage, legal expense, and other items to which it was subjected by Allied's default. . . .

Wilson Trading Corp. v. David Ferguson, Ltd.
244 N.E.2d 685 (N.Y.) 1968

JASEN, J. The plaintiff, Wilson Trading Corporation, entered into a contract with the defendant, David Ferguson, Ltd., for the sale of a specified quantity of yarn. After the yarn was delivered, cut and knitted into sweaters, the finished product was washed. It was during this washing that it was discovered that the color of the yarn had "shaded"—that is, "there was a variation in color from piece to piece and within the pieces." This defect, the defendant claims, rendered the sweaters "unmarketable."

This action for the contract price of the yarn was commenced after the defendant refused payment. As a defense to the action and as a counterclaim for damages, the defendant alleges that "[p]laintiff has failed to perform all of the conditions of the contract on its part required to be performed, and has delivered . . . defective and unworkmanlike goods."

The sales contract provides in pertinent part:

> 2. No claims relating to excessive moisture content, short weight, count variations, twist, quality or shade shall be allowed *if made after weaving, knitting, or processing,* or more than 10 days after receipt of shipment. . . . The buyer shall within 10 days of the receipt of the merchandise by himself or agent examine the merchandise for any and all defects. [Emphasis supplied.]
>
> 4. This instrument constitutes the entire agreement between the parties, superseding all previous communications, oral or written, and no changes, amendments or additions hereto will be recognized unless in writing signed by both seller and buyer or buyer's agent. It is expressly agreed that no representations or warranties, express or implied, have been or are made by the seller except as stated herein, and the seller makes no warranty, express or implied, as to the fitness for buyer's purposes of yarn purchased hereunder, seller's obligations, except as expressly stated herein, being

limited to the *delivery of good merchantable yarn of the description stated herein.* [Emphasis supplied.]

Special Term granted plaintiff summary judgment for the contract price of the yarn sold on the ground that "notice of the alleged breach of warranty for defect in shading was not given within the time expressly limited and is not now available by way of defense or counterclaim." The Appellate Division affirmed, without opinion.

The defendant on this appeal urges that the time limitation provision on claims in the contract was unreasonable since the defect in the color of the yarn was latent and could not be discovered until after the yarn was processed and the finished product washed.

Defendant's affidavits allege that its sweaters were rendered unsaleable because of latent defects in the yarn which caused "variation in color from piece to piece and within the pieces." This allegation is sufficient to create a question of fact concerning the merchantability of the yarn (Uniform Commercial Code, § 2-314, subd. [2]). Indeed, the plaintiff does not seriously dispute the fact that its yarn was unmerchantable, but instead, like Special Term, relies upon the failure of defendant to give notice of the breach of warranty within the time limits prescribed by paragraph 2 of the contract.

Subdivision (3) (par. [a]) of section 2-607 of the Uniform Commercial Code expressly provides that a buyer who accepts goods has a reasonable time after he discovers or should have discovered a breach to notify the seller of such breach. . . . Defendant's affidavits allege that a claim was made immediately upon discovery of the breach of warranty after the yarn was knitted and washed, and that this was the earliest possible moment at which the defects could reasonably be discovered in the normal manufacturing process. Defendant's affidavits are, therefore, sufficient to create a question of fact concerning whether notice of the latent defects alleged was given within a reasonable time. . . .

However, the Uniform Commercial Code allows the parties, within limits established by the code, to modify or exclude warranties and to limit remedies for breach of warranty. The courts below have found that the sales contract bars all claims not made before knitting and processing. Concededly, defendant discovered and gave notice of the alledged breach of warranty after knitting and washing.

We are, therefore, confronted with the effect to be given the time limitation provision in paragraph 2 of the contract. Analytically, paragraph 2 presents separate and distinct issues concerning its effect as a valid limitation on remedies for breach of warranty (Uniform Commercial Code, § 2-316, subd. [4]; § 2-719) and its effect as a modification of the express warranty of merchantability (Uniform Commercial Code, § 2-316, subd. [1]) established by paragraph 4 of the contract.

Parties to a contract are given broad latitude within which to fashion their own remedies for breach of contract. Nevertheless, it is clear from the official comments to section 2-719 of the Uniform Commercial Code that it is the very essence of a sales contract that at least minimum adequate remedies be available for its breach. "If the parties intend to conclude a contract for sale within this Article they must accept the legal consequence that there be at least a fair quantum of remedy for breach of the obligations or duties outlined in the contract. Thus any clause purporting to modify or limit the remedial provisions of this Article in an *unconscionable manner* is subject to deletion and in that event the remedies made available by this Article are applicable as if the stricken clause had never existed." [Emphasis supplied.]

It follows that contractual limitations upon remedies are generally to be enforced unless unconscionable. . . .

Whether a contract or any clause of the contract is unconscionable is a matter for the court to decide against the background of the contract's commercial setting, purpose, and effect, and the existence of this issue would not therefore bar summary judgment. . . .

Reversed.

National Compressor Corp. v. Carrow

417 F.2d 97 (1969)

A railroad sold an assortment of goods located upon railroad property under a "bill of sale" which provided that such goods would become the property of the buyers, Carrow and McGee, upon removal from the railroad premises. It was further provided that if the goods were not removed by a specified date, the railroad could sell them free of any claim of the buyers. One of the items was a compressor which the buyers resold to one Davis, who in turn sold it to the plaintiff, National Compressor Corporation. The plaintiff, in turn contracted to sell it to another party, who was to inspect it before paying the purchase price. A fire allegedly caused by the railroad company and the other defendants destroyed the compressor while it was still on the railroad premises. The lower court gave judgment for the plaintiff, and the defendants appealed contending that plaintiff did not have a sufficient interest in the compressor to entitle it to bring suit.

VAN OOSTERHOUT, J. . . . We reject appellants' contention that plaintiff did not have title or sufficient interest in the compressor to give it standing to bring this action. This issue turns upon the interest acquired by Carrow and McGee by the bill of sale from the Missouri Pacific Railroad. It is undisputed that Carrow and McGee conveyed and delivered their full interest in the compressor to Davis for a valuable consideration and that Davis in turn transferred his full interest to the plaintiff for value received. By such transfers, plaintiff acquired all interest in the compressor, acquired by Carrow and McGee from the railroad.

.   .   .

. . . Section 400.2-722 (of the Uniform Commercial Code) provides:

Who can sue third parties for injury to goods.
Where a third party so deals with goods which have been identified to a contract for sale as to cause actionable injury to a party to that contract
    (a)   a right of action against the third party is in either party to the contract for sale who has title to or a security interest or a special property or an insurable interest in the goods; and if the goods have been destroyed or converted a right of action is also in the party who either bore the risk of loss under the contract for sale or has since the injury assumed that risk as against the other. . . .

Section 400.2-501 reads:

"Insurable interest in goods—manner of identification of goods.
(1) The buyer obtains a special property and an insurable interest in goods by identification of existing goods as goods to which the contract refers even though the goods so identified are non-conforming and he has an option to return or reject them. Such identification can be made at any time and in any manner explicitly agreed to by the parties. In the absence of explicit agreement identification occurs.
    (a)   when the contract is made if it is for the sale of goods already existing and identified. . . . "

It is entirely clear that the compressor here involved as described in the bill of sale constitutes goods already existing and identified within the meaning of § 400.2-501 and hence as a minimum Carrow and McGee obtained a special property and insurable interest in the compressor by the bill of sale. Upon the basis of such special or insurable interest, plaintiff is a person authorized to bring suit for the injury of the compressor under § 400.2-722.

Appellants' further contention that plaintiff had no interest in the compressor at the time of the fire because they had contracted to sell the compressor to Earl E. Knox Company lacks merit. The Knox purchase order was subject to "inspected good condition." Neither the inspection nor payment was made before the fire. Knox cancelled after the fire. Plaintiff accepted the cancellation. Thus plaintiff had a right to sue under § 400.2-722(a) as a party who has "since the injury assumed the risk (risk of loss) against the other." Further, if the contract was not legally cancelled, it would have a right to sue by reason of having a security interest in the unpaid purchase price. . . .

Affirmed.

CHAPTER 21
REVIEW QUESTIONS AND PROBLEMS

1. *A* sold an advertising sign to *B* on credit. Seven days later *B* filed a petition in bankruptcy, and the trustee in bankruptcy took possession of the sign. Three weeks later *A* demanded that the sign be returned to him. Is he entitled to the sign?
2. *A* contracted to sell cosmetics to *B*. *A* refused to perform and *B* brought suit for specific performance on the ground that the goods were purchased at close-out prices and that they could not be otherwise obtained at the agreed price. Has *B* selected the correct remedy?
3. *A* sold goods to *B* and received payment in full. *B* became bankrupt, and *A* claimed that he could retain possession of the goods because *B* still owed him for goods previously sold and delivered. Is *A* entitled to retain possession?
4. *A* sold a number of coin-operated dry-cleaning machines to *B*. The machines were not as warranted. What is the measure of *B*'s damages?

5. *A* sold and delivered skateboard components to *B*. *B*, without justification, returned a quantity of the goods. *A* rebuilt the components and sought to recover from *B*. Does *A* have a claim against *B*?

6. *A* sold and delivered a horse to *B*. Subsequently *B* discovered that the condition of the horse had been misrepresented to him, and he notified *A* that the sale was rescinded. *A* contends that *B* cannot rescind since he had already accepted the horse. Is *A*'s contention correct?

7. *A* Furnace Company on June 1, 1963, sold a furnace to *B* and warranted that it would heat well in sub-zero weather. *B* brought action for breach of warranty on November 1, 1967. Was the action timely?

8. *A*, a clothing manufacturer, had a contract to purchase all of his wool cloth requirements from *B*. *B* repudiated the contract. Can *A* require *B* to abide by the terms of the contract?

9. *A* contracted to manufacture specially designed valves for *B*. After he had manufactured a considerable number and at a time when others were being assembled, *B* repudiated the contract. What should *A* do?

10. *A* sold goods to *B* under a contract which required *B* to pick up the goods at *A*'s place of business and which allowed *B* 30 days in which to pay for the goods. When *B* came to get the goods, *A* refused to let *B* have them unless he paid cash. Under what circumstances would *A*'s conduct be justified?

chapter

22

Warranties
and Product
Liability

3-55. Introduction. The word "warranty" has a variety of meanings. As used in the law of sales of goods, it means the obligation of the seller with respect to the goods that have been sold. The seller is responsible for transferring to the buyer a good title and goods which are of the proper quality and free from defects. He may also be responsible for the proper functioning of the article sold and for its suitability to the needs of the buyer. Thus a warranty may extend not only to the present condition of goods but may also extend to the performance which is to be expected of them.

A seller may make a variety of statements about his goods, and it is necessary to evaluate these to determine whether they are warranties or simply part of his salesmanship, which does not impose legal responsibility.

A warranty is a matter of contract, but it may take on the aspects of tort if a seller fraudulently misrepresents the goods. The buyer can either sue for breach of warranty or for fraud and deceit where the goods are misrepresented.

The responsibility of a seller has been recognized since ancient times, but the degree of his obligation to the buyer has been subject to reevaluation by the courts and legislatures over the years. In early times, a buyer could reasonably evaluate the goods and make an intelligent decision as to whether they were of good quality and suitable for his needs. The items were uncomplicated and could be readily inspected in the presence of the seller. The two parties were usually in fairly equal bargaining positions, and the law did not regard the seller as having any very substantial obligation to the buyer. Nor did it impose a high degree of responsibility upon a seller in these circumstances. He was allowed to make many representations about his goods, and the buyer was expected to regard these with skepticism—to be shrewd enough to make his decision without taking this "seller's talk" or "puffing" at face value. The parties thus dealt in terms of the goods and not the statements made by the seller about the goods. Of course, as part of the bargaining process the seller might give a guarantee to the buyer, and the buyer could insist upon it as a condition to making the purchase, but the general concept was that statements were not warranties unless it was clear that such were intended.

As the nature of the sales transaction changed over the years, the need for more protection to the buyer was recognized. Usually he was no longer dealing directly with the seller but was now buying from a representative of the seller, and the goods were often not such as could be readily evaluated upon inspection. The buyer had to rely upon statements about the goods and upon the seller's responsibility for their truth. The outlook of society also had changed. *Caveat emptor* (let the buyer beware) was gradually replaced by *caveat venditor* (let the seller beware). If the goods were defective, the seller should be held responsible, and the buyer should justifiably expect that what he purchased was at least sound and merchantable.

Related to the expansion of the warranty obligation is the subject of products liability, which is discussed later in this chapter. Manufacturers and sellers are held liable to persons who are injured as a result of defects in the products manufactured and sold. Warranties are often the basis for the injured persons' claims for damages.

The early law generally required that there be *privity of contract* before one person could bring legal action against another. This meant that there had to be a direct contractual relationship between a buyer and a seller so that in the case of manufactured goods, if the goods were defective, a buyer could only sue the retailer and could not bring action against the manufacturer. This privity is no longer required in most states, so direct action can be maintained against the manufacturer, especially in cases of personal injury.

The Code has several provisions relating to warranties. It draws a distinction, as did prior law and cases, between express warranties made by a seller and those implied from the transaction. The seller may guarantee the product directly, in which case it is an *express* warranty, or the warranty may be *implied* from the transaction and the surrounding circumstances. The Code classifies warranties as (1) express warranties, (2) implied warranties, and (3) warranties of title. It should be noted that, when the seller is a merchant, special treatment is sometimes afforded to the warranty. This is also true with respect to modifications or exclusions of warranties.

3-56. Express Warranties.   An express warranty is one which is made as a part of the contract for sale and which becomes a part of the basis of the bargain between the buyer and the seller. Such a warranty, as distinguished from an implied warranty, is part of the contract because it has been included as part of the individual bargain. To create an express warranty, the seller does not have to use formal words such as "warrant" or "guarantee," nor must he have the specific intention to make a warranty. An express warranty comes into existence by virtue of any *affirmation of fact* or *promise* made by the seller to the buyer which relates to the goods and becomes part of the basis of their bargain. These statements by the seller create an express warranty that the goods will conform to his affirmation or promise. A distinction is drawn between statements of fact and promises on the one hand, and statements of value or commendation on the other. As a general rule, a mere affirmation of the value of the goods or a statement purporting to be merely the opinion of the seller or his commendation of the goods does not give rise to a warranty. This is obviously a difficult distinction to make in some cases, but the basic factor is whether the statement is fact or opinion. The buyer is not justified in relying upon opinions expressed by the seller or commendatory remarks made by him, and they do not usually become part of the bargain. For example, a seller who states that an article is worth twice the asking price would not have made a warranty. It should be stressed again that a key element of express warranties is that they rest on negotiated aspects of the individual contract and that they are part of the basis for the bargain that is made.

Expressions of opinion or commendation by the seller may, however, be part of the basis of the bargain in some situations. The question is whether the buyer was justified in relying upon them. Thus the opinion of an expert with regard to the value of a gem might be considered as justifying the reliance of the buyer, and thus the opinion becomes part of the basis of the bargain.

The test with regard to what statements of the seller are warranties is primarily an objective one. Statements are warranties if they can properly be considered as terms of the agreement ultimately reached by the parties. The seller makes warranties in order to induce the sale of goods, and for this reason, warranties are regarded as essential parts of the contract. It should be remembered that warranties made after the sale has been consummated are binding without any new consideration.

An express warranty may be made in a variety of ways. One of these is for the seller to specifically make a factual statement about the goods, such as "this engine will produce 500 horsepower" or "this fabric is 100 percent nylon." Another is for him to make a direct promise with respect to the goods, such as "this grass seed is free from weeds." Generally, words which are descriptive of the product are warranties that the goods will conform to the description. Descriptions may also be in the form of diagrams, pictures, blueprints, and the like. Technical specifications of the product would constitute warranties. If part of the basis for the bargain, all of these are express warranties that the goods will conform to them.

Just as the seller may describe the goods, he may inform the buyer by showing him a model or a sample of what is being sold. For example, fabrics or clothing might be purchased on the basis of samples shown to the buyer, or a seller might display a working model of an engine. In either event, there would be an express warranty that the goods shall conform to the sample or model if the parties have made this a part of their bargain. It is arguable that a sample or model is intended only to suggest the nature of the goods and not to be a part of the bargain. This raises a question of fact, but in general the presumption would be that literal compliance with the sample or model would be required—that they were descriptive and therefore warranties.

3-57. Implied Warranties.   The two implied warranties under the Code are (1) the warranty of merchantability and (2) the warranty of fitness for a particular purpose. Whereas express warranties come into existence by virtue of the bargaining of the parties, implied warranties come into being as a matter of law, without any bargaining, and as an integral part of the normal sales transaction. Express warranties are said to rest on "dickered" or negotiated aspects of the bargain between seller and buyer; implied warranties are legally present, unless clearly disclaimed or negatived. Implied warranties are included for the benefit and protection of the buyer and are of particular importance in the modern setting of a consumer-conscious society. Implied warranties exist even if a seller is unable to discover the defect involved or to cure it if it could be ascertained.[1] Liability for breach of warranty is not based on fault but on the public policy of protecting the buyer of goods.

Merchantability. A warranty that the goods shall be merchantable is implied in a contract for sale if the seller is a merchant who deals in goods of the kind involved in the contract. This important warranty imposes a very substantial obligation upon the merchant-seller. It has a broad application and specifically includes within the framework of a sale the serving for value of food or drink on the seller's premises or elsewhere. Prior to the Code the serving of food had been regarded as the rendering of a service rather than as a sale of goods, and implied warranties were therefore not applicable.

The Code provides that goods to be merchantable must be at least such as

(a) pass without objection in the trade under the contract description; and

(b) in the case of fungible goods, are of fair average quality within the description; and

(c) are fit for the ordinary purposes for which such goods are used; and

(d) run, within the variations permitted by the agreement, of even kind, quality and quantity within each unit and among all units involved; and

(e) are adequately contained, packaged, and labeled as the agreement may require; and

(f) conform to the promises or affirmations of fact made on the container or label if any. (U.C.C. 2-314)

It will be noted that the foregoing provides the minimum acceptable standards of merchantability. Fungible goods (b) are those usually sold by weight or measure such as grain or flour. The term "fair average quality" generally relates to agricultural bulk commodities and means that they are within the middle range of quality under the description. Fitness for ordinary purposes (c) is not limited to use by the immediate buyer. If a person is buying for resale, the buyer is entitled to protection, and the goods must be honestly resalable by him. They must be of such nature that they are acceptable in the ordinary market without objection. With reference to (d), it should be noted that usages of the trade sometimes permit substantial variations and considerable leeway. Subsection (e) is applicable only if the nature of the goods and of the transaction require a certain type of container, package, or label. Where there is a container or label and there is a representation thereon, the buyer is entitled to protection under (f) so that he will not be in the position of reselling or using goods delivered under false representations appearing on the package or container. He obtains this protection, even though the contract did not require either the labeling or the representation. Other implied warranties, you should note, may arise from "course of dealing or usage of trade."

It can be stated generally that the implied warranty of merchantability imposes a very broad responsibility upon the merchant-seller to furnish goods which are at least of average acceptable quality. In any given line of business, the word "merchantable" may have a meaning somewhat different from the

[1] Vlases v. Montgomery Ward & Co., page 447

Code definition, and the parties by their course of dealing may indicate a special meaning for the term.

Fitness for a particular purpose. It was noted above that, under the warranty of merchantability, the goods must be fit for the *ordinary purposes* for which such goods are used. An implied warranty of fitness for a particular purpose is created if, at the time of contracting, the seller has reason to know any particular purpose for which the buyer requires the goods and that the buyer is relying on the seller's skill or judgment to select or furnish suitable goods. This means that the seller must in these circumstances select goods which will in fact accomplish the purpose for which they are being purchased. This appears to be a fair burden, especially in view of the great range of sizes and models, and the presumably superior knowledge of the seller. Thus, when a buyer intending to purchase a furnace which will heat his building approaches a merchant, he is entitled to rely upon the seller to furnish a unit which will accomplish that particular purpose.

By its very nature, the implied warranty of fitness, does not ordinarily apply to nonmerchants, although the Code does not so restrict it. Also, the buyer need not specifically state that he has a particular purpose in mind or that he is placing reliance upon the seller's judgment if the circumstances are such that the seller has reason to realize the purpose intended or that the buyer is relying on him.[2] Reliance in fact is required by the buyer, however, and if such reliance is not proved the warranty would not apply.

There is a difference between merchantability and fitness for a particular purpose, although both may be included in the same contract. In many instances the net result would be the same regardless of which warranty applied. This would be true of many items such as food and clothing. The particular purpose involves a specific use by the buyer; whereas the ordinary use as expressed in the concept of merchantability means the use which would ordinarily be made of the goods. Thus an appliance such as a dishwasher would ordinarily be used to wash dishes but might not be suited for the specific dishwashing needs of a restaurant. The warranty of fitness for a particular purpose may arise even though the goods are sold under a trade name. If the buyer mentions a trade name in telling the seller what he wants, this does not necessarily mean that he is insisting upon a particular brand. If the seller recommends a particular article which bears a brand name as adequate for the buyer's purposes, the warranty may be applicable. The buyer's insistence on a particular brand would counteract the warranty because he would not then be relying on the seller's judgment.

Many cases have dealt with the subject of this implied warranty, and the questions raised include whether the seller was chargeable with knowledge of the buyer's special purpose and whether the buyer relied upon the seller's skill and judgment.

3-58. Warranty of Title. Although title is warranted by implication in the sale of goods, it is treated as a separate warranty under the Code. One reason for this is that title is intangible and is probably less in the mind of the buyer than warranties relating to the physical aspects of what he is buying.

[2] Southwest Distributors, Inc. v. Allied Paper Bag Corp. page 448

A seller warrants that he is conveying good title to the buyer and that he has the right to sell the goods. He further warrants that there are no encumbrances or liens against the property sold and that no other person can claim a security interest in them. In effect, the seller impliedly guarantees to the buyer that he will be able to enjoy the use of the goods free from the claims of any third party. Of course, property may be sold to a buyer who has full knowledge of liens or encumbrances, and he may buy such property subject to such claims. In this event there would not be a breach of the warranty of title. The purchase price would, however, reflect that he was obtaining something less than complete title.

Warranty of title can be excluded or modified only by specific language or by circumstances which make it clear that the seller is not vouching for the title. Judicial sales and sales by executors of estates would not imply that the seller guaranteed the title. Also, a seller could directly inform the buyer that he is selling only the interest that he has and that the buyer takes it subject to all encumbrances.

A seller who is a merchant regularly dealing in goods of the kind that are the subject of the sale makes an additional warranty. He warrants that the goods are free of the rightful claim of any third person by way of infringement of such person's interests—that the goods sold do not, for example, infringe upon a patent. But a buyer may furnish to the seller specifications for the construction of an article, and this may result in the infringement of a patent. Not only does the seller not warrant against such infringement, but the buyer must protect the seller from any claims arising out of such infringement.

3-59. Disclaimers and Inconsistencies.   A seller will often seek to avoid or restrict warranty liability. He may include in the contract for sale a provision that purports to exclude "all warranties express or implied." As noted in the preceding section, the warranty of title cannot be excluded in this fashion. In connection with the other implied warranties, the Code imposes requirements for disclaimers in order to protect the buyer from unexpected and unfair disclaimers. This is in keeping with the need to protect the consumer against a loss of his right to redress should the goods he buys be defective or unsatisfactory for his needs. The seller may have given the buyer an express warranty and then include in the contract a disclaimer of all warranties. In this situation the disclaimer will not be given effect, and the express warranty will be enforceable.

Implied warranties can be excluded or modified, but rigid rules apply to disclaimers. The implied warranty of merchantability can be excluded only by language expressly mentioning "merchantability," and if the disclaimer is in writing, it must be conspicuous. The exclusion of or modification of any implied warranty of fitness must be in writing *and* must be conspicuous. The exclusion of all implied warranties of fitness can be accomplished by the use of such expressions as "There are no warranties which extend beyond the description on the face hereof." Thus, in general, it is possible to disclaim the implied warranties, but the seller must take necessary measures to bring to the buyer's attention the fact that such warranties have been excluded or modified.

There are other situations in which implied warranties may be wholly or partially excluded. The seller may specifically indicate that he is selling goods "as is," "with all faults," or statements of similar import. Such language calls the buyer's attention to the exclusion and makes it plain to him that the sale involves no implied warranty.

The buyer's examination of the goods also has a bearing upon whether implied warranties are present. If he has examined the goods as fully as he desired, there is no implied warranty as to defects which an examination ought to have revealed to him. If the seller has requested that the buyer examine the goods and the buyer refuses to do so, there would be no implied warranty as to those defects that an examination would have revealed. The buyer is thus required to examine the goods if the seller so demands, and his failure to do so will place upon him the burden of the defects that would have been revealed. But the buyer's failure to inspect the goods will not exclude warranties, unless he has refused to examine them upon the seller's request that he do so.

A course of dealing between the parties, course of performance, or usage of trade can also be the basis for exclusion or modification of implied warranties. Thus, these factors can be important in determining the nature and extent of implied warranties in any given transaction.

Just as the parties can exclude or modify warranties, they can limit the remedies for breach of warranty. Warranty remedies are subject to the limitations discussed in the previous chapter with reference to contractual modifications or limitations of remedies generally. (See Section 3-51.)

Another warranty problem relates to the situation in which there is a conflict between warranties. Any transaction may involve both express and implied warranties, and there may be an inconsistency between them. Then, the warranties are construed as consistent with each other to the extent that this is possible, and they are treated as cumulative—each will be given effect. If this cannot be reasonably done, the intention of the parties will control as to which warranty is dominant. The intention will be determined on the basis of these rules:

1. Exact or technical specifications prevail over an inconsistent general description or sample or model.
2. A sample prevails over general language of description.
3. Express warranties prevail over inconsistent implied warranties except the implied warranty of fitness for a particular purpose. (U.C.C. 2-317)

The general concept is that effect shall be given to all warranties and that inconsistencies be handled in such a fashion that a reasonable adjustment can be made.

3-60. Extent of Warranties. Historically, the warranties of a seller extended only to his immediate buyer. A contractual connection, known as privity of contract, was required before suit could be brought. As will be discussed in the sections which follow, the requirement of privity of contract has been the subject of substantial litigation and change in recent years.

The privity of contract issue has two aspects which may be described as horizontal and vertical. The *horizontal* privity issue is: To whom does the warranty extend? Does it only run in favor of the actual purchaser, or does it extend to others who may use or be affected by the product? The *vertical* privity issue is: Against whom can action be brought for breach of warranty? Can the party only sue the seller, or will direct action lie against wholesalers, manufacturers, producers, and growers?

The Code does not contain any provisions on the vertical issue[3] but does contain provisions relating to the horizontal issue. It provides that express or implied warranties extend to any person who is in the family or household of the buyer or who is a guest in his home, if it is reasonable to expect that such person would use, consume, or be affected by the goods. If such a person is personally injured because of a defect in the goods, he may bring an action against the seller. This provision for a third-party beneficiary of a warranty is quite restricted in that it does not provide for suit against anyone but the seller.

The subject of product liability involves much more than breach of implied warranty. In addition to the breach of warranty theory as a basis of recovery for injury caused by a product, the theories of negligence and strict liability are available.[4] These are discussed in the sections which follow, and the problems caused by lack of privity of contract will also be further explored.

PRODUCT LIABILITY

3-61. Introduction.   One of the consequences of manufacturing or selling a product should be responsibility to a consumer or user if the product is defective and causes injury to a person or property. As previously noted, a seller makes implied warranties and often express warranties to the buyer, and the buyer is entitled to recover consequential damages for personal injury or property damage proximately resulting from a breach of these warranties. Limitation of consequential damages for injury to the person in the case of consumer goods is regarded as prima facie unconscionable. A seller's liability to a buyer for breach of warranty is rather clearly established in the law.

However, the Code does not provide specifically for liability of anyone other than the seller or liability to anyone other than the buyer and his family or guests in his home. Product liability issues encompass the broad questions of liability which a manufacturer or seller or anyone in the chain of sale may have to any consumer or user. Thus, they encompass not only the liability of the immediate seller but also that of the manufacturers, producers, growers, packers, and others in the chain of distribution. They extend beyond the immediate buyer to all users of the product and all persons who may be injured by someone else's use of the product.

The Code takes a neutral position with regard to product liability and leaves the way open for the courts to develop the law. The trend of the law on product liability is clearly in the direction of extending greater protection to consumers. This tendency is evidenced in the cases which impose liability on manufacturers and which extend the right of recovery to persons other than the buyer. Naturally this has added a new dimension to the problems of business manage-

[3] Kassab v. Central Soya et al., page 450
[4] Lonzrick v. Republic Steel Corp. page 452

ment. The financial burden of defending damage suits brought by persons injured because of allegedly defective products is often substantial. The court dockets are receiving a growing number of such cases and large verdicts are often awarded by juries.

The trend in the law is the result of social as well as legal and financial considerations. A manufacturer has an obligation to the public to put on the market a product which is safe to use and free from defects. The consumer is entitled to protection from injuries. In furtherance of these policies, some cases have imposed liability when the facts indicate that the product was not defective but that the injury was caused by the way in which the product was used. Should the manufacturer be held liable if the user is careless? It is arguable that industry is best able to absorb the costs and that it in turn can pass them on by increasing the price of the product. Product liability has been imposed because of defects in design as well as defects in manufacture. For example, a manufacturer of power lawn mowers was held liable to a person whose hand was injured when he reached under the machine to remove a rock which had obstructed the blades. The ruling of the court was that the company was negligent in failing to install a guard which would have made it impossible to put a hand into the blade compartment.

3-62. The Demise of the Privity Requirement. Historically, manufacturers were relatively free from direct responsibility to injured consumers and users. There were many reasons for this, some of which were of a legal nature and others which reflected the social attitudes of a different era and the relative strength and bargaining power of a consumer versus a manufacturer. From the standpoint of the law, the principle of privity of contract prevented direct action against a manufacturer on a cause of action based on breach of warranty. The rule was well established that one who was not a party to a contract could not bring an action for its breach. There may be several contracts as the product moves from the manufacturer to the ultimate consumer or user. The manufacturer may sell to a wholesaler, the wholesaler to the retailer, and the retailer to the consumer. Under early contract law the consumer who suffered an injury could not bring an action against the manufacturer; his only recourse was against the retailer with whom he had a contract.

There was a gradual erosion of the privity requirement in cases of personal injuries caused by defective products. The early cases which abandoned the privity requirement involved personal injury and sickness caused by food and drugs. As a matter of social policy, a packer, grower, or manufacturer of a product consumed by human beings should be liable if that product caused injury. Liability would be a deterrent to the sale of dangerous food and drug products, and the loss would be on the party best able to afford it. Privity of contract had never been required for a negligence action, and the elimination of the requirement in breach of warranty actions was a recognition of the similarity of the two theories and of the difficulty of proving negligence of the seller of such products as canned goods. The breach of warranty theory eliminated the need to prove fault, and the elimination of privity of contract made the new theory realistically available and workable. It also avoided multiplicity of suits.

Various courts have used different justifications to eliminate the privity requirement. Some have employed the dangerous instrumentality theory in nonfood cases.[5] These courts said that privity was not required in such cases because food was inherently dangerous, and therefore if another product was inherently dangerous, the same rationale would be applied, and privity of contract would not be required. The law in effect fed on itself and expanded. Other courts stated that "warranties run with goods" in much the same way that a warranty involving the title to land runs with the land. A warranty is an invisible appendage that is a part of the goods, and as such, it belongs to anyone who is affected by the goods. Regardless of the reason given, the trend has been to eliminate privity of contract as a requirement in product liability cases.

The latest development in product liability is the natural extension of the erosion of privity. Known as the doctrine of *strict liability,* this development imposes liability wherever damage or injury is caused. It is the logical result of the elimination of the need to prove negligence and of the demise of the privity requirement. In states which have adopted the strict liability theory, the theories of negligence and breach of warranty are becoming less significant.

It should be noted that the law of product liability is not uniform among the states and that such law is primarily the product of the courts. Some states still retain the privity rule. Also, in many states there is a distinction drawn between cases involving personal injuries as opposed to those concerned with injury to property. Relaxations of the requirements for suit are primarily for the purpose of allowing suits for personal injuries,[6] but damage to property is included by some courts.

Just as the Restatement of the Law of Contracts has great weight and influence in litigation involving contracts, the Restatement of the Law of Torts (second) is often cited, quoted, and relied upon by courts in cases involving product liability. This Restatement has several sections which summarize the law of product liability. The Restatement is not *the law,* but it is highly regarded and has a strong persuasive force.

The following sections discuss in more detail the various theories or bases upon which liability for injuries caused by defective products has been sustained.

3-63. Negligence.   The leading case on a manufacturer's liability for a defective product is *McPherson* v. *Buick Motor Co.,* decided in 1916. In that case the plaintiff was injured when a defective wheel on his car collapsed causing an accident. The wheel had not been manufactured by the motor company but was furnished by a supplier. The court held the company liable on the ground that it was negligent in assembling a car with a defective wheel. The court ruled that a car with a defect of this sort is dangerous to human life and thus extended a previous rule which gave a right to sue in cases involving foods and other products for human consumption. The rationale of this rule was that direct action against a producer or packer of food should be allowed when the product if defective would be dangerous to human life and safety.

---

[5] Suvada v. White Motor Company, page 453
[6] State ex. rel. Western Seed Production Corp. v. Campbell, page 455

The application of the inherently dangerous doctrine to an automobile was a significant breakthrough in the law of product liability. However, this was a tort case and not one based upon breach of warranty. In order to recover, the plaintiff had to establish the negligence of the defendant—its failure to exercise reasonable care. The burden of proving negligence is a substantial one, and while the case established an important precedent, it was only a step in the direction of imposing product liability upon manufacturers.

In a tort action based upon negligence, privity of contract is not required. Hence, an action could be maintained not only by the person who purchased the defective product but also by any person who suffered an injury on account of a defect in the product if the defect was the proximate cause of his injury. Thus, in the case of an automobile with defective brakes, it is reasonably forseeable that other drivers would be placed in jeopardy if the brakes failed. The Restatement of Torts (second), Section 395, states the rule as follows:

> A manufacturer who fails to exercise reasonable care in the manufacture of a chattel which, unless carefully made, he should recognize as involving an unreasonable risk of causing physical harm to those who use it for a purpose for which the manufacturer should expect it to be used and to those whom he should expect to be endangered by its probable use, is subject to liability for physical harm caused to them by its lawful use in a manner and for a purpose for which it is supplied.

The plaintiff, of course, must by appropriate evidence prove that the manufacturer was negligent—failed to exercise reasonable care. However, he may be able to rely on the doctrine of *res ipsa loquitur*—the thing speaks for itself. This means that in some situations the very happening of the accident creates a presumption of negligence. This is, however, a very restricted doctrine, and its application to product liability cases has been limited.

Another method of establishing negligence is to prove that the manufacturer violated some statutory regulation in the production and distribution of his product. Some industries are subject to regulation under state or federal laws with regard to product quality, testing, advertising, and other aspects of production and distribution. Proof of a violation of the statute may be sufficient to establish negligence in the case of a manufacturer in such industries, although there is a division of authority on this point. Negligence established by proof of violation of a statute is called *negligence per se*.

3-64. Misrepresentation. If the seller has advertised the product through newspapers, magazines, television, or otherwise and in so doing made misrepresentations with regard to the character or quality of the product, tort liability may be imposed on him. The Restatement of Torts (second), Section 402B summarizes the liability of a seller for misrepresentation as follows:

> One engaged in the business of selling chattels who, by advertising, labels, or otherwise, makes to the public a misrepresentation of a material fact concerning the character or quality of a chattel sold by him is subject to liability for physical harm to a consumer of the chattel caused by justifiable reliance upon the misrepresentation, even though
>   (a) it is not made fraudulently or negligently, and
>   (b) the consumer has not bought the chattel from or entered into any contractual relation with the seller.

It is to be noted that such misrepresentation may also be a violation of statutes in some cases. The rationale of the Restatement position is that a great deal of what the consumer knows about a product comes to him through the various media, and sellers should be held responsible and accountable for misrepresentations made to the public. Truth in advertising is a subject of interest and concern to courts and legislatures alike.

3-65. Breach of Warranty Liability.   In most states the requirement of privity has been relaxed or abolished, and in such states an action can be maintained on the basis of the breach of implied warranties. An action based upon such breach, being a contract action, does not require proof of negligence on the part of the manufacturer or seller. This is a great advantage to the injured plaintiff, as he must only prove that the product was defective and that such defect was the proximate cause of his injury. The philosophy of this rule is that the warranty in effect runs with the goods and that, if breached, it is available as the basis for a cause of action by the injured consumer. However, in states which retain the privity rule, a breach of warranty action against anyone other than the immediate seller is not permitted.

An express warranty may also be the basis of a claim for injuries. It has been held that advertising constitutes an express warranty by the seller and that the affirmations and promises made to the consumer in radio, television, or through the printed media can be relied upon by him and can be the basis for a suit by one not in privity with the advertiser.

3-66. Strict Liability.   The concept of *strict liability* is new, its ramifications are being explored by the courts, and its exact dimensions remain to be determined. At the outset, it should be noted that it is a tort rather than contract cause of action. However, its result is similar to breach of warranty suits in those states which have abolished privity and extended implied warranties to all parties. It is the logical extension of the other developments in the field.[7]

Clearly this imposes a very substantial liability upon sellers and manufacturers. The Restatement of Torts (Second) has been cited and followed in a number of cases. The Restatement takes a neutral position on the question of whether anyone other than a *user* or *consumer* is entitled to bring an action predicated upon strict liability. Some courts have allowed suits by bystanders on this theory, and others have refused to do so.[8]

It will be noted that under the Restatement definition strict liability will be imposed only upon a seller who is engaged in the business of selling an unreasonably dangerous product. Basically, a consumer or user who is injured by a product in a defective condition may recover damages if he can prove that the product was defective; that the defect was the proximate cause of a personal injury; and that the defect made the product unreasonably dangerous. He is not required to prove that the seller was negligent. This liability imposed upon a seller has been applied both to personal injuries and to damage to the

[7] Greeno v. Clark Equipment Company, page 457
[8] Mitchell v. Miller, page 459

property of the user or consumer. Some courts, however, have refused to extend it to property.

The Restatement has other provisions which are related to strict liability. One of these imposes liability upon a seller of goods manufactured by a *third person,* if he fails to give proper warning that a product is or is likely to be dangerous of if he fails to exercise reasonable care to inform buyers of the danger or to otherwise protect them against it. This applies to a product which may have inherently dangerous qualities. A similar duty to give warning applies to the manufacturer. This relates in part to the requirement that a warning must be placed on a container or label if a product is explosive, poisonous, etc. Some cases extend the liability to the manufacturer of a component part of a product which fails. For example, the manufacturer of the jet engine as well as the manufacturer of the airplane may be liable to the victims of a plane which crashes due to mechanical failure.

It should be emphasized that the provisions of the Restatement do not have the force of a statute; they are simply an authoritative exposition on the subject. The courts decide cases on the basis of law and facts, and many courts have not followed the Restatement.

The concept of strict liability as developed by the courts furnishes another example of the way in which law changes and evolves in conformity with social needs and pressures. The concern for the safety of the consumer is clearly evidenced by placing a burden upon manufacturers and sellers. As a result of this increased liability and expense, many businesses and industries are searching for ways in which to increase the safety of their products and to give adequate warning of any dangers connected with them. At the same time legislative bodies are setting standards that must be complied with in connection with safety and freedom from defects. All of this is part of a changing scene in which more and more emphasis is placed upon the needs and requirements of consumers.

WARRANTIES AND PRODUCT LIABILITY CASES

Vlases v. Montgomery Ward & Co.
377 F.2d 846 (1967)

The plaintiff purchased 2,000 chickens from the defendant in order to start a chicken-raising business. After a few weeks the chickens showed signs of illness and were found to be suffering from avian leukosis, or bird cancer. The plaintiff brought an action based upon breach of implied warranties. The defendant contended that there was no way of detecting the disease in baby chicks, and the testimony bore this out. It was the defendant's position that the birds might have contracted the disease subsequent to the sale, but the jury returned a verdict in favor of the plaintiff. The defendant appealed.

MC LAUGHLIN, J. . . . The two implied warranties before us are the implied warranty of merchantability and the implied warranty of fitness for a particular purpose. Both of these are designed to protect the buyer of goods from bearing the burden of loss where merchandise, though not violating a promise expressly guaranteed, does not conform to the normal commercial standards or meet the buyer's particular purpose, a condition upon which he had the right to rely.

Were it to be assumed that the sale of 2,000 chickens infected with avian leukosis transgressed the norm of acceptable goods under both warranties, appellant's position is that the action will not lie in a situation where the seller is unable to discover the defect or cure the damage if it could be ascertained. That theory does not eliminate the consequences imposed by the Code upon the seller of commercially inferior goods. It is without merit. . . .

. . . The entire purpose behind the implied warranty sections of the Code is to hold the seller responsible when inferior goods are passed along to the unsuspecting buyer. What the Code requires is not evidence that the defects should or could have been uncovered by the seller but only that the goods upon delivery were not of a merchantable quality or fit for their particular purpose. If those requisite proofs are established the only exculpatory relief afforded by the Code is a showing that the implied warranties were modified or excluded by specific language under Section 2-316. Lack of skill or foresight on the part of the seller in discovering the product's flaw was never meant to bar liability. The gravamen here is not so much with what precautions were taken by the seller but rather with the quality of the goods contracted for by the buyer. . . .

Affirmed.

Southwest Distributors, Inc. v. Allied Paper Bag Corp.

384 S.W.2d. 838 (Mo.) 1964

SPERRY, Commissioner. . . . Plaintiff sued defendant for damages growing out of a breach of an implied warranty of fitness for intended use. Defendant counterclaimed. Trial to the court resulted in a judgment for plaintiff, on its petition, for $3,200.00, and for plaintiff on defendant's counterclaim. Defendant appeals. . . .

Plaintiff has its offices in Kansas City. It is engaged in the business of manufacturing and selling mixed feeds, fertilizers, and other products. It maintains a plant in Verdun, Nebraska, where it processes corncobs for various commercial uses. Among its corncob products is a mulch which is adapted to agricultural uses. It is beneficial to soil, as an aid to moisture retention, aeration, fertilization, and the addition of humus. It is a dry, bulky material and is shipped, as are other products of plaintiff, in fifty (50) pound paper bags. Prior to the occurrence of this controversy, plaintiff had purchased bags from defendant for shipment of its other products, and the bags furnished were satisfactory. . . .

Defendant was engaged in the business of manufacturing and selling bags for use in the shipment of various commercial products. Its factory and place of business is located in Kansas City.

Sometime prior to June, 1959, defendant's salesman called on Mr. Harris (plaintiff's manager). Mr. Harris stated that he told the salesman about the new product that he intended to produce, the name of which was "Magic Mulch." He stated that he told him, generally, of its nature and purposes; that he wanted to bag it for shipment in "nice, new, fancy bags"; that the bags were to contain fifty (50) pounds of the product, to be sold chiefly in California, where there was a good demand because of the nature of the climate and soil;

that he asked defendant to produce a "dummy" sample that could be shown to California customers engaged in distributing such products; that the defendant produced such a sample bag; that witness went to Los Angeles, where he contacted one Cal Erwin and sold him two carloads of the product. He also sold an order to another dealer at Van Nuys, California. He stated that, upon his return, he interviewed defendant's agent and told him that such products were, universally, stored in the open, on the ground, in California; that defendant's representative then recommended that the bag should contain an inner liner of asphalt, so as to protect its contents from moisture; that plaintiff ordered five thousand (5,000) bags; that plaintiff did not specify to the defendant any quality required of the bags except size—that they weigh fifty (50) pounds when filled, that they were to be stored outside of sheds, and the lettering that was to go on them; that he wanted them as quickly as possible because he had orders ready to be filled; that, before the bags were made, plaintiff saw and inspected the plate (the lettering) and changed one word therein; that he was present when an extra workman, at defendant's plant, was ready to print the lettering on the bags; that the workman was having trouble with the ink; that the workman said the trouble was with the steam; that the workman, eventually, told him that they had the matter corrected; that witness left the plant after having seen some bags that "looked good." He stated that the bags were shipped to Nebraska, where they were filled and shipped to dealers in California, in box cars; that he did not see the bags prior to their shipment; that he left the making of the bags to the judgment of defendant, who was skilled in that business.

Mr. Harris stated that, about four (4) weeks after shipment, he received telephone complaints from dealers regarding the bags; that they were fading; that Mr. Erwin, a customer who had ordered and received two carloads, had then only paid for one car; that he went to California to see Erwin to collect, but that he could not collect; that, later, he made another trip to California and brought back samples of the bags, one of which was placed in evidence as an exhibit. It is before us. The advertising matter appears in red, green, and black. The red and green coloring is badly faded and the colors have "run," so that the entire bag is unsightly. It gives the appearance of being stale, shopworn. Mr. Harris stated that several hundred bags sold to Erwin were in this condition; that he had previously purchased from defendant from five to ten times the number of bags herein involved, which were used for shipment of ground corncobs and which were stored in the open by purchasers . . . that these bags had been satisfactory and had been paid for. He also stated that one shipment of "Magic Mulch" went to B. & E. Enterprises, Van Nuys, California; that the customer refused to pay therefore, because of the above conditions, and that plaintiff took the shipment back; that Erwin had returned to him much of this merchandise that they had sold; that the complaints were based on colors fading and running; that at no time did plaintiff suggest or specify the type of ink to be used in the printed matter on the bags. . . .

Plaintiff ordered these bags from defendant for the specific purpose of shipping its "Magic Mulch" to customers in California. Plaintiff told defendant, generally, what type and size of container it wanted. It wanted an attractive bag printed in multicolors, describing the contents and stating its purposes and uses. It wanted bags that could safely be stored in the open. It was not in the business of manufacturing bags but only produced merchandise for shipment therein. It had no facilities for chemically testing the paints, inks, and other materials that went into or on the bags. It left all of that to the judgment and discretion of defendant who specialized in that business and had access to such information. It had previously ordered many thousands of bags from defendant for shipment of similar merchandise under similar conditions. . . .

Defendant is bound by the well-settled law on this subject, to wit: that a manufacturer-seller of an article for a particular purpose impliedly warrants that such article will be reasonably fit for that purpose for which it is intended to be used, *if the buyer communicates to the manufacturer-seller the specific purpose for which he wants the article, and if he relies, and has reason to rely, on the producer-seller's skill, judgment, and experience to produce an article that will answer the purpose.*

The doctrine does not apply to well-known or commonly used articles. It rests in part upon the principle of superior knowledge and experience of the producer-seller. However, if the purchaser has, or acquires by testing and analysis, knowledge equal to that of the seller the rule does not apply because the seller has no superiority of knowledge of the facts.

The evidence in this case supports the court in its finding of the issues for plaintiff against defendant. The evidence was to the effect that plaintiff relied wholly on defendant to produce bags for a specific purpose; that that purpose was communicated to defendant; that plaintiff did not specify the types of materials to be used but relied on defendant's judgment and skill in producing an article reasonably fit for its purposes; that plaintiff had reason to rely on defendant's skill and judgment to produce for it a bag reasonably fit for its intended use; that the bags produced were not reasonably fit for that use; and that by reason thereof, plaintiff suffered damages as adjudged by the court. . . .

The judgment is affirmed.

Kassab v. Central Soya et al.

246 A.2d 848 (Pa.) 1968

The plaintiff placed an order for cattle feed with defendant Pritts, a feed dealer. Pritts blended the feed in accordance with a formula previously used by the plaintiff. One of the ingredients was a feed supplement, Cattle Blend, manufactured by the defendant, Central Soya. The feed was fed to the plaintiff's cattle, and "Shortly thereafter the cows in the herd began to abort and the breed bull began behaving in a manner which tended to cast doubt upon his masculinity." The bull was eventually pronounced sterile. Tests showed that Cattle Blend contained a drug, stilbestrol, which could cause the plaintiff's cattle to be unable to reproduce.

The plaintiff brought action for breach of warranty against both the seller and Central Soya. Central Soya contended that it cannot be liable for breach of warranty because of lack of privity of contract. The trial judge found for the defendants. The plaintiff appealed.

ROBERTS, J. . . . [A]ppellants maintain that the Court below . . . had no choice but to find for them on the issue of liability, since the tainted feed constituted a clear breach of the implied warranty of merchantability and of the warranty of fitness for a particular purpose. With this contention we agree. . . .

. . . Appellee Central Soya, the feed supplement manufacturer, argues that it cannot be liable for breach of any implied warranty because it was not in privity with appellants. . . . Soya disclaims liability because appellants purchased the feed from Pritts and cannot therefore maintain an action . . . against Soya, a remote manufacturer.

Indeed, were we to continue to adhere to the requirement that privity of contract must exist between plaintiff and defendant in order to maintain an action . . . for injuries caused by a breach of implied warranty, there would be no doubt that Soya could escape liability. . . .

. . . [T]his Court is now of the opinion that Pennsylvania should join the fast-growing list of jurisdictions that have eliminated the privity requirement . . . [in suits] by purchasers against remote manufacturers for breach of implied warranty. . . .

As far back as 1931 the seeds of discontent were sown in the field of privity. . . .

Courts and scholars alike have recognized that the typical consumer does not deal at arm's length with the party whose product he buys. Rather, he buys from a retail merchant who is usually little more than an economic conduit. It is not the merchant who has defectively manufactured the product. Nor is it usually the merchant who advertises the product on such a large scale as to attract consumers. We have in our society literally scores of large, financially responsible manufacturers who place their wares in the stream of commerce not only with the realization, but with the avowed purpose, that these goods will find their way into the hands of the consumer. Only the consumer will use these products; and only the consumer will be injured by them should they prove defective. . . .

Under the Uniform Commercial Code, once a breach of warranty has been shown, the defendant's liability, assuming of course the presence of proximate cause and damages, is absolute. Lack of negligence on the seller's part is no defense.

. . . Under the Restatement, if an action be commenced in tort by a purchaser of a defective product against a remote manufacturer, recovery may be had without a showing of negligence, and without a showing of privity, for any damage inflicted upon the person or property of the plaintiff as a result of this defective product.

. . . [W]e are convinced that on this issue [of privity], the Code must be coextensive with Restatement section 402a in the case of product liability. . . .

The explanation offered . . . for not abolishing "vertical" privity of contract in breach of warranty actions brought under the U.C.C. was that section 2-318 of the code, limiting the persons benefited by an express or implied warranty to the buyer himself, to members of the buyer's family or household, and to guests in his home, impliedly prohibited any further relaxation of privity strictures. However, although the code sets an absolute limit on those injured parties who may seek shelter under the umbrella of a manufacturer's warranty, section 2-318 says nothing whatsoever about the second problem. . . . That is: how far back up the distributive chain may an injured party go in seeking to enforce an implied warranty? Must he be satisfied with recovery only against his immediate seller, or may he also hold liable the manufacturer with whom he had no personal contact? In short, given the code's pronouncement on "horizontal privity" (who, besides the purchaser, has a right of action against the manufacturer or seller of a defective product), what, if anything, does this signify concerning the code's complete silence on the issue of "vertical privity" (who, besides the immediate seller, is liable to the consumer for injuries caused by the defective product)?

The answer to this question is provided in the clearest of language by the drafters of the code in comment 3 to section 2-318. . . . The comment recites that: "This section [2-318] expressly includes as beneficiaries within its provisions the family, household, and guests of the purchaser. Beyond this, the section is neutral and is not intended to enlarge or restrict the developing case law on whether the seller's warranties, given to his buyer who resells, extends to other persons in the distributive chain." Thus it is clear beyond peradventure that the drafters of the code never intended 2-318 to set any limits on vertical privity. . . .

Moreover, it would not take a comment such as the one cited above to demonstrate that 2-318 does not cover problems of vertical privity. Merely to *read* the language is to demonstrate that the code simply fails to treat this problem. Therefore, just as is the rule for any area of contract law not covered by the code, general principles of law control. There thus is nothing to prevent this Court from joining in the growing number of jurisdictions which, although bound by the code, have nevertheless judicially abolished vertical privity in breach of warranty cases.

Curiously, the imagined limits on the Court's power under the code to discard vertical privity have not prevented us from eliminating the privity requirement in cases involving tainted food. We now believe that the time has come to recognize that the same policy reasons underlying the food cases also underlie cases involving defective non-edibles which cause injury. When it is considered that continued adherence to the requirements of vertical privity results merely in perpetuating a needless chain of actions whereby each buyer must seek redress for breach of warranty from his own immediate seller until the actual manufacturer is eventually reached . . . [v]ertical privity can no longer commend itself to this Court.

We therefore hold that the lack of privity between appellants and Soya cannot insulate the latter from liability for breach of warranty.

.   .   .

The judgment of the Court of Common Pleas of Washington County is vacated, and the record remanded for further proceedings consistent with this opinion.

Lonzrick v. Republic Steel Corp.

205 N.E.2d 92 (Ohio) 1965

SKEEL, J. This appeal comes to this court from a judgment entered for the defendant. . . . The action is one for money only. The plaintiff alleges in his petition that he suffered certain personal injuries when "steel bar joists" manufactured by the defendant, which had been placed in a building, collapsed and fell down upon him. The plaintiff was a construction worker employed by a *subcontractor,* the Valley Steel Erectors, Inc. The joists were purchased from the defendant by the *general contractor.* The cause of action, as stated by the plaintiff, is based on a claim of a breach of the duty imposed by law on the defendant to furnish *merchantable* joists to the general contractor. *No claim of privity between the plaintiff and defendant is stated in the petition,* and under the facts stated no such claim could be made.

We are, therefore, confronted with the question whether the petition states a cause of action. . . .

There are . . . three methods by which one who suffers injury or damage in using a chattel delivered by the manufacturer or the vendor in a defective condition may proceed to seek redress against the manufacturer:

1. Where the ultimate purchaser stands *in a contractual relation* with the producer or vendor, an action (if justified by the facts) for breach of express or implied warranty may be maintained as provided by the Uniform Commercial Code.

2. By an action charging *negligence* in producing the chattel . . . *regardless of privity.*

3. By an action seeking to enforce *strict tort liability without privity.* . . .

In the case now before us, the plaintiff states facts which show that he had no contractual relations with the defendant and that he bases his claim on "strict tort liability." While the words "implied warranty" are used, they are intended to mean and describe the duty and representation of a producer of chattels to the buying public that his goods may be used for the purposes intended without danger to the purchaser from latent defects making their use dangerous to the user. The use of the word "warranty" is probably improper; however, the courts, in describing causes of action for strict tort liability in product cases, seem to have continued to use it for want of a better word, not intending it to mean anything more than the manufacturer putting his goods into the stream of commerce, thereby representing that they are of merchantable quality, unless a different intention is clearly expressed. . . .

For the foregoing reasons, the judgment . . . is reversed, and the cause is remanded with instructions to overrule the demurrer and for further proceedings.

Judgment reversed.

Suvada v. White Motor Company
201 N.E.2d 313 (Ill.) 1964

A truck belonging to the plaintiffs, partners in a milk distributing business, collided with a bus as a result of the failure of the brakes on the truck.

In 1957 plaintiffs purchased from White the 1953 motor vehicle for use in plaintiffs' business of distributing milk. White installed a brake system in the reconditioned motor vehicle which brake system was manufactured and supplied by Bendix. The plaintiffs allege that the collision was caused by an inherently dangerously made brake system in the tractor-trailer, and that the unit was purchased from White and the brake system was manufactured by Bendix; that as a result of the collision the tractor-trailer unit was damaged and numerous persons were injured; that plaintiffs expended money for investigation of the collision and in the defense of lawsuits arising out of the collision; that they made compromise settlements of some of the personal injury claims and property damage claims, and that they expended money in repair of their tractor-trailer. The complaint alleges that the failure of the braking system to operate was because of an inherently dangerous and defectively made linkage bracket. The plaintiffs sued both the seller, White, and manufacturer of the brake system, Bendix, for recovery of property damage to their tractor-trailer unit and, additionally, for indemnification of expenditures made by them in settlement, investigation and defense of claims that arose out of the collision.

BURKE, J. . . . Plaintiffs state that the amounts paid by them for settlement, investigation and defense of personal injuries and property damage claims constitute proper elements of damage for indemnification from defendants; that these expenditures are reasonably probable and foreseeable as a direct result of the sale and manufacturing of an inherently dangerous or defectively made product and that the expenditures under the facts pleaded do not make them volunteers.

In the recent case of *Goldberg* v. *Kollsman Instrument Corp.,* the court said: "A breach of warranty, it is now clear, is not only a violation of the sales contract out of which the warranty arises but is a tortious wrong suable by a noncontracting party whose use of the warranted article is within the reasonable contemplation of the vendor or manufacturer. . . . As we all know, a number of courts . . . have for the best of reasons dispensed with the privity requirement. . . . Very recently the Supreme Court of California imposed 'strict tort liability' (surely a more accurate phrase) regardless of privity on a manufacturer in a case where a power tool threw a piece of wood at a user who was not the purchaser. The California court said that the purpose of such a holding is to see to it that the costs of injuries resulting from defective products are borne by the manufacturers who put the products on the market rather than by injured persons who are powerless to protect themselves and that implicit in putting such articles on the market are representations that they will safely do the job for which they were built." . . .

The cases in Illinois . . . support . . . the proposition that the manufacturer who places in the stream of commerce a product that becomes dangerous to life and limb of the public is liable to a subpurchaser because of the nature of the product and that the liability is not based upon a contractual relationship. In *Lindroth* v. *Walgreen Co., and Knapp-Moncharch Co.* (329 Ill. App. 105, 67 N.E.2d 595), the court held that where the product is inherently dangerous a cause of action by the subpurchaser against the manufacturer exists in the absence of privity. Today's manufacturer, selling to distributors or wholesalers, is still interested in the subsequent sales of the product. His advertising is not aimed at his distributors. The historical relative equality of seller and buyer no longer exists. A product that is inherently dangerous or defectively made constitutes an exception to the requirement of privity in an action between the user of the product and its manufacturer. We cannot say from the allegations of the complaint that Bendix is beyond the immediate distributive chain. The complaint alleges that Bendix manufactured an inherently dangerous or defectively made brake system which was installed by White into a motor vehicle as part of its renovation. Bendix is charged with manufacturing and supplying that brake system. The complaint does not charge that the brake system was reconditioned.

The exception to the privity requirement is not superseded nor is it modified by the provisions of the Uniform Commercial Code. In Comment 3 to Sec. 2-318 of the Code, the drafters state that: "The section is neutral and is not intended to enlarge or restrict the developing case law on whether the seller's warranties, given to his buyer who resells, extend to other persons in the distributive chain." In *Henningsen* v. *Bloomfield Motors, Inc.* (32 N.J. 358, 161 A2d. 69, 75 A.L.E.2d 1), the court held that the subpurchaser is entitled to recover from a manufacturer of an automobile that is inherently dangerous or defectively manufactured in the absence of privity. The court said that it could find no distinction between an unwholesome food case and a defective car. This position was taken in *B. F. Goodrich Co.* v. *Hammond* (269 F.2d. 501) (10th Circuit Kansas). In that case the administrator of an estate of a subpurchaser and wife who were occupants of an automobile sued the tire manufacturer for breach of implied warranty. Goodrich sold blowout-proof tires. The mishap resulted because of a defect in the manufacture of a tire that caused a sudden blowout. In deciding that the subpurchaser and his wife had a cause of action against the manufacturer based upon breach of warranty, the court said (269 F.2d. p. 502): "[P]rivity is not essential where an implied warranty is imposed by law on the basis of public policy."

A motor vehicle that is operated on the highways with a braking system that is inoperative is obviously dangerous to life and limb. The State of Illinois recognizes the necessity for a proper braking system in motor vehicles and has declared it to be public policy of the State that all motor vehicles manufactured and sold within the State shall be equipped with brakes adequate to control the movement of the vehicle. The manufacturer of the braking system is in the best position to provide and insure an adequate braking system of motor vehicles that are driven on the public highways. (Ill. Rev. State. 1963, Chap. 95-1/2, 211.) We think that the court erred in striking the counts based on the theory of an implied warranty. . . .

For these reasons the judgment is reversed and the cause is remanded with directions to reinstate the counts that were dismissed and for further proceedings not inconsistent with these views.

Judgment reversed and cause remanded with directions.

State ex. rel. Western Seed Production Corp. v. Campbell

442 P.2d 215 (Oreg.) 1968

The plaintiffs, Oregon sugar-beet growers, purchased beet seed from a local supplier. They contended that the seed, furnished by an Arizona corporation, was defective and that it did not produce a crop. The Arizona corporation was not engaged in business in Oregon but was sued under the Oregon "long-arm" statute. The plaintiff's action was based on two theories: (1) breach of implied warranty and (2) negligence. The defendant contended that the breach of warranty action would not lie because of lack of privity of contract. The lower court dismissed the suit, and the plaintiff appealed.

GOODWIN, J. . . . In *Price* v. *Gatlin* (241 Or. 315, 405 P.2d 502 (1965)), we held that a purchaser of a defective tractor could not hold the wholesaler, with whom he had no contract, strictly liable where the defect had resulted only in a loss of profits to the purchaser's business. In the present case, plaintiffs lost the profits they expected to derive from a normal sugar-beet crop. There was no damage to their land; there was only a loss of use thereof. The alleged damage is, therefore, essentially of the same character as that suffered in *Price* v. *Gatlin.*

The pending action . . . is against a producer rather than against a wholesaler. But since each case involved a remote seller, there is no substantive basis on these facts for distinguishing *Price* v. *Gatlin.* In either situation, the question is whether a purchaser of a defective product who suffers only economic loss should be allowed to maintain an action for breach of warranty against one with whom he has had no dealings.

. . . The code provides a scheme of warranty recovery, in which fault is irrelevant, for all types of loss resulting from "unmerchantable" products. . . . The code is silent . . . as to privity requirements for breach-of-warranty actions. This aspect of sales law has been left to the courts in jurisdictions adopting the code.

Because of social pressure to compensate innocent victims of personal injuries, and because remedies for such injuries have traditionally been provided by tort law, this court has joined those which have abolished privity requirements in actions for personal injuries from defective products. We have assumed that such a cause of action sounds in tort and thus is unhampered by the statutory impediments to relief for breach of warranty. Where a product is defective within the meaning of the Restatement (Second) of Torts § 402A (1965) and causes personal injury, the injured party can recover for his injuries against any seller of the defective product. . . .

Where the damages sought do not involve personal injury, . . . the application of Section 402A to property damage is, in this state, an open question.

The risk that a product may not perform as it should exists in every purchase transaction. A buyer who chooses his seller with care has an adequate remedy should any warranties be breached. A buyer whose seller proves to be irresponsible will understandably seek relief further afield. But to allow a nonprivity warranty action to vindicate every disappointed consumer would unduly complicate the code's scheme, which recognizes the consensual elements of commerce. Disclaimers and limitations of certain warranties and remedies are matters for bargaining. Strict-liability actions between buyers and remote sellers could lend themselves to the proliferation of unprovable claims by disappointed bargain hunters, with little discernible social benefit. Because the buyer and his seller will normally have engaged in at least one direct transaction, litigation between these parties should ordinarily be simpler and less costly than litigation between buyer and remote seller. For these reasons we retain the rule stated in *Price* v. *Gatlin, supra:* Where the purchaser of an unmerchantable product suffers only loss of profits, his remedy for the breach of warranty is against his immediate seller unless he can predicate liability upon some fault on the part of a remote seller.

Plaintiffs, therefore, have not stated a cause of action for breach of warranty against Western Seed, a remote seller.

Affirmed on this issue.

Greeno v. Clark Equipment Company

237 F.Supp. 427 (1965)

The plaintiff was injured when a forklift truck, which he was operating while working for his employer, failed to operate properly due to an alleged defect. He brought an action for damages against the manufacturer of the truck, which had been leased by his employer from an equipment handling company. He claimed to be entitled to relief on the basis of strict liability of the manufacturer. The defendant moved to dismiss the complaint.

ESCHBACH, J. . . . This opinion will consider the theory of strict liability only in the context of products liability. When so confined, its least ambiguous definition appears in Restatement (Second), Torts 402A (Approved May 1964), set out as follows:

> 402A. Special Liability of Seller of Product for Physical Harm to User or Consumer.
> (1) One who sells any product in a defective condition unreasonably dangerous to the user or consumer, or to his property, is subject to liability for physical harm thereby caused to the ultimate user or consumer, or to his property, if
>   (a) the seller is engaged in the business of selling such a product, and
>   (b) it is expected to and does reach the user or consumer without substantial change in the condition in which it is sold.
> (2) The rule stated in Subsection (1) applies although
>   (a) the seller has exercised all possible care in the preparation and sale of his product, and
>   (b) the user or consumer has not bought the product from or entered into any contractual relation with the seller.

Without attempting an exhaustive explanation, it may fairly be said that the liability which this section would impose is hardly more than what exists under implied warranty when stripped of the contract doctrines of privity, disclaimer, requirements of notice of defect, and limitation through inconsistencies with express warranties. . . . The conditions of liability which may not be self-evident in the above text are a "defective condition" at the time the product leaves the seller's control and which causes harm to a user or consumer. A "defective condition" is a condition not contemplated by the consumer/user and which is "unreasonably dangerous" to him or his property, that is, more dangerous than would be contemplated by the ordinary consumer/user with the ordinary knowledge of the community as to its characteristics and uses. An axe is not unreasonably dangerous because, as in negligence law, users would contemplate the obvious dangers involved. But a farm combine with a weak lid over the auger would constitute an unreasonable danger because such a danger is beyond the contemplation of ordinary users. . . . Recovery in strict liability is not conditioned on privity of contract, or reliance or notice to the seller of a defect, and the seller cannot disclaim or by contract alter a duty which the law would impose upon him. Nor can inconsistent express warranties dilute the seller's duty to refrain from injecting into the stream of commerce goods in a "defective condition." . . .

It is generally recognized that implied warranty is more properly a matter of public policy beyond the power of the seller to alter unilaterally with disclaimers and inconsistent express warranties. . . . Where there is implied in law a certain duty to persons not in contract privity, it seems preposterous that the seller should escape that duty by inserting into a non-contractual relationship a contractual disclaimer of which the remote injured person would be unaware. Even as between parties to a contract, where the law would imply in a sale the reasonable fitness of the product for ordinary purposes, it seems unconscionable that the seller should by disclaimers avoid the duty of selling merchantable products or shift the risk of defect, unless the total circumstances of the transaction indicate the buyer's awareness of defects or acceptance of risk. This warranty imposed by law, irrespective of privity and based on public policy is more aptly called "strict liability."

As the Indiana courts have escaped the rigors of privity in negligence through the doctrine of "imminently dangerous," other courts have invoked various exceptions which in time have devoured the requirement of privity in both negligence and implied warranty. Some cases hold that privity is not required in a products liability case based on implied warranty, while others reach the same result by expanding the old common law concept of privity. . . . Food and beverages are well known products where privity is no longer required. . . . In the recent case of *Putman* v. *Erie City Manufacturing Co., supra,* the Court of Appeals for the Fifth Circuit extended to all defective products unreasonably dangerous to the user the reasoning of *Decker & Sons, Inc.* v. *Capps,* . . . The latter was an implied warranty food case which dispensed with privity on the grounds that implied warranty arises from public policy rather than contract and that the rights and duties it creates cannot be limited to the contracting parties. *Henningsen* v. *Bloomfield Motors, Inc., supra,* did likewise, stating at p. 379 of 32 N.J., at p. 80 of 161 A.2d. at p. 17 of 75 A.L.R.2d,

> The limitations of privity in contracts for the sale of goods developed their place in the law when marketing conditions were simple, when maker and buyer frequently met face to face on an equal bargaining plane and when many of the products were relatively uncomplicated and conducive to inspection by a buyer competent to evaluate their quality. With the advent of mass marketing, the manufacturer became remote from the purchaser, sales were accomplished through intermediaries, and the demand for the product was created by advertising media. In such an economy it became obvious that the consumer was the person being cultivated. Manifestly, the connotation of "consumer" was broader than that of "buyer." He signified such a person who, in the reasonable contemplation of the parties to the sale, might be expected to use the product. Thus, where the commodities sold are such that if defectively manufactured they will be dangerous to life or limb, then society's interests can only be protected by eliminating the requirement of privity between the maker and his dealers and the reasonably expected ultimate consumer.

The reasoning of . . . the many other cases striking down the requirement of privity in implied warranty seems eminently sound. As Judge Wisdom so aptly recognized in *Putman, supra,* at 919 of 338 F.2d, "Since 1958, almost every court which has considered the question has expanded the doctrine of strict liability to cover all defective products, regardless of lack of proof of negligence." Various means have been applied to reach this result without naming the rule "strict liability" and without the furor which that label has created. . . .

The direction of the law is clear. . . . If the Restatement correctly states the conditions of recovery now in practice, let those elements have a fresh name and abandon the old entanglements of "warranty."

Already the Restatement, *supra,* is being followed and shaped. The recent case of *Delaney* v. *Towmotor Corp.* (339 F.2d, 4, 2d Cir., December 3, 1964) held the Restatement word "sells" is merely descriptive and that the product need not be sold, if it has been placed "in the stream of commerce by other means." . . .

The question is now squarely before this court and must be decided. It is perhaps fortuitous that the Indiana Supreme Court has not yet passed on this issue, but doubtlessly that forward-looking court would embrace the Restatement (Second), Torts 402A, and the many recent cases and authors who have done likewise, as eminently just and as the law of Indiana today.

Accordingly, defendant's motion to dismiss . . . is hereby denied.

Mitchell v. Miller

214 A.2d 694 (Conn.) 1965

The plaintiff brought action to recover damages for the death of her husband. A Buick automobile belonging to one of the defendants was parked on an incline near a golf course with the gearshift lever in the "park" position. The gears did not lock but became disengaged; as a result, the car rolled down the incline and struck the plaintiff's husband. The plaintiff sued the owner of the car and General Motors Corporation, alleging negligence and breach of warranty.

KLAU, J. . . . In imposing liability upon manufacturers to ultimate consumers in terms of implied warranty even though no privity exists, the courts have used a convenient legal fiction to accomplish this result. Ordinarily, there is no contract in a real sense between a manufacturer and an expected ultimate consumer of his product. As a matter of public policy, the law has imposed on all manufacturers a duty to consumers irrespective of contract or of privity relationship between them. The search for correct principles to delineate manufacturers' responsibility to consumers has found expression in the doctrine of tort and strict liability. The "strict tort liability" doctrine is "surely a more accurate phrase" than breach of implied warranty of suitability for use.

The second Restatement of the Law of Torts adopts the basis of strict liability, in the case of the seller of products, for occasioning physical harm to a user or consumer. See Restatement (Second), 2 Torts § 402A. The rule is one of strict liability, making the seller subject to liability to the user or consumer even though the seller has exercised all possible care in the preparation and sale of the product. The product, of course, must be not only defective but unreasonably dangerous to the user or consumer.

The question, then, is whether strict liability ought to be extended to one who is not in the category of one who is a user or consumer of the product, or whether it is to be confined solely to commercial transactions where injury results only to the user or ultimate consumer. In a caveat, the American Law Institute in its second Restatement of the Law of Torts expresses no opinion as to whether the rules stated in § 402A may not apply to harm to persons other than users or consumers. In commenting upon this caveat, the Restatement states: "Thus far the courts, in applying the rule stated in this Section, have not gone beyond allowing recovery to users and consumers, as those terms are defined in Comment *l.* Casual bystanders, and others who may come in contact with the product, as in the case of employees of the retailer, or a passer-by injured by an exploding bottle, or a pedestrian hit by an automobile, have been denied recovery. There may be no essential reason why such plaintiffs should not be brought within the scope of the protection afforded, other than that they do not have the same reasons for expecting such protection as the consumer who buys a marketed product; but the social pressure which has been largely responsible for the development of the rule stated has been a consumers' pressure, and there is not the same demand for the protection of casual strangers. The Institute expresses neither approval nor disapproval of expansion of the rule to permit recovery by such persons." Restatement (Second), 2 Torts § 402A, comment o.

In the only reported case involving an injury to a nonuser in this state, the court refused to find that a cause of action, based on a warranty of fitness, existed, as against the used-car dealer from whom the car was purchased, in favor of a pedestrian who was injured as a result of a defect in the car existing at the time of the sale. The court, as a matter of public policy, was unwilling to extend the doctrine of strict liability in favor of a pedestrian against a used-car dealer. Since the decision in the *Kuschy* case, the Michigan Supreme Court has applied the doctrine of strict liability in favor of an innocent bystander who was injured when the barrel of a shotgun being fired by another party exploded because of a defective shell.

The trend toward applying the doctrine of strict liability in the case of an injury arising from the manufacture of a product which may be unreasonably dangerous and from which the likelihood of injury arising from its use is reasonably foreseeable is expanding. Foreseeable or reasonable anticipation of injury from the defect is becoming the test. Reliance on representations or notice of injury are no longer absolute conditions precedent. . . . The attempt to predicate liability on the law of sales or contract is being abandoned in an increasing number of jurisdictions. In *Piercefield* v. *Remington Arms Co.* . . . the court thrust aside all fictions as to the basis of the manufacturer's liability, and liability was imposed on the basis of a tort committed by the defendant. Issues should not be determined by labels, which serve only to confuse.

A defective automobile manufactured as alleged in this complaint by the defendant General Motors constitutes a real hazard upon the highway. . . . The likelihood of injury from its use exists not merely for the passengers therein but for the pedestrian upon the highway. The public policy which protects the user and consumer should also protect the innocent bystander. In the instant case, an innocent bystander, while playing golf, was killed by a car defectively manufactured, insofar as the allegations of the complaint go, by the defendant automobile corporation. There seems to be no sound public policy to bar a trial upon the issues raised in the complaint. Accordingly, the demurrer of the General Motors Corporation to the third count of the complaint is overruled.

CHAPTER 22
REVIEW QUESTIONS AND PROBLEMS

1. *A* was considering the purchase of a used crane from *B*. The crane was demonstrated to *A* but did not do any actual lifting in the demonstration. *A* decided to purchase the crane and was assured that it would lift thirty tons. If the crane is not capable of lifting thirty tons, would *A* have a cause of action against *B*?

2. *A*, an employee of BCD Company, was injured by a machine manufactured by the X Company and sold to BCD. The statute of limitations has outlawed any tort claim for personal injuries. Is there any other theory upon which *A* could bring a court action for his injuries?

3. *A* sold skins to *B* with knowledge that *B* would make leather jackets from them. Nothing was said about warranties. Has *A* made any warranties to *B*?

4. *A*, while driving his station wagon, rammed into the rear of a car driven by *B*. *B* brought action against the Ford Motor Company, claiming that a defective accelerator caused the accident. Would the manufacturer have any liability?

5. *A* was a pallbearer at a funeral. The casket handle he was holding broke and caused the casket to fall and injure him. *A* brought action against the funeral parlor and the manufacturer of the casket. Upon what basis could *A* obtain recovery?

6. *A* was in the business of selling electric power. *A* purchased a generator from the B Electric Company. The generator did not function properly, and *A* claimed several million dollars in consequential damages. The warranty provision of the contract, however, relieved *B* from any liability for consequential damages. Will the warranty restriction be upheld?

7. *A* operated a restaurant. He purchased clams from *B*. *C*, a customer at *A*'s restaurant, in April, 1964, ordered clams, ate them, and claimed that he contracted hepatitis. *C* brought an action against *A*, and *A* sought to have *B* included as a party to the case in August, 1969. *B* demurred to the complaint, and the demurrer was sustained. Why was the demurrer sustained?

8. *A* bought a farm tractor from *B*, a dealer. The tractor was defective and not suited for use on a farm. *A* was unable to harvest his crop because of the defective tractor, and he brought an action for damages against the manufacturer. The manufacturer contended that *A* could not maintain the action. Upon what basis would such an action be justified?

9. *A* sold *B* a car which had been mortgaged to the X Finance Co. *B* was not aware of the mortgage. The contract contained a clause which excluded all warranties. If X Finance Company repossesses the car, does *B* have any rights against *A*?

10. *A* purchased diving equipment from *B.* He told *B* that he intended to dive to depths of 200 feet. *B* selected the gear from his stock. *A* suffered from the bends when he dove to that depth. Can *A* recover damages from *B*?

chapter 23

Introduction to Commercial Paper

3-67. In General. The term "commercial paper" is used by the Code to describe certain types of negotiable instruments. The adjective "negotiable" has long been used to describe special types of written contracts used to represent credit and to function as a substitute for money. The term is derived from the Latin word *negotiatus*, consisting of the prefix, *neg*, meaning *not* or *negation*, plus the root *otium*, meaning leisure—making the combination *not-leisure* or *non-leisure*—plus the suffix *able*, meaning capable of. This idea was easily applicable to business and came to mean the capacity of certain kinds of paper to pass, like money, from person to person. Paper designated as "negotiable" became a medium of exchange.

The overwhelming importance of negotiable instruments to our business community and to our economy is readily apparent. It is obvious that business could not expand and develop its full potential if it were necessary to rely only upon money—coin and currency—for its transactions. Checks are used in settling about nine-tenths of all business transactions. Accumulations of wealth in the form of commercial paper far exceed wealth represented by actual money.

Commercial paper consists of two basic types of instruments—promissory notes and bills of exchange, frequently called drafts. A note is a *promise* to pay money; a bill of exchange is an *order* directed to another person to pay money to a third party. A check is a typical bill of exchange—it is an order by the drawer directing the drawee (bank) to pay money to the payee of the check.

3-68. History of the Promissory Note. The origin of the modern promissory note may be traced to an early writing called *scripta obligatoria* or *writing obligatory*. The debtor made a promise, formally under seal or informally without a seal, to pay a sum of money to the creditor, his attorney, or a nominee, someone designated by the creditor as entitled to receive payment. The attorney or nominee of the creditor as well as the creditor himself could thus sue the debtor if he failed to pay the note. Sometimes the paper would read "payable to the creditor or the producer of the document." Early cases tried in the "Fair Courts" in England in the sixteenth century disclose suits by persons other than the original creditor, such as an attorney or assignee or the "bearer or producer of the paper." Thus the idea of a transferable writing, either as order or bearer paper, was conceived. In buying and selling goods and wares from overseas, *bills of debt* or *billes obligatories* were given for merchandise by one merchant to another merchant. By transferring the "billes obligatories," the merchant as creditor could empower another to collect a debt, or the merchant as debtor could use the paper to pay a debt owed by him to another. Thus these notes served as a medium of exchange and could be used to discharge debts. By statute and by recognition of the law merchant by the king's court, these written obligations took on many of the present characteristics of negotiable promissory notes.

Bills obligatory were not only used to pay for goods but were issued by goldsmiths to merchants who left their surplus funds for safekeeping with the goldsmiths. These instruments were transferable; it may be said that they were the forerunners of our modern bank notes.

Bank notes issued by an individual goldsmith as a banker were subject to the risk of the bankruptcy of the goldsmith. It was not until 1694, when the Bank of England was established, that a quasi-government institution gave credit to bank notes. The Bank of England was authorized to issue "bills obligatory and of credit"—bank notes—which would pass from one person to another, by assignment or indorsement, for the payment of debts. In 1704, the English Parliament passed a statute known as the Promissory Note Act which gave to promissory notes the attributes of negotiability according to the custom of merchants.

Another early source of modern promissory notes now recognized as government obligations, such as bonds and paper money, was the English Exchequer Bill. The English government was authorized by statue in 1696 to borrow money and issue interest-bearing demand bearer bills therefor. The act authorized that these bills pass from one person to another and be accepted for the payment of debts. Soon, by necessity, these instruments—as government paper money—took on all the attributes of negotiability.

3-69. History of the Bill of Exchange.   The origin or source of the bill of exchange rests in antiquity. There is evidence of its use in ancient Assyria, Egypt, Greece, and Rome. The bill of exchange was invented for the purpose of effecting an exchange of money—coin, silver, and gold—in distant parts without running the risk of its physical transportation. Italian merchants are said to have introduced the efficient use of modern bills of exchange. As trade and commerce increased, a safe and effective method for the exchange of money became a necessity. Goldsmiths and money exchangers in the different countries established a system whereby a merchant who owed money in a foreign country could pay his debt. The merchant delivered his money to his local exchanger, and the local exchanger drew a bill upon his foreign correspondent, directing that the creditor merchant be paid or that the foreign merchant collect from the foreign correspondent exchanger. The exchangers met from time to time at the local merchant fairs and settled the accounts. The type of instrument they used is the ancestor of our modern bill of exchange, bank draft, and check.

Not only were drafts drawn on money exchangers, acting as bankers, but merchants in foreign countries also became drawees (the person who is required to pay a draft) when their credit was well established. The following situation illustrates how the modern trade acceptance developed: *D*, a silk merchant in London, had his purchasing agent *A*, in Brussels, purchase silk from a merchant in Brussels. In order to pay for the silk, *A* drew a bill of exchange on *D* in London, payable to the order of the Brussels merchant. The Brussels merchant cashed the bill with a money exchanger, who sent it, in turn, to London for collection. Instead of making the seller in Brussels the payee, *A* might, "by way of exchange, as is done by common custom of merchants," cash the bill of exchange with an exchanger and pay the Brussels seller with coin. By the close of the seventeenth century, these instruments were in general use but not yet recognized by the common law courts of England.

Thus, the law of negotiable instruments developed first in the law merchant based upon customs and usages of the merchant. Later it was absorbed by the common law and a great body of case law developed which was replete with conflicts and contradictions. Subsequently, it was codified by the Uniform Negotiable Instruments Law (NIL) and finally the NIL was replaced by Article 3—Commercial Paper—of the Uniform Commercial Code.

3-70. The Concept of Negotiability. Commercial paper serves a dual function: It is used as a substitute for money by supplementing the supply of currency, and it serves as a credit device—representing money to be paid in the future. These basic functions are illustrated by common commercial paper transactions. If *A* buys goods from *B* and pays with a check, the parties have used commercial paper as a substitute for money. If *A* buys goods from *B* and gives him a negotiable note payable in thirty days, *A* has in effect received thirty days' credit. Also, *B* may now negotiate the note in payment of his own obligation, or if he is in need of cash he could discount the note, i.e., sell it to someone else.

The legal theory which forms the basis for the use of commercial paper to represent credit and to serve as a substitute for money is the same under the Code as it was under the law merchant and prior statutes. Negotiable instruments developed because of the commercial need for something that would be readily acceptable in lieu of money and that would accordingly be readily transferable in trade and commerce. The person to whom the instrument was payable would need a ready market for it so that he could use it in much the same fashion as he could use money. This would require that substantial protection and assurance of payment be given to any person to whom the paper might be transferred. To accomplish this, it would be necessary to insulate the transferee from most of the defenses which the primary party, e.g., maker of a note, might have against the payee, so that the primary party could not assert them against the person to whom the paper was transferred. Further assurance could be given by requiring each party who transferred the instrument to assume liability to pay in the event that the maker or other primary party failed or refused to do so. Finally, the transferring party could make warranties to the transferee that the instrument transferred was in all respects genuine.

Article 3 of the Code encompasses all of the foregoing principles. A person to whom commercial paper is negotiated takes it free of personal defenses of the maker or drawer; the party who transfers it by indorsement assumes an obligation to pay if the primary party fails or refuses to do so; and an indorser makes warranties that the paper is genuine.

This basic theory of negotiability can be further explained by noting the difference between the *assignment* of a contract and the negotiation of a negotiable instrument. As was discussed in Chapter 14, Book Two, on Contracts, contract rights are transferable by assignment. For example, suppose *A* owed *B* $100 for goods sold by *B* to *A*, or for services rendered by *B* for *A*. *B* has a right that *A* pay him $100. *A* is under duty to *B* to pay this $100. This type of contract right owned by *B* is called a *chose in action*. *B* may sell and assign to *C* his right to collect $100 from *A*. Assume that *A* has a defense in the nature of a counterclaim against *B* for $35, either because the goods sold were not as required by contract or the services rendered by *B* were not satisfactory. The right that *C* purchased from *B* would be subject to *A*'s defense of failure of consideration and *C* could collect only $65 from *A*. *C,* the assignee, would secure no better right against *A* than the original right held by *B,* the assignor.[1] *C,* the assignee, would "stand in the shoes" of *B,* the assignor.

In the example given above, if the evidence of the debt is not a simple contract for money but a negotiable promissory note given by *A* to *B* and it is properly negotiated to *C, C* is in a superior position to that which he occupied when he was an assignee. Assuming that *C* is a "holder in due course," *C* has a better title because he is free of the personal defenses that are available against *B,* the payee, and the original party to the paper. Therefore, *A* cannot use the defense of failure of consideration, and *C* can collect the $100 note.

Transfer of the instrument free of personal defenses is the very essence of negotiability. Three requirements must be met before a holder is free from defenses. First, the instrument must be negotiable, i.e., it must comply with the statutory formalities and language requirements. An instrument that does not qualify is nonnegotiable, and any transfer is an assignment subject to defenses. These requirements are discussed in the next chapter.

Second, the instrument must be properly *negotiated* to the transferee. The method of negotiation depends upon whether the instrument is payable to "order" or payable to "bearer." If it is the latter, it may be negotiated by delivery; if the former, an indorsement is required for negotiation. The person who negotiates paper, especially an indorser, assumes greater responsibility than does one who assigns a nonnegotiable instrument. An indorser will be responsible to pay the holder of a negotiable instrument if the maker or other primary party fails to do so. Transferors of bearer negotiable instruments as well as indorsers warrant that the instrument is genuine.

Third, the party to whom negotiable commercial paper is negotiated must be a *holder in due course* or have the rights of a holder in due course. A

[1] Universal C.I.T. Credit Corporation v. Hudgens, page 470

holder in due course is a holder who takes an instrument (1) for value, (2) in good faith, and (3) without notice that it is overdue, or has been dishonored or of any defense against it or claim to it on the part of any person. This concept is fully discussed in Chapter 25.

The defenses that cannot be asserted against a holder in due course are called personal defenses. Real defenses, on the other hand, may be asserted against anyone including a holder in due course. Real defenses include forgery, fraud in the execution, and other matters that go to the existence of the instrument; personal defenses such as failure of consideration involve less serious matters.

Freedom from personal defenses coupled with the right of recourse against prior indorsers are the distinguishing features of commercial paper. They are the attributes that enable it to pass freely from person to person and to serve its purpose as a money supplement and credit device. Business convenience requires these characteristics. A businessman would be reluctant to take a note or a check from a holder if he thereby incurred the risk of an assignee of an ordinary contract right.

A result comparable to negotiability can be obtained if a contract expressly provides that upon assignment the party who is obligated to pay agrees to waive defenses as against assignees. Such a provision is often included in contracts for the purchase of such items as appliances. The seller often sells these contracts to banks or finance companies. The courts have recognized such provisions to the extent that a bona fide (good faith) purchaser takes the contract free from many of the personal defenses. Although these contracts do not qualify as commercial paper, they nevertheless may be transferred free of defenses much as if they were commercial paper.

3-71. Types of Instruments. Article 3—Commercial Paper—is restricted in its coverage to the draft (bill of exchange), the check, the certificate of deposit, and the note. A writing which complies with the statutory requirements is:

(a) a "draft" (bill of exchange) if it is an order;

(b) a "check" if it is a draft drawn on a bank and payable on demand;

(c) a "certificate of deposit" if it is an acknowledgment by a bank of receipt of money with an engagement to repay it;

(d) a "note" if it is a promise other than a certificate of deposit. (U.C.C. 3-104(2))

A note is two-party paper as is the certificate of deposit. The parties to a note are the *maker,* who promises to pay, and the *payee* to whom the promise is made. The draft and the check are three-party instruments. A draft presupposes a debtor-creditor relationship between the *drawer* and the *drawee,* or some other obligation on the part of the drawee in favor of the drawer. The drawee is the debtor; the drawer the creditor. The drawer-creditor orders the drawee-debtor to pay money to a third party who is the payee. The mere execution of the draft does not obligate the drawee on the paper. His liability on the paper arises when he formally *accepts* the obligation to pay in writing upon the draft itself, and by so doing he becomes primarily liable on the paper. Thereafter the drawee is called an *acceptor,* and his liability is similar to the liability of the maker of a promissory note.

A check is a draft drawn on a bank (drawee) by the drawer (who has an account with the bank) to the order of a payee.

Checks are paid by the bank in due course without an acceptance in the usual sense, but the holder of a check may have it certified which is the equivalent of an "acceptance" by the bank.

The various types of commercial paper are tailored to meet the needs of particular types of business transactions and to serve particular needs as credit devices and substitutes for money. Among the more common types of commercial paper are:

Checks.   A check drawn by a bank upon itself is a *cashier's* check. A *certified* check is a check that has been "accepted" by the drawee bank. *Traveller's checks* are like cashier's checks in that the financial institution issuing such instruments is both the drawer and the drawee. Such instruments are negotiable when they have been completed by the identifying signature.

Drafts.   A *bank draft* is a banker's check; that is, it is a check drawn by one bank on another bank, payable on demand. Such drafts are often used in the check collection process and are called "remittance instruments" in this connection. As noted, Article 4—Bank Deposits and Collections—deals with this phase of commercial paper.

Drafts are often used as an instrument for payment of goods shipped by a seller to a buyer—e.g., a manufacturer shipping goods to a distributor. The draft in payment for the goods may be drawn on the buyer's bank and may provide, for example, that it is payable in ninety days. The bill of lading which will enable the buyer to obtain the goods from the carrier may be attached to the draft with instructions to the bank to surrender the bill of lading to the buyer after the bank has "accepted" the draft. The name given to this arrangement is *banker's acceptance.*

The business situation in which a banker's acceptance is used may be described as follows: The seller of goods often refuses to deliver to the buyer upon the buyer's credit alone; or the seller of the goods may wish to secure in payment for his goods a negotiable instrument that has a ready sale. A draft accepted by a bank would have stronger credit than an instrument signed by the buyer. *B* informs his banker that he expects to purchase goods from *S* and requests the bank to accept a draft drawn on it by *S. B* presents collateral to the bank or agrees to keep a certain amount on deposit in order that the bank will be assured of funds at the time of payment. By this means the bank does not make a loan, but merely lends its credit to the buyer. *S* can dispose of his paper readily and on better terms than if the negotiable instrument were a trade acceptance accepted only by the buyer, *B.*

The above arrangement may be formalized through the use of a *letter of credit* and the *documentary draft* as explained in the previous chapter. The documentary draft is one which can be honored by the issuer of the credit (bank) only upon presentation of documents such as bills of lading as specified in the agreement between the bank and its customer.

A draft drawn by the seller in reliance upon a letter of credit creates a binding obligation of the bank. Letters of credit, although used in domestic trade, are more frequently employed in international trade. In domestic commerce, letters of credit are employed in automobile marketing to assure the manufacturer of prompt payment by the distributor. Such paper is also used to obtain credit to finance the manufacture of articles which are made for a particular buyer.

Another special type of draft is the *trade acceptance.* It is often used as a part of a transaction for the sale of goods. The seller takes the trade acceptance in payment for the goods. He draws the instrument payable to his order and presents it to the buyer. The buyer *accepts* it by placing his signature on it and thereby assumes liability to pay. The trade acceptance is often used when the buyer and seller are at different places, and the goods are to be shipped to the buyer. The seller can draw a draft on the buyer payable to his order and obtain a bill of lading from the carrier which will transport the goods. The bill of lading will enable the buyer to obtain the goods from the carrier. The seller will then send the draft with bill of lading attached to a bank at the buyer's location with instructions to deliver the bill of lading to the buyer when he accepts the trade acceptance. The trade acceptance is then returned to the seller. It may be payable at a future date, and the seller can await that date and present the trade acceptance to the buyer for payment or he can *discount* it and obtain the funds earlier. It will be noted that the buyer has been given a credit period during which he may sell the goods and obtain the funds with which to pay off the trade acceptance when it matures. The seller, on the other hand, has an instrument that can be converted into cash should he need it. A buyer may accept a trade acceptance before he receives the goods. If the goods are defective, the buyer, of course, has a defense against the seller and could refuse to pay. However, if the seller has negotiated the trade acceptance to a holder in due course, this defense could not be asserted, and the buyer would have to pay the holder. The buyer would then seek his remedy against the seller. The seller often *discounts* trade acceptances at a bank or uses them as collateral for loans.

The process of discounting is extremely important in business and commercial transactions. Typically, it involves the situation in which the holder of an instrument desires to obtain money on the strength of the instrument prior to the time when it matures. Thus, the holder may be in need of funds presently, and if he is the owner of a trade acceptance which matures six months in the future, he may by discounting obtain funds for his present needs. If the trade acceptance is discounted at a bank, for example, the bank would compute the interest that would accrue during the life of the trade acceptance, subtract this amount from the face of the instrument, and pay the borrower the net sum, less any other charges.

Promissory notes.   Notes may be used in many different ways. The purpose for which they are used and the nature of the security for the promise given by the maker to support his promise are often used to designate the type or kind of note. A note which on its face carries only the promise of the maker and is limited to his personal security may be called a simple promissory note. However, business convenience often requires a high degree of certainty that the money promised will be paid; hence the personal promise of the maker is often supported by other contracts which make property available as collateral security. The payee may require the obligation of another person. Such person may be a cosigner or an accommodation party.

A note may be secured by personal property in the nature of other notes, bonds, stock certificates, etc. temporarily placed within the control of the payee. The property transferred is called *collateral,* and such a note a *collateral note.* Many kinds of property may be used as collateral security for a note.

The maker may sign a contract which permits the payee or holder to confess a judgment against the defaulting maker without a trial. This form of note is called a *judgment note.* It is not permitted in most states, however.

The security for a note may be a mortgage. There are two kinds of mortgages, depending upon the character of the property used as security. When the maker conveys to the payee as security a right in the title of chattels, the note so secured is called a *chattel mortgage note.* When the right in the title conveyed is in real property, the note is called a *real estate mortgage note.*

It is noted that the Code (Article 9) has consolidated all security devices involving personal property into a device known as the "security interest." However, the term "chattel mortgage" is still frequently used to describe this instrument.

Certificate of deposit. The classification of different types of promises to pay money is sometimes controlled by the character of the maker. This is true of the certificate of deposit. A certificate of deposit is an acknowledgment given by a bank to a depositor, as a receipt for a deposit which the bank engages to repay with interest. Care must be taken to distinguish certificates of deposit from the usual receipt given by the bank when a depositor deposits sums to his checking account. This receipt is called a "deposit slip," which evidences the deposit to the account.

3-72. Other Negotiable Instruments. Many instruments other than commercial paper may be negotiable. The negotiability of stocks and bonds is covered by Article 8 of the Code—Investment Securities. Bills of lading and warehouse receipts are covered by Article 7—Documents of Title. The chapters that follow cover only those instruments which fall within Article 3—Commercial Paper.

INTRODUCTION TO COMMERCIAL PAPER CASE

Universal C.I.T. Credit Corporation v. Hudgens
356 S.W.2d 658 (Ark.) 1962

SMITH, J. On May 21, 1959, the appellees, Anson Hudgens and his daughter, bought a used Ford car from E. W. Mack, doing business as West Memphis Auto Sales. The conditional sales contract executed by the purchasers was transferred by Mack to the appellant finance company the next day. None of the monthly payments were made by the purchasers, who insist that they were defrauded. The appellant brought this action in replevin to recover the car. The case was transferred to equity, where the chancellor canceled the contract for fraud in its procurement and for usury. We do not reach the issue of usury, for we have concluded that the decree must in any event be affirmed upon the finding of fraud.

It should be stated at the outset that the appellant does not and cannot invoke the protection afforded to the holder of a negotiable instrument. No promissory note is involved, and the conditional sales contract is not negotiable, as it does not contain an unconditional promise payable to order or bearer.

Gale & Co. v. *Wallace* (210 Ark. 161, 194 S.W.2d 881). Hence, as we held in the case cited, the appellant holds the contract subject to defenses available against the original seller.

If the execution of the contract was induced by fraud it was properly canceled. *Gentry* v. *Little Rock Road Mach. Co.* (232 Ark.—339 S.W.2d 101). Here, as in the *Gentry* case, the purchasers testified that the seller represented the vehicle to be in good condition, when in fact it needed extensive repairs. Mack's salesman gave the appellees a signed memorandum stating that the seller had given a 30-day guarantee on the motor, transmission, and rear end; but when the dissatisfied purchasers brought the car back within a few days Mack refused to repair it unless the buyers would bear half the expense.

A more serious charge of fraud is the appellees' assertion that Mack's salesman, Harris, induced them to sign the contract in blank and then filled it in for $300 more than the agreed purchase price of $1,095. As a witness for the appellant, Harris admitted that the contract was signed in blank and was left with him for completion, but he insisted that the figure which he inserted as the purchase price, $1,395, was in accordance with the parties' agreement.

No useful purpose would be served by a detailed discussion of the conflicting testimony. Hudgens, his daughter, and his son were all present when the car was bought, and all three testified to facts amply supporting the charge of fraud. Their version of the matter is contradicted only by the salesman, Harris. After studying the record we cannot say that the evidence adduced by one side is essentially more credible than that adduced by the other. The chancellor had the great advantage of observing the witnesses as they testified. His findings do not appear to us to be against the weight of the evidence.

Affirmed.

CHAPTER 23
REVIEW QUESTIONS AND PROBLEMS

1. Why does Article 3 of the Code not include within its coverage other negotiable documents such as stock certificates and bonds?

2. *A* has $1,000 which he would like to invest for a period of one or two years. It may be necessary for him to get the money on short notice. Would a bank offer investment possibilities that would suit his needs?

3. *P* is the payee of a note for $1,000 executed by *M. P* indorses the note to *H* for $900. Why was *P* willing to sell the note at a discount?

4. *A* sold *B* a TV set on an installment contract. *A* then sold the contract to *X.* When *X* sought to recover the payments from *B, B* refused to pay on the ground that the set was defective. Can *B* successfully defend on this ground? Does *X* have any recourse against *A* ?

5. *M* executed a note payable to the order of *P. P* indorsed the note to *H* at a time when the note was overdue. Does the late transfer affect *H*'s rights against *M*?

6. *M* executed a note: "I promise to pay $500 to *P* on June 1, 1966." *P* indorsed the note to *A* in payment for goods. If *M* is unable to pay the note, can *A* hold *P* liable?

7. *A* purchased a car from *B* and gave a negotiable note in payment. The note provided that title to the car would remain in *B* until the note was paid. If the car were destroyed without fault of *A* prior to maturity of the note, would *A* be relieved of liability?

8. *A* is indebted to *B* in the amount of $500. *B* drew a draft on *A* in that amount payable to the order of *P*. *P* presented the draft to *A* for payment and *A* refused to pay. Can *P* sue *A* on the draft?

9. *A* is the holder of a check drawn by *B* on X Bank. Under what circumstances might *A* wish to have the check certified?

10. *S*, seller, drew a trade acceptance on *B*, buyer, for the price of goods sold. *B* accepted the instrument and *S* then discounted it at X Bank. The goods were never delivered to *B*. Can X Bank force *B* to pay the amount of the acceptance?

Commercial Paper: Creation and Transfer

REQUIREMENTS OF COMMERCIAL PAPER

3-73. In General. The negotiability of an instrument is determined by the terms written on the face of the instrument. The Code (Article 3) requires that the instrument satisfy certain formal requirements; deviation from these requirements prevents the instrument from being negotiable.

In order for an instrument to be negotiable, it must satisfy four basic requirements. (It is stressed that these requirements relate to *negotiability* of the instrument and not to its validity, enforceability, or transferability.) The instrument must: (a) be signed by the maker or drawer; (b) contain an unconditional promise or order to pay a sum certain in money; (c) be payable on demand or at a definite time; and (d) be payable to order or to bearer. The sections that follow discuss these basic requirements in detail.

3-74. Writing and Signature. The requirement of the Code is simply that there be a writing signed by the maker or drawer. It is not required that any particular type or kind of writing be used, nor is it necessary that the signature be at any particular place upon the instrument. The instrument may be in any form which includes "printing, typewriting, or any other intentional reduction to tangible form." (U.C.C. 1-201(46)) A symbol is a sufficient signature if it was "executed or adopted by a party with present intention to authenticate a writing." (U.C.C. 1-201(39)) The use of the word "authenticate" in the definition of "signed" makes it clear that a complete signature is not required. The authentication may be printed or written and may be placed on the instrument by stamp.

3-75. The Necessity of a Promise or Order. A negotiable note must contain a *promise* to pay. It is not required that the exact word "promise" be used;

a word or words expressing an undertaking to pay may be substituted. However, as a practical matter the word "promise" is used in almost all notes. The promise must be derived from the language, not from the fact that a debt exists. For example, the words in an instrument "due X, $500 for value received" would not satisfy the requirement of a promise. A mere acknowledgment of a debt in writing is not promissory. The simplest form of an instrument which merely acknowledges a debt is an IOU. Though such a written memorandum is sufficient to evidence and create a valid enforceable instrument upon which recovery may be had, it is not negotiable.

A draft must contain an *order* to pay. The purpose of the instrument is to order the drawee to pay money to the payee or his order. The drawer must use plain language to show an intention to make an order. The language must signify more than an authorization or request. It must be a direction to pay. Thus, an instrument in the following form would not be negotiable: "To John Doe. I wish you would pay $1,000 to the order of Richard Roe. (Signed) Robert Lee." This would nevertheless be a valid authorization for John Doe to make payment to Richard Roe.

3-76. The Promise or Order Must Be Unconditional.

Negotiable instruments serve as a substitute for money and as a basis for short-term credit. If these purposes are to be served, it is essential that the instruments be readily received in lieu of money and freely transferable. Conditional promises or orders would defeat these purposes, for it would be necessary for every transferee to make a determination with regard to whether or not the condition had been performed prior to his taking the instrument. The instruments would not freely circulate. In recognition of the functions which are served by negotiable instruments and the need for certainty if the instruments are to serve as a substitute for money and a basis for credit, the law requires that the promise or order be unconditional. If the promise or order is a conditional one, the instrument would not be negotiable even though it satisfied all of the other requirements.

The question whether or not the promise or order is conditional arises when the instrument contains language in addition to the promise or order to pay money. The Code specifies those situations in which the additional language renders the promise or order conditional and also sets forth a number of situations in which the additional language does not impair negotiability.

The promise or order is conditional if the language of the instrument provides that payment is controlled by or is subject to the terms of some other agreement. Clearly, a promise or order is conditional if reference to some other agreement is *required* and where payment is *subject to* the terms of another contract. Negotiability is also destroyed if reference to another writing would be necessary in order to determine the exact nature of the promise or order. However, a mere *reference* to some other contract or agreement does not condition the promise or order and does not impair negotiability.[1] A distinction, then, is to be drawn between additional language which imposes the terms of some other agreement and language which simply gives information as to the transaction which gave rise to the instrument. Thus, the use of the words "subject to contract" conditions the promise or order, while the words "as per contract" would not render the promise or order conditional. The latter is

[1] D'Andrea v. Feinberg, page 485

informative rather than restrictive. A recital "as per contract" might disclose an executory promise as the return for which an instrument was given. Implied or constructive conditions, such as the implication that no obligation would arise until an executory promise has been performed, do not render a promise or order conditional.

Statements of the consideration for which the instrument was given and statements of the transaction out of which the instrument arose are simply informative. A draft may have been drawn under a letter of credit, and a reference to this fact does not impose a condition. Notes frequently contain a statement that some sort of security has been given, such as a mortgage on property, or that title to goods has been retained as security for the payment of the note. In either case the purpose is to make clear to the holder that the promise to pay is secured by something in addition to the general credit of the maker, and as a consequence a mere reference to the security does not destroy negotiability.

Notes given in payment for property purchased on installment often provide that title to such property shall not pass to the maker of the note until all payments called for have been made. A statement to this effect in a note does not condition the promise to pay.

3-77. The Particular Fund Concept.   A statement that an instrument is to be paid only out of a particular fund imposes a condition. Such an instrument does not carry the general personal credit of the maker or drawer and is contingent upon the sufficiency of the fund on which it is drawn. An illustration of such promise or order is as follows: "To *A*. Pay to *B* or order $500 out of the proceeds of the sale of my store building. (Signed) *Y.*" Even though there is a sufficient fund in existence when the instrument falls due, the instrument is nonnegotiable.

There are two exceptions to the foregoing rule with regard to a limitation to payment out of a particular fund. An instrument issued by a government or government agency is not deemed nonnegotiable simply because payment is restricted to a particular fund. Second, an instrument issued by or on behalf of a partnership, unincorporated association, trust, or estate may be negotiable, although it is limited to payment out of their entire assets.

A mere *reference* to a particular fund does not impair negotiability. Such references are often made for purposes of record keeping and accounting, and they do not in any way limit liability to payment out of the fund mentioned. Thus, a check which provides "charge to agent's disbursing account" would not be deemed to contain a conditional order, but would simply indicate the account to be debited.

3-78. The Sum Must Be Certain.   The language used in creating commercial paper must be certain with respect to the amount of money promised or ordered to be paid. Otherwise, its value at any period could not be definitely determined. If the principal sum to be paid is definite, negotiability is not affected by the fact that it is to be paid with interest, in installments, with exchange at a fixed or current rate, or with cost of collection and attorney's fees in case payment shall not be made at maturity. If at any point of time during the term of the paper its full value can be ascertained with certainty, the requirement that the sum must be certain is satisfied. The obligation to pay costs and attorney's fees is part of the security contract, separate and distinct from the primary promise to pay money and does not, therefore, affect the requirement as to a sum certain. The certainty of amount is not affected if the instrument specifies different rates of interest before and after default; neither is the certainty affected by a provision for a stated discount for early payment or an additional charge if payment is made after the date fixed.

3-79. Instruments Must Be Payable in Money.   An instrument, to be negotiable, must be payable in money. Instruments payable in chattels, such as one hundred bushels of wheat or one ounce of platinum, are therefore not negotiable. "Money" is defined as "medium of exchange authorized or adopted by a domestic or foreign government as a part of its currency." (1-201(24)) The amount payable may be stated in foreign as well as domestic money, provided the medium specified has government approval. Thus, the amount payable may be stated in sterling, francs, lire, or other foreign currency. If the sum payable is stated in foreign currency, the instrument may be satisfied by payment of the dollar equivalent, that is, the number of dollars that could be purchased by the foreign currency at the "buying sight rate" on the day payable, or if it is demand paper at the rate on the date of demand. However, if it is specified in the instrument that a foreign currency is the medium of payment, payment would have to be made in that currency. An instrument expressed in terms of foreign currency but payable in dollars is negotiable, even though the exchange rate fluctuates. It might be argued that the sum is not certain since the number of dollars required to satisfy the instrument could not be determined until the date of payment or demand, but what is really involved is simply the "buying power" of money.

Negotiable instruments are sometimes made payable in "currency" or "current funds." Such terms mean that the instrument is payable in money.

3-80. Time of Payment.   As a substitute for money, negotiable instruments would be of little value if the holder were unable to determine at what time he could demand payment. It is necessary, therefore, that there be certainty as to the time of payment. A negotiable instrument must be payable on demand or at a "definite time."

Demand paper.   An instrument is payable on demand when it so states, when payable at sight or on presentation, or *when no time of payment is stated.* In general, the words "payable on demand" are used in notes and the words "at sight" in drafts. If nothing is said about the due date, the instrument is demand paper.[2] A check is a good illustration of such an instrument. The characteristic of demand paper is that the holder of such paper can require payment at any time by making a demand upon the person who is obligated on the paper.

Payable at a definite time.   The requirement of a definite time is in keeping with the necessity for certainty in instruments. It is important that the value of an instrument at any given time be capable of determination. This value will be dependent upon the ultimate maturity date of the instrument. If an instrument is payable only upon an act or event, the time of whose occurrence is uncertain, it is not payable at a definite time even though the act or

[2] Liberty Aluminum Products Co. v. John Cortis et ux., page 486

event has occurred. Thus, an instrument payable "thirty days after my father's death" would not be negotiable.

The requirement of certainty as to the time of payment is satisfied if it is payable on or before a specified date.[3] Thus, an instrument payable on June 1, 1974, is payable at a definite time, as is one payable "on or before" June 1, 1974. In the latter situation, the obligor on the instrument has the privilege of making payment prior to June 1, 1974, but is not required to pay it until the specified date. An instrument payable at a fixed period after a stated date, or at a fixed period after sight, is payable at a definite time. The expressions "one year after date" or "sixty days after sight" are definite as to time.

There are two types of provisions appearing on the face of instruments which affect the definite time. The first is called an acceleration clause. An acceleration clause hastens or accelerates the maturity date of an instrument. Accelerating provisions may be of many different kinds. One kind, for example, provides that in case of default in payment of interest or of an installment of the principal, the entire note shall become due and payable. Another kind gives the holder an option to declare the instrument due and payable when he feels insecure with respect to ultimate payment. An instrument payable at a definite time subject to *any acceleration* is negotiable. If, however, the acceleration provision permits the holder to declare the instrument due when he feels insecure, the holder must act in good faith in the honest belief that the likelihood of payment is impaired. The presumption is that the holder has acted in good faith, placing the burden on the obligor-payor to show that such act was not in good faith.

The second type of provision affecting time is an extension clause. An extension clause is the converse of the acceleration provision. It provides for the extension of the time for payment beyond that specified in the instrument. For example, a note payable in two years might provide that the maker has the right to extend the time of payment six months. An instrument is payable at a definite time if it is payable "at a definite time subject to extension at the option of the holder, or to extension to a further *definite time* at the option of the maker or acceptor, or automatically upon or after a specified act or event." (U.C.C. 3-109(1)(d)) It is to be noted that in an extension at the option of the holder, no time limit is required. The holder always has the right to refrain from undertaking collection. An extension at the option of the maker or acceptor, or an automatic extension, must provide for a definite time for ultimate payment.

The primary importance of the provision for extension at the option of the holder is that it preserves the liability of indorsers and other secondary parties. In the absence of such a provision an extension of time granted by the holder would discharge their liability to the holder in the event of nonpayment by the maker. It is to be noted that the holder must permit payment at maturity if a tender of payment is made. He cannot over the objection of the maker or acceptor extend the time in order to continue to earn interest.

3-81. Words of Negotiability.   The words of negotiability express the intention to create negotiable paper. The usual words of negotiability are "order" and "bearer." For example, "Pay to the order of John Doe" or "Pay to John

---

[3] Ferri v. Sylvia, page 486

Doe or order" creates order paper; "Pay to bearer" creates bearer paper. The words "order" and "bearer" are used in recognition of the fact that the instrument is expected to be transferred by the person receiving it. Order paper and bearer paper are in effect payable to more than one person. Bearer paper is payable to anyone who *bears* or possesses it. An instrument payable to the order of *"X"* is payable to *"X"* or anyone to whom *"X"* orders it paid.

3-82. Order Paper. An instrument is payable to order when by its terms it is payable to the order of any person specified with reasonable certainty, or to him or his order. Order paper requires an indorsement for negotiation.

An instrument may be payable to the order of the maker or drawer or the drawee. It may be payable to two or more payees together such as *"A and B"* or in the alternative such as *"A or B."* An instrument payable to *"A and B"* must be indorsed by both, but one payable to the order of *"A or B"* may be negotiated by either.

An instrument may be payable to the order of an estate, trust, or fund, in which case it is payable to the order of the representative of such estate, trust, or fund or his successors. It may also be payable to the order of an office, or an officer by his title as such in which case it is payable to the principal but the incumbent of the office or his successors may act as if he or they were the holder of the instrument. An instrument payable to the order of a partnership or unincorporated association is payable to the partnership or association and may be transferred by any person authorized by the partnership or association.

Instruments payable to the order of a person sometimes have additional words which are added to describe such person. The descriptive words may show that the payee is an agent of a named principal or an officer of a specified company or organization—"John Smith, Treasurer of *X* Corp." They may indicate that he is a fiduciary for a specified person or entity—"Henry Rose, Trustee of the Ford Trust." The words may, on the other hand, simply describe the status of the payee without tying in any other specified person—"John Doe, Agent." In the first example the instrument is payable to the company —the additional words are not merely for identification—and the officer is named only for convenience in enabling him to cash the check.

In the second example, "Henry Rose, Trustee," the instrument by reason of the law of fiduciaries is payable to the individual named. He is the real party in interest. He has power to negotiate, enforce, or discharge the paper. As a trustee he is liable for breach of trust, but this does not impinge upon his power to negotiate. (The person receiving an instrument from a trustee may not qualify as a holder in due course, however. This will be discussed in the next chapter.)

In the last example, "Pay to John Doe, Agent," where the descriptive words do not disclose a principal or beneficiary, the person named is the payee and real party in interest. Such person may negotiate, enforce, or discharge the paper. Any person dealing with such payee may in effect disregard the description and will be protected unless he has notice of some irregularity.

An instrument which is not payable to order may contain a statement such as "payable upon return of this certificate properly indorsed." Since the purpose of such language is usually to have the indorsement serve as a receipt, the addition of such clause does not make the instrument payable to order and the instrument would not be negotiable.

Paper which is on its face payable to order becomes bearer paper if it is indorsed in blank—by signature alone without specification of the indorsee.

It sometimes happens that in filling in a printed form a person will execute an instrument in such form as "Pay *to the order of* John Smith or bearer," without noticing the word "bearer," and the italicized words are typed or written by the person drawing the instrument. This is considered as order paper because the insertion of the name of the payee shows such an intent. On the other hand, if the word "bearer" is added either in typewriting or handwriting, this indicates an intent that the instrument be payable to bearer.

3-83. Bearer Paper. An instrument is payable to bearer and can be negotiated by delivery if it is payable to:

(a)   bearer or the order of bearer; or

(b)   a specified person or bearer; or

(c)   "cash" or the order of "cash," or any other indication which does not purport to designate a specific payee. (U.C.C. 3-111)

The basic characteristic of bearer paper as distinguished from order paper is that it can be negotiated by delivery without indorsement. However, in most cases the person to whom bearer paper is negotiated will require an indorsement in order to obtain a right against the transferor in case the instrument is not paid.

Whether an instrument is bearer paper may be determined either by what appears on the face of the paper, e.g., "Pay to bearer" or by the last indorsement. A "special indorsement"—one which designates the name of the indorsee, e.g., "Pay to John Doe"—transforms bearer paper into order paper. On the other hand, a blank indorsement, one consisting simply of the indorser's signature, transforms order paper into bearer paper. The last indorsement on paper is controlling. For example, a check payable "to the order of John Doe" becomes bearer paper if it is indorsed "John Doe." Since bearer instruments are much like cash in that they can be negotiated by delivery, caution in their care is necessary.

A check drawn payable to the "order of cash" is bearer paper.

ADDITIONAL TERMS: OMISSIONS

3-84. Terms and Omissions Not Affecting Negotiability. Some additional terms may be added to commercial paper without impairing negotiability. For example, some provisions for the benefit of the payee or other holder are permitted. Statements with respect to collateral given to secure the paper including the right to sell the collateral if the maker defaults are allowed. The drawer may stipulate on a check that the payee by cashing or indorsing it acknowledges full satisfaction of the maker's obligation.

Many words which would appear to be essential are, in fact, nonessential. The validity and negotiable character of an instrument otherwise negotiable are not destroyed by the fact that it is not dated, that the words "value" or "value received" are omitted, or that it does not state what consideration was given for it.

3-85. Date.   The dating of an instrument is not an essential of negotiability. Whether there is no date, an antedate, or a postdate is not important from the standpoint of negotiability. Any date which does appear on the instrument is presumed correct until evidence is introduced to establish a contrary finding. Even though the date on the instrument is not proper, it has no effect on the negotiability. Any fraud or illegality connected with the date of the instrument does not affect its negotiability, but merely gives a defense.

If a date is necessary in order to ascertain maturity, an undated instrument is an incomplete instrument. The date, however, may be inserted by the holder.

If an instrument is payable on demand or at a fixed period after date, the date which is put on the instrument controls even though it is antedated or postdated.

3-86. Incomplete Instruments.   A person may sign an instrument which is incomplete in that it lacks one or more of the necessary elements of a complete instrument. Thus, a paper signed by the maker or drawer in which the payee's name or the amount is omitted, is incomplete.

An incomplete instrument cannot be enforced until it is completed. If the blanks are subsequently filled in by any person in accordance with the authority or instructions given by the party who signed the incomplete instrument, it is then effective as completed. A person might, for example, leave blank signed checks with an employee with instructions to complete the checks as to amounts and payee in payment of invoices as goods are delivered. When the employee completes the checks in accordance with these instructions, they are perfectly valid.

A blank date can be supplied in similar fashion and this may be important in order to constitute a "complete instrument," e.g., where it is payable "sixty days after date."

If the completion of the blanks is not in conformity with the signer's authority, the unauthorized completion is treated as a material alteration of the instrument, but a holder in due course can enforce the instrument as completed. The loss is placed upon the person who signed the incomplete paper because he made wrongful completion possible. A person not a holder in due course is subject to the defense of improper completion.

3-87. Instruments "Payable Through" a Bank—"At a Bank."   Instruments representing insurance payments, payroll checks, dividends, and other instruments are sometimes made "payable through" a designated bank. The words, "payable through," do not make the bank the drawee; they do not authorize or order the bank to pay the instrument out of funds in the account of the drawee; neither do they order or require the bank to take the paper for collection. The bank's authority in this situation is extremely limited; the bank is merely a funnel through which the paper is to be properly presented to the drawee or maker.

A related situation is that in which a note or acceptance of a draft contains the language: "Payable at" a designated bank. In recognition of varying banking practices in different sections of the country, the Code provides two alternatives either of which could be adopted by a state in enacting the Code, namely (1) that a note or an acceptance of a draft "payable at a bank" is like a draft on the bank, and upon its due date the bank is authorized, without consultation, to make the payment out of any available funds of the maker or acceptor; or (2) such words *are not* an order or authorization, but a mere direction for the bank to request instructions from the maker or acceptor.

3-88. Other Writings Affecting Instrument.   Often a transaction will involve both a negotiable instrument and another contract where both are executed as a part of the same transaction. The separate written agreement may be, for example, an installment contract for consumer goods, a contract for the purchase of a house by way of a note secured by a mortgage, or a contract for the purchase of heavy equipment.

Negotiable instruments are also contracts between the immediate parties such as the maker and the payee. Under a general rule of construction and interpretation of contracts, courts will look to the *entire contract* and all writings executed as part of the same transaction and construe them as a single agreement.[4] Therefore, if the writing separate from the note provided for an acceleration of payment, a court would construe the acceleration as applicable to the note.

As noted previously, a reference to a separate agreement does not affect the negotiability of a note or other instrument. A holder in due course is not affected by any limitation of his rights arising out of a separate agreement if he took the instrument without notice thereof. With this limitation the terms of a negotiable instrument may be affected by another written agreement executed as part of the same transaction.

3-89. Ambiguous Terms and Rules of Construction.   In view of the millions of negotiable instruments that are made and drawn daily, it is to be expected that a certain number of them will be ambiguously worded. The rules for the interpretation and construction of instruments are:

(a) Where there is doubt whether the instrument is a draft or a note, the holder may treat it as either. A draft drawn on the drawer is effective as a note.

(b) Handwritten terms control typewritten and printed terms, and typewritten control printed.

(c) Words control figures except that if the words are ambiguous, figures control.

(d) Unless otherwise specified, a provision for interest means interest at the judgment rate at the place of payment from the date of the instrument, or if it is undated from the date of issue.

(e) Unless the instrument otherwise specifies two or more persons who sign as maker, acceptor or drawer or indorser and as a part of the same transaction, are jointly and severally liable even though the instrument contains such words as "*I* promise to pay."[5]

(f) Unless otherwise specified, consent to extension authorizes a single extension for not longer than the original period. A consent to extension, expressed in the instrument, is binding on secondary parties and accommodation makers. A holder

---

[4] Merchants National Bank & Trust Company v. Indianapolis Professional Men's Association, Inc., page 487

[5] Ghitter v. Edge, page 488

may not exercise his option to extend an instrument over the objection of a maker or acceptor or other party who . . . tenders full payment when the instrument is due. (U.C.C. 3-118)

The purpose of the extension clause is to continue the liability of indorsers and other secondary parties who would otherwise be discharged.

TRANSFER AND NEGOTIATION

3-90. In General. The rights which a person has in an instrument may be transferred by either "negotiation" or "assignment." Transfer is an encompassing word which means the process by which the owner of property delivers it to another intending thereby to pass his rights in it to the other. The transfer of an instrument vests in the transferee such rights as the transferor has. Negotiation is defined as a specific type of transfer by means of which the transferee becomes a "holder." A "holder" is a person who is in possession of an instrument "drawn, issued, or indorsed to him or to his order or to bearer or in blank." (U.C.C. 1-201(20))

3-91. Negotiation. There are two methods of negotiating an instrument so that the transferee will become a holder. If the instrument is payable to bearer, it may be negotiated by delivery alone; if it is order paper, indorsement and delivery are required. A thief or finder can transfer bearer paper but not order paper. The indorsement must be placed on the instrument itself or on a paper so firmly affixed to it as to become a part thereof. Such paper is called an *allonge.* The indorsement must be made by the holder or by some one who has the authority to do so on behalf of the holder.

The indorsement must be for the entire amount of the instrument. *A* cannot indorse to *B* $50 out of a $100 check. However, a holder can negotiate the unpaid balance due on an instrument.

If the name of the payee is misspelled, the payee may negotiate by indorsing either in the name appearing on the instrument or in his true name, or both. A person who pays the instrument or gives value for it may require that both names be indorsed. The desirable practice is to indorse in both names.

It sometimes happens that an order instrument, or one which is specially indorsed, is transferred without indorsement. Thus, a purchaser may pay for an instrument in advance of the time when it is delivered to him, and the seller either inadvertently or fraudulently may fail to indorse the paper. Of course, an indorsement would be necessary for negotiation. If the transferee has given value for the instrument, and if there was no contrary agreement between the parties, the transferee can demand an indorsement. The negotiation is not effective until the indorsement is given. The transferee is not a holder, and he cannot qualify as a holder in due course if he receives notice of a defense or claim prior to obtaining such indorsement.

NEGOTIATION BY INDORSEMENT

3-92. Kinds of Indorsement. Indorsements are either special or blank. These are the ordinary indorsements used in negotiating paper. If other terms are added which condition the indorsement, it is a restrictive indorsement. Such terms restrict the indorsee's use of the paper. Also, the indorser may *limit* or qualify his liability as an indorser by adding such words as "without recourse." This qualified indorsement has the effect of relieving the indorser of his contractual liability as an indorser—that he will pay if the primary obligor refuses to do so. These indorsements are discussed in the sections that follow.

3-93. Blank Indorsement. A blank indorsement consists of the indorser's name written on the instrument and is a form of indorsement commonly used. It does not specify any particular indorsee. If an instrument has been drawn payable to order and is indorsed in blank, it becomes payable to bearer and may be negotiated by delivery, without indorsement. However, if such instrument is thereafter indorsed specially, it reverts to its status as order paper and indorsement is required for further negotiation. For example, a check on its face payable to "Henry Smith or order," if indorsed "Henry Smith," carries a blank indorsement. As bearer paper, it can be negotiated by mere delivery, and a thief or finder could by such delivery pass title to the instrument.

3-94. Special Indorsement. A special indorsement specifies the person to whom or to whose order it makes the instrument payable. When an instrument is specially indorsed, it becomes payable to the *order of* the special indorsee and requires his indorsement for further negotiation. Thus an indorsement "Pay to John Jones" or "Pay to the order of John Jones" is a special indorsement and requires the further indorsement by John Jones for negotiation. If a bearer instrument is indorsed specially, it requires further indorsement by the indorsee.

The holder of an instrument may convert a blank indorsement into a special indorsement by writing above the blank indorser's signature "any contract consistent with the character of the indorsement." Thus, Richard Roe, to whom an instrument has been indorsed in blank by John Doe, could write above Doe's signature "Pay to Richard Roe." The paper would now require Roe's indorsement for further negotiation.

3-95. Restrictive Indorsements. A person who indorses an instrument may impose certain restrictions upon his indorsement, that is, the indorser may protect or preserve certain rights in the paper and limit the rights of the indorsee. There are four types of restrictive indorsements, the most important of which is the indorsement for deposit or for deposit and collection. By indorsing "For Deposit" the indorser is not negotiating the check but is simply prohibiting any further use of the check other than to deposit it to his account. Stores which cash checks for their customers often instruct their clerks to stamp each check "For Deposit" as it is received.

A second type is the conditional indorsement whereby the indorser specifies that the indorsee is entitled to payment only upon a condition. This type of indorsement is not used frequently. An example is an indorsement: "Pay John Doe if Generator XK-711 arrives by June 1, 1972."

The third indorsement is one in which the indorser stipulates that the transfer is for the benefit of the indorser or some other designated person. For example: "Pay John Doe in trust for Richard Roe."

The Code also lists as a fourth type of restrictive indorsement one which purports to prohibit further transfer of the instrument. For example, an indorsement "Pay John Doe only" would appear to prevent John Doe from indorsing to any other person. However, no effect will be given to such an attempted restriction, and the indorsement will have the same effect as if the restrictive language had not been used.

The Code provides that no restrictive indorsement prevents further transfer or negotiation of the instrument and sets forth the obligations of the parties with reference to compliance with the restrictions imposed. The effect of restrictive indorsements is substantially limited as applied to banks which are involved in the process of deposit and collection of instruments. This process is described in Article 4-Bank Deposits and Collections. The process and terminology can best be illustrated by considering a typical banking transaction.

> *D* owes $100 to *P* for an article of merchandise which he has purchased from *P*. *D* draws a check on the bank ("payor bank") of which he is a "customer" and mails it to his creditor in another city. The creditor ("depositor") deposits the check in his own bank ("depositary bank"). *P*'s bank then forwards the check to *X* Bank which may in turn forward it to *Y* Bank. *X* Bank and *Y* Bank are called "intermediary banks" and along with the depositary bank are called "collecting banks." *Y* Bank ("presenting bank") presents the check to the payor bank. The payor bank honors the check, charges it to the customer's account and finally returns it to the customer along with his other canceled checks and monthly statement. Even a simple transaction such as this involves a multiplicity of legal relationships.

Because of the tremendous volume of such transactions, banks do not have any practicable opportunity to consider the effect of restrictive indorsements. Therefore the Code provides that intermediary banks or a payor bank which is not a depositary bank can disregard restrictive indorsements. Such banks are concerned only with the indorsement of the bank's immediate transferor. This limitation does not affect whatever rights the restrictive indorser may have against the bank of deposit or his rights against parties outside the bank collection process.

3-96. Negotiation Subject to Rescission.   Negotiation by an infant or other person lacking in contractual capacity is effective to transfer the instrument notwithstanding the lack of capacity. A transfer is effective even though it was obtained by fraud, duress, or mistake; in violation of a duty on the part of the transferor; or as part of an illegal transaction. This reflects the philosophy of negotiability that any person in possession of an instrument which by its terms runs to him is a holder and that anyone may deal with him as a holder. Thus, the indorsee who has received the instrument under the above circumstances is nonetheless a holder and can in turn negotiate the paper as long as he is in possession of it. Certainly the party who lacks capacity or who was imposed upon can rescind the transfer and recover the paper, but until he does so the transferee is in a position where he can negotiate the paper to a holder in due course. The right to rescind is not available against a holder in due course, but

may be exercised against other parties.[6] The remedies available against such
parties are determined by local law—e.g., the law relating to an infant's rights.
The foregoing relates only to the effectiveness of the transfer and does not
impose liability on the infant, or other party who lacks capacity to contract,
from negotiating the instrument. Such party may take advantage of various
defenses which are available under the Code and which will be discussed later
in Chapter 26.

CREATION AND TRANSFER CASES

D'Andrea v. Feinberg
256 N.Y.S.2d 504 (N.Y.) 1965

DILLON, J. The plaintiff as a holder in due course of a promissory note
in the face amount of $4,000 has moved for summary judgment. . . . The maker
of the note is Sain Builders, Inc., and the note is executed on behalf of the
maker by Samuel Feinberg as President. The note is endorsed by Samuel
Feinberg in his capacity as President of the corporation and individually. The
action was commenced against the corporation and against Samuel Feinberg
individually. The note was duly presented for payment, was dishonored and
protested. The corporate defendant is involved in bankruptcy proceedings in
the Federal District Court and in connection therewith an order has been
signed staying all actions against it until a final decree has been entered in the
bankruptcy proceedings. Accordingly, the motion for summary judgment as
against the corporation is denied.

On behalf of the individual defendant, it is urged that plaintiffs are not
holders in due course because at the time they acquired the note they were
aware of the existence of a contract between the corporate defendant and the
payee of the note. This fact cannot be disputed because the note itself has
endorsed thereon, in the lower left-hand corner the legend "as per contract."
It is argued that the endorser should not be held liable on the note until such
time as the primary obligation between the maker and the payee has been
resolved. The court is thus faced with two questions: (1) whether the note is
a negotiable instrument; and (2) whether the plaintiffs are holders in due
course.

The note meets all the requirements of section 3-104 of the U.C.C. with the
possible exception that it does not contain an unconditional promise because
of the legend "as per contract." Section 3-105(1)(c) expressly states that an
unconditional promise "is not made conditional by the fact that the instrument
(c) refers to or states that it arises out of a separate agreement or refers to a
separate agreement for rights as to prepayment or acceleration."

The official comment on the above quoted provision . . . is that it was
"intended to resolve a conflict, and to reject cases in which a reference to a
separate agreement was held to mean that payment of the instrument must be
limited in accordance with the terms of the agreement, and hence was conditioned by it." The court is satisfied that the legend "as per contract" does not
affect the negotiability of an instrument as would a statement that the instru-

---

[6] Snyder v. Town Hill Motors, Inc., page 489

ment "is subject to or governed by any other agreement" (Uniform Commercial Code, Sec. 3-105(2)(a); *Enoch* v. *Brandon,* 249 N.Y. 263, 164 N.E. 45).

The court determines that the note being sued upon is a negotiable instrument and that the plaintiffs are holders in due course. Since a cause of action against "an indorser of any instrument accrues upon demand following dishonor of the instrument" (Uniform Commercial Code, Sec. 3-122(3)), it is clear that the plaintiffs need not first recover judgment against the maker as the individual defendant urges.

Motion Allowed as to Individual Defendant.

Liberty Aluminum Products Company v. John Cortis

14 D.&C.2d 624. (Pa.) 1958

The plaintiff, holder of a note executed by the defendants obtained a judgment on the note. The defendants filed a motion to have the judgment set aside on the ground that the note did not contain a schedule of installments and set out no date of maturity.

CUMMINS, J.... The first alleged deficiency is the one which must be explored a little further. The defendants' motion to strike completely overlooks the Uniform Commercial Code.... This Code states categorically that "instruments payable on demand include those payable at sight or on presentation and *those in which no time for payment is stated"* [italics added]—that under the Commercial Code this instrument is a demand note by virtue of its tenor....

The parties have the right to use a blank and tailor it to their needs. And the failure to include installment payments simply and clearly means that none were intended....

The face of the record will support the judgment.

Ferri v. Sylvia

214 A.2d 470 (R.I.) 1965

JOSLIN, J. The question is whether the note is payable at a fixed or determinable future time. If the phrase "within ten (10) years after date" lacks explicitness or is ambiguous then clearly parol evidence was admissible for the purpose of ascertaining the intention of the parties....

At the law merchant it was generally settled that a promissory note or a bill of exchange payable "on or before" a specified date fixed with certainty the time of payment.... The same rule has been fixed by statute first under the Negotiable Instruments Law ... and now pursuant to the Uniform Commercial Code. The Code in 6A-3-109 (1) reads as follows: "An instrument is payable at a definite time if by its terms it is payable (a) on or before a stated date or at a fixed period after a stated date.... "

The courts in the cases we cite were primarily concerned with whether a provision for payment "on or before" a specified date impaired the negotiability of an instrument....

On principle no valid distinction can be drawn between an instrument payable "on or before" a fixed date and one which calls for payment "within" a stipulated period....

We . . . equate the word "within" with the phrase "on or before." So construed it fixes both the beginning and the end of a period, and insofar as it means the former it is applicable to the right of a maker to prepay, and insofar as it means the latter it is referable to the date the instrument matures. We hold that the payment provision of a negotiable instrument payable "within" a stated period is certain as well as complete on its face and that such an instrument does not mature until the time fixed arrives.

For the foregoing reasons it is clear that the parties unequivocally agreed that the plaintiff could not demand payment of the note until the expiration of the ten-year period. It is likewise clear that any prior or contemporaneous oral agreements of the parties relevant to its due date were so merged and integrated with the writing as to prevent its being explained or supplemented by parol evidence. . . .

Judgement for the defendants.

Merchants National Bank and Trust Company v. Indianapolis Professional Men's Association, Inc.

409 F.2d 600 (1969)

The bank brought suit to recover possession of collateral under a security agreement on the ground that a note from the Indianapolis Professional Men's Association (IPMA) was due and payable. The nature of IPMA's business was to collect bills for professional people. IPMA executed a note to the bank and also a security agreement covering accounts receivable held by it. IPMA had taken over a former collection agency which was obligated to pay $140,000 to the bank. The contract for purchase of the collection agency provided that the obligation to the bank was to be repaid only from IPMA profits, and the bank was a party to the contract. IPMA never did make a profit but continually operated at a loss. The primary question was whether the IPMA note was due and this turned upon whether the contract should be construed as a part of the note. The federal district court ruled that the terms of the contract applied to the note so that no payment was due. The bank appealed.

PITTMAN, J. . . . This case arose after the adoption by Indiana of the Uniform Commercial Code. Prior to the adoption of this Code the Indiana courts had held:

> Where two instruments are executed as parts of a single transaction and pertain to the same matter, they must be construed together in order to ascertain the intention of the person executing such instruments. *Stair* v. *Oswalt*, 121 Ind.App. 382, 97 N.E.2d 375 (1951).

Factually, the instruments in these cases were all executed on the same date, but this factor does not appear to be crucial nor do the cases hold that this be true as a prerequisite in an application of the rule. The emphasis is (1) whether or not the instruments relate to the same subject matter and not necessarily whether they refer to each other, and (2) whether or not the instruments were executed as parts of a single transaction. Where several instruments executed contemporaneously or at different times pertain to the same transaction, they will be read together although they do not expressly refer to each other. . . . The applicable portion of the Uniform Commercial

Code which was in effect in Indiana at the time these transactions occurred is Indiana Annotated Statutes, Sec. 19-3-119 (Burns Replacement 1964).

> As between the obligor and his immediate obligee or any transferee the terms of an instrument may be modified or affected by any other written agreement executed as a part of the *same transaction.* . . . [Emphasis added.]

The official comment states:

> Purposes: . . . It is intended to resolve conflicts as to the effect of a separate writing upon a negotiable instrument. . . . This section is limited to the effect of a separate written agreement executed as a part of the same transaction. . . . It may . . . be any type of contract, including an agreement that upon certain conditions the instrument shall be discharged or is not to be paid. . . .

Considering the applicable principle of law in Indiana prior to the Uniform Commercial Code and the purposes as stated in the official comment to the Uniform Commercial Code, it seems clear the April 23 contract, the cover letter, the May 3 note and security agreement, and the renewals are all part and parcel of the same transaction.

We hold the district court was correct in admitting the April 23 contract and subsequent cover letter and in its holding that: "It is the intention of the parties that the advances of Merchants shall be repaid only from profits and from excess cash obtained from the liquidation of certain documents receivable, which cash shall not otherwise be needed in the purchase of new outstanding accounts receivable. . . . " [A]nd "that IPMA has never at any time earned a profit nor has said corporation at any time had any excess cash obtained from the liquidation of accounts receivable or otherwise."

Judgment affirmed.

Ghitter v. Edge
165 S.E.2d 598 (Ga.) 1968

The plaintiff brought action on notes which recited "We promise to pay" and were signed by the defendant, Edge, and two other persons. The notes were in the amount of $2,100 and Edge contended that he should be required to pay only $700. The other two signers were not parties to this action. The court ruled in favor of the defendant and plaintiff appealed.

WHITMAN, J. . . . [T]he promissory notes sued upon were executed after the effective date of the Uniform Commercial Code and are governed thereby. Code Ann. § 109A-3-118(e) (Ga.L.1962, pp. 156, 245), provides that: *"Unless the instrument otherwise specifies* two or more persons who sign as maker . . . as a part of the same transaction are *jointly and severally liable* even though the instrument contains *such words* as 'I promise to pay.' "* [Emphasis supplied.] Appellee contends that the use of the words "We promise to pay" in the notes is a sufficient specification of the manner in which the makers agreed to be held liable. We can not agree. Such is but an indirect specification by reference to the meaning which the words "we promise" held in the prior law. We understand the Code section to mean that whenever two or more persons sign as maker they are jointly and severally liable unless the instrument in its own language specifies the obligation differently, e.g., "we jointly promise . . . " or "we promise severally. . . . "

Each of the three makers of the notes sued upon was jointly and severally liable. Therefore an action can be maintained against appellee alone and the fact that the other two makers were not joined or legally accounted for affords no basis for a dismissal of the action. . . .

Judgment reversed with direction that an order be entered granting plaintiff's motion for summary judgment with regard to liability only.

Snyder v. Town Hill Motors, Inc.

165 A.2d 293 (Pa.) 1960

A minor (Snyder) entered into a contract with a friend (Rhea) whereby he agreed to trade his 1946 Pontiac plus $1,000 for Rhea's Chrysler. The two thereupon went to the place of business of the defendant (Town Hill Motors) where Rhea negotiated for the purchase of a Lincoln. Rhea instructed Snyder to assign the title of the Pontiac to the Motor Company and to indorse to the company a $1,000 check which was payable to Snyder's order and drawn by a third party, as the down payment by Rhea on the Lincoln. (Snyder had intended to use the check in payment for the Chrysler.) Snyder complied with Rhea's instructions and Rhea gave him a receipt:

"Received of Richard Snyder one-thousand dollars and 1946 Pontiac coupe in exchange for a 1955 Chrysler Windsor."

Snyder accepted delivery of the Chrysler, but a month or so later he returned it to the motor company and demanded the return of his Pontiac and the $1,000. He contended that Rhea had misrepresented the amount of the encumbrance against the Chrysler.

The motor company which had cashed the check and received the proceeds refused his demand. Snyder then sued the motor company for $1,000 on the theory that he had the right to rescind the negotiation of an instrument. The jury returned a verdict for the defendant and Snyder appealed.

MONTGOMERY, J. . . . Appellant's . . . theory is . . . without merit. The rescission of a negotiable instrument by an infant against a subsequent holder in due course is not permitted by Section 3-207 of the Uniform Commercial Code, on which appellant relies. Having received the instrument by negotiation from Rhea for value, in good faith, and without notice that it was overdue or had been dishonored or that there was any defense against it, the Motor Company was a subsequent holder in due course. The jury has found that there were no dealings between Snyder and the appellees.

Appellant's argument that the Motor Company was not a "subsequent" holder in due course is not supported by the evidence. The fact that the check was not manually transferred from Snyder to Rhea and then to the Motor Company would be immaterial under the definition of "delivery" contained in the Negotiable Instruments Law of 1901 . . . which provides that transfer of possession may be actual or constructive. Although the Uniform Commercial Code repealed the Negotiable Instruments Law, it nevertheless did not prescribe any new definition of the term "delivery." We are of the opinion, therefore, that the established definition should prevail. The generally recognized meaning of "delivery" set forth in Corpus Juris Secundum is as follows:

"What constitutes delivery depends largely on the intent of the parties. It is not necessary that delivery should be by manual transfer. A constructive delivery is sufficient if made with the intention of transferring the title, and this rule is recognized by the definition of delivery in Negotiable Instruments Act . . . as the transfer of possession, 'actual or constructive.' "

.   .   .

The facts previously stated show clearly the intention of these parties. Together, Snyder and Rhea took the check to the Motor Company, where it was exhibited and where Rhea exercised dominion over it by directing Snyder to hand it over to the Motor Company. Snyder agreed to this and accepted Rhea's receipt, which acknowledged that Rhea had received the proceeds of the check. This was sufficient to constitute constructive delivery from Snyder to Rhea and "subsequently" from Rhea to the Motor Company.

Orders affirmed. . . .

CHAPTER 24
REVIEW QUESTIONS AND PROBLEMS

1. *A* made a note dated 1967 and payable ninety days after date. In 1969 action was brought on the note, and *A* sought to introduce evidence of an agreement that payment would not be due until construction of a certain building had been started. Would this evidence be admissible?

2. *A* drew a check payable to the order of *B* and *C* jointly. *C* indorsed the check and deposited it to his account in the X Bank. X Bank sent the check to the drawee bank for collection. Can *B* recover from X Bank?

3. *A* signed his name to a note in connection with a mortgage of property and made reference to the mortgage in the note. Does this affect the negotiability of the note?

4. *M* executed a note to *P* in the sum of $500. The note did not contain words of negotiability. Can *P* recover on the note from *M*? If *P* transferred the note to *X,* could *X* recover from *M*?

5. A note contained a provision: "This note is payable from the proceeds of the sale of the Douglas Building." Is the note negotiable?

6. A note provides: "Payable on January 1, 1967, or sooner in the event that the *A-B* partnership is dissolved." Is the note negotiable?

7. *P* signed a check but left the designation of the payee in blank. The check was stolen and the word "cash" inserted in the blank. The check was honored by the bank. *P* seeks to recover the amount of the check from the bank. What result?

8. *M* made a note payable to the order of *P*. *P* indorsed to *A* by writing his name "*P*" on the back of the note. *A* transferred the note to *B* without indorsement. Can *B* be a holder in due course?

9. *H,* the holder of a check, wishes to protect himself against its loss or theft. It has been indorsed to him in blank. How may he gain this protection?

10. *A* purchased merchandise from B Chemical Company and "accepted" a trade acceptance drawn to the order of B Chemical Company. The company indorsed the instrument to F Finance Company. F Finance Company now seeks to recover on the instrument, which states, "The transaction which gives rise to this instrument is the purchase of goods from the drawer by the acceptor." *A* claims the merchandise was defective. Is this defense good against F Finance? Does F Finance have recourse against B Chemical Company?

chapter 25

Holders and
Holders in
Due Course

3-97. Definitions.   A *holder* is a person in possession of an instrument payable to him or to his order or to bearer. It may be so payable either on original issue or as a result of an indorsement. A holder of an instrument may transfer it or negotiate it. A holder can with certain exceptions, enforce payment on the instrument or discharge it. A holder who does not qualify as a holder in due course is in a position equivalent to that of an assignee, in that he cannot enforce payment in the event a defense to the instrument legally exists.

A *holder in due course* is a holder who because he meets certain requirements is given a special status and a preferred position in the event that there is a claim or a defense to the instrument. If there is no claim or defense to the instrument, it is immaterial whether the party seeking to enforce it is a holder or a holder in due course. A holder in due course can enforce payment, notwithstanding the presence of a personal defense to the instrument. (As will be discussed more fully later, defenses fall into two categories—personal and real.) A holder in due course will not be able to enforce the instrument in the event a real defense is asserted. The preferred status of a holder in due course over the status of a holder exists only where the defense to the instrument is in the category of a personal defense.

3-98. Requirements.   In order to qualify as a holder in due course, a holder must have taken the instrument for value and in good faith. In addition, he must not have notice that the instrument is overdue, that it has been dishonored, or that any other person has a claim to it or a defense against it. These requirements are discussed in detail in the sections which follow.

A purchaser of a limited interest in paper can be a holder in due course only to the extent of the interest purchased. For example, if a negotiable instrument is transferred as collateral for a loan, the transferee may be a holder in due course, but only to the extent of the debt which is secured by the pledge of the instrument.[1]

A payee may be a holder in due course. Since the payee of an instrument usually deals directly with the primary party, he would ordinarily be aware of any defense that the maker or drawer may have. However, if the payee is able to satisfy the requirements, he may become a holder in due course in the same fashion as any other holder.

To illustrate a situation in which the payee is a holder in due course, assume that *M* signs his name to an instrument which is complete except for the amount, and which is payable to the order of *P*. *M* then directs his agent, *A,* to purchase a certain quantity of merchandise from *P* and pay for the same by filling in the proper amount. The agent, *A,* in violation of this authority, completes the check in a larger sum than authorized, delivers it to *P*, obtains the merchandise, and appropriates the balance. *P* has no knowledge of the unauthorized act of *M's* agent. *P* has satisfied all of the requirements of a holder in due course, in that he has taken the check in good faith, for value, and without notice of any wrongdoing.

3-99. Value.   A holder must pay value for an instrument in order to qualify as a holder in due course. One to whom an instrument is transferred as a gift does not qualify.

An *executory* promise to give value does not make the holder a holder for value.[2] It is required in general that the consideration agreed upon by the parties must actually have been given. When an instrument is negotiated presently under an arrangement that the transferee will pay for it later or perform the required services at a later date, such transferee has not given "value." If a purchaser has not yet paid value when he becomes aware of a defense to the instrument, he does not have to pay for it but is free to rescind the transaction. Accordingly, there is not the same necessity to give him the standing of a holder in due course, free from claims and defenses, as in the case of a holder who has actually parted with value. A holder who purchases an instrument for less than its *face value* can be a holder in due course to the full amount of the instrument; but, if the discount is exceedingly large, it may, along with other factors, be evidence of bad faith on the part of the holder.

A holder who takes an instrument in payment of an antecedent claim may be a holder for value. The same is true of a holder who takes the instrument as security for an antecedent debt. Thus, if *A* owed *B* $500 on a past-due account and transferred a negotiable instrument to *B* in payment of such account or as security for its payment, *B* would qualify as a holder for value. In this regard it is to be noted that "value" is not synonymous with "consideration."

As noted above, a mere promise to pay for negotiable paper does not make one a holder for value. If the promise to pay is negotiable in form, however, the purchaser immediately becomes a holder for value. For example, a drawer who issues his check in payment for a negotiable note which he is purchasing from the holder becomes a holder for value even before his check is cashed. The reason for this rule is that there is a possibility that the check might be

[1] Wood v. Willman, page 497.
[2] Korzenik v. Supreme Radio, Inc., page 498

negotiated to a holder in due course, in which event such person could require payment.

3-100. Good Faith and Without Notice. *Good faith* is defined as "honesty in fact in the conduct or transaction concerned." (U.C.C. 1-201(19)) In many situations it is obviously difficult to evaluate good faith, but there are circumstances in which the very nature of the situation precludes a person from becoming a good faith holder.[3]

The usual method of financing consumer purchases is for the purchaser to sign an installment note for the purchase price. The note is often attached to the installment contract by a perforation. The seller often does much of his business through installment notes, and he needs to obtain the purchase price in order to replenish his inventory. Accordingly, he often sells and negotiates the note to a finance company. If the finance company is a holder in due course, it would take the paper free of the personal defenses which the consumer has against the seller. This means that the consumer would have to pay the finance company, even though the goods were defective. The only recourse of the consumer would be against the seller, and this remedy would be of little value if the seller were not financially responsible.

Recent decisions have questioned the status of the finance company as a holder in due course, although the decisions are conflicting on this point. The basis for decisions which deny holder in due course status have been predicated upon a close relationship between the finance company and the seller. The finance company may finance most of the sales of a particular company; it may provide the note and contract forms and make the note payable at its office; and it may make a check on the buyer's credit before the sale. Under such circumstances it is questionable as to whether the finance company should be insulated against the defenses of the buyer.[4]

Consumer advocates have been concerned about the abuses inflicted upon consumers as a result of the holder in due course principle. Consumers have been required to pay for defective merchandise and even for merchandise and services not received. As a result, a campaign has begun to eliminate the holder in due course status for purchasers of negotiable paper made payable to a seller by a consumer. Massachusetts has enacted such a statute and the Consumer Federation of America has endorsed such legislation in all states. The Office of Economic Opportunity contends that there are many abuses in the home improvement field which are made possible by the holder in due course concept and its repeal has been urged for such contracts. In the 1970's, the classical protection given a holder in due course may be substantially changed or even eliminated by statute as a part of the desire to give consumers greater protection. Lack of good faith by a seller would in effect be imputed to its financial backer by law if the consumer protection advocates are successful in their campaign. The field of commercial paper law developed centuries ago may well fall in the 1970's.

Closely related to good faith is the requirement that the transferee must not have notice of any claim or defense to the instrument and that he not have notice either that the instrument is overdue or has been dishonored. A person

[3] Jaeger and Branch, Inc. v. Pappas, page 499
[4] American Plan Corp. v. Woods, page 499.

has notice of a fact when he is actually aware of it or when, from all the facts and circumstances, he has reason to know that it exists.

A purchaser has notice of a claim or defense if the instrument is so incomplete, bears such visible evidence of forgery or alteration, or is otherwise so irregular as to call into question its validity. Also, notice of a claim or defense is given if the purchaser has notice that the obligation of any party is voidable in whole or in part. A *voidable obligation* is one in which a party, such as the maker of a note, has the right to avoid his original obligation on the instrument, as in the case of a fraud perpetrated by the payee.

A purchaser has notice of a claim against the instrument if he is aware that a fiduciary, such as a trustee or agent, has negotiated the instrument in payment of or as security for his own debt or in any transaction for his own benefit. Thus, if a trustee negotiates a trust instrument in payment of his own personal debt, this would give notice of misappropriation of the funds. However, the mere fact that a transferee has knowledge of the fiduciary relation would not prevent him from being a holder in due course. One is entitled to assume that the fiduciary acted properly in the absence of special circumstances.

There are a number of situations in which knowledge of certain facts does *not* of itself give the purchaser notice of a defense or claim.[5] Knowledge that an instrument is antedated or postdated does not prevent a holder from taking in due course. Notice of a defense or claim is not imparted by virtue of knowledge that an instrument was issued or negotiated in return for an executory promise or that the instrument was accompanied by a separate agreement, nor does the fact that the purchaser of the instrument was engaged in financing the payee of the instrument. Of course if the purchaser is aware that the contract has been breached or repudiated or that the separate agreement has been violated, he would not qualify as a holder in due course.

Knowledge that an incomplete instrument has been completed does not give notice of a defense or claim. However, if the purchaser has notice that the completion was improper, he cannot be a holder in due course.

The filing or recording of a document which gives notice of a defense does not of itself constitute notice to a person who would otherwise be a holder in due course. Instruments would not pass freely as money if persons receiving them were required to check the public records to ascertain if a defense existed.

To be effective, notice must be received at such time and in such manner as to give a reasonable opportunity to act on it. For example, a notice received by the president of a bank one minute before the bank's teller cashes a check is not effective to prevent the bank from becoming a holder in due course.

3-101. Before Overdue.   A holder in due course must be a holder who has purchased the paper before it is due. The law presumes that every person under a duty will perform on the date that performance is due, and, if such person fails to perform—that is, fails to pay the instrument—it is presumed that he has some defense or valid reason for not performing. Consequently, a purchaser of overdue paper would be charged with knowledge that some defense may exist. Where an instrument is payable on a fixed date, any purchaser thereafter would not be a holder in due course.

---

[5] Factors & Note Buyers, Inc. v. Green Lane, Inc., page 500.

Where the instrument is due upon a fixed date, but subject to an earlier maturity by reason of an accelerating clause, the instrument would not be overdue until the option to mature the paper had been exercised by the holder. If an acceleration of the instrument has been made, the purchaser with notice of such fact is a purchaser of overdue paper. However, a purchaser may take accelerated paper as a holder in due course if he takes without notice of the acceleration.

If the instrument is payable on demand, it is said to be overdue an unreasonable length of time after issue. A purchaser has notice that an instrument is overdue if he has reason to know "that he is taking a demand instrument after demand has been made or more than a reasonable length of time after its issue." (U.C.C. 3-304(3)(c))

What is a reasonable or an unreasonable time is determined by a consideration of the nature of the instrument, the usage of the trade or business, and all of the circumstances and facts involved in each case. With regard to a check, however, the time is specified. "A reasonable time for a check drawn and payable within the states and territories of the United States and the District of Columbia is presumed to be thirty days." (U.C.C. 3-304(3)(c)) "Presumption" or "presumed" mean that "the trier of fact must find the existence of the fact presumed unless and until evidence is introduced which would support a finding of its nonexistence." (U.C.C. 1-201(31))

If an instrument is payable in installments it may be transferred at a time when one or more of the installments is past due. A purchaser who has reason to know of an overdue installment on principal has notice that the instrument is overdue and therefore could not be a holder in due course. Past-due interest, on the other hand, does not impart notice of any defect in the instrument. It is recognized that interest payments are frequently in arrears without a defense existing.

3-102. Holder from a Holder in Due Course.   Since a transferee obtains the rights of a transferor, a person who does not himself qualify as a holder in due course but who derives his title through a holder in due course has the rights and privileges of a holder in due course.[6] This is often referred to as the "shelter provision." While this may seem to detract from the basic holder in due course philosophy, it is in reality in keeping with the underlying concept of marketability of commercial paper. The shelter provision which affords an extension of the holder in due course benefits is designed to aid the holder in due course so that he may readily dispose of the paper. The paper in the hands of the holder in due course is free from personal defenses and such holder should have the privilege of transferring all of his rights in the paper. Thus the transfer of an instrument vests in the transferee such rights as the transferor has therein.

The shelter provision is subject, however, to the limitation that a person who formerly held the paper cannot improve his position by later reacquiring it from a holder in due course. If a former holder was himself a party to any fraud or illegality affecting the instrument, or if he had notice of a defense or claim against it as a prior holder, he cannot claim the rights of a holder in due course by taking from a later holder in due course. This reflects the philosophy

[6] Canyonville Bible Academy v. Lobmaster, page 502.

that a holder in due course should have a free market for his paper but one who was a party to any fraud or who had notice of a claim or defense against an instrument should not be allowed to improve his status by repurchasing from a later holder in due course. A person should not be allowed to wash the paper clean by passing it into the hands of a holder in due course and then repurchasing it.

A *reacquirer* may reissue or further negotiate the instrument. He is not, however, entitled to enforce payment against any intervening persons to whom he was liable. Such intervening indorsers are also discharged as to subsequent parties except subsequent holders in due course.

The following examples illustrate the shelter provision. *P* fraudulently induces *M* to execute a note payable to the order of *P.* (1) *P* indorses to *A* who takes in good faith and otherwise satisfies the requirements of a holder in due course. *A* indorses in blank and delivers it to *B* who has notice of the fraud but did not participate in it. *B* obtained the rights of *A*, the holder in due course. (2) *P* indorses to *A* who has notice of the fraud. *A* negotiates it to *B* who takes without notice of the fraud and is a holder in due course. *A* repurchases the note from *B. A* remains subject to *M*'s defense of fraud and does not acquire *B*'s rights as a holder in due course.

HOLDERS AND HOLDERS IN DUE COURSE CASES

Wood v. Willman
423 P.2d 82 (Wyo.) 1967

The defendant was the maker of notes which the payee had pledged to the plaintiff as security for a loan. The defendant alleged that he had a defense against the payee and that the plaintiff could be a holder in due course only to the extent of the loan which was secured. The lower court ruled in favor of the defendant, and the plaintiff appealed.

PARKER, J. . . . When the Commercial Code was adopted in this jurisdiction, relatively few changes in the law of negotiable instruments as applied to commercial paper were effectuated. Indeed, it is commonly recognized that the Code merely sought to modernize, clarify, and consolidate various provisions of the Uniform Negotiable Instruments Act.

. . . [W]here the obligor proves a defense good as against the pledgor, the pledgee will be allowed to recover only to the extent of the debt for which he holds the collateral as security. . . . As heretofore noted, under the provisions of § 34-3-302(4), the plaintiff was a purchaser of a limited interest and a holder in due course to the extent of the interest purchased; but he could enforce the notes over defenses only to the extent of his interest, defenses good against the pledgor remaining available insofar as the pledgor retained an equity in the instrument. Thus, aside from the limited interest, the defense of want or failure of consideration was open to the defendant here. . . .

Affirmed.

Korzenik v. Supreme Radio, Inc.

197 N.E.2d 702 (Mass.) 1964

Defendants delivered two trade acceptances to the Southern New England Distributing Corporation. Southern delivered them to the plaintiff as part payment on a retainer for legal services to be performed. Southern was guilty of fraud in the original transaction, but the plaintiff was unaware of the fraud.

The plaintiff did some legal work between October 25 and October 31, 1961. There was no proof as to the value of these services. The plaintiff had paid cocounsel part of the money he had collected.

The trial court found for the defendant, and the plaintiff appealed, contending that he is a holder in due course. The appellate court affirmed.

WHITTEMORE, J. . . . Decisive of the case is the correct ruling that the plaintiffs are not holders in due course under G.L. c. 106, § 3-302; they have not shown to what extent they took for value under § 3-303. That section provides: "A holder takes the instrument for value (a) to the extent that the agreed consideration has been performed or that he acquires a security interest in or a lien on the instrument otherwise than by legal process; or (b) when he takes the instrument in payment of or as security for an antecedent claim against any person whether or not the claim is due; or (c) when he gives a negotiable instrument for it or makes an irrevocable commitment to a third person."

Under clause (a) of § 3-303 the "agreed consideration" was the performance of legal services. It is often said that a lawyer is "retained" when he is engaged to perform services, and we hold that the judge spoke of "retainer" in this sense. The phrase that the judge used, "retainer *for services*" [emphasis supplied], shows his meaning as does the finding as to services already performed by Korzenik at the time of the assignments. Even if the retainer had been only a fee to insure the attorney's availability to perform future services, there is no basis in the record for determining the value of this commitment for one week.

The Uniform Laws Comment to § 3-303 points out that in this article "value is divorced from consideration" and that except as provided in paragraph (c) "[a]n executory promise to give value is not . . . value. . . . The underlying reason of policy is that when the purchaser learns of a defense . . . he is not required to enforce the instrument, but is free to rescind the transaction for breach of the transferor's warranty."

General Laws c. 106, § 3-307(3), provides: "After it is shown that a defense exists a person claiming the rights of a holder in due course has the burden of establishing that he or some person under whom he claims is in all respects a holder in due course." The defense of fraud having been established this section puts the burden on the plaintiffs. The plaintiffs have failed to show "the extent . . . [to which] the agreed consideration . . . [had] been performed."

The only other possible issue under § 3-303 is whether, because of or in connection with taking the assignments, Korzenik made "an irrevocable commitment to a third person." There is no evidence of such a commitment. The finding as to a payment to cocounsel shows only that some of the proceeds of other assigned items have been expended by Korzenik.

Order dismissing report affirmed.

Jaeger and Branch, Inc. v. Pappas

433 P.2d 605 (Utah) 1967

The defendant, Pappas, ordered carpeting from Allo, a manufacturer. Impatient over a delay in the shipment of the carpeting, he telephoned the plaintiff, Jaeger, who was a creditor of Allo, to enlist his aid in getting the shipment released. The telephone conversation concerned the trouble the defendant was having with Allo. The next day the defendant mailed a check for $6,500 payable to Allo. The carpeting was shipped, but the defendant stopped payment on the check. Meanwhile Allo had indorsed the check to the plaintiff in payment of a preexisting debt. The check was returned to the plaintiff, who brought action against the defendant as drawer. The lower court ruled for the plaintiff, and the defendant appealed.

CROCKETT, J. . . . . We have no disagreement with certain postulates inherent in plaintiff's position: that when one who takes a negotiable instrument is aware of any fact which should alert him that there is a defense, he cannot close his eyes and ignore it. He must act in good faith and exercise such caution as a reasonable person would under those circumstances and is chargeable with knowledge of such facts as reasonable inquiry would disclose. However, the converse of that proposition is equally true, that in the absence of anything to warn him to the contrary, he may assume that persons with whom he deals are themselves acting honestly and in good faith. A very high proportion of the commerce of the world is carried on through credit, which is necessarily based on confidence in the honesty and integrity of those who engage in it. To impose upon one who is offered commercial paper the duty of inquiring in each instance whether obligations have been satisfactorily performed by prior holders would so burden such transactions as to create insuperable impedimenta to the free exchange of negotiable paper, an indispensable part of modern business.

From our survey of the facts in this case in the light of the principles we have discussed herein, we have discovered nothing which would compel the finding contended for by the defendant: that the plaintiff was aware of facts which precluded him from being a holder in due course. To the contrary, the evidence provides ample support for the trial court's rejection of that contention in favor of what impresses us as a reasonable view of the situation: that what the defendant Pappas attempted to do was to get the shipment of carpet released by the use of this check, and that when he accomplished that purpose, he sought to renege on his commitment by stopping payment on the check.

Affirmed. Costs to plaintiff (respondent).

American Plan Corp. v. Woods

240 N.E.2d 886 (Ohio) 1968

Crystal Clear, Inc. was engaged in the business of selling water softener equipment. In 1962 Crystal Clear approached the American Plan Corporation and offered to sell it notes which Crystal Clear expected to receive from purchasers of water softeners. American Plan agreed to this arrangement. A water softener was sold to the defendant, who claimed that the salesman had made fraudulent misrepresentations. The note which she gave in payment was sold and assigned to the plaintiff. Plaintiff brought suit on the note, and the defendant asserted fraud as a defense. The lower court found for the plaintiff, and the defendant appealed.

DUFFEY, J. . . . Section 1303.31, Revised Code, defines a holder in due course as one who, among other prerequisites, took the instrument "in good faith." In *Unico* v. *Owen* ((1967), 50 N.J. 101, at 109, 232 A.2d 405, at 410), the court said:

> In the field of negotiable instruments, good faith is a broad concept. The basic philosophy of the holder in due course status is to encourage free negotiability of commercial paper by removing certain anxieties of one who takes the paper as an innocent purchaser knowing no reason why the paper is not as sound as its face would indicate. It would seem to follow, therefore, that the more the holder knows about the underlying transaction, and particularly the more he controls or participates or becomes involved in it, the less he fits the role of a good faith purchaser for value; the closer his relationship to the underlying agreement which is the source of the note, the less need there is for giving him the tension-free rights considered necessary in a fast-moving, credit-extending commercial world.

The New Jersey court denied the status of holder in due course "where the financer maintains a close relationship with the dealer whose paper he buys; where the financer is closely connected with the dealer's business operations or with the particular credit transaction; or where the financer furnishes the form of sale contract and note for use by the dealer, the buyer signs the contract and note concurrently, and the dealer endorses the note and assigns the contract immediately thereafter or within the period prescribed by the financer."

In *Local Acceptance Co.* v. *Kinkade* ((Mo., 1962), 361 S.W.2d 830), the court held that it was not necessary that the financer know in advance of the execution of this specific note and of the contemporaneous execution of the particular contract. It was sufficient that the plaintiff knew in advance of any sales that they were to be made exclusively upon that method, and assented to the method.

There is conflicting authority in other jurisdictions. However, in our opinion, the doctrine so well stated in *Unico* strikes the proper balance between the protection of the commercial need for negotiability and the individual's need for relief against fraud. As that court stated, we are impelled to "join those courts which deny holder in due course status in consumer goods sales cases to those financers whose involvement with the seller's business is as close, and whose knowledge of the extrinsic factors—i.e., the terms of the underlying sales agreement—is as pervasive, as it is in the present case." *Unico* v. *Owen* ((1967), 50 N.J. 101, at 116, 232 A.2d 405, at 413).

The judgment of the Common Pleas Court will be reversed, and the judgment of the Municipal Court will be affirmed.

Judgment reversed.

Factors & Note Buyers, Inc. v. Green Lane, Inc.

245 A.2d 223 (N.J.) 1968

YANCEY, J. This is a motion for summary judgment on three notes executed by defendant Green Lane, Inc. and signed by defendant George Gottesman, its secretary.

The notes were signed May 15, 1964 to the order of Comfort Cooling Co. Defendants claim in their affidavit by Gottesman that the notes were made with the express agreement that they would not be discounted "but would merely be exhibited for the purpose of obtaining supplies in order to complete the contract." Unfortunately, this was nowhere indicated on the instruments.

Defendants claim that on May 18, 1964, when the corporation learned of Comfort Cooling's intent to discount the notes to plaintiff, and again on May 19, Gottesman telephoned plaintiff, spoke to Alexander Matathias, its vice-president, and "advised him of Green Lane's position, and emphatically requested that the notes not be discounted." Nevertheless, plaintiff acquired the notes. . . .

Defendants say Comfort Cooling did not complete performance and subsequently went bankrupt. They do not say how soon this was after the discounting and do not specifically allege plaintiff had knowledge of Comfort's financial troubles and of its incomplete performance. However, Gottesman does allege his "firm belief" that "plaintiff corporation had complete knowledge of the surrounding circumstances." . . .

In *N. J. Mtge. and Inv. Corp.* v. *Calvetti, supra,* at p. 36, 171 A.2d at p. 330, the court, in a case very similar to the case at bar, noted:

> All we are shown is an ordinary commercial financing transaction by a company in the legal business of discounting commercial paper. While the possibility of guilty knowledge on plaintiff's part cannot be categorically excluded, defendants, even on a motion for summary judgment, must provide at least some small ray of light indicating eventual illumination of that possibility as a probability. This they have not done. They are not "entitled to go to trial on the vague supposition that something may turn up. 6 *Moore, supra,* § 56.15, p. 2148."

In the case at bar defendants apparently consider Gottesman's telephone calls to plaintiff not only a "ray of light" but a beacon. However, even if it be assumed that plaintiff purchased the notes on May 21, 1964 and that Gottesman's telephone calls to Matathias thus should be considered, I hold as a matter of law that the information communicated by Gottesman in those calls in ineffective to preclude plaintiff from becoming a holder in due course.

The only provision of N.J.S. 12A:3-304, N.J.S.A., "Notice to Purchaser," that might be applicable in the case at bar is section 4(b). It reads as follows:

> (4) Knowledge of the following facts does not of itself give the purchaser notice of a defense or claim

> .   .   .

> (b) that it was issued or negotiated in return for an executory promise or accompanied by a separate agreement, unless the purchaser has notice that a defense or claim has arisen from the terms thereof;

> .   .   .

The import of this provision is explained by paragraph 9 of the Comment following 3-304, as follows:

Mere notice of the existence of an executory promise or a separate agreement does not prevent the holder from taking in due course, and such notice may even appear in the instrument itself. If the purchaser has notice of any default in the promise or agreement which gives rise to a defense or claim *against the instrument,* he is on notice to the same extent as in the case of any other information as to the existence of a defense or claim. [Emphasis added.]

The breach by Comfort Cooling of its agreement not to negotiate the notes would not give rise to a defense or claim against the notes but only against Comfort Cooling. Thus plaintiff took the notes "without notice that it is overdue or has been dishonored or of any defense against or claim to it on the part of any person." N.J.S. 12A:3-302(1), N.J.S.A. . . .

Motion for plaintiff allowed.

Canyonville Bible Academy v. Lobemaster

247 N.E.2d 623 (Ill.) 1969

The defendants executed an installment note to a trailer sales company in payment for a trailer. The trailer company indorsed the note to a bank. Following a default in payments on the note, the Bank assigned all of its interest in the note to the plaintiff. The defendants contended that the plaintiff was not a purchaser for value and not a holder in due course and therefore subject to personal defenses of the defendant. The lower court rendered judgment for the defendants, and the plaintiff appealed.

TRAPP, J. . . . Under Section 3-201 of the Uniform Commercial Code (Ill.Rev.Stat.1963, ch. 26, § 3-201) transfer is provided for as follows:

(1) Transfer of an instrument vests in the transferee such rights as the transferor has therein except that a transferee who has himself been a party to any fraud or illegality affecting the instrument or who as a prior holder had notice of a defense or claim against it cannot improve his position by taking from a later holder in due course.

In the Illinois Annotated Statute, the Illinois Code Comment under this section is the following interpretation:

The first clause of this subsection changes the rule under the first part of § 49 of the Illinois NIL (§ 49 of the NIL with variations), which provided, "where the holder of an instrument payable to his order transfers it *for value* without indorsing it, the transferer vests in the transferee such title as the transferee [transferer] had therein" [emphasis supplied]. This subsection eliminates the requirement of value for purposes of transferring the rights of the holder. It is in accord with Illinois case law indicating that a valid transfer may be made by way of gift.

Additionally, under the Uniform Commercial Code Comment in the Illinois Annotated Statute is the following:

2. The transfer of rights is not limited to transfers for value. An instrument may be transferred as a gift, and the donee acquires whatever rights the donor had.

Under Section 3-201 of Ch. 26, Ill.Rev.Stat. (1963), it is quite clear that any transfer of an instrument transfers all rights of the transferor, except in the specific case noted as an exception. Since the Bank was a holder in due course and plaintiff was not a prior holder, the plaintiff by transfer from the Bank acquired the rights of a holder in due course irrespective of the question of value. . . .

We conclude that the transfer of the defendant's note by the Bank to plaintiff gave plaintiff the Bank's status as a holder in due course, and the note is enforceable by plaintiff against defendant.

The cause is reversed and remanded with directions to enter judgment in favor of plaintiff and against the defendants in the amount of $9,674.30 with interest at 7 percent per annum from June 16, 1966, and reasonable attorneys' fees not to exceed 15 percent of the amount due at the time of suit and costs.

Reversed and remanded.

CHAPTER 25
REVIEW QUESTIONS AND PROBLEMS

1. A salesman of the A Contracting Company called upon an uneducated widow and suggested repairs to her house. He persuaded her to sign a note, and the note was sold to the BCD Finance Company. The work performed on her house was of no value to the widow. The finance company purchased the note for 50 percent of its face value. Would BCD Finance Company be a holder in due course?

2. *A* was an officer and stockholder of a corporation. He executed a note payable to the B Bank and had the proceeds placed in the corporation's account at the bank. The corporation failed, and the bank brought action against *A*. *A* contended that there was a failure of consideration. Would this defense be good against the bank?

3. *A* was the holder of a $3,000 note which had been indorsed to him. He had taken the note at a $200 discount and had paid $1,000 of the price. The maker of the note has a defense. Can he assert it against *A?*

4. *A* drew a check to the order of *B*. *B* indorsed it to *C* in payment of an existing indebtedness which *B* owed to *C*. *A* stopped payment on the check before *C* deposited it. *A* seeks to assert his defense of failure of consideration against *C*. Should he succeed?

5. *A* signed a conditional sales contract and note in blank in connection with the purchase of a car from *B*. *B* was to retain the note and contract until title to the car sold could be cleared. Instead *B* took the note and contract to the C Finance Company, where an employee of the company typed in the blanks as directed by *B*. *A* did not get title to the car and asserts this as a defense against the *C* company, which purchased the note from *B*. Should *A* succeed in this defense?

6. Jones induces Smith to sign a note in payment for worthless securities which Jones fraudulently claimed had great value. Jones indorses the note to Black in payment of a long-standing obligation. Black indorses to White who has knowledge of the fraud, having read about it in a newspaper account of the criminal prosecution of Jones. Can White recover on the note from Smith?

7. *M* executed a note to *P,* who promised to paint *M's* building. *P* indorsed the note in blank to *H. H* sued *M* on the note, and *M* alleged that the building had not been painted. He also alleged that *H* knew that the note had been given in return for *P's* promise to paint. *H* contends that he is entitled to a judgment because *M* has not alleged a valid defense. Decide.

8. *A* gave *B* a check in the amount of $500 in payment for linoleum installed in *A's* home. The check was dishonored, and *B* brought action to recover on the check. *A* contended that the linoleum was not satisfactory. The trial judge instructed the jury that the check was not subject to any defenses arising from claimed breaches of the contract. Was this instruction correct?

9. The X Finance Company furnished a dealer with printed forms of notes and contracts. The dealer, after making sales to customers and using these forms, would sell the paper to the finance company. On one such note the customer-maker of the note refused to pay, contending that the merchandise he bought was defective. Is this defense good against the X Finance Company?

10. *A* fraudulently induced *B* to execute a check for $2,495. *B* discovered the fraud and stopped payment on the check. In the meantime *A* cashed the check at Perfect's Market. The market seeks to recover from *B.* How would you decide?

chapter 26

Defenses

3-103. Introduction. As noted in Chapter 25, a holder in due course takes commercial paper free from the *personal* defenses of the parties to the paper. One who is not a holder in due course or who does not have the rights of one under the shelter provision is subject to such defenses. The law of commercial paper does not purport to relieve a holder in due course from all risks involved in a commercial paper transaction, however, and even a holder in due course is subject to what are referred to as *real* defenses.

In general, real defenses are those which relate to the existence of any obligation on the part of the person who asserts them. The most obvious real defense is the forgery of the signature of the maker of a note or the drawer of a check. The person whose signature was forged has not entered into any contract, and he should have an absolute defense even against a holder in due course.

The Code specifies which defenses are real and which are personal. Those that are real may be used against a holder in due course; those that are personal are available only against a person who does not have that status. Some defenses, however, are real in some states and personal in others; this is true, for example, of the defense of infancy. The chart on page 506 indicates various defenses and their usual status.

3-104. Unauthorized Signature. It is obvious that a person whose signature was placed upon an instrument, in whatever capacity, without permission or consent should not be liable to any holder. The term which describes this situation is "unauthorized signature." This means either a signature or an indorsement which was made without actual, implied, or apparent authority. It includes a forgery and a signature by an agent in the name of his principal when the agent lacked authority to sign. Unless the person whose signature

Commercial Paper: Typical Defenses

Personal Defenses		*Real Defenses*	
1.	Lack or failure of consideration	1.	Unauthorized signature
2.	Nonperformance of a condition precedent	2.	Material alteration
3.	Nondelivery of an instrument or delivery for a special purpose	3.	Infancy, if it is a defense to a simple contract
4.	Payment	4.	Lack of capacity
5.	Slight duress	5.	Extreme duress
6.	Fraud in the inducement	6.	Fraud in the inception
7.	Theft by the holder or one through whom he holds	7.	Illegality
8.	Violation of a restrictive indorsement	8.	Discharge in bankruptcy
9.	Unauthorized completion	9.	Discharge of which the holder has notice
10.	Other defenses to a simple contract.		

was placed upon the paper without authority has ratified the signature or is estopped [1] from asserting the lack of authority, he can assert this defense against any holder. A forger or other unauthorized signer has personal liability on an instrument. In the absence of ratification, estoppel, or negligence, any loss resulting from an unauthorized signature is placed upon the holder in due course.

3-105. Material Alteration. Similar to unauthorized signature is the defense of material alteration of an instrument. The most common example of an alteration is the "raising" of a check. For example, a check drawn in the amount of $50 might be raised by alteration to $500. Such alteration is a real defense to the extent of the alteration. A subsequent holder in due course could enforce the check in the amount of its original tenor—$50.

Material alteration includes the completion of an incomplete instrument otherwise than as it was authorized and changing the writing as it was signed, either by adding to it or by removing any part of it. A holder in due course is not subject to the defense of unauthorized completion of an incomplete instrument. In this instance, the defense is personal. The person who left the blank space must bear the risk of wrongful completion as against such a holder. As a general rule, a person should not be charged on a contract he has not made. However, certain words may be added or deleted which do not affect the paper or in any way affect the contract of any previous signer. For example, addresses of parties may be changed or information about the parties added without any legal operative effect.

Changes in the amount of money due, adding persons as additional payees, changing the interest rate, unauthorized completion of blanks, mutilating or cutting away nonperforated related contracts are illustrations of material alterations which change the legal effect of the instrument and make a different contract than that originally intended.

---

[1] Huber Glass Co. v. First National Bank of Kenosha, page 511.

Commercial paper is often printed as part of formal written contracts. Such instrument may or may not provide for the detachment of the commercial paper. To evidence implied authority to detach, perforations or dotted lines are set out between the negotiable portion and the contract. In absence of authority to detach either expressed or implied, unauthorized detachment from a formal written contract constitutes a material alteration. A holder in due course of a detached instrument, however, may recover according to the original tenor of the paper as it was with the contract attached.

It can be said in general that a material alteration results in a discharge of the person whose contract is changed. However, for this result to obtain, the alteration must have been made by a holder and for a fraudulent purpose. Interference with the paper by third party strangers can in no way affect the holder's rights nor impair the instrument in its original form. Likewise, if an alteration is made innocently with an honest belief that it is authorized or for the benefit of an obligor, such note is not discharged. If the alteration is not material, no party is discharged. Thus a discharge of a party results only from a fraudulent, material alteration by a holder which affects the contract of the party claiming the discharge—only the party whose contract was changed can assert this defense.

Alterations which do not qualify under the above specifications will not result in the discharge of any parties, and the altered instrument may be enforced against them in accordance with its original tenor. If the instrument was incomplete and thereafter wrongfully completed, it can be enforced in accordance with the authority in fact given.

The defense of discharge by alteration is quite restricted, and a party whose contract would have been discharged may nevertheless be bound if he has previously assented to the alterations or his conduct has been such as to estop him from asserting this defense.

3-106. Lack of Capacity, Duress, Illegality.

These three defenses are considered together because their status as real defenses is, in the main, dependent upon state law. In Chapter 10 it was noted that the treatment accorded to the contracts of minors is not uniform among the states. The law of each state must be consulted in order to determine when infancy is available as a defense to a simple contract or the conditions under which it may be asserted. For example, in some states an infant who has misrepresented his age may be precluded from asserting his infancy as a defense. To the extent that it is a defense to a contract, infancy is a real defense.

With respect to other incapacity, duress, or illegality, the defense is personal if state law renders a contract voidable, as opposed to void, when these factors are involved. Contracts which are void under state law give rise to real defenses.

The effect of duress upon a contract depends upon the degree of the duress.[2] Each state has its own standards for measuring it and determining its effect. As a general proposition, an instrument signed at gunpoint would be void even in the hands of a holder in due course, whereas one signed under threat to prosecute the son of the maker for theft may be merely voidable.

[2] Smith v. Lenchner, page 513.

Illegality of a contract may make it null and void. Each state has many statutes relating to illegal transactions and the status of such transactions. Gambling and usury statutes are two of the most common. Contracts involving usury in particular are treated quite differently in the various states. If state law makes obligations of a usurious nature null and void, the defense of usury can be asserted against a holder in due course. If the statute does not have this effect, the defense would be personal.

3-107. Fraud and Misrepresentation.   A distinction exists between fraud in the *inducement* or *consideration* and fraud in the *inception*. The former pertains to the consideration for which an instrument is given. The primary party intended to create an instrument but was fraudulently induced to do so. Such a defense is personal and is not available against a holder in due course. Fraud in the *inception* exists where a negotiable instrument is procured from a party when circumstances are such that the party does not know that he is giving a negotiable instrument. Fraud in the inception, sometimes called fraud in the *factum,* may be available as a defense against a holder in due course. The theory is that since the party primarily to be bound has no intention of creating an instrument, none is created. For example: *A,* intending to sign a lease at the request of *B,* unknowingly, and by trickery on the part of *B,* signs a negotiable instrument. *B* negotiates the instrument to *C,* a bona fide purchaser. Upon presentation of this instrument by *C* to *A* for payment, *A* may have a real defense against *C.* Carelessness on the part of the maker which facilitates the fraud will deprive him of this defense against a holder in due course.[3] Thus, in the above illustration, if *A* had signed the so-called lease without reading it and had allowed himself to be deceived into thinking the negotiable instrument he signed was a lease, he would have been liable to a holder in due course of the instrument. In such a case he cannot throw the loss occasioned by his negligence on the holder in due course.

3-108. Discharge.   A person who is unable to meet his obligations may become involved in bankruptcy or other insolvency proceedings. " 'Insolvency proceedings' includes any assignment for the benefit of creditors or other proceedings intended to liquidate or rehabilitate the estate of the person involved." (U.C.C. 1-201(22)) A discharge in bankruptcy or other insolvency proceedings will be available as a defense against a holder in due course. Thus, if *A* owed *B* $500 on a negotiable note and thereafter filed a petition in bankruptcy and received his discharge, *A* could assert his discharge in bankruptcy as a defense against *B* or a holder in due course to whom *B* had negotiated the note.

A purchaser is not a holder in due course if he has notice that all the parties to an instrument have been discharged. However, if the notice does not include all of the parties, the holder may still be a holder in due course. Suppose that *M* has made a note payable to the order of *P. P* has indorsed to *A, A* has indorsed to *B,* and *B* has indorsed to *C.* If *C* discharges *B* from his liability as an indorser and then negotiates the paper to *H, H* could be a holder in due course and could hold the maker and prior indorsers liable. If he does not have

---

[3] Burchett v. Allied Concord Financial Corp., page 515.

notice of the discharge of *B,* such discharge would not be effective against him, and the discharge is treated as a personal defense.

3-109. Lack or Failure of Consideration.   Consideration is essential to make promises binding in commercial paper and its want or failure is a defense as against all persons except holders in due course. Unlike general contract law, consideration is *not* required in connection with the issuance or transfer of commercial paper if the paper is given in payment of or as security for an antecedent obligation such as payment of an existing debt.[4]

As noted in connection with the requirements for a holder in due course, another term, "value," is used in the law of negotiable instruments. The two terms must be distinguished. "Consideration" has significance only in determining whether a binding contractual obligation has been created; it refers to what the obligor—here, the maker of a note—has received for his obligation and is important only in its bearing on the question of whether his obligation is enforceable against him. "Value" is used to determine whether a holder has given something in payment for an instrument as an element of his acquiring the status of a holder in due course. To illustrate: *M* executes a note in favor of *P* in return for merchandise which is never delivered. As against *P, M* has a defense of failure of consideration. *P* indorses the note to *H* in payment of an obligation. H has furnished value and can enforce the note against *M* in spite of his defense.

A holder in due course takes free from the defense of failure or absence of consideration. However, want or failure of consideration is a defense between immediate parties and against those not holding in due course.

3-110. Lack of Delivery.   The defenses of nondelivery, conditional delivery, or delivery for a special purpose may be asserted against one who is not a holder in due course, but a holder in due course takes the instrument free of these personal defenses. For example, *A* executed a note in favor of *B,* intending to deliver it to *B* only after *B* had performed certain services. *B* managed to obtain possession of the note without *A*'s knowledge and negotiated it to *C. A* can assert the defense of nondelivery against *C* only if *C* is not a holder in due course. As between immediate parties and parties other than holders in due course, the delivery may be shown to be conditional or for some special purpose only. To illustrate: *A* drew a check in favor of *B* and delivered it to him with the express understanding that it was to be negotiated only on condition that *B* first redecorate the main floor of *A*'s department store. *B* negotiated the check to *C* in violation of this understanding. If *C* is not a holder in due course, *A* can assert the conditional delivery and *B*'s failure to perform as a defense against *C.*

3-111. Theft.   A person who does not have the rights of a holder in due course is subject to the defense that a person through whom he holds the instrument acquired it by theft. On the other hand, such defense cannot be asserted against one who has holder in due course rights.

[4] Insdorf v. Wil-Avon Merchandise Mart, Inc., page 517.

3-112. Claims of Third Persons.   A holder in due course is not subject to the defense that a third party has a claim to the instrument. He is entitled to be paid in spite of such claim. One who does not have the rights of a holder in due course is subject to the defense that such claims exist with reference to instruments acquired by theft and failure to comply with restrictive indorsements, but other third-party claims are not available as a defense against one not a holder in due course unless the third person who has the claim to the instrument defends the action in which enforcement of the instrument is sought.

3-113. Order and Burden of Proof.   When a written document becomes involved in litigation, there is a general presumption that the signatures which it contains are genuine. In most states a pleading denying the execution of a written instrument must be under oath. Therefore, a plaintiff suing on commercial paper establishes a prima facie case when he files the paper with his complaint. Unless the defendant's answer establishes a defense, the plaintiff is entitled to a summary judgment.

If the defendant raises a defense in his answer, the burden of coming forth with evidence to prove the defense is on the defendant, as is the burden of persuading the trier of fact of the validity of the defense. If the defense is a real defense, a finding that it is valid will result in a judgment for the defendant. If the defense is a personal defense, the plaintiff then has the burden of proving that he or some person under whom he claims is a holder in due course.[5] If the plaintiff successfully establishes that he has the rights of a holder in due course, a judgment will be entered for the plaintiff, because the defense, as a matter of law, does not defeat the plaintiff's claim. The issue as to whether or not the plaintiff is a holder in due course does not arise until a defense is shown to exist.

3-114. Negligence as a Factor in Asserting Defenses.   Negligence of a party will reduce a real defense to a personal defense. Negligent conduct is frequently present in situations of fraud and material alteration. For example, in the case of material alteration, that which otherwise might have resulted in a discharge will not have that result if the negligence of the party claiming the discharge contributed to or facilitated the alteration. Thus one who writes a check and leaves a large blank space in front of the amount on the check renders it easier for a wrongdoer to raise the check and constitutes negligence reducing the defense to a personal one.

Negligence in failing to detect forged indorsements precludes the careless party from asserting his defense against a holder in due course or from asserting the defense against a drawee or payor such as a bank who pays the instrument in good faith and "in accordance with the reasonable commercial standards of the drawee's or payor's business."[6]

The reasoning behind the negligence rule is that if checks or other commercial paper are to pass current as money, the careless creator of paper should suffer the loss as against holders in due course and the innocent drawees and

[5] Northside Bank of Tampa v. Investors Acceptance Corp., page 517.
[6] Gresham State Bank v. O & K Construction Co., page 519

other payors who pay the instrument in good faith. How negligent and careless the drawer must be is a fact question, but the negligence must be *substantial.*

Insofar as checks are concerned, the debtor-bank is under a duty to pay those drawn by the depositor in accordance with the contract. It is therefore proper that the depositor should be bound to exercise care in drafting checks in order to prevent the bank from being deceived. Drawing a check in a manner which facilitates fraud constitutes a breach of duty to the bank. For example, *A* as a practice has permitted his secretary to issue checks by means of a mechanical device and rubber stamps. Unauthorized checks issued and delivered by reason of the careless control and supervision of such equipment would prevent *A* from denying liability. Likewise, inadvertency in mistakenly mailing checks, particularly to persons of the same name as the intended payee, is negligent conduct contributing to the use of an unauthorized signature, so that the loss must be borne by the drawer. The question is, what conduct is "negligent" so that it can be said that it has "substantially contributed to a material alteration" or to the making of "an unauthorized signature." It is believed that reasonable care would not demand the use of sensitized paper, fast inks, and "checkographs" by drawers in order to avoid negligent conduct.

A person placing current paper in the channels of business owes a duty to future users to so create paper that it cannot be altered. The holder, drawee, and other good faith takers should not be deterred in its use. The negligent drawers and makers must seek recovery from the wrongdoer. Of course, when the instrument has been altered by a mechanical process or erasure or chemical change, another instrument has been created, and no negligent conduct can be attributed to the issuer of the paper.

DEFENSES CASES

Huber Glass Co. v. First National Bank of Kenosha
138 N.W.2d 157 (Wis.) 1965

Huber Glass Company maintained a checking account with First National Bank of Kenosha. R. C. Huber, president, and his wife, Bertha, were the only ones authorized to sign checks. Kenneth Miller, bookkeeper for the company since 1959, was discharged in 1963 and committed suicide the next day. It was later discovered that certain checks signed "R. C. Huber" and made out to and indorsed by Miller had been drawn on the account since August, 1960. Huber denied actually signing any of the checks. Huber Glass Company, plaintiff, brought suit against the bank, defendant, to recover $23,875.42 which had been paid within the prior year on the checks allegedly forged by Miller. (The statute outlawed claims on checks more than a year old.) Judgment was rendered for the plaintiff, and the defendant bank appealed.

WILKIE, J. The law concerning the duty of a bank towards its depositor was summarized in *Wussow* v. *Badger State Bank.* Since their relationship is grounded in contract, a bank can only make payments from a depositor's account in accordance with proper authorization and is bound to restore any amount paid out on forged checks. A bank can only avoid this strict liability where the "depositor is in equity estopped to assert that the bank is absolutely liable." To do this successfully, the bank must show (1) that it was without fault in failing to detect the forgeries, and (2) that the depositor was negligent in causing the money to be paid. In the instant case the trial court found as a matter of fact that (1) the bank "was negligent in not detecting the forgeries," and (2) that the depositor "was not negligent." To enable the bank to prevail against the depositor's claim it must, on this appeal, demonstrate that both of these findings are against the great weight and clear preponderance of the evidence.

Thus, the two issues presented on this appeal are:

1. Is the finding of negligence on the part of the bank against the evidence?
2. Is the finding of no negligence on the part of the depositor against the evidence?

.   .   .   .

The record establishes that the bank used a reasonable method to inspect and process the checks presented to it, and that the forgeries were not palpable or flagrant. . . . Consequently there is no evidence to support the finding that the bank was negligent.

Even if the bank is not guilty of negligence in failing to uncover the forgery, the depositor is nonetheless entitled to a restoration of the funds paid out in the absence of negligence on its own part. Thus, the crucial question here is whether or not the depositor was negligent.

A depositor is bound to examine the checks and statements returned by the bank, and this duty is violated when it neglects to do those things dictated by ordinary business customs and which, if done, would have prevented the wrongdoing.

In *Wussow,* the court held that the depositor had a duty to examine his checks and the statements and discover whether the balance stated was correct and whether any forgeries were included and report any discrepancies in balance and any forgeries to the bank at once.

It had been held that the reconciliation should include, as a minimum, the following steps: (1) A comparison of the cancelled checks with the check stubs, (2) a comparison of the statement balance with the check book balance, and (3) a comparison of the returned checks with the checks listed on the statement.

There is no question that in the case at bar the procedure employed by the respondent [plaintiff] in checking the returned checks and bank statements did not comply with these suggested steps. On the contrary, the undisputed evidence showed that the checks returned to respondent by appellant were received by Miller who made a preliminary examination of the statement. Presumably, the forged checks were removed from the others at this point. Then another employee of the bookkeeping department listed the checks numerically and determined the ones that were outstanding. After this, Miller would reconcile the bank statement with the check ledger. Huber got the checks at this point, but he testified that he never attempted to reconcile the bank statement with the books but left this task entirely up to Miller. . . .

. . . Under the circumstances, entrusting Miller alone with the job of reconciling the statements for three years, when a simple spot check of the records would have uncovered the forgeries, was unreasonable and the trial court's finding of no negligence is contrary to the great weight and clear preponderance of the evidence. Huber, however, takes the position that the president of a company which employs between 50 and 75 people, and which writes almost 13,000 checks a year, cannot be expected to personally examine and/or reconcile the books. But the president himself is not required to do this; the task can be delegated to another employee. Modern business practice dictates at least some semblance of internal control. Estoppel from claiming against the bank is the price of blind reliance on a single employee.

The earliest checks forged on the depositor's account by Miller appeared in August in 1960. Respondent's negligence in failing to employ proper reconciliation methods preceded the one-year period—April, 1962-1963—embraced by the depositor's claim, and he is estopped from asserting a claim against the bank for any check embraced in the lower court's judgment. . . .

Judgment reversed.

Smith v. Lenchner
205 A.2d 626 (Pa.) 1964

WRIGHT, J. . . . The note in question is dated July 6, 1962, in amount of $1,200.00 payable on demand, and is under seal. The petition . . . alleges that the maker of the note is not indebted to the payee, and requests that the judgment be opened because (a) the note was given "under duress of a threat made by the plaintiff to maliciously and falsely interfere with and disrupt a business transaction which the petitioner was then negotiating"; and (b) no consideration was received for the execution and delivery of the note. Appellant's answer denies that the note was given under duress of a threat, and avers to the contrary that the note was voluntarily negotiated as "the result of a good-faith, arm's-length business transaction." The answer further denies want of consideration, and alleges to the contrary (1) that the presence of the seal imports consideration and (2) that the transaction which gave rise to the note "was a sale of stock by plaintiff to defendant." . . . A brief summary of this testimony is as follows:

Joseph S. Lenchner, the appellee, testified that he was a college graduate, admittedly experienced in business transactions. In the month of June, 1962, negotiations were pending for the sale of the Lenchner-Corvato Company, a security business in which he was financially interested. Martin B. Smith, [plaintiff] an employe and owner of one share of stock, demanded the sum of $1,200.00, "and if I didn't give it to him he was going to try to do everything and anything he could to kill our deal . . . I suggested a note which he agreed to take." Although he had ample time to do so, Lenchner did not consult his attorney before the note was executed and delivered. . . .

Martin B. Smith, the appellant, testified that he was manager of the underwriting department of Lenchner-Corvato Company, and had paid $1,200.00 for the one share of stock which he owned. He had doubts as to the financial status of the proposed purchaser of the business, and objected to the sale "because I didn't think we'd ever get paid." He proposed that Lenchner buy his share of stock for the cost price. Lenchner did not have the cash available, and said "that he would give me a note." The stock certificate was endorsed, but was retained as collateral. Smith flatly denied making any threats, and testified that the transaction was purely a business deal.

We perceive no merit in appellee's contention that he was under duress when he executed and delivered the note in question. The threat purportedly made by appellant was not of physical violence or of criminal process, indeed not even of civil process. The case of *McDermott* v. *Bennett* (213 Pa. 129, 62 A. 637) cited in the brief, involved the relationship of client and attorney and is readily distinguished. Duress has been defined as that degree of restraint or danger, either actually inflicted or threatened and impending, which is sufficient in severity or apprehension to overcome the mind of a person of ordinary firmness. The quality of firmness is assumed to exist in every person competent to contract, unless it appears that by reason of old age or other sufficient cause he is weak or infirm. Where persons deal with each other on equal terms and at arm's length, there is a presumption that the person alleging duress possesses ordinary firmness. Moreover, in the absence of threats of actual bodily harm, there can be no duress where the contracting party is free to consult with counsel.

Appellee also contends that he may raise his alleged defense of want of consideration despite the fact that the note was executed under seal. Reliance is placed upon Section 3-113 of the Uniform Commercial Code, which reads as follows: "An instrument otherwise negotiable is within this Article even though it is under a seal." It is argued that the Code Comment under this section, as well as the Pennsylvania Bar Association Notes, indicate that the defense of want of consideration is now available despite the presence of a seal. This question was raised but expressly not decided in *Thomasik* v. *Thomasik* (413 Pa. 559, 198 A.2d 511). Howbeit, the note in the instant case is not "an instrument otherwise negotiable" because it *authorizes confession of judgment as of any term.* Prior to the enactment of the Code, a note containing a warrant of attorney to confess judgment at *any time* was held to be a non-negotiable instrument. This rule was applied to a demand note. The same result has been reached in cases subsequent to the enactment of the Code. Since the instant note is *non-negotiable,* it follows that the seal imports consideration.

We should perhaps here mention that Section 3-112(1) of the Code provides that the negotiability of a note "is not affected by . . . (d) a term authorizing a confession of judgment on the instrument if it is not paid when due." The Pennsylvania Bar Association Notes under the section point out that most judgment notes in use in this Commonwealth are not negotiable because judgment may be entered before the amount is due. To the same effect is the Code Comment that "paragraph (d) is intended to mean that a confession of judgment may be authorized only if the instrument is not paid when due, and that otherwise negotiability is affected." The Code did not change prior law in this respect.

Appellee contends finally that appellant may not rely upon the seal because he affirmatively pleaded independent consideration. It is argued that appellant "should now be estopped from relying upon the seal as a substitute for consideration." The doctrine of estoppel has no application in the instant case. We perceive no reason which would prevent appellant from utilizing both theories.

Order reversed.

Burchett v. Allied Concord Financial Corp.

396 P.2d 186 (N.M.) 1964

The plaintiffs (Burchett and Beevers) purchased an aluminum siding installation for their home upon the false representation of the salesman that they would receive a 100-dollar credit for every other job contracted in the area. Without reading the forms, they signed notes and mortgages, which were transferred to the defendant finance corporation by the siding company. On discovering their predicament, the plaintiffs brought suit to have the notes and mortgages canceled. The lower court found for the plaintiffs, and the defendant appealed.

CARMODY, J. . . . The only real question in the case is whether, under the facts, appellees, by substantial evidence, satisfied the provisions of the statute relating to their claimed defense as against a holder in due course.

. . . The provision of the code applicable . . . is as follows:

> To the extent that a holder is a holder in due course he takes the instrument free from . . .
> (2) all defenses of any party to the instrument with whom the holder has not dealt except . . .
> (c) such misrepresentation as has induced the party to sign the instrument with neither knowledge nor reasonable opportunity to obtain knowledge of its character or its essential terms; and . . .

Although fully realizing that the official comments appearing as part of the Uniform Commercial Code are not direct authority for the construction to be placed upon a section of the code, nevertheless they are persuasive and represent the opinion of the National Conference of Commissioners on Uniform State Laws and the American Law Institute. The purpose of the comments is to explain the provisions of the code itself, in an effort to promote uniformity of interpretation. We believe that the official comments following § 3-305 (2) (c), Comment No. 7, provide an excellent guideline for the disposition of the case before us. We quote the same in full:

> (7) Paragraph (c) of subsection (2) is new. It follows the great majority of the decisions under the original Act in recognizing the defense of "real" or "essential" fraud, sometimes called fraud in the essence or fraud in the factum, as effective against a holder in due course. The common illustration is that of the maker who is tricked into signing a note in the belief that it is merely a receipt or some other document. The theory of the defense is that his signature on the instrument is ineffective because he did not intend to sign such an instrument at all. Under this provision the defense extends to an instrument signed with knowledge that it is a negotiable instrument, but without knowledge of its essential terms.
> The test of the defense here stated is that of excusable ignorance of the contents of the writing signed. The party must not only have been in ignorance, but must also have had no reasonable opportunity to obtain knowledge. In determining what is a reasonable opportunity all relevant factors are to be taken into account, including the age and sex of the party, his intelligence, education and business experience;

his ability to read or to understand English, the representations made to him and his reason to rely on them or to have confidence in the person making them; the presence or absence of any third person who might read or explain the instrument to him, or any other possibility of obtaining independent information; and the apparent necessity, or lack of it, for acting without delay.

Unless the misrepresentation meets this test, the defense is cut off by a holder in due course.

We observe that the inclusion of subsection (2) (c) in § 3-305 of the Uniform Commercial Code was an attempt to codify or make definite the rulings of many jurisdictions on the question as to the liability to a holder in due course of a party who either had knowledge, or a reasonable opportunity to obtain the knowledge, of the essential terms of the instrument, before signing. . . .

The reason for the rule, both as it was applied under the Negotiable Instruments Law and as is warranted under the Uniform Commercial Code, is that when one of two innocent persons must suffer by the act of a third, the loss must be borne by the one who enables the third person to occasion it.

We believe that the test set out in Comment No. 7 above quoted is a proper one and should be adhered to by us. (By giving approval to this Comment, we do not in any sense mean to imply that we thereby are expressing general approval of all the comments to the various sections of the Uniform Commercial Code.) Thus the only question is whether, under the facts of this case, the misrepresentations were such as to be a defense as against a holder in due course.

The facts and circumstances surrounding each particular case, both under the Negotiable Instruments Law and the Uniform Commercial Code, require an independent determination. . . .

We recognize that the reasonable opportunity to obtain knowledge may be excused if the maker places reasonable reliance on the representations. The difficulty in the instant case is that the reliance upon the representations of a complete stranger (Kelly) was not reasonable, and all of the parties were of sufficient age, intelligence, education, and business experience to know better. In this connection, it is noted that the contracts clearly stated, on the same page which bore the signatures of the various appellees, the following:

> No one is authorized on behalf of this company to represent this job to be "A SAMPLE HOME OR A FREE JOB."

The conduct of the Beevers in signing the additional form some weeks after the initial transaction, without reading it, is a graphic showing of negligence. This, however, is merely an added element and it is obvious that all of the parties were negligent in signing the instruments without first reading them under the surrounding circumstances. See *First National Bank of Philadelphia* v. *Anderson, supra,* which held that the mere failure to read a contract was not sufficient to allow the maker a defense under § 3-305 of the Uniform Commercial Code. In our opinion, the appellees here are barred for the reasons hereinabove stated.

Although we have sympathy with the appellees, we cannot allow it to influence our decision. They were certainly victimized, but because of their failure to exercise ordinary care for their own protection, an innocent party cannot be made to suffer.

Reversed.

Insdorf v. Wil-Avon Merchandise Mart, Inc.

8 Ches. Co. Rep. 341 (Pa.) 1958

The defendant executed a check payable to the order of the plaintiff in settlement of accounts owing to the plaintiff. The check was made and delivered on January 11, 1958, but dated January 23, 1958. The plaintiff presented the check after January 23, but the bank refused payment because the defendant had stopped payment. The plaintiff attempted to recover the amount of the check, and the defendant resisted, claiming that the plaintiff's complaint failed to allege with particularity the accounts between the parties for which the check was allegedly given in payment.

GAWTHROP, J. . . . Defendant's second contention is without merit. Under the Negotiable Instruments Law . . . Section 24, every negotiable instrument was deemed, prima facie, to have been issued for valuable consideration. There was no necessity to plead in detail the terms of the contract in connection with delivery of a check . . . The Uniform Commercial Code, . . . Section 3-408, supplies and replaces, *inter alia,* Section 24 of the Act of 1901, and by its terms provides that "no consideration is necessary for an instrument or obligation given in payment of or as security for an antecedent obligation of any kind." We cannot conclude that the enactment of the Code has altered the law or the practice to require Plaintiff to aver the details of the contract which gave rise to making the check. Moreover, Section 3-408 of the Code, by making consideration unnecessary where the instrument is given for an antecedent obligation, makes it equally unnecessary to plead consideration in such circumstances. Therefore, the averment may be regarded as surplusage.

Furthermore, the same section of the Code makes want or failure of consideration a matter of defense as between the original parties. Both such defenses must . . . be pleaded under New Matter in Defendant's Answer, and if not so pleaded are waived. . . . In our view the detailed nature of the consideration pleaded need not be set forth, especially since Defendant must make any defense of want or failure of consideration by pleading it affirmatively as New matter.

The preliminary objection is dismissed. Defendant is allowed twenty days to file an answer.

Northside Bank of Tampa v. Investors Acceptance Corp.

278 F.Supp. 191 (1968)

MARSH, J. In this diversity action, plaintiff, a bank, sues the defendant as the drawer of three checks, each dated August 22, 1966, and drawn to the order of Style-Rite, Inc., a corporation, having its checking account in plaintiff's bank in Tampa, Florida. Each check was drawn on the Western Pennsylvania National Bank, Pittsburgh, Pennsylvania.

On August 25th, the plaintiff bank cashed one check and on August 24th and 25th accepted the other two for deposit, crediting Style-Rite's account; the plaintiff thereupon applied a part of this credit to Style-Rite's overdrawn balance in the sum of $2,046.13, and permitted Style-Rite to withdraw a substantial part of the remaining credit before it received notice that the defendant had ordered the drawee bank in Pittsburgh to stop payment.

Defendant admits to the issuance of the three checks and to the deposit of two, while pleading no knowledge as to the truth of plaintiff's averment that it cashed the third. The genuineness of the signatures is not denied. In paragraphs 13 and 14 of a verified Answer, defendant avers that it was induced to draw those checks by Style-Rite's false and fraudulent representation as to its financial ability to perform certain home improvement contracts and to fulfill certain other promises which were the bargained consideration for which defendant issued the checks involved.

Seeking to cut off this defense, the plaintiff bank has moved for summary judgment, averring that the affidavits attached demonstrate that the plaintiff bank is a holder in due course; that the defenses alleged are not defenses against a holder in due course; and that there is no genuine issue of material fact. We think that the plaintiff's motion should be denied.

The parties agree that plaintiff's right to enforce payment of these checks against the defendant drawer is governed by Pennsylvania law as expressed in the relevant provisions of the Uniform Commercial Code, 12A Purdon's Pa. Stat. Ann. § 1-101 et seq.

Under the Code a holder of a check is entitled to recover on it unless the defendant establishes a defense. When a defense exists, the plaintiff holder has the burden of establishing that it is in all respects a holder in due course, if it claims such rights. See: 12A Purdon's Pa.Stat.Ann. § 3-307(2) (3).

Unquestionably, the defendant's verified Answer and affidavit show that it has a defense against the payee, Style-Rite, which defense is not controverted by the plaintiff bank. Thus the bank has the burden of establishing by credible evidence to the satisfaction of the jury that it is "in all respects" a holder in due course.

A holder in due course is a holder who takes the instrument (a) for value; and (b) in good faith; and (c) without notice that it is overdue or has been dishonored or of any defense against or claim to it on the part of any person. 12A Purdon's Pa.Stat.Ann. § 3-302, as amended.

It is our opinion that unless the circumstances of the holder's taking the checks were free of all doubt, the court would not be in a position to direct a verdict in favor of the plaintiff bank because the elements constituting a holder in due course are questions of fact for the triers of fact to determine. The court conceives of situations in which it could direct a verdict in favor of defendant for insufficiency of evidence that plaintiff bank was a holder in due course, but it is otherwise as to directing a verdict for plaintiff, who has the burden of persuading the jury by the preponderance of evidence on all material issues of fact. . . .

. . . In such circumstances, we think the defendant has the right to require plaintiff to prove by a preponderance of the credible evidence that it is a holder in due course to the satisfaction of the jury.

An appropriate order will be entered.

Gresham State Bank v. O & K Construction Co.

370 P.2d 726 (Oreg.) 1962

F. C. McKenna was employed by O & K Construction Company as a bookkeeper. He was authorized to receive checks payable to the company and to deposit these checks in the First National Bank of Gresham. The company furnished him with a rubber stamp, "For deposit only at the First National Bank." The office supplies also included another stamp, "O & K Construction Co., Route 1, Gresham, Oregon," which was intended to be used in marking statements and other items. During the years 1957, 1958, 1959, McKenna indorsed thirty checks which had been made payable to the company and cashed them at Zimmerman's Store. He indorsed the checks with the latter rubber stamp followed by his own name and the designation, "Office Manager" or "Bkpr." Zimmerman's Store deposited the checks in its account in the plaintiff bank. The checks were sent through the regular banking channels and paid by the drawee banks. In May, 1959, McKenna's defalcations were discovered. The construction company obtained the canceled checks from the various drawers and made a demand for payment from all of the drawee banks. These banks in turn made demand upon the plaintiff bank. As these demands were made on it, the plaintiff withdrew from the account of Zimmerman's Store an amount equal to the check and placed it in a "suspense account." After the last check had been presented, the bank filed an interpleader suit naming O & K Construction Co. and Zimmerman's Store as defendants. The bank paid the money represented by the checks into court and was discharged from liability. The lower court entered a judgment for Zimmerman's Store.

O'CONNELL, J. . . . The defendant O & K Construction Company relies upon the rule that one who makes payment upon an unauthorized endorsement of the payee's name is liable to the payee for conversion.

Defendant Zimmerman contends that the loss falls upon the defendant construction company on the basis of any one of the following grounds: (1) that McKenna had implied or apparent authority to endorse the checks and to present them to Zimmerman's for payment on behalf of the construction company; (2) the construction company is precluded from recovery by its negligence; (3) where one of two innocent parties must suffer, the loss should fall upon the one whose acts made the loss possible.

The third contention adds nothing to the first two. There is no legal principle which places the loss upon one of two innocent parties merely because one acted and the other did not. The law makes the choice upon the basis of fault or some other consideration warranting the preference. In the present case we must decide upon some such rational ground which of the two defendants should be favored.

We begin with the well established rule that one who obtains possession of a check through the unauthorized endorsement of the payee's name acquires no title to it and is liable to the payee for the amount of the check unless the payee is precluded from setting up the want of authority. . . .

The mere fact that an employee has charge of a company's office does not entitle third persons dealing with the employee to assume that he has the authority to execute or endorse the company's negotiable paper. We find no evidence to support a finding that McKenna was clothed with apparent authority.

The contention that defendant O & K Construction Company was precluded from recovery because of its negligence presents a more difficult legal problem. There was evidence to support a finding that Osburn and Kniefel were negligent in failing to scrutinize the records of the company over the three-year period during which the defalcation occurred. They made little individual effort to examine their books during that period and no audit was made. . . .

The pattern for decision in cases such as the one before us is found in Section 3-406 of the Uniform Commercial Code which . . . provides as follows:

> Any person who by his negligence substantially contributes to a material alteration of the instrument or to the making of an unauthorized signature is precluded from asserting the alteration or lack of authority against a holder in due course or against a drawee or other payor who pays the instrument in good faith and in accordance with the reasonable commercial standards of the drawee's or payor's business.

. . . It is apparent that this section requires a weighing process in choosing between the owner of the forged instrument and the payor in allocating the loss. Translating the section in terms of the factual situation before us, the O & K Construction Company is not precluded from asserting McKenna's lack of authority unless two conditions exist: (1) That O & K Construction Company's negligence "substantially contributes" to the making of the unauthorized signature, and (2) that Zimmerman made payment on the instrument in good faith "and in accordance with the reasonable commercial standards of the . . . payor's business." . . .

Ordinarily the customary practices of a business must be established by evidence. However, it has been judicially recognized in many adjudicated cases that one who cashes a check endorsed by an agent has the duty to inquire as to the agent's authority to make the endorsement. We can, therefore, take judicial notice of this duty to make inquiry as a part of the "reasonable commercial standards" of a business. . . .

In testing Zimmerman's conduct by the standard of ordinary commercial practice, it is to be noted that the checks were not cashed by McKenna in connection with any purchase of items in the store on behalf of the construction company. McKenna received the whole amount of the check. Moreover, the amounts paid to him were substantial, including several checks for $300 or more.

Ordinarily, it is the usual practice for a company to deposit checks received by it and to pay for its expenditures by checks drawn on its own account. . . .

We hold that, as a matter of law, Zimmerman did not make payment of the checks in accordance with the reasonable commercial standards of his business. . . .

We hold that, because of defendant Zimmerman's negligent failure to act in accordance with the reasonable commercial standards of its business, the defendant O & K Construction Company, although negligent, is not precluded from recovering upon the forged checks. . . .

Reversed and remanded.

CHAPTER 26
REVIEW QUESTIONS AND PROBLEMS

1. *A* operated a check cashing service in the vicinity of *B*'s manufacturing plant. Many of *B*'s employees cashed their paychecks through *A*. *B* arranged for one of his employees to spend time at *A*'s place of business to approve checks presented for cashing. A forged check drawn on *B* was cashed by *A*. *A* seeks to recover the amount of the check from *B*, who contends that forgery is an absolute defense. Who should prevail?

2. *A* purchased a car from *B* and signed a negotiable instrument in payment. *B* assigned the papers to the C Finance Company. When C attempted to collect, *A* refused to pay on the grounds that she had been told she was buying a new car when it was in fact used, and that she had signed the papers in blank. Are these defenses good against the C Company?

3. A salesman for the A Company demonstrated a water softening device to *B* in his home. The salesman told *B* that he could use it for six months without charge if he would allow demonstrations in his home. He asked *B* to sign some papers so that he could satisfy his company as to the location of the machine. Unknown to *B* he had signed a note which was subsequently discounted by the X Bank. Does *B* have a defense against the X Bank?

4. The A Company installed aluminum siding for *B*. *B* gave a note in payment, with the understanding that *A* would hold the note and that *B* could pay by obtaining siding jobs for *A*. *B* obtained the jobs, but *A* refused to return the note and indorsed it to *C* in payment of an obligation. Can *B* assert his defense against *C*?

5. The A Corporation, a wholesale jeweler, sold jewelry to *B*, a retailer, and *B* gave notes in payment. *A* then discounted the notes with the X Bank. The A Corporation had failed to qualify to transact business in the state. Does *B* have a defense against X Bank?

6. *M* executed a note to *P* with interest at the rate of 25 percent. *P* indorsed the note to *H*. Can *H* enforce the note against *M*?

7. *M*, the maker of a note, filed a petition in bankruptcy. Prior to bankruptcy he had executed a note in the amount of $10,000 to *A*, and *A* had indorsed it to *H*. Can *H* recover on the note from *M*?

8. *M* arranged to have a new furnace installed in her home and signed several papers including a note, at the request of *P*, a heating contractor, without knowledge or reason to believe that any one of the papers was a note. *P* indorsed the note to X Bank. *M* never received the furnace. Is *M* liable to the bank?

9. *M* is the drawer of a check. After giving the check to *P* in payment for merchandise, he discovered that the merchandise is worthless. To what extent can *M* protect himself by stopping payment on the check?

10. The X Finance Company furnished an automobile dealer with printed forms of notes and contracts and did credit investigations prior to approval of a transaction. The dealer, after making sales to customers and using these forms, would sell the paper to the finance company. The form for assignment was a part of the contract. Are defenses of car purchasers good against X Finance Company?

27

Liability
of Parties

3-115. Introduction. The liability of a person in a transaction involving commercial paper may be predicated either on the instrument itself or on the underlying contract. No person is liable on the instrument itself unless his signature appears thereon, but the signature may be affixed by a duly authorized agent. Persons whose signatures appear on instruments may have different types of liability depending on their status. In studying the subject of liabilities, we shall assume except when otherwise noted that no defense exists on behalf of the party being sued.

3-116. Liability Based on the Nature and Location of the Signature. The general principles of the law of agency are applicable in the field of commercial paper. A principal is bound by the duly authorized acts of his agent, but if the agent does not possess the requisite authority, the principal in most instances will not be bound. Just as in the general law of agency and contracts, an agent who fails to bind his principal because of failure to name him or due to lack of authority will usually be personally liable to third parties. The agent will also be liable if he fails to show his representative capacity. Thus, the correct way for an agent to execute commercial paper is to affix the name of his principal followed by his own signature and the capacity in which it is made. For example, *"P"* Principal, by *A.* as agent.

The liability of the agent on commercial paper is limited to persons other than those with whom the agent dealt, assuming that the person with whom he dealt knew of the representative capacity and that the principal's name appeared on the instrument. The liability to third persons is based on the premise that a purchaser of commercial paper is entitled to know by looking at the face of the paper whose obligation is evidenced by the paper, and on the presumption that a person who signs intends to be bound in the absence of evidence to the contrary.[1] Special circumstances may give notice to third parties that a signature was in a representative capacity.[2] The chart on page 525 shows the liability that results from various methods of execution. Assume that the principal's name is Paul Principal and the agent's name is Art Servant and that the agent has authority.

There are two exceptions to the rule that an unauthorized signature does not bind the principal. These were mentioned in the preceding chapter. The principal may ratify the signature or he may be estopped from asserting lack of authority. When the agent did not have authority he may actually be a forger and may be prosecuted for the crime of forgery notwithstanding the ratification.

Another issue concerning signatures relates to the capacity in which the signature is affixed. As will be discussed later in this chapter, the liability of primary parties such as makers of notes is different from the liability of secondary parties such as indorsers. The capacity of a signature may be ambiguous because of its physical location or because of the language used. The rule for resolving ambiguous signatures is that unless the instrument clearly indicates that a signature is made in some other capacity it is an indorsement.

The place of the signature is the usual method of indicating capacity. If the place of signature indicates that the signer intended to be bound other than as an indorser (on the face), parol evidence is not admissible to show that he intended to be an indorser. However, if the signer's name appears on the front of the paper after the word "indorser," he is an indorser in spite of the fact that he signed on the face of the paper. A note might provide: "I, John Doe, promise to pay . . . " and be signed by both John Doe and Richard Roe. This would indicate that Roe signed as an indorser even though his signature is on the face of the paper.

The intention to be bound in some capacity other than that of indorser may be indicated by the language used. Thus the signatures "John Jones, Maker," "Henry Brown, Acceptor," "Pete Smith, Surety" indicate an intention to be bound, but not as indorsers. When the back of an instrument contains a long list of notations of interest payments followed by an entry, "Interest paid to Aug. 1, 1972, J. B. Brown," Brown's indication of the purpose for which his signature was placed on the paper, namely, receipt for an interest payment, clearly indicates that he did not sign as an indorser or intend any liability on the paper.

3-117. Liability of Banks in Cases of Forgery.   A special problem exists in connection with forgeries insofar as banks are concerned. Checks presented to drawee banks for payment may bear forged signatures of drawers or forged indorsements. If the bank pays on such paper it incurs liability to the person whose name was forged. If the drawer's signature was forged, the bank that honors the check has not followed the order of the drawer and cannot charge his account. If charged, it must be recredited. Likewise, the bank will have to make restitution to the party whose name was forged on the check as an indorsement. In either case, the loss initially is that of the bank, and in the case

[1] Fanning v. Hembree Oil Co., page 532.
[2] Pollin v. Mindy Mfg. Co., page 533.

Form of Signature	Principal is		Agent is				
	Liable	Not Liable	Liable to Third Parties	Not Liable to Third Parties	Liable to Immediate Party	Not Liable to Immediate Party	Not Liable to Anyone
Paul Principal	X			X		X	X
Art Servant		X	X		X		
Art Servant, Agent		X	X			X	
Paul Principal / Art Servant	X		X			X	
Paul Principal, by Art Servant, Agent	X			X		X	X
Paul Principal, by Art Servant, as Agent	X			X		X	X

Liability resulting from various methods of execution

of a forged drawer's signature, the so-called *"Rule of Price* v. *Neal"* pre-cludes the bank from shifting the loss to the person who received payment, but it can recover from a person who received payment of a check bearing a forged indorsement. This is subject to the limitation that recovery may be had from the person who dealt with the forger if it can be established that such person was negligent.[3] Also, the person whose name was forged will suffer the loss if his negligence made the forgery possible.

Banks may also cash checks indorsed by agents who lack authority. In such cases, the bank will be held liable to the payee if the bank is charged with knowledge of the lack of authority and the principal can recover from the bank the amount paid out on such indorsements, which are, in effect, forgeries. Just as in the case of forgery by a stranger, the drawer can insist that the drawee recredit his account with the amount of any unauthorized payment.

3-118. Impostors: Fictitious Payees.   A situation that is comparable to for-gery arises when an instrument is made payable to a fictitious person,[4] or where one person impersonates another and the instrument is made payable to the impostor in the name he has assumed. In each of these situations the drawer's signature is genuine but the instrument is indorsed in the fictitious name or the name of the person who is being impersonated. Who should bear the loss in such fraudulent schemes?

An example of a fraudulent scheme is one in which a person poses as someone else and induces the drawer to issue a check payable to the order of the person who is being impersonated. In such situations the indorsement by the impostor is effective and the loss falls on the drawer rather than the person who took the check or the bank which honored it.

The loss, regardless of the type of fraud which the particular impostor has committed, should fall upon the maker or drawer. However, "impostor" refers to impersonation, and does not extend to a false representation that the party is the authorized agent of the payee. The maker or drawer who takes the precaution of making the instrument payable to the principal is entitled to have his indorsement.

A typical situation of a fictitious payee is one in which a dishonest employee is either authorized to sign his employer's name to checks or draws checks which he presents to his employer for the latter's signature. Thus the employee may draw payroll checks or checks payable to persons with whom the em-ployer would be expected to do business. He either signs the checks or obtains his employer's signature and then cashes the checks indorsing the name of the payee. If he is in charge of the company's books, he is able to manipulate the books when the canceled checks are returned and may thus avoid detection. The Code imposes this loss on the employer—the dishonest employee can effectively indorse in the payee's name.

LIABILITY BASED ON STATUS

3-119. In General.   Code provisions determine the liability of the various parties because the parties would ordinarily not do so themselves. The parties

---

[3] White v. First National Bank of Scotia, page 534
[4] Snug Harbor Realty Co. v. First National Bank of Toms River, page 536

are divided into two groups—primary parties and secondary parties. The primary parties are the makers of notes and the acceptors of drafts. These parties have incurred a definite obligation to pay and are the parties who, in the normal course of events, will *actually* pay the instrument. They understand that this is their responsibility and that no conditions need be satisfied as a prerequisite to this responsibility. A primary party engages that he will pay the instrument according to its tenor—the terms of the instrument—at the time of his engagement. The maker thus assumes an obligation to pay the note as it was worded at the time he executed it, and the acceptor assumes responsibility for the draft as it was worded when he gave his acceptance.

There are some instances in which makers and acceptors are treated to some extent as secondary rather than primary parties. This relates to what is called "domiciled paper," i.e., an instrument which is payable at a particular place on the date of its maturity. In most instances "domiciled" notes and drafts are made payable at a specified bank—the bank specified is the place where the note or draft must be presented for payment.

The secondary parties are drawers of drafts, drawers of checks, and indorsers of any instrument. These parties do not expect to pay the instrument but assume rather that the primary parties will fulfill their obligations. The drawer and indorsers expect that the acceptor will pay the draft. The indorsers of a note expect that the maker will pay when the note matures. Drawers and indorsers have a secondary responsibility; i.e., an obligation to pay if the primary parties do not, *provided* that certain conditions precedent are satisfied. The drawer and the indorser are, in effect, saying that they will pay if the primary party—acceptor or maker—does not, but only if the party entitled to payment has made proper demand upon the primary party, and due notice of the primary party's dishonor of the instrument has then been given to them —the secondary parties.

3-120. Liability of Maker.   The maker of a note is primarily liable. He is obligated to pay the instrument according to its terms. If a maker signs an incomplete note, such note when thereafter completed, even though the completion is unauthorized, can be enforced against him by a holder in due course. On the other hand, if an instrument is materially altered after it is made, the maker has a real defense in the absence of negligence. The maker admits as against all subsequent parties the existence of the payee and his capacity to indorse.

3-121. Liability of Acceptors.   An acceptor of a draft is also primarily liable. By accepting the instrument, an acceptor engages that he will pay according to the tenor of his acceptance; and admits (1) the existence of the drawer; (2) the genuineness of the drawer's signature; (3) the drawer's capacity and authority to draw the instrument; (4) the existence of the payee, and (5) his then capacity to indorse. The instrument may be drawn by the drawer and negotiated before its acceptance by the drawee. The instrument may be accepted by the drawee before it is signed by the drawer or completed. This, of course, involves some risk on the part of the drawee-acceptor.

One who draws a draft (drawer) is usually a creditor of the drawee or has arranged with the drawee for authority to draw on him. For instance, John Doe enters into an agreement with the First National Bank whereby the latter agrees to accept drafts for a certain amount drawn on the bank by John Doe.

The bank is not liable to the payee of the draft until it "accepts" the draft. If the bank refuses to accept, it is liable to John Doe, the drawer, for breach of its contract to accept. It is only after acceptance that the bank is liable to the payee.

The acceptance must be in writing on the draft and signed by the drawee-acceptor. Acceptance is usually made by the drawee's writing or stamping the word "Accepted," with his name and the date, across the face of the instrument. Promises to accept and acceptances upon separate instruments and other collateral acceptances are not effective *as acceptances.* Danger of separation from the draft or check and ambiguous language leading to dispute as to whether an acceptance was or was not made dictate the necessity for certain and accurate evidence of the drawee's liability.

The drawee's signature as acceptor on incompleted paper binds him to all subsequent parties to the extent of its completion as authorized. He is also subject to the risks and duties imposed by the Code as to wrongful completion and, if by his negligent conduct he contributes to materially altered paper which gets into the stream of commerce, he is liable to any person with the rights of a holder in due course for all loss caused by such negligence. It is to be noted that the acceptance relates to the instrument as it was at the *time of acceptance.* If the draft were "raised" or otherwise altered before acceptance, the acceptor is bound to pay the raised amount—his responsibility is not limited to the original tenor of the draft. However, as noted in a later section, the acceptor would have recourse against the party who presented the paper for acceptance, since that party warrants that the draft has not been materially altered.

A check or other draft does not of itself operate as an assignment of any funds in the hands of the drawee and the drawee is not liable *on the instrument* until he *accepts* it.

Even if the drawee by previous contract is under a duty to accept, such duty gives no cause of action to a holder upon refusal of the drawee to accept. The drawee's liability is to the drawer. The failure of the drawee to accept or his breach of other arrangements with the drawer will expose the drawee to liability to the drawer, but not to a holder. A holder's recourse is against prior indorsers or the drawer. A drawee bank's unwarranted refusal to pay a check, which thereby impairs the credit of the drawer, may subject the bank to liability to the drawer for failure to comply with its obligations to him, as may its failure to live up to other promises to pay or accept.

It is the acceptance of the paper by the drawee that gives rights to the holder *on the paper.* The acceptance makes the drawee-acceptor the primary obligor; the drawer and all other parties become secondary parties. By such method paper is created which can function freely in the channels of commerce as a substitute for money.

3-122. Liability of Drawees of Checks.   The certification of a check by the bank upon which it is drawn, at the request of a holder, is equivalent to an acceptance. The bank thereby becomes the principal debtor upon the instrument because it appropriates the funds required from the depositor's account. The liability of the bank is the same as the liability of an acceptor of any other draft.

Certification may or may not change the legal liability of the parties upon the instrument.[5] When the *drawer* has a check certified, such a certification merely acts as additional security and does not relieve the drawer of any liability. On the other hand, when the *holder* of a check secures certification by the drawee bank, he thereby accepts the bank as the only party liable thereon. Such an act discharges the drawer and all prior indorsers from liability. The effect of such certification is similar to a payment by the bank and redeposit by the holder. Note that in the case of other drafts, acceptance does not ordinarily give a discharge to the drawer or indorsers.

The refusal of a bank to certify a check at the request of a holder is held not to be a dishonor of the instrument. The bank owes the depositor a duty to pay but not necessarily the duty to certify checks which are drawn on it, unless there is a previous agreement to certify. A drawer cannot countermand a check after the bank has certified it.

A check may also come to the drawee bank without proper indorsement. The bank *may* certify the check before returning the same through channels for indorsement, in order to relieve the drawer from liability that might arise because of loss occurring before the check is returned. Such certification discharges the drawer.

3-123. Nature of the Acceptance.   When a draft is created and placed in the channels of trade, the payee and all future holders are entitled to an *unqualified acceptance* by the drawee. Any other acceptance changes the original contract between the parties. Thus, when the drawee offers an acceptance which in any manner varies or changes the direct order to pay or accept, the holder may refuse the acceptance. The paper is dishonored, and upon notice of dishonor or protest the holder may hold all prior parties on the paper back to and including the drawer. An acceptance is at variance with the order when the drawee-acceptor accepts for only a part of the specified sum, or specifies a different time of *payment* from that required by the draft. If the drawee places a condition on his obligation to pay or stipulates that he will perform a service in payment of the draft in lieu of a money payment, he has deviated from the duty to pay money as ordered by the drawer.

Tender of a different kind of acceptance by the drawee is an offer to give a substituted performance. If the holder wishes to accept such nonconforming performance, he may do so. This, however, creates a new contract, and all prior parties including the drawer are discharged unless a consent for substituted performance has been given. If the drawee refuses to perform the varied acceptance, he is liable for breach of contract to the holder.

The draft is not varied by an acceptance to pay at a particular bank or place in the United States unless acceptance states that the draft is to be *paid only* at such bank.

3-124. Liability of the Drawer.   The drawer engages that upon *dishonor* of the draft and any necessary notice of dishonor or protest he will pay the amount of the draft to the holder or to any indorser who takes it up. In effect, the drawer assumes a conditional liability on the instrument—that he will pay if the instrument is dishonored and he is properly notified of this fact. Such

[5] Sam Goody, Inc. v. Franklin Nat. Bank of Long Island, page 536

liability can be disclaimed, however, if the draft is drawn "without recourse." The party who draws a draft or check like one who makes a note or accepts a draft, admits as against all subsequent parties the existence of the payee and his then capacity to indorse.

3-125. Liability of Indorsers.   Indorsers are secondarily liable on instruments by virtue of their *contract* of indorsement. If an indorser adds the words "without recourse" to his indorsement, he thereby disclaims liability on the *indorsement contract*.[6] The contract of indorsement is conditional, that is, the indorser obligates himself to pay only if the instrument is properly presented to the primary party, is dishonored, and notice of dishonor is given to him. This obligation of the indorser runs to any holder and to a subsequent indorser who has reacquired the instrument. The engagement of the indorser is to pay the instrument according to its tenor at the time of his indorsement. The indorser of an altered instrument thus assumes liability as indorser on the instrument as altered.

As noted previously, a person who indorses in a representative capacity can indorse in such terms as to negative personal liability.

In addition to this conditional liability, an indorser, if he is a transferor, makes *warranties* with reference to the instrument which is transferred. Thus the indorser in addition to his conditional contract liability has unconditional liability as a warrantor. This is discussed in Section 3-129.

Unless they otherwise agree, indorsers are liable to one another in the order in which they indorse. This is presumed to be the order in which their signatures appear on the instrument, but parol evidence is admissible as between indorsers to show that the indorsers did not actually indorse in the order in which their names appear or that they may have agreed among themselves as to the nature and order of their liability.

3-126. Liability of Accommodation Parties.   One who signs an instrument for the purpose of lending his name and credit to another party to an instrument is an "accommodation" party. His function is that of a surety or guarantor, and he may be motivated to assume this liability for a variety of reasons. He may sign as an indorser, maker, or acceptor or as a comaker or coacceptor. The accommodation party is liable in the capacity in which he signed.[7] As an indorser he does not indorse for the purpose of transferring the paper but rather to lend security to it.

There is some significance to the surety status of an accommodation party. In some situations he is entitled to discharge under the general law and may exercise this right against one who is not a holder in due course. He is not liable to the party accommodated, and if he is required to pay he can obtain reimbursement from such party.

3-127. Liability of Guarantors.   The preceding sections dealt with the contract of the maker, the drawer, the acceptor, the indorser, and the accommodation party. This section relates to a guarantor's contract and to the effect to be attributed to *words* of guaranty. This should be distinguished from the

---

[6] The Union Bank v. Joseph Mobilla, page 538
[7] Seaboard Finance Company v. Dorman, page 539

accommodation situation in which the obligation arises without express words designating its specific nature.

If the words "Payment guaranteed" or their equivalent are added to a signature, the signer engages that if the instrument is not paid when due, he will pay it *without previous resort by the holder to other parties on the paper.* If the words "Collection guaranteed" are added to a signature, the signer becomes secondarily liable on the instrument and can be required to pay only if the holder has obtained a judgment against the primary party, and execution on the judgment has been returned unsatisfied, unless the primary party has become insolvent or unless it is otherwise apparent that it is useless to proceed against him.

If words of guaranty are used but it is not specified whether "of payment" or "collection," they will be deemed to constitute a guaranty of payment.

Words of guaranty by a sole maker or acceptor are without effect; but if such words are added to the signature of one of two or more makers or acceptors, such words create a presumption that the party who added such words signed for the accommodation of the others.

If an indorser guarantees payment, he waives the conditions precedent of presentment, notice of dishonor, and protest. The words of guarantee do not affect the indorsement as a means of transferring the instrument, but impose upon such indorser the liability of a comaker. If the indorser guarantees collection, he likewise waives the performance of the conditions precedent.

3-128. Presentment Warranties.   A note is presented to the maker for payment; a draft is presented to the drawee for either acceptance *or* payment; and a check is presented to a bank ordinarily for payment but sometimes for certification. In the case of each of these presentment situations, the presenting party makes certain warranties. These warranties give some measure of protection to the party who pays or accepts.[8] Liability for breach of warranty exists without performance of any conditions precedent. It is therefore called unconditional liability.

The person who presents the instrument warrants that no indorsements are forged, that so far as he knows the signature of the maker or drawer is genuine, and that it has not been materially altered—e.g., raised. Thus the person who pays or accepts will have recourse against the presenting party and prior indorsers if the warranties are breached. The warranty with regard to the drawer's signature is not absolute—it is only that the warrantor has no knowledge that such signature is forged or unauthorized. A holder in due course has a lesser warranty liability with respect to unauthorized signatures and material alterations.

3-129. Transfer Warranties.   A party who transfers commercial paper by indorsement also makes warranties to the transferee. If such warranties are breached, he has liability. He warrants that he has good title to the instrument, that all signatures are genuine or authorized, that the instrument has not been materially altered, and that no defense of any party is good against him. These warranties are similar to the presentment warranties but are somewhat more extensive. There is an additional warranty that the transferor does not have

[8] Kirby v. First & Merchants Nat. Bank, page 540

knowledge of any insolvency proceeding with respect to the maker or acceptor, or in the case of an instrument that has not been accepted, of the drawer. This does not mean that the transferor guarantees the solvency of these parties, but simply that to his knowledge no insolvency proceedings such as bankruptcy have been instituted.

The warranties are made whether the transfer is by delivery, by qualified indorsement (without recourse), or by unqualified indorsement. The qualified indorser's warranty about defenses is simply that he has no *knowledge* of any defense. In the case of delivery of bearer paper without indorsement, the warranties run only to the immediate transferee, whereas the indorser's warranties extend to subsequent holders. Often an indorsement will be required even though the instrument is in bearer form.

3-130. Conversion of Instrument.   In tort law a conversion is any act in relation to personal property inconsistent with the owner's interest in the goods. There is a conversion of an instrument if (1) a drawee to whom it is delivered for acceptance refuses to return it upon demand, (2) any person to whom it is delivered for payment refuses on demand either to pay it or return it, or (3) it is paid on a forged indorsement. The payment over a forged indorsement is a conversion as against the true owner, the party whose indorsement was forged. He can recover from the party who made payment, and the paying party then has recourse against other parties for breach of the presentment warranty as discussed in Section 3-128. Ordinarily, the measure of damages for conversion will be the face amount of the instrument.

LIABILITY OF PARTIES CASES

Fanning v. Hembree Oil Co.
434 S.W.2d 822 (Ark.) 1968

The plaintiff oil company, to whom Razorback Asphalt, Inc. was indebted on open account for over $2,000 threatened to discontinue supplying oil unless the president and secretary of Razorback give a "personal note" in the amount of the indebtedness. They executed a note which they signed under the typed name "Razorback Asphalt, Inc." and did not indicate their representative capacity. The president, Fanning, claimed that the note was drawn in the name of the company because he had refused to assume personal liability. The lower court gave judgment against Fanning personally and he appealed.

BROWN, J. . . . The single point for reversal is that the judgment in favor of Hembree "is not supported by a preponderance of the evidence."

. . .

As we interpret the Uniform Commercial Code, the burden was on Fanning to affirmatively show there was an understanding between him and Hembree that Fanning was signing the note in a representative capacity.

> Unless the instrument clearly indicates that a signature is made in some other capacity it is an indorsement. Ark.Stat.Ann. § 85-3-402 (Add.1961).

. . .

(2) An authorized representative who signs his own name to an instrument

(b) except as otherwise established between the immediate parties, is personally obligated if the instrument names the person represented but does not show that the representative signed in a representative capacity, or if the instrument does not name the person represented but does show that the representative signed in a representative capacity. Ark.Stat.Ann. § 85-3-403 (Add.1961).

In light of the quoted statutes we think the burden was on Fanning to affirmatively show an understanding between him and Hembree that Fanning would not be personally liable on the note. . . .

In addition to the evidence, the trial court made mention of some significant circumstances: A note which bound only Razorback would have been of little value considering its financial condition; after the note was signed, Hembree extended substantial credit to Razorback; Hembree had little education and was not a good reader; "Mr. Fanning had a secretary, typewriter, had charge of making out the note and he was perfectly capable of putting president, secretary, or anything he wanted in it, so I can't ignore that fact."

Viewing the evidence and circumstances in light of the law and the circumstances we have recited, we find there was substantial evidence to support the verdict.

Affirmed.

Pollin v. Mindy Mfg. Co.
236 A.2d 542 (Pa.) 1967

The defendant was the president of Mindy Mfg. Co. In that capacity he signed payroll checks for the company. Some of these checks were cashed by plaintiff who operates a check-cashing business. Because of insufficient funds in the corporate payroll account, the drawee bank refused to honor the checks. The plaintiff sought to impose personal liability on the president. The name and address of the corporation were printed on the top of each check, along with "Payroll check no.—." The corporate name was also printed at the lower right corner of the checks, above the space for the authorized signature. The lower court held for the plaintiff and defendant appealed.

MONTGOMERY, J. . . . Summary judgment against appellant was entered by the lower court on the authority of Section 3-403 of the Uniform Commercial Code, the Act of April 6, 1953, P.L. 3, § 3-403, 12A P.S. § 3-403, which provides, "An authorized representative who signs his name to an instrument . . . (b) except as otherwise established between the immediate parties, is personally obligated if the instrument names the person represented but does not show that the representative signed in a representative capacity . . . ," and our decisions thereunder. . . .

The issue before us, therefore, is whether a third party to the original transaction, the endorsee in the present case, may recover against one who affixes his name to a check in the place where a maker usually signs without indicating he is signing in a representative capacity, without giving consideration to other parts of the instrument or extrinsic evidence. This appears to be a novel question under the Uniform Commercial Code.

If this were an action brought by the payee, parol evidence would be permitted to establish the capacity of the person affixing his signature under Section 3-403 (b), previously recited. . . .

However, since this is an action brought by a third party our initial inquiry must be for the purpose of determining whether the instrument indicates the capacity of appellant as a signer. Admittedly, the instrument fails to show the office held by appellant. However, we do not think this is a complete answer to our problem, since the Code imposes liability on the individual only " . . . if the instrument . . . does not show that the representative signed in a representative capacity. . . . " This implies that the instrument must be considered in its entirety.

Although Section 3-401(2) of the Uniform Commercial Code provides that "A signature is made by use of any name, including any trade or assumed name, upon an instrument, or by any word or mark used in lieu of a written signature," which would be broad enough to include the printed name of a corporation, we do not believe that a check showing two lines under the imprinted corporate name indicating the signature of one or more corporate officers would be accepted by any reasonably prudent person as a fully executed check of the corporation. It is common to expect that a corporate name placed upon a negotiable instrument in order to bind the corporation as a maker, especially when printed on the instrument, will be accompanied by the signatures of officers authorized by the by-laws to sign the instrument. . . . While we do not rule out the possibility of a printed name being established as an acceptable signature, we hold that such a situation is uncommon, and in the present case the two lines under the printed name dictate against a valid corporate signature. Corporations act through officers.

Next, we must give consideration to the distinction between a check and a note. A check is an order of a depositor on a bank in the nature of a draft drawn on the bank and payable on demand. It is revocable until paid or accepted for payment. A note is an irrevocable promise to pay on the part of the maker. The maker of a check impliedly engages not only that it will be paid, but that he will have sufficient funds in the bank to meet it. In the present instance the checks clearly showed that they were payable from a special account set up by the corporate defendant for the purpose of paying its employees. This information disclosed by the instrument of itself would refute any contention that the appellant intended to make the instrument his own order on the named bank to pay money to the payee. The money was payable from the account of the corporation defendant over which appellant as an individual had no control.

Considering the instrument as a whole, we conclude that it sufficiently discloses that appellant signed it in a representative capacity. . . .

Judgment reversed and entered for appellant-defendant.

White v. First National Bank of Scotia

254 N.Y.S.2d 651 (N.Y.) 1964

REYNOLDS, J. Stanley G. White, who had a joint checking account with his wife, Emma C. White, in appellant bank, purportedly wrote his name as "S. G. White" and included his address on the *back* of one of his *blank* checks and gave it to a stranger. Thereafter someone allegedly filled out the *face of the check* in the amount of $300 naming Emma J. White as *payee* and S. G. White as *drawer.* On the reverse side of the instrument appears the name of the payee, Emma J. White, above that of S. G. White. The instrument in this form was cashed at the Ticonderoga branch of the State Bank of Albany and forwarded to the appellant [defendant-drawee bank] which paid the State Bank and charged White's account. When the canceled check was received by White he immediately notified appellant and demanded reimbursement to his account. The appellant refused and White brought an action to recover the balance in his account including the disputed $300 debited therefrom by appellant. The court below granted summary judgment for White and this determination is brought here on appeal. *Appellant in turn commenced a third-party action against the State Bank of Albany* [cashing bank]. The State Bank without answering appellant's complaint moved to dismiss it on the grounds it did not state facts sufficient to constitute a cause of action. The instant appeal is also brought from an order granting this motion and the subsequent judgment dismissing appellant's complaint.

We do not think respondent White was entitled to summary judgment. While it is true that *as a general rule a bank which makes payment on forged paper cannot debit its depositor's account for the amount improperly paid out . . . it is also true that conduct of the depositor may preclude his recovery. . . .* Here White alleges that his signature as drawee is also forged and that his "endorsement" was not intended as such. At least the last and perhaps, most crucial of these assertions, however, is exclusively within his knowledge and clearly not within the knowledge of appellant. Under these circumstances summary judgment should not have been granted. . . . *If the record as finally developed supports White's assertions he may well be entitled to recovery.* However, appellant is entitled to subject him to cross examination in the hope of eliciting a variance in his account of what transpired which might preclude his recovery.

With respect to the third-party action, it is clear that appellant would be entitled to a recovery from the State Bank of Albany except for the long established rule of *Price* v. *Neal* (3 Burrows 1354) that the drawee cannot recover payment when it has paid on the forged signature of its depositor. . . . This doctrine, however, is subject to the exception that the drawee may recover from a presenter or cashing bank which itself acts in bad faith or negligently. . . . It should be noted that *the Uniform Commercial Code while retaining the bad-faith exception abandons unanswered questions of fact as to respondent's conduct in receiving the check which requires a plenary trial.* Appellant may well be able to establish that respondent contributed to the fraud by its negligence in purchasing the check from a stranger or other third person without adequate inquiry, although in good faith and for value. . . . [Emphasis supplied]

Judgments and orders reversed, on the law and the facts, and motions denied, without costs.

[The case was returned to the trial court for a trial at which time the defendant bank will be allowed to offer proof concerning the "indorsement" and negligence on the part of the Albany Bank.]

Snug Harbor Realty Co. v. First National Bank of Toms River

253 A.2d 581 (N.J.) 1969

LEWIS, J. . . . Snug Harbor, a construction company, maintained a system under which parties asserting claims against it would submit invoices which were then given to its superintendent, Joseph Magee, for investigation. It was Magee's responsibility to make the necessary inspection and, upon being satisfied that the alleged work was done or materials furnished, to initial the invoices and forward them to the company's bookkeeper for verification of the contract obligations and the preparation of checks payable to the claimants. Checks drawn on First National were then signed by the company's authorized official. Certain checks were picked up by Magee for delivery to the respective payees who authorized the "pickup." Between January 10, 1964 and August 13, 1965, Magee converted to his own personal use 132 checks, totaling $27,-516.27, by forging the endorsements of the payees and cashing the checks.

The trial court found as a matter of law that a provision of the Uniform Commercial Code was "dispositive" and, accordingly, that the bank should be relieved of any liability to plaintiff. The pertinent section of the Code, N.J.S. 12A:3-405(1) (c), N.J.S.A., provides:

> (1) An indorsement by any person in the name of a named payee is effective if . . . (c) an agent or employee of the maker or drawer has supplied him with the name of the payee intending the latter to have no such interest.

We find, in the circumstances here presented, that plaintiff proved a *prima facie* case and that the cited Code provision is inapplicable.

Magee, an unfaithful employee of the construction company, did not supply to his employer "the name of the payee intending the latter to have no such interest." To the contrary, the payees were *bona fide* creditors of the company who had respectively submitted their invoices for work performed or materials furnished.

It is thus plain that judgment was improvidently entered. The matter should proceed to a plenary hearing for a judicial determination of the merits of plaintiff's complaint in light of any defenses appropriately raised by the defendant bank. . . .

Reversed and remanded for new trial.

Sam Goody, Inc. v. Franklin Nat. Bank of Long Island

291 N.Y.S.2d 429 (N.Y.) 1968

FARLEY, J. Motion by plaintiff for summary judgment . . . in the sum of $1,600.00 or for partial summary judgment in the sum of $16.00, and cross motion by the defendant for judgment dismissing the action.

The unusual facts of this case give rise to the application of law that is rarely invoked. A check in the amount of $16.00, made payable to the plaintiff, was presented to the defendant bank for certification either by the depositor or by an accomplice of the depositor. The bank's certification stamp did not show the amount for which the check was certified and after the certification was procured, the amount was altered to read $1,600.00. The check was then presented to the plaintiff in payment of merchandise by a customer who represented the instrument was given to him by his employer as a bonus. The customer, on the previous day, had ordered the merchandise and stated he would secure from his employer a certified check drawn directly to the plaintiff to pay the balance owing. The plaintiff, upon consulting the telephone directory, found the name, address, and phone number given by the person corresponded with a listing in the directory. The check, upon presentment to the bank for payment, was not honored due to the alteration.

The fraudulent scheme perpetrated in this case was obviously made possible by the knowledge that the certification stamp of the defendant bank would not disclose the amount for which the check was certified. The plaintiff claims the negligence of the bank in this respect caused the loss and that the bank is estopped from asserting the defense of alteration under section 3-406 of the Uniform Commercial Code. The plaintiff also points to the practice of at least one bank that follows a policy of showing the amount for which an instrument is certified. Whether or not this practice is a custom that prevails in banking circles cannot be determined from the evidence presented and that question appears immaterial to the issues raised in view of the provision of the Code that appears to control the disposition of this case (see U.C.C., §§ 3-413; 3-417 [1] [c] iv; 4-207 [1] [c] iv).

Section 3-406 of the Code relied on by the plaintiff states:

> Any person who by his negligence substantially contributes to a material alteration of the instrument . . . is precluded from asserting the alteration . . . against the holder in due course or against a drawee or other payor who pays the instrument in good faith and in accordance with reasonable commercial standards of the drawee's or payor's business.

This section represents a ratification of the English rule pronounced in *Young* v. *Grote,* 4 Bing. 253, 130 Eng.Rep. 764, which was contrary to New York law as it existed prior to the adoption of the Code.

In the opinion of the Court, however, the provisions of section 3-406 have no application in this case.

A bank, when certifying a check, does no more than to affirm the genuineness of the signature of the maker, that he has funds on deposit to meet the item, and that the funds will not be withdrawn to the prejudice of the holder. The certification constitutes an acceptance of the check to this extent (U.C.C., § 3-411), but the bank by its certification does not guaranty the body thereof and engages only to pay the item according to its tenor at the time certification is procured (U.C.C., § 3-413). Furthermore, a holder of a check, by having it certified, is deemed to have warranted to the bank that the instrument has not been materially altered (U.C.C., § 3-417, subd. (1) [c]; see also § 4-207, subd. (1) [c]). The Code makes one exception to this rule by providing that the same warranty is not given by a holder in due course whether the alteration is made before or after certification (U.C.C., §§ 3-417 subd. (1) [c.iii, iv]; 3-413). Consequently, under the Code, where a check is certified after the amount has been altered, the bank runs the risk of sustaining the loss if the instrument passes into the hands of a holder in due course. The Code in this respect changes the law which previously obtained in New York.

The rule, however, is otherwise where the certification of the check is procured by the maker. In such case, the bank does not incur the risk of an alteration prior to its acceptance, and only agrees to pay the instrument according to its tenor at the time of certification even as to a holder in due course (U.C.C., § 3-413 [1]).

The evidence in this case does not disclose whether the maker or his accomplice procured certification of the check, but the controlling fact that alteration occurred after certification of the instrument is not disputed. The bank, in checking its records, discovered the alteration and refused payment. Under these circumstances, the negligence of the bank, if any, is not a substantial or proximate cause of the loss, and in accordance with the rules mentioned above, it is not liable to the plaintiff except for the amount for which the check was originally drawn.

The alternative request of plaintiff's motion is granted, and defendant's cross motion is granted to the extent of dismissing plaintiff's action insofar as it seeks recovery in excess of $16.00.

The Union Bank v. Joseph Mobilla

43 Erie Co. Leg. J. 45 (Pa.) 1959

LAUB, J. . . . On January 15, 1958, the defendant, a used car dealer, represented to the plaintiff bank that he had sold a used Ford automobile to one Theresa Piotrowski of 650 East 24th Street. For finance purposes, he exhibited an installment sales contract and a judgment note allegedly signed by Theresa Piotrowski as maker. There was nothing on the face of either instrument to indicate that the signatures had not been placed there by the maker or that either had been signed by someone else acting in the maker's behalf. . . . The note which was payable to defendant was endorsed by him "without recourse," and the security agreement, which was in defendant's favor as a seller of a chattel, was assigned to the bank. Both instruments, as well as the title to the vehicle in question, were turned over to the bank as part of the finance transaction.

. . . After default the bank importuned both the purported maker and the defendant to discharge the obligation but without avail, the maker having denied executing either document or having bought the vehicle from the defendant. In consequence, plaintiff instituted this action, alleging that defendant is guilty of a breach of warranty, and as part of its action, alleging a written warranty in the security agreement "that the above instrument is genuine and in all respects what it purports to be." Plaintiff also claims upon an implied warranty of the genuineness of the note.

The defendant in his answer admits that he endorsed the note and assigned the security agreement to the plaintiff. He also admits that the maker did not sign either document. It is his defense, however, that Theresa Piotrowski's signature was affixed by an authorized agent named Edward Rogalia and that he (the defendant) is not liable in any event because his indorsement of the note was "without recourse."

We can see no merit whatever in the defenses offered and consider that plaintiff is entitled to the judgment which it seeks. The defendant's conception of the litigation as being a suit against an endorser who signed "without recourse," misses the point. Plaintiff is not suing on the note, but as noted above, is claiming upon a breach of warranty. If it were true that the suit was against the defendant on the sole basis that he was an endorser, there might be some value to the defenses offered, but the pleadings reveal an entirely different situation. As the pleadings now stand, it is admitted on the record that the defendant in writing warranted the security agreement to be all that it purported to be, and it is clear that it was not. Further, the admission that defendant endorsed the note as part of his finance dealings with the plaintiff and that the note was not signed by the maker is a clear admission of a breach of the implied warranty which accompanies situations of this character. While no statute is required to establish the common sense conclusion that one who presents a document for discount or otherwise impliedly warrants its genuineness when he accepts a consideration for its transfer, the Uniform Commercial Code has such a provision. In Section 3-417 (2) (a) of that Act . . . it is provided that the transferor of an instrument for consideration warrants, among other things, that all signatures are genuine or authorized. This certainly does not imply that a transferor, with knowledge that a signature is not that of the person it purports to belong to and there is no qualifying or descriptive language indicating that the signature was made by someone other than the maker, may remain silent and suppress such knowledge to the detriment of the transferee.

Judgment for the plaintiff.

Seaboard Finance Company v. Dorman

227 A.2d 441 (Conn.) 1966

KINMONTH, J. This action was brought on a promissory note made by Kenneth W. Dorman and his wife, Geraldine Dorman, and payable to the plaintiff. The defendants denied the allegations of the complaint and alleged lack of consideration. The court found the issues for the plaintiff, and the defendant Geraldine Dorman has appealed, assigning as error the court's refusal to correct the finding and that the conclusions are not supported by the facts found. As the first assignment is not pursued in her brief, it is considered abandoned.

The court's finding may be summarized as follows: The defendants are husband and wife. The defendant Kenneth W. Dorman was interested in photography and was negotiating with Colonial Industries to purchase equipment and to receive training but needed money for that purpose. Both defendants went to the plaintiff's office and executed a note, as makers, and the plaintiff made out a check payable to Kenneth W. Dorman, in the presence of his wife, Geraldine Dorman. The defendant Geraldine Dorman received no consideration from the plaintiff for signing the note, but she signed the note for the purpose of lending her name to her husband. The court concluded that the defendant Geraldine was an accommodation maker and was thus liable on the note.

The sole issue in the case is whether the court erred in finding that Geraldine was an accommodation maker. "An accommodation party is one who signs the instrument in any capacity for the purpose of lending his name to another party to it." General Statutes § 42a-3-415(1). In the instant case, Geraldine's signature on the note was admitted, although she did not testify, but she claims she received no consideration. "The motive with which an act is done may be, and often is, ascertained and determined by inference from the proofs of facts and circumstances connected with the transaction and the parties to it." In the absence of direct evidence, the trier is entitled to draw reasonable and logical inferences, and its conclusion must stand unless no reasonable person could reach it.

The court found that Geraldine signed the note for the purpose of lending her name to her husband. A wife may be an accommodation maker for her husband and, as in other cases, the consideration which supports her promise to pay is that moving to the accommodated party, her husband. Geraldine had full knowledge of the meaning and purpose of the transaction which involved her husband, and the court properly concluded that she was an accommodation maker. The want of consideration is the peculiar characteristic of accommodation paper. Thus the defense of no consideration is ineffective.

When the instrument has been taken for value before it is due, the accommodation party is liable in the capacity in which he has signed, even though the taker knows of the accommodation. General Statutes § 42a-3-415(2).

As the court's conclusions must be tested by the subordinate facts found, we cannot say the court erred in concluding that the defendant was an accommodation maker.

There is no error.

Kirby v. First & Merchants Nat. Bank

168 S.E.2d 273 (Va.) 1969

The defendant handed a $2,500 check drawn to the order of her and her husband to the teller at the plaintiff bank. The check was drawn on the same bank. The teller handed her $200 and credited her account with the balance. The following day the bank discovered that the check was drawn against insufficient funds. The bank then charged $2,500 to her account leaving an overdraft of $543.47. The bank brought suit for this amount. The trial court gave judgment for plaintiff and the defendants appealed.

GORDON, J. . . . The trial court, sitting without a jury, entered judgment for the plaintiff First & Merchants, and the defendants Mr. and Mrs. Kirby appeal. The question is whether the bank had the right to charge Mrs. Kirby's account with $2,500 on January 10 and to recover from Mr. and Mrs. Kirby the overdraft created by that charge ($543.47).

U.C.C. § 4-213 provides:

> (1) An item is finally paid by a payor bank when the bank has done any of the following, whichever happens first:
> (a) paid the item in cash. . . .

So if First & Merchants paid the Neuse check in cash on December 30, it then made final payment and could not sue Mr. or Mrs. Kirby on the check except for breach of warranty.

When Mrs. Kirby presented the $2,500 Neuse check to the bank on December 30, the bank paid her $200 in cash and accepted a deposit of $2,300. The bank officer said that the bank cashed the check for $2,500, which could mean only that Mrs. Kirby deposited $2,300 in cash.

And the documentary evidence shows that cash was deposited. The deposit of cash is evidenced by the word "currency" before "2,300.00" on the deposit ticket and by the words "Cash for Dep." on the back of the check. The bank's ledger, which shows a credit of $2,300 to Mrs. Kirby's account rather than a credit of $2,500 and a debit of $200, is consistent with a cashing of the Neuse check and a depositing of part of the proceeds. We must conclude that First & Merchants paid the Neuse check in cash on December 30 and, therefore, had no right thereafter to charge Mrs. Kirby's account with the amount of the check.

The trial court apparently decided that Mr. and Mrs. Kirby were liable to the bank because they had indorsed the Neuse check. But under U.C.C. § 3-414(1) an indorser contracts to pay an instrument only if the instrument is dishonored. And, as we have pointed out, the bank did not dishonor the Neuse check, but paid the check in cash when Mrs. Kirby presented it.

As a practical matter, the contract of an indorser under U.C.C. § 3-414(1) does not run to a drawee bank. That contract can be enforced by a drawee bank only if it dishonors a check; and if the bank dishonors the check, it has suffered no loss.

The warranties that are applicable in this case are set forth in U.C.C. §§ 3-417(1) and 4-207(1): warranties made to a drawee bank by a presenter and prior transferors of a check. Those warranties are applicable because Mrs. Kirby presented the Neuse check to the bank for payment. U.C.C. § 3-504(1). And those warranties do not include a warranty that the drawer of a check has sufficient funds on deposit to cover the check.

The rule that a drawee who mistakenly pays a check has recourse only against the drawer was firmly established before adoption of the Uniform Commercial Code:

> The drawer of a check, and not the holder who receives payment, is primarily responsible for the drawing out of funds from a bank. An overdraft is an act by reason of which the drawer and not the holder obtains money from the bank on his check. The holder therefore in the absence of fraud or express understanding for repayment, has no concern with the question whether the drawer has funds in the bank to meet the check. The bank is estopped, as against him, from claiming that by its acceptance an overdraft occurred. A mere mistake is not sufficient to enable it to recover from him. Banks cannot always guard against fraud, but can guard against mistakes.
>
> It is therefore the general rule, sustained by almost universal authority, that a payment in the ordinary course of business of a check by a bank on which it is drawn under the mistaken belief that the drawer has funds in the bank subject to check is not such a payment under a mistake of fact as will permit the bank to recover the money so paid from the recipient of such payment. To permit the bank to repudiate the payment would destroy the certainty which must pertain to commercial transactions if they are to remain useful to the business public. Otherwise no one would ever know when he can safely receive payment of a check.

(Zollman, The Law of Banks and Banking § 5062 (1936).) . . .

For the reasons set forth, the trial court erred in entering judgment for First & Merchants against Mr. and Mrs. Kirby.

Reversed and final judgment.

CHAPTER 27
REVIEW QUESTIONS AND PROBLEMS

1. *A* purchased an automobile from *B* and gave a check in payment. He then discovered that there were liens against the car and stopped payment on the check. In the meantime *B* had deposited the check and received cash and credit. The bank was unable to collect the full amount of the check from *B* and seeks to hold *A* liable for the balance. Is *A* liable?

2. A group of individuals formed a joint venture for the purpose of developing a residential tract. One of the members of the joint venture executed a note that bore only his name. The note was not paid, and action was brought against all members of the joint venture. They claimed that they were not liable because their names did not appear on the note. Do these parties have any liability?

3. *A*, an agent of X Corporation, wished to obtain a loan for the benefit of a corporation in which he had an interest. He signed a note payable to the order of B Bank, and the bank made funds available to the corporation's account. *A* contends that he is an accommodation party. Why does he wish to have this status?

4. *A* was one of two signers of a note. The word "guarantor" followed his signature. The holder of the note brought action against *A*, and *A*'s only defense was that the holder must sue the other signer before bringing action against *A*. Is *A*'s contention correct?

5. A promissory note was signed:
    "*A* and *B* Distributing, Inc.
    Albert Jones"
    The payee of the note seeks to collect from Jones. Can Jones introduce evidence that he signed only on behalf of *A* and *B* Distributing, Inc.?

6. *A*, the holder of a note, indorses it to *B* "without recourse." The maker of the note had filed a petition in bankruptcy prior to the indorsement. Can *B* hold *A* responsible for the payment of the note?

7. *M*, the bookkeeper for X Corporation, prepared payroll checks to the order of persons not on the payroll. The checks were presented to the company's treasurer, who signed them as a matter of course. *M* indorsed the checks in the name of the purported payees and cashed the checks at various stores. The checks were honored by the drawee bank. X Corporation seeks to recover from (1) the stores which cashed the checks (2) the drawee bank. How would you decide this case?

8. Smith introduced himself to Brown as "Professor Weinstein," a noted psychologist, and claimed to be raising funds for a study of juvenile delinquency. Brown drew a check for $10,000 payable to the order of

"Professor Weinstein." Smith (alias Weinstein) indorsed the check in the name of Weinstein and cashed it at the bank. Is the bank liable to Brown?

9. *D* drew a check payable to the order of *P. P* indorsed to *A, A* indorsed to *B*, and *B* indorsed to *H. H* obtained certification of the check after which the drawee bank failed. What are *H's* rights against *D, P, A,* and *B*?

10. *H* holds a note which, unknown to him, has been forged. He, by an indorsement "without recourse," indorses it to *A*, a holder in due course. It is presented and payment is refused. *A* desires to hold *H* liable on his indorsement. May he do so?

chapter 28

Commercial Paper: Conditions Precedent, Discharge

PRESENTMENT, NOTICE OF DISHONOR, AND PROTEST

3-131. Introduction. In the preceding chapter the liability of the secondary parties, namely drawers and indorsers of negotiable paper, was discussed. It was pointed out that their conditional (contractual) liability to the holder does not arise until the performance of certain *conditions precedent,* namely due presentment for payment, dishonor by the primary party, and the giving of due notice of dishonor to the drawer or indorser. These conditions may be waived by the parties to a negotiable instrument. A waiver set forth in the body of a note is effective as to all parties whose names appear on the instrument, while a waiver which is part of an indorsement applies only to the particular indorser, unless the language used is broad enough to cover later indorsers.[1] *Protest* is a very formal act or procedure for complying with the conditions precedent.

The importance of presentment and notice of dishonor should be stressed —failure to comply may result in either the complete or the partial discharge of the secondary parties. Thus, a holder who fails to properly present a note to the maker will have thereby discharged the indorsers from their conditional liability. If the maker does not pay, the holder will not have recourse against the indorsers. Performance of conditions precedent is necessary to charge secondary parties unless excused.

It must be remembered that secondary parties also have *unconditional liability* which stems from the warranties which they make upon transfer of an instrument. Such warranty liability exists without regard to the performance of conditions precedent. Likewise, it must be noted that even though a secondary party is discharged from his liability as a secondary party, he may

[1] Fett Developing Co. v. Garvin, page 553

still be liable on the underlying obligation which was the basis of the transfer of the instrument. (See Section 3-147 for a discussion of this concept.) Thus a secondary party may incur liability on his contract as indorser or drawer, his warranty obligation, or the underlying obligation.

Performance of conditions precedent is not necessary to impose liability on a primary party—maker or acceptor—except as noted hereafter for "domiciled paper," i.e., notes and drafts payable at a bank. The secondary parties, however, engage to pay only if there has been presentment, dishonor, and any necessary notice of dishonor or protest.

Attention will now be given to the various conditions precedent that normally must be fulfilled to establish secondary liability. It is necessary to carefully distinguish drawers from indorsers and also to differentiate between drawers of drafts as compared to drawers of checks. A distinction is also to be noted as between indorsers of notes on one hand and indorsers of checks and drafts on the other.

3-132. Presentment in General. Presentment is defined as a "demand for acceptance or payment made upon the maker, acceptor, drawee or other payor by or on behalf of the holder." (U.C.C. 3-504(1))

Exhibition of the instrument is not an essential element of a proper presentment. Presentment may be made by mail, by telephone, or in some other way. If the presentment is made by mail, it is effective on the date when the mail is *received*. Presentment may be made through a "clearing house," an association of banks in a community. It may be made to any person who has authority to make or refuse the payment or acceptance. If there are two or more makers, acceptors, drawees, or other payors, presentment can be made to any one of them.

An instrument may be presented for payment (in the case of a note or draft) or may be presented for acceptance (in the case of a draft). Thus, there are two basic types of presentment—for acceptance and for payment.

3-133. Presentment for Acceptance. Presentment for acceptance is not applicable to promissory notes, but it is often *required* in the case of drafts. The drawee of a draft is not bound upon the instrument as primary party until he accepts it. The holder will, in many cases, wait until maturity and present his draft to the drawee for payment, but he may present it to the drawee for acceptance before maturity in order to give credit to the instrument during the period of its term. The holder may present the draft to the drawee for acceptance at any time. The drawee is under no legal duty to the *holder* to accept; but if he refuses, the draft is dishonored by nonacceptance; a right of recourse arises immediately against the drawer and the indorsers, and no presentment for payment is necessary.

In most instances it is not necessary to present an instrument for *acceptance.* Presentment for *payment* alone is usually sufficient, but in the following cases *presentment for acceptance must be made in order to charge the drawer and indorsers of a draft.*

> 1. Where the *draft* expressly stipulates that it must be presented for acceptance.
> 2. Where the *draft* is payable elsewhere than at the residence or place of business of the drawee. Otherwise the drawee may not know of his obligation to be present at the place designated for payment.

3. Where the date of payment depends upon such presentment as where the draft is payable after sight. For example, "Thirty days after sight pay to the order of *X,*" requires that the draft be presented to the drawee for acceptance in order to determine the maturity date of the instrument.

3-134. Presentment for Payment.   Failure to make a presentment results in the complete discharge of indorsers. A limited discharge is accorded to drawers and also to makers and acceptors of "domiciled paper." They are discharged only to the extent that the delay in presentment caused them a loss. Thus, if the bank becomes insolvent subsequent to the date upon which presentment should have been made, the loss from such insolvency will fall upon the tardy holder. The liability in the event of such insolvency can be discharged by assigning to the holder the rights to receive such funds from the bank.

3-135. How Presentment Is Made.   A draft accepted or a note made payable at a bank must be presented at such bank. If the place of payment or acceptance is specified in the instrument, presentment may be made at such place. If no place is specified, it may be made at the place of business or residence of the party who is to accept or pay. If there is no one authorized to accept or pay "present or accessible" at the place of payment specified, or at the place of business or residence of the party to accept or pay, presentment is excused. Ordinarily, presentment would be made at the place of business of the primary party or drawee.

The party to whom presentment is made may without dishonor require the exhibition of the instrument, and reasonable identification of the person making presentment and evidence of his authority to make it if made for another. In addition, he may require that the instrument be produced for acceptance or payment at a place specified in it, or if there be none at any place reasonable in the circumstances, and he has the right to a signed receipt on the instrument for any partial or full payment and its surrender upon full payment.

If the primary party does not avail himself of these rights, the presentment is perfectly valid no matter how the presentment is made or where it is made. If he does require that the presentment be made in accordance with the above provisions, a failure to comply invalidates the presentment and the instrument is not dishonored. However, the time for presentment is extended to give the person presenting a reasonable opportunity to comply. The requirement of identification of the presenting party applies to bearer paper as well as order paper.

3-136. Time of Presentment.   In general, an instrument must be presented for payment on the day of maturity. If such day is not a full business day for either party, it is due on the next following day. The presentment must be made at a reasonable hour and, if at a bank, during banking hours. Several rules govern the time for presentment. Where the instrument is to be presented for acceptance, the presentment must be made on or before the date it is payable. When an instrument is payable after sight, it must be presented for acceptance or negotiated within a reasonable time after the date on the instrument or the date of issue, whichever is later. If the maturity date has been accelerated, presentment for payment must be made within a reasonable time after the acceleration. In all other situations it is required, in order to fix liability upon all secondary parties, that presentment for acceptance or payment be made within a reasonable time after such secondary party became liable, e.g., after his indorsement. Thus, in the case of a demand note an indorser would be discharged if presentment were not made within a reasonable time after he indorsed the note.

Note that presentment within a "reasonable time" is required in those situations when a definite maturity date is not included in the instrument— i.e., sight and demand instruments. Certain rules are to be applied in determining what constitutes a "reasonable time." A reasonable time for presentment is determined by the nature of the instrument, any usage of banking or trade, and the facts of the particular case. Though this is of some help in resolving the question of reasonableness—and possibly as much as can be accomplished by statute—it was deemed desirable to provide more definite rules for checks.

With respect to the liability of the drawer of a check, a reasonable time within which to present for payment or to initiate bank collection is presumed to be thirty days after date or issue, whichever is later. As to an indorser's liability, the presumed reasonable time is seven days after his indorsement. Thus, the drawer must "back up" a check for a longer period than an indorser, but the drawer having issued the check is not being imposed upon by the requirement that he keep funds on hand for thirty days to cover it. Thirty days is also the period after which a purchaser has notice of the staleness of a check. But an indorser is in a different position and is entitled to notice promptly, so that he may take adequate steps to protect himself against his transferor and prior parties if the check is dishonored. The drawer of a check is protected as to funds on deposit by Federal Deposit Insurance.

3-137. Dishonor.   The party who presents an instrument is entitled to have the instrument paid or accepted, as the case may be. If the party to whom the instrument is presented refuses to pay or accept, the instrument is dishonored. The presenting party then has recourse against indorsers or other secondary parties, provided he has given notice of such dishonor.

3-138. Time Allowed for Acceptance or Payment.   The drawee to whom a draft is presented for *acceptance* may defer without dishonoring the draft until the close of the next business day following presentment. Also, the holder who made the presentment may allow an additional business day and still retain the liability of the secondary parties. It should be stressed that strict compliance with the time requirements is essential—otherwise a discharge is granted to secondary parties.

Where the presentment is for *payment* the party to whom presentment is made is allowed time within which to examine the instrument to determine whether it is properly payable, but payment must be made not later than the close of business on the day of presentment.

3-139. Notice of Dishonor.   In the preceding sections two of the conditions precedent to the enforcement of liability against secondary parties have been discussed—presentment and dishonor. This section deals with the third requirement.

When an instrument has been dishonored on proper presentment, the holder must give prompt notice of the dishonor and by so doing has an immediate right of recourse against the secondary parties who have been notified. Failure to give prompt and proper notice of dishonor results in discharge of indorsers. Drawers of checks are discharged to the same extent as in the case of slow presentment. Likewise, makers, drawers, and acceptors of "domiciled paper" are entitled to notice of dishonor, but are released only to the extent that they are injured by the failure of the holder to give prompt notice of dishonor.

Generally, notice is given to secondary parties by the holder or by an indorser who has himself received such notice. The Code permits any party who may be compelled to pay the instrument to notify any party who may be liable on it.

Except for banks, notice must be given before midnight of the third business day after dishonor. In the case of a person who has received notice of dishonor and wishes to notify other parties, notice must be given by him before midnight of the third business day after receipt of the notice of dishonor. A person thus has sufficient time to determine what he is supposed to do and then get out a business letter in relation thereto.

In the case of banks, any necessary notice must be given before its "midnight deadline"—before midnight of the next banking day following the day on which a bank receives the item or notice of dishonor.[2] Article 4 provides further exceptions with respect to collecting banks, which are discussed in Chapter 29.

Notice may be given in any reasonable manner which would include oral notice, notice by telephone, and notice by mail. Such notice must identify the dishonored instrument and state that it has been dishonored. The Code approves the general banking practice of returning the instrument bearing a stamp that acceptance or payment has been refused as a sufficient notice of dishonor.

Written notice is effective when *sent* although it is not received, assuming proper address and postage. Note that when *presentment* is made by mail, the time of *presentment* is determined by time of *receipt* of mail.

If a party to whom notice is to be given is involved in insolvency proceedings, e.g., assignment for benefit of creditors, the notice may be given either to such party or to the representative of his estate.

Proper notice preceded by any necessary presentment and dishonor imposes liability upon secondary parties to whom such notice of dishonor is given, including makers and acceptors of "domiciled paper." Proper notice operates for the benefit of all parties who have rights on the instrument against the party notified. Thus, it is only necessary to notify a party once for his liability to be fixed. For example, if *A, B, C,* and *D* are indorsers in that order, and the holder gives notice only to *A* and *C, C* will not be required to give additional notice to *A,* and if *C* is compelled to pay, he would have recourse against *A.* *B* and *D* are discharged if they are not notified by the holder or one of the indorsers. Neither presentment, notice of dishonor, nor protest is necessary to charge an indorser who has indorsed an instrument after maturity.

[2] Samples v. Trust Co. of Georgia, page 553

3-140. Protest. Protest is a certificate which sets forth that an instrument was presented for payment or acceptance, that it was dishonored, and the reasons, if any, given for refusal to accept or pay. It is a formal method for satisfying the conditions precedent. It is required only for drafts which are drawn or payable outside the United States. The protest requirement is in conformity with foreign law in this respect. In other cases protest is optional with the holder. Protest serves as evidence both that presentment was made and that notice of dishonor was given—it creates a presumption that the conditions precedent were satisfied.

3-141. Delay and Excuse. An unexcused delay in making any *necessary* presentment or in giving notice of dishonor discharges secondary parties and other parties who are entitled to performance of the conditions precedent. As noted previously, indorsers are completely discharged by such delay, and drawers, makers of notes payable at a bank, and acceptors of drafts payable at a bank receive only a limited discharge.

Delay in making presentment, in giving notice of dishonor, or in making protest is excused when the holder has acted with reasonable diligence, and the delay is not due to any fault of the holder. He must, however, comply with these conditions or attempt to do so as soon as the cause of the delay ceases to exist. Also, delay in complying with the conditions precedent is excused if the holder did not know that the time for compliance had arrived. Thus, if an instrument has been accelerated, but the holder did not know of this fact, his late presentment would be excused. He would not know that the time for presentment had arrived.

The performance of the conditions precedent is entirely excused if the party to be charged, e.g., the indorser, upon whom liability is sought to be imposed, has *waived* the condition either before or after it is due. The waiver may be express as when it is set forth in the instrument or in the indorsement or it may be by implication. When such waiver is stated on the face of the instrument it is binding on all parties; when it is written above the signature of the indorser it binds him only.

Implied waivers are not defined but the test evolved by the courts is whether the secondary party's (e.g., indorser) conduct was such as to induce the holder to forego the usual procedures to fix liability on the indorser or was such as to otherwise indicate an intention to waive.

The words "Protest Waived" contained in an instrument mean that presentment, notice of dishonor, as well as technical protest are waived. This is true even though technical protest is not required.

The performance of the conditions precedent is also excused if the party to be charged has himself dishonored the instrument or has countermanded payment or otherwise has no reason to expect or right to require that the instrument be accepted or paid. This provision is illustrated by the situation in which a drawer of a check has stopped payment on the check. Such drawer is aware that the bank will dishonor the check in accordance with his order and certainly is not in a position to complain about slow presentment or any lack of notice of dishonor. Similarly, the rule applies to an accommodated party who has failed to pay. Even though he may nominally appear as an indorser he is in reality a primary party and the accommodation maker is really a surety.

Performance of the conditions precedent is also excused if by reasonable diligence the presentment or protest cannot be made or the notice given. This means that if the circumstances which gave rise to the "excuse" persist, the performance of the conditions is "entirely excused."

When a draft has been dishonored by *nonacceptance,* a later presentment for payment is excused unless of course the drawee has in the meantime accepted the instrument. This means that a holder who has presented a draft for acceptance is not, if acceptance is refused, required to make a subsequent presentment for payment. The refusal to accept is in itself a dishonor of the instrument.

DISCHARGE AND FINALITY

3-142. In General.   There are two facets to the ultimate termination of liability of parties to commercial paper. One of these relates to finality of payment or acceptance. Once an instrument has been paid or accepted, a holder in due course no longer has any liability to the payor or acceptor, except for his presentment warranties. If these warranties have not been breached, the holder in due course is insulated from any further liability and is entitled to retain the payment or to enforce the liability of the acceptor. This means that even though a bank discovers that it has paid on a forged check, it cannot recover a payment made to a holder in due course.

The other aspect is the discharge of any or all parties from their liability on the paper. Here again the special treatment accorded the holder in due course is evidenced. No discharge of any party is effective against a subsequent holder in due course unless he had notice of it at the time he took the instrument.

The following are methods whereby any party may be discharged from liability on an instrument.

1. By payment or satisfaction.[3]
2. By tender of payment.
3. By cancellation or renunciation.
4. By impairment of right of recourse or collateral.
5. By reacquisition of the instrument by a prior party.
6. By fraudulent and material alteration.
7. By certification of a check.
8. By acceptance varying a draft.
9. By unexcused delay in presentment or notice of dishonor or protest.

In addition a party may be discharged from liability on an instrument *to another party* by any other act or agreement with such party which would discharge his simple contract for the payment of money.

[3] Balmoral Arms v. Rutkin, page 554

3-143. Payment or Satisfaction. The usual method for obtaining a discharge is for the primary party to pay the holder the amount of the instrument. The primary party can safely do this even when he is aware that some third party has a claim on the paper. The third party can, however, bring court action to enjoin the payment or to supply the holder with indemnity against his liability for refusing to pay the holder.

It would not be proper to require the party who is obligated to make payment to pass judgment on whether the third party's claim was justified or not.

3-144. Tender of Payment. A tender is an offer to pay or perform a contractual obligation. A tender does not discharge the debt or obligation, but it does stop the running of interest. If the creditor thereafter brings legal action to recover the amount of the debt, the costs of suit and attorney's fees will be imposed on him.

This generally accepted rule of tender is adopted by the Code to give a limited discharge to the obligor on an instrument. If he tenders to the holder full payment when or after it is due, he is discharged to the extent of all subsequent liability for interest, costs, and attorney's fees.

Further, if the maker or acceptor is ready and able to pay at every place specified in the instrument when it is due, an equivalent of tender has been made. Thus, makers and acceptors of notes and drafts payable at a bank have made a proper tender if they maintain an adequate balance in the bank as of the due date of the instruments.

If the holder refuses to accept a proper tender, indorsers and other parties who have a right of recourse against the party making the tender are discharged.

Thus, if the maker of a note tendered payment which was refused by the holder, indorsers prior to the holder would be discharged because they have a right of recourse against the maker.

3-145. Cancellation and Renunciation. The holder of an instrument may even without consideration discharge any party in any manner apparent on the face of the instrument or the indorsement. This can be accomplished by intentionally canceling the instrument or the party's signature by destruction or mutilation, or by striking out the party's signature. He can renounce his rights by a writing signed and delivered or by surrender of the instrument to the party to be discharged.

He may strike out the signature of one or more of the parties or of all of them.

3-146. Impairment of Right of Recourse or of Collateral. An indorser who is required to pay an instrument has the right to recover in turn from indorsers prior to him and from the primary party whose refusal to pay placed this burden upon him. Likewise, if the instrument is a draft, he would have recourse against the drawer. The indorser is entitled to rely upon this right of recourse and also to rely upon any collateral that may have been given as security for the instrument by the primary party. The indorser's obligation is like that of a surety—he promises to pay if the primary party refuses to do so.

If the holder interferes with his right of recourse or if he does not utilize the collateral properly, the indorser has been harmed and he should be discharged from his liability.[4] The same can be said of an accommodation party who is a surety no matter what his capacity on the paper. Certain principles of the law of suretyship produce this result and are applicable to discharge of parties to commercial paper.

A party is discharged to the extent that the holder, without his consent: (1) releases or agrees not to sue any person against whom the party has recourse; (2) agrees to suspend his rights in the collateral; (3) impairs any collateral; or (4) otherwise discharges a party against whom there is a right of recourse. A common example is the striking out of one indorser's name on an instrument. This act discharges not only that indorser, but also those parties who have a right to recourse against the indorser whose name was stricken out.

3-147. Discharge of Underlying Obligations.   In most situations pertaining to the issuance or transfer of an instrument, there is an obligation involved for which the instrument was issued or transferred. It is the usual understanding of the parties that the *obligation* itself is not discharged until the instrument is paid, and that action on the debt or obligation is simply held in abeyance pending the exhaustion of efforts to collect on the instrument. By the same token the parties could agree otherwise—that is, that the instrument *is* received as final payment. However, it is not often that the parties spell out their intention in this regard. An instrument is said to be only conditional payment —the person who receives it gives up the right to sue on the obligation until the paper is due, but if it is not paid upon proper and timely presentment, the right to sue on the obligation is reinstated.[5]

When an instrument is taken for an underlying obligation, the obligation is suspended until the instrument is due; and if it is dishonored, action can be brought either on the instrument or the obligation.[6]

A question arises as to the position of the parties when an instrument has been indorsed to another, and the holder was late in presenting the instrument or in giving notice of dishonor. Here the holder initially had rights against the indorser on the indorsement contract and the underlying debt. If because of slow presentment or tardy notice of dishonor, the indorser is discharged from the former, is he also discharged from the latter? The Code provides that discharge of the underlying obligor on the instrument also discharges him on the obligation. As noted previously, failure to satisfy the conditions precedent discharges indorsers of checks, drafts, and notes irrespective of any injury to them. On the other hand, *drawers* are discharged on the instrument only to the extent of injury caused by the delay, so that they would continue to be liable on the underlying obligation except to the extent that the delay caused them a loss. Therefore, if the holder of a check indorses it to a creditor in payment of an underlying obligation and the creditor does not make a proper presentment, the indorser is discharged *both* on the instrument and on the underlying debt. The indorser does not have to prove any injury. If a person draws a draft or a check in payment of an obligation, he remains liable on the

[4] Reeves v. Hunnicutt, page 555.
[5] Mansion Carpets, Inc. v. Marinoff, page 556.
[6] In re Eton Furniture Co., page 557.

underlying obligation in the event of dishonor of the check or draft in spite of late presentment.

These provisions emphasize the importance of proper compliance with the conditions precedent.

3-148. Lost, Destroyed, or Stolen Instrument. The owner of an instrument which is lost, whether by destruction, theft, or otherwise, may maintain an action in his own name and recover from any party liable thereon upon due proof of his ownership, the facts which prevent his production of the instrument and its terms. The court may require security indemnifying the defendant against loss by reason of further claims on the instrument.[7]

Since it is possible that the instrument might at a later date actually turn up in the hands of a holder in due course, the court may require security to indemnify the obligor against double liability.

CONDITIONS PRECEDENT, DISCHARGE CASES

Fett Developing Co. v. Garvin
168 S.E.2d 212 (Ga.) 1969

BELL, J. . . . In this suit on a note plaintiff, as first indorsee, obtained a judgment against the indorsing payee. . . .

The [defendant] alleges error in overruling defendant's motion to dismiss the complaint. This contention, based on the failure of the complaint to allege presentment and notice of dishonor, is without merit. The note sued on and incorporated in the complaint contained an express waiver of presentment and notice. The Commercial Code, Code Ann. § 109A-3-511(6), provides: "Where a waiver of presentment or notice or protest is embodied in the instrument itself it is binding upon all parties. . . . " We do not decide whether a complaint, in order to withstand a motion to dismiss, must allege presentment and notice of dishonor where necessary under Code Ann. § 109A-3-501 *et seq.*

Judgment affirmed.

Samples v. Trust Co. of Georgia
163 S.E.2d 325 (Ga.) 1968

The defendant, Samples, received a check drawn on the plaintiff bank. He indorsed the check and received payment from another bank. That bank sent the check for collection to plaintiff bank and the check was paid. Later, the plaintiff discovered that the drawer of the check did not have an account and that it had mistakenly charged the check to one of its customers. Plaintiff then sought to recover from the defendant indorser. Defendant contended that the check had not been dishonored within the time allowed by law. The lower court gave judgment for plaintiff and defendant appealed.

BELL, J. . . . "Unless excused . . . notice of any dishonor is necessary to charge any indorser. . . . " Code Ann. § 109A-3-501(2). "Any necessary notice must be given by a bank before its midnight deadline. . . . " Code Ann. § 109A-3-508(2). That is, "midnight on its next banking day following the

---

[7] Dluge v. Robinson, page 558

banking day on which it receives the relevant item." Code Ann. § 109A-4-104(h). "Where without excuse any necessary presentment or notice of dishonor is delayed beyond the time when it is due ... any indorser is discharged.... " Code Ann. § 109A-3-502(1). "Delay by a ... payor bank beyond time limits prescribed or permitted by this Act or by instructions is excused if caused by interruption of communication facilities, suspension of payments by another bank, war, emergency conditions or other circumstances beyond the control of the bank provided it exercises such diligence as the circumstances require." Code Ann. § 109A-4-108. The plaintiff bank's failure to give notice of dishonor within the prescribed time was not due to "circumstances beyond the control of the bank" and was not excused by any provision of the Code, but was due to the bank's error in mistaking the signature on a check drawn on a fictitious account for the signature of one of its customers with a similar name. A bank is bound to know the signatures of its depositors. ... § 109A-4-302 also demands a reversal. That sections provides: "In the absence of a valid defense such as breach of a presentment warranty ... settlement effected or the like, if an item is presented on and received by a payor bank the bank is accountable for the amount of ... a demand item other than a documentary draft whether properly payable or not if the bank ... does not pay or return the item or send notice of dishonor until after its midnight deadline. ... "

The trial court erred in rendering judgment for the plaintiff bank.

Judgment reversed.

Balmoral Arms v. Rutkin

250 A.2d 50 (N.J.) 1969

The plaintiff brought suit to foreclose a mortgage which secured a note, signed by the defendants. The March 1 interest payment was mailed but not received by the plaintiff. Plaintiff accelerated the note as provided in the mortgage. The defendant claimed that the check was payment even though not received.

LANE, J. . . . Plaintiff argues that even assuming the check was received, receipt of the check by itself would not be payment. It is true that under common law a check received for the payment of a debt is not in fact payment unless the check is paid, "except in cases where it is positively agreed to be received as payment." *State* v. *United States Steel Corp.* 12 N.J. 38, 45, 95 A.2d 734 (1953). Although there was no agreement to receive a check in and of itself as payment unless the check was paid, the mortgagee did agree to receive payments of interest by check through the mail. The receipt of such a check would suspend the obligation *pro tanto* until the presentment of the check. N.J.S. 12A:3-802(1) (b), N.J.S.A. Here the mortgagor drew the check on March 4, 1968 and deposited it that day in the United States mail. This was in accordance with plaintiff's implied consent. There was no negligence, inadvertence or other conduct on the part of the mortgagor that led to the failure of plaintiff to receive the check. By reason of the fact that plaintiff consented to the payment of the interest by mail, the risk of loss in the event of nondelivery fell upon plaintiff and not the mortgagor. 40 Am.Jur., Payment, § 36, p.737. Under the facts of this case the failure of plaintiff to receive the March

1 payment through the mail does not result in the loss of the mortgagor's rights through nonpayment and will not sustain this action.

An almost identical situation was before the court in *Console* v. *Torchinsky,* 97 Conn. 353, 116 A. 613 (Sup.Ct.Err.1922). There it was held that the risk of the nonreceipt of a check mailed in payment of interest on a mortgage fell upon the mortgagee and not upon the mortgagor.

In view of the holding above, it is not necessary to deal with the counterclaim filed by defendants Barnett and Elman.

Upon payment to plaintiff within ten days of the March and May payments of interest in the amount of $562.50 each, the complaint will be dismissed.

Reeves v. Hunnicutt

168 S.E.2d 663 (Ga.) 1969

Reeves, as payee of a note, transferred it to Hunnicutt. The note was secured by office and shop equipment. Thereafter one of the makers transferred all of the equipment to one Griffin who assumed all of the obligations of the note in a separate written instrument. The collateral was in turn transferred to another person. Payments were made on the note to Hunnicutt, but subsequently there was a default and Hunnicutt sued Reeves. The lower court gave summary judgment to the plaintiff, Hunnicutt. Defendant appealed.

QUILLIAN, J. . . . The defendant, Reeves, contends that acts of Hunnicutt unjustifiably impaired the collateral for the note within the meaning of Code Ann. § 109A-3-606(b) (Ga.L.1962, pp. 156, 278), thereby discharging him as a matter of law. The defendant contends: that Hunnicutt without his knowledge or consent allowed the original maker of the note to transfer the collateral securing the note to another party; that the collateral was then transferred several times without his knowledge or consent. The defendant insists that this action by Hunnicutt completely divorced him from the collateral, which has been dissipated, and destroyed his right of contribution from the transferees.

The defendant's contentions are without merit because of the provisions of the note in question which provide in part: " . . . the surrender or release of any collateral held by the payee or holder hereof, shall not affect the liability of any indorser, guarantor, surety or other party to this note or release or relieve them or either of them, from liability to pay the full amount of this note, and the holder or payee may proceed against any party to this note without first proceeding against the maker or other party. The payee or holder hereof shall be under no duty to enforce payment of the collateral securing this note. Should any payee or holder undertake to collect upon said collateral or any part thereof, it shall not be liable for any negligence or mistake in judgment in making such collection, and shall have the full right and authority to adjust, compromise and receive less than the amount due upon any of said collateral, and otherwise to enter into any accord and satisfaction with respect to same as may to said payee or holder seem advisable, without liability of any nature to any party to this paper, except to duly credit the amount received, less expenses upon this note."

Code Ann. § 109A-3-606 provides that: "The holder discharges any party to the instrument to the extent that *without such party's consent* the holder . . . (b) unjustifiably impairs any collateral for the instrument given by or on behalf of the party or any person against whom he has a right of recourse." [Emphasis supplied.] As pointed out in 2 ULA-UCC § 3-606, Offical Comment 2: "Consent may be given in advance and is commonly incorporated in the instrument. . . . It requires no consideration, and operates as a waiver of the consenting party's right to claim his own discharge." This is precisely what transpired in this situation.

It is clear that under the terms of the note knowledge on the part of Hunnicutt of transfers of the collateral would not affect the defendant's liability for payment of the note.

The granting of the summary judgment was not error.

Judgment affirmed.

Mansion Carpets, Inc. v. Marinoff

265 N.Y.S.2d 298 (N.Y.) 1965

PER CURIAM. . . . Plaintiff sued to recover upon a check issued by defendants for carpeting and floor tile installed by plaintiff in defendants' residence. Defendants counterclaimed for breach of warranty based on work not encompassed by the check. At the time of trial, plaintiff's claim on the check had been reduced to $415 by payment made after suit was begun. In defense, defendants offered proof of failure of consideration. The jury found for plaintiff on the $415 claim and awarded defendants $200 on their counterclaim. There must be a new trial because of the *reversible error committed in instructing the jury that the check represented an unconditional promise to pay and was not subject to any defenses arising from claimed breaches of the contract pursuant to which payment was made by check.* The requirement of the Uniform Commercial Code, 3-104(1) (b) that a check contain an unconditional promise to pay applies only to the matter of the *form* of a negotiable instrument. *As between the original parties payment by check is conditional* (UCC 2-511); and if the instrument is dishonored, action may be maintained *on either the instrument or the obligation* (UCC 3-802 (1) (b). [Emphases added.] Want or failure of consideration is a defense as against any person not having the rights of a holder in due course (UCC 3-408). Although UCC 3-302 (2) states a payee may be a holder in due course, it is obvious that plaintiff herein does not fall within the category of the type of payee contemplated by that Section. Thus, the jury should have been permitted to consider defenses to the check based upon the original transaction. It would, however, be appropriate for defendants to amend their answer to plead failure of consideration as a defense. Moreover, the jury was apparently confused by the charge for it originally returned to announce a verdict for defendants on plaintiff's cause of action and for defendants on their counterclaim in the sum of $100. Only after the Trial Judge reiterated his direction that plaintiff was entitled to a verdict on the cause of action based on the check and sent the jury back for further deliberation, did the jury return with the verdict appealed from. In view of our conclusion as to the prejudicial effect of the erroneous charge, we are of the opinion that the interests of justice dictate a new trial as to defendants' counterclaims as well. Submission of the case on an erroneous theory may well have influenced the jury in its deliberations on the entire case.

Reversed and remanded for new trial.

In re Eton Furniture Co.

286 F.2d 93 (1961)

The general manager of the Eton Furniture Company, Huntington, on several occasions borrowed money from the bank, giving his personal note to the bank, and arranged for the proceeds to be credited to Eton's account. When Eton's deposits produced a balance deemed to be sufficiently ample, the bank appropriated Eton's funds to pay off the loans. On November 6, 1957, Eton was adjudged a bankrupt and the trustee in bankruptcy asked for a turnover order against the bank alleging that the bank had in its possession $6,600 belonging to the bankrupt estate. The trustee contended that "the loans negotiated by Huntington from the bank, and for which he gave his personal notes to the bank were loans to him and not to Eton." His position was that the money in the account was Eton's and that as an asset of the estate it should be turned over to him as trustee. The bank, in effect, contended that the loan was really to Eton and that the amount in the account, therefore, could be set off against Eton's deposit account thereby satisfying Eton's debt to the bank. The referee and the lower court held that the primary obligation was that of the company and ruled in favor of the bank.

BIGGS, C. J. . . . It was argued that Eton received the proceeds of the loans from Huntington and not from the bank, and that therefore the satisfaction of the obligations from Eton's account with the bank constituted an unjustified appropriation of Eton's funds by the bank to pay the debts of another. . . .

The single issue which this court must determine is whether Eton was indebted to the bank in the amounts of the loans negotiated by Huntington, its general manager. The trustee makes two arguments which we must consider. First, relying on Section 3-401 (1) of the Uniform Commercial Code, applicable in Pennsylvania, 12A P.S. Section 3-401 (1), he contends that *since Huntington's signature alone appears on the notes* given by him to the bank, Huntington alone can be held liable by the bank for repayment of the loans. Second, he argues that Huntington was not authorized to borrow money for Eton and that therefore, regardless of any understanding that may have existed between Huntington and the bank, Eton, not being bound, could not be liable for repayment of the loans. . . .

Section 3-401 (1) provides that "[N]o person is liable on an instrument unless his signature appears thereon." On the basis of this provision the trustee contends that Eton, not having signed the notes given to the bank, cannot be held liable for repayment of the loans. This argument finds no support in the words of the statute which provides merely that one who does not sign a note cannot be liable *on the note.* Contrary to the trustee's argument, the provision quoted cannot be read to mean that no person is liable on a debt whose signature does not appear on a note given as collateral security for that debt. Indeed, it has long been settled in Pennsylvania and elsewhere that the one to whom money is loaned or property advanced is liable for the debt regardless of the fact that his name may not appear on the security taken if that security was regarded by the parties purely as collateral. That Section 3-401 (1) was not intended to change this rule is demonstrated clearly by the comment to that section which states in pertinent part: "Nothing in this section is intended to prevent any liability arising apart from the instrument itself." The party who does not sign may still be liable on the original obligation for which the instrument was given. . . .

In the present case, the evidence of Huntington, adopted "as verity" by the referee, similarly shows that the loans were for Eton's use, that the bank, Eton and Huntington understood this to be so, and that the money was in fact used by the company for its own benefit. We hold that the finding of the referee and that of the court below that the debts were incurred by Eton is supported by the evidence and that their rulings are in accordance with the applicable law. . . .

The judgment of the court below will be affirmed.

Dluge v. Robinson
204 A.2d 280 (Pa.) 1964

FLOOD, J. This is an appeal from a judgment for the plaintiffs in an action against J. Robinson as endorser of two checks, brought by Isaac Dluge, the endorsee. The checks were dishonored by the drawee bank because of insufficient funds in the maker's account. Dluge died after instituting suit and the executors of his estate have been substituted as plaintiffs.

The complaint sets forth that immediately after the bank refused payment and returned the checks to Dluge, he returned them to the defendant with a demand for payment which the defendant refused. The defendant, both in his answer and on the witness stand, denied any demand for payment at the time Dluge returned the checks. When called by the plaintiffs for cross examination, Robinson testified that the checks had been returned to him by Dluge "for insufficient funds, to give them back to Mr. Wapner [the maker]" and that he turned them over to Wapner and never got them back. Wapner testified that he paid the amount of the checks to Dluge and then tore them up. The trial judge, who heard the case without a jury, overruled an objection to the admission of Wapner's testimony at the trial, but later reconsidered that ruling. Concluding that Wapner was an incompetent witness under the Dead Man's Act she excluded his testimony from consideration in reaching the decision that plaintiffs were entitled to recover on the checks.

If the plaintiffs [executors of Dluge estate] were holders in due course, they would have to prove only (1) that the defendant [Robinson] endorsed the checks and delivered them to Dluge, and (2) that they had been presented to the endorser for payment within a reasonable time. (Uniform Commercial Code, § 3-501(1) (b).) In the case of an uncertified check this is presumed to be within seven days after the endorsement. (U.C.C., § 3-503(1)(e), § 3-503(2)(b).)

> Presentment is a demand for acceptance or payment . . . by or on behalf of the holder. (U.C.C., § 3-504(1).)

The only evidence of any demand was the admission by defendant that he received a letter from Dluge's attorney demanding payment. The defendant did not state when he received this letter. The plaintiffs did not offer the letter in evidence and there is no way to determine from the record when it was sent except that it was presumably sent before the complaint was filed on September 12, 1960, seven months after the checks were dishonored by the drawee bank. Since the defendant denied any demand at the time the checks were returned to him, and the record is otherwise barren of any evidence of demand within seven days, or any reasonable time, after endorsement, the plaintiffs did not establish any right to recover even if they had been holders in due course.

The plaintiffs are not holders in due course. Dluge gave the checks to the defendant without any demand for payment, so far as the record shows, and was not in possession of them when the suit was brought. Therefore he was not the holder. "'Holder' means a person who is in possession of a document of title or an instrument or an investment security drawn, issued or endorsed to him or to his order or to bearer or in blank." (U.C.C., § 1-201(20).) A fortiori, he was not a holder in due course. (U.S.C., § 3-302(1).)

The plaintiffs argue that they may nevertheless recover from the defendant, as the endorser of a "lost" check owned by them, under § 3-804 of the Uniform Commercial Code. This section provides: "The owner of an instrument which is lost, whether by destruction, theft or otherwise, may maintain an action in his own name and recover from any party liable thereon upon due proof of his ownership, the facts which prevent his production of the instrument and its terms. . . . "

There is, however, neither allegation nor proof that the checks were destroyed, stolen, or otherwise lost. If the plaintiffs had proved that Dluge had returned the checks with a demand for payment, or that they later demanded that defendant return the checks, they might argue that his failure either to pay or return them constituted a theft or a *conversion.* (U.C.C., § 3-419.) There was no evidence of such demand and therefore no proof of conversion or theft. The maker, Wapner, testified that he paid Dluge and then destroyed the checks. This testimony was stricken from the record, following the plaintiffs' objection. Therefore there is no evidence in the record of the destruction of the checks. Finally, there is no evidence that they were otherwise lost. "A note cannot be considered to have been lost so as to permit action on it as a lost note if the party in possession of it is known to plaintiff and the ownership is in dispute." (54 C.J.S. Lost Instruments § 1.) "An article is 'lost' when the owner has lost the possession or custody of it, involuntarily and by any means, but more particularly by accident or his own negligence or forgetfulness, and when he is ignorant of its whereabouts or cannot recover it by an ordinary diligent search." (*Black's Law Dictionary*, 4th ed., p.1096 and cases cited.)

Moreover, to recover under § 3-804 of the Code, the plaintiffs must prove ownership of the checks. Such proof of ownership must be clear and convincing. In the absence of possession, ownership would usually depend upon proof that the holder did not voluntarily surrender possession unless he did so conditionally upon payment of the checks. Surrender of the checks to a prior party, without payment, and without even a demand for payment, tells against the retention of ownership, and indicates, if anything, an intention not to hold such party liable on the instrument. (Cf. U.C.C., § 3-605(1)(b).)

The plaintiffs did not prove that the checks were "lost" as that word is used in § 3-804 of the Code, or that they were still the owners of the checks when suit was brought. More importantly, there is no proof of *demand for payment* by the plaintiffs when the checks were returned to the defendant. Plaintiffs have therefore failed to prove their right to recover against Robinson whether they are holders or owners of the checks.

The burden upon one not a holder who seeks to recover on a negotiable instrument is a heavy one. The plaintiffs have not sustained it. They must recover, if at all, upon the underlying obligation for which the checks were given.

Judgment reversed and entered for the defendant n.o.v. [Notwithstanding the verdict.]

CHAPTER 28
REVIEW QUESTIONS AND PROBLEMS

1. *A* was the holder of a note made by *B.* He is unable to locate the note and fears that it may have been inadvertently destroyed. Is there any possibility that *A* could enforce payment of the note?

2. A Corporation is the maker of a note that was indorsed by *B,* an officer of the corporation along with other officers. *C,* the holder of the note, waited eighteen months before presenting the note for payment to the corporation. Will *B* be held liable as an indorser?

3. *A,* the holder of a note, brought action against *B,* an indorser. The note contained a provision on its face, "Protest Waived." *B* contends that he is discharged from liability because the note was not presented for payment and no notice of dishonor was given to him. Is *B* discharged?

4. *A* performed services for *P* and gave him in payment a third-party note of which *P* was payee. *P* indorsed the note to *A* "without recourse." If the note is not paid, does *A* have any remedy against *P*?

5. *A* is the holder of a bill of exchange drawn by *X* on *Y. A* presents the instruments to *Y* for the acceptance and *Y* refuses to accept. What should *A* do to protect his rights? May he wait until the bill matures before taking any action?

6. *A* executed a note in favor of *B.* The note was indorsed by *B* to the holder. Prior to the maturity of the note, *A* became insolvent and for this reason the holder did not present the note to *A* for payment. Is *B* relieved of his liability as an indorser?

7. *A* executed a note in favor of *B,* the note containing an automatic acceleration clause. Several days after the event that accelerated payment had occurred, the holder of the note presented it to *A* for payment. Payment was refused. Can the holder look to *B* as indorser?

8. *A* is the maker of a note drawn in favor of *B. B* indorses to *C,* and *C* indorses to *H. H* presents the note to *A* and receives a worthless check in payment. Is the note discharged?

9. *H* is the holder of a negotiable bill of exchange upon which there are six indorsers. *H* desires to release the fourth on the list. If he does, what will be the effect?

10. At the office of a real estate broker *X, M* gave his negotiable note and mortgage to *P* in return for the conveyance of land. *M* paid annual interest on the note to the broker *X* under *P*'s instructions. A year later,

P assigned the note to *H* but did not deliver the same. Thereafter *M* paid all the principal and interest in a lump sum to *X*, *X* retaining possession of the note. *X* absconded with the payments. Whose loss?

chapter 29

Bank Deposits
and Collections

3-149. Introduction. Article 4 of the Code—Bank Deposits and Collections —provides uniform rules to govern the collection of checks and other instruments for the payment of money. These rules govern the relationship of banks with each other and with depositors in the collection and payment of *items.* (An item is any instrument for the payment of money, whether it is negotiable or not). There is some overlapping between Article 3—Commercial Paper— and Article 4; in case of conflict, the provisions of Article 4 prevail.

The following terminology of Article 4 is significant, especially with regard to the designation of the various banks in the collection process:

(a) "Depositary bank" means the first bank to which an item is transferred for collection even though it is also the payor bank;

(b) "Payor bank" means a bank by which an item is payable as drawn or accepted;

(c) "Intermediary bank" means any bank to which an item is transferred in course of collection except the depositary or payor bank;

(d) "Collecting bank" means any bank handling the item for collection except the payor bank;

(e) "Presenting bank" means any bank presenting an item except a payor bank;

(f) "Remitting bank" means any payor or intermediary bank remitting for an item. (U.C.C. 4-105)

It will be recalled that a holder of a check should present it to the drawee-payor bank or initiate the collection process without delay; that a check becomes stale after thirty days; and that to charge indorsers, presentment must be made within seven days. Since timing is very important, there are two time terms which are defined: (1) A *banking day* means "that part of any day on which a bank is open to the public for carrying on substantially all of its banking functions." (U.C.C. 4-104(c)) A bank is permitted to establish a cutoff

562

hour of 2 P.M. or later so that the bank may have an opportunity to process items, prove balances, and make the necessary entries to determine its position for the day. If an item is received after the cutoff hour—if one be fixed—or after the close of the banking day, it may be treated as having been received at the opening of the next banking day. (2) *Midnight deadline* with respect to a bank means midnight on its next banking day following the banking day on which the bank receives the check or notice with regard to it.

Another important term is "clearing house," which means an association of banks which engages in the clearing or settling of accounts between banks in connection with checks.

A customer who deposits an item for collection should indorse it, but quite frequently a customer overlooks doing so. The depositary bank may supply the missing indorsement. If the bank states on the item that it was deposited by a customer or credited to his account, such a statement is effective as the customer's indorsement. This is a practical rule intended to speed up the collection process by making it unnecessary to return to the depositor any items he may have failed to indorse.

3-150. Collection of Items: Depositary and Collecting Banks.

The collection process is initiated when the customer deposits a check to his account; his account is provisionally credited by the bank at that time. (See Section 3-95.) The check then passes through the collecting banks, each of which provisionally credits the account of the prior bank, and finally when the check reaches the payor (drawee) bank, that bank debits the drawer's account. The payor bank then credits the account of the presenting bank, remits to it, or if both belong to the same clearing house, includes the check in its balance there. If the payor bank honors the check, the settlement is final. Transactions prior to this final settlement by the payor bank are called "provisional settlements" because until final settlement, it is not known whether the check is "good." If the payor bank dishonors the check, each provisional settlement is *revoked,* and the depositary bank which had given its provisional credit to the customer for the deposit cancels it. The dishonored check is then returned to the customer.

Unless a contrary intent clearly appears, a collecting bank is an agent for the owner of a check. Until settlement becomes final, the depositor bears the risk of loss as owner of the check in the event of its nonpayment or the insolvency of one of the collecting banks before final settlement.

When a bank has received a check for collection, it has the duty to use ordinary care in performing its collection operations. These operations include presenting the check or forwarding it for presentment, sending notice of dishonor or nonpayment or returning the check after learning that it has not been paid, and settling for the check when it receives final payment. Failure of the collecting bank to use ordinary care in handling a check or other item subjects the bank to liability to the depositor for any loss or damage sustained. And depositary banks have additional responsibilities.[1]

In order to act seasonably, a bank is generally required to take proper action before the midnight deadline following the receipt of a check, a notice, or a payment. Thus, if a collecting bank receives a check on Monday and presents

---

[1] Salsman (formerly Odgers) v. National Community Bank of Rutherford, page 568

it or forwards it to the next collecting bank any time prior to midnight Tuesday, it has acted seasonably.

Each customer or collecting bank who obtains payment or acceptance of an item makes substantially the same warranties to the payor bank as the warranties on presentment and transfer of commercial paper.

During the collection process a bank has the right to claim a security interest in an item or its proceeds so that the bank may protect itself against the depositor and his creditors with respect to advances and payments it has made in connection with the item. Where an item has been deposited in an account, the bank has a security interest to the extent that withdrawals have been made against the credit. The depositary bank may hold the item as security as against the depositor or his creditors. The security interest continues until the bank receives a final settlement or surrenders the instrument for purposes other than collection.

For purposes of determining the status of a bank as a holder in due course, a security interest constitutes value. Thus, a bank can qualify as a holder in due course and can enforce an instrument even though its depositor or other transferor could not. In this connection it is to be noted that an intermediary bank or a payor bank which is not a depositary bank is not affected by a restrictive indorsement except that of the bank's immediate transferor. Notice of claim or defense is not imparted by such indorsement. Depositary banks, however, may be liable to the owner of an item who had indorsed it restrictively.

If an item has been dishonored, as in the case of an "N.S.F." check, the presenting bank will revoke its provisional settlement and charge the item back to the account of the next prior collecting bank. Likewise, other banks in the chain of collection will charge back. The final step is a charge-back to the customer's account by the depositary bank. Each of the collecting banks must return the item or send notification of the facts by its midnight deadline. The right to charge back by the depositary bank is not affected by the fact that the depositor may have drawn against the provisional credit.

A depositor does not have the right to draw against uncollected funds. Accordingly, he is not entitled to draw against an item payable by another bank until the provisional settlement which his depositary bank has received becomes final.

Where the deposit is an item *on which the depositary bank is itself the payor* ("on us" items), the credit becomes final on the second banking day following receipt of the item.

3-151. Collection of Items: Payor Banks. An item may be presented to a payor bank for payment *over the counter,* but most items will be presented through a clearing house or by mail. The payor bank will make a provisional settlement for them on the banking day they are received. In this event, it has until final payment of the check, but not later than the midnight deadline on the following day, to decide whether or not the item is good. Within this time the bank may revoke the settlement and return the item or, if this is not possible, send written notice of dishonor or nonpayment. This enables the bank to defer posting until the next day. Where a check drawn by one customer of a bank is *deposited by another customer of the same bank* for credit on its books, the bank may return the item and revoke any credit given at any time on the following day.

Failure of a payor-drawee bank to take action within the prescribed time limits may make it accountable to the person who deposited a check, although the check is not paid and the drawer of the check did not have sufficient funds to cover it. This liability is imposed if (1) the bank retains a check presented to it by another bank beyond midnight of the banking day of receipt without settling for it or (2) the bank does not pay or return the check or send notice of dishonor within the period of its midnight deadline.[2] If the payor bank is also the depositary bank; i.e., the check deposited by the customer is one which is drawn on his bank, settlement on the day of receipt is not required, but the bank must return the check or send notice of dishonor before its midnight deadline. Thus, failure on the part of the payor bank to take the necessary action within the proper time renders it liable to the depositor, even though the check was not properly payable.

Following the receipt of a check, the payor bank must process it. This involves a series of acts which are initiated by receipt of the check—from the clearing house, by mail, or over the counter. The check passes to the sorting and proving department, after which it may be photographed. It then moves to the bookkeeping department, where it is examined as to form and signature. Here it is also determined whether the drawer's account is sufficient to cover the check. If it is found to be proper in all respects, it will be posted to the drawer's account. The entire process may require considerable time and may extend into the next banking day.

During the period of processing a check or prior thereto, the payor bank may receive actual or constructive notice or acquire knowledge which affects the check or other item. Such knowledge or notice may be that the drawer has filed a petition in bankruptcy;[3] that the drawer has stopped payment on a check; or that the drawer's account has been attached by a creditor. These circumstances raise questions as to (1) when a stop order becomes effective so that the bank is under a duty to refuse to pay the check and (2) when an attachment is effective so as to preclude the bank from paying checks which are drawn on the account. Any notice or stop order received by a bank, any legal process such as attachment served on it, or any set-off exercised by the bank comes too late to prevent payment of a check by the bank if the bank has done any one of the following:[4]

1. Accepted or certified the item.

2. Paid the item in cash.

3. Settled for the item without reserving or having the right to revoke the settlement.

4. Completed the posting of the check to the customer's account or otherwise has evidenced its decision to pay the check by examining the customer's account and has taken some action to indicate an intention to pay.

5. Become liable for the check or other item because of failure to settle for or return the check in time.

[2] Rock Island Auction Sales v. Empire Packing Co., page 570
[3] Bank of Marin v. England, Trustee, page 571
[4] Gibbs v. Gerberich, page 573

Another problem relates to the *order of payment of checks.* There is no priority as among checks drawn on a particular account and presented to a bank on any particular day. The checks and other items may be accepted, paid, certified, or charged to the indicated account of its customer in any order convenient to the bank.

3-152. Relationship Between Payor Bank and Its Customer.   It is basic to the banking function that upon proper payment of a draft or check the drawee (payor bank) may charge the account of the drawer (customer). This fundamental proposition applies even though the check or draft is an *overdraft,* since the check itself authorizes the payment for the drawer's account and carries with it an implied promise to reimburse the drawee. This promise is only by the drawer and does not extend to a joint owner of the account.

It will be recalled that a holder in due course is protected against the defense of discharge by reason of material alteration and that he is able to enforce the instrument according to its original tenor. Likewise, protection is afforded to a drawee who pays a subsequently completed instrument in good faith according to the instrument as completed. Therefore if a bank in good faith makes payment to a holder, it may charge the account of its customer according to (1) the original tenor of the altered check or (2) the tenor of a completed item. Thus, if a check is raised, the bank can charge its customer's account with the original amount of the check. In addition, if a person signs his name to a check in blank and loses it, after which an unauthorized person completes the check, and is paid by the drawee bank, the bank may charge the customer's account the full amount of such check, if it pays in good faith and does not know that the completion was improper. A bank is under a duty to honor checks drawn by its customer when there are sufficient funds in his account to cover the checks. If a bank wrongfully dishonors a check, it is liable in damages to its customer for damages proximately caused by the wrongful dishonor. When the dishonor occurs by mistake, as distinguished from a malicious or willful dishonor, liability is limited to the *actual damages* proved. Provision is also made for *consequential damages* proximately caused by the wrongful dishonor and may include damages for arrest or prosecution of the customer. The Code rejects decisions which have held that if the dishonored item were drawn by a merchant, he is defamed in his business because of the reflection on his credit and accordingly could recover substantial damages on the basis of defamation per se without proof of actual damages.

A customer has the right to stop payment on checks drawn on his account. Only the drawer has this right; it does not extend to holders—payees or indorsees. In order to be effective, a stop payment order must be "received at such time and in such manner as to afford the bank a reasonable opportunity to act on it prior to an action by the bank with respect to the item. . . . " (U.C.C. 4-403) It has been held that if a check has been certified, the depositor cannot stop payment whether he or the payee procured the certification. An oral stop order is binding on the bank for only fourteen days, unless confirmed in writing within that period. Unless renewed in writing, a written stop order is effective for only six months.

If a bank pays a check upon which payment has been stopped, it will be liable to its customer for resulting damages. However, the burden is on the customer to prove the fact and the amount of loss. If the customer cannot prove that he has suffered a loss, he cannot recover against the bank for paying the check. Exculpatory provisions in a stop order form are invalid.

A bank is not *obligated* to pay a check that is over six months old. The bank, however, is entitled to pay a check which has been outstanding more than six months and may charge it to the customer's account. Certified checks do not fall within the six months' rule—they are the primary obligation of the certifying bank, and the obligation runs directly to the holder of the check.

As a general proposition, the death or incompetency of a person terminates the authority of others to act on his behalf. If this principle were applied to banks, a tremendous burden would be imposed upon them to verify the continued life and competency of drawers. Accordingly, the death of a customer does not revoke the bank's authority to pay checks drawn by him until the bank knows of the death and has a reasonable opportunity to act on it. The same rule applies to an adjudication of incompetency.

Even though the bank knows of the death of its customer, it *may* pay or certify checks for a period of ten days after the date of his death. This is intended to permit holders of checks drawn and issued shortly before death to cash them without the necessity of filing a claim in probate. This is subject to the proviso that a stop order may be made by a relative or other person who claims an interest in the account.

Generally, a bank makes available to its customer a statement of his account and his canceled checks. Within a reasonable time after they are returned to the customer or made available to him, he is under a duty to examine them for forgeries of his signature and for raised checks. He is further obligated to report any irregularities to the bank. The bank does not have the right to charge his account with forged checks, but the customer's failure to examine and notify will prevent him from asserting the forgery (or alteration) against the bank if the bank can establish that it suffered a loss because of this failure. Thus, the bank may be able to prove that a prompt notification would have enabled the bank to recover from the forger.

The Code does not specify the period of time within which the customer must report forgeries or alterations, but it does specify that if the same wrongdoer commits successive forgeries or alterations, the customer's failure to examine and notify within a period not to exceed fourteen days after the first item and statement were available to him will bar him from asserting the forgeries or alterations of subsequent checks by the same person paid by the bank in good faith. This rule is intended to prevent the wrongdoer from having the opportunity to repeat his misdeeds. If the customer can establish that the bank itself was negligent in paying a forged or altered item, the bank cannot avail itself of a defense based upon the customer's failure to promptly examine and report.[5]

A customer is precluded from asserting a forged signature or alteration on a check after one year from the time the check and statement were made available to him, even though the bank was negligent. Forged indorsements

[5] Jackson v. First National Bank of Memphis, Inc., page 574

must be reported within three years. If a payor bank, as a matter of policy or public relations, waives its defense of tardy notification by its customer, it cannot thereafter hold the collecting bank or any prior party for the forgery.

In some situations a payor bank is subrogated to, or takes over, the rights of other parties in order to prevent unjust enrichment and to prevent loss to the bank by reason of its payment of a check or other item. This right arises in those cases in which the bank has made an improper payment, such as a payment in violation of a stop order. Three aspects of a payor bank's subrogation rights are important.

1. The bank is subrogated to the rights of any holder in due course on the item against the drawer. When a bank is sued for wrongful payment over a stop order, it can assert the defense that its customer, the drawer, did not suffer a loss because he would have been liable to a holder in due course whether the stop order was obeyed or not. Thus, even if payment had been stopped, the drawer would have had to make good to a holder in due course. To the extent necessary, the Code places the bank in the position of such holder as against the drawer.

2. The bank is subrogated to the rights of the payee or any other holder of the item against the drawer-customer. This relates to rights of the payee in the check or his rights under the transaction for which the check was issued. Again, assuming payment of a check over a stop order, the payee may have received the check in payment for defective goods. If the drawer retains the goods, he is probably obliged to pay at least a part of the agreed price. If the bank has paid the check, it is subrogated to the payee's claim against the drawer for a portion of the contract price and can recoup its loss to this extent.

3. The bank is subrogated to the rights of the drawer against the payee or any other holder in connection with the transaction which gave rise to the item. Here the bank, having improperly paid a check, takes over the rights of its own customer—the drawer—against the payee. If the drawer had been defrauded by the payee, for example, the bank, upon reimbursing the drawer, is subrogated to the latter's right to get back the money from the fraudulent payee.

BANK DEPOSITS AND COLLECTIONS CASES

Salsman (formerly Odgers) v. National Community Bank of Rutherford
246 A.2d 162 (N.J.) 1968

The plaintiff, a widow, retained a lawyer to handle matters relating to her husband's estate. She was the beneficiary of a profit sharing plan in a company in which her late husband had an interest. In payment of benefits under the plan, she received a cashier's check for $159,770.02, made out to her order by the First National City Bank. Her lawyer informed her that the check was not hers but belonged to the estate and that it must be kept in a separate estate account. He wrote on the back of the check"Pay to the order of the Estate of Arthur J. Odgers." At his request the plaintiff signed her name to complete the indorsement. After the plaintiff left the office, the lawyer added the words "Estate of Arthur J. Odgers—for deposit Harold Breslow, Trustee." Under this purported indorsement, Breslow's secretary wrote "For deposit Harold Breslow, Trustee." The lawyer then sent the check to the defendant bank for collection, and the proceeds were deposited in Breslow's account. There was no estate account in the defendant bank.

The lawyer later confessed and pleaded guilty to the charge of embezzlement. Some moneys were recovered, but the balance not yet recovered was $117,437.43. The plaintiff sought to recover this amount from the defendant bank.

BOTTER, J. . . . In the absence of defenses such as negligence, estoppel or ratification, the payee of a check is entitled to recover against a bank making collection from the drawee based upon a forged or unauthorized indorsement of a check. . . .

The check in question was indorsed by the payee, Mrs. Odgers, to the order of the Estate of Arthur J. Odgers. There was no valid indorsement thereafter by the estate of Arthur J. Odgers. . . .

The check in question could not be negotiated without an authorized indorsement of the special indorsee, the estate of Arthur J. Odgers. . . . "Any unauthorized signature is wholly inoperative as that of the person whose name is signed unless he ratifies it or is precluded from denying it . . . ." There is no evidence in this case which shows a ratification by Mrs. Odgers of the conduct of Breslow; there has been nothing shown to preclude her from denying the indorsements in question, and there is no evidence of any negligence on her part which contributed to the misapplication of the funds. . . .

Receiving the funds without a proper indorsement and crediting the funds to one not entitled thereto constitutes a conversion of the funds. A holder is one who receives an instrument which is indorsed to his order or in blank. The bank cannot be a holder, or a holder in due course without a valid indorsement of this check by the estate of Arthur J. Odgers. N.J.S. 12A:3-419(1) (c), N.J.S.A. provides that an instrument is converted when it is paid on a forged indorsement. N.J.S. 12A:1-201(43), N.J.S.A. provides that an unauthorized signature or indorsement is one made without authority (actual, implied or apparent) and includes a forgery. . . .

N.J.S. 12A:3-419(3), N.J.S.A. clearly implies the liability of a depositary or collecting bank in conversion when it deals with an instrument or its proceeds on behalf of one who is not the true owner, where the bank does not act in accordance with "reasonable commercial standards." Defendant did not act in accordance with reasonable commercial standards. . . .

In the present case there are sufficient facts to justify the conclusion that defendant bank is liable regardless of how we view the conduct of Mrs. Odgers in giving the check to Breslow. The bank was negligent in allowing funds to be deposited in Breslow's attorney's trust account without inquiry as to his authority to indorse the check as trustee on behalf of the estate. There were no circumstances to suggest any apparent authority in Breslow to do this. Moreover, the indorsement purportedly made on behalf of the estate was a "for deposit" indorsement, a restrictive indorsement. (N.J.S. 12A:3-205(c), N.J.S.A.) This is another fact which should have alerted the bank to a misapplication of the funds.

. . . N.J.S. 12A:3-419(3) and (4), N.J.S.A. clearly imply liability in conversion when a depositary bank fails to honor a restrictive indorsement, even though made by a party who is not that bank's immediate transferor. Thus, even if the indorsement for the estate had been authorized, defendant bank would be liable for failing to deposit the proceeds to the credit of the estate as required by that indorsement....

. . . It is sufficient to hold that the bank is liable for paying the instrument on an unauthorized indorsement, whether or not a forgery; that the alleged negligence of Mrs. Odgers cannot excuse the bank, since the bank did not comply with the reasonable standard of making inquiry into Breslow's authority to sign for the estate as a trustee; that, in any case, Mrs. Odgers was not negligent, and that even if the indorsement had been authorized the bank is liable for violating a restrictive indorsement.

For the foregoing reasons judgment shall be entered in favor of plaintiffs against defendant bank in the sum of $117,437.43, plus interest and costs.

Rock Island Auction Sales v. Empire Packing Co.

204 N.E.2d 721 (Ill.) 1965

The plaintiff sold cattle to the Empire Packing Co. and received a check in payment. The check was drawn and deposited on September 24, in the plaintiff's bank in Iowa. The check was received by the payor bank on September 27. The payor bank held the check for five days on assurance by Empire that sufficient funds would be deposited to cover it. Finally, on October 2 the bank marked the check "Insufficient Funds" and returned it by mail. The check was never paid, and a petition in bankruptcy was filed against Empire on November 7. The plaintiff filed action against the payor bank (Illinois National Bank and Trust Company) and Empire. The lower court ruled for the plaintiff, and the defendants appealed.

SCHAEFER, J. . . . The plaintiff's case against Illinois National Bank and Trust Company of Rockford (hereafter defendant) rests squarely on the ground that as the payor bank it became liable for the amount of the check because it held the check without payment, return or notice of dishonor, beyond the time limit fixed in section 4-302 of the Uniform Commercial Code....

Section 4-302 of the Uniform Commercial Code provides: "In the absence of a valid defense such as breach of a presentment warranty (subsection (1) of Section 4-207), settlement effected or the like, if an item is presented on and received by a payor bank the bank is accountable for the amount of (a) a demand item . . . if the bank . . . retains the item beyond midnight of the banking day of receipt without settling for it or . . . does not pay or return the item or send notice of dishonor until after its midnight deadline. . . . " Section 4-104 (h) of the Code defines the "midnight deadline" of a bank as midnight on the banking day following the day on which it received the item.

The important issues in the case involve the construction and validity of section 4-302. The defendant argues that the amount for which it is liable because of its undenied retention of the check beyond the time permitted by section 4-302 is not to be determined by that section, but rather under section 4-103 (5) which provides that "[t]he measure of damages for failure to exercise ordinary care in handling an item is the amount of the item reduced by an amount which could not have been realized by the use of ordinary care. . . ."

But the statute provides that the bank is accountable for the amount of the item and not for something else. "Accountable" is synonymous with "liable . . . ", and Section 4-302 uses the word in that sense. . . . The circuit court correctly held that the statute imposes liability for the amount of the item.

[Defendant contends] . . . that section 4-302 is invalid because it imposes a liability upon a payor bank for failing to act prior to its midnight deadline that is more severe than the liability which section 4-103(5) imposes upon a depositary bank or a collecting bank for the same default. Of course there are no such separate institutions as depositary, collecting and payor banks. All banks perform all three functions. The argument thus comes down to the proposition that the failure of a bank to meet its deadline must always carry the same consequence, regardless of the function that it is performing.

But the legislature may legitimately have concluded that there are differences in function and in circumstance that justify different consequences. Depositary and collecting banks act primarily as conduits. The steps that they take can only indirectly affect the determination of whether or not a check is to be paid, which is the focal point in the collection process. The legislature could have concluded that the failure of such a bank to meet its deadline would most frequently be the result of negligence, and fixed liability accordingly. The role of a payor bank in the collection process, on the other hand, is crucial. It knows whether or not the drawer has funds available to pay the item. The legislature could have considered that the failure of such a bank to meet its deadline is likely to be due to factors other than negligence, and that the relationship between a payor bank and its customer may so influence its conduct as to cause a conscious disregard of its statutory duty. The present case is illustrative. The defendant, in its position as a payor bank, deliberately aligned itself with its customer in order to protect that customer's credit and consciously disregarded the duty imposed upon it. The statutory scheme emphasizes the importance of speed in the collection process. A legislative sanction designed to prevent conscious disregard of deadlines can not be characterized as arbitrary or unreasonable, nor can it be said to constitute a legislative encroachment on the functions of the judiciary. . . .

Judgment affirmed.

Bank of Marin v. England, Trustee

352 F.2d 186 (1965)

Between August 27, 1963, and September 17, 1963, Marin Seafoods drew five checks in favor of Eureka Fisheries, payee, upon its account with the Bank of Marin, drawee-defendant, totaling $2,318.82. On September 26, before these checks had been presented for payment, Marin Seafoods filed a voluntary petition in bankruptcy. John M. England was appointed receiver and subsequently trustee in bankruptcy. He is the plaintiff in this lawsuit.

On the date of the filing of the petition, sums of money in excess of $3,200 were due and owing Marin Seafoods from customers for merchandise previously delivered. Beginning on the day after the filing of the petition, and continuing for several days, Marin Seafoods collected portions of these outstanding accounts receivable and deposited them in the company's commercial account at the bank. On October 2, 1963, the checks which Marin Seafoods had drawn and delivered to Eureka Fisheries prior to the filing of the petition were duly presented to the bank by Eureka Fisheries for payment and were paid.

At the time the bank paid these checks it had received no notice and had not otherwise obtained knowledge of the filing of the petition in bankruptcy. The bank was not informed of the pending bankruptcy proceeding until October 3, 1963, when it received a letter, dated October 2, 1963, from the receiver (England, plaintiff). This was one day after the bank had honored the checks referred to above.

The trustee applied to the referee for a "turnover order" to require the bank to pay over to him the amount paid to Eureka on October 2, or in the alternative to require Eureka to pay this amount. The referee held that the bank and Eureka were *jointly liable.* Eureka *paid* and demanded *contribution* from the bank. The bank appealed from the referee's ruling.

HAMLEY, J. . . . In seeking recovery of the stated amount from the bank, the trustee relied upon section 70, sub. a of the Act, (52 Stat. 879 (1938)), as amended, (11 U.S.C. 110, sub. a (1964)). This section provides, in pertinent part, that, upon his appointment and qualification, a trustee in bankruptcy shall be vested "by operation of law" with the title of the bankrupt as of the date of the filing of the petition initiating a proceeding in bankruptcy, with exceptions not here material, to described kinds of property wherever located. Among the kinds of property so described, the statute includes:

> . . . (5) property, including rights of action, which prior to the filing of the petition he (bankrupt) could by any means have transferred or which might have been levied upon and sold under judicial process against him, or otherwise seized, impounded, or sequestered: Provided, . . . (not here material).

This provision of the Act, considered by itself, would appear to support the trustee's application for a turnover order against the bank. The bank, however, contends that notwithstanding this statute, it should be held that a bank is not liable to a trustee in bankruptcy when, in good faith, and without actual knowledge of the bankruptcy proceedings, it honors the checks of a bankrupt depositor in the regular course of business after the adjudication of bankruptcy. . . .

The bank further argues that a court of bankruptcy is governed by equitable principles and, applying those principles to this case, must protect the bank from incurring liability for honoring checks of a depositor where it had no notice of the bankruptcy of the depositor.

Under the trustee's theory of the case the bank must, in order to avoid liability, keep itself informed of the possibility of bankruptcy proceedings involving a depositor. According to the bank, this will require it to keep advised momentarily of bankruptcy filings. This burden is enhanced by the fact that filing in any district court in the United States will have the same effect. The steps demanded for protection are cited as impractical and otherwise burdensome. . . .

Upon considering the respective arguments, we think the bank makes out a strong case for hardship and impracticability insofar as the timely discovery of bankruptcy proceedings involving depositors is concerned. We are not as certain that the problem is one which threatens great and unprotectable financial liability. The fact that our case, and *Rosenthal,* appear to be the only reported cases dealing with this particular problem is some indication that it is not one which will frequently confront banks. Moreover, it would seem that the risk, such as it is, may ordinarily be taken into account as a cost of the business and financed as such.

It is true that courts of bankruptcy exercise certain equity powers. But there is no room for equitable relief of a kind which is expressly foreclosed by the Act. . . .

The bank characterizes its position as analogous to a garnishee who has paid his creditor without notice of garnishment. A garnishee is not liable to the garnisher in such circumstances. . . . But, the analogy is inapplicable in our case because, in bankruptcy proceedings, the filing of the petition and the adjudication is deemed *notice to the world,* except where the Act requires more specific notice.

Affirmed.

Gibbs v. Gerberich

203 N.E.2d 851 (Ohio) 1964

The defendants, realtors, had sold property belonging to the plaintiffs but had allegedly failed to account to the plaintiffs for the proceeds of the sale. The money had been deposited in an escrow account at the bank. Plaintiffs brought suit for an accounting and the appointment of a receiver. The court issued an order on the bank restraining it from making payment from the escrow account. Prior to notice of the restraining order, the bank had received a check drawn on the account payable to one Hewit. This check was for the entire balance of the account. The bank had charged the check to defendant's account, but upon receipt of the restraining order, the bank restored the credit to the account. Hewit's check was returned to him unpaid. The lower court ruled that Hewit's check had not been paid and that the money in the escrow account belonged to the receiver for the purposes of distribution to the plaintiff and other creditor clients of the realtors.

DOYLE, J. In brief, we must determine whether a certain check cleared The First National Bank of Wadsworth, Ohio, and was or was not paid within the meaning of the provisions of the Uniform Commercial Code adopted by the Ohio Legislature; . . .

In the appeal of Hewit, the first assignment of error relates to this check. It is claimed that: "The check for . . . $9,579.76 was paid by the bank to the Hewits within the meaning of the Uniform Commercial Code of Ohio prior to the receipt of the restraining order and the receiver, therefore, has no right to said funds." . . .

The Ohio Code further provides:

(A) An item is finally paid by a payor bank when the bank has done any of the following, whichever happens first:
(3) completed the process of posting the item to the indicated account of the drawer, maker, or other person to be charged therewith; . . .

As we view the statutes in their bearing upon the assignment of error, the question for decision appears to be whether the check was paid prior to the bank's notice of the restraining order of the court, and one of the measuring points for determining whether the check was paid is whether the "process of posting" was completed.

In Section 4-109 of the Uniform Commercial Code—Bank Deposits and Collections (not incorporated in the Ohio Code)—the experts, whose combined talents created the Code, gave the following definition:

> The "process of posting" means the usual procedure followed by a payor bank in determining to pay an item and in recording the payment including one or more of the following or other steps as determined by the
> (a) verification of any signature;
> (b) ascertaining that sufficient funds are available;
> (c) affixing a "paid" or other stamp;
> (d) entering a charge or entry to a customer's account;
> (e) correcting or reversing an entry or erroneous action with respect to the item.

It is generally thought, and this court so holds, that the "process of posting" involves two basic elements: (1) a decision to pay, and (2) a recording of the payment.

In brief summary, we find that the check had been charged against the Gerberich escrow account undoubtedly prior to the receipt of the restraining order, but that before any decision to pay was made by the bank, the restraining order was served, and the bank then recredited the account. The check had not been perforated or otherwise cancelled.

Under these circumstances, we conclude that the check had been posted, but that the "process of posting" had not been completed, as there is no evidence indicating a decision of the bank to pay. The mere debiting of a customer's account does not per se indicate a decision to pay. The key point in a bank's completion of the "process of posting" is the completion of all of the steps followed in the particular bank's payment procedure. In the instant case, the "posting run" was not completed, and the day's posting had not been found to be in balance prior to the receipt of the restraining order. The check had not been "voided or cancelled," as it would have been if the "process of posting" had been completed. It appears, therefore, that the statutory "process of posting" had not been completed, and, as a consequence, the check had not been paid.

We reject the claim of the appellant Hewit "that the restraining order was of no avail and that this money belongs to the Hewits just as though it had been paid to them in cash over the counter."

It is obvious from the foregoing that we affirm that part of the trial court's judgment holding that this fund belongs to the receiver for the purposes of distribution.

Jackson v. First National Bank of Memphis, Inc.
403 S.W.2d 109 (Tenn.) 1966

This is an action to recover money from a bank, money which had been paid out on forged instruments. The suit was brought by Jackson, Trustee of a church, on behalf of the Church against the Bank. In 1963 the church opened an account which required two signatures for withdrawal—those of Cleve Jordan, Financial Secretary, and Jackson. For a period of about one year, Jordan forged Jackson's name on some fifty checks and used the money to gamble at the dog races. The Bank sent monthly statements to Jordan in his capacity as Financial Secretary. The Church discovered the fraud and brought suit against the Bank for the money. The trial court found for the Church, and the Bank appealed.

BEJACH, J. . . . [A] drawee bank which pays the check on a forged signature is deemed to have made the payment out of its own funds and not the depositor's, provided the depositor has not been guilty of negligence or fault that misled the bank. . . .

In the instant case, the negligence of the depositor relied on by the Bank is its failure to examine the checks and report the forgery, thus preventing a repetition thereof. The fallacy of this argument is that the checks were mailed to Cleve Jordan, Financial Secretary of the Church, who was the forger. He was an unfaithful servant, and obviously his knowledge and information on the subject would not be reported by him to the Church, nor imputed to it. He had been a faithful and trusted member of the Church and one of its officers for about twenty years, and, consequently, the Church cannot be held guilty of negligence in employing an unfaithful agent. The contention is made, however, that the church officials, other than Cleve Jordan, himself, should have called on Jordan for an accounting from time to time, and that the Church was negligent in its failure to perform this duty. The proof shows that the Church did from time to time call on Cleve Jordan for production of the checks and records of the Church, but that he made excuses, said he forgot to bring them, or made other excuses. Under these circumstances, in view of his previous good record and reputation, we cannot say that the Bank carried the burden of showing negligence on the part of the Church.

. . . Under the provisions of section 47-4-406, T.C.A. (Section 4-406 of the Uniform Commercial Code) subsection 2(b), a depositor is precluded by failure to examine the checks within fourteen days from asserting liability against the bank on account of unauthorized signature or alteration of a check paid by the bank in good faith, but subsection (3) of the same Code section provides: "The preclusion under subsection (2) does not apply if the customer establishes lack of ordinary care on the part of the bank paying the item(s)."

In *Farmers' and Merchants' Bank* v. *Bank of Rutherford* (905, 115 Tenn. 64, 88 S.W. 939, 112 Am.St.Rep. 817), the Supreme Court held that, "It is negligence in a drawee bank to pay a forged check drawn on it in the name of its customer, whose signature is well known to it, where the cashier does not examine the signature closely, but relies on the previous endorsements." It is argued on behalf of the Bank that such examination of the signature card, which admittedly was not made in the instant case, is not practical under modern banking methods. Such may be true as a practical matter, but, if so, the Bank, because of that fact, cannot escape the consequences and must, under that decision, be held guilty of negligence.

We think, however, that the Bank must be held to be guilty of negligence in another and much stronger aspect of the instant case. The Bank account here involved was that of a church, which obviously involved trust funds, and the countersignature of Milton Jackson, Trustee, whose signature has been forged, was required on all checks. In the case of *Fidelity and Deposit Co. of Maryland* v. *Hamilton Nat'l Bank* 23 Tenn.App. 20, 126 S.W.2d 359), . . . [we] . . . held that one who takes paper from a trustee importing upon its face its fiduciary character, is bound to inquire of the transferor the right to dispose of it. . . . Any adequate inquiry made in the instant case by the Bank would have disclosed the situation that Cleve Jordan was forging the name of Milton Jackson, Trustee, and would have prevented a repetition of such forgery.

There is another and a stronger reason why the Bank must be held guilty of negligence and held responsible for the result of the forgery here involved. All of the checks, recovery for which was granted in the instant case, were made payable to Cleve Jordan, personally; and many of them bear the endorsement of the Southland Racing Company, which is the corporation operating the dog racing track in Arkansas across the Mississippi River from Memphis. These circumstances, and especially the one that the checks were made payable to Cleve Jordan, personally, should have put the Bank on inquiry as to whether or not the funds represented by these checks were being withdrawn for unauthorized purposes. Any inquiry would have disclosed the true situation and prevented further depletion of the Church's bank account. The bank account being a trust fund, and the checks withdrawing same being made to one of the authorized signers of checks, was sufficient to put the Bank on notice that the funds were being improperly withdrawn, or should at least have required the Bank to make inquiry as to whether or not the withdrawals involved were authorized. . . .

Affirmed.

CHAPTER 29
REVIEW QUESTIONS AND PROBLEMS

1. *A* was a depositor in the B bank. Certain indorsements on checks drawn by him were forged, but he did not call the bank's attention to this until more than three years later. *A* claimed that he was excused from giving earlier notice. Would the bank be liable for honoring checks with forged indorsements?

2. *A*'s bank wrongfully dishonored two small checks which she had drawn. She brought action against the bank and recovered a judgment of $631.50 as follows: $1.50 for a telephone call to one of the payees; $130.00 for two weeks' lost wages; and $500.00 for illness, embarrassment, and incovenience. Would this judgment be upheld on appeal?

3. The A Construction Company had a checking account with the B Bank. A check was drawn on the company's account by an unauthorized person, and the bank honored the check. The same person had one time previously drawn a check without objection from A Company. The check in question was several months old when presented. Is the bank liable?

4. *A*, a used car dealer, had a checking account with the B Bank. The bank wrongfully dishonored three checks drawn by *A*. Is *A* entitled to

recover damages from his bank?

5.   *A,* a depositor in the B Bank, drew a check for $29.00 and had it certified. *A* then altered the check to make it read $2900.00 and gave it to a jeweler, *X,* in payment for a ring. As between *X* and the bank, who must suffer the loss?

6.   *A* is the holder of a check drawn by *B* on the Last National Bank. (*A* also has an account at Last National.) The check is deposited at the bank on a Monday. On that day *B's* account is overdrawn, but *B* has promised to make a substantial deposit, so the bank holds the check until Thursday. *B* does not make the deposit, and on Friday the bank returns the check to *A* marked "Insufficient Funds." Can *A* require the bank to make good on the check?

7.   *A* is the drawer of a check drawn on the Last National Bank. The check was drawn to the order of *B* in payment for a TV set. The set is defective, and *A* stops payment on the check. However, the bank by mistake honors the check. Would it matter whether the check was presented by *B* rather than one to whom *B* had indorsed it, insofar as the bank's position is concerned?

8.   *A* draws on the D Bank a check for $150 in favor of *P. P* holds the check for ninety days, and when he presents it, he finds that *A* has no money in his account. At the time the check was drawn, *A* had more than sufficient funds there to meet it. May *P* recover from *A* on the check?

9.   A check was sent to the X Bank for collection. X Bank, through the negligence of one of its employees, delayed in forwarding the check to the drawee bank. When the check was finally forwarded, the drawer's account was overdrawn, and the check was returned. Would the X Bank be liable to the depositor of the check?

10.   The drawer's signature to a check was forged. Neither the depositor nor any of the collecting banks has knowledge of the forgery. The payor bank honored the check. Against whom does the payor bank have recourse?

chapter 30

Secured Transactions: Security Interest

3-153. Introduction.   A secured transaction is one in which a borrower or a buyer gives security to a lender or seller that an obligation will be satisfied. Secured transactions occur at all levels of commerce. For example, manufacturers finance raw materials, retailers and wholesalers finance inventory, and consumers finance their purchases. In each of these cases the party who is in need of financial assistance might borrow the money needed for the purchase or obtain the needed financing from the seller. Although it is possible that the financing might be obtained simply on the credit of the buyer, it is most likely that the seller or lender would demand some security for the debtor's promise to pay.

There are many examples of secured transactions. One simple illustration is a *pledge* in which a borrower gives the physical possession of his property, e.g., a watch, to a lender as security for a loan. If the loan is not repaid, the lender can sell the watch in order to satisfy the debt. Stocks and bonds are frequently used as collateral in pledge transactions. However, in many transactions the pledge is not satisfactory as a security arrangement because it requires that possession must be delivered to the creditor. Therefore, security devices that allow the debtor to retain the possession and use of the property were developed. These devices give a creditor a security interest in the debtor's personal property so that the creditor can dispose of the debtor's property and thereby obtain satisfaction of a debt in the event of nonpayment. The names given to these devices such as chattel mortgages, conditional sales contracts, trust receipts, factor's liens, and assignment of accounts receivable continue to be used even though they have been replaced by a single security device under the Code: the *security interest.*

Article 9 of the Code—Secured Transactions—deals with the security interest in personal property. Its basic policy is to provide a simple, effective, and unified arrangement to meet the needs of modern secured financing transactions. The Code provides rules that are tailored to meet the financing requirements which will vary according to the type of property and the relationship between the parties to the transaction. In particular, consumers and farmers for reasons of established public policy are afforded some special considerations in their role as debtors who give security interest in their personal property, and the rules pertaining to these groups should be carefully noted.

3-154. The Scope of Article 9. Article 9 has replaced all of the former security devices with a single device—the security interest. It did not repeal such state laws as those regulating consumer installment sales and consumer loans. And although the Code covers consumer transactions, it does not purport to cover the field of consumer protection, which is left to other legislation such as the Uniform Consumer Credit Code.

Although Article 9 deals primarily with secured transactions, it also covers outright sales of certain types of property, namely accounts, contract rights, and chattel paper. Thus, a sale of the accounts receivable of a business must comply with the Code requirements to the same extent as would be the case if the accounts were used as security for a loan. One of the reasons for this inclusion is that a transfer of such items is most often made for security purposes.

Except for sales of accounts, contract rights, and chattel paper, the main test to be applied to determine whether a given transaction falls within the purview of Article 9 is whether it was intended to have effect as security.[1] Every transaction with such intent is covered. For example, a lease with option to buy is considered a security transaction rather than a lease if the requisite intent is present.

Certain transactions are expressly excluded from Article 9 coverage. The exclusions in general are transactions that are not basically of a commercial character. One important exclusion is liens given by state law for services and materials, as for example, the artisan's lien given to a man who repairs a car. The repairman has a lien on the car, but except to the extent that a question of its relative priority with security interests is involved, it is outside the scope of Article 9.

3-155. General Terminology. A "Security interest" is an interest in personal property or fixtures which secures either payment of money or performance of an obligation. The reference to fixtures is included because personal property is often affixed to real property in which event it is called a fixture. The security interest results from the execution by the parties of a "security agreement" covering the debtor's "collateral"—the personal property in which a security interest exists. The parties to the security agreement are the "debtor" who owes the obligation and is giving the security and the "secured party," lender, seller, or other person in whose favor there is a security interest. Before a security interest is effective as between the parties, it must *attach* to the collateral, and before it is effective to give priority over the rights of third parties, the security interest must be *perfected*. Attachment (Section 3-161) is the means whereby the secured party acquires rights in the collateral; perfec-

[1] In re Wheatland Electric Products Co., page 590

tion (Section 3-163) is the method whereby the secured party is given priority over claims of third parties and is often accomplished by a public filing.

3-156. Classifications of Collateral.   Collateral may be classified according to its physical makeup into (1) tangible, physical property or goods, (2) purely intangible property such as an account receivable, and (3) property which has physical existence, such as a negotiable instrument, but which is simply representative of a contractual obligation. Each type of collateral presents its own peculiar problems and the framework of Article 9 is structured on the peculiarities of each type. There may be a security interest not only in the collateral itself, but also in the proceeds of the collateral—that which the debtor receives when he sells or otherwise disposes of it. If the collateral is returned to the debtor or repossessed by him, the security interest which existed originally may be reinstated. The method of perfecting the security interest will depend upon the classification of the collateral.

3-157. Tangible Property: Goods.   Four classifications are established: consumer goods, equipment, farm products, and inventory. In determining the classification of any particular item of collateral in the form of goods, it is necessary to take into account not only the physical attributes but also the status of the debtor who is either buying the property or using it as security for a loan and the use the debtor will make of the goods.

    Consumer goods.   Goods fall into this classification if they are used or bought primarily for personal, family, or household purposes. The particular significance of the consumer status in a secured transaction stems from the public policy of protecting a person who is not generally accustomed to analyzing carefully all aspects of his transactions and reading carefully all the papers and documents involved. As noted previously, this public policy is reflected in a variety of state statutes regulating small loans and retail installment sales. The perfection of a security interest in such goods may be by attachment without the requirement of filing. Note should also be taken that special treatment is afforded upon default by a consumer.

    Equipment.   Goods which are used or bought for use primarily in a business, in farming, in a profession, or by a nonprofit organization or government agency fall within this category.[2] Also included are goods which do not meet the above specifications but also do not qualify as consumer goods, inventory, or farm products. Thus, the category is something of a "catchall" so that goods which otherwise defy classification will be treated as equipment. It is important to note that equipment as well as other goods may become attached to realty so as to constitute a "fixture." There may thus be questions of priority as between the holder of a security interest in the fixture and the party, such as a mortgagee, who has security in the land. Special rules relate to the method of perfecting a security interest in fixtures (See Section 3-174).

    Inventory.   Inventory consists of goods which are held by a person for sale or lease or to be furnished under a contract of service, whether they be raw materials, work in process, completed goods, or material used or consumed in a business. The basic test to be applied in determining whether

---

[2] National Bank of Commerce v. First National Bank & Trust Co., page 591

goods are inventory is whether they are held for immediate or ultimate sale or lease, but the test must be applied with caution. The reason for the inclusion of materials used or consumed in a business, e.g., supplies of fuel and boxes and other containers to be used in packaging the goods, is that they will soon be used up or consumed in a course of production which results in an end product which will be sold. Most often the inventory will be goods offered for sale by a merchant who is financing his business through the medium of a security interest in the inventory.

Farm products. This category includes: crops and livestock, supplies used or produced in farming operations, the products of crops or livestock in their unmanufactured state (e.g., ginned cotton, wool, milk, and eggs)—provided that such items are in the possession of a debtor who is engaged in farming operations. Farm products are *not* equipment or inventory. Note that goods cease to be farm products and must therefore be reclassified when: (1) they are no longer in the farmer's possession, or (2) they have been subjected to a manufacturing process. Thus, when the farmer delivers his farm products to a marketing agency for sale or to a frozen-food processor as raw materials, the products in the hands of the other party are inventory. Likewise, if the farmer maintained a canning operation, the canned product would be inventory even though it remained in his possession.

The proper classification of goods in other instances as well is to be determined on the basis of their nature and intended use to be made of them by the debtor. For example, a television set in a dealer's warehouse is inventory to the dealer and as such may be covered by an inventory-financing arrangement. When the set is sold on a conditional sale contract to a consumer-customer, it is a consumer good in the consumer's hands. The customer is the debtor; the dealer is the secured party; and the collateral is the specific television set. If an identical set were sold on the same terms to the owner of a tavern to be used for entertaining his customers, the set would be equipment in the hands of the tavern owner.

3-158. "Semi-intangible" Collateral. Three types of property-paper are included for convenience under this heading: documents of title, chattel paper, and instruments. They comprise various categories of paper used in commerce which are either negotiable or to some extent dealt with as though negotiable. They are all evidenced by an "indispensable writing," and are representative of obligations and rights.

Documents of title. Included under this heading are bills of lading, warehouse receipts and any other document which in the regular course of business or financing is treated as sufficient evidence that the person in possession of it is entitled to receive, hold, and dispose of the document and the goods it covers.

Chattel paper. Chattel paper refers to a writing or writings which evidence both (1) an obligation to pay money, and (2) a security interest in or a lease of specific goods. The chattel paper is *itself* a security agreement. A security agreement in the form of a conditional sale contract, for example, is often executed in connection with a negotiable note or a series of notes. The group of writings—the contract plus the note—taken together as a composite constitute "chattel paper." A typical situation involving chattel paper as collateral is one in which a secured party who has obtained it in a transaction with his customer may wish to borrow against it in his own financing. To illustrate: A dealer sells an electric generator to a customer on a conditional sales contract, and the customer signs a negotiable installment note. At this point the contract is the security agreement: the dealer is the secured party; the customer is the debtor; and the generator is the collateral-equipment. The dealer needing funds for working capital transfers the contract and the note to a finance company as security for a loan. In the transaction between dealer and finance company, the contract and note are the collateral-chattel paper; the finance company is the secured party; the dealer is the debtor; and the customer is now designated as the "account debtor."

     Instrument. To be distinguished from chattel paper, an instrument means (1) a negotiable instrument, (2) a security such as stocks and bonds, or (3) any other writing which evidences a right to the payment of money and which is not itself a *security agreement or lease.* In order to qualify as an instrument, the "other writing" must also be one which is in ordinary course of business transferred by indorsement or assignment. Thus, the classification includes in addition to negotiable instruments those which are recognized as having some negotiable attributes. Instruments are frequently used as collateral and they present certain problems in this connection because of their negotiable character.

3-159. Intangibles. Under this heading are three items: (1) accounts, (2) contract rights and (3) "general intangibles." They are distinguished from the "semi-intangibles" discussed in the preceding section by virtue of the fact that they are not represented by an indispensable writing.

     Account. Account means any right to payment arising out of the sale of goods or the rendition of services which is not evidenced by either an instrument or chattel paper. It is an account receivable and represents a right to payment earned by the seller's performance—the sale of goods or services actually rendered.

     Contract right. This is a right to payment under a contract, which right has not yet been earned, but rather is to be earned by performance under an existing contract. A contract does exist and when the party performs his obligations under the contract, his potential account becomes an account receivable.

     General intangibles. This heading includes miscellaneous types of intangible personal property and contractual rights which may be used as commercial security and which do not fall within any of the preceding five classifications of intangible or semi-intangible property. Examples are goodwill, literary rights, patents, and copyrights.

3-160. The Security Agreement. The security agreement must be in writing, unless the security arrangement is a possessory one and the secured party is in possession of the collateral. The only other formal requirement is that the agreement be signed by the debtor and that it contain a description of the collateral sufficient to reasonably identify it. The security agreement may contain many other provisions and the forms in general use include also a statement of the amount of the obligation and the terms of repayment, the debtor's duties in respect to the collateral such as insuring it, and the rights of the secured party on default. In general, the parties can include such terms and provisions as they may deem appropriate to their particular transaction, but there are a few limitations on this freedom to contract in the interest of fairness to the debtor.

3-161. Attachment.   It is not sufficient to merely create a security interest; it must "attach" to the collateral. A security interest attaches only after three events have occurred: (1) the security agreement has been executed, (2) the secured party has given value, and (3) the debtor has rights in the collateral. They may occur in any order. For example, a security agreement may be executed and the secured party may give value, e.g., loan money, to the debtor before the debtor acquires rights in the collateral. "Attachment" is the legal term used to describe the phenomenon whereby the secured party acquires rights in the collateral.

Value for purpose of attachment is defined somewhat differently than it is in commercial paper. Basically, value means that a secured party has furnished to the debtor any consideration sufficient to support a simple contract. The secured party also gives value if his rights are acquired in return for a binding commitment to extend credit to the debtor, or if he acquires his rights as security for, or in total or partial satisfaction of, a preexisting claim which he has against the debtor. In most cases the giving of value by the secured party will be quite obvious. A dealer sells a piece of equipment to a merchant: the delivery of the equipment is the value. A bank loans $10,000 to a merchant and takes a security interest in his inventory: the loan of money constitutes the value.

The third requirement for attachment is that the debtor have *rights in the collateral.* A debtor has no rights: (1) in crops until they are planted or otherwise become growing crops, or in the young of livestock until they are conceived; (2) in fish until they are caught; (3) in oil, gas, or minerals until they are extracted; (4) in timber until it is cut. A debtor has no rights in an account until it comes into existence—until goods have been sold there could not be an account receivable. While a merchant could enter into an agreement to assign future accounts to a secured party, the latter's security interest could not *attach* until the accounts actually came into existence.

The security agreement may provide that property acquired by the debtor at any later time shall also secure the obligation covered by the security agreement. This means that if such a clause were included in the security agreement, *after-acquired property* of the debtor would be additional security for the secured party—i.e., as soon as the debtor acquires rights in other property a security interest would attach to such property in favor of the secured party. This obviously binds a debtor quite severely and the Code places a limitation on the effect of after-acquired property clauses in relation to crops and to consumer goods on the theory that such clauses are best suited to commercial transactions and might work an undue hardship on a consumer or a farmer. Thus, no security interest can attach under an after-acquired property clause: (1) to crops which become such more than one year after the execution of the security agreement; or (2) to consumer goods which are given as additional security unless the consumer obtains the goods within ten days after the secured party gives value.

3-162. The "Floating Lien." As noted above, the security agreement entered into between the secured party and the debtor may provide that property acquired in the future by the debtor will also be collateral in which the secured party will have a security interest.[3] The agreement may also provide that future advances to the debtor will be covered by the collateral in which the secured party has a security interest. In addition the debtor may be allowed to have absolute control over the collateral without impairing the security interest of the secured party. Thus a secured party may have a security interest in the debtor's future and existing assets even though the debtor has the freedom to use or dispose of the collateral. The secured party and the debtor can enter into a security agreement which provides for these features and, as will be discussed later, can give public notice that they will be dealing on these terms. This means that the secured party who is financing a retailer can maintain a security interest in the debtor's constantly changing inventory and also have a security interest in the proceeds of the sale of inventory in the debtor's ordinary course of business. His security interest will be protected against the claims of third parties by virtue of the public notice that such financing arrangement has been made. This concept is referred to as a "floating lien." The amount of the debt and the actual collateral can be constantly changing if the security agreement is so worded as to include after-acquired property and future advances of money. This sort of arrangement could have the effect of tying up most of the assets of a debtor by the secured party. This possibility is considered to be acceptable with regard to business financing but is restricted insofar as consumers and farmers are concerned. Businessmen can encumber property to be obtained in the future, but farmers and consumers are limited as noted above.

PERFECTION OF THE SECURITY INTEREST

3-163. In General. The security agreement provides for the creation of the security interest in the debtor's collateral as between the secured party and the debtor, provided that the security interest has attached to the collateral. This is not sufficient, however, to give the secured party the protection he desires. He is not necessarily protected against other persons who may claim an interest in the collateral. Such claims could arise in a variety of circumstances and might well defeat the secured party's interest. The debtor's creditors might attach the collateral in his possession and have it sold to satisfy their claims against him. The debtor may subsequently give a security interest in the collateral to another person. The debtor might sell the collateral to another person who was not aware of the security interest. Another possibility is that the debtor would become bankrupt, and the collateral would become an asset of his bankrupt estate. In any of these situations the secured party stands to lose the security in the collateral.

In order to achieve maximum protection of his security interest, the secured party must "perfect" his security interest. The concept of perfection is primarily based upon giving notice that the secured party may have a security interest in the debtor's collateral. If such notice is given, persons dealing with

---

[3] Grain Merchants of Indiana v. Union Bank & Savings Co., page 593

the debtor would be aware of the fact that his property may be encumbered, and they could take this into account in their dealings with him.

The simplest way to give notice of a security interest is for the secured party to take possession of the collateral. If the collateral is a negotiable instrument, the only way in which complete protection could be afforded the secured party would be for him to possess it. The pledge of property is one method of perfecting a security interest.

A second method of perfection and the most usual one is for the secured party to file a "financing statement" in the proper central or local office designated for that purpose. This has the effect of giving notice that the debtor and the secured party have made an arrangement for secured financing. Any person interested can determine from the public records that the debtor may have encumbered his property, and if he desires more explicit information could contact the debtor for further details.

The third method of perfection is that which is accomplished simply by the attachment of the security interest without any further action being required. This method is restricted to transactions involving installment sales to consumers and to sales of farm equipment that has a purchase price of $2,500 or less.

Several factors must be taken into account in determining which of the three methods of perfection is appropriate in any given transaction: (1) the kind of collateral in which a security interest was created, (2) the use the debtor intends to make of the collateral, and (3) the status of the debtor in relation to the secured party.

It should be noted that even a perfected security interest is subordinate to some third-party rights. For example, a person who repairs or improves the collateral may have a lien for his services and materials that will be superior to the secured party's interest. In general, a security interest will be inferior to a prior perfected security interest in the same collateral. In the case of inventory collateral, a buyer from the debtor in the ordinary course of business will obtain clear title to the goods.[4]

In the main, however, the holder of a perfected security interest will prevail in his rights in the collateral. On the other hand, an unperfected security interest is in general subordinate to the claims of others who acquire an interest in the collateral without knowledge of the unperfected security interest, even though it is subsequently perfected. Also, a "lien creditor" is preferred over the unperfected interest if he becomes such without knowledge of the security interest and before it is perfected.

A "lien creditor" is to be distinguished from an ordinary creditor. He is a creditor who by legal process has attached or levied upon the collateral and thereby acquired a lien against it. Trustees in bankruptcy, equity receivers, and assignees for the benefit of creditors are included within the definition.

3-164. Perfection by Possession. The possession of the collateral by the secured party gives notice of his security interest—hence no public filing is required. As noted previously, the possessory security interest does not require a written security agreement. Therefore, this is the simplest method of handling a secured transaction, but it has very definite limitations in practice. In

---

[4] Al Maroone Ford, Inc. v. Manheim Auto Auction, Inc., page 595

most secured transactions the debtor will want to use the collateral either as a consumer or as a manufacturer or merchant. Accordingly, the possessory security interest is appropriate primarily in those situations where the debtor does not need or desire the use of the collateral; where the collateral is of such nature that it does not have a practical utility to the debtor; or where it is the only feasible method of giving the required notice and protection.

Possession is the required method of perfection of a security interest in instruments and is the optional method in the case of collateral consisting of goods, negotiable documents of title, and chattel paper. However, possession is the only method whereby complete protection in documents and chattel paper can be obtained since: (1) the rights of holders to whom a document has been negotiated by the debtor will prevail over the secured party, even though there has been a filing; and, (2) the purchaser of chattel paper from the debtor is given such protection if he takes without *actual notice* of the security interest, gives new value, and takes possession in the ordinary course of his business.

However, in the case of instruments the secured party has a perfected security interest for a period of 21 days after the security interest attaches even though he does not take possession. The grace period applies only if the secured party gave new value to the debtor—it would not apply if the security interest in the instrument were given to buttress an existing obligation. Also, for the grace period to apply it is necessary that there be a *written* security agreement. The grace period is a substantial benefit to the parties and is in keeping with normal commercial necessity, but, unless he takes possession of the instrument, the secured party's rights will be defeated if the debtor transfers the instrument to a holder in due course during the 21-day period. It is to be recalled that the basic characteristic of instruments is their negotiability.

A 21-day grace period during which the security interest is protected against creditors of the debtor without possession or filing is also provided in the case of *negotiable documents.* The same risk exists that the documents may be negotiated to a good faith holder, who, of course, would prevail and the same requirements of a written security agreement and new value by the secured party apply.

Special considerations are required if a negotiable document of title has been issued covering goods, since there could theoretically be a security interest in both the *goods* and a *document* such as a warehouse receipt or bill of lading which *represents the goods.* This problem is resolved by a provision that no separate security interest can exist in the goods and at the same time in the document, during the period that the goods are in the *possession of the issuer* of a negotiable document. Therefore the creditor with a security interest in the document prevails. Possession of goods by a bailee gives notice to any potential financer or purchaser that a document of title may be outstanding and that he should proceed with caution.

A different rule applies if the goods in the hands of a bailee are covered by a *nonnegotiable* document or if no document has been issued. In these circumstances, a security interest in goods in the hands of a bailee may be perfected: (1) by issuance of a document in the name of the secured party, (2) by giving the bailee proper notice of the secured party's interest, or (3) by filing as to the goods themselves.

For a variety of commercial reasons it may be necessary or desirable that the secured party temporarily release possession of the collateral to the debtor. Since the release is of short duration, it would be cumbersome to require a filing. The Code therefore provides that a security interest *remains perfected* for a period of 21 days without filing where a secured party having a *perfected security interest* releases the collateral to the debtor. This grace period applies only to (1) an instrument, (2) a negotiable document, and (3) goods in the hands of a bailee and not covered by a negotiable document of title. It applies only to a secured party who already has a perfected security interest. The purposes for which the collateral may be released to the debtor, in the case of *goods* or *documents* representing the goods, are limited to making them available to the debtor (1) for the purpose of ultimate sale or exchange, or (2) for purposes such as of loading, unloading, storing, shipping, transshipping, manufacturing, processing, or otherwise dealing with them in a manner preliminary to their sale or exchange.

In the case of a temporary release of an *instrument* to the debtor, the purpose must be to enable the debtor to make a presentation of it, collect it, renew it, obtain registration of a transfer or to make an ultimate sale or exchange. The risk attendant upon such a release—an improper or unauthorized negotiation to a holder or sale to a bona fide purchaser by the debtor— has been previously discussed.

3-165. Perfection by Filing—the "Financing Statement." The most common method of perfecting a security interest is by filing a "financing statement." The financing statement, which is to be distinguished from the *security agreement,* is a document signed by both the debtor and the secured party which contains a description of the collateral and indicates that debtor and secured party have entered into a security agreement and gives their addresses. Simple forms are available which contain spaces for additional provisions as agreed upon by the parties, but this basic information is all that is required. If crops or fixtures constitute the collateral, then the financing statement must include a description of the real estate concerned.

A financing statement is not a substitute for a security agreement, but a security agreement may be filed as a financing statement if it contains the required information and is signed by both parties, but the converse is not true.[5] However, filing the security agreement would make public, information which the parties might prefer to have remain confidential, and for this reason there will usually be a separate financing statement.

The Code is based upon a system of "notice filing," which means that the purpose of filing is only to give notice that the secured party who filed it may have a security interest in the described collateral. A person searching the records therefore obtains minimal information, and further inquiry from the parties to the financing statement would be required to obtain more complete information. A procedure is established for such disclosure by the secured party at the request of the debtor.

The financing statement may provide a maturity or expiration date, but more often it is silent on this point, since the statement usually will not mention the debt or obligation. In the absence of such date, the filing is effective for

[5] American Card Co. v. H.M.H. Co., page 597.

a period of five years, subject to being renewed by the filing of a continuation statement signed by the secured party. If so renewed, it continues the effectiveness of the original statement for another five years. The presence in the records of a financing statement constitutes a burden upon the debtor since it reveals to all persons with whom he may be dealing that his property is or may be subject to the claims of others. Therefore, the Code provides for the filing of a *termination statement* to clear the record when the secured party is no longer entitled to a security interest, as where the debtor has completely satisfied the obligation for which the security interest was given. Failure of the secured party to send a termination statement within ten days after written demand by the debtor subjects him to a $100 penalty and also renders him liable for any loss occasioned to the debtor.

As noted previously, filing a financing statement is *required* in order to perfect a nonpossessory security interest in most secured transactions. However, filing is not required to perfect a security interest in transactions concerning certain purchase-money security interests involving consumers and farmers. This exemption is discussed in the next section dealing with perfection by attachment. Filing is also not required in the case of an assignment of accounts or contract rights where assignments to the same assignee are not a significant part of the outstanding accounts or contract rights of the assignor. Thus, the isolated transaction is exempted.[6]

The Code provides three alternative methods in regard to the place where the financing statement is to be filed. Filing is either central, which means one place of filing in each state, or local, which refers to a county filing, or a combination of both. Each state selects one of the three alternative filing systems.

One system is to have all financing statements filed centrally except for local filing where the collateral is or is to become a fixture. A second system is local filing for fixtures, local filing for farm-related collateral and consumer goods, and central filing for all other collateral. The third alternative is like the second except that local filing is required *in addition* to central filing for certain statements that are required to be filed centrally.[7]

The Code makes special provisions for goods that have a certificate of title. The filing requirements of the Code do not apply and the usual method of indicating a security interest is to have it noted on the certificate of title.

3-166. Perfection by attachment.   Perfection based upon attachment of the security interest to the collateral is a very restricted concept. It is limited to transactions involving installment sales to consumers and sales of farm equipment having a purchase price of $2,500 or less. The transaction must be a purchase-money security interest. In such transactions the secured party obtains a perfected security interest without filing a financing statement. The reason for this rule is a practical one. The volume of transactions within this category is so great that a filing requirement would be extremely burdensome. The protection afforded the secured party is limited in this type of perfection. He is protected against the claims of creditors of the debtor and from others to whom the farmer or consumer debtor may give a security interest in the

---

[6] Citizens & Southern Nat. Bank v. Capital Const. Co., page 598
[7] Sequoia Machinery, Inc. v. Jarrett, page 599

collateral, but he is *not* protected against the rights of a good-faith purchaser from the debtor. If a person buys the collateral from the debtor without knowledge of the security interest and for his own family or household purposes or his own farming operation, he will take the collateral free of the security interest. The secured party can obtain protection against this risk by filing a financing statement if he wishes to do so. The exemption from the filing requirement does not apply if the collateral is a motor vehicle which is required to be licensed.

3-167. Purchase-Money Security Interests.   The purchase-money concept has application to transactions other than in consumer goods and farm equipment. It relates to any transaction in which a security interest is taken or retained in collateral in connection with the purchase thereof. Such interest is available to either the seller or the party who makes the funds available for the purchase, provided the funds are actually so used. Several characteristics are peculiar to the purchase-money transaction. A ten-day grace period, following the date upon which the debtor receives possession of the collateral, is provided, during which a secured party has some protection without filing, in those cases where filing is required for perfection. The secured party must, however, file *within* the ten-day period. The protection during such prefiling period is limited: it gives priority only over the rights of (1) transferees in bulk from the debtor, and (2) lien creditors to the extent that such rights arise between the time the purchase-money security interest attaches and the time of filing. It is to be noted that the secured party is *not* protected against: (1) a sale by the debtor to another party, or (2) a secured transaction wherein the collateral is given as security for a loan. Other significant features of the purchase-money security interest will be discussed in the next chapter.

3-168. Proceeds.[8]   The debtor may sell or otherwise dispose of the collateral with or without the authority, (as provided in the security agreement) to do so. In such event the secured party has an interest in the "identifiable proceeds"—that which the debtor receives when he sells, exchanges, collects, or otherwise disposes of the collateral. The proceeds are either (1) "cash proceeds"—money, checks, etc., or (2) "noncash proceeds." In the latter category is the account receivable the debtor obtained when he sold the collateral on credit.

Two situations must be considered: (1) where the debtor has the authority under the security agreement to dispose of the collateral as in the case of inventory, and (2) where the debtor unauthorizedly disposes of it as in the case of a sale of equipment. In either situation, the secured party has an interest in the *proceeds;* but in the former he loses his security interest in the *collateral* which is sold in the ordinary course of business, while in the latter he retains a security interest in the collateral and thus has a security interest in *both* the collateral *and* the proceeds.

The security interest in proceeds is based upon the interest in the primary collateral, hence it comes into existence whether or not provision is made therefore in the security agreement; and even though the security agreement may have prohibited disposition.

[8] Quigley and Federation Agricultural Credit Corporation v. Caron et al., page 601.

The financing statement may provide for a security interest in proceeds in which event no further filing is required; the original filing constitutes all that is necessary for *perfection* of a security interest in the proceeds. If (1) the financing statement covering the original collateral did *not* provide for proceeds, or (2) if the security interest was perfected by possession or attachment rather than by filing, a perfected security interest in proceeds continues for ten days provided the secured party: (1) files a financing statement covering the proceeds *within* the ten-day period, or (2) he takes possession of the proceeds.

The debtor may in the course of his business have sold the collateral (inventory) and then received it back either (1) by voluntary act on the part of his customer who was not satisfied with it, or (2) by repossession from a defaulting customer, or (3) by exercising the rights given to him under Article 2-Sales—to reclaim the goods or stop them in transit. (See Section 3-44.) In general, the secured party's security interest attaches to the returned or repossessed goods and continues to be perfected in such goods without further action. However, there are significant priority problems in connection with returned or repossessed goods. Other persons may be financing the seller's business besides the party who has a security interest in his inventory—e.g., one who purchases the chattel paper arising from the sale and one who purchases the account receivable arising therefrom. These problems will be discussed in the next chapter.

Special provisions relate to the secured party's interest in proceeds if the debtor becomes involved in bankruptcy or other insolvency proceedings. In general, the secured party is entitled to reclaim from the trustee in bankruptcy proceeds which can be identified as relating to the original collateral, including cash proceeds which are identifiable—i.e., have not been commingled with other money or deposited in a bank account prior to the insolvency proceedings. Checks which have not been deposited by the debtor can also be reclaimed. If the cash (money and checks) proceeds are no longer identifiable because they have been commingled or deposited, the secured party nonetheless has a perfected security interest in the debtor's cash or bank account, but subject to the following limitations: (1) it is limited to a maximum of the amount of any cash proceeds received by the debtor within ten days prior to the commencement of the bankruptcy proceedings, (2) less the amount of any cash proceeds which the debtor may have paid to the secured party during the ten-day period, and (3) subject to any existing right of set-off, as where an obligation may be owing from the secured party to the debtor.

The foregoing constitutes a general picture of the secured transaction including the creation, attachment, and perfection of a security interest. The specific application of the rules of Article 9 as well as a delineation of the rights, duties, and obligations of the secured parties and debtors is determined largely by (1) the nature of the collateral and the use to be made of it by the debtor, and (2) the type of transaction. The next chapter is concerned with priorities, default, and the remedies of the parties.

SECURED TRANSACTIONS: SECURITY INTEREST CASES

In re Wheatland Electric Products Co.
237 F.Supp. 820 (1964)

Burroughs Corp. leased a machine to Wheatland Electric Products Co. for a term of one year and to continue thereafter until terminated. In the lease, the list price was stipulated and a monthly rental was set. The lease contained an option to purchase with a provision that 75 percent of the rentals would be applied toward the purchase. The lease was subsequently extended. Wheatland filed a petition in bankruptcy and Burroughs filed a petition for reclamation of the machine in the bankruptcy proceedings. The referee refused the petition on the ground that the lease was a security agreement and since it had not been filed was invalid against the trustee in bankruptcy.

MILLER, J. . . . The question presented by the Petition for Review is whether the lease was intended as security and is to be determined by the facts of the case. In determining the intent of the parties, we may look only to the language of the lease itself, which provided that "there are no understandings, agreements, representations or warranties, express or implied, not specified herein, respecting this lease or the equipment . . . hereinabove described."

The Code provides that "the inclusion of an option to purchase does not of itself make the lease one intended for security." . . .

This language of the Code describes what was formerly known in Pennsylvania as a bailment lease, a security device by which one desiring to purchase an article of personal property, but not wishing to pay for it immediately, could secure possession of it with the right to use and enjoy it as long as the rental was paid and with the further right to become the owner, upon completing the installment payments, by the payment of an additional nominal sum.

The Courts, in referring to the term "nominal consideration," frequently use it interchangeably with the sum of $1.00 or some other small amount.

In the instant case, the additional amount which Wheatland was to pay to secure ownership of the machinery should it choose to exercise the option was a minimum of 25 percent of the list price, or $2,006.25. That amount is not a nominal consideration for the right to become the owner of the equipment, but represents a substantial proportion of the purchase price. . . .

Because we find that the leasing agreement between Burroughs and Wheatland was not one intended for security within the terms of the Uniform Commercial Code, Burroughs was not required to file a financing statement to perfect its interest and to maintain its right to reclamation.

For this reason, the Order of the Referee in Bankruptcy will be reversed and the case remanded to the Referee for proceedings consistent with this Opinion.

National Bank of Commerce v. First National Bank & Trust Co.

446 P.2d 277 (Okla.) 1968

One Leigh requested Case, proprietor of an auto repair shop in Tulsa, to help him obtain an Avanti sports car and agreed to pay him $100 plus expenses for his aid. Case located such a car in Kansas and purchased it with his own check. He brought it back to Tulsa and Leigh gave him his check in the amount of the purchase price plus $100. The check was dishonored for insufficient funds and Case repossessed the car. Case borrowed money from the First National Bank (FNB) to cover the check he had given to the Kansas dealer.

He informed the bank that the car would be used in his business. On October 20, the loan was made and the bank centrally filed a financing statement covering "equipment." (In Oklahoma there is central filing for "equipment" and local filing for "consumer goods.")

At the same time Leigh arranged with the National Bank of Commerce (NBC) a loan to pay for the car with the understanding that the bank would issue a cashier's check payable to Leigh and Case jointly. This arrangement was confirmed by a telephone conversation with Case who thereupon released the car to Leigh.

However, the National Bank of Commerce made a mistake and instead of issuing a joint cashier's check credited the proceeds of the loan to Leigh's account. The bank made a local filing of its financing statement on October 30. Leigh withdrew his account from NBC and departed to parts unknown. The lower court held that the claim of the FNB was superior to that of NBC and the latter appealed.

HODGES, J. . . . Several sections of 12A O.S.1961, the Uniform Commercial Code, are involved in this case. . . .

§ 9-307 provides that a buyer in ordinary course of business takes free of a security interest created by his seller even though the security interest is perfected and even though the buyer knows of its existence (with certain exceptions not applicable here).

§ 9-312(4) provides that a purchase money security interest in collateral other than inventory has priority over a conflicting security interest in the same collateral if the purchase money security interest is perfected at the time the debtor receives possession of the collateral or within ten days thereafter. . . .

§ 9-109 provides in pertinent part that goods are "consumer goods" if they are used or bought for use primarily for personal, family or household purposes; that they are "equipment" if they are used or bought for use primarily in business; and that they are "inventory" if they are held by a person who holds them for sale. In the Uniform Commercial Code comments following § 9-109, it is said of "inventory" that "Implicit in the definition is the criterion that the prospective sale is in the ordinary course of business." Under this section, the terms defined are mutually exclusive—that is, goods may belong to only one class at a given time. Also, "equipment" is a sort of residuary classification, in that goods that are not included in the definitions of inventory, farm products or consumer goods are classified as "equipment."

It is agreed that the primary issue in this case is the classification of the Avanti as equipment, consumer goods or inventory, to determine the proper place of filing. If it was equipment, then FNB perfected its security interest by properly filing in Oklahoma County on October 20th. If it was consumer goods, FNB filed in the wrong county on October 20th, and its interest is inferior to the NBC security interest which was perfected by the filing in Tulsa County on October 30th. If it was inventory, even though the FNB financing statement was properly filed in Oklahoma County on October 20th, still the NBC interest is superior if Bill Leigh was a buyer in the ordinary course of business, under § 9-307. . . .

. . . NBC argues that the court erred in classifying the Avanti as equipment, and not as consumer goods or inventory, under § 9-109. In this connection, the only direct evidence as to the use to which the Avanti would be put after the Cases repossessed it from Leigh on October 15th was the testimony of Mrs. Case that they already had two family cars, and planned to use the Avanti as a company car in their business. This puts the Avanti squarely within the definition of "equipment" found in § 9-109. NBC argues with some force that it is unreasonable and illogical to suppose that a man engaged in an automobile repair business would buy a "very fancy Studebaker," an "unusual type of car," such as the Avanti, for use as a company car. This argument would bear more weight if the record showed that the Cases voluntarily and intentionally acquired the Avanti, but such is not the case. They originally intended only to earn a "finder's fee" by locating the Avanti in Hutchinson, Kansas, for Leigh to purchase from the Bevan Motor Co. Their subsequent repossession of the Avanti from Leigh was a matter of self-protection, and since they already had two family automobiles, their decision to use the Avanti as a company car may be characterized as making the best of a bad bargain. Their resale of the Avanti to Leigh on October 19th furnishes no basis for classifying the Avanti as "inventory," since implicit in the definition of "inventory" found in § 9-109 is the criterion that the prospective sale is in the ordinary course of business. The October 19th sale was not in the ordinary course of business because on that day Case was not a Studebaker dealer, did not have either a new car dealer's license or a used car dealer's license, and had never before sold a Studebaker, new or used, in his business. . . .

Since the Avanti was properly classified as "equipment" under § 9-109, the FNB financing statement was properly filed in Oklahoma County under § 9-401, and became a perfected purchase money security interest. Also, because Leigh was not a buyer in the ordinary course of business under § 1-201(9), in the October 19th sale from Case to Leigh, NBC cannot claim priority for its lien under § 9-307. Since the FNB lien is based upon a perfected purchase money security interest upon collateral other than inventory, it has priority both from the standpoint of filing time and under § 9-312(4).

The judgment is therefore affirmed.

Grain Merchants of Indiana, Inc. v. Union Bank & Savings Co.
408 F.2d 209 (1961)

CUMMINGS, J. In September 1965, Grain Merchants of Indiana, Inc., commenced its business of buying and selling grain and feed ingredients. On the 17th of that month, Grain Merchants entered into a security agreement with Union Bank and Savings Company of Bellevue, Ohio. Pursuant to Section 9-302 of the Uniform Commercial Code (5 Burns Ind.Stats.Ann., Title 19, § 19-9-302), appropriate financing statements were filed in the office of the Indiana Secretary of State and of the Allen County, Indiana, Recorder that same month. The security agreement granted the bank a security interest in all of Grain Merchants' accounts receivable "now or hereafter received by or belonging to Borrower [Grain Merchants] for goods sold by it or for services rendered by it." This security interest was to secure loans to be made by the bank to Grain Merchants, but the loans were not to exceed 60 percent of the total of said accounts receivable which were not more than 60 days old.

During the October 1965—September 1966 period that the bank was lending working capital to Grain Merchants, on or about the 20th day of each month Grain Merchants submitted to the bank a financial statement as of the end of the previous month, a list of all accounts receivable, and a promissory note in the sum of 60 percent of the outstanding accounts receivable as of the last day of the previous month. As the proceeds of accounts receivable were collected by Grain Merchants, they were deposited in an account with the bank, and, prior to October 3, 1966, Grain Merchants was permitted to draw on this account in order to satisfy its day-to-day expenses of doing business.

For the purposes of this case, three promissory notes executed by Grain Merchants in the bank's favor are pertinent. Two notes in the amounts of $30,000 and $20,000 were executed in December 1965, and a $100,000 note was executed on September 20, 1966. Upon receipt of this last note, the bank canceled a note for a like amount which had been executed by Grain Merchants the previous month. All parties concede that the cancellation of this August note on September 20 constituted the last formal extension of new value to Grain Merchants.

On September 30, 1966, Grain Merchants, which had become insolvent in June of that year, ceased doing business. On October 27, 1966, it filed its petition in bankruptcy.

On October 3, the bank took various steps to apply assets in the hands of Grain Merchants toward payment of the $152,255.55 balance, including interest, owed on these three notes. Out of an October 3 deposit by Grain Merchants with the bank, $13,575.53 appropriated by the bank represented collections on accounts receivable which came into existence after September 20, 1966. On October 3, Grain Merchants turned over to the bank its then outstanding uncollected accounts receivable. The bank then proceeded to collect these accounts, and $38,865.96 of these collections were on accounts receivable which arose after September 20, 1966.

In Grain Merchants' bankruptcy proceedings, the referee ordered the bank to turn over to the bankruptcy trustee the aforesaid amounts totaling $52,-441.49, less $7,116.52, which represents an excess over the total indebtedness to the bank and is in escrow. Therefore, the present proceeding involves $45,324.97.

The bankruptcy referee held that the transfer of accounts receivable to the bank took place at the time that the individual accounts came into existence and that therefore the transfer of accounts receivable post September 20, 1966, were transfers on account of an antecedent debt. He concluded that the transfers of such accounts receivable constituted preferences within Section 60a of the Bankruptcy Act (11 U.S.C. § 96(a)). He also concluded that at the time of the transfers of such accounts the bank had reasonable cause to believe that Grain Merchants was insolvent, so that the preferences were voidable under Section 60b of the Bankruptcy Act (11 U.S.C. § 96(b)). The district court set aside the referee's turnover order, holding that the transfers to the bank of these accounts receivable did not constitute a preference. . . .

The agreement between Grain Merchants and the bank was executed on September 17, 1965, and granted the bank "a security interest" in all of Grain Merchants' accounts receivable "now or hereafter received." The parties thus intended to accomplish a transfer to the bank of a security interest in Grain Merchants' present and future accounts receivable. In conformity with Section

9-302 of the Commercial Code, appropriate financing statements were duly filed later that month.

Reference to state law is necessary to determine whether a secured creditor has "so far perfected" his lien as to cut off the rights of a subsequent lien creditor under Section 60a(2) of the Bankruptcy Act. . . . Since the Uniform Commercial Code was in effect in Indiana at the time of this transaction, this question must be answered by reference thereto. Section 9-204(3) of the Commercial Code validates a floating lien by providing that "a security agreement may [as here] provide that collateral, *whenever acquired,* shall secure all obligations covered by the security agreement." [Emphasis supplied.] This Section obviously permits a security agreement to create a lien in after-acquired accounts receivable.

Under Section 9-301(1) (d) of the Code, the bank's unperfected security interest in the future accounts receivable would be subordinate to the rights of "a person [lien creditor] who is not a secured party and who is a transferee to the extent that he gives value without knowledge of the security interest and *before it is perfected.*" [Emphasis supplied.] A lien creditor is defined in Section 9-301(3) as a "a creditor [including a bankruptcy trustee] who has acquired a lien on the property involved by attachment, levy or the like. . . ." Thus we are presented with a situation where as soon as an account receivable comes into existence and is sought to be attached by a lien creditor, it has already become subject to a perfected security interest—here that of the bank. The very occurrence which gives rise to the full perfection of the security interest prevents the subsequent lien creditor from obtaining a priority as to the property. Although the Code does not explicitly resolve this problem, we are persuaded by virtue of Section 9-301(1) (d), taken in conjunction with Section 9-204(3), that a secured creditor who has duly filed a financing statement covering after-acquired collateral is entitled to priority over a subsequent lien creditor seeking to levy on the same property. Thus by promptly filing the financing statements required by the Code, the bank's security interest in the future accounts receivable then became superior to subsequent liens obtainable by "proceedings on a simple contract" as prescribed in Section 60a(2) of the Bankruptcy Act.

Al Maroone Ford, Inc. v. Manheim Auto Auction, Inc.

208 A.2d 290 (Pa.) 1965

Brown bought a new car from a New York dealer, Al Maroone Ford Inc., under an installment sales contract under which the seller retained title. The car was driven to Pennsylvania and sold to Manheim Auto Auction, Inc. Brown executed a New York certificate of sale. The New York dealer assigned the contract to the Bank of Buffalo and it was immediately recorded. Manheim claimed the car free of the security interest as a buyer in the ordinary course of business. Under New York law the reservation of title was effective even though no notation of the sellers' interest appeared on the title certificate. The lower court ruled in favor of Manheim.

FLOOD, J. . . . [T]he court below held that the appellee [Manheim Auto Auction, Inc.] was a "[b]uyer in ordinary course of business" under 1-201(9) of the Uniform Commercial Code and therefore took the car free of the seller's perfected security interest under 9-307(1) of the Code.

A buyer in ordinary course of business is defined in 1-209(9) of the Code as a "person who in good faith and without knowledge that the sale to him is in violation of the ownership rights or security interest of a third party in the goods buys in ordinary course from a person in the business of selling goods of that kind. . . . " The appellant raises no question as to the appellee's good faith or knowledge of the appellant's rights. Therefore we shall assume its good faith and ignorance of the appellant's rights and confine our consideration to the question of whether it bought "in ordinary course from a person in the business of selling goods of that kind."

There is no evidence that the appellee purchased from one "in the business of selling goods of that kind," i.e., a dealer in automobiles. . . . The car was a new automobile when the Browns bought it the day before in New York. While the certificate of sale executed by Brown to appellee indicates that the car was used, the word "New" was inserted in the box for the listing of the last plate number of the vehicle.

Under these circumstances, we cannot find from the agreed statement that the appellee purchased from a dealer or a "person in the business of selling goods of that kind." The recitals in the certificate of sale give rise, at most, to an inference that Gordon Brown was the owner of the car and was trading it as a dealer in used cars. These self-serving recitals do not constitute proof that Brown owned the car or was a dealer. The evidence is that he and his wife were the owners. The transaction with the appellee appeared to be a sale to a dealer, not a consumer.

The definition of "buyer in ordinary course" as one who buys "in ordinary course" from a dealer is in part circular. Under our cases a sale in the ordinary course normally means a sale from inventory. The comment of the draftsmen of the Code likewise states that the definition of " [b]uyer in ordinary course of business," restricts it, for practical purposes, almost exclusively to inventory. It also states that in most of the cases covered the goods will in fact be inventory. Nothing in the case stated indicates that there was a sale from inventory here.

We conclude that the appellee was not a buyer in ordinary course. Moreover, the facts that the car was a substantially new car, purchased for resale many miles away from the place of business of the sellers by an auctioneer who has had experience with foreign security interests in automobiles, without any inquiry, so far as the agreed facts show, as to existence of any such interest, all tell against the contention that the appellee was a buyer in ordinary course.

Since Manheim is not a buyer in ordinary course under the Code, it may take against the appellant, the holder of a security interest, only "to the extent that (it) gives value and receives delivery of the collateral without knowledge of the security interests and before it is perfected." (Uniform Commercial Code, 9-301(10) (c). . . .) Here the security interest of the appellant was perfected when the appellee bought the car . . . and the appellee's purchase was subject to the security interest. Therefore, the sale of the car by the appellee was a conversion of the car as against the appellant. . . .

The judgment is reversed and is entered in favor of the use-plaintiff, Bank of Buffalo, against the defendant, Manheim Auto Auction, Inc.

American Card Company v. H.M.H. Co.

196 A.2d 150 (R.I.) 1963

CONDON, J. This is a partnership creditors' claim for priority as a valid security interest under the Uniform Commercial Code. . . .

The sole question for our determination is whether the superior court erred in holding that 6A-9-203(1) (b) of the Code requires in a case of this kind a written security agreement between the debtor and the secured party before a prior security interest in any collateral can attach. The claimants, Oscar A. Hillman & Sons, a co-partnership, contend that a separate agreement in writing is not necessary if the written financing statement which was filed contains the debtor's signature and a description of the collateral. In support of that position they point out that . . . 6A-9-402 recognizes that a security agreement and a financing statement can be one and the same document. They further argue that "under the unique circumstances that exist in this case" the minimum requirements of 6A-9-203 are satisfied. . . .

Those circumstances may be summarized as follows. On February 21, 1962 the debtor corporation executed a promissory note in the sum of $12,373.33 payable to claimants. On March 14, 1962 the corporation as debtor and claimants as secured parties signed a financing statement form provided by the office of the Secretary of State and filed it in that office in accordance with the provisions of the Uniform Commercial Code. . . . (6A-9-402)

On July 2, 1962 Melvin A. Chernick and George F. Treanor were appointed co-receivers of the debtor corporation. On October 6, 1962 claimants duly filed their proof of debt and asserted therein a security interest against certain tools and dies of the debtor which were mentioned in the financing statement as collateral. . . .

The claimants argue that the Code requires no " ' magic words,' no precise, formalistic language which must be put in writing in order for a security interest to be enforceable." And they further argue that "the definition of a security agreement indicates, the question of whether or not a security interest is 'created or provided for' is a question of fact which must be decided upon the basis of the words and deeds of the parties." They rely on the definition of "agreement" in 6A-9-105(1) (h) for support of this latter contention.

Upon consideration of those provisions of the Code, we are of the opinion that they are not decisive of the special problem posed in the instant case. The receivers contend here, as they did successfully before the superior court, that the controlling section of the Code is, in the circumstances, 6A-9-203(1) (b) and that in order to establish a security interest in any collateral the secured party must show that "the debtor has signed a security agreement which contains a description of the collateral. . . . " They concede that such a signed agreement may serve as a financing statement if it also contains the requirements thereof, but they deny that a financing statement, absent an agreement therein, can be treated as the equivalent of a security agreement.

The pertinent language of 6A-9-402 in this regard is, "A copy of the security agreement is sufficient as a financing statement if it contains the above information and is signed by both parties." In other words, while it is possible for a financing statement and a security agreement to be one and the same document as argued by claimants, it is not possible for a financing statement which does not contain the debtor's grant of a security interest to serve as a security agreement.

In our opinion there is merit in the receivers' contention, and since the financing statement filed here contains no such grant it does not qualify as a security agreement. . . .

In an article . . . (42 B.U.L.Rev. 187) entitled "Accounts Receivable Financing: Transition from Variety to Uniform Commercial Code," it is stated at page 189: "The financing statement does not of itself create a security interest. An agreement in writing signed by the debtor 'which contains a description of the collateral' is required." In the absence of any judicial precedent this commentary on the Code is worthy of consideration in the solution of the question here.

The financing statement which the claimants filed clearly fails to qualify also as a security agreement because nowhere in the form is there any evidence of an agreement by the debtor to grant claimants a security interest. . . .

The claimants' appeal is denied and dismissed, the decree appealed from is affirmed, and the cause is remanded to the superior court for further proceedings.

Citizens & Southern Nat. Bank v. Capital Const. Co.

144 S.E.2d 465 (Ga.) 1965

One Mozley, doing business as Briarcliff Plumbing and Heating Co., assigned to the plaintiff bank an account owing him by the defendant. Mozley had written to the defendant, Capital, as follows:

> Re: Work completed at Buick, Oldsmobile, Pontiac Plant.
> Gentlemen: The work completed and billed to you in the amount of $13,809.00 has been assigned to the Citizens And Southern National Bank. Please issue your checks payable to them and us when remitting.

This letter contained a notation that it was "Accepted by: Capital Construction Company, Guy H. Miles" and dated 8/31/64.

The money was not paid by defendant and plaintiff brought suit. Defendant alleged that it had defenses and counterclaims against Mozley. The bank alleged that it had loaned Mozley more than the amount of money due under the contract; that it had not been aware of defenses or counterclaims; and that it had relied on defendant's "acceptance."

The lower court ruled in favor of the defendant and the plaintiff appealed.

NICHOLDS, J. Under Code Ann. 109A-9-302(1) (e), the assignment of an account not embracing a loan or in connection with other assignments to the same assignee, a significant part of the outstanding accounts or contract rights of the assignor does not have to be perfected by the filing of a financing statement under the Uniform Commercial Code, and under Code Ann. 109A-9-203 the security agreement must be in writing but not in any particular form. The writing relied upon in the instant case stated that the "account" (right to payment for goods sold or services rendered, Code Ann. 109-A-106), had been assigned to the plaintiff, the defendant acknowledged such assignment, and the writing was delivered to the plaintiff who on the strength thereof loaned money to the debtor (the defendant's creditor).

Under the decision of the Supreme Court in *Southern Mutual Life Insurance Ass'n* v. *Durdin* (132 Ga. 495, 64 S.E. 264, 131 Am.St.Rep. 210), the language used in the letter addressed to the defendant and "accepted" by it was sufficient to constitute as assignment of the indebtedness so as to create a security interest under the terms of the Uniform Commercial Code and there had been value given (the loan to the defendant's creditor) so as to bring it under the terms of Code Ann. 109-A-9-204 before the present action was filed.

As between the plaintiff and the defendant the petition set forth a cause of action and the trial court erred in sustaining the defendant's general demurrer and dismissing the petition.

Judgment reversed.

Sequoia Machinery, Inc. v. Jarrett

410 F.2d 1116 (1969)

DUNIWAY, J. This bankruptcy case involves the interpretation of § 9401(1) of the California Uniform Commercial Code. Appellants sold combines to James C. Clark by conditional sales contracts which were filed in the office of the California Secretary of State, but not in the office of the County Recorder. The combines are specialized equipment usable only for harvesting grain. Clark was not a farmer. He owned no land. Instead, he was a "custom harvester" who used the combines in harvesting the crops of various farmers in Tulare and King Counties on a contract basis.

After Clark filed a voluntary petition in bankruptcy, appellants repossessed and sold the combines for $30,200, which has been stipulated to be their present fair value. Appellee trustee in bankruptcy then petitioned for an order that the moneys received from the sale be turned over to him. The referee held that the harvesting combines were "equipment used in farming operations," and that the trustee was therefore entitled to the moneys, because the appellants' failure to record their security interests in the office of the County Recorder rendered them invalid as against the trustee. The District Court affirmed. So do we.

Appellants contend that the phrase "equipment used in farming operations" should be interpreted in light of the occupational status or contractual arrangements of the debtor-purchaser, rather than as referring to the actual intended use of the equipment itself. They claim that the grain harvesting combines, even though only usable for harvesting grain, were not "equipment used in farming operations" in *this* case, because Clark was not a farmer.

Appellants' argument is based on the language of various provisions of the Code. They point out that § 9109 classifies goods as "equipment" if, *inter alia,* they are not included in the definition of "farm products," and defines "farm products" as including supplies only "if they are in the possession of a debtor engaged in raising, fattening, grazing, or other farming operations." Appellants conclude that the term "farming operations" is therefore to be restricted to activities in the nature of "raising, fattening, or grazing," under the maxim "expressio unius est exclusio alterius" and the concept "ejusdem generis." Appellants also argue that Clark's operations were not "essentially local," since he worked in two different counties, and point out that, according to a Uniform Commercial Code comment,

It is thought that sound policy requires a state-wide filing system for all transactions except the essentially local ones covered in subsection (1) (a). . . .

They point out that another Code section indicates that the drafters of the Code did not regard commercial harvesting equipment as of an "essentially local" type. Consequently, they conclude that the Clark financing statements were properly filed in the office of the Secretary of State.

We are not persuaded. If the drafters of the Code had intended such a result, they could merely have written § 9401 (1) to refer to "equipment of a farmer used in his farming operations." We doubt that they expected anyone to divine such a result from the references to which appellants refer. And even if the overall rationale for the local filing of financing statements covering equipment used in farming operations is that such transactions are "essentially local," it would be unworkable to tell secured sellers to file all financing statements centrally unless the transaction is "essentially local." How does one determine what is or is not "essentially local"?

We think that the drafters of the Code carefully avoided defining "equipment used in farm operations" in terms of the occupational status or contractual arrangements of the debtor-use. In many cases it would be difficult to determine whether or not the debtor was a "farmer." One who owns or leases agricultural land, who raises crops thereon, and who purchases harvesting equipment solely for his own use on his own land, would clearly be a farmer within appellants' construction. But what of a person who owns or leases agricultural land, and farms it, but purchases harvesting equipment with the intention of using it on his own land some of the time, and using it at other times to harvest the crops of his neighbors on a contract basis? Under appellants' rationale he would be using the equipment *as a farmer* only when he was using it on his own land. In such a situation, would the equipment dealer have to determine what its "primary" intended use would be? Or would the intended use on a particular day or hour control? According to § 9401(3), a filing made in the proper place continues effective even though the use of the collateral should later change. But the Code does not say at what point one determines what the use is. Should it be when the security interest attaches, when the financing statement is filed, or when? Cf. In re Pelletier, D. Maine, 1968, 5 UCC Rep. 327, 330.

The phrase "equipment used in farming operations" is clear and unambiguous. That was the only use to which this equipment could be or was put. We decline to resort to a construction that would raise more problems than it would solve.

Finally, the California Equipment Dealers Association as amicus curiae suggests that § 9401(1) is ambiguous, and that we should therefore hold that any good faith attempt by a conditional seller to file a financing statement in the proper place should be sufficient to protect the security interest against a trustee in bankruptcy. But the Code does not allow this result. Section 9401(2) provides:

A filing which is made in good faith in an improper place . . . is nevertheless effective . . . against any person who has knowledge of the contents of such financing statement.

Section 9301(1) provides, *inter alia,* that

> ... [A]n unperfected security interest is subordinate to the rights of ... (b) A person who becomes a lien creditor. ...

Under section 70c of the Bankruptcy Act, 11 U.S.C. § 110(c), the trustee in bankruptcy has the status of an ideal hypothetical lien creditor, similar to a creditor without notice—even if the trustee has actual notice. Collier, Bankruptcy, 14th ed., § 70.53. And even apart from the Bankruptcy Act provision, the secured party would, under § 9401(2), have to prove that either the trustee in bankruptcy or perhaps all the unsecured creditors had actual knowledge of the contents of the financing statement.

Affirmed.

Quigley and Federation Agricultural Credit Corporation v. Caron et al.

247 A.2d 94 (Maine) 1968

This was a suit to determine the right to proceeds of fire insurance resulting from the destruction of the defendant's potato crop.

In 1966 Caron gave a security interest to Federation on his 1966 crop. The crop was destroyed by fire in January 1967. The loss was covered by insurance. In February 1967 Quigley obtained a judgment against Caron. Quigley claimed the insurance money in satisfaction of his judgment; Federation claimed it as "proceeds" of the collateral. The lower court ruled in favor of Quigley and Federation appealed.

WILLIAMSON, C. J. . . . The basic issue is whether under the Uniform Commercial Code-Secured Transactions (11 M.R.S.A. § 9-101 *et seq.*) the proceeds of the insurance are security for the potatoes destroyed by fire. The pertinent provisions of the Code are set forth below. In the words of the presiding Justice, "We come then to whether the bald assertion of a perfected security interest in the collateral personal property extends to 'identifiable proceeds ... received by the debtor' ... (11 M.R.S.A. § 9-306(2) when the 'identifiable proceeds' constitute money paid by reason of a fire loss under the circumstances found here." . . .

In the Uniform Commercial Code-Secured Transactions the only references to insurance appear to be in Sections 9-104(7) and 9-207(2) (b). In each instance it is plain that the Code does not create an interest in the insurance for a security holder under the facts of this case. . . .

We are satisfied that payments (or the right thereto) for fire losses often referred to as "insurance proceeds," are not "proceeds" of the collateral security, that is, of the potatoes, as that term is defined in Section 9-306(1). " 'Proceeds' include whatever is received when collateral or proceeds is sold, exchanged, collected or otherwise disposed of." The insurance monies plainly do not come from a sale or exchange or collection of the security.

Were the potatoes "otherwise disposed of"? We answer in the negative. In our view, the Code covers voluntary disposal and not a change from destruction by fire.

Inasmuch as the insurance monies (or as here the claims against the insurance companies) are not "proceeds" of collateral under the Code, it follows that the monies may not be classed within "identifiable proceeds" in Section 9-306(2).

The Rhode Island Court has reached a like result. In holding that insurance payments for losses are not "proceeds" under Section 9-306(1), the Court said: "Insurance moneys or proceeds flow from the insurance contract and not from the property insured." Again, in passing upon the "or otherwise disposed of" clause, the Court said of a tractor demolished in an accident, "This involuntary conversion of the tractor is not a disposition within the meaning of [Section 9-306(1)]." *Universal C.I.T. Credit Corp.* v. *Prudential Invest. Corp.* (R.I.) 222 A.2d 571 (1966).

No other cases covering the question of whether the proceeds of secured collateral under the Code include proceeds of insurance have been called to our attention.

An additional factor, apart from the persuasive Rhode Island case, gives strength to our view. The statute under which a lien on insurance may be created for the benefit of a mortgagee has not been changed or altered with the passage of the Uniform Commercial Code. This is evidence to us that the Legislature in enacting the Code and in particular the sections relating to Secured Transactions, did not intend to change the existing law relating to fire insurance and the interests of owner and security holder therein.

Federation places its claim on the ground that under the Uniform Commercial Code-Secured Transactions it would be inequitable for the insurance monies to go to Caron and through him via the trustee process to a creditor, and not to Federation which had loaned money on the strength of the potatoes.

The facts are inescapable, however, that the insurance was taken to benefit Caron and not Federation, and that Federation has no interest therein.

The entry will be appeal denied.

CHAPTER 30
REVIEW QUESTIONS AND PROBLEMS

1. *A,* a farmer, obtained fertilizer and other supplies from *B* and gave *B* a note which stated that the note was covered by a security agreement. In fact no security agreement had been entered into, but the parties had signed and filed a financing statement. Subsequently, *A* sold his corn crop to *C,* and *B* claims the right to the corn by virtue of his security interest. Is *B*'s right in the corn superior to *C*'s?

2. *A* had a business in Texas and also a mining business in New Mexico. A Texas bank has a security interest in a compressor that was used in the mining operations. How would the bank perfect its security interest?

3. A bank had a security interest in a machine that *B,* the debtor, was building for *C* and also in its proceeds. Does the bank have a security interest in the contract right which *B* has against *C* when the machine is delivered to *C*?

4. *A* was a cattle buyer, trader, and feeder, but he was mainly engaged in purchasing and fattening cattle on behalf of X Company. *A* entered into a financing agreement with B Bank whereby the bank was given a

security interest in his cattle. Some of *A*'s cattle had been purchased on behalf of X Company. How would the cattle be classified? What difference would it make?

5. *A* entered into a security agreement with *B.* The agreement provided that *A* was to have a security interest in all of *B*'s inventory and accounts receivable. The financing statement described the collateral as "all inventory" plus proceeds. Does *A*'s security interest include accounts receivable arising from the sale of inventory?

6. A Company, wishing to obtain equipment, entered into an agreement with B Leasing Company whereby the latter purchased the equipment from the manufacturer and leased it to A. A Company made a substantial initial payment and agreed to make fixed monthly payments for five years, the total payments equaling the cost of the equipment plus 7 percent interest. Shortly thereafter, A Company filed in bankruptcy, and B Leasing Company wishes to obtain the equipment. Can B recover it from the trustee in bankruptcy?

7. *A* loaned *B* $500 to enable him to purchase a color TV set. *A* and *B* entered into a security agreement whereby *A* was given a security interest in the set. *A* wishes to know whether or not he should file a financing statement. Advise him.

8. *A* sold a TV set to a dentist for the waiting room in the dentist's office. What should *A* do to perfect a security interest in the set?

9. *A* is negotiating with *B* to furnish financing for *B*'s retail business. What should he do in order to determine the status of *B*'s assets?

10. *A* is arranging with *B* to finance *B*'s business. It will be a secured financing plan and *A* will have a security interest in inventory, equipment, and accounts receivable belonging to *B.* What provisions should *A* require for inclusion in the security agreement? In the financing statement?

chapter 31

Secured Transactions: Priorities, Default and Remedies

3-169. Introduction. Collateral is frequently the subject of conflicting claims. Conflicts as to the right to collateral may arise (1) when the debtor gives more than one security interest in the collateral, (2) when a trustee in bankruptcy claims the collateral under the "strong-arm clause" of the Bankruptcy Act (see Section 4-29), (3) when the collateral is sold to a good faith purchaser,[1] (4) when the collateral becomes attached to real property so that it is a fixture, (5) when it becomes attached to personal property which belongs to another or in which another has a security interest, (6) when it has been repaired or improved by the services or materials of another, and (7) when it has been processed, as where raw material in which there is a security interest is converted into a finished product. In all of the foregoing situations, as well as many others, it becomes necessary to sort out the conflicting interests and determine a priority among them. Also, rules must be provided for determining the rights as between the debtor and the secured party.

There are two important sources for the rules used in determining the priority among conflicting claimants and also the rights and duties of the debtor and the secured party. One source is the security agreement of the debtor and the secured party. Provisions concerning (1) the rights and duties of the debtor and secured party in connection with the collateral, (2) the rights of the secured party upon default or in the event that he has cause for concern as to the ability of the debtor to perform his obligations under the agreement, and (3) the course of action to be taken in fulfillment of the agreement are important in determining the rights when one of the claimants is the debtor or someone claiming through the debtor, such as a trustee in bankruptcy.

The other source, the Code, contains three types of provisions which affect priorities and other rights. First of all, in order to protect the debtor, some

---

[1] United States v. McCleskey Mills, Inc. page 612

provisions limit the freedom of contract of the parties. These debtor protection provisions prohibit the inclusion of certain terms in the security agreement or give the debtor certain rights notwithstanding the agreement. Secondly, some Code provisions are so worded that they become a part of the security agreement if there is no actual provision to the contrary. If the parties do not spell out their respective rights and duties in the agreement, the Code supplies them. Thirdly, the Code has developed a "notice filing" system, which provides a means by which third parties may determine if a debtor has entered into a security agreement. This notice system was discussed in detail in the previous chapter under the heading, "Perfection of the Security Interest."

PRIORITIES

3-170. Priorities—In General. The secured party who has not filed a financing statement or otherwise perfected his security interest has an interest as against the debtor but has only a very limited protection as against third parties. He will, however, generally have priority over persons who acquire the property with *knowledge* of his interest or become lien creditors with such knowledge. However, a fundamental proposition of the Code is that a buyer in the ordinary course of business takes free of a security interest in the seller's inventory. Where two secured parties are involved, one may agree to subordinate his interest to that of the other.

The Code provides rules to determine priorities of perfected security interests where more than one party has or claims an interest in the same collateral. Priorities are based on the nature of the collateral, its intended use, and the relationship of the parties. The following sections discuss specific priority issues.

3-171. Chattel Paper as Proceeds. More than one interest may exist in the same proceeds. For example, a merchant whose inventory is financed under a security agreement with a secured party may sell items from inventory to a customer on an installment sale contract. Such contract (chattel paper) is now the collateral in place of the item sold, since it is the proceeds derived from the sale. If the secured party does not take possession of the chattel paper, the debtor could sell the paper to a third party, and a question would arise as to the right to the paper as between the secured party and the third party. If the third party gave new value and took the paper in the ordinary course of his business, he will prevail. This is true even though the purchaser of the chattel paper knew that it was subject to a security interest.

The situation is different if the secured party's interest in the chattel paper is not based upon its status as proceeds of the sale of inventory. If the chattel paper itself was the original collateral, a transferee will not prevail over the secured party if he had knowledge of the prior security interest. Thus, if the secured party under these circumstances entrusts the paper to the debtor for collection purposes, the wrongful disposition by the debtor will not subordinate the interest of the secured party.

It is to be noted that the secured party who allows the debtor to have possession of the paper could stamp or designate on the paper that it has been assigned or sold. In this way he could impart knowledge of his interest and prevent the conflict from arising.

3-172. Returned or Repossessed Goods.   Another conflict of claims to collateral may arise when a debtor's inventory is being financed, and the debtor sells **an** item from inventory, receiving in return either chattel paper or an account receivable, and the goods are subsequently reacquired. The debtor may have reacquired the goods under several circumstances. The buyer may have returned them because of his dissatisfaction; the seller may have repossessed them because of a default by the buyer; or the seller may have stopped the goods in transit, as allowed under Article 2, upon discovery of the buyer's insolvency. In any event, the goods are now again in the possession of the debtor. There may be a conflict between the inventory secured party and the transferee of the chattel paper or account receivable related to the returned goods.

The original security interest of the inventory secured party attaches to the returned or repossessed goods. The security interest in the goods continues to be perfected provided it has not lapsed or terminated. As between the inventory secured party and the transferee of the chattel paper, the person holding the chattel paper has priority. This is not the result if an account receivable was transferred; then the transferee of the account is subordinate to the party having a security interest in inventory with respect to goods which were returned or repossessed.

3-173. Purchase-Money Security Interest.   It will be recalled that a purchase-money security interest is one which is either taken or retained by the seller as collateral to secure the price, or taken by one who makes advances which enable the debtor to acquire the collateral The secured party who has a purchase-money security interest enjoys a preferred status in some situations. As previously noted, a security agreement may contain an after-acquired property clause. This means that in a commercial transaction (as opposed to one involving consumers or farmers) the lender who has a security interest in the debtor's collateral with an after-acquired clause will also have a security interest in subsequent inventory purchases. However, this result can be avoided by one who is furnishing inventory to a dealer if the proper steps are taken. The party who is going to furnish inventory on a purchase-money basis can notify the prior secured party that he has or expects to obtain a purchase-money security interest in inventory. The notice must be given prior to the time that the debtor obtains possession of the goods and must set forth the type of collateral which will be involved. If such notice is given, the secured party who furnishes the inventory will prevail.

Because of the prevalence of the "floating lien" with its after-acquired aspects, it would behoove one who is furnishing inventory to check the records with regard to the persons with whom the potential debtor is doing his financing. Notice should be sent to all such parties. Instead of using the notice procedure, it is also possible to make an agreement with a prior secured party that the latter's security interest will be subordinate to that of the inventory party.

For collateral other than inventory a purchase-money security interest is superior to conflicting security interests in the same collateral, provided the purchase-money security interest is perfected at the time the debtor receives the collateral or within ten days thereafter.

3-174. Fixtures. Goods that are collateral for a security agreement may be attached to real property, in which event such goods are fixtures.[2] This raises a question of priority as between the secured party and one who has a security interest in the real property, e.g., one who has a mortgage upon the real property. An example of a fixture would be a heating system installed in a building. Article 9 does not determine the circumstances under which goods become fixtures, but it does provide rules for determining priorities when a fixture is involved.

A security interest which attaches to goods before they become fixtures will be given priority—if it is *perfected* before they become fixtures—over existing and subsequent interests in the real property. Even if it is not so perfected it will have priority over prior mortgages because of the value added, but it will be inferior to subsequent purchasers or mortgagees because it was not perfected. It is possible to obtain a security interest in goods after they have become fixtures, in which event the secured party will not prevail over prior claimants to the real property, unless such prior party agrees in writing to the security interest or is willing to state in writing that he disclaims any interest in the goods as fixtures.

The secured party who has priority is entitled, upon default, to remove his property from the real estate. He is required to reimburse any encumbrancer or owner other than the debtor for the cost of repair of any physical damage caused by the removal.

As noted previously filing is required to perfect a security interest in fixtures regardless of the classification of the goods as consumer goods, farm equipment, etc. The filing should be done in the office where real estate mortgages are filed or recorded.

3-175. Accessions. Goods, in addition to being affixed to real estate, may become installed in or affixed to other goods. The goods so installed or affixed are called "accessions." In general, a perfected security interest which attaches to goods *before* they become accessions has priority as to such goods over a security interest in the whole and subsequent purchasers of the whole. A security interest may attach to goods after they have become affixed. The secured party has the same priorities as those stated above, but his security interest will prevail over another security interest in the whole only if the holder of the security interest in the whole has consented in writing to the security interest. As in the case of fixtures, the secured party can upon default remove his collateral from the whole, but he must make payment for the cost of repair of any physical damage caused by removal.

3-176. Commingled and Processed Goods. In a manufacturing process several items, including raw materials and components, each of which may be subject to different security interests, combine to make a finished product. The security to which the financing party is entitled will ultimately be the product which results from the combination of the materials in which he has a security interest. If a security interest in the raw materials was perfected, the security

---

[2] Cain v. Country Club Delicatessen of Saybrook, Inc. page 613

interest continues in the product if (1) the identity of the goods is lost, or (2) the original financing statement provided for a security interest which covered the "product." In a situation where component parts are assembled into a machine, the secured party would have a choice of either (1) claiming a security interest in the machine or (2) claiming an interest in a component part as provided for security interests in accessions. If he stipulates "products" in the financing statement, he cannot claim an accession. Where more than one security interest exists in the product, the secured parties share in the product in proportion to the costs of their materials used.

3-177. Liens on Goods.   The common-law lien on goods which is allowed for repair, improvement, storage, or transportation is superior to a perfected security interest as long as the lien claimant retains possession of the property. Statutory liens also have such priority unless the statute expressly subordinates them. Even though a lien is second in point of time, it will be granted priority over a perfected security interest in the goods, unless the statute creating the lien provides that it is subordinate.[3] The reason for this is that the service rendered by the lienholder has added to or protected the value of the property.

3-178. Miscellaneous.   The foregoing is a compilation of rules for determining priorities among conflicting security interests in particular situations and involving particular collateral. The following general rules apply to all other situations: (1) If the conflicting interests are perfected by filing, the *first to file* will prevail, even though the other interest attached first and whether it attached before or after filing; (2) Unless both are perfected by filing, the *first to be perfected* will have priority regardless of which one attached first; and (3) If neither of the security interests is perfected, priority will be given to the *first to attach.*

RIGHTS AND REMEDIES OF THE SECURED PARTY

3-179. Before Default.   A secured party has certain rights in the collateral during the period prior to default. These rights and duties of the parties are those set forth in the security agreement and those provided by the Code. The Code also contains limitations on the rights of the secured party and imposes certain duties upon him in respect to the collateral. The secured party who is in possession of the collateral is required to exercise reasonable care of it, and the duty to do so may not be disclaimed. Reasonable care in the case of an instrument or chattel paper includes taking necessary steps to preserve rights against prior parties—e.g., in the case of a negotiable instrument, making a timely presentment to the primary party and giving notice of dishonor.[4] The parties can agree, however, that this obligation shall rest with the debtor. *Unless the security agreement provides otherwise:* (1) all reasonable expenses related to the collateral are chargeable to the debtor and are secured by the collateral; (2) the risk of accidental loss or damage is on the debtor to the extent that it is not covered by insurance; (3) the secured party is entitled to hold as additional security any increase or profits, except money, received

[3] Manufacturers Acceptance Corp. v. Gibson, page 614
[4] Grace v. Sterling, Grace & Co., page 615

from the collateral—money so received shall be applied to reduce the secured obligation or remitted to the debtor; (4) the secured party is entitled to re-pledge—i.e., use the collateral as security in his own financing—but only on such terms as do not impair the debtor's right to redeem it, but (5) the secured party must keep the collateral identifiable except that fungible goods can be commingled. Should the secured party fail to meet his obligations in these respects, he is liable for any loss, but he does not thereby lose his security interest. The security agreement may provide, when the collateral is accounts, chattel paper, contract rights, instruments, or general intangibles, that the arrangement be on a "notification" basis or that it be on a "nonnotification" basis. The former means that the secured party can notify the account debtor, for example, that the account has been transferred and can instruct such person to make payment directly to the secured party. With a nonnotification basis, the debtor collects on the accounts and remits to the secured party; the party owing the account is not notified.

In most situations the collateral will remain in the possession of the debtor, and he may be given wide latitude in using commingling, or disposing of the property without thereby rendering the security interest invalid or fraudulent against creditors. The Code lists the following additional specific privileges which a debtor may exercise without infringing upon the validity of the security interest: He may (1) collect or compromise accounts, contract rights, or chattel paper; (2) accept the return of goods or make repossessions; or (3) use, commingle, or dispose of proceeds. The security interest is not affected by reason of the failure of the secured party to require the debtor to account for proceeds or replace collateral. Note that the foregoing are permissive and that the security agreement may, and usually will, substantially restrict the debtor in possession. He may, for example, be required to obtain the secured party's permission prior to a sale of the collateral and be required to account for and surrender to the secured party all proceeds as they are received. Also, the security agreement should make appropriate provisions for insuring the collateral and for all other matters relating to its preservation and protection.

Usually the financing statement will state only that a secured party may have a security interest in specified types of collateral owned by the debtor. Nothing is said about either the amount of the secured debt or the particular assets covered. The debtor, for various reasons, may need a detailed statement as to both the present amount of the obligation and the collateral which is covered. The Code provides that the secured party is obligated to furnish such information when so requested by the debtor.

3-180. After Default.   In most respects the parties can specify in their agree-ment what steps are to be taken upon default. The Code sets forth applicable rules where the parties have not so specified.

When the debtor is in default under the security agreement—has failed to pay or satisfy the obligation which is secured—the secured party is given several remedies. What the secured party can do, as well as the protection afforded the debtor in connection with the default procedures, is determined by the terms of the security agreement and the rules set forth in the Code. The Code therefore both supplements the security agreement and limits it. The limitations are designed to protect not only the defaulting debtor but also other creditors of the debtor. The basic remedies of the creditor—secured party—on default are to repossess the collateral and to dispose of it. It is also possible for the secured party to accept the collateral as discharge of the obligation and retain it rather than sell it. This remedy is discussed in the next section.

If the secured party is already in possession of the collateral, as in the case of a possessory security interest, or has acquired possession in accordance with the security agreement or by other arrangement prior to default, he is of course entitled to retain possession. If he does not have possession, the right to take possession is specifically granted. The secured party can simply take the collateral into his possession without any judicial process if he can do so without "breaching the peace."[5] If he meets with resistance in his effort to repossess, he can, of course, obtain judicial assistance in accomplishing it. The security agreement may contain provisions for possession by the secured party, before or after default, and may require the debtor after default to gather the collateral together and voluntarily make it available to the secured party at a place designated by the secured party. In some situations it is not practical to take possession or remove the collateral, as where it is heavy equipment installed in the debtor's plant. The Code then authorizes the secured party to render the equipment unusable pending resale or other disposition.

Somewhat different problems arise when the collateral is accounts, chattel paper, contract rights, instruments, or general intangibles. The Code in recognition of this provides that the secured party or assignee can simply proceed to collect whatever may become due on the collateral, e.g., direct the person who owes the account receivable to make payment directly to the secured party. Prior to default, the payments may have been coming to the debtor-assignor, who was under a duty to remit collections to the secured party. In addition, the secured party is entitled to take control of any proceeds. (See Section 3-168). As noted previously, Article 9 covers both outright sales and secured transactions where the property (collateral) is chattel paper, accounts, or contract rights. If such collateral has been assigned to a secured party as security for a *loan,* then the secured party, upon collection, must account to the debtor for any surplus, and the debtor (absent a contrary provision in the security agreement) is liable for any deficiency if the amount collected is not sufficient to satisfy the obligation. On the other hand, if the transaction is a *sale* of such items, the assignee can retain any surplus, and the assignor is not liable for any deficiency in the event that the items prove uncollectible. The purchase agreement can, however, provide for a different result.

If the secured party has repossessed the collateral or is otherwise in possession of it, the Code gives him broad powers to dispose of it in order to obtain satisfaction of the obligation. He may sell or otherwise dispose of it in its present condition, or he may within "commercially reasonable" limits prepare the goods for sale. Any sale of the goods is subject to the provisions of Article 2—Sales. The sale may be either public or private and is subject to the requirement that it be accomplished in a commercially reasonable manner. In general, the secured party is required to notify the debtor of the time and place of any public sale or of the time after which a private sale is to be made. The notification is not required where (1) the collateral is perishable or threatens

[5] Morris v. First National Bank & Trust Co. of Ravenna, Ohio, page 616

to decline speedily in value, or (2) it is of a type "customarily sold on a recognized market." Notice must also be sent (except in the case of consumer goods) to any other person who has filed a financing statement covering the same collateral and who is known to have a security interest in the collateral. The secured party may buy at the public sale if he so desires. If the sale is private, the secured party's right to purchase is substantially restricted. The person who buys the collateral at a sale thereof receives it free of the security interest under which the sale was made and free, also, of any subordinate security interest. Thus, the good faith purchaser at a disposition sale receives substantial assurance that he will be protected in his purchase. After the sale has been made, the proceeds of the sale will be distributed and applied as follows and in that order: (1) the expenses of the secured party in connection with the repossession and sale including (if provided for in the security agreement) attorney's fees and legal expenses, (2) the satisfaction of the debt owing to the secured party, (3) satisfaction of the indebtedness owing to persons who have a subordinate security interest in the collateral; finally, if any surplus remains after satisfaction of all of the above, the secured party shall account for it to the debtor. Note that the debtor is liable for any deficiency unless the security agreement otherwise provides.

3-181. Acceptance in Discharge. The secured party may prefer to simply keep the collateral in satisfaction of the obligation rather than dispose of it. He is entitled to make such a proposition in writing and send it to the debtor. Except in the case of consumer goods, the proposal must also be sent to all persons who have filed a financing statement covering the collateral or who are known to have a security interest in it. Within prescribed time limits, the debtor, a secured party entitled to receive notification, or any other secured party can object in writing to the proposal, in which event the collateral would have to be sold. If no such notice is forthcoming, the matter is closed and the secured party can retain the collateral in satisfaction. Special provisions relate to consumer transactions. Disposition of the goods is *compulsory,* and a sale must be made within ninety days after possession is taken if, in the case of: (1) a purchase-money security interest in consumer goods, 60 percent of the cash price has been paid; or (2) a security interest based upon a loan against consumer goods, 60 percent of the loan has been repaid. The consumer can, however, waive this right by signing a statement to that effect after default.

3-182. Debtor's Right to Redeem. Except for the ninety-day period for consumer goods, the secured party is not required to make disposition of the repossessed goods within any time limits. The right to redeem the property by the debtor or another secured party exists until such time as (1) the property has been sold or contracted to be sold, or (2) the obligation has been satisfied by the retention of the property. The redeeming party must, as a condition to redemption, tender the full amount of the obligation secured by the collateral, plus the expenses incurred by the secured party in connection with the collateral, and if so provided in the agreement, attorney's fees and legal expenses.

3-183. Compliance by Secured Party. If the secured party fails to comply with provisions of the Code relating to default, a court may order disposition or restrain disposition as the situation requires. If the sale has already taken

place, the secured party is liable for any loss resulting from his noncompliance
and may lose his right to recover any deficiency. If the collateral is consumer
goods, the consumer-debtor is entitled to recover *in any event* an amount not
less than the (1) credit service charge plus 10 percent of the principal amount
of the debt or (2) the time-price differential plus 10 percent of the cash price.
The secured party is protected against claims that he did not obtain the best
possible price for the goods if he has made the sale in a commercially reasonable manner. The Code gives substantial latitude to the secured party in selecting the time for and method of the sale.

PRIORITIES, DEFAULT, AND REMEDIES CASES

United States v. McCleskey Mills, Inc.
409 F.2d 1216 (1969)

McCleskey Mills is in the business of buying and selling farm products
including peanuts. The company advances cash to the farmers with whom it
deals. In 1963 an advance was made to Steve Smith, a farmer, and there was
no security for the advance. The Farmers Home Administration (henceforth
called FHA) also loaned money to Smith under the Farm Tenant Act. In
February, 1964, Smith executed a security agreement to FHA, including his
1964 peanut crop. The agreement was perfected by filing. In October, 1964,
Smith transfered 12,000 pounds of his crop to McCleskey Mills to be credited
against his account. McCleskey Mills did not know of FHA's security interest
and had been assured by Smith that the crop was free and clear. McCleskey
Mills resold the peanuts, and the Government brought this action against
McCleskey for conversion of the peanuts and sought to recover their value.
The lower court ruled that McCleskey's undisputed good faith in buying the
peanuts precluded recovery by the Government. The Government appealed
from this ruling.

WISDOM, J. . . . Under the scheme imposed by Article Nine of the Code,
the United States obtained a perfected security interest in Steve Smith's 1964
peanut crop on February 5, 1964, the day that it filed its financing statement,
or whenever the crop was planted thereafter, whichever came last. That perfected security interest would not, it is true, withstand challenge by most
"buyer[s] in ordinary course of business." Such buyers . . . take free of previously perfected security interests, for the sake of untrammeled commercial
dealing. Section 109A-9-307(1) specifically excepts from that exalted class of
buyers in the ordinary course of business, however, "a person buying farm
products from a person engaged in farming operations." It can hardly be
denied that McCleskey Mills here fits the description of the excluded class of
buyers. McCleskey cannot therefore invoke the strong protection afforded a
buyer in the ordinary course of business.

. . . [A] security interest continues in collateral notwithstanding sale, exchange, or other disposition by the debtor unless his action was authorized by
the secured party in the security agreement or otherwise.

. . . [T]he secured party may in such cases maintain an action for conversion
against the subsequent purchaser. This principle underlies the effective operation of any recording system: subsequent transferees, unless they are entitled

to special protection, must be on notice of any recorded and hostile interest in the land or chattels they receive. Subjective innocence will not ward off liability. Since the Code makes no exceptions for buyers such as McCleskey Mills, and since the Government had perfected its security interest prior to the purchase from Smith by McCleskey, "the secured party . . . [has] the right to follow collateral into the hands of good faith purchasers for value and to have recovery, by an action in replevin or conversion the law of the relevant state may allow."

The decision of the district court is accordingly reversed and remanded for further proceedings consistent with this opinion.

Cain v. Country Club Delicatessen of Saybrook, Inc.

203 A.2d 441 (Conn.) 1964

This is a motion of the receiver, Cain, for a determination of priority between two secured creditors. The First Hartford Fund, Inc., and General Electric Credit Corporation were both secured creditors of Country Club Delicatessen of Saybrook, Inc. By court order the assets of the delicatessen were sold, and the entire proceeds were ordered held by the receiver until a determination of the parties' rights was made by the court. The funds held are not sufficient to satisfy both creditors. The delicatessen borrowed $35,000 from First Hartford, giving a promissory note secured by a chattel mortgage covering "All goods, personal property, equipment, machinery, fixtures, inventory, leasehold rights, including, but not limited to, the property described below, *including all after-acquired property* of like kind, [and there followed a description of specific property]." First Hartford had filed a financing statement with the Secretary of State, showing the defendant-delicatessen as debtor and itself as creditor. First Hartford also filed a similar statement with the clerk in the town of Old Saybrook. The financing statements were filed August 15, 1962.

Hewitt Engineering, Inc., sold the defendant on August 30, 1962, goods hereinafter described as "Hewitt goods" on a conditional sale contract and assigned the contract to General Electric. General Electric then filed a financing statement with the clerk of the city but not with the Secretary of State, Uniform Commercial Code Division. Some of the same property was described in both parties' financing statements. First Hartford claims priority, since it was the first to file. General Electric claims priority on the ground that Hewitt was the seller of the Hewitt goods and that First Hartford Fund, Inc., could not have a security interest in the collateral on August 15, 1962, because the debtor had none on that date. The receiver requested a ruling so that he would be able to distribute the funds.

PASTORE, J. . . . Under Section 9-204(3), after-acquired property of the kind described in the conditional sale contract of Hewitt can become subject to the security agreement of First Hartford. . . . The retention or reservation of title by a seller of goods notwithstanding delivery to the buyer is limited in effect to a reservation of a "security interest." Also, the delivery of the "Hewitt goods" under the conditional sale contract with retention of title in Hewitt does not, in and of itself, affect the rights of First Hartford.

The conditional sale contract of August 30, 1962, between defendant corporation and Hewitt created a security interest in favor of Hewitt which attached to the property thereby sold. . . . To perfect this security interest, a financing statement was required to be filed . . . , which, as to goods which at the time the security attached were or were to become fixtures, would be filed in the office where a mortgage on the real estate would be filed, and in all other cases would be filed in the office of the Secretary of State. . . .

The question of the priority of such of the Hewitt goods as at the time the security interest of Hewitt may have attached were fixtures is next considered. . . .

The question when and whether personal property becomes fixtures is determined by the law of the state other than the Uniform Commercial Code. . . . The conditional sale contract of Hewitt, assignor of General Electric, provided in part as follows: "The equipment shall remain personal property regardless of any affixation to the realty and title thereto shall not pass to buyer until the . . . balance has been fully paid in cash." The parties to the contract were competent to make such an agreement, which was binding as between them, even though any such equipment were to be permanently affixed to the realty. . . . On August 30, 1962, the "rights in the collateral" which defendant-debtor had . . . with respect to any such fixtures were as personal property. When on that date, therefore, the rights of the defendant in the Hewitt collateral and said collateral came under the coverage of the after-acquired property clause of the First Hartford security agreement, the Hewitt goods were still personal property. On this basis, the failure of Hewitt and General Electric to file with the Secretary of State makes their security interest subordinate to that of First Hartford, whose prior filing gives First Hartford priority over that of General Electric. . . . Moreover, there is nothing to indicate that General Electric has any interest in the pertinent real estate which would subordinate the First Hartford security interest to the benefit of General Electric. . . .

In accordance with the foregoing, it is hereby found and adjudged that the secured claim of The First Hartford Fund, Inc., in its full amount has priority over the secured claim of General Electric Credit Corporation and is entitled to payment in priority to said General Electric Credit Corporation.

Manufacturers Acceptance Corp. v. Gibson
422 S.W.2d 435 (Tenn.) 1967

A used car was taken by the buyer to Gibson's transmission repair shop for repairs. The finance company had a security interest in the car, which was perfected by notation on the certificate of title. The repairs were not paid for, and Gibson claimed a lien upon the car for the amount of the repair bill. He retained possession of the car. The finance company instituted legal action to obtain the car. The court ruled in Gibson's favor, and the finance company appealed.

CRESON, J. . . . The sole and only issue presented on this appeal is the question of the priority of liens upon a motor vehicle as between (1) the common law possessory lien of an artisan, and (2) the prior perfected security interest of the finance company. . . .

The subject of priority of liens is specifically covered by T.C.A. § 47-9-310, which provides as follows:

> *Priority of certain liens arising by operation of law.*—When a person in the ordinary course of his business, furnishes services or materials with respect to goods subject to a security interest, a lien upon goods in the possession of such person given by statute or rule of law for such materials or services takes priority over a perfected security interest unless the lien is statutory and the statute expressly provides otherwise. (Acts 1963, ch. 81, § 1(9-310). . . .

It is obvious that the draftsmen of this section adopted the view that claims arising from work intended to enhance or preserve the value of the collateral would take priority over an earlier security interest, even though perfected, and even though the artisan's services or materials were furnished without the knowledge or approval of the secured party.

The language of the statute, so far as critical here, makes it clear that an artisan's lien has priority; (1) when based upon the common law, and (2) when based upon a statute which does not expressly provide for its subordination. The subsequent artisan's lien is subordinate only when it is created by statute; and the statute expressly declares it to be subordinate. . . .

Applying the language of T.C.A. § 47-9-310 to the situation here, Alert did furnish services and materials in the ordinary course of business to goods which were subject to a security interest. Alert exercised a lien upon the goods while in its possession. Consequently, this lien takes priority over the perfected security interest held by M.A.C. . . .

The judgment of the lower court is affirmed. The costs of this appeal are assessed against the plaintiff in error.

Grace v. Sterling, Grace & Co.

289 N.Y.S.2d 632 (1968)

Plaintiff owned some convertible debentures which she pledged to secure a debt. They were repledged by the creditor. During the period of the pledge, the issuer of the debentures gave proper notice that the debentures would be called for redemption. If the pledgee and sub-pledgee had converted the debentures to common stock prior to the redemption date as they had a right to do, the stock would have been worth approximately twice as much as the redemption price. Plaintiff sued for her loss alleging negligence by the pledgees. The lower court held for the plaintiff, and the defendants appealed.

EAGER, J. . . . Under the common law and by statutory provision, Cleveland, holding the debentures as a pledgee, albeit a sub-pledgee from a pledgee, was under the duty to exercise reasonable care for the preservation and protection of their value.

Section 9-207 of the Uniform Commercial Code provides as follows:

> (1) A secured party must use reasonable care in the custody and preservation of collateral in his possession. . . .
> (3) A secured party is liable for any loss caused by his failure to meet any obligation imposed by the preceding subsections but does not lose his security interest.

Cleveland, repledgee of the debentures from Sterling, was a lender of money in whose favor there existed a security interest and, therefore, was a "secured party" under the duty of exercising reasonable care for the preservation and protection of the collateral held by it (Uniform Commercial Code, § 9-105(1) (i)).

Furthermore, at common law, and independent of the statutory provisions aforesaid, a pledgee, considered a bailee, is held bound to exercise ordinary care for the protection and preservation of the subject matter of the pledge.

Where commercial paper or other securities are placed in the custody and control of the pledgee, it is clear that his responsibility is not limited solely to the physical preservation of the same. His responsibilities extend to the exercise of such care as a reasonably prudent pledgee would exercise under like circumstances to protect and preserve the validity and value of the securities. This is the rule at common law and also under the Uniform Commercial Code. Thus, where bearer or negotiable instruments, taken as collateral, mature before the payment of the secured indebtedness, the pledgee is required, prior to, on or following the due date, to take such action as reasonable prudence suggests to preserve the value of the collateral, such as the giving of proper notice to parties contingently liable and the taking of necessary steps to collect the instruments. . . .

By analogy, it follows that where pledged convertible debentures are called at par and thereby become payable while in the control of a pledgee, he may be required in the exercise of reasonable care to do more than just stand by and wait for payment of the face value of the securities. . . .

Morris v. First National Bank & Trust Co. of Ravenna, Ohio
254 N.E.2d 683 (Ohio) 1970

The bank loaned money to Morris to enable him to purchase a rotary mower. Morris executed a promissory note and security agreement and thereafter defaulted on his payments. An agent of the bank went to Morris's premises and demanded possession of the mower, which was refused. Morris ordered the agent to leave the premises. Later, when Morris was not at home, the mower was repossessed over the strenuous objections of plaintiff's son, who said that he was placed in fear. Morris filed action for damages. The lower court granted summary judgment to the bank, and Morris appealed.

HERBERT, J. . . . Section 1309.46, Revised Code [CC § 9-503], provides:

> Unless otherwise agreed a secured party has on default the right to take possession of the collateral. In taking possession, a secured party may proceed without judicial process if this can be done without breach of the peace. . . .

The judgments below and appellee's position at bar are mainly based upon the conclusion that, as a matter of law, the evidence before the trial court upon the motion for summary judgment failed to show a breach of the peace.

In his disagreement with this conclusion, appellant argues that the evidence before the trial court raised a genuine question of whether an assault was committed by appellee's agents, and that if an assault was found the peace was thereby breached, and § 1309,46, Revised Code would be no defense to his action.

Research of Ohio cases involving the question of what constitutes a breach of the peace discloses that our courts have previously dealt with this subject in instances where a statute or ordinance was violated. The controversy in those cases stemmed from whether it was necessary that the particular violation be felonious or treasonous in order to constitute a breach of the peace. The courts have uniformly held that *included* in "breach of the peace" are not only treason and felony violations, but misdemeanors as well. However, we have found no case which requires the conclusion that unless or until some statute or ordinance has been violated no breach of the peace can occur. On the contrary, in an exhaustive interpretation of § § 2331.11 to 2331.14, Revised Code, relating to immunity of certain persons from arrest, Justice Matthias quoted from 7 Ohio Jurisprudence 2d 689, Section 1, as follows:

> In general terms, *a breach of the peace is* a violation of public order, *a disturbance of the public tranquility, by any act* or conduct inciting to violence or *tending to provoke or excite others to break the peace,* or, as is some times said, it includes any violation of any law enacted to preserve peace and good order. *It may consist of* an act of violence or *an act likely to produce violence.* [Emphasis added.] *Akron* v. *Mingo* (1959), 169 Ohio St 511, 513, 9 OO2d 7,8,160 NE2d 225.

We do not quarrel with appellee's position that the Ohio Uniform Commercial Code, of which § 1309.46 is a part, has as its main purpose the uniform expansion and encouragement of commercial transactions in this state, and that the statutes therein should be liberally construed to effectuate that purpose. However, such construction cannot be permitted to defeat our fundamental public policy of discouraging extrajudicial acts by citizens when those acts are fraught with the likelihood of resulting violence.

In the instant case, a citizen was "surrounded" by two men and placed in fear of "being beaten." Must a citizen so treated physically lash out, whether justifiably or not, before the peace is breached? To so hold would be to wrongly relegate relationships among citizens to the after-the-fact status of the dog which formerly was permitted its first bite.

It appears clear, therefore, that no assault need have been committed by appellee's agents in order for them to have committed a breach of the peace, as that term is employed in Section 1309.46, Revised Code.

Appellant's petition is based upon alleged trespass and conversion. While we leave the question of conversion to be determined in future proceedings below, we are constrained to hold that when appellee's agents were physically confronted by appellants's representative, disregarded his request to desist their efforts at repossession and refused to depart from the private premises upon which the collateral was kept, they committed a breach of the peace within the meaning of Section 1309.46, Revised Code, lost the protective application of that section, and thereafter stood as would any other person who unlawfully refuses to depart from the land of another.

While it is not involved in the case at bar, the parties agreed in oral argument that sound public policy should also dictate that a repossessor, proceeding without judicial process, should not enter or attempt to enter any private structure without the express consent of the person in charge thereof We view the conclusion of the parties in that respect with favor.

The judgment of the Court of Appeals is reversed and the cause is remanded for further proceedings.

Judgment reversed.

CHAPTER 31
REVIEW QUESTIONS AND PROBLEMS

1. *A* had furnished services and materials for the repair of an airplane. The B Bank had a prior perfected security interest in the plane. Does *A* have priority over the bank's security interest?

2. *A* purchased an automobile and gave his note for $1,400 in payment. Shortly thereafter he went to the office of the finance company, said that he did not want the car, and authorized the company to sell it. The finance company sold the car for $750 to a used car dealer and now seeks to recover the balance due on the note. *A* claims that the $750 selling price was not reasonable and that he should not be required to pay the balance. Is *A*'s contention correct?

3. *A*, the debtor, complained that *B*, the secured party, had not conducted a sale of the collateral in a commercially reasonable manner. He claimed that the property was worth $750,000 and was sold by the secured party for $19,000. Does *A* have any recourse?

4. The A bank had a perfected security interest in *B*'s property. *C*, a creditor of *B*, obtained a judgment against him. Both the A Bank and *C* are seeking to obtain possession of the property. Who prevails?

5. *A* had a security interest in *B*'s airplane. *A* repossessed the airplane; it was later found that the repossession was wrongful. Is *B* entitled to punitive damages?

6. *X* sold goods to *Y* and has a security interest in *Y*'s inventory. The financing statement provides for a security interest in after-acquired property. *Y* is now negotiating for the purchase of additional inventory items from *Z* and wishes to give *Z* a security interest in the new inventory. *Z* is concerned over the status of his security interest if he sells goods to *Y*. Advise *Z* as to proper course of action.

7. *R*, a retail automobile dealer, at times borrowed money from the X Company and the Y Company, each of whom had filed the necessary statements, X Company being first to file. Thereafter on October 1, *R* borrowed $10,000 from Y Company and used four cars as security. He later borrowed $8,000 from X Company and used the same cars as security. *R* is now insolvent, and X Company took possession of the cars. Is this lien superior to that of Y Company?

8. *R*, a retail farm implement dealer, sold a used tractor to *F*, a farmer, for $2,200, payable in installments, and retained a security interest in the tractor to secure the payments. After *F* had reduced the indebtedness to $1,800, he became bankrupt. *R* had not perfected his lien by filing. Is *R*'s security interest good as against the trustee in bankruptcy?

9. *A,* a furniture dealer, by a valid security agreement retained a security interest in a $750 sofa sold to *B* on credit. No financing statement was filed. *B* resold the sofa to *C,* another consumer. If *A* is not paid, may he repossess the sofa?

10. K Piano Company consigned pianos to *R,* a retailer dealer. *R* sold one of the pianos to *X* for cash but did not account to the K Company for the proceeds of the sale. K Company had filed a financing statement. It claims to be entitled to possession of the piano. Can K Company recover the piano from *X*?

BOOK FOUR

Creditors' Rights

The Debtor-Creditor
Relationship

4-1. Introduction. Each of the parties to the debtor-creditor relationship possesses a variety of rights and duties. These rights and duties are the result of a multitude of statutes and cases interpreting them. The simple common-law right of a creditor to be paid, along with the duty of a debtor to pay, has been superseded by a highly complex and technical relationship which is the subject of constant consideration by most legislative bodies.

The laws regulating debtors and creditors may be divided into three categories. Some statutes, such as the federal Truth-in-Lending Act, are designed primarily to protect debtors. Other laws, such as those creating liens, are primarily concerned with protecting creditors. The third category consists of laws, such as those relating to bankruptcy, which give substantial rights and impose major duties on both parties.

Books Two and Three of this text discussed matters which to a substantial degree are designed to protect creditors. The Uniform Commercial Code contains numerous references to the rights of creditors and, in fact, Article 6 (Bulk Transfers) and many sections of Article 9 (Secured Transactions) are exclusively concerned with providing protection for creditors. Article 6 will be discussed later in this chapter in Section 4-3. All of the materials in this chapter should be considered in juxtaposition to the Code provisions, as they are often intimately connected therewith.

Later chapters of this text will also be concerned with laws that provide support for creditors. For example, subjects such as mortgages, trust deeds, and the mechanic's lien will be discussed. Each of these gives the creditor an interest in the real property of the debtor. A *mechanic's lien* gives a creditor who has performed services on real property or furnished supplies and materials for such services a means of enforcing his claim.

Two additional legal subjects involving basic rights of creditors are the law of artisan's liens and suretyship. An *artisan's lien* is a security interest in personal property in favor of one who has performed services on the personal property, usually in the form of a repair. Some of the priority problems in this connection were discussed in the material on secured transactions. However there are many other basic legal principles relating to artisan's liens which will be discussed in the next section. *Suretyship* deals with the security of a creditor resulting from a contract in which a third party, the surety, agrees to assume responsibility for the debt or other obligation in the event of a default by the principal debtor. This has been discussed previously in connection with accommodation parties to commercial paper and the statute of frauds. Suretyship is the subject matter of the next chapter.

The rights of a creditor may be classified (1) with regard to those which require suit before they can be effectively used to collect the debt and (2) those which are effective as a means of collection without suit. The rights of the secured party in a secured transaction under the Uniform Commercial Code provide an example of the latter. The unsecured debt that the debtor fails to pay is a typical example of one which requires suit. Where suit is required, the law provides certain methods of collection after a judgment is obtained. The rights of judgment creditors will be discussed in Section 4-5.

LAWS ASSISTING CREDITORS

4-2. Artisan's Liens.   From a very early date, the common law permitted one who expended labor or material upon the personal property of another to retain possession of such property as security for his compensation.[1] The right arose when the task was completed and was not assignable since it was personal. The lien did not arise where the parties had agreed to extend credit. The lien also existed in favor of public warehousemen and common carriers of goods entrusted to their care; it has been extended by statute to cover all cases of storage or repair.

The artisan's lien may be superior to prior liens of record or the claim of a party with a security interest in the goods. Since it is based on possession, voluntary surrender of possession terminates the lien, unless the surrender is only temporary, with an agreement that the property will be returned. Even in such case, if the rights of a third party arise while the lienholder is not in possession of the property, the lien is lost. Surrender of part of the goods will not affect the lien on the remaining goods. Surrender of possession will not terminate the lien if a notice of lien is recorded in accordance with state lien and recording statutes.

At common law, the lienholder retained the property until a judgment was obtained, at which time he levied execution on the property. Modern statutes permit the lienholder to foreclose, and the property is sold to satisfy the claim. Any surplus proceeds after the claim is satisfied are paid to the owner of the property.

4-3. Bulk Transfers.   Article 6 of the Uniform Commercial Code is concerned with bulk transfers. A *bulk transfer* occurs when a business or a substantial

[1] Beck v. Nutrodynamics, Inc., page 630

portion of it is sold. The sale of a business usually includes such assets as inventory, equipment, furniture, and fixtures. The creditors had presumably extended credit on the strength of these assets and the sale of them could jeopardize the ability of the creditor to collect the debt, since the debtor might fail to pay the debt after receiving the proceeds of the sale. The various states have for many years, by statute, attempted to remedy this situation by imposing certain requirements on debtors and those who purchase businesses from them, if the sale is to pass title to the property free of the claims of creditors. As between the parties, a contract of sale of a business is valid without compliance,[2] but if the statutory requirements are not met, the property in the hands of the purchaser is subject to the claim of the seller's creditors. Article 6 of the Code has not only provided uniformity in this area, it has also simplified the procedures to be followed on the sale of a business.

Article 6 is not limited to the sale of an entire business. It covers sales of less than an entire business if: (1) the sale is in bulk and not in the ordinary course of business; (2) it is of the major part of the materials, supplies, merchandise, or other inventory; and (3) the seller's principal business is the sale of merchandise from stock. Ordinarily a manufacturing concern would not be included; it would be if it maintained a retail outlet which it was selling. Enterprises that manufacture what they sell, certain bakeries for example would be included. Enterprises whose principal business is the sale of services rather than merchandise are not included.

In addition to a sale of inventory, Article 6 is applicable to transfers of a substantial part of the equipment of an enterprise if it is made in connection with a bulk transfer of inventory, but not otherwise.

Basically, Article 6 imposes two requirements: (1) a scheduling of the property and a listing of the creditors of the seller, (2) a notification of the proposed sale to the seller's creditors. An optional provision of Article 6 provides for mandatory application of the proceeds of the transfer to the debts of the *transferor*. The states are free to adopt or not to adopt this provision which gives additional protection to the seller's creditors.

It is the duty of the *transferee* to obtain from the transferor a schedule of the property transferred and a sworn list of the transferor's creditors, including their addresses and the amount owed to each. The transferee can rely on the accuracy of this listing. The transferee must keep this information for six months and have it available for creditors, or, in the alternative, file it at the designated public office.

The transferee must then give notice personally or by registered mail to all persons on the list of creditors and all other persons known to the transferee to assert claims against the transferor. The notice must be given at least ten days before the transferee takes possession of the goods or pays for them (whichever happens first) and must contain the following information: (1) that a bulk transfer is about to be made; (2) the names and business addresses of both transferor and transferee; (3) whether the debts of the creditors are to be paid in full as a result of the transaction and, if so, the address to which the creditors should send their bills. If no provision is made for payment in full of the creditors, the notice must contain the following additional information: (1) estimated total of transferor's debts; (2) location and description of prop-

2 Macy v. Oswald, page 632

erty to be transferred; (3) address where creditor list and property schedule may be inspected; (4) whether the transfer is in payment of or security for a debt owing to transferee and, if so, the amount of the debt; (5) whether the transfer is a sale for new consideration and, if so, the amount of the consideration and the time and place of payment.

In states which have adopted the optional provision of Articles 6, the transferee is obligated, in effect, to see that creditors are paid in full or pro rata from the "new consideration" paid by the transferee. Failure to do so creates personal liability for the value of the property.[3]

If the required procedure have been followed, the transferor's creditors will have had ample opportunity to take any necessary steps to protect their interests. Such steps might include the levying of execution against the property, obtaining a writ of attachment or a temporary injunction to stop the sale. If the Code procedures have not been followed, the transfer is ineffective as to the creditors, and they may use any appropriate remedy to collect the debt from the property. The creditors must act within six months after the transferee took possession unless the transfer was concealed, in which case they must act within six months after they learn of the transfer. A purchaser who buys for value and in good faith from the transferee obtains the property free of objection based on noncompliance with the Code.

Article 6 is applicable to bulk sales by auction. The auctioneer is required to obtain a list of creditors and of the property to be sold. (All persons who direct, control, or are responsible for the auction are collectively called the *auctioneer*.) The auctioneer is also required to give ten days notice of sale to all persons on the list of creditors. Failure to do so makes the auctioneer liable, up to but not exceeding the proceeds of the auction, to the creditors as a class.

4-4. Legal Procedures to Obtain a Judgment.   As previously noted, there are many rights of creditors (i.e., creditors who have a security interest) which are not based upon and do not require litigation for enforcement. Creditors who do not have a security interest in property are at a substantial disadvantage and must resort to litigation to collect if the debtor fails to pay. These lawsuits do not differ substantially from other lawsuits, but there are a few special concepts which are significant in suits by creditors against debtors.

Frequently there is a problem of obtaining jurisdiction if the defendant-debtor resides in a different state. Jurisdiction may be obtained by "attaching" property of the defendant within the state.[4] Since the court does not have personal jurisdiction over the defendant, attachment will serve to give jurisdiction only to the value of the property attached. Personal jurisdiction may also be obtained by using "long-arm" statutes when the contract creating the debt was entered into in the creditor's state of domicile. (For a further discussion of "long-arm" statutes, see Chapter 4, Section 1-29.)

In addition to the usual methods for obtaining a judgment, in a few states, the law provides for judgments by confession. Judgments by confession were mentioned in the material dealing with commercial paper, where it was noted that a provision in an instrument allowing the holder to confess a judgment does not impair negotiability. This special remedy for creditors in the few

[3] Darby v. Ewing's Home Furnishings, page 633
[4] Hobgood v. Sylvester, page 635

states which allow it may be included in many types of contracts and agreements other than commercial paper. At the time of the agreement and as a part thereof, the debtor agrees that if he becomes in default, a judgment may be entered against him without service of process or even notice of the suit. He usually also waives his right to appeal. A confessed judgment includes principal, interest, costs, and a reasonable attorney's fee for the creditor's attorney.

It should be noted that in most states a confession of judgment is not an allowable procedure. Also, it will be recalled that several of the cases studied previously involved attempts on the part of a defendant against whom a judgment has been confessed to have it opened up for a hearing on the merits.

The right to confess a judgment is an extremely powerful tool for the creditor—one that, it is readily apparent, creates difficult problems for debtors, for the courts, and for society. And the difficult problems raised by this procedure have yet to be satisfactorily resolved.

The debtor usually will satisfy the judgment. However, he may be unwilling or unable to do so, in which event the creditor is then in a position to bring a battery of ancillary remedies into action against the debtor and his property.

4-5. Enforcement of Judgments.   The various techniques for enforcing judgments and decrees were discussed in Book One, Section 1-37. Writs of execution, garnishment, and citation proceedings are used by judgment creditors to collect judgments which are not voluntarily paid by the judgment debtor. In all the states there are certain limitations on garnishment, and certain property of the debtor is exempt from execution. These exemptions and limitations are discussed in Section 4-6 as part of the laws protecting debtors.

In spite of the remedies the creditor may use, it frequently develops that the judgment is of little value because of the lack of assets which can be reached or because of other judgments. It must be remembered that a judgment standing alone has little value. In many cases, the debtor may file a voluntary petition in bankruptcy or may commit an "act of bankruptcy," which allows his creditors to file a petition in involuntary bankruptcy against him. Bankruptcy will be discussed in Chapter 34.

LAWS PROTECTING DEBTORS

4-6. State Laws.   Every state has laws which have been enacted for the purpose of protecting debtors not only from the unconscionable conduct of creditors but also from their own folly. Some of these laws, for instance, those pertaining to usury and wage assignments, have been previously discussed with the material on contracts. Laws like those pertaining to usury are protective in nature and are necessary because of the unequal bargaining power between debtors and creditors. Social policy and the public interest have dictated that such laws are desirable.

Typical of other state laws protecting debtors are those exempting property from debts. In most states the exemption statutes cover both real and personal property. The real property exemption is called the *homestead exemption,* and it usually provides that upon the sale of the family home to satisfy a judgment debt, a certain amount of the sale price shall be paid to the judgment debtor to be his property free of the debt. For example, assume a homestead exemption of $5,000 and that the family home is sold for $26,000 at public auction to satisfy a judgment for $10,000. Assume also that the house was mortgaged for $15,000 prior to the judgment. The debtor would receive $5,000, the mortgagee $15,000, and the creditor $6,000 leaving the judgment unsatisfied to the extent of the $4,000. Of course, the judgment creditor could collect the balance from other nonexempt property, if any. The reason for the homestead exemption is to provide sufficient funds to the debtor for another home. Public policy favors the debtor and his family's having a home rather than the creditor's being able to collect his entire debt. In some states the homestead exemption is not available to debtors who do not have a family, thus evidencing the policy of protecting the family.

Statutes exempting personal property usually provide that the following are exempt from attachment, execution, and distress for rent:

1. Wearing apparel and other personal possessions such as family pictures, books, and Bible.
2. A certain dollar value of household furniture.
3. Money which was received as a bonus or pension from any government on account of military service.

By statute, the various states and the federal government limit the amount of disposable earnings of an employee which may be subject to garnishment. These statutes also frequently prohibit the discharge of an employee because of garnishment for any one indebtedness. The federal law, which is part of the Consumer Credit Protection Act, covers all places of employment.

A garnishment proceeding cannot be commenced until a judgment is obtained. Statutes restricting these proceedings limit the amount of earnings which may be subject to garnishment, and the term "earnings" includes wages, salaries, commissions, bonuses, and periodic payments pursuant to a pension retirement program. The federal law affords a good illustration of typical limitations on garnishment. It provides that for an individual, the maximum part of the total disposable earnings subject to garnishment in any week *may* not exceed the *lesser* of

1. 25 percent of the disposable earnings for that week or
2. The amount by which his disposable earnings for that week exceeds thirty times the federal minimum hourly wage prescribed by Section 6(a)(1) of the Fair Labor Standards Act in effect at the time earnings are payable (currently this is $1.60 an hour, or $48 a week).

Disposable earnings means earnings after deductions for income taxes and social security taxes. The table on page 629 illustrates the application of the federal statute. Among the exceptions to the federal law are child support, orders of a bankruptcy court, and debts due for state or federal taxes.

Many employers in the past have discharged employees who were the subject of garnishment proceedings; the federal law has prohibited this practice in situations involving only one garnishment proceeding. The federal law does not preempt the field of garnishment or affect any state law. Many state laws exempt larger amounts than does the federal law, and the net effect of the

Weekly Gross Earnings	Taxes	Disposable Earnings	25%	Minimum Wage	Amount Subject to Garnishment
$ 48	$ 4	$ 44	$11	$48	$ 0
55	7	48	12	48	0
70	10	60	15	48	12
115	15	100	25	48	25

federal law is to exempt the larger amount that either provides. Both the state and federal laws illustrate a public policy against using a wage earner's income to pay judgment debts.

4-7. Federal Laws. In recent years several federal laws have been enacted to protect consumers. Some have been directed at the labeling of products; others have been concerned with the quality of goods. In 1969 a law designed to assist debtors, commonly known as the "Truth-in-Lending" Act, was enacted. This law gives protection both to people who buy property on credit and to people who borrow money. Its terms and provisions apply not only to those who lend money or sell on credit in the ordinary course of business but also to anyone who arranges for the extension of credit. It applies only to natural persons who borrow money or obtain credit for personal, family, household, or agricultural purposes. If a purchaser or borrower is other than a natural person (for example, a corporation or partnership) or if the purchase or loan is for business rather than household, etc. use, the law is not applicable. It covers real estate transactions as well as personal property transactions. In the latter case, it is not applicable if the loan or purchase exceeds $25,000. The law does not apply to a sale by one consumer to another consumer, since the sale is not in the seller's ordinary course of business. Typical of transactions covered are installment loans and sales, short-term notes, real estate loans, home improvement loans, and farm loans.

The Federal Reserve Board was given responsibility to develop regulations to implement the purpose of the law. For this reason, most of the procedures developed to implement the law are based on the regulations of the Federal Reserve Board, and like all rules of administrative agencies, they are periodically changed. Because of this, businesses subject to the law should make sure that they comply with the current regulations.

The purpose of the Truth-in-Lending Act is to disclose certain figures to a prospective purchaser or borrower so that he may shop for credit. The theory is that he may then obtain disclosure statements from several dealers or financers, compare them, and determine whether or not he wishes to go ahead with his purchase or loan. But whether this works in practice is subject to debate.

The goals of the Truth-in-Lending Act are accomplished by the use of disclosure statements. A copy of the disclosure statement is given to the borrower and the original is retained by the lender for two years or until the debt is paid, whichever is longer. Separate disclosure statements are required for each transaction including refinancing. These statements inform the borrower of the amount financed, the finance charge, and the annual percentage rate. They also disclose the amount of each payment and the number of payments. It is important to realize that the annual percentage rate generally will not be the same as the interest rate. One important reason for this difference is that the annual percentage rate is based upon the finance charge, and the finance charge includes all charges imposed by the creditor, only one of which is interest. For example, the finance charge may include the cost of credit reports, credit life insurance, health insurance, appraisals, etc. Other reasons for the difference in annual percentage rate and interest rate are that interest is sometimes prepaid and principal may be repaid in installments.

Any creditor subject to the law who fails to make the required disclosure may be sued by the debtor within one year from the date of the violation for *twice the amount of the finance charge.* This may not be less than $100 nor more than $1,000. If the creditor has made an incorrect disclosure, he must, within fifteen days after discovering the error, notify the debtor and make whatever adjustments are necessary to ensure that the debtor will not be required to pay a finance charge in excess of the amount of the percentage rate actually disclosed. If he is to avoid the penalty, the creditor must discover the error and give notice to the debtor before notification by the debtor or before the debtor institutes action against him.

The Commissioners on Uniform State Laws have prepared a Uniform Consumer Credit Code designed to accomplish the same purposes as the federal Truth-in-Lending Act. The Uniform Consumer Credit Code also attempts to protect consumers by utilizing the technique of full disclosure. The coverage of this Code is much broader in its application than that of the federal Truth-in-Lending Act. The state law is applicable to practically every transaction involving credit, whereas the federal law is limited in its application.

THE DEBTOR-CREDITOR RELATIONSHIP CASES

Beck v. Nutrodynamics, Inc.

186 A.2d 715 (N.J.) 1962

The plaintiff, Beck, procured a writ of attachment and levied upon certain goods owned by the defendant, Nutrodynamics, Inc. These goods were in the possession of Ivers-Lee Company. Ivers-Lee filed a motion with the court, claiming a paramount and prior property right in the goods, based on an artisan's lien for materials, labor, and services furnished. The goods involved were 193 cases of pills that Ivers-Lee had packaged for the defendant. The sheriff seized the pills, and Ivers-Lee filed the motion to determine the priority of its claim vis-a-vis that of Beck's attachment.

YANCEY, J. . . . In New Jersey there is no statute with reference to an artisan's lien. Such lien stands as at common law. The only statute having any applicability to an artisan's lien in New Jersey is N.J.S. 2A:44-32, N.J.S.A., which states:

> A lien held by a person upon chattels in his possession for labor or materials furnished in the repair or construction thereof, shall not be waived, merged or impaired by the recovery of a judgment for the moneys due for such labor or material, but the lien may be enforced by levy and sale under execution upon the judgment. . . .

N.J.S. 2A:44-32, N.J.S.A., being merely declaratory of the common law, must be interpreted in accordance with common law principles.

A common law lien is the right to retain the possession of personal property until some debt due on or secured by such property is paid or satisfied. This lien is one that arises by implication of law and not from express contract. It is founded on the immemorial recognition of the common law of a right to it in particular cases, or it may result from the established usage of a particular trade or from the mode of dealing between the parties.

The right to this common law lien applies to a bailee, to whom goods have been delivered. To entitle a bailee to a lien on the article bailed, more is necessary than the mere existence of the bailment relationship. The bailee must, by his labor and skill, contribute to the improvement of the article bailed. The bailee having thus performed, the well-settled rule of the common law is that a bailee (artisan) who receives in bailment personal property under an express or implied contract to improve, better, manufacture or repair it for remuneration, and enhances the value of such property by his skill, labor, or materials employed in such undertaking, has a specific lien on such property. This lien may be enforced against the bailor while the property remains in the bailee's possession, and until the reasonable value of his labor, skill, and expenses is paid.

The first question before the court, therefore, is whether the kind of work done by Ivers-Lee is such as to support its assertion to an artisan's lien. The undisputed facts set forth are that Nutrodynamics Inc. delivered to the claimant a huge quantity of loose, unpackaged capsules so that the same could be rendered saleable amount the claimant prepare, mark and package the capsules and place the packages in cardboard mailing containers suitable for delivery to the customers of Nutrodynamics, Inc. The claimant, Ivers-Lee, agreed to render the service and labor and to supply the materials necessary to accomplish the foregoing. The claimant did in fact supply such labor and packaging materials. This work and materials have become assimilated into the final product, and have enhanced the value of the heretofore loose unpackaged pills.

In the case of *O'Brien* v. *Buxton,* 9 N.J.Misc. 876, 156 A. 17 (Cir.Ct.1931), the case dealt with a lien on goods for personal services rendered and for repairs to the goods. The court stated:

> A workman who by his skill and labor has enhanced the value of a chattel, under an employment . . . has a lien on the chattel for his reasonable charge . . . .

The lien arises from the rendering of the service, and if such service be not paid for, there is a right to detain. The court further stated:

> . . . It is the natural outcome of the transaction wherein one takes his chattel to another with whom he contracts for the performance by the latter of some service upon it for its betterment.

It is to be concluded from the foregoing that the work done by Ivers-Lee did enhance the value of the product.

Counsel for plaintiff contends that a common law lien does not attach where the contract makes payment a condition precedent to delivery, and that no possessory lien exists in an artisan where payment is a condition of redelivery. True, the existence of an artisan's lien is inconsistent with a credit relationship between the parties. But the voluntary extension of credit for some deliveries under an entire contract does not negate an artisan's lien against other property withheld because of nonpayment.

The question as to whether a lien could exist where the relationship of the parties was one based on a contract for credit was settled in the case of In the Matter of *Tele King Corp. Debtor,* 137 F.Supp. 633 (S.D.N.Y.1955), where the court stated:

> The voluntary extension of credit for some deliveries under an entire contract does not vitiate an artisan's lien against other property withheld because of nonpayment.

In the case at bar Ivers-Lee was to receive payment before shipment of the completed product. The fact that some payment was made in advance, the balance to be paid at a later date, did not destroy the lien. Ivers-Lee, after having performed the work as per the agreed contract, was entirely within its rights in demanding payment before delivering to Nutrodynamics, Inc. the foil-packed pills. The rule is that an artisan is entitled to retain the property serviced, the lien attaching to the goods to the extent of the whole amount due for work done upon all of the goods.

As to the contention that the lien was lost when the goods were given over to the sheriff under the writ of attachment, it is to be noted that a lien is lost only by the lienholder's voluntary and unconditional surrender of possession or control of the property. For Ivers-Lee to resist would have placed it in contempt of the order of the court.

For the reasons above stated and in the absence of express language in our lien statute, I find that the work and labor expended by Ivers-Lee did enhance the value of the product, and I further find that Ivers-Lee has a valid common law lien to the goods for the balance now due and owing.

Macy v. Oswald

182 A.2d 94 (Pa.) 1962

The plaintiff, Macy, confessed a judgment against the defendant, Oswald, on a note. The defendant filed a petition to open the judgment on the ground that the plaintiff had failed to comply with the bulk sales provision of the Uniform Commercial Code.

MONTGOMERY, J. . . . On and prior to June 4, 1957, William Macy and Michael Macy were, as partners, the owners and operators of a service station located in Johnstown, Pennsylvania. The business was operated and conducted under a fictitious name, "Corner Service Station," but the name was not registered as a fictitious one.

On June 4, 1957, William Macy alone negotiated with James Oswald alone and entered into an oral agreement whereby James Oswald agreed to purchase said service station business for the sum of $1,500. Oswald paid the appellee the sum of $125 cash and it was agreed that the balance of $1,375 should be secured by a judgment note, payable six months after date, without interest. The parties together went to the office of an alderman who prepared the note, deleting the printed provision "with interest." The alderman suggested that

Theresa Oswald, wife of James Oswald, should likewise sign the note, which she did. At the time Macy told Oswald that "everything was okay," indicating that he could convey a good unencumbered title to the business.

On June 5, 1957, Oswald commenced operating the business, but, on that same day the sheriff of Cambria County levied on the various items of personal property and equipment connected with the service station upon a writ of execution based upon a judgment against William J. Macy and Michael R. Macy. On June 28, 1957, the sheriff posted sale notices on the service station premises which were removed by Oswald within a few hours. The debt underlying the execution was paid by Macy within a few days after June 28, 1957.

Oswald alleges that he complained to Macy about the execution notices and that he asked Macy to take back the business, return his money and cancel the deal, but Macy refused. Macy denied that Oswald asked him to take the station back. Oswald closed the station on June 30, 1957, and reopened on July 29, 1957, remaining in business until September 30, when he closed the business finally and sold the remaining personal property for $300. . . .

The provisions of the Uniform Commercial Code regulating bulk sales are . . . inapplicable. A sale of goods in bulk may be valid as between the parties although there has been no compliance with the act.

The bulk transfers provisions of the Code requires that the transferee obtain from the transferor a sworn schedule of the property and a list of existing creditors. Where compliance with the bulk sales provisions of the Code is expressly made a condition of the contract, failure to comply may justify rescission. Here, there was no such provision and the appellants themselves did not comply with the Code. Therefore, they have no standing to complain. . . .

Order affirmed.

Darby v. Ewing's Home Furnishings

278 F.Supp. 917 (1967)

Plaintiff, a trustee in bankruptcy, sued the defendant for $13,052.50, which is alleged to be the value of merchandise purchased by the defendant from the bankrupt. The defendant did not require the bankrupt to furnish a list of his existing creditors before the sale was consummated, and defendant failed to give notice to the creditors of transferor as required by the bulk transfer provision of the Uniform Commercial Code. The defendant asked for a summary judgment on the ground that the transaction was the result of bona fide negotiations and was an "arm's-length" deal with a fair price. Defendant contended that the bulk transfer law does not create personal liability but only a right to avoid the contract or to attach the property.

EUBANKS, J. . . . Pertinent provisions of the Uniform Commercial Code now in effect in Oklahoma are:

12A OSA § 6-104 which provides in part that

Except as provided with respect to auction sales (Section 6-108), a bulk transfer subject to this Article is ineffective against any creditor of the transferor unless: [a] The transferee requires the transferor to furnish a list of his existing creditors prepared as stated in this section; and [b] the parties prepare a schedule of the property transferred sufficient to identify it.

12A OSA § 6-105 provides:

In addition to the requirement of the preceding section, any bulk transfer subject to this Article except one made by auction sale (Section 6-108) is ineffective against any creditor of the transferor unless at least ten days before he takes possession of the goods or pays for them, whichever happens first, the transferee gives notice of the transfer in the manner and to the persons provided in Section 6-107.

12A OSA § 6-107 provides:

The notice to creditors provided for in Section 6-105 shall state: [a] that a bulk transfer is about to be made; and [b] the names and business addresses of the transferor and transferee, and all other business names and addresses used by the transferor within three years last past so far as known to the transferee; and [c] whether or not all the debts of the transferor are to be paid in full as they fall due as a result of the transaction, and if so, the address to which creditors should send their bills.

12A OSA § 6-106 provides that in addition to the requirements of § 6-104 and § 6-105:

(1) Upon every bulk transfer subject to this Article for which new consideration becomes payable except those made by sale at auction it is the duty of the transferee to assure that such consideration is applied so far as necessary to pay those debts of the transferor which are either shown on the list furnished by the transferor (Section 6-104) or filed in writing in the place stated in the notice (Section 6-107) within thirty days after the mailing of such notice. This duty of the transferee runs to all the holders of such debts, and may be enforced by any of them for the benefit of all.
(2) If any of said debts are in dispute the necessary sum may be withheld from distribution until the dispute is settled or adjudicated.
(3) If the consideration payable is not enough to pay all of the said debts in full, distribution shall be made pro rata.

The 1964 edition of *Forms and Procedures Under the Uniform Commercial Code,* by William F. Willier, Professor of Law, Boston College Law School, and Frederick M. Hart, Professor of Law, Boston College Law School, says in Section 61.03

Even when Article 6 applies, the Code does not make the transfer illegal or automatically void because the parties have failed to act in accord with the provisions of the Article, and, *except* in those states which have adopted the optional Section 6-106, no personal liability attaches to the transferee for want of compliance. Since the results flowing from noncompliance are limited, and evaluation of the risks involved in not following the required procedure of Article 6 may be worthwhile in those situations where an otherwise profitable transaction would be rendered impractical by the delays and paper work required by Article 6. For example, the necessity of waiting ten days after giving notice of the sale before taking possession might interfere with the transferee's plans for a quick resale. If the transferee has complete confidence in the solvency of the transferor and his willingness to pay creditors, he may be satisfied that compliance is unnecessary. However, this decision should be made *cautiously as the mere failure to follow the requirements of*

Article 6 opens even an honest transfer to attack and may, where Section 6-106 has been enacted, impose personal liability on the transferee, [Italics mine]

Section 6-106, makes the transferee *personally liable* to holders of debts owed by the transferor if there is a failure to comply with this provision. A limited degree of protection is afforded the transferee by Section 6-109 which gives the transferee credit for sums paid to creditors in good faith even though these payments were not correctly made.

From the foregoing it is abundantly clear that a "Bulk Sales" transferee who fails to comply with the sections of the Uniform Commercial Code above cited renders himself personally liable to creditors of transferor for the value of the property purchased or the amount he paid therefor.

I am of the further opinion that the suit in this case is properly brought by the Trustee.

Since defendant makes no contention of compliance with the cited provisions of the Uniform Commercial Code but only contends that he paid a fair consideration for the goods at an "arm's-length" transaction, the motion for summary judgment and motion to dismiss are without merit and accordingly are overruled. Defendant will have fifteen days from the date hereof in which to answer.

Hobgood v. Sylvester

408 P.2d 925 (Oreg.) 1965

GOODWIN, J. Plaintiff commenced an action to recover an alleged debt from nonresident defendants. To obtain *quasi in rem* jurisdiction over the defendants, plaintiff sought to attach a debt owed them by third-party Oregon residents. From an order quashing the return of service upon motion made by way of a special appearance, plaintiff appeals.

The debt sought to be attached in these proceedings was the unpaid balance of the purchase price of land, which debt had been evidenced by a negotiable promissory note and secured by a mortgage on the land. In answer to the notice of garnishment, the garnishees eventually acknowledged the installment debt, described the note, and correctly stated that no payment was due as of the date of the return. (The first return had stated: "Nothing due now.")

The issue is whether, for jurisdictional purposes, a debt which is evidenced by a negotiable instrument can be attached under ORS 29-170 (manner of executing writ).

> The sheriff to whom the writ is directed and delivered shall note upon the writ the date of such delivery, and shall execute the writ without delay, as follows:
>
> (1) To attach real property. . . .
>
> (2) Personal property capable of manual delivery to the sheriff and not in the possession of a third person, shall be attached by taking it into . . . (the sheriff's) custody.
>
> (3) Other personal property shall be attached by leaving a certified copy of the writ, and a notice specifying the property attached, with the person having possession of the same, or if it be a debt, then with the debtor . . .

by simply serving the debtor with the notice described in subsection (3). The alternative would require the instrument itself to be brought under a sheriff's control as "property" described in subsection (2). The plaintiff was unable to effect the seizure of the note, which reposed in a California bank.

The underlying theory of *quasi in rem* jurisdiction does not contemplate a typical personal judgment against the defendant, but only a judgment to the extent of the defendant's property within the state. The concept is that, where the court controls the disposition of a defendant's property through attachment, as an exercise of the sovereign's power over property found within its borders, the court can also adjudicate unrelated personal rights of the nonresident property owners, and enter judgment up to the value of their property within the court's control. Due process is satisfied by the presumption that a person ordinarily keeps track of his property, and will come in and defend the case. The property may be tangible or intangible, but it must be brought under the control of the court so that it can be sold, if need be, on execution. . . .

The inquiry involves two questions: (1) whether the attachment attempted . . . which did not effect a change in the possession of the negotiable instrument was an effective attachment of the debt; and (2) if not an effective attachment, was it nonetheless sufficient to confer jurisdiction?

If the court should, in a case like the one now pending, enter judgment against the defendants, it would be asked to order execution of the judgment. The purchaser of the debt at the execution sale would, presumably, demand payment of the next installment to fall under the terms of the note. . . . Assuming that the garnishee should pay an installment under the compulsion of such an execution, however, such a payment would not be a defense to an action against the garnishee by a holder in due course.

If a holder in due course acquires a negotiable instrument, he takes it free of all defenses of any party to the instrument with whom the holder has not dealt (except for certain statutory defenses not relevant here). Even payment is no defense against a holder in due course, and a maker of a negotiable instrument who pays the original payee all or part of the debt evidenced thereby may be compelled by a holder in due course to pay again. . . . [W]hen a debt is evidenced by a negotiable instrument, attempted levy of execution against the debt without reduction of the instrument to the sheriff's possession gives the judgment creditor no interest in the note as against a holder in due course of the note. This rule seems to be in harmony with authority elsewhere. . . .

. . . We believe that when a debt has been evidenced by such an instrument, because of the peculiar incidents of negotiability, the debt cannot be attached effectively without bringing the instrument under the court's control. The reason given for this rule in other jurisdictions is that without obtaining control of the instrument, the court cannot protect the maker against double liability.

An attempted attachment under subsection (3) obviously is not effective to enable the court to issue a writ of execution upon the note. If execution is attempted upon the debt without surrender of the instrument, the execution would be either an empty gesture or, if it produced a payment, the payment could work substantial injustice upon the garnishee. The garnishee is, between the litigants, an innocent third person. Accordingly, we hold that where the return of a garnishee shows that a debt has been evidenced by a negotiable instrument, an attachment of the debt does not confer *quasi in rem* jurisdiction upon the court until the instrument itself is reduced to the possession of the sheriff. The only purpose of *quasi in rem* jurisdiction is defeated if the court cannot dispose of the property sought to be attached without invading the rights of innocent third persons. . . .

The order quashing the return of service is affirmed.

CHAPTER 32
REVIEW QUESTIONS AND PROBLEMS

1. *B* repaired *A*'s automobile and installed a new engine. He wished to retain a lien on the car for parts and labor. How can he accomplish this?
2. *G* held a security interest in a certain automobile. The owner of the car took it to *H*'s garage for repairs. The owner paid neither *G nor H*, and *H* is now in possession of the car. *G* seeks to obtain possession of the car from *H*. Will he succeed?
3. Debtor *A* lives in Illinois but owns property in Oregon. Creditor *B* wishes to bring legal action to recover from *A*. In what state may he bring his legal action?
4. *H* and *W,* husband and wife, have a joint bank account at the Last National Bank. *X* has a judgment against *H* resulting from a tort action for negligence. Can *X* garnish the Last National Bank? To what extent?
5. *A* has a $10,000 judgment against *B*. A writ of execution has been issued on the judgment. Can the sheriff levy upon and sell all of *A*'s real property?
6. *X* owned a shoe store and purchased his stock from the ABC Shoe Co. *X* was approximately a year behind in paying for his stock. The ABC Co. is contemplating suit to recover the funds. *X*'s only property is the shoe store and its stock. The president of the ABC Co. learns that *X* is about to sell the store and its stock to *Y* at a rather substantial loss. May the ABC Co. bring an action for injunction? What steps must *Y* follow?
7. *X,* the owner of a grocery store, owes *Y,* a grocery retailer, $20,000 for stock purchased.
      a. How may *Y* reach *X*'s store and stock before trial? Under what circumstances?
      b. How may *Y* reach *X*'s bank account? Under what circumstances?
      c. How may *Y* reach *X*'s home, worth $20,000? What limitations are there on such action?
      d. How may *Y* reach *X*'s income from second job which he holds? What limitations exist?
8. Why do we have laws protecting debtors?
9. What is the purpose of the federal law of garnishment? How does it work?
10. What are the goals of truth-in-lending legislation?

chapter 33

Suretyship

4-8. Introduction. Several methods of providing "security" for creditors have been previously discussed. Chapters 30 and 31 dealt with security interests in the personal property of the debtor, and Chapter 32 with the lien on property as a method of assuring collection of a debt. This chapter is concerned with suretyship, a method of providing security for a creditor which does not involve an interest in property. In suretyship the security for the creditor is provided by a third person's promise to be responsible for the debtor's obligation.

In the law of suretyship the person who borrows money or assumes direct responsibility to perform is called the *principal, principal debtor,* or *obligor,* the party who promises to be liable for the principal's obligation is called the *surety* or *guarantor;* and the party entitled to performance or payment is customarily called the *creditor,* or *obligee.* The term "surety" has both a broad and a narrow meaning. In the broad sense, it is used to describe those third persons who are liable for the debts or obligations of another person. In this sense, a surety may be primarily, as well as secondarily liable. Surety in this broad sense includes guarantors. A contract of guaranty is one in which a third party, the guarantor, promises the person who is the creditor that he will pay the debt or fulfill the obligation only *if the debtor does not.* The obligation of a guarantor is secondary to that of the principal debtor. Surety in the narrow sense of the word does not include a guarantor but is limited to one who is primarily liable. In modern law, the distinction between a surety and a guarantor is of little significance. The Restatement of Security treats suretyship and guaranty as synonymous.[1] However, surety is still used by a few courts in the narrow sense. Unless otherwise noted, the legal principles of suretyship discussed in this chapter include guaranty contracts.

[1] Timberlake v. J. R. Watkins Company, page 647

A contract of suretyship can be distinguished from a contract of indemnity. Both provide security for a promisee but a surety makes a promise to a person who is *to receive* performance of an act on payment of a debt by another, whereas in a contract of indemnity, the promise is made to one who is promising *to do* an act or *to pay* a debt. Suretyship provides security to creditors, whereas indemnity provides security to debtors. Indemnity is a promise to the debtor, or obligor, to save him harmless from any loss that he may incur as a result of the debt or promise.

Performance bonds and fidelity bonds are also contracts of suretyship. A performance bond provides protection against losses that may result from the failure of a contracting party to perform the contract as agreed. The surety (bonding company) promises the party entitled to performance to pay losses caused by nonperformance by the principal in an amount not to exceed the face of the bond. Fidelity bonds give protection against the dishonest acts of a person. For example, they protect employers from losses caused by embezzlement by an employee—the bonding company promises to repay the employer any loss caused by defalcation of the covered employees not to exceed a stated amount. Thus, bonding companies are sureties in the sense that the term "surety" includes security either for the payment of money or for the faithful performance of some other duty.

4-9. The Suretyship Contract. Suretyship usually results from an agreement of the parties, but it may also result by operation of law. For example, assume that Jones sells his retail lumber business to Smith. The latter assumes and agrees to pay, as part of the purchase price, all of Jones's outstanding liabilities. As between Smith and Jones, Smith has now become the primary debtor, and Jones is secondarily liable. As soon as the creditors are notified of the sale, they are obligated to respect the new relationship. However, this does not require that the creditors first attempt to recover from Smith before looking to Jones.

Suretyship most often results from an express contract between the surety and the creditor whereby the surety assumes responsibility for the principal's performance for the creditor. The surety agrees that he may be called upon to pay or to perform in case the principal defaults. Like other contracts, the contract of suretyship requires consideration. In the majority of instances the consideration that supports the surety's promise is the same as that received by the principal.

Thus, if *S* promises *C* to pay for goods that *C* supplies to *P* in case *P* fails to pay for them, *S* does not in one sense directly receive a benefit. However, the creditor, *C,* supplies the goods to *P* on the strength of the promises of both *P* and *S,* and the requisite consideration is supplied to support both promises. In reliance upon the two promises, the creditor did an act he was not otherwise obligated to do. However, if the goods had been delivered before the surety made his promise, some new consideration would have been essential to bind the surety because past consideration[2] will not support a present promise.

As with other contracts, there is a need for rules to interpret contracts of suretyship when the terms of such contracts are ambiguous. For example, assume that a surety in guaranteeing payment states: "Let *P* have what

[2] Vaccaro v. Andresen, page 649

supplies he needs, and if he fails to pay for them, I will." This promise is capable of being construed as an offer to guarantee payment for a single purchase or as a continuing guaranty of credit. In the absence of a time or an amount limitation, the courts tend to limit the liability to one transaction and construe the guaranty as for a single purchase rather than a continuing offer. Where there is a time limitation in the guaranty, the courts tend to construe the guaranty as continuous for the period stated, in a reasonable amount. When there is limit on amount but not time, the guaranty is likewise continuous,[3] with the maximum liability being the amount stated. A continuing guaranty of credit is effective until it is withdrawn, in the same manner as any continuing offer. Therefore, receipt of a withdrawal notice or death of the guarantor terminates liability for credit thereafter extended to the principal.

Courts are not in agreement as to whether a creditor who relies upon an offer of guaranty is obligated to notify the guarantor that he accepts the offer; or that he has acted or will act in reliance upon it. If it is a general offer addressed "to whom it may concern," the better view according to the Restatement is that the creditor must notify the guarantor within a reasonable time after credit has been extended. Because of the uncertainty in the law, it is a wise business policy in *all* cases to give notice that the guaranty has been or will be relied upon.

Agreements to become secondarily liable for the debt or default of another are required by the statute of frauds to be evidenced by writing. (See Chapter 13, Sec. 2-77.)

The contract of suretyship is of ancient origin. The original surety was the human hostage who was subject to imprisonment or death unless redeemed. The Bible contains references to suretyship, which illustrate the basis for many of our modern legal views toward sureties. In Proverbs 11:15 it is stated: "He that is surety for a stranger shall smart for it; and he that hateth suretyship is sure." This recognition that sureties are likely to regret coming to the aid of a friend and that the prudent person will not do so has resulted in several special rights and defenses for uncompensated sureties. Many cases distinguish between the protection afforded an uncompensated surety and that afforded a compensated surety. Most compensated sureties are bonding and insurance corporations. It is important that particular attention be paid to the differences in treatment of compensated as opposed to uncompensated sureties.

One major difference in the treatment afforded compensated as contrasted with uncompensated sureties is in the interpretation of the contract. Ambiguous provisions of surety agreements are construed in favor of the unpaid surety and against the creditor. Ambiguous provisions of surety agreements involving compensated sureties are resolved against the surety. This distinction results from the fact that ambiguous language is generally construed against the party using it. In the case of unpaid sureties, the language is usually framed by the creditor and signed by the surety. In the case of compensated sureties, the contract is usually prepared by the surety.

4-10. Fiduciary Aspects.   The suretyship relation is, within limits, fiduciary in character, involving special trust and confidence between the parties. For this reason, a creditor possessing information affecting the risk must communi-

---

[3] Frell v. Dumont-Florida, Inc., page 649

cate such information to the surety before the contract is made. This duty applies only to information that is significant to the risk.

Since the contract is between the surety and the creditor, any misconduct of the principal which induces the surety to become such does not permit the surety to avoid the contract. However, if at the time of the contract the creditor is aware of the principal's misrepresentation, the creditor is obligated to inform the surety of the misrepresentation. For example, an employer who has knowledge of past defalcations of an employee and who seeks a bond assuring faithful performance by the employee of his duties is obligated to notify the surety at the time the contract is being formed of such misconduct. Similarly, a creditor who learns that the principal has misrepresented his financial condition to a prospective surety is obligated to warn the surety of the unanticipated risk. If the creditor fails to warn the surety, the surety's promise is not enforceable.

An employer who discovers that bonded employee has been guilty of misappropriation of funds should immediately discharge the employee unless the surety assents to his continued employment. To continue the employee at his task subjects the surety to a risk not contemplated. Rehabilitation of the employee by "giving him a second chance" can only be undertaken with the consent of the surety. If the surety does not consent, and if the employee is guilty of misappropriation a second time, the surety is not liable on the surety bond.

THE LIABILITY OF SURETIES

4-11. General Principles. The surety, or absolute guarantor, becomes liable to the creditor as soon as the principal defaults in the performance of his obligation. The creditor need not exhaust his remedies against the principal before looking to the surety. This rule is applicable even though the creditor is in possession of collateral provided by the principal debtor. The creditor may resort to the surety to collect without disposing of the collateral, unless the surety demands the sale of the collateral in order to avoid unreasonable hardship.

In most states, a creditor is not required to give notice of default by the debtor to the surety prior to commencing suit against the surety. Notice of default by the debtor is not a condition precedent to the creditor's right to enforce the promise of the surety. It is the duty of a surety to keep informed and to act when the principal fails, unless the contract of surety requires that notice of default by the debtor be given to the surety. In those cases in which the contract does require that notice of default by the debtor be given to the surety, an uncompensated surety will be released if the notice is not given. A compensated surety will not be released unless there is proof that the rights of the compensated surety have been prejudiced by the delay in giving notice.[4]

A guaranty of collectibility guarantees the solvency of the debtor at the time the obligation matures. In such a case, the guarantor is not liable unless the creditor first sues the debtor and is unable to collect or presents convincing

---

[4] Ireland's Lumber Yard v. Progressive Contractors, page 650.

evidence that a suit to collect would have been futile. The creditor is also obligated to notify such a guarantor, usually called a conditional guarantor, of a default by the debtor. Failure to do so releases the guarantor to the extent he is injured by failure to receive prompt notice of default.

When there is more than one surety on an obligation, the liability of the sureties is described as joint and several. This means that the creditor may sue them jointly for the debt or he may sue each surety separately for the total debt. If the sureties are sued jointly, the entire judgment against them can be collected from one debtor just as if the debtor had been sued separately. The problem of allocating shares of the obligation between the sureties does not concern the creditor and this matter is left exclusively to the sureties as a result of this joint and several liability. Of course, a creditor may agree to limit the liability of any surety either in amount or in percentages.

A guarantor, or surety, for a particular debt continues liable until the obligation has been satisfied, unless released by the statute of limitations. Similarly, a guarantor or surety who agrees to be liable for the default of an employee or an elected official continues liable as long as the employee works under his original contract or the official remains in office, unless the contract sets its own period of liability.

Whenever two or more sureties become secondarily liable for the same obligation of the principal, they become cosureties. This is true even if one surety does not know of the existence of the other. If the creditor compels one surety to meet the obligation in full, that particular surety takes on the burden of recovering from his cosureties the portion they should contribute.

An extension of time to or a release of one surety releases other sureties only to the extent the released surety would have been obligated to contribute. There is an implied contract between cosureties that they will share any loss equally unless they have agreed otherwise or have fixed different maximum amounts for their liability. In the latter event, they are assumed to have agreed to share in proportion to their maximum liability. This right to contribution from cosureties provides initially for a sharing between solvent cosureties within the state. Each contributing surety then possesses an independent action against the insolvent or nonresident surety for the amount which he paid on behalf of the insolvent or nonresident surety.

So long as the balance of a claim remains outstanding and unpaid, a cosurety has no right to contribution unless he has paid more than his share of the claim, and then only to the extent of the excess. This he may recover from any cosurety unless it compels the latter to pay more than his full share.

No surety has a right to profit at the expense of a cosurety. Neither has he a right to reduce his personal risk by secretly procuring collateral from the principal debtor. Any such collateral, obtained either before or after he became a surety, must be held for the benefit of all the sureties. It is possible, of course, for all the sureties at the time they become such to agree that one of them may be favored by receiving collateral for his protection, but in the absence of such an arrangement, all have a right to share in the collateral held by one.

The liability of a surety may be released and the surety discharged upon the happening of several events. Among these are changes in the contract terms, extension of the time of payment, payment of the obligation, and any other act that materially prejudices the rights of the surety. These matters are discussed in the sections that follow.

4-12. The Effect of an Extension of the Time of Payment on Liability.

Debtors frequently seek an extension of time for payment from the creditor. In cases where the debt is secured by a promise of a surety, the creditor should be careful not to extend the time for performance without the surety's consent. As a general rule, a binding contract between the principal and the creditor, which definitely extends the time within which performance may be demanded, releases the unpaid surety absolutely. A similar contract will also release the compensated surety if the compensated surety can show actual injury as a result of the extension agreement.[5] Injury is shown when the ability of the principal to perform has perceptibly weakened during the period of extension.

A contract of extension releases the unpaid surety because the surety's right to proceed against the principal has been postponed and the financial status of the principal may become less sound during the period of the extension.

The extension agreement must be a binding enforceable contract. As such, it must be for a definite time and must be supported by consideration. Consideration for an extension may take the form of an advance payment of interest or the giving of a note promising to pay it or an increase in the interest rate. Merely promising to pay the original debt at a future date will not supply the consideration for the promise to extend the time of payment and will not discharge the surety. However, some courts have held that a promise to pay interest at the same rate for the extended time supplies the consideration. This reasoning is questionable.

Mere indulgence upon the part of the creditor or passively permitting the debtor to take more time than the contract calls for does not release the surety.[6] The latter is in no sense injured by such conduct, because he is free at any time to perform and immediately start suit against the principal.

The consent of the surety may be obtained either before or after the extension has been granted. Consent given after the extension amounts to a waiver of the right to rescind and is valid, although it is not based upon any new consideration. Notice to the surety that an extension has been granted or a failure on the part of the surety to reply to a request seeking permission to extend is not equivalent to consent. In the latter case, silence should act as a warning not to grant the extension since the surety is apparently unwilling to extend the risk.

An extension of time by the creditor, in which the extension agreement stipulates reservation of rights against the surety, does not release the surety. Such an extension binds only the creditor. It does not bind the surety. He is free at any time to complete performance for the principal and immediately to sue him for damages suffered, since to him the arrangement is quite similar to mere indulgence. To illustrate: *S* becomes surety for *P* on a note in favor of *C*. The note falls due on a certain date, and *P* requests from *C* an extension of ninety days. The extension is granted with the express stipulation that *C* reserves all rights against *S*. *S* is not released, although he receives no notice

[5] Bayer & Mingolia Const. Co. v. Deschens, page 652.
[6] Fireman's Fund Insurance Company v. Richard, page 653.

of the extension. His right to pay the debt at any time he desires and to turn to P for reimbursement is not impaired.

To the extent that a surety is protected by securities placed with him by his principal debtor, an extension of time does not effect a discharge. An extension of time cannot injure a fully secured surety, and one who is only partially secured is released to the extent the security is inadequate.

An extension of time on an obligation arising out of a continuous guaranty does not release the guarantor except that the maximum liability is not thereby extended. To illustrate, let us assume that G guaranteed payment of goods sold to P by C up to a maximum of \$10,000. If a claim for \$3,000 falls due, an extension of time by C will not release G. C is still protected by the \$10,000 maximum liability of G.

4-13. The Effect of a Change in Contract Terms on Liability.   Any material change in the terms of the contract between the principal and the creditor, without the consent of the surety, discharges him.[7] Inasmuch as the principal contract governs the surety's liability, any change in its terms must be assented to by him. Likewise, the creditor's failure to comply with the terms of the contract of suretyship will result in the discharge of the surety.[8]

A discharge of the principal debtor, or any one of them if there are two or more, unless assented to, releases the surety. This rule is subject to those exceptions existing in the case of an extension of time; that is, the surety is not released if the principal debtor is discharged with reservation of rights against the surety, or if the surety is protected by securities or is a paid surety and is not injured.

4-14. The Effect of Payment on Liability.   Payment of the principal obligation by the debtor or someone in his behalf discharges the surety, although a payment later avoided causes the surety's liability to revive. This situation is likely to occur in bankruptcy, where a creditor may be compelled in certain cases to surrender a preference received.

A valid tender of payment by either the principal or the surety that is rejected by the creditor releases the surety. In such a case it is not necessary that the tender be kept good or continuously available in order for the surety to be released. Since the creditor has had an opportunity to receive his money, the surety is no longer liable.

Whenever payment is made by a debtor who owes several obligations to the creditor, unless the debtor has indicated where it is to be applied, the creditor is free to apply it on any matured obligation. However, if the money is in reality supplied by the surety, and this fact is known to the creditor, he must apply it on the one for which the surety is liable. If the creditor makes no specific application, in court the money will be applied where the court feels it is equitable, but a tendency to apply it on the unsecured obligations is reasonably clear from court decisions.

The mere receipt of a note or check of the principal debtor by the creditor does not release the surety, as the debt is not paid until the note or check is honored. If a new note is given in settlement of an old one, the old one being

---

[7] Magazine Digest Pub. Co., Limited v. Shade et al., page 655
[8] George E. Failing Co., v. Cardwell Investment Co., page 656

canceled and returned, an extension of time has taken place, which releases the surety. Where both notes are retained by the creditor, the courts hold that the second is merely collateral to the first and the surety is not released.

4-15. The Surety's Defenses.   There are numerous defenses available to a surety to avoid liability. Some of these defenses are available only to the surety, and others belong to the principal but are also available to the surety. The previous sections have discussed situations in which a surety is discharged, and discharge is perhaps the most important of a surety's defenses. Another important defense is that of lack of a principal obligation. In other words, the surety is not bound if the principal is not bound. This may occur when the principal fails to sign the contract although expected to do so. A similar defense arises when the signature of a person shown by contract to be a cosurety is missing. Since failure of a cosurety to sign affects the right of contribution, the signature is a condition precedent to liability.

A similar defense to lack of signature by principal or cosurety exists when the principal's signature is forged. The creditor has a duty to obtain the genuine signature of the principal, and failure to do so is an absolute defense for the surety. The same rule is not used when the cosurety's signature is forged and this fact is unknown to the creditor. The burden is on the surety to ascertain if the cosurety's signature is genuine. Many other defenses available to the principal may be asserted by the surety against the creditor, particularly when the principal is willing to have the defenses so used. Such defenses as mutual mistake, fraud, illegality, lack or failure of consideration, or undue influence, if available to the principal, may be used by the surety.

There are three important exceptions to the general rule that defenses available to the principal may be used by the surety to avoid liability to the creditor. These defenses are infancy, bankruptcy, and the statute of limitations. Infancy and bankruptcy are not available to the surety as a defense since the surety is employed in the first instance to protect the creditor against the inability of the debtor to perform. If a minor avoids a contract and, in so doing, fails to return all of the consideration which he had received, the surety is required to make up any deficiency between the value of the item returned and the amount of the indebtedness.

The statute of limitations available to the principal debtor may not be used by the surety.[9] Each has his own period after which he is no longer liable to the creditor, and the period may be longer for one than for the other. Thus, the debtor may be liable on an oral contract while the surety is liable on a written contract, or the debtor may have made a part payment which extends the period of his liability but which has no effect upon the liability of the surety.

Set-offs and counterclaims of both the principal and surety may be used as a defense by the surety under certain circumstances. The surety can set off any claim it has against the creditor and use the set-off to reduce or eliminate the liability. If the debtor is insolvent, if the principal and surety are sued jointly, or if the surety has taken an assignment of the claim of the debtor, the surety is entitled to use as a defense, any set-off that could be used by the principal debtor in a suit by the creditor.

[9] Bomud Company v. Yockey Oil Company and Osborn, page 657

RIGHTS OF THE PARTIES

4-16. Rights of the Surety Against the Principal.   One who becomes a surety at the request, or with the approval, of the principal is entitled to reimbursement for any loss caused by the principal's default. Normally, the surety is not permitted to add any attorney's fees that he has been compelled to pay on his own behalf by way of defense or fees paid to the creditor's attorney. All attorney's fees can be avoided by performance of contract terms; when the principal fails to perform, it becomes the immediate duty of the surety to act. Attorney's fees incurred in a bona fide attempt to reduce the amount of the recovery form an exception to this general rule.

The surety may recover only the amount paid by him. Thus, if he settles a claim for less than the full amount owing the creditor, his right to recover is limited to the sum paid under the settlement. Furthermore, bankruptcy on the part of the principal, although it takes place before the surety is called upon to perform, releases the principal from further liability to the surety.

Any securities falling into the possession of the surety at the time he settles his principal's obligation may be disposed of as far as is necessary to extinguish the surety's claim for indemnity.

The surety also possesses the right to be exonerated, which makes it possible for him to go into court and compel the principal to perform in order to save the surety harmless. Naturally, this right of exoneration has little value where the principal is financially unable to make payment or to take such other action as his contract requires.

4-17. Subrogation Rights of Creditors.   Literally, subrogation means the substitution of one person in place of another, and as used in this section, it refers to the creditor's right to step into the shoes of the surety and to enforce the surety's rights against the principal. For example, the principal may deliver corporate stock to the surety in order to protect the surety in the event of the principal's default. This is actually a means of providing "security" for the party securing the original obligation. The original creditor, to the extent of his claim, may substitute his position for that of the surety, with reference to the stock. In the event of the return of the stock by the surety to the principal, the creditor is entitled to follow the stock into the hands of the debtor and subject it to a lien. This rule applies only where the rights of innocent third parties have not intervened. The creditor may also secure an injunction against return of the stock to the principal, thus having it impounded by the court until the principal debt falls due, at which time the stock may be sold for the benefit of the creditor.

Collateral posted with a surety to protect him against loss on any one of several obligations upon which he is surety does not necessarily give a particular creditor the right of subrogation. In the event of the surety's insolvency, the collateral is apportioned among the various creditors to whom the surety was obligated.

The right of subrogation does not exist where the security is left with the surety by some third party. The theory is that security placed with the surety forms a trust of that portion of the principal's estate which he sets aside for the payment of his debt. Securities belonging to third parties do not form part of the principal's estate, and, therefore, are not subject to subrogation.

4-18. The Surety's Right of Subrogation.   This is another aspect of subrogation to be distinguished from the subrogation rights of the creditor in collateral held by the surety for the latter's protection. The surety who fully performs the obligation of his principal is subrogated to the creditor's rights against the principal. The surety who pays his principal's debt becomes entitled to any security that the principal has placed with the creditor to secure that particular debt. Likewise, if the creditor has obtained a judgment against the principal, the surety receives the benefit of the judgment when he satisfies the principal's debt. Where the creditor has collateral as general security for a number of obligations, the surety's right of subrogation does not arise unless all of the obligations are satisfied. It should be noted that subrogation applies only to rights of the creditor against the principal. If some third person, to secure the principal's debt, also pledges collateral to the creditor, the surety has no equity in the security, although the creditor calls upon him to satisfy the debt.

A creditor in possession of collateral given to him by the principal is not at liberty to return it without the consent of the surety. Any surrender of security releases the surety to the extent of its value, his loss of subrogation damaging him to that extent. Failure of the creditor to make use of the security, however, does not relieve the surety, since the latter is free to pay the indebtedness and to obtain the security for his own protection. However, if the creditor loses the benefit of collateral by inactivity—failure to record a mortgage or notify an indorser—the surety is released to the extent he is injured. In general, if the person who is entitled to protection under the contract of suretyship does anything that will materially prejudice the rights of the surety, the surety will to that extent, at least, be discharged.[10]

SURETYSHIP CASES

Timberlake v. J. R. Watkins Company
209 N.E.2d 909 (N.Dak.) 1965

The Watkins Company, plaintiff, entered into a written agreement with Timberlake whereby he became a distributor of the company's products. Timberlake, defendant, purchased the products from the plaintiff, and his wife, Stella, also a defendant, signed an agreement to guarantee payment by her husband of amounts due to the company up to $3,000. In the agreement she was called "surety." Timberlake received credit and did not pay; and the company brought action against both him and his wife. The lower court entered judgment for the plaintiff and the Timberlakes appealed.

WICKENS, J. Appellants [defendants] declare that the second agreement is a "suretyship agreement" and is void because . . . there is "lack of mutuality, want of consideration, failure to create a valid suretyship agreement for the reason that no tripartite relation of principal creditor, principal debtor or obligor, and surety, existed at the time the alleged Suretyship Agreement was signed; . . . "

[10] Board of Education v. Hartford Accident & Ind. Co., page 657

Appellants' demurrer and most of appellants' argument on the merits hinge on the question of whether these agreements create a "suretyship" as appellants use this term. Appellants contend that when Stella signed an agreement in 1952 no obligation then existed on the part of Everett [Timberlake] moving to appellee. It is insisted that this situation constitutes a failure to establish the tripartite relationship essential to a surety agreement.

We find that similar agreements have been construed by the courts of this State to be those of suretyship. . . .

It is a frequent general holding that suretyship involves a tripartite arrangement, that is, a principal debtor or obligor and a valid subsisting debt or obligation for which the principal is responsible and an undertaking by the surety to make himself collaterally liable. . . .

No reason has been advanced to show that the agreement in question cannot be more than merely one of suretyship, as that word has been used in a limited or strict sense. We think it is capable of being a contract of suretyship under certain facts (i.e., where a debt already exists) and under a different set of facts, being one of guaranty or one of indemnity. It appears that was the theory on which the trial court proceeded.

Authorities have attempted with some success to differentiate between contracts of suretyship, guaranty, indemnity, and in some instances, insurance. At the same time we have not found any that indicate a contract might not be capable of having the attributes of more than one of these classifications. In fact the Restatement of the Law of Security, sec. 82, p. 231, says "the term 'guaranty' is used in this Restatement as a synonym for suretyship." It further says:

> The possible convenience of having certain terms denote only particular types of surety obligations has resulted in some jurisdictions in the use of "suretyship" as a general term and "suretyship" with a restricted meaning. There has never been general agreement as to which term is to be the broader and which the narrower. Moreover, if both of the two terms are used with a restricted meaning, they do not suffice to cover even the main types of surety obligations.
> Suretyship obligations are contractual, and the important point of inquiry should be the precise undertaking of the surety and the duty of the principal. The recognition of the existence of different forms of contractual suretyship and the emphasis upon the obligation assumed in a particular case, are of greater significance than the distribution of labels to the various types of contracts.

Following that suggestion, we proceed to ignore the label and place emphasis on the obligation assumed. Stella Timberlake executed an agreement which appellee accepted. This contract specified that if appellee would extend credit to Everett Timberlake, in consideration thereof, she promised to pay up to $3,000 of the indebtedness thereafter incurred and owing by Everett. Such an agreement is not contrary to public policy; it contravenes no statute known to us; being in writing it is not within the statute of frauds. In this case it is not being attacked for fraud and no question was properly raised affecting its execution. We conclude with the trial court that it is a valid and enforceable agreement.

As to the consideration for the contract, the extension of credit to Everett

Timberlake constitutes sufficient consideration. Consideration need not be of benefit to the party making the promise. . . .

We find no merit in appellant's argument that there is no tripartite relationship here. As we understand that arrangement, all elements are present except an existing obligation which we hold to be unnecessary since after incurred indebtedness is covered by the agreement.

Finding no error, the judgment is affirmed.

Vaccaro v. Andresen

201 A.2d 26 (D.C.) 1964

HOOD, C. J. Michael P. Vaccaro [plaintiff], one of the appellants here, and appellee [defendant] Andresen were officers and stockholders in a corporation engaged in the florist business. The corporation was in financial difficulties and on March 31, 1961, Vaccaro and his wife executed an "installment discount" note to a bank in the sum of $2,556. The net proceeds of the note amounted to $2,009.54 and Vaccaro paid $2,000 of it to the corporation. According to Vaccaro the note was executed and the money paid to the corporation at the request of Andresen, who orally guaranteed payment of the note. According to Andresen, he merely asked Vaccaro "to put some money in the corporation." After receiving $2,000 the corporation carried the note on its books as a corporate liability and the corporation made some payments on it.

In June 1961 Andresen executed a paper guaranteeing payment of the Vaccaro note, promising to make the future installment payments on it and agreeing to reimburse Vaccaro for payments he had made on the note. In October 1961 the corporation went into bankruptcy and Vaccaro filed a claim against the bankrupt estate for money loaned "to the bankrupt corporation on March 31, 1961." The present action was brought by Vaccaro and his wife against Andresen on the guaranty agreement of June 1961, alleging that Andresen had paid $568 on the note and seeking recovery of the balance of $1,988. The trial court found that Vaccaro made a loan to the corporation on March 31 and that the guaranty agreement of June 7 lacked consideration, and the court denied recovery.

An enforceable contract of guaranty or suretyship requires, as do all contracts, a valid consideration; and where the guaranty is given subsequent to the original contract, the guaranty must be supported by a new consideration, separate and independent from the original contract. Here there was no evidence of any new consideration to Andresen for execution of the agreement of 1961. . . .

Affirmed.

Frell v. Dumont-Florida, Inc.

114 S.2nd 311 (Fla.) 1959

PEARSON, J. The appellant [Frell] was defendant in an action on a written guaranty. He appeals from a final judgment for the plaintiff which was based upon a jury verdict. The letter of guaranty contained the following:

> You have been requested to open a line of credit not to exceed Ten Thousand Dollars ($10,000.00), in favor of: Best Appliance Sales & Service Ltd.

You have indicated that you are unwilling to extend this line of credit to this dealer without other, and further, security of payment thereof.

In consideration of this agreement to extend this dealer a line of credit in question, the undersigned, hereby undertakes to, and does guarantee payment of any, and all, credit granted by you not to exceed Ten Thousand Dollars ($10,-000.00). . . .

The appellant contends first that the guaranty was, by its terms, limited to $10,000 and after that total amount had been purchased the guaranty did not cover new purchases even though the indebtedness was not as much as $10,-000. This argument overlooks the ordinary meaning of "a line of credit," which is a limit of credit to cover a series of transactions.

It is further argued that the guaranty was rendered ineffective as to purchases from the plaintiff after the date that the principal-debtor changed its name and one of the partners withdrew. The trial judge correctly found that the appellant as guarantor was estopped to claim this defense because the guarantor (1) participated in the change of name, (2) participated in the profits (if any) of the original debtor after the change, which business both before and after the name change was dependent upon the purchases made under the continuing guaranty, and (3) the guarantor at no time disclaimed responsibility under the guaranty until suit. . . .

The judgment of the trial court is therefore affirmed.

Affirmed.

Ireland's Lumber Yard v. Progressive Contractors

122 N.W.2d 554 (N.D.) 1964

TEIGEN, J. Plaintiff, Ireland's Lumber Yard, Inc., a materialman, instituted this suit against the prime contractor, Progressive Contractors, Inc., and its two payment and performance bond sureties for materials furnished. The bonds were executed to secure payment for all labor and materials furnished in the prosecution of the work covered by the principal contract calling for the construction of 744 housing units for military personnel at the United States Air Force Base at Grand Forks, North Dakota. . . .

The district court tried the case without a jury. It found in favor of the plaintiff and awarded judgment against the prime contractor and the defendant sureties in the amount of $9,723.03, plus interest at 4% per annum from May 21, 1960. The sureties have appealed and demand trial *de novo*.

The defendant sureties specify it was error for the court to hold . . . (that) the plaintiff was entitled to recover the additional sum of $8,045.69 as it had failed to comply with the terms of the bond with respect to timeliness in giving notice of claim. . . .

We shall now consider the last error charged, that the written notice of claim was not timely given. The bond provides:

"4. No suit or action shall be commenced hereunder by any claimant.

"(a) Unless claimant shall have given written notice to any two of the following: The Principal, any one of the Obligees, or the sureties above named, before the expiration of the period referred to in condition 2 above, stating with substantial accuracy the amount claimed and the name of the party to whom the materials were furnished, or for whom the work or labor was done or performed. . . . "

. . . It is . . . from the language of the bonds that no notice need be given the sureties at all as a condition precedent to bringing suit against them.

Part 4 of the bond, quoted above, provides that no suit or action shall be commenced unless claimant shall have given written notice to any two of the following: The principal, any one of the obligees, or the surety. Thus, a claimant giving notice to the principal and one of the obligees is permitted to sue the surety on the bond without prior written notice to the surety. We have no statute requiring notice to surety before suit on a suretyship bond in North Dakota. Generally, in the absence of statute to the contrary or provisions in the contract so requiring, notice of default need not be given to the sureties before they can be sued on the obligation, since it is their duty to make inquiry and ascertain whether the principal is discharging the obligations resting on him. . . .

Section 22-03-06, N.D.C.C., provides a surety is exonerated:

"4. To the extent to which he is prejudiced by an omission of the creditor to do anything when required by the surety which it is his duty to do."

We said in *Long* v. *American Surety Company*, 23 N.D. 492, 137 N.W. 41, that where a surety has paid a premium for issuing its bond, it will usually be treated rather as an insurer than according to the strict law of suretyship. This rule, however, does not exempt the beneficiary from living up to the terms of the agreement and the bond provisions are not to be construed strictly for or against either party, but reasonably as to both. In that case the court held that notice was required to be given within the time described in the bond. In a later case, *Mountrail County* v. *Farmers' State Bank*, 53 N.D. 789, 208 N.W. 380, the rule of *Long* v. *American Surety Company, supra*, was followed. However, the majority of the court in a special concurring opinion, agreed to the application of the rule in those two cases but questioned the broad statement of the rule in the *Long* v. *American Surety Company* case in the following language:

"I concur in the order of reversal and in the opinion as prepared by Mr. Justice Burke, particularly wherein it is stated that this case is controlled by that of *Long* v. *American Surety Company*, 137 N.W. 41, 23 N.D. 492, but I am not prepared to say that sureties are or should be held to be released in every case where there has been a failure to give a notice of default as required by the terms of the bond. In other words, I question the application of the rule, broadly stated in the *Long* case, to a situation in which the prejudice sustained by the sureties would not extend to the obligation previously fixed and determined. To illustrate the distinction in mind: Suppose the first default on a depository bond to have been coincident with the closing of a bank. The bank passes into the hands of a receiver. The insured depositor presents its claim to the receiver, and obtains a receiver's certificate, which it can readily assign to the sureties, but it neglects for more than 90 days to notify the sureties on the depository bond. The failure to notify in such case could scarcely operate prejudicially to the bondsmen as to the liability which became fixed at the failure of the bank. A notice promptly given would not enable the sureties to reduce the liability or cancel the bond, and they would continue to have the same rights against indemnitors that they had at the time of the failure. As applied to such a situation, it is difficult to see why the failure to give the notice should operate as a complete release. Rather, it seems to me, where there has been a breach of a bond, resulting in a liability for a fixed or determinable amount, the failure to give the notice stipulated for should not wipe out this liability to any greater extent than the prejudice suffered. I think the principle of exoneration to the extent of prejudice, as stated in section 6681 of the Compiled Laws for 1913, is applicable in such a situation. In my opinion, the rule is too broadly stated in the *Long* case, but I nevertheless concur in holding that that case is decisive of the present on the facts here involved. . . ."

In the instant case defendant surety companies had knowledge that there were unpaid bills for materials furnished when the first notice was timely given. Furthermore, the indebtedness to the claimant was fixed and did not increase in amount. It does not appear the sureties could have been prejudiced by the omission to serve the second notice of claim within the 90-day period provided in the bond. No fraud or dishonesty is shown. Suit was brought within the one year period as provided by the bond. The obligation placed upon the claimant by the terms of the bond was not broken until the loss had already occurred for which a liability has ensured. We do not believe the surety was in any way prejudiced by the delay in sending notice. A breach of such an obligation should not release the surety from liability but should exonerate him only to the extent to which he is prejudiced by the failure of the claimant to give the required notice, if any. Section 22-03-06, *supra*.

We would affirm the judgment on the record before us but, because the issue on the question of prejudice to the sureties was not litigated in the lower court, we deem it necessary to the accomplishment of justice that an opportunity be given the defendant sureties to offer evidence, if any they have, on this question. For this reason, we grant a new trail.

Bayer & Mingolia Construction Co. v. Deschenes
205 N.E.2d 208 (Mass.) 1965

The plaintiff, Bayer, was the general contractor on a State highway contract and the defendant, Deschenes, was a subcontractor engaged by plaintiff to do certain excavation work as specified in the prime contract. Under the subcontract all work was to start not later than November 24, 1958, and be completed on or before March 1, 1959. Deschenes was required to furnish a bond of $91,000 for faithful performance. The bond was written by Aetna Insurance Co. Deschenes did not start work until December 1, 1958, and on June 22, 1959, when he quit, he had completed only about half of the work. During this time Bayer made efforts to get Deschenes to do the work but finally completed the job himself. He brought action against Aetna on the bond and the lower court rendered judgment for the plaintiff. The defendants appealed.

CUTTER, J. Aetna contends that it is discharged as surety by the extensions of time for performance given by Bayer to Deschenes, despite Aetna's knowledge of these extensions, and the absence of any finding of injury to Aetna caused thereby. Aetna, however, "is a compensated surety and is not entitled to invoke the ancient doctrine of *strictissimi juris*. . . . "

In the case of an *accommodation* surety, "where the principal and creditor, without the surety's consent, make a binding agreement to extend . . . time . . . the surety is discharged unless the creditor in the extension agreement reserves his rights against the surety. . . . " The modern rule, however, with respect to a *compensated* surety (see Restatement: *Security,* 129 (2)) is that such a surety "is discharged only to the extent that he is harmed by the extension."

In any event, it is only by a binding, enforceable agreement for new consideration for an extension, which cannot be rescinded or disregarded, that the discharge of a surety will be effected. . . . The auditor's finding concerning the extensions of time for performance is merely that they were made "by mutual agreement of Bayer . . . and Deschenes." This finding does not import to us an enforceable agreement for consideration but merely Bayer's effort to obtain even dilatory performance by Deschenes.

We hold that Aetna, which has not shown itself to have been harmed by the extensions of time, was not thereby discharged as surety.

The order for judgment against Aetna is affirmed.

Fireman's Fund Insurance Company v. Richard

209 So.2d 95 (La.) 1968

LANDRY, J. From a judgment in favor of Fireman's Fund Insurance Company (Fireman's) casting defendant E. R. Richard in the sum of $2,025.00 on a written surety contract wherein Richard agreed to pay the debt of a third party, defendant has appealed. . . .

It is shown that a Mrs. Sylvia Veronica Stacey became indebted to Fireman's as a result of her embezzlement of funds of a former employer having no connection with the present litigation. Fireman's, surety on a fidelity bond issued Mrs. Stacey's prior employer, made good the amount of her defalcation and thus became subrogated to the employer's rights against the errant employee. Subsequently, Mrs. Stacey became associated with defendant Richard who owned a cleaning and pressing establishment in Houma, Louisiana. Upon being advised by local police authorities of an outstanding warrant for Mrs. Stacey's arrest on embezzlement charges, defendant discussed the situation with Mrs. Stacey who agreed to a compromise settlement of her obligation to plaintiff herein. Negotiations led to the confection of a contract wherein Mrs. Stacey acknowledged an indebtedness to Fireman's in the amount of $2,-200.00, which she agreed to pay in monthly installments of $100.00 commencing May 1, 1962. Appended to said document is a surety agreement signed by defendant, Richard, the pertinent portion of which reads as follows:

"(A) Should Sylvia Veronice [sic] Stacey default in the above agreed monthly payments of One Hundred Dollars ($100.00) on the first day of each month during the payment period, then endorser, E. R. Richard, P. O. Box 950, Houma, Louisiana, upon written notice form [sic] Fireman's Fund Insurance Company, will make up such payment within five days of notification.

(B) Should Sylvia Veronica Stacey default in payment of said note for a period of three (3) consecutive months, and endorser be notified in writing of such default, then it would and will become the duty of said endorser, E. R. Richard, to assume the monthly payments of One Hundred Dollars ($100.00) until the amount past due and/or payable be paid in full according to terms agreed upon by Sylvia Veronica Stacey and Firemans Fund Insurance Company. . . . ''

On May 4, 1962, Mrs. Stacey's first payment in the form of a check for $100.00 was received by Fireman's but was subsequently returned by the drawee bank as the drawer's account was insufficient to pay said amount. In June, 1962, Mrs. Stacey sent Fireman's a money order in the amount of $100.00 to cover the check dishonored upon presentment for payment. Thereafter Mrs. Stacey made two payments of $37.50 each on her obligation to Fireman's making her credits total $175.00. In September, 1962, Mrs. Stacey left Houma, Louisiana, and concerted efforts by both plaintiff and defendant to locate her failed to reveal her whereabouts. By letter dated November 14, 1962, plaintiff advised defendant that plaintiff would be compelled to look to defendant for payment pursuant to the hereinabove mentioned surety contract.

Appellant maintains the trial court wrongly rejected his claim that an extension or extensions of payment dates were granted Mrs. Stacey without appellant's knowledge or consent thereby releasing appellant from liability under the indemnification agreement.

Plaintiff counters . . . by denying that any extension or extensions of payments were granted. In this regard appellee acknowledges indulgence or forbearance on its part in collecting past due installments owed by Mrs. Stacey but that no extension either express or implied was ever granted the prime obligor.

Both parties hereto agree that the law of the instant case is stated in *O'Banion* v. *Willis,* 14 La.App. 638, 129 So. 440, to the effect that to constitute an extension of time which releases the surety of his obligation, there must be an agreement between obligor and obligee whereby, for sufficient consideration, the obligor foregoes his right of action against the obligee during the extension period. The litigants likewise agree that such an extension need not necessarily be express but may be implied from the circumstances attending the transaction between obligor and obligee. . . .

Appellant does not contend that a written extension was granted by Fireman's but in effect maintains acceptance of partial payments by Mrs. Stacey constituted an extension of time. . . .

The difference between indulgence which does not affect the release of the surety and an extension of time which terminates the surety's obligation is defined in the *O'Banion* case, as follows:

> The agreement between the maker and the holder of the note in this case was not the mere gratuitous indulgence or forbearance on the part of the holder not to force collection without fixing a definite period and without the giving of any consideration, as we find was the case in some decisions, notably *John M. Parker & Co.* v. *Guillot et al.,* 118 La. 223, 42 So. 782, and cases therein cited, but it was a valid and binding agreement during the life of which plaintiff had precluded himself from suing the maker of the note. As such was the situation, if either of the sureties had paid the holder after the part payment had been made and the extension granted, he could have exercised no greater right than the holder of the note, and would have been successfully met by the same plea of prematurity on the part of the maker.

We unhesitatingly conclude, as did the trial court, that circumstances of the instant case merely disclose plaintiff's gratuitous forbearance for an unspecified time as differentiated from an extension for a definite interval predicated upon consideration paid therefor. . . .

Accordingly, the judgment of the trial court is affirmed at appellant's cost. *Affirmed.*

Magazine Digest Pub. Co., Limited v. Shade et al.

199 A.2d 190 (Pa.) 1938

DREW, J. This suit in assumpsit was brought [by Magazine Digest] to recover money alleged to be due under a contract between plaintiff and Mutual Magazine Distributors, Inc., on which contract defendants were guarantors. In their affidavit of defense defendants denied liability on the ground that they were discharged by a subsequent oral agreement which altered the original contract without their knowledge or consent. . . .

Under its original contract Mutual Distributors agreed to buy plaintiff's magazines at 14.5 cents a copy for resale to retailers at 16.5 cents. Defendants guaranteed Mutual's obligation to pay plaintiff, with the additional stipulation that:

> . . . the publisher (plaintiff) may in his absolute discretion and without diminishing the liability of the guarantors (defendants), grant time or other indulgence to the distributor and may accept or make any composition or arrangements when and in such manner as the publisher may think expedient.

The parties continued under this contract until September 19, 1933, when Mutual was in arrears to the extent of $1,162.12. On that date it was orally agreed between plaintiff's president and the president of Mutual that if plaintiff refrained from terminating the contract, Mutual would pay the increased price of 15 cents a copy for the magazines. . . .

We cannot agree that defendants are liable for Mutual's debts under the substituted agreement of September 10, 1933. Even compensated guarantors —and defendants are not shown to be such—are not liable when the original contract on which their undertaking was made is materially changed without their assent. A gratuitous or accommodation guarantor is discharged by any change, material or not, and "even if he sustains no injury by the change, or if it be for his benefit, he has a right to stand upon the very terms of his obligation and is bound no farther." But there can be no doubt here the alteration was material. To the distributor it meant 25 per cent less in its sale profit, to the plaintiff it made the difference between the terminating and continuing contractual relations with the distributor, and to the defendants it meant an increase in their obligation of $1,118.05 on 223,609 magazines received from the publisher after the new contract was in force. . . . Nor can the legal effect of alteration be escaped by limiting recovery against guarantors to the rate set in the original contract. The very theory of their defense is that after the change there is a new contract on which the guarantor has not agreed to be liable to any extent. . . .

Defendants are not relieved, however, from Mutual's debts which accrued while the original contract remained in force. The subsequent variation of that contract had no effect upon the liability that had already become fixed. Consequently defendants were not discharged as to it.

George E. Failing Co. v. Cardwell Investment Co.

376 P.2d 892 (Kans.) 1962

The defendant, Cardwell Investment Co., was guarantor of the payment of McPeters, drilling contractors, purchasers from the plaintiff. The guaranty agreement required plaintiff to submit all invoices to the contractor for approval and at the same time mail to defendant copies of all invoices. The plaintiff delayed seven months in mailing a copy of a particular invoice to defendant. The lower court ruled that the guarantor was discharged from liability and the plaintiff, Failing Co., appealed.

SCHROEDER, J. Even compensated guarantors are not liable when the original contract on which their undertaking was made is materially changed without their assent. A gratuitous or accommodation guarantor is discharged by any change, material or not, and even if he sustains no injury by the change, or if it be for his benefit, he has a right to stand upon the very terms of his obligation and is bound no further. The guarantor is at least entitled to notice of change and the attempt to increase his burden and his chances of loss. . . .

In the instant case the terms of the guaranty contained in the letters are neither ambiguous nor inconsistent. The law views with a jaundiced eye any attempt to vary by parol evidence the terms of a written contract. This is particularly true with respect to a written contract of guaranty, inasmuch as the nature of the transaction makes it subject to the statute of frauds. . . . If the language of the contract of guaranty is clear and leaves no doubt as to the parties' intention concerning the measure of the guarantor's liability, the guarantor cannot be held liable in excess of the limitations that the contract language imposes. The character of the credit given in a written guaranty which is complete in itself cannot be explained by parol evidence. . . .

By the terms of the contract Failing agreed to submit all invoices to Mr. McPeters for his approval, and at the same time mail copies of all invoices to Cardwell "as made" for Cardwell's knowledge of McPeters' purchases through Failing.

We hold that Failing was required under the written terms of the guaranty to make a reasonably prompt submission of all invoices by sending a copy to Cardwell for his knowledge of McPeters' purchases through Failing, if Failing sought to obligate Cardwell on the guaranty.

It may be conceded that the contract of guaranty specified no limitation as to the amount McPeters might purchase through the Failing Company or the time during which such purchases could be made, but this does not preclude a reasonably prompt submission of copies of invoices for which purchases were made through Failing.

An analogous situation is found with respect to the time for presentment of a check for payment which has been drawn upon a bank. . . . A check must be presented for payment within a reasonable time after its issuance or the drawer will be discharged from liability thereon to the extent of the loss caused by the delay.

Accordingly, the judgment of the trial court is affirmed.

Bomud Company v. Yockey Oil Company and Osborn

142 P.2d 148 (Kans.) 1958

Osborn in a letter guaranteed payment by Yockey of oil well supplies which the plaintiff, Bomud, in reliance on the letter sold to Yockey on credit. Yockey is no longer liable because of the short statute of limitations for oral agreements but the five-year statute applying to written accounts has not run. Osborn contends that he is released because Yockey is no longer liable and the lower court awarded judgment in favor of Osborn, against whom the plaintiff has taken this appeal.

FATZER, J. A guarantor, to be relieved from his obligation to pay, must establish one of three facts: (1) the debt has been paid or extinguished; (2) a valid release or discharge; or (3) the bar of the statute of limitations as to himself. It is conceded that the debt has not been paid. The fact that the statute bars recovery against Yockey does not extinguish the debt. . . . It is also conceded that the statute of limitations has not run as to Osborn's individual liability on his written contract if he has not been released or discharged. Did the failure to bring the action upon the open account, until the statue had run in favor of Yockey, release or discharge Osborn from his guarantee to pay under his written contract? We think it did not. . . . The contract of a guarantor is his own separate contract. It is in the nature of a warranty by him that the thing guaranteed to be done by the principal shall be done, and is not an engagement jointly with the principal to do the thing. A guarantor, not being a joint contractor with the principal, is not bound like a surety to do what the principal has contracted to do, but answers only for the consequence of the default of the principal. . . . When default occurs on the part of the principal, the guarantor's liability becomes primary and is absolute. . . .

Osborn's contract with Bomud was based upon a valid consideration. It was a separate undertaking to pay if Yockey defaulted. When Osborn's liability became primary and absolute, the open account was then enforceable against Yockey, and it is of no consequence to Osborn if since that time the statute has run in Yockey's favor. Osborn's liability was fixed and determined by his written guaranty and that obligation has not been discharged. That the statute of limitations (G.S.1949, 60-306, *First*) had not run in Osborn's favor when suit was filed is conceded. The debt has not been paid. Bomud is entitled to recover from Osborn in accordance with the terms and conditions of his contract.

The judgment is *reversed* with directions to set aside the order entering judgment for Osborn on the pleadings, and to proceed in accordance with the views expressed in this opinion. It is so ordered.

Board of Education (Anning-Johnson Co.) v. Hartford Accident & Ind. Co.

208 N.E.2d 51 (Ill.) 1965

Anning-Johnson Co., plaintiff, was a subcontractor on a project for the Board of Education. The prime contractor was bonded by Hartford by arrangement of the Board of Education. The parties stipulated as to the following facts: plaintiff upon completion of the subcontract delivered waivers of lien to the general contractor certifying that he had been paid $6,840 on his claim of $9,600, that plaintiff to the extent of $6,840 released the Board of his right of lien against public money in its hands; that in fact he had been paid nothing; that the general contractor was thereby enabled to receive a payment of $6,840 from the Board. Anning-Johnson sought to recover $9,600 from Hartford. In an action on the bond, the court held that Hartford, surety, was obligated to pay only $2,760. The plaintiff appealed.

CORYN, J. The judgment held, in effect, that plaintiff is barred from recovery against Hartford on the performance bond to the extent of amounts for which plaintiff delivered partial waiver of lien. The trial court found that by reason of plaintiff's conduct, its claim, to the extent of $6,840, was not a just claim within the meaning of the act in relation to bonds of contractors entering into contracts for public construction.

Defendant, Hartford, argues that the ruling of the trial court is correct, in that the partial waivers of lien delivered by plaintiff induced payment by the School District as plaintiff intended; that these waivers therefore operated as a relinquishment of rights to which defendant was entitled to be *subrogated* in the event of its payment to plaintiff; *that defendant's position was materially prejudiced by this conduct of plaintiff which reduced the amount of public moneys available as security for defendant's commitment as surety;* and that plaintiff's claim is not therefore a just claim within the meaning of said Payment Bond Statute.

In *Alexander Lumber Co.* v. *Aetna Co.* (296 Ill. 500, 129 N.E. 871), it was held that where the bond of a building contractor covers obligations for material furnished for the building, a subcontractor supplier of material who refrained from filing a lien against a building fund for a portion of his claim, so that the right thereto was lost, to that extent released the surety on the bond. Such failure was held to be a violation of a duty arising from the relationship of surety and assured. "It is an equitable rule," said the court at page 509, 129 N.E. at page 874, "that, where a creditor releases or permits to be lost a security for a debt, other sureties are thereby released to that extent." In *Northbrook Supply Co. et al.* v. *Thumm Construction Co. et al.* (39 Ill.App.2d 267, 188 N.E.2d 388), plaintiff was a supplier to a subcontractor and had delivered lien waivers to the subcontractor by which the latter was enabled to obtain payment from the general contractor. When the subcontractor subsequently failed to pay the plaintiff, a complaint was filed against the surety on the general contractor's performance bond delivered in compliance with 15 and 16 of ch. 29, Ill. Rev.Stat. Although the facts of this case are substantially different from those in the case at bar, the Appellate Court there held plaintiff's claim barred, not because the general contractor had paid the claim once and had not defaulted, but because plaintiff was estopped by its conduct and its claim was not therefore a just one. At 50 Am. Jur., Suretyship, 109, 110, it is stated that a surety by operation of principles of equity is entitled to be subrogated to the benefit of all the securities and means of payment under a creditor's control.

Defendant, Hartford, in the case at bar, by reason of the relationship of the parties here as surety and assured, had a right exercisable at any time, to pay plaintiff's claim and to be subrogated thereby to its rights of lien against public moneys in the hands of the School District. By extinguishing this right through the delivery of partial waivers certifying payment, which induced the release of public moneys, as plaintiff intended, plaintiff is estopped by its own conduct, *pro tanto,* from recovering against Hartford. We agree with the finding of the trial court that plaintiff's claim is not a just one within the meaning of the statute. Irrespective of whether the statute contemplates liability on the part of a surety in cases where final settlement may have been made, and rights of subrogation therefore lost, it is also evident that the claim asserted must be a just one. The statute does not contemplate liability, in our judgment, in a case where a claimant has voluntarily prejudiced the rights of the surety.

The judgement of the trial court is accordingly affirmed.

CHAPTER 33
REVIEW QUESTIONS AND PROBLEMS

1. *S* wrote a letter to *C,* a materialman, saying he would be liable for "any bill my son makes for material." A dispute arose later as to whether this covered one purchase or a series of purchases. What is your answer?

2. *G,* by contract, guaranteed prompt payment of a certain note owing by *P* to *C.* The note fell due at a time when the maker was solvent, but *C* made no attempt to collect and gave *G* no notice of the default. Later *P* became insolvent and *C* desires to collect of *G.* May he do so?

3. Davis was surety for his brother on a $1,152 note in favor of Bank, the brother giving Davis a mortgage on real property to protect him against loss. Davis and his brother are insolvent and are thinking about releasing the mortgage. The court held Bank could have the mortgage impounded for its benefit. Why?

4. *S* was surety upon *P's* obligation to *C.* Some time after the debt fell due, *P,* with the knowledge and consent of *S,* made a payment on the obligation. Did this payment toll the statute of limitations for *S* as well as *P?*

5. *C, A, E,* and *M* were sureties upon a $4,000 obligation of *B* to *W.* The obligation provided for attorney fees of 10 per cent if placed with an attorney for collection. *B* defaulted and *C,* upon demand, paid the $4,000 note to *W.* He then sued *A, E,* and *M* for $3,000 and attorney fees in an action against them jointly. The court refused to allow any attorney fees and refused to give a joint judgment against the three. Why?

6. The mother and wife of *P* became cosureties on *P's* note for $5,000, the note being secured by a chattel mortgage on *P's* household furniture. The wife settled the claim for $3,500 and released the chattel mortgage on furniture worth $2,500. She now seeks contribution from the mother, her mother-in-law. How much should she recover?

7. *C* Company loaned *J* Company $68,000, $59,280 of the amount being guaranteed in writing by *W* and his wife. As security for the guaranty, they pledged a note for $59,280 owing to them as joint tenants by *X.* The $68,000 debt fell due, and in settlement a new note for a lesser amount and a different rate of interest was given *C* Company by *J*

Company. *W* guaranteed the new debt and repledged the $59,280 note as security, his wife not joining in the guaranty or pledge. *J* Company is again in default and *C* Company proposes to use the $59,280 note as a means of collection, when *W*'s wife claims one-half of it because she did not join in the pledging. Was her original pledge still good?

8.   *X* had a credit card from the ABC Oil Company, which he often used to purchase gasoline and oil. One provision of the contract underlying the card was that the holder of the card, *X*, remained liable for all purchases made with the card up to the time he reported it lost or stolen. *X* lost his card and did not discover that fact for over three weeks. *Y* found the card, and purchased over $2,000 worth of automotive supplies during the three weeks. The ABC Company sues *X* for the value of those services. What result?

9.   *X* hired *Y*, a general contractor, to build a house. *Y* in turn hired *Z*, a subcontractor to paint the house. However, knowing *Z* to be a rather irresponsible person, *Y* required *Z* to obtain a bond from an insurance company, the ABC Company, to insure his performance. *Z* left town, and *Y* brought an action against the ABC Company alone. May he do so?

chapter 34

Bankruptcy

4-19. Introduction. The law of bankruptcy is of ancient origin and is concerned with the problems which arise when a person, firm, or corporation is unable to satisfy obligations due to creditors. Bankruptcy has its roots in the law of the Roman Empire and has been a part of English jurisprudence since 1542. Laws relating to bankruptcy have been enacted or amended in the United States after each major economic depression. The current statute was originally enacted in 1938, and while there are almost annual minor amendments, the last major one was in 1952. This statute as amended provides various methods for relieving debtors of their debts or postponing the time of their payment, and for protecting some of the rights of their creditors.

Bankruptcy proceedings are predicated on federal laws and are conducted in the federal courts. Bankruptcy laws contain provisions relating to voluntary and involuntary bankruptcy—the former being at the instigation of the debtor and the latter at the instigation of creditors. In addition, the modern federal statute contains provisions on arrangements, wage-earner plans, compositions of creditors, and corporate reorganizations. These latter procedures, which are also concerned with the affairs of insolvent debtors, will be discussed in this chapter as part of the law of bankruptcy in the broad sense.

The law of bankruptcy is designed to accomplish several purposes. Historically, the major purpose was to provide a method of applying a debtor's assets in an equitable distribution among his creditors. It prevented the debtor from preferring one creditor over another and minimized the losses of all creditors to the extent possible. A second purpose of the modern bankruptcy provisions is found in the sections relating to voluntary bankruptcy, the purpose of which is to relieve honest debtors of the weight of oppressive indebtedness in order that they may start afresh, free of their former obligations. This purpose recognizes that misfortune and poor judgment often create a situation in which a debtor will never be able to discharge his debts by his own efforts. Public policy dictates that such debtors should be able to obtain a fresh start not only in their personal lives but in business as well. The procedures for arrangements and reorganizations are similar in purpose. Their function is the rehabilitation of debtors, whether businesses or individuals.

4-20. Bankruptcy Proceedings. Bankruptcy proceedings are relatively simple. A petition is filed (by the debtor if voluntary and by creditors if involuntary) with the federal district court. A petition filed by a partnership as a firm is not a petition on behalf of the partners as individuals, and if they intend to obtain individual discharges, separate petitions are required. The proceedings are conducted by an officer of the court known as the *referee in bankruptcy.* Referees are used in lieu of judges because of the large volume of cases. The decisions and orders of the referee are the orders of the court, and while they are subject to review by the judges, the referee is for all intents and purposes a judicial officer, and he exercises judicial powers.

The voluntary petition in bankruptcy constitutes an adjudication of the debtor as a bankrupt and consists of essentially four items—a list of creditors, secured and unsecured; a list of property or assets; a list of property claimed by the debtor to be exempt; and a statement of affairs of the bankrupt. The petition is filed on official forms designated by the Supreme Court for that purpose. Great care must be exercised in the completion of these forms. Concealing assets is a crime under the bankruptcy laws, as is the willful making of a false oath. The schedules are sworn to, and knowingly supplying false information is the making of a false oath.

Involuntary petitions are filed by creditors to have the debtor adjudged a bankrupt. The special aspects of involuntary bankruptcy are discussed in the next section, but it is noted here that the petition must allege, among other things, that the debtor has committed an act of bankruptcy. (Acts of bankruptcy are discussed in Section 4-22.) The debtor answers the petition, and if adjudged a bankrupt by the referee, the debtor will be required to complete the same schedules as the debtor in a voluntary proceedings.

After the adjudication of the debtor as a bankrupt, which is the formal decision by which jurisdiction over the debtor's property is obtained, the proceedings in voluntary and involuntary bankruptcy are identical. After the adjudication of the debtor as a bankrupt, the referee notifies each creditor of the proceeding, of the date by which all claims are to be filed, and of the date of a meeting of the creditors with the debtor.

If upon the filing of the petition, it appears to the referee that it is necessary to have control over the debtor's property prior to the first meeting of creditors, the referee may appoint a receiver. A *receiver* is a temporary officer designated to take charge of property and to care for it to prevent waste and loss. Receivers are usually appointed to operate a business until the first meeting of creditors can be conducted.

At this first meeting, a *trustee* in bankruptcy is elected by the creditors, unless the bankrupt's estate has "no assets." A majority in number and amount of claims held by those present at the meeting is necessary for election. The trustee takes title to all nonexempt property, both real and personal, owned by the bankrupt at the time the petition was filed. It becomes his duty to dispose of the property as best he can, under the supervision of the court, for the benefit of creditors. Personal property purchased from the bankrupt by an innocent party, after the filing of the petition but before the trustee or receiver takes possession, remains with the purchaser. Any property received by the bankrupt after the filing of the petition belongs to his new estate, except that all devises, bequests, or inheritances received within six months thereafter belong to the trustee. Executory contracts of the debtor may be accepted or rejected by the trustee within sixty days after the petition in bankruptcy has been passed upon. If the trustee chooses to reject a contract, the other party is then permitted to file a claim for damages against the bankrupt estate. In case of leases, however, the landlord may file a claim for all past-due rentals and for damages caused by breach of the lease agreement, but the latter claim shall not be in excess of one year's rental as will be hereinafter discussed.

At the meeting of creditors, the debtor may be examined by the creditors to ascertain if property has been omitted from the list of assets, if property has been conveyed in defraud of creditors, and about other matters which may effect the right of the debtor to have his obligations discharged. In many voluntary bankruptcies, after this meeting of creditors, the proceedings are essentially over. This is true in "no asset" cases because there is no property to be sold and nothing to be used to pay creditors. The only issues remaining are possible grounds for denying a discharge. If there are nonexempt assets, the trustee in bankruptcy will take control of them, sell them for cash, pay all expenses, and use the balance to pay dividends to creditors in accordance with the rules on claims and priority discussed later.

During the proceedings, creditors will file their claims, and some creditors may object to the discharge. These matters will be heard and decided by the referee. The legal principles involved are discussed in subsequent sections.

4-21. Bankruptcy Jurisdiction. Any person, firm, or corporation may become a *voluntary* bankrupt, with five exceptions. Railway, banking, insurance, and municipal corporations, and building and loan associations may not become voluntary bankrupts. However, an insolvent railway may petition a bankruptcy court for confirmation of a reorganization plan, provided the plan has first been approved by the Interstate Commerce Commission.

Any natural person, except a farmer or wage earner; any partnership and any moneyed business or commercial corporation, except the five previously mentioned, may be adjudged an *involuntary* bankrupt for proper cause. Thus, three groups are exempt from involuntary bankruptcy—farmers, wage earners, and nonbusiness corporations.

A farmer is defined as anyone engaged in the tillage of the soil, raising poultry or livestock and their products, or operating a dairy. If he spends most of his time on the farm and expects to derive most of his income from it, he is deemed a farmer although he is incidentally engaged in other enterprises. A wage earner, for the purpose of involuntary bankruptcy, is one who works for another at a rate of pay of $1,500 a year or less. A worker who earns over $1,500 per year is not exempt from involuntary bankruptcy.

Involuntary bankruptcy proceedings require that the debtor's liabilities equal at least $1,000. If twelve or more creditors exist, at least three of them must sign the petition; if there are fewer than twelve creditors, only one need sign. The petitioning creditors as a group must also own definite unsecured claims totaling $500 or more. Relatives, persons holding fully secured claims, and other biased creditors are not counted in determining the number of creditors required to sign the petition.

4-22. Acts of Bankruptcy. The purpose of involuntary bankruptcy is to force an equitable distribution of an insolvent debtor's assets. Mere insolvency affords no basis for a petition in involuntary bankruptcy. Unless a debtor has committed some act which indicates an intention to abuse his creditors or to prefer certain creditors, or has done something which shows a willingness to have his assets distributed, he may not be adjudged an involuntary bankrupt. The bankruptcy law sets forth six acts; one of them must be alleged to have been committed within four months prior to the petition before involuntary bankruptcy proceedings may be commenced.

Acts of bankruptcy consist of a debtor's having:

1. Conveyed, transferred, concealed, or removed, or permitted to be concealed, or removed, any part of his property with intent to hinder, delay, or defraud his creditors, or made a fraudulent transfer under the fraudulent transfer provisions.[1]

2. Made a preferential transfer of property to a creditor in payment of an antecedent debt at a time when he was insolvent.

3. Allowed, while insolvent, any creditor to obtain a lien upon his property through court action and having failed to discharge such lien within thirty days from the date it was entered or at least five days before the date set for any sale or other disposition of the property.

4. Made a general assignment for the benefit of creditors.

5. A receiver appointed, voluntarily or involuntarily, to take charge of his property because of insolvency or inability to pay debts as they mature.

6. Admitted in writing his inability to pay his debts and his willingness to be adjudged a bankrupt.

The first act of bankruptcy consists of conduct amounting to a fraudulent conveyance. The property that was fraudulently conveyed may be recovered and used to pay the debts under certain circumstances. This subject is discussed more fully in Section 4-29.

Attention is called to the fact that the second, third, and fifth acts require insolvency. The first, fourth, and sixth acts, do not require it. However, solvency at the time the petition is filed is a good defense to the first act of bankruptcy, and proof of solvency will cause a denial of the creditors' petition. Insolvency, where required, refers to the financial condition at the time the act is committed. Except for the fifth act, *insolvency,* as used in bankruptcy, refers only to the situation in which the debtor's assets, valued on the basis of a voluntary sale, fail to equal his liabilities. It differs from insolvency in the "equity sense," which means that a debtor is unable to pay his debts in the ordinary course of business. In accounting terms, insolvency in the "equity sense" means that current liabilities exceed current assets, while insolvency in the bankruptcy sense means that total liabilities exceed total assets. By definition, the fifth act encompasses both concepts of insolvency.

---

[1] Marshall v. Showalter, page 674 , see also Section 4-29.

It should be emphasized, concerning the third act, that it is not the *lien* which constitutes the act of bankruptcy, but it is the *failure to vacate it* within the time allotted to the debtor.

The petition in involuntary bankruptcy must be filed within four months of the commission of one of the acts of bankruptcy. Transfers of property are frequently not fully effective as to third parties until a document is recorded and made a matter of public record. For example, a conveyance of real estate is not complete until the deed is recorded. Whenever recording is required, the four months' period is calculated from the date of recording and not from the date of the transfer.

CLAIMS

4-23. Introduction.   Not all claims of creditors are allowed to participate. Not all claimants against a bankrupt may share in his assets. There are many technical terms in the Bankruptcy Act which are significant to an understanding of the rights of persons who may have claims against a bankrupt.

The term "provable claim" is used to describe those claims which are entitled to share in the bankrupt's estate. The term "dividend" describes payments by the trustee to creditors. A "dischargeable claim" is one that will be barred to the extent that it is not paid in the proceedings. Not all claims are discharged; many will continue to be binding obligations even though the bankrupt has received a discharge.

Before a claim is dischargeable, it must meet the statutory requirements to qualify as a provable claim, because claims which are not provable are not dischargeable and, therefore, are not properly before the bankruptcy court. As previously noted, the mere fact that a claim qualifies as provable does not necessarily mean that it is also dischargeable. Some debts continue after the conclusion of the bankruptcy proceedings.

The sections which follow will discuss the requirements for a claim to qualify as provable, those which are not dischargeable, and the priority for the payment of claims.

4-24. Provable Claims.   To qualify as a provable claim, the claim must be filed by the creditor within six months of the date first set by the referee for the first meeting of creditors. However, claims of the United States, and claims of persons under a disability, such as infants and insane persons without guardians, are not subject to this requirement. In the latter case, an additional six months is granted for filing the claim.

A trustee may sue a third party to recover property for the estate or to set aside a lien on property of the estate. If the trustee is successful in recovering such property or setting aside the lien, the third party may have a claim against the bankrupt's estate. If the third party has such a claim, he is given thirty days, after turning the property or money over to the trustee or from the date the lien is avoided, in which to file the claim.

In order to qualify as provable, the claim must be liquidated or certain in amount. Among the typical claims which are not liquidated are those involving contracts in dispute, tort claims, and claims of several creditors where the security may be of lesser value than the amount of the claim. If a suit on a contract is pending at the time of the petition, the claim may be made certain by agreement with the trustee as to the amount of damages, or by judicial decision either in the court in which the suit is pending or by proof before the referee. The claim must still be filed within the six months' period. The provability of tort claims will be discussed later in this section, but as a general rule, tort claims not reduced to judgment are not provable. A claim of a secured creditor will be allowed to the extent that the claim exceeds the security. This amount can be determined by selling the security or by compromise or litigation with the trustee.

Most provable claims are fixed liabilities based on judgments or instruments in writing such as commercial paper. All judgments, including those arising in tort, are provable. Claims may also be based on open accounts and on any contract, express or implied, including anticipatory breach of executory contracts.

"Implied contracts," as the term is used in bankruptcy, include the remedy of quasi contract as well as implied in fact contracts. This is important in those states which allow the remedy of quasi contract to be used as a basis of recovering damages for such torts as trespass to goods or conversion. In these states, quasi-contract claims are provable though not reduced to judgment if liquidated, in the same manner as other contracts because the action is considered to be contractual rather than tortious. The same is true of suits for personal injuries based on product liability because of the contractual nature of such actions. This is not a serious problem because of the treatment of negligence cases as provable claims which will be discussed below.

If the breach of contract action is for the breach of an unexpired lease, the claim is limited to one year's future rent plus unpaid accrued rent. Thus, landlords' claims are limited to the rent due to the date of surrender of possession plus one year, provided the lease runs for that period.

Tort claims are not provable unless they have been made certain by contract or judgment prior to the petition in bankruptcy. An exception exists for claims based on a theory of negligence. In such cases, the injured party may prove his claim if he has instituted suit prior to the filing of bankruptcy proceedings. For example, assume that *A* has sued *B* for a willful tort, such as assault and battery, and that the case has not proceeded to judgment when *B* files a petition in bankruptcy. *A* cannot file a claim and will not share in *B*'s bankrupt estate. However, the claim is not discharged and may be enforced against any new assets *B* may acquire. On the other hand, if *A*'s cause of action is based on negligence, *A* is entitled to share in the estate, and his claim is discharged. If *A* has not filed his negligence suit, the claim is not provable and not dischargeable.

Other provable claims that are exceptions to the general principle of certainty are workmen's compensation awards based on injuries, sickness, or death occurring prior to the adjudication of bankruptcy; claims for costs in suits started against the bankrupt or in cases started by him and abandoned by the trustee; and tax claims.

If a creditor has illegally received preferential treatment from the bankrupt, the trustee can set aside the preference and demand the return of that which was received. Thus, if a creditor has knowingly received payment of a claim from an insolvent debtor within four months of bankruptcy, the creditor must return the payment. Having done so, he may file a claim, but so long as he retains the preference, he is precluded from proving any claim whether related to the preference or not. See Section 4-30 for a further discussion of preferences.

4-25. Claims That Are Not Discharged. Provable claims are dischargeable, but discharge may be denied either because of the nature of the claim or because of conduct of the debtor. The debtor's conduct that may result in a denial of discharge may occur before the proceedings are commenced or during the proceedings.

Among provable claims that are not discharged are (1) claims for taxes due any governmental body; (2) debts created by fraud, embezzlement, misappropriation, or defalcation of a debtor acting in any fiduciary capacity; (3) alimony and child support, (4) liability resulting from willful or malicious torts;[2] (5) wages earned within three months of filing the petition in bankruptcy; (6) liabilities for property or money obtained under false pretenses or by fraudulent representations; and (7) claims for money of an employee which had been retained by his employer to secure the faithful performance of the employment contract.

In regard to taxes, a recent amendment makes dischargeable, in bankruptcy, debts for taxes which became legally due and owing more than three years preceding bankruptcy. The discharge does not release or affect any tax lien, however.

Because of the extremely large number of automobile accident cases and the rapidly increasing size of the verdicts, the question of discharge of claims arising out of automobile accidents is of substantial importance. It has already been noted that tort claims on which litigation has not been commenced are not discharged. Accordingly, a person faced with potential tort liability should not file a petition to eliminate this potential liability until suit is brought against him. It has also been noted that an intentional tort is not dischargeable even though it is provable if reduced to a judgment, but a claim based on the tort of simple negligence is both provable and dischargeable. For example, suppose that A has a $50,000 judgment against B and is paid $10,000 as a dividend in the bankruptcy proceedings. If the judgment is based on an intentional tort, A still has a valid judgment against B for $40,000 after the discharge in bankruptcy; but if the suit is based on a theory of negligence, A's judgment is discharged. A difficult issue is presented when the theory of the lawsuit lies between simple negligence on the one hand and a clearly intentional tort on the other. Such lawsuits proceed on a theory known as *willful and wanton misconduct.* Modern cases tend to hold that judgments based on willful and wanton misconduct are not dischargeable.[3]

As previously noted, it is the duty of the bankrupt to file a schedule of all creditors and the amount due each. Notice of the proceedings is then given each creditor in order that he may attend the meetings of creditors and file claims. The claim of any creditor who is not listed or who does not learn of the proceedings in time to file his claim is not discharged. The bankrupt, under such circumstances, remains liable. In the case of nonlisted creditors, the

[2] First National Bank of Lansing v. Padjen, page 676.
[3] Perrett v. Johnson, page 678.

burden of proof to establish that the creditor had knowledge of the proceedings in time to file a claim rests with the bankrupt. Proof of actual knowledge is required, and while such knowledge is often present, care should be taken to list all creditors so that all claims will unquestionably be discharged. In certain cases, the schedules may be amended to correct errors, but this is discretionary with the referee.[4]

4-26. Bankrupts Who Are Not Discharged.

A discharge in bankruptcy is a privilege and not a right. Therefore, in addition to providing that certain *claims* are not discharged, the Act lists seven grounds for denying a *bankrupt* a discharge. These grounds must be specifically set forth by a creditor as an objection to discharge and must be proven to the satisfaction of the referee at a hearing on the objection. When a discharge is denied, the assets are distributed among the creditors, but the debtor remains liable for the unpaid portion of all claims. The Act provides that discharge will be denied if the bankrupt has:

(1) committed a "bankruptcy crime" (one that is created by the Bankruptcy Act itself rather than by the general criminal law) punishable by imprisonment; (2) destroyed, mutilated, falsified, concealed, or failed to keep or preserve books of account or records, from which his financial condition and business transactions might be ascertained, unless the court deems such acts or failure to have been justified under all the circumstances of the case;[5] or (3) while engaged in business as a sole proprietor, partnership, or as an executive of a corporation obtained for such business money or property or credit,[6] or obtained an extension or renewal of credit, by making or publishing or causing to be made or published, in any manner whatsoever, a materially false statement in writing respecting his financial condition or the financial condition of such partnership or corporation; or (4) at any time subsequent to the first day of the twelve months immediately preceding the filing of the petition in bankruptcy, transferred, removed, destroyed, or concealed or permitted to be removed, destroyed, or concealed, any of his property, with intent to hinder, delay, or defraud his creditors; or (5) has within six years prior to bankruptcy been granted a discharge . . . ; or (6) in the course of a proceeding under this Act refused to obey any lawful order, or to answer any material question approved by the court; or (7) has failed to explain satisfactorily any losses of assets or deficiency of assets to meet his liabilities.

Any of the circumstances mentioned may be set up by a creditor as a bar to a discharge, or they may be set up by the trustee, when he has been authorized to do so by the creditors. Furthermore, if any creditor can show reasonable cause for believing that the bankrupt has done any of the things mentioned, the burden shifts to the bankrupt to show that he has not committed an act that will bar discharge.

It should be noted that the third ground for barring the discharge is limited to businessmen. Persons not in business who furnish false financial statements to obtain property or credit may nevertheless be discharged. Such false statements will not bar discharge but will prevent discharge of the debt which arose out of the transaction in which the fraudulent financial statement was submit-

[4] Robinson v. Mann, page 680
[5] Gross v. Fidelity & Deposit Company of Maryland, page 682
[6] Branch v. Mills & Lupton Supply Company, page 684

ted. Therefore, a false financial statement by a businessman is a complete bar
to a discharge, but a false financial statement by a person not engaged in
business is only a bar to discharge of the debt involved.

4-27. Priority of Claims.   Creditors are either secured or unsecured. Since the
trustee's title to property is only the title previously held by the bankrupt, any
valid lien or security interest against the property continues after bankruptcy.
The secured creditor can collect the debt by enforcing his security interest. If
the total value of the property securing the secured creditor is greater than the
debt, the trustee may pay off the debt and then use the property to satisfy the
unsecured creditors. A secured creditor who forecloses his security interest
without accepting the property in full satisfaction is an unsecured creditor to
the extent of any deficiency.

The law relating to priority of claims is concerned with the order in which
unsecured creditors are paid. Unsecured creditors are paid dividends from any
assets remaining after secured creditors have exercised their rights. The Bankruptcy Act creates six classes of unsecured creditors and directs that each class
be paid in full before anything is paid to the next class. If funds are insufficient
to pay in full any particular class of creditors, the funds available for such
group are distributed in proportion to the amount of each claim; in this
situation all classes falling lower in the list receive no payment. For example,
if the assets are not sufficient for paying in full the claims of wage earners
amounting to $600 per person and earned within the previous three months,
the wage earners would share proportionately the amount available, but the
claims for taxes and general creditors would not share. The order of priority
of the classes of unsecured creditors is as follows:

1. Cost of preserving and administering the bankrupt estate. This includes
such items as court costs, receiver, trustee and attorney's fees, and appraisal
fees. It also includes rent of property occupied by the receiver or trustee during
the administration of the bankrupt's estate.

2. Claims of wage earners not exceeding $600 to each claimant, provided
the wages have accrued within the three months preceding bankruptcy. Wage
earners include workmen, clerks, servants, and salesmen. These people were
dependent on the bankrupt for their support and are thus preferred. Claims
in excess of $600 are treated as a sixth-class claim, as are wages earned before
the three-month period.

3. Claims for money expended in defending suits against or setting aside
arrangements of the bankrupt debtor.

4. Claims for taxes.[7] The priority accorded to taxes in the distribution of
bankrupt estates applies to those taxes which became legally due and owing
within three years preceding bankruptcy. Other taxes are a sixth-class claim.

5. Claims for rent granted priority by state statute and any claims allowed
priority by federal law. Many of the claims held by the federal government
have been given priority under this provision. The law restricts the priority for
rent to not more than three months' rent owing at the time of bankruptcy and
further restricts this priority to rent accruing for actual use of the premises.

---

[7] In Re Connecticut Motor Lines, Inc., page 685

This priority is given because of the limitations imposed on landlords' liens under the statute.

6. Claims of general creditors.

4-28. Exemptions.   The debtor may claim property as exempt from his bankrupt estate if an exemption is provided by either the laws of the United States or the laws of the state of his domicile. State law usually exempts certain personal property not to exceed a specified value and in addition provides that a certain sum out of the value of the homestead shall be paid to the debtor free of the debts. These exemptions were discussed in Chapter 32, Section 4-6.

The Bankruptcy Act provides that no exemption shall be allowed out of property which a bankrupt has transferred or concealed and which is recovered by the trustee for the estate. The debtor is required to prepare a list of property claimed to be exempt. Failure to claim the exemptions or to list property may result in the use of property otherwise exempt to pay the creditors.

4-29. Voidable Transfers.   A trustee in bankruptcy may bring suit to avoid transfers of property by the debtor on several grounds. First, the trustee may do so on any ground which could have been used by the debtor to obtain a return of his property. Since the trustee has stepped into the debtor's shoes, grounds such as fraud, mutual mistake, and lack of capacity may be used by the trustee to obtain a return of property.

Second, a trustee may avoid a transfer which constitutes a preference by the debtor for one or more creditors over others. Preferences are discussed in the next section.

Third, the trustee may avoid any judicial lien (judgment) or judicial sale that is obtained or conducted within four months of the filing of the bankruptcy petition if the lien or sale was obtained or conducted while the debtor was insolvent. The reasons for not allowing liens to be treated as valid secured claims if perfected within four months immediately preceding the filing of the petition in bankruptcy are the same as those for allowing the recovery of payments or transfers which constitute preferences.

Fourth, the trustee may set aside any transfer made by the debtor, or any obligation incurred by the debtor which is fraudulent under either federal or state law. The Bankruptcy Act has substantially incorporated the Uniform Fraudulent Conveyance Act in its provisions. Fraudulent transfers will be discussed in Section 4-31.

Besides having several grounds for avoiding a transfer of property, the trustee has several statuses or capacities in which to act. As previously noted, the trustee stands in the shoes of the debtor and may avoid any transfer which the debtor could have avoided. A provision of the Bankruptcy Act sometimes referred to as the "strong-arm" clause gives the trustee two additional statuses in which to act to set aside fraudulent or voidable transfers of property.

The "strong-arm" clause gives the trustee the rights and powers of a judgment creditor who obtained a judgment against the bankrupt on the date of the adjudication of bankruptcy and who had an execution issued against the bankrupt which was returned unsatisfied. The trustee has these rights of a judgment creditor whether or not any judgment creditor actually exists.

The clause also gives the trustee the status of a lien creditor with a lien on all of the bankrupt's property on which any creditor could have obtained a lien, whether or not a lien creditor actually exists. Thus, the "strong-arm" clause gives the trustee the status of both a judgment creditor and a lien creditor. It allows the trustee to avoid any transfer of property made by the debtor which any creditor would have been able to avoid under any state law.

For example, assume that the debtor has made a bulk transfer of property and that the parties did not comply with the provisions of Article 6 of the Uniform Commercial Code. The trustee in his status as a lien creditor could avoid the transfer notwithstanding the fact that the debtor could not have done so. If the law merely placed the trustee in the shoes of the debtor, the transferred property would be beyond the control of the trustee. But in the area of voidable transfers, the "strong-arm" clause has greatly expanded the power of the trustee. He possesses not only all of the rights and powers of the debtor-bankrupt but all of the rights and powers of the creditors as well. These may be exercised independently and inconsistently, depending on the needs and decisions of the trustee.

The status of the trustee as a judgment creditor is also important in determining the priority of claimants. It gives the trustee representing general creditors a priority over an unfiled federal tax lien. Unfiled federal tax liens are subject to prior judgments, and the "strong-arm" provision in effect gives all general creditors a judgment for this purpose.

4-30. Preferences.   One of the goals of bankruptcy proceedings is to provide an equitable distribution of a debtor's property among his creditors. In order to accomplish this goal, the trustee in bankruptcy is allowed to recover payments which constitute a preference of one creditor over another. To constitute a recoverable preference, the payment must have been made (1) by an insolvent debtor;[8] (2) to a creditor for, or on account of, an antecedent debt; (3) within four months of the filing of the bankruptcy petition; and (4) to a creditor who, at the time of the payment, knew, or had cause to believe, that he was obtaining a greater percentage of his claim than other creditors could recover. The term "payment" includes transfers of property. The distinction between a transfer which constitutes the second act of bankruptcy and one which constitutes a recoverable preference is found in the fourth requirement for a recoverable preference. As noted in Section 4-22, a payment or transfer may be the second act of bankruptcy, but it may not be a recoverable preference if the creditor does not know that he is being preferred. In such cases, a petition in involuntary bankruptcy may be successfully filed, but the creditor receiving the payment need not return it.

As noted previously, recoverable preferences include not only payments of money but also the transfer of property as payment of, or as security for, a prior indebtedness. A mortgage or pledge may be set aside as readily as payment, providing it is received by the creditor with knowledge of the debtor's insolvency. Such pledge or mortgage can be avoided, however, only if it was received within the immediate four months prior to the filing of the petition in bankruptcy and was obtained as security for a previous debt. In the

[8] Riccio v. General Motors Acceptance Corporation, page 687

case of the mortgage, the four months' period dates from the recording of the mortgage rather than from its signing.

If the property received by a preferred creditor has been sold to an innocent third party, recovery of the property may not be had, but its value may be obtained from the creditor. A creditor, however, who in good faith extends additional credit after having received a preference, may deduct from the recoverable preference the amount of any new credit extended. In this manner, a creditor who attempts to help an insolvent debtor out of financial difficulty is not penalized if, after obtaining payment, he extends no greater credit than the amount of the old claim.

Payment of a fully secured claim does not constitute a preference and, therefore, may not be recovered.

Transfers of property for a present consideration may not be set aside because there is a corresponding asset for the new liability. A mortgage given to secure a contemporaneous loan is valid although the mortgagee took the security with knowledge of the debtor's insolvency. An insolvent debtor has a right to attempt to extricate himself, as far as possible, from his financial difficulty.

Any debtor of a bankrupt may set off against the amount he owes the bankrupt estate any sum which the estate owes him. To the extent of his set-off, he becomes a preferred creditor, but he is legally entitled to this preference. This, however, does not apply when the claim against the bankrupt has been purchased or created with the express purpose of taking advantage of the rule relating to set-offs. For example, a bank that has loaned a bankrupt $2,000 and happens to have $1,500 of the bankrupt's on deposit at the time of bankruptcy, is a preferred creditor to the extent of the deposit. This set-off will be allowed unless the evidence discloses that the deposit was made with the express purpose of preferring the bank. In such a case, the deposit becomes a part of the bankrupt estate.

4-31. Fraudulent Conveyances. A transfer of property by a bankrupt-debtor may be fraudulent either under federal or state law.[9] The trustee may proceed under either to set aside a fraudulent conveyance. Under federal law, a fraudulent conveyance is a transfer within one year of the filing of the petition, with the intent, actual or implied, to hinder, delay, or defraud creditors. Under state law, the period may be longer and is usually within the range of two to five years.

An actual intent to hinder, delay, or defraud creditors may be present. If so, the trustee will be successful in setting aside the conveyance. The intent to hinder, delay, or defraud creditors may also be implied. Such is the case when debtor is insolvent and makes a transfer for less than a full and adequate consideration.[10] The intent will also be implied when the transfer results in insolvency. *Implied intent* means that the law conclusively supplies such intent regardless of the actual intent of the debtor. A conveyance of property to a relative or a friend is a typical situation in which the intent will be implied.

[9] Priebe v. Svehlek, page 689
[10] Robinson v. Mann, supra, page 680

A special provision relating to the intent factor by a debtor who is in business provides that the intent will be implied where the transfer is without fair consideration and leaves the businessman with an unreasonably small amount of capital. The businessman may be solvent, but he has, nevertheless, made a fraudulent transfer if the net result of the transfer is such that he is left with an unreasonably small amount of capital, provided the transfer was without fair consideration. Whether or not the remaining capital is unreasonably small is a question of fact.

Fraudulent intent sufficient to avoid a transfer without fair consideration may be implied from the state of mind of the debtor at the time of the transfer. For example, assume that *A* is about to enter business and that he plans to incur debts in the business. Because of *A's* concern that he may be unable to meet these potential obligations, he transfers all his property to his wife without consideration. Such a transfer may be set aside as fraudulent, and the requisite intent is supplied by the factual situation at the time of the transfer and the state of mind of the transferor. The actual financial condition of the debtor in such a case is not controlling but does shed some light on the intent factor and state of mind of the debtor.

Of course, transfers are fraudulent in which the actual intent to hinder, delay, or defraud creditors exists. Actual fraudulent intent may be inferred from the fact that the consideration is unfair, inadequate, or nonexistent. Solvency or insolvency at the time of the transfer is significant, but it is not controlling. Actual fraudulent intent exists when the transfer makes it impossible for the creditors to be paid in full or impossible for the creditors to make use of the legal remedies that would otherwise be available.

Bona fide purchasers, lienors, and obligors who acquire property from the immediate transferee in good faith and for a fair consideration are protected under the Bankruptcy Act. The trustee may not proceed against such parties. However, if property has been fraudulently transferred to an innocent third party, the transfer can be avoided if the consideration given for it was inadequate. In such a case, the third party is reimbursed to the extent he gave consideration. Property may also be recovered from any person who receives it with knowledge of the fraud. Such person becomes an ordinary creditor of the debtor to the extent of the consideration which he gave for the property.

OTHER PROCEEDINGS

4-32. Arrangements and Reorganizations. The previous sections have discussed ordinary bankruptcies. The Bankruptcy Act also contains provisions that are for the purpose of debtor relief rather than the liquidation of assets. These debtor relief provisions are designed to assist debtors by developing some plan to enable them to pay their debts and avoid the stigma of bankruptcy. Most plans involve an extention of time for payment and such other relief as cancellation of executory contracts and determination of the priorities of claims so that the pressure by creditors is alleviated. In addition to aiding the debtor, arrangement and reorganization provisions also aid the majority of creditors by allowing them to work with the debtor in attempting to straighten out his affairs.

The arrangement and reorganization chapters of the Act recognize four distinct situations for granting assistance to a debtor. Under each situation the rules differ, as does the power of the court. The four situations are (1) where the arrangement will affect only the claim of unsecured creditors; (2) where the debtor is an individual, and not a corporation, and there are no debts secured by real estate; (3) where the debtor is a wage earner; and (4) where the debtor is a corporation. In this latter situation, the corporation is usually permitted to continue operation under court supervision until some plan of reorganization is approved or it is determined that no plan can secure the requisite support for its approval. If such support cannot be obtained, the court proceeds to liquidate the corporation as in any other case of bankruptcy.

The procedures are somewhat similar in the four situations. Each plan must be approved by the court and by a stipulated percentage of the creditors who are affected by the plan. The percentage varies from a simple majority in number and amount to two-thirds of the claims in each class affected, depending on the type of arrangement which is involved. Secured creditors are not affected by extension arrangements and wage earner plans.

4-33. Wage-earner Plans.   One section of the federal Bankruptcy Act provides an arrangement whereby a wage earner who qualifies can work out a plan to pay off his unsecured creditors over a period of time in lieu of filing an ordinary petition in bankruptcy. In this connection a "wage earner" is a person whose principal income is derived from wages, salary, or commissions. Such a plan enables a person having financial problems and being pressed by his creditors to work out a long-range program to pay off his debts. The debtor submits his future earnings to the supervision and control of the court for the purpose of carrying out the approved plan. If the plan is not carried out, the wage earner may be entitled to convert it to straight bankruptcy.[11]

BANKRUPTCY CASES

Marshall v. Showalter

375 F.2d 529 (1967)

KERR, J. In this appeal, Everette Marshall, the bankrupt, challenges the decision of the District Court affirming the Order of the Referee in Bankruptcy by which appellant was adjudicated a bankrupt. The case involves the construction of Sections 3(a) (1) and 67 of the Bankruptcy Act, defining what constitutes an act of bankruptcy and what amounts to insolvency.

On July 5, 1963, appellant, Everette Marshall, and his wife, Harriet Marshall, sold their farm to a group of individuals who thereupon formed the Marshall Land and Cattle Co., Inc. In consideration for the sale, the corporation agreed to pay Marshall's personal indebtedness which was approximately $213,000.00, and executed its promissory note to the Marshalls and their son, Robert, in the face amount of $300,000.00. The principals of the corporation individually guaranteed the payment of the note. Shortly thereafter, Robert Marshall assigned his interest in the note to his parents. On June 1, 1964, Everette Marshall transferred his one-half interest in the note to his wife,

---

[11] In the Matter of R. C. Hendren, page 690

Harriet. At that time $15,000.00 had been paid by the Corporation and the balance due on the note was $285,000.00.

On September 4, 1964, appellant's creditors filed a petition to have him adjudicated bankrupt on the ground that he committed an act of bankruptcy on June 1, 1964, by the assignment of his interest in the promissory note to his wife. Appellant denied that he was insolvent at the time of the transfer and that he was rendered insolvent thereby, contending that his equitable interest in the note and his contract rights with the Marshall Land and Cattle Company constituted assets sufficient to prove his solvency. After a hearing on the creditors' petition and appellant's answer, the Referee prepared and filed a Memorandum Opinion, Findings of Fact and Conclusions of Law and ruled that Everette Marshall was an involuntary bankrupt under the Bankruptcy Act. The Referee's holding was affirmed by the District Court which held that on June 1, 1964, appellant performed an act of bankruptcy under Sections 3(a)(1) and 67 of the Bankruptcy Act by transferring his one-half interest in the note to his wife without fair consideration, thereby rendering himself insolvent.

As the District Court found, appellant's assets on June 1, 1964, were a $14,000.00 claim against the Marshall Land and Cattle Co., Inc., for personal expenses, and another claim against that company for unpaid salary. He had a life interest subject to a second mortgage on his home, some small insurance policies, some equity in a tractor, and the equity, if any, in the note which he had assigned to his wife. His liabilities on June 1, 1964, were approximately $157,500.00, which was the balance due his personal creditors whom the Marshall Land and Cattle Company agreed to pay as part of the consideration for the sale of appellant's farm, and a $15,000.00 liability to the Brighton National Bank secured by a mortgage on a tractor.

Under the facts and circumstances of this case, the District Court correctly found that on June 1, 1964, appellant was personally indebted to his creditors in the amount of $157,500.00. Appellant's creditors were not parties to the agreement between Marshall and the Marshall Land and Cattle Company; they did not consent to an assumption by the Company of the obligation to pay appellant's debts. At no time was the Corporation substituted as the debtor in place of appellant. As shown by the record, appellant's contract right to hold the Marshall Land and Cattle Company liable for the payment of his debts had no monetary value and did not amount to discharge of his personal liability to his creditors. Since appellant had not been released by his creditors from his obligation to pay his debts, the debtor-creditor relationship continued. As between appellant and his creditors, appellant remained personally and solely liable for the payment of the $157,500.00.

Likewise without merit is appellant's contention that he retained an equity in his one-half interest in the promissory note, and that such equitable interest constituted an asset on and after June 1, 1964. On that date, appellant assigned to his wife "all of his right, title and interest" in the $300,000.00 note. Appellant concedes that the assignment was, on its face, absolute. He attempts to explain, however, that the transfer was made merely to expedite the collection of the note from the individual members of the corporation. The District Court correctly found that, according to the evidence, Harriet Marshall did not take and hold appellant's interest in the note in trust for him and his creditors. The transfer of his interest was absolute and unrestricted. There was no agreement requiring Harriet Marshall to give appellant and his creditors the proceeds which might be realized from any collection suits. We accept the conclusion of the District Court that under the law of Colorado, a wife is not under a legal or equitable duty to apply her funds to her husband's debts.

Having concluded that the assets of appellant do not include the contractual right to recover over against the Marshall Land and Cattle Company for the payment of his personal debts, nor the alleged equity in his one-half interest in the promissory note, we turn now to the question of whether the transfer of appellant's right, title and interest in the promissory note on June 1, 1964, constituted an act of bankruptcy under Section 3(a) (1) of the Bankruptcy Act. The second phrase of that section is applicable to the facts of this case, for the crucial issue is whether appellant fraudulently transferred his property. Section 3(a) (1) refers to Section 67 for the determination of that question. Under Section 67(d) (2) (a) a transfer of property is fraudulent if made without fair consideration, and also if made by a debtor who is or will be thereby rendered insolvent. The intent of the debtor is expressly eliminated from consideration. The record indisputably supports the District Court's finding that the consideration of One Dollar for the transfer of the $300,000.00 note was less than fair consideration.

The final issue to be resolved is whether the creditors must prove appellant's insolvency at the time of the transfer, or whether it is sufficient to prove that he was rendered insolvent by the transfer. A person is insolvent "when the present fair salable value of his property is less than the amount required to pay his debts; . . . " To come within the provisions of Section 67(d) (2) (a) the transfer is fraudulent if the debtor is insolvent at the time of the transfer, or if he is rendered insolvent as a result of the transfer. These are alternative provisions. They are unambiguous. The District Court correctly construed the law as not requiring a finding of insolvency at the date of the transfer. The facts and the law support the court's conclusion that appellant's transfer to his wife of all his right, title and interest in the promissory note of the face value of $285,000.00, was made without fair consideration, and that said transfer rendered appellant insolvent. The act of bankruptcy under Section 3(a) (1) occurred upon the transfer within the meaning of Section 67(d) (2) (a) on June 1, 1964, within one year prior to September 4, 1964, the date of the creditors' petition for involuntary bankruptcy of appellant.

Affirmed.

First National Bank of Lansing v. Padjen

210 N.E.2d 332 (Ill.) 1965

BURKE, J. This action was brought by plaintiff-mortgagee (First National Bank) against defendants-mortgagors for the conversion of chattels covered by a chattel mortgage. The defense of discharge in bankruptcy was raised, which was sustained by the trial court. The mortgagee appeals.

On April 7, 1962, defendants executed a chattel mortgage covering restaurant equipment to plaintiff. The mortgage was duly recorded and covered, among other items, two heat lamps and a glass chiller. Defendants later filed a petition in bankruptcy, individually and in their business capacity, in the United States District Court. A receiver was appointed and plaintiff obtained an order from the federal court directing that the receiver turn over to plaintiff all chattels in his possession which were covered by the chattel mortgage. All of the chattels were turned over except the two heat lamps and the glass chiller; it was at this time that plaintiff first learned that these chattels had been previously disposed of by defendants. It appears that on July 30, 1963, the glass chiller was returned to the seller from whom it had been purchased and $300 credited to defendants' account; when and to whom the two heat lamps were disposed of does not appear on record.

Plaintiff thereupon filed this action in the Circuit Court for damages for the conversion of the chattels. Judgment was rendered in favor of the defendants on the ground that the defendants' act of disposing of the chattels did not constitute a conversion within the meaning of Section 17 of the Bankruptcy Act (11 U.S.C.A. 35) and consequently was not within those debts of a bankrupt not discharged by bankruptcy. The trial court certified the following question to this court: whether or not the return of the chattel-mortgaged property to the original seller for which money is received by the chattel-mortgagors, without securing the release or consent of the chattel-mortgage holder, is tantamount to willful conversion of property which would not be discharged under Section 17 of the Bankruptcy Act (11 U.S.C.A. 35). It does not appear that this matter was presented in the bankruptcy court so that the question of *res judicata* does not arise. . . .

Section 17 of the Bankruptcy Act states:

> (a) A discharge in bankruptcy shall release a bankrupt from all of his provable debts, whether allowable in full or in part, except such as . . . (2) are liabilities for . . . willful and malicious injuries to the person or property of another. . . . (11 U.S.C.A. 35.)

The question certified to this court and raised by this appeal is one of first impression in the State of Illinois. Only two other states have passed upon this question. . . .

The United States Supreme Court has held that to deprive another of his property by deliberately disposing of it without semblance of authority is an injury thereto within the common meaning of the words used in the Bankruptcy Act. . . . Furthermore, the converter need not act with actual malice or ill will, nor with the specific intent to injure a particular person, but only that he act without legal cause or justification. . . .

The Illinois Commercial Code provides that the conversion of the security of a loan by a mortgagor without the assent of the mortgagee will subject the mortgagor to criminal penalties. . . . The same was true under the statutes predating the present Code. . . . The purpose of these criminal penalty provisions is to prevent the disposition of the security by the mortgagor to the injury of the mortgagee. . . . That the mortgagee's interest in the chattel securing a loan is a protectible property cannot be doubted.

In the instant case, defendants disposed of the chattels in question without the consent of the plaintiff. In so doing, they deprived plaintiff of property to which it had a right to look in the event that defendants failed to meet the payments on the loan. It would be an absurd result to say that plaintiff, upon defendants' bankruptcy, has a right to those chattels covered by the mortgage which are still in defendants' possession, but has no right to seek the value of those chattels covered by the mortgage wrongfully disposed of, on the grounds that the liability for the wrongful disposition was discharged by the bankruptcy proceedings. We are of the opinion that the unauthorized disposition of the two heat lamps and the glass chiller constituted a "willful and malicious injury to property" within the meaning of Section 17 of the Bankruptcy Act. The question certified to this court by the trial court is answered in the affirmative.

The judgment is reversed and the cause is remanded with directions to enter judgment for plaintiff and against defendants in the amount of $550 and costs.

Judgment reversed and cause remanded with directions.

Perrett v. Johnson

175 So.2d 497 (Miss.) 1965

JONES, J. This case arises from an automobile accident which occurred July 22, 1963, on Highway No. 55, an interstate four-lane highway presently completed from Jackson nearly to Crystal Springs. The highway has a median strip between the two southbound lanes and the two northbound lanes. While traveling south, appellant struck from the rear a car occupied by Jones B. Johnson, which was traveling south ahead of the appellant's car. As a result of the collision Johnson died. A suit for the wrongful death of deceased was filed in the Circuit Court of Copiah County, Mississippi, by the deceased's widow and children. After trial, judgment was rendered for the sum of $23,-000. There was no appeal from this judgment.

About a week after the judgment was rendered, appellant filed voluntary bankruptcy proceedings. A writ of garnishment was issued against the appellant's employer, who answered admitting indebtedness; and the appellant made his appearance and pleaded his bankruptcy discharge as a full and final discharge of the judgment debt. After a hearing on the issue, the circuit judge held that the judgment had not been discharged and gave judgment on the writ of garnishment against the appellant's employer for the amount due by him to the appellant. The case comes here on appeal and we affirm the decision of the lower court.

Section 17 sub. a(2) of the Bankruptcy Act provides: "A discharge in bankruptcy shall release a bankrupt from all of his provable debts, whether allowable in full or in part, except such as . . . liabilities . . . for willful and malicious injuries to the person or property of another . . . " 11 U.S.C.A. § 35, sub. a (Supp.1964). The question presented here, therefore, is whether the injury to the decedent was a willful and malicious injury within the meaning of section 17, sub. a(2) of the Bankruptcy Act.

A more detailed discussion of the facts is pertinent to this issue. It was shown that after the collision, the appellant's automobile came to a stop 471 feet from the place of the accident, traveling on the highway after the accident 336 feet and continuing after it left the paved surface of the road, for an additional 135 feet. Decedent's car traveled 384 feet after impact, 180 feet on the highway and 204 feet beyond the highway, turning over, and finally coming to rest. After the accident a portion of a bottle of vodka was found in appellant's automobile. Appellant admitted having taken a drink of vodka that afternoon. The accident occurred about 9:00 or 9:30 P.M. Although decedent's car was traveling on the proper side of the highway with a lane to the left in which another car could easily pass, appellant's car struck the car in which decedent was riding. The pictures of the automobiles which were introduced showed signs of a terrific impact, appellant's car being damaged in the front about the center, and decedent's car being heavily damaged in the rear more to the center and right of the center.

.   .   .

The determination whether an injury resulting from an automobile accident is "willful and malicious" within the meaning of section 17, sub. a(2) of the Bankruptcy Act has caused the courts considerable difficulty.

What constitutes willful and malicious injury growing out of an automobile accident, within the provision of the Bankruptcy Act relating to discharge, depends in each case upon the particular facts. Whether a claim arising out of an automobile accident survives a discharge in bankruptcy because it involves a willful and malicious injury depends upon the facts and circumstances surrounding the injury and the specific acts of misconduct charged against the tortfeasor. It is clear, however, that liability for simple negligence in the operation of a motor vehicle which results in an injury to another is not excepted from a discharge in bankruptcy as a willful and malicious injury. Neither reckless nor unlawful operation of the vehicle brings liability for an injury resulting therefrom within the exception, unless the conduct appears to have been so in disregard of consequences to another that it can be said to have been wanton as well as willful. Malice, or its equivalent, is essential for an exception from a bankruptcy discharge, but if the conduct causing the injury, though not done with actual malice, is willful and wanton, done intentionally, and in willful disregard of known duty, that is sufficient, according to many decisions, to categorize it as "malicious" within the intendment of the Bankruptcy Act.

In order to fall within the exception to bankruptcy discharge, the injuries must have been both willful and malicious. The word "willful" means "nothing more than intentionally doing an act which necessarily leads to injury." 1 Collier, *Bankruptcy* § 17.17, at 1631 (14th ed. 1964). A "malicious" act, under this provision, is an "unlawful or wrongful act done intentionally without just cause or excuse." 9 Am.Jur.2d *Bankruptcy* § 786, at 588 (1963).

The word "wilful" means intentional or deliberate. It is not, as used in the exception, restricted to the meaning which it may have in criminal prosecutions. Any act that is done unlawfully and maliciously is necessarily wilfully done.
A "malicious" act, within the meaning of the exception, is an unlawful or wrongful act done intentionally without just cause or excuse. While a wilful act is not a malicious act unless the intent is to do harm or to act in utter disregard of another's rights, it is not necessary that one be incited by a malevolent or malicious motive, such as is required to give color to a criminal act, in order that his act may be malicious within the meaning of the exception. "Wilful and malicious" is equivalent in meaning to "wilful and wanton." It is sufficient to supply the element of a malicious injury if the act be such that malice may be implied therefrom. An act may be wilful and malicious even in the absence of hatred or ill will, and it is not necessary, in order to invoke the exception, to show special or express malice. (9 Am.Jur.2d *Bankruptcy* § 786 (1963)).

In *Wegiel* v. *Hogan,* 28 N.J.Super. 144, 100 A.2d 349, 353 (1953) it was stated that:

"Wanton and reckless conduct," that is, acts done with an utter disregard of rights and safety of others, may constitute "willful and malicious injury" to person and property of another within meaning of Bankruptcy Act provision exempting from discharge liabilities of bankrupt for "willful and malicious injury" to person or property of another.

In *Breeds* v. *McKinney,* 171 Ohio St. 336, 170 N.E.2d 850 (1960), defendant unsuccessfully pleaded discharge in bankruptcy as a defense to a proceeding by a judgment creditor in aid of execution of a default judgment in an automobile accident case in which defendant had been alleged to have "carelessly, negligently, recklessly, willfully and wantonly" while under the influence of intoxicating liquor and while driving at an unlawful speed crossed over the center lane of the highway and collided with the plaintiff. It was held that plaintiff's injuries had been willfully and maliciously caused within the meaning of the Bankruptcy Act.

In *McClure* v. *Steele,* 326 Mich. 286, 40 N.W.2d 153, 13 A.L.R.2d 160 (1949), a discharge in bankruptcy was not a bar to the collection of a judgment in which there was a stipulation between the parties and the personal injuries occasioned to the plaintiff's wife by the car of the defendant being driven over the curb and sidewalk were the result of the defendant's "wilful and wanton negligence." It was held tantamount to an admission that the defendant was guilty of causing "willful and malicious injuries to the person or property of another" within the meaning of the exception in the Bankruptcy Act.

And In re *Papale,* D.C., 17 F.Supp. 146 (1936), a debt against a father resulting from a judgment for his thirteen year old son's wilfully and maliciously putting out the eye of a playmate with a pellet from an air rifle was held not dischargeable in bankruptcy, where the bankrupt knew that his son used the air rifle indiscriminately in shooting at cats, birds, and playmates.

In this case the circuit judge heard the evidence, and after considering the matter, he held that the judgment was the result of wilful and malicious injuries within the meaning of the Bankruptcy Act. We find nothing in the record which would justify us in saying that the lower court was in error, and the case is therefore affirmed.

Affirmed.

Robinson v. Mann

339 F.2d 547 (1964)

GRIFFIN, J. . . . On June 1, 1961, appellant executed a deed conveying his house and lot at Fort Valley, Georgia, for no consideration to his three minor children. On October 9, 1961, he filed a voluntary petition in bankruptcy. The trustee in bankruptcy then filed a petition seeking to set aside the June 1 conveyance as in fraud of creditors. . . . At the date of bankruptcy, appellant had debts in excess of $30,000. Aside from the house conveyed to the minor children (found by the Referee to be worth $15,500), his only asset was an automobile worth $1,291. He testified that his financial condition was even worse on June 1, the date of the conveyance, although he did not realize it at the time.

Section 67, sub. d(2) of the Bankruptcy Act provides in pertinent part:

Every transfer made . . . by a debtor within one year prior to the filing of a petition initiating a proceeding under this title . . . is fraudulent (a) as to creditors existing at the time of such transfer . . . if made . . . without fair consideration by a debtor who is or will be thereby rendered insolvent, without regard to his actual intent. . . .

The Referee found that the conveyance was made within one year prior to bankruptcy, without consideration, and that appellant was insolvent at the time. . . . Consequently, we hold that the Referee was correct in setting aside the conveyance. It is insisted that the conveyance was not made with intent to defraud creditors, but this of course is no defense. By the express terms of § 67, sub. d(2), intent is irrelevant.

. . . . .

When the creditors schedules were drawn up in October 1961, appellant informed his attorney of a note owing to the Citizens & Southern National Bank in the amount of $1,100. The debt had been assigned to the bank by the Home Roofers & Builders, Inc., and arose in connection with repair work performed on his house. The attorney erroneously concluded that the debt was only a lien against the property, i.e., that there was no personal liability. Since the property had been conveyed to the minor children, the attorney intentionally failed to list the debt on the creditors schedules. In point of fact, the bank has no lien and appellant is personally liable on the note.

The first meeting of creditors was held on October 26, 1961. From this date up until December 19, 1962, appellant was apparently without the services of an attorney. At the suggestion of the Referee, he then employed a second attorney, and on December 28, 1962, this attorney petitioned the bankruptcy court to amend the creditors schedules so as to include the debt owed the Citizens & Southern National Bank. The Referee denied the amendment on the grounds that amendments more than six months after the first meeting of creditors were barred by § 57, sub. n of the Bankruptcy Act, 11 U.S.C.A., § 93, sub. n. The District Court affirmed, and this ruling is now challenged.

Section 57, sub. n of the Bankruptcy Act provides:

. . . Claims which are not filed within six months after the first date set for the first meeting of creditors shall not be allowed. . . .

This section has generally been held to operate as an absolute bar against creditors who seek to present their claims beyond the six months deadline. The section has also often been applied to prevent the bankrupt from amending his schedules after six months. . . .

We do not think that § 57, sub. n deprives the courts of power to allow amendments by the bankrupt more than six months after the first meeting of creditors. That section is addressed to creditors, not to the bankrupt. Its primary purpose is to prod creditors to seasonably present their claims, not to force bankrupts to seasonably present their amendements. A bankruptcy court is a court of equity, and in an appropriate case its inherent equity powers may be invoked to allow amendment after six months. However, amendments should not be allowed as a matter of course. Section 57, sub. n evinces a statutory purpose to achieve speed and certainty in bankruptcy proceedings, and this purpose could be defeated by excessive amendments which disrupt and prolong administration of the bankrupt's estate. Consequently, we hold that the proper rule is that amendment by the bankrupt may be allowed more than six months after the first meeting of creditors, but only in exceptional circumstances appealing to the equitable discretion of the bankruptcy court. In exercising this discretion, the Referee should, of course, consider such factors as may be offered in justification of the failure to originally list the creditor in question. In this case these will also include the circumstances attendant to the failure of counsel to have originally listed the creditor, the degree of disruption which would result from allowing the amendment, and whether any creditor including the unlisted creditor would be prejudiced thereby.

From the present record, we are unable to determine with certainty whether the Referee denied the amendment on the ground that he had no power to allow it under § 57, sub. n or on the ground that this was not an appropriate case for the exercise of his discretion. In view of the conflict in authority and lack of a controlling decision by this court heretofore, the Referee's decision could have been based on either ground. Therefore, we hold that this case should be remanded to allow the Referee to reconsider the application to amend in the light of the equitable discretion which we have here held that he possesses.

Affirmed in part; vacated and remanded in part for further proceedings not inconsistent herewith.

Gross v. Fidelity & Deposit Company of Maryland

302 F.2d 338 (1962)

MATTHES, J. In this bankruptcy proceeding the broad question on appeal is whether Everett W. Gross is entitled to be discharged as a bankrupt in accordance with the provisions of § 14 of the Bankruptcy Act, 11 U.S.C.A. § 32. This section provides that the adjudication of a bankrupt shall operate as an application for a discharge; for the filing of objections to the discharge; and that the court shall grant the discharge unless satisfied that bankrupt has "(2) destroyed, mutilated, falsified, concealed, or failed to keep or preserve books of account or records, from which his financial condition and business transactions might be ascertained, unless the court deems such acts or failure to have been justified under all the circumstances of the case;" or "(6) in the course of a proceeding . . . refused to . . . answer any material questions approved by the court."

The three creditors of the bankrupt who appear here as appellees filed objections to the discharge. Two of the objections have relevancy here. For sake of brevity, they will be referred to as objection 1 and objection 2. Objection 1 is that "The Bankrupt has failed to keep books of account or records, from which his financial condition and business transactions might be ascertained." Objection 2 is "At the examination of the Bankrupt, the Bankrupt was un-cooperative and evasive and refused to give direct and factual answers to the interrogatories propounded to him." After a hearing on the objections, the referee overruled them; however, on petitions to review, the United States District Court reversed the action of the referee on objections 1 and 2, and entered an order denying the discharge. . . . Bankrupt has appealed from the order denying the discharge.

Before proceeding to further consideration of the issue before us, it is pertinent to observe that statutory provisions regulating discharges are remedial in nature; they should be construed liberally with the purpose of carrying into effect the legislative intent, and that the statutory grounds for opposing a discharge should not be extended by construction. . . .

> It is settled law that the Bankruptcy Act, 11 U.S.C.A. § 1 et seq., is to be liberally construed in favor of a bankrupt. A bankrupt is entitled to a discharge unless it clearly appears that he has committed some act which precludes his right thereto. And the initial burden rests upon the one objecting to establish reasonable basis for believing that the bankrupt has committed an act or acts which prevent his discharge. But when a prima facie case has been made by the one objecting to the granting of the discharge, the burden shifts to the bankrupt to clear himself of the charge established by such prima facie case.

In light of the foregoing principles, we are satisfied from careful examination and consideration of the record that the findings of the referee were not clearly erroneous and that the trial court improperly set aside the findings and denied an order of discharge in bankruptcy.

It is unnecessary, in view of the factual summary appearing in the trial court's opinion, to again deal extensively with the evidence. Suffice to say that Gross filed a voluntary petition in bankruptcy on January 9, 1958. No assets were listed and a trustee was not appointed. However, on December 23, 1958, and on December 17, 1959, hearings were held before the referee, at which the bankrupt was examined rather extensively. He had been connected with the Gross Oil Company which sold petroleum products at wholesale and retail. Books and records consisting largely of "invoices of purchases and sales" and social security tax records were maintained. The firm did business with a bank in Decorah, Iowa. Gross testified, without direct contradiction, that the records, stored in boxes, were left in a service station previously occupied by his company and that when "we moved from the service station over to where I am presently located, the new owners were very impatient and they hauled out and destroyed a whole bunch of records before I was able to stop them or recover them;" that the Colonial Oil Company, which had taken over the station, "allowed us to keep this one room, office room, for a period of a month until these other office quarters were completed . . . and it was during this period of moving, . . . that they helped it along;" that "there was never any records destroyed by me or at my direction, or with my knowledge or consent." In considering and disposing of the objections, the referee found "[t]he bankrupt explained that the books of his business were destroyed after the business of the Gross Oil Company was discontinued. In 1956 the building where the business was located was taken over by someone else and a small area reserved for storage for the books, but the new occupant destroyed the books. . . . No one denies it or is in a position to deny it. The Court can hardly be expected to say it is not true. The objection as to books must be overruled." The trial court concluded that under the circumstances existing, particularly with respect to bankrupt's prior financial condition, the bankrupt had not exercised reasonable care to preserve his books and records and that his failure to do so was not justified.

As we have seen, objection 1 was that bankrupt had failed "to keep books of account or records." Assuming that the "failure to keep books" is sufficiently broad to encompass "failure to preserve," we are of the view that this issue was, under the facts and circumstances developed by the evidence, an issue of fact for the referee to decide. On this record we cannot say that the evidence was all one way or was so overwhelmingly one way as to compel a finding that, as a matter of law, bankrupt has failed to preserve books and records. The referee could have decided that the bankrupt's failure to preserve was not justified, but certainly he was not compelled to so find. All of the facts and circumstances were before him—resolution of the issue depended in large measure on the credibility and the weight to be given to bankrupt's testimony. The referee chose to believe his version of the destruction of the records. In this situation, and since there is authority for the proposition that a discharge should not be refused if the destruction of books and records is the result of an accident, or the act of a stranger or third person over whom bankrupt has no control, we must conclude that there was no justification in the record nor any legal basis for overturning the referee's finding and to reach independent findings based upon what the trial court apparently felt the result should be.

Neither are we warranted in affirming the trial court's action in reversing the referee's finding and conclusion as to objection 2. It is vitally important to observe that the statutory ground for a denial of a discharge is a refusal "to obey any lawful order of, or to answer any material question approved by, the court." Appellees did not in their objections and do not on appeal assert that bankrupt *refused* to answer any questions, material or otherwise. Rather, their objection was that he was "un-cooperative and evasive and refused to give direct and factual answers. . . . " While the referee "thought the bankrupt was evasive" he concluded that this was not a ground for denying discharge. This conclusion finds support not only in the statute but in the case of *In re Fanning* (D.C.E.D.N.Y, June 18, 1907), 155 F. 701, where the court stated: "The bankrupt apparently gave evasive and disrespectful answers, but there was nothing to show that he willfully concealed testimony. . . . Ordinary questions of contumacy or contempt of court can be disposed of directly, and of themselves are not to be corrected by the withholding of a discharge."

. . . We do not believe that the statute should be amended by judicial fiat to include evasiveness in answering questions as a ground for refusing discharge. In our view, equivocal and evasive answers may very properly be considered in evaluating the weight and credibility to be accorded the bankrupt's testimony, but since such conduct is not a statutory ground for refusing discharge, the trial court should have sustained the referee's finding and conclusion as to objection 2.

The order appealed from denying the discharge in bankruptcy is reversed.

Branch v. Mills & Lupton Supply Company
348 F.2d 901 1965

Branch had made false statements in writing for the purpose of obtaining a loan from a creditor. Thereafter he was involved in bankruptcy proceedings and a creditor objected to his receiving a discharge. The referee allowed the objection and his decision was upheld by the federal district court. Branch appealed.

PER CURIUM. The bankrupt, who was engaged in the business of building shell homes, admitted that he furnished false affidavits for the purpose of obtaining a loan. One of the creditors filed specifications of objections to his discharge.

The referee in bankruptcy sustained the objections to the discharge in a memorandum opinion containing findings of fact and conclusions of law, saying:

> One of the objects of the Act is to release an honest and insolvent person from his debts. From this evidence it does not appear that this bankrupt was honest in his dealings with his creditors and the public. While he claims that it was a recognized practice of the trade and that he had made this same affidavit in many other cases, that does not cure the fact that he swore falsely to a material fact for the purpose of obtaining a loan. The giving of an oath, either written or oral, should be treated as sacred. This bankrupt's act of swearing falsely for the purpose of obtaining a loan is not indicative of such honesty as Congress intended to protect.
>
> I find as a fact that the bankrupt swore falsely, or made a false statement in writing, to material fact for the purpose of obtaining credit or property from Family Pride Homes, Inc., in Atlanta, Georgia, and that they knew at the time these statements were made they were false. I further find that Family Pride Homes, Inc., to whom the statements were made, relied upon them in extending the credit.

We find that the pertinent facts and applicable law are correctly set forth in the opinion of the district court.

Affirmed.

In re Connecticut Motor Lines, Inc.

336 F.2d (1964)

In this bankruptcy proceeding, claims for wages within three months were allowed as a second-class claim. Other wages were a sixth-class claim. The trustee deducted withholding taxes and the employee's share for social security on the wages actually paid as dividends. The issue before the court is whether the amounts due the federal government on account of these taxes are to be paid as a first-, second-, fourth- or sixth-class claim. The district court held that the payroll taxes on accrued wages were an expense of administration and a first-class claim. The trustee appealed.

FORMAN, J. . . . Though novel for this court, the issue presented on appeal is a recurring one, *viz.,* what status in the order of creditors' priorities is to be given a Government claim for income withholding and social security taxes arising from wages accrued prior to bankruptcy, but paid during bankruptcy as a second priority matter, or as a dividend to general creditors?

It is well settled that taxes arising from transactions completed in all respects prior to bankruptcy are to be treated as fourth priority items. The problem faced here, however, is a hybrid—there has been an accrual of wages prior to bankruptcy, but their payment was held in abeyance until the second priority and general creditor distributions under the Bankruptcy Act.

. . .

Most post-bankruptcy taxes have been placed into the category of costs and expenses of administration, and as such, these taxes have been entitled to first priority status. This position is the natural consequence of the broad principle that "the cost of protecting a fund in court is everywhere recognized as a dominant charge on that fund." Section 64, sub. a(1) of the Bankruptcy Act also recognizes that costs associated with the distribution of the fund are expenses of administration.

> . . . If the tax [on wages accruing prior to bankruptcy but allotted in bankruptcy] were on the distribution of the wage claim, the tax could be a valid expense of administration since distribution is a part of administration; but the tax in question is not a tax on distribution but a tax on wages paid.

Thus, as the tax on such wages as is before us neither has a relationship to the cost of protecting or developing the bankrupt's assets, nor can be reasonably considered a tax on the mere distribution of the wages, Section 64, sub. a(1) of the Bankruptcy Act is distorted by attempting to create a fiction. . . .

The Government is willing to concede that any claim it might have, for withholding and social security taxes based on wages paid prior to the filing in bankruptcy, is merely entitled to Section 64, sub. a(4) status. It reasons that payment of wages prior to filing establishes a figure "legally due and owing by the bankrupt," a figure certain in amount. Thus, the language of Section 64, sub. a(4) clearly governs in such circumstances. It is further argued by the Government that when wages are not paid until after a bankruptcy proceeding arises, such taxes cannot be "legally due and owing by the bankrupt" at the time of filing, for under the Internal Revenue Code the tax only attaches at the time the wage payment is made. And until such payment is made, the amount due cannot be definitively ascertained. Thus, says the Government, such a tax as is here before us cannot fit into Section 64, sub. a(4) as a tax "legally due and owing by the bankrupt," and, therefore, must be a post-bankruptcy Section 64, sub. a(1) cost and expense of administration. The Government's position falls on several grounds.

The Government makes the initial assumption that taxes must attach prior to the filing of the petition in bankruptcy before they may be considered as falling into Section 64, sub. a(4). . . .

Certainly the Government's view that no post-bankruptcy matters can fit into Section 64, sub. a(4) is, at the very least, questionable.

Secondly, the Government's reliance on the phraseology of Section 3102 of the Internal Revenue Code is faulty. . . .

A third concern with the Government's position is that it fails to recognize the conditions that do exist here which allow the income withholding and social security taxes to attach as fourth priority items. The Government's contention that taxes are not certain in amount, and on this ground cannot be "legally due and owing" at the time of filing, if their basis, the wages, are paid after filing, is not meritorious. A maximum wage due would certainly be discernible from the bankrupt's records. Thus, a maximum tax due, albeit *in futuro,* could also be established. This amount is as certain as the tax which falls into the fourth priority when wage claims are paid prior to filing. Unexpected post-filing expenses can certainly reduce that fourth priority distribution. Thus, the mere fact that wages had only accrued, but had not been paid until bankruptcy, in no way heightens the uncertainty which the Government claims will arise if wages have not been paid at the time, for bankruptcy purposes, the tax becomes "legally due and owing." The mere fact of payment after the filing does not, for bankruptcy purposes, lessen the ability of the Government to file a proof of claim. Because a maximum figure is ascertainable, though subject to reduction, an adequate proof of claim can be filed. . . .

Inherent in the Government's position is a fourth basis for argument which we also reject. The Government contends that the phrase "legally due and owing *by the bankrupt"* indicates that only pre-bankruptcy tax matters were contemplated as falling within Section 64, sub. a(4), because the payment of wages by trustees, as a second priority matter or to general creditors, would result in a tax owing by the Trustee rather than the Bankrupt. But in asserting this position the Government overlooks the fact that to establish its right to the contested taxes it most persuasively argued that, for purposes of the Internal Revenue Code, the Trustee stands in the position of the Bankrupt. Thus, the wage payment by the Trustee fell within the provisions of the Code and was a valid claim by the Government. The whole basis for the equation of employer with trustee is that the employer, in a case in which he was not involved in a bankruptcy proceeding, would have had to pay the wages as employer, under the Internal Revenue Code, even if he were no longer, in actuality, employer. And he would, at the time of payment, have had to pay the accrued taxes, despite his no longer being employer. Thus, based on this reasoning, if the Trustee can be Bankrupt-employer for the purpose of wage payments, it is difficult to see why he may not be Bankrupt-employer, rather than Trustee, for the payment of the taxes on those wage distributions. We find that he may consistently be considered in that light, and that his liability to the Government for Section 64, sub. a(4) taxes "legally due and owing" is a liability for taxes "owing by the bankrupt."

In retrospect then, we find that both the history of the development of the Section 64, sub. a(4) priority and the practical mechanics of the Bankruptcy statute, were meant to effectuate a movement of tax claims, clearly not costs and expenses of administration, to a fourth priority status.

.   .   .

We hold, therefore, that such taxes based on wage claims accruing prior to bankruptcy, but paid during bankruptcy, are not Section 64, sub. a(1) "costs and expenses of administration," but are Section 64, sub. a(4) "taxes legally due and owing by the bankrupt."

Riccio v. General Motors Acceptance Corporation

203 A.2d 92 (Conn.) 1963

This is an action by the trustee in bankruptcy, Riccio, to recover the proceeds of the sale of an automobile.

In 1960 Jamarc entered into a contract with Michael J. Cozy, Inc., for the purchase of a new 1960 Oldsmobile. The terms called for payment of $100.76 monthly in twenty-four installments. To secure payment, the seller reserved the title and retained a security interest in the automobile until the amount due was fully paid in cash. The seller assigned the contract to the defendant, G.M.A.C. Jamarc defaulted in the payment due on January 21, 1961, and continued to be in default. On February 3, 1961, the defendant exercised its rights under the contract and repossessed the automobile. The car was then sold. On February 7, 1961, Jamarc was adjudicated a bankrupt. The bankrupt's trustee brought this suit to recover the money on the grounds that it was a preferential transfer. The trial court found for the defendant and the trustee appealed.

JACOBS, J. . . . Briefly stated, the elements of a preference under Sec. 60a consists of the following: a debtor (1) making or suffering a transfer of his property, (2) to or for the benefit of a creditor, (3) for or on account of an antecedent debt (resulting in a depletion of the estate), (4) while insolvent, and (5) within four months of bankruptcy . . . , (6) the effect of which will enable the creditor to obtain a greater percentage of his debt than some other creditor of the same class. The creditor's knowledge or reasonable cause to believe that a preference is effected by a transfer to him is no longer an element in determining whether such transfer constitutes a preference under subdivision a or Sect. 60. However, under subdivision b a preference is voidable by the trustee in bankruptcy only upon proof of the additional element that (7) the creditor receiving or to be benefited by the preference had reasonable cause to believe that the debtor was insolvent. If any one of the elements of a preference as enumerated in Sect. 60a is wanting, there is no necessity of considering an avoidance of the transfer under Sect. 60b, since a preference under the terms of Sect. 60 itself has not been established.

In order to prove that a preference be effected under Sect. 60 of the Act, a transfer of property must be made or suffered by the debtor "while insolvent." . . . As in the other elements of a preference, the burden of proof is on the trustee to show insolvency at the time of the transfer. . . . The transfer may be voluntary or involuntary. The term "suffered," as used in the Act, does not require any conscious participation by the debtor. . . . The insolvency must be in the bankruptcy sense, as defined by Sect. 1(19) of the Bankruptcy Act (30 Stat. 544, Sect. 1(15), as amended, 11 U.S.C. Sect. 1(19), which reads as follows: "A person shall be deemed insolvent within the provisions of this title whenever the aggregate of his property, exclusive of any property which he may have conveyed, transferred, concealed, removed, or permitted to be concealed or removed, with intent to defraud, hinder, or delay his creditors, shall not at a fair valuation be sufficient in amount to pay his debts.

Applying the foregoing principles to the controverted issue of insolvency at the time of the transfer in the present case, we point out that it was incumbent on the trustee to introduce into evidence a statement of the assets and liabilities of the bankrupt. . . . There is nothing in the record before us showing the financial condition of the bankrupt; such as inventories, bankruptcy appraisals, trustee's reports, orders confirming bankruptcy sales, or even the bankrupt's own schedules. . . . It was the duty of the trustee not only to plead but to prove, and for the court to make a finding, that on February 3, 1961—the date of the alleged transfer—the bankrupt's debts exceeded the aggregate fair value of its assets. A failure to prove and find this indispensable and essential element must result in a finding that the preference, if any, is not voidable. It becomes unnecessary, in the view which we have taken of his case, to consider other legal propositions argued and briefed by the trustee.

Judgment for Defendant affirmed.

Priebe, Trustee of Estate of Giles Svehlek, Bankrupt v. Svehlek

245 F.Supp. 743 (1965)

This is an action by the trustee in bankruptcy to set aside as fraudulent a transfer of $10,000 made by the bankrupt to his wife. The bankrupt and his wife were joint tenants in a piece of real estate which served as their homestead. The defendant-wife was given a weekly allowance for running the household while the home was occupied. The house was sold in 1961, and the defendant and her husband received $19,000 after all encumbrances were paid; the husband transferred $10,000 to his wife. Shortly thereafter he declared bankruptcy. It is the position of the plaintiff-trustee that the bankrupt made, without fair consideration, the transfer of $10,000 which left him without sufficient funds to pay his debts and was therefore fraudulent as to his creditors. The defendant contends that the bankrupt was solvent when he purchased the property and that he made a gift at the time of the purchase by virtue of the fact that she acquired a one-half interest in the property as joint tenant. She does not contest the fact that her husband was insolvent at the time the property was sold and when he paid her $10,000 from the proceeds of the sale. She contended merely that the $10,000 simply represented the proceeds of the sale of property in which she had a one-half interest.

GRUBB, D. J. The Wisconsin Supreme Court recently discussed the interests of joint tenants in the case of *Jezo* v. *Jezo* (23 Wis.2d 399, 406, 127 N.W.2d 246, 250 (1964) as follows:

> The rule is, therefore, that the interests of joint tenants being equal during their lives, a presumption arises that upon dissolution of the joint tenancy during the lives of the cotenants, each is entitled to an equal share of the proceeds. This presumption is subject to rebuttal, however, and does not prevent proof from being introduced that the respective holdings and interests of the parties are unequal. The presumption may be rebutted by evidence showing the source of the actual cash outlay at the time of acquisition, the intent of the cotenant creating the joint tenancy to make a gift of the half interest to the other cotenant, unequal contribution by way of money or services, unequal expenditures in improving the property or freeing it from encumbrances and clouds, or other evidence raising inferences contrary to the idea of equal interest in the joint estate.

Considering the facts of this case in light of the principle expressed in the *Jezo* case, it is clear that the defendant did not have an interest in the property which would be sufficient consideration for $10,000. In this regard, it should be noted that the $10,000 is more than half of the $19,000 realized from the sale of the property.

The record in this case does not support the contention that a gift of one-half interest in the property was made in 1958 when the deed was executed to the defendant and her husband as joint tenants. The record does not demonstrate that the property was placed in joint tenancy for any reason other than mere convenience and in accordance with common practice.

The conveyance by the bankrupt of the $10,000 was one made without fair consideration. It is now necessary to decide whether the conveyance was one which left the bankrupt without sufficient funds to pay his debts as they matured.

In the latter part of 1960, the bankrupt decided to go into the restaurant business. As a result of this decision, he negotiated a lease of a building and personally guaranteed performance of the lease. He also entered into contracts for the purchase of equipment for the restaurant, which contracts were also guaranteed personally. The restaurant was operated for approximately three months before a gas explosion ended operations. At the time of the transfer of the $10,000, the total amount of these obligations from the restaurant, together with federal tax liabilities for 1958 and 1960, was approximately $55,000.

At the time of the transfer involved here, the assets of the bankrupt consisted of the equity in the home and stock in two corporations—Golden Chicken, Inc., and Golden Chicken Products, Inc. After the restaurant explosion and in February 1961, these two corporations had no income and paid no salary or dividends to the bankrupt. In March 1963, when the petition in bankruptcy was filed by the defendant, this stock was listed as worthless.

The conveyance of the $10,000 by the bankrupt to the defendant was one without fair consideration, which left the bankrupt without sufficient funds to pay his debts as they matured, and was fraudulent as to his creditors under Chapter 242, Wisconsin Statutes.

Judgment for the plaintiff.

In the Matter of R. C. Hendren, Debtor

240 F.Supp. 807 (1965)

This is an appeal from the referee's decision denying a debtor the conversion from a wage-earner plan to a straight bankruptcy. The debtor had filed in 1962. He, at that time, chose to proceed under the Wage-Earner Plan pursuant to Chapter XIII of the Bankruptcy Act, in which he made regular payments to a trustee in order to pay off his creditors on a long-term basis. When Hendren found himself unable to continue making the monthly payments, he petitioned to convert to a straight bankruptcy. The referee denied the petition and the debtor appealed.

PECK, J. . . . Chapter XIII was intended as a rehabilitating device by which a debtor could be sheltered from his creditors while applying his future earnings to the payment of his debts. Straight bankruptcy envisages the liquidation of the bankrupt's estate for the payment of his creditors. The Act provides that a wage-earner is not subject to involuntary proceedings (11 U.S.C. Sec. 22, sub. b), so a debtor in financial difficulty may only seek relief under Chapter XIII or in voluntary bankruptcy proceedings.

The question presented here is whether a debtor who is in arrears in making payments pursuant to his confirmed Wage-Earner Plan has the right, under the provisions of the Act, to convert his plan to straight bankruptcy or whether such conversion lies within the discretion of the Referee. . . .

As relevant here, Section 1066 provides for certain failures of a plan " . . . if after confirmation a debtor defaults in any of the terms of the plan . . . the court shall . . . (2) where the petition has been filed under (Chapter XIII), enter an order dismissing the proceeding under this chapter or, with the consent of the debtor, adjudging him a bankrupt and directing that bankruptcy be proceeded with pursuant to the provisions of this title." . . .

In the case at bar . . . the debtor has fallen behind on his payments made pursuant to his plan and must be held to be in default. In view of the mandatory language of 11 U.S.C. Sect. 1066 . . . it is here concluded that when a debtor is in default under the provisions of his plan and the Referee does not dismiss it on his own motion, the debtor may convert to straight bankruptcy as a matter of right. . . .

To deny one who has sought to honorably pay his creditors in full under a Chapter XIII proceeding the right to convert to voluntary bankruptcy when the obligations of a wage-earner plan become intolerable would be inconsistent with the intent of the Bankruptcy Act, repugnant to the philosophy of this Court, and would substantially destroy the attraction of such a plan to the foundering but well-intentioned wage earner. Accordingly,

It is ordered that the petition for review should be and it hereby is granted and sustained. . . .

CHAPTER 34
REVIEW QUESTIONS AND PROBLEMS

1. *A* is insolvent. His assets are $50,000 in value and his liabilities are $100,000. State whether the following transactions would (1) justify the filing of a petition in involuntary bankruptcy by his other creditors and (2) if so, they would be recoverable preferences:

    a. *A* paid creditor *X* in full on an open account.

    b. *A* gave creditor *Y* a mortgage on part of *A*'s property.

    c. *A* paid creditor *Z* in full a debt secured by a mortgage on property owned by *A*.

    d. *A* borrowed $10,000 from creditor *R* and gave a mortgage on *A*'s property to secure a loan.

2. *C* sued *T* to recover on an indebtedness of $500, which *T* claimed was discharged in bankruptcy. *K* had sold the goods to *T* but had assigned the $500 claim to *C* and *T* had received notice of the assignment to *C*. *T* listed *K* as a creditor and notice of bankruptcy was sent to *K* but not to *C*. Consequently, *C*, not learning of bankruptcy, failed to file a claim. Because of this, *C* contends the claim is not discharged. Is *C* correct in his contention?

3. A petition in involuntary bankruptcy was filed against *K* on November 29. On November 30 *K* sold to *M* $16,000 in accounts receivable for $15,600, *M* knowing of the petition in bankruptcy. *K* used these funds to meet payroll and taxes. On December 10, *K* was adjudicated a bankrupt, and the trustee sought to obtain the return of the accounts. The court allowed the trustee to recover. Was this decision sound?

4. An insurance agent collected premiums but failed to remit to the com-

pany. The agent became a bankrupt and obtained his discharge. Is he still liable to the company for the premiums? Was the agent a fiduciary?

5. *A* staged a fireworks display at which *B* was injured due to *A*'s negligence. *B* sued *A* and obtained a judgment against him. Before *B* could execute his judgment, *A* deeded all of his real property to his wife approximately three days after the judgment. Does *B* have a remedy?

6. The ABC Company had outstanding liabilities of $250,000 and assets of $300,000. However at the insistence of its three major creditors the company made a general assignment of its property for the benefit of creditors. Is this an act of bankruptcy?

7. *X,* a Russian immigrant, ran a one-man shoe store. He kept his papers, what there were of them, on a nail on the wall. The business made about $6,500 per year, mostly in cash trade. *X* filed a voluntary petition in bankruptcy, and *Y,* a creditor, objected on the grounds of failure to keep books. What result?

8. The XYZ Company was adjudicated bankrupt on July 15, 1970, on proceedings initiated on May 20, 1969. Its assets totaled $250,000. It had the following liabilities:

   State property taxes of $22,000 for 1969 and 1970.

   Attorney's fees of $5,000 for successfully recovering property fraudulently conveyed by the president of the firm.

   Claims for wages—To *A,* $750; To *B,* $600; and to *C,* a part-time watchman, $500, $100 per month for the months of January through May, 1969.

   A loan to the corporation of $200,000 made August 1, 1968 by the ABC Bank.

   A loan of $100,000 made by the DEF Bank, secured by a mortgage on the realty owned by the corporation made on July 1, 1968.

   How much would each claimant recover?

9. *A* is a farmer and owes many creditors. He has made some unwise investments and is now insolvent. One of his large creditors, *B,* is pressing for payment, and in order to relieve this pressure, *A* gave *B* a mortgage on his farm. May *A*'s other creditors force him into involuntary bankruptcy?

10. *B* owed *C* a past-due indebtedness of $500 and induced the latter to extend the maturity of the indebtedness three years at 6 percent interest by giving a chattel mortgage as security. Sixty days after the mortgage was given, *B* filed a petition in voluntary bankruptcy. Under what conditions, if any, will the trustee in bankruptcy be able to avoid the mortgage?

11. *A* became a voluntary bankrupt. At the time the petition was filed, he owed *B* the sum of $2,000, which was to fall due sixty days later. *B* owed *A,* on a separate transaction, the sum of $1,000, which was due at the time the petition was filed. May the trustee collect the $1,000 and force *B* to become an ordinary creditor as to the $2,000?

12. What are the duties of the following?
    a. The trustee
    b. The referee
    c. The bankrupt

13. What are the six acts of bankruptcy?
14. List five claims that are not discharged in bankruptcy?
15. List five situations in which discharge will be denied a bankrupt.

BOOK FIVE

Agency and
Employment

chapter 35

Introduction to Agency and Employment

5-1. Scope of the Subject Matter. The law of agency and employment not only has application in the private law subjects of contracts and torts but also in such public law subjects as administrative law and labor relations. The issues in the private sector of the law generally involve questions of liability on contracts entered into by an agent, or for torts committed by a servant. In the public sector, the issues involve such matters as hiring, firing, terms of employment, and collective bargaining.

The principles of agency law are essential for the conduct of business transactions. A corporation, as a legal entity, can function only through agents. The law of partnership is to a large degree a special application of agency principles to that particular form of business organization. The law of employment is also an essential part of our society in which law is used as a scheme of social control. The standard of living of workers, working conditions, and other aspects of the employer-employee relationship are regulated and improved when society uses its legal system as an instrument of change.

A study of the law of agency and employment requires some mention of the role of government at all levels. For example, the Civil Rights Act of 1964 is directly concerned with the selection and discharge of employees. The rights of employees *must* be analyzed in light of this statute. While it is not the intention to cover all of the legal aspects of employment that are affected by public statutes, many of them will be mentioned in order that the legal environment of employment may be more fully understood.

The law of agency and employment is in part statutory but is based primarily on case law. Statutes provide the basic legal principles in such areas as labor-management relations, minimum wages, and civil rights. Case law provides most of the basic principles of agency law in the fields of torts and contracts. The American Law Institute has prepared a Restatement of Agency,

697

and references to that source will be found in many of the cases appearing in this book.

Agency issues are usually discussed within a framework of three parties: the principal *(P)*, the agent *(A)*, and the third party *(T)* with whom *A* contracts or against whom *A* commits a tort while in *P*'s service. These letters—*P, A,* and *T*—will often be used to describe these parties in the sections and chapters that follow.

There are a variety of situations in which these three parties may be involved in litigation. The following examples illustrate the problems involved and indicate the chapter in which each will be discussed.

1. *T* v. *P.* Third party sues principal for breach of a contract which *T* entered into with *A* (Chapter 36), or for damages because of a tort committed by *A* (Chapter 37).

2. *T* v. *A.* Third party sues agent personally for breach of the contract entered into by the agent (Chapter 36), or for committing a tort (Chapter 37).

3. *P* v. *T.* Principal sues third party for breach of a contract which *A* entered into with *T* for *P* (Chapter 38).

4. *A* v. *T.* Agent sues third party for some loss suffered by *A*. For example, the loss of a commission due to *T*'s interference with a contract (Chapter 38).

5. *P* v. *A.* Principal sues agent for loss caused by latter's failure to follow his duties, such as to obey instructions (Chapter 39).

6. *A* v. *P.* Agent sues principal for injuries suffered in course of employment, for wrongful discharge, or for sums due for services or advancements (Chapter 39).

Most of the litigation usually involves suits against the principal and agent for torts. Most of these suits are defended by the insurance carrier of the principal. The insurance usually covers the agent as well.

5-2. Terminology. The Restatement of Agency[1] defines "agency" as follows:

> Agency is the fiduciary relation which results from the manifestation of consent by one person to another that the other shall act on his behalf and subject to his control, and consent by the other so to act.

In a comment to the foregoing statement it is said:

> The relation of agency is created as the result of conduct by two parties manifesting that one of them is willing for the other to act for him subject to his control, and that the other consents so to act. The principal must in some manner indicate that the agent is to act for him, and the agent must act or agree to act on the principal's behalf and subject to his control.

Traditionally, the term "agency" has been used to describe the legal relationship that arises when one party (the principal) authorizes another party (the agent) to create, to modify, or to terminate contractual relations between the principal and third parties. This traditional and technical definition ex-

---

[1] Restatement of the Law, Agency (2d), p.7,sec.1(1).

cludes the relationship of master and servant because a servant does not have power to create or to modify contractual relations for his master. The terms "master" and "servant" are used in the field of torts when the issue is generally not one of authority but rather whether the person that committed the tort was acting within the scope of his employment. These terms are frequently considered to be synonymous with "employer" and "employee." In recent years, the tendency for some courts has been not to observe these classical and technical distinctions between the master-servant and principal-agent relationships. Many tort cases describe the parties as principal and agent, and some contract cases, especially when the authority to contract is greatly limited, will describe the employee as a servant. As the cases are studied, the trend away from strict terminology is apparent. However, as will be noted later, the historical distinctions cannot be ignored.

Agents are frequently classified by the functions they perform and by the rights and powers they possess. Two common terms are *broker* and *factor*. A broker is an agent with special and limited authority to procure a customer in order that the owner can effect a sale or exchange of property. For example, a real estate broker has authority to find a buyer for another's real estate. The real estate remains under the control of the owner. A factor is a person who has possession and control of another's property, usually personal property such as goods, and is authorized to sell such property. A factor has a property interest and may sell the property in his own name, whereas a broker may not.

Agents are also classified as *general* or *special* agents. A general agent has much broader authority than does a special agent. Some cases define a general agent as one authorized to conduct a series of transactions involving a continuity of service, whereas a special agent conducts a single transaction or a series of transactions without continuity of service. Third parties should always ascertain the exact nature of the agency.[2]

The term *employee* has various meanings in the law depending on the context in which it is being used. It may include persons who are not agents or servants, and it may or may not include all agents and servants. For example, for withholding-tax purposes, insurance agents are usually looked upon as agents but not as employees.

Some persons who perform services for others are known as *independent contractors*. A person may contract for the services of another in such a way as to have full and complete control over the details and manner in which the work will be conducted, or he may simply contract for a certain end result. If the agreement provides merely that the second party is to accomplish a certain result and has full control over the manner and methods to be pursued in bringing about the result, he is deemed an independent contractor, and the one receiving the benefit of his services is generally not responsible to third parties for the independent contractor's actions, either in contract or tort. On the other hand, if the second party places his services at the disposal of the first in such a manner that the action of the second is generally controlled by the former, an agency relation is established.[3]

An agent may act on behalf of a designated principal, in which case the latter is called a *disclosed principal*. If the agent purports to act for himself

---

[2] Farm Bureau Mutual Insurance Company v. Coffin, page 703
[3] King v. Young, Brown, and Beverly, Inc., page 705

and keeps his agency a secret, the principal is called an *undisclosed principal.*
A third term, *partially disclosed principal,* is used to describe the situation
in which the agent acknowledges that he is acting for a principal but does not
disclose his identity.

5-3. Capacity of Parties.   It is generally stated that anyone who may act for
himself may act through an agent. To this rule there is one well-recognized
exception. An infant may enter into a contract, and so long as he does not
disaffirm, the agreement is binding. However, there is considerable authority
to the effect that any appointment of an agent by an infant is void, and not
merely voidable. Under this view any agreement entered into by such an agent
would be ineffective, and an attempted disaffirmance by the minor would be
superfluous. Many recent cases hold, however, that a contract of the agent on
behalf of a minor principal is voidable only and is subject to rescission or
ratification by the minor the same as if the minor had personally entered into
the contract.

An infant may act as an agent for an adult, and agreements he makes for
his principal while acting within his authority are binding on the principal.
Although the infant agent has a right to terminate his contract of agency at
his will, as long as he continues in the employment his acts within the scope
of the authority conferred upon him become those of his principal.

5-4. Formal Requirements.   As a general rule, no particular formalities are
required to create an agency. The appointment may be either written or oral
and the relationship may be expressed or implied.

There are, however, two situations in which formalities are required. First,
when the purpose of the agency can be exercised only by the signing of a formal
document under seal, the agency must be created under seal. Where a formal
sealed instrument is used for conferring authority upon the agent, he is said
to possess a *power of attorney,* and the agent is called an "attorney in fact"
to distinguish him from an "attorney at law,"the term used to describe lawyers.
A power of attorney may be general, giving the agent authority to act in all
respects as the principal could act, or it may be special, granting to the agent
only restricted authority. A power of attorney is customarily acknowledged
before a notary public whose seal is affixed thereto. Second, the statute of
frauds in the majority of the states requires that any agent who is given power
to sell or to convey any interest in or concerning real estate must obtain such
power by a written authorization from the principal.[4] The ordinary real estate
broker, however, in most states would not need a written agreement, as his
authority is merely to find a buyer with whom the seller is willing to contract.
Normally, he has no authority to enter into a binding contract to convey the
property. However, in many states a "listing agreement" is required to be in
writing.

A third exception exists in a few states where it is required that the act which
confers authority must possess the same dignity as the act to be performed.
In these states an agent who possesses authority to sign a contract which is
required to be in writing must receive his appointment by an instrument in
writing.

[4] Dineff v. Wernecke, page 706

When an agent signs a simple contract or commercial paper he should execute it in such a fashion as to clearly indicate his representative capacity. If the signatures are ambiguous in that they fail to indicate the actual relationship of the parties and to identify the party intended to be found, the agent may be personally liable on the instrument. Many states permit the use of parol evidence to show the intention of the agent and the third party when the signature is ambiguous—the agent is allowed to offer proof that it was not intended that he assume personal responsibility. As previously noted, the Code contains express provisions on the liability of an agent who signs commercial paper. Also, in contracts in general, the agent may be liable if he fails to clearly indicate his representative capacity. If he does so indicate, liability may be avoided.[5]

5-5. Statutory Aspects of Employment. There are many legislative enactments which affect the employment relationship. First, there are the federal statutes which regulate labor-management relations and especially collective bargaining. These statutes, the judicial decisions interpreting them, and the actions of the administrative agency which enforces and administers them compose a major segment of the law relating to employment.

Secondly, there are both federal and state statutes which regulate wages, hours, and working conditions. The Fair Labor Standards Act which controls such matters as minimum wages, hours, and the records to be kept by employers is an example of such a statute. State laws control such matters as child labor, safety devices, workmen's compensation, unemployment compensation, and fair employment practices. While most of these matters will not be discussed in detail, it must be recognized that many of the rights and duties of both employers and employees are determined by these statutes and the administrative agencies operating pursuant to them. The businessman must be familiar with these statutes and the regulations related to them and must comply with those applicable to his business.

5-6. Labor-Management Relations. An examination of employment and the employer-employee relationship necessarily includes some mention of labor-management relations. Since many, if not most, employment contracts are entered into by unions on behalf of their members, a general understanding of the laws affecting labor-management contracts is important to an understanding of the problems involved.

While there had been several earlier statutes which had attempted to encourage collective bargaining by unions on behalf of workers, it was not until the adoption of the so-called Wagner Act in 1935 that the legal environment which would encourage the growth of unions and collective bargaining was provided. An administrative agency, the National Labor Relations Board (N.L.R.B.) was established to enforce the law and decide disputes relating to collective bargaining.

The Wagner Act, to encourage collective bargaining and give equality of bargaining power to labor, declared certain activities of employers to be unfair labor practices. These included interference with efforts of employees to form, join, or assist labor unions; domination of labor organizations (company un-

---

[5] Guillory v. Courville, page 707.

ions); discrimination in hiring or tenure because of union affiliation; discrimination against employees who filed charges or testified under the Act; and refusing to bargain collectively with a duly designated union. These unfair labor practices have been the subject of numerous judicial decisions interpreting the Act and a whole body of labor law has developed concerning the duties of employers in bargaining with unions. While it is not the purpose of this discussion to cover these matters in detail, the student is cautioned that the common-law principles discussed herein are subject to the limitations of these statutes as are the contracts entered into in the areas covered by them.

Unions, encouraged by the Wagner Act and the increased demand for labor caused by World War II, grew in power and importance until by the mid-1940s there was a feeling that laws were needed to curb the power of unions and to balance once again the bargaining power of labor and management. The Wagner Act had encouraged the union movement and had sought to give unions equal bargaining power with management but it had failed to create equality because the result was that labor had superior bargaining power. In 1947, the Taft-Hartley Act was enacted with the same goal, to wit, to equalize the bargaining power of the parties and to protect the public interest. It declared that certain activities by unions were unfair labor practices and, in addition, to protect the public interest, created legal machinery to postpone nationwide strikes where the public interest would be adversely affected. This latter provision provides for an eighty-day cooling-off period during which federal mediators attempt to resolve the differences between management and labor. Activities which are unfair labor practices by unions include coercing employees into joining a union, causing discrimination against nonunion employees, refusing to bargain with the employer, engaging in secondary boycotts for illegal purposes, causing an employer to pay for work not performed, and picketing where the union is not certified. While this list is not complete, it indicates the type of activity which is prohibited in order to encourage collective bargaining and fair treatment. The avowed purpose of both statutes is to create equality of bargaining power between labor and management, while protecting the interest of the public, to the end that collective bargaining will settle disputes and controversies concerning employment.

In 1959, Congress enacted the Labor-Management Reporting and Disclosure Act, usually referred to as the Landrum-Griffin Act. This statute was adopted in order to protect union members from wrongful conduct by their officers. The statute also clarified and tightened the restrictions of the Taft-Hartley statute on secondary boycotts, hot cargo contracts, and organizational picketing. The statute is designed to give the rank and file union members control over the union affairs and to ensure that their rights are protected by federal intervention if necessary. The information which unions must furnish the Department of Labor concerning their activities is very substantial.

5-7. Job Discriminations.   Many cities, most states, and the federal government have enacted statutes which are designed to prevent discrimination in hiring, promotion, pay, or layoffs because of race, color, creed, sex, or national origin. These statutes have modified the basic common-law concept that an employer had a free choice in selecting his employees and in the absence of a contract, a free choice in discharging them. They have been enacted as a part of the general philosophy of government that all persons should have equality of opportunity. These statutes frequently contain criminal sanctions and authorize civil suits for damages. Usually, administrative agencies called Fair Employment Practices Commissions are established to enforce these statutes.

These anti–job-discrimination laws are an example of private contract rights being superseded by an overriding public policy. Freedom of contract has given way to laws regulating the employment relationship because of the economic loss to the country caused by discrimination and because of the adverse effect it has on the minority groups directly affected.

The federal statute is applicable to all employers of twenty-five or more employees, all employment agencies, and all labor organizations maintaining a hiring hall. Exceptions are created where there is a bona fide occupational qualification. For example, a university desiring to hire a football coach could legally limit the job to males without being subject to a suit for discrimination based on sex.

Most statutes require the keeping of records by employers which establish the reason for various actions in respect to employee relations. While testing is specifically allowed under the federal law, tests should not be used to defeat the goal of equal opportunity and if a test is more difficult than necessary to select qualified persons for a particular job, the employer may be guilty of discrimination.

INTRODUCTION TO AGENCY AND EMPLOYMENT CASES

Farm Bureau Mutual Insurance Company v. Coffin

186 N.E.2d 180 (Ind.) 1962

PFAFF, J. This action was begun by the appellee, Bonnie Eugene Coffin, to recover on an alleged oral contract of insurance between the appellee and the appellant through its employee, James R. Pierson, in which contract appellee's liability and property damage insurance was transferred to a new car and comprehensive and collision coverages were added to the policy. The appellant's answer denied that appellee had his automobile insured with the appellant except for bodily injury and property damage. . . . [A] trial resulted in a finding and judgment for the appellee in the sum of $1760.00, plus costs. . . .

The evidence discloses that the appellee, Bonnie Eugene Coffin, who was an assigned risk to the appellant, Farm Bureau Mutual Insurance Company, called the appellant's home office on December 13, 1955. When a girl answered the telephone, appellee stated that he wanted to transfer the insurance on his car. The call was switched to a second girl who in turn stated that she would connect appellee with Dick Pierson (James R. Pierson). When the appellee told James R. Pierson that he wanted to transfer the liability and property damage insurance on his 1953 Chevrolet to a new 1956 Buick and get additional collision and comprehensive insurance, the reply was: "O.K. you are covered. . . . "

Pierson also told the appellee that his application papers would be in the morning mail and the appellee should fill them out and return them. In completing these forms, appellee, Coffin, did not properly mark the application to indicate that he desired the comprehensive and collision coverages.

The testimony indicates that James R. Pierson was not an insurance agent. At the time in question, he was Typing Supervisor in the Auto Underwriters Department. Transfers of insurance were routine matters; however, evidence revealed the home office would only give additional coverage on written directives. The usual practice was to deal through an agent. There is no contrary testimony to the statements that Pierson had no authority to give collision coverage to an assigned risk.

The appellee had an accident one day after he talked to Pierson, that is, on December 14, 1955. This action was begun to recover for damage to the appellee's car which damage was caused by that accident.

． ． ．

The appellant alleges that Pierson is a special agent; therefore appellee, Coffin, had a duty to inquire as to the extent of his authority. The appellee contends that regardless of the actual authority of Pierson he had the appearance of a general agent; therefore it was unnecessary for the appellee to inquire as to his specific authority.

The problem is whether the law applicable to special agents or that applicable to general agents should be followed in this case.

> The distinction between a general and special agent is very accurately and correctly stated by Mr. Wait, in his work on Law and Practice, vol. 1, p. 215, where it is said: "A general agent is one who is authorized to transact all the business of his principal, or all his business of some particular kind, or at some particular place. The principal will be bound by the acts of a general agent, if the latter acted within the usual and ordinary scope of the business in which he was employed, notwithstanding he may have violated the private instructions which the principal may have given him, provided the person dealing with such agent was ignorant of such violation and that the agent exceeded his authority. The authority of an agent being limited to a particular business does not make it special; it may be as general in regard to that, as though its range were unlimited. A special agent is one who is authorized to do one or more specific acts, in pursuance of particular instructions or within restrictions necessarily implied from the act to be done. The principal is not bound by the acts of a special agent, if he exceeds the limits of his authority. And it is the duty of every person who deals with a special agent to ascertain the extent of the agent's authority before dealing with him. If this is neglected, such person will deal at his peril, and the principal will not be bound by any act which exceeds the particular authority given."

． ． ．

. . . [T]he trial judge . . . concluded that Pierson was clothed with such authority that the appellee was justified in assuming that Pierson was a general agent. . . . The appellee called the appellant's home office and stated that he desired to transfer his insurance. He talked to two different girls who did not have authority to make such a transfer. Finally he was connected with James R. Pierson, who told the appellee that he had collision coverage as of that moment. We think that these facts are sufficient to sustain a finding that James R. Pierson had apparent authority to transfer the appellee's liability and property damage insurance and to add collision coverage.

When one has the appearance of a general agent the law is clear that a third person dealing with him is not bound to inquire into his specific authority, nor is the principal protected by secret limitations upon the authority of such an agent. The reason for the rule is that where one of two innocent persons must suffer because of the betrayal of a trust reposed in a third, the one who is most at fault should bear the loss. Since the principal put the agent in the position of trust, he is the one who should suffer the detriment. . . .

Judgment affirmed.

King v. Young, Brown, and Beverly, Inc.

107 S.2d 751 (Fla.) 1958

King, the plaintiff, brought suit against Young, a trucker, Brown, a transportation broker, and Beverly, Inc., a supplier of vegetables, to recover for losses sustained in a two tractor-trailer collision caused by the negligence of Young's driver. The plaintiff alleged that Young was the agent of the other defendants.

Beverly, Inc., had called Brown to obtain transportation for a load of beans to a destination in Georgia, and Brown in turn called Young. Young picked up the beans and upon the return of the receipted bill of lading was to receive from Brown $234.79, less a brokerage commission of 7 per cent. Brown and Beverly, Inc., both contend that Young was an independent contractor and that no agency relationship existed. The lower court found in favor of defendants, Beverly, Inc., and Brown. King, the plaintiff, appealed on his claim against Brown. Young was held liable and no appeal was taken from the judgment against him.

KANNER, J. . . . The term *agency* may be defined as "a contract either express or implied upon a consideration, or gratuitous undertaking, by which one of the parties confides to the other the management of some business to be transacted in his name or on his account, and by which that other assumes to do the business and render an account of it." (2 Am. Jur., *Agency,* Section 2, p. 13) In an agency relationship, the party for whom another acts and from whom he derives authority to act is known and referred to as a principal, while the other party who acts for and represents the principal and who acquires his authority from him is known and referred to as an agent. Thus, the agent steps into the shoes of his principal and acts for him pursuant to the grant of authority vested in him by the principal. (2 Am. Jur., *Agency,* Section 2, p. 13)

In the instant case, Brown was merely the intermediary in the transaction between the shipper and the transportation medium. What he did was to procure transportation for the shipper through the trucker, Young, for which he, Brown, was to receive as his brokerage commission a percentage of the total transportation price. Although Brown arranged for Young to haul the beans, Young was to pay his own expenses; he had the control and choice of routes to follow; and he was completely independent of Brown after the load was arranged, except that Young had to bring back a receipt so as to show delivery of the beans before he could collect his freight charge.

The status of an independent contractor, as distinguished from that of an agent, consists of a contractual relationship by one with another to perform something for him, but the one so engaged is not controlled or subject to the control of the other in the performance of the engagement but only as to the result. Conversely, a principal in an agency relationship retains the right to control the conduct of an agent in regard to the engagement intrusted to him. It may be said that the recognized distinction between an agent and an independent contractor relationship is determined by whether the person is subject to or whether he is free from control with regard to the details of the engagement. . . .

The position assumed by appellant is inconsistent, because the agency relationship as applied to the instant case can only contemplate that one person, that is, the principal, is superior and that the other person, the agent, is subordinate. There is no indication whatever that Brown was a principal to either the shipper of the commodity or of the trucker. He was called upon by the shipper as a transportation broker to procure transportation and he then arranged with the trucker to haul the load, for which he was only to receive a commission for his services. . . .

Judgment affirmed.

Dineff v. Wernecke

190 N.E.2d 308 (Ill.) 1963

Plaintiffs, prospective purchasers of realty, brought suit for specific performance and for damage for breach of an alleged contract to sell property jointly owned by the defendants. The defendants were brother and sister. The contract had been signed by the sister individually and as agent for her brother. The brother had not authorized his sister in writing to enter into the contract on his behalf but had orally agreed to its terms. The defendants pleaded the statute of frauds, and the lower court sustained the plea. Plaintiffs appeal.

HERSHEY, J. . . . The record is clear that Louis R. Wernecke did not sign any contract or letter of acceptance of an offer from Dineff. Nor is there in evidence any writing signed by any agent in behalf of Louis R. Wernecke. Further, there is no evidence that Louis R. Wernecke in writing authorized Elsie Wernecke or anyone else to act as his agent in selling or signing any contract. Section 2 of the Illinois Statute of Frauds provides: "No action shall be brought to charge any person upon any contract for the sale of lands, tenements or hereditaments or any interest in or concerning them, for a longer term than one year, unless such contract or some memorandum or note thereof shall be in writing, and signed by the party to be charged therewith, or some other person thereunto by him lawfully authorized in writing, signed by such party." As we stated in *Fletcher* v. *Underwood* (240 Ill. 554, 88 N.E. 1030): "Where an agent sells real estate for another, in order to bind the principal it is not only necessary that the authority of the agent should be in writing, but also that the contract made by the agent, or some memorandum thereof, should be in writing and signed by the agent."

Thus, it is clear that Louis R. Wernecke is in no way bound as to the plaintiff.

The fact that Louis R. Wernecke did not sign any contract with the plaintiffs makes the contract unenforceable against Elsie Wernecke since the negotiations for the purchase of the property were intended to be with Elsie

Wernecke and Louis R. Wernecke jointly. Plaintiffs intended to purchase the interests of both parties, not separate interests. The instant case is like that in *Madia* v. *Collins* (408 Ill. 358, at page 362, 97 N.E.2d 313, at page 315), wherein we said: "It is obvious that plaintiff knew with whom he was dealing; that he was not misled as to the ownership; and that his offer of purchase was made to both owners for the entire title. Without the signature of both owners, no contract was formed, and there could be no breach upon which plaintiff could base an action for specific performance. . . . One cannot have specific performance in such case where the contract contemplates the sale of all the interests in the property contracted for, or none. *(Spadoni* v. *Frigo,* 307 Ill. 32, 138 N.E. 226)"

The complaint nowhere alleges a separate price for the interests of each and there is no prayer for partial performance against Elsie Wernecke. At all times plaintiffs treated the Werneckes as a unit.

Decree affirmed.

Guillory v. Courville

158 So.2d 475 (La.) 1963

CULPEPPER, J. This is a suit on an open account. From an adverse judgment the plaintiff appeals.

The substantial issue is whether the defendant has proved his defense that he was acting as a disclosed agent of a corporation.

There is no dispute as to the law. An agent is responsible to those with whom he contracts when he does not disclose that he is acting as an agent. Furthermore, the special defense of agency, cannot be proved by the mere testimony of defendant. He must be corroborated by other evidence.

The facts show that in January of 1958 the defendant, Claude Courville, and several other parties formed a corporation known as "Basile Flying Service, Inc.," domiciled in Evangeline Parish, Louisiana, for the purpose of engaging in the business of providing flying services to farmers. This concern purchased gasoline from the plaintiff at various times, from February 1958 down through July of 1959, on an open account. Although occasionally delinquent, the account was paid except for the sum of $1,834.48 for purchases made during the period July 4, 1959, through July 30, 1959. Plaintiff's statements of account were addressed to "Basile Flying Service."

Plaintiff testified that he did not know the business was incorporated and that he was relying on the credit of defendant, with whom he had done satisfactory business before. Defendant testified that he personally told plaintiff before the purchases in question were made, that the business was incorporated. At least one other witness corroborated defendant in this respect. Furthermore, several checks received by plaintiff's office, in payment of previous amounts on this open account, were clearly marked "Basile Flying Service, Inc.," although plaintiff denied seeing any of these checks.

The record amply supports the following finding of facts by the district judge:

> The court is of the opinion that plaintiff was informed by the defendant and other stockholders of the corporation of the fact that he was doing business with the corporation; that plaintiff cashed checks from the corporation; that an account was

opened for the corporation and a credit check was made on the corporation. It is further the opinion of the court that the present action against defendant is a result of plaintiff's inability to effect collection against the corporation to whom the gasoline was originally billed or charged. The court is of the opinion that no action of defendant in this matter created a personal obligation toward plaintiff.

For the reasons assigned the judgment appealed is affirmed.
Affirmed.

CHAPTER 35
REVIEW QUESTIONS AND PROBLEMS

1. *M,* a minor, appoints *S,* a stockbroker, as his agent to buy and sell stock. *M* deposits $10,000 with *S.* The investments are later worth $3,000. Can *M* recover the other $7,000 from *S*?

2. *D,* an 81-year-old woman, clearly senile, gives *X* a general power of attorney. *X* enters into several contracts on *D's* behalf. *D's* executor upon her death seeks to rescind those contracts. Should rescission be granted?

3. *A,* duly authorized by *P* to sign promissory notes, signs five separate notes in the following manner:
    a) "*P*"
    b) "*A*"
    c) "*P,* by *A,* agent"
    d) "*A,* agent"
    e) "*P, A*"
    P then becomes insolvent, and all five creditors come to *A* for payment. In which cases does *A* have liability?

4. On the day an election is to be held to determine whether or not *A's* employees will organize and become members of a labor union, *A* grants all employees a bonus of $100. Is *A* guilty of an unfair labor practice?

5. *X,* a black, applied for a job at the ABC Company. *X* was given an interview and the company failed to hire him. Does *X* have any recourse?

6. *Y,* a singer on military duty, customarily loaned his car to *F,* who gratuitously arranged publicity for *Y.* Returning from one such errand, *F* negligently ran over *K.* May *K* recover from *Y*?

7. "Newsboys" who work at newstands in large cities are provided with advertising material, and are subject to the publisher's standards of diligence, conduct, and time on the job. They are paid only a certain percentage of each paper sold, with no base salary. Are such persons employees within the language of the Wagner Act so that they are entitled to bargain collectively?

8. John Jones, the President of XYZ Company, signed a note payable to the ABC Bank as follows: "John Jones, President." He intended for the company to pay the note, but the company became insolvent. Is John Jones personally liable on the note?

chapter 36

Contractual Liability of Principals and Agents

LIABILITY OF PRINCIPAL IN GENERAL

5-8. Introduction. A principal is liable on all contracts properly executed and entered into by an agent possessing actual or apparent authority to enter into the contract, provided that the third party knows that the agent is contracting for the principal. A principal is also liable on unauthorized contracts entered into by a purported agent, if the principal with knowledge of all of the facts, ratifies the contract. Therefore, a principal is not liable upon a contract that he has not actually or apparently authorized and has not ratified. The burden of proving the requisite authority or ratification is on the party dealing with the agent; the principal does not have the burden of proving lack of authority or lack of ratification.

5-9. Actual Authority. Actual authority is that authority which a principal confers upon the agent, or unintentionally by want of ordinary care, allows the agent to believe himself to possess. Actual authority includes express authority and implied authority. The term "express authority" describes the authority explicitly given to the agent by the principal. Implied authority is used to describe authority which is necessarily incidental to the express authority or which arises because of business custom and usage or prior practices of the parties. Implied authority is sometimes referred to as "incidental authority"; it is required or reasonably necessary in order to carry out the purpose for which the agency was created.

Implied authority based on custom and usage varies from one locality to another and among different kinds of businesses. To illustrate: P appoints A as his agent to sell a certain used automobile for $900. As an incident to his authority to sell, A has authority to enter into a written contract with the purchaser and to sign P's name to the contract. Whether he has implied or incidental authority to sell on credit instead of cash or to warrant the condition of the car sold depends upon local custom. If it is customary for other agents in this locality to make warranties or sell on credit, this agent and the third party with whom he deals may assume he possesses such authority in the absence of knowledge to the contrary. Custom, in effect, creates a presumption of authority.

Implied authority must be distinguished from apparent or ostensible authority, which is authority predicated on the theory of estoppel. Implied authority cannot be derived from the words or conduct of the agent. A third person dealing with a known agent may not act negligently in regard to the extent of the agent's authority or blindly trust his statements in such regard, but must use reasonable diligence and prudence in ascertaining whether the agent is acting within the scope of his authority. Similarly, if persons who deal with a purported agent desire to hold the principal liable on the contract, they must ascertain not only the fact of the agency but the nature and extent of the agent's authority. Should either the existence of the agency or the nature and extent of the authority be disputed, the burden of proof regarding these matters is upon the third party.

All agents, even presidents of corporations, have limitations on their authority.[1] Authority is not readily implied. For example, possession of goods by one not engaged in the business of selling such goods does not create the implication of authority to sell. Authority to sell does not necessarily include the authority to extend credit, although custom may create such authority.

5-10. Apparent or Ostensible Authority.   The terms "apparent authority" and "ostensible authority" are synonymous and describe the authority a principal, intentionally or by want of ordinary care, causes or allows a third person to believe the agent to possess. Liability of the principal for the ostensible agent's acts rests on the doctrine of estoppel. The estoppel is created by some conduct of the principal that leads the third party to believe that a person is his agent or that an actual agent possesses the requisite authority. This conduct must be known to and justifiably relied upon[2] by the third party to his injury or damage. The injury or damage may be a change of position, and the facts relied upon must be such that a reasonably prudent person would believe that the authority of the agency existed. Thus, three usual essential elements of an estoppel—conduct, reliance, and injury—are required to create apparent authority.

The theory of apparent or ostensible authority is that if a principal by his words or conduct has led others to believe that he has conferred authority upon an agent, he cannot be heard to assert, as against third persons who have relied thereon in good faith, that he did not intend to confer such power. The acts may include words, oral or written, or may be limited to conduct which reasonably interpreted by a third person causes that person to believe that the principal consents to have the act done on his behalf by the purported agent. An agent's apparent authority to do an act for a principal must be based on the principal's words or conduct and cannot be based on anything the agent himself has said or done. An agent cannot create his own authority.

---

[1] North American Sales A., Inc. v. Carrtone Lab., Inc., page 721
[2] Movie Films, Inc. v. First Security Bank of Utah, N.A., page 722

Apparent or ostensible authority may exist where no agency in fact exists, or it may exceed the actual authority possessed by one who is in fact an agent. In other words, an agency may be created by an estoppel or it may be expanded by an estoppel. Ostensible authority gives an agent power to bind a principal when he has no right to do so.

An agency by estoppel or additional authority by estoppel may arise from a course of dealing on the part of an agent, which is constantly ratified by the principal, or it may result from a person's holding himself out as an agent without any dissent on the part of the purported principal under conditions where the principal owed a duty to speak. To illustrate: Upon several occasions *A* indorses his principal's name to checks and has them cashed at the bank. The principal has never given the agent such authority, but no protest is lodged with the bank until the agent appropriates to his own use the proceeds from one of the checks. The principal then attempts to recover from the bank. By approval of the agent's previous unauthorized action, the principal has led the bank to reasonably assume that the agent possesses authority to indorse checks.

5-11. Authority Created by Necessity or Emergency. An existing emergency which necessitates immediate action adds sufficiently to the agent's powers to enable him to meet the situation. However, if time permits and the principal is available, any proposed remedy for the difficulty must be submitted to the principal for approval.[3] It is only when the principal is not available that the powers of the agent are extended. Furthermore, the agent receives no power greater than that sufficient to solve the difficulty. Thus, the power of an agent to borrow money on the strength of his principal's credit is rarely implied. Suppose, however, that a C.O.D. shipment arrives for the principal during his absence and money is not available to pay for the goods. Clearly, his representative in charge of the business may borrow sufficient funds to pay for the goods and avoid demurrage charges and other possible losses. The principal would not be liable for any excess borrowed beyond that required to pay for the particular shipment.

5-12. Secret Limitations. It is said that limitations imposed upon the usual and ordinary powers of an agent do not prevent the principal from being liable to third parties where the agent acts in violation of such limitations, unless the attention of the third parties has been drawn to them.[4] In other words, the third party, having established that an agency exists and having determined in a general way the limits of the authority, is not bound to explore for unexpected and unusual restrictions. He is justified in assuming, in the absence of contrary information, that the agent possesses those powers which like agents customarily have.

For example, an instruction to a sales agent not to sell to a certain individual or not to sell to him on credit, when credit sales are customary, cannot affect the validity of a contract made with this individual, unless the latter was aware of the limitation at the time the contract was made. The principal, by appointing an agent normally possessed of certain authority, is estopped to set up the

---

[3] Carlson v. Hannah et al., page 723
[4] Zager v. Gubernick, page 725

limitation as a defense, unless the limitation is made known to the third party prior to the making of the contract.

5-13. Ratification.   As previously noted in Section 5-8, a principal may become bound on an unauthorized contract by ratifying it.[5] Ratification is an express or implied adoption or confirmation, with knowledge of all material matters, by one person of a contract performed in his behalf by another, who at that time assumed to act as his agent but lacked authority to do so. Ratification relates back to and is the equivalent of authority at the commencement of the act or time of the contract and is the affirmance of the contract already made. It cures the defect of lack of authority.

Various conditions must exist before a ratification will be effective to bring about a contractual relation between the principal and the third party. First, since ratification relates back to the time of the contract, ratification can be effective only where both the principal and the agent were capable of contracting at the time the contract was executed and are still capable at the time of ratification. For this reason a corporation may not ratify contracts made by its promoters on the corporation's behalf before the corporation was formed. For the corporation to be bound by such agreements, a novation or an assumption of liability by the corporation must occur.

Second, an agent's act may be ratified only when he holds himself out as acting for the one who is alleged to have approved the unauthorized agreement. In other words, the agent must have professed to act as an agent. A person who professes to act for himself and who makes a contract in his own name does nothing that can be ratified, even though he intends at the time to let another have the benefit of his agreement. Therefore, an undisclosed principal may not ratify an unauthorized contract and hold the third party to it. In addition, the undisclosed principal cannot be held liable by the third party on the contract. However, it should be noted that an undisclosed principal who receives the benefits of a contract is liable in quasi contract for the benefits actually received.

Third, as a general rule, ratification does not bind the principal unless he acts with full knowledge of all the material facts attending negotiation and execution of the contract. Of course, when there is express ratification and the principal acts without any apparent desire to know or to learn the facts, he may not later defend himself on the ground that he was unaware of all the material facts. When, however, ratification is to be implied from the conduct of the principal, he must act with knowledge of all important details.

The states are in some conflict as to whether the third party may withdraw before ratification takes place. The better view, which has the support of most of the states, is that the third party may withdraw from the transaction at any time before it is ratified by the principal. If the third party were not allowed to withdraw, the unique situation in which one party is bound and the other is not would exist. Fair and equal treatment dictates the majority rule allowing the third party to withdraw prior to ratification. However, it must be kept in mind that ratification does not require notice to the third party. As soon as conduct constituting ratification has been indulged in by the principal, the third party loses his right to withdraw.

[5] David v. Serges, page 726

5-14. Conduct Constituting Ratification.   Ratification may be either express or implied. Where certain formalities, such as a writing or an authorization under seal, are required to create a particular agency, the ratification must follow the form required for the creation of the agency. Aside from this, any conduct that definitely indicates an intention on the part of the principal to adopt the transaction will constitute ratification. It may take the form of words of approval to the agent, a promise to perform, or actual performance, such as delivery of the product called for in the agreement. Accepting the benefits of the contract or basing a suit on the validity of an agreement clearly amounts to ratification. Ratification may be implied by any facts and circumstances from which it can be reasonably inferred that the party to be charged, with knowledge of facts, acquiesced in and accepted the transaction as his own, or which are inconsistent with any other intention. The intent to ratify an unauthorized act or contract may be implied from circumstances, and this implication may be made even though the person to be charged as principal may have had an intention not to ratify. The issue of whether or not ratification has occurred, if there is any dispute as to the facts or to the inference to be drawn from the facts, is a question to be decided by the jury.

On the issue of ratification, it is sufficient to make a question for the trier of fact, if all of the facts and circumstances justify the reasonable inference that the party charged as principal accepted the transaction as his own. It is not necessary that each separate act, fact, or circumstance stands on its own as sufficient proof to justify such inference.

Among the facts to be considered by the jury are the relationship of the parties, prior conduct, and circumstances surrounding the transaction, and the action or inaction of the alleged principal upon learning of the contract. Inaction or silence by the principal creates difficulty in determining if ratification has occurred. Failure to speak may mislead the third party, and courts frequently find that a duty to speak exists where silence will mislead. Silence and inaction by the party to be charged as a principal, or failure to dissent and speak up when ordinary human conduct and fair play would normally call for some negative assertion within a reasonable time, tends to justify the inference that the principal acquiesced in the course of events and accepted the contract as his own. Acceptance and retention of the fruits of the contract with full knowledge of the material facts of the transaction is probably the most certain evidence of implied ratification.[6] As soon as a principal learns of an unauthorized act by his agent, he should promptly repudiate it, if he is to avoid liability on the theory of ratification.

At this point it should be mentioned that an unauthorized act may not be ratified in part and rejected in part. The principal cannot accept the benefits of the contract and refuse to assume its obligations. Because of this rule, a principal by accepting the benefits of an authorized agreement, ratifies the means used in procuring the agreement unless, within a reasonable time after learning the true facts, he takes steps to return, so far as possible, the benefits he has received. Therefore, if an unauthorized agent commits fraud in procuring a contract, acceptance of the benefits not only ratifies the contract but the fraudulent acts as well, and the principal is liable therefor.

---

[6] Wilks v. Stone, page 727

LIABILITY OF PRINCIPAL—SPECIAL SITUATIONS

5-15. Introduction.   Many special problems arise in the law of agency as it relates to contractual liability and authority of agents. Some of these problems are founded on the relationship of the parties. For example, a spouse is generally liable for the contracts of the other spouse when such contracts involve family necessities. In most states this liability is statutory. Other issues involve such matters as whether or not notice to an agent or knowledge possessed by him is imputed to the principal. Some of these questions are covered by statutes. For example, civil practice statutes contain provisions on service of a summons on an agent. They specify who may be an agent for the service of process and in effect provide that notice to such agents constitutes notice to the principal. The general principals relating to notice and to some of the other special issues of authority are discussed in the sections that follow.

5-16. Notice to Agent.   Notice to or knowledge acquired by an agent while acting within the scope of his authority binds the principal.[7] This is based on the theory that the agent is the principal's other self, and, therefore, what the agent knows, the principal knows. However, it must be recognized that while *knowledge* possessed by an agent is *notice* to the principal, the principal may not have actual knowledge of the particular fact at all. Knowledge acquired by an agent acting outside the scope of his authority is not effective notice unless the party relying thereon has reasonable ground to believe that the agent is acting within the scope of his authority (similar to apparent authority). To illustrate, assume that an agent who is acquiring property for his principal has knowledge of certain unrecorded liens against the property. The principal purchases the property subject to those liens. Equal knowledge possessed by another agent who did not represent the principal in the particular transaction and who did not obtain the knowledge on behalf of his principal, is not imputed to the principal.

A question exists as to whether or not notice acquired by an agent before he became such can bind the principal. One view is that notice which is acquired by a person before the creation of the agency is notice to the principal who later hires the person as his agent. There is considerable authority to the contrary.

Notice or knowledge received by an agent under circumstances where the agent would not be presumed to communicate the information to the principal does not bind the principal. This is an exception to the general rule that will be observed in cases when the agent is acting in his own behalf and adversely to the principal[8] or when the agent is under a duty to some third party not to disclose the information.

Furthermore, notice to the agent, combined with collusion or fraud between him and the third party that would defeat the purpose of the notice, would not bind the principal. Thus, an agent who learns of an unrecorded mortgage from the mortgagor, with request that the fact not be made known to the principal,

---

[7] Ivers & Pond Piano Co. v. Peckham, page 729
[8] Joel Strickland Enterprises v. Atlantic Discount Co., page 730

has not received notice which is binding on the principal. If the principal purchases the property, it will not be subject to the mortgage.

As a general rule, an agent or person ostensibly in charge of a place of business has apparent authority to accept notices in relation to the business. In addition, an employee in charge of the receipt of mail may accept written notifications.

5-17. Agent's Power to Appoint Subagents. Agents are usually selected because of their personal qualifications. Owing to these elements of trust and confidence, a general rule has developed that an agent may not delegate his duty to someone else and clothe the latter with authority to bind the principal.[9] An exception has arisen to this rule in those cases in which the acts of the agent are purely ministerial or mechanical. An act that requires no discretion and is purely mechanical may be delegated by the agent to a third party. Such a delegation does not make the third party the agent of the principal or give him any action against the principal for compensation unless the agent was impliedly authorized to obtain this assistance. The acts of such third party become in reality the acts of the agent and bind the principal, if they are within the authority given to the agent. Acts which involve the exercise of skill, discretion, or judgment may not be delegated without permission from the principal.

The case of authorized salesmen for local insurance agents seems to offer a slight exception to this rule. The local agent of an insurance company often authorizes his salesmen to accept fire insurance risks. Even though such action seems to involve a certain amount of judgment and discretion, the insurance companies are bound by the subagent's act, although they are in no respect obligated to compensate him, for the salesman must obtain his compensation from the local agent.

An agent may, under certain circumstances, have the actual or implied authority to appoint other agents for the principal, in which case they become true employees of the principal and are entitled to be compensated by him. Such a power on the part of the agent is not often implied, but if the situation is such that the major power conferred cannot be exercised without the aid of other agents, the agent is authorized to hire such help as is required. Thus, a manager placed in charge of a branch store may be presumed to possess authority to hire the necessary personnel the size of the business demands.

5-18. Agent's Authority to Collect. An agent who delivers goods sold for cash has the implied authority to collect all payments due at the time of delivery. A salesman taking orders calling for a down payment has implied authority to accept the down payment. However, salesmen by the very nature of their jobs have no implied authority to receive payments on account, and any authority to do so must be expressly given or be implied from custom. Thus, a person in his capacity as salesclerk in a store has authority to collect any payment made at the time of sale but no authority to receive payments on account. A payment to a sales agent without authority to collect that is not delivered to the principal may be collected by the principal from either the agent or from the party who paid the agent.

[9] State ex rel. Kendrick v. Thormyer, page 732

Possession of a statement of account on the billhead of the principal or in the principal's handwriting does not create implied or apparent authority to collect a debt. Payment to an agent without authority to collect does not discharge the debt.

Authority to collect gives the agent no authority to accept anything other than money in payment. Unless expressly authorized, he is not empowered to accept negotiable notes or property in settlement of an indebtedness. It is customary for an agent to accept checks as conditional payment. Under such circumstances the debt is not paid unless the check is honored. If the check is not paid, the creditor-principal is free to bring suit on the contract which gave rise to the indebtedness or to sue on the check, at his option.

5-19. Agent's Authority to Purchase on Credit or to Borrow.   A general agent placed in charge of a business has implied or apparent authority to purchase for cash or on credit. The implied authority is based on the nature of his position and on the fact that the public rightly concludes that a corporation or an individual acting through another person has given him the power and authority that naturally and properly belong to the character in which the agent is held out. Consequently, the public may rely upon his having such authority as is suggested by the ordinary habits and past experiences encountered in the business world. If this were not the case, commercial relations would constantly break down and chaos would result. Apparent authority is based on estoppel; therefore, the power is limited to purchases of the character or line of merchandise carried by the business. For example, the manager of a men's clothing store could not purchase a quantity of drugs on credit. A principal may defend a suit based on the extension of credit to an agent on the ground that the third party knew, or in the exercise of ordinary care and prudence should have known, that the agent did not have authority.

Authority to borrow money is not easily implied.[10] Such authority must be expressly granted or qualify as incidental authority to the express authority, or the principal will not be bound. The authority to borrow should always be confirmed with the principal.

5-20. Authority to Buy and Sell.   An agent who is given *special* authority to purchase goods is not authorized to contract for goods beyond the quantity authorized by the principal. A *general* purchasing agent will bind the principal even if he exceeds the quantity authorized because the authorization would constitute a secret limitation and would not be effective against third parties. The distinction between a general and special agent were discussed in Section 5-2 of Chapter 35. This material and the case referred to therein should be reviewed at this time.

A selling agent's authority differs depending on whether the subject matter of the sale is real estate or personal property. The ordinary real estate broker possesses no authority, implied or apparent, in the absence of an express grant, to enter into a contract for the sale of property listed with him. It is his business to find a party who is ready, willing, and able to purchase the property upon the terms set forth in the "Listing Agreement." The owner reserves the right to contract, or not, as he sees fit, at the time the broker presents a prospective

[10] Bank of America, Nat. Trust & Sav. Ass'n. v. Horowytz, page 732

buyer. For an agent to possess such power, it would require a power of attorney to comply with the provisions of the statute of frauds in most states.

An agent has authority to do everything necessary or proper and usual, in the ordinary course of business for effecting the purpose of the agency. When the purpose is to make a sale of personal property, the agent's authority to sell means that he is authorized to find a purchaser, to enter into a contract of sale, to make a delivery of title to the purchaser, and, if a writing is required, to execute the writing. If the agent's authority is limited to finding a purchaser, the agent may not enter into the contracts or execute the writings involved.

If a salesman is limited to obtaining orders for goods, the orders being subject to approval of the principal, no contract exists until the approval of the seller has been secured.

UNDISCLOSED PRINCIPAL

5-21. Undisclosed Principal's Contracts.   For various reasons a principal may desire to hide his identity. To achieve this secrecy, he will direct an agent to enter into all contracts in the agent's own name, leaving the third party either unaware of the existence of the principal (undisclosed principal) or unaware of the principal's *identity* (partially disclosed principal). The law relating to partially disclosed principals is the same as that relating to undisclosed principals and they are here treated together. Such agreements are always entered into on the strength of the agent's credit, and the agent is liable thereon until such a time as the third party elects to hold the principal. The third party, upon learning of the principal's existence or identity, may elect to enforce the contract against the principal rather than against the agent. The undisclosed principal is responsible for all contracts entered into by the agent within the scope of the agent's actual authority and he may be sued when his existence becomes known. Being unknown, the principal could not have created any apparent authority, consequently his liability is limited to actual authority— that which is expressly given and that which may be implied as incidental thereto.

The undisclosed principal is never liable upon a negotiable instrument signed by his agent since his name does not appear thereon. However, the third party can waive the note and sue the principal upon the agreement that furnished the consideration for the note and thus avoid the lack of liability on the note itself.

5-22. Settlement Between Principal and Agent.   In the preceding section it was stated that the third party, after learning of a previously undisclosed principal's interest in a transaction, might elect to look to the principal rather than to the agent for performance. Suppose, however, that the undisclosed principal supplied the agent with money to purchase the goods, but the agent purchased on credit and appropriated the money. In such a case the principal would be relieved of all responsibility. The same result obtains when the undisclosed principal *settles* with the agent after the contract is made and the goods are received, but before his disclosure to the third party. Any bona fide settlement between principal and agent before disclosure releases the principal. A settlement cannot have this effect, however, when it is made after the third party has learned of the existence of the principal, and the principal is aware that his identity is known. The settlement rule is based on equitable principle. It is fair to the third party, in that it gives him all the protection he originally bargained for, and it is fair to the principal, in that it protects him against a second demand for payment.

5-23. Election.   Election means choice, and a choice becomes possible only when the third party learns of the existence and identity of the principal. If a settlement has taken place previously, no election is possible; otherwise, the third party, when he learns of the existence of a previously undisclosed principal, may look either to the agent or to the principal for performance until such time as he definitely elects to hold one or the other. The election to hold one party releases the other from liability. No conduct by the third party which precedes the disclosure of the principal can constitute an election. Because of this rule, it has been held that an unsatisfied judgment obtained against the agent before disclosure of the principal will not bar a later action against the principal.

After disclosure, the third party may evidence his election by obtaining a judgment against one of the parties, or by making an express declaration of his intention. It has been held that sending a bill to one of the parties does not indicate an election. Most states also hold that the receipt of a negotiable instrument from either principal or agent does not show an election. The mere starting of a suit has been held insufficient to constitute an election, but if the case does not involve an issue of liability and proceeds to judgment against either the agent or the principal, election has taken place although the judgment remains unpaid. Many jurisdictions allow both parties to be joined in the same suit and allow either of them to make a motion to require the plaintiff to elect one or the other prior to proceeding to trial. The motion will not be allowed if both deny liability because it would be unfair to require an election until the jury has determined the issue of liability. If the lawsuit does not involve questions of liability, the motion to elect will be allowed. If it does involve the liability issue, the motion to elect will be made as a part of the posttrial proceedings, and the election will be required at that time. From these illustrations it can be seen that definite action is essential to constitute an election. The third party is usually free at any time to sue the particular party, principal or agent, whose credit is best.

LIABILITY OF AGENT

5-24. Contractual Liability.   As a general rule, an agent is not personally liable on contracts which he has entered into on behalf of his disclosed principal and the liability is solely that of the principal.[11] To this rule, there are certain well-recognized exceptions. First, if the agent carelessly executes a written agreement, he may fail to bind his principal and incur personal liability. To use an illustration suggested previously, the agent who signs a negotiable instrument for his principal, but fails to execute it in the principal's name by himself as agent or otherwise fails to show his representative capacity, is personally liable under the Uniform Commercial Code.

[11] Henderson v. Phillips, page 734

Second, the third party may request the agent to be personally bound because of the agent's credit rating or some other personal reason. Where the agent voluntarily assumes the burden of performance in his personal capacity, he unquestionably becomes liable in the event of nonperformance by his principal.

Third, if the agent does not disclose his agency and name his principal, he binds himself and becomes subject to all liabilities, express and implied, created by the contract and transaction, in the same manner as if he were the principal in interest.[12] The fact that the agent is known to be a commission merchant, auctioneer, or other professional agent, is immaterial. Any agent for an undisclosed or partially disclosed principal assumes personal liability.

If the agent wishes to avoid liability, it is his duty to disclose the name or identity of his principal clearly and in such a manner as to bring such adequately to the actual notice of the other party. It is not sufficient that the third person has knowledge of certain facts and circumstances that would, if reasonably followed by inquiry, disclose the identity of the principal. Disclosure of the principal is required in order to give the third party the opportunity to verify the authority of the agency and to allow the third party to decide if he wants to extend credit to the principal. As was previously noted, the third party may elect to hold either the agent or the principal, provided he acts within the proper time after he learns of the existence of the undisclosed principal. If the agent is held liable, he in turn has recourse against the principal.

5-25. Warranty of Authority. An agent may attempt to act for a principal even though the agent has no authority to do so. The agent may or may not be aware of this lack of authority and he may honestly believe that he possesses the requisite authority. Awareness of lack of authority and honesty is immaterial. If an agent exceeds his authority, he becomes liable to third parties for the damages resulting from his failure to bind the principal. His liability is said not to rest upon the contract itself, but to result from breach of an implied warranty of authority. As a general rule, an agent impliedly warrants to third parties that he possesses power to affect the contractual relations of his principal. If in any particular transactions the agent fails to bear such a relation to his principal, the agent violates this implied warranty. In addition, an agent who intentionally misrepresents his authority may be liable in an action of deceit. In such a case all the elements of fraud are present. Presumably, in either event, the damages would be those suffered because the agent failed to possess the authority that he attempted to exercise.

The agent may escape liability for damages arising from lack of authority by a full disclosure to the third party of all facts relating to the source of the agent's authority. Where all the facts are available, the third party is as capable of judging the limits of the agent's powers, as is the agent. In other words, the third party must rely upon the warranty in order to hold the agent for its breach. Where he has full knowledge of all particulars, he relies upon his own judgment and not upon the agent's representation of authority.[13]

The liability of the agent is qualified in one other respect. He is not liable

---

[12] Anderson v. Smith, page 736
[13] Fuller v. Melko, page 737

when, unknown to him, his agency has been cut short by the death of the principal. Death of the principal terminates an agency; this will be discussed in Chapter 40. Such an event as death is usually accompanied by sufficient publicity to reach third parties. As indicated earlier, the facts are equally available to both parties, so that no warranty arises.

5-26. Competent Principal.

Every agent who deals with third parties warrants that his principal is capable of being bound. Consequently, an agent who acts for a minor or a corporation not yet formed may find himself liable for the nonperformance of his principal. The same rule enables the third party to recover from the agent where his principal is an unincorporated association. In such a case, since there is no entity capable of being bound, a breach of the warranty results. The third party has a right to insist that the principal be a person, a firm, or a corporate entity capable of entering into an enforceable agreement. An unincorporated body has no legal entity, and only those voting for the particular transaction, or later adopting it, are liable.

Where, however, the third party is fully informed that the principal is an unincorporated organization, and he agrees to look entirely to it for performance, the agent is relieved. The evidence must clearly indicate such an agreement, as the normal presumption is that the third party expects to look to one party and not to the membership for performance.

In case the principal is a corporation, the agent does not warrant that his principal has legal capacity to enter into the particular transaction. In other words, the agent is not responsible if the contract made by him exceeds the authorized powers of the corporation. The limits of a corporation's powers are governed by its charter. Since charters are usually made a matter of public record, the powers of the corporation are equally available to the agent and to the third party.

5-27. To Account for Money Received.

An agent who, in the course of his employment, receives money from third parties for the benefit of the principal owes no duty to account to the third parties. If such money does not find its way into the principal's hands, it may be recovered in an action by the principal against the agent. This rule adequately protects all parties. On the other hand, money paid to an agent who has no authority to collect it, and who does not turn it over to the principal, may be recovered from the agent in an action by the third party. To illustrate: A traveling salesman normally has no authority to collect open accounts for his principal. Should he do so, he is subject to an action by the third party.

A different problem is presented when money is paid to an agent in error, such as occurs by overpayment of an account. If the agent has passed the money on to his principal before the mistake is discovered, it is clear that only the principal is liable. Nevertheless, money that is still in the possession of the agent when he is notified of the error should be returned to the third party. The agent does not relieve himself of this burden by subsequently making payment to his principal.

Any payment made in error to an agent and caused by the agent's mistake or misconduct may always be recovered from him, although he may have surrendered it to his principal. Also, any overpayment may be recovered from the agent of an undisclosed principal because the party dealing with the agent was unaware of the existence of the principal.

CONTRACTUAL LIABILITY OF PRINCIPALS AND AGENTS CASES

North American Sales A., Inc. v. Carrtone Lab., Inc.
214 So.2d 167 (La.) 1968

The president of a drug manufacturing company (Mr. Carr), without the express authority of the Board of Directors, entered into a contract to purchase the stock of a totally unrelated company and to hire the sole former shareholder (Mr. Ostrich) of said company, the plaintiff herein, for a minimum of five years at a compensation that could exceed $100,000 (the compensation was based on a formula). The drug company defendant when sued for breach of contract contended that it was not bound on the agreement because the president had not been authorized to enter into the agreement. From a judgment in favor of the drug company the plaintiff appeals.

CHASEZ, J. . . . No evidence was presented to sustain that the president of Carrtone was authorized, either by its charter, or bylaws, to execute on its behalf, an instrument of the character and with the import of the contract with Mr. Ostrich. There was no resolution of the Board of Directors, specifically or generally, empowering Mr. Carr to enter into such an agreement with Mr. Ostrich for the acquisition of NASA. Nor, was his action in this regard over expressly or tacitly ratified by the Board of Directors.

As its president, Mr. Carr, possessed the inherent power and authority to perform these administrative and other related acts normally exercised by a corporate officer, of equal status in the ordinary course and scope of managing the day-to-day affairs of a corporation engaged in identical pursuits with those of Carrtone and not expressly prohibited by the charter or bylaws. Any act of a corporate officer, which exceeds these standards, is beyond the scope of his authority and is not binding upon the corporation, unless it is subsequently ratified, consented to, or acquiesced therein.

The court cannot construe Mr. Carr's action of purchasing a totally unrelated business and contractually binding Carrtone for a period of five years, with a potential financial obligation in excess of $100,000.00, as being a routine, normal act in the ordinary scope and course of managing the day-to-day affairs of a corporation engaged in the manufacturing of drugs. Nor does the evidence warrant the conclusion that the Board of Directors, by their inaction or acquiescence in similar transactions in the past, clothed Mr. Carr with the apparent authority to bind the corporation, as he attempted to do in this agreement. The record does not reflect a single instance where Mr. Carr previously entered into a contract of this nature on behalf of Carrtone, with the board's tacit consent and approval. There is no basis, in law or fact, to assume that Mr. Carr possessed the implied or apparent authority to bind the corporation to this agreement.

The mere fact, that the document was drafted by the general counsel for Carrtone, who also expressed the opinion, in the presence of the plaintiff, that Mr. Carr did not need the authorization of the directors, is not in itself sufficient to vest apparent authority in Carr to bind the corporation. Nor, does it produce the legal consequence of relieving the plaintiff of the duty of ascertaining the agents authority to act for his principal.

Finally, did the corporation ratify the contract by the failure of its directors to repudiate it? This query must be answered in the negative.

There is no testimony tending to establish that the directors had any knowledge of the negotiations between Carrtone and Ostrich, or of the contents of the agreement dated February 3, 1963, until after its execution. Upon learning of this transaction, the directors convoked a meeting of its Board on March 23, 1963, and discharged Mr. Carr, as president of Carrtone. . . .

It is the opinion of the Court, that Mr. Carr's action of entering into the agreement with Ostrich, was beyond the scope of his authority as president and was not authorized by the charter, bylaws, or Board of Directors. It was manifestly an *ultra vires* act of a corporate officer, and as such, is not binding on the corporation. Accordingly, the plaintiff's demand against Carrtone Laboratories, Inc. is rejected. . . .

Affirmed.

Movie Films, Inc. v. First Security Bank of Utah, N.A.

447 P.2d 38 (Utah) 1968

CROCKETT, C. J. Plaintiff Movie Films, Inc., sues the defendant First Security Bank to recover funds which it claims the bank disbursed on checks not bearing the signatures of the two corporate officers as required by the signature card which fixes the agreement for withdrawals. Upon a trial to the court without a jury judgment was given for the plaintiff in the amount of $5,450.93.

Defendant bank appeals, contending:

(1) that Shawn D. Patterson, president and director of the plaintiff, had ostensible authority to effect a change of signature cards and to withdraw the funds solely on his signature; and

(2) That even if contention (1) above fails, the judgment should be reduced by $3,170.34 because that amount of money actually went to the benefit of the corporation.

In July, 1966, Shawn D. Patterson as president and Rex L. Jensen as vice president formed the plaintiff corporation, Movie Films, Inc., for the purpose of marketing movie cameras and accessories by direct sales to customers in Utah. Mr. Jensen, who resided in Las Vegas, Nevada, and was carrying on a similar business there, advanced the initial capital to get the business started, including $1,000 as working capital, $500 for attorney's fees and incorporation costs, and furnished a beginning inventory of one and one-half dozen cameras. Mr. Patterson as president of the new corporation was to manage the Salt Lake business, employing salesmen on a commission basis.

The corporation bank account was opened in defendant bank. The signature card and a corporate resolution left with the bank required that checks were to be paid only on the signatures of both Patterson and Jensen. Shortly thereafter, when the bank refused to honor checks bearing only the signature of Patterson as president, he went into the bank and talked to Mr. Clair McKell, Assistant Manager. He said there had been some misunderstanding;

that he could not conduct the business in Salt Lake with Mr. Jensen in Las Vegas if he had to go through the cumbersome procedure of getting both signatures on the checks. It was suggested that Patterson execute a new signature card and obtain another resolution of the corporation authorizing withdrawals on his signature only; and he took forms furnished by the bank to accomplish that purpose. Although neither the forms nor the resolution were returned to the bank, it proceeded to pay the several checks bearing Patterson's signature only on which this lawsuit is based.

Within a month after the business was started Patterson absconded with the cash and inventory belonging to the corporation.

The cases which hold that when the president of a corporation deals exclusively for the corporation, and the corporation takes the benefit of the transaction, it may be bound on the basis of ostensible authority and/or estoppel are not controlling in the instant situation. The evidence does not compel a conclusion that in drawing the checks Patterson was either acting exclusively for the corporation or that it derived benefit from the transactions. Indeed it seems reasonable to believe to the contrary, since it is now apparent that he was in the process of cheating the corporation, and shortly absconded with its money and its assets. There is a further consideration which lends support to the trial court's refusal to find that the bank could place reliance on Patterson's "ostensible" authority to sign the checks for the plaintiff corporation. The evidence shows plainly that the bank was not relying on any such "ostensible" authority. The bank's contention in that regard is squarely inconsistent with the express arrangement it had with the plaintiff corporation: there was an agreement in writing that the bank would honor checks of the corporation only upon both signatures; and the bank had itself insisted on the need of a resolution of the corporation authorizing the change. It is the duty of the drawee bank not to disburse funds except upon checks or orders signed properly by the drawer in accordance with the bank's agreement with him. . . .

Affirmed.

Carlson V. Hannah et al.

6 N.J. 202 (1951)

During the year 1940 Carlson and Galler Beverages, Inc., entered into a contract whereby the former was to act as distributor for "7-Up" in Paterson and certain territory north of the city. He was to supply his own truck, and was not to assign his contract without the approval of Galler. In 1942, Carlson, the plaintiff, was called into the service of the United States Army, so he made an agreement with the defendant, Hannah, to operate his route, with a certain amount being paid to the plaintiff for use of his truck. He then gave one McHugh power of attorney to act for him in those matters requisite and necessary to the distributorship. Business increased and the company demanded an additional truck, and a driver was found for it, he being given the outside city route. In 1944, the defendant threatened to quit unless he were protected when the plaintiff returned from the service, so McHugh agreed that the northern route was to be his upon the plaintiff's return, the latter being limited to the city route. This agreement had the approval of Galler. After plaintiff's return, he refused to approve the contract made by McHugh and demanded his entire territory although the defendant continued to operate the northern route as though it was his own. The plaintiff then instituted this suit to determine the effect of McHugh's contract and for an accounting. The lower court determined that McHugh exceeded his authority and gave plaintiff a judgment of $4,000.

ACKERSON, J. . . . The power of attorney which accompanied the contract made between Carlson personally and Hannah on May 22, 1942, conferred upon McHugh authority to act for the plaintiff during his absence " . . . in all matters pertaining to my distributorship of a carbonated beverage known as "7-Up," . . . giving my said attorney full power to do everything whatsoever, requisite and necessary to be done in said distributorship, . . . " McHugh's authority with respect to the operation of the accompanying contract itself is expressed in paragraph 8 thereof, hereinabove quoted, giving him power "to alter" the contract when deemed necessary with the consent of the other party thereto.

Attorneys in fact created by formal letters of attorney are merely agents and their authority and the manner of its exercise are governed by the principles of the law of agency. Such actual authority may be express or implied. Implied authority may be inferred from the nature or extent of the function to be performed, the general course of conducting the business, or from the particular circumstances of the case. Implication is but another term for meaning and intention; express authority given to an agent includes by implication, whether the agency be general or special, unless restricted to the contrary, all such powers as are proper and necessary as a means of effectuating the purposes for which the agency was created. Accordingly, it is well settled that, unless otherwise agreed, the authority of an agent to manage a business extends no further than the direction of the ordinary operations of the business, including authority to make contracts which are incidental to such business, are usually made in it, or are reasonably necessary in conducting it. But prima facie authority to manage a business does not include authority to dispose of it in whole or in part.

What, then, was the purpose of the instruments executed by plaintiff on the eve of entering the armed forces? Obviously he desired to preserve his business intact until his return and appointed McHugh to supervise it during his absence. Logically it is impossible to imply from the evidence before us any authority in the agent McHugh to dispose of any part of his principal's business by gift, sale or otherwise, and thereby defeat the very purpose for which such instruments were created. The grant of power was intended to aid and facilitate the operation of the distribution during plaintiff's absence and not to authorize its partition upon his return.

Appellant further contends that McHugh's authority to contract for the assignment of the territory in question was implied under the doctrine of "emergency power." This principle is defined in the Restatement (*Agency*) § 47, as follows:

> Unless otherwise agreed, if after the authorization is given, an unforeseen situation arises for which the terms of the authorization make no provision and it is impracticable for the agent to communicate with the principal, he is authorized to do what he reasonably believes to be necessary in order to prevent substantial loss to the principal with respect to the interests committed to his charge.

It is important to note, however, that this rule is expressly qualified in the Restatement as applicable only where it is "impracticable for the agent to communicate with the principal" and ascertain his wishes before acting.

The claimed emergency relied upon the invocation of the foregoing rule is said to be the choice with which McHugh was confronted of either abandoning the entire route because of the uncertainty of replacing Hannah due to wartime shortage of manpower, or acceding to his demand for a part of the territory on plaintiff's return. We find no merit in this contention. Emergency in this connection means "a sudden or unexpected occurrence or condition calling for immediate action." The evidence discloses that continuous pressure to procure the questioned contract had been exerted on McHugh by both Hannah and Galler for upwards of two months before it was finally signed. During all of this period and resistance, however, no attempt was made to communicate with Carlson and it was not impracticable to have done so. Furthermore there is no proof that Hannah could not have been replaced. While McHugh testified that he did not know where he could have picked up another driver, nevertheless it does not appear that he made any effort to do so. Significantly, only a month before the execution of the questioned contract, another driver was procured to help Hannah service the territory. No immediate urgency or necessity was presented other than an opportunity to demand a part of plaintiff's capital and that situation was of Hannah's own making.

We therefore conclude that the defendant McHugh was not authorized to make the executory assignment of territory attempted to be accomplished by the agreement of September 2, 1944. . . .

Judgment of the lower court affirmed.

Zager v. Gubernick

208 A.2d 45 (Pa.) 1965

Plaintiff sued an insurance adjuster (Gubernick) and an insurance company to recover on a settlement for an accident claim. After the accident, plaintiff's attorney wrote the owner of the car at fault for the name of the insurance company. Gubernick then advised that he was handling the claim. A $4,200 settlement was negotiated and plaintiff signed releases prepared by the adjuster which were forwarded to the company with the request for payment. Payment was not made because the company contended the settlement was too high and that the adjuster had exceeded his authority. The company indicated that Gubernick was a good adjuster but that the authority of outside adjusters was limited. The company contended that the releases were executed subject to acceptance or rejection by the company. The trial court found for the plaintiff holding that the adjuster was authorized.

FLOOD, J. . . . The circumstances clearly warrant the conclusion that the company in authorizing Gubernick to handle this case for it, authorized him to make adjustment of the claims.

So far as the plaintiffs are concerned, the appellant had clothed Gubernick with all the appearances of authority to negotiate a settlement.

. . . [E]ven if Gubernick did not have actual authority to settle the claim, and we think there is evidence that he did, he had at least apparent authority to deal with the plaintiffs and make the settlement. Under such circumstances, the plaintiffs have the same rights with reference to the appellant as if Gubernick had been authorized.

Even if there were a limitation as to the amount for which Gubernick could settle, and he was aware of this, the appellant would still be bound. A limitation on his authority as to amount only, which was communicated to Gubernick but not to the parties with whom he is authorized to deal, does not affect his principal's liability. Such "secret instructions" have no effect upon dealings with a third person who had no notice of them.

. . . Moreover, there is no evidence that even Gubernick knew of any such limitation on his authority until the appellant attempted to repudiate it, or that the settlement or its amount was so far beyond what had been previously negotiated by him in other cases on behalf of the appellant as to negate the natural inference that his authority extended to it.

All the circumstances of the case taken together show that Gubernick had at least apparent authority to conclude the settlement and bind the company so far as the plaintiffs were concerned. An adjuster may occupy such a relation to the company by virtue of long continued employment, and long continued custom with relation to the conduct of certain matters, that his acts will bind it. When an insurance company delegates the power of adjustment an adjuster so employed has the power to make arrangements with the insured after loss, and to bind the insurer thereby.

An affirmance of even an unauthorized transaction can be inferred from a failure to repudiate it. Here, there was a total failure to communicate to the plaintiffs or their attorney any dissent from, or repudiation of, the settlement for almost three months after Gubernick had made it on the appellant's behalf. . . .

The plaintiffs have performed their part of the accord by executing and delivering the releases, and therefore have the right to enforce the settlement instead of suing in trespass for their damages in the accident.

Judgment affirmed.

David v. Serges
129 N.W.2d 882 (Mich.) 1964

SOURIS, J. When an agent purporting to act for his principal exceeds his actual or apparent authority, the act of the agent still may bind the principal if he ratifies it. The Restatement of Agency 2d, § 82, defines ratification thusly:

> Ratification is the affirmance by a person of a prior act which did not bind him but which was done or professedly done on his account, whereby the act, as to some or all persons, is given effect as if originally authorized by him.

"Affirmance" is defined in § 83 of the Restatement:

> Affirmance is either
> (a) a manifestation of an election by one on whose account an unauthorized act has been done to treat the act as authorized, or
> (b) conduct by him justifiable only if there were such an election.

Although Michigan cases in which ratification has been discussed usually have involved receipt of direct benefits by the ratifying principal, evidence of receipt of benefits, while it lends plausibility to an allegation of ratification and, indeed, may in itself constitute ratification, is not a *sine qua non* of ratification. Paragraph (d) of the comment to § 82 of the Restatement, *supra,* discusses the matter in these terms:

> That the doctrine of ratification may at times operate unfairly must be admitted, since it gives to the purported principal an election to blow hot or cold upon a transaction to which, in contract cases, the other party normally believes himself to be bound. But this hardship is minimized by denying a power to ratify when it would obviously be unfair. See §§ 88-90. Further, if the transaction is not ratified normally the pseudo-agent is responsible; if not, it is because the third party knew, or agreed to take the risk, of lack of authority by the agent. In many cases, the third person is a distinct gainer as where the purported principal ratifies a tort or a loan for which he was not liable and for which he receives nothing. This result is not, however, unjust, since although the creation of liability against the ratifier may run counter to established tort or contract principles, the liability is self-imposed. Even one who ratifies to protect his business reputation or who retains unwanted goods rather than defend a law suit, chooses ratification as preferable to the alternative. . . .

In this case the only testimony taken was plaintiff's, who testified that defendant's managing agent had borrowed from him $3,500 upon defendant's behalf and for use in defendant's business, a retail meat market. Plaintiff further testified that defendant subsequently had paid to him $200 on the alleged loan and had upon several occasions stated to plaintiff that the full sum would eventually be paid. With this testimony in the record plaintiff rested his case and defendant, without likewise resting, moved for a judgment of no cause on the theory that plaintiff had failed to prove a prima facie case.

The trial court erred in granting defendant's motion. Defendant not having rested, the procedural posture of the case then was such that the court was required to consider the defendant's motion as if it had been a motion for directed verdict made at conclusion of plaintiff's proofs in a trial to a jury. Only if plaintiff's testimony, viewed in its most favorable light, could be said to be insufficient as a matter of law to support a judgment in his favor would the judgment of no cause be permissible under our former practice.

Even if borrowing money were not within the agent's actual or apparent authority, plaintiff's evidence, viewed favorably, was legally sufficient to establish defendant's liability for the alleged loan upon a theory of ratification. Thus, plaintiff's evidence was sufficient to require defendant to be put to his proofs.

Reversed and remanded. Costs to plaintiff.

Wilks v. Stone

339 S.W.2d 590 (Mo.) 1960

Plaintiff Wilks brought an action of replevin to recover a 1957 Plymouth which plaintiff's minor son Larry had traded to defendant auto dealer on the purchase of a 1959 Chevrolet. Larry Wilks subsequently sold the Chevrolet and kept the money. Plaintiff had title to the 1957 Plymouth and was aware of her son's actions. Larry had agreed that the title would be delivered to defendant and stated that he was authorized to make the trade. The trial court refused to allow defendant to offer evidence to prove the son's authority on the mother's ratification. Defendant appeals from a decision for plaintiff.

RUARK, J. . . . The principal issue and dispute is whether respondent Wilks was bound to the contract of exchange because she ratified the acts of her son Larry, who purported to act as her agent (if such be proved) in making the purchase of the 1959 Chevrolet and in trading the 1957 Plymouth in as a part of the purchase price.

As relates to agency, "ratification" is an express or implied adoption or confirmation, with knowledge of all material matters, by one person of an act performed in his behalf by another who at that time assumed to act as his agent but lacked authority to do so. Ratification relates back and is the equivalent of authority at the commencement of the act. It is the affirmance of a contract already made. The existence of agency and the authority of the agent can be and often is implied by proof of facts, circumstances, words, acts, and conduct of the party to be charged. As applied to the agency or authority which is created or related back by means of ratification, it may be implied by any facts and circumstances from which it can be reasonably inferred that the party to be charged (with knowledge of the facts) acquiesced in and accepted the transaction as his own, or which are inconsistent with any other intention. The intent to ratify may be implied from the circumstances, and this implication may be made even though the person to be charged as principal may have had an intention *not* to ratify.

As to what facts, circumstances, and conduct will justify the inference of agency, no fixed rule can be stated. There is no particular mode by which it must be established. It depends upon the situation in each individual case. One of the circumstances to be considered is the relationship of the parties. Although the bare relationship of parent and child is not, in and of itself, sufficient to justify the inference, such relationship is a factor of "considerable weight" to be considered along with all other circumstances as tending to establish the fact. The prior conduct of the parties is also a factor to be taken into account if such conduct is a part of the "chain of circumstances" surrounding the transaction. Under some conditions the mere silence and inaction of the party to be charged, a failure to dissent or speak up when ordinary human conduct and fair play would normally call for some negative assertion within a reasonable time, tends to justify the inference that the principal acquiesced in the course of events and accepted the contract as his own.

Probably the most certain evidence of implied ratification is the acceptance and retention of the fruits of the contract with full knowledge of the material facts of the transaction. Although this ratification by acceptance of the fruits does not necessarily apply where the benefits went to the assumed agent or some third party, nevertheless we think the party to be charged as principal should not be permitted to escape if she, with full knowledge of the facts, knowingly channels the benefits into the hands of another, or assists, aids, and abets the benefited party in making away with the fruits of the transaction so that the *status quo* cannot be restored. Such conduct is inconsistent with a good faith claim of no authority at the outset.

Since ratification may be established by facts and circumstances, it is sufficient to make a question for the trier of the fact if the whole sum total of the facts and circumstances justifies *the reasonable inference* that the party charged as principal accepted the transaction as his own. It is not necessary that each separate act, fact or circumstance stand on its own as proof sufficient to justify the inference. Each separate fact, act or circumstance is admissible if it *tends to establish* the agency, even though only remotely relevant. Consequently a wide latitude is permitted in the introduction of evidence as to the circumstances, and objections to the reception of such evidence are not viewed with favor. If there is any dispute as to the facts, or if different inferences can reasonably be drawn, ratification is a question of fact to be determined by the trier of the fact and not by the court.

In this case the defendant offered and attempted to prove (*a*) the son Larry acquired the 1959 Chevrolet with consent and approval of his mother, the plaintiff; (*b*) plaintiff knew her son had traded in the 1957 Plymouth on another car which he brought home and she did not object or express dissent at that time; (*c*) after the purported trade had been made but the balance of the purchase price had not been paid (because of a no funds check) she stated to the defendant that "the matter would be consummated"; (*d*) she consented and "authorized" her son to go to Joplin to obtain financing so that the balance of the purchase price could be paid; (*e*) she affirmatively consented to and approved of her minor son's sale of the 1959 Chevrolet received in the transaction to another dealer, for which sale the son received $2,200 in cash. By such conduct it could be found that she assisted in and made possible a transaction whereby the fruit of the transaction was appropriated and the return of the parties to *status quo* was made impossible.

We think these facts and circumstances, some of which were denied by the plaintiff, had they been permitted in evidence, would have permitted a finding by the trier of the fact that Mrs. Wilks ratified the sale or exchange of her automobile, and that consequently the trial court was in error in excluding such evidence. We believe that, under the situation here involved, justice to all parties requires that the whole circumstances of the transaction be revealed. For such reason the judgment is *reversed and the case is remanded for retrial.*

Ivers & Pond Piano Co. v. Peckham
139 N.W.2d 57 (Wis.) 1966

The defendant, Peckham, entered into a contract with plaintiff by which defendant (father) guaranteed payment for pianos delivered to his son not to exceed $2,000. The son's account rose to $5,200 and an agent of plaintiff Hoyman contacted the son about collecting the $2,000 from the defendant. Defendant gave his son a $2,000 check, payable to the son, which the son deposited in his own account. The son then mailed a check to the plaintiff for $2,000. Plaintiff's agent knew that the defendant had furnished the $2,000. The son and plaintiff continued business on a cash basis for a year at which time the balance of the account was discharged in bankruptcy. Plaintiff sued defendant on the guaranty and the defendant answered alleging payment. The trial found for the defendant and the plaintiff appeals.

HEFFERNAN, J. The trial court found that Robert H. Hoyman, agent for the piano company, knew that the $2,000 paid on May 12, 1961, originating with the defendant, Ellsworth L. Peckham, was for the purpose of satisfying the guaranty contract and, therefore, held that the defendant discharged his guaranty by payment. We deem that the court applied the correct rule of law. Where a creditor accepts payment from a third person knowing it came from the guarantor, the payment must be applied in satisfaction of the guaranty.

> . . . if the creditor is aware of the source of the payment, he should apply it to the note guaranteed by the surety. . . .

However, though Hoyman, the agent, knew that the father in fact made the payment, was that knowledge imputable to the principal . . . ? We conclude that it was. . . .

Where an agent has authority to deal in general with the subject matter of a transaction, knowledge that he gives in the course of that transaction is imputable to the principal, and he is charged with the consequences of that knowledge. . . .

The knowledge of an agent may be imputed to a principal irrespective of whether the agency is founded on express or implied authority.

. . . It is not denied that the representative . . . was the agent for sales purposes. It is equally obvious that his duties entailed the collection of past-due accounts. . . .

. . . Hence, we conclude that Hoyman was an agent whose knowledge that the payment was made by the father was imputable to Ivers & Pond.

We therefore conclude that Ellsworth Peckham's contract of guaranty was discharged by payment.

Judgment affirmed.

Joel Strickland Enterprises v. Atlantic Discount Co.
137 So.2d 627 (Fla.) 1962

RAWLS, J. Atlantic Discount Company, Inc., brought this action for a declaratory decree to determine the ownership of two automobiles. From a decree in favor of Atlantic, Joel Strickland Enterprises, Inc., defendant below, appealed.

David Saye, a used car dealer d/b/a Dave's Southern Servicecenter, in Fort Lauderdale, Florida, had possession and title to a 1958 Cadillac, and sold the same to Horace and Helen Neely on November 12, 1959, under a conditional sales contract agreement. On January 15, 1960, David Saye sold a 1957 Buick Roadmaster to his father and mother, the L. D. Sayes, also under a conditional sales contract. Immediately after each sale the respective conditional sales contracts were assigned to Atlantic Discount Company.

At the time of each sale the used car dealer had possession of the automobile sold and had the title certificate for each which had been assigned to him in blank. The purchasers of both of the automobiles and Atlantic relied upon the used car dealer to apply for new title certificates, and to cause to be noted thereon Atlantic's lien. Some time subsequent to each sale, Atlantic received a notice from the used car dealer to the effect that he had made application for new title certificates, though he had in fact not done so.

During this time the used car dealer, Saye, had an agreement with Joel Strickland Enterprises, Inc., whereby Saye was as agent authorized to purchase automobiles in the name of his principal and to pay for same by signing a draft in favor of the seller on the Orlando Auto Auction—one of three wholesale automobile auctions owned by Strickland. If the title certificate and draft attached thereto were acceptable to Strickland, Saye was then required to bring the automobile to one of the auctions to be sold. The purpose of this agreement was to stimulate business at the auctions.

In February 1960, Saye, purporting to buy the two automobiles in question for Strickland, drew drafts on the Orlando auction. The February 16 draft on the Buick was made payable to Florence L. Henry (Saye's sister) although the title certificate attached was in the name of Witt Brothers, the record title holder. The February 23 draft on the Cadillac was payable to J. R. Rees although the title certificate attached was in the name of Cobb and Warner, the record title holder. These drafts were honored by Strickland who applied to the Motor Vehicle Commissioner for certificates of title.

Thereafter, Atlantic obtained possession of the Cadillac on April 28, 1960, and the Buick in mid-March. Upon nonpayment of the installments due under its conditional sales contract, Atlantic applied to the Motor Vehicle Commissioner for repossessed titles, and discovered for the first time Strickland's interest in the automobiles.

When the automobiles were not delivered to the auction, Strickland also began investigating. To prevent further depreciation both parties agreed to sell the automobiles, to place the proceeds in escrow and to determine ownership by a suit for declaratory decree. In this action brought by Atlantic the lower court found that the knowledge of the agent Saye was imputed to his principal, Strickland, and Atlantic was entitled to summary final decree as a matter of law.

The first question presented here is whether the knowledge of the agent Saye is imputed to the principal Strickland.

The general rule is well settled that a principal is chargeable with notice or knowledge received by his agent while acting within the scope of his authority.

There is, however, a well-established exception to this general rule, where the conduct of the agent is such as to raise a clear presumption that he would not communicate to the principal the facts in controversy, as where an agent is in reality acting in his own business or for his own personal interest and adversely to the principal. Knowledge acquired by officers or agents of a corporation while not acting for the corporation but while acting for themselves, is not imputable to the corporation.

.   .   .

The agent Saye in this case had an established used car business and was clearly acting for himself in his own business and not on behalf of his principal Strickland when he first sold the automobiles to the purchasers and assigned the conditional sale contracts to Atlantic. When thereafter Saye delivered the assigned title certificates to Strickland and received payment for the automobiles with knowledge of the outstanding conditional sale contracts held by Atlantic, he was acting fraudulently in his own interest and adversely to the interest of his principal. The record shows that the agent Saye did not reveal the true facts to his principal Strickland. . . .

Reversed.

State ex rel. Kendrick v. Thormyer
155 N.E.2d 66 (Ohio) 1958

This was a mandamus action brought against the defendant, Thormyer, by Kendrick to compel reinstatement of the latter as a state employee. Kendrick had been released by a notice signed with Thormyer's name by one Reiners, his assistant. By statute power of appointment and dismissal rested in the head of the department Thormyer, and plaintiff alleges that the dismissal was ineffective because action was taken without the personal knowledge of Thormyer.

MILLER, J. . . . The question presented is whether or not the suspension was by Thormyer, who had no personal knowledge of the transaction, even though his name appeared on the letter to the relator, which in fact was signed by his alleged authorized agent, Fred G. Reiners. Now, if there had been a proper delegation of authority to Reiners, clearly, the suspension order would have been that of Thormyer, but it is our opinion that such powers may not be delegated for the reason that the authority imposed upon Thormyer involved personal judgment or discretion. We are supported in our conclusion by 2 O. Jur.2d., 134, which says:

> It is a well-established general rule that when authority delegated to an agent involves personal trust or confidence reposed in the agent, and especially when the exercise of that delegated authority involves personal judgment, skill, or discretion, such authority cannot be delegated by the agent to another as subagent to represent the principal, unless the principal has given express authority to the agent to delegate the authority conferred upon him. Ordinarily authority to conduct a transaction does not include authority to delegate the performance of the acts incidental to that transaction which involve the agent's discretion or skill, unless it is otherwise agreed as between the principal and the agent.

And in 9 C. Jur.2d, 420, it is said:

> Where the whole power of appointment to, and removal or suspension from, a particular position rests in one officer, an order of suspension issued by another officer is absolutely void and of no effect. An action for wrongful suspension of a civil service employee must be brought against the employing authority who made the actual suspension and not against a supervisor who caused the suspension.

In our case the sole power of appointment was in Thormyer who also possessed the sole power of suspension or removal under Section 143-26, Revised Code. . . .

For the foregoing reasons we hold that the order of suspension was void and since the relator has no adequate remedy at law the writ of mandamus will be allowed in accordance with the prayer of the petition.

Judgment for the plaintiff.

Bank of America, Nat. Trust & Sav. Ass'n. v. Horowytz
248 A.2d 446 (N.J.) 1968

O'BRIEN, J. This is a suit on a promissory note, dated October 26, 1961, signed in the name of defendant, "Carol Horowytz d/b/a E. D. S. by J. Pearl," and endorsed on the reverse side by "Jack Pearl."

Defendant has admitted in the pretrial order that J. Pearl is her father and that he engaged in business in defendant's name from time to time.

It appears from the exhibits introduced into evidence that on April 8, 1957, a checking account was opened with plaintiff bank in the name of defendant doing business under the tradename E. D. S., as a men's clothing business at 957 Market Street, San Francisco, California. The signature card, containing defendant's authorized signature, also contains the statement, "J. Pearl power of attorney attached." The original of this "signature card: power of attorney" was received into evidence and defendant admits signing it.

No oral testimony was offered by either party. The evidence consisted of the admissions contained in the pretrial order and the instruments introduced into evidence. The question presented is whether J. Pearl had the authority to obligate defendant on the note in question. Plaintiff relies solely upon the power of attorney as establishing such authority.

Thus the court is called upon to determine whether the power of attorney can be construed as clothing the attorney-in-fact with the authority to borrow on behalf of defendant principal.

A power of attorney is an instrument in writing by which one person, as principal, appoints another as his agent and confers upon him the authority to perform certain specified acts or kinds of acts on behalf of the principal. The primary purpose of a power of attorney is not to define the authority of the agent as between himself and his principal, but to evidence the authority of the agent to third parties with whom the agent deals.

The authority to borrow money on the credit of the principal is among the most important and also dangerous powers which a principal can confer upon an agent, since manifestly there is a great possibility of the abuse of the power. For this reason, in the absence of express authority, the authority of an agent to borrow on the principal's credit will not be inferred unless it is necessarily implied by the scope and character of the authority which is expressly granted. Unless otherwise agreed, an agent is not authorized to borrow unless such borrowing is usually incident to the performance of acts which he is authorized to perform for the principal.

These principals have been well expressed by the court in *Williams* v. *Dugan*, 217 Mass. 526, 105 N.E. 615, L.R.A.1916C, 110 (1914):

> The power to borrow money or to execute and deliver promissory notes is one of the most important which a principal can confer upon an agent. It is fraught with great possibilities of financial calamity. It is not lightly to be implied. It either must be granted by express terms or flow as a necessary and inevitable consequence from the nature of the agency actually created.

Courts are reluctant to find an authority to borrow where such authority is not explicitly conferred. . . .

It is apparent that the authority to borrow money is not given to the attorney-in-fact in so many words. Thus, it becomes necessary to determine whether such authority may be implied by a reasonable construction and interpretation of the instrument, or whether such power may be inferred or necessarily implied by the scope and character of the authority which is expressly granted. . . .

The instrument delegates power "to sign and endorse checks, notes and drafts and transact all business with your Day and Night Branch San Francisco Calif." The delegation is in both specific and general terms. If the power to borrow money is necessarily to be implied by the terms of the instrument, it must be expressed by the specific terms "sign . . . notes" rather than by the general term "and transact all business." For, by the law of California:

> When authority is given partly in general terms and partly in specific terms, the general authority gives no higher powers than those specifically mentioned.

Focusing, therefore, on the words "sign . . . notes," plaintiff construes that language to mean "make and deliver promissory notes as evidence of a debt," i.e., the power to borrow money. Defendant, on the other hand, construes the same language to mean "endorse notes presented for payment" or "sign notes payable at the bank," which amounts to an authorization to the bank to pay such notes from funds credited to the checking account. . . .

The power does not expressly authorize the agent to borrow money and requires construction and interpretation of the language used. Therefore, it is this court's opinion that the instrument must be construed most strongly against the party supplying it—plaintiff bank.

. . . [T]he court concludes that it cannot be any reasonable construction or interpretation construe the language used in the power of attorney supplied by plaintiff bank to authorize the attorney-in-fact to borrow money on the defendant's credit nor can the court find that such authority is to be necessarily implied by the scope and character of the authority expressly granted. . . .

In addition to the authority to borrow which may be directly granted or which may be indispensable to the execution of the powers actually conferred, an agent may have an apparent authority to borrow money on the credit of his principal—for example, where such borrowing has been approved by a long course of dealing of such a nature as must inevitably have become known to the principal. . . .

Accordingly, for the reasons herein stated the court concludes that the power of attorney does not contain an express or implied grant of power to borrow money; nor may such power be inferred as necessarily implied by the scope and character of the authority which is expressly granted; nor has any evidence been adduced of any apparent or ostensible power given to the attorney-in-fact sufficient to bind defendant principal.

Judgment will therefore be in favor of defendant.

Henderson v. Phillips

195 A.2d 400 (D.C.) 1963

MYERS, J. The sole question upon appeal is whether appellee Phillips, president of Metropolitan Designed for Living, Inc., was personally liable under two contracts for plumbing services rendered by appellant.

Metropolitan Designed for Living, Inc., was a corporation engaged in the construction of new houses. Phillips was president of the company. Henderson was engaged in the plumbing business. Phillips telephoned Henderson requesting an estimate on the cost of doing some plumbing work on a particular house, identifying himself as president of the construction firm. Henderson admitted he might have so identified himself. After inspecting the house under construction, Henderson prepared two written contracts addressed to "Design for Modern Living" and mailed them to the corporation. Each was accepted under the signature of "James O. Phillips" and remailed to Henderson in an envelope bearing in the upper left corner the name "Designed for Living, Inc., 2814 Pennsylvania Avenue, N.W., Washington 7, D.C.," within the outline of a picture of a house. Thereafter, payment on account was made by checks mailed in a similar envelope. Printed on the first check in the upper lefthand corner was "Metropolitan Designed for Living, Inc.," showing the Pennsylvania Avenue address. It was signed by two persons, one of whom was Phillips, under the printed name of the corporation, with no indication as to the capacity of either signor. A second check, similarly drawn, was not paid upon presentment. Henderson then sued both the corporation and Phillips.

Phillips and Henderson had had one previous business dealing when Henderson completed plumbing work on another house built by the same corporation. On that occasion, three similar checks, drawn on the corporate account and signed by the same two persons, without identification of their official authority to co-sign the checks, were received in payment.

Upon this evidence, the trial judge, sitting without a jury, found that Phillips was not individually liable for the balance due under the contracts with Henderson.

In this jurisdiction, when an agent enters into a contract without disclosing both the identity of his principal as well as the fact of his agency relationship, he becomes personally liable on the contract. On the other hand, when his principal is disclosed and words are absent from the contract expressly binding him, the agent ordinarily does not incur personal liability. The law is well settled that when an agent acts in good faith on behalf of a disclosed principal, he is not held responsible in the event of his principal's default. A principal is disclosed if "at the time of a transaction conducted by an agent, the other party thereto has notice that the agent is acting for a principal and of the principal's identity. . . . " (Restatement (Second) *Agency,* § 4 (1958))

The prior dealing between appellant and Phillips was sufficient to impute notice of the agency relationship of Phillips. The checks in payment for the work performed by Henderson were definitely revealing as to the corporate identity of the builder. The present contracts were again negotiated through Phillips who identified himself as president of the corporation. It is true that he "accepted" the written contracts without indicating his agency capacity, but he did the same when co-signing the corporation checks in payment for both jobs by Henderson. Henderson recognized that he was dealing with a corporate entity when he addressed his contracts to "Design for Modern Living." It is also significant that Henderson never testified that he thought he was dealing only with Phillips and intended to rely upon him for payment and not upon the corporate builder. Neither contract contained any words expressly binding Phillips personally or indicating any intent by him to be responsible for payment in the event the corporation defaulted.

The identity of the principal being known and the agency of Phillips being established at the time of the transaction, upon default of the disclosed principal, personal liability could not be imposed upon its agent.

The decision of the trial judge was substantiated by competent evidence, and we find no error requiring reversal.

Affirmed.

Anderson v. Smith

398 S.W.2d 635 (Tex.) 1966

Plaintiff architects sued contractor defendant for services rendered under a written contract. Defendant Anderson claimed that the contract was not made with him individually but with the corporation known as Hal Anderson, Inc. The contract, in the form of a letter, set forth the terms and was signed by defendant individually and returned to plaintiffs. The services were rendered in connection with the design of a house for a Mr. Lay who contracted with Hal Anderson, Inc., for the construction of a house. Five thousand dollars had been paid plaintiffs by check drawn on the corporation, but plaintiffs had not seen the construction contract. The lower court held that the defendant was individually liable and he appealed. Defendant conceded that until plaintiffs received the $5,000 from the corporation, he was personally liable as an agent for an undisclosed principal, but contended on appeal that after appellees had actual knowledge of his agency or were put upon inquiry, which if pursued would have revealed such agency, only the corporation was liable.

BATEMAN, J. . . . Some of the well-established rules of law applying to this situation are as follows:

> Unless the parties have agreed otherwise, a person making or purporting to make a contract with another as agent for a disclosed principal is not himself a party to the contract and is not liable thereon. However, if he purports to act on his own account, but is in fact contracting on account of an undisclosed principal, or even if it be known that he is acting as an agent but the identity of his principal remains undisclosed, the agent is a party to the contract and is personally bound thereby.

If the agent would avoid personal liability, the duty is on him to disclose his principal; it is not upon the party with whom the agent deals to discover the principal.

The agent is not relieved from personal liability merely because the person with whom he dealt had a means of discovering that the agent was acting in a representative capacity. Knowledge of the real principal is the test, and this means actual knowledge, not suspicion.

It is not sufficient that the seller may have the means of ascertaining the name of the principal. If so, the neglect to inquire might be deemed sufficient. He must have actual knowledge. There is no hardship in the rule of liability against agents. They always have it in their own power to relieve themselves, and when they do not, it must be presumed that they intend to be liable.

If an agent who negotiates a contract in behalf of his principal would avoid personal liability, the burden is upon him to disclose his agency to the other contracting party. And his disclosure must include not only the fact that he is an agent, but also the identity of his principal. . . .

Applying these well-settled principles of law to the facts of this case leads us to the inescapable conclusion that, since it was never established that appellees had actual knowledge that appellant was acting as agent for the corporation, if in fact he was, appellees were entitled to recover from appellant the amounts earned by them under the schedule of hourly rates of pay agreed upon between them. . . .

Affirmed.

Fuller v. Melko
76 A.2d 683 (N.J.) 1950

WACHENFELD, J. This is an appeal from a judgment of $5,212.67 plus interest for fees and expenses allegedly due to the plaintiff by reason of an investigation which he undertook at the behest of the defendant, the Middlesex County Prosecutor. The appeal was taken to the Superior Court, Appellate Division, and brought here on our own motion.

The plaintiff in 1947 was a licensed detective. On March 3 of that year, the defendant, in his official capacity as County Prosecutor, asked the plaintiff to undertake an undercover investigation of gambling activities in Middlesex County. There is a factual conflict as to what comprised the schedule of fees and expenses. . . .

Investigatory activities were immediately commenced after the meeting of March 5 and continued until April 20, when the plaintiff was ordered to quit because a Special Attorney General had been appointed to take charge of all gambling investigations in the County. He thereafter completed his reports and submitted his bill in the amount of $5,212.67, the subject of this action.

The Prosecutor forwarded the bill to Justice Colie, pursuant to R.S. 2:182-7, N.J.S.A., which provides that amounts expended by the prosecutor "shall not exceed the amount fixed by the board of chosen freeholders in its regular or emergency appropriation, unless such expenditure is specifically authorized by order of the supreme court justice presiding in such county." The Justice refused to approve the bill as he thought it exorbitant.

The plaintiff submitted his bill to the County, which denied payment, asserting the contract was void as to the County, being in excess of the amount appropriated for the purpose of special investigations. It also lacked the approval of the justice. . . . This suit was thereupon initiated against the Prosecutor individually, based on the theory that he became personally liable by reason of having exceeded his authority in making the contract.

The case was tried before a jury and a verdict in favor of the plaintiff was returned for the full amount plus interest. . . .

The true test of the defendant's personal liability in the present case is whether or not the plaintiff, in making the contract with him, had full knowledge of the facts regarding his authority to bind the County for the expenses incurred.

It is not disputed that the Prosecutor acted as the agent of the County in making the contract with the plaintiff and that it was for a public purpose in pursuance of the duties and obligations of his office.

One who assumes to act as agent for another impliedly warrants his authority to do so, but where he fully discloses the facts constituting his authority, he may not be held liable either on the contract or for breach of implied warranty. 1 Williston on Contracts, Rev. Ed. 1936, Sec. 282: "Fraud on the part of the agent is not essential to his liability, but if he fully discloses the facts on which his assumption of authority is based, or if the other party has actual or presumptive knowledge thereof, he will not be a warrantor."

In *Mott* v. *Kaldes,* 288 Pa. 264, 135 A. 764 (1927), the rule is stated in these words: "Neither agent nor principal is bound by unauthorized exercise of agent's authority, where parties knew the facts but misconceived applicable law."

In *Mickles* v. *Atlantic Brokerage Co., Inc.,* 209 App.Div. 182, 204 N.Y.S. 571, 572 (1924), the defendant, as agent, sold certain goods which its principal refused to deliver because the agent had exceeded its authority. In an action seeking to hold the agent personally liable, the court said:

> The plaintiffs invoke the principle of law which gives one a right of action against an agent who assumes to make a contract on behalf of his principal, which he in fact is not authorized to make. The basis of such action is a breach of an implied warranty of authority. . . .
>
> To the general rule giving such right of action there is an exception, to the effect that an agent cannot be held liable if he fully discloses to the person with whom he is dealing the limitations upon his authority, and discloses all the facts and circumstances with reference to the authority under which he assumes to act.

Similar language was used in *Michael* v. *Jones,* 84 Mo. 578: "Where all the facts are known to both parties, and the mistake is one of law as to the liability of the principal, the fact that the principal cannot be held is no ground for charging the agent with liability."

And in *Equitable Trust Co.* v. *Taylor,* 330 Ill. 42, 161 N.E. 62, 64 (1928): "Where the contract is made in good faith, and both parties are fully cognizant of the fact as to the agent's authority, the result is to exonerate the principal from liability because the agent had no lawful authority to make the contract, and the agent cannot be held liable either ex contractu or ex delicto."

The facts as developed in the case *sub judice* definitely qualify it within the rule enunciated in the cited authorities.

. . . The plaintiff vigorously asserts that he did not know the unexpended amount of the appropriation available to the Prosecutor for special investigations. He did know, however, according to his own bill of particulars, that the appropriation was insufficient to cover the cost of the investigation upon which he was about to embark. He also admittedly knew that the payment for services and expenses, in so far as they exceeded whatever unexpended appropriation remained, was contingent upon securing the authorization of the presiding Supreme Court Justice. He had considerable experience in this field of endeavor, having worked for a prosecutor for fifteen years and, according to his own testimony, had heard this procedure "discussed many times." He must have been cognizant that the certification of the Supreme Court Justice would be forthcoming only if the bill for services submitted was in his opinion, reasonable and proper. . . .

There was a full and complete disclosure of the facts regarding the defendant's authority, its limitation, the budgetary statutes and the procedure to be followed to secure payment for the services rendered. Under these circumstances there was no personal liability.

The judgment below is reversed without costs.

CHAPTER 36
REVIEW QUESTIONS AND PROBLEMS

1. *P*, the owner of a grocery store chain, hires *A* to manage one store. *P* tells *A* to stock the store himself. Assume that *P* tells *A* :
   a. "Be sure to buy soup."
   b. "Don't buy soup."
   c. Nothing about soup.
   A then proceeds to buy forty cases of soup from *T.* In which case is *P* liable to *T*?
2. *X* hires *Y*, an attorney, to sue *Z* for a debt. While *X* is out of town, *Y* settles the case with *Z*, and *Y* forges *X*'s name to a release. When *X* returns, he accepts *Z*'s check. May *X* claim *Y* acted without authority and avoid the release?
3. *T*, while purchasing weed killer from *A*, the XYZ Company's salesman, asks *A* whether the weed killer will injure lilies. *A* replies, without authority, that it will not. *T* purchases the weed killer, and after using it, the weed killer injuries his lilies. May *T* recover from the XYZ Company?
4. *T* enters a private parking lot owned by *P. A, P*'s parking lot attendant, tells *T,* "Give the keys to Joe. He will park it for you." Joe, unknown to *T,* was not *P*'s employee, and *A* had no actual authority to obtain assistance in his work. Joe steals *T*'s car and demolishes it. May *T* recover from *P*?
5. *W,* president of XYZ Packing Company, calls ABC Company, identifies himself and asks whether ABC Company has olives for sale. An agent of ABC Company replies in the affirmative. *W* orders forty cases. In reality, *W* was not buying for XYZ Company, but was placing the order as a favor for the RST Company, with whom ABC had refused to deal.
   a. Is XYZ Company liable on the contract?
   b. Is RST Company liable on the contract?
   c. Can ABC Company refuse to perform?
6. *X* purchased an insurance policy on his own life. He paid the premiums directly to the insurance agent, *Y. Y* appropriated the premiums to his own use. *X* died. May the beneficiaries recover from the insurance company?
7. *X* made a contract with *Y* for the purchase of lumber. Unknown to *Y, X* was acting on *Z*'s behalf. *Z* paid the contract price plus a commission to *X*, prior to *Y*'s discovery of *Z*'s existence. *X* misappropriated the funds to pay a personal debt. Does *Y* have any recourse against *Z*?
8. *X* gave *Y* a power of attorney to "do and perform all and every act which I may do, including mortgaging my property." *Y* sold *X*'s property to *Z. X* brought an action against *Z* for return of the property. May *X* recover?

9. *A* owned a life insurance policy, on which he made quarterly payments. One such payment was due on April 1. On March 1, *A* delivered the payment to *B,* the company's local agent. *B* refused the payment, saying he was not authorized to collect premiums. On five previous occasions, *B* had accepted the premiums and forwarded them to the home office. On April 11, *A* died. Assuming that there was no grace period for the payment of premiums, may the beneficiaries recover from the company?

10. *A,* thinking he had authority to do so, signed *P*'s name to a contract whereby *T* was to drill an oil well for $7,000. Later, *A* and *T* learned *P* had not given *A* authority to do so. Is *A* liable if the contract was signed "*P* per *A*"?

11. *A* was authorized by *P* to purchase bowling alley equipment on credit. He told the seller he was acting as an agent, but was not at liberty to disclose his principal's name. The bill remaining unpaid and *P* being now disclosed, may the seller recover of *A*?

12. *A,* an insurance salesman for *X* Company without authority to adjust losses, learned that *T*'s car had been badly damaged in an accident, and because he knew the car was covered by insurance, he had it towed to *G*'s garage for immediate repairs. Some time later, the adjuster for *X* Company visited the garage to see the car and noticed that *G* was engaged in repairing it. He made no comment, and the company later refused to pay the repair bill, alleging lack of authority by *A.* Is *X* Company liable?

13. *A* was the purchasing agent of *P* for the purpose of buying poultry and farm produce. In all his transactions with the farmers, *A* acted as the principal and purchased on the strength of his own credit. *A* failed to pay for some of the produce purchased. The farmers, having ascertained that *P* was the true principal, seek to hold him. May the do so? Suppose *P* had previously settled with *A*?

14. *A,* acting for a corporation that is soon to be formed, orders two delivery trucks from *T.* The corporation is formed, but refuses to ratify the contract. Under what circumstances is *A* liable to *T*?

15. *T,* by reason of an error on the part of *A,* an agent for *P,* overpays to the extent of some $300 his account with *P.* Before *A* pays the money over to *P, T* discovers the error and demands the excess amount from *A.* Is *A* under a duty to return the money to *T,* or may he turn it over to *P*?

16. *A* was a traveling salesman for *P.* He sold and delivered to *T* goods amounting to $300. At the time of delivery, he collected the sale price, but failed to turn the money over to *P.* Will *T* have to pay again? Would the result be the same if *P* had shipped the goods and *A* had collected at the end of the month? Suppose *A* had sold the goods in exchange for groceries and had used the groceries. Would *P* have been able to collect again of *T*?

chapter 37

Liability for Torts

5-28. Introduction. As was discussed in the prior chapter, an agent is someone that contractually represents another known as a principal. The terms
"principal" and "agent," while frequently used in the law of torts, are not
helpful or technically accurate in deciding issues of tort liability because an
agent for contractual purposes is either a servant or independent contractor
for purposes of tort liability. The following is a summary of the fundamental
principles of tort liability in the law of agency and an indication of the section
in which each will be discussed:

1. Agents and servants are personally liable for their own torts. (Section
5-29)
2. A master is liable under the doctrine of *respondeat superior* for the torts
of his servant if the servant is acting within the scope of his employment.
(Section 5-30)
3. A principal is not liable for the torts of an agent who is not also a servant
in the performance of his duties. (Section 5-28)
4. A principal, proprietor, employer, or contractee (each of these terms is
sometimes used) is not as a general rule liable for the torts of an independent
contractor. (Section 5-32)

While the terms "master" and "servant" are technically more accurate than
the terms "principal" and "agent" in describing the parties when tort liability
is based on the doctrine of *respondeat superior,* courts nevertheless frequently
describe the parties as "principal" and "agent." A careful analysis of cases
imposing liability upon a principal under the doctrine of *respondeat superior*
will indicate that the agent involved is actually a servant also. Many such cases
involve factual situations where the "agent's" act was done in the manner
"authorized" by the principal or the result was "authorized." While the use

of contract terminology in torts is apparent, it should not be overlooked that the agent is actually a servant and that discussions of authority actually are discussions about control. Authority is not the actual test of tort liability—control is. A principal is liable for torts of only those agents who are subject to that kind of control which establishes the master-servant relationship.

As the cases and materials in this chapter are studied, the fact that some courts use the terms "agent" and "servant" almost interchangeably should not obscure the technical distinction nor change the basic principles of law applicable to the master-servant relationship. Regardless of the label used, for the purposes of the doctrine of *respondeat superior,* a servant is a person who is employed with or without pay to perform personal services for another in his affairs, and who, in respect to the physical movements in the performance of such service, is subject to the master's right or power of control. A person who renders services for another but retains control over the manner of rendering such services is not a servant but an independent contractor.

As a general rule, a principal or master is not criminally liable for the criminal conduct of agents or servants. There are several well-recognized exceptions to this rule, such as the criminal liability of a corporation under the antitrust laws. Corporate employers can be fined for criminal acts of employees, and this area of the law is rapidly expanding as legislative bodies increase the role of government in regulating business activity. Criminal liability of employers is generally beyond the scope of this text.

5-29. Tort Liability of Agents and Servants.   Every person who commits a tort is personally liable to the individual whose person or property is injured or damaged by the wrongful act. One is not relieved of tort liability by establishing that the tortious act was committed under the direction of someone else or in the course of employment by another. The fact that the employer or principal may be held liable does not in any way relieve the employee or agent from his liability. The agent's, or servant's, liability is joint and several with the liability of the principal.

In the event that *A* commits a tort against *T, T* can bring action against *A* or against *P,* or *T* can sue *A* and *P* jointly. Assume that *T* sues and collects from *P,* as is typically the case, because *P's* financial standing is usually better than *A's.* Can *P* upon paying the judgment recover his loss from *A*? The answer is Yes if the tort arose from *A's* negligence and there was no contributing fault on *P's* part. As will be discussed more fully in Chapter 39, Section 5-43, a servant is liable for his own misconduct either to others or to his employer. He is required to exercise that degree of skill and diligence ordinarily expected of those who perform like undertakings. A servant who agrees to perform a particular task implies that he possesses the requisite skill and training. However, his duty requires only that he exercise a reasonable degree of care; he is not liable for a failure to use the highest degree of care possible. Suits by masters against servants are not common because the servant's financial situation seldom warrants an action against him. In most instances *P's* liability will be covered by insurance so that the loss is actually as borne by the insurer and the servant will not be required to reimburse the master.

Just as *P* may have a right to reimbursement or indemnity from *A*, under certain situations *A* may successfully maintain an action for reimbursement or indemnity against *P*. Such is the case when *A* commits a tort in conformity with instructions given to him by *P*, without knowledge that his conduct is tortious. For example, *P*, a retail appliance dealer, instructs *A* to repossess a TV set from *T* who had purchased it on an installment contract. *P* informs *A* that *T* is in arrears in his payments. Actually, *T* is current in his payments, and a bookkeeping error had been made by *P*. In accordance with his instructions and over protest from *T*, *A* makes the repossession. *A* *has* committed a tort, but *P* must indemnify him and satisfy *T's* claim against *A*, if *T* elects to collect from *A*.

A question that has not been fully resolved relates to the relatively infrequent situation in which the principal has immunity from suit. Is the agent or servant who commits a tort while serving such an employer likewise immune from legal action brought against him by an injured third party? For example, assume that under the law of a particular state a municipality is immune from suit and that a policeman in that city commits a tort. The usual view is that the servant is not protected by such immunities and the policemen would be liable. It should be noted, however, that the immunity granted governmental and other bodies has been substantially reduced in scope.

5-30. *Respondeat Superior.* A master is liable to third persons for the torts committed by his servants *within the scope of their employment.* This concept frequently known as *respondeat superior* (let the master respond) imposes vicarious liability on employers as a matter of public policy. While negligence of the servant is the usual basis of liability, the doctrine of *respondeat superior* is also applicable to intentional torts, such as trespass, assault, libel, and fraud, which are committed by a servant acting within the scope of his employment. It is applicable even though the master did not direct the willful act or assent to it.[1]

This vicarious liability imposed on masters, which makes them pay for wrongs they have not actually committed, is not based on logic and reason but on business and social policy and the theory that the master is in a better position to pay for the wrong than is the servant. This concept is sometimes referred to as the "deep pocket" theory. The business policy theory is that injuries to persons and property are hazards of doing business, the cost of which the business should bear rather then have the loss borne by the innocent victim of the tort or society as a whole.

There are two major difficulties in applying the doctrine of *respondeat superior.* The first involves the issue as to whether the party at fault is a servant as contrasted with an independent contractor. The tort liability of one engaging an independent contractor for the acts of an independent contractor is discussed in Section 5-32 of this chapter, but it must be noted that, as a general rule, the doctrine of *respondeat superior* is not applicable to this relationship.

---

[1] Lockhart v. Friendly Finance Co., page 749

The second problem is whether the servant is *acting within the scope of his employment* at the time of the commission of the tort. The law imposes liability on the master only when the master's business is being carried on or where the wrongful act was authorized or ratified by the principal.[2] The master's liability does not arise when the servant steps aside from his employment to commit the tort or does the wrongful act to accomplish some purpose of his own. If the tort is activated by a purpose to serve the master or principal, then he is liable. Otherwise he is not. Although the scope of employment is considerably broader than explicitly authorized acts of the employee, it does not extend to cases in which the servant has stepped aside from his employment to commit a tort which the master neither directed in fact nor could be supposed, from the nature of the servant's employment, to have authorized or expected the servant to do. It is not possible to state a simple test to determine if the tort is committed within the scope of the employment. However, factors which are considered in determining the scope of employment include the nature of the employment; the right of control, "not only as to the result to be accomplished but also as to the means to be used";[3] the ownership of the instrumentality such as an automobile; whether the instrumentality was furnished by the employer; whether the use was authorized; and the time of the occurrence. Most courts inquire into the intent of the servant and the extent of deviation from expected conduct involved in the tort. The issue is usually one of fact and is left to the jury.

A servant is not acting within the scope of his employment if he is on a "frolic" of his own. The deviation may sometimes be described as a "detour," in which case, a problem is presented as to the point at which the detour ends and the course of employment resumes.[4] Another difficult situation is presented when the servant combines his own business with that of his master. As a general rule, this fact does not relieve the master of liability. The doctrine of *respondeat superior* has been extended to create liability for negligence of strangers while assisting a servant in carrying out the master's business, where the authority to obtain assistance is given or is required as in the case of an emergency.

Intentional or willful torts are not as likely to occur within the scope of the servant's employment as are those predicated upon a negligence theory. If the willful misconduct of the servant has nothing to do with his master's business and is animated entirely by hatred or a feeling of ill will toward the third party, the master is not liable. Where the predominant motive is not to work off a personal grudge, but rather to advance his master's interests, it has been held that the master is liable.

The doctrine of *respondeat superior* has been extended to borrowed servants under what is usually referred to as the "borrowed servant" doctrine. Under this doctrine, an employee, while generally employed by one party, may be loaned to another in such a manner that the special employer may be responsible for actions of the employee under the doctrine of *respondeat superior* and the general employer will not be liable. In determining who is the master of an employee in a case in which it is contended that the borrowed

[2] Fisher v. Carrousel Motor Hotel, Inc., page 750
[3] Konick v. Berke, Moore Company, page 751
[4] Fiocco v. Carver, page 752

servant doctrine is applicable, it becomes necessary to ascertain who was the master at the time of the tortious act of the employee. This requires an inquiry into whose work was being performed at that time—a matter ascertained by finding who has the power to direct and control the work being performed and the right to control it. It is not who actually controlled the actions of the servant that determines the applicability of the borrowed servant doctrine, but who has the right to control them.

As a general rule, the master cannot avoid liability by showing that he has instructed the servant not to do the particular act complained of, although many states have a well-recognized exception insofar as automobile guests are concerned.[5] In addition, the master is not released by evidence that the servant was not doing the work his master had instructed him to do, when the servant had misunderstood the instruction. As long as the servant is attempting to further his master's business, the master is liable.

A minor may be a servant but cannot be held to a master's liability. The master-servant relationship cannot as a general rule be established by estoppel, but liability may be based on ratification of the tort. Ratification requires a positive act rather than mere silence or inaction. For example, suppose a bartender assaults a customer as a result of a private quarrel. If the master fails to discharge the bartender, has he ratified the tort? Common sense and most courts would say No.

5-31. Procedure.   As previously noted, the law of torts in most states, unlike the law of contracts, allows joinder of the master and servant as defendants in one cause of action or permits them to be sued separately. While the plaintiff is limited to one recovery, the master and servant are jointly and severally liable. The party may collect from either or both in any proportion until the judgment is paid in full. If the servant is sued first and a judgment is obtained, which is not satisfied, such a suit is not a bar to a subsequent suit against the master, but the amount of the judgment against the servant fixes the maximum limit of potential liability against the master.

If the servant is found to be free of liability, either in a separate suit or as a codefendant with the master, then the suit against the master on the basis of *respondeat superior* will fail. The master's liability is predicated upon the fault of the servant, and if the servant is found to be free of fault, the master has no liability as a matter of law.

The granting of a "release" or a "covenant not to sue" by the third party to either the servant or principal but not to the other raises significant issues. A release eliminates liability, and if given to either the master or servant, it will operate to discharge the other from any further liability. A "covenant not to sue" is not a release of liability but is simply a promise not to sue to impose liability. The several states take differing viewpoints on the legal effect of a covenant not to sue. Most hold that giving such a covenant to a servant by the third party operates to bar a suit based on *respondeat superior* against the master.[6] A significant number of states hold that a covenant not to sue a servant is not a bar to a suit against the employer but that the employer's liability is entitled to be credited with any sum paid by the servant to the third

[5] Klatt v. Commonwealth Edison Company, page 754
[6] Holcomb v. Flavin, page 755

party. On the other hand, in almost every state, a covenant not to sue the master does not release the servant.

5-32. Independent Contractors.   An independent contractor is a person performing a service for one who employs him under an arrangement by which the person engaged has the power to control the details of the work being performed.[7] Since the performance is within the control of such person, he is not a servant, and his only responsibility is to accomplish the result contracted for. To illustrate: *A* contracts to build a boat for *P* at a cost of $1,000 and according to certain specifications. In such a case it is clear that *A* is an independent contractor, with the completed boat as the result. However, had *P* engaged *A* by the day to assist in building the boat under *P*'s supervision and at *P*'s direction, the master-servant relationship would have resulted. As previously discussed, it should be kept in mind that an agent with authority to represent his principal contractually will, at the same time, be either a servant or independent contractor for the purpose of tort liability.

The distinction between servants and independent contractors is important because, as a general rule, the doctrine of *respondeat superior* and the concept of vicarious liability in tort are not applicable to independent contractors. There is no tort liability, as a general rule, because the theories which justify liability on the master for the servant's tort are not present when the person engaged to do the work is not a servant.

The hallmark of a master-servant relationship is that the master not only controls the result of the work but has the right to direct the manner in which the work shall be accomplished; the distinguishing feature of an independent contractee-contractor relationship is that the person engaged in the work has exclusive control of the manner of performing it, being responsible only for the result and not the means. In ascertaining whether a person is a servant or independent contractor, the basic inquiry is whether such person is subject to the alleged employer's control or right to control with respect to his physical conduct in the performance of services for which he was engaged. If the facts as to alleged master-servant relationship are in dispute, the precise nature of the relationship is for the decision of a jury, but where the facts are not in dispute, the question of the relationship is for court determination. Contracts frequently provide that the relationship is that of independent contractor. Such a provision is not binding on third parties, and the contract cannot be used to protect the contracting parties from the actual relationship as shown by the facts.

The rule of insulation from liability in the independent contractor situation is subject to several well-recognized exceptions. The most common of these is where the work involved is inherently dangerous to the public. The basis of this exception is that it would be contrary to public policy to allow one engaged in such an activity to avoid his liability by selecting an independent contractor rather than a servant to do the work.

Another exception to insulation from vicarious liability exists where the work being done is illegal, although the logical connection between illegality and fault is frequently not present. A common exception involves employee's duties which are considered to be nondelegable. In the law of contracts, it was

---

[7] Jaramillo v. Thomas, page 757

noted that personal rights and personal duties could not be transferred without consent of the other party. Many statutes impose strict duties on parties such as common carriers and innkeepers. If an attempt is made to delegate these duties to an independent contractor, it is clear that the employer upon whom the duty is imposed has liability for the torts of the independent contractor.

Tort liability is also imposed where the employer is himself at fault, as when he negligently selects the employee. For example, if a young boy without qualifications is hired to break a horse, the employer would be liable to third parties injured by the horse. Fault may also exist where the employer actively participates in the work, such as inspecting during performance or giving unsolicited advice.

Just as a servant is personally liable for his own torts, it should be remembered that the independent contractor has liability for his own torts.

5-33. Injuries to Employees—Common Law. Another problem is whether the master must compensate the servant for injuries to the servant caused by third parties or fellow employees. At common law and except as modified by statute (see next section), a master is not an insurer of the safety of his servant.[8] It is the duty of a master to use ordinary care in providing a safe place to work and reasonably fit appliances for his servant's use. Where the master fails to discharge his duties and injury to the servant proximately results therefrom, the master is liable absent some special defense. For example, an employer is liable to an injured employee if the injury is a result of an assault and battery by a fellow employee known by the employer to have such vicious and dangerous propensities as to constitute a hazard to fellow workers.

5-34. Workmen's Compensation. At common law, an employee who was injured at work could sue his employer but was confronted with overcoming three defenses available to the employer, one or all of which usually barred recovery. The first of these defenses was that the employee was *contributorily negligent.* If the employee was even partially at fault, this defense was successful though the majority of the fault was the employer's. Second, if the injury was caused in part by some other employee, the "fellow servant" doctrine excused the employer and limited recovery to a suit against the other employee who was at fault. Finally, in many jobs which by their very nature involved some risk of injury, the doctrine of "assumption of risk" would allow the employer to avoid liability.

The common-law rules resulted for the most part in imposing on employees the burdens that resulted from accidental injuries, occupational diseases, and even death. Through the legislative process, society has rather uniformly determined that this result is undesirable as a matter of public policy, and statutes usually known as Workmen's Compensation have been enacted to balance the interest of the parties by creating liability without fault (eliminated the defenses), but limiting the amount of the liability by creating definite and detailed schedules of amounts due for various injuries. At the federal level, there is a Federal Employers' Liability Act, which accomplishes similar results for businesses engaged in interstate and foreign commerce such as railroads. F.E.L.A.,

[8] Hopkins v. Hacker, page 759.

however, requires proof of negligence but does not limit the amount of recovery. Basically, F.E.L.A. merely eliminates the common-law defenses.

The purpose of Workmen's Compensation is to compensate the employee for losses due to accidental injuries, occupational diseases, and death "arising out of and in the course of employment." This purpose is achieved either by the employer's paying directly or the state's paying from a fund created by employers all medical expenses of the employee and, in addition, periodic payments for support. These support payments are usually paid weekly during periods of disability; they are based on prior earnings and the size of the family to be supported.

Many statutes provide for a specific number of weekly payments for specific losses such as an arm, finger, leg, or eyes. In addition, a fixed death benefit depending on earnings and number of dependents is provided. For permanent total disability, a lifetime pension may be allowed. Disfiguration and injuries such as those to the back create difficult questions as to the amount due. These are decided by the administrative agency, such as an industrial accident commission, which administers the compensation laws and fixes the benefits.

In recent years, the administrative agencies and the courts have tended to broaden the coverage and scope of Workmen's Compensation. For example, an employee who suffers a heart attack may have incurred a compensable injury based on recent standards.[9] Broken legs incurred in athletic contests during lunch periods have also been held to be compensable.

In some states, Workmen's Compensation is the exclusive remedy available to an injured employee. In others he may bring a common-law tort action against his employer but the common-law defenses are available. Some states have provisions comparable to F.E.L.A., which eliminate common-law defenses of employers. In these states the employer can elect to reject Workmen's Compensation and carry private insurance. When the injury is caused by a third party, the employee may bring a tort suit in all states, but the employer is subrogated to the extent of the Workmen's Compensation payments.

5-35. Trends in Tort Liability.   In recent years, the law has been expanding the concept of vicarious liability. Some of this expansion has been by judicial decision, but most of the expansion has been by statute. Liability for automobile accidents has been a major area of concern. Some states have adopted what is known as the "family car doctrine." Under it, if the car is generally made available for family use, any member of the family is presumed to be an agent of the parent-owner when using the family car for his or her convenience or pleasure. The presumption may be rebutted, however. Other states have gone further and provided that anyone driving a car with the permission of the owner is the owner's agent, and the owner has vicarious liability to persons injured by the driver. These laws greatly expand the liability of automobile owners, who should take precautionary measures to make sure that this potential risk is adequately covered by insurance.

Another area of expanding liability involves parental liability for the malicious mischief and destruction of property by minors. In an attempt to prevent such conduct, legislative bodies have created liability on parents but have

---

[9] Fattore v. Police and Firemen's Retirement System of N.J., page 760

usually limited the liability to a relatively small amount such as $500. Courts reviewing these statutes are finding them to be constitutional.

Another trend is to find liability on some legal theory other than *respondeat superior*. Such liability is based on contract principles or because of some other relationship, such as that between a passenger and a common carrier.[10]

LIABILITY FOR TORTIOUS CONDUCT CASES

Lockhart v. Friendly Finance Co.

110 S.2d 478 (Fla.) 1959

The plaintiff, Lockhart, purchased a television set from a third party, after which the defendant claimed to have security interest in it. It was orally agreed between plaintiff and defendant that plaintiff would pay $100 at the rate of $15 a week. The plaintiff failed to pay, so the defendant sent its agent out to collect the account or repossess. Plaintiff, when approached by the agent and two detectives, told them not to enter since his wife was ill and very nervous. Nevertheless, they entered and threw a small radio and lamp on the floor, breaking them, and slamming a door so hard the glass in it was broken. They carried the television set away, and the plaintiff sued for trespass and damages sustained. The lower court directed a judgment for the plaintiff, but later ordered a new trial because he thought he erred. The plaintiff appealed from the order for a new trial.

WIGGINGTON, J. . . . We are now called upon to determine whether the undisputed facts recited above, construed in a light most favorable to the defendant, were reasonably susceptible of but the single conclusion that defendant was liable as a matter of law.

The problem here presented has been passed upon by our Supreme Court on many occasions. Basically it has been held that the determination of this question must turn upon the facts and circumstances of each case.

Actions for trespass committed by an agent are based upon the doctrine of *respondeat superior*. The master's liability does not arise unless the tortious act was committed as an incident to the master's business and while acting within the range of employment, or that the master directed the wrongful act or ratified it afterwards. The test of liability is whether the act constituting the trespass was within the general scope of the servant's employment while engaged in the employer's business, and was done with the view of furthering that business.

The latest decisions on this subject have followed the modern view that the liability of the master for intentional acts which constitute legal wrongs can only arise when that which is done is within the real or apparent scope of the master's business. It does not arise where the servant has stepped aside from his employment to commit a tort which the master neither directed in fact nor could be supposed, from the nature of his employment, to have authorized or expected the servant to do.

It is appellee's contention that the issues of whether its agent's act of trespass was committed within the real or apparent scope of defendant's

---

10 St. Michelle v. Catania, page 761

business; whether the agent stepped aside from his employment to commit the act complained of; and whether defendant directed or could be supposed to have authorized or expected the agent to commit the tortious act, were all questions for the jury to determine. It is upon this premise that appellee insists the trial court committed error in directing a verdict on these issues in plaintiff's favor, and that the court's subsequent order granting a new trial because of such error is correct and should be sustained. . . .

The manager's instruction to the agent to go to plaintiff's house and get the television receiver, knowing as he did that the agent was not then armed with judicial process entitling him to lawfully take the security claimed by defendant, is susceptible of but one reasonable interpretation. These instructions, unqualified as they were, contemplated that the agent would take such action as he deemed necessary in order to carry them out. That the agent did not misinterpret these instructions is evidenced by the fact that he reinforced himself with the assistance of two city detectives before arriving at plaintiff's home with the obvious intention of retaking the receiver by whatever means appeared necessary. Defendant's manager knew, or is presumed to have known, that television receivers are customarily if not invariably kept inside people's homes, and cannot be seized by a lienor over the objection of the owner without the commission of a trespass. Defendant accepted and benefited from its agent's activities by retaining the receiver without offering to return it to its owner, knowing or being presumed to have known the manner in which possession of the instrument was obtained.

It is our view that the undisputed evidence established defendant's liability for the tortious act of its agent, and any contrary view that may have been taken by the jury could not have been sustained. There was no genuine issue of any material fact touching upon defendant's liability in this case, and the trial court was correct as a matter of law in directing a verdict in plaintiff's favor. It therefore follows that the court committed error by entering its order granting a new trial. . . .

The order granting a new trial is reversed.

Fisher v. Carrousel Motor Hotel, Inc.

424 S.W.2d 627 (Tex.) 1967

Plaintiff brought suit for actual and exemplary damages growing out of an alleged assault and battery. The defendants were a motor hotel corporation, a corporation operating a restaurant in the motor hotel, and the restaurant manager who committed the assault and battery. The jury found for the plaintiff, but the court entered a judgment notwithstanding the verdict because the defendants had not authorized the assault and battery.

GREENHILL, J. . . . The rule in Texas is that a principal or master is liable for exemplary or punitive damages because of the acts of his agent, but only if:

(a) the principal authorized the doing and the manner of the act, or

(b) the agent was unfit and the principal was reckless in employing him, or

(c) the agent was employed in a managerial capacity and was acting in the scope of employment, or

(d) the employer or a manager of the employer ratified or approved the act.

... At the trial of this case, the following stipulation was made in open court:

It is further stipulated and agreed to by all parties that as an employee of the Carrousel Motor Hotel the said Robert W. Flynn was manager of the Brass Ring Club.

We think this stipulation brings the case squarely within part (c) of the rule ... as to Flynn's managerial capacity. It is undisputed that Flynn was acting in the scope of employment at the time of the incident; he was attempting to enforce the Club rules by depriving Fisher of service.

The rule ... set out above has four separate and disjunctive categories as a basis of liability. They are separated by the word "or." As applicable here, there is liability if (a) the act is authorized, or (d) the act is ratified or approved, *or* (c) the agent was employed in a managerial capacity and was acting in the scope of his employment. Since it was established that the agent was employed in a managerial capacity and was in the scope of his employment, the finding of the jury that the Carrousel did not authorize or approve Flynn's conduct became immaterial.

.   .   .

The judgments of the courts below are *reversed,* and judgment is here rendered for the plaintiff. ...

Konick v. Berke, Moore Company
245 N.E.2d 750 (Mass.) 1969

Plaintiffs sued the defendant, Prescott, and his employer, Berke, Moore Company, to recover for injuries sustained in an automobile accident. The jury found that Prescott was negligent, but the court directed a verdict for the defendant company, holding, as a matter of law, that it was not liable under the doctrine of *respondeat superior.*

SPALDING, J. ... We summarize the evidence as follows: The accident occurred on Charles Street, Boston, on July 9, 1959. At that time Prescott was working for the Company as a salaried employee. The Company was a general contractor and was engaged on a "job" in Chelsea. Prescott was a timekeeper on that job. During the morning Prescott was instructed by one Moore, his supervisor, to "jump in the car and get the payroll" at the Company's office on Newbury Street in Boston. He was not told what car to take, but other than his own, there was only one car at the job site and that belonged to Moore. Prescott drove in his own car from Chelsea to Boston by way of the Mystic River Bridge, which he considered was the "most direct route." The route chosen and the speed of the car were determined by Prescott. The accident occurred before he reached the office in Boston. The Company, as was its practice, later reimbursed him for the toll fee which he paid to cross the bridge.

In addition, the Company paid for gas and oil used by Prescott. The car was registered in Prescott's name, and both the registration fee and the operator's license were paid for by him. When he was first employed in 1950, he was not required to own a car as a condition of employment.

The Company may be liable under the doctrine of *respondeat superior* only if Prescott was its servant. The general rule laid down by our cases is that in order for the relation of master and servant to exist, "the employee must be subject to control by the employer, not only as to the result to be accomplished but also as to the means to be used." Restatement 2d: *Agency,* § 220(1), also stresses the importance of control by defining a servant as "a person employed to perform services in the affairs of another and who with respect to the physical conduct in the performance of the services is subject to the other's control or right to control."

. . . .

. . . An employee while driving his own car may be an independent contractor, even though he would be a servant when performing other jobs. Our decisions, however, have recognized that there may be sufficient evidence of a master-servant relationship to go to the jury if an officer of the company has instructed the employee what route to follow and could have told him how to drive his car en route. . . .

. . . Other cases, in holding that a master-servant relationship may have existed, do not even mention whether the employer had a right to control the actual operations of the car, and thus imply that there is no such requirement.

Some of the decisions . . . suggest that the crucial question is the right to control the driver's general activities, not the physical control of the car. In other words, if there is a right to control the employee's general activities, he is a servant, even though the master may not have the right to control the details of the operation of the car when the servant is carrying out an errand for his master. Thus, as was said by the Court of Appeals for the Fifth Circuit in *Hinson* v. *United States,* 257 F.2d 178, 181, "Control or the right to control the manner or means of performing the task hardly seems decisive. If the relationship of master and servant exists and if what the employee is doing is in the furtherance of the master's business, i.e., in the scope of his employment, the law gives the master the right of direction and control."

We are of opinion that we should no longer follow our cases to the extent that they indicate that a master-servant relationship does not exist unless the employer has a right to control the manner and means (the details, in other words) of operating the car. In the circumstances here, where Prescott clearly was a servant in relation to his duties as a timekeeper, where he was instructed to do a specific job, and where he had at least implicit permission to use his own car, the fact that he chose the route and his speed does not change his status to that of an independent contractor. Accordingly, the verdicts for the Company should not have been directed, and the plaintiffs' exceptions to this action must be sustained.

Fiocco v. Carver

137 N.E. 309. (N.Y.) 1922

CARDOZO, J. The defendants, engaged in business in the city of New

York, sent a truckload of merchandise from Manhattan to Staten Island. The duty of the driver when he had made delivery of the load was to bring the truck back to the garage at Twenty-third street and Eleventh avenue on the west side of the city. Instead of doing that, he went, as he tells us, to Hamilton street on the east side, to visit his mother. A neighborhood carnival was in progress in the street. A crowd of boys, dressed in fantastic costumes, as Indians, Uncle Sam, cowboys, and the like, were parties to the frolic. They asked the driver for a ride, and in response to the request, he made a tour of the district, going from Hamilton street to Catherine, then through other streets and back again to Catherine. At this point he stopped in front of a pool room, and left his truck for a moment to say a word to a friend. It is here that the plaintiff, a child of eleven years, arrived upon the scene. The merrymakers were still crowding about the truck. The plaintiff with a playmate tried to join them. While he was climbing up the side, the driver came back and three times ordered him to get off. As the third order was given, the plaintiff started to come down, but before he could reach the ground, the truck, as he tells us, was started without warning, and his foot was drawn into a wheel. The driver gives a different story, insisting that the boy ran after the moving truck and climbed on the side when it was impossible to see him. All the witnesses agree that the truck as it left Catherine street was still carrying the boys. The driver adds that his purpose then was to go back to the garage. Upon these facts a jury has been permitted to find that he was in the course of his employment. The ruling was upheld at the Appellate Division by the divided court.

We think the judgment may not stand.

The plaintiff argues that the jury, if it discredited the driver's narrative of the accident, was free to discredit his testimony that there had been a departure from the course of duty. With this out of the case, there is left the conceded fact that a truck belonging to the defendant was in the custody of the defendant's servant. We are reminded that this without more sustains a presumption that the custodian was using it in the course of his employment. But the difficulty with the argument is that in this case there *is* more, though credit be accorded to the plaintiff's witnesses exclusively. The presumption disappears when the surrounding circumstances are such that its recognition is unreasonable. We draw the inference of regularity, in default of evidence rebutting it, presuming, until otherwise advised, that the servant will discharge his duty. We refuse to rest upon presumption, and put the plaintiff to his proof, when the departure from regularity is so obvious that charity can no longer infer an adherence to the course of duty. . . .

We turn, then, to the driver's testimony to see whether anything there, whether read by itself or in conjunction with the plaintiff's narrative, gives support for the conclusion that the truck was engaged at the moment of the accident in the business of the master. All that we can find there, when we view it most favorably to the plaintiff, is a suggestion that after a temporary excursion in streets remote from the homeward journey, the servant had at last made up his mind to put an end to his wanderings and return to the garage. He was still far away from the point at which he had first strayed from the path of duty, but his thoughts were homeward bound. Is this enough, in view of all the circumstances, to terminate the temporary abandonment and put him back into the sphere of service? We have refused to limit ourselves by tests that are merely mechanical or formal. Location in time and space are circumstances that may guide the judgment, but will not be suffered to control it, divorced from other circumstances that may characterize the intent of the transaction. The dominant purpose must be proved to be the performance of the master's business. Till then there can be no resumption of a relation which has been broken and suspended.

We think the servant's purpose to return to the garage was insufficient to bring him back within the ambit of his duty. He was indisputably beyond the ambit while making the tour of the neighborhood which ended when he stopped at Catherine street upon a visit to a pool room. Neither the tour nor the stop was incidental to his service. Duty was resumed, if at all, when ending the tour, he had embarked upon his homeward journey. It was in the very act of starting that the injury was done. The plaintiff had climbed upon the truck while it was at rest in front of the pool room, still engaged upon an errand unrelated to the business. The negligence complained of is the setting of the truck in motion without giving the intruder an opportunity to reach the ground. The self-same act that was the cause of the disaster is supposed to have ended the abandonment and reestablished a relation which till then had been suspended. Act and disaster would alike have been avoided if the relation had not been broken. Even then, however, the delinquent servant did not purge himself of wrong. The field of duty once forsaken, is not to be re-entered by acts evincing a divided loyalty and thus continuing the offense. . . .

The judgment of the Appellate Division and that of the Trial Term should be reversed, and the complaint dismissed, with costs in all courts.

Klatt v. Commonwealth Edison Company
211 N.E.2d 720 (Ill.) 1965

Plaintiff Bonnie Klatt was injured while riding as a guest in an automobile owned by the defendant, Edison, and driven by one of its employees, Herbert Klatt, plaintiff's father. The defendant had a company rule which, in substance, provided that unauthorized persons unconnected with the employer's business were not to be transported in the employer's vehicles. Defendant contended that the driver was not acting within the scope of his employment. The jury found for the plaintiffs, but the trial judge granted a new trial. Plaintiff appealed and the appellate court affirmed in part and reversed in part. The Supreme Court granted leave to appeal.

UNDERWOOD, J. . . . . Defendant Edison next contends that Klatt was not acting within the scope of his employment at the time of the accident, and vigorously urges that, even if Klatt was within the general scope of his employment at the time of the accident, liability should nevertheless not attach under the doctrine of *respondeat superior*. Much reliance for this proposition is placed upon section 242 of the Restatement of the Law, *Agency,* (2d) vol. III, which states: "A master is not subject to liability for the conduct of a servant towards a person harmed as the result of accepting or soliciting from the servant an invitation, not binding upon the master, to enter or remain upon the master's premises or vehicle, although the conduct which immediately causes the harm is within the scope of the servant's employment."

A company rule of defendant Edison in force at the time of the accident in substance provides that unauthorized persons unconnected with company business are not to be transported in company vehicles. The record establishes that Klatt had received a copy of this rule. Under these circumstances there can be no question that defendant Edison would be relieved of liability under the Restatement rule. The question for decision here is whether that rule in substance should be followed in Illinois.

The basic reason underlying this view, as stated in the Restatement reporter's notes, is " . . . that by accepting the hospitality of the servant and causing him to commit a breach of duty, the intruder had so identified himself with the servant that it is just that his claim against the master should be forfeited. Further, although the servant drives 'in scope of employment,' he is also driving for the benefit of the intruder." Restatement, *Agency* (2d) vol. III, sec. 242, at pages 384-385. (Reporter's Notes).

There is, however, a clear line of authority contrary to the view expressed by the Restatement. The Supreme Court of Errors of Connecticut, for example, in rejecting the Restatement view, observed: "The Connecticut doctrine rests on the broader ground that every man, who prefers to manage his affairs through others, remains bound to so manage them that third persons are not injured by any breach of legal duty on the part of such others, while they are engaged upon his business and within the scope of their authority. [Citation]. Public policy requires that the master shall be held liable for negligent acts of the servant performed in the course of his employment even though they are not specifically authorized or at times contrary to instructions. [Citing cases.] . . . '[T]he law is not so futile as to allow a master by giving secret instructions to his servant to discharge himself from liability.' "

.　　　　.　　　　.

After thorough consideration of the foregoing divergent authority, we conclude that the Restatement embodies the more sound reasoning and logic. We accordingly adopt that view. Defendant Edison thus cannot be held responsible to plaintiff here for the defalcations of the former's errant servant under the doctrine of *respondeat superior.*

Since our adoption of the Restatement rule wholly relieves defendant Edison of any liability herein, there exists no reason for its continued presence as a party to this cause, and the trial court is hereby directed to dismiss defendant Edison as a party defendant at the new trial.

Reversed in part and affirmed in part, and remanded, with directions.

Holcomb v. Flavin

216 N.E.2d 811 (Ill.) 1966

Plaintiff brought an action for personal injuries sustained in an automobile accident with one Barnard. Plaintiff had settled his claim against Barnard for $16,000 and given him a covenant not to sue. This action was against Barnard's employers on the theory of *respondeat superior.* The defendants sought to join Barnard as a third-party defendant on the ground that if the defendants were liable to the plaintiff, Barnard was liable to the defendants. This motion was allowed in a prior appeal. Defendants moved for summary judgment on the ground that the covenant not to sue Barnard discharges defendants. The trial court allowed the motion and the appellate court reversed. The Supreme Court granted leave to appeal. The sole issue before this court is whether the execution of a covenant not to sue an agent or servant serves to extinguish a claim against his principal or employer whose liability, if any, arises under the doctrine of *respondeat superior.*

SULFISBURG, J. . . . The covenant herein is a standard covenant not to sue containing no reservations of rights against others and provides that "this instrument is and shall be construed as a covenant not to sue as distinguished from a release." No mention is made in the covenant of the defendants in this suit.

The appellate court specifically rejected the view recognized by a number of cases from other jurisdictions. In those cases the courts, although recognizing the distinction between a release and a covenant not to sue as applied to joint tort-feasors generally, have taken the view that where the only liability of a master or principal arises under the doctrine of *respondeat superior,* the injured person's covenant not to sue the servant operates to release the master or principal from liability. The rationale of these cases is based either upon the theory that such a result will avoid circuity of action or that since the liability of the master or principal is merely derivative and secondary, exoneration of the servant removes the foundation upon which to impute negligence to the master or principal.

A leading case on the subject is *Karcher* v. *Burbank,* 303 Mass. 303, 21 N.E.2d 542, 124 A.L.R. 1292, where the court stated:

> The company's [employer's] liability is of a derivative or secondary character, resting solely upon the doctrine of *respondeat superior.* The company was, in effect, the plaintiff's [employee's] surety, and could, therefore, recover over against him if compelled to pay damages for his negligence while he was acting as its agent within the scope of his authority. It is a principle of the law of suretyship that a release or covenant not to sue the person known by the covenantor to be the principal will discharge the surety.

In *Stewart* v. *Craig,* 208 Tenn. 212, 344 S.W.2d 761, the court in a similar situation involving a covenant not to sue the servant pointed out that if a judgment were obtained against the employer based upon the employee's negligence, the employer would be entitled to sue the employee and obtain the same judgment against him. Since the plaintiff had given the employee the covenant not to sue, the employee would be then entitled to judgment against the plaintiff as was originally obtained in the action against the employee, thus completing the circuit and the parties would come out in the same position as when they started. The court, therefore, held that a covenant not to sue the servant extinguishes the cause of action against the wrongdoer and therefore extinguishes the cause of action against his superior.

.   .   .

In the case at bar the trial court recognized that if the defendants would have to respond in damages, they could sue their alleged employee, the covenantee, for the amount they had to pay. The employee would then have to respond in the very damages which the covenant was supposed to guard against. The contrary result reached by the appellate court herein would certainly involve an undesirable circuity and multiplicity of actions.

The appellate court stated that when Barnard paid for the covenant, he is presumed to know that if the plaintiff recovered from his employers they, in turn, would seek indemnity from him. Considering the conflict in the cases we do not believe that the appellate court could fairly indulge in such a presumption. If the appellate court conclusion is correct, there is a serious question as to what Barnard got for his $16,000, for he certainly did not buy his peace if he may still ultimately by liable to his employer. We believe a more logical and satisfactory result is reached by our holding in accordance with the majority view, that the covenant not to sue the servant or agent releases the master or principal and we so hold. In line with the cases hereinbefore cited a circuity of action will be avoided and since the liability of the master or principal is merely derivative and secondary, the exoneration of the servant or agent prevents the imputing of negligence to the master or principal. . . .

Appellate court reversed; circuit court affirmed.

Jaramillo v. Thomas

409 P.2d 131 (N. Mex.) 1965

MCINTOSH, J. Plaintiff's complaint alleged that Thomas, while driving an automobile in the course and scope of his employment with American Trust Life Insurance Company, negligently struck and killed plaintiff-decedent Urbano Jaramillo. At the time, Thomas was returning to his home in Albuquerque, after calling on prospective insurance customers in Estancia and Mountainair, and going by to see one man for personal reasons. He was working under an employment contract with defendant insurance company which provided for his solicitation of applications for insurance to be submitted to defendant insurance company.

Under his contract he was assigned territory in "New Mexico as directed," on a non-exclusive basis. He was free to choose any means of transportation he desired and worked only at such times and places as suited his convenience. The contract was immediately terminable by the company upon non-compliance therewith and was further terminable by either party without cause upon thirty days' written notice. It also specifically provided in paragraph 14:

> . . . that the Agent is an independent contractor and his sole compensation is through the commission provided herein. Agent shall pay all expenses incurred by him in performance of this contract. . . .

Judgment by default was entered against defendant Thomas and the complaint was dismissed as to the defendant insurance company on its motion for summary judgment.

Plaintiff contends that the relationship of master and servant existed between Thomas and the insurance company and the doctrine of vicarious liability applied to render the insurance company liable for the acts of its servant.

On the other hand, the defendant insurance company maintains that the defendant Thomas was an independent contractor and no liability attached to it.

The deposition of defendant Thomas was taken and written interrogatories were submitted to and answered by the defendant insurance company, after which defendant's motion for summary judgment was filed.

There being no controversy on the facts, the only question for decision here is the legal one of whether defendant Thomas was an independent contractor or the servant of the insurance company. If the relationship of master and servant existed then the insurance company is liable, but if the relationship was that of independent contractor then no liability attaches.

It is generally agreed that the determinative factor in situations similar to that presented here is the right to control and this court has on numerous previous occasions adhered to that general doctrine.

.   .   .

A right to control the physical details as to the manner and method of performance of the contract usually but not always establishes a master and servant relationship, but control only of the ultimate results to be obtained usually results in an independent contractor relationship.

Section 250, Restatement, *Agency* 2d, which was cited with approval by this court, not only in *Stambaugh* v. *Hayes, supra,* but also in *Romero* v. *Shelton, supra,* reads in part as follows:

> a. A principal employing another to achieve a result but not controlling or having the right to control the details of his physical movements is not responsible for incidental negligence while such person is conducting the authorized transaction. Thus, the principal is not liable for the negligent physical conduct of an attorney, a broker, a factor, or a rental agent, as such. In their movements and their control of physical forces, they are in the relation of independent contractors to the principal. It is only when to the relation of principal and agent there is added that right to control physical details as to the manner of performance which is characteristic of the relation of master and servant that the person in whose service the act is done becomes subject to liability for the physical conduct of the actor. . . .

In *Burruss* v. *B.M.C. Logging Company, supra,* it was held that the relationship was that of master and servant principally because of the power of discharge, and in *Bland* v. *Greenfield Gin Company, supra,* we held that the relationship was that of independent contractor principally because there was no power of termination or discharge, except for non-compliance with the contract.

The "power of discharge" is, however, only one of the elements to be considered; it may be of primary importance in one case and of no consequences in another depending on the circumstances. Many other elements have been considered by the courts in determining the relationship between the parties and this led Mr. Justice Sadler in *Huff* v. *Dunaway, supra,* to comment:

> . . . . . what in many cases are considered satisfactory tests, in other cases and under different circumstances, are not satisfactory. . . . .

There are many similarities and some minor differences between the facts in this case and those in *Burruss* and *Bland* and it must be observed that here the parties by their agreement in paragraph 14 specifically agreed that their relationship was that of independent contractor with compensation payable solely on a commission basis.

In *Romero* v. *Shelton,* supra, the employer had no power of control over the agent's mode of transportation and it was held that while the agent was traveling from one town to another he was neither the servant nor the agent of the employer and no liability attached to the employer as a result of his operation of an automobile.

In the instant case the insurance company had no control of Thomas' mode of transportation and *Romero* v. *Shelton,* supra, would appear to be controlling.

We conclude that the relationship was that of independent contractor and the lower court was correct in sustaining the motion for summary judgment.

Appellee also argues that at the time of the accident the agent was not engaged upon the master's business and there accordingly could not be any liability. From what has been said and in view of our disposition of the first point we need not consider this argument.

The decision of the district court in sustaining the motion for summary judgment will be affirmed.

Hopkins v. Hacker
195 A.2d 587 (N.H.) 1963

DUNCAN, J. . . . The disputed issues relate to the verdict for Hopkins as defendant in the cross action of *Hacker* v. *Hopkins,* in which Hacker sought damages for personal injuries suffered in an assault by a third person.

As agent for Hopkins, Hacker leased certain premises at Seabrook Beach for the latter part of the summer of 1957, at a rental of $400, $100 of which was deposited with Hacker in advance. The tenant or tenants, who were residents of Massachusetts, took possession on July 27, paying the $300 balance by check. They were immediately dissatisfied with the condition and furnishings of the premises, and complained to Hacker. At Hacker's request Hopkins visited the premises on July 28 and 29 to adjust the oil burner and to repair a lock. The tenants occupied the premises through Labor Day.

On July 28, Hacker delivered the $300 check to Hopkins, and there was evidence that on the same day the tenants demanded their money back. However Hopkins deposited the check on July 29, and later in the week was notified by the bank that payment had been stopped. The agent was advised by letter of the tenant, received on July 29, that payment of the check had been stopped. On August 3, 1957, however, the $300 balance of the rental, was paid to Hopkins on behalf of the tenant, in cash, at Hopkins' residence.

On the evening of July 30, it came to the attention of Hacker, who resided nearby, that a trailer was being driven onto the Hopkins property. He went to the premises and advised the driver of the trailer that zoning requirements forbade trailers at this location. While he was so engaged, he was assaulted by one or more of the occupants of the rented cottage, as he stood by the highway.

There was conflict in the testimony as to whether the principal Hopkins was aware of any prior threat to the safety of the agent. The agent testified that he repeatedly asked the principal to refund the $300 paid, and that the principal refused to do so.

The liability of a principal for injuries suffered by his agent in carrying out the agency is defined in the Restatement (Second), *Agency,* s. 471 as follows:

"A principal is subject to liability in an action of tort for failing to use care to warn an agent of an unreasonable risk involved in the employment, if the principal should realize that it exists and that the agent is likely not to become aware of it, thereby suffering harm." In the absence of special agreement, the principal is under no duty to indemnify his agent against the torts of third persons.

In this case the testimony of the agent plainly indicated that as early as July 28, 1957, he was apprehensive of violence at the hands of the tenants, and that his knowledge of the risk was at least as great as the principal's.

Hacker, as plaintiff, contends that Hopkins was under a duty to have refunded the rent, and that had he done so the assault would not have occurred. The answer to this contention is that payment of the $300 check had been stopped before July 30, so that the principal then had no rent which could be refunded. The down payment of $100 was made to the agent, and had not been paid over to the principal before the assault occurred. Further, there was evidence from which the Court could find that the agent himself resisted the principal's suggestion made on July 28, that the deposit should then be refunded and the letter of the tenant received by the agent on July 29 stated that the tenant would vacate the premises and forfeit the deposit.

We are satisfied that the verdicts returned by the Court were fully warranted by the law and the evidence. . . .

Judgment on the verdicts.

Fattore v. Police and Firemen's Retire. Syst. of N.J.

80 N.J. Super. 541 (1963)

Fattore, a fireman, was assisting in the replacement of a fire hose on a pumper apparatus. He was pulling and folding lengths of hose weighing 225 lbs. handed him by others. While doing the work, he felt a pain in the upper part of his chest which went down his left arm. This was later diagnosed as a myocardial infarction. He was off work some time and later tried to return to work but slight work caused precardial distress, and he applied for a retirement pension. His doctor diagnosed his condition as an acute myocardial infarction due to arteriosclerotic heart disease and coronary arteriosclerosis. The medical board for the retirement system agreed with the diagnosis but did not believe that it was precipitated by the work. An independent doctor was consulted who agreed that the work could have caused the condition.

CONFORD, J. . . . Of controlling effect in this case are the two prior decisions of this court in *Roth* v. *Board of Trustees, etc.* (49 N.J. Super, 309,), and *Kochen* v. *Consolidated Pol., etc., Pension Fund Comm.* (71 N.J. Super. 463). In construing cognate public employee disability pension legislation, we held in these cases that such legislation was social in nature and purpose, should be liberally construed in favor of employees, and, specifically, that the principles of the Workmen's Compensation Act as construed should be applied in passing upon the issue of causal connection between the work effort and the alleged accidental injury. There is no reason why those decisions should not be held controlling here, the legislation in question being of the same general nature and purposes as that construed in the *Roth* and *Kochen* cases.

Viewed from this perspective, it is clear that the attitude and approach of the medical board in the present case, upon which the board of trustees substantially relied for its determination, was erroneous. The essence of the position of the medical board and of its testimonial representative, Dr. Eckstein, was that the work incident could not be taken to be the natural and proximate cause of the heart attack and disability because the work Fattore was then doing was an effort of the type to which he was accustomed. Also stressed is the fact that he had a pre-existing arteriosclerosis. This approach is the equivalent of the rule of "unusual strain," once accepted as a prerequisite criterion of compensable heart attacks, but in effect discarded as incorrect in *Ciuba* v. *Irvington Varnish & Insulator Co.* (27 N.J. 127). As most recently restated in *Dwyer* v. *Ford Motor Co.* (36 N.J. 487, at p. 493), the heart attack is compensable if the actual work effort (whether or not unusual for the workman) did in fact materially contribute to the precipitation, aggravation or acceleration of the heart attack, or of any pre-existing heart or circulatory disease, thereby culminating in an attack. The former presumption that a heart attack is the result of natural physiological causes is also rejected in that case.

The difficulty of deciding the issue of causality in a particular case does not excuse the adjudicating tribunal from making the effort. The claim cannot automatically be rejected because the work effort was such as the worker was accustomed to, or because of the contribution to the attack of pre-existing disease, factors clearly constituting the ratio decidendi of the medical board and the adjudicating agency in this case.

. . . The predominance of the credible proofs sustains the conclusion in terms of probability that the work effort caused the heart attack.

. . . *Reversed, with directions to the board of trustees to grant the accidental disability retirement allowance.*

St. Michelle v. Catania

250 A.2d 874 (Md.) 1969

Plaintiff, a passenger in a taxicab operated by defendant carrier, brought suit for damages incurred when the cab driver and another passenger allegedly assaulted, battered, raped, robbed, and kidnapped her. Plaintiff alleged that the injuries were received during performance of the contract of carriage but did not allege that the cab driver was acting within the scope if his employment when the acts occurred. The trial court dismissed the complaint and the plaintiff appealed.

SINGLEY, J. . . . The only question before the lower court and before us is whether the facts alleged in the St. Michelle declaration, if true, would set out a cause of action against Mrs. Catania.

Mrs. Catania argues that Maryland has always applied the doctrine of *respondeat superior* to cases involving assaults on passengers by the employees or agents of a common carrier, and has relieved the carrier from responsibility for assaults committed by employees who were acting outside the scope of their employment, . . . and that a common carrier is not an insurer of its passengers.

Miss St. Michelle, on the other hand, argues that a common carrier can be held liable to a passenger who is assaulted by an employee of the carrier before the contract of transportation has been completely executed, irrespective of whether the employee was acting without the scope of his employment. While the decisions of this Court have not been entirely consistent, the well-reasoned cases and the weight of modern authority support Miss St. Michelle's contention.

A taxicab is a common carrier. A common carrier is not an insurer of the safety of its passengers, but is bound to employ the highest degree of care for their safety, consistent with the nature of the undertaking. It owes its passengers a duty to deliver them to their destination as expeditiously as possible, consistent with safety.

Some of our prior decisions in this area have turned on the question of whether the assault on the passenger occurred before or after the contract for safe carriage had ended. For example, in *Central Ry. Co.* v. *Peacock,* 69 Md. 257, 14 A. 709 (1888), the carrier was held not to be liable for an assault by its driver on a passenger who had alighted from a streetcar to report the driver for misconduct.

In denying liability, this Court cited *New Jersey Steamboat Co.* v. *Brockett,* 121 U.S. 637, 7 S.Ct. 1039, 30 L.Ed. 1049 (1887) as authority for the proposition that a carrier must protect his passengers from the violence of the carrier's employees and from that of other passengers but added that to bring a case within the operation of the *Brockett* rule, it must appear that the claimant was a passenger, and that the employee was executing the contract of transportation at the time of the assault.

The Court then concluded:

> ... The carrier had a right to regard [Plaintiff's] contemplated trip as ended, and contract executed. He was no longer being carried as a passenger, but was walking on the street. ... True, he had been insulted in the car; but was not assaulted in the car. ... [The driver] actually stopped his team, and left it in the street with the passengers unguarded, in order that he might pursue his victim and knock him down. In doing this, he cannot be regarded as acting within the sphere of his duty or scope of his authority.

Balto. & Ohio R.R. Co. v. *Barger,* 80 Md. 23, 30 A. 560, 26 L.R.A. 220 (1894), which held the railroad answerable to a passenger who had been assaulted on the train by a conductor, amplified the holding in *Peacock:*

> ... If [the conductor] has the opportunity to prevent an assault on a passenger in his charge, it is his duty to do so, and his failure to make a reasonable effort to protect the passenger from such assault, would make the company responsible. If that be a correct statement of the law, as it undoubtedly is, then, *a fortiori,* the company must be liable if the conductor makes an assault on one who is still a passenger, as Barger was.

In *Rosenkovitz* v. *United Rys. & Electric Co.,* 108 Md. 306, 70 A. 108 (1908), plaintiff was a newsboy, either a trespasser or an intended passenger according to the opposing contentions, and was ejected from the streetcar. The Court held:

> There can be no reasonable dispute as to the law, applicable to a case of this character, upon either theory as herein stated. If the assault was made, and the

plaintiff was ejected, whilst a passenger, and whilst the conductor, was in its employ, executing "the contract of transportation" (provided the jury found these facts), the company would clearly be responsible.

The existence of a contract of transportation as the element which determines liability is the modern view.

We conclude that under the Maryland cases involving a carrier's liability to its passengers, the crucial test should be whether the assault occurred before the contract of transportation or of safe carriage had ended, and that concepts of "scope of employment" or "line of duty," although relied upon in some cases, simply provide an additional base for the grounding of liability, and are not the only reasons why liability may be imposed.

> Besides the duty of avoiding negligent misconduct, the carrier is under an absolute duty to protect his passengers from the misconduct of its servants or agents. The decisions are often rested on the ground that the action of the servant or agent was within the scope of his employment, and in many cases this may be true; but when the act in question had no relation to the carrier's business and, though occurring in the carrier's vehicle or station was due wholly to private interests or motives of the servant, the carrier's liability must be rested on the broader ground previously discussed in connection with innkeepers. [*i.e.,* strict liability] 10 Williston, *Contracts* § 1123 (3d Ed. 1967) at 300.

Professor Prosser similarly reasons that the carrier's responsibility to its passenger is a classic example of vicarious liability, Prosser, *Torts* § 69 (3d Ed. 1964) at 477-78, while Restatement, *Agency* 2d (1958) § 214 adopts the idea that the carrier's responsibility to the passenger is a non-delegable duty, for the breach of which the carrier is liable:

> A master or other principal who is under a duty to provide protection for or to have care used to protect others or their property and who confides the performance of such duty to a servant or other person is subject to liability to such others for harm caused to them by the failure of such agent to perform the duty.

Comment e to § 214 says, " . . . In situations coming within the rule stated in this Section, the fact that the one to whom the performance of the duty is delegated acts for his own purposes and with no intent to benefit the principal or master is immaterial," thus laying to rest the idea that the doctrine of *respondeat superior* is controlling in such situations.

.   .   .

Since Miss St. Michelle's declaration alleged facts which, if proved to the satisfaction of the jury, would support a finding that the contract of transportation had not ended, the omission of an affirmative allegation that the driver was acting within the scope of his employment did not make the declaration demurrable.

.   .   .

Reversed and remanded.

CHAPTER 37
REVIEW QUESTIONS AND PROBLEMS

1. *X,* an employee of ABC Company, was driving a truck owned by the XYZ Car Rental Company and leased by the ABC Company. While making a delivery for ABC in the leased vehicle, *X* negligently hit *Y'*s car. *X* then fled and *Y* gave chase. *Y* enlisted the aid of a policeman, *Z. X* pulled out a gun and shot *Y* and injured him. *Z* then shot and killed *X.*

   a. Is ABC Company liable to *Y* for damage to the car and for *Y's* injuries?

   b. Is ABC Company liable to *Z* for his injuries?

   c. Is XYZ liable to either *Y* or *Z*?

   d. To whom is *X's* estate liable?

   e. Is *X's* widow entitled to Workmen's Compensation?

2. A construction company engaged a subcontractor to procure fill dirt. The subcontractor's employee, operating a bulldozer, scraped a high pressure gas line under the surface of the ground. The gas line exploded, damaging the plaintiff's property. May the plaintiff recover from the construction company?

3. The *Daily Bugle* customarily dropped several bundles of newspapers at a certain corner where *X,* a newsboy, picked them up. *X* then folded the newspapers, throwing the bundling wire on the sidewalk. *Y* tripped over the wire, injuring himself. Assuming that *X* is an independent contractor, may *Y* recover from the *Daily Bugle?*

4. Giantburger, Inc., sold a franchise to *X* to operate a Giantburger business. *X* owns the lot and building. Giantburger controls the products which *X* sells, and prescribes the advertising, layout of the building, hiring policies, and bookkeeping practices. *X* receives 65 percent of the net profits and Giantburger receives the other 35 percent. *Y,* a business visitor, is injured as a result of *X's* negligence. May *Y* recover from Giantburger, Inc.?

5. *X,* a salesman for the *Z's* company, stopped at a hotel while on a business trip. After an argument, *X* hit *Y,* the bellboy, with his fist and injured him. When told of the injury, *Z* exclaims "I'm glad you hit him. I would have hit him again." May *Y* hold *Z* liable?

6. *X,* a driver for the ABC Brick Company, was instructed to deliver a load of bricks to *T.* They were to be placed only at the curb. When *X* arrived, *T* persuaded him to deliver the bricks to *T's* garage. *T* directed *X* as he backed the truck into the garage. *T* then left, but *X* on leaving the garage crashed into the door. Was *X* a "borrowed servant" to *T,* thereby defeating *T's* claim?

7. *A,* working under contract to paint an outdoor movie screen for the XYZ Theater Company, had almost finished at quitting time. He induced *B,* an employee of the XYZ Company to stay later to operate a scaffold winch so that *A* might finish the job. *B* negligently operated the winch, causing *A* to fall and injure himself. May *A* recover from the XYZ Theater Company?

8.　*A,* a doctor, was employed at a regular salary by the QRS Shipping Lines to serve aboard ship and treat passengers. *A* treated *B,* a passenger, and *B* died as a result of *A's* negligence. May *A's* heirs recover from the QRS Lines?

9.　*X,* an employee of the ABC Company, was put in charge of a construction project in the desert. One day after working hours, *X* was returning in his car with drinking water for the crew when he negligently injured *Y.* The ABC Company had not told him to procure drinking water, but none was available at the job site. May *Y* recover from the ABC Company?

10.　*A,* a mechanic for XYZ Airlines, decided to fly with *B* on a test run of a new plane. Due to the negligence of *B,* the plane crashed on takeoff and *A* was injured. May *A* recover from XYZ?

11.　*N,* a nurse employed by Charity Hospital, was asked by *D,* a doctor, to inject a patient, *P,* with some medication. *N* was negligent in giving the injection, and *P* was injured. May *P* recover from *D*? From the hospital?

12.　*M,* driving a gasoline truck, negligently ran into and killed *Z. M* was driving the truck for his brother, a distributor of T oil and gas products. The contract with T Company provided that the truck carry the words "T Company" in certain places, that it be used for delivery of T Company products to designated filling stations, and that the driver, in collecting for deliveries made, sign the receipt in the name of T Company. For these services *M's* brother received a commission. When sued by *Z's* executor for wrongful death, T Company claimed that *M's* brother was an independent contractor rather than an agent. What result?

13.　*S,* a bus driver for X Company, was operating his bus when it was struck by a truck of T Company, driven by *F. S* stopped the bus and attempted to get the name of the truck driver and license number of the truck. At this point, *F* kicked and beat him up very badly. *S* sued T Company for damages. What result?

14.　*A* was employed by *D* as a laundry-route salesman. He was furnished a truck and uniform. After his usual working hours, *A* used his personal car to make a delivery he had forgotten to make before returning *D's* truck. While making the delivery, *A* negligently injured *P. P* sues *D.* What result?

15.　*P* sued *X* and *Y* for damage to his automobile caused by a faulty oil filter installed by *X. Y* had leased *X* his station, and *X* honored *Y's* credit cards. Is *Y* liable?

chapter 38

Liability of
Third Parties

5-36. Introduction. Previous chapters have discussed the contractual and tort liability of principals, masters, proprietors, agents, servants, and independent contractors. In this chapter the rights of these parties against third persons are discussed.

5-37. Contractual Liability to Principal. A disclosed principal may enforce any contract made by an authorized agent for the former's benefit. This right applies to all contracts in which the principal is the real party in interest, including contracts that are made in the agent's name. Furthermore, if a contract is made for the benefit of a disclosed principal by an agent acting outside the scope of his authority, the principal is still entitled to performance, provided the contract is properly ratified before withdrawal by the third party.

An undisclosed principal is entitled to performance by third parties of all assignable contracts made for his benefit by an authorized agent. It is no defense for the third party to say that he had not entered into a contract with the principal.[1] However, if the contract is one which involves the skill or confidence of the agent and which would not have been entered into but for this skill or confidence, its performance may not be demanded by the undisclosed principal, since the contract would not be assignable because personal rights and duties are not transferable without consent.

In cases other than those involving commercial paper, the undisclosed principal takes over the contract subject to all defenses which the third party

[1] Kelly Asphalt Block Co. v. Barber Asphalt Paving Co., page 768

could have established against the agent. For example, if the third party contracts to buy from such an agent and has a right of set-off against the agent, he has this same right of set-off against the undisclosed principal. The third party may also pay the agent prior to discovery of the principal,[2] and such payment will discharge his liability.

5-38. Contractual Liability to Agent.   Normally the agent possesses no right to bring suit on contracts made by him for the benefit of his principal, because he has no interest in the cause of action. Where the agent binds himself to the third party, either intentionally or ineptly by a failure properly to express himself, he may, however, maintain an action. An agent of an undisclosed principal is liable on the contract and may sue in his own name in the event of nonperformance by the third party. Thus, either the agent or the undisclosed principal might bring suit, but in case of a dispute, the right of the previously undisclosed principal is superior.

Custom has long sanctioned an action by the agent based upon a contract in which he is interested because of anticipated commissions. As a result, a factor may institute an action in his own name to recover for goods sold. He may also recover against a railroad for delay in the shipment of goods sold or to be sold.

Similarly, an agent who has been vested with title to commercial paper may sue the maker thereof. The same is true of any claim held by the principal that he definitely places with the agent for collection and suit, where such is necessary. In all cases of this character, the agent retains the proceeds as a trust fund for his principal.

5-39. Tort Liability.   Irrespective of other legal relationships, any person injured by the commission of a tort has a cause of action against the wrongdoer. As previously noted, if an employee is injured by a third party, the principal is entitled to recover any Workmen's Compensation payments from the sum which the employee recovers from the wrongful third party.

There are three rather unusual tort situations which have a direct relation to the employment contract. First, any third party who maliciously or wrongfully influences a principal to terminate an agent's employment thereby commits a tort.[3] The wrongful third party must compensate the agent for any damages which result from such conduct. Second, any third person who wrongfully interferes with the prospective economic advantage of an agent has liability to the agent for the loss sustained.[4] Third, any person who influences another to breach a contract in which the agent is interested thereby renders himself liable to the agent as well as to the principal. To illustrate: The agent has sold goods to T upon which he is entitled to a commission. Anyone who causes T to refuse to carry out the agreement thereby damages the agent and is correspondingly liable.

---

[2] Darling-Singer Lumber Co. v. Commonwealth et al., page 769
[3] Herron v. State Farm Mutual Insurance Company, page 770
[4] Fitt v. Schneidewind Realty Corp., page 772

LIABILITY OF THIRD PARTIES CASES

Kelly Asphalt Block Co. v. Barber Asphalt Paving Co.

105 N.E. 88 (N.Y.) 1914

CARDOZO, J. The plaintiff sues to recover damages for breach of an implied warranty. The contract was made between the defendant and one Booth. The plaintiff says that Booth was in truth its agent, and it sues as undisclosed principal. The question is whether it has the right to do so.

The general rule is not disputed. A contract not under seal, made in the name of an agent as ostensible principal, may be sued on by the real principal at the latter's election. . . . The defendant says that we should establish an exception to that rule, where the identity of the principal has been concealed because of the belief that, if it were disclosed, the contract would not be made. We are asked to say that the reality of the defendant's consent is thereby destroyed, and the contract vitiated for mistake.

The plaintiff and the defendant were competitors in business. The plaintiff's president suspected that the defendant might refuse to name him a price. The suspicion was not based upon any previous refusal, for there had been none; it had no other origin than their relation as competitors. Because of this doubt the plaintiff availed itself of the services of Booth, who, though interested to the defendant's knowledge in the plaintiff's business, was also engaged in a like business for another corporation. Booth asked the defendant for a price and received a quotation, and the asphalt blocks required for the plaintiff's pavement were ordered in his name. The order was accepted by the defendant, the blocks were delivered and payment was made by Booth with money furnished by the plaintiff. The paving blocks were unmerchantable, and the defendant, retaining the price, contests its liability for damages on the ground that if it had known that the plaintiff was the principal, it would have refused to make the sale.

We are satisfied that upon the facts before us the defense cannot prevail. A contract involves a meeting of the minds of the contracting parties. . . . Neither of the supposed parties was wanting in this case. The apparent meeting of the minds between determinate contracting parties was not unreal or illusory. The defendant was contracting with the precise person with whom it intended to contract. It was contracting with Booth. It gained whatever benefit it may have contemplated from his character and substance. . . . An agent who contracts in his own name for an undisclosed principal does not cease to be a party because of his agency. . . . Indeed, such an agent, having made himself personally liable, may enforce the contract though the principal has renounced it. . . . As between himself and the other party, he is liable as principal to the same extent as if he had not been acting for another. It is impossible in such circumstances to hold that the contract collapses for want of parties to sustain it. The contractual tie cannot exist where there are not persons to be bound, but here persons were bound, and those the very persons intended. If Booth had given the order in his own right and for his own benefit, but with the expectation of later assigning it to the plaintiff, that undisclosed expectation would not have nullified the contract. His undisclosed intention to act for a principal who was unknown to the defendant was equally ineffective to destroy the contract in its inception. . . .

The judgment should be affirmed, with costs. . . .

Darling-Singer Lumber Co. v. Commonwealth & Others

290 Mass. 488 (1953)

RUGG, J. This is a petition . . . to enforce a lien for the collection of the price of lumber furnished to Attilio D. Daddario, hereinafter called the defendant, who used it pursuant to two contracts with the Commonwealth for the construction of sections of the Metropolitan sewer. . . .

The facts pertinent to the grounds of this decision are: On November 3, 1950, the defendant purchased from one A. C. Place, doing business in Boston as the Place Lumber Company, 50,000 feet of fir plank to be shipped from the Pacific Coast, to be consigned to the defendant and to be delivered at site of job by Place. . . . In fact, Place was acting as agent for the plaintiff, Darling-Singer Lumber Co. of Portland, Oregon. He was authorized by it to sell lumber on commission and had been notified to have purchasers remit directly to F. P. Gram Co., Inc., of said Portland, to which corporation at that time the plaintiff was assigning its accounts receivable. Place, in conducting his business in Boston, used his own stationery, memoranda of sales, and held himself out to the defendant as conducting business on his own account. Place solicited the orders for this lumber from the defendant, and the defendant believed and had every reason for believing that he was dealing with Place as principal. . . . This lumber was delivered by Place at the location indicated by the defendant. Accompanying the bill of lading was an invoice on the letterhead of Darling-Singer Lumber Co., Portland, Oregon. Also accompanying the invoice and bill of lading was a notice headed from F. P. Gram Co., Inc., reading "We enclose herewith duly assigned to us invoice and bill of lading covering cars containing lumber sold and shipped to you by Darling-Singer Lumber Company amounting to $1,459.36. We are entitled to the proceeds under this assignment and look to you for payment of the same. Please remit directly to us." . . . The defendant has paid Place in full for all this lumber shipped by the plaintiff and has paid all freight charges. Place deposited the checks thus received to his own credit and has not accounted for them to the plaintiff. In making these payments to Place, the defendant acted entirely in good faith. He regarded Place as the only one with whom he had contracted and the only one to whom he owed any obligation of payment. He failed to understand the legal significance of the documents mailed to him by F. P. Gram Co., Inc. . . . The trial judge found, "under the facts herein set forth," that the payments by the defendant to Place constituted payments of the accounts for which this petition was brought and denied a ruling to the contrary, requested by the plaintiff, subject to its exception. A final decree was entered dismissing the bill as to the defendant, with costs. The plaintiff appealed. . . .

The plaintiff was the undisclosed principal of Place in the sales of lumber to the defendant. Although Place purported to act as principal, he was in fact the agent for the plaintiff in making those sales. An undisclosed principal may sue on a single contract not under seal made by his agent even though the agent appeared as principal in the transaction without disclosing his agency. This rule is equally applicable to foreign and domestic principals. (*Barry* v. *Page,*

10 Gray, 398, 399.) When property is sold by an agent purporting to act as principal but in truth as agent for an undisclosed principal, if before payment the undisclosed principal gives notice to the purchaser to pay to him and not to the agent, the purchaser is bound to pay the principal subject to any equities of the purchaser against the agent. . . . The purchaser, however, is protected in making payment to the agent at any time previous to notice of the agency, but not in making payment after notice of the agency. . . . Difficulty may arise in determining under what circumstances the purchaser has notice of the agency so that thereafter at his own risk he pays the agent, and whether such notice means actual knowledge or reasonable cause to know. . . . That point need not here be determined.

. . . The invoice and bill of lading thus indicating the plaintiff as seller were accompanied by notice from F. P. Gram Co., Inc., as assignee of the invoice demanding payment for the lumber. This was express notice to the effect that the plaintiff was principal in the sale. It was given to the defendant before payment by him to Place. The question of reasonable cause to know that the plaintiff was principal in the transaction does not arise because the notice was direct and unequivocal. The circumstance that Place had told the defendant that he had a western mill or office from which the lumber would be shipped does not dull the effect of the notice. The documents sent by F. P. Gram Co., Inc., were unmistakable in their import that the plaintiff was the seller of the lumber and had assigned to F. P. Gram Co., Inc., the amount due for such lumber, and that payment must be made to F. P. Gram Co., Inc., alone. That the defendant failed to understand them does not exonerate him from the legal effect upon him of the terms of those documents. . . .

The result is that upon the facts found the decree in favor of the defendant could not rightly have been entered. The plaintiff was entitled to prevail. *The exceptions are sustained and the decree is reversed.* . . .

Herron v. State Farm Mutual Insurance Company

363 P.2d 310 (Cal.) 1961

GIBSON, J. Plaintiffs, attorneys at law, brought this action against Mr. and Mrs. Donald Halverson for breach of contract and against State Farm Mutual Insurance Company and its agent, Anthony Caruso, for intentional interference with contractual relations. The Halversons were not served, and a demurrer of State Farm and Caruso (who will be referred to as defendants) was sustained without leave to amend. Plaintiffs have appealed from the ensuing judgment.

The following is a summary of plaintiffs' allegations: The Halversons entered into a contingent fee contract with plaintiffs concerning claims reasonably worth $60,000 for personal injuries sustained in an automobile accident caused by the negligence of a person insured by State Farm. Plaintiffs were to advance all expenses necessary for the preparation of the case and for court costs and were to receive one-third of the amount of the recovery remaining after deduction of the costs. No settlement was to be made without the consent of plaintiffs and the Halversons, and in the event there was no recovery plaintiffs were to receive nothing for their services or for costs advanced. Plaintiffs notified defendants of the agreement immediately after its execution, and they proceeded to hire private investigators, photographers, and a draftsman, make an investigation, and incur expenses in the amount of $1,250. Defendants, by telling the Halversons that they did not need an attorney and that a satisfactory settlement would be made, induced them to breach the contingent fee contract and to discharge plaintiffs and deprive them of the benefits of the contract and the expenses incurred for investigation and preparation. Defendants assisted the Halversons in preparing letters which informed plaintiffs of their dismissal. The conduct of defendants was maliciously designed to injure plaintiffs' rights and lawful business, and it violated the rules of the National Conference Committee on Adjusters of which State Farm or its agents are members. The rules provide, in part, that an insurance company will not deal directly with any claimant represented by an attorney without the consent of the attorney and will not advise the claimant to refrain from seeking legal advice or retaining counsel to protect his interest. As a result of the conduct of defendants, plaintiffs suffered the loss of the expenses incurred in investigation and preparation and did not receive their one-third contingent fee.

Plaintiffs prayed for judgment against defendants for $20,000 or one-third of the judgment or settlement recovered by the Halversons, whichever is the lesser, and, in addition, for $25,000 punitive damages.

An action will lie for the intentional interference by a third person with a contractual relationship either by unlawful means or by means otherwise lawful when there is a lack of sufficient justification. . . . There is no valid reason why this rule should be applied to an attorney's contingent fee contract. Such an agreement is a legal and valid contract entitled to the protection of the law, and an attorney who is wrongfully discharged is generally entitled to the same amount of compensation as if he had completed the contemplated services. . . . While a client is permitted to discharge his attorney without cause, this is allowed not because the attorney's interest in performing his services and obtaining his fee is unworthy of protection but because of the importance of the client's interest in the successful prosecution of his cause of action. . . . An attorney's interest in his contingent fee agreement is greater than that if a party to a contract terminable at will, as to which it has been held that an intentional and unjustifiable interference is actionable. . . .

. . . . .

Whether an intentional interference by a third party is justifiable depends upon a balancing of the importance, social and private, of the objective advanced by the interference against the importance of the interest interfered with, considering all circumstances including the nature of the actor's conduct and the relationship between the parties. . . . Justification is an affirmative defense and may not be considered as supporting the trial court's action in sustaining a demurrer unless it appears on the face of the complaint. . . . The only allegation relied upon by defendants as showing justification is that State Farm had issued an automobile public liability insurance policy to the person whose negligence caused the injuries to the Halversons. In our opinion this allegation does not establish justification.

The conduct of an insurance company in inducing an injured person to repudiate his contract with an attorney may be detrimental not only to the interests of the attorney but also to the interests of the client since, as we have seen, the client, in addition to being deprived of the aid and advice of his attorney, may also be liable for the full contract fee. Defendants argue that the policy of the law is to encourage settlement, that an insurance company has a legal duty to effect a settlement of a claim against its insured in an appropriate case . . . and that furtherance of the actor's own economic interests will justify an intentional interference with a contractual relationship in some circumstances where his interests are threatened by the contract. However, these considerations standing alone cannot justify inducing the Halversons to repudiate the contract and to deprive plaintiffs of its benefits. So far as appears from the complaint, no cause for the dismissal of plaintiffs existed, no efforts were made to negotiate with them, and there is no indication that State Farm could not have protected its interests and obtained a satisfactory settlement without interfering with the contract.

The judgment is reversed with directions to overrule the demurrer.

Fitt v. Schneidewind Realty Corp.

196 A.2d 26 (N.J.) 1963

The plaintiff, Fitt, a real estate broker, employed Decker as a real estate agent. Decker was requested by an agent of the defendants to ascertain if certain property owned by Oiljak was for sale and, if so, the price. Decker contacted Oiljak and was informed that the property was for sale and that several agents were trying to sell it. The information was transmitted to the defendants, and several later contacts were made between Decker and the defendants' agents.

Later, defendants' agents contacted Oiljak directly. Oiljak inquired whether a real estate commission would be due, and defendants' agent said No. This resulted in a lowering of the price by Oiljak, and a contract of sale was entered into, which included a clause providing that the purchaser would pay any commissions that might come due. Plaintiff sued for the commissions. Defendants deny the allegations and assert further that they retained the plaintiff's employee Decker as a consultant to investigate the particular piece of property; consequently, defendants are liable only for the fair value of the services actually performed but not for the brokerage commission from the sale.

GIULIANO, J. . . . The cause of action which plaintiff alleges here, interference with prospective economic advantage, must be clearly distinguished from another and similar tort commonly referred to as interference with contractual or business relations. Under an allegation of interference with contractual relations recovery may only follow a showing that there was a wrongful interference with some contractual or business relationship. In the instant matter there is no need for the plaintiff to make a showing of interference with an *existing* business relationship. The tort here asserted is interference with the opportunity to enter into an advantageous business relationship. Consequently, the plaintiff need not establish an existing business relationship between himself and the seller Oiljak.

It is well settled that the right to pursue any lawful business and to enjoy the fruits and advantages of one's industry are rights which the law protects against unjustified or wrongful interference. The business of real estate brokerage is such a lawful business and is protected against unjustified interference. The essence of the protection the courts afford those claiming to have been interfered with is in adjudging whether what defendant has done is actionable and not in the exercise of an equal or superior right. The ultimate inquiry for the court is whether the conduct was:

> ... "both injurious and transgressive of generally accepted standards of common morality or of law." ... In other words, was the interference by the defendant "sanctioned by the 'rules of the game.' " There can be no tighter test of liability in this area than that of the common conception of what is right and just dealing under the circumstances. Not only must defendants' motive and purpose be proper but so also must be the means.

The wrongful act must however be found to have interfered with some expectancy on the part of the plaintiff who, in the present case is a real estate broker. A broker's chief stock-in-trade lies in his knowledge of available properties. Development of interests in these properties is his chief activity, and he frequently does this with no more than an expectation that if he produces a buyer, the seller will pay a commission. The expectancy of a commission may arise from a written or oral agreement between the broker and seller, or it may arise, as in the instant matter, out of an offer to the public or to brokers generally. . . .

The action lies, therefore, for the wrongful interference with the conduct of negotiations which might culminate in a commission. In order for the plaintiff to prevail in an action such as this, the court must find from the evidence that but for defendants' wrongful acts it is reasonably probable that plaintiff would have effected the sale of the property and recovered a commission, but it is not necessary to show that the commission was actually earned. When the broker has brought together a customer and an owner and there is no substantial break in the ensuing negotiations, the broker is considered to have been the efficient cause of the sale and to have entitled himself to a commission. . . .

Granting all the factors necessary to recovery indicated above have been established, the court must also find that the act of interference was wrongful. A wrongful act is one which in the ordinary course of events will infringe upon the rights of another to his damage, or one which is done with the purpose of benefiting the acting party at the other's expense and is not done in the exercise of an equal or superior right. The mere doing of an act which is damaging to another and to the actor's benefit is wrongful and not within the "rules of the game."

. . . An act is wrongful under the law if it be done for the purpose of benefiting the acting party at the expense of the person who is interfered with. Not only must the defendants' motive and purpose be proper, but so also must be the means. It is apparent from the evidence that the defendants were taking advantage of the plaintiff soon after the first inquiry was made about the property. They accepted the efforts and interest of Decker. Thereafter they attempted to lull plaintiff into a false sense of security by assuring him that he would not be let down. Further, they represented to Oiljak that no broker was interested in the sale, and it was not until plaintiff approached Oiljak that the activity of a broker was acknowledged by them. It is clear that the representation by defendants that no broker was involved in the sale resulted in the reduction of the asking price. In short, defendants attempted to benefit themselves at the expense of plaintiff while not acting in the exercise of an equal or superior right. This kind of activity will not be sanctioned by the court. Defendants' actions are far from the common conception of just dealing and fall far short of the "rules of the game."

The court therefore finds in favor of plaintiff and against defendants in the amount of the commission on the sale of the Oiljak property, stipulated to be $8700, plus interest from the date of the transfer of the property, November 17, 1961.

An appropriate order for judgment may be submitted.

CHAPTER 38
REVIEW QUESTIONS AND PROBLEMS

1. *A,* acting on *B*'s behalf, and *C,* acting on *D*'s behalf, make a contract in which *B* is to convey certain real property to *C. C* and *D* know of *B*'s existence, but *A* and *B* do not know of *D*'s existence. May *D* obtain specific performance from *B*?

2. *X,* owner of a building, leased the building to *Y.* Unknown to *X, Y* was acting on *Z*'s behalf. When *X* learned of *Z*'s existence, *X* refused to give possession to *Z.* May *Z* obtain specific performance?

3. As well as selling his own home-grown seed, *A,* the owner of a seed store, acted as agent for the XYZ Seed Company. *A* made a contract with *T* for the sale of seed. The seed sold to *T* was the seed of the XYZ Company; *T* was not told this. If *T* fails to pay, may *A* maintain an action for the XYZ Company's seed?

4. *X,* while driving an automobile negligently struck an automobile in which six key employees of *Y* were riding. May *Y* recover from *X* for the loss to *Y*'s business?

5. *X* was the exclusive dealer for the ABC Auto Parts Company in a three-state area. *Y* had a similar dealership in a neighboring two-state area. Both contracts were terminable at will. *Y* convinces the ABC Company to terminate *X*'s contract and give him, *Y,* the dealership for the entire five-state area. May *X* recover from *Y*?

chapter 39

Duties of Principal and Agent to Each Other

DUTIES OF AGENT TO PRINCIPAL

5-40. Introduction. The nature and extent of the duties imposed upon agents and servants are governed largely by the contract of employment. In addition to the duties expressly designated, certain others are implied by the fiduciary nature of the relationship and by the legal effects on the principal of actions or omissions by the agent. The usual implied duties are (1) to be loyal to his principal; (2) to obey all reasonable instructions; (3) not to be negligent; (4) to account for all money or property received for the benefit of the principal; and (5) to inform the principal of all facts which materially affect the subject matter of the agency. As will be more fully discussed in the sections which follow, these implied duties are essential to the employer-employee relationship. There is a correlation between these implied duties and the legal principles relating to liability of the parties previously discussed. This correlation will be observed in the sections that follow.

5-41. Duty of Loyalty. An agent stands in a fiduciary relationship to his principal and thus has a duty of undivided loyalty to the principal. Because of the duty of loyalty it is held that he should undertake no business venture that competes or interferes in any manner with the business of his employer nor make any contract for himself when he should have made it for his principal. The same rule forbids a sales agent to sell his principal's property to himself, unless the principal assents to the sale. The rule also prevents a purchasing agent from buying his own property or that in which he has an interest. Transactions violating these rules may always be rescinded by the principal, if he so desires, despite the fact the agent acted for the best interests of his principal and the contract was as favorable as could be obtained elsewhere. The general rule is applied without favor in order that every possible motive or incentive for unfaithfulness may be removed.

In addition to the remedy of rescission, a principal is entitled to treat any profit realized by the agent in violation of this duty as belonging to the principal. Such profits include rebates, bonuses, commissions, or divisions of profits received by an agent for dealing with a particular third party. Here again the contracts may have been favorable to the employer, but the result is the same, since the agent should not be tempted to abuse the confidence reposed in him.

An agent may deal with himself only if he obtains the permission of the principal. In any case in which the agent obtains the consent of the principal to deal with himself, the agent must disclose fully all facts which materially influence the situation. In such a case, agent and principal do not deal at "arm's length," and the circumstances demand the utmost good faith on the part of the agent.

The duty of loyalty denies a broker the right to represent both the seller and the buyer in the same transaction unless both have been informed of his dual relationship.[1] His desire to earn the commission is apt to cause him to disregard the best interests of one of his principals. Either party who is without knowledge of the dual representation may rescind the agreement, and the agent is not entitled to any fee or commission.

Loyalty demands that information of a confidential character acquired while in the service of the principal shall not be used by the agent to advance his interests in opposition to those of the principal. An employee who learns of secret processes or formulas or comes into possession of lists of customers may not use this information to the detriment of his employer. The employer may obtain an injunction to prevent its use. The rule relating to trade secrets is applied with equal severity whether the agent acts before or after he severs his connection with the principal. The knowledge must in fact be a trade secret. Knowledge that is important but which does not amount to a trade secret may be used, although it affects the agent's former employer injuriously. For this reason there is nothing to hinder a person who has made the acquaintance of his employer's customers from later circularizing those whom he can remember. His acquaintanceship is part of his acquired skill. The employer may protect himself in the later case by a clause in the employment agreement to the effect that the employee will not compete with the employer or work for a competitor for a limited period of time after his employment is terminated, as discussed in the book on contracts.

"Moonlighting" has in recent years become quite common. Many people work at two jobs in order to improve their standard of living. While such initiative may be very laudable, certain legal problems arise. If the second job is conducted during the time the agent is supposed to be working for the principal, the duty of loyalty is breached, and the principal may recover any amounts paid to the agent. If the work is performed after hours or during a period when he is not expected to be working for his principal, the gain or money received unquestionably remains the property of the agent.

---

[1] Taborsky v. Mathews, page 782

5-42. Duty to Obey Instructions. It is the duty of an agent to obey all instructions issued by his principal as long as they refer to duties contemplated by the contract of employment. Burdens not required by the agreement cannot be indiscriminately imposed by the employer. An instruction may not be regarded lightly merely because it departs from the usual procedure and seems fanciful and impractical to the employee. It is not his business to question the procedure outlined by his superior. Any loss which results while he is pursuing any other course makes him absolutely liable to the principal for any resulting loss.

Furthermore, an instruction of the principal does not become improper merely because the motive is bad. He may be well aware of the agent's distaste for certain tasks, yet, if those tasks are such as may be called for under the employment agreement, it becomes the agent's duty to perform them. Failure to perform often results in proper grounds for his discharge.

This obligation on the part of the agent to follow carefully his principal's orders applies to an agent who acts gratuitously, as well as to one who receives pay for his services. Although the former is under no duty to perform, even though he has promised to do so, yet if he undertakes to carry out his commission, he must follow explicitly the instructions received.

Closely allied to the duty to follow instructions is the duty to remain within the scope of the authority conferred. Because of the doctrine of estoppel, it often becomes possible for an agent to exceed his authority and still bind his principal. In case of such a violation of his contract, the employee becomes responsible for any resulting loss.[2] He is in this instance failing to follow the instructions set forth in his contract with his employer. These instructions, as well as those issued later by the principal, must be fully complied with.

Occasionally circumstances arise that nullify instructions previously given. Because of the new conditions, the old instructions would, if followed, practically destroy the purpose of the agency. Whenever such an emergency arises, it becomes the duty of the agent, provided the principal is not available, to exercise his best judgment in meeting the situation.

An instruction to do an illegal or immoral act, or an act that will impair the security or position of the agent, may be disregarded. To illustrate: A factor has a lien on goods in his possession for all money advanced to his principal. An order from the principal to return the goods or to sell them on credit could be disregarded until such time as all advances had been paid.

5-43. Duty Not to be Negligent. As was discussed in Chapter 37, the doctrine of *respondeat superior* imposes liability upon a principal or master for the torts of an agent or servant acting within the scope of his employment. The agent or servant is primarily liable, and the principal or master is secondarily liable.

It is an implied condition of employment contracts, if not otherwise expressed, that the employee has a duty to act in good faith and to exercise reasonable care and diligence in performing his tasks. Failure to do so is a breach of the employment contract. Therefore, if the employer has liability to third persons due to the employee's acts or omissions of negligence and the

[2] Crawford v. DiMicco, page 783

application of the doctrine of *respondeat superior,* the employer may recover his loss from the employee. This right will be transferred by the doctrine of subrogation to the liability insurance carrier of the employer when the liability policy does not cover the employee.

5-44. Duty to Account.   Money or property entrusted to the agent must be accounted for to the principal. Because of this fact, the agent is required to keep proper records showing receipts and expenditures, in order that a complete accounting may be rendered. Any money collected by an agent for his principal should not be mingled with funds of the former. If they are deposited in a bank, they should be kept in a separate account and so designated that a trust is apparent. Otherwise, any loss resulting from an insolvent bank must be borne by the agent.

The principal may follow any funds misappropriated by the agent until they fall into the hands of a third party. Even then, the principal may follow the proceeds and impress a trust upon them, so long as they have not reached an innocent third party. Furthermore, if such proceeds can be shown to have increased the estate of the agent, a trust may be imposed upon the agent's estate to that extent.

5-45. Duty to Give Notice.   Section 5-16 of Chapter 36 discussed the legal effect of knowledge possessed by an agent. It should be reviewed at this time. It was noted that knowledge acquired by an agent within the scope of his authority binds the principal, or more succinctly, knowledge of an agent is notice to the principal. Therefore, the law imposes on the agent the duty to inform his principal of all facts which affect the subject matter of the agency and which are obtained within the scope of the employment. Information learned while outside the scope of employment and beyond the agent's authority need not be communicated to the principal.

This rule extends beyond the duty to inform the principal of conflicting interests of third parties or possible violations of the duty of loyalty in a particular transaction. It imposes upon the agent a duty to give his principal all information that materially affects the interest of the principal. For example, knowledge of facts which may have greatly advanced the value of property placed with an agent for sale must be communicated before the property is sold at a price previously established by the principal.

DUTIES OF PRINCIPAL TO AGENT

5-46. Duty to Compensate in General.   The agent is entitled to be compensated for his services in accordance with the terms of his contract of employment. If no definite compensation has been agreed upon, there arises a duty to pay the reasonable value of such services. Whenever the party performing the services is a stranger to the employer, the obligation to compensate exists. However, where relatives are working for one another and no express agreement has been formulated, the courts are likely to infer that the services so rendered should be considered gratuitous. This question frequently arises in claims against an estate for the value of care given the deceased prior to his death by a relative. Following this rule, the claims are usually denied in the absence of an express contract to pay for the care.

If the contract is silent on the amount of compensation, the reasonable value will be the customary rate in the community, if any. If no customary rate is available, opinion evidence is received in determining the value of the services.

Many employment contracts include provisions for paying a percentage of profits to a key employee. In the absence of a detailed enumeration in the employment contract of the items to be considered in determining net income, it will be computed in accordance with generally accepted accounting principles, taking into consideration past custom and practice in the operation of the employer's business. It is assumed that the methods of determining net income will be consistent and that no substantial changes will be made in the methods of accounting without the mutual agreement of the parties. The employer cannot unilaterally change the accounting methods, nor can the employee require a change in order to effect an increase in his earnings.

5-47. Duty to Compensate Real Estate Brokers.　The right of a real estate broker or agent to a commission is frequently the subject of litigation. In the absence of an express agreement, the real estate broker earns a commission in either of two situations. First, he will be entitled to it if he finds a buyer who is ready, willing, and able to meet the terms outlined by the seller in the listing agreement. The owner cannot deprive the agent of a commission by refusing to deal with the prospective purchaser or by withdrawing the property from sale. The owner cannot relieve himself of the duty to pay the commission by terminating the agency and later contracting directly with the broker's prospect. The fee is earned if it is shown that the broker was the inducing cause of the sale.[3]

The commission is also earned if the owner contracts with the purchaser (whether or not the price is less than the listed price), even though it later develops that the buyer is unable to meet the terms of the contract. The owner assumes the risk of performance upon executing the contract with the buyer presented by the broker. This is true even if the law allows the buyer to avoid liability, as for example, where the property is destroyed.[4] The broker's commission is contingent on payment by the purchaser only when his contract of employment so states. An owner who lists property with several brokers is obligated to pay the first one to find a satisfactory purchaser, at which time the agency of other brokers is automatically terminated, assuming a simple listing.

There are three distinct types of real estate listings—placing of property with real estate brokers for sale. First is the simple listing of the property for sale on the terms set forth by the seller, in which case the listing may be with several brokers and the right to withdraw or terminate the relationship at any time is reserved by the seller. Under such circumstances, the seller pays the commission to the first broker who finds a buyer. The owner is free to sell on his own behalf without a commission. The second type consists of an exclusive listing which usually gives to the broker the exclusive right to find a buyer for an agreed period of time. In this case the seller is not free to list the property with other brokers, and a sale through other brokers would be a violation of the contract of listing, although the seller himself is free to find a buyer of his

---

[3] Haymes v. Rogers, page 784
[4] Hecht v. Meller, page 786

own. Third, a listing in which the broker is given an exclusive right to sell. In this case even the seller is not free to find a buyer of his own choosing. If the seller does sell on his own behalf, he is obliged to pay a commission to the broker holding an exclusive right to sell.

In recent years, there has developed what is known as a "Multiple Listing Agreement." This is a method of listing property with several brokers simultaneously. These brokers belong to an organization, the members of which share listings and divide the commissions. For example, a typical commission would be split, 60 percent to the selling broker, 30 percent to the listing broker and 10 percent to the organization for operating expenses. These multiple listing groups give homeowners the advantage of increased exposure to potential buyers. In return for this advantage, most multiple listing agreements are of the exclusive right to sell type.

The right to a real estate commission is subject to statutory limitations in several states. Some of these require a written contract and others require a license before a person may engage in this activity. Some courts have gone so far as to hold that a broker selling property in a state in which he is licensed is not entitled to a fee if the buyer is found or the sale completed in another state. Strict adherence to the licensing statutes is usually required. The cases referred to earlier in this chapter indicate that a broker may forfeit his right to compensation by improper conduct, breach of the duty of loyalty, or lack of good faith. A real estate broker is a fiduciary and his actions must be for the sole benefit of his principal.

As directed to obtaining equality of opportunity in housing, the civil rights movement has frequently caused difficult problems for real estate brokers. Discrimination in the sale and leasing of housing has been and still is widespread. As an agent for the owner, the broker is faced with a dilemma. The owner may want to discriminate; assuming that the agent does not, must the agent follow the owner's instructions? The financial ramifications are obvious.

During the 1960s many state and local legislative bodies passed laws which forbid a broker to engage in any discriminatory practices. Discrimination by a broker will result in the loss of his license. Since the broker is not permitted to discriminate, neither can the owner. Also, some statutes are applicable to owners as well as to brokers. As a result of various statutes, the owner-broker relationship has become a three-party relationship, with the public the third party. Such duties as that to obey instructions and that of undivided loyalty have been changed by statute because of the overriding public policy against discrimination and in favor of equal access to housing.

5-48. Duty to Compensate Sales Representatives.   Salesmen who sell merchandise on a commission basis are confronted by problems similar to those of the broker, unless their employment contract is specific in its details. Let us assume that X Company appoints *A* as its exclusive sales representative in a certain territory on a commission basis and that the employer is engaged in producing and selling electrical equipment. *T,* a businessman in the area involved, sends a large order for merchandise directly to the home office of X Company. Is *A* entitled to a commission on the sale? It is generally held that such a salesman is entitled to a commission only on sales solicited and induced by him, unless his contract of employment gives him greater rights.

The salesman usually earns his commission as soon as an order from a responsible buyer is obtained, unless his contract of employment makes payment contingent upon delivery of the goods or collection of the sale's price. If payment is made dependent upon performance by the purchaser, the employer cannot deny the salesman his commission by terminating the agency prior to collection of the account. When the buyer ultimately pays for the goods, the seller is obligated to pay the commission.

An agent who receives a weekly or monthly advance against future commissions is not obligated to return the advance if commissions equal thereto are not earned. The advance, in the absence of a specific agreement, is considered by the courts as a minimum salary.

5-49. Duty to Reimburse and Indemnify. Those situations in which a servant will be indemnified for tort losses have been mentioned previously. They are limited to factual situations in which the servant is not at fault and his liability results from following the instructions of the master. An agent or servant is justified in presuming that instructions given by the principal are such as he lawfully has a right to give, and that performance resulting from such instructions will not injuriously affect third parties. Where this is not the case, and the agent incurs a liability to some third party because of trespass or conversion, the principal must indemnify the agent against loss. There will ordinarily be no idemnification for losses incurred in negligence actions, because the servant's own conduct is involved. The idemnification is usually of the master by the servant in tort situations.[5]

An agent has a general right to reimbursement for money expended on behalf of his principal. It must appear that the money was reasonably spent and that its expenditure was not necessitated by the misconduct or negligence of the agent. It is the duty of the principal to make performance by the agent possible whenever the latter has entered into a contract in his own name for the former's benefit. The undisclosed principal must fully protect his agent by making the funds available to perform the contract as agreed.

5-50. Duty to Protect from Injury. An employer is not an insurer of the safety of his employees. At common law, the duty of an employer is to use that degree of care which an ordinary prudent man engaged in the same business would use in providing a safe place to work and proper tools. Failure to do so is negligence. Common-law tort actions against employers by employees are subject to the defenses of contributory negligence, assumption of risk, and the fellow servant doctrine. The issues of negligence of the employer and of the defenses such as contributing negligence are questions of fact unless the facts admit of only one conclusion, in which event, the issues become a matter of law.[6]

Assumption of risk will bar a common-law recovery where the employee knows of the danger arising from an act either of himself or another, and understands the risks arising therefrom, but nevertheless voluntarily exposes himself to it. An employee assumes all risks incident to the services in which he is engaged. Before an employee can be said to have assumed a risk which

[5] Stawasz v. Aetna Insurance Company, page 787
[6] Ferguson v. Lounsberry, page 789

may not necessarily be a common one incident to employment, the employee must know or should know that danger exists.

As was discussed in Chapter 37, most common-law actions by employees against employers have been replaced by Workmen's Compensation and F.E.L.A. statutes. A major activity that is not covered by these statutes is agricultural employment as the *Ferguson* case illustrates.

DUTIES OF PARTIES CASES

Taborsky v. Mathews

121 So.2d 61 (Fla.) 1960

SHANNON, J. This is an appeal taken by the defendants in a foreclosure suit from a summary final decree based upon the order of the chancellor below striking the defendants' affirmative defense and dismissing their counterclaim.

The defense and the counterclaim attempted to raise the fact that the real estate agent who acted for the defendants was also the agent for the plaintiff in this transaction; that the agent had received a commission from both parties; and that the defendants had no knowledge of the dual agency. By their counterclaim the defendants sought to recover the portion of the purchase price which had been paid.

In this appeal the defendants have raised three points. Inasmuch as the first point comprehends all that is necessary to support our opinion, the only question which we will consider is:

> In an action to foreclose a purchase-money mortgage upon certain real property where a real estate broker without disclosing the dual nature of his agency to the purchasers, acted as agent for both parties in negotiating the sale of the property, have the purchasers the right, upon discovering the dual agency, to avoid the sale and purchase-money mortgage?

. . .

In our jurisprudence it is well established that an agent for one party to a transaction cannot act for the other party without the consent of both principals. Where an agent assumes to act in such a dual capacity without such assent, the transaction is voidable as a matter of public policy. Florida has unequivocally aligned itself with this principle . . . saying . . .

> "No principle is better settled than that a man cannot be the agent of both the seller and the buyer in the same transaction, without the intelligent consent of both. Loyalty to his trust is the most important duty which the agent owes to his principal. Reliance upon his integrity, fidelity, and ability is the main consideration in the selection of agents; and so careful is the law in guarding this fiduciary relation that it will not allow an agent to act for himself and his principal, nor to act for two principals on opposite sides in the same transaction. In such cases the amount of consideration, the absence of undue advantage, and other like features are wholly immaterial. Nothing will defeat the principal's right of remedy, except his own confirmation, after full knowledge of all the facts. Actual injury is not the principle upon which the law holds such transactions voidable. The chief object of the principle is not to compel restitution where actual fraud has been committed, or

unjust advantage gained, but it is to prevent the agent from putting himself in a position in which to be honest must be a strain on him, and to elevate him to a position where he cannot be tempted to betray his principal."

It is evident from all these authorities that in cases of double agency the relief granted to the principal against the agent, or against the third party who has compromised the agent, is not made to depend upon the intention to defraud, the presence of actual misrepresentation or non-disclosure, or the presence of injury.

The law, in the words of Judge Cardozo, " . . . stops the inquiry when the relation is disclosed; and sets aside the transaction or refuses to enforce it . . . without undertaking to deal with the question of abstract justice in the particular case. . . . "

The law being well established, this court need only determine whether the allegations of the defendants' affirmative defense and counterclaim set forth facts sufficient to raise the issue of dual agency. Essentially, the defendants allege the dual agency, and the fact that they were not aware of the agent's status with the plaintiff, and we find that this is sufficient to bring the rule into play. Hence, the order of the chancellor below striking the defendants' affirmative defense and dismissing their counterclaim was in error. Therefore, the final summary decree, which was based upon this order, is also in error.

·   ·   ·

Reversed.

Crawford v. DeMicco

216 So.2d 769 (Fla.) 1968

Plaintiff sued an insurance company to recover the value of a boat lost in a storm. The agent that issued the binder on the boat had been instructed not to issue coverage on boats more than three years old or worth more than $5,000, without a condition survey. The boat in question was thirteen years old and insured for $5,000. The defendant insurance company filed a cross claim against its agent. The lower court found for the agent on the indemnity claim, and the defendant insurance company appealed.

CROSS, J. (After discussing other issues) . . . Turning now to the action by the cross-plaintiff-insurer against the cross-defendant-agency, we are to determine if an insurance agent binds a contract of insurance which he is not authorized to do, is such agent liable to indemnify the company for its losses arising from the enforcement of the insurance contract so bound.

The facts as alluded to above are simple, and the law is equally so. It has long been well settled that an agent owes to his principal the obligation of high fidelity, and that he may not proceed without or beyond his authority, particularly where he has been forbidden to act and that so proceeding, his actions caused loss to his principal, the agent is fully accountable to the principal therefor. 2d Restatement of Agency, § 401. An elementary factor in the principal-agent relationship is control. As stated in 2d Restatement of Agency, § 14B(f), "An agent acts for and on behalf of his principal and subject to his control. . . . The agent owes a duty of obedience to his principal."

The record in this case reveals that the agency through its employee proceeded without and went beyond its authority. . . .

The record further indicates that the agent's employee was informed on a prior occasion when dealing with insurance being placed on another vessel, that as a matter of course the insurer specifically instructed the agent's employee that a survey is required on vessels that are valued at $5,000 or over or are more than three years old, if the vessel was to be submitted to the insurer for insurance.

Under the facts of the instant case and the settled law applicable thereto, unless and until the principal with full knowledge of all the applicable facts waived the breach of its instructions, ratified or adopted the agent's act as its own, or facts otherwise raising an estoppel against the principal, the agent became and remained liable to the principal for the damages incurred in acting without authority to the disadvantage of its principal. The facts herein reveal no adoption, ratification or estoppel on the part of the principal-insurer.

The cross-defendant-agency through its employee, acted precipitatively, unreasonably and without authority. The testimony reveals vividly that the agency's employee admittedly and grievously breached his duty to the insurer by his initial unauthorized act in binding the vessel, and therefore the cross-defendant-agent cannot escape the loss or any part thereof and throw such loss upon the principal-insurer.

Reversed.

Haymes v. Rogers

222 P.2d 789 (Ariz.) 1950

DECONCINI, J. In our former opinion, June 12, 1950 (70 Ariz. 257, 219 P.2d 339), we held that as a matter of law there was bad faith shown on the broker's part which precluded him from recovery of his commission. In the light of the motion for rehearing and a re-examination of the evidence and instructions, we are constrained to change our view.

Kelley Rogers, hereinafter called appellee, brought an action against L. F. Haymes, hereinafter referred to as appellant, seeking to recover a real estate commission in the sum of $425.00. The case was tried before a jury which returned a verdict in favor of appellee. The said appellant owned a piece of realty which he had listed for sale with the appellee, real estate broker, for the sum of $9,500. The listing card which appellant signed provided that the commission to be paid appellee for selling the property was to be five (5%) per cent of the total selling price. Tom Kolouch was employed by the said appellee as a real estate salesman, and is hereinafter referred to as "salesman."

On February 4, 1948 the said salesman contacted Mr. and Mrs. Louis Pour, prospective clients. He showed them various parcels of real estate, made an appointment with them for the following day in order to show them appellant's property. The salesman then drew a diagram of the said property in order to enable the Pours to locate and identify it the next day for their appointment. The Pours, however, proceeded to go to appellant's property that very day and encountering the appellant, negotiated directly with him and purchased the property for the price of $8,500. The transcript of evidence reveals that the appellant knew the Pours had been sent to him through the efforts of appellee's salesman, but whether he knew it before they verbally agreed on a sale and appellant had accepted a $50 deposit was in dispute. Upon learning that fact he told the Pours that he would take care of the salesman.

Appellant makes several assignments of error and propositions of law directed against the appellee's requested instructions given by the trial court and the court's refusal to grant his requested instructions and a motion for an instructed verdict in favor of the defendant.

The trial court correctly refused defendant's motion for an instructed verdict in his favor, because the matter of bad faith on the part of the appellee broker should have been submitted to the jury.

The important proposition of law relied upon by the appellant is as follows:

The law requires that a real estate broker employed to sell land must act in entire good faith and in the interest of his employer, and if he induces the prospective buyer to believe that the property can be bought for less, he thereby fails to discharge that duty and forfeits all his right to claim commission and compensation for his work.

There is no doubt that the above proposition of law is correct. A real estate agent owes the duty of utmost good faith and loyalty to his principal. The immediate problem here is whether the above proposition is applicable to the facts in this instance.

The facts here are as follows: The salesman informed the purchasers that he had an offer of $8,250 for the property from another purchaser which he was about to submit to appellant. He further told them he thought appellant would not accept the offer, but they might get it for $8,500.

Mr. Rogers, the appellee broker, testified that appellant phoned him after he had accepted the $50 deposit from the purchasers and informed him that he had closed the deal himself and felt that he owed no commission but would split the commission with him, which he, the appellee, refused to do. He further testified that the appellant told him that if their other offer from a third person had been $8,500 he would have accepted it and paid a full commission.

The evidence in this case presents a close question as to good or bad faith on the part of the broker. The trial court should have submitted that matter for the jury to decide. This court has held in negligence cases where the question is close or is in the "shadow zone" that the trial court should not as a matter of law decide those things but rather submit the question to the jury. (*Dillon* v. *City of Yuma,* 55 Ariz. 6, 97 P.2d 535) We feel that while the facts are not analogous, yet the principle of law is the same and decline to decide what is bad faith as a matter of law because that is within the province of the triers of fact. The appellant is entitled to have the jury weigh the evidence and inferences therefrom as to whether or not appellee acted in bad faith in the light of the foregoing.

We wish to reiterate that a broker or salesman owes the utmost good faith to his principal as does any other person acting as agent or in a fiduciary capacity. If an agent betrays his principal, such misconduct and breach of duty results in the agent's losing his right to compensation for services to which he would otherwise be entitled. . . .

In this case the appellant sold the property to a purchaser whom he knew was sent to him by the appellee's salesman. Therefore, in the absence of bad faith the broker is entitled to his commission when he is the procuring cause of sale. . . .

Judgment is reversed and the case remanded for a new trial with directions to submit the question of bad faith on the part of the appellee to the jury.

Judgment reversed.

Hecht v. Meller

244 N.E.2d 77 (N.Y.) 1968

KEATING, J. This appeal presents a question of first impression: Is a real estate broker entitled to commissions on the sale of real property if the purchaser asserts a statutory privilege to rescind the contract of sale because the property has been substantially destroyed by fire after the contract was executed, but before the buyer took title or possession?

.   .   .

Briefly, the facts submitted were the following: Helen Hecht, plaintiff-appellant, entered into a written contract with Herbert and Joyce Meller, defendants-respondents, by which she became the exclusive selling agent for the sale of their personal residence and an adjacent lot which they wished to sell for $75,000. Through the plaintiff's efforts suitable buyers were introduced to the Mellers, and on May 30, 1963 a contract for the sale of the property was signed which acknowledged that Mrs. Hecht had brought the parties together, established a sale price of $60,000, and set August 1 as the closing date.

On July 20, without fault of either the vendors or vendees, the dwelling house on the property was substantially destroyed by fire. The buyers elected to rescind the contract, as provided for by statute and the Mellers, therefore, returned the buyers' down payment. The present action was commenced by the real estate broker when the sellers refused to pay the $3,600 brokerage commission allegedly earned by the broker in bringing the contracting parties together.

The statutory provision applicable to the realty contract under consideration provides that any contract for the purchase and sale of realty shall be interpreted, unless the contract expressly provides otherwise, as including an agreement that the vendor cannot enforce the contract of sale if the property is substantially destroyed and the vendee has taken neither the legal title nor possession of the property. This section was enacted to alter the common-law rule which, absent any agreement to the contrary, cast the risk of destruction of the property between the time the contract of sale was entered into and passing of title upon the vendee. . . .

The force of the enactment, however, did not render realty contracts unenforcible but, rather, simply bestowed a privilege on vendees to rescind the contract.

Examination of the legislative history of the Uniform Vendor and Purchaser Risk Act (General Obligations Law § 5-1311, subd. 3) discloses no evidence that the Legislature intended to shift the risk of payment of earned brokerage commissions, because of the assertion of a vendee's privilege, from the seller to a business loss of the broker. . . .

This court has consistently stated that a real estate broker's right to commissions attaches when he procures a buyer who meets the requirements established by the seller.

At the juncture that the broker produces an acceptable buyer he has fully performed his part of the agreement with the vendor and his right to commission becomes enforcible. The broker's ultimate right to compensation has never been held to be dependent upon the performance of the realty contract or the receipt by the seller of the selling price unless the brokerage agreement with the vendor specifically so conditioned payment. As we stated in *Gilder v. Davis* (supra, 137 N.Y. p. 506, 33 N.E. p. 600): "If from a defect in the title of the vendor, or a refusal to consummate the contract on the part of the purchaser for any reason in no way attributable to the broker, the sale falls through, nevertheless the broker is entitled to his commissions, for the simple reason that he has performed his contract."

Since the vendee may elect to fully perform the contract even though the contingency contemplated by the statute has occurred, it would be an unwarranted construction of the section to find that it gave a seller a privilege not to compensate his broker. . . .

The vendor can protect against the risk by either conditioning the brokerage contract, so that commissions would only be paid out of the proceeds of the sale, or contracting with the vendee that he would either have to purchase the property irrespective of its condition on the closing date or pay the broker's earned commission if he elected to rescind the contract.

. . . Neither the section's legislative history nor its language support a privilege to the seller not to pay an earned brokerage commission. The fact that our decisions decided before and after the enactment of the section have consistently held that a broker is entitled to commissions when he brings the parties together compels a finding in this case that the expense of the brokerage commission must be paid by the vendor who has contracted for the broker's services, even though the Legislature has given the vendee the privilege of rescinding the contract which the broker helped bring about. The sellers in this case, having failed to shift the possible loss, must be deemed to have assumed the risk themselves.

The order of the Appellate Division should be reversed and the judgment of Special Term reinstated, with costs.

Reversed.

Stawasz v. Aetna Insurance Company

240 N.E.2d 702 (Ill.) 1968

SEIDENFELD, J. Defendants, Aetna Insurance Company and Publicker Chemical Corporation, separately appeal from summary judgments entered against them.

Publicker operated a "tank farm," an industrial operation in which inflammable substances such as naptha, alcohol, and ketones were blended into various products and shipped out in steel drums. Stawasz was a foreman for Publicker. An employee of Publicker had given a drum, which had contained a chemical shipment to Publicker, to one Morgan. Stawasz was not present on the day this was done and had not authorized it. The drum given to Morgan exploded at his home causing injuries which later resulted in his death.

The conservator of Morgan's estate, before his death, filed a suit against Publicker and Stawasz. Aetna, as the liability carrier for Publicker, entered a defense for both defendants, but as to defendant Stawasz, defended under a reservation of rights. However, this suit was voluntarily dismissed and, subsequently, a wrongful death was instituted joining Publicker and various employees, including Stawasz, as defendants. The charges of negligence against both Publicker and Stawasz were essentially the same. Both were charged with negligence in the storage, handling, possession, labelling and transfer of possession of the drum without warning of the dangerous contents. Aetna's attorneys entered a defense for Publicker but not for Stawasz, and refused various tenders by the latter during the course of litigation. Stawasz defended by his personal attorney. The trial resulted in a damage judgment on a jury verdict against Publicker; with Stawasz being found not guilty.

Stawasz filed this suit to recover his expenses of defense from Aetna, later adding a second count against Publicker and asking the same relief. . . . Publicker's motion to strike the complaint was denied. Thereupon issues were joined on Stawasz's motion for summary judgment, which the trial court granted as to both defendants and from which the defendants appeal. . . .

THE CASE AGAINST AETNA

Plaintiff's theory against Aetna is that, although he is not a named insured, he is covered by the policy issued to his employer, Publicker, as a third-party beneficiary. Arguing from the premise that an employer is required to indemnify an employee for his cost of defense, plaintiff claims that the provisions of the employer's policy providing that the insurer shall pay all sums which the insured shall be legally obligated to pay, warrants recovery of his expenses of defense.

The premise is false and unsupported by authority. Absent, a contract between the employer and employee to that effect, an employer has no obligation under the circumstances present here either to defend or to indemnify an employee charged with a negligent act whether charged jointly with his employer or not. No such contract of indemnity or agreement to provide a defense is present in this case. An employer may be liable jointly with the employee to a third person for the negligent acts of his employee while acting within the scope of the employment. But the indemnity runs in the opposite direction from the course charted by the plaintiff: the employer becomes liable under the doctrine of *respondeat superior* or agency for the negligent acts of his employee, and the employer, in turn, may seek to be indemnified by his employee for his loss for the reason that an employee owes to his employer the duty of exercising reasonable care in the performance of his duties. Stawasz, here, defended to disclaim his personal negligence, and in so doing was acting in his own interest; and, in establishing his freedom from negligence, was doing no more than that required of him as an employee.

.   .   .

We hold that the court erred in granting plaintiff's motion for summary judgment against Aetna, and remand for further proceedings in accordance with this opinion.

THE CASE AGAINST PUBLICKER

Stawasz's case against Publicker proceeds on the admittedly novel theory that since both the employer and the employee were charged with the same wrongful conduct, and the employer was found at fault while the employee was found free of fault, the employee is entitled to be indemnified for any expense he has been put to because of the "primary" fault of the employer.

The fatal flaw in this argument is that no possible act of Publicker placed Stawasz in a position of liability. Stawasz was not found guilty of negligence, which, under any theory, could have allowed him to place that burden on one more at fault. Stawasz incurred no liability for any conduct of Publicker. The positions are reversed, in fact. If Stawasz had been found to be negligent, and Publicker then burdened with damages for its derivative liability based on the fault of its employee, Publicker could have secured indemnity from its employee. It, of course, could not logically be said that Publicker would have to assume Stawasz's cost of defense because the latter was an employee. Stawasz is liable for his own misconduct—to others or to Publicker. If he is wrongfully charged with negligence he must defend at his own expense unless he has contracted with someone else to assume such defense. No such contract is expressed or implied in the circumstances of this record.

We hold that the court erred in denying the motion to strike the complaint of Stawasz against Publicker and remand with directions to strike the complaint and dismiss this portion of the case with prejudice.

Ferguson v. Lounsberry

207 N.E.2d 309 (Ill.) 1965

SMITH, J. While operating a power-driven corn elevator on the farm of his defendant employer, plaintiff's clothes became entangled in its mechanism and he sustained injuries. The jury returned a verdict in his favor for $65,000.00 Defendant's post-trial motion for judgment notwithstanding the verdict or in the alternative for a new trial was denied. From this judgment entered on the verdict and the denial of his post-trial motion, the defendant appeals.

Defendant first asserts that the plaintiff was guilty of contributory negligence which bars his recovery. This requires our scrutiny of the situs, the circumstances and the conduct of the plaintiff at and immediately before the occurrence. It likewise requires a consideration of the respective proper functions of court and jury in the factual picture presented by the evidence. The occurrence events come almost exclusively from plaintiff's lips, as the only other eyewitness was the 3 1/2 year old daughter of the defendant.

It is abundantly clear from the evidence that plaintiff was a 29 year old farm hand and experienced in the operation of mobile farm grain elevators. He was employed by the defendant when the particular equipment was purchased three years before, had operated it many times and had been operating it a week or more before the accident. He had "spotted" or placed the equipment for the unloading process and had repaired the knuckle to which reference will be made later. The day in question was cold and somewhat damp. The plaintiff had on two pair of long underwear, a wool slipover sweater and was generally warmly and heavily clothed. It seems clear from the evidence that it was this sweater which first became entangled in the mechanism.

The corn elevator was generally typical in design and operation, is commonly called a corn dump, and is used to elevate corn from its hopper into an adjacent corncrib. . . .

There is some spillage in this operation and on this day some 5-6 bushels of corn were on the ground. With the equipment in operation, plaintiff was picking up this corn and he states the sequence of events in this language:

> Well, I was squatted down and I had the elevator in motion running and I was picking it up by hand and was throwing it in and I had cleaned up pretty well all right along the hopper and I was squatted down and I made a left hand turn towards the shaft and reached over to pick up some corn and it got hold of my clothing. After it got hold of my clothes, I remember it jerked me up and started taking me around, flopping me through the air, and I guess I hit my head on the ground or something and I just passed out from shock. That's all I remember until I regained consciousness. I woke up and I could see Mr. Lounsberry's little daughter standing there in a blur, haze, and so I told her to go get her mother. I had just a little piece of clothing here and there. . . .

It is but the assertion of a ritualistic truism, hoary with age and dog-eared from repetition, to say that contributory negligence is ordinarily a question of fact for the jury. Where the underlying facts, factors conduct and circumstances, together with their reasonable inferences and implications, are beclouded or uncertain from conflicting or divergent testimony, it becomes the time-honored function of the jury to sort the wheat from the chaff and to seek out and find the truth and to express that truth in its verdict. This is hallowed ground properly barred from invasion by either the trial or reviewing courts. It is when the underlying facts, factors, conduct and circumstances, together with their reasonable inferences and implications, present a clear, sharp and vivid picture of conduct that a pungent question of judicial intervention rears its ugly head. Two schools of thought are extant: One is the Holmes view which prompted him to say that "every time that a judge declines to rule whether certain conduct is negligent or not he avows his inability to state the law, . . ." The antithesis of this view is one which permits the jury to meander within broad general principles of law and by its verdict label certain conduct negligent or non-negligent. A like set of facts before one jury imposes liability and before another jury denies it. Standards of conduct vary from week to week, from jury to jury and from community to community. . . .

    . . . [W]e are not dealing with a non-functioning or mal-functioning piece of equipment. . . . Everything about it now known to anybody was known or should have been known to the plaintiff. We think all minds would reasonably agree that a square shaft and a knuckle revolving at a rate in excess of 500 revolutions a minute telegraphed to one with even less expertise then plaintiff that it was an area of danger. His employer was in the field picking corn—plaintiff had a specific job to do—its manner and method rested in his sole judgment—he was in full charge of the operation. He could have shut off the equipment and picked up without incident. He chose not to do so. He could have picked up without bringing himself in contact with the moving equipment. If fact, he testified that he had many times picked up with the equipment moving. Obviously, it was without previous incident and without personal contact with the equipment. The conclusion is inescapable that he inadvertently, unthinkingly, heedlessly, or carelessly brought his clothing into contact with the equipment. We do not facetiously say that he reached out toward it; it did not reach out toward him; his was an affirmative and voluntary action. The facts are undisputed. We would abjure our responsibilities if we did not say as a matter of law that the plaintiff was not in the exercise of due care and caution for his own safety.

... [T]here are proper cases for jury determination where the facts are disputed, where reasonable inferences from known facts are divergent or where the conduct of the plaintiff is not free from doubt. Merely to read them is to readily distinguish them from the case at bar.

... There being a total want of proof of an essential element of plaintiff's cause of action, the trial court erred in not directing a verdict or in failing to enter a judgment notwithstanding the verdict. Its judgment must be and it is accordingly reversed.

Reversed.

CHAPTER 39
REVIEW QUESTIONS AND PROBLEMS

1. *A,* a real estate agent, while attempting to sell *P*'s property, loaned *T* funds from his commission, which *T* used as a down payment on *P*'s property. Is *A* entitled to his commission? Assuming a contract was signed, may *T* specifically enforce the contract?

2. *X,* a real estate broker, had listing agreements with both *Y* and *Z* to sell their respective homes. After some difficulty in procuring buyers, *X* discovered that *Y* and *Z* were interested in each other's home. He effected a trade of homes. May *Y* and *Z* refuse *X*'s commission because he represented adverse parties?

3. *A* told *B* that *A* would find a renter for *B*'s property at a rent of $500 per month, and that *A* would manage the building for $100 per month. *B* agreed. *A* rented the property to *C* at a rate of $550 per month. *A* kept the $50 difference when he collected the rent. May *B* recover the extra profits from *A*?

4. *X,* owner of a retail store, agreed that *Y,* an advertising agency, was to place a large ad in the first section of a certain newspaper. It is the custom in the advertising business that the agency places the ad in the section selected by the agency. *Y* placed the ad in the last section of the paper, near the want ads. May *X* refuse to pay *Y*?

5. *X,* while delivering goods for *Y,* negligently ran into a train, damaging *Y*'s automobile. May *Y* recover from *X*?

6. *X,* a widow, owned a small "country store." *Y,* her son, managed the store. Although she had no proof since *Y*'s books were very confused, *X* suspected that *Y* was stealing funds. May *X* compel *Y* to give an accounting?

7. *X* agreed to pay *Y* $10,000 if he would find a lessor for a particular oil well. *Y* expended great amounts of time and effort in an attempt to find one, but was unable to do so. May *Y* recover his expenses from *X*?

8. *A*, a real estate agent, was engaged by *B* to procure a buyer, "payment on closing of sale." *A* found *C*, who was ready, willing, and able to purchase. However on the day of closing, the property burned down. May *A* obtain his commission from *B*?

9. *A*, at *B*'s instruction, repossessed *C*'s car. *B* had no right to repossess the car. *A* seeks to join *B* in the suit and attempts to impose any liability on *B*, which he, *A*, may have to *C*. May he do so?

10. P Company was engaged in a wholesale business supplying goods to hospitals and novelty stores, *A* being its manager. *A*, while still working for P Company, agreed with a salesman of the company and a third party to enter a competing business and arranged to handle two lines for which the P Company previously held the exclusive agency. *A* quit and entered the competing business, but P Company seeks to enjoin it from operation. What result?

11. *P* employed *A* as manager of his business and authorized him to buy such supplies and merchandise as were needed. Being a member of CO-OP, *A* purchased all of his supplies through it. At the end of the year, he received a personal dividend of $900 because of the purchases. Is he entitled to retain it? Assume that he purchased the supplies as advantageously as he could have at any other place.

12. *B*, appointed to sell merchandise in a certain area for *S*, was to receive a commission of 2 percent on all sales. He received a weekly advance of $750 for ten weeks, but his commissions averaged only $40 a week. Does he owe *S* the $350 difference?

13. *P*, a real estate broker, sold *D*'s house to *X*. *P* prepared a real estate contract to be executed by the parties. *P* sued *D* for his commission. *D* defended on the ground that *P*'s action in preparing the contract constituted unauthorized practice of law; therefore, the whole transaction was illegal, and *P* could not collect a commission. What result?

Termination

5-51. Introduction. There are two basic issues involved with the subject of termination of an agency relationship. First, what acts or facts are sufficient to terminate the authority of the agent insofar as the immediate parties are concerned? Second, what is required to terminate the agent's authority insofar as third parties are concerned? The latter question recognizes that an agent may continue to have the *power* to bind the principal but not the *right* to do so. The methods of termination are usually divided into termination by act of the parties and termination by operation of law. The discussion which follows is limited to termination of the agency relationship. It should be remembered that termination of the master and servant relationship will frequently be subject to the terms of an applicable collective bargaining agreement, and the employer does not necessarily have the right to terminate all employment relationships at will. In addition, the provisions of the civil rights laws relating to hiring, firing, promotion, and tenure regulate the employment contract and the rights and duties of the parties. Their provisions are beyond the scope of this text, but it should always be the policy of employers to provide equal employment opportunities and to avoid discrimination based on race, creed, color, sex, or national origin.

5-52. By Act of the Parties. Termination by act of the parties includes termination by force of their agreement or by the act of one or both of the parties. An example of the former is an agency which is created to continue for a definite period of time. It ceases, by virtue of the terms of the agreement, at the expiration of the stipulated period. If the parties consent to the continuation of the relationship beyond such period, the courts imply the formation of a new contract of employment. The new agreement contains the same terms as the old one and continues for a like period of time, except that no implied contract can run longer than one year because of the statute of frauds.

Another example is an agency created to accomplish a certain purpose, which automatically ends with the completion of the task assigned. In such case third parties are not entitled to notice of the termination. Furthermore, when it is possible for one of several agents to perform the task, such as selling certain real estate, it is held that performance by the first party terminates the authority of the other agents without notice of termination being required.

Many, if not most, agency contracts do not provide for the duration of the agreement. Such agencies are terminable at the will of either party at any time.[1]

Any contract may be terminated by mutual agreement; therefore, the agency relationship may be canceled in this manner. Furthermore, as a general rule, either party to the agreement has full *power* to terminate it whenever he desires, although he possesses no *right* to do so. Wrongful termination of the agency by either party subjects him to a suit for damages by the other party.[2]

5-53. Wrongful Termination and Its Effect. An employment which continues at the will of the parties may be rightfully terminated by either party at any time. On the other hand, if the employer wrongfully terminates a contract which was to continue for an agreed period, he becomes liable for damages. If the agent is discharged for cause, such as failure to follow instructions or to exercise proper care or for nonperformance of various other duties, he may not recover damages from his employer.

The employee whose employment has been wrongfully cut short is entitled to recover compensation for work done before his dismissal and an additional sum for damages. Most of the states permit him to bring an action either immediately following the breach, in which he recovers prospective damages,[3] or after the period has expired, in which event he recovers the damages actually sustained. In the latter case, he is compelled to deduct from the compensation called for in the agreement the amount which he has been able to earn during the interim.[4] Under such circumstances, the employee is under a duty to exercise reasonable diligence in finding other work of like character. Apparently this rule does not require him to seek employment in a new locality or to accept work of a different kind or more menial character. His duty is to find work of like kind, provided it is available in the particular locality.

5-54. Termination by Law. Certain acts are held by law to terminate the agency. Among these are death, insanity, bankruptcy of either of the parties, or destruction of the subject matter of the agency. Bankruptcy has such an effect only in case it affects the subject matter of the agency.

It is said of such cases that the agency is immediately terminated and that no notice need be given to either the agent or the third parties. However, with reference to insanity, unless the principal has been publicly adjudged insane, it is believed that an agent's contracts are binding on the principal unless the third party is aware of the mental illness, especially where the contract is beneficial to the insane principal's estate.

[1] Brekken v. Reader's Digest Special Products, Inc., page 796.
[2] Shumaker v. Hazen, page 797.
[3] Cornell v. T. V. Development Corp., page 798.
[4] People v. Johnson, page 800.

5-55. Agency Coupled with an Interest.   As a general rule, an agency contract can be terminated at any time by either party. As previously noted, the power to terminate exists without the right to do so, and if the power is exercised wrongfully, a suit at law for damages may be brought. Agency contracts are not specifically enforceable against the principal because of the lack of mutuality in the remedy, even though equity courts will restrain violation of an express or implied covenant not to compete. Since the principal could not require the agent to work (involuntary servitude), the agent cannot, as a general rule, compel the principal to continue the agency.[5]

To the general rule, however, there is one well-recognized exception known as "an agency coupled with an interest." The term, "an agency coupled with an interest" describes the relationship which exists when the agent has an actual beneficial interest in the property which is the subject matter of the agency. For example, a mortgage which contains a provision naming the mortgagee as agent to sell the property in the event of default creates an agency coupled with an interest in property. An agency coupled with an interest in property cannot be terminated unilaterally by the principal and is not terminated by events (such as death or bankruptcy of the principal) which otherwise terminate agencies by operation of law. The net effect is that an agency coupled with an interest in property cannot be terminated without the consent of the agent.

An agency coupled with an interest in property must be distinguished from *an agency coupled with an obligation.* This latter term describes the situation in which the agency is created as a source of reimbursement to the agent. For example, an agent who is given the right to sell a certain automobile and to apply the proceeds on a claim against the principal is an agency coupled with an obligation. Such an agency is a hybrid between the usual agency and the agency coupled with an interest in property. The agency coupled with an obligation cannot unilaterally be terminated by the principal, but death or bankruptcy of the principal will terminate the agency by operation of law.

Under either type of agency, it should be clear that the interest in the subject matter must be greater than the mere expectation of profits to be realized or in the proceeds to be derived from the sale of the property. The interest must be in the property itself. For example, a real estate broker is not an agent coupled with an interest, even though he expects a commission from the proceeds of the sale. Likewise, a principal who has appointed an agent to sell certain goods on commission has the power to terminate the agency at any time, although such conduct might constitute a breach of the agreement.

5-56. Notice in Event of Termination.   Termination of the agency, as explained above, may take place by act of the parties or by operation of law. If the parties by their own action have terminated the agency, it is the duty of the principal to notify all third parties, who have learned of the existence of the agency, of its termination. Without such notice the agent would still possess apparent authority to act for his principal. Those persons entitled to such notice may be divided into two groups: (1) those who have previously relied upon the agency by dealing with the agent; and (2) those who have never

[5] Sarokhan v. Fair Lawn Memorial Hospital, Inc., page 801

previously dealt with the agent, but who, nevertheless, have learned of the agency. The principal's duty to the first class can be satisfied only by the actual receipt of notice of the termination by the third party. The principal satisfies his duty to the second group by giving public notice, such as newspaper publicity, in the location involved. If any one of the second group, not having seen the newspaper account of the termination, relies upon the continuation of the agency to his detriment, he has no cause of action against the principal. If a member of the first group has not received direct notice from the principal, but has learned indirectly of the severance of relation or of facts sufficient to place him on inquiry, he is no longer justified in extending credit to the agent or otherwise dealing with him as a representative of the principal.

Where the agency is terminated by action of law, such as death, insanity, or bankruptcy, no duty to notify third parties is placed upon the principal. Such matters receive publicity through newspapers, official records, and otherwise, and third parties normally become aware of the termination without the necessity for additional notification. If the death of the principal occurs before an agent contracts with a third party, the third party has no cause of action against either the agent or the estate of the principal unless the agent is acting for an undisclosed principal. In the latter case, since the agent makes the contract in his own name, he is liable to the third party. Otherwise, the third party is in as good a position to know of the death of the principal as is the agent.

Two additional problems of notice need be considered. Must an undisclosed principal give notice of termination? The answer is "No." Since the failure to give notice allows liability on a theory of apparent authority and there is no apparent authority in cases involving undisclosed principals, notice of termination is not required.

The other problem involves notice in cases of special agents as distinguished from general agents. Ordinarily, notice is not required to revoke the authority of a special agent, since the agent possesses no continuing authority and no one will be in a habit of dealing with him. However, if the principal has directly indicated that the agent has authority in a certain matter or at a certain time, notice will be required to prevent reliance on the principal's conduct by a party dealing with the agent. This is especially true if the agent is acting under a special power of attorney. Actual notice of termination is required in these cases.

TERMINATION CASES

Brekken v. Reader's Digest Special Products, Inc.

353 F.2d 505 (1965)

MERCER, J. Summary judgment was entered in this suit for damages arising out of the alleged improper termination by defendant of the plaintiffs' contracts of employment. This appeal followed:

Each of the plaintiffs was employed by defendant as a regional manager pursuant to the provisions of a written, form contract executed by the parties. Each plaintiff was discharged from employment within one year after his contract had been signed.

The controversy relates to the construction of the following provisions of the contracts, to-wit:

> This agreement shall be effective from the date of execution and shall remain in effect for a period of twelve months and will be automatically renewed for twelve-month terms unless sooner terminated.
>
> This agreement may be terminated by either party upon written notice or by Manager's death.

Plaintiffs do not question the adequacy of the notice given if defendant had the legal right to terminate the contracts within the first year of their life.

Plaintiffs argue that the words "unless sooner terminated" apply only to renewal periods subsequent to the expiration of the initial term. That argument is born from the contemplation of the plaintiffs' frustrated hopes, not from any tenable legal foundation.

The well-established principles guiding the construction of ambiguous contract provisions are of no help to plaintiffs in the light of the plain provisions of these contracts. An employment contract for a stated term, which is expressly terminable by either party upon notice, must be recognized as a valid contract and its provisions must be given effect.

It cannot be doubted as plaintiffs assert that they expected their employment to continue for at least one year, but that was merely an expectation and not a right guaranteed by the contracts which they signed. The courts cannot rewrite the contracts which they made. Clearly the phrase "unless sooner terminated" relates to the whole sentence of which that phrase is a part. The court below correctly construed each of these contracts as being terminable at will.

Affirmed.

Shumaker v. Hazen

372 P.2d 873 (Okla.) 1962

Plaintiff sued defendant, alleging that defendant had employed plaintiff to sell 12,700 shares of stock in the Utex Exploration Co. at stated percentage commissions, that plaintiff could have sold the stock but defendant refused to allow him to do so. Plaintiff had been given an irrevocable power of attorney for one year, but defendant had canceled it during the year. Plaintiff contended that defendant had by this act prevented the performance of the contract.

JOHNSON, J. . . . . The power of attorney in this case provided that it should be "irrevocable" for a period of one year. The law is well settled that a principal may revoke an agent's authority at any time and is not at all affected by the fact that there is an express or implied contract that the agency is irrevocable unless the power is coupled with an interest.

We hold that . . . this was not a power coupled with an interest.

Therefore, the power to revoke is beyond question but it is subject to the following qualification . . .

The principal, having the power to revoke an agency, is liable in damages if, by the revocation, substantial injury is sustained by the agent.

*The defendant was therefore answerable in damages.
Affirmed.*

Cornell v. T. V. Development Corp.

215 N.E.2d 349 (N.Y.) 1966

SCILEPPI, J. Plaintiff was hired as General Manager by the defendant T. V. Development Corp. for a five-year period starting in March, 1962, at an annual salary of $20,000. The employment contract contained covenants not to compete and that all inventions by the plaintiff would be assigned to the corporation. The action arises out of defendant's breach of this employment contract.

In the first cause of action, plaintiff sought to recover money earned but not paid prior to his unlawful discharge in August, 1963; in the second, his prospective salary loss resulting from the wrongful discharge; in the third, damages for malicious interference with his employment contract; and in the fourth, sought to recover a share of the corporate defendant's profits; stock in defendant's Colorgrams, Inc.; a declaration that plaintiff was the sole owner of an invention called Colorgrams; and an injunction restraining all of the defendants from using this invention.

The answer contained two counterclaims, one by T. V. Development Corp. for breach of contract; and the other by that corporation, Renrac Corp., Colorgrams, Inc., and Richard Zatzkin for malicious disclosure of damaging, confidential information about the defendants.

The trial court (1) granted plaintiff judgment against T. V. Development Corp. on the first cause of action in the sum of $2,100, and against T. V. Development Corp. on the second cause of action in the sum of $5,000; (2) dismissed the third cause of action; (3) declared plaintiff inventor and sole owner of the product "Colorgrams" subject to T. V. Development's nonexclusive right to practice and use the invention; (4) denied the injunctive relief sought in the fourth cause of action, and (5) dismissed the counterclaims.

The plaintiff appealed, contending that the damages awarded him were inadequate and should be increased from $5,000 to $70,000, the difference representing the salary accruing after the date plaintiff organized his own business venture. The Appellate Division affirmed, . . . holding that, once plaintiff formed a corporation to market Colorgrams, he "removed himself from every field of employment [and] must be deemed to have made an irrevocable election to forego the damages ordinarily recoverable, and he must be deemed to have accepted the profits of his new venture—whether they be more or less—in lieu of his damages and in full satisfaction thereof. The corporation, which must fend off his competition, should not also be required to stand as his surety against any loss thus voluntarily incurred by him. It is quite inequitable, to say the least, to permit him to take all the possible profits of his competitive venture but to have the corporation bear all his possible losses to the extent of the damages to which he otherwise might have been entitled."

Mr. Justice Benjamin, dissenting, said: "I believe it is improper to limit plaintiff's damages for his wrongful discharge to the period prior to his entry into business. I believe he is entitled to his contract salary for the unexpired period of the contract, less whatever he has so far earned and can reasonably be expected hereafter to earn from his business up to the end of the contract period. . . .

"There is a finding by both lower courts that the defendant wrongfully discharged the plaintiff. The only question presented is whether the plaintiff is then entitled to a judgment for the salary called for in the contract to its termination date. The breach of contract action is an action at law and the principles applicable thereto must be applied.

"The plaintiff is entitled to damages which will compensate him for the defendant's breach of contract. *Prima facie* the measure of such damage is 'the wage that would be payable during the remainder of the term'; but this is only the *prima facie* measure. The actual damage is measured by the wage that would be payable during the remainder of the term reduced by the income which the discharged employee has earned, will earn, or could with reasonable diligence earn during the unexpired term. The discharged employee's damages may be measured *prima facie* by the unpaid wage, but it is the present worth of the obligation to pay the wages at a time in the future that fixes the damages. Indeed, in the case of breach of contract of employment, not only time but the uncertainty of human life may be taken into consideration in fixing the present worth of an obligation to pay money due at some time in the future, after the trial." . . .

Here the proof shows that the plaintiff was borrowing funds to form a corporation for the purpose of going into the electronic business. At the time of trial, the corporation had no bank account; it owned no assets; and the plaintiff received no employment income after his discharge, but did receive $600 in unemployment insurance payments.

Defendant appears to have offered no proof of what, if anything, plaintiff earned or could have earned after his wrongful discharge. Instead, defendant makes the bare, and from the authorities above cited, incorrect assertion that plaintiff had the burden of showing his prospective income from his newly formed corporation. From this incorrect premise, defendant concludes that, because plaintiff chose to form his own business venture, he is barred from further recovery.

The record shows that the plaintiff attempted to obtain employment after his wrongful discharge, and, failing to do so, started his own business with the intention of promoting his invention, if upon trial he was awarded the right to use the invention. Under these circumstances, we fail to see how it could be held that the plaintiff's entry into corporate business barred his right to damages accruing after that date.

. . .

After the plaintiff's failure to obtain employment, his decision to form a corporation from which he might reasonably expect to derive some financial benefit was consonant with his obligation to mitigate damages. . . . Therefore, the mere fact that plaintiff organized a corporation should not bar recovery on the ground that he took himself out of the employment field. By so holding, we avoid the absurdity of one rule of law calling upon the plaintiff to make reasonable efforts to mitigate his damages "while another rule required him to remain idle in order that he may recover full wages." . . .

In sum, the lower courts improperly concluded that plaintiff was barred from recovering anything for the period following formation of his corporation. Although defendant offered no proof of mitigation of damages, on this record, it would be needlessly harsh for us to require the defendant to pay over the balance due on the employment contract. Rather, we remit this case for a new trial on the question of damages only, at which trial the defendant will now be in a better position to show, if it can, the actual and prospective earnings of plaintiff from his corporate business. Plaintiff's corporation was just created about the time of trial. Enough time has now elapsed to permit an evaluation of his potential income from the corporation and the ascertainment of the income so far actually received by plaintiff therefrom.

We conclude that, in addition to the amount already paid, plaintiff is entitled to receive the present value of the money that would have been due him under the original contract, less what he has earned and can reasonably be expected to earn in his new corporate venture during the unexpired term of the contract. . . .

Order reversed, etc.

People v. Johnson

205 N.E.2d 470 (Ill.) 1965

A writ of mandamus was sought to compel City of Chicago officials to pay the back salary accrued during a period of wrongful discharge of one Jack F. Bourne, referred to as Relator. Relator was a civil service employee who was suspended from city employment because of his debts. The debts were incurred during the illness and death of his wife and the wrongfulness of the discharge had been established in a separate adminstrative hearing.

From March 5, 1962 to January 4, 1963, Relator worked from 5:00 P.M. to 2:00 A.M. at a liquor store for $105 a week. These hours were not during the hours of his city employment, and he also worked the same hours at the liquor store prior to his discharge. The city had no rule against "moonlighting."

UNDERWOOD, J. . . . The defendant officials contend the courts erred in holding the monies earned in the liquor store employment should not be set off against the back salary. . . . Relator concedes that the right of setoff exists as to earnings by an employee during the period of wrongful discharge, but contends that this rule embraces only those earnings which would have been incompatible with the prior employment. The precise question for our consideration is, therefore, whether an employer who wrongfully discharges an employee is entitled to credit on a back-pay award for subsequent earnings of the employee from a secondary job, compatible with, and held by the employee in conjunction with the principal employment.

We have previously and specifically held the employer entitled to set off the employee's earnings from other employment against the salary accruing during the period he was improperly prevented from performing his duties.

The theory underlying a suit for back salary is to make the employee whole —to compensate him to the extent that the wrongful deprivation of salary has resulted in financial loss. For that reason the amount recoverable is to be reduced by his other earnings during the period of separation insofar as such income would have been incompatible with performance of his duties to his erring employer. But this does not necessitate mitigation of the recoverable salary by earnings compatible with and being received during the employment from which the employee is wrongfully discharged. There is in this record no hint of incompatibility between relator's liquor store employment and his obligation to the municipality, either in the form of regulatory proscriptions or conflicting hours or duties. In fact, relator held both jobs for a substantial period of time prior to his wrongful discharge. As was aptly observed by the Appellate Court, the industrious holder of two compatible jobs who is wrongfully discharged from one should not be penalized by permitting the wrongdoer to deduct from the damages for which he is liable the earnings of the second job during the period of wrongful discharge.

Embraced in defendants' argument is the contention that relator must establish his use of reasonable diligence to secure substitute employment before he may recover damages in the form of back salary, but we believe defendants misplace the burden. The defendants were here the wrongdoers, and the obligation to produce whatever proof existed in diminution of damages rested on them. The overwhelming weight of authority, in this State and elsewhere in this country, is that an employer in an action for lost wages must affirmatively show in order to reduce damages that the discharged employee could or did have other earnings subsequent to the wrongful discharge. There is here no proof that Relator regarded his liquor store employment as a substitute for his municipal employment, except such probative value as may attach to the fact that the former terminated about the time of his reinstatement to the latter, and this scarcely serves to outweigh the fact that he performed the duties of both for a substantial period prior to the municipal discharge. Nor is there any showing of lack of diligence in seeking additional employment during the hours formerly occupied by the municipal work. We therefore conclude that where an employee simultaneously holds two compatible jobs and is wrongfully discharged from one, his employer may not set off the earnings from the remaining job against liability for lost wages in the absence of proof of a lack of diligence by the employee in seeking additional employment or that the remaining job was regarded as a complete substitute for the prior dual employment.

(Writ Issued).

Sarokhan v. Fair Lawn Memorial Hospital, Inc.

199 A.2d 52 (N.J.) 1964

A doctor brought suit to enjoin a hospital from terminating his services as medical and surgery director and for other relief. Plaintiff had no financial investment in the hospital but had a written contract for ten years. The agreement provided that it could not be revoked or altered during the period. Plaintiff had organized the hospital and was given rather complete control over it. A controversy developed, and the Board of Directors of the hospital sought to discharge the plaintiff.

KILKENNY, J. The contract herein was one for the rendition of personal services. This is so even though the duties of the job required a person "knowledgeable in the medical arts and in the process of medical administration," as the contract noted. Personal service contracts are generally not specifically enforceable affirmatively. Equity will not compel performance of the personal services, even where the contract involves a "star" of unique talent, because equity will not make a vain decree. At most, equity will restrain violation of an express or implied negative covenant, thus precluding the performer from performing for somebody else.

So, too, it is a general rule that agency contracts are not specifically enforceable in a suit brought by the agent against his principal. Courts are not wont to force a principal to keep an agent against his will, "because the law has allowed every principal a power to revoke his deputation at any time." To do so would violate the basic concept in the law of agency, *viz.,* the right of the principal to select his own *alter ego,* to exercise his *delectus personarum.*

The mere fact that the appointment recites that it will be irrevocable during the term of the appointment does not preclude the principal from exercising the power to revoke it. So, too, "it is not necessary for the principal to have any good reasons for his action in revoking the agency, and he may cancel the agent's authority at his caprice, even though the instrument creating the agency contains an express declaration of irrevocability." This does not mean that the principal may breach such a contract with impunity. For a wrongful breach, the agent may sue at law and recover money damages. Normally, that is the only remedy available to him. The same rule is applicable to a partnership agreement, a mutual agency relationship in which co-owners carry on a business for profit. . . .

The trial court was concerned about the possible injury to plaintiff's professional reputation that might result from termination of the contract. This possible impairment of the agent's reputation, as a basis for ordering specific performance of a personal service contract, was considered by our then highest court in *Fiedler, Inc.* v. *Coast Finance Co., Inc., supra,* and rejected. Such an element of damage can be proved "with as much accuracy as any unliquidated claim can be ascertained." *(Ibid)* Similarly rejected in *Hewitt* v. *Magic City Furniture & Mfg. Co., supra,* was plaintiff's contention therein that specific performance would give him the opportunity to make a reputation for efficiency in the superintendence of defendant's business that would be of great future advantage to him in the business world.

Specific performance of personal services contracts is refused for the further reason that they lack mutuality of enforcement. The employee or agent, reinstated by judicial decree, might abandon his duties on the next day, and a court of equity could not compel him to perform. The wronged principal's only remedy would be an action at law for money damages. *Fiedler, Inc.* v. *Coast Finance Co., Inc., supra,* noted that a want of mutuality in the remedy warrants denial of specific performance. "If the enforcement of the obligation may not be granted to both contracting parties, it should not be enforced against one party."

The law has recognized, as an exception to the general rule, that "an agency coupled with an interest" cannot be revoked by the principal during the term fixed for its existence. Even the death of the principal does not terminate it. The best known case setting forth this exception is *Hunt* v. *Rousmanier* (8 Wheat. (U.S.) 174, 5 L.Ed. 589 (1823)). In that case, Hunt loaned money to Rousmanier and to secure repayment of the debt the borrower gave the lender a power of attorney to sell a vessel, with authority to deduct from the proceeds the balance due on the loan and turn over the residue to the borrower. The issue was whether the power survived the death of Rousmanier, the giver of the power. The rule was laid down that the death of the principal does not revoke an agency coupled with an interest.

Defendants concede that, if the contract herein created an agency coupled with an interest, they would not have the power to revoke it. They maintain that such an agency was not created. We agree. The test of an agency coupled with an interest is stated in 2 Williston, *Contracts* (3rd Ed.), § 280, pp. 301-302, as follows:

> Does the agent have an interest or estate in the subject matter of the agency independent of the power conferred, or does the estate or interest accrue by or after the exercise of the power conferred?
> If the former, it is an agency coupled with an interest, or as has been suggested, a proprietary power; if the latter, it is not.

If the agency is given as security for a debt or obligation, it is regarded as an agency coupled with an interest. "In order that a power may be irrevocable because coupled with an interest, it is necessary that the interest shall be in the subject matter of the power, and not in the proceeds which will arise from the exercise of the power." (3 Am.Jur.2d, *Agency,* § 62). The agency herein was not given as security for some obligation due plaintiff. He had no interest in the subject matter of the power independent of the power conferred. The power conferred by defendant hospital was not one "coupled with an interest." Accordingly, it is not irrevocable, despite the terminology used by the parties.

We conclude that the contract in issue did not create an agency coupled with an interest and that defendants had and have the *power* to terminate it. It becomes unnecessary for us to decide whether the contract contravenes public policy. We make no determination as to whether defendants breached any contractual *right* of plaintiff in terminating his relationship with the hospital. Those reserved issues will require a plenary trial for resolution, as will the tort claims set forth in the first two counts of the complaint.

The order under review is reversed and the injunction pendente lite *is dissolved. The matter is remanded to the Chancery Division for further proceedings not inconsistent herewith.*

CHAPTER 40
REVIEW QUESTIONS AND PROBLEMS

1. *A,* the owner of a small insurance agency, agreed to represent the XYZ Insurance Company. Three years later the company revoked *A*'s authority. Does *A* have any rights against the XYZ Company?

2. *X,* a physician, was hired by a hospital to serve as hospital administrator for a term of ten years. After three years, the hospital discharged *X.* May *X* obtain specific performance of the contract? Does *X* have any remedy against the hospital?

3. *P*, the owner of a drive-in grocery store, signed an exclusive "listing agreement" with *A*, a licensed real estate broker. After three months, *P* leased the store to *T*, and revoked *A*'s authority. Does *A* have any remedy against *P*?

4. For years, *X*, housekeeper in *Y*'s home, had ordered fuel oil for *Y* from *Z*. On January 15, *Y* died. On February 15, *X* ordered a tankful of oil for *Y*'s home, which *Z* delivered. Can *Z* collect from *Y*'s estate? Can *Z* collect from *X*?

5. *A*, a real estate agent, was authorized by *P* to sell several lots at a specified price. *A* was to receive a 5 percent commission on each lot sold. Before any lots were sold, *P* revoked the authorization. Was *A*'s authority irrevocable as a "power coupled with an interest"?

6. *A* was employed by *P* to manage a farm. *A* lived in a house on the land and took care of all the details of running the farm. Customarily *A* hired *T* to bale the hay in a certain field. Unknown to *T*, *P* revoked *A*'s authority, though *A* continued to live in the house. *A* gave *T* permission to cut the hay "as usual." Is *P* liable to *T*?

7. *X* managed a store owned by his brother, *Y*, and for several years made purchases from *Z* of clothing and other goods for the store. *Z* customarily extended credit for these purchases. After an argument, *Y* revoked *X*'s authority. *X* then purchased from *Z* on credit a large order of goods similar to those sold in the store. May *Z* recover from *Y*?

8. *A* represented the XYZ Pickle Company in purchasing pickles and peppers from farmers. After a dispute, XYZ resolved to discharge *A*, but because of a mistake, *A* was not notified. *A* made several contracts with farmers for the purchase of their crops. Do the farmers have any rights against the XYZ Company?

9. After her divorce, *P* retained *A*, an attorney, to represent her in an action to recover some real estate from her ex-husband. As his compensation, *A* accepted *P*'s assignment of a one-third interest in the land if *P* should win the lawsuit. *P* then attempted to discharge *A*. Does *A* have a "power coupled with an interest"?

10. *P* engaged *A* to operate a retail lumber business in the latter's name. *A* sold merchandise to *T* on credit. Later *P* notified *T* that *A*'s agency was terminated and directed *T* to pay the debt to *P*. *T* disregarded instructions and paid the obligation to *A*, who failed to account to *P*. May *P* collect from *T*?

11. *X* and *Y* had an employment contract which provided that it would remain in effect for twelve months and would be automatically renewed for twelve-month periods unless sooner terminated. It also provided that the agreement could be terminated by either party on written notice or by the employee's death. *X* gave written notice of termination within the initial twelve-month period. *Y* sued *X* for breach of contract. What result?

12. *X* signed a note which contained a confession of judgment clause. *X* died and *P*, the noteholder, thereafter confessed judgment on the note. *X*'s executor moved to set the judgment aside on the ground that the death of *X* terminated the authority of any attorney to confess judgment

against him. *P* contended that the agency was coupled with an interest and therefore survived. What result?

13. *A* gave two real estate brokers, *X* and *Y*, simple listings on his house. *X* found a ready, willing, and able buyer one day, and before *A* could notify the other broker, *Y*, *Y* also found a buyer. Is *Y* entitled to a commission?

14. *A*, a buyer for the *X* department store, was discharged. *Y* had never sold to *A* but knew that *A* was *X*'s buyer. After *A* was discharged, an article about his changing jobs was in the newspaper, but *Y* did not read it. If *A* purchases goods on credit from *Y*, charging them to *X*, is *X* liable therefor?

BOOK SIX

Business
Organizations

Choosing the Form
of Organization

6-1. Introduction. Business organizations may operate under a variety of legal forms. The most common ones are sole proprietorships, partnerships, limited partnerships, and corporations. In the last category there are some specialized organizations known as professional service corporations. In addition to the usual forms of organization, other forms are sometimes used, such as joint-stock companies, business trusts, and joint ventures.

This chapter will examine the various forms of organization and the factors that influence the actual selection of a particular form. The factors involved in this selection are applicable to all businesses from the smallest to the largest, but the relative influence of the various factors varies greatly depending on the size of the business. For example, as a practical matter, the very large business must be incorporated because this is the only method that can bring a large number of owners and investors together for an extended period of time. The difficulty of deciding which is the best form of organization to select is most often encountered in the closely held business. It should also be kept in mind that taxation is usually the most significant contributing factor. Although a detailed discussion of the tax laws is beyond the scope of this text, some of the general principles of taxation will be presented in order to illustrate the influence taxation brings to bear in choosing diverse organizational forms.

6-2. General Partnerships. Partnerships developed logically in the law merchant, and the common law of partnerships has been codified in the Uniform Partnership Act. A partnership is an association of two or more persons to carry on as co-owners, a business for profit. It is the result of an agreement.

This form of organization has many advantages: (1) since it is a matter of contract between individuals to which the state is not a party, it is easily formed; (2) the costs of formation are minimal; (3) it is not a taxable entity; (4) each owner as a general rule has an equal voice in management; (5) it may operate in more than one state without being required to comply with many legal formalities; and (6) partnerships are generally subject to less regulation and less governmental supervision than corporations. The fact that a partnership is not a taxable entity does not mean that partnership income is tax free. A partnership files an information return allocating its income among the partners and each partner pays income tax on the portion allocated to him.

There are several aspects of partnerships that may be considered disadvantageous in many cases. First, only a limited number of people may own such a business. Second, a partnership is dissolved any time a member ceases to be a partner either by withdrawal or death. Although dissolution is the subject matter of Chapter 44, it should be observed here that the perpetual existence of a corporation is often a distinct advantage as compared to easily dissolvable partnerships.

Third, the liability of a partner is unlimited as contrasted with the limited liability of a shareholder. The unlimited liability of a partner is applicable to both contract and tort claims. Fourth, since a partner is taxed on his share of the profits of a partnership, whether distributed to him or not, a partner may be required to pay income tax on money that is not received. This burden is an important consideration in a new business which is reinvesting its profits for expansion. A partner in such a business would have to have an independent means of paying the taxes on such income.

The greater advantages of corporate organization found in the tax laws have substantially reduced the significance of partnerships as a form of business organization. In the 1970s, the number of businesses using this form of organization will continue to decrease.

6-3. Limited Partnerships.

6-3. Limited Partnerships.   A limited partnership, just as other partnerships, comes into existence by virtue of an agreement. However, a limited partnership is like a corporation in that it is authorized by statute and the liability of one or more of the partners, but not of all, is limited to the amount of capital contributed at the time of the creation of the partnership. This latter characteristic supplies the name for this type of business organization, which is in effect a hybrid between the partnership and the corporation. A limited partnership may be formed by two or more persons, having one or more general partners and one or more limited partners. To create a limited partnership under the Uniform Limited Partnership Act, the parties must sign and swear to a certificate containing the following information: the name of the partnership; the character of the business, its location; the name and place of residence of each member; those who are to be the general and those who are to be the limited partners; the term for which the partnership is to exist; the amount of cash or the agreed value of property to be contributed by each partner; the additional contributions, if any, to be made from time to time by each partner; the time that any such contributions are to be returned to the limited partner; the share of profit or compensation each limited partner shall receive; the right that a limited partner has to substitute an assignee of his interest; the right to admit additional limited partners; the right given to one or more of the limited partners to priority over other limited partners as to contributions, and compensation by way of income; the right of a limited partner to demand property rather than cash in return for his contribution; and the right of the remaining general partners to continue the business on the death, retirement, or incapacity of other partners.

The certificate must be recorded in the county where the partnership has its principal place of business, and a copy must be filed in every community where it conducts business or has a representative office. In addition, most states require notice by newspaper publication. In the event of any change in the facts contained in the certificate as filed, such as a change in the name of the partnership, the capital, or other matters, a new certificate must be filed. If such a certificate is not filed and the partnership continues, the limited partners immediately become liable as general partners.

The statutes of most states require the partnership to conduct its business in a firm name which does not include the name of any of the limited partners or the word "Company." Some states specify that the word "Limited" shall be added. In some jurisdictions no liability will attach to the limited partners unless creditors are misled or injured by the failure of the firm to use the word "Limited" or by the use of the word "Company." A limited partner is not liable beyond his contribution to creditors of the partnership in the pursuit of the partnership business, unless the limited partner participates in the management and control of the business.[1] Participation in management makes the limited partner a general partner with unlimited liability, notwithstanding the certificate. A limited partnership cannot be dissolved voluntarily before the time for its termination as stated in the certificate, without the filing and publication of the notice of the dissolution. Upon dissolution, the distribution of the assets of the firm is prescribed in the statute which gives priority to limited partners over general partners after all creditors are paid.

The limited partnership is of special value in many new businesses and especially in real estate ventures such as shopping centers and apartment complexes. It gives the investor limited liability and the operators control of the venture. It allows the maximum use of the tax advantages of accelerated depreciation due to the fact that a partner can deduct losses as shown on the partnership tax return. Accelerated depreciation usually results in a tax loss in the early years but with a cash-flow gain. The limited partnership allows this loss to be immediately deducted instead of carried forward while the cash-flow gain is being paid out, as in the case of a corporation. When such ventures start to show a taxable gain, the limited partnership is often dissolved and a corporation formed.

The obvious disadvantage in a limited partnership is the fact that the limited partner cannot participate in management without a change of status to that of a general partner. However, he does have a right to inspect the books of the business and to receive an accounting, so that his situation, despite the restrictions imposed upon it, is not entirely undesirable.

6-4. Joint Venture. A joint venture, or joint adventure, occurs when two or more persons combine their efforts in a particular business enterprise and agree to share the profits or losses jointly or in proportion to their contributions. It is to be distinguished from a partnership in that the joint venture is a less

---

[1] *Filesi v. United States*, page 817

formal association and contemplates a single transaction or a limited activity whereas a partnership contemplates the operation of a general business.[2] It is a specific venture without the formation of a partnership or corporation.

While a partnership in most states is a legal entity, apart from the partners, a joint venture is not. A joint venture cannot sue or be sued except by or on behalf of the joint venturers individually.

Joint ventures file a partnership tax return and have many of the other legal aspects of partnerships. For example, the parties stand in a fiduciary relationship with each other and are agents for purposes of tort liability.

6-5. The Business Corporation.   A corporation comes into existence by an act of the state. It is a legal entity which usually has perpetual existence. The liability of the owners is limited to their investment.[3]   A corporation is a taxable entity paying a tax on its net profits. In addition, dividends paid to stockholders are also taxable, giving rise to the frequently made observation that corporate income is subject to double taxation. The accuracy of this observation will be discussed later.

The advantages of the corporate form of organization may be briefly summarized as follows: (1) it is the only method that will raise substantial capital from a large number of investors; (2) the investors have limited liability; (3) the organization can have perpetual existence; (4) it is possible for control to be vested in those with a minority of the investment by using such techniques as nonvoting or preferred stock; (5) ownership may be divided into many separate and unequal shares; (6) the investors, notwithstanding their status as owners, may also be employees entitled to such benefits as Workmen's Compensation, etc.; (7) certain laws such as those relating to usury are not applicable to corporations; and (8) the tax laws have several provisions that are favorable to corporations.

Among the frequently cited disadvantages of the corporate form of organization are (1) the cost of forming and maintaining the corporate form with its rather formal procedures; (2) expenditures such as license fees and franchise taxes that are assessed against corporations but not against partnerships; (3) the double taxation of corporate income and the frequently higher rates; (4) the requirement that it must be qualified to do business in a state;[4] (5) the fact that corporations are subject to more regulation by government at all levels than other forms; and (6) that a corporation must use an attorney in litigation, whereas a layman can proceed on his own behalf.[5]

The fact that taxation was listed as both an advantage and a disadvantage of the corporate form illustrates the overwhelming importance of the tax factor in choosing this particular form of organization. The corporate tax law provisions that most encourage incorporation are those relating to qualified profit sharing and pension plans. These provisions allow a corporation to deduct from taxable income its payments under a qualified plan. These payments are invested and the earnings are not subject to taxation when earned. Income tax is paid by the recipients on retirement and if received in a lump sum, the tax

[2] Fredrickson v. Kluever, page 820
[3] Shaw v. Bailey-McCune Company, page 822
[4] Eli Lilly and Company v. Sav-On-Drugs, Inc., page 823
[5] Tuttle v. Hi-Land Dairyman's Association, page 824

is at capital gains rates. To illustrate the advantages of such plans, assume that *A, B,* and *C* are shareholders and employees of the ABC Company. Assume also that the company has five additional employees and that the net income of the company is $100,000. If ABC Company pays $10,000 under a qualified plan, the income tax reduction is $4,800 (assuming no surtax and a 48 percent rate). The net cost of the payment to the company is $5,200. The $10,000 is credited to the accounts of the employees by a formula based on wages and years of service. The amounts credited to *A, B,* and *C* may exceed the $5,200, giving them an initial net gain and a tax-free investment. In addition, the employees have received benefits and security. *A, B,* and *C* would receive their savings upon retirement at a time when their tax rates would be lower and exemptions increased. Such plans have given the impetus to the incorporation of hundreds of thousands of small businesses.

Other advantages of the tax laws to corporations are (1) health insurance payments are fully deductible and not subject to the limitations applicable to individuals; (2) deferred compensation plans may be adopted; (3) earnings up to $25,000 are taxed at a rate of 22 percent, which is often lower than the individual investor's tax rate; (4) income that is needed in the business is not taxed to a person who does not receive it; and (5) accumulated income can be taken out as a capital gain on dissolution.

The corporate form is frequently at a disadvantage from a tax standpoint because of the double taxation aspect and because the 48 percent rate often exceeds the individual rate of the owners of the business. In addition, some states impose a higher tax on corporate income than on individual income; there are also many taxes that are imposed on corporations but not on individuals or partnerships.

In connection with the double taxation of corporate income, it should be noted that there are certain techniques which may be used to avoid, in part, the double taxation of corporate income. First of all, reasonable salaries paid to corporate employees may be deducted in computing the taxable income of the business. Thus, in a closely held corporation, in which all or most shareholders are officers or employees, this technique can be used to avoid double taxation of much of the corporate income. However, the Internal Revenue Code disallows a deduction for excessive or unreasonable compensation, and such payments are taxable as dividends. Therefore, the determination of the reasonableness of corporate salaries is an ever-present tax problem in the closely held corporation.

Secondly, the capital structure of a corporation may include both common stock and interest-bearing loans from shareholders. For example, assume that a company needs $200,000 to commence business. If $200,000 of stock is purchased, there will be no expense to be deducted. However, assume that $100,000 worth of stock is purchased and $100,000 is loaned to the company at 8 percent interest. In this case $8,000 of interest each year is deductible as an expense of the company, and thus subject to only one tax as interest income to the owners. Just as in the case of salaries, the Internal Revenue Code contains a counteracting rule relating to corporations that are undercapitalized. If the corporation is undercapitalized, interest payments will be treated as dividends and disallowed as deductible expenses.

The third technique for avoiding double taxation, at least in part, is simply not to pay dividends and to accumulate the earnings. After the earnings have been accumulated, the shareholders can sell their stock or dissolve the corporation. In both situations, the difference between the original investment and the amount received is given capital gains treatment. Here again, we have tax laws designed to counteract the above technique. There is a special income tax imposed on "excessive accumulated earnings" in addition to the normal tax, and rules relating to collapsible corporations.

Finally, there is a special provision in the Internal Revenue Code that allows small, closely held business corporations to be treated similarly to partnerships for income tax purposes. These corporations, known as Sub-Chapter S corporations, are discussed more fully in the next section.

6-6. The Sub-Chapter S Corporation.   The limited partnership is a hybrid between a corporation and a partnership in the area of liability. A similar hybrid known as a tax-option or Sub-Chapter S corporation exists in the tax area of the law.

The tax-option corporation is one that elects to be taxed in a manner similar to that of partnerships—i.e., to file an information return allocating income among the shareholders for immediate reporting regardless of dividend distributions, thus avoiding any tax on the part of the corporation.

Sub-Chapter S corporations cannot have more than ten shareholders, each of whom must sign the election to be taxed in the manner similar to a partnership. Corporations with more than 20 percent of their income from rents, interest, dividends, or royalties do not qualify. There are many technical rules of tax law involved in Sub-Chapter S corporations, but, as a rule of thumb, this method of taxation has distinct advantages for a business operating at a loss because the loss is shared and immediately deductible on the returns of the shareholders. It is also advantageous for businesses capable of paying out net profits as earned. In the latter case, the corporate tax is avoided. If net profits must be retained in the business, Sub-Chapter S tax treatment is disadvantageous because income tax is paid on earnings not received. There is also a danger of double taxation to the individual because undistributed earnings that have been taxed once are taxed again in the event of the death of a shareholder. Such corporations have the advantage of the corporate form without the double taxation of income. However, a recent change in the tax laws relating to pension plans has greatly reduced the advantages of such corporations. This change has given them equal status with partnerships and sole proprietorships for pension and profit sharing plan purposes. This status is discussed more fully in the next section.

6-7. The Professional Service Association.   Traditionally, professional services, such as those of a doctor, lawyer, or dentist, could only be performed by an individual and could not be performed by a corporation because the relationship of doctor and patient or attorney and client was considered a highly personal one. The impersonal corporate entity could not render the personal services involved.

The tax advantages of profit sharing and pension plans previously discussed in connection with corporations are not available to private persons and partnerships to the same extent that they are available to corporations. (An individual is limited to a $2,500 deduction under what is usually referred to as the H.R. 10 pension plan provision.) Therefore, in recent years professional persons have desired to incorporate or to form a professional association in order to obtain these tax advantages. As a result, almost every state has enacted statutes authorizing professional associations. These associations are legal entities similar to corporations. The IRS in a series of cases challenged these statutes and attempted to deny deductions for payments to pension plans by these professional service associations. However, in late 1969, the IRS conceded that organizations of professional people, organized under state professional association statutes, will generally be treated as corporations for tax purposes. The law of the state in which the professional service is being rendered must be consulted prior to the decision to form and operate such an association.

6-8. Joint-Stock Companies. A joint-stock company is a business arrangement which provides for the management of the business to be placed in the hands of trustees or directors. Under the constitution or bylaws of the organization, shares represented by certificates are issued to the various members who are joint owners in the enterprise. These shareholders elect the board of directors or trustees. The shares are transferable, the same as the shares of a corporation, and such transfer does not cause dissolution. Likewise, the death of one of the shareholders does not dissolve the organization as it does in the case of a partnership.[6] It exists for the period of time designated in the bylaws. Such an association is a partnership, even though the primary purpose of such an arrangement is to secure many of the advantages of a corporation. Unlimited liability continues, but in many other respects the features of a corporation are present. In many states by statute a suit may be brought against a joint-stock company as an entity.

6-9. Business Trusts. The business trust is an organization formed by trustees under a contract, called a declaration of trust, executed by the trustees. Under the agreement, the trustees issue certificates of beneficial interest, which are sold to investors.

The trustees take the capital in compliance with the agreement and operate the business, whatever it may be, as principals, for the benefit of the shareholders. Business Trusts have many of the characteristics of corporations, in that the trustees elect officers from among themselves, and in some states the shareholders at stated meetings, by virtue of the trust agreement, are permitted to elect the trustees.

Such an organization avoids the statutory regulations of a corporation, in that it is not a creature of the state, and seeks as well to avoid partnership liability on the part of the investors. The courts in most of the states, however, have held that if the investors under the trust agreement have a right to exercise some control over the management of the business, by way of election of trustees or otherwise, such shareholders are liable as partners. It is clear, on the other hand, that if such shareholders have no control over, or no right to

---

[6] Hammond et al. v. Otwell et al., page 825

interfere in any way with, the management of the business, they are beneficiaries under a trust agreement and are not liable as partners.[7] This business organization has been called different names, such as "Business Trust," "Massachusetts Trust," and "The Common Law Trust." As a substitute for a corporation, it has lost many of its advantages, owing to statutory regulation by the various states; as a method to avoid partnership liability, it is ineffective, in that a shareholder whose money is being risked in a business venture naturally desires to have some control over the policy and conduct of the business, and such reservations carry with them the obligation of partnership.

The trustees are usually held to have unlimited liability for all obligations of the business trust unless the contracts restrict the rights of the creditors to the assets of the trust. It is customary for business trusts to place this limiting clause in all contracts, particularly if there is any possible question about the solvency of the trust. Generally, those organizations known as "Business Trusts" engage in the investment business. Investors purchase shares or certificates which entitle the holders to income from and increased value of stocks and bonds purchased by the trustees or directors of trust.

6-10. Making the Decision.   The business with substantial capitalization will be a corporation for the reasons previously noted. If the business is to be owned and operated by relatively few persons, the decision as to the form of organization involves a consideration of the factors previously discussed, the most significant of which are (1) taxation, (2) liability, (3) control, (4) continuity, and (5) legal capacity. Legal capacity is the power of the business to sue and be sued in its own name and the power to own and dispose of property as well as to enter into contracts in its own name.

In evaluating the impact of taxation, an accountant or attorney will look at the projected profits or losses of the business, the ability to distribute earnings, and the tax brackets of the individuals involved as owners. A computation of the estimated total tax burden under the various forms of organization will be made. The results will be considered along with the other factors in making the decision as to the form of business organization to be used.

The generalization that partners have unlimited liability and stockholders limited liability must be qualified in the case of a closely held business. A small closely held corporation with limited assets and capital will find it difficult to obtain credit on the strength of its own credit standing alone, and as a practical matter, the shareholders will usually be required to add their own individual liability as security for the debts. For example, if the XYZ Company seeks a loan at a local bank, the bank will require the owners X, Y, and Z to personally guarantee repayment of the loan. This is not to say that closely held corporations do not have some degree of limited liability. The investors in those types of businesses are protected with limited liability for contractlike obligations that are imposed as a matter of law (such as taxes) and for debts resulting from torts that are committed by company employees while engaged in company business.

If the tax aspects dictate a partnership, and limited liability is desired by some investors, the limited partnership will be considered.

[7] Commercial Casualty Insurance Co. v. North et al., page 827

Issues of liability are not restricted to the investors in the business or to financial liability. Corporation law has developed several instances in which the directors and officers of the corporation will have liability to shareholders or to the corporation for acts or omission by such directors or officers in their official capacity. These matters will be discussed more fully in Chapter 46.

The significance of the law relating to control will be apparent in the discussions on formation and operation of partnerships and corporation in the chapters that follow. The desire of one or more individuals to control the business is a major factor in selecting the form, and the control issues are second only to taxation in importance.

The table on pages 818   and 819   summarizes the factors that are considered in choosing a form of organization.

CHOOSING THE FORM OF ORGANIZATION CASES

Filesi v. United States

352 F.2d 339 (1965)

BOREMAN, C. J. The Commissioner of Internal Revenue, asserting that the Jolly Tavern had been operated as a cabaret because dancing had been permitted to the music of a jukebox, assessed deficiencies in cabaret excise taxes, penalties, and interest in the amount of $46,567.28 against the taxpayer, Alfred Filesi, based on the receipts from the operation of the tavern. . . .

In the District Court, Filesi . . . contended that he was not liable for excise tax for the period from the first quarter of 1954 through the first quarter of 1956, as he was a "limited partner" during this period and did not become a general partner until a written partnership agreement was executed on April 4, 1956. . . .

At the close of all the evidence the District Court ruled as a matter of law that Filesi was a general partner for the period in dispute. . . .

. . . From 1949, when Filesi first became associated with the management of the Jolly Tavern until April 14, 1951, Filesi along with Muller and John Marshall were the only shareholders of a corporation organized to operate the tavern. Marshall wanted out of the business, and on April 14, 1951, the corporation was dissolved and Muller assumed to purchase Marshall's interest, but to do so Muller borrowed money from an outside source, and the loan was subsequently repaid from the profits of the Jolly Tavern before Filesi and Muller received their shares as partners. The effect of this transaction was that Filesi became the purchaser of one half of Marshall's interest. According to Filesi, Muller did not have funds to buy Filesi's interest also, so Muller persuaded him to leave his investment in the tavern. In return, Felesi testified, it was orally agreed that he was to manage the business at a stipulated salary and receive 50 percent of all profits but was not to be liable for any losses. The liquor license was transferred to Muller's name and the business was operated under this arrangement until April 4, 1956. On that date Muller and Filesi executed a written partnership agreement under which both were to share gains and losses equally. From April 4, 1956, to April 4, 1957, the tavern was operated under this written agreement. On the latter date the partnership was dissolved and Muller sold his interest to Filesi who has since owned and operated the tavern.

Filesi argues that he was a limited partner from April 14, 1951, to April 4,

Comparison of Characteristics of Business Organizations

Characteristic	Corporations		Partnerships	
	General	Sub-Chapter S	General	Limited
1. Method of Creation	Charter issued by state	Same + file agreement with IRS	Created by agreement of the parties	Same + file statutory form in public office
2. Liability of members	Shareholders have limited liability	Same	Partners have unlimited liability	General partners—unlimited liability; limited partners—limited liability
3. Duration	May be perpetual	Same	Termination by death, agreement, bankruptcy, or withdrawal of a partner	The term provided in the certificate
4. Transferability of interest	Generally freely transferable subject to limits of contacts between shareholders	Same	Not transferable	General partner—not transferable; limited partner—transferable
5. Management	Shareholders elect directors who set policy	Same	All partners in absence of agreement have equal voice	General partners have equal voice; limited partners have no voice
6. Taxation	Income taxed to corp.; dividends taxed to shareholders	Net income taxed to shareholders whether distributed or not	Not a taxable entity—net income taxed to partners whether distributed or not	Same

Characteristic	Corporations		Partnerships	
	General	Sub-Chapter S	General	Limited
7. Legal Entity for progress of: a. suit in firm name b. owning property in firm name c. bankruptcy d. limiting liability	Is a legal entity in all states. For all purposes	Same	By modern law is an entity for a. Yes b. Yes c. Yes d. No	Same
8. Transact business in other states	Must qualify to do business and obtain certificate of authority	Same	No limitation	Copy of certificate must be filed in all counties where doing business
9. Organization fee annual license fee and annual reports	All required	Same	None	None
10. Modification of amendment of articles	Must obtain state approval	Same	No requirement	Must file changes
11. Agency	A shareholder is not an agent of the corporation	Same	Each partner is both a principal and agent of his copartners	Limited partners are not principals or agents. General partners are the same as in general partnership.

1956, and as such he was not liable for any losses of the partnership during this period; that, as the excise tax from the first quarter of 1954 through the first quarter of 1956 would constitute a loss he should not be held accountable for the tax. We cannot agree. It is well settled that to obtain the protections and privileges of limited liability a person must comply with the statutory requirements regulating the formation of limited partnerships or otherwise be held liable as a general partner. The Annotated Code of Maryland specified the acts which must be performed by a person desiring to become a limited partner in the operation of a business within that State. It was clearly shown that Filesi did not comply with these provisions and, therefore, he cannot now claim the protection of a limitation of liability. It is clear from the evidence generally and from Filesi's own testimony that he openly and publicly took an active part in the management and control of the business. We think the District Court was correct in holding as a matter of law that Filesi was liable as a general partner for any excise tax properly assessed for the period in dispute.

Even assuming that Filesi was a limited partner his argument is unsound. According to applicable law, a limited partner is liable for any losses of the partnership to the extent of his investment in the assets of the business. On this point, however, no evidence was produced to show what Filesi's investment was for the period, although in 1951 it was slightly in excess of $10,000.

Cause reversed for other reasons.

Fredrickson v. Kluever

152 N.W.2d 346 (S. Dak.) 1967

HANSON, J. This action for personal injuries and property damage followed a collision of motor vehicles. The jury returned a verdict for defendant and plaintiff appeals.

Plaintiff, Russell Fredrickson, lives in Cherokee, Iowa. He is a cattle commission buyer for the Spencer Packing Company. His older brother, Eldon Fredrickson, lives on a farm nearby where he feeds cattle, and trucks in partnership with his son.

On October 18, 1962, Russell, Eldon, Eldon's wife, and Henry Anderson left Cherokee to attend a cattle sale at Highmore, South Dakota. The purpose of the trip was to purchase cattle. Although plaintiff owned the 1960 Oldsmobile car used for the trip, Eldon drove as he was in the habit of doing whenever the brothers were together. They arrived in Highmore around noon. Eldon took his wife to Holabird to visit a sister and immediately returned to the sale barn. The afternoon was spent at the sale. No cattle were purchased. Eldon left the sale to get his wife and the party left Highmore about 5:30 or 6:00 o'clock in the evening. Eldon again drove, with his wife riding in the front seat and Henry Anderson and plaintiff in the rear seat.

The defendant, Douglas Kluever, is a trucker from Bigelow, Minnesota. He was in Highmore on the day of the accident to truck cattle purchased by a Dale Robison. He drove a 1959 International semi-truck and trailer. After the cattle were loaded, defendant started east on Highway 14, the same route plaintiff's car was traveling.

U.S. Highways 14 and 281 run together south of Wolsey for approximately three miles at which point 14 curves off east toward Huron, and 281 continues straight south. The Fredrickson car followed defendant's truck through Wolsey. Somewhere south of town the Fredrickson car passed the truck. Eldon testified he was not familiar with the road and the intersection of Highways 14 and 281 was bigger than expected so he applied his brakes to prevent swerving. He didn't know anyone was behind him and did not observe the headlights from defendant's truck which collided with the rear end of the car.

According to defendant he had been proceeding south out of Wolsey between 50 and 55 miles per hour. As he approached the intersection in question he reduced his speed. Just before or right at the curve the Fredrickson car passed his truck. After passing, the driver of the Fredrickson car pulled back into the right lane and applied brakes. Defendant immediately applied his brakes, but was unable to avoid a collision.

Plaintiff was riding in the back seat of his car and was asleep at the time of the accident. He contends the negligence of the driver of his car could not be imputed to him as a matter of law and it was error to submit the issues of imputed contributory negligence and joint enterprise to the jury.

Imputed negligence means that by some legal relationship existing between two or more persons the negligence of one is charged to another. It is applied to bar recovery of a master for the negligence of his servant and to bar recovery by members of a joint adventure or joint enterprise for the negligence of one member. Section 491 Restatement of Torts seemingly establishes a two-way test for determining when the contributory negligence of one member of a joint enterprise will be imputed to bar recovery of another member against third persons. It provides "Any one of several persons engaged in a joint enterprise, such as to make each member of the group responsible for physical harm to other persons caused by the negligence of any member, is barred from recovery against such other persons by the negligence of any member of the group."

A partnership is statutorily defined as an association of two or more persons to carry on as co-owners a business for profit. This is ordinarily a formal association of a continuing nature for the conduct of a general business. Although a joint venture, or joint adventure as it is otherwise called, is sometimes compared to a partnership, it is usually a less formal association entered into to perform a more limited business function for a more limited time.

A "joint enterprise," on the other hand, is not easily defined. It is frequently used interchangeably with the term "joint adventure." In fact there is no significant difference. In *Scheuring* v. *Northern States Power Co.,* 67 S.D. 484, this court said: "To constitute a joint enterprise there must be both a community of interest in the object and purpose of the undertaking in which the automobile is being driven and an equal right in the occupants to direct each other in relation to the management of the vehicle." The court went on to quote with approval from *Farthing* v. *Hepinstall,* 243 Mich. 380, as follows: "To constitute a joint enterprise between a passenger and the driver of an automobile, within the meaning of the law of negligence, there must be such a community of interest in its operation as to give each an equal right of control. There must be a common responsibility for its negligent operation, and there can be no common responsibility unless there is a common right of control. It must be held that the driver is acting as the agent of the other members of the enterprise. The rule of joint enterprise in negligence cases is found on the law of principal and agent. On no other theory could the negligence of the driver be imputable to a passenger. Being parties to the same enterprise, they are assumed to have common control and possession of the machine. Otherwise, each could not be charged with the negligence of the other."

The elements necessary to constitute a joint enterprise are seldom found in purely social arrangements or matters of friendly accommodation between friends, neighbors, and relatives. As pointed out in Prosser, *Law of Torts,* 3rd ed., p. 490, "it is generally agreed that something more is required for a joint enterprise than the mere showing of a contract or agreement to travel together to a destination for a common purpose. Something in the nature of a common business, financial or pecuniary interest in the objective of the journey is said to be essential." The essential elements are generally considered to be: (1) an agreement, express or implied, among the members of the group; (2) a common purpose to be carried out by the group; (3) a community of pecuniary interest in that purpose among the members; and (4) an equal right to a voice in the direction and control of the enterprise, which gives an equal right of control."

The evidence in the present action falls short of showing the Fredrickson brothers were involved in a joint enterprise on their cattle buying trip. Apparently they went to the livestock sale at Highmore to purchase cattle separately; consequently, the element of a common financial interest in the purpose of the trip is lacking.

Reversed.

Shaw v. Bailey-McCune Company

355 P.2d 321 (Utah) 1960

The defendant, Bailey-McCune Company, leased real property from the plaintiffs and also purchased certain items of merchandise on credit. The individual defendants are stockholders in the corporation. The corporation failed financially and the plaintiffs contending that the corporate structure is a sham, seek to hold the stockholders personally liable for the unpaid rent and merchandise. The plaintiffs contend that the corporation was undercapitalized. The lower court dismissed the action against the individual defendants. The plaintiffs appealed.

CALLISTER, J. . . . The mere relation of being a stockholder in a debtor corporation does not under the law make a stockholder liable for the debts and obligations of the corporation. A corporation is a statutory entity which is regarded as having an existence and personality distinct from that of its stockholders even though the stock is owned by a single individual.

Under some circumstances the corporate entity may be disregarded in the interest of justice in such cases as fraud, contravention of law or contract, or public wrong. However, great caution should be exercised by the courts in disregarding the entity.

Moreover, the conditions under which the corporate entity may be disregarded or the corporation be regarded as the alter ego of the stockholders vary according to the circumstances in each case inasmuch as the doctrine is essentially an equitable one and for that reason is particularly within the province of the trial court.

The lower court found that the corporation was not a sham or the alter ego of the Baileys and refused to disregard the corporate entity. These findings of the trial court should not be overturned unless the evidence clearly preponderates against them. We have carefully examined the record and find no reason to reverse the trial court's determination.

Affirmed.

Eli Lilly and Company v. Sav-On-Drugs, Inc.

366 U.S. 276 1961

BLACK, J. The appellant Eli Lilly and Company, an Indiana corporation dealing in pharmaceutical products, brought this action in a New Jersey state court to enjoin the appellee Sav-On-Drugs, Inc., a New Jersey corporation, from selling Lilly's products in New Jersey at prices lower than those fixed in minimum retail price contracts into which Lilly had entered with a number of New Jersey drug retailers. . . . Sav-On moved to dismiss this complaint under a New Jersey statute that denies a foreign corporation transacting business in the State the right to bring any action in New Jersey upon any contract made there unless and until it files with the New Jersey Secretary of State a copy of its charter together with a limited amount of information about its operations and obtains from him a certificate authorizing it to do business in the State.

Lilly opposed the motion to dismiss, urging that its business in New Jersey was entirely in interstate commerce and arguing, upon that ground, that the attempt to require it to file the necessary information and obtain a certificate for its New Jersey business was forbidden by the Commerce Clause of the Federal Constitution. Both parties offered evidence to the Court in the nature of affidavits as to the extent and kind of business done by Lilly with New Jersey companies and people. On this evidence, the trial court made findings of fact and granted Sav-On's motion to dismiss, stating as its ground that "the conclusion is inescapable that the plaintiff [Lilly] was in fact doing business in this State at the time of the acts complained of and was required to, but did not, comply with the provisions of the Corporation Act." On appeal to the Supreme Court of New Jersey, this constitutional attack was renewed and the State Attorney General was permitted to intervene as a party-defendant to defend the validity of the statute. The State Supreme Court then affirmed the judgment upholding the statute, relying entirely upon the opinion of the trial court. We noted probable jurisdiction to consider Lilly's contention that the constitutional question was improperly decided by the state courts.

The record shows that the New Jersey trade in Lilly's pharmaceutical products is carried on through both interstate and intrastate channels. Lilly manufactures these products and sells them in interstate commerce to certain selected New Jersey wholesalers. These wholesalers then sell the products in intrastate commerce to New Jersey hospitals, physicians and retail drug stores, and these retail stores in turn sell them, again in intrastate commerce, to the general public. It is well established that New Jersey cannot require Lilly to get a certificate of authority to do business in the State if its participation in this trade is limited to its wholly interstate sales to New Jersey wholesalers. Under the authority of the so-called "drummer" cases, such as *Robbins* v. *Shelby County Taxing District,* Lilly is free to send salesmen into New Jersey to promote this interstate trade without interference from regulations imposed by the State. On the other hand, it is equally well settled that if Lilly is engaged in intrastate as well as interstate aspects of the New Jersey drug business, the State can require it to get a certificate of authority to do business. In such a situation, Lilly could not escape state regulation merely because it is also engaged in interstate commerce. We must then look to the record to determine whether Lilly is engaged in intrastate commerce in New Jersey.

The findings of the trial court, based as they are upon uncontroverted evidence presented to it, show clearly that Lilly is conducting an intrastate as well as an interstate business in New Jersey. . . .

We agree with the trial court that "[t]o hold under the facts above recited that plaintiff [Lilly] is not doing business in New Jersey is to completely ignore reality." Eighteen "detailmen," working out of a big office in Newark, New Jersey, with Lilly's name on the door and in the lobby of the building, and with Lilly's district manager and secretary in charge, have been regularly engaged in work for Lilly which relates directly to the intrastate aspects of the sale of Lilly's products. These eighteen "detailmen" have been traveling throughout the State of New Jersey promoting the sales of Lilly's products, not to the wholesalers, Lilly's interstate customers, but to the physicians, hospitals and retailers who buy those products in intrastate commerce from the wholesalers. To this end, they have provided these hospitals, physicians and retailers with up-to-date knowledge of Lilly's products and with free advertising and promotional material designed to encourage the general public to make more intrastate purchases of Lilly's products. And they sometimes even directly participate in the intrastate sales themselves by transmitting orders from the hospitals, physicians and drugstores they service to the New Jersey wholesalers. . . .

Lilly also contends that even if it is engaged in intrastate commerce in New Jersey and can by virtue of that fact be required to get a license to do business in that State, New Jersey cannot properly deny it access to the courts in this case because the suit is one arising out of the interstate aspects of its business. In this regard, Lilly relies upon such cases as *International Textbook Co. v. Pigg,* holding that a State cannot condition the right of a foreign corporation to sue upon a contract for the interstate sale of goods. We do not think that those cases are applicable here, however, for the present suit is not of that kind. Here, Lilly is suing upon a contract entirely separable from any particular interstate sale and the power of the State is consequently not limited by cases involving such contracts.

Affirmed.

Tuttle v. Hi-Land Dairyman's Association

350 P.2d. 619 (Utah) 1960

The credit manager of a dairy association brought suit against Tuttle in the small claims court without the assistance of an attorney. Judgment was entered and garnishment proceedings commenced. Tuttle then brought this suit to enjoin the proceedings since the association proceeded without an attorney. From a finding for Tuttle, the association appeals.

WADE, J. . . . As to the contention that the court erred in finding that a corporation cannot proceed in a small claims court except through a licensed attorney, appellants argue, and we agree, that a corporation is a "person" within the meaning of the provisions of Sec. 78-6-2, U.C.A. 1953. That section provides that actions may be maintained in the small claims court by any person who executes an affidavit setting forth the nature of the claim. However, from the fact that a corporation is a "person" which can maintain an action in a small claims court, it does not follow that any officer or employee of such corporation can properly institute such an action by executing such affidavit and appearing in behalf of the corporation at the hearing provided in the Small Claim Courts Act. Corporations are different in that respect from natural persons. A corporation cannot practice law and must have a licensed attorney representing it in court matters.

As stated in *Paradise* v. *Nowlin, . . .*

> A composite of the rule in the decided cases, overwhelmingly sustained by the authorities, may be thus stated: A natural person may represent himself and present his own case to the court although he is not a licensed attorney. A corporation is not a natural person. It is an artificial entity created by law and as such it can neither practice law nor appear or act in person. Out of court it must act in its affairs through its agents and representatives and in matters in court it can act only through licensed attorneys. A corporation cannot appear in court by an officer who is not an attorney and it cannot appear *in propria persona. . . .*

. . . Affirmed.

Hammond et al. v. Otwell et al.

170 Ga. 832 (1930)

The plaintiffs, Hammond and others, brought this action against the defendants who were allegedly members of a joint-stock association, People's Bank. The plaintiffs all have claims against the now defunct bank. The defendants contended that the bank was a partnership which had been dissolved by the prior death of some of the partners. The lower court granted a nonsuit as to all of the defendants except one, and the plaintiffs excepted.

HINES, J. . . . The question whether a joint-stock company can be legally created in this state by agreement of parties, without legislative action, has been discussed by counsel for the defendants; but in the view which we take of this case we deem it unnecessary to pass upon this question. The controlling question is whether the articles of association, the substance of which is above set out, created a partnership or a joint-stock company. It is difficult to frame an exact definition of a joint-stock company, one sufficiently comprehensive to embrace every essential element, and sufficiently exclusive to exclude every irrelevant factor. It has been held that at common law joint-stock companies are regarded as partnerships. It has been said that unincorporated joint-stock companies are governed by the same general principles as are applicable to partnerships. It has been said that such companies are partnerships except in form. It has been held that they are partnerships with some of the powers of corporations. But such companies are not entirely controlled by the legal rules and principles which govern ordinary partnerships. (*Spotswood* v. *Morris,* 12

Idaho 360, 85 Pac. 1094, 6 L.R.A. (N.S.) 665.) In a joint-stock company there is no *delectus personae* as in the ordinary partnership. It has been declared that one distinction between a joint-stock company and a partnership is that the death of a member of the former does not ordinarily dissolve a joint-stock company, whereas it does have that effect in an ordinary partnership. Another distinction is that in a partnership each member speaks and acts as the agent of the firm, while this is not true in a joint-stock company. It has been declared that a joint-stock company at common law lies midway between a corporation and a partnership, and partakes of the nature of both. The changeability of membership or transferability of shares is often used as a determining criterion between ordinary partnerships and joint-stock companies. . . . "The fundamental distinction between ordinary partnerships and joint-stock companies is that the partnership consists of a few individuals known to each other, bound together by ties of friendship and mutual confidence, and who therefore are not at liberty, without the consent of all, to retire from the firm, and substitute other persons in their places, and the decease of a member works a dissolution of the firm; whereas, a joint-stock company consists of a large number of individuals not necessarily or indeed usually acquainted with each other at all, so that it is a matter of comparative indifference whether changes are made among them or not, and consequently the certificates and shares in such associations may be transferred at will, without the consent of other members, and the decease of a member does not work a dissolution of the association or entitle the personal representative to an accounting. In joint-stock companies there is no *delectus personae.*"

In view of these fundamental distinctions between ordinary partnerships and joint-stock companies, in which class does the association with which we are dealing fall? The answer to this question is not entirely free from doubt. We cannot say that this association consisted of such a large number of individuals as to hold that it falls within the class of joint-stock companies. The articles of association limit the transferability of the shares of the members of the association. In the first place, a member desiring to withdraw from the business must give 60 days notice in writing of his intention to do so. In the second place, a member can only sell, transfer, and convey his interest in the bank to some individual, corporation, or firm who is acceptable to the finance committee in charge of said business, as a shareholder in the bank. Here the right of *delectus personae* is reserved to the members composing the association. In joint-stock companies the members have no right to decide what new members shall be admitted; on the other hand, the right of *delectus personae* is an inherent quality of an ordinary partnership. The provision that the shares shall be of the par value of $100, and that certificate shall be issued to the members, indicating the amount paid and the amount of interest that each subscriber has in the business of the bank, is not conclusive of the fact that the association is a joint-stock company. Such provision is consistent with the formation of a partnership. The shares are issued to indicate the amounts paid in by the members and the amount of interest the subscriber has in the bank. Of course, this provision can be looked to in determining the character of the association. Again, the provision that the business shall be conducted by a finance committee to be elected or appointed by the subscribers and that each subscriber shall be entitled to one vote for each $100 or for each share paid in by him, does not conclusively establish the character of the association as a joint-stock company. It can be looked to in the solution of this question. All of the above provisions are consistent with the view that the association established by this agreement was a partnership and not a joint-stock company. The articles of association expressly declare that it is the purpose of the members signing the same to establish a partnership. Again, the articles of association declare that the committee appointed to conduct the business of the bank shall select a cashier and general manager who shall "be in charge of disbursing the funds belonging to the partnership hereby formed."

. . . We hold that under the articles of association a partnership was formed by the defendants for the purpose of conducting a banking business.

Having reached the conclusion that the association formed by the defendants under the articles of agreement constituted a partnership, we are next to consider the question whether the death of three of the members of the partnership dissolved it; these deaths occurring prior to the contraction of the debts upon which the plaintiffs sue in this case. Every partnership is dissolved by the death of one of the parties. A dissolution puts an end to all the powers and rights resulting from the partnership. As to third persons, it absolves the partners from all liability for future contracts and transactions, but not for transactions that are past. After dissolution, a partner has no power to bind the firm by a new contract, or to revive one already for any cause extinct, nor to renew or continue an existing liability. When one of the partners dies, it is not necessary that notice should be given to third persons or to the world of the dissolution of the partnership. The death of a partner supplies such notice. So, when the debts sued on in this case were contracted, the partnership doing business as the People's Bank had been dissolved by the death of several of its members; and members of the partnership who had no part in creating these debts could not be held liable by reason of their membership in the dissolved partnership.

Applying the principles above ruled, the trial judge did not err in granting a nonsuit as to all the defendants except M. W. Webb.

Commercial Casualty Insurance Co. v. North et al.

320 Ill. App. 221 (1943)

The plaintiff brought this action against the defendants, who were the beneficiaries of a business trust in the construction business. The plaintiff had furnished a performance bond for the business trust and had been required to defend a legal action for an alleged breach of the construction contract. The plaintiff seeks to recover the expenses incurred in defending the suit. The lower court ruled in favor of the defendants and the plaintiff appealed.

DOVE J. . . . Appellant invokes the rule that when the beneficiaries of an alleged trust are given control over the management of the trust property, the so-called trust agreement, as a matter of law, creates a partnership.

. . . In *Schumann-Heink* v. *Folsom* (328 Ill. 321, 327), the court sets out in the opinion the well-established rule in such cases, in the following language: "There are also essential differences between a business trust and a partnership, but there are times when it is difficult to determine whether the declaration of trust relieves the trustees and shareholders from liability as partners.

A partnership is, in effect, a contract of mutual agency, each partner acting as a principal in his own behalf and as agent for his copartner. Where, under the declaration of trust, the unit holders retain control over the trustees and have authority to control the management of the business the partnership relation exists. On the other hand, where the declaration of trust gives the trustees full control in the management of the business of the trust and the certificate holders are not associated in carrying on the business and have no control over the trustees, then there is no liability as partners."

We agree with the claim of appellees that the trust agreement in this case goes further than a positive vestiture of powers in the trustees, and negatives any right of control in the beneficiaries. After generally and in detail vesting complete control of the business and the property in the trustees, too voluminously set out to be repeated here, Paragraph Fourth (F) concludes with these words: "and the right of said Trustees to manage, control and administer the said trust estate shall be absolute and unconditional, free from the control or management of the Certificate Holders." And Paragraph Ninth (C) provides: "The ownership of interests hereunder shall not entitle the Certificate Holder to any title in or to the trust property whatsoever, or . . . for an accounting, or for any voice or control whatsoever of the trust property or of the management of said property or business connected therewith by the trustees."

. . . Our conclusion is that the trust agreement is valid, and appellees are not liable to appellant individually or as partners for any of the reasons urged.

Affirmed.

CHAPTER 41
REVIEW QUESTIONS AND PROBLEMS

1. The Green River Club, a voluntary unincorporated recreational club, brought an action to enjoin the enforcement of a state civil rights statute against the club, maintaining the statute was inapplicable. May the club bring the action?

2. *A, B,* and *C,* three physicians, operated the Sunnyhill Sanitarium as partners. As a result of *C's* medical negligence, *X,* a patient, died. May *X's* wife recover for wrongful death from *A* and *B?*

3. *A,* the owner of an automobile dealership, and *B,* signed and recorded a limited partnership agreement in which *A* was the general partner, and *B* the limited partner. *B* contributed $10,000 and worked, under *A's* control, as manager of the service department. *C,* a creditor of the partnership, obtained a judgment for $25,000 against the partnership. This amount exceeded the partnership's assets and *A's* personal assets combined. May *C* reach *B's* personal assets?

4. *A* and *B* orally agreed to purchase and to operate a motel-restaurant, although no formal partnership agreement was ever executed. *B* purchased the motel-restaurant personally, without informing *A* of the transaction. Does *A* have a remedy against *B?*

5. *A, B,* and *C* filed articles of incorporation with the state of Ohio, but failed to perfect the corporation by fulfilling all of the statutory require-

ments. They proceeded to operate a warehouse together. *X* entered the warehouse and because of *A*'s negligence fell down an abandoned elevator shaft. May *X* recover from the personal assets of *B* and *C*?

6. Seventy persons gave $10,000 each to *M* under a declaration of trust, whereby *M* was to use the money to organize and operate a movie production business. *M* and four other trustees were given full powers of control, title to all property, and the authority to fill all vacancies on the board of trustees. *X*, a creditor of the firm, sues the shareholders in their personal capacities. May he recover?

7. John Doe and Richard Roe wish to enter the camping equipment manufacturing business. Assume that each of the following facts exist. In each case which type of business association would be most advantageous?

    a.   Doe is an expert in the field of camping gear production and sale, but has not funds. Roe knows nothing about such production, but is willing to contribute all necessary capital.

    b.   Camping gear production requires large amounts of capital, much more than Doe and Roe can raise personally or together, yet they wish to control the business.

    c.   Some phases of production and sale are rather dangerous, and a relatively large number of tort judgments may be anticipated.

    d.   Sales will take place on a nationwide basis.

    e.   Doe and Roe are both sixty-five years old. No profits are expected for at least five years, and interruption of the business before that time will make it a total loss.

    f.   Several other persons wish to put funds into the business, but are unwilling to assume personal liability.

    g.   The anticipated earnings over cost, at least for the first few years, will be approximately $70,000. Doe and Roe wish to draw salaries of $25,000 each; they also want a hospitalization and retirement plan, all to be paid from these earnings.

    h.   A loss is expected for the first three years, due to the initial capital outlay and the difficulty in entering the market.

Formation of
Partnerships

6-11. Introduction. A *partnership* is an association of two or more persons to carry on as co-owners a business for profit. It is the result of an agreement between competent parties, either expressed or implied, to place their money, effects, labor or skill, or a combination of them in a business and to divide the profits and losses.[1] Express partnership agreements may be either oral or written, but such agreements should be reduced to writing and be carefully prepared. The provisions usually contained in articles of partnership will be discussed later in this chapter.

Issues concerning the existence of a partnership may arise between the parties or between the alleged partnership and third parties. The legal issues in these two situations are substantially different. When the issue is between the alleged partners, it is essentially a question of intention. This is discussed more fully in the next section. When the issue concerns liability to a third person, the question involves not only intention as to the actual existence of the partnership but issues of estoppel as well. This matter is discussed more fully in Section 6-13.

6-12. Implied Partnerships. As previously noted, a partnership between the parties may be implied from the conduct of the parties. The basic question is whether the parties intend a relationship which includes the essential elements of a partnership, not whether they intend to be partners.

If the essential elements of a partnership are present, the mere fact that the parties do not think they are becoming partners is immaterial. If the parties agree upon an arrangement that is a partnership in fact, it is immaterial whether they call it something else or that they declare that they are not partners. On the other hand, the mere fact that the parties themselves call the

[1] Grau v. Mitchell, page 835

830

relation a partnership will not make it so, if they have not, by their contract, agreed upon an arrangement which by the law is a partnership in fact.

The essential attributes of a partnership are a common interest in the business and management and a share in the profits and losses. However, if there is a sharing of profits, a partnership may be found to exist even though there is no sharing of losses.

The presence of a common interest in property and management is not enough to establish a partnership by implication. Also, an agreement to share the gross returns of a business, sometimes called gross profits, does not of itself prove an intention to form a partnership. However, the Uniform Partnership Act provides that the receipt by a person of a share of the real or net profits in a business is prima facie evidence that he is a partner in the business.[2] The presumption that a partnership exists by reason of sharing net profits is not conclusive and may be overcome by evidence that the share in the profits is received for some other purpose such as payment of a debt by installments, wages, rent, annuity to a widow of a deceased partner, interest on a loan, or as payment for goodwill by installments.[3] For example, bonuses are frequently paid as a percent of profit, and such a payment does not make the employee a partner.

6-13. Partner by Estoppel.   Insofar as third persons are concerned, partnership liability may be predicated upon the legal theory of estoppel. Where a person by words, spoken or written, or by conduct, represents himself or consents to another's representing him to another to be a partner in an existing partnership, or a partner with other persons not in a partnership, he is not a partner but is liable to any party to whom such representation has been made.[4] Such liability, created by estoppel, does not arise, however, unless the third party gives credit to the firm or other persons in reliance upon such representation. If the facts in any particular case indicate that such party knew the true facts, or should reasonably have known them, no liability on the basis of partnership is created. If the representation is made in a public manner either personally or with consent, the apparent partner is liable if credit is extended to the partnership, even if the creditor did not actually know of the representation. This is a statutory exception to the usual estoppel requirement of actual reliance.

If the estoppel creates a partnership liability, the apparent partner is liable as though he were an actual member of the firm. If no partnership liability results from the conduct or representation of one not a partner, the party making the representation may nevertheless be liable jointly with other persons, if any, so consenting to the contract or representation as to incur liability.

Liability based on estoppel is similar to that of a principal based on the apparent authority of an agent or an ostensible agent. If a person not a partner holds himself out to be a partner and all members of the firm consent to it, a partnership obligation results. If less than all members consent, it is the joint obligation of the person holding himself out to be a partner and those partners consenting to it.

[2] Troy Grain & Fuel Co. v. Rolston et al., page 836.
[3] Trojnar v. Bihlman, page 837.
[4] Brown & Bigelow v. Roy, page 838.

The courts are not in accord as to whether a person is under a duty to affirmatively disclaim a reputed partnership where the representation of partnership was not made by or with the consent of the person sought to be charged as a partner. Some court cases hold that if a person is held out as a partner and he knows it, he should be chargeable as a partner unless he takes reasonable steps to give notice that he is not, in fact, a partner. Other cases indicate that there is no duty to deny false representations of partnership where the ostensible partner did not participate in making the misrepresentation.

The doctrine of estoppel is used not only to impose liability on one not a partner but also to impose liability on a partner for acts of another partner beyond his authority. For example, if one partner, with the knowledge but not the consent of the other partner, accepts promissory notes in matters outside the scope of the partnership business and negotiates them by endorsing the partnership name, the partnership will be bound on the unauthorized endorsement of the negotiable paper by the partner, under the doctrine of estoppel, if the course of conduct is allowed to continue sufficiently long to supply the requirement of justifiable reliance.

ARTICLES OF PARTNERSHIP

6-14. Introduction. The articles of partnership will vary from business to business, but among the subjects usually contained in such agreements are the following: the names of the partners and of the partnership; its purpose and duration; the capital contributions of each partner; the method of sharing profits and losses; the effect of advances; the salaries, if any, to be paid the partners;[5] the method of accounting and the fiscal year; the rights and liabilities of the parties upon the death or withdrawal of a partner; and the procedures to be followed upon dissolution.

The Uniform Partnership Act or other partnership statute is a part of the agreement as if it had actually been written into the contract or made part of its stipulations. The Uniform Partnership Act is not in derogation of the common law and is not strictly construed. The sections which follow discuss some of the more important provisions of partnership agreements and indicate the effect of the Uniform Act on the agreement.

6-15. The Profit and Loss Provision. Unless the agreement is to the contrary, each partner has a right to share equally in the profits of the enterprise, and each partner is under a duty to contribute equally to the losses. Capital contributed to the firm is a liability owing by the firm to the contributing partners. If, on dissolution, there are not sufficient assets to repay each partner his capital, such amount is considered as a loss and must be met like any other loss of the partnership. For example, a partnership is composed of *A, B,* and *C. A* contributed $20,000, *B* contributed $10,000, and *C* contributed $4,000. The firm is dissolved, and upon the payment of firm debts there remains only $10,000 of firm assets. Since the total contribution to capital was $34,000, the operating loss is $24,000. This loss must be borne equally by *A, B,* and *C,* so that the loss for each is $8,000. This means that *A* is entitled to be reimbursed to the extent of his $20,000 contribution less $8,000, his share of

---

[5] Chambers v. Sims, page 840

the loss, or net of $12,000. *B* is entitled to $10,000, less $8,000, or $2,000. Since *C* has contributed only $4,000, he must now contribute to the firm an additional $4,000 in order that his loss will equal $8,000. The additional $4,000 contributed by *C*, plus the $10,000 remaining, will now be distributed so that *A* will receive $12,000 and *B* $2,000.

Occasionally articles of copartnership specify the manner in which profits are to be divided, but neglect to mention possible losses. In such cases, the losses are borne in the same proportion that profits are to be shared. In the event that losses occur when one of the partners is insolvent and his share of the loss exceeds the amount owed him for advances and capital, the excess must be shared by the other partners. They share this unusual loss, with respect to each other, in the same ratio that they share profits.

Thus in the above example, if *C* is insolvent, *A* and *B* would each bear an additional $2,000 loss.

In addition to the right to be repaid his contributions, whether by way of capital or advances to the partnership property, the partnership must indemnify every partner in respect of payments made and personal liabilites reasonably incurred by him in the ordinary and proper conduct of its business, or for the preservation of its business or property.

6-16. The Partnership Capital Provision.   Partnership capital consists of the total credits to the capital accounts of the various partners, provided the credits are for permanent investments in the business. Such capital represents that amount which the partnership is obligated to return to the partners at the time of dissolution, and it can be varied only with the consent of all the partners. Undivided profits which are permitted by some of the partners to accumulate in the business do not become part of the capital. They, like temporary advances by firm members, are subject to withdrawal at any time unless the agreement provides to the contrary.

The amount which each partner is to contribute to the firm, as well as the credit he is to receive for assets contributed, is entirely dependent upon the partnership agreement.

A person may become a partner without a capital contribution. For example, he may contribute services to balance the capital investment of the other partners. Such a partner, however, has no capital to be returned at the time of liquidation. Only those who receive credit for capital investments—which may include goodwill, patent rights, and so forth, if agreed upon—are entitled to the return of capital when dissolution occurs.

If the investment is in a form other than money, the property no longer belongs to the contributing partner. He has vested the firm with title and he has no greater equity in the property than any other party. At dissolution he recovers only the amount allowed to him for the property invested.

6-17. Provisions Relating to Partnership Property.   It is obvious that a partnership may use its own property, the property of the individual partners, or the property of some third person. It frequently becomes important, especially on dissolution and where claims of firm creditors are involved, to ascertain exactly what property constitutes partnership property in order to ascertain the rights of partners and firm creditors to specific property.

As a general rule, the agreement of the parties will determine what property is properly classified as partnership property. In absence of an express agreement, what constitutes partnership property is ascertained from the conduct of the parties, and from the purpose for and the way in which property is used in the pursuit of the business.[6] The Uniform Partnership Act, in general terms, states: (1) All property originally brought into the partnership stock, or subsequently acquired by purchase or otherwise on account of the partnership, is partnership property. (2) Unless the contrary intention appears, property acquired with partnership funds is partnership property.

Since a partnership has the right to acquire, own, and dispose of personal property in the firm name, legal documents affecting the title to partnership personal property may be executed in the firm name by any partner. The Uniform Partnership Act also treats a partnership as a legal entity for the purposes of title to real estate which may be held in the firm name. Title so acquired can be conveyed in the partnership name; though without words of inheritance a deed passes the entire estate of the grantor, unless a contrary intent appears. Where title to real property is in the partnership name, any partner may convey title to such property by a conveyance executed in the partnership name. To be effective such a conveyance must be within the terms of the partnership agreement or within the pursuit of the partnership business.

6-18. The Name Provision. Since a partnership is created by the agreement of the parties, they select the name to be used. This right of selection is subject to two limitations by statute in many states. First, a partnership may not use the word "company" or other language that would imply the existence of a corporation. Secondly, if the name is other than that of the partners, they must comply with an assumed name statute which requires the giving of public notice as to the actual identity of the partners. Failure to comply with this assumed name statute may result in the partnership's being denied access to the courts to sue its debtors, or it may result in criminal actions being brought against those operating under the assumed name. The firm name is an asset of the firm, and as such it may also be sold, assigned, or disposed of in any manner the parties agree upon.[7] Also it should be recognized that the firm can sue and be sued in its firm name in most states and can go through bankruptcy as a firm. To this extent and to the extent previously discussed in Section 6-17 relating to property, a partnership is a legal entity. It is not a legal entity to the same extent as a corporation, however.

6-19. Provisions Relating to Goodwill. Goodwill, which is usually transferred with the name, is based upon the justifiable expectation of the continued patronage of old customers and the probable patronage of new customers resulting from good reputation, satisfied customers, established location, and past advertising. Goodwill is usually considered in an evaluation of the assets of the business, and it is capable of being sold and transferred. Upon dissolution caused by the death of one of the partners, it must be accounted for by the surviving partner to the legal representative of the deceased partner, unless otherwise agreed upon in the Buy and Sell Agreement.

[6] Sanderfur v. Ganter, page 841
[7] O'Hara v. Lance et ux., page 842

When goodwill and the firm name are sold, an agreement not to compete is usually part of the sales agreement.[8] Such an agreement may be implied, but should be a part of the buy and sell provisions.

6-20. The "Buy and Sell" Provisions. Either as part of the partnership agreement or by separate contract, the partners should provide for the contingency of death or withdrawal of a partner. This contingency is covered by a buy and sell agreement, and it is imperative that the terms of the buy and sell provisions be agreed upon before either party knows whether he is a buyer or a seller. Agreement after the status of the parties becomes known is extremely difficult, if not impossible. If such agreement is lacking, many additional problems will arise upon the death or withdrawal of a partner, and there are many possibilities of litigation and economic loss to all concerned. Many of these problems can be avoided by providing a method whereby the surviving partner can purchase the interest of the deceased partner or the remaining partner can purchase the interest of the withdrawing partner. A method of determining the price to be paid for such interest should be provided. The time and method of payment should be stipulated, and the buy and sell agreement should specify whether a partner has an option to purchase the interest or has a duty to do so.

It is common for partners to provide for life insurance on each other's lives. In the event of a partner's death, proceeds of the insurance are utilized to purchase the deceased partner's interest. Premiums on such life insurance are not deductible for tax purposes but are usually treated as an expense for accounting purposes. There are a variety of methods for holding title to the insurance. It may be individually owned or business owned. The provisions of the policy should be carefully integrated into the partnership agreement; each partner's estate plan should also properly consider the ramifications of this insurance and of the buy and sell agreement.

FORMATION OF PARTNERSHIPS CASES

Grau v. Mitchell
397 P.2d 488 (Colo.) 1964

DAY, J. . . . Plaintiff filed suit alleging a copartnership with the defendant in the operation of a business in Parshall, Colorado. He sought dissolution of the partnership, appointment of a receiver, an accounting of the partnership assets, liabilities and profits, and distribution to the partners according to their respective rights and interests. . . .

Trial was to the court which entered findings of fact and conclusions of law and judgment of dismissal in favor of defendant. It held that the evidence failed to support this claim. . . .

No good purpose would be served in detailing the complete history of plaintiff's work in and around defendant's business establishment for the period involved. A reading of the record fails to disclose any of the elements of a partnership between the parties.

[8] Bergum v. Weber, page 844

The real estate was owned by defendant, and there is nothing in the record to establish plaintiff's interest in the real property and improvements thereon. As to the operation of the business, the defendant kept the books, maintained the bank account in her name, paid all the bills, and compensated plaintiff either in cash or "in kind" for all the work that he did. No partnership returns were filed with either the federal or state government. Plaintiff's remuneration had no relationship with the business making or losing money. He was not able to establish any agreement for a share of the profits, and there was nothing to make him liable for any of the debts.

At one time in the relationship there was some talk of a partnership, and pursuant thereto, an agreement drawn up which plaintiff refused to consummate because, as he said, "he wasn't going to assume any part of the indebtedness; also, he wanted a half interest in the entire real estate." This evidence in itself would be sufficient to defeat the claim of a partnership.

This court has stated that a partnership is a contract, express or implied, between two or more competent persons to place their money, effects, labor or skill, or some or all of them, into a business, and to divide the profits and bear the losses in certain proportions.

In reading the record one cannot find any evidence of an agreement, oral or written, express or implied, wherein the parties were joined together to carry on the business for a profit and to share the losses. The . . . claim was properly dismissed. . . .

Affirmed.

Troy Grain & Fuel Co. v. Rolston et al.

227 S.W.2d 66 (Mo.) 1950

The plaintiff, Troy Grain & Fuel Co., brought this action against Miller Howard and Jackson Rolston, as partners, for the unpaid balance due for corn and oats delivered. Howard owned two trucks, and it was agreed that he would furnish the trucks and Rolston the labor in hauling grain. The profits from the operation were to be divided equally. A judgment was rendered in favor of the plaintiff, and defendant Howard appealed.

SPERRY, Comm. . . . Howard stated that he and Rolston verbally agreed that Rolston should furnish the labor and use his trucks in hauling grain; that Rolston should keep books on the transactions, pay all expense of operation, and give Howard half of the profits as rent on the trucks; that Rolston kept books and delivered same to him, which he then had in court (but they were not offered in evidence); that Rolston kept the bank account in his own name and wrote all checks thereon; that they operated under this arrangement until shortly after these transactions occurred. He denied the existence of a partnership or that he was to bear any losses occuring in the operation.

The evidence made a submissible case on the question of partnership between Howard and Rolston. Partnership is a relation arising out of contract expressed or implied whereby two or more parties agree to engage in a common enterprise, each contributing capital or services and each sharing in the profits and losses. In the absence of proof of an express contract a partnership may be proved by evidence of the entire transaction, and construed from that, in the light of surrounding circumstances. The testimony of both Howard and

Rolston was to the effect that they agreed that Howard should furnish his trucks, Rolston furnish the labor, and that Rolston should buy, transport, and sell grain, the profits thereof to be equally divided after payment of expenses. Sharing the profits of a business venture, where one furnishes capital and the other labor, constitutes prima facie evidence of the existence of a partnership. While an agreement to share profits in such a venture is not conclusive proof of the existence of a partnership, it is prima facie proof thereof and raises a presumption of partnership. If such presumption is not overcome by other evidence tending to prove that, in fact, the parties intended there to be no partnership, such prima facie proof of the existence of a partnership becomes conclusive. It is true that there was no direct proof that the partners were to share the losses accruing in the venture, nevertheless their agreement to share profits implies a sharing of loss; and that presumption can only be overcome by evidence tending to prove the contrary. While a partnership relationship necessarily rests on contract, as between the parties themselves, the contracting parties are not required to know and fully understand all of the legal incidents flowing therefrom. Parties "entering into agreements and transactions which, by the law of the land constitute them partners, whatever they may please to say or think about it, or by whatever name they may choose to call it," will be held to be partners. We hold that there was substantial evidence tending to prove that Howard and Rolston were partners; and the determination of that question was for the jury.

    ... *The judgment should be affirmed.*

Trojnar v. Bihlman

200 N.E.2d 227 (Ind.) 1964

HUNTER, J. This is an appeal from the Lake Circuit Court wherein the trial judge sustained a motion for a directed verdict filed by the defendant-appellee at the close of the plaintiff-appellant's evidence. The appellant alleged as a basis for the cause of action in the lower court that the appellee was liable to the appellant for additional compensation for overtime work in excess of forty (40) hours per week during the two and one-half (2 1/2) years that the appellant was employed by the appellee, and further alleged that the appellee was liable to the appellant for a share of the profits of appellee Bihlman Enterprises, Inc., based upon the existence of a partnership agreement between the appellant and the appellee Bihlman. The defendant-appellee in his answer alleged full payment of any debt due the appellant, and denied the existence of a partnership agreement. . . .

In the pleadings filed in the trial court, the appellant inferentially alleged that a partnership agreement existed between the plaintiff-appellant and the defendant-appellee. The theory was raised also in the brief filed by the appellant in this court. The existence or non-existence of a partnership is controlled by the provisions of the Uniform Partnership Act. . . . Under this act, specific rules have been formulated to determine whether or not a partnership exists. . . . The following provisions have been established:

> In determining whether a partnership exists, these rules shall apply:
> (1) Except as provided by section 16, persons who are not partners as to each other are not partners as to third persons.

(2) Joint tenancy, tenancy in common, tenancy by the entireties, joint property, common property, or part ownership does not of itself establish a partnership, whether such co-owners do or do not share any profits made by the use of the property.

(3) The sharing of gross returns does not of itself establish a partnership, whether or not the persons sharing them have a joint or common right or interest in any property from which the returns are derived.

(4) The receipt by a person of a share of the profits of a business is prima facie evidence that he is a partner in the business, but no such inference shall be drawn if such profits were received in payment:

(a) As a debt by installments or otherwise,

(b) As wages of an employee or rent to a landlord,

(c) As an annuity to a widow or representative of a deceased partner,

(d) As interest on a loan, though the amount of payment vary with the profits of the business,

(e) As the consideration for the sale of a goodwill of a business or other property by installments or otherwise. . . .

To afford himself the remedy of recovery under the theory of partnership, the appellant necessarily should have proved the existence of a partnership . . . by the evidence presented at the trial. The appellant failed, however, to bring himself within the provisions of the Uniform Partnership Act, by the testimony presented. The record does not show the existence of a written partnership agreement, nor does it show the existence of an implied agreement, nor does it show a periodic sharing of the profits of the appellee's business, which would raise a presumption in favor of the appellant's allegation of the existence of a partnership agreement. The plaintiff-appellant having failed to prove a prima facie case of partnership, the directing of a verdict on the part of the trial court was correct with respect to the issue of partnership.

The appellant contends that the terms of his employment contract were based upon a forty-hour work week, and that any labor in excess of the forty hours constituted overtime, which required additional compensation. There is, however, no evidence of the existence of an hourly wage. The evidence further shows that the appellant worked varying numbers of hours in separate weeks while still receiving an identical salary for each week's labor. The appellant's salary was increased on two occasions during his two and one-half year term of employment, but the evidence introduced in the trial court fails to show any discussion between the appellant and appellee concerning an overtime rate and the actual number of hours of overtime labor. At no time during the term of employment did the appellant demand overtime compensation. At the termination of the employment, the appellant requested only his compensation for his final week's labor, and further that the appellee purchase a truck which the appellant had used in the business. No demand was made for compensation for alleged overtime labor during the two and one-half years that the appellant had been employed. In addition, there was no evidence of a demand for a sharing of the profits, which the appellant alleges was promised to him by the appellee at the inception of the term of employment. . . .

Judgment affirmed.

Brown & Bigelow v. Roy

132 N.E.2d 755 (Ohio) 1955

MILLER, J. This is a law appeal from the judgment of the Municipal Court rendered in favor of the plaintiff-appellee for the sum of $413.66 and interest and costs. The action was one on an account for goods and merchandise sold and delivered to the F. & M. Truck Stop, an alleged partnership consisting of Clarence F. Roy, the appellant, and H. Fay Lucas, who was not a party to the action.

The answer was a general denial. Upon request being made, the court filed separate findings and conclusions of law and fact. Those pertinent to the issues presented are:

(1) The merchandise was "purchased by the partnership, and sold to it."

(2) That the defendant-appellant "held himself out or permitted himself to be held out as a partner in the F. & M. Truck Stop."

(3) That the defendant-appellant is estopped from denying such partnership; and

(4) That no notice or publication pertaining to termination or dissolution of said partnership was made by the defendant.

All of the errors assigned relate to the sufficiency of the evidence to sustain the judgment, the appellant urging that his motion to dismiss at the close of plaintiff's case, and again at the conclusion of all of the evidence, should have been sustained.

No direct proof of a partnership was offered, but the same was based upon the conduct of the appellant at the place of business; that a sum of money was advanced by the appellant which he testified was a loan to the other alleged partner and upon the further fact that a vendor's license was secured from the State of Ohio in the name of "Henry F. Lucas and Clarence F. Roy, DBA F. & M. Truck Stop." The application for this license was signed by both of the alleged partners and the license issued in response thereto was posted at the place of business of the alleged partnership. It is urged that the evidence does not disclose that the appellee had any knowledge of the information contained in the license and therefore there could have been no reliance placed on the statements it contained; that the doctrine of estoppel has no application. We concur with counsel for the appellant upon his factual conclusion and are of the opinion that his views as to the law would be correct were it not for the fact that out statutory law modifies the common-law rule. Section 1775-15 of the Revised Code provides:

> When a person, by words spoken or written or by conduct, represents himself, or consents to another representing him to anyone, as a partner in an existing partnership or with one or more persons not actual partners, he is liable to any such person to whom such representation has been made, who has, on the faith of such representation, given credit to the actual or apparent partnership, and if he has made such representation or consented to its being made in a public manner he is liable to such person, whether the representation has or has not been made or communicated to such person so giving credit by or with the knowledge of the apparent partner making the representation or consenting to its being made.

Clearly the defendant represented that he was a partner in the business when he signed the application for a vendor's license and the posting of the license at the place of business was notice to the public of the nature of the business being conducted on the premises. The Court did not err in holding that the defendant was a partner.

Affirmed.

Chambers v. Sims

374 P.2d 841 (Utah) 1962

CALLISTER, J. Plaintiff commenced this action seeking a partnership accounting. Defendant, Sims, filed a counterclaim and impleaded. Mrs. Chambers as a cross-defendant, asking damages from her for alleged improper bookkeeping. Mrs. Chambers is the wife of plaintiff and sister of the defendant.

By time of trial all accounting differences had been reconciled except those relating to salaries. The lower court, sitting without a jury, at the conclusion of the trial dismissed defendant's counterclaim and cross-claim and awarded plaintiff judgment for the reasonable value of his services to the partnership. Both the plaintiff and the defendant appeal.

. . . [A] limited partnership, known as South East Ready Mixed Concrete Company, was formed on May 8, 1948. Plaintiff and defendant were the general partners and L. H. Sims, father of defendant and Mrs. Chambers, was the limited partner. . . .

At the outset, it was agreed that important decisions would be referred to defendant, and that he was to give only such time to the partnership as was necessary. Plaintiff, on the other hand, was to devote his full time to the business. Mrs. Chambers was made office manager and was, at all times pertinent hereto, in charge of the firm's books and records.

The two general partners did not draw money from the business at regular intervals, but instead drew out money as they needed it. Mrs. Chambers allowed part of her salary to remain in the partnership and added to her husband's capital account. Entries were made in the capital accounts for salaries by either Mrs. Chambers or a bookkeeper under her direction. . . . The books reflected that from 1948 to 1958 no salary was credited to defendant, while rather large salaries were entered in favor of the plaintiff. . . . It was understood that the plaintiff intended to prove the salary due him by the specific practice of the partnership as evidenced by the books and records. Defendant, on the other hand, claimed that the salary entries were unauthorized and that the salaries of both partners had been fixed by an oral agreement entered into on the same day the articles of partnership were executed.

The articles of partnership contained the following pertinent provisions:

XII. That the General Partners shall have the sole management of the business and business activities, and shall be entitled to compensate themselves for their services as an expense of operation of the business before computation of profits, to the extent that such compensation for services of General Partners is reasonable under the circumstances.

XIII. That the General Partners at the present time are equal owners and shall share equally in the profits; provided, that their interests shall be readjusted as they make additional contributions to the partnership in property, money or services, or by adjustment of property value by mutual agreement.

After the respective parties had put on their case and rested, the trial judge submitted a memorandum decision in which he held that partners had orally agreed, at the time the partnership was formed, that the defendant was to receive $400 per month as salary and the plaintiff $350. However, he held that this agreement never became operative. He further determined that a specific practice, of which defendant had notice, had been established of compensating plaintiff for full-time services (including his wife's) and allowing nothing by way of salary to defendant from 1951 to 1959. The trial judge rejected the salary entries in the books as being insufficient and conflicting. He held that in light of the provisions of paragraphs XII and XIII of the partnership agreement the plaintiff was entitled to a reasonable compensation and suggested that a master be appointed to hear testimony and determine the matter. This suggestion was opposed by the defendant and plaintiff's motion to reopen was granted. Whereupon, evidence was taken relating to the reasonable value of the services rendered by plaintiff. At the conclusion judgment of $29,314.66 was awarded to plaintiff, which was $22,000 less than plaintiff claimed the books showed.

.   .   .

As previously stated, the record before us is lengthy and complex. However, we have carefully examined the same and find that it contains substantial evidence to support the findings of the lower court.

Generally, a partner is not entitled to any remuneration for his services in the absence of an agreement by the partners to that effect. However, the lower court correctly held that articles of partnership contemplated compensation, and that a practice of remunerating plaintiff, of which defendant had knowledge, had been established.

That the books and records did not support plaintiff's claim is clearly shown by the evidence and the exhibits. Where the partnership agreement or a specific practice, acquiesced to by the partners, contemplates the payment of salary to one or more partners, but no amounts are specified, it is presumed that payment of reasonable salaries is intended. Therefore, the trial court correctly permitted the plaintiff to reopen and receive evidence relating to the reasonable value of his services.

Affirmed. No costs awarded.

Sanderfur v. Ganter

259 S.W.2d 15 (Ky.) 1953

The plaintiff, Dr. Fred Ganter, is seeking to recover possession of office space from the defendant Dr. B. D. Sanderfur. Plaintiff's father had secured a ten-year lease on the space for the practice of optometry. Plaintiff was called into military service, and during his absence, the father entered into a partnership agreement with the defendant which gave the latter an option to purchase an interest in the office equipment, but which did not mention the lease or the office space. The office space was actually used for partnership purposes. Plaintiff's father died and the executrix assigned all interests in the lease to the plaintiff. The defendant continued in possession, claiming under the right of a surviving partner. The trial court ruled in favor of the plaintiff and defendant appealed.

CULLEN, J. This is an appeal by Dr. B. D. Sanderfur from a judgment which held that Dr. Fred Ganter is entitled to the exclusive possession of certain office space in a building in Glasgow, and which mandatorily enjoined Dr. Sanderfur to surrender possession of the office to Dr. Ganter.

... The only basis upon which Dr. Sanderfur claims to be entitled to occupy the offices is that the lease (or at least Dr. George Ganter's interest in the lease) was a partnership asset. The trial court found that it was not, so our concern is with the correctness of that finding.

... The question of whether property which was owned by a partner prior to the formation of the partnership has been contributed by him to the firm so as to become partnership property, is a question of the intention of the parties, and the mere fact that the property is used in the firm business will not of itself show that it is firm property. [Cases cited] As concerns real estate owned by a partner, it has been held that there is a presumption against its inclusion in the partnership, and in order that it be treated as belonging to the partnership, the intention must be clearly manifested. While a lease is technically not real estate, we think that the reasons behind the rule with respect to real estate may be equally as applicable to a lease.

We find nothing in the partnership agreement here, or in the conduct of the parties, to show that the lease was intended to be contributed by Dr. George Ganter to the partnership as an asset. The agreement shows clearly that Dr. Ganter was not contributing his equipment, and there is no reason to conclude that he intended to contribute or donate the lease, which, as evidenced by this lawsuit, was a valuable item of property.

It is our opinion that the trial court correctly found that the lease was not a partnership asset, and therefore Dr. Sanderfur has no basis for his claim of right to occupy the office.

O'Hara v. Lance et ux.

77 Ariz. 84, 1954

The defendant, General W. Lance, established a business known as the Ace-Lance Refrigeration Company in Phoenix in 1942. In 1946 the defendant and the plaintiff entered into a partnership agreement and continued in the same business as "Ace-Lance & O'Hara Refrigeration Company." In 1949 the partnership was dissolved, Lance selling all partnership assets, including goodwill, to O'Hara. Lance agreed not to compete for a period of two years and granted to O'Hara the exclusive right to the firm name except for the condition that after December 21, 1950, O'Hara might not further use Lance's name without his consent. In 1951 the plaintiff sued to enjoin the defendant from competing and to restrain him from using the word "Ace" in the firm name of any refrigeration business in Arizona. The lower court denied this relief and held that the defendant alone had the right to use the word "Ace." The plaintiff appealed.

TULLAR, J. . . . The first and primary step is to determine what was bought and sold at the time of the dissolution of the partnership. Happily, the agreement of the parties is explicit. Lance, "the retiring partner," is being paid, "for his share in the business and the capital, stock, equipment, effects and good will thereof." The agreement recites that valuations and estimates have been placed upon these items, and agreed to, specifically including the good will, and a balance has been struck.

In the law of partnership, it is the rule that, in the absence of agreement to the contrary, a sale of assets and good will of a commercial partnership carries with it the right to use the partnership name. We are not here dealing with a "professional" partnership, wherein the law is quite different.

A conveyance of the good will of a business carries with it an implied covenant to do nothing which would derogate from the grant. If the vendor of the good will re-engage in business, it is his duty to conduct his new business in such a way that it will not appear to be a continuation of the business that he has sold. The vendor has a duty not only to his vendee, but to the public, not to confuse or deceive the customer into thinking he is in one place of business when he is in another. This type of confusion and deceit is the keystone of unfair competition. And, we have previously pointed out, this is the universal test for the presence of unfair competition: Is the public likely to be deceived?

So in this case, when Lance included in his sale the good will of the business, he sold to O'Hara the right to the use of the firm name, Ace-Lance & O'Hara Refrigeration Company. And, as the agreement recites, this was "to hold the same unto O'Hara absolutely."

This does not necessarily mean, in law, that Lance has parted with the right henceforth to use his own personal name. Indeed, there is a presumption that no one intends to part with this right, and that an assignment of good will does not, ipso facto, confer upon the assignee the exclusive right to the use of assignor's personal name. While one may sell his own name as a trade name servient to the business to which it is attached, the intent so to divest oneself must clearly be shown.

Lance . . . sold to O'Hara the exclusive use of his personal name as a trade name in the refrigeration business, but only for a limited time. The time limit having expired, there is now no restraint upon Lance's use of his personal name for any lawful purpose he may desire, so long as he does not transgress his obligation not to interfere with O'Hara's right to receive the benefits of his purchase.

. . . Fact and law conclusively show O'Hara's right in and to the use of the word "Ace," in the refrigeration business in his trade area. Lance does not have the same right.

O'Hara has prayed for state-wide restraint. He is, however, entitled to protection only in the territory from which he received business or might reasonably be expected to receive business in the future. His protection should extend as far as his business reputation and his goods have become known.

The judgment of the trial court is reversed with directions to dissolve the restraining order and enter judgment in favor of plaintiff, . . . granting to plaintiff the right to use the name, "Ace," and granting to plaintiff an injunction restraining the defendants, and all persons acting for them or under them, from using the name, "Ace," in any refrigeration business within the area served by the Phoenix metropolitan area telephone directory.

Bergum v. Weber

136 Cal. App.2d 389, 1955

Plaintiff, Bergum, bought the entire interest of the defendant, his former partner, in the partnership including goodwill. The defendant thereafter solicited business from customers of the old partnership, and the plaintiff sought to enjoin such solicitation. The trial court dismissed the action and plaintiff appealed.

NOURSE, J. pro tem. . . . Did the defendant, by the contract alleged in the complaint, impliedly covenant not to directly solicit the customers of plaintiffs who had been customers of the business he had sold to them[?]

We have come to the conclusion that this question must be answered in the affirmative.

The goodwill of a business is property and may be transferred. The customers of a business are an essential part of its goodwill. In fact, without their continued custom goodwill ceases to exist, for goodwill is the expectation of continued public patronage.

When the goodwill of a business is sold, it is not the patronage of the general public which is sold, but that patronage which has become an asset of that business. It follows that one who has sold his interest in the goodwill of a business can no more act directly to destroy that asset than he could to destroy or make useless any other asset which he had for value transferred to the purchaser.

The law implies in every contract a covenant that neither party will do anything that will deprive the other of the fruits of his bargain.

The direct solicitation by the seller of the customers of the business, the goodwill of which he has sold, is a violation of this covenant.

This implied covenant does not prevent the seller from engaging in a competing business and by fair means soliciting the business of the public generally. It does prevent him from directly soliciting the patrons of the business he has sold.

Relief sought by plaintiff was granted.

CHAPTER 42
REVIEW QUESTIONS AND PROBLEMS

1. *A,* a 65-year-old woman, approached *B,* a 77-year-old man, asking for employment milking *B's* cows. *B* countered with the offer that if *A* would live on his farm, clean his house, milk the cows, and assume one-half of his indebtedness, she would be entitled to one-half the profits of the farm. Are *A* and *B* partners?

2. *A* and his son *B* operated a dairy farm. The farm consisted in reality of two farms, one owned by each *A* and *B.* A telephone was installed under the name "*A* and son," bills being sent to *A* and son. *B* made several long-distance calls. Is *A* liable for these?

3. *A* and *B* formed a partnership to do kitchen remodeling work pursuant to an oral agreement. It was agreed that *A* was to invest $10,000 and

manage the business affairs; *B,* who would invest $1,000, was to work as job superintendent and manage the work. Profits were to be split fifty-fifty, but possible losses were not discussed. The business proved unprofitable, and *A* brought action for contribution from *B.* May he recover?

4. *X* and *Y* operated an automobile agency as partners for over twenty years. At the outset, they had prepared a written agreement containing the provision that in the event of either partner's death, the surviving partner would purchase the deceased partner's share for $40,000. *X* died, and *Y* tendered the $40,000. *X*'s executor refused to sell on the basis that $40,000 was insufficient. The executor contends that *Y* is required to proffer the amount of *X*'s share of capital and accumulated profits. Should *Y* succeed in an action for specific performance against the executor?

5. *A* was the principal stockholder in the XYZ Stockyards Corporation, and *B* was his secretary-bookkeeper. They were married, and in the same year the XYZ Corporation was dissolved. *A* continued to operate the business as sole owner. *B* continued to work in the same capacity as before, though without salary, and she testified that *A* orally made her a partner. Twenty years later *B* divorced *A* and asked for a one-half interest in all partnership property. Should she recover?

6. *A* and *B* as partners rented a cannery for one season. They entered into a contract with *P,* a broker, whereby it was agreed to label all products with *P*'s label, to allow *P* the exclusive right to sell their entire output, and to pay him 5 percent of gross sales. *P* guaranteed the cannery a supply of cans and other material and promised to advance money for operating expenses and payroll. For this advance *P* was to receive as "extra compensation" one-half the net profits of the cannery for the season. *P* also had the right to control wages and the payroll for the cannery. Is *P* a partner?

7. *M* wished to purchase a tract of land, plat it, and sell the lots. He needed capital, and *P* loaned him $6,000. *M* gave *P* a note and it was understood that when the lots were sold, the proceeds would first be used to pay the $6,000 to *P.* Any profits above the $6,000 would be divided equally. Was there a partnership?

8. *P* and *D* entered into an agreement for trading in grain futures. *P* furnished the funds for margin requirements, and profits and losses were to be shared. No partnership income tax return was ever filed. The authorization for *D* to trade on *P*'s account with the brokerage company referred to *D* as *P*'s "agent." Do these last two facts prevent holding that a partnership existed?

9. Give reasons for including buy and sell provisions in the articles of partnership.

10. *A,* a grain broker, and *B,* his brother, a farmer, entered into an agreement whereby each was to pay to the other one-half the profits of his business annually for three years and also to make good one-half the losses that might be suffered by the other. The ownership of each individual business was to be distinct. *B* became bankrupt. To what extent, if any, could *A* be made to satisfy the claims of *B*'s creditors?

11. *A* and *B* formed a partnership, and *A* contributed an unpatented invention. He later took out the patent in his own name. Upon dissolution of the partnership to whom does the patent belong?

12. *A* and *B* are partners. *A* dies and *B* continues the business in his own name. In accounting for the firm assets, he refuses to make any allowance for goodwill. May the executrix of *A*'s estate recover an additional sum for the goodwill of the business? Give a definition of goodwill.

chapter 43

Operating the
Partnership

6-21. Introduction. The operation of a partnership is governed by the provisions of the partnership agreement and by the applicable statutory law, which in most states is the Uniform Partnership Act. Thus the rights, duties, and powers of partners are both expressed (those in the agreement) and implied (those created by law). Many of the expressed rights, duties, and powers were discussed in the previous chapter, which covered the typical subjects found in articles of partnership. Those that are implied will be discussed in this chapter, along with some additional observations about the partnership agreement as it affects operations. Throughout the discussion, it should be kept in mind that a partner is essentially an agent for the other partners and that the general principles of the law of agency are applicable.

The terms "general" and "limited," as used to modify "partner," have been previously discussed. Before examining the rights, duties, and powers of partners, certain additional terminology should be understood. A *silent partner* is one that does not participate in management. However, if the silent partner is to have limited liability, the provisions of the Uniform Limited Partnership Act would have to be complied with. A *secret partner* is unknown to third parties. He may advise management and actually participate in decisions, but his interest is not known to third parties. A *dormant partner* is both secret and silent.

RIGHTS OF PARTNERS

6-22. Right to Participate in Management. All partners have equal rights in the management and conduct of the firm business. The partners may, however, by agreement, place the management within the control of one or more partners. The right to an equal voice in the management and conduct of the business is not determined by the share that each partner has in the business.

In regard to ordinary matters arising in the conduct of the partnership business, the opinion of the majority of the partners is controlling. If the firm consists of only two persons, and they are unable to agree, and the articles of partnership make no provision for the settlement of disputes, dissolution is the only remedy.

The majority cannot, however, without the consent of the minority, change the essential nature of the business by altering the partnership agreement or by reducing or increasing the capital of the partners; or embark upon a new business; or admit new members to the firm.

There are certain acts other than those enumerated above which require the unanimous consent of the partners in order to bind the firm, namely: (1) assigning the firm property to a trustee for the benefit of creditors; (2) confessing a judgment; (3) disposing of the goodwill of the business; (4) submitting a partnership agreement to arbitration; and (5) doing any act which would make impossible the conduct of the partnership business.

6-23. Partner's Right to Be Compensated for Services.   It is the duty of each partner, in absence of an agreement to the contrary, to give his entire time, skill, and energy to the pursuit of the partnership affairs. No partner is entitled to payment for services rendered in the conduct of the partnership business, unless an agreement to that effect has been expressed or may be implied from the conduct of the partners.[1] Often one of the partners does not desire to participate in the management of the business. The partnership agreement in such case usually provides that the active partners receive a salary for their services in addition to their share in the profits. A surviving partner is entitled to reasonable compensation for his services in winding up the partnership affairs, unless he is guilty of misconduct in winding up the affairs.[2]

6-24. Partner's Right to Interest.   Contributions to capital are not entitled to draw interest unless they are not repaid when the repayment should be made. The partner's share in the profits constitutes the earnings upon his capital investment. In absence of an expressed provision for the payment of interest, it is presumed that interest will be paid only on advances above the amount originally contributed as capital. Advances in excess of the prescribed capital, even though credited to the capital account of the contributing partners, are entitled to draw interest from the date of the advance.

Unwithdrawn profits remaining in the firm are not entitled to draw interest. Such unwithdrawn profits are not considered advances or loans by the mere fact that they are left with the firm. However, custom, usage, and circumstances may show an intention to treat such unwithdrawn profits as loans to the firm.

6-25. Right to Information and to Inspection of Books.   Each partner, whether active or inactive, is entitled to full and complete information concerning the conduct of the business and may inspect the books to secure such information. The partnership agreement usually provides for a bookkeeper, and each partner is under a duty to give the bookkeeper whatever information is necessary to carry on the business efficiently and effectively. It is the duty

[1] Waagen v. Gerde et ux., page 853
[2] Lee v. Dahlin, page 854

of the bookkeeper to keep the books at the firm's place of business and to allow each partner access to them. No partner has a right to remove the books without the consent of the other partners. Each partner is entitled to inspect the books and make copies therefrom, provided he does not make such inspection or copies to secure an advantageous position or for fraudulent purposes.

6-26. Partner's Right to An Accounting. The partners' proportionate share of the partnership assets or profits, when not determined by a voluntary settlement of the parties, can only be ascertained by a *bill in equity* for an accounting. As a general rule, a partner cannot maintain an *action at law* against other members of the firm on the partnership agreement, because until there is an accounting and all partnership affairs are settled, the indebtedness between the firm members is undetermined.[3] This general rule is subject to a few commonsense exceptions.[4]

Since partners ordinarily have equal access to the partnership books, there is usually no need for formal accountings to determine partnership interests. A suit for an accounting is not permitted for settling incidental matters or disputes between the partners. However, if a dispute is of such grievous nature as to make impossible the continued existence of the partnership, a suit for an accounting in equity is allowed.

In all cases a partner is entitled to an accounting upon the dissolution of the firm. In addition he has a right to a formal accounting without a dissolution of the firm in the following situations:

1. Where there is an agreement for an accounting at a definite date.

2. Where one partner has withheld profits arising from secret transactions.

3. Where there has been an execution levied against the interest of one of the partners.

4. Where one is in such a position that he does not have access to the books.

5. Where the partnership is approaching insolvency and all parties are not available.

Upon an agreement between themselves, the partners may make a complete accounting and settle their claims, without resort to a court of equity.

6-27. Property Rights of Partners. The Uniform Partnership Act enumerates the property rights of a partner as (1) his rights in specific partnership property and (2) his interest in the partnership. A partner is a co-owner with his partners of specific partnership property and subject to any agreement between the partners, a partner has an equal right among his partners to possess partnership property for partnership purposes. He has no right to possess specific partnership property for other purposes without the consent of the other partners. A partner has a right that the property shall be used in the pursuit of the partnership business and to pay firm creditors. A partner does not own any specific item of the partnership property. He, therefore, has no right in specific partnership property that is assignable, and any sale by him, as an individual, of a particular part of the partnership property does not pass title

---

[3] Weiser v. Burick, page 855

[4] Smith v. Hensley, page 856

to the specific property. He has no right to use firm property in satisfaction of his personal debts[5] and he has no interest in specific partnership property that can be levied upon by his personal creditors.

When a partner dies, his right in specific partnership property passes to the surviving partner or partners who possess the property only for partnership purposes subject to the partnership agreement and the rights of the estate of the deceased partner. The surviving partner may sell the property, real and personal, of the partnership in connection with winding up the business.

A partner's interest *in the firm* consists of his rights to share in the profits which are earned and, after dissolution and liquidation, to the return of his capital and such profits as have not been distributed previously. This assumes, of course, that his capital has not been absorbed or impaired by losses.

The Act provides that a partner can assign his interest in the partnership and that such an assignment will not of itself work a dissolution of the firm. The assignee is not entitled to interfere in the management of the business or to require that the books of the firm be made available for his inspection. The only right of the assignee is to receive the profits to which the assignor would otherwise have been entitled and, in the event of dissolution, to receive his assignor's interest.

At common law a partner's interest could be levied upon by his separate creditors and sold at public sale, but under the Act a separate creditor of a partner must proceed by way of a "Charging Order," which is obtained by a judgment creditor who applies to the court for an order charging the interest of the debtor partner with the unsatisfied amount of the judgment debt.[6] The court will ordinarily appoint a receiver who will receive the partner's share of the profits and any other money due or to fall due to him in respect of the partnership and apply the same upon the judgment. Likewise, the court may order that the interest charged be sold. Neither the charging order nor the sale of the interest will cause a dissolution of the firm.

THE DUTIES AND POWERS OF PARTNERS

6-28. Duties in General.   A partnership is a fiduciary relationship,[7] and each partner owes the duty of undivided loyalty to the other. Therefore, every partner must account to the partnership for any benefit, and hold as a trustee for it any profits gained by him without consent of the other partners from any transaction connected with the formation, conduct, or liquidation of the partnership, and account for any use by him of the partnership property. This duty also rests upon representatives of deceased partners engaged in the liquidation of the affairs of the partnership.

The partnership relation is a personal one, and each partner is under duty to exercise good faith and to consider the mutual welfare of all the partners in his conduct of the business. If one partner attempts to secure an advantage over the others, he thereby breaches the partnership relation, and he must account for all benefits that he obtains. This includes transactions with partners and with others.

---

[5] Windom National Bank et al. v. Klein et al., page 858
[6] Shirk v. Caterbone, page 859
[7] Hurst v. Hurst, page 860

6-29. Powers in General. A partner is an agent of the partnership for the purpose of its business and the general laws of agency are applicable to his conduct. (It is suggested that Chapter 36 be reviewed.) He has the power to bind the partnership both in tort and in contract. The Uniform Partnership Act provides for contractual liability whenever the partner is apparently carrying on, in the usual way, the business of the partnership of which he is a member, unless the partner so acting has in fact no authority to act for the partnership in the particular matter, and the person with whom he is dealing has knowledge of the fact that he has no such authority. An act of a partner which is not apparently for the carrying on of the business of the partnership in the usual way does not bind the partnership unless authorized by the other partners.[8]

However, unless authorized by the other partners or unless they have abandoned the business, one or more but less than all the partners have no authority to do those things set forth in Section 6-22.

The Act imposes tort liability upon the partnership for all wrongful acts or omissions of any partner acting in the ordinary course of the partnership and for its benefit.[9]

The rules of agency relating to authority, ratification, and secret limitations on the authority of a partner are applicable to partnerships, but the extent of implied authority is generally greater for partners than for ordinary agents. Each partner has implied power to do all acts necessary for carrying on the business of the partnership. The nature and scope of the business and what is usual in the particular business determine the extent of the implied powers. Among the common implied powers are the following: to compromise, adjust, and settle claims or debts owed by or to the partnership; to sell goods in the regular course of business and to make warranties; to buy property within the scope of the business for cash or upon credit;[10] to buy insurance; to hire employees; to make admissions against interest; to enter into contracts within the scope of firm; and to receive notice. In a trading partnership, a partner has the implied authority to borrow funds and to pledge the assets of the firm. Some of these implied duties are discussed more fully in the sections which follow.

6-30. Powers over Property. Each partner has implied authority to sell to good-faith purchasers personal property that is held for the purpose of resale and to execute such documents as are necessary to effect a transfer of title thereof.[11] Of course, if his authority in this connection has been limited and such fact is known to the purchaser, the transfer of title will be ineffective or voidable. A partner has no power to sell the fixtures and equipment used in the business unless he has been duly authorized. Such acts are not a regular feature of the business and a prospective purchaser of such property should make certain that the particular partner has been given authority to sell. The power to sell, where it is present, gives also the power to make such warranties as normally accompany similar sales.

---

[8] Bole v. Lyle et al., page 860
[9] Phillips v. Cook, page 861
[10] Rodgers v. Saunders, page 862
[11] Lankford v. State, page 863

The right to sell firm real property is to be inferred only if the firm is engaged in the real estate business. In other cases, there is no right to sell and convey realty, except where such sale has been authorized by a partnership agreement.

Under the Uniform Partnership Act, title to real property may be taken in the firm name as a "tenancy in partnership," and any member of the firm has power to execute a deed thereto by signing the firm name. In such a case, what is the effect of a wrongful transfer of real estate that has been acquired for use in the business and not for resale? The conveyance may be set aside by the other partners, since the purchaser should have known that one partner has no power to sell without the approval of the others. However, if the first purchaser has resold and conveyed the property to an innocent third party, the latter takes good title.

If the title to firm property is not held in the firm name, but is held in the names of one or more of the partners, a conveyance by those in whose names the title is held passes good title, unless the purchaser knows or should know that title was held for the firm. There is nothing in the record title in such a situation to call the buyer's attention to the fact that the firm has an interest in the property.

The power to mortgage or pledge firm property is primarily dependent upon the power, later discussed, to borrow money and bind the firm. A partner with authority to borrow may, as an incident to that power, give the security normally demanded for similar loans. Since no one partner, without the consent of the others, has the power to commit an act that will destroy or terminate the business, the power to give a mortgage on the entire stock of merchandise and fixtures of a business is usually denied. Such a mortgage would make it possible, upon default, to liquidate the firm's assets and thus destroy its business. Subject to this limitation, the power to borrow carries the power to pledge or mortgage.

6-31. Financial Powers. For the purpose of determining the limit of a partner's financial powers, partnerships may be divided into two general classes —trading and nontrading partnerships. A trading partnership is one which has for its primary purpose the buying and selling of commodities. In such a trading firm, each partner has an implied power to borrow money and to extend the credit of the firm, in the usual course of business, by signing negotiable paper.[12]

A nontrading partnership is one that does not buy and sell commodities, but that has for its primary purpose the production of commodities or is organized for the purpose of selling services, for example, professional partnerships. In such partnerships a partner's powers are more limited and a partner does not have implied power to borrow money or to bind the firm on negotiable paper. However, where the act is within the scope of the partnership business, a member of a nontrading partnership may bind the firm by the exercise of implied authority just as a partner in a trading partnership may.

6-32. Notice and Admissions. Each partner has implied authority to receive notice for all of the other partners concerning matters within the pursuit of the

[12] Holloway v. Smith et al., page 864

partnership business; and knowledge, held by any partner in his mind but not revealed to the other partners, is notice to the partnership. Knowledge of one partner is knowledge of all. This knowledge, however, must be knowledge obtained within the scope of the partnership business. If the partner could have and should have communicated knowledge to the other partners and fails to do so, his failure would be chargeable to the firm. This rule does not apply, however, if fraud is perpetrated on the partnership by the partner having such knowledge.

Admissions or representations pertaining to the conduct of the partnership business and made by a partner may be used as evidence against the partnership.

OPERATING THE PARTNERSHIP CASES

Waagen v. Gerde et ux.

36 Wash.2d 563 (1950)

The plaintiff and the defendants were partners in the ownership and operation of a fishing vessel. The plaintiff brought this action for an accounting and alleged that the defendants had wrongfully withheld partnership earnings from the plaintiff. The defendant Karl Gerde perfected a new type of net for catching sharks and contended that he was entitled to compensation for the time and effort expended in constructing the shark nets. The lower court held in favor of the plaintiff and the defendants appealed.

DONWORTH, J. . . . . Appellant's final assignment of error is that the trial court erred in refusing to allow appellant any credit for work done by him in constructing the shark nets.

The evidence shows that appellant with some help from his two sons designed and built the shark nets. Respondent did not in any way assist him in this job. According to appellant, the value of this work was $2,500 and he claims that he should be compensated for this work.

The general rule is clear that one partner is not entitled to extra compensation from the partnership, in the absence of an express or an implied agreement therefor. Each case must depend largely upon its own facts, and thus other cases are generally of little or no assistance in deciding the case at hand.

The exception to the general rule is well stated in 1 Rowley, *Modern Law of Partnership* 412, § 354, as follows: "Where it can be fairly and justly implied from the course of dealing between the partners, (or from circumstances of equivalent force, that one partner is to be compensated for his services, his claim will be sustained." The partnership may be of such a peculiar kind, and the arrangements and the course of dealing of the partners in regard to it may be such as pretty plainly to show an expectation and understanding, without an express agreement upon the subject, that certain services of a copartner should be paid for. Such cases, presenting unusual conditions, are exceptions to the general rule.

While appellant's ingenuity and industry were largely responsible for the success of the *Princess* in shark fishing, we cannot find anything in the record from which an agreement to pay him special compensation could be implied. Appellant did inform respondent that he was busy getting the nets ready and that it would "be lots of work to fix" them, but never at any time did he inform respondent what the work actually entailed or that he expected any compensation for it. Since respondent had so little knowledge of the conduct of the net operations, there could not be any implied agreement for compensation. The trial court found no factual basis for such an allowance, and we can find none in the record.

Affirmed.

Lee v. Dahlin

159 A.2d 679 (Pa.) 1960

COHEN, J. Dahlin Bros. Coal Mining Company was a partnership owned by A. Vern Dahlin and George T. Dahlin, which mined coal in Clearfield County. At the death of George T. Dahlin on May 31, 1951, the partnership was dissolved, but A. V. Dahlin, the surviving partner, continued to operate the mine for eighteen months, after which time he gradually began to liquidate the partnership. A. V. Dahlin died on January 8, 1956, and because the partnership still had not been fully liquidated, a receiver was appointed.

The receiver filed a complaint in equity against the Estate of A. V. Dahlin for a full accounting of the partnership affairs and liquidation from the date of the death of the first deceased partner. The administrator of the estate filed a partial accounting which was not satisfactory and the court directed the receiver to investigate and make a report. After the receiver filed his account and the court below filed an adjudication to which exceptions were made, a decree was entered finding the estate liable to the receiver for $7,221.44. This is an appeal by the administrator of the estate from this final decree.

The appellant contends that the A. V. Dahlin estate is entitled to credit for payment of a bank overdraft which existed at the time of the first partner's death in 1951. There was a great deal of confusion as to what bookkeeping method was employed by the partnership—cash or accrual; however, this is of no import since the real issue is what money was legitimately received and spent by A. V. Dahlin. Appellant produced no testimony or proof as to this overdraft. The burden is on the liquidating partner or his estate to furnish proof of any credits claimed, and this was not done. The account filed by the receiver was prepared by a certified public accountant appointed by the court, and in the absence of evidence of a mistake in its computation and because of its acceptance by the lower court, we are inclined to give this audit substantial weight.

The appellant next contends that A. V. Dahlin was entitled to compensation as a surviving partner. The Uniform Partnership Act of March 26, 1915, provides that a partner is not entitled to compensation "except that a surviving partner is entitled to *reasonable* compensation for his services in winding up the partnership affairs." At common law in Pennsylvania a liquidating partner was entitled to compensation only for *extraordinary* services performed in the liquidation. In *Murdock* v. *Murdock,* 1930, 300 Pa. 280, the court held that "though partners, in the absence of special agreement, receive no compensation, yet 'a surviving partner is entitled to reasonable compensation for his services in winding up the partnership affairs.' " There is no question that ordinarily A. V. Dahlin would have been entitled to some compensation;

however, on the facts of this case, he has forfeited this right. A surviving partner is in a fiduciary capacity as regards the estate of his deceased partner. Since the death of one partner leaves the survivor in a position of absolute control with only the duty to account, it is apparent that the survivor must proceed with utmost caution and use the highest degree of care in the liquidation of the partnership. This was not done. There is ample evidence on the record that A. V. Dahlin, after the death of George Dahlin, took a truck belonging to the partnership for which he failed to account; used partnership funds for personal expense and failed to account to George Dahlin's estate even after a lapse of approximately five years. A trustee who breaches his fiduciary duty with a resultant loss to the estate forfeits his rights to compensation. For this reason it is evident that A. V. Dahlin was not entitled to the monies which he withdrew from the partnership as compensation, and the final decree of the court below requiring its return is correct.

Decree affirmed at appellant's cost.

Weiser v. Burick

263 N.Y.S.2d 506 (1965)

DEMPSEY, J. Plaintiff sued defendant in the County Court to receive $2000 alleged to have been advanced by plaintiff for the partnership and on behalf of the same. Defendant, in addition to denying the alleged partnership agreement, has interposed an affirmative defense plus several counterclaims. . . .

(The court has challenged its jurisdiction over the subject matter of the suit.)

The test of jurisdiction of a cause must be resolved by the nature of the action. Though the prayer for relief seeks recovery of purported money damages, the documentation of jurisdiction stands or falls upon the factual allegations in the complaint. . . .

For resolution is the question whether the complaint is based in equity or at law. Distinctions in pleadings on equity and law actions have been abolished by the Legislature. Jurisdictional questions of equity actions, however, persist. The County Court is a court of limited equity jurisdiction. . . .

The instant action is, as heretofore stated, a suit by one partner against another. The pleading is replete with reference (Paragraphs "Second, Third, Fourth, Fifth and Sixth") with claim of a partnership and an advance for the benefit of the partnership. It is almost universally recognized that absent statutory authorization one partner may not maintain an action at law based upon partnership transactions which involves an accounting of the partnership affairs until there has been a final settlement of the business of the partnership. In the absence of an accounting, one partner cannot maintain a suit at law for contributions or advances made by him to the firm, or for money paid on debts (or assumption of obligations as herein alleged) settled by him for the firm out of his private funds. Breach of special covenants may give rise to law actions under special circumstances, but these are not here present.

This is an equity action before our court. This court does not have jurisdiction of the dissolution and accounting of partnerships. The procedures should be utilized for removal of the case to the proper forum. . . . The application should be made in thirty days. *If no such application is made, this Court will then entertain a motion to dismiss for lack of jurisdiction over the subject matter.*

Smith v. Hensley
354 S.W.2d 744, (Ky.) 1962

STANLEY, Comm. The action is by Clyde Hensley, one of eight partners constituting the firm of Mary Gail Coal Company, against all the partners, including himself by name, to recover damages for the value of a motor truck owned individually by the plaintiff, which he alleges was destroyed by the negligence of employees of the partnership.

The partnership operated a coal mine near Hyden and had its production transported by a fleet of thirty or more trucks to a tipple on a railroad at Manchester. Sometimes the trucks made several round trips a day. They were serviced by their several drivers at a gasoline filling station owned and operated by the company at the mine scales. Hensley's personally owned truck was one of the fleet. The evidence is skimpy. There is no evidence as to the contractual relationship, but the appellants do not question appellee's statement that his truck and driver had been "hired" by the company.

On June 10, 1958, plaintiff's driver had filled his gasoline tank preparatory to hauling a load of coal to the tipple when gasoline became ignited and fire destroyed the truck. The plaintiff alleged this was caused by the defendants' negligently permitting gasoline to be spilled from the pumps and to remain exposed on the ground. The defendants pleaded sole or contributory negligence of the plaintiff's driver or that the loss was an unavoidable casualty. Upon a verdict, judgement for $4,000 was entered for the plaintiff against his seven partners.

The defendants have contended that the plaintiff may not maintain the action against his co-partners. Specifically, they say the manager and other employees of the mining partnership were agents of the plaintiff as well as agents of the defendants, and their negligence, if any, was imputable to the plaintiff as well as to the defendants. The record fails to disclose the articles or contract of partnership, but we may assume that it was a general, ordinary partnership, without limitations or reservations inter se.

The situation presents a novel question in the field of partnership law.

Various legalistic concepts could be invoked as a basis for denying a right of recovery to the plaintiff. One would be that a partner cannot sue the partnership because a litigant cannot sue himself. Another would be that if negligence of the partnership employees is to be imputed to the defendant partnership to establish a basis for liability, by the same token the negligence must be imputed to the plaintiff so as to bar recovery.

It is our opinion, however, that under a realistic approach, seeking to achieve substantial justice, the plaintiff should be held entitled to maintain the action.

It is true that an action at law *ordinarily* is not maintainable between a partner and his firm. . . . But the situation here presented is not an ordinary one. The law is well settled that a partner who has paid an obligation of the firm out of his own funds may obtain contribution from his co-partners. Also, a partner is entitled to reimbursement from the firm for losses suffered by him in the ordinary and proper course of the firm affairs.

As concerns use of the doctrine of imputable negligence, courts have recognized that the doctrine is of artificial creation and must in particular cases yield to reason and practical considerations. As with the related doctrine of *respondeat superior,* it had its origin in considerations of public policy, convenience and justice, and has been developed and extended out of the necessities of changing social and economic conditions. It has been held by this Court that the doctrine of imputed negligence is inapplicable in an action between members of a joint enterprise or partnership.

Clearly, if negligence of the partnership had caused damage to the property of a stranger, the partnership would be liable. We do not find any just reason for denying recovery where the damaged property is that of a partner. It seems to us that the damage should be considered an ordinary business loss.

It perhaps could be argued that while public policy imposes liability upon a partnership for damages to property of strangers, there is no public policy requiring partners to share the loss from damages to property of one of their number sustained in carrying on the partnership business. However, in both instances the considerations of public policy grow out of the realities of the economic world, and we find in those realities no basis for saying that if there is damage to property of a stranger, or to property owned by the partnership, the partners must share the loss, but not so if the property is owned by one partner.

The law is well settled that if one partner negligently damages the property of another partner, the latter may recover from the former. Thus there is no basic public policy or rule of law to the effect that a partner who uses his own property in connection with the partnership business does so completely at his own risk. Why then, should he be held to assume the sole risks when the damage is done by a partnership *employee* rather than by another member of the partnership? It is a common practice for partnerships to carry on their business through employees. The practical realities of the business world dictate that the partners should share the loss of damage to property resulting from the negligence of the partnership employees, regardless of who owns the property.

If it be considered, as appears actually to have been the case here, that the use of the plaintiff's truck was not *in* the partnership business but was a collateral use in connection with an independent contract between the plaintiff and the partnership, then there is more reason to impose a duty on the partners to share the loss, because there is no basis upon which it could be said that the plaintiff contributed his truck to the use of the partnership with an intent of the parties that he would assume all risk of loss.

We hold the action is maintainable.

The judgment is against the plaintiff's seven co-partners by name "doing business as Mary Gail Coal Company." This recognizes that the liability was that of the partnership firm, even though the plaintiff was a partner. The negligence was that of the firm's employees, acting within the scope of their employment. The partners, who are liable jointly and severally for obligations of the firm should bear their respective proportionate shares as may be determined by the contract of partnership. The plaintiff, Hensley, must bear his part. So the judgement should provide that satisfaction be out of the assets of the partnership, as an "association," before resorting to the individual members thereof.

The judgment may be so modified and as modified it is affirmed.

Windom National Bank et al. v. Klein et al.

191 Minn. 447 (1934)

Four brothers owned and operated, as partners, a dairy farm under the firm name of Bender Bros. The plaintiff bank had an unsatisfied personal judgment against two of the brothers and, in conformity with the provisions of the Uniform Partnership Act, had a receiver appointed over all the right and interest of the two brothers in the partnership. The court also gave an order charging *their interest* in the firm with payment of the judgment debt. The two brothers had mortgaged certain specific partnership property to the defendants, Klein and others, and this action by the bank was for the purpose of annulling these mortgages. The defendants demurred and the lower court sustained the demurrer. Plaintiffs appealed.

STONE, J. . . . The tenancy in partnership created by the statute is an innovation on the common law. Its genesis was in the "inequitable results" of the long-established judicial habit of applying to partnership property the analogies of joint tenancy. Some of them (particularly a joint tenant's unrestrained power of disposition) did not fit. The result was "very great confusion" where separate creditors of a partner tried to reach specific partnership property or where a partner attempted to dispose of it for his own purposes.

Thus it appears that tenancy in partnership is a restricted adaptation of common-law joint tenancy to the practical needs of the partnership relation. One of those needs arose from the formerly conflicting claims to specific partnership property of (1) separate creditors of a partner and (2) assignees of a partner's share in an aliquot part of the firm assets. To meet that need, two simple "incidents" have been attached to the tenancy in partnership: (1) Expressly, the interest of each tenant or partner in specific partnership property is put beyond reach of his separate creditors; and (2) it has been made nonassignable. That means simply that the partner owner is deprived of all power of separate disposition even by will.

All a partner has now, subject to his power of individual disposition, and all that is subject to the claims of his separate creditors, is his interest, not in specific partnership property, but in the partnership itself. Plain is the purpose that all partnership property is to be kept intact for partnership purposes and creditors. The statutory incidents of the partnership cotenancy are attached thereto for that purpose, which will be *pro tanto* thwarted as effect is given to an attempted disposition of a partner's interest in specific partnership property. The aim of the statute is to prevent such an assignment.

. . . Dean William Draper Lewis, one of the commissioners who drafted the Uniform Partnership Act, has said, in explanation of its purpose to "avoid the consequences of regarding partners as joint tenants" that "while any partner has an equal right with his copartners to possess partnership property for partnership purposes" and while he "may assign partnership property for a partnership purpose, . . . if he attempts to assign the property for his own purposes he makes no assignment at all, because the act destroys the quality of assignability for any but a partnership purpose."

. . . It follows that a receiver, such as plaintiff Gillam, of a partner's "share of the profits," acting under a charging order and § 28 (Mason's Minn. St. 1927, § 7411), has the right in a proper action to have adjudicated the nullity of any mortgage or other assignment by some but not all of the partners of their interest in specific property of the partnership less than the whole. Such a receiver is entitled to any relief under the language of the statute "which the circumstances of the case may require" to accomplish justice under the law. Obviously, a part of such relief is the avoidance of any unauthorized attempt to dispose of partnership property. Such a receiver is entitled to the "share of profits and surplus" of the partner who happens to be the judgment debtor. While he is not entitled to share in the management of the firm as a partner, the receiver would be of little use if he could not protect "profits and surplus" by preventing such unauthorized and illegal dissipations of firm assets as the complaint alleges in this case.

The complaint states a cause of action. It was error to sustain the demurrer.

The order sustaining the demurrer was reversed because the partners could not lawfully mortgage partnership property to secure personal indebtedness.

Shirk v. Caterbone

193 A.2d 664 (Pa.) 1963

FLOOD, J. . . . We have examined the question raised in the appeal and find no merit in the appellant's position. The appellant seeks priority for a charging order entered in his favor upon a judgment against a member of a partnership, as against a levy, made later, upon personal property of the partnership under a judgment obtained against the partnership by the plaintiff. The court below properly held that the charging order has priority. The levy against the partnership reached all the tangible personal property of the partnership levied upon, and was a lien upon the property. The charging order, on the other hand, reached only the distributive share of the judgment-defendant Caterbone, one of the partners, in the assets of the partnership after all its debts had been paid and was not a lein upon any specific property of the partnership.

Section 28 of the Uniform Partnership Act provides that upon due application to a competent court by any judgment creditor of a partner the court which entered the judgment may "charge the interest of the debtor partner with payment of the unsatisfied amount of such judgment debt with interest thereon; and may then or later appoint a receiver of his share of the profits, and of any other money due or to fall due to him in respect of the partnership. . . . " It is obvious from this language that the creditor of the individual partner is entitled only to his debtor's share of the profits or of the net assets upon liquidation. It is equally obvious that the amount due a partnership creditor is a liability that must be discharged before the amount of net assets is determined out of which profits are due to a partner. The partnership creditor who has obtained judgment is entitled to be paid out of partnership assets and may levy upon its tangible property. The creditor of the individual partner, on the other hand, can be paid only out of what remains to the individual partner as his share of the profits after the partnership obligations, including those of any judgment creditor of the partnership have been satisfied. He cannot reach partnership property in execution.

Appeal quashed.

Hurst v. Hurst

405 P.2d 913 (Ariz.) 1965

HATHAWAY, J. . . . We shall consider the question of certain "unidentified deposits" in appellee's bank account prior to dissolution. Appellee Lee Hurst had deposited both partnership funds and personal funds in his own personal account. The accounting report prepared for the trial court excluded these unidentified deposits in computing the undistributed cash assets belonging to the dissolved partnership. We hold that this was partially erroneous.

A partner stands in a fiduciary relationship to his co-partner. If a trustee mixes trust funds with his own, the entire commingled mass should be treated as trust property except in so far as the trustee may be able to distinguish what is his. The evidence having established that part of the money deposited in Lee Hurst's account was partnership or trust funds, it was incumbent upon the trustee-partner, Lee Hurst, to distinguish his personal funds. He failed to do this and the unidentified deposits for 1951, 1952, and 1953 should have been treated as a partnership cash asset.

So ordered.

Bole v. Lyle et al.

287 S.W.2d 931 (Tenn.) 1956

Lyle, Peters, and Barton were partners operating a business which manufactured packing crates and other wood products. The partnership had purchased a tract of timber and were cutting it into lumber to supply their needs. Barton, the managing partner, entered into a contract to sell lumber to the plaintiff and received payment therefor. The lumber was never delivered to plaintiff, and Barton never accounted to the partnership for the money received. Plaintiff sought to hold the partnership accountable. The lower court held that Lyle and Peters were not liable. The plaintiff appealed.

MC AMIS, J. . . . The general rule is that each partner is a general agent of the firm but only for the purpose of carrying on the business of the partnership. Any sale by a partner to be valid must be in furtherance of the partnership business, within the real scope of the business or such as third persons may reasonably conclude, from all the circumstances, to be embraced within it. If the act is embraced within the partnership business or incident to such business according to the ordinary and usual course of conducting it, the partnership is bound regardless of whether the partner, in performing the act, proceeds in good faith or bad faith toward his copartners.

Sales made by a partner in a trading firm are, of course, not viewed with the same strictness as in nontrading firms such as here involved, because in trading firms sales are usually within the scope of the business while in nontrading firms they are exceptional and only incidental to the main business. A priori, in determining whether an act is within the scope of the business it is of importance, first, to determine the character of the partnership operations. (Cases cited.)

We think the case here presented is simply that of a nonresident, unfamiliar with the partnership operations, being defrauded by one of the partners acting in a matter beyond both the real and apparent scope of the business and beyond the real or apparent scope of the agency. There was nothing in the firm name to suggest that it was in the business of selling lumber. Complainant chose to deal with one of the partners without knowing anything of the nature of the partnership operations and we agree with the Chancellor that the nonparticipating partners were in no way responsible for his loss and that recovery should be against Barton alone.

Affirmed.

Phillips v. Cook

210 A.2d 743 (Md.) 1965

Daniel Phillips and Isadore Harris were partners doing business as Dan's Used Cars. While driving home in a car which was part of the inventory of the business, Harris injured the plaintiffs. They sued the partners individually and the partnership. Neither of the partners owned a personal automobile, but both, whenever they desired to, drove partnership automobiles with dealer licenses. The defendant Phillips appealed from a verdict for the plaintiffs, contending that there was insufficient evidence that Harris was acting within the scope of the partnership business and for its benefit.

MARBURY, J. . . . If there was any evidence, no matter how slight, viewed in the light most favorable to appellees, that Harris, in using the partnership vehicle, was acting within the scope of the partnership agreement and business, i. e., the use was of some benefit or incidental to the partnership arrangement, then the question was for the jury's determination. Appellant contends that because Harris was on his way home from the used car lot at the time of the accident, the evidence was insufficient to support a finding by the jury that he was acting within the scope of the partnership arrangement or that such use of the vehicle was of benefit to the partnership.

In a case involving a partnership, the contract of partnership constitutes all of its members as agents of each other and each partner acts both as a principal and as the agent of the others in regard to acts done within the apparent scope of the business, purpose and agreement of the partnership or for its benefit. It is clear that the partnership is bound by the partner's wrongful act if done within the scope of the partnership's business. Code (1957), Article 73A, Section 13 provides:

> Where, by any wrongful act or omission of any partner acting in the ordinary course of the business of the partnership, or with the authority of his copartners, loss or injury is caused to any person, not being a partner in the partnership, or any penalty is incurred, the partnership is liable therefor to the same extent as the partner so acting or omitting to act.

The test of the liability of the partnership and of its members for the torts of any one partner is whether the wrongful act was done within what may reasonably be found to be the scope of the business of the partnership and for its benefit. The extent of the authority of a partner is determined essentially by the same principles as those which measure the scope of an agent's authority. Partnership cases may differ from principal and agent and master and servant relationships because in the nonpartnership cases, the element of control or authorization is important. This is not so in the case of a partnership for a partner is also a principal, and control and authorization are generally within his power to exercise.

In the past, we have held both in workmen's compensation cases and others that where an employer authorizes or furnishes the employee transportation to and from his work as an incident to his employment, or as a benefit to the employer, the employee is considered in the course of his employment when so traveling. This is so whether it be to his place to eat, sleep or to the employee's home. . . . Other jurisdictions have held that the question of agency or scope of employment is for the jury where the use of a motor vehicle by an employee or agent to go to and from the place of his employment, to his home or to get his meals, is dictated by the nature of the services to be performed, part of the contract of employment, or whether such use is beneficial to both principal and agent or master and servant.

Here, the fact that the defendant partners were in the used car business; that the very vehicle involved in the accident was one of the partnership assets for sale at all times, day or night, at any location; that Harris was on call by Phillips or customers at his home—he went back to the lot two or three times after going home; that he had no set time and worked irregular hours, coupled with the fact that he frequently stopped to conduct partnership business on the way to and from the lot; drove partnership vehicles to the Department of Motor Vehicles, and to dealers in Baltimore to view and buy used cars while on his way to or from his home; that one of the elements of the partnership arrangement was that each partner could have full use of the vehicles; that the use of the automobile by Harris for transportation to and from his home was admittedly "essential" to the partnership arrangement and the most practical and convenient way to operate; and that Harris conducted partnership business both at the used car lot and from his home requires that the question of whether the use of the automobile at the time of the accident was in the partnership interest and for its benefit be submitted to the jury. We find that the lower court did not err in refusing to grant appellant's motions for a directed verdict as to him in the capacity of a co-partner trading as Dan's Used Cars. . . .

Judgment affirmed.

Rodgers v. Saunders

396 P.2d 817 (Mont.) 1964

Plaintiffs Rodgers sued defendant Saunders, on an open account, for service station products. The defendant was a partner in the operation of a dance studio with one Farrell. Farrell had charged the gasoline products and had also paid prior accounts by using partnership checks. Farrell had abandoned the business and was not a party to the lawsuit.

Plaintiffs contended that Farrell had used his car in promoting the dance studio and that the debt was therefore a partnership obligation. The lower court found no liability, and the plaintiffs appealed.

HARRISON, J. . . . There is general agreement in the law that each partner may be considered agent for the partnership and thereby bind the partnership if he is acting within the scope of the partnership business. This is, in fact, manifested in the instant case by the fact that Saunders went to Glasgow when Farrell abandoned the business in order to take care of the dancing students still entitled to instruction. Farrell had obligated the partnership to these students because he was acting within the scope of the partnership business in making the contracts.

The record does not show that the gasoline purchases were purchased pursuant to partnership business. There is some indication that Farrell drove in and about the Glasgow area to promote the studio, but the gasoline purchased was not related to such tours. By the nature of the set-up, Farrell had control over the management of the Glasgow studio. He was free to use the studio account as his own. Purchase of items for the studio would, of course, obligate the partnership. Since Farrell alone maintained the account he could use it to write checks for personal items as well. In a sense all items benefit the partnership as they tend to support Farrell, but this is not sufficient to make the partnership liable for all charge accounts. The purchase of gasoline, at best, tendered an incidental benefit to the partnership. It is generally agreed that,

> . . . a partner has no implied authority to make a purchase not within the scope of the business as ordinarily conducted, and, in the absence of authorization, the other partners will not be liable therefor unless they have adopted or ratified it or unless the purchase was made for the protection of the firm against a liability incurred.

And further:

> [T]he mere fact that a firm receives a benefit from a contract or transaction entered into by a partner in his individual capacity has been held insufficient to impose liability on the firm.

Therefore, we feel the service station charges are not the liability of Saunders or of the partnership but of Farrell personally. . . .

Affirmed.

Lankford v. State

144 S.E.2d 463 (Ga.) 1965

This action upon an open account was brought by Universal Creditors Association, Inc., as assignee of a firm composed of several medical doctors, against Leonard R. Wood and Joan C. Wood. The defendants except to the trial court's judgment overruling their general demurrer. Defendants contend . . . that the petition fails to state a cause of action because plaintiff is not a real party in interest due to the assignment by only one doctor of the firm.

BELL, J. . . . Defendants argue that the assignment of the claim to plaintiff fails to show that the assignor is a legal entity; and that the plaintiff corporation "can stand in no better position than its transferor." The assignment of the claim, a copy of which is annexed to the petition as an exhibit, shows that it was executed by one member of a named "firm" composed of several medical doctors, on behalf of the firm. In common acceptation the word "firm" is synonymous with "partnership." Any member of a partnership may in its behalf transfer in writing choses in action belonging to the firm. The assignment to the corporation, the plaintiff in this case, being valid, there is no merit in the defendants' contention that the plaintiff is not a real party in interest.

The trial court properly overruled defendants' general demurrer to plaintiff's petition.

Judgment affirmed.

Holloway v. Smith et al.

197 Va. 334 (1955)

The defendants Smith and Ten Brook were partners in the automobile business under the name of Greenwood Sales and Service. Defendant Ten Brook borrowed $6,000 from the plaintiff and gave a partnership note in return. It is contended by the Smiths that Ten Brook borrowed the money to make his initial capital contribution to the partnership and that the obligation to repay was solely that of Ten Brook. They also contended that Ten Brook lacked the authority to bind the partnership on the note. The lower court held that the Smiths were not liable on the note.

SPRATLEY, J. Greenwood Sales & Service was a trading or commercial partnership, and in the course of its business, it borrowed money for carrying on its business in the usual way.

. . . It is settled law in Virginia, both by statute and in numerous decisions that a partner is an agent of the firm for the purpose of the partnership business, and may bind all partners by his acts within the scope of such business. It is of no consequence whether the partner is acting in good faith with his copartners or not, provided the act is within the scope of the partnership's business and professedly for the firm, and third persons are acting in good faith.

. . . Pertinent here is this statement from 40 Am. Jur., *Partnership*, § 11 at p. 134:

> The character and nature of partnerships ordinarily determine the powers and liabilities of different classes of partners. In this connection, the most important distinction exists between trading or commercial partnerships and those which are not organized for the purpose of trade or commerce. Greater powers are impliedly given to members of the former as compared with the second type of partnerships, such as in the matter of drawing or endorsing negotiable instruments.

The Smiths selected Ten Brook as their partner. The partnership was a going concern when the $6,000 note was executed. In the absence of a restriction on his authority, known to Mrs. Holloway, Ten Brook had the same power to bind the partnership as his copartners had. Ten Brook, as the agent of the partnership, solicited the loan professedly for the firm, and executed the note evidencing it, for "apparently carrying on in the usual way the business of the partnership" of which he was a member.

The court held that the Smiths as well as Ten Brook were liable on the note.

CHAPTER 43
REVIEW QUESTIONS AND PROBLEMS

1. *A* and *B* operated a law firm as partners. A personality conflict arose, and they agreed to dissolve the partnership. Each individually would continue in practice. After dissolution, *A* took most of the client files with him without *B*'s knowledge or consent. Does *B* have a remedy?

2. *A, B,* and *C* orally agreed to operate a refuse collection service as partners. Each contributed $2,000 toward the purchase of a truck and refuse cans. *A* was to manage the business affairs, and *B* and *C* were to do the outside pickup work. Profits were to be divided equally, but nothing was said about wages. A dispute arose and the partnership was dissolved. *B* and *C* claim an additional payment of back wages for services. Should the claim be allowed?

3. *A, B,* and *C* operated a trucking firm as partners. While driving the firm truck on partnership business, *A* had motor trouble. *A* decided to sleep in the cab until morning, and the night was foggy, he placed no warning lights on the truck. A motorist, *D,* struck the rear of the unlighted truck and suffered severe injuries, totaling $150,000. The firm owns assets of $25,000; *A* has $3,000; *B* is insolvent; and *C,* their rich uncle, has $200,000. From whom may *D* recover?

4. *X, Y,* and *Z* operated a poultry farm as partners. The nature of the business was buying, raising, and selling poultry. *X,* the managing partner, borrowed money from *A* and signed notes in his individual capacity. *A*'s intent was to use the money for firm purchases, but it was not so applied. Is the partnership liable on the notes?

5. *A* trained several horses for other persons, including a horse owned by *A* and *B* as partners. *A* gratuitously loaned one of the stalls assigned to the partnership at a racetrack to *C* to groom a horse. Sometime thereafter, *A* told *C* that this stall was needed for an additional horse. An argument ensued; it ended with *A* attacking *C* with a pitchfork, seriously injuring him. May *C* recover from *B*?

6. *A* and *B,* brothers, purchased a parcel of land on which they constructed a service station. They shared the down payment and both signed the mortgage. Later they deeded the property to *C,* their mother, who was helping to pay off the mortgage. *A* and *B* continued to operate the gasoline station together, sharing the profits and work. Some time later, *C* deeded the property to *A,* reserving a life estate for herself. The common use of the property remained the same though *B* knew of the deed. In time the mother died, and disputes arose between *A* and *B*. *A,* claiming he was sole owner, ejected *B* from the property. Does *B* have a remedy?

7. *A* advances to a partnership, for a period of sixty days, the sum of $19,000 in addition to his agreed capital. Is he entitled to interest on the advance?

8. *A* and *B* have been partners for a number of years. Upon *A*'s death, *B* spent considerable time in winding up the partnership affairs. Is he legally entitled to compensation for his services?

9. *A* and *B* are partners in a retail clothing business. Being short of funds in the business, *A*, without the consent or knowledge of *B*, borrowed $500 from *C* and signed a security agreement. Is the partnership property subject to the debt?

10. *X*, a partner in an accountancy firm, borrowed $10,000 in the firm name and used the proceeds to pay an individual debt. Is the firm liable for the debt?

Dissolution of
Partnerships

6-33. Introduction. The term "dissolution" is used to describe the legal destruction of the partnership relationship that occurs whenever, for any reason, a partner ceases to be a member of the firm. Dissolution of an existing partnership also occurs when a new partner is admitted.[1] That dissolution of a partnership is not the same as a termination will be discussed more fully later.

Dissolutions will occur without violation of the partnership agreement: *(a)* by the termination of the stipulated term or particular undertaking specified in the agreement; *(b)* by the express will of any partner when no definite term or particular undertaking is specified;[2] *(c)* by the express will of all the partners who have not assigned their interests or suffered them to be charged for their separate debts either before or after the termination of any specified term or particular undertaking; or *(d)* by the expulsion, in good faith, of any partner from the business, in accordance with such a power conferred by the partnership agreement.[3]

Dissolution may also occur in violation of the partnership agreement. Although the agreement stipulates the length of time the partnership is to last, dissolution is always possible because the relationship is essentially a mutual agency not capable of specific performance and, therefore, each partner has the *power*, but not the *right* to revoke the relationship. In the event of wrongful dissolution, the wrongdoer is liable for damages.

6-34. By Operation of Law. If during the period of the partnership, events occur that make it impossible or illegal for the partnership to continue, it will be dissolved. Such events or conditions are: death or bankruptcy of one of the

[1] Johnson v. Hill, page 873
[2] Johnson v. Kennedy, page 875
[3] Fisher v. Fisher, page 876

partners, or a change in the law that makes the continuance of the business illegal.

A partnership is a personal relationship existing by reason of contract. Therefore, when one of the partners dies, the partnership is dissolved. However, it is not terminated on dissolution but continues for the purpose of winding up partnership's affairs. The process of winding up is, in most states, the exclusive obligation and right of the surviving partner or partners. The executor or administrator of the deceased partner has no right to participate unless the deceased was the last surviving partner or unless specifically authorized by a court to do so.[4] As a general rule, the estate of the deceased partner is not bound on new contracts unconnected with winding up which are entered into after dissolution, even though the partnership agreement provided that the partnership be continued. This subject is discussed further in Section 6-36.

A partnership agreement may provide that the personal representative of the deceased partner is to continue in the firm. Such provisions are not binding on the personal representative. As a matter of fact, he has a choice and may participate in the firm during the period of administration if he elects to do so. Occasionally articles of partnership provide that a deceased partner's interest in the firm may be retained by the survivors for a limited period. Such provision may be enforced and the partnership extended beyond the death of a partner. Although the authorities are not unanimous, it has been held that the estate of a deceased partner is liable for further transactions in such cases.

The bankruptcy of a partner will dissolve the partnership, because the control of his property passes to his assignee or trustee for the benefit of the creditors in somewhat the same way that the control of the property passes to the legal representatives upon the death of a partner. The mere insolvency of a partner will not be sufficient to justify a dissolution, unless there has been an assignment of his assets. The bankruptcy of the firm itself is a cause for dissolution, as is also a valid assignment of all the firm assets for the benefit of creditors.

6-35. Dissolution by Court Decree. When a partnership, by its agreement, is to be continued for a term of years, circumstances may arise that might make the continued existence of the firm impossible and unprofitable. Therefore, upon the application of one of the partners to a court of equity, the partnership may be dissolved. The following are the circumstances and situations in which a court of equity may order dissolution:

1. Total incapacity of a partner to conduct business and to perform the duties required under the contract for partnership.

2. A declaration by judicial process that a partner is insane.

3. Gross misconduct and neglect or breach of duty by a partner to such an extent that it is impossible to carry out the purposes of the partnership agreement. The court will not interfere and grant a decree of dissolution for mere discourtesy, temporary inconvenience, differences of opinion, or errors in judgment.[5] The misconduct must be of such gross nature that the continued operation of the business would be unprofitable.

[4] Niagara Mohawk Power Corporation v. Silbergeld, page 878
[5] Lunn v. Kaiser, page 879

4. Willful and persistent commitment of breach of the partnership agreement, misappropriation of funds, or commitment of fraudulent acts.

5. A partnership that was entered into by reason of fraud may be dissolved on the application of an innocent party. But, if the defrauded partner continues in the partnership with the knowledge of the fraud, no decree of dissolution will be granted.

DISSOLUTION: ITS EFFECT ON THE PARTNERS

6-36. Effect of Dissolution on Powers of Partners. Since upon dissolution a partnership is not terminated, the process of winding up, except when the agreement provides for continuation by purchase of a former partner's share, involves the liquidation of the partnership assets so that cash may be available to pay creditors and to make a distribution to the partners. When the agreement provides for continuation and purchase of a deceased partner's interest, the technical dissolution is followed by valuation and payment, and the new firm immediately commences business.

As a general rule, dissolution terminates the actual authority of any partner to act for the partnership except so far as may be necessary to wind up partnership affairs, to liquidate the assets of the firm in an orderly manner, or to complete transactions begun but not then finished. This termination of authority eliminates actual authority as it relates to the partners; but when it concerns third persons who had dealings with the firm, apparent authority still exists.

The effect of dissolution on the power of a partner to bind the firm depends upon the cause of the dissolution. If the dissolution is caused by (1) the act of a partner, (2) bankruptcy of the partnership, or (3) the death of a partner, each partner is liable to the other partner for his share of any liability incurred on behalf of the firm after dissolution, just as if there had been no dissolution, unless: *(a)* the dissolution was caused by the *act* of any partner and the partner incurring the liability had knowledge of the dissolution; *(b)* the dissolution being by the *death* or *bankruptcy* of a partner, the partner acting for the partnership had knowledge or notice of the death or bankruptcy. In these situations, where knowledge of the dissolution is present, the partner incurring the liability is solely responsible and he cannot require his fellow partners to share the burden of his unauthorized act. If the dissolution is not caused by the act, bankruptcy, or death of a partner, no partner has authority to act and therefore no right to contribution from other partners for liabilities incurred after dissolution.

When dissolution results from the death of a partner, title to partnership property remains in the surviving partner or partners for purposes of winding up and liquidation. Both real and personal property is, through the survivors, thus made available to a firm's creditors. All realty is treated as though it were personal property; it is sold and the surviving partners finally account, usually in cash, to the personal representative of the deceased partner for the latter's share in the proceeds of liquidation.

Upon dissolution, it is the duty of the remaining partner or partners to wind up the affairs. If they fail to do so and instead continue the business, they have liability to the withdrawing partner, his assignee, or personal representative for use of partnership assets. The liability may include interest if the value of the former partner's portion of the partnership can be ascertained.

6-37. Right of Partners After Dissolution. Where the dissolution is caused in any way other than the breach of the partnership agreement, each partner, as against his copartners or their assignees, has a right to insist that all the partnership assets be used first to pay firm debts. After firm obligations are paid, remaining assets are used to return capital investments, proper adjustments for profits and losses having been made. All of the partners, except those who have caused a wrongful dissolution of the firm, have the right to participate in the winding up of the business. The majority may select the method or procedure to be followed in the liquidation, but the assets, other than real estate, must be turned into cash unless all the partners agree to distribution in kind.

If a partnership which is to continue for a fixed period is dissolved by the wrongful withdrawal, in contravention of the partnership agreement, of one of its members, the remaining members may continue as partners under the same firm name for the balance of the agreed term of the partnership, if they have settled with the withdrawing partner for his interest in the partnership. The remaining partners, in determining the interest of the withdrawing partner, have the right to pay him his share in cash, less the damages caused by his wrongful withdrawal. In the calculation of his share, the goodwill of the business is not taken into consideration. If no accounting is made at the time that the partner withdraws, the remaining partners may continue the business for the agreed period by securing the payment of the ascertained value of such withdrawing partner's interest by a bond approved by the court, covering not only the partner's interest at the time of the withdrawal, but also indemnifying him against any future liabilities of the continuing partnership.

The right of the partners to expel one of their number is determined entirely by the partnership agreement. Thus, the right to continue after expulsion, as well as the amount which the expelled partner is to receive, depends exclusively upon the articles of copartnership.

DISSOLUTION: ITS EFFECT ON THIRD PARTIES

6-38. Liability Existing Prior to Dissolution. Although the dissolution of a partnership terminates the authority of the partners to create future liability, it does not discharge the existing liability of any partner. An agreement between the partners themselves that one or more of the partners will assume the partnership liabilities and that a withdrawing partner will be discharged does not bind the firm creditors. However, upon dissolution, a partner who withdraws may be discharged from any existing liability by an agreement to that effect with the creditors. If upon dissolution of a partnership, an incoming partner or the remaining partners promise to assume the liabilities of the dissolved partnership, such liabilities will be discharged as to the withdrawing partner if any creditor of the partnership, knowing of the agreement, changes or alters the character of the liability or the time of its payment by agreement with the new firm.

The individual estate of a deceased partner, where firm assets are insufficient to pay firm debts, is liable to third parties for all debts created while he was a partner, subject, however, to the payment of his separate debts.

6-39. Notice. Transactions entered into with former creditors of the firm who have not received actual knowledge of the dissolution continue to bind any partner who has withdrawn.[6] Notice of dissolution is required whether the dissolution is caused by an act of the parties or by law, except where a partner becomes bankrupt or the continuation of the business becomes illegal. Therefore, upon death of a partner, his personal representative must give immediate notice in order to avoid further liability.

Where the dissolution is caused by an act of the parties, the partners will continue to be liable to all persons who formerly dealt with the firm but who are not creditors, unless public notice of such dissolution is given. Notice by publication in a newspaper in the community where the business has been transacted or notice of the dissolution by a properly addressed envelope placed in the mailbox is sufficient.

Where a partner has not actively engaged in the conduct of the partnership business and creditors had not learned that he was a partner and had not extended credit to the firm on the faith of such partner, he is under no duty to give notice to either of the groups mentioned above.

6-40. New Partners and New Firms. A person admitted as a partner into an existing partnership is, as a member of the firm, liable to the extent of his investment for all obligations created before his admission, as though previously he had been a partner. His separate estate is not liable for such obligations, and the creditors of the old firm can look only to the firm assets and to the members of the old firm.

If a business is continued without liquidation of the partnership affairs, creditors of the first, or dissolved, partnership are also creditors of the partnership continuing the business. Likewise, if the partners assign all their interest to a single partner, who continues the business without liquidation of the partnership affairs, creditors of the dissolved partnership are also creditors of the single person so continuing the business. Likewise, when all the partners or their representatives assign their rights in the partnership property to one or more third persons who promise to pay the debts and to continue the business, the creditors of the dissolved partnership are also creditors of the person or persons continuing the business.

DISTRIBUTIONS ON DISSOLUTION

6-41. Solvent Partnerships. Upon the dissolution of a solvent partnership and a winding up of its business, an accounting is had to determine its assets and liabilities. Before the partners are entitled to participate in any of the assets, whether such partners are owed money by the firm or not, all firm creditors other than partners are entitled to be paid. After firm creditors are paid, the assets of the partnership are distributed among the partners, as follows:

[6] Letellier-Phillips Paper Co. v. Fiedler et al., page 880

1. Each partner who has made advances to the firm, or has incurred liability for or on behalf of the firm, is entitled to be reimbursed.

2. Each partner is then entitled to the return of the capital which he has contributed to the firm.[7]

3. Any balance is distributed as profits, in accordance with the partnership agreement.

6-42. Insolvent Partnerships.   When the firm is *insolvent* and a court of equity has acquired jurisdiction because of a bill for accounting, a petition by creditors, or an insolvency proceeding, etc., over the assets of the partnership, together with the assets of the individual partners, the assets are distributed in accordance with a rule known as "marshaling of assets."

Persons entering into a partnership agreement impliedly agree that the partnership assets shall be used for the payment of the firm debts before the payment of any individual debts of the partners. Consequently, a court of equity, in distributing firm assets, will give priority to firm creditors in firm assets as against the separate creditors of the individual partners and will give priority to private creditors of individual partners in the separate assets of the partners as against firm creditors. Each class of creditors is not permitted to use the fund belonging to the other until the claims of the other have been satisfied. Since the firm creditors have available two funds out of which to seek payment—firm assets and the individual assets of the partners—and individual creditors of the partners have only one fund, the personal assets of the partners, equity' compels the firm creditors to exhaust firm assets before having recourse to the partners' individual assets.[8] This rule does not apply, however, if a partner conceals his existence and permits the other member of the firm to deal with the public as the sole owner of the business. Under these circumstances, the dormant partner by his conduct has led the creditors of the active partner to rely upon firm assets as the separate property of the active partner, and by reason of his conduct, the dormant partner is estopped from demanding an application of the equity rule that firm assets shall be used to pay firm creditors in priority, and individual assets to pay individual creditors. Thus the firm assets must be shared equally with firm creditors and the individual creditors of the active partners. In such a case, since the firm assets may not be sufficient to pay all the firm debts when depleted by payments to individual creditors, there may be unpaid firm creditors, and dormant partners will be personally liable. Since the firm creditors' right to firm property rests upon the partners' right that firm assets be used to pay firm debts, the conduct that estops a dormant partner also denies the creditors such a preference. Furthermore, the creditors who relied upon the assets in the hands of the sole active partner cannot claim a preference when later they learn such assets were partnership assets.

Just as the individual creditors are limited to individual assets, firm creditors are limited to firm assets. Therefore, firm creditors are not entitled to payment out of the individual assets of the partners until the individual creditors have been paid. This rule applies, even though the firm creditors may, at

---

[7] Gordon v. Ginsberg, page 880
[8] Casey et al. v. Grantham et al., page 881

the same time, be individual creditors of a member of the firm. There are two main exceptions to this general rule: (1) Where there are no firm assets and no living solvent partners. The rule for the limit of firm creditors to firm assets applies only where there are firm assets. If no firm assets or no living solvent partner exists, the firm creditors may share equally with the individual creditors in the distribution of the individual estates of the partners. (2) If a partner has fraudulently converted the firm assets to his own use, it follows that the firm creditors will be entitled to share equally with individual creditors in such partner's individual assets.

The doctrine of marshaling of assets was not applicable to tort claims at common law and is not applicable to tort claims under the Uniform Partnership Act. Partners are individually liable in tort for the acts of the firm, its agents and servants. The liability is joint and several. Thus, the injured party may sue the partners individually or as a partnership. The firm assets need not be first used to collect a judgment and direct action may be taken against individual assets.

DISSOLUTION OF PARTNERSHIPS CASES

Johnson v. Hill

402 P.2d 225 (Ariz.) 1965

KRUCKER, C. J. This appeal involves a dispute arising out of a medical partnership. The appellant (plaintiff below), Dr. Johnson, sought an accounting for his share of the net worth of the partnership from the defendants, Doctors Holbrook, Stephens, Hill, and Goodin. The lower court, sitting without a jury, found for the defendants. No written findings of fact or conclusions of law were made by the court.

A chronological sequence of events will be discussed in order to understand the nature of the dispute.

In 1934, Dr. Holbrook entered into a medical partnership with Dr. Hill in Tucson, Arizona. Dr. Stephens was admitted into the partnership in 1946. In 1950, Dr. Johnson, the plaintiff, was employed on salary by the then existing partnership. In 1960, Dr. Johnson became the fourth member in the partnership. Articles of partnership were drawn up, giving Dr. Johnson a 23.5 percent share of net profits. Dr. Goodin was made a partner on January 1, 1961, by oral agreement with the unanimous consent of the other partners. It was this oral agreement that caused the dispute in the settling of accounts when Dr. Johnson left the partnership. Plaintiff contends that this oral agreement revoked the written articles, and therefore he is entitled to a percentage of the net worth of the partnership. Defendants contend that plaintiff is entitled only to certain insurance policies and the amount shown in his capital account, in accordance with the written articles. The plaintiff received the policies and the amount in his capital account. These payments are not the subject of this appeal.

On May 1, 1961, a meeting was held in which percentages of profits were discussed. Doctors Johnson and Goodin were requested to acquiesce to a reduction of their percentage to approximately 19 percent. It was a short time after this meeting that Dr. Johnson terminated his relationship with the partnership.

Two provisions of the articles of partnership of 1960 are of importance in this case:

> Article III—Contingencies
> 1. With the unanimous consent of the then existing partners, new partners may be admitted into the partnership at any time. Each new partner shall adopt and subscribe to these Articles by affixing his signature to "Schedule A—Partnership Interests" (hereunto annexed and by reference made a part hereof, and shall adopt and subscribe to any other terms and conditions which may then be imposed).
> 2. . . . Upon such withdrawal, he shall be entitled to receive, and there shall be assigned to him forthwith in full payment for his interest in the partnership, only such policy or policies of life insurance as is or are then being carried on his life by the partnership, . . .

On January 1, 1961, when Dr. Goodin was unanimously accepted as a partner, he did not sign the articles of 1960, nor were they ever signed by him. Plaintiff thus contends that as of January 1, 1961, there was a new partnership based on the oral agreement, and the formation of this new partnership revoked the written articles of partnership. It is further contended by plaintiff that provision 2 of the articles dealing with withdrawal is not applicable inasmuch as the articles were revoked. Defendants claim, and they prevailed in the lower court, that the articles were never revoked but that the partnership continued to operate under the 1960 articles, as modified only to the extent of adjusting profit percentages so that Dr. Goodin could receive his share.

Article III, dealing with admission of new partners, specifically states that the new partner shall adopt and subscribe to the articles by affixing his signature thereto. The evidence is clear that this was not done by Dr. Goodin.

It is a well-established general rule that an existing partnership is dissolved and a new partnership is formed whenever a partner retires or a new one is admitted. In other words, every change in the personnel of a firm works a dissolution. This general rule would apply unless something in the agreement provides otherwise. The written agreement in this case did provide for admission of new partners, but said provision was not complied with.

This leads us to the conclusion that upon Dr. Goodin's admittance the old partnership of January 1, 1960 to January 1, 1961, consisting of Doctors Holbrook, Hill, Stephens, and Johnson, was terminated as a matter of law. Thereafter, a new partnership was formed consisting of Doctors Holbrook, Hill, Stephens, Johnson, and Goodin. There is no argument that a partnership may be formed by oral agreement, in absence of statutory regulation.

The question therefore remains, was there evidence at the trial to show that the new partnership by oral agreement was to exist and abide by the written articles of the terminated partnership. . . .

[W]e must look to the evidence to see if the five partners to the oral agreement did intend to adopt the old articles of partnership for determining their rights and duties in their new partnership. . . .

In the present case, the plaintiff, Dr. Johnson, testified that the written agreement was not discussed at the meeting in which Dr. Goodin was admitted to the partnership. He also testified that there was no conversation that under the oral agreement they would operate according to the provisions of the written agreement. He testified that a new paper was handed around but that he only noticed the new percentages.

In contrast, Dr. Goodin testified that a new written agreement (after Dr. Johnson had departed) was the same as they had always been under as far as he knew. Dr. Holbrook testified that he brought a copy of the old written agreement to the meeting to point out that under the new arrangement they would continue to operate under the written agreement. Doctors Stephens and Hill corroborated Dr. Holbrook in that the latter did have a copy of the written agreement with him. They also testified that all the old partners were to bring their copy in so that Dr. Goodin could sign them.

It is thus apparent to the Court that there is conflicting evidence as to the Doctors' intention concerning the written Articles. The lower court chose to believe the defendants. Upon a reading of the transcript of testimony, we find ample evidence to support the finding of the lower court. . . .

The judgment of the lower court is affirmed.

Johnson v. Kennedy

214 N.E.2d. 276 (Mass.) 1966

Plaintiff brought suit in equity for an accounting and for damages based on an alleged wrongful dissolution of an oral partnership. The issue was whether the dissolution was wrongful. The lower court found that it was not and entered a decree for the defendants.

KIRK, J. . . . In April, 1961, the plaintiffs Johnson and Walker joined with the defendant Donald C. Kennedy (Kennedy) in forming an insurance agency partnership to be known as the Triangle Insurance Agency (Triangle). The arrangement was oral. There was no agreement as to how long the partnership would continue. It was agreed that each would have a one-third interest in the partnership. . . .

In August, 1963, the partners retained counsel to prepare a written partnership agreement. By December 7, 1963, the agreement was drawn. It provided that the partnership was to last for twenty-five years from January 1, 1964. The three partners were to meet, discuss, and sign the agreement on December 16, 1963.

Meanwhile, early in December, 1963, Kennedy secretly consulted an attorney about owning the business himself, and, without consulting Johnson and Walker, arranged that the Triangle bank accounts be held jointly with his wife. In November, Kennedy drew more than twice his salary from the agency. This caused some dispute among the partners, and Johnson took the agency's books to his home for review. On December 13, Kennedy transferred the agency funds to two Boston banks, concealing their location from the other partners, opening one account in his wife's name alone, and the other in the name of Triangle with his wife having the right to withdraw. On the night of December 14, 1963, Kennedy secretly removed all books, records, and furniture from the office to another office a block away where he opened for business under the Triangle name. On December 17, Johnson and Walker brought this bill, claiming wrongful dissolution and a right to damages. Kennedy denied, *inter alia,* that the dissolution was wrongful or that damages were due. . . .

In his initial report . . . , the master concluded generally that the dissolution of the firm caused by Kennedy's actions was wrongful, and that damages should be assessed against Kennedy in the amount of $8,333.33 in favor of each plaintiff, that amount being one-third of what the master found to be the firm's fair market value, namely, $25,000.

The defendant Kennedy objected to various parts of the report, and specifically asked that the case be recommitted for an accounting. The case was recommitted for that purpose. . . .

The final decree adjudged that the dissolution was not wrongful and that the plaintiffs were not entitled to damages for breach of the agreement. Kennedy was ordered to pay Johnson $1,330.15 and to pay Walker $980.15. Johnson and Walker were ordered to convey all of their interest in the physical property of the partnership to Kennedy. . . .

We consider the final decree. There was no error in the rulings that the dissolution of the partnership was not wrongful and that the plaintiffs were not entitled to damages for breach of the agreement. Inasmuch as the oral agreement did not specify the life of the agency, the partnership was at the will of the partners. As G.L. c. 108A, § 31, provides, "Dissolution is caused: (1) Without violation of the agreement between the partners . . . (b) By the express will of any partner when no definite term or particular undertaking is specified." Thus, in a partnership of indefinite duration, any partner may lawfully dissolve the firm at any time. The unexecuted agreement specifying a duration of twenty-five years did not affect the nature of the existing partnership. Because the firm was a partnership at will, Kennedy's termination of it, however unseemly in manner and method, was not a legal wrong. . . .

Affirmed.

Fisher v. Fisher

212 N.E.2d 222 (Mass.) 1965

SPIEGEL, J. This is a bill in equity for dissolution of a partnership and a partnership accounting. The defendants filed a counterclaim for breach of the partnership agreement. The case was referred to a master. . . . A final decree was entered dismissing the plaintiff's bill from which the plaintiff appealed.

The master found the following facts.

In 1897 George E. Fisher established George E. Fisher & Co. Over a period of years, from 1919 to around 1930, he took into his business as partners his brother Carlos (plaintiff) and sons Allen, George Ellis, and Donald (defendants). When George E. Fisher died, his widow was taken in as a nominal partner until her death in 1956.

The parties operated under ten year term partnership agreements covering business in insurance, real estate, and mortgage loans. However, their last agreement, made in 1960, covered only insurance business. Under the 1960 agreement the plaintiff was to work half time and to draw $65 per week plus an auto allowance, life insurance premiums, and one quarter of the net profits. Provision was made for the payment of specified sums on death or withdrawal of a partner. All of the agreements required each partner to contribute to the partnership fifteen percent of all fees and commissions received for acting in any fiduciary capacity. In April of 1961 the defendants discovered that Carlos had been receiving moneys for which he failed to properly account to the partnership. An accountant's report showed that the plaintiff owed about $380 to the partnership for money received after execution of the 1960 partnership agreement and several thousand dollars for money received on earlier dates. The defendants suspended the plaintiff from the partnership as of May 1, 1961, and stopped his drawing account, auto allowance, and insurance premiums. The plaintiff wrote a letter protesting the stopping of his drawing account and claiming his rights as a partner. On June 23, 1961, the plaintiff was notified that he was "permanently suspended" from the partnership because of his failure to account to the partnership. In October, 1961, he brought this bill for a partnership accounting.

The master also found that if Carlos was wrongfully excluded from the partnership, he was entitled to $34,469.51 on liquidation, and he should be charged for $4,983.03 withheld from the firm. On recommittal on the issue of the plaintiff's share of the profits after October 1, 1962, the master found the plaintiff's share to be $4,682.80.

The plaintiff contends that he is not barred from maintaining this suit by his conduct toward the partnership. "The doctrine of clean hands is not one of absolutes. It is to be so applied as to accomplish its purpose." Its purpose is to prevent a party from benefiting by his dishonesty. In the instant case the plaintiff's claims do not arise out of his improper conduct. "A partner does not lose his rights in the accrued profits of a firm by reason of breaches of the partnership articles, whether or not committed in bad faith, although of course he will be subject to charges for all unexcused breaches in the final accounting."

The defendants argue that by his actions the plaintiff withdrew from the partnership, and the provisions of the partnership agreement on withdrawal govern him. There is no provision in the agreement or in the Uniform Partnership Act that a breach is equivalent to withdrawal from the partnership, and we will not imply one. This bill cannot be construed as a withdrawal, since the plaintiff had already been excluded from the partnership.

The plaintiff's failure to properly account to the partnership for moneys received by him constituted a breach of the agreement. This breach furnished grounds for the defendants to seek a decree of dissolution of the partnership under the provisions of G.L. c. 108A, § 32(1) (d). Instead of following the procedure under the statute and without any provision in the agreement authorizing what the defendants called a "permanent suspension," they ousted the plaintiff from the partnership and divided his interest in the partnership among themselves. This wrongful action furnished the plaintiff with grounds to obtain dissolution under the same provisions of the statute.

We believe that in justice to the defendants they should not be required to continue to pay the plaintiff moneys beyond June 23, 1961, the date the plaintiff was notified in writing that he was suspended from the partnership because of his failure to account to the partnership. Equity and the furtherance of justice require that the partnership be dissolved as of June 23, 1961. Such a decree may be entered *nunc pro tunc*.

It follows, therefore, that the plaintiff is entitled to receive from the partnership such sums as may be determined to be due him if the partnership had been dissolved as of June 23, 1961, in accordance with the provisions of G.L. c.

108A, § 38, with interest from that date.... The ... is remanded to the Superior Court for further proceedings in accordance with this opinion.

So ordered.

Niagara Mohawk Power Corporation v. Silbergeld

294 N.Y.S.2d 975 (1966)

JOSEPH P. KUSZYNSKI, J. . . . This is a motion for summary judgment brought by the defendants, Abraham R. Kushner and Molly Silbergeld, as Executors of the estate of Rose Silbergeld, deceased, on the ground that with respect to the estate, the plaintiff's cause of action is without merit. The facts are as follows:

On December 13, 1963 a contract between Niagara Mohawk Power Corporation and a partnership known as H. Silbergeld and composed of Arthur Silbergeld and his mother, Rose Silbergeld, now deceased, was executed. The contract provided that the partnership would demolish and salvage an obsolete power generating station owned by plaintiff in Niagara Falls, New York, and known as the Adams Station. In return for the salvage recovered by the partnership, the partnership was to pay plaintiff the sum of $175,000 subject to certain adjustments in accordance with a schedule set forth in the agreement. The agreement called for the work to be completed by December 15, 1964 and contained a forfeiture clause operable at the option of the plaintiff upon the occurrence of a number of contingencies including default in payment by the partnership or its failure to proceed diligently with the work. If the plaintiff decided to avail itself of the forfeiture clause, it was required to give three days' written notice exclusive of the day of mailing to the partnership at 209 13th Street, Niagara Falls, New York.

The contract not having been completed on December 15, 1964, an extension agreement was negotiated allowing the completion date of June 15, 1965, to be substituted for the original completion date. The partnership failed to complete its work or its payment on June 15, 1965. On June 5, 1965, one of the partners, namely Rose Silbergeld, died.

Written notice of intention to forfiet the agreement was mailed to the partnership at the address indicated on August 3, 1965, and received by it on August 4, 1965.

In the fall of 1965 the plaintiff awarded the job for completion of the work to the lowest bidder at a cost of $28,317.00.

The attorneys for the estate on this motion argue that the estate was entitled to come in and complete the work unless the plaintiff gave specific notice to it of the intent to terminate the agreement because the Company knew of the death of Rose Silbergeld.

This Court is of the opinion that the contention of the estate is without merit. The Partnership Law provides under Section 62 that upon the death of one partner, the partnership is dissolved. Furthermore, the rights of a deceased partner are governed by the Partnership Law rather than by the Decedents Estate Law. While the partnership is not terminated on dissolution, it continues merely for the purpose of winding up the partnership affairs and the processes of winding up is an exclusive obligation and right of the surviving partner. The executors of the dead partner have no right to participate in or interfere with the winding up processes by the surviving partner. The only right of the executors of a deceased partner is to demand an accounting from the surviving partner upon completion of the winding up of its affairs.

Under the terms of the contract the exercise of the forfeiture clause was at the option of the plaintiff upon failure to comply with the agreement. This Court finds that the plaintiff has complied with the requirements of notice to the partnership as provided under the terms of the agreement. Therefore this motion is in all respects denied.

Lunn v. Kaiser
72 N.W.2d 312 (S. Dak.) 1955

Plaintiff and defendant were partners in the farming and livestock business. They became involved in a series of arguments over matters of a trivial nature and plaintiff brought this action to dissolve the partnership. The lower court ruled in favor of the plaintiff and the defendant appealed.

RUDOLPH, J. . . . The evidence also discloses several minor incidents such as arguments about walking across the lawn, the amount of cream furnished plaintiff, the pounding on the house being remodeled while defendant's children were asleep, and perhaps other similar incidents.

It may be conceded that the relationship between the parties was not that of bosom friends but nevertheless the purpose for which the contract was entered into succeeded and the personal animosity, if such it may be called, existing between the parties did not detract from the successful conduct of the business.

. . . We find nothing in the record to support any determination that plaintiff was deprived of any right of direction he had under the contract. The real dispute here relates to discord over trivial matters, for which both parties were responsible. No doubt the bringing of this action only added to the discord, as plaintiff testified the parties were only on speaking terms during the two months preceding the trial, but defendant cannot be charged with commencing these proceedings.

The agreement expires by its own terms on March 1, 1956. It does not clearly appear that the plaintiff will suffer any loss by the continuation of the relationship during the existence of the agreement. The trial court stated in his memorandum opinion, "I am unable to determine that one is more responsible for this situation than the other. . . . " Under these circumstances we believe the harsh remedy of dissolution is unnecessary.

We are inclined to agree with the Pennsylvania court, "Differences and discord should be settled by the partners themselves by the application of mutual forbearance rather than by bills in equity for dissolution. Equity is not a referee of partnership quarrels. A going and prosperous business will not be dissolved merely because of friction among the partners; it will not interfere to determine which contending faction is more at fault."

Reversed.

Letellier-Phillips Paper Co. v. Fiedler et al.

32 Tenn. App. 137 (1949)

The plaintiffs brought this action to recover from the defendants as individuals and members of a partnership for merchandise sold and delivered to them. A corporation had been formed by the defendants which took over their individual and partnership assets. The plaintiffs alleged that they were not aware that the partnership had been converted into a corporation. From a judgment in favor of the plaintiffs, defendants appealed.

SWEPSTON, J. The suit is on account for merchandise sold and delivered and the essential question in the trial below was whether there was partnership liability or corporate liability, the partners having operated as such for about a year and having later formed a corporation.

... The bill alleges that about December 24, 1945, complainant agreed to extend credit to defendants, Fiedler & Sullivan, individually and as partners trading as Fied-Sul Paper Mills. That upon the pledge of the individual credit of the defendants complainant began shipping them merchandise.

That the account about January 1, 1947, was current and amounted to $6,855.26. That subsequently the balance began to grow larger until on August 1, 1947, it amounted to $26,890.70, which later upon demand was reduced to $24,060.74 at which figure it has remained, because all purchases lately have been for cash.

That about August 1, 1947, complainant learned for the first time that a corporation had been formed by defendants and that it had taken over certain assets of the individuals and of the partnership all without notice to complainant.

That it had never dealt with the corporation and had relied upon the credit of the partnership and the individuals composing it and that said transfer of assets was fraudulent, etc.

... The cases show that the notice may be an express notice or may be implied from sufficient circumstances. However obtained, it must be sufficient to amount to actual knowledge where one who has been dealing with the firm before dissolution is involved. The knowledge may be constructive as to those who have not dealt with the firm before dissolution.

Affirmed.

Gordon v. Ginsberg

255 N.Y.S.2d 966 (1964)

PER CURIAM. In an action for the dissolution of a partnership and for an accounting, defendant appeals from an interlocutory judgment of the Supreme Court, Kings County, entered July 30, 1963, after a nonjury trial, upon the opinion and decision of the court in plaintiff's favor. ...

The parties, concededly, were partners in a leather goods business known as Ginsberg Brothers. The principal dispute between them is whether they were also partners in certain real estate ventures into which defendant entered in his own name. We are of the opinion that the proof was sufficient to support the finding of the learned trial court that the parties were partners in the real estate transactions. Each party, on the accounting which has been directed, may establish the amount of his capital contributions to the various ventures and each will be entitled to the return of such contributions before any division is made of the remainder of the assets.

We are also of the opinion, however, that an accounting of the leather goods business should have been ordered. Both parties requested such an accounting in their pleadings; the business allegedly was the source, at least in part, of the funds used for the purchase of the real estate; and, under the circumstances presented by this record, we believe such an accounting is required in order to determine, adequately, the respective rights of the parties.

Casey et al. v. Grantham et al.

239 N.C. 121 (1954)

The plaintiff, Casey, brought this action against the defendant Harold J. Grantham, his partner in the sawmill and cotton gin business, for a partnership accounting and against the defendant Clarence Grantham to enjoin the foreclosure of a deed of trust on partnership property and on the home and farm of the plaintiffs until a partnership accounting is had. The deeds of trust had been given to secure a loan made to the partnership by the defendant Clarence Grantham. The plaintiffs contend that the partnership property is well worth the amount of the debt owed by the partnership to Clarence Grantham. The lower court sustained a demurrer to the complaint and the plaintiffs appealed.

PARKER, J. . . . G.S. § 59-68 (1) reads:

> When dissolution is caused in any way except in contravention of the partnership agreement, each partner, as against his copartners and all persons claiming through them in respect of their interest in the partnership, unless otherwise agreed, may have the partnership property applied to discharge its liabilities, and the surplus applied to pay in cash the net amount owing to the respective partners.

. . . It is said in 68 C.J.S., *Partnership,* § 185, p. 639, "The right, in equity, to have the partnership and individual assets marshaled is for the benefit and protection of the partners themselves, and, therefore, the equity of a creditor, to the application of this doctrine, is of a dependent and subordinate character, and must be worked out through the medium of the partners or their representatives"—citing in support of the text *Dilworth* v. *Curts* (139 Ill. 508, 29 N.E. 861, 865), where it is said "the right in equity to have the partnership and individual assets marshaled is one resting in the hands of the partners, and must be worked out through them."

Each partner has the right to have the partnership property applied to the payment or security of partnership debts in order to relieve him from personal liability.

It appears that under the general rule as to marshaling partnership and individual assets, or under the application of a principle of equity similar to that rule, the rule that partnership debts may be paid out of individual assets is subject to the modification that the individual assets may be so applied where, and only where, there are no firm assets, or where the firm assets have become exhausted. It would seem that the rationale for this modification to the rule rests upon the fact that the partners occupy the position of sureties in respect to their individual property being liable for the payment of partnership debts.

    . . . It may be that the property of the partnership conveyed in the deed of trust may not sell for enough at a forced sale to pay Clarence Grantham's debt in full—though the demurrer admits that it will—but that Harold J. Grantham may be indebted to the partnership in an amount to make up such deficiency, if such a deficiency should exist. How can that be determined, until there is an accounting between the parties of the partnership affairs?

    Under the rules laid down above it would seem to be plain that the plaintiffs have alleged sufficient facts to enjoin a foreclosure sale under the deed of trust until there has been an accounting and settlement of the partnership affairs between the partners, Casey and Harold J. Grantham. Under such circumstances it is the rule with us that an injunction should be granted where the injury, if any, which the defendant Clarence Grantham, would suffer from its issuance would be slight as compared with the irreparable damage which the plaintiffs would suffer from the forced sale of their home and farm from its refusal, if the plaintiffs should finally prevail.

    Reversed.

CHAPTER 44
REVIEW QUESTIONS AND PROBLEMS

1.   *A* and *B* formed a partnership to operate a restaurant. *A* contributed a building and fixtures worth $8,500, and *B* contributed $3,000 cash. *A* obtained a dissolution of the firm on account of *B*'s wrongful withholding of *A*'s share of the profits in the amount of $5,500. After dissolution but before final judgment on the accounting and termination of the partnership, *A* formed another partnership with *X* and *Y* which made a profit operating the restaurant. Is *B* entitled to a share therein?

2.   *A* agreed with *B* to share the profits and losses of a farming operation. *B* was to supervise the operation and also to furnish a tractor and $2,500. *B* failed to furnish the tractor or the money; he was insolvent. There were no other joint funds available to pay the cost of harvest. *A* had already contributed more than he had agreed to contribute. What are *A*'s rights?

3.   *A, B, C,* and *D* formed a partnership to drill oil and gas wells. In 1960 it was dissolved by mutual consent. In 1961, still during the period of liquidation of partnership assets, *A,* who was in charge of liquidation, signed a note purporting to bind the partnership. This note was payable to *X,* who knew of the dissolution, and was given for an insurance premium payment that had become due in 1959. Against whom may *X* obtain a judgment on the note if it is not paid when due?

4.   *A* and *B* formed a partnership under written articles which provided that if either partner desired to dissolve the firm he was to give written notice to the other partner. The notice was to include a statement of the amount the partner was willing to pay for the interest of the other partner. The partner who received the notice was then to have his option

of selling his interest for the sum so stated or else of buying the interest of the notifying partner for the same amount. *A* gave notice to *B*, and *B* elected to sell. *A* refused to pay *B* for his share, and *B* sued for specific performance. What results?

5. *A* and *B* were owners of two cattle ranches. *A* and *B* married and formed a partnership pursuant to an oral agreement for the operation of the ranches. Marital discord developed and *A* left *B*'s home and dissolved the partnership. *B*, in the hope of a reconciliation, continued to make purchases of feed and grain in the name of the partnership, and used partnership assets in purchasing additional land. What are *A*'s rights?

6. *A*, *B*, and *C*, architects, were in partnership. *D*, a consulting engineer, did considerable work for the firm in the past, and was always paid promptly. *A*, the senior member of the firm, decided to withdraw from the partnership and retire. The partners executed an indemnity agreement, whereby a new partnership of *B* and *C* was formed, and in which the new firm expressly assumed all debts of the old partnership. *D* was given express notice of *A*'s withdrawal. Without *A*'s services the firm began to falter and was unable to meet *C*'s bill. A debt in the amount of $5,000 remained from the old partnership, and a new debt of $15,000 was accrued by the new firm. How much may *D* collect from *A*?

7. *X* and *Y* operated a drugstore under a written partnership agreement. A provision in the agreement stated that in the event of one of the partner's death, the remaining partner might continue the business as sole owner by paying one-third of the value of the business to the legal representative of the deceased partner. *X* died after being in the business fifteen years. The assets included $6,300 worth of stock and inventory, including a lease on the building. However, the real worth of the drugstore lay in the fact that both *X* and *Y* were extremely sociable, and had through their friendliness built up a substantial clientele. *X*'s executor refuses the tender of $2,100, and asks for $5,000 as a one-third share, contending the goodwill was worth at least $8,700. Must *Y* pay something for goodwill?

8. *A*, *B*, and *C* are partners, and by the terms of the agreement the partnership is to continue for a period of five years. At the end of the third year prevailing conditions indicate that the firm cannot continue to operate except at a loss. *B* and *C* refuse to quit, and *A* files a bill to obtain an order for dissolution. Should he succeed?

9. *A*, *B*, and *C* are partners under an agreement whereby the firm is to continue in business for ten years. *A* causes a wrongful dissolution of the partnership and demands his interest therein. May he demand that firm assets be liquidated? Is there any asset in which he is not entitled to share?

10. *A*, *B*, and *C* take a new partner, *D*, into their business. He invests $3,000. What is the extent of his liability, if any, to creditors of the old firm? What are the rights of creditors of the old firm, in comparison with creditors of the new firm, in the firm assets?

chapter 45

Formation of
a Corporation

6-43. Introduction. Corporations may be classified in a variety of ways. Public corporations may be contrasted with private corporations. Corporations for profit, or business corporations, are distinguished from not-for-profit corporations. Each state classifies corporations doing business within that state as foreign or domestic to denote the state where incorporation took place. Moreover, each state has a variety of statutes relating to such specialized corporations as cooperatives, church and religious corporations, and fraternal organizations. In this chapter and those which follow, we are primarily concerned with the private business corporation. It should be noted that the statutes relating to business corporations vary from state to state; yet they are quite similar. For our discussion, the basic principles of the Model Business Corporation Act will be used as the basic statute.

Before discussing the steps in the formation of a corporation, it is helpful to examine the status of a corporation in our legal system. A *corporation* is an artificial, intangible being, created by law. It is a method by which individuals unite under a common name, for common purposes as long as the entity continues to exist. As a legal entity, the corporation is not affected by the death, incapacity, or bankruptcy of a member. It owns property and can sue or be sued the same as a natural person.

In most statutes when the word "person" is used, a corporation is considered a person. Of course, it is not a person under some statutes, such as those allowing the appointment of suitable persons as parole officers. A corporation is a person for purpose of the due process clause of the Fifth and Fourteenth Amendments to the United States Constitution. For purposes of the privilege against compulsory self-incrimination, it is not a person.

A corporation is not a citizen within the privileges and immunities clause of the federal Constitution. Therefore, a state may lawfully prevent a foreign corporation from coming within its boundaries to engage in *intrastate* business. Moreover, since a state has the power to prevent entry altogether, it may impose any conditions on entry that it sees fit.

6-44. Procedure for Incorporation.   The general law authorizing the formation of a corporation defines the purposes for which corporations may be formed and prescribes the steps to be taken for the creation of the corporation. Such general law prescribes that any number of adult persons, usually not less than three, who are citizens of the United States and at least one of whom is a citizen of the state of incorporation, may file an application for a charter. The application contains the names and addresses of the incorporators; the name of the corporation; the object for which it is formed; its duration; the location of its registered office; the name of its registered agent; the total authorized capital stock, preferred and common; the number of shares with their value; and if the statute provides for stock without par value, the number of shares of such stock.

Some states also require the names and addresses of the subscribers to the capital stock and the amount subscribed and paid in by each. All applications contain a statement as to the amount and the character of capital stock proposed to be issued at once. It is usually indicated whether the stock is to be paid for in cash or in property.

The application, signed by all the incorporators and acknowledged by a notary public, is forwarded to a state official, usually the secretary of state. The official then issues a charter which contains the application. Upon receipt of the charter, it is filed by the incorporators in the proper recording office. The receipt of the charter and its filing are the operative facts that bring the corporation into existence and give it authority and power to operate.

A fee is charged, payable in advance, for filing an application for a charter, and no charter will be issued until such fee is paid. When the application is for a corporation, not for profit, no detailed information is required relating to issues of stock, shares, and so forth. Requirements for securing a charter vary in the different states, and sometimes for different types of business in the same state. The requirements of the statute must be satisfied and complied with in detail for the formation of a *de jure* corporation. This is the responsibility of the attorney assisting in the formation of the corporation.

After the charter has been received and filed, the incorporators and all preincorporation subscribers to stock meet and elect a board of directors. They may also approve the bylaws of the corporation if the applicable law so provides. In most instances, the bylaws must be approved by the board but not by the shareholders. The board of directors which has been elected then meets, approves the bylaws, elects the officers, calls for the payment of the subscription price for the stock, and makes whatever decisions are necessary to commence business.

The charter of a corporation is a contract and cannot be repealed or amended by the legislature unless such power has been reserved by the state when the charter was granted. The charter may be amended, however, by the consent of all the stockholders or a certain portion thereof, as provided by the statute of the state of incorporation.

6-45. The Bylaws.   As previously noted, the original bylaws are usually approved by the board of directors. The power to alter, amend, or revoke the bylaws is also vested in the board unless reserved to the shareholders by statute or by the articles of incorporation. As a general rule, the shareholders have the power to alter, amend, or revoke the bylaws to the same extent that they have power to create bylaws in the first instance. A bylaw change must be passed as a bylaw and not as a mere resolution.[1] The board cannot, however, repeal, amend, or add to the bylaws, where such change will affect the vested rights of a stockholder.

A bylaw is a rule for governing and managing the affairs of the corporation which is binding upon all stockholders, but the provisions of the bylaws are not binding on third parties unless the third parties have knowledge of them. The bylaws contain provisions establishing the corporate seal and the form of the stock certificate to be used. They also contain provisions providing for the number of officers and directors, the method of electing them and removing them from office, as well as the enumeration of their duties. They also specify the time and place of the meetings of the directors and the stockholders. If the corporation is a nonstock corporation, the bylaws specify the requirements and the method for membership. Together with the articles of incorporation and the applicable statute, the bylaws provide the rules for operating the corporation. (The operation of the corporation is the subject of the next chapter, and many of the matters discussed there have to do with bylaws.) The bylaws are subservient to the articles of incorporation and the statute but are of greater authority than, for instance, a single resolution of the board. And failure to follow the bylaws constitutes a breach of the duties of a director or officer.

The bylaws may be used to expand the power of the board of directors or officers. Since such expansion reduces the protection of the shareholders, the bylaws should be carefully studied by investors, especially in closely held corporations. Even though the board of directors is usually given the right to adopt new bylaws or to repeal or add to them, it cannot change the bylaws with respect to limitations of board powers or eliminate a duty imposed upon the board by the shareholders. Neither can the board fail to follow the bylaws because they are, in effect, a contract with the shareholders.[2]

6-46. *De Jure* and *De Facto* Corporations.   A *de jure* corporation is a corporation which has been formed in compliance with the law authorizing such a corporation. A *de facto* corporation is one which operates as a corporation for all practical purposes, but which has failed to comply with some provision of the law with respect to its creation and thus has no legal right to its corporate existence. Its corporate existence can be challenged only by the state itself, and not by third parties. A *de facto* corporation results where there is a valid law authorizing such a corporation; a bona fide attempt to organize and comply with the statute; and the exercise of corporate power. The *de facto* corporation can make contracts, purchase and hold real estate, sue and be sued in its corporate name, and do any and all things necessary to its corporate existence that a *de jure* corporation may do, but the state may challenge its continued existence or impose other penalties.

[1] Model, Roland & Co., v. Industrial Acoustics Co., page 898
[2] Chadwick v. Cross, Abbott Company, page 898

If persons hold themselves out as a corporation and create liability, and such organization is less than a *de facto* corporation, they are generally held liable as partners. In some jurisdictions the stockholders even of a *de facto* corporation are held personally liable like partners for debts incurred by the corporation. Some courts, however, hold that the liability rests not upon partnership relationship but upon the theory that such persons are agents for the other members of a pretended corporation.

6-47. Entity Disregarded.   A problem similar to that of *de facto* corporations arises when a suit is brought to hold the shareholders personally liable for an obligation of a corporation. Such suits attempt to "pierce the corporate veil" and ask the court to look behind the corporate entity and take action as though no entity separate from the members existed. However, the corporate entity may not be disregarded simply because all of the stock is owned by the members of a family or by one person.[3] One of the basic advantages of the corporate form of business organization is the limitation of liability, and corporations are formed for the express purpose of limiting one's risk to the amount of his investment in the stock.

There are certain situations in which the corporate entity is often disregarded. First, if the use of the corporation is to defraud or to avoid an otherwise valid obligation, the court may handle the problem as though no corporation existed.[4] To illustrate, let us assume that *A* and *B* sold a certain business and agreed not to compete with the buyer for a given number of years. Desirous of reentering business, in violation of the contract term, they organize a corporation, becoming the principal stockholders and managers. The buyer may have the corporation enjoined from competing with him as effectively as he could have enjoined *A* and *B* from establishing a competing business. Likewise, if the corporate device is used to evade a statute, the corporate entity may be disregarded.[5]

A parent corporation owning a controlling interest in a subsidiary often completely dominates the activity of the latter so that it becomes purely an agent or arm of the parent company. Under such circumstances, the courts have often held the parent company liable for torts committed by the subsidiary. Occasionally, if the finances of the two companies have been used somewhat indiscriminately to meet the obligations of either company, ordinary contract creditors of the subsidiary are permitted to sue the parent company.

FOREIGN CORPORATIONS

6-48. Introduction.   A corporation organized under the laws of a particular state or country is called, within that particular state or country, a "domestic corporation." When such a corporation does business within another state or country, it is called a "foreign corporation" in such state or country. (Section

[3] Marks v. Green, page 901
[4] Diamond Fruit Growers, Inc. v. Goe Co., page 902
[5] New Hampshire Wholesale Beverage Assn. v. New Hampshire State Liquor Comm., page 903

6-50 of this chapter sets forth the circumstances in which a corporation is deemed to be "doing business.") Domestic corporations become qualified to do business upon receipt and recording of their charter, but foreign corporations doing business in *intrastate* commerce must "qualify" to do business in each state in which they are doing business and obtain a certificate of authority from such state. A foreign corporation engaged wholly in *interstate* commerce need not qualify in each state, but there are usually sufficient local activities to require qualification. Failure to qualify usually results in a denial of access to the courts as a plaintiff and other penalties.

6-49. Qualification Procedures.   Most state statutes require foreign corporations to register by filing a copy of their articles with the secretary of state, to appoint an agent upon whom service of process may be served, to pay license fees, to designate and maintain an office in the state, to keep books and records. Some states further require the corporation to deposit bonds or securities with the treasurer of the state for the purpose of protecting any individual who might suffer loss by reason of the corporation's conduct. Refusal or failure by a foreign corporation to comply with these requirements justifies the state in denying the corporation the right of access to the courts. This has the net effect of preventing them from conducting business, since the corporation contracts are not enforceable by suit and debtors would thus be able to avoid payment of their debts to the corporation. It must be noted that a corporation which has not qualified may still be sued, and noncompliance cannot be used as a defense by the corporation when sued by a third party. If a contract is fully performed, neither party may seek restitution. Transacting business within the state without complying with the statute also subjects the corporation or its officers to statutory penalties.

While a state may require compliance with the above requirements by a foreign corporation, it may not impose arbitrary and unreasonable requirements and may not discriminate against foreign corporations in favor of domestic corporations in the fees and taxes charged and other burdens imposed on commerce. Foreign corporations are protected in this regard by the commerce clause of the federal Constitution.

6-50. What Constitutes "Doing Business."   The term "doing business" is not reducible to an exact and certain definition. State statutes do not define this term. The Model Business Corporation Act has provisions to aid in determining whether a corporation is "doing business" within a state. It sets forth basic principles heretofore established by the courts. The Act defines the term to mean that a foreign corporation is "doing business" when "some part of its business substantial and continuous in character and not merely casual or occasional" is transacted within a state. The Act states that a corporation is *not* "doing business" in a state merely because:

> it participates in litigation, holds meetings of directors or shareholders, maintains bank accounts and offices for the transfer of its stock, makes sales through independent contractors, solicits orders which will be accepted out of state, creates debts or collects debts, transacts interstate commerce, or conducts an isolated transaction which is completed within thirty days.

The issue of what constitutes doing business is not limited to corporate qualification to do business. It is also important in deciding whether a corporation is subject to the jurisdiction of the courts of a particular state. Today most states have "long-arm" statutes authorizing service of summons beyond the borders of the state if the corporation or other defendant has enough contacts with the state so that requiring it to defend the lawsuit in that jurisdiction does not transcend our traditional notions of justice and fair play. Employees of corporations may also be served within the state, and issues concerning the validity of the process to obtain jurisdiction over the corporate employer are raised.

For purposes of jurisdiction, establishing a beachhead for the conduct of business within a state, retaining open lines of communication, and owning property have all been held to amount to doing business within a state. The mere presence of a wholly owned subsidiary is not enough, however.[6] The test is simple and pragmatic; it is, Is the corporation here? Maintaining offices, leasing real estate, receiving money, doing public relations work have been held sufficient to make a corporation present within a state for the service of process.

The general rule is that a foreign corporation is doing business within a state when it transacts some substantial part of its ordinary business therein—which must be determined largely by the facts of each individual case. Necessarily, this requires careful consideration of the nature and extent of the business activities conducted by or on behalf of the foreign corporation in the forum state.

Many of the cases involving out-of-state service of a summons on a corporation arise in tort litigation, especially in the field of product liability. The trend of the cases is to hold that if a product causes injury in a state, the state has jurisdiction of the action arising from the injury. In effect, the manufacturer of a product must defend suits in all states where his product is sold or used.

6-51. The Delaware Corporation. The state of Delaware has encouraged incorporation in that state in much the same way as Nevada has encouraged gambling. As a result of laws favorable to corporations, thousands of closely held businesses are Delaware corporations, even though they only transact business outside Delaware and frequently only in one other state. Such businesses, in effect, are foreign corporations in the states in which they do business.

Some of the reasons for incorporating in Delaware may be summarized as follows:

1. Delaware has no securities law.

2. A corporation may incorporate in Delaware and still have no income tax liability in Delaware if it does not transact business there.

3. Delaware corporations may issue no-par common and preferred stock for a price fixed by the directors.

4. All corporate meetings may be held outside the state, and all records may be kept outside the state.

[6] Bolger v. Dial-A-Style Leasing Corporation, page 904

5. Stock may be issued in series and may be nonvoting.

6. Action may be taken by unanimous consent in lieu of formal meetings, and board meetings may be conducted by telephone.

7. Stock may be issued for property, services, or cash at a value fixed by the directors in the absence of fraud.

8. A majority vote is all that is required to merge or to dissolve the corporation or to sell all or substantially all of the corporate assets. (A two-thirds vote is required in most states.)

9. Management powers may be vested in persons other than the board if this will help establish the most appropriate internal organization and structure for the enterprise. In fact, the board of directors may have a single member.

10. There are no preemptive rights except where granted by the certificate of incorporation.

11. All classes of stock may be convertible, and either the security holder or the corporation may be given the right to convert.

While the foregoing is not a complete list, it is apparent that there are many reasons for incorporating in Delaware. The costs are not large, relatively speaking, and there are businesses whose sole activity is assisting in the formation of Delaware corporations and serving as registered agent for them. These businesses also assist in filing annual reports and in record keeping.

POWERS OF CORPORATIONS

6-52. Introduction.   The application for a charter includes a statement of the powers desired by the corporation, and these are usually quite broad. A corporation has only such powers as are conferred upon it by the state which creates it. States may grant corporations any power requested that is not prohibited by the federal Constitution or a state constitution. The charter, together with the statute under which it is issued, sets forth the express powers of the corporation. In addition, all powers reasonably necessary to carry out the expressed powers are implied.[7]

In addition to the power of conducting its usual business, the following general powers are ordinarily granted to the corporation by statute: (1) to have perpetual existence, (2) to sue and be sued, (3) to have a corporate name and corporate seal, (4) to own, use, convey, and deal in both real and personal property, (5) to borrow and lend money other than to officers and directors, (6) to purchase, own, and dispose of securities, (7) to enter into contracts of every kind, (8) to make charitable contributions, (9) to pay pensions and establish pension plans, and (10) all powers necessary or convenient to effect any of the other purposes. Some of these powers will be discussed more fully in the sections which follow. Note that the power to make charitable contributions is a fairly recent development, evidence of the growing acceptance of the social responsibilities of business corporations.

6-53. Power to Borrow.   In connection with the power to borrow money, it should be noted that a corporation may give a mortgage or security interest

---

[7] Elward v. Peabody Coal Co. et al., page 907

in its property to secure a debt created for a corporate objective. In addition, the officers may, with the consent of a majority of the stockholders, when the corporation is insolvent, make an assignment of all the property for the benefit of creditors. In the absence of statutory authority, a corporation cannot sell or mortgage its franchise or charter. In addition, corporations vested with the public interest, such as public utilities, cannot mortgage or sell their property without authority from the state creating them.

A corporation has the power, in the absence of an express restriction, to borrow money and to evidence the same with bonds. The statute usually specifies the procedure necessary for issuing such bonds, and if the statute is not complied with, the bonds are invalid.

A corporation likewise has implied power to take or to endorse promissory notes and to accept or to endorse bills of exchange in the usual course of its business. A corporation has no implied power to lend money or become a surety or guarantor, in absence of express statutory authority, unless it is necessary for the purpose of carrying out the objectives of the corporation. Statutes in some states authorize a corporation to enter into contracts of guaranty without limitation; others allow it only when the corporation has a direct interest in the subject matter of the contract guaranteed.

6-54. Other Powers.   A corporation, unless its charter specifically authorizes it to do so, is without power to enter into a partnership or combination with other corporations for the purpose of bringing the management of the partnership or corporations under one control. A corporation does not have authority to share its corporate management with natural persons in a partnership because it would expose the stockholders to risks not contemplated by the stockholders' contracts, although it may enter a joint venture.

A corporation, in absence of statutory authority, has no implied power to subscribe to, purchase, or hold the stock of another corporation whose chartered purpose is totally foreign to its own. Many states allow such stock transactions; those who do not, feel that to permit such action would subject the stockholders to risks not anticipated by them. By court decision or statute, the corporations of most states are now empowered to subscribe for, or purchase, the stock of other corporations for the purpose of furthering their own objectives. They may invest idle funds in the stock of other corporations or accept such shares in settlement of an indebtedness owing to them. A certain phase of a corporation's business may be transacted by means of a subsidiary for whose organization it is responsible or whose control it has acquired by stock purchase. In such cases, the parent company may, or may not, be a holding company organized for the express purpose of acquiring stock of other corporations.

Acquisitions of stock of other corporations are subject to the provisions of section 7 of the Sherman Antitrust Act as amended by the Celler-Kefauver Amendment, which prohibits the acquisition by one corporation of assets or stock of another, where, in any line of commerce, the effect may be substantially to lessen competition, or tend to create a monopoly. This will be discussed more fully in Chapter 48.

6-55. The Power to Acquire Treasury Stock.   A corporation is somewhat restricted in its power to purchase its own previously issued stock, because the purchase of its own stock might effect a reduction of its capital to the detriment of creditors and stockholders. In most states a corporation is permitted to purchase shares of its own stock only out of accumulated profits or surplus.[8] This retains an investment in the corporation by stockholders equivalent to the original capital as a protective cushion for creditors in case subsequent losses develop. A few states, however, permit a corporation to acquire treasury stock as long as the corporation is not insolvent. A corporation may also acquire its own stock in payment of, or in security for, an antecedent debt due the corporation. It may also take its own stock for nonpayment of an authorized assessment made by the company on the stock, or it may take it as a gift. A corporation that has issued preferred stock has the power to redeem such stock, where there is no injury to, or objection by, creditors. Here again, many of the states require the preferred stock to be redeemed out of surplus or demand that authority to reduce the capital stock be obtained from the state.

Treasury stock—stock of its own issue acquired by a corporation—is not automatically canceled. It lies dormant in the treasury of the corporation without the right to vote or to share in dividends until it is again sold and transferred to a stockholder. It is to be noted that the capitalization of a corporation can be reduced only with the approval of the state of incorporation, and the procedure outlined in the state corporation laws must be followed in effecting the reduction.

6-56. Ultra Vires.   Any acts of a corporation that are beyond the authority, express or implied, given to it by the state are said to be *ultra vires* acts— "beyond the authority." If a corporation performs acts or enters into contracts to perform acts which are *ultra vires,* the state creating such a corporation may forfeit its charter for misuse of its corporate authority. The extent of the misuse is controlling in determining whether the state will take away its franchise or merely enjoin the corporation from further *ultra vires* conduct.

While third parties have no right to object to the *ultra vires* acts of a corporation, a stockholder may bring court action to enjoin a corporation from performing an *ultra vires* contract. In addition, the corporation may recover from the directors who approved the *ultra vires* contracts any losses or damages sustained because of the *ultra vires* venture. When they exceed corporate powers, the directors may become personally liable for resulting losses.

At common law, a corporation had no liability on contracts beyond its corporate powers because the corporation has capacity only to do those things expressly authorized within its charter or which were incidental thereto. However, most modern statutes, including the Model Business Corporation Act, provide that all *ultra vires* contracts are enforceable. Neither party to such a contract may use *ultra vires* as a defense. *Ultra vires* conduct on the part of the corporation may be enjoined by the state or any stockholder as previously noted, but otherwise contracts previously made are binding whether they be wholly executory, partially executed, or fully performed. In such cases, the directors are liable for losses suffered as a result of engaging in *ultra vires* activities.

[8] Jarroll Coal Co., Inc. v. Lewis et al., page 908.

6-57. The Power to Commit Torts and Crimes. A corporation is a person for purposes of both tort and criminal law. As an impersonal entity it can act only through agents and servants, but the corporation is subject to the doctrine of *respondeat superior* and may be punished for certain criminal acts of its agents or servants. *Ultra vires* is no defense to a tort action or criminal prosecution. All aspects of agency law relating to torts apply to corporations.[9] Corporations are not only liable for acts committed by their agents in the pursuit of the corporate business but they are also liable for injury caused by the failure of their agents to perform duties of the corporation. Thus a corporation is liable for acts or omissions such as the negligence of an agent in failing to keep corporate property in safe condition. Corporate tort liability includes actions for fraud committed by officers or agents within the scope of their actual or apparent authority.

Modern criminal statutes recognize that a corporation may commit a crime; and they provide for fines as the method of punishment, incarceration being impossible. The criminal law specifies those crimes for which the legislature intends corporate liability to be imposed. These are generally limited to cases where an agent is acting within the scope of his employment or where the activity is authorized, requested, or performed by the board of directors. A common defense to a criminal charge against a corporation is that a high managerial agent having supervisory responsibility over the conduct which is the subject matter of the offense exercised due diligence to prevent commission of the crime.

Most corporate crimes involve a law which imposes a duty upon the corporation to do, or not to do, an act. For example, a corporation may be fined for failure to comply with some statute that specifies that certain things be done by the corporation—such as supplying protection for employees or making reports—and for the violation of regulatory statutes under the police power of the state. A corporation may also be indicted for improperly performing an act that it may lawfully do. For example, a corporation may be indicted for conducting a perfectly legal business in such a manner as to be guilty of maintaining a nuisance. Many of the criminal actions involving corporations arise out of violations of the antitrust laws. These laws are discussed more fully in Chapter 48.

OTHER ASPECTS OF CORPORATE FORMATION

6-58. Promoters. A promoter, as the name implies, is one who promotes the corporation and assists in bringing it into existence. One or more promoters will be involved in making application for the charter, holding the first meeting of shareholders, entering into preincorporation subscription agreements, and engaging in other activities necessary to bring the corporation into existence. Promoters are responsible for compliance with the applicable blue-sky laws (statutes relating to the sale of securities), including the preparation of a prospectus if required.

Many of these activities involve the incurring of contractual obligations or debts. For example, the preparation of the application for a charter usually

---

[9] Poledna v. Bendix Aviation Corporation, page 909.

requires the assistance of a lawyer, and it must be accompanied by the required filing fee. Legal questions as to who has liability for these obligations and debts frequently arise. Is the promoter liable? Is the corporation after formation liable? Are both liable?

Certain general principles of contract and agency law prevent simple answers to these questions. First of all, a promoter is not an agent prior to incorporation because there is no principal. A party who purports to act as an agent for a nonexistent principal is generally liable as a principal. Second, the corporation technically cannot ratify the contracts of promoters because ratification requires capacity to contract both at the time of the contract and at the time of the ratification.

In order to avoid the difficulties caused by these legal theories, the law has used some fictions to create an obligation on the part of the corporation. One fiction is that a novation occurs. This theory proceeds on the premise that when the corporation assents to the contract, the third party agrees to discharge the promoter and to look only to the corporation. The discharge of the promoter by the third party is consideration to make binding the corporation's promise to be bound upon the contract. Such a theory infers that in the absence of evidence to show that such a novation has occurred, the promoter will continue to be personally liable on the contract. Since the contract made with the promoter was made in anticipation of the formation of a corporation, the acceptance of the contract by the corporation after its creation is some evidence from which to draw an inference that a novation has occurred. Establishing a novation, however, often fails because of a lack of proof of any agreement to release the promoter.

The novation theory overlooks the fact that the parties frequently do not intend the promoter to be liable on a preincorporation contract, and that promoters are not always liable on them. A promoter may avoid personal liability by informing the other party that he does not intend to be liable and that he is acting in the name of and solely on the credit of a corporation to be formed.[10] But if the promoter represents that there is an existing corporation when there is none, the promoter is liable. A promoter should make sure that contracts entered into by him on behalf of the proposed corporation are so worded as to relieve him from personal liability.

Another theory which is used to determine liability on preincorporation obligations may be described as the offer and acceptance theory. Under this theory, a contract made by a promoter for the benefit of the corporation is an offer which may be accepted by the corporation after it comes into existence. Acceptance of the benefits of the contract constitutes an adoption of it, or an acceptance of the offer.[11] In cases where the corporation does not accept the offer, the corporation is not liable. The promoter may or may not be liable, depending on the degree of disclosure as indicated above.

Corporations have also been held liable on promoters' contracts on theories that may be called the *consideration theory* and the *quasi-contract theory.* Under the consideration theory, a promise made after incorporation by the directors to pay for the expenses and services of promoters will be binding and supported by sufficient consideration, on the theory of services previously

[10] Stewart Realty Co. v. Keller, page 910
[11] Knox et al. v. First Security Bank of Utah et al., page 911

rendered. The quasi-contract theory holds that corporations are liable by implication for the necessary expenses and services incurred by the promoters in bringing them into existence, because such expenses and services accrue, or inure, to the benefit of the corporation. Finally, it should be noted that some states have abandoned trying to justify corporate liability with a legal theory and have simply provided by statute that corporations are liable for the reasonable expenses incurred by promoters.

Promoters occupy a fiduciary relationship toward the prospective corporation and have no right, therefore, to secure any benefit or advantage over the corporation itself or over other stockholders, because of their position as promoters. A promoter cannot purchase property and then sell it to the corporation at an advance, nor has he a right to receive a commission from a third party for the sale of property to the corporation. In general, however, he may sell property acquired by him prior to the time he started promoting the corporation, provided he sells it to an unbiased board of directors after full disclosure of all pertinent facts.

A promoter who enters into a contract that is subsequently ratified by the corporation cannot later sue on that contract. Such a contract can only be enforced by the corporation. This result is consistent with the offer and acceptance theory of promoters' contracts and with the fiduciary nature of the promoter's activities.[12]

6-59. Stock Subscriptions Before Incorporation. A stock subscription is an agreement to purchase stock in a corporation. It is a binding agreement (a subscriber cannot revoke his subscription) created among the subscribers for stock in a corporation to be formed. The subscription may be drafted in such a manner as to create a contract, and some states by statute have provided that a preincorporation subscription constitutes a binding, irrevocable offer to the corporation, by reason of the mutual promises of the parties, which offer is accepted when the corporation is formed. Other states regard the subscription as a mere continuing offer which may be revoked at any time prior to acceptance by the corporation.

Certain conditions are inherent in the subscription contract. The subscriber will not be liable unless the corporation is completely organized as a *de jure* corporation; the full amount of the capital stock has been subscribed in absence of an express agreement to the contrary; and the purpose, articles, and bylaws of the corporation are as originally stated and relied upon by the subscriber. Conditions, express or implied, in the stock subscription agreement are often waived by the subscriber if, with knowledge of the nonperformance, he participates in stockholders' meetings, pays part or all of his subscription, or acts as an officer or director of the corporation.

Subscriptions for shares are often made subject to the happening of certain expressed conditions precedent. For example, the subscriber agrees to take shares conditional upon the promoter's securing certain other persons to take shares, or upon a certain number of shares being subscribed. As between the corporation after it is chartered and the subscriber, the subscriber has no liability for the subscription if the conditions are not met. However, if the rights of third parties, such as creditors of the corporation, who do not have

---

[12] *Speedway Realty Company v. Grasshoff Realty Corp.*, page 913

knowledge of the failure of the condition become involved, the subscription is enforceable under the doctrine of estoppel,[13] and the subscriber's oral testimony of such condition and its nonperformance is not admissible. Therefore, for the protection of the subscriber, any conditions should be made a part of the subscription agreement.

A distinction must be made between a subscription on a condition and a conditional delivery of a subscription contract. In an action against the subscriber to enforce the subscription agreement, oral evidence may be introduced by the subscriber to prove that the subscription contract was conditionally delivered and that in absence of the happening of the condition no subscription contract was to come into existence. Such evidence, however, cannot be introduced to show that the delivery of the subscription agreement was a conditional one if other parties, such as creditors of the corporation, have been misled thereby. These parties must occupy a position similar to that of a holder in due course of commercial paper if the conditional delivery is to be ignored.

6-60. Subscriptions After Incorporation. A subscription to stock of a corporation already in existence is a contract between the subscriber and the corporation, and such a contract may come into existence by reason of an offer either made by the corporation and accepted by the subscriber or made by the subscriber and accepted by the corporation. If the corporation opens subscription books and advertises its stock, it is seeking for an offer to be made by the subscriber. The corporation may, however, make a general offer to the public, which may be accepted by the subscriber in accordance with the terms of the general offer.

One must exercise care in distinguishing between a present subscription to stock, by which contract the subscriber immediately becomes liable as a stockholder, and a contract to purchase stock. Where the contract is for the purchase of stock, the purchaser does not become a stockholder until a certificate of stock has been delivered to him. Upon the breach of such contract and the tender of the stock certificate by the corporation, recovery is limited to damages for failure to purchase. Under a present subscription contract, however, the subscriber is liable upon his promise to pay for the full amount of the stock subscribed, even though the corporation has not tendered the stock certificate.

An underwriter's contract to place a certain block of stock or, if unable to dispose of it, to purchase it himself is not a subscription contract. Such an underwriter may, however, be held liable for as much of the stock as he guaranteed to dispose of but was unable to place. For his services in this connection, the underwriter receives a certain commission on stock sold.

6-61. The Corporate Name. One of the provisions in the application for a corporate charter is the proposed name of the corporation. In order that persons dealing with a business will know that it is a corporation and that the investors therefore have limited liability, the law requires that the corporate name include one of the following words or end with an abbreviation of them: "corporation," "company," "incorporated," or "limited." In addition, a corporate name must not be the same as or deceptively similar to the name of any

[13] Hoppe v. Rittenhouse, page 914

domestic corporation or that of a foreign corporation authorized to do business in the state to which the application is made.

Most states have procedures for reserving a corporate name for a limited period. Inquiry is usually made as to the availability of a name, and if it is available it is reserved while the articles are being prepared. The name may be changed by charter amendment at any time without affecting corporate contracts or title to corporate property in any way.

6-62. The Blue-sky Laws.   Both the federal and state securities laws are known as *blue-sky laws* because they act to prevent the sale of "blue sky," i.e., worthless emptiness. More specifically, their purpose is to protect the public, particularly the innocent investor, from the dishonesty, incompetence, ignorance, and irresponsibility of persons engaging in the business of disposing of securities of uncertain value whereby the inexperienced and confiding are likely to suffer. Since their objective is to protect innocent persons from investing their money in speculative enterprises over which they have little or no control, the laws are paternalistic in character and are liberally construed to protect the public. The result of this liberal construction is that the securities laws cover not only stocks and bonds but every kind of investment in which one person invests money and looks to others for the success of the venture. The laws are applicable to every investment in which a person receives some evidence of indebtedness or a certificate of interest or participation in a profit sharing agreement. As a result, sales of oil well interests, interests in limited partnerships and even savings and loan investments have been held to come within the scope of the blue-sky laws.

The goals of the blue-sky laws are accomplished primarily by requiring the registration of security issues and full disclosure to investors. There are two major methods for registration. Some securities are registered simply by notifying the state involved of the sale. For example, securities which are registered under the Federal Securities Act may be registered in a state by merely notifying the state of the sale. Other issues of securities are registered by qualification. Qualification requires filing detailed information and preparing a prospectus for approval of the state. The prospectus is the vehicle for ensuring full disclosure to potential investors.

The securities laws contain both criminal and civil sanctions. Violations may be a felony or misdeameanor. In addition, a sale in violation of the law is voidable by the buyer. Under certain circumstances, the buyer is also entitled to attorney's fees and interest.

You should always obtain legal advice as to the requirements of the blue-sky laws prior to the sale of any investment. Liability to refund money is placed not only on the issuer of the security but also on anyone who assists in the sale. The effect of the blue-sky laws must be considered in the formation of any business.

6-63. The Corporate Buy and Sell Agreement.   The importance of a buy and sell agreement between partners was previously mentioned. Frequently a buy and sell agreement between shareholders in a closely held corporation is also desirable. It is equally as important to have a means of getting money out of a business as it is to have a means of getting money into the business.

Shareholder buy and sell provisions should be worked out before any shareholder knows whether he is a buyer or seller. While withdrawal from active participation will not effect a dissolution, it can have the serious effect of precipitating a lawsuit, or a shareholder may continue to participate in management when he does not desire to do so. Frequently, a withdrawing shareholder will be forced to sell his stock for less than it is worth because a buy and sell agreement was not worked out in advance.

Corporate buy and sell provisions are similar to those in a partnership, except the corporation as an entity is frequently a party to them. Many contracts provide that before a shareholder can sell his stock to an outsider, it must first be offered to the corporation. Some contracts also require that it be offered to other shareholders. Such rights of first refusal are legal.

Corporations may buy life insurance on the life of an officer-shareholder and use the proceeds to buy stock. Stock redemptions on the death of a shareholder are an integral part of estate planning, and the various alternatives and plans to redeem such stock should be carefully studied at the time the corporation is formed.

FORMATION OF A CORPORATION CASES

Model, Roland & Co., v. Industrial Acoustics Company
16 N.Y.2d 703 (1965)

MEMORANDUM: Order of the Appellate Division directing judgment for the plaintiff-respondent affirmed. Defendant-appellants are correct in their contention that the provisions of article VIII of the corporate by-laws are ineffective to the extent that they require a two-thirds majority shareholder vote to amend certain of the by-laws—in particular the by-law which sets the number of directors on the board. The Business Corporation Law clearly provides that a simple majority vote of the shareholders is sufficient to amend the by-laws, unless the certificate of incorporation provides otherwise. The provision here involved would have been valid were it placed in the certificate of incorporation, but as a by-law it is invalid. However, the single question submitted . . . was whether or not a simple majority resolution of the stockholders, increasing the number of directors from four to five, was valid and effective. This question was correctly answered in the negative. . . . Subdivision (b) of section 702 of the Business Corporation Law provides that the shareholders may change the number of directors (1) by an amendment to the by-laws embodying the change, or (2) by a simple resolution, *if* there is a by-law in effect which provides for the change by such a resolution. In either case the change is effected by means of a by-law. Here the shareholders acted by resolution alone, and not under the provisions of a by-law. It is clear, therefore, that, even though a simple shareholder vote could have effected a change in the number of directors if such a by-law had been adopted authorizing such a vote, their naked resolution to do so cannot be enforced.

Chadwick v. Cross, Abbott Company
205 A.2d 416 (Vt.) 1964

Plaintiff brought suit to determine the value of his minority stock interest in a closely held corporation. The corporate books used the double declining balance method of depreciation, and the company had taken an additional 20 percent first year depreciation. This fact was known to the plaintiff, who had been president of the company. The bylaws provided that minority shareholders would be paid book value, and that book value shall be determined according to sound and accepted accounting rules and practice. The certified public accountant who furnished the opinion on book value used the straight line method of depreciation. The lower court held that the book value was correctly determined by the straight line method, notwithstanding the fact that the actual records had used a different method.

SHANGRAW, J. . . . The defendant places considerable emphasis in its brief on paragraph 7 of the findings which reads:

> 7. That the provisions of Article 18 of the By-laws constitutes a contract between the parties in entering into the corporate relations represented by the pooling of assets in the Randolph Red & White, Inc. and provides a fair and equitable means for the minority stockholder to withdraw from the Corporation and receive for his stock-equity a sum of money equal to his share of ownership as the books of the Corporation showed such value to be.

By this finding the defendant contends that it gives no latitude for the plaintiff to go outside the books of Randolph Red & White, Inc., and adopt for his then current purpose a new approach to depreciation write-off; and further, that before the plaintiff may be heard to say that he was entitled to use a straight line depreciation method he was under the compelling duty of establishing the fact that the double declining method was not a sound and accepted accounting practice, which defendant claims the plaintiff failed to do.

To this end the evidence discloses that there are several methods of taking depreciation for various purposes. It is not disputed that the depreciation method adopted by the defendant may have been proper for some purpose, such as income tax accounting. The purpose of Article 18 was to permit plaintiff to arrive at the just and actual value of his stock. Whether plaintiff's or defendant's method is preferable is not the point. By Article 18 plaintiff was given the choice of methods to be employed provided his determination of book value was determined from the books of the corporation, which was done, and according to sound and accepted accounting rules and practice. The evidence reveals that the straight line method of depreciation is a sound and accepted accounting practice, and by its use reflected a realistic and sound value of plaintiff's stock.

As bearing upon plaintiff's adherence to Article 18, the trial court made the following finding.

> 17. The Court further finds that the plaintiff observed every requirement under Article 18 of the By-laws of the Corporation at the time of his withdrawal from the same in the ascertaining of the book value of his stock according to sound and accepted accounting principles.

This finding is amply supported by the evidence.

By finding No. 6 the trial court found that the written opinion of a certified public accountant, referred to in Article 18, which accompanied plaintiff's notice to withdraw from the corporation, " . . . was inserted in the By-laws to the end that the withdrawing minority stockholder might be fully protected against any errors, non-feasance, mis-feasance or mal-feasance in the keeping of the corporate records by the accounting department of the defendant Cross, Abbott Company." By this finding the defendant urges that plaintiff was not allowed the privilege of determining the book value of his stock by a method of his own choice. We do not view the above quoted provisions of the finding, or Article 18 to which it is addressed, as a binding limitation of the method of depreciation to be adopted by the plaintiff in arriving at the book value of his stock, provided sound and accepted accounting rules and practice were adopted. Reading the finding in support of the judgment, as we are required to do, it is clear that the trial court correctly regarded that sound and accepted accounting practices was the only requirement imposed.

Lastly, the defendant in its answer pleaded the affirmative defense of estoppel. It now claims that the evidence establishes this defense. It urges that the plaintiff is estopped from utilizing the straight line method of depreciation in determining the book value of the corporate stock, and is bound as a matter of law by the method used by the defendant. It is claimed by the defendant that the accounting method adopted by the plaintiff is detrimental to the position of the defendant; that up to plaintiff's withdrawal it had been led to believe the accounting used by the corporation was acceptable to the plaintiff as a basis of evaluating the stock; and further, that plaintiff by his conduct accepted the benefit of the double declining method of accounting.

On the assumption that plaintiff as director, president, treasurer, and manager had knowledge of the corporation's accounting system, this did not foreclose him from invoking the provisions of Article 18 in establishing the book value of his stock. This Article constituted a contract between plaintiff as the minority stockholder, and the defendant as the majority stockholder—not a contract between plaintiff and the Randolph Red & White, Inc. This article might well have disregarded the actual book value and placed an arbitrary price on the stock for transfer purposes. In such event neither party could have complained notwithstanding the accounting method used by the corporation. By Article 18 the defendant has given the plaintiff the right to adopt a fair and accepted practice in determining the book value of his stock.

.   .   .

As stated in *Boston & Maine R. R.* v. *Howard Hardware Co.,* 123 Vt. 203, 211, 186 A.2d 184, 191, "The fundamental basis for estoppel in the law of contracts is the justification for the conduct of the party claiming it," citing 3 Williston, *Contracts* § 692, at 1998 (Rev.Ed.). Estoppel involves the conduct of both parties, since it is based upon some misleading conduct or language of one person and reliance thereon by another who is misled to his prejudice. The test of an estoppel is whether, in all circumstances of the case, conscience and duty of honest dealing should deny one the right to repudiate the consequences of his representations or conduct.

Estoppel is an affirmative defense. One who invokes the doctrine of equitable estoppel has the burden of establishing all of its constituent elements.

Defendant has produced no evidence from which it may be inferred that it relied upon the accounting method adopted by the corporation as a basis upon which plaintiff's stock was to be purchased. Its book value was governed by Article 18 of the By-laws as a matter of contract between the parties. The essential elements of estoppel are not present in this case.

The findings are supported by the evidence, and the judgment is supported by the findings.

The judgment is affirmed.

Marks v. Green

122 So.2d 491 (Fla.) 1960

The plaintiff is the sole owner of all the outstanding shares in Sa-Rey-Mar, Inc., a Florida corporation whose assets consist principally of intangible property. The corporation paid an intangible tax on this property, but the defendant did not include his stock in Sa-Rey-Mar in his personal return. The taxing authorities ordered him to do so. He refused to do so and brought this suit for equitable relief against imposition of the tax. The defendants include the state comptroller, the county tax assessor and the county tax collector. From a judgment in favor of the defendants plaintiff appealed.

WIGGINGTON, C. J. . . . The principal ground for relief is predicated upon the premise that the intangible tax assessment against appellant's ownership of all outstanding shares of stock in the corporation duplicated the tax assessment in the same amount levied against the corporation based upon the value of the intangible property owned by it, and as such amounted to a four mill levy on intangible property within the prohibition of the Constitution and laws of Florida. . . .

Appellant does not dispute that the capital stock owned by him in Sa-Rey-Mar, Inc., falls within the classification of Class B intangible property as defined by the statute. He contends, however, that since he is the sole owner of the corporation and the corporation has already paid the intangible tax assessed against it on its capital assets, that he should be relieved of the burden of again paying an intangible tax on the value of the same property for which the corporation has already once paid the identical tax. Such reasoning falsely assumes that there exists an identity between the property owned by appellant as represented by his shares of stock in Sa-Rey-Mar, and the property owned by the corporation on which it has already paid the intangible tax. Appellant asks the court to indulge in this assumption on the theory that for tax purposes the separate identity of the corporation should be disregarded, and he as an individual should be adjudged the owner of the intangible property held by the corporation on which the tax has already been paid.

Appellant fortifies his position by citing a number of decisions in which courts of equity have under particular circumstances disregarded the corporate entity, pierced the corporate veil, or regarded the corporation as the alter ego of its stockholders. Such principles, when properly applied, are sound and entitled to respect. The cited authorities indicate, however, that such course has been followed as a matter of necessity only for the purpose of promoting justice or preventing injustice or fraud. We do not conceive that such principles may logically be applied in resolving the issue raised by this appeal. . . . It is our judgment that a sounder concept of the principles which should be followed in making an equitable distribution of the tax burden among the property owners of this state requires that for purposes of taxation, the identity of the corporate entity must be kept separate and distinct from the identity of its stockholders, unless otherwise provided by statute. . . .

Appellant has seen fit to organize a domestic corporation and own all its outstanding capital stock. He has elected to do business through this corporate entity. The benefits of conducting one's business in such manner are obvious and too numerous to mention in this opinion. Having so elected, appellant is in no position to claim all benefits accruing to him by virtue of doing business as a corporation, and at the same time seek to disregard the existence of the corporate entity in order to avoid payment of a tax otherwise chargeable to him. If payment of the intangible tax on the value of his stock in the corporation is considered to be an onerous burden, appellant . . . may dissolve the corporation and distribute to himself in kind the intangible property held by it.

. . . In adopting the latter course appellant would lose the many benefits he now enjoys by conducting his business through a fictitious legal entity. The choice of alternatives is the appellant's, but he cannot eat his cake and have it too.

Affirmed.

Diamond Fruit Growers, Inc. v. Goe Co.

400 P.2d 909 (Oreg.) 1966

PERRY, J. The plaintiff Diamond Fruit Growers, a cooperative association, brought this suit against the defendants to have a standard cooperative growers contract entered into with Goe Brothers, a partnership consisting of Joe, Merle and Donald Goe, specifically enforced.

The trial court entered its decree enforcing the provisions of the contract, and the defendants appeal.

The record discloses that the partnership was the owner of four separate parcels of land upon which fruit was produced; that on September 4, 1957, the partnership and the individual members of the partnership entered into a growers contract with the plaintiff association. This contract provided that:

> The said Grower hereby transfers and agrees to deliver to the Association his entire crop of merchantable apples, pears, strawberries and other fruit for the year 1957 and every year thereafter, continuously, provided that the Grower may cancel this contract on March 31st of any year by giving written notice to the Association on or before March 20th of such year that he desires the same cancelled, and delivering his copy of the contract to the Association and paying any indebtedness due to the Association from the Grower. The failure of the Grower to so notify the Association and comply with the provisions aforesaid shall operate to continue this contract in force until such notification shall be given at the proper time, and other stipulations aforesaid shall likewise be complied with.

Subsequently, and on the 4th day of February, 1963, a corporation known as "Goe Co." was organized by the Goe brothers and all of the real property except one parcel was conveyed by the partnership to the corporation. On February 28, 1963, the partnership notified the plaintiff association that they had sold the other three parcels of land and as to these properties the marketing agreement would no longer be recognized.

After the formation of the corporation and the transfer of the three parcels of land from the partnership to the corporation, the real property was managed and operated in exactly the same manner by the Goe brothers as they had under the partnership, and the income therefrom was used to pay personal bills of the brothers as they had done when operating as partners.

The trial court found "that the principal purpose of forming the corporation and transferring the partnership interest in three of the four partnership ranches to the corporation was to avoid the obligation to market through the plaintiff as required in the contract of September 4, 1957." With this finding we agree.

Since the trial court held in effect that the creation of the corporation was but a subterfuge to avoid the marketing contract, and we agree, that a court of equity will look through the form of the transaction to the substance and enforce the contract sought to be avoided.

The decree of the trial court is affirmed.

New Hampshire Wholesale Beverage Assn. v. New Hampshire State Liquor Comm.

116 A.2d 885 (N.H.) 1955

The plaintiff is an association of individuals who hold wholesaler's liquor permits issued by the defendant commission under authority of a statute (R.C.L. 170). Sec. 76 of the statute provides, "No person shall directly or indirectly hold more than two off-sale permits at one time." The plaintiff alleges that the defendant has violated the statute by issuing one or two off-sale permits to each of certain corporations, with knowledge that such corporations are owned, operated, or controlled by the same person or the same group of persons. The plaintiff seeks an injunction and a declaratory judgment. The trail judge referred the case to the Supreme Court.

GOODNOW, J. . . . In applying this limitation to a corporation, the commission has treated the corporation as a separate entity, without regard to whether the person or persons who own or control it are the owners or in control of other corporate off-sale permittees. The plaintiffs contend that the same person or group of persons have thereby been permitted to hold "directly or indirectly . . . more than two off-sale permits at one time," in violation of § 76.

The fiction that the corporation is a being independent of those who are associated as its stockholders is not favored in this state.

It is to be disregarded "when justice demands it." In this case, it is not entitled to recognition as the basis for the issuance of off-sale permits if a means is thereby provided of avoiding a clear legislative purpose.

The defendants, relying on the fact that § 58 specifically authorizes the issuance of off-sale permits to corporations and that the word "person" in the statute in question should be construed as "corporation" in accordance with § 1, subd. III, contend that the Legislature did not intend that the issuance of off-sale permits to a corporation should in any way depend upon the identity of its stockholders. They further urge that if such had been the legislative purpose, that fact could have been spelled out as it is in the prohibitions concerning interlocking stock ownership between the holder of a wholesaler's permit and the holder of an on-sale or off-sale permit. We are unable to adopt this view of the Legislature's intention.

Chapter 170 has repeatedly been construed by this court as "intended to provide a complete and well-rounded system for the regulation and control of all intoxicating liquors."

By its terms, manufacturers, wholesalers and retailers of alcoholic beverages are separated into classes and "no control, direct or indirect and no interest, financial or otherwise, shall be exercised by one over the other." The statute now in question was designed to impose a similar regulation within one class of retailers.

The maximum number of off-sale permits is not only fixed at two but the limitation is to be applied so that "no person" shall hold more than that number either "directly or indirectly." By so limiting the number of off-sale permits we believe that the Legislature intended to prevent a concentration of such permits in the hands of the same persons. Not every case of interlocking stock ownership results in an indirect holding of an off-sale permit. Before the issuance of such permits to a corporation the facts must be determined by the commission as to whether the person or persons owning or controlling the corporation are also the holders of other off-sale permits, either individually or as the owners or those in control of other corporate off-sale permittees.

The relief sought by plaintiffs was granted.

Bolger v. Dial-A-Style Leasing Corporation
409 P.2d 517 (Colo.) 1966

SUTTON, J. The sole question presented for our determination on this writ of error is whether the defendants in error, two New York corporations, were "transacting business" in Colorado of a sufficient nature to make them amenable to the civil jurisdiction of our courts through the use of substituted service of process on foreign corporations. . . . We shall hereafter refer to the parties by name or as plaintiff and defendants.

Bolger filed an action against Dial-A-Style Leasing Corporation, a wholly owned subsidiary, and its parent company, Beauty Industries Incorporated. He sought a rescission and damages for alleged false representations arising out of a contractual relationship entered into between the plaintiff and Dial-A-Style on February 8, 1963 whereby Bolger became the latter's "agent" in promoting and selling its services and equipment to beauty parlors in Colorado.

Service of process was obtained on the two defendants in the statutory manner. Thereafter, the defendants made a special appearance through their attorneys and moved to set aside and quash the service of process based on affidavits that Dial-A-Style had not transacted sufficient business in Colorado to render it subject to service in this State and that Beauty Industries had not transacted any business here. The trial court granted the motion to quash and improperly, thereafter, dismissed Bolger's complaint without prejudice. It found that service had been made on July 5, 1963 in accordance with the statute, that both defendants were foreign corporations and "That neither . . .

has transacted business within the State of Colorado so as to render either or both of them amenable to service of process in Colorado," and that it had no jurisdiction over these two corporations. By writ of error, Bolger seeks to reverse the judgment. We note, in connection with the above mentioned dismissal of the complaint, that the proper procedure is not to dismiss a complaint because of improper or invalid service of process; the trial court should, in such a case, merely hold the service invalid and allow the action to stand so that the plaintiff can continue to seek proper service. To do otherwise could, for example, prevent the tolling of a statute of limitations or harm a plaintiff in some other manner.

The district court had before it the complaint, the two affidavits of the New York companies and the counter-affidavit of Bolger. A reading of these instruments reveals that both defendants have their principal place of business in New Jersey and that the plaintiff first became acquainted with them through an advertisement which appeared in the *Wall Street Journal* signed by one Herman Perl, the chairman of the board of Beauty Industries. Bolger contacted Perl's office, and was thereafter called upon in Denver by Arthur J. Waldorf, who admittedly was Dial-A-Style's West Coast representative. Dial-A-Style, a separate corporate entity, appears to be the franchising and servicing company for Beauty Industries.

Bolger's complaint and counter-affidavit show that he was made the sole agent of Dial-A-Style. No other persons were hired in Colorado by either of the defendants. It appears that Bolger was to lease certain cameras and processes to beauty salons in Colorado and to sign the agreements as the *agent* of Dial-A-Style. Copies of the signed leases, which did not require the defendant's prior ratification to become binding, were then sent to the corporation's home office. Title to the machines remained in Dial-A-Style and it was to pay the Colorado taxes thereon. In addition, Dial-A-Style was to supply Bolger with other materials upon request. It appears, however, that at least one billing to plaintiff was made on Beauty Industries' stationery. Dial-A-Style's affidavit admits the appointment of Bolger as "its sole distributor in Colorado"; that Bolger was required "to lease out certain machines"; and that "pursuant to that (its) agreement" it shipped "three sets of equipment plus miscellaneous supplies" from New Jersey to Bolger in Colorado.

It is asserted that Waldorf had been informed by Bolger's attorney, at the time the franchise agreement was signed, that the defendants would have to qualify to do business in Colorado. In a telephone call at that time this requirement was relayed to the officers and counsel of the two companies in New Jersey. It is alleged that they agreed so to qualify their companies; their promises, however, were never fulfilled.

One further item in the record is that it appears from an exhibit that some public relations work may have been carried on by Beauty Industries in Colorado when it distributed a progress circular printed under its name. The extent of the distribution of this circular is not clear, nor is it clear whether anyone in Colorado except Bolger was exposed to this advertising.

Although Dial-A-Style was totally owned by Beauty Industries, the mere presence in Colorado of this wholly owned subsidiary, standing alone, does not in and of itself subject the absent parent corporation to our state's jurisdiction, where the two companies are operated as distinct entities, as appears here. We thus conclude that Bolger had the burden of proving the necessary "presence" in Colorado of both companies.

The question of what constitutes sufficient minimal contacts within a particular state so as to hold that a foreign corporation has subjected itself to *in personam* jurisdiction without violating the due process clause under the 14th Amendment of the Federal Constitution has been developing over the years in decisions of the United States Supreme Court. . . .

In *International Shoe* . . . noting that in order to subject a foreign corporation to a state's jurisdiction, certain minimal contacts in that state are required so that "traditional notions of fair play and substantial justice" are not offended by the bringing of the suit, the court said:

> But to the extent that a corporation exercises the privilege of conducting activities within a state, it enjoys the benefits and protection of the laws of that state. *The exercise of that privilege may give rise to obligations; and, so far as those obligations arise out of or are connected with the activities within the state,* a procedure which requires the corporation to respond to a suit brought to enforce them can, in most instances, hardly be said to be undue. . . . [Emphasis supplied.]

And, in *McGee* . . . the court extended the *International Shoe* case concept to a situation where the only contact by the corporation in the forum state was the assumption of a single insurance contract, which became the subject of the questioned suit. Noting the increasing expansion of commercial transactions in the United States, it was held that that corporation's contact was sufficient to meet the test of due process because the suit was based on a contract which had substantial connection with the state and "It cannot be denied that California has a manifest interest in providing effective means of redress for its residents when their insurers refuse to pay claims."

In Colorado, it has been recognized that each case of this type rests upon its own facts. . . .

Turning first to the question of Beauty Industries' amenability to substituted service, we hold that the trial court's finding that it lacked jurisdiction over the parent corporation is supported by the record. Bolger alleged that the two defendant companies had common officers and that they carried on certain correspondence with him, but that alone certainly does not prove these were other than two distinct corporate entities, nor does it make Beauty Industries a party to the dealership contract with plaintiff. The "contacts" that Beauty Industries had in Colorado appear to be the advertisement of Dial-A-Style franchises published in the *Wall Street Journal* which is sold in Colorado; that it allowed at least one of Dial-A-Style's billings to be made on Beauty Industries' stationery; and that it sent one written notice publicizing the beauty aid process in question to Colorado. We agree with the trial court that these are insufficient minimal contacts and that Bolger did not carry his burden of proof as to that company to establish its legal "presence" in Colorado for substituted service.

We cannot, however, come to the same conclusion as to Dial-A-Style as we do as to the parent company. An examination of the undisputed facts set out in the record shows that this company was "doing business" in Colorado in the sense of at least minimal contacts through Bolger as its agent. He was the sole distributor of its process and products. Machines, taxable to Dial-A-Style and to which it retained title, plus additional supplies were sent by it to Colorado. Leasing contracts were consummated in Colorado for it through its agent; and it appears that no prior approval by Dial-A-Style was required to make such leases binding. Establishing such a beachhead and retaining open lines of communication, as well as strings of ownership as evidenced by its title, is "doing business" within a state. This is so because the activities complained of were not irregular and casual but rather by their nature were continuous and systematic with the claim in question itself being generated by Dial-A-Style's corporate activity in Colorado.

The judgment is reversed with directions to reinstate the complaint as to both parties and to proceed in accordance with the views expressed herein.

Elward v. Peabody Coal Co. et al.

9 Ill. App.2d 234 (1956)

The plaintiff, a stockholder in the defendant corporation, brought this suit against the corporation and its seven directors for a declaratory decree that a stock option was invalid and for injunctive relief. The directors by resolution gave one of the employees of the corporation an option to purchase 40,000 shares at $3 per share. On the day that the option was given, the market price of the common was $3 per share; in June, 1955, it was $8 per share. The plaintiff contended that under the corporate laws of Illinois, the corporation was not authorized to grant the option. The lower court dismissed the complaint and plaintiff appealed.

BURKE, J. . . . The plaintiff asserts that the Business Corporation Act does not empower a corporation to issue a stock option; that this power is not granted in express terms or by implication; that a shareholder is entitled under the common law to preemptive rights; and that the Act should be construed strictly so as not to impair the preemptive rights of stockholders. The public policy of this state is found in the Constitution, the statutes and the decisions of the courts. Plaintiff cites cases pointing out the distinction between the power to sell and the power to give an option. The preemptive right of shareholders to share pro rata in any new issue of corporate stock, so that their interest will not be diluted, but continue proportionately, is part of the common law of this State. Section 24 of the Business Corporation Act, reads:

> The preemptive right of a shareholder to acquire additional shares of a corporation may be limited or denied to the extent provided in the articles of incorporation. Unless otherwise provided by its articles of incorporation, any corporation may issue and sell its shares to its employees or to the employees of any subsidiary corporation, without first offering the same to its shareholders, for such consideration and upon such terms and conditions as shall be approved by the holders of two-thirds of its shares entitled to vote with respect thereto or by its board of directors pursuant to like approval of the shareholders.

The first sentence of § 24 provides that the charter of an Illinois corporation may limit or deny the preemptive right of a shareholder to acquire additional shares of stock. The second sentence of the section allows a corporation which does not have an express charter denial or limitation of preemptive rights, to issue and sell stock to its employees free of preemptive rights for such consideration and upon such terms and conditions as shall be approved by the holders of two-thirds of its shares entitled to vote with respect thereto or by its board of directors pursuant to like approval of the shareholders. Plaintiff inquires that, keeping in mind the doctrine that corporate powers are to be construed strictly and that no power is to be implied unless reasonably necessary to an express power, under what section or sections could the power to issue stock options be regarded as implied? Section 5 of the Business Corporation Act states that each corporation shall have power to make contacts and incur liabilities, to elect or appoint officers and agents of the corporation, to define their duties and fix their compensations, and to exercise all powers necessary or convenient to effect any or all of the purposes for which the corporation is formed. It cannot be doubted that Illinois corporations are empowered to enter into contracts relating to employment. The implied powers which a corporation has in order to carry into effect those expressly granted and to accomplish the purposes of its creation are not limited to such as are indispensable for these purposes, but comprise all that are necessary in the sense of appropriate and suitable, including the right of reasonable choice of means to be employed. (13 Am. Jur., *Corporations*, § 740). We are of the opinion that there is ample implied power in §§ 5 and 24 of the Business Corporation Act and in Article 9 of the amended charter to sustain the action of the defendant corporation in entering into a valid contract with an officer or employee for a stock option.

Reversed and remanded, however, for other reasons.

Jarroll Coal Co., Inc. v. Lewis et al.

210 F.2d 578 (1954)

On March 1, 1949, E. L. Jarroll, Sr., and the members of his family owned all the stock of the mining company, defendant in this action. On that day he entered into a contract with the company by the terms of which the company purchased all of the stock from him, paying him $4,000 in cash and giving him its note in the sum of $20,000. There was testimony that the note was to be secured by a chattel deed of trust, but this was not executed until two years later. In March, 1949, the assets of the company, exclusive of good will, exceeded its liabilities, exclusive of the note by less than $15,000.

The plaintiffs, trustees of the United Mine Workers Welfare and Retirement Fund, had obtained a judgment against the company on a contract of March 1, 1949, whereby the company agreed to pay into the Welfare and Retirement Fund a certain amount per ton on coal mined by the company. This matter was brought before the court at the instance of the United States Marshal to have the court determine the conflicting claims to property of the coal company upon which he had levied execution. The trustees claimed it under their judgment and Mr. Jarroll claimed it under his trust deed.

. . . From a judgment in favor of the plaintiffs, execution creditors, holding the note and chattel deed of trust void as against them because violative of the West Virginia statute, Code of 1949, § 3051 (31-1-39), forbidding a corporation to use its funds to purchase its own stock, where this results in an impairment of capital, the coal company has appealed.

PARKER, C. J. . . . The pertinent portion of § 3051 of the West Virginia Code of 1949 (31-1-39), which was taken from the general corporation law of the State of Delaware, is as follows:

> Every corporation organized under this chapter, or existing under the laws of this State, shall have the power to purchase, hold, sell and transfer shares of its own capital stock: Provided, that no such corporation shall use its funds or property for the purchase of its own shares of capital stock when such use would cause any impairment of the capital of the corporation.

Accepting, as we think we should, the finding of the trial judge that the good will of the company was without value, there can be no question but that payment of the $4,000 in cash and the execution of the $20,000 note on March 1, 1949, not only impaired the capital of the corporation but rendered it insolvent. Appellant contends that, even so, the trustees of the welfare and retirement fund were not creditors at that time and cannot complain of the transaction for that reason. It appears, however, that the contract under which the claim of the trustees arises was executed on the very day that the note was given and that the indebtedness had been incurred before the execution of the chattel deed of trust, two years later, transferring the assets of the corporation to secure the note. It was the transfer under this deed which was relied upon to defeat the levy under the execution; and there can be no question but that such transfer, made at a time when the corporation was insolvent and made to secure stockholders for the purchase price of stock theretofore purchased from them, is void as to claims of creditors existing at the time it was made. As said by this court . . .

> While, in the absence of charter or statutory prohibition, it is well settled that a corporation may purchase its own stock, it can only do so provided the act is in good faith and without intent to injure its creditors. . . . The authorities are unanimous to the effect that, even though a corporation be solvent when it contracts to purchase its own stock, it may not later, upon insolvency, pay for it, until after the existing creditors have been paid. . . .

We think, also, that, even though the trustees be regarded as subsequent creditors, they are in a position to attack the transaction here under consideration. It is a fraud on subsequent as well as upon existing creditors for the stockholders of a corporation to cause it to purchase their stock at a price rendering it insolvent, take an unrecorded lien upon all of its assets and allow it to continue doing business in its corporate name as if nothing had happened. Such creditors are unquestionably entitled to treat as void, because in fraud of their rights, a transaction which in effect gives stockholders a secret lien on corporate assets.

    . . . *There was no error and the judgment appealed from will be affirmed.*

Poledna v. Bendix Aviation Corporation

103 N.W.2d 789 (Mich.) 1960

EDWARDS, J. Plaintiff Robert Poledna brought a libel and slander action against defendants Bendix Aviation Corporation and Walter Bare for certain allegations of theft made against him. After trial before Berrien County Circuit Court, the jury returned a verdict of $10,000 "past damage" and $2,500 "punitive" damage. . . .

Defendants appeal claiming . . . that defendant corporation may not be held responsible for slander by an employee. . . .

The action was occasioned by the circumstances of plaintiff's discharge from the employment of defendant Bendix Aviation Corporation by defendant Walter Bare, at that time the employment manager for Bendix' plant at St. Joseph, Michigan.

. . . The next of appellants' issues pertains to the claim that defendant corporation is not liable for the actions of defendant Bare. . . .

The facts in our current record leave no doubt that Bare was functioning in his official capacity as employment manager of defendant corporation on the occasion of the slanderous utterance. The trial judge's charge included these words:

> And by the way, the defendant, Bendix Aviation Corporation, is responsible for any act of its personnel officer, who is the other defendant, Walter Bare, in this case.

Whatever the state of the law of libel and slander when [the] *Flaherty* [case] was decided, it seems apparent that the trial judge's charge comes far closer to representing the majority rule today. There is no longer any doubt that a corporation may be held liable for slander uttered by an agent while in the discharge of his duty as agent, and in relation to the matter about which his duty as agent permits or requires him to act, in the same way and to the same extent as an individual could be held liable for the same slander. . . .

Fletcher's *Cyclopedia Corporations* (Perm. Ed.) § 4888, says:

> The doctrine of nonliability based on the proposition that there can be no agency in slander has long been exploded.

We approve the charge of the trial judge on this issue. . . .

The corporation was held to be liable.

Stewart Realty Co. v. Keller

193 N.E.2d 179 (Ohio) 1962

GUERNSEY, J. This is . . . an action for damages brought by the plaintiff, as vendor in a contract for the sale of real estate, against Gerald D. Keller, who the plaintiff claims is personally liable on the contract.

The vendee named in the contract, "Avon Brand, Inc., an Ohio corporation," was never organized in accordance with the representations of Keller. The contract was signed, "Avon Brand, Inc., by Gerald D. Keller, Pres." It is undisputed in evidence that the contract was executed by plaintiff with full knowledge that Avon Brand, Inc., did not have any corporate existence at the time, *de jure* or *de facto,* and that Keller expressly declined to execute any contract naming him as a party individually.

Under the contract, title to real estate therein described was not to be conveyed to the vendee until June 30, 1964, after certain payments. A down payment of $5,000 and two monthly payments of $350 each were made, and other prescribed monthly payments have long been in default. It appears further that a corporation named Byrnes Rest, Inc., of which Keller was president, took possession of the premises; that it yielded possession after several months to Avon Brand, Inc., a *Kentucky* corporation organized by Keller and others; and that at the time action was brought neither Keller nor any corporation with which he was connected was in possession of the subject real estate, the keys for the building thereon having been returned to plaintiff several months beforehand.

. . . The action was on the contract for the sale of real estate, and to prevail it was necessary that plaintiff prove that the defendant was personally liable under the contract. The defendant was in the category of a promoter, and as stated in 18 C.J.S. *Corporations* § 132, p. 533, "[p]romoters are not personally liable on contracts made in the name and solely on the credit of the future corporation, and not on an express or implied representation that there is an existing corporation, where such intention is known to the other contracting party. . . . Whether or not a contract was made by the promoters personally or on the credit of the corporation only, may be a question of fact or one of law according to circumstances."

Considering the contract herein in its entirety, there is nothing on the face thereof which indicates, as a matter of either fact or law, that it was anything other than a contract to bind plaintiff and the corporation named therein. There were no promises made in the contract by defendant as an individual or any benefits to be received by him individually under the provisions of the contract. As to the knowledge of the plaintiff that the corporation only was to be bound and not the defendant personally, plaintiff proved this by its own witnesses, in particular plaintiff's attorney, and offered no evidence of any probative value to the contrary. Notwithstanding plaintiff's claim that the defendant represented that he would invest certain personal funds in the corporation, there is no evidence that the contract was made except in the name of and solely on the credit of the future corporation. Such being the case, there was no issue of fact for the jury respecting the personal liability of defendant, either by express provisions of the contract or by estoppel.

There being no evidence of any probative value of defendant's personal liability on the contract, the plaintiff was not entitled to judgment as a matter of law. . . .

Affirmed.

Knox et al. v. First Security Bank of Utah et al.

196 F.2d 112 (1952)

As surviving heirs of Frank Knox, the plaintiffs brought this action against the bank, as executor of the estate of A. C. Milner, deceased, and the Milner Corporation as defendants to recover damages for breach of contract. In 1909 Milner, as a promoter, entered into an agreement with the deceased Frank Knox whereby it was stipulated that the Milner Corporation would be organized and that when chartered the corporation would pay to Knox $25,000 from the first net profits derived by the corporation from the sale of the mining properties involved in the agreement. The corporation was subsequently organized, and in 1924 Milner, as president of the defendant corporation, wrote a letter to the plaintiff, DeWitt Knox, stating that the corporation would live up to the terms of the agreement made with his father. The lower court sustained defendant's motion to dismiss, and the plaintiffs appealed.

BRATTON, J. . . . The first contention urged by plaintiffs is that the complaint stated a cause of action against the defendant Milner Corporation, and that the court erred in dismissing the action as against that defendant. It is argued in support of the contention that the original undertaking entered into in 1909 was a promoter's contract; that it was accepted and adopted by the defendant Milner Corporation; and that therefore such defendant is liable. It is well-settled law in Utah that promoters or those contemplating the organization of a corporation do not have power to enter into a contract with binding effect upon the corporation after it is organized. They lack that power, either as agents or otherwise. But promoters or those contemplating the formation of a corporation may make a contract in furtherance of the corporation and for its benefit; and if the corporation after it comes into existence accepts or adopts the contract, it thereupon becomes the contract of the corporation and may be enforced against it.

Under the law of Utah, a contract made by and with promoters which is intended to inure to the benefit of a corporation about to be organized is to be regarded as an open offer which the corporation may after its formation accept or adopt, as it chooses. And if it does in the exercise of its own judgment accept or adopt the contract and retain the benefits of it, it cannot reject liability under it. In the absence of acceptance or adoption of a contract of that kind, the corporation is not liable even though it may have been entered into with the understanding that the corporation would be bound. But it is not necessary that acceptance or adoption of a contract of that kind be by express action of the corporation entered in the minutes of the directors, or that it be effectuated in any other like formal manner. It may be inferred from acts, conduct, and acquiescence.

The original undertaking was an agreement in the nature of a promoter's contract. And from what has been said it is manifest that defendant Milner Corporation is not bound by it to make payment of the $25,000 unless it was accepted or adopted in an effective manner. Assuming for the moment that Milner, in his capacity as president of the corporation, was clothed with authority to act for it in accepting and adopting the undertaking, there can be little doubt that the letter written in 1924 constituted an effective acceptance and adoption. The letter referred at the beginning to the undertaking to pay $25,000 from the sale of the property or from profits derived from its operation. It stated in clear terms that the time when liquidation of the obligation would begin was dependent upon the volume of business done and the payment of advances made to an operating company. And it further stated without condition or qualification that the agreement was being kept in mind and would be reached at the proper time. Plainly, the last statement was intended to mean that the obligation would be reached for payment at the proper time. The letter constituted recognition of the original undertaking as an obligation on the part of the corporation to pay the amount specified in the contract at the proper time. And in the circumstances, that recognition amounted to an effective acceptance and adoption of the undertaking.

The judgment insofar as it dismissed the action against the defendant Milner Corporation is reversed.

Speedway Realty Co. v. Grasshoff Realty Corp.

216 N.E.2d 845 (Ind.) 1966

RAKESTRAW, J. . . . The appellee Herbert F. Grasshoff rented certain real estate from the appellant Lemon H. Trotter beginning in 1940. Over a period of years, a drive-in restaurant was operated on the rented premises. In about 1955, the appellee and the appellants started discussing arrangements concerning some additional land, a new building, and a 99 year lease arrangement. In the negotiations, there were discussions about the formation of a corporation. The corporation, Grasshoff Realty Corporation, was organized. A detailed written lease was prepared, but the lease was never executed by the appellants Lemon Trotter or the Speedway Realty Company. Various steps were taken including the partial completion of a building. The parties then fell out, and the entire arrangement was terminated.

The Grasshoff Realty Corporation filed a suit against the appellants asking for damages in the sum of $50,000.00 and that the appellants be compelled to execute and deliver a 99 year lease of the real estate. In the alternative, a judgment for $125,000.00 was requested. After this case was taken to Hancock County on a change of venue, it was ultimately tried and a judgment of $1,000.00 was rendered in favor of Grasshoff Realty Corporation on December 9, 1960.

In that action, the appellee Herbert F. Grasshoff represented the Grasshoff Realty Corporation. The suit was brought at his initiative and was directed by him at all times. He was its president, principal stockholder, and manager. . . .

On January 18, 1961, the appellee Herbert F. Grasshoff individually filed his action for damages against the appellant. It is this second suit that is now the subject of this appeal. In this action the Grasshoff Realty Corporation was made a party defendant, and essentially the same facts were alleged as had been alleged in the previous action. The appellee alleged "Defendant Speedway Realty Company and Lemon H. Trotter agreed with plaintiff that defendants would *lease said above described real estate to plaintiff's corporation* for 99 years . . . ."

The trial court found that the Grasshoff Realty Corporation had no interest in the action and rendered judgment for the appellee Herbert F. Grasshoff for $83,000.00.

From the record, it appears that the evidence was substantially the same in both suits. The undisputed evidence does show that the Grasshoff Realty Corporation was formed, that it did ratify and accept all the acts of its president, the appellee. . . .

It is fundamental that "Every action must be prosecuted in the name of the real party in interest, . . . " In the case of *Cutshaw et al. v. Fargo* (1893), 8 Ind.App. 691, 696, 34 N.E. 376, the Appellate Court held that the stockholders of a corporation had no standing to sue in their individual names for breach of a contract made with the corporation. . . .

It is true that in the present case, the Grasshoff Realty Corporation was not in existence at the time of the preliminary negotiations. However, it is well settled that,

> If, after it comes into existence, a corporation expressly or impliedly ratifies a contract made for its benefit by its organizers before it was formed, such contract becomes the contract of the corporation and it is entitled to the benefits thereof and is liable thereon.

This court has held in the case of *Smith* v. *Parker* (1897), 148 Ind. 127, that a promoter's contract made on behalf of a corporation to be formed became the contract of the corporation when subsequently approved by it and afterwards the promoter-stockholder has no standing to sue. This court said:

> The second paragraph sufficiently shows that the new corporation had knowingly received some of the benefits of said contract. And therefore it sufficiently appears that the new corporation had accepted and adopted the contract sued on, and, as that contract is the obligation of the defendant to the new corporation, and to nobody else, the question arises whether the appellant, though a stockholder in the new corporation, has any right of action for a breach of that contract; or, in other words, does a breach of that contract make a cause of action in his favor against the defendant? That question has been answered in the negative by this court in Tomlinson v. Bricklayers' Union, [etc.] 87 Ind. 308. It was there held that a cause of action in favor of a private corporation could not constitute a cause of action in favor of one of its stockholders. . . .

The authorities are uniform that a contract of a corporation, or a contract made by the promoters and subsequently adopted by the corporation can be enforced only through an action brought by the corporation.

Under the pleadings and the evidence in this case, a personal judgment for the appellee Herbert F. Grasshoff cannot be sustained, therefore the judgment of the trial court must be reversed. *This cause is therefore reversed and remanded to the trial court with instructions to enter judgment below for appellant.*

Hoppe v. Rittenhouse

279 F.2d 3 (1960)

The Trustee in Bankruptcy (Hoppe) challenged, as a voidable preference, a secured creditor's claim filed by one of the creditors. The creditor, Gammill, had assigned his claim to Rittenhouse. The bankrupt, Los Gatos Lumber Products, Inc., had been hampered by lack of adequate working capital. Morton, president of the bankrupt, had advanced substantial sums of money to it but this had not been sufficient. The creditor had also advanced money and had obtained a mortgage on the property of the bankrupt. The Trustee's contention was that the corporation was insolvent at the time the mortgage was given and that this was known to the creditors. The creditor contends that the corporation was not insolvent because Morton was not a creditor—that his advances were not "as loans but as equity capital in the form of subscriptions to the capital stock." The lower court ruled in favor of the creditor and the Trustee appealed.

KOELSCH, C. J. . . . The undisputed evidence is thus that the Mortons had orally agreed to exchange their notes for stock in the corporation on the condition that additional working capital be obtained from some outside source, and that the corporation, through its president, Carl Morton, not only agreed to this proposal but actively sought additional financing from prospective lenders by positively asserting that the apparent indebtedness of the corporation to the Morton family would be erased as a liability when additional financing was obtained. There is little doubt that the Mortons intended to and did enter into a conditional subscription agreement. The critical question, then, is whether this agreement was binding and enforceable, for on it hinges the validity of the referee's finding that the Mortons' advances were "subscriptions," not "loans." . . .

Under California law an agreement by prospective shareholders to purchase stock in a proposed corporation, or unissued shares in an existing corporation, is a binding and enforceable contract. . . . The proposal made by such subscribers must be accepted by the corporation before they are finally bound, and it is clear in the present case that Carl Morton, acting on behalf of the corporation, did so accept. . . .

The trustee argues that because no stock was issued to the Mortons, they remained creditors and did not become subscribers of stock; but as in most cases, their status as subscribers is determined by the intention of the parties to the agreement. . . . Here the intention to convert notes into stock if additional capital was obtained is established by an abundance of testimony, and it is clear that the mere mechanical act of issuing stock certificates is not necessary to constitute the subscribers shareholders. . . .

It is true that the agreement was subject to a condition precedent, i.e., obtaining additional working capital, but that condition occurred when the Gammills began advancing considerable sums, which eventually exceeded $29,000.00, to the corporation. The condition thus having occurred, the contract became binding and constituted the Mortons shareholders instead of creditors, and as such "beneficial owners" of the corporate assets. . . .

Moreover, should we assume that the agreement was subject to some infirmity rendering it invalid, it is clear under California law that as between the Gammills and the Mortons, the latter would be estopped to deny their status as subscribers where, as here, the Gammills relied upon the agreement in making loans. . . .

The fact that the Mortons presented creditors' claims in the bankruptcy proceeding is not conclusive but at most creates a conflict in the evidence. Indeed, such behavior by subscribers follows a familiar pattern where efforts to continue the corporation in operation have failed: subscribers oftentimes endeavor to salvage something of their investment by attempting to qualify as creditors. . . .

Affirmed.

CHAPTER 45
REVIEW QUESTIONS AND PROBLEMS

1. *X,* an employee of the ABC Powder Company, parked a truck loaded with dynamite next to a wooden building and left it unattended. While he was away, the building caught fire; the truck exploded, killing a bystander, *Y.* May the state charge the ABC Powder Company with manslaughter on the theory that a corporation is a person, and is therefore covered by a statute defining manslaughter as "reckless, wilful or wanton conduct by any person resulting in the death of another? "

2. *A* is the sole stockholder of the A Company, a corporation engaged in construction work. *A* has complete control over the business and manages all operations; all profits flow to *A;* and the company is undercapitalized. As president of A Company, *A* makes a contract for the purchase of building supplies and subsequently fails to pay. May *A* be held personally liable?

3. The ABC Country Club, Inc., had a bylaw requiring ten days' notice of any special stockholders' meeting. *X,* president of the country club had made a contract with *Y* to purchase land for use as a golf course, subject to acceptance by the shareholders. Seven days before the meeting was to be held, *X* sent notice of the special meeting to consider the contract. At that meeting the contract was accepted. The country club later refused to purchase, setting up the invalidity of the acceptance as a defense. May *Y* obtain specific performance?

4. The ABC Company, an Indiana corporation, was not qualified to do business in New Jersey. ABC had a contract with the XYZ Company, a New Jersey corporation. XYZ breached the contract. Under New Jersey statutes, to bring suit on a contract made in New Jersey, a corporation must qualify to do business in that state. The evidence shows that the ABC Company conducts both intrastate and interstate business in New Jersey, and the contract sued on resulted from ABC's intrastate activities. May the XYZ Company set up the New Jersey statute as a defense to the contract?

5. The P Company, a corporation, owns real and personal property in state *X. X* has a statute requiring qualification by foreign corporations, but the P Company has not qualified. P Company leases its property to *D,* the lease being executed in state *Y.* If *D* fails to pay the rent, may the P Company sue him in state *X*?

6. *X* Company was formed but failed to have its charter recorded locally. The company leased space to *D,* and *D* failed to pay the rent. When *X* Company sued *D* for the rent, *D* challenged the legality of *X*'s organization and contended that *X* Company had no standing to sue. What result?

7. A Company was the parent company and B Company, a subsidiary. A Company extended credit to B Company. The latter became insolvent and the other creditors objected to A Company's sharing equally in the assets. Is A Company entitled to its pro rata share of B's assets?

8. *P* sued D Company for a percentage of the net earnings of the company pursuant to an employment contract. D Company had commingled its

records and funds into a corporate maze. *P* seeks to hold liable all companies of the "maze" and to disregard the various corporate entities. May he do so?

9. A manufacturing concern, X Company, purchased some stock in the A Bank from another stockholder. The bank refused to issue a new stock certificate, contending that X Company had no power to own stock and that the bank wanted only individual stockholders. X Company sued A Bank to require the issuance of new stock certificates. What result?

10. The L & S Lumber Company was a corporation operating a mill in the woods. A high-voltage line used in the mill extended across a road. This highline had fallen once. *B*, a stockholder-director and officer of the corporation who worked at the mill, knew this and knew of the continuing danger that the line might again fall. The line fell again, and *X* was struck. Is *B* liable to *X*? Is the corporation liable to *X*?

11. *A*, a promoter for the proposed XYZ Company, signed a contract for the purchase of some real estate from *B* as "The XYZ Company by *A*." The XYZ Company was never formed. May *B* obtain specific performance against *A*?

12. *A*, an air traffic specialist, contracted with *B*, a promoter for the proposed XYZ Air Line Corporation, to provide advice and management for the corporation. He performed his part of the contract, but upon incorporation, the board of directors of the XYZ Corporation refused to pay. May *A* recover from the company?

13. List five reasons for incorporating in Delaware.

14. Who may be held liable under the blue-sky laws?

15. What are the steps required in forming a corporation? In qualifying it to do business in a foreign state?

16. The XYZ Company was organized as a real estate business by *X, Y,* and *Z*. By a good faith mistake, the amount of paid-in capital was only $4,500, whereas a state statute required $5,000 before a corporation came into existence. The XYZ Company sold a parcel of realty to *A*. May *A* rescind the contract?

chapter 46

Operating
the Corporation

6-64. Introduction. The previous chapter was concerned with the legal aspects of forming a corporation. Many of the legal principles that were discussed there are also applicable to the operation of a corporate entity. For example, many bylaw provisions are directly concerned with operations. Some of the subjects dealt with in this chapter, such as stock and the rights of shareholders, have a bearing on formation problems. Therefore, the discussion in the prior chapter and the materials in this chapter should be considered complementary to each other.

There are three distinct groups which participate in the management of a corporation. The *shareholders* comprise the basic governing body. In some states the law uses the term "shareholder," and in other states the term in use is "stockholder." These terms are synonymous and may be used interchangeably. The Model Business Corporation Act uses "shareholder," and that term is probably in more common usage today. Shareholders exercise their control by electing the *board of directors,* by approving the bylaws, and by voting on such matters as merger, consolidation, or dissolution. The board of directors is the policy-making group, and, in addition, has the responsibility for electing the *officers* who carry out the policies. The duties and powers of the shareholders, the board of directors, and the various officers are regulated by statute and by the bylaws of the corporation. These duties and powers will be discussed in this chapter.

SHAREHOLDERS

6-65. Meetings. Action by the shareholders normally binds the corporation only when taken in a regular, or properly called, special meeting after such notice as is required by the bylaws or statute has been given. However, it is generally conceded and some states so provide by statute that action approved informally by *all shareholders* will bind the corporation.

Notice of a special meeting must include a statement concerning the matters to be acted upon at the meeting, and any action taken on other matters will be ineffective. If unusual action, such as a sale of corporate assets, is to be taken at a regular annual meeting, notice of the meeting must call specific attention to that fact; but otherwise any business may be transacted at the annual meeting.

Failure to give proper notice of a meeting generally invalidates the action taken at the meeting. A stockholder who, having failed to receive notice, attends and participates in a meeting is said to waive the notice by his presence.

A quorum of shareholders must be present in order to transact business, such quorum being a majority of the voting shares outstanding, unless some statute or the bylaws provide for a larger or smaller percentage. Affirmative action is approved by majority vote of the shares represented at a meeting, provided a quorum exists. There are certain unusual matters, such as merger or sale of all corporate assets, which at common law required unanimous vote. Today, statutes usually provide that such action can be taken by vote of two-thirds or three-fourths of the stockholders. Many of these statutes also provide that the dissenting shareholders have the right to surrender their shares and receive their fair value if they disapprove of the action taken. These matters are discussed in the next chapter.

6-66. Voting. As a general rule, every shareholder is entitled to vote. In nonstock companies the members are entitled to one vote. In stock companies the members are entitled to as many votes as they own shares of stock. The stockholder whose name appears upon the corporate record is usually designated by the bylaws as the person entitled to vote. Preferred stockholders, by their contract with the corporation, may not be entitled to vote.

Some jurisdictions also authorize nonvoting common stock. Voting stock cannot be made nonvoting by bylaw changes, but an original issue of stock may be nonvoting. In such case a corporation issues stock, either common or preferred, and specifies that the holder shall not vote.

The statutes of some states provide that a shareholder, in the election of directors by cumulative voting, may cast as many votes for one candidate for a given office as there are offices to be filled, multiplied by the number of his shares of stock, or he may distribute this same number of votes among the candidates as he sees fit.

A stockholder is entitled to vote only by virtue of his ownership in the stock, and under the common law, this right can only be exercised in person. However, by statute or the charter or the bylaws, a stockholder may specifically authorize another to vote his stock. This authorization is made by power of attorney and must specifically state that the agent of the stockholder has power to vote his principal's stock. This method of voting is called *voting by proxy.* It is a personal relationship, and may be revoked at any time by the stockholder before the authority is exercised. The laws relative to principal and agent control this relationship.

A stockholder, unlike a director, is permitted to vote on a matter in which he has a personal interest. In certain respects he represents the corporation welfare in his voting, whereas in other respects he votes in such a manner as he thinks will best serve his interest. The majority of stockholders may not take action, however, that is clearly detrimental to the corporation and minority interests. This becomes particularly significant when the majority of the shareholders also own most of the stock of an allied or related enterprise and seek to operate the first corporation in such a manner as to profit the second at the expense of the first. If it is clear that the affairs of the first corporation are being mishandled in order to benefit the second, such action may be enjoined by the minority interests.

6-67. Voting Pools and Trust Agreements.   Various devices have been used whereby minority interests or a group of stockholders may effectively control a corporation. The creation of a holding company; the issuance of nonvoting shares or the issuance of shares with voting rights but with a small or nominal par value; voting pools; and voting trusts have all been utilized for this purpose, and in general all of them are effective means for obtaining control. A voting pool arises whenever a number of stockholders agree to vote their stock as a unit in accordance with a certain plan. Such an agreement is enforceable unless the purpose to be accomplished is illegal.

A voting trust develops from the transfer of title of their shares by various stockholders to a trustee for the purpose of voting the stock. The stock is then registered in his name, he votes at the meetings of shareholders, and receives dividends as they are declared. He issues to each stockholder whose stock he holds, a certificate of beneficial interest, which entitles the owner thereof to have his shares returned at the termination of the trust and to receive dividends within a given time after they are paid. In the early law, some courts held voting trusts unenforceable because they tend to separate ownership from control and management. Today courts enforce the trust agreement, unless its objectives are improper or the period of its continuance unreasonably long.[1] The Model Business Corporation Act sets a limit of ten years upon voting trusts.

RIGHTS OF SHAREHOLDERS

6-68. In General.   A shareholder has the following rights usually created by statute and reiterated in the bylaws: (1) the right to inspect the books and papers of the corporation, (2) the right to attend stockholders' meetings and to vote for directors and on certain other matters such as dissolution or merger, (3) a right to share in the profits when a dividend is declared, (4) the preemptive right, and (5) the right to bring a shareholder's derivative suit. In some states, a stockholder has the additional right of cumulative voting or voting all of his votes for one or more directors by accumulating them.

The right to inspect the books and papers is limited to inspections for proper purposes at the proper time and the proper place. The inspection, however, must be made with a justifiable motive and not through idle curiosity or for purposes which in any way interfere with the corporate management. The business hours of the corporation are the reasonable and proper hours in which a stockholder is entitled to inspect the books. Some courts hold that the motive

---

[1] Alderman et al. v. Alderman et al., page 933

of inspecting the books is immaterial and that the corporation has no right to question the reason for which the books are being inspected.

6-69. Dividends. While a stockholder has a right to his share of dividends when declared, whether or not a dividend is declared is within the discretion of the board of directors. The stockholders of a corporation are not entitled to the payment of a dividend simply because earned surplus exists. The board of directors, at its discretion, may see fit to continue the profits in the business for the purpose of extension and improvements. A board of directors, however, must act reasonably and in good faith. Where such is not the case and there are profits out of which dividends may be declared, the stockholders may compel the board of directors to declare dividends.[2] It must be clear, however, that the board of directors has, illegally, wantonly, and without justification, refused to declare a dividend before the stockholders have a right to interfere.

When a dividend is declared, it becomes a debt of the corporation and will be paid to the person whose name appears on the corporate stock records as the owner of the share, unless the corporation has received notice of a transfer. A cash dividend, once its declaration has been made public, may not be rescinded, although there is some authority for rescinding a stock dividend.

The statutes of the various states governing the declaration of dividends appear to follow two distinct patterns. The first group of states, apparently codifying the common law, provide that dividends can be declared only out of net profits. Under this rule it seems safe to say that dividends may be declared out of current profits, even though a deficit has arisen from the operation of previous years. Capital surplus or surplus arising from the appreciation of fixed assets would not appear to be available for dividends under the law of these states.

The other group of states, representing perhaps a majority, determine the legality of a dividend by its effect upon the capital stock. A declaration of dividends is proper so long as it does not impair the capital stock. Any declaration, however, which reduces the net assets of the corporation below the outstanding capital stock is illegal. Under this view it would seem that capital or paid-in surplus is available for dividends. The law in this regard is not at all definite, but the Model Business Corporation Act, which has accepted the majority view, makes capital surplus available for dividends. However, it limits the use of surplus arising from appreciation of fixed assets to stock dividends.

Under either theory, dividends are permissible only after provision has been made for all expenses, including depreciation. In those industries dealing with wasting or depleting assets, such as mines and oil wells, it is not necessary to allow for the depletion before declaring dividends.

In many states the directors are personally liable to creditors for dividends improperly declared. Also, the stockholders who receive such dividends may be compelled to return them. In a few of the states, statutes make the stockholders liable only if they received them in bad faith and directors liable only if they acted carelessly or in bad faith.

[2] Knapp et al. v. Bankers Securities Corporation, et al., page 935

Dividends may be paid in cash; property other than cash including the stock of another corporation; or scrip, which is a certificate representing property which will later be redeemed in cash from the sale of the property or stock.

A stock dividend is a transfer of surplus to capital and is used where the earnings are required for growth of the business. Stock dividends of the issuing company are not taxable income to stockholders. A stock split differs from a stock dividend in that in the former there is no transfer of surplus to capital but only a reduction in par value and an increase in the number of shares.

6-70. Preemptive Right.   The capital stock of a corporation is fixed by the charter, and it cannot be increased except by express authority from the state creating the corporation. The shareholders, and not the directors, must authorize an increase in the capital stock. Such an authorization must be made by amendment of the charter in compliance with the statute providing for changes in the corporation.

When an increase in the capital stock has been properly authorized, the existing stockholders have a prior right against third parties to subscribe to the increased capital stock. This right is called the stockholder's *preemptive right* and is based upon the stockholder's right to protect and maintain his proportionate control and interest in the corporation.[3] Thus, if a class of stock has no voting power and is nonparticipating, it is questionable whether such preemptive right exists. This right may be limited or waived by contract and by provisions in the charter or bylaws of the corporation. In many states it is not applicable to treasury stock.[4] It is applicable to new authorizations of stock and perhaps to new allotments of stock previously authorized, particularly if the new allotment of an original authorization takes place some time after the original issue. Some states approve the issuance of stock to employees without regard to the preemptive right. Whether or not a stockholder must pay more than par value for the increased stock varies among the different states. Some states hold that he can be compelled to pay more, and other states hold that he cannot.

6-71. Derivative Suits.   A stockholder cannot maintain an *action at law* for injuries to the corporation, because the corporation is a legal entity and by law has a right to bring a suit in its own name. A stockholder cannot bring a suit at law for and in behalf of the other stockholders for injury to the corporation. Neither can a stockholder bring a suit in law against the directors or other officers of the corporation for negligence, waste, and mismanagement in the conduct of the corporate business, although such conduct is injurious to the stockholder. The right to sue for injuries to the corporation rests strictly with the corporation itself.

A stockholder may, however, bring a *suit in equity* known as a shareholder's derivative suit to enjoin the officers of a corporation from entering into *ultra vires* contracts or from doing anything that would impair the stockholders' rights in the corporate assets. Likewise, the stockholder has a right to bring suit in equity for, or on behalf of, the corporation itself if the officers are acting outside the scope of their authority; are guilty of negligent conduct; or are

[3] Ross Transport, Inc. et al. v. Crothers et al., page 936
[4] Runswick et al. v. Floor et al., page 937

engaging, or about to engage, in fraudulent transactions with other stockholders in such a way as to be injurious to the corporation itself.[5]

Before a stockholder may enter into a suit in equity for and on behalf of the corporation, he must show that he has done everything possible to secure action by the managing officers and directors and that they have refused to act. Any judgment received in such an action benefits the corporation and only indirectly the stockholder who initiates the action. He is permitted, however, to recover the expenses involved in the suit.

It has been held that mere dissatisfaction by some of the stockholders as to the management of the corporation will not justify a derivate suit.

DIRECTORS

6-72. Qualifications and Powers.　The directors of a corporation are elected by the stockholders. In the absence of a provision in the charter, bylaws, or statute, it is not essential that directors hold stock in the corporation. Since they are to supervise the business activities, select key employees, and plan for the future development of the enterprise, they are presumably elected because of their business ability.

The directors have power to take such action as is necessary or proper consistent with the charter in the ordinary business activities of enterprises of the type being managed. They may not amend the charter, approve a merger, or bring about a consolidation with another corporation without the approval of the stockholders.

Directors are presumed to be free to exercise their independent judgment upon all matters presented to them. Consequently, their management of the business cannot be interfered with by action on the part of the stockholders.[6] Similarly, any contract made by a director with a stockholder concerning a particular matter before the board is contrary to public policy and unenforceable. Free and independent action by directors is required for the best interests of the corporation itself as distinct from the interests of a few stockholders.

6-73. Meetings.　The statute, charter, and bylaws usually provide for the number of directors. In most cases, not less than three directors are required. Since the board of directors must act as a unit, it is usually necessary that it assemble at board meetings.[7] The bylaws usually provide for the method of calling directors' meetings and for the time and the place of meeting. A record is usually kept of the activities of the board of directors, and the evidence of the exercise of its powers is usually stated in resolutions kept in the corporate record book. A majority of the members of the board of directors is necessary to constitute a quorum. Special meetings are proper only when all directors are notified or are present at the meeting. Directors may not vote by proxy, having been selected as agents because of their personal qualifications.

Modern statutes make informal action possible by a board of directors (usually by telephone), provided the action taken is subsequently reduced to

---

[5] Ramsburg et al. v. American Investment Company of Illinois et al., page 938.

[6] Petition of Avard, page 939.

[7] Tuttle v. Junior Bldg. Corporation, page 941.

writing and signed by the directors. This gives a board the flexibility and capability to make decisions when needed without delay.

6-74. Compensation.   In the absence of a stipulation in the charter or bylaws or resolution of the stockholders, directors receive no compensation for their services as such. If they do work not recognized as falling within the duties of a director, they may recover for the reasonable value of their services. Directors who are appointed as officers of the corporation should have their salaries fixed at a meeting of the shareholders or in the bylaws. Since directors are not supposed to vote on any matter in which they have a personal interest, director-officers of small corporations usually vote on salaries for each other but not their own, and the action to determine salaries should be ratified by the stockholders in order to ensure the validity of the employment contracts.

6-75. Liabilities of Directors.   Directors are said to stand in a fiduciary relation to the corporation.[8] They are not trustees in the strict sense, they are agents with more than the usual authority of an agent. Therefore, a director occupies a position of trust and confidence with respect to the corporation, and cannot, by reason of his position, directly or indirectly derive any personal benefits that are not enjoyed by the corporation or the stockholders.[9] All secret profits obtained by a director in the pursuit of the corporate business must be accounted for to the corporation.

A director may contract with the corporation that he represents, but he is subject to the same limitations as an agent is in dealing with his principal. He is required to disclose his interest in all contracts and, because of his fiduciary relation, to volunteer all pertinent information regarding the subject matter involved. Furthermore, he is forbidden to vote as a director on any matter in which he has a personal interest. Even though his vote is not necessary to carry the proposition considered, most courts would regard any action taken as a result of that vote to be voidable. Some courts go so far as to hold that, if he is present at the meeting, favorable action will not be binding. Clearly, if his presence is required to make a quorum, no transaction in which he is interested should be acted upon. These rather severe rules are enforced so that directors will not be tempted to use their position to profit at the expense of the corporation.

Directors are personally liable when they willfully misuse their power and misapply the funds of the corporation. They are also personally liable when they issue stock as fully paid when it is not paid in full. Directors are required to perform the duties of their office in a reasonable manner and in good faith. The standard of care required of directors cannot be exactly defined. It is generally held that directors are bound to exercise that degree of care which men of prudence exercise in the management of their own affairs. The standard of care varies with the size and type of the corporation. In large corporations many duties must be delegated, thus intimate knowledge of details by the directors is not possible. In corporations invested with a public interest—such as insurance companies, banks, building and loan associations, and public utilities—rigid supervision and specific obligations are imposed upon direc-

[8] Mardel Securities, Inc. v. Alexandria Gazette Corp., page 942
[9] Vulcanized Rubber & Plastics Company v. Scheckter, page 943

tors. If a director fails to exercise the requisite degree of care and skill, the corporation will have a right of action against him for resulting losses. When directors by their negligent misconduct involve the corporation in an *ultra vires* transaction which causes a loss, the directors may be liable to the corporation. They are not liable, however, for accidents and mistakes of judgment or for losses, if they have acted in good faith and have exercised ordinary care, skill, and diligence. The corporation must pay the expense of defending unfounded claims against officers and directors.

The directors, although holding a fiduciary relation to the corporation, have no such relationship with the individual stockholders. In a sale of stock by a stockholder to a director, they deal at arm's length. The director who, because of his relation to the corporation, is in a position to know many factors which affect the value of the stock, is not obligated to volunteer such information to the stockholder. However, there is a strong minority view and a tendency in recent decisions to support a fiduciary relationship in such cases. The rules of the S.E.C. also regulate insider transactions and sales and purchases of stock by a director may be voidable under these regulations.

CORPORATE STOCK

6-76. Introduction.   Membership in a corporation is acquired by a contract with the corporation; this membership is evidenced by a certificate showing ownership of shares of stock. The right to membership may be acquired by a stock subscription before the corporation is created or by a purchase of shares of stock from the corporation after it is organized or by a transfer of shares from some person who owns the stock.

The term *"capital stock"* creates confusion because the term *"capital"* and *"stock"* have a distinct meaning when not joined together. Technically, *capital stock* is the expressed equity of the stockholders in corporate assets resulting from their investments before the latter have been influenced by profits or losses. It should equal the amount of money, services, and property paid in or subscribed by the shareholders for the purposes of carrying on the corporate business. However, if a subscriber pays more than par value, as stated on the face of the certificate, to the corporation for his stock, the excess is usually credited to capital surplus or paid in surplus, rather than to the corporation's capital stock account. Capital stock is the sum fixed as such in the corporate charter. The capital stock would therefore always remain the same unless changed by an amendment of the charter. This viewpoint is generally considered to express the true meaning of "capital stock," but the term is sometimes loosely used to describe other concepts, such as the total assets of the corporation.

The term "capital" means the net assets of the corporation, including not only the original investment but also all gains and profits realized from the conduct of the corporate business. For example, if a corporation is incorporated with a capital stock of $50,000, fully paid, and it makes a profit of $20,000, which is kept in the business and is not distributed as dividends, it has a capital of $70,000. Its capital stock, however, is the $50,000 originally placed in the business.

The term "stock" refers to the ownership of rights in the corporation. These rights are primarily three in number: the right to share in profits, the right to participate indirectly in the control of the corporation, and the right to receive a portion of the assets at time of dissolution. A share of stock is representative of an investment made in the corporation, but it gives the holder no right to share in the active management of the business, and the general rules of law applicable to personal property are applicable to stock.

A certificate of stock is written evidence of the ownership of a certain number of shares of stock of a corporation, which shows upon its face the character of the interest and the method of transfer and may state a part of the contract existing between the shareholder and the corporation or between him and the other shareholders. A subscriber often becomes a stockholder before the certificate is issued. The certificate is merely the physical evidence and indicates that the corporation recognizes a certain person as being a stockholder.

The term "stock" must be distinguished from the term "bond." A bond, unlike stock, is an obligation of the corporation to pay a certain sum of money in the future at a specified rate of interest. It is comparable to a promissory note of which the corporation is the maker. Corporate bonds are often secured by a mortgage on the assets of the corporation, but many corporate bonds called *debentures* do not have such security. A bondholder is a creditor of the corporation, whereas a stockholder is not. A stockholder has a right to receive dividends if they are declared by the board of directors and to participate in the assets of the corporation after all creditors have been paid. A bondholder has no right to vote or to participate in the management and control of a corporation, unless, upon insolvency, such rights are given by contract; whereas a shareholder, in the absence of contractual limitations, has a right to participate in the corporate control.

6-77. Terminology.   *Common stock* is the simplest type of corporate stock; it entitles the owner to share in the control, profits, and assets of the corporation in proportion to the amount of common stock he holds. Such a stockholder has no advantage, priority, or preference over any other class of stockholders unless otherwise specified as to any particular class.

Preferred stock is stock that has a prior claim to dividends, or to assets on dissolution, over other classes of stock. The most important right given to a preferred stockholder is the right to receive a certain specified dividend, even though the earnings are not sufficient to pay a like dividend to common stockholders.

Preferred stock may be provided for by the charter, but, if no provision is made for the issuance of preferred stock by the charter or statute, such stock cannot be issued without the unanimous consent of the common stockholders.

Preferred stock may be *cumulative* or *noncumulative.* If the certificate of the preferred stock evidencing the contract provides not only that the preferred shares shall be entitled to a dividend of a certain percentage annually when earned but also that the arrears, if any, in one year or more are payable out of the earnings of the subsequent years, before payment of dividends on the common stock, the dividends are said to be cumulative. If the dividends are to be paid out of current profits only, without provision for payment of arrearages, the preferred stock is said to be noncumulative. Whether preferred stock is cumulative or noncumulative depends upon the statute, the charter, or the contract set forth on the face of the certificate of stock. However, if nothing is said about the payment of the dividends, the preferred stock is cumulative,[10] and preferred dividends and all arrears thereon must be paid before a dividend is declared on common stock.

Preferred stock may be *participating* or *nonparticipating*. If the preferred stock is given the right to share in dividends equally with other classes of stock after the payment of the preferred dividends, it is designated as participating preferred stock. Such participating preferred stock is entitled to additional dividends, however, only after the common stock has received a dividend equal to the preferred dividend for the current year. If, however, the preferred stock is limited in its dividend to a fixed amount, it is designated as nonparticipating preferred stock. The term "participating preferred stock" is also used to designate a preferred stock which receives a preference in the corporate assets on dissolution and liquidation of the corporation and may, in addition, enable the holder to share with other classes of stock in the assets that remain after the common and preferred stock have been fully satisfied by repayment of the stockholder's original investment. To determine whether preferred stock has equality in the participation in dividends and assets with other classes of stock after the payment of its fixed dividend or return of investment, it is necessary to examine not only the contract evidenced by the stock certificate but also the articles of incorporation, the bylaws, and the state corporation statutes. In the absence of an agreement or other provision, preferred stock has no preference in corporate assets at dissolution.

The statutes of most states provide that a corporation may issue stock with *no par* value, the value of the stock being determined by its sale value in the open market or by the price set by the directors as a "stated value." Stockholders, creditors of the corporation, and the public will not be misled or prejudiced by this type of stock, because there is no holding out that the stock has any particular face value, and all persons dealing in such stock are put on notice that they should investigate the corporation's assets and its financial condition. Stock with no par value represents the proportionate part of the total assets of the corporation it stipulates but does not indicate the monetary value or par value of the share. The state law usually permits the directors to determine what portion of the amount received from the sale of no par stock shall be credited to the capital stock account and how much, if any, shall be credited to capital or paid-in surplus.

A *stock warrant* is a certificate which gives to the holder thereof the right to subscribe for and purchase a given number of shares of stock in a corporation at a stated price. It is usually issued in connection with the sale of other shares of stock or of bonds, although the law of some states permits the issuance of stock warrants entirely separate and apart from the sale of other securities. Usually the warrants are transferable, although in some cases they are personal only. The option to purchase contained in the warrant may or may not be limited as to time or otherwise conditioned. A warrant has value and can readily be sold on the market in the same fashion as other securities.

[10] Arizona Power Co. v. Stuart, page 944

6-78. Watered Stock.   Watered stock is stock that has been issued as fully paid, when in fact its full par value has not been paid in money, property, or services.[11] The capital stock of a corporation represents the total par value of all the shares of the corporation (plus the stated value of no par stock), and the public, including corporate creditors, has a right to assume that the capital stock issued has been paid for in full. The corporation represents that assets have been received in payment equal in amount to its issued capital stock. If stock is issued in excess of the actual assets in money value received for it by the corporation, it is said to be *watered stock,* and original holders of such stock are liable to corporate creditors for the difference between its par value and the amount they actually paid for the stock.

In suits by creditors against stockholders to force payment on watered stock, it is maintained by many jurisdictions that the capital stock is a "trust fund" for the payment of the corporate debts and that the law implies a promise by the original stockholders to pay their stock in full when called upon by the creditors.

Another basis upon which creditors seek recovery against holders of such stock is called the "holding out" theory. Under this doctrine the right of creditors to compel the holders of bonus stock to pay for it, contrary to their actual agreement with the corporation, rests not upon an implied contract or upon any trust fund doctrine but simply upon the ground of fraud. This right applies only to those creditors who have relied upon the stock as representing actual capital paid in; therefore, payment cannot be enforced against stockholders in favor of those creditors who became such before the bonus stock was issued. In either case, only the original purchaser of the stock is liable. One who acquires it in good faith from the original stockholder has no additional liability.

6-79. Treasury Stock.   *Treasury stock* is that which has been issued by the corporation for value and returned by gift or purchase to the corporation or to trustees for the corporation to sell. It may be sold below par and the proceeds returned to the treasury of the corporation for working capital. It differs from stock originally issued below par, in that the purchaser is not liable for the difference between par and the sale price. It may be sold at any price the company sees fit to charge.

TRANSFER OF STOCK AND OTHER INVESTMENT SECURITIES

6-80. In General.   A share of stock is personal property, and the owner has the right to transfer it just as he may transfer any other personal property. A share of stock is generally transferred by an indorsement and the delivery of the certificate of stock. A share may be transferred or assigned by a bill of sale or by any other method that will pass title to a chose in action or other intangible property. Whenever a share of stock is sold and a new stock certificate issued, the name of the new owner is entered on the stock records of the corporation. In a small corporation the secretary of the corporation usually

---

[11] Bing Crosby Minute Maid Corp. v. Eaton, page 945

handles all transfers of stock and also the canceling of old certificates and issuing of new. Large corporations, in which there are hundreds and even thousands of transactions employ transfer agents. The transfer agents transfer stock, cancel old certificates, issue new ones, prepare and keep up to date the names of the stockholders of the corporation, distribute dividends, mail out stockholders' notices, and perform many functions to assist the corporation secretary. Stock exchange rules provide that corporations listing stock for sale must maintain a transfer agency and registry, operated and maintained under exchange regulations. The registrar of stock is an agent of the corporation whose duty is to see that no stock certificates are issued in excess of the authorized capitalization of the corporation.

The volume of transactions in stock sold publicly is so large that many techniques have been developed to reduce the cost and confusion of transfers. One such technique is for the title to the stock to be held in the "house" name of a brokerage firm. If the firm has transactions with both buyers and sellers in the same stock, a transfer can be effected by a bookkeeping entry, and new certificates need not be issued. The firm will, however, solicit proxies and vote the stock in accordance with the instructions of the actual owner. As another means of reducing transfers many companies are discouraging small share-holders from investing. For example, a company may try to purchase back the stock of every holder of ten shares or less. Such a policy will greatly reduce corporate administrative expenses.

Many people are advocating replacing stock certificates with "punch cards" which can be easily transferred by computer. It is anticipated that in the near future, formal stock certificates may disappear from use by large corporations.

6-81. Article 8 of the Uniform Commercial Code—In General.

The subject matter of Article 8 is investment securities. The term "investment security" is defined as an instrument which

1. is issued in bearer or registered form; and

2. is a type commonly dealt in upon securities exchanges and markets or is commonly recognized as a medium for investment; and

3. evidences a share, participation or other interest in property or in an enterprise or evidences an obligation of the issuer.

A security is in registered form when it specifies the name of the owner and when it may be transferred by registration upon books maintained by or on behalf of the issuer. A security is in bearer form when it is made out to bearer and not by reason of any indorsement.

The definition of "security" is functional—based upon its use as a medium of investment—rather than formal as in the case of commercial paper. As a result, the term includes stock certificates; bonds, both registered and bearer; warrants; debentures; investment paper; scrip; and any other instrument which evidences a share of or participation in an interest in an enterprise. The size of the organization issuing the securities is not significant.

The general principle of Article 8 is that securities are negotiable instruments and that bona fide purchasers thereof have greater rights than they would have "if the things bought were chattels or simple contracts." The principles of Article 3 that relate to the establishment of preferred status for commercial paper are applied to securities. Defenses of the issuer are generally not effective against a purchaser for value who has taken without notice of the particular defense. It should be recognized that negotiability is not affected, under Article 8, by expressions that the instrument is "subject to" another agreement.

A bona fide purchaser is one who purchases in good faith and without notice of any adverse claim. He takes delivery of a security in bearer form or of one in registered form issued to him or indorsed to him or in blank. One who takes from a bona fide purchaser is given the rights of a bona fide purchaser. This is comparable to the "shelter provision" of Article 3—Commercial Paper. A bona fide purchaser takes free of "adverse claims," which include a claim that a transfer was wrongful or that some other person is the owner of, or has an interest in, the security.

6-82. The Issue of Securities.   The power of a corporation to issue securities is controlled by statute, and the charter limits the number of shares that can be issued. Issuing securities in excess of the authorized amount is prohibited. An *overissue* is defined as "the issue of securities in excess of the amount which the issuer has corporate power to issue." If a person is entitled to securities and if by issuing them to him the corporation would exceed its authorized limit, he may insist that when identical shares are reasonably available on the market or by purchase from other shareholders the corporation purchase the shares in order to fulfill its obligation to him. As an alternative, the party entitled to the shares can recover damages for failure of the corporation to provide the shares.

A corporation may entrust its securities to an employee or transfer agent to prepare them for issue. This process includes affixing the corporate seal and adding a signature necessary for issue. If the person entrusted with the securities or who has access to them forges a signature or signs without authority "prior to or in the course of issue," such signature is ineffective except that "the signature is effective in favor of a purchaser for value and without notice of the lack of authority. . . . " The purpose of this is to place upon the issuer the duty to avoid negligent entrusting of securities to employees or others in the course of issue. This rule deals with signatures placed upon securities prior to or in the course of issue and does not apply to forged indorsements. A related problem is that of completion or alteration of an instrument. A purchaser for value without notice can enforce an incorrectly completed instrument. A complete security which is wrongfully altered is enforceable but only according to its original terms. Nondelivery of an incomplete instrument is not a defense against a holder for value without notice.

When a security in registered form is transferred, the new owner should present it to the issuer for registration of the transfer. Prior to such presentment, the issuer may "treat the registered owner as the person exclusively entitled to vote, to receive notifications, and otherwise to exercise all the rights and powers of an owner." Stock that is being paid for by installments that fall due at the demand or call of the board of directors may be sold before all of the calls have been made. In such cases the purchaser is deemed to have assumed responsibility for all future calls, and the transferor is relieved of liability.

As to calls made previous to the transfer, but that remain unpaid at that time, the transferor remains liable. The liability of the transferee in such a case doubtless depends upon his knowledge or lack of knowledge of the unpaid calls. If the corporation issues a certificate prior to the time when all calls are made, it should not be marked "fully paid and nonassessable." An innocent purchaser of stock thus erroneously marked takes it free from any liability to the corporation for unpaid calls. The Code does not affect the liability of the registered owner of a security for calls, assessments, or the like. Likewise, the Code does not preclude a holder of record from denying ownership when assessments are levied if he is otherwise entitled to do so under state law.

6-83. Transfer.　A person who transfers a security for value warrants that his transfer is effective and rightful; that the security is genuine and has not been materially altered; and that he knows of no fact which might impair the validity of the security. A broker makes all the warranties of a transferor.

A transfer is accomplished when the transferor delivers the security to the purchaser. Such transfer is complete upon delivery. If the security is in registered form and has been transferred without any necessary indorsement, the purchaser has a specifically enforceable right to have any necessary indorsement supplied. He does not attain the status of a bona fide purchaser until the indorsement is received.

Indorsement.　The transfer may be accomplished by the signature of the transferor on the back of a security or by a separate document signed by the transferor. An indorsement may be in blank or special; an indorsement to bearer is a blank indorsement. A special indorsement specifies the person to whom the security is transferred. A holder may convert a blank indorsement into a special indorsement. The indorser does not assume any obligation that the security will be honored by the issuer unless the indorser has agreed to assume this obligation. A security, unlike commercial paper, may be transferred in part. Thus, if the certificate represents 100 shares, an indorser may transfer 50, 25, etc. shares. There are two steps in the transfer—indorsement and delivery. The transfer is not accomplished until delivery has taken place. Since the concept of indorsement is applicable to registered securities, the indorsement of a security in bearer form is normally of no effect.

If an indorsement is forged, the owner may assert the ineffectiveness of the indorsement to deprive the owner of his ownership against the issuing corporation or any purchaser other than a bona fide purchaser who has in good faith received a new, reissued, or reregistered security on registration of transfer. The issuer who registers the transfer of a security upon a forged indorsement is subject to liability for improper registration.[12] Any person guaranteeing a signature of an indorser of a security makes certain warranties.[13]

The right to transfer freely one's share in the ownership of the business is inherent in corporations. It is one of those features of corporate life which distinguishes it from a partnership. However shareholders of "close" corporations often attempt by agreement or bylaw to limit the group of potential

[12] *Lesavoy Industries v. Pennsylvania General Paper Corp.*, page 946
[13] *Love v. Pennsylvania Railroad Co.*, page 947

purchasers. A corporate bylaw which provides that the shares of stock can be transferred only to the corporation or to those approved by the board of directors is unenforceable. It places too severe a restraint upon the alienation of property. Society is best protected when property may be transferred freely. However, an agreement or bylaw, approved by all stockholders, to the effect that no transfer of stock shall be made until it has first been offered to the other shareholders or to the corporation is generally enforced. Notice of the bylaw or agreement should be set forth in the stock certificate, since an innocent purchaser without notice of the restriction on alienation receives ownership free from the restriction.

6-84. Registration.   Though a transfer, as between transferor and purchaser, is complete when a registered security is indorsed and delivered, the remaining step is to register the transfer. This means that the new owner's name is placed on the stock register and the transferor's name is removed. Registration is of vital importance to the purchaser. When a security in registered form is presented to the issuer with a request to register transfer, the issuer is under a duty to do so provided: the security is properly indorsed; reasonable assurance is given in a manner satisfactory to the corporation at the time of presentment that the indorsements are genuine; tax requirements have been satisfied; and the transfer is in fact rightful or is to a bona fide purchaser.

When a security has been lost, apparently destroyed, or wrongfully taken, the owner must notify the issuer of such fact within a reasonable time. Should he fail to do so and the issuer registers a transfer, the owner is precluded from asserting the ineffectiveness of a forged indorsement and the wrongfulness of the registration of the transfer. If the lost security had been indorsed by the owner the registration is not wrongful unless notice has been given to the issuer.

Where the owner of a security claims that the security has been lost, destroyed or wrongfully taken, the issuer must issue a new security in place of the original security if the owner

(a) so requests before the issuer has notice that the security has been acquired by a bona fide purchaser; and

(b) files with the issuer a sufficient indemnity bond; and

(c) satisfies any other reasonable requirements imposed by the issuer.

If, after the issue of the new security, a bona fide purchaser of the original security presents it for registration of transfer, the issuer must register the transfer unless registration would result in overissue, in which event the issuer's liability is governed by the provisions previously discussed as to overissue. In addition to any rights on the indemnity bond, the issuer may recover the new security from the person to whom it was issued or any person taking under him except a bona fide purchaser.

Dividends on stock belong to the person who is owner of the stock at the time the dividends are declared. As to the corporation, ownership of the stock is determined by the stock register, and the dividends will be paid to the person whose name appears upon the stock book. In the absence of an agreement to the contrary, dividends declared before a transfer of stock, although not payable until a future time, belong to the transferor. But dividends declared after the transfer of the stock, although earned before the transfer, belong to the transferee. However, by agreement between the transferor and the transferee, upon notice to the corporation, the corporation must pay the dividends in compliance with the agreement.

Dividends are often declared as of a certain date and payable to stockholders of record as of a later date. In such cases a transfer after declaration but before the record date carries the dividends to the transferee. There is also some authority to the effect that a stock dividend passes to the transferee unless the contract of sale provides otherwise. Dividends normally become a debt as of the time they are declared, but stock dividends may be rescinded, according to many courts, after they have been declared. Consequently, in the case of cash dividends, the debt is owed to the stockholder at the date of declaration, or record date, whereas in reference to stock dividends, no debt exists, since the new issue of stock is transferred to the owner at the time it is issued. "No interference is intended with the common practice of closing the transfer books or taking a record date for dividend, voting, and other purposes as provided for in bylaws, charters, and statutes."

OPERATING THE CORPORATION CASES

Alderman et al. v. Alderman et al.

178 S.C. 9 (1935)

The plaintiffs had assigned their stock in the D. W. Alderman & Sons Company to the defendants, R. J. and Paul R. Alderman, in a voting trust. The plaintiffs sought to have the trust declared null and void. The lower court ruled in favor of the defendants, and the plaintiffs appealed.

BAKER, J. . . . It is a universally known fact to lumbermen that the operation of a sawmill and lumber plant, small or large, is a business in which one can lose heavily unless well managed. Indeed, this is so well recognized that it has become an adage among lumbermen, "Never to wish an enemy in torment but wish such enemy owned a sawmill."

Realizing, no doubt, that the success of the corporations, especially D. W. Alderman & Sons Company, depended upon the management, D. W. Alderman, Sr., requested that upon his death R. J. and Paul R. Alderman should be continued in the active management and control of the corporations in order that his well-known policies would be continued, and therefore, in deference to the wishes of the said D. W. Alderman, Sr., and having little if any experience with the operation and management of the business of said corporations, Mrs. Rice, Mrs. Shaw, Miss Martha Alderman, and D. W. Alderman, Jr., severally executed trust deeds or contracts conveying their stock in trust in the said corporations to the said R. J. and Paul R. Alderman.

. . . The position of appellants is that the instruments placing R. J. and Paul R. Alderman in the control of the corporation constituted what is known to the law as "voting trusts"; that they are void and voidable; being without consideration, illegal, and against public policy.

Therefore, the natural approach to a decision is to first inquire what constitutes a voting trust. There are various definitions of a voting trust given by the textbook and text-writers, among such definitions being as follows:

> A voting trust agreement is an agreement which cumulates in the hands of a person or persons the shares of several owners of stock in trust for the purpose of voting them in order to control the corporate business and affairs.
>
> A voting trust may be comprehensively defined as one created by an agreement between a group of the stockholders of a corporation and the trustee, or by a group of identical agreements between individual stockholders and a common trustee, whereby it is provided that for a term of years, or for a period contingent upon a certain event, or until the agreement is terminated, control over the stock owned by such stockholders, either for certain purposes or for all, shall be lodged in the trustee, with or without a reservation to the owner or persons designated by them of the power to direct how such control shall be used.

The definitions given by the various leading text-writers are practically in accord, and the whole theory of voting trusts is built up on the idea that a group or a portion of the stockholders of a corporation unite and execute an instrument to a trustee for the purpose of voting and controlling the policies of the corporation, but in no definition, nor reported case, do we find the entire stock of the corporation pooled in the same trustee or trustees. The instruments executed in the case at bar, while containing practically every element going to make up what is commonly known as a voting trust, in fact go farther, and constitute in addition thereto a managing trust and trust deed, and the voting power given under the instruments has been treated as only one of the many powers conveyed by the instruments and as incidental to governing the management of the corporations. The instruments before the court convey the certificates of stock in the corporations to these trustees with full power and authority to control the corporations, and for a definite time, the lifetime of the trustees or the survivor. On their face, the instruments have all the earmarks of a complete contract. The parties thereto were competent to contract. There was a subject-matter, there was a legal consideration, and there was mutuality of agreement and mutuality of obligation.

We come then to the question first if the instruments before the court are void or voidable as being against public policy.

... If the instruments create nothing more than voting trusts, are they void as against public policy? There are two distinct lines of cases, the one holding that the separation of the voting power in stock from its beneficial ownership is contrary to public policy and void, the other, that any voting trust which is entered into in good faith and for the promotion and good of the corporation, and thereby necessarily for the welfare and good of all of the stockholders, is valid and enforceable.

> ... It is very generally held or said that voting trusts are not per se unlawful; and one of the most familiar illustrations of a voting trust which may be lawful is where the object is to carry out a particular policy, with a view to promote the best interest of all of the stockholders. It is said that the validity of the trust is to be determined by the propriety and justness of the ultimate purposes sought to be accomplished ... (14 C. J. 915).

The instruments herein sought to be declared null and void are not against the public policy of the state, not contravening any statute, and there being a total lack of evidence that they were entered into to serve any illegal purpose, but, to the contrary, to better serve the interests of all of the stockholders and benefit them and the corporations.

Judgment affirmed.

Knapp et al. v. Bankers Securities Corporation et al.

230 F.2d 717 (1956)

The plaintiffs, shareholders in the defendant corporation, brought this action against the corporation and its directors to compel the declaration of dividends. The lower court held in favor of the plaintiffs.

MARIS, C. J. . . . The present action was brought in the district court for the eastern district of Pennsylvania by shareholders, New York residents, against the Bankers Securities Corporation, a Pennsylvania corporation, and its directors, charging that Albert M. Greenfield, one of the directors and the majority shareholder, and the other directors were acting unreasonably in failing to eliminate accumulated arrearages of dividends of approximately $3,000,000 on the common stock in order that the preferred and common stockholders might participate in the earnings of the corporation, that the distribution of earnings was being arbitrarily withheld for the benefit of the majority shareholder.

. . . It is an elementary principle of corporation law that the declaration of dividends out of net profits rests in the discretion of the board of directors. However, there are circumstances under which shareholders may compel the declaration of dividends. If directors have acted fraudulently or arbitrarily in refusing to declare a dividend when the corporation has a surplus which it can divide among the shareholders without detriment to the business, a shareholder may invoke the equitable powers of a court for relief. It is just such equitable power which the plaintiffs seek to invoke in this case. The question then is whether in such an action the shareholder is seeking relief from a personal wrong done to him and thus is enforcing a primary or personal right of his own or is seeking to redress a wrong done to the corporation and thus is enforcing a secondary right derived from the corporation.

. . . The right to dividends is an incident of the ownership of stock. The fact that the distribution of profits cannot ordinarily be enforced until after a dividend has been declared does not detract from the shareholders' fundamental right to share in the net profits of the corporation. This right is the basis of his suit to compel the declaration of dividends. If the directors have wrongfully withheld the declaration of dividends the shareholder is the injured party. He shows an injury to himself which is quite apart from any which the corporation might be thought to suffer. Even if the corporation might under some circumstances have a right of action that fact would not affect the authority of its shareholders to enforce by suit their personal and individual rights to the declaration of a dividend.

It is suggested that the right here asserted must be regarded as one vested in the corporation because the mechanics of relief have to be worked out by a decree against the directors rather than against the corporation. Our answer to this proposition was made by Judge Goodrich, when he said:

> It is to be observed that when a court steps in and orders the payment of a dividend, the corporate affairs have reached the point where the judgment of the directors is no longer controlling. The set of facts presented is such that the court substitutes its judgment, based on a rule of law, for the ordinary business judgment of those in charge of the business enterprise. . . .
>
> In such a case, even though the individual directors are joined as parties, they are not called upon to exercise any business discretion. The case has passed that point. As said before, the court is declaring rights protected by a rule of law, not calling upon the directors to exercise judgment. . . . The duty of a corporation to pay dividends then and there has been imposed by the judgment of the court, not by the ayes and nays of the members of the board. The situation becomes in substance the same as that in which any corporate creditor sues the enterprise in the corporate name to recover from it what it owns him; he does not need any meeting of the corporation's board to make his judgment good. Nor does a shareholder whose claim to dividends is based on his showing of fiduciary mismanagement need a directors' meeting to make his rights good. The judgment of a court is enough in either case.

. . . The order of the district court will be affirmed.

Ross Transport, Inc. et al. v. Crothers et al.

185 Md. 573 (1946)

The plaintiff, Crothers and other stockholders, brought this action against the corporation, its directors, and certain stockholders to set aside the issuance of certain shares of stock. The stock was sold to a director and to the family of the president and director. The lower court decreed that the stockholders who had received the additional stock must repay to the corporation the dividends received by them. The stock was declared to be illegally issued and ordered cancelled. The defendants appealed.

MARBURY, C. J. . . . The sale of this additional stock to a director and to the family of the president and director . . . without opportunity to buy given to other stockholders, is sought to be justified on the ground that it was originally planned, and that the money was needed to purchase additional buses at a cost of about $16,000. The facts, however, show no such need. The company was an immediate financial success.

. . . The appellees give two reasons for their contention that the stock sales of August 26th were void: First, because they deprive them and the other original stockholders of their pre-emptive rights to purchase a proportionate amount of the remaining shares, and, second, because, in selling to themselves and their nominees, Williams and Ross have abused their trust as officers and directors. They claim to be injured in two ways. Their voting powers have been proportionately lessened, and the control of the company has passed to Williams and Ross. And the amount paid in dividends has to be divided among 365 more shares of stock to the consequent financial loss of the holders of the original shares.

. . . The doctrine known as the pre-emptive right of shareholders is a judicial interpretation of general principles of corporation law. Existing stockholders are the owners of the business, and are entitled to have that ownership continued in the same proportion. Therefore, when additional stock is issued, those already having shares, are held to have the first right to buy the new stock in proportion to their holdings. This doctrine was first promulgated in 1807 in the case of *Gray* v. *Portland Bank,* 3 Mass. 364, 3 Am. Dec. 156. At that time, corporations were small and closely held, much like the one before us in this case. But in the succeeding years, corporations grew and expanded. New capital was frequently required. New properties had to be acquired for which it was desirable to issue stock. Companies merged, and new stock in the consolidation was issued. Stock was issued for services. Different kinds of stock were authorized—preferred without voting power but with prior dividend rights—preferred with the right to convert into common—several classes of both common and preferred with different rights. Some stock had voting rights. Other stock did not. Bonds were issued, convertible into stock. All of these changes in the corporate structure made it impossible always to follow the simple doctrines earlier decided. Exceptions grew, and were noted in the decisions.

Only one of these exceptions is involved in the present case. It has been held that pre-emptive rights do not exist where the stock about to be issued is part of the original issue. This exception is based upon the fact that the original subscribers took their stock on the implied understanding that the incorporators could complete the sale of the remaining stock to obtain the capital thought necessary to start the business. But this gives rise to an exception to the exception, where conditions have changed since the original issue. The stock sold the Williams family and Ross was part of the original issue and it is claimed by the appellants that it comes within the exception, and the appellees and the other stockholders have no pre-emptive rights.

The appellees, on the other hand, contend, and the chancellors found that changed conditions made it unnecessary to use the remaining unsold stock to obtain capital, and pre-emptive rights exist in it just as they would exist in newly authorized stock.

It is unnecessary for us to decide which of these two conflicting points of view applies to this cause, because another controlling consideration enters. The doctrine of pre-emptive right is not affected by the identity of the purchasers of the issued stock. What it is concerned with is who did not get it. But when officers and directors sell to themselves, and thereby gain an advantage, both in value and in voting power, another situation arises, which it does not require the assertion of a pre-emptive right to deal with.

It has long been the law in this State that trustees cannot purchase at their own sale, and trustees, in this sense, include directors of corporations.

... *The decree will be affirmed.*

Runswick et al. v. Floor et al.

116 Utah 91 (1946)

The plaintiff and other stockholders of the New Quincy Mining Company, a corporation, brought this action against Floor and other defendants to set aside the sale of treasury stock to the defendant Floor. The lower court ruled in favor of the defendants and the plaintiffs appealed.

LATIMER, J. . . . The principal issue to be decided by this court is as to the validity or invalidity of the sale of the treasury shares to defendant Floor. In proceeding to determine this question, it should initially be pointed out that the shares of stock involved had been once fully paid for and had been returned to the treasury of the company. Officers of a corporation may reissue this type of stock for value and in good faith without first offering it pro rata to existing shareholders. We quote from *Borg* v. *International Silver Co.* (D.C.S.D.N.Y., 11 F.2d 143, 11 F.2d 147): "The distinction may appear tenuous, but rests upon the effect which a new issue has upon the voting control of the company. When a person buys into a company with an authorized capital, he accepts that proportion of the voting rights which his purchase bears to the whole. This applies certainly so far as the other shares are issued at the same time, and perhaps, also, though they are issued much later. But treasury shares have by hypothesis once been issued, and have diluted, as it were, the shareholder's voting power *ab initio.* He cannot properly complain that he is given no right to buy them when they are resold, because that merely restores the status he originally accepted. All he can demand is that they shall bring to the corporate treasury their existing value. If they do, his proportion in any surplus is not affected. However, when the capital stock is increased beyond the original amount authorized, the voting power is diluted along with it; the shareholders who had not originally bought into so large an issue may insist that the old proportions be observed. To deprive them of their right of pre-emption is to change their contract. At any rate it is only on this theory that any right of pre-emption exists, and since the shares at bar were never bought to be retired, and the capital was not increased, the right does not exist."

Hence, the sale of the 150,000 shares to Floor was not objectionable by reason of the fact that the shares were not first offered to existing shareholders on a pro rata basis.

Affirmed.

Ramsburg et al. v. American Investment Company of Illinois et al.

231 F.2d 333 (1956)

The plaintiffs, as stockholders of defendant Domestic Finance Corporation, brought this suit for an injunction to restrain a proposed merger of that company with defendant American Investment Company of Illinois. Both are incorporated under the laws of Delaware. The complaint averred that American had, through divers means, obtained some 80 percent of the common stock of Domestic, thereby gaining control; that American had utilized its stock to effectuate election of a board of directors of Domestic composed of officers of American who were serving as Domestic's officers; and that American, through its control, had so operated Domestic as to reduce its effective position as a competitor of American in various cities and states where both corporations transact business. On August 17, 1955, Domestic mailed to its stockholders a notice of a special meeting to be held September 15, 1955, to consider and vote on a proposed merger of the two corporations. The complaint herein was filed September 7, 1955, charging that the merger would constitute a violation of § 7 of the Clayton Act, in that its effect would be to lessen substantially competition in commerce. It was further averred that Domestic would be seriously injured by the proposed action.

The complaint prayed a preliminary injunction restraining American from voting its Domestic stock in favor of the merger at the September 15 meeting or at any other time, and that, after hearing on the merits, the temporary injunction be made final, and a decree entered directing American to divest itself of the Domestic stock it owns and granting such other and further relief as to the court might seem just. The lower court denied the injunction and plaintiffs appealed. The defendants moved to dismiss the appeal on the ground that the cause was moot since the merger had been accomplished.

LINDLEY, C. J. . . . The question before us is reduced to an inquiry as to whether a stockholders' derivative suit will lie under § 7 of the Clayton Act. We frame our answer to that question on the teachings contained in a recent opinion by the Court of Appeals for the Second Circuit in *Fanchon & Marco, Inc.* v. *Paramount Pictures, Inc.* (202 F.2d 731, 36 A.L.R.2d 1336), which involved an appeal from a judgment dismissing a stockholders' derivative, antitrust suit for treble damages and injunctive relief. The court held that the action would lie and reversed the judgment of dismissal, saying (202 F.2d at p. 734): "Now there does not seem real doubt but that an antitrust derivative suit will lie; indeed, that seems to follow from the nature of such suits. ' . . . Equity . . . traditionally entertains the derivative or secondary action by which a single stockholder may sue in the corporation's right when he shows that the corporation on proper demand has refused to pursue a remedy, or shows facts that demonstrate the futility of such a request. . . . The cause of action which such a plaintiff brings before the court is not his own but the corporation's. . . .' Mr. Justice Jackson in *Koster* v. *(American) Lumbermen's Mutual Casualty Co.* (330 U.S.518, 522, 523, 67 S.Ct. 828, 91 L.Ed. 1067)." After discussing the applicable authorities, the court continued (202 F.2d at p. 735): "There is an occasional flat statement . . . that no derivative antiturst suit will lie, as in *Kalmanash* v. *Smith* (291 N.Y. 142, 157, 51 N.E.2d 681, 688); but, as indicated, the precedents actually look the other way and we can see no reason for such a view." We agree with this reasoning and hold that plaintiffs were competent parties when this suit was brought and have remained so throughout pendency of the litigation.

Motion to dismiss appeal denied.

Petition of Avard

144 N.Y.S.2d 204 (1955)

The petitioners, minority stockholders of Oneita Knitting Mills, a corporation, brought this action against the corporation to recover the value of their stock in the corporation. The corporation, which manufactured knit goods, was operating at a loss in its plant in New York and it desired to shift its operations to a low-cost plant in South Carolina, where it was believed that the business could be profitably conducted. The petitioners contended that the sale by the company of its property in New York could not be made without the consent of two-thirds of the stockholders. The lower court dismissed the petition, and the stockholders appealed.

GORMAN, J. . . . Section 20 of the Stock Corporation Law in substance requires the approval of two-thirds of the stockholders entitled to vote if a corporation desired to sell or convey its property, rights, privileges and franchises, or any interest therein or any part thereof, if such sale, lease or exchange is not made in the regular course of its business and involves all or substantially all of its property, rights, privileges and franchises, or an integral part thereof essential to the conduct of the business of the corporation. Section 21 of the same law prescribes the procedure to be followed by duly objecting stockholders. If, in view of the purposes and objects of a corporation, a particular sale may be regarded as within the regular and normal course of the business of the corporation and as not involving an integral part thereof, it is not within the purview of the statute. If the sale is such as to deprive the corporation of the means of accomplishing the ends for which it was incorporated; that is, if the business, and assets sold were essential to the ordinary conduct of the business, it is within the statute.

The present controversy squarely poses the question of whether the conduct of the respondent was such as to bring it within the scope of § 20. The management of a corporation is entrusted to its board of directors. It is well established that the directors have power, in the ordinary course of business, to do any act permitted by the charter or certificate of incorporation. There is no serious suggestion that the actions of the board of directors were tainted by fraud, deceit or bad faith in any of the contested transactions. Although the statute has been held inapplicable to the actions of a corporation pursuing a business advantage, the courts have rarely been called upon to construe the applicability of its terms to the actions of a solvent corporation motivated by business conditions to pursue somewhat far-reaching measures in the manipulation of its assets in an effort to continue its business.

If corporate management determines that a business is unprofitable, it may dispose of the property or business to eliminate further loss without the consent of its stockholders.

The time-honored test to determine the need for stockholder consent "is not the amount involved, but the nature of the transaction, whether the sale is in the regular course of the business of the corporation and in furtherance of the express objects of its existence, or something outside of the normal and regular course of the business."

The instant transactions do not involve the investment of respondent's assets in a substantially different business of a kind in which it was not authorized to engage, nor the exchange of its stock for the stock of another corporation, nor were they *pro tanto* going out of business in any vital department or branch of respondent's business.

"What in the instance of one corporation may be a sale or lease of all its assets requiring consent of stockholders, may, in the case of another corporation, depending upon its purposes, methods of operation and past history, and the industry practices and pattern, represent usual, normal and ordinary activity which does not require consent." Respondent has shown that it has long been the custom in the knit goods industry in general and its own operations in particular to discontinue unprofitable production and to sell equipment and machinery no longer needed in the ordinary course of its business. Subsequent to 1920, respondent found it expedient to reduce the production of men's and, particularly, women's heavy-weight underwear, the volume of which had previously been much greater than the aggregate of all its other production. This procedure constituted a normal operation of its business and was affected without specific stockholder approval. Respondent's present decision to concentrate upon the profitable production of light-weight underwear, T-shirts and outerwear would seem to be in accord with accepted business practice. Respondent has not relinquished any of its franchises nor has it prohibited itself from engaging in any branch of the knitted goods business which may now, or in the future, prove acceptable to consumers and profitable to it. None of the acts of the respondent can practicably be called acts of complete or partial self-destruction. It has not deprived itself of its ability to carry out its corporate purposes as exemplified in its amended charter by alienating an integral part of its business and has not altered the avowed purpose of the corporation—to manufacture, process, sell and otherwise deal in knit goods of any character. Since the charter further specifically provides that the corporate purpose is to do all acts and things as may be necessary, convenient or incidental to the foregoing, the board of directors may not be held to have acted in excess of their declared powers.

Affirmed.

Tuttle v. Junior Bldg. Corporation
228 N.C. 507 (1948)

The directors and stockholders of the defendant Junior Building Corporation met informally and discussed plaintiff's offer to purchase the building owned by the corporation. It was informally agreed to sell to the plaintiff, and the defendant's attorney, who was also a director, was instructed to prepare a deed. There was no formal vote, and no record of the meeting was entered in the corporate minutes. The deed was delivered to the bank in escrow and later withdrawn without the consent of the plaintiff and before he tendered the balance of the purchase price. The plaintiff brought this suit to compel specific performance of the contract of purchase and sale. From a judgment for defendant, plaintiff appealed.

BARNHILL, J. . . . A corporation is bound by the acts of its stockholders and directors only when they act as a body in regular session or under authority conferred at a duly constituted meeting. "As a rule authorized meetings are prerequisite to corporate action based upon deliberate conference, and intelligent discussion of proposed measures."

. . . "The separate action, individually, without consultation, although a majority in number should agree upon a certain act, would not be the act of the constituted body of men clothed with corporate powers." Angel & Ames on Corporations, § 504. "Indeed, the authorities upon this subject are numerous, uncontradicted, and supported by reason."

. . . If stockholders and directors cannot bind the corporation by their individual acts and declarations, *a fortiori* an unauthorized act performed in the name of the corporation by its officers cannot thereafter be ratified by such acts or declarations. Hence the court below properly excluded the evidence of declarations made by stockholders and directors after the sale had been repudiated and the deed withdrawn from escrow.

Affirmed.

Mardel Securities, Inc. v. Alexandria Gazette Corp.

183 F.Supp. 7 (1960)

HOFFMAN, J. Mardel Securities, Inc. has instituted this secondary action in its capacity as a 48 percent minority stockholder of the Alexandria Gazette Corporation, publishers of a newspaper advertised as "America's Oldest Daily Newspaper," against the Gazette and its principal officer, Charles C. Carlin, Jr., the latter being the owner of 52 percent of the outstanding stock issued by the Gazette. Plaintiff contends that Carlin is indebted to the Gazette in substantial amounts allegedly occasioned by reason of Carlin's ownership and operation of a newspaper known as the "Arlington Daily Sun," hereinafter referred to as the "Sun," which said newspaper Carlin caused to be printed at, and partially operated from, the physical plant of the Gazette at Alexandria, Virginia, only a few miles from Arlington where the Sun had its principal office but possessed no facilities for printing the newspaper. Plaintiff contends that the amounts charged to the Sun by the Gazette resulted in substantial losses to the Gazette for which Carlin, by reason of his fiduciary capacity, is liable to the Gazette. In short, the action, while maintained by the minority stockholder, is actually for the use and benefit of the Gazette corporation.

. . . We have no difficulty applying the controlling principles of law to the facts here presented. As was said in *Rowland* v. *Kable* (174 Va. 343, 6 S.E.2d 633, 642):

> The authorities are agreed that a director of a private corporation cannot directly or indirectly, in any transaction in which he is under a duty to guard the interests of the corporation, acquire any personal advantage, or make any profit for himself, and if he does so, he may be compelled to account therefor to the corporation. This does not mean that he may not deal with his corporation or sell his property to the corporation if the transactions are open, fair and honest, and the corporation is represented by competent and authorized agents. The unbending rule is that the director must act in the utmost good faith, and this good faith forbids placing himself in a position where his individual interest clashes with his duty to his corporation. The purpose of the law is to secure fidelity in the director. If, in violation of the general rule, he places himself in a position in which he may be tempted, by his own private interest, to disregard that of the corporation, his transactions are voidable at the option of the corporation and may be set aside without showing actual injury. One who is entrusted with the business of another cannot be allowed to make that business an object of interest to himself.

To the same effect will be found . . . *Wight* v. *Heublein* (4 Cir., 238 F. 321, 324). In the last cited case, the Court pointed out that directors are:

> . . . (precluded) from doing any act, or engaging in any transaction in which their own private interest will conflict with the duty they owe to the stockholders and from making any use of their power or of the corporation property for their own advantage.

In *Solimine* v. *Hollander* (128 N.J.Eq. 228, 16 A.2d 203, 217), we are told that a director or officer of a corporation cannot use corporate assets to acquire, finance, or develop his own individual business project or venture and insist that either the venture or the profits thereof are his own property.

It is clear that Carlin, in his fiduciary capacity as officer and director of the Gazette, has violated the cardinal rules applicable to his position.

Vulcanized Rubber & Plastics Company v. Scheckter

162 A.2d 400 (Pa.) 1960

COHEN, J. On August 20, 1959, the appellee corporation moved for and was granted a temporary order restraining the appellants, two of whom had been both lawyers and accountants of the appellee and a third a former director, from voting any of appellee's stock owned, held or controlled by appellants at any future stockholders' meeting. After holding several hearings, the chancellor, finding that certain stock was acquired by appellants in breach of their fiduciary responsibilities, decreed that the restraining order be continued as a preliminary injunction pending final hearing and determination of the case. From this order appellants have taken these appeals.

The instant suit involves another round in the struggle between the present management group of the appellee, Vulcanized Rubber & Plastics Company, and a group headed by the individual appellants, Scheckter, Fish and Redland, for managerial control of the appellee corporation. . . .

The chancellor found that from about March 1, 1956, until approximately the commencement of this action, a Weatherly Steel Castings Company and its successor, the appellant Dutron Plastics, Inc., made numerous purchases of the appellee's common stock, causing the price of the stock to increase from about $25 per share to more than $60 per share. Throughout this period, appellants Scheckter and Fish held majority control of both Weatherly Steel Castings Company and Dutron Plastics. They did not reveal their interest in these companies to the appellee. . . .

. . . Generally speaking, a corporation as such has no interest in its outstanding stock, or in dealings by its officers, directors, or shareholders with respect thereto. As a result, in and of itself, there can be nothing improper so far as the corporate entity is concerned with one of its fiduciaries, be he officer, director or otherwise, buying up a controlling number of shares. . . . Nor can it be of any consequence, therefore, if the control is secretly acquired (which as a practical matter will usually be the case, for to do so otherwise will result in a rise in the market price).

On the other hand, if there should exist some reason or necessity for the corporation to purchase its outstanding shares, the situation is necessarily altered. There is no doubt that the relationship between a corporation and its officers and directors, as well as its lawyers and accountants, is such that these "fiduciaries" cannot act contrary to or compete with the interests of the corporation. Predominantly for the protection of shareholders, there has developed in corporation law a doctrine of "corporate opportunity" under which a corporation has the right to legal redress where one of its fiduciaries has in some way usurped some advantageous opportunity in which the corporation has an existing interest or where the opportunity is necessary for corporate existence or prosperity. . . .

It becomes evident that the basis of appellee's action here must be that the appellant fiduciaries, in purchasing the stock in issue, regardless of the secrecy in doing so, have acted in competition with some existing corporate interest in the stock, or have pre-empted a corporate purchase which was necessary for the appellee's prosperity or existence. . . . Upon an examination of the record, and upon analysis of the applicable doctrines of corporate law, we find that the appellee corporation, as a corporate entity separate and apart from its management group, had no interest in purchasing the stock in issue . . . which could result in the appellee being legally harmed by the conduct of the appellants. . . .

There being no indication in the record that the board of directors as a body ever considered purchasing any stock, there could not be any existing corporate interest therein. Accordingly, it cannot be held that appellants' purchases were in competition with the corporation itself. . . .

The order granting the preliminary injunction is reversed.

Arizona Power Co. v. Stuart

212 F.2d 535 (1954)

The plaintiff corporation brought this action against the defendant, the Collector of Internal Revenue, to recover income taxes allegedly overpaid. The question presented to the court was whether the plaintiff could deduct dividends paid on preferred stock for the purpose of computing the corporate surtax. This in turn depended upon whether the stock fell within the definition of preferred stock in the Internal Revenue Code as being stock the dividends of which are cumulative. The lower court ruled against the plaintiff and the plaintiff appealed.

LEMMON, J. . . . A preferred stockholder is not creditor of the corporation in which he holds his stock. The dividends thereon are not payable absolutely but only out of the net earnings or net assets in excess of capital and only when and as declared. A dividend is that which the corporation has set aside from its net earnings or profits to be divided among the stockholders. The preference is limited to profits when earned. The agreement to pay dividends on preferred stock is to be construed as an agreement to pay them from profits. This is the rule unless corporations are expressly authorized by statute to resort to capital in payment of such dividends.

Dividends on preferred stock are ordinarily regarded as cumulative.

. . . This brings into focus the distinction between a cumulative and a non-cumulative dividend. A cumulative dividend survives as a senior charge on earnings. A non-cumulative dividend disappears if not declared and ceases to be a preferential right.

. . . Appellee [Collector of Internal Revenue] reminds us that there is no specific statement in the articles that the preferred stock is cumulative. But references are made in the articles to "accumulated and unpaid dividends" on the preferred stock.

. . . It is unnecessary that the word "cumulative" be used. It is sufficient if the stipulated preferences make it such.

. . . *Reversed and remanded with directions to enter judgment in favor of appellant.*

Bing Crosby Minute Maid Corp. v. Eaton

297 P.2d 5 (Cal.) 1956

The plaintiff corporation was a judgment creditor of a corporation in which the defendant, Eaton, was the principal stockholder. The judgment was not paid, and the plaintiff brought this action to recover from the defendant. The defendant had received 4,500 shares of stock having a par value of $10 in return for consideration from the defendant of $34,780.83. The lower court rendered a judgment against the defendant in the amount of $10,219.17. The lower court granted a new trial and the plaintiff appealed.

SHENK, J. . . . In this state a shareholder is ordinarily not personally liable for the debts of the corporation; he undertakes only the risk that his shares may become worthless. (Cases cited.) There are, however, certain exceptions to this rule of limited liability. For example, a subscriber to shares who pays in only part of what he agreed to pay is liable to creditors for the balance.

. . . The plaintiff seeks to base its recovery on the only other exception to the limited liability rule that the record could support, namely, liability for holding watered stock, which is stock issued in return for properties or services worth less than its par value. Accordingly, this case calls for an analysis of the rights of a creditor of an insolvent corporation against a holder of watered stock. Holders of watered stock are generally held liable to the corporation's creditors for the difference between the par value of the stock and the amount paid in.

. . . The liability of a holder of watered stock has been based on one of two theories; the misrepresentation theory or the statutory obligation theory. The misrepresentation theory is the one accepted in most jurisdictions. The courts view the issue of watered stock as a misrepresentation of the corporation's capital. Creditors who rely on this misrepresentation are entitled to recover the "water" from the holders of the watered shares. (Cases cited.)

Statutes expressly prohibiting watered stock are commonplace today. In some jurisdictions where they have been enacted, the statutory obligation theory has been applied. Under that theory the holder of watered stock is held responsible to creditors whether or not they have relied on overvaluation of corporate capital.

. . . In his answer the defendant alleged that in extending credit to the corporation the plaintiff did not rely on the par value of the shares issued, but only on independent investigation and reports as to the corporation's current cash position, its physical assets and its business experience. At the trial the plaintiff's district manager admitted that during the period when the plaintiff extended credit to the corporation, (1) the district manager believed that the original capital of the corporation amounted to only $25,000, and (2) the only financial statement of the corporation that the plaintiff ever saw showed a capital stock account of less than $33,000. These admissions would be sufficient to support a finding that the plaintiff did not rely on any misrepresentation arising out of the issuance of watered stock. The court made no finding on the issue of reliance. If the misrepresentation theory prevails in California, that issue was material and the defendant was entitled to a finding thereon. If the statutory obligation theory prevails, the fact that the plaintiff did not rely on any misrepresentation arising out of the issuance of watered stock is irrelevant and accordingly a finding on the issue of reliance would be surplusage.

It is therefore necessary to determine which theory prevails in this state. The plaintiff concedes that before the enactment of § 1110 of the Corporations Code in 1931, the misrepresentation theory was the only one available to creditors seeking to recover from holders of watered stock.

. . . In view of the cases in this state adopting the misrepresentation theory, it is reasonable to assume that the Legislature would have used clear language expressing an intent to broaden the basis of liability of holders of watered stock had it entertained such an intention. In this state the liability of a holder of watered stock may only be based on the misrepresentation theory.

The plaintiff contends that even under the misrepresentation theory a creditor's reliance on the misrepresentation arising out of the issuance of watered stock should be conclusively presumed. This contention is without substantial merit. If it should prevail, the misrepresentation theory and the statutory obligation theory would be essentially identical. This court has held that under the misrepresentation theory a person who extended credit to a corporation (1) before the watered stock was issued, or (2) with full knowledge that watered stock was outstanding, cannot recover from the holders of the watered stock. These decisions indicate that under the misrepresentation theory reliance by the creditor is a prerequisite to the liability of a holder of watered stock. The trial court was therefore justified in ordering a new trial because of the absence of a finding on that issue.

. . . *The order granting the new trial is affirmed.*

Lesavoy Industries v. Pennsylvania Gen. Paper Corp.
404 Pa. 161 (1961)

The owner of all the stock in Lesavoy Industries, plaintiff, executed a general power of attorney to Allen Daniels. Plaintiff corporation was the owner of all the outstanding stock in the defendant corporation. Daniels entered into an agreement with one Price whereby Price was to receive 52 percent of the stock in defendant corporation, and a certificate was to be issued in the name of Price. Plaintiff corporation contends that it did not give the power to Lesavoy (its sole shareholder) or to Daniels to enter into this agreement. A certificate was issued to Price and is now in his possession. Plaintiff asked the court to declare null and void the transfer of shares from defendant corporation to Price and that defendant corporation be ordered to reassign and retransfer to plaintiff the shares of stock. The lower court ruled for plaintiff.

COHEN, J. . . . The lower court, in order to support its finding that the defendant corporation was a principal defendant, ruled that the plaintiff had alleged a proper cause of action against the defendant corporation on the theory that the defendant corporation breached its duty to protect its stockholder from an unauthorized transfer of shares.

It is generally accepted that a corporation owes its shareholders the duty to protect them from fraudulent transfers. A corporation also owes its shareholders a duty to protect them from unauthorized transfers. This court impliedly recognized such a duty where a corporation had been informed in advance of conflicting claims to the stock in question. We need not now decide if this duty extends beyond cases involving forgeries or notice to the corporation of irregularities, since here a wholly owned subsidiary relied upon a general power of attorney given to an agent by the parent corporation's sole shareholder. There can be no greater justification for a finding that the agent was clothed, at least, with apparent authority, thus effectuating an estoppel against the principal (plaintiff corporation).

Plaintiff has failed to allege a cause of action against the defendant corporation and thus that defendant is only a passive party in a dispute between two claimants to the same stock. As such the defendant corporation is not a principal defendant (cases cited).

The situs of the stock in question is determined by the Uniform Stock Transfer Act (now embodied in the Uniform Commercial Code), the policy of which is to make the certificate represent the shares of stock.

In *Crane* v. *Crane* (1953, 373 Pa. 1, 95 A.2d 199), this court did consider the situs of stock to be that of the corporation and permitted an action against the corporation to transfer shares on its books. However, such actions will be permitted only where the outstanding certificates are either seized, surrendered or their transfer enjoined unless it is unnecessary to enjoin transfer; e.g., the defendant cannot convey title of the certificate without the joinder of the attaching creditor. It is admitted that the outstanding shares in this case are located in New York and that they have not been seized or surrendered nor their transfer enjoined. We must therefore find that property which is the subject matter of the action is not within the jurisdiction of the court below.

Extra-territorial service upon Price, failing to qualify under either of the criteria set forth in Pa. R.C.P. 1504 (b), was unauthorized and ineffectual to subject him to the jurisdiction of the court below.

Decree reversed.

Love v. Pennsylvania Railroad Co.
200 F.Supp. 563 (1961)

The plaintiff and her father jointly owned stock, with the right of survivorship, in the Pennsylvania Railroad Company. The father prepared an assignment whereby the stock was transferred to him individually and forged plaintiff's name to the assignment. The railroad transferred the shares from the joint names of plaintiff and her father to the sole name of the father. Plaintiff sued the railroad, and two banks were added as defendants on the basis that they had guaranteed the signatures of plaintiff and her father on a stock assignment and dividend request. Plaintiff seeks to amend her complaint to assert a claim against the additional defendants.

KRAFT, J. . . . Plaintiff relies in part upon Section 8-312 of the Uniform Commercial Code, as that section provided at the time of the guarantee:

Section 8-312. Effect of Guaranteeing Signature or Indorsement

(1) Any person guaranteeing a signature as being that of an indorser of a security warrants to any person taking or dealing with the security in reliance on the guaranteed signature that

(a) the signature is not forged; and

(b) the signer is the holder or has authority to sign in the name of the holder; and

(c) the signer has legal capacity to sign.

But the guarantor does not warrant the rightfulness of the particular transfer.

(2) . . .

(3) The guarantor of a signature or an indorsement shall be liable to any person, including an issuer who registers a transfer in reliance on the guarantee, for any loss resulting from breach of the warranties stated in this section but no issuer may require an indorsement guarantee as a condition to registration or transfer of a security.

Plaintiff emphasizes the phrase "to any person" in subsection (3), and contends that these words establish the third-party defendants' liability to her for her loss resulting from the breach of the warranty that "the signature is not forged." While a literal reading of the provision lends some support to the plaintiff's contention, we think it clear that its language must be read in conjunction with that contained in subsection (1). So read, the signature guarantor's liability "to any person" must be deemed co-extensive merely with his warranty, which runs only "to any person taking or dealing with the security in reliance on the guaranteed signature." That this was the real meaning of subsection (3) seems apparent from the fact that the subsection was amended in 1959 to express, in clear and unequivocal language, that precise meaning. Since, under the averments of the complaint, plaintiff did not take or deal with the security in reliance on the guaranteed signature, the third-party defendants' warranty did not extend to her, and they are not liable to her for any loss resulting from its breach.

The industry of counsel and our own research have disclosed a singular dearth of authority on the precise question. However, the few cases in point establish the principle that the guarantee of a signature does not run to the owner of the security unless the signature guarantor had actual knowledge of the impropriety of the transaction. It was so held in *Eulette* v. *Merrill, Lynch, Pierce, Fenner and Beane* (101 So. 2d 603, 606, Fla. App. 1958).

> The guarantee of the forged signature of the appellant (owner) on the stock certificate could not, in our opinion, afford the appellant any basis for recovery. The guarantee would run only to those persons who, subsequent to the guarantee, dealt with the stock in reliance upon the guarantee. There has been no showing that the appellant acted to his detriment, or, for that matter, acted at all, in reliance upon the appellee's guarantee.

It is the uniform rule in Pennsylvania that a person making a general guarantee to warranty is liable only to those parties who have acted in reliance thereon (cases cited).

We conclude, therefore, that the averments of the proposed amended complaint fail to state a legal claim against either third-party defendant, and the motion for leave to amend must be denied.

CHAPTER 46
REVIEW QUESTIONS AND PROBLEMS

1. *A* bought stock in X Corporation from the corporation. He did not receive certificates at the time, but did pay the purchase price. Is *A* a stockholder if the transaction was entirely oral?

2. *P* was a stockholder in X Corporation. He desired to obtain a list of stockholders before the annual stockholders' meeting so that he could contact and try to persuade them to vote for a corporate merger which board of directors of X Corporation opposed. Is *P* entitled to inspect the books and records of the company and prepare a list of stockholders?

3. *P* sued D Company under a contract. *P* was a director of D Company, and his presence and vote were necessary to the approval of the contract. D Company contends that the contract is not binding. Is the company correct?

4. *X*, a promoter of the ABC Corporation purchased a parcel of land. A few days later he sold it to the corporation at a grossly inflated profit, obtaining a mortgage which he now is attempting to foreclose. *X* completely dominated the corporation, was chairman of the board and majority stockholder. Does *Y*, a minority shareholder, have any right to relief?

5. The XYZ Company owned all the stock of a subsidiary corporation, the ABC Company. The ABC Company purchased materials from *Y* under a contract. The ABC Company is now insolvent. May *Y* recover from the XYZ Company?

6. *A* sold *B* some stock of the XYZ Company. *A* gave the stock to *B* and received the funds, but he did not indorse the stock. *A* died, and *A*'s executor now claims that the stock, which has greatly increased in value, should be returned since it was not indorsed. Should it be?

7. *A* purchased ten shares of stock in the XYZ Company from *B*. *A* surrendered the stock, asking reissue in his name. The corporation failed to reissue. Does *A* have a remedy?

8. *A* was a vice-president of the XYZ Company. In his contract of employment was a provision saying that if he remained an employee for forty-eight months he would have an option to purchase stock. After thirty-nine months *A* resigned to take the position of director. Will *A* be entitled to the option if he remains a director for nine months?

9. The ABC Company authorized a director, *Z*, to negotiate the purchase of some land. Instead, *Z* secretly bought the land himself and sold it to the corporation at a profit. After learning of the deceit, the corporation failed to act. Does *B*, a minority shareholder, have any cause of action?

10. The X Company has issued both preferred and common stock. The preferred stock is 7 percent stock. The company declares a 7 percent dividend on the preferred stock and then a 10 percent dividend on the common stock. Under such conditions, have the preferred stockholders a right to demand 10 percent?

11. On March 1 Y Company declared a cash dividend of 5 percent, payable on June 1 to all stockholders of record on May 1. On April 10, *A* sold ten shares of Y Stock to *B,* but the transfer was not recorded on the corporation's books until May 15. To whom will the company pay the dividend? Who is entitled to the dividend?

12. X Company adopted the policy of allowing employees to purchase treasury stock in the company at its par value, which was 50 percent of its actual value. *P,* a 10 percent shareholder, files suit to enjoin the sale on the alternative that he be allowed to purchase, at the same price, 10 percent of all stock sold. What result?

47

Corporate Dissolutions, Mergers, and Consolidations

6-85. Introduction. Corporate existence terminates upon the expiration of the period set forth in the charter and upon the voluntary or involuntary dissolution of the corporation. In a consolidation, corporate existence technically ceases for both corporations; in a merger, it does so for one of the corporations involved. This chapter will discuss these various methods of terminating the corporate existence.

Most corporate charters provide for perpetual existence. However, where the charter stipulates that the corporation shall exist for a definite period, it automatically terminates at the expiration of the period, unless application to continue the corporation is made and approved by the authority granting the charter.

6-86. Voluntary Dissolutions. A corporation that has obtained its charter but that has not commenced business may be dissolved by its incorporators. The incorporators file articles of dissolution with the state, and a certificate of dissolution is issued if all fees are paid and the articles are in order.

A corporation that has commenced business may be voluntarily dissolved either by the written consent of *all* of its shareholders or by corporate action instituted by its board of directors and approved by two-thirds of the shareholders. The board action is usually in the form of a recommendation, and it directs that the issue be submitted to the shareholders. A meeting is called to consider the dissolution issue, and if the vote is at least two-thirds in favor of it, the officers follow the statutory procedures for dissolution.

These procedures require that the corporate officers file a statement of intent to dissolve with the state of incorporation. This statement of intent includes the consent of all shareholders if that method is used, or the resolutions, if the dissolution was instituted by board action. Upon filing the statement of intent, the corporation must cease to carry on its business, except for winding up its affairs, but its corporate existence continues until a certificate of dissolution is issued by the state.

In winding up its affairs, the corporation must give notice to all creditors of the corporation. Directors become personally liable for any debt about which notice is not given.[1]

Corporate assets are first used to pay debts. After all debts are paid, the remainder is distributed proportionately among the shareholders. If there are insufficient assets to pay all debts, a receiver will be appointed by a court and the proceedings will be similar to those of involuntary dissolutions, discussed later. It should be noted that receivers have authority to perform executory contracts.

When all funds are distributed, the corporation will prepare duplicate "articles of dissolution" and forward them to the state for approval. When signed by the appropriate state official, usually the secretary of state, one copy is filed with state records, and one copy is returned to the corporation to be kept with the corporate records.

The filing of a statement of intent to dissolve is not irrevocable. If the shareholders change their minds before the articles of dissolution are issued, the decision may be revoked by filing a statement of revocation of voluntary dissolution proceedings. When such a statement is filed, the corporation may resume its business.

INVOLUNTARY DISSOLUTIONS

6-87. Proceedings Commenced by the State.   The state, having created the corporation, has the right to institute proceedings to cancel the charter. Suits by a state to cancel or forfeit a charter are known as *quo warranto* proceedings. They are filed only by the attorney general and usually at the request of the secretary of state, although they are sometimes filed at the request of a private party. In quo warranto suits the term "relator" is used to describe the person who has requested the suit; *ex rel.* (on the relation of) is used in the title of the case to indicate the party asking the attorney general to file the suit for the people.

Quo warranto proceedings may be brought by the attorney general if a corporation (1) fails to file its annual report; (2) fails to pay its franchise tax and license fees; (3) procured its charter by fraud; (4) abuses and misuses its authority; (5) fails to appoint and maintain a registered agent for the service of notices and process, or fails to inform the state of the name and address of its registered agent; or (6) ceases to perform its corporate functions for a long period of time. The attorney general may also, without charter forfeiture, by proper proceedings enjoin a corporation from engaging in a business not authorized by its charter.

6-88. Proceedings Commenced by Shareholders.   Involuntary dissolution may be ordered by a court of equity at the request of a shareholder when it is established that the directors are deadlocked in the management of the corporate affairs or that the shareholders are deadlocked in voting power and

---

[1] People v. Parker, page 955

unable to elect a board of directors. Deadlocks require proof that irreparable injury is likely and that the deadlock cannot be broken.

Courts will also liquidate a corporation at the request of a shareholder when it is proved that those in control of the corporation are acting illegally, oppressively, or fraudulently, that corporate assets are being wasted or looted,[2] or that the corporation is unable to carry out its purposes. A corporation will not be dissolved by a court for errors of judgment or because the court confronted with a question of policy would decide it differently than would the directors. Dissolutions by decree at the request of a shareholder are rare.

6-89. Proceedings Commenced by Creditor.   A corporation is in the same position as a natural person insofar as its creditors are concerned. A suit may be brought against it, and upon judgment being obtained, an execution may be levied against its property, which may then be sold. Also, corporate assets may be attached, and if the corporation has no property subject to execution, its assets may be traced by a bill in a court of equity.

The creditors have no right, because they are creditors, to interfere with the management of the business. A creditor who has an unsatisfied judgment against a corporation, because there is no corporate property upon which a levy can be made, may bring a bill in equity to set aside conveyances and transfers of corporate property which have been fraudulently transferred for the purpose of delaying and hindering creditors. Creditors may also, under the above circumstances, ask for a receiver to take over the assets of the corporation and to apply them to the payment of debts.

When there is an unsatisfied execution and it is established that the corporation is insolvent, a court may order a dissolution. The same is true if the corporation admits its insolvency. Dissolution in such cases proceeds in the same manner as if instituted by the state or by voluntary proceedings when insolvent. These procedures are discussed in the next section.

6-90. Procedure on Involuntary Dissolution.   In liquidating a corporation, courts have the full range of judicial powers at their disposal. They may issue injunctions, appoint receivers, and take whatever steps are necessary to preserve the corporate assets for the protection of creditors and shareholders. The receiver will usually collect the assets including any amount owed to the corporation for shares. The receiver will then sell the assets, pay the debts and expenses of liquidation, and, if any funds are left, divide them proportionately among the shareholders. Courts usually require creditors to prove their claims in court in a manner similar to that in bankruptcy proceedings. When all funds in the hands of a receiver are paid out, the court issues a decree of dissolution that is filed with the secretary of state. Funds due persons who cannot be located are deposited with the state treasurer and held for a stated number of years. If not claimed within the stated period by the creditor or shareholder, the funds belong to the state.

6-91. Liability of Shareholders on Dissolution.   As a general rule, shareholders are not liable for the debts of the firm. However, a shareholder who has not paid for his stock in full is liable to the receiver or to a creditor for the unpaid balance. In addition, many states have increased by statute the liabili-

----

[2] *Kruger v. Gerth,* page 956

ties of shareholders to corporate creditors. These statutes provide that the shareholders shall be liable for a sum in addition to the par value of their stock. In a few states, this statutory liability is applicable to manufacturing corporations. Some states attach liability equal to the par value of the shares in banking and trust companies. This is done in order to insure the solvency of banks and to encourage shareholders to participate in management. The statutory liability laws allow creditors to reach the assets of the corporation in the hands of the shareholders on the theory that the assets have been transferred in fraud of creditors. Some statutes limit the liability to particular types of debts, such as employees' salaries.[3]

Most states have statutory provisions that provide for survival for a two-year period of remedies against a corporation, its directors, officers, and shareholders for claims existing prior to dissolution, if the dissolution is by a certificate issued by the state, by expiration of the charter, or is by court decree which does not conform with the corporation law. Suits against the corporation may be prosecuted or defended in the corporate name. The two-year period is not a statute of limitation, but is simply the period during which claims survive. A judgment on such a claim may be collected from property distributed to shareholders on dissolution or the creditor may proceed directly against the shareholder receiving the property.[4]

It should also be noted that the directors and officers will have liability if they fail to follow the statutory procedures on dissolution.

CONSOLIDATIONS AND MERGERS

6-92. Definitions.   Consolidation is the uniting of two or more corporations, whereby a new corporation is created and the old entities are dissolved. The new corporation takes title to all the property, rights, powers, and privileges of the old corporations, subject to the liabilities and obligations of the old corporations.

In a merger, however, one of the corporations continues its existence, but absorbs the other corporation, which ceases to have an independent existence. The continuing corporation may expressly or impliedly assume and agree to pay the debts and liabilities of the absorbed corporation. If so, such creditors become third-party creditor beneficiaries. By statute in most states, the surviving corporation is deemed to have assumed all the liabilities and obligations of the absorbed corporation.[5]

Mergers and acquisitions comprise a major segment of the antitrust laws. This aspect will be discussed more fully in the next chapter.

6-93. Procedures.   The procedures for consolidations and mergers are statutory. The usual procedure is for the board of directors of each corporation to approve the plan by resolution. The resolution will set forth in detail all of the facts of the planned merger or consolidation. The plan is then submitted to the shareholders of each corporation for approval. Notice is given of the meeting and the resolution passed by the directors is usually a part of the

[3] Stull v. Bellefonte Stone Products Corporation, page 958
[4] State et al. v. Simmer Oil Corporation et al., page 958
[5] State ex rel. Safeguard Ins. Co. v. Vorys, page 959

notice. The shareholders must approve the plan by a two-thirds vote[6] of all shares and two-thirds of each class if more than one class of stock is voting. If the consolidation or merger is approved by the shareholders of both corporations, articles of consolidation or articles of merger will be prepared and filed with the state. If the papers are in order and all fees are paid, a certificate of consolidation or a certificate of merger will be issued.

A shareholder who dissents to a consolidation or merger and who makes his dissent a matter of record by serving a written demand that the corporation purchase his stock is entitled to be paid the fair market value of his stock on the day preceding the vote on the corporate action. Procedures are established for ascertaining the fair market value and for a judicial decision of that issue if necessary. It is noted that a shareholder who dissents from a sale or exchange of all or substantially all of the assets or property of the corporation, other than in the usual course of business, has the same right to be paid for his stock.

CORPORATE DISSOLUTION, CONSOLIDATION AND MERGER CASES

People v. Parker
197 N.E.2d 30 (Ill.) 1964

HERSHEY, J. The People of the State of Illinois recovered a judgment of $1,024.40 against Paul A. Parker, a former director of the dissolved corporation, Parker Laundry Company, for unpaid personal property taxes levied against the corporation for the years 1953 and 1954. Parker appeals . . . urging that the action was barred by the two-year limitation contained in section 94 of the Business Corporation Act.

Parker Laundry Company, an Illinois corporation, with offices in the city of Rock Island, on December 31, 1954, filed with the Secretary of State a statement of intent to dissolve. The defendant, Parker, was a director at the time, as well as the sole stockholder. The corporation was then liable for personal property taxes for the year 1953 in the amount of $295.46, and for the year 1954, $286.27. Although section 79 of the Business Corporation Act requires that notice of intent to dissolve be given each known creditor, no such notice was given the county treasurer for Rock Island County. The corporation was dissolved February 15, 1955.

The State's Attorney for Rock Island County on October 16, 1961, filed the complaint which initiated this civil action. The basis for recovery was section 42(f) of the Business Corporation Act, which imposes liability on directors of a corporation which has filed a statement of intent to dissolve and fails to mail notice of such action to known creditors of the corporation to the extent of "all loss and damage occasioned thereby." A motion to dismiss the complaint on the basis that the action was outlawed by section 94 of the Business Corporation Act was denied. . . .

Section 94 reads as follows: "The dissolution of a corporation either (1) by the issuance of a certificate of dissolution by the Secretary of State, or (2) by the decree of a court of equity when the court has not liquidated the assets and

---

[6] Rath v. Rath Packing Company, page 960

business of the corporation, or (3) by expiration of its period of duration, shall not take away or impair any remedy available to or against such corporation its directors, or shareholders, for any right or claim existing, or any liability incurred, prior to such dissolution if action or other proceeding thereon is commenced within two years after the date of such dissolution. . . . "

The foregoing provision appears to be a survival statute rather than a statute of limitation. . . .

Unless the liability imposed on corporate directors by section 42(f) abates upon dissolution of the corporation involved, section 94 has no application. Defendant offers no authority for the necessary premise that dissolution of a corporation abates liability incurred by its directors, and we do not know of any principle that requires that result. . . .

Logic . . . suggests that the liability created by section 42(f) does not abate upon dissolution of the corporation involved. It would be anomalous that the occasion giving rise to the liability, dissolution of the corporation, would also cause it to abate.

. . . Section 94 has no application to the directors' liability imposed by section 42(f), and it is conceded that the general statute of limitations has no application to plaintiff. . . .

Judgment affirmed.

Kruger v. Gerth

255 N.Y.S.2d 498 (1964)

Minority stockholders brought suit to compel dissolution of a corporation on the ground of waste. The alleged waste occurred in the payment of bonuses to one director who was an individual defendant and to two employees. The trial court ordered two of the three directors to dissolve the firm.

MEMORANDUM BY THE COURT. . . . During the relevant period of time in issue, the defendant Arthur A. Gerth was the only party to the action in the corporation's employ; he owned 53 percent of the corporation's common stock and half of its preferred stock; his brother, defendant Harry J. Gerth, owned 1 percent of its common stock; and plaintiffs owned the remainder of its common and preferred stock. The corporation is in the retail lumber business.

The gist of the first cause of action to compel dissolution of the corporation is that Arthur A. Gerth has dominated and controlled the affairs of the corporation; that he has taken salaries and bonuses in such amounts as to leave little net profit annually; that no dividends have ever been paid on the common stock; that the dividend payments on the preferred stock, which began only in 1958, gave plaintiffs a meager return for their capital interest in the corporation; that, because of various conditions that affect the business of the corporation, the corporation cannot be operated so as to increase its profits; that the said Gerth has a personal interest in continuing the business of the corporation, namely, to provide himself with employment, at substantial salaries and bonuses, and thereby has been exploiting the corporation to the detriment of the other stockholders.

The corporation's net profit in each of the years 1958 to 1961, both inclusive, has been less than $2,000, before provision for income taxes. In each of the first three of those years Arthur A. Gerth's salary was $9,000; and in 1961 it was $9,374.94. His bonus for each of the four years was, respectively, $5,857.20, $7,153.20, $6,480, and $6,120. Throughout these years the corporation has had a net worth of substantially more than $100,000 and total annual sales ranging from about $245,000 to about $275,000.

More is required to sustain an action to compel the dissolution of a corporation than to sustain a derivative stockholder's action for waste. Dissolution will not be compelled unless it be found that the dominant stockholders or directors have been "looting" the corporation's assets and impairing the corporation's capital or maintaining the corporation for their own special benefit, thereby enriching themselves at the expense of the minority stockholders; and the fact that the corporation is operating profitably or that the complaining stockholders may have a right to relief by way of derivative suits or otherwise is not in itself a bar to compelling dissolution.

In the instant case there was no evidence from which it could be found that there was any looting and impairment of capital or maintenance of the corporation for the special purpose of the individual defendants at the expense of the other stockholders. The plaintiffs acquired their stock in a bequest under the last will and testament of Henry M. Kruger, who died in August 1961. In 1950 both he and Arthur A. Gerth were employees of the corporation, receiving equal salaries of $6,000. In that year the said Kruger became ill and retired from active participation in the business. Thereupon, the only stockholder in active participation in the business carrying the responsibilities of the business was Arthur A. Gerth, but he had to employ another person to replace Henry M. Kruger. Nevertheless, said Kruger continued to receive a salary from the corporation for about eleven years, that is, from 1950 to 1961, when he died.

In 1951 Arthur A. Gerth's salary was increased to $7,500; and he began taking a bonus. Since then there have been increases in his salary and bonus. There was no evidence that anyone complained that the said Gerth did not deserve the salaries and bonuses he received during the eleven years up to August 1961 during which he operated the business while Kruger remained on the sidelines. There was no material difference between the total of Gerth's salaries and bonuses annually from 1955 to 1961, both years inclusive. As a matter of fact, at the conclusion of the trial, plaintiffs' counsel expressly admitted that no proof had been offered to the effect that Gerth's salaries had been excessive.

In sum, plaintiffs' claim rests only on the fact that the amount of the bonus for each of the four years up to and including 1961, though varying from year to year, served so to reduce the net profit as to leave an insufficient amount to provide a fair return to plaintiffs on their stock in the corporation. We have found no case in which dissolution of a corporation was directed on such a meager showing. . . . [N]o claim was made in this action that there has been a calculated deflation or impairment in the value of the capital stock in order to coerce the minority stockholders to sell their shares at depressed prices.

Reversed.

Stull v. Bellefonte Stone Products Corporation

205 A.2d 677 (Pa.) 1964

ERVIN, J. This appeal is concerned with the right of a president of a corporation to recover unpaid salary from stockholders of the corporation. The court below, by its order, entered judgment for Harold R. Stull, president of Bellefonte Stone Products Corporation, against the defendants, E. R. Scheuner and Joseph Mills, two stockholders of the corporation, in the respective amounts of $2,574.00 and $3,332.00, with interest, for unpaid salary due to Stull as president of the corporation. The two stockholders have appealed.

The Act of May 5, 1933, provides: "A. A shareholder of a business corporation shall not be personally liable for any debt or liability of the corporation, except salaries and wages due and owing to its laborers and employes, for services rendered to the corporation. In such event, every shareholder shall be personally liable in an amount equal to the value of the shares of the corporation owned by him."

The appellants argue that the above provision does not "apply to the chief executive officer who has complete control of the corporation."

The act of June 25, 1864, provided for individual liability of the stockholders "for debts due mechanics, workmen and laborers employed" by the company. By the Act of April 29, 1874, the liability of shareholders was limited to "all work or labor done to carry on the operations of each of said corporations." Section 514 of the Business Corporation Law of 1933, above quoted, enlarged the language theretofore used by the use of the phrase "*salaries* and wages due and owing to its laborers and *employes.*" [Emphasis supplied] The word "wages" is commonly used with reference to pay of laborers and workmen, whereas the word "salary" may be used with reference to the pay of any employee, no matter how big his position or how large his pay. We are of the opinion that the legislature intended, by the 1933 law, to include any employee of the company, whether he be president or common laborer.

While the 1933 act does not expressly include officers, we believe their inclusion is implicit from the words "salaries" and "employees." Construing the words in their popular sense, the inference to be made is that salaried employees include officers of the corporation. . . .

Judgment Affirmed.

State et al. v. Simmer Oil Corporation et al.

231 Iowa 1041 (1942)

The plaintiff, State of Iowa, obtained a judgment against the defendant corporation. This judgment was not paid and the plaintiff is seeking to set aside certain transfers of property made by the corporation in order that the property may be made available to satisfy the plaintiff's claim. The corporation deeded the property to Leonard Simmer and his wife, the principal stockholders of the defendant corporation. The trial court ruled that the transfer would not be set aside and the plaintiff appealed.

SAGER, J. . . . Appellants insist that they are entitled to have these properties subjected to the unpaid debts of the oil corporation. Appellees deny, urging that they legally have claim to these properties because transfers were made in satisfaction of money advanced by them to the corporation; and they say that even though the corporation deeded to Leonard, president and director, this was a valid legal transaction. The trial court took this view and we think therein erred. It must be admitted that some of our earlier cases tend to support the decision below.

These cases do declare generally the right to give such preference but our later cases, while not overlooking the prior decisions, have limited their apparent scope. In discussing the so-called trust-fund doctrine we said in *Luedecke* v. *Des Moines Cabinet Co.* (140 Iowa 223):

> We do not recognize the trust-fund doctrine to the extent that it has obtained in some of the courts; but are of opinion that corporate creditors are entitled in equity to the payment of their debts before any distribution of corporate property is made among the stockholders, and recognize the right of a creditor of a corporation to follow its assets or property into the hands of any one who is not a good-faith holder in the ordinary course of business.

Certainly the appellees Simmer are not good-faith holders "in the ordinary course of business." We do not wish to be understood as charging that they were guilty of any actual or intentional fraud. The record excludes this. Agnes Simmer put into this corporation upwards of twenty thousand dollars, even mortgaging the homestead to keep the business going. If there be any fraud in the transaction it is in a strictly legal sense and not actual fraud with which we are dealing.

. . . Under the authorities cited, the properties above described should be made subject to the debts held by appellants and other creditors, if any there be.

. . . As to these, any equities there may be above existing mortgages should be applied to the payment of unpaid creditors of the Simmer Oil Corporation.

It follows that the cause must be and it is remanded for further proceedings in accordance herewith. Other creditors, if there are any, should be brought in as parties so their interest may be protected.

State ex rel. Safeguard Ins. Co. v. Vorys
167 N.E.2d 910 (Ohio) 1960

The relator (Safeguard Ins. Co.) brought an action in mandamus against Vorys, Superintendent of Insurance, to require the latter to turn over to relator $53,000 in securities which had been deposited by an indemnity company which had since merged into relator. Safeguard had deposited with the superintendent for the security and benefit of all its policy holders the requisite amount of securities required for the combined companies.

TAFT, J. . . . Generally, where there is an assumption by one legal entity of the liability or obligation of another legal entity, such assumption will not represent a payment or an extinguishment of such liability or obligation. However, the extent of the liability or obligation of a corporation may be dependent upon and measured by the law which establishes its existence as a legal entity. Thus, that law may authorize the substitution, for the liability and obligation of a corporation that it has created as a corporate entity, of the liability of another solvent legal entity into which it lawfully merged. . . .

Certainly, a creditor who voluntarily deals with such a corporation in the light of constitutional provisions such as "corporations may be formed under general laws: but all such laws may, from time to time, be altered or repealed" is in no position to complain where the law which created the corporation provides that (on the happening of certain events and without interfering with any pending legal proceedings) such corporation's obligations and liabilities shall cease to be the obligations and liabilities of such corporation and instead shall become the obligations and liabilities of a solvent legal entity into which said corporation merges. . . .

Thus, after the merger, any obligations and liabilities secured by the $53,000 deposits made with the respondent superintendent by the indemnity company, which were not the subject of pending legal proceedings (none apparently were) were no longer obligations and liabilities of the indemnity company as a legal entity separate from relator but were obligations and liabilities of relator, although still secured by those $53,000 of deposits; and those deposits belong to relator, subject to any claims or liens against such deposits in favor of those to whom the indemnity company had been before the merger and to whom relator was thereafter obligated or liable. . . .

It follows that relator's demurrer to the amended answer must be sustained. . . .

Writ allowed.

Rath v. Rath Packing Company

136 N.W.2d 410 (Iowa) 1965

GARFIELD, C. J. The question presented is whether an Iowa corporation may carry out an agreement with another corporation, designated "Plan and Agreement of Reorganization," which amounts to a merger in fact of the two without approval of holders of two-thirds of its outstanding shares. . . .

Plaintiffs, minority shareholders of Rath, brought this action in equity to enjoin carrying out the agreement on the ground . . . it provides for a merger in fact with Needham Packing Co., which requires approval of two-thirds of the holders of outstanding Rath shares and that was not obtained. The trial court adjudicated . . . in favor of defendants Rath and its officers, and entered judgment of dismissal on the pleadings. It held approval of the plan by holders of a majority of Rath shares was sufficient. Plaintiffs appeal.

Plaintiffs own more than 6,000 shares of Rath Packing Co., an Iowa corporation with its principal plant in Waterloo, Iowa. Rath has 993,185 shares outstanding held by about 4,000 owners. It is engaged in meat packing and processing, mostly pork and allied products.

Needham Packing Co. is a corporation organized in 1960 under Delaware law with its principal plant in Sioux City, Iowa. Its total shares outstanding, including debentures and warrants convertible into stock, are 787,907, held by about 1,000 owners. Both Rath and Needham stock is traded on the American Stock Exchange. Needham is also engaged in meat packing, mostly beef. . . .

Pursuant to authority of Rath's board prior to April 2, 1965, it entered into the questioned agreement with Needham, designated "Plan and Agreement of Reorganization," under which Rath agreed to: (1) amend its articles to double the number of shares of its common stock, create a new class of preferred shares and change its name to Rath-Needham Corporation; (2) issue to Needham 5.5 shares of Rath common and two shares of its 80-cent preferred stock for each five shares of Needham stock in exchange for all Needham's assets, properties, business, name and goodwill, except a fund not exceeding $175,000 to pay expenses in carrying out the agreement and effecting Needham's dissolution and distribution of the new Rath-Needham stock to its shareholders, any balance remaining after 120 days to be paid over to Rath; (3) assume all Needham's debts and liabilities; and (4) elect two Needham officers and directors to its board.

Under the plan Needham agreed to: (1) transfer all its assets to Rath; (2) cease using its name; (3) distribute the new Rath-Needham shares to its stockholders, liquidate and dissolve; and (4) turn over to Rath its corporate and business records.

If the plan were carried out, assuming the new preferred shares were converted into common, the thousand Needham shareholders would have about 54 percent of the outstanding common shares of Rath-Needham and the four thousand Rath shareholders would have about 46 percent.

Under the plan the book value of each share of Rath common stock, as of January 2, 1965, would be reduced from $27.99 to $15.93, a reduction of about 44 percent. Each share of Needham common would be increased in book value, as of December 26, 1964, from $6.61 to $23.90, assuming conversion of the new Rath-Needham preferred.

In the event of liquidation of Rath-Needham, Needham shareholders would be preferred to Rath's under the plan, by having a prior claim to the assets of Rath-Needham to an amount slightly in excess of the book value of all Needham shares. Needham shareholders are also preferred over Rath's under the plan in distribution of income by the right of the former to receive preferred dividends of 80 cents a share—about five percent of Needham's book value. Shortly prior to the time terms of the plan were made public, Rath and Needham shares sold on the American Exchange for about the same price. Almost immediately thereafter the price of Needham shares increased and Rath's decreased so the former sold for 50 percent more than latter.

At a meeting of Rath shareholders on April 26, 1965, 60.1 percent of its outstanding shares, 77 percent of those voted, were voted in favor of these two proposals: (1) to amend the articles to authorize a class of 80 c preferred stock and increase the authorized common from 1,500,000 shares ($10 par) to 3,-000,000 shares (no par); and (2) upon acquisition by Rath of the assets, properties, business and goodwill of Needham to change Rath's name to Rath-Needham Corporation and elect as its directors Lloyd and James Needham. Holders of 177,000 shares voted against these proposals and 218,000 shares were not voted. The plan was not approved by the shareholders except as above stated.

         .   .   .

I. We will summarize the provisions of Code chapter 496A, I.C.A., so far as material to the appeal. . . .

Section 496A.70 provides for approval of the plan of merger by the shareholders of each merging corporation and "[a]t each such meeting, a vote of the shareholders shall be taken on the proposed plan. . . . The plan . . . shall be approved upon receiving the affirmative vote of the holders of at least two-thirds of the outstanding shares of each such corporation. . . . "

Section 496A.77 states that any shareholder shall have the right to dissent from any merger to which the corporation is a party.

Section 496A.78 gives a dissenting shareholder, by following the procedure there outlined, the right to be paid the fair value of his shares as of the day prior to that on which the corporate action was approved.

The above sections are those on which plaintiffs rely. They contend these statutes specifically provide for effecting a merger and the same result cannot legally be attained at least without approval of the holders of two-thirds of the shares and according to dissenters "appraisal rights"—i.e., the right to receive the fair value of their stock by compliance with the specified procedure.

Defendants contend and the trial court held compliance with the above sections was not required and defendants could legally proceed under other sections of chapter 496A which merely authorize amendments to articles of incorporation and issuance of stock. The sections just referred to provide that a corporation may amend its articles in any respects desired and in particular: change its name, change the number of shares of any class, change shares having a par value to those without par and create new classes of shares with preferences over shares then authorized.

Section 496A.56 states articles may be amended by giving shareholders notice of a meeting at which the amendments are to be considered, with a summary of the proposed changes, and upon receiving the affirmative vote of holders of a majority of the stock entitled to vote. . . .

II. The principal point of law defendants asked to have adjudicated . . . is that the provisions of chapter 496A last referred to are legally independent of, and of equal dignity with, those relating to mergers and the validity of the action taken by defendants is not dependent upon compliance with the merger sections under which the same result might be attained. The trial court accepted this view. . . .

III. The "Plan and Agreement of Reorganization" clearly provides for what amounts to a merger of Rath and Needham under any definition of merger we know.

We have approved a statement that a merger exists where one corporation is continued and the other is merged with it, without the formation of a new corporation, from a sale of the property and franchises of one corporation to another. "A merger of corporations consists of a combination whereby one of the constituent companies remains in being—absorbing or merging in itself all the other constituent corporation. . . . "

If, as we hold, this agreement provides for what amounts to a merger of Rath and Needham, calling it a Plan and Agreement of Reorganization does not change its essential character. A fundamental maxim of equity, frequently applied, is that equity regards substance rather than form. . . .

At common law no merger could take place without unanimous consent of the stockholders. However, statutes in all jurisdictions now authorize mergers upon a vote of less than all stockholders. A shareholder who dissents to a merger may obtain the value of his stock if the right thereto is provided by statute, if procedure is established therefor and is followed by him. Sections 496A.77, 496A.78 confer such right and provide such procedure.

The merger sections of chapter 496A clearly and expressly confer the necessary power to merge. Section 496A.74, *supra,* expressly requires compliance "with the provisions of this chapter with respect to the merger . . . of domestic corporations." Nothing in the sections dealing with amending articles and issuing stock purports to authorize a merger. They make no reference to merger. The most that may fairly be claimed is that they impliedly confer the required power to merge. But this is insufficient. . . .

It is apparent that if the sections pertaining to amending articles and issuing stock are construed to authorize a merger by a majority vote of shareholders, they conflict with the sections specifically dealing with the one matter of mergers which require a two-thirds vote of shareholders. The two sets of sections may be harmonized by holding, as we do, that the merger sections govern the matter of merger and must be regarded as an exception to the sections dealing with amending articles and issuing stock, which may or may not be involved in a merger.

The construction we give these sections is in accord with the cardinal rule that, if reasonably possible, effect will be given to every part of a statute. . . .

The merger sections make it clear the legislature intended to require a two-thirds vote of shareholders and accord so-called appraisal rights to dissenters in case of a merger. It is unreasonable to ascribe to the same legislature an intent to provide in the same act a method of evading the required two-thirds vote and the grant of such appraisal rights. The practical effect of the decision appealed from is to render the requirements of a two-thirds vote and appraisal rights meaningless in virtually all mergers. It is scarcely an exaggeration to say the decision amounts to judicial repeal of the merger sections in most instances of merger.

It is obvious, as defendants' counsel frankly stated in oral arguments, that corporate management would naturally choose a method which requires only majority approval of shareholders and does not grant dissenters the right to be paid the fair value of their stock. The legislature could hardly have intended to vest in corporate management the option to comply with the requirements just referred to or to proceed without such compliance, a choice that would invariably be exercised in favor of the easier method. . . .

IX. We hold . . . that defendants should be enjoined from carrying out the "Plan and Agreement of Reorganization" until such time, if ever, as it is approved by the holders of at least two-thirds of the outstanding shares of Rath. . . .

Reversed and remanded.

CHAPTER 47
REVIEW QUESTIONS AND PROBLEMS

1. *D* owed X Corporation $10,000. X Corporation's directors and shareholders voted to dissolve. Thereafter, X Corporation sued *D*, and *D* contended that he had no liability because of the dissolution. What result?

2. *A* owned a minority share of the stock in X Corporation. He did not agree with the majority who desired to merge with another corporation. What are *A*'s rights?

3. X Corporation entered into a contract to purchase linseed oil from *Y.* Subsequently, X Corporation merged with Z Corporation and the latter refused to purchase linseed oil from *Y.* Does *Y* have a cause of action against Z Corporation?

4. A Corporation had not made a profit for twenty years and no dividends had been paid for that period. The preferred stockholders brought suit to obtain a decree of dissolution. What result?

5. *P* owned stock in X Bank. *P* went to the bank, informed the officers of his desire to sell his stock and inquired as to its value. He was informed that the stock was worth its par value, $100 per share. The book value was $149 and a merger was in process. *P* signed his certificates in blank and delivered them to the officers. On merger, the stock brought $187 per share. *P* seeks to rescind the sale. May he do so?

6. *A,* the owner of all of the capital stock of the XYZ Corporation, a newspaper business, sold all of his shares to *B* and promised to serve as adviser to the newspaper for a period of five years, in return for $11,000. After three years, *B* petitioned for dissolution, which was obtained. Only $4,000 had been paid to *A.* Does *A* have a remedy against the corporation?

7. *A, B,* and *C* were owners of some orange groves in Florida. *X* wished to enter the orange-growing business and approached *A, B,* and *C* with an offer to form a corporation. The corporation was formed and the land owned by *A, B,* and *C* was transferred to the corporation. *X* was to manage the corporation, and *A, B,* and *C* were to retire, leaving the operation of the groves to *X. X* failed to manage the groves; in fact he did nothing. May *A, B,* and *C* dissolve the corporation?

8. *A* and *B,* father and son, entered into an agreement whereby each was a 50 percent stockholder of a close corporation, operating a luncheonette. The agreement provided that in the event of the death of either party, this would constitute an automatic option to the survivor to purchase, at book value, the shares of stock of the deceased. Upon *A*'s death, *C, B*'s brother and administrator of *A*'s estate, refuses to sell for the value shown on the books and creates a deadlock in management. *C* then petitions for dissolution. Should it be granted?

9. What steps are required for a voluntary dissolution?

10. List four grounds on which the state may obtain involuntary dissolution.

Government Regulation of Business Organizations

6-94. Introduction. The business environment is the product of political, social, economic, and legal forces. While each of these forces has its own substantial impact on our society, it is the law that possesses the cohesive quality to unite them and make our private property system and competitive economic system workable. The law not only creates and protects property rights, it also regulates business activity in an infinite variety of ways. It ensures that the system is viable and strives to be of maximum benefit to the society it serves.

In earlier periods of history, the law was primarily concerned with enforcing contracts, and protecting property, and maintaining order. Today, the role of law is much broader, with primary emphasis on government regulation of business. The contemporary legal climate of business may be described in terms of bigness—big business, big unions, and big government and the inter-relationships between them. Government regulations affecting every aspect of business, including labor relations, are a major part of "business law" today. Many of the significant problems confronting society in the 1970s will be solved by the interaction of law with business, labor, and society. As business has become a social as well as an economic institution, it has by its own volition and by the force of law become more concerned with the effect of its decisions on the public and has more often considered the public interest in the formulation of policy.

Early attempts by government to regulate business were challenged under the due process clauses of the Constitution of the United States and were often considered an infringement upon freedom of contract. The twentieth century has seen the elimination of due process and freedom of contract as bases for challenging government regulation of business.

By 1934, liberty of contract and the right to use one's property as one pleases, even though admitted to be fundamental rights, became amenable to social needs and subject to legislative control. An explanation of this principle and its implication are set out by Justice Roberts in the case of *Nebbia* v. *People of the State of New York* (291 U.S. 502, 1934), in the following language:

> ... Under our form of government the use of property and the making of contracts are normally matters of private and not of public concern. The general rule is that both shall be free of governmental interference. But neither property rights nor contract rights are absolute; for government cannot exist if the citizens may at will use his property to the detriment of his fellows, or exercise his freedom of contract to work them harm. Equally fundamental with the private right is that of the public to regulate it in the common interest.
>
> The Fifth Amendment, in the field of federal activity, and the Fourteenth, as respects state action, do not prohibit governmental regulation for the public welfare. They merely condition the exertion of the admitted power, by securing that the end shall be accomplished by methods consistent with due process. And the guaranty of due process, as has often been held, demands only that the law shall not be unreasonable, arbitrary, or capricious, and that the means selected shall have a real and substantial relation to the object sought to be attained. It results that a regulation valid for one sort of business or in given circumstances, may be invalid for another sort, or for the same business under other circumstances, because the reasonableness of each regulation depends upon the relevant facts.
>
> The reports of our decisions abound with cases in which the citizen, individual or corporate, have vainly invoked the Fourteenth Amendment in resistance to necessary and appropriate exertion of the police power.
>
> The court has repeatedly sustained curtailment of enjoyment of private property, in the public interest. The owner's rights may be subordinated to the needs of other private owners whose pursuits are vital to the paramount interests of the community. The state may control the use of property in various ways; may prohibit advertising billboards except of a prescribed size and location, or their use for certain kinds of advertising; may in certain circumstances authorize encroachments by party walls in cities; may fix the height of buildings, the character of materials, and methods of construction, the adjoining area which must be left open, and may exclude from residential sections offensive trades, industries and structures likely injuriously to affect the public health or safety; or may establish zones within which certain types of buildings or businesses are permitted and others excluded. And although the Fourteenth Amendment extends protection to aliens as well as citizens, a state may for adequate reasons of policy exclude aliens altogether from the use and occupancy of land.
>
> Laws passed for the suppression of immorality, in the interest of health, to secure fair trade practices, and to safeguard the interest of depositors in banks, have been found consistent with due process. These measures not only affected the use of private property, but also interfered with the right of private contract. Other instances are numerous where valid regulation has restricted the right of contract, while less directly affecting property rights.
>
> The Constitution does not guarantee the unrestricted privilege to engage in a business or to conduct it as one pleases.

In this chapter, we will be concerned with the legal bases for the role government plays in the operation of business, and we will briefly examine one aspect of government regulation of business—the field of antitrust law.

Regulation of business is the result of action by both the legislative and executive branches of government. Many regulations ensue from statutes enacted by the legislative branch and are executed by administrative agencies exercising their rule-making, enforcing, and quasi-judicial powers. The determination of the constitutionality and legality of all regulatory activities as well as the application of the rules issued ultimately rests with the courts. Therefore, as a practical matter, all branches of government are actively engaged in placing limitations on business activity.

6-95. The Federal Power to Regulate Business.   The power of the federal government to regulate business activity is found in the commerce clause of the Constitution which provides: "Congress shall have the power to regulate commerce with foreign nations, among the several States and with the Indian tribes." The key language is the phrase "among the several States." This language has been construed to give Congress power to enact laws covering any business activity in *interstate* commerce, and any *intrastate* business activity that has a substantial effect on interstate commerce. The effect on interstate commerce may be positive or negative. For example, Congress may pass a law prohibiting a specific activity and thereby prevent interstate commerce. The effect of any individual business on interstate commerce need not be substantial, if the cumulative effect of all similar businesses is substantial.

The net effect of the decisions has been to make the federal power to regulate business illimitable. In recent years, this power has been used in a variety of ways. One of the more important pieces of legislation is the Civil Rights Act of 1964, particularly its provisions pertaining to public accommodations.[1] The purpose of this statute is to obtain equal protection of the laws and equal treatment for all citizens regardless of race, creed, color, sex, or natural origin. It is significant that the bill was enacted by Congress as an exercise of its power to regulate interstate commerce and not under the provisions usually associated with civil rights. In the 1970s, this power will be used to attack other problems facing society, such as pollution and poverty.

The broad interpretation of the commerce clause has aided the development of a strong central government and has fostered and encouraged the regulation of activities which, while local in nature, have effect on the country as a whole. Such regulations have assisted in obtaining a degree of national uniformity in business activities and have tended to downgrade the role of state and local governments in regulating business.

6-96. State Regulation of Business.   State and local governments use their "police power" to enact laws to promote the public health, safety, morals, and general welfare. Of necessity, such laws frequently result in the regulation of business activity. The commerce clause does not expressly prohibit the use of a state's police power merely because one aspect of a given law has this result, but as interpreted by the courts, the commerce clause does impose several restrictions on the use of police power as it affects business.

The first restriction is that state and local governments cannot enact laws on subjects that are considered to be exclusively federal. For example, a state could not pass a law establishing the width of a railroad track or a law

[1] Heart of Atlanta Motel, Inc. v. United States, page 972

concerning air traffic because such subjects require national uniformity. For this reason, any state law concerning a subject that is exclusively under the federal government's jurisdiction is unconstitutional under the commerce clause. This is true even if there is no federal law on the subject.

The second limitation concerns subject matters over which the federal government has taken exclusive jurisdiction by enacting legislation. Federal laws that assert exclusive jurisdiction over a subject are said to preempt the field. Preemption may result from express language or by comprehensive regulation showing an intent by Congress to exercise exclusive dominion over the subject matter. When a federal statute has preempted the field, *any* state or local law pertaining to the same subject matter is unconstitutional and the state regulation is void.

Not every federal regulatory statute preempts the field. When a federal law does not preempt the field and the subject matter is not exclusively federal, state regulation under the police power is permitted, but when a state law is inconsistent or irreconciably in conflict with the federal statute, it is unconstitutional and void. Moreover, state laws are invalid if they discriminate against interstate commerce or impose an undue burden on it.

In addition to the commerce clause limitations previously discussed, a state's exercise of police power may be challenged under the constitutional provisions relating to "due process," "equal protection of the laws," and under all provisions of the Bill of Rights. Challenges to the constitutionality of a law based on "due process" and "equal protection" are most frequently used to challenge a tax imposed on interstate commerce, but may also be used to challenge a regulation or licensing statute. The Bill of Rights provisions are employed to challenge such laws as "Sunday Closing" statutes or censorship of movies ordinances.

It should be observed that every tax is to some extent regulatory. The commerce clause also imposes limitations on the taxing power of state and local governments. Although the issues involved are varied and complex, it may be said as a general rule that a state may impose a tax such as an income tax or a property tax on a business engaged in interstate commerce provided that the tax is *apportioned* by some reasonable formula to local activities within the state and does not discriminate against interstate commerce in favor of intrastate commerce. There must be a connection between the tax and the local enterprise being taxed *(nexus)*, or the tax will violate the commerce clause. The concepts of nexus and apportionment are used to ensure that interstate commerce pays its fair share for benefits received from the state.

THE ANTITRUST LAWS

6-97. The Sherman Act. In 1890, under its power to regulate interstate commerce Congress passed the Sherman Antitrust Act. The Sherman Act was directed essentially at two areas: (1) contracts, combinations, or conspiracies in restraint of trade, and (2) monopoly and attempts to monopolize. The law sought to preserve competition. This was to be achieved by imposing four sanctions for the violation of the law. First of all, violation was made a federal crime punishable by fine or imprisonment or both. Originally, the fine was set at $5,000. In 1955, Congress raised it to $50,000 and as of this writing, it is being proposed to increase it to $500,000. Second, the Sherman Act authorizes injunctions to prevent and restrain violations or continued violations of the Act. Failure to obey may be punished by contempt proceedings. Third, a remedy is given to those persons who have been injured by violation of the act. Such persons are given the right, in a civil action, to collect treble damages plus court costs and reasonable attorney's fees.[2] Normally, the objective of money damages is to place the injured party in the position he would have enjoyed, as nearly as this can be done with money, had his rights not been invaded. The treble-damage provision serves not only as a means of punishing the defendant for his wrongful act but also of compensating the plaintiff for his actual injury. Finally, if any property owned in violation of the restraint of trade provisions of the Act is being transported from one state to another, it is made subject to seizure by and forfeiture to the United States. This latter sanction has rarely been used.

The philosophy underlying the Sherman Act was clearly discernible: A system of small producers, each dependent for his success upon his own skill and character, is preferable to one in which the great mass of those engaged in commerce must accept the direction of a few. It reflected the belief that great industrial concentrations are inherently undesirable, regardless of their economic results. It was the purpose of Congress to put an end to great aggregations of capital because of the helplessness of the individual before them.

From its adoption, the Sherman Act proved unable to accomplish all of its goals. This resulted from its very broad language and from the favorable treatment given "big business" by the courts early in this century. Various amendments designed to make the act more specific have been enacted through the years. These amendments and some other statutes are discussed more fully in the sections that follow.

6-98. The Clayton Act. In 1914, Congress enacted the Clayton Act which was designed to make the Sherman Act more specific. The Act declared illegal certain practices which might have an adverse effect on competition, but which were something less than contracts, combinations, or conspiracies in restraint of trade, and which did not constitute actual monopolization or attempts to monopolize. The practices it enumerated were outlawed if their effect *might* be to substantially lessen competition, or tend to create a monopoly.

The Clayton Act contained four major provisions. Section 2 made it unlawful for a seller to discriminate in price between purchasers of commodities when the prohibited effect or tendency might result. Price discrimination is lawful if due to differences in the grade, quality, or quantity of the product sold, or differences in cost of transportation. In addition, no violation exists if the seller discriminates in price in order to meet competition in good faith.

Section 3 made it unlawful for a person engaged in commerce to lease or sell commodities (whether patented or unpatented) or fix a price charged, on the condition that the lessee or purchaser shall not use or deal in the commodities of a competitor of the lessor or seller when the prohibited effect or tendency might result. This section concerning tying and exclusive contracts prevents a seller of a product that is in high demand from forcing a purchaser to purchase a less desirable product in order to obtain the former. It results

---

[2] Klor's Inc. v. Broadway-Hale Stores, Inc., page 974

in every product standing on its merits. For example, a seller or lessor of a computer could not require that the buyer or lessee purchase all punch cards from him. Such a requirement is an unreasonable restraint that might substantially lessen competition, by foreclosing competitors from a substantial market.

Section 7 prohibited the acquisition of all or part of the stock of other corporations, where the effect *might* be to lessen competition substantially or to *tend* to create a monopoly. This section was substantially amended and its provisions will be discussed in Section 6-102.

Section 8 of the Clayton Act was aimed at interlocking directorates. It prohibits a person from being a member of the board of directors of two or more corporations at the same time, when one of them has capital, surplus, and undivided profits totaling more than $1,000,000, where elimination of competition by agreement between such corporations would amount to a violation of any of the antitrust laws.

6-99. The Federal Trade Commission Act.   Congress enacted a second antitrust law in 1914. This law created the Federal Trade Commission as one of the expert "independent administrative agencies." The Federal Trade Commission was given jurisdiction over cases arising under Sections 2, 3, 7, and 8 of the Clayton Act. The commission is composed of five members appointed by the President, with the advice and consent of the Senate, in staggered terms of seven years each. They are not permitted to engage in any other business or employment during their terms, and may be removed from office by the President only for inefficiency, neglect of duty, or malfeasance in office. The Federal Trade Commission has executive, legislative, and judicial functions.

Section 5 of the Federal Trade Commission Act declared that "unfair methods of competition in commerce" were unlawful, and empowered and directed the commission (exclusively) "to prevent persons, partnerships, or corporations . . . from using unfair methods of competition in commerce." This provision was amended later to make "unfair methods of competition in commerce and *unfair or deceptive acts or practices in commerce* " unlawful. The Commission has to determine what methods, acts, or practices are "unfair" or "deceptive" and thus illegal.[3] The majority of the Commission's activities are in this field, with special emphasis on labeling of furs and textiles. Great deference is given to the decisions of the Commission as they affect the marketing of goods. An activity may be an unfair method of competition without being a violation of the Sherman or Clayton Acts.[4]

6-100. The Robinson-Patman Act.   From 1914 to 1936, there was no major federal legislation in the antitrust field. In 1936, Congress enacted the landmark Robinson-Patman amendment of Section 2 of the original Clayton Act, dealing with price discrimination. This amendment, sometimes referred to as "the chain-store act" was designed to ensure equality of treatment to all buyers of a seller, in those cases when the result of unequal treatment might substantially lessen competition or tend to create a monopoly in any line of commerce. Section 2 of the Clayton Act had not accomplished this end, partly due to the

---

[3] F.T.C. v. Mary Carter Paint Co., page 976
[4] F.T.C. v. Brown Shoe Co., page 977

legality of quantity discounts under it, and partly because some buyers were able to obtain indirect benefits such as promotional or brokerage allowances. Such allowances were actually discounts which gave competitive advantage to one buyer over other buyers dealing with the same seller.

The Robinson-Patman Act made it a crime for a seller to sell at lower prices in one geographical area than in another in the United States in order to eliminate competition or a competitor, or to sell at unreasonably low prices to drive out a competitor. In addition, the Federal Trade Commission was given jurisdiction and authority to eliminate quantity discounts and to forbid brokerage allowances, except to independent brokers. The statute also prohibited promotional allowances, except on an equal basis.

6-101. The Fair Trade Laws.

In 1937, Congress passed the Miller-Tydings Act which amended the Sherman Act to permit fair trade contracts where legal under state law. In any state that adopts the requisite enabling fair trade statute, a manufacturer of a brand or trade name product is permitted to enter into a contract with a retailer whereby the retailer agrees to sell the product at not less than the minimum prices specified without having the agreement constitute a violation of the Sherman Act. If a state has no fair trade legislation, any such contract is unenforceable and a violation of the Sherman Act. The purpose of "Fair Trade" is to allow a manufacturer of a brand or trade name product to protect that brand name and the aura of quality carried with it by a higher price and to protect his scheme of distribution by preventing one retailer from discouraging other retailers from selling the product by use of cutthroat price competition and loss leaders.

In most states, the fair trade laws have non-signers clauses that make the contract setting minimum retail prices enforceable against both parties to the contract, and against non-signers as well. The McGuire Fair Trade Act of 1952, which has been upheld by the Supreme Court, provided that such statutes and the contracts pursuant thereto are legal and constitutional. Fair trade contracts that did not cover non-signers would not be an effective method of resale price maintenance.

6-102. The Celler-Kefauver Act.

This Act, passed in 1950, amends Section 7 of the Clayton Act so that it prohibits the acquisition of the stock *or assets* of other corporations, when the effect may be or tend to create a monopoly *in any line of commerce* in any section of the country. Section 7 as originally written covered horizontal mergers—those between competitors. It did not cover vertical (those between a buyer and seller) or conglomerate mergers. Moreover, a major gap existed in the language concerning stock of another company but not its assets. Acquisitions could occur simply by the purchase of a plant instead of the corporate stock. The Celler-Kefauver amendment plugged this loophole by adding "assets to stock." It also was broadened to cover vertical and conglomerate mergers with the deletion of the language "of a competitor" and the insertion of the language "any line of commerce."

Section 7 only requires a finding and conclusion that a given acquisition or merger have a reasonable probability of lessening competition or tending toward monopoly. It does not deal with certainties, only with probabilities.

The goal of the law is to arrest anticompetitive effects and trends toward undue concentration of economic power at their incipiency.[5] In judging cases brought under Section 7 of the Clayton Act as amended by the Celler-Kefauver Act, courts consider not only the probable effects of the merger upon the economics of the particular markets affected but also its probable effects upon the economic way of life sought to be preserved by Congress. Congress is desirous of preventing the formation of further oligopolies with their attendant adverse effects upon local control of industry and upon small business. Its aim was primarily to arrest apprehended consequences of intercorporate relationships before those relationships could work their evil, which may be at or any time after the acquisition, depending upon the circumstances of the particular case.

The majority of antitrust litigation in the 1970s falls under Section 7. Recent years have seen a rash of corporate mergers since growth by acquisition or merger is usually deemed easier than internal growth. In addition to creating antitrust problems, these mergers have also caused problems for accountants and financial experts. For example, financial reporting for conglomerates is obviously difficult when one considers that such statements may combine the sales of a distillery and an airline, for example. Solving the numerous problems raised by mergers will be a matter of concern for many years to come.

GOVERNMENT REGULATION OF BUSINESS ORGANIZATIONS CASES

Heart of Atlanta Motel, Inc. v. United States
85 S.Ct. 348 (1964)

A motel operator in Atlanta, Georgia, sued for a declaratory judgment that the public accommodation provision of the Federal Civil Rights Statutes of 1964 were unconstitutional. The government counterclaimed for enforcement. Plaintiff had refused to rent rooms to Negroes. The facts of the case were not in dispute, and it was admitted that plaintiff's operations were within the provisions of the Act. Therefore, the sole question before the court was the constitutionality of the Act, which the lower court upheld. The motel operator appealed.

CLARK, J. . . . The appellant contends that Congress in passing this Act exceeded its power to regulate commerce under Art. 1, § 8, c.l. 3, of the Constitution of the United States; . . .

The appellees counter that the unavailability to Negroes of adequate accommodations interferes significantly with interstate travel, and that Congress, under the Commerce Clause, has power to remove such obstructions and restraints. . . .

Section 201(C) . . . declares that "any inn, hotel, motel or other establishment which provides lodging to transient guests" affects commerce per se. . . .

While the Act as adopted carried no congressional findings, the record of its passage through each house is replete with evidence of the burdens that discrimination by race or color places upon interstate commerce. . . . This

[5] United States v. Von's Grocery Company, page XXX.

testimony included the fact that our people have become increasingly mobile with millions of all races traveling from State to State; that Negroes in particular have been the subject of discrimination in transient accommodations, having to travel great distances to secure the same; that often they have been unable to obtain accommodations and have had to call upon friends to put them up overnight, and that these conditions had become so acute as to require the listing of available lodgings for Negroes in a special guidebook which was itself "dramatic testimony of the difficulties" Negroes encounter in travel. These exclusionary practices were found to be nationwide, the Under Secretary of Commerce testifying that there is "no question that this discrimination in the North still exists to a large degree" and in the West and Midwest as well. This testimony indicated a qualitative as well as quantitative effect on interstate travel by Negroes. The former was the obvious impairment of the Negro traveler's pleasure and convenience that resulted when he continually was uncertain of finding lodging. As for the latter, there was evidence that this uncertainty stemming from racial discrimination had the effect of discouraging travel on the part of a substantial portion of the Negro community. This was the conclusion not only of the Under Secretary of Commerce but also of the Administrator of the Federal Aviation Agency who wrote the Chairman of the Senate Commerce Committee that it was his "belief that air commerce is adversely affected by the denial to a substantial segment of the traveling public of adequate and desegrated public accommodations." We shall not burden this opinion with further details since the voluminous testimony presents overwhelming evidence that discrimination by hotels and motels impedes interstate travel.

The Power of Congress Over Interstate Travel

The power of Congress to deal with these obstructions depends on the meaning of the Commerce Clause. . . .

The determinative test of the exercise of power by the Congress under the commerce clause is simply whether the activity sought to be regulated is "commerce which concerns more than one state" and has a real and substantial relation to the national interest. . . .

"Commerce among the states, we have said, consists of intercourse and traffic between their citizens, and includes the transportation of persons and property. . . . "

That Congress was legislating against moral wrongs in many of these areas rendered its enactments no less valid. In framing Title II of this Act Congress was also dealing with what it considered a moral problem. But that fact does not detract from the overwhelming evidence of the disruptive effect that racial discrimination has had on commercial intercourse. It was this burden which empowered Congress to enact appropriate legislation, and, given this basis for the exercise of its power, Congress was not restricted by the fact that the particular obstruction to interstate commerce with which it was dealing was also deemed a moral and social wrong.

It is said that the operation of the motel here is of a purely local character. But, assuming this to be true, "[i]f it is interstate commerce that feels the pinch, it does not matter how local the operation which applies the squeeze." As Chief Justice Stone put it in *United States* v. *Darby:*

> The power of Congress over interstate commerce is not confined to the regulation of commerce among the states. It extends to those activities intrastate which so affect interstate commerce or the exercise of the power of Congress over it as to make regulation of them appropriate means to the attainment of a legitimate end, the exercise of the granted power of Congress to regulate interstate commerce.

Thus, the power of Congress to promote interstate commerce also includes the power to regulate the local incidents thereof, including local activities in both the States of origin and destination, which might have a substantial and harmful effect upon that commerce. One need only examine the evidence which we have discussed above to see that Congress may—as it has—prohibit racial discrimination by motels serving travelers, however "local" their operations may appear.

We, therefore, conclude that the action of the Congress in the adoption of the Act as applied here to a motel which concededly serves interstate travelers is within the power granted it by the Commerce Clause of the Constitution, as interpreted by this Court for 140 years. It may be argued that Congress could have pursued other methods to eliminate the obstructions it found in interstate commerce caused by racial discrimination. But this is a matter of policy that rests entirely with the Congress not with the courts. How obstructions in commerce may be removed—what means are to be employed—is within the sound and exclusive discretion of the Congress. It is subject only to one *caveat* —that the means chosen by it must be reasonably adapted to the end permitted by the Constitution. We cannot say that its choice here was not so adapted. The Constitution requires no more.

Affirmed.

Klor's, Inc. v. Broadway-Hale Stores, Inc.

359 U.S. 207 (1959)

BLACK, J. Klor's, Inc., operates a retail store on Mission Street, San Francisco, California; Broadway-Hale Stores, Inc., a chain of department stores, operates one of its stores next door. The two stores compete in the sale of radios, television sets, refrigerators and other household appliances. Claiming that Broadway-Hale and ten national manufacturers and their distributors have conspired to restrain and monopolize commerce in violation of §§ 1 and 2 of the Sherman Act, 26 Stat. 209, as amended, 15 U.S.C. §§ 1, 2, 15 U.S.C.A. §§ 1, 2, Klor's brought this action for treble damages and injunction in the United States District Court.

In support of its claim Klor's made the following allegations: George Klor started an appliance store some years before 1952 and has operated it ever since either individually or as Klor's, Inc. Klor's is as well equipped as Broadway-Hale to handle all brands of appliances. Nevertheless, manufacturers and distributors of such well-known brands as General Electric, RCA, Admiral, Zenith, Emerson and others have conspired among themselves and with Broadway-Hale either not to sell to Klor's or to sell to it only at discriminatory prices and highly unfavorable terms. Broadway-Hale has used its "monopolistic" buying power to bring about this situation. The business of manufacturing, distributing and selling household appliances is in interstate commerce. The concerted refusal to deal with Klor's has seriously handicapped its ability to compete and has already caused it a great loss of profits, goodwill, reputation and prestige.

The defendants did not dispute these allegations, but sought summary judgement and dismissal of the complaint for failure to state a cause of action. They submitted unchallenged affidavits which showed that there were hundreds of other household appliance retailers, some within a few blocks of Klor's who sold many competing brands of appliances, including those the defendants refused to sell to Klor's. From the allegations of the complaint, and from the affidavits supporting the motion for summary judgment, the District Court concluded that the controversy was a "purely private quarrel" between Klor's and Broadway-Hale, which did not amount to a "public wrong proscribed by the [Sherman] Act." On this ground the complaint was dismissed and summary judgment was entered for the defendants. The Court of Appeals for the Ninth Circuit affirmed the summary judgment. . . . It stated that "a violation of the Sherman Act requires conduct of defendants by which the public is or conceivably may be ultimately injured." . . . It held that here the required public injury was missing since "there was no charge or proof that by any act of defendants the price, quantity, or quality offered the public was affected, nor that there was any intent or purpose to effect a change in, or an influence on, prices, quantity, or quality. . . . " The holding, if correct, means that unless the opportunities for customers to buy in a competitive market are reduced, a group of powerful businessmen may act in concert to deprive a single merchant, like Klor, of the goods he needs to compete effectively. . . .

We think Klor's allegations clearly show one type of trade restraint and public harm the Sherman Act forbids, and that defendants' affidavits provide no defense to the charges. Section 1 of the Sherman Act makes illegal any contract, combination or conspiracy in restraint of trade, and § 2 forbids any person or combination from monopolizing or attempting to monopolize any part of interstate commerce. . . .

Group boycotts, or concerted refusals by traders to deal with other traders, have long been held to be in the forbidden category. . . .

Plainly the allegations of this complaint disclose such a boycott. This is not a case of a single trader refusing to deal with another, nor even of a manufacturer and a dealer agreeing to an exclusive distributorship. Alleged in this complaint is a wide combination consisting of manufacturers, distributors and a retailer. This combination takes from Klor's its freedom to buy appliances in an open competitive market and drives it out of business as a dealer in the defendants' products. It deprives the manufacturers and distributors of their freedom to sell to Klor's at the same prices and conditions made available to Broadway-Hale and in some instances forbids them from selling to it on any terms whatsoever. It interferes with the natural flow of interstate commerce. It clearly has, by its "nature" and "character," a "monopolistic tendency." As such it is not to be tolerated merely because the victim is just one merchant whose business is so small that his destruction makes little difference to the economy. Monopoly can as surely thrive by the elimination of such small businessmen, one at a time, as it can be driving them out in large groups. In recognition of this fact the Sherman Act has consistently been read to forbid all contracts and combinations "which 'tend to create a monopoly,' " whether "the tendency is a creeping one" or "one that proceeds at full gallop." . . .

The judgment of the Court of Appeals is reversed and the cause is remanded to the District Court for trial.

Reversed.

F.T.C. v. Mary Carter Paint Co.
382 U.S. 46(1965)

BRENNAN, J. Respondent manufactures and sells paint and related products. The Federal Trade Commission ordered respondent to cease and desist from the use of certain representations found by the Commission to be deceptive and in violation of § 5 of the Federal Trade Commission Act. The representations appeared in advertisements which stated in various ways that for every can of respondent's paint purchased by a buyer, the respondent would give the buyer a "free" can of equal quality and quantity. The Court of Appeals for the Fifth Circuit set aside the Commission's order. We granted certiorari. We reverse.

Although there is some ambiguity in the Commission's opinion, we cannot say that its holding constituted a departure from Commission policy regarding the use of the commercially exploitable word "free." Initial efforts to define the term in decisions were followed by "Guides Against Deceptive Prices." These informed businessmen that they might advertise an article as "free," even though purchase of another article was required, so long as the terms of the offer were clearly stated, the price of the article required to be purchased was not increased, and its quality and quantity were not diminished. With specific reference to two-for-the-price-of-one offers, the Guides required that either the sales price for the two be "the advertiser's usual and customary retail price for the single article in the recent, regular course of his business," or where the advertiser has not previously sold the article, the price for the two be the "usual and customary" price for one in the relevant trade areas. These, of course, were guides, not fixed rules as such, and were designed to inform businessmen of the factors which would guide Commission decisions. Although Mary Carter seemed to have attempted to tailor its offer to come within their terms, the Commission found that it failed; the offer complied in appearance only.

The gist of the Commission's reasoning is in the hearing examiner's finding, which it adopted, that . . . the usual and customary retail price of each can of Mary Carter paint was not, and is not now, the price designated in the advertisement ($6.98) but was, and is now substantially less than such price. The second can of paint was not, and is not now, "free," that is, was not, and is not now, given as a gift of gratuity. The offer is, on the contrary, an offer of two cans of paint for the price advertised as or purporting to be the list price or customary and usual price of one can.

In sum, the Commission found that Mary Carter had no history of selling single cans of paint; it was marketing twins, and in allocating what is in fact the price of two cans to one can, yet calling one "free," Mary Carter misrepresented. It is true that respondent was not permitted to show that the quality of its paint matched those paints which usually and customarily sell in the $6.98 range, or that purchasers of paint estimate quality by the price they are charged. If both claims were established, it is arguable that any deception was limited to a representation that Mary Carter has a usual and customary price for single cans of paint, when it has not such price. However, it is not for courts to say whether this violates the Act. "[T]he Commission is often in a better position than are courts to determine when a practice is 'deceptive' within the meaning of the Act." There was substantial evidence in the record to support the Commission's findings; its determination that the practice here was deceptive was neither arbitrary nor clearly wrong. The Court of Appeals should have sustained it. . . .

Judgment of Court of Appeals reversed. . . .

F.T.C. v. Brown Shoe Co.
384 U.S. 316 (1966)

BLACK, J. Section 5(a) (6) of the Federal Trade Commission Act empowers and directs the Commission "to prevent persons, partnerships, or corporations . . . from using unfair methods of competition in commerce and unfair or deceptive acts or practices in commerce." Proceeding under the authority of § 5, the Federal Trade Commission filed a complaint against the Brown Shoe Co., Inc., one of the world's largest manufacturers of shoes with total sales of $236,946,078 for the year ending October 31, 1957. The unfair practices charged against Brown revolve around the "Brown Franchise Stores' Program" through which Brown sells its shoes to some 650 retail stores. The complaint alleged that under this plan Brown, a corporation engaged in interstate commerce, had "entered into contracts or franchises with a substantial number of its independent retail shoe store operator customers which require said customer to restrict their purchases of shoes for resale to the Brown lines and which prohibit them from purchasing, stocking or reselling shoes manufactured by competitors of Brown." Brown's customers who entered into these restrictive franchise agreements, so the complaint charged, were given in return special treatment and valuable benefits which were not granted to Brown's customers who did not enter into the agreements. In its answer to the Commission's complaint Brown admitted that approximately 259 of its retail customers had executed written franchise agreements and that over 400 others had entered into its franchise program without execution of the franchise agreement. Also in its answer Brown attached as an exhibit an unexecuted copy of the "Franchise Agreement" which, when executed by Brown's representative and a retail shoe dealer, obligates Brown to give to the dealer but not to other customers certain valuable services, including among others, architectural plans, costly merchandising records, services of a Brown field representative, and a right to participate in group insurance at lower rates than the dealer could obtain individually. In return, according to the franchise agreement set out in Brown's answer, the retailer must make this promise:

In return I will:
1. Concentrate my business within the grades and price lines of shoes representing Brown Shoe Company Franchises of the Brown Division and will have no lines conflicting with Brown Division Brands of the Brown Shoe Company.

Brown's answer further admitted that the operators of "such Brown Franchise Stores in individually varying degrees accept the benefits and perform the obligations contained in such franchise agreements or implicit in such Program," and that Brown refuses to grant these benefits "to dealers who are dropped or voluntarily withdraw from the Brown Franchise Program. . . . " The foregoing admissions of Brown as to the existence and operation of the franchise program were buttressed by many separate detailed fact findings of a trial examiner, one of which findings was that the franchise program effectively foreclosed Brown's competitors from selling to a substantial number of retail shoe dealers. Based on these findings and on Brown's admissions the Commission concluded that the restrictive contract program was an unfair method of competition within the meaning of § 5 and ordered Brown to cease and desist from its use.

On review the Court of Appeals set aside the Commission's order. In doing so the court said:

> By passage of the Federal Trade Commission Act, particularly § 5 thereof, we do not believe that Congress meant to prohibit or limit sales programs such as Brown Shoe engaged in in this case. . . . The custom of giving free service to those who will buy their shoes is widespread, and we cannot agree with the Commission that it is an unfair method of competition in commerce.

In addition the Court of Appeals held that there was a "complete failure to prove an exclusive dealing agreement which might be held violative of Section 5 of the Act." We are asked to treat this general conclusionary statement as though the court intended it to be a rejection of the Commission's findings of fact. We cannot do this. Neither this statement of the court nor any other statement in the opinion indicate a purpose to hold that the evidence failed to show an agreement between Brown and more than 650 franchised dealers which restrained the dealers from buying competing lines of shoes from Brown's competitors. Indeed, in view of the crucial admissions in Brown's formal answer to the complaint we cannot attribute to the Court of Appeals a purpose to set aside the Commission's findings that these restrictive agreements existed and that Brown and most of the franchised dealers in varying degrees lived up to their obligations. Thus the question we have for decision is whether the Federal Trade Commission can declare it to be an unfair practice for Brown, the second largest manufacturer of shoes in the Nation, to pay a valuable consideration to hundreds of retail shoe purchasers in order to secure a contractual promise from them that they will deal primarily with Brown and will not purchase conflicting lines of shoes from Brown's competitors. We hold that the Commission has power to find, on the record here, such an anticompetitive practice unfair, subject of course to judicial review.

In holding that the Federal Trade Commission lacked the power to declare Brown's program to be unfair the Court of Appeals was much influenced by and quoted at length from this Court's opinion in *FTC* v. *Gratz,* 253 U.S. 421. That case, decided shortly after the Federal Trade Commission Act was passed, construed the Act over a strong dissent by Mr. Justice Brandeis as giving the Commission very little power to declare any trade practice unfair. Later cases of this Court, however, have rejected the *Gratz* view and it is now recognized in line with the dissent of Mr. Justice Brandeis in *Gratz* that the Commission has broad powers to declare trade practices unfair. This broad power of the Commission is particularly well established with regard to trade practices which conflict with the basic policies of the Sherman and Clayton Acts even though such practices may not actually violate these laws. The record in this case shows beyond doubt that Brown, the country's second largest manufacturer of shoes, has a program, which requires shoe retailers, unless faithless to their contractual obligations with Brown, substantially to limit their trade with Brown's competitors. This program obviously conflicts with the central policy of both § 1 of the Sherman Act and § 3 of the Clayton Act against contracts which take away freedom of purchasers to buy in an open market. Brown nevertheless contends that the Commission had no power to declare the franchise program unfair without proof that its effect "may be to substantially lessen competition or tend to create a monopoly" which of course would have to be proved if the Government were proceeding against Brown under § 3 of the Clayton Act rather § 5 of the Federal Trade Commission Act. We reject the argument that proof of this § 3 element must be made, for as we pointed out above, our cases hold that the Commission has power under § 5 to arrest trade restraints in their incipiency without proof that they amount to an outright violation of § 3 of the Clayton Act or other provisions of the antitrust laws. This power of the Commission was emphatically stated in *FTC* v. *Motion Picture Advertising Co.,* 344 U.S. 392, at pp. 394-395:

> It is ... ... clear that the Federal Trade Commission Act was designed to supplement and bolster the Sherman Act and the Clayton Act ... to stop in their incipiency acts and practices which, when full blown, would violate those Acts ... as well as to condemn as "unfair methods of competition" existing violations of them.

We hold that the Commission acted well within its authority in declaring the Brown franchise program unfair whether it was completely full blown or not.

Reversed.

United States v. Von's Grocery Company

86 S.Ct. 1478 (1966)

The United States brought action for an injunction charging that the acquisition by Von's Grocery Company of Shopping Bag Food Stores violated Section 7 of the Clayton Act. The District Court entered judgment for the defendants, ruling as a matter of law that there was "not a reasonable probability" that the acquisition would tend "substantially to lessen competition" or "create a monolopy." The Government appealed.

BLACK, J. ... The record shows the following facts relevant to our decision. The market involved here is a retail grocery market in the Los Angeles area. In 1958 Von's retail sales ranked third in the area and Shopping Bag's ranked sixth. In 1960 their sales together were 7.5 percent of the total two and one-half billion dollars of retail groceries sold in the Los Angeles market each year. For many years before the merger both companies had enjoyed great success as rapidly growing companies. From 1948 to 1958 the number of Von's stores in the Los Angeles area practically doubled from 14 to 27, while at the same time the number of Shopping Bag's stores jumped from 15 to 34. During that same decade, Von's sales increased fourfold and its share of the market almost doubled while Shopping Bag's sales multiplied seven times and its share of the market tripled. The merger of these two highly successful, expanding and aggressive competitors created the second largest grocery chain in Los Angeles with sales of almost $172,488,000 annually. In addition the findings of the District Court show that the number of owners operating a single store in the Los Angeles retail grocery market decreased from 5,365 in 1950 to 3,818 in 1961. By 1963, three years after the merger, the number of single-store owners had dropped still further to 3,590. During roughly the same period from 1953 to 1962 the number of chains with two or more grocery stores increased from 96 to 150. While the grocery business was being concentrated into the hands of fewer and fewer owners, the small companies were continually being absorbed by the larger firms through mergers. According to an exhibit prepared by one of the Government's expert witnesses, in the period from 1949 to 1958 nine of the top 20 chains acquired 126 stores from their smaller competitors. Figures of a principal defense witness, set out below, illustrate the many acquisitions and mergers in the Los Angeles grocery industry from 1953 through 1961 including acquisitions made by Food Giant, Alpha Beta, Fox and Mayfair, all among the 10 leading chains in the area. Moreover, a table prepared by the Federal Trade Commission appearing in the Government's reply brief, but not a part of the record here, shows that acquisitions and mergers in the Los Angeles retail grocery market have continued at a rapid rate since the merger. These facts alone are enough to cause us to conclude contrary to the District Court that the Von's-Shopping Bag merger did violate § 7. Accordingly, we reverse. . . .

Like the Sherman Act in 1890 and the Clayton Act in 1914, the basic purpose of the 1950 Celler-Kefauver Bill was to prevent economic concentration in the American economy by keeping a large number of small competitors in business. In stating the purposes of the bill, both of its sponsors, Representative Celler and Senator Kefauver, emphasized their fear, widely shared by other members of Congress, that this concentration was rapidly driving the small businessman out of the market. The period from 1940 to 1947, which was at the center of attention throughout the hearing, and debates on the Celler-Kefauver bill, had been characterized by a series of mergers between large corporations and their smaller competitors resulting in the steady erosion of the small independent business in our economy. . . .

The facts of this case present exactly the threatening trend toward concentration which Congress wanted to halt. The number of small grocery companies in the Los Angeles retail grocery market had been declining rapidly before the merger and continued to decline rapidly afterwards. This rapid decline in the number of grocery store owners moved hand in hand with a large number of significant absorptions of the small companies by the larger ones. In the midst of this steadfast trend toward concentration, Von's and Shopping Bag, two of the most successful and largest companies in the area, jointly owning 66 grocery stores merged to become the second largest chain in Los Angeles. This merger cannot be defended on the ground that one of the companies was about to fail or that the two had to merge to save themselves from destruction by some larger and more powerful competitor. What we have on the contrary is simply the case of two already powerful companies merging in a way which makes them even more powerful than they were before. If ever such a merger would not violate § 7, certainly it does when it takes place in a market characterized by a long and continuous trend toward fewer and fewer owner-competitors which is exactly the sort of trend which Congress, with power to do so, declared must be arrested.

Appellee's primary argument is that the merger between Von's and Shopping Bag is not prohibited by § 7 because the Los Angeles grocery market was competitive before the merger, has been since, and may continue to be in the future. Even so, § 7 "requires not merely an appraisal of the immediate impact of the merger upon competition, but a prediction of its impact upon competitive conditions in the future; this is what is meant when it is said that the amended § 7 was intended to arrest anticompetitive tendencies in their 'incipiency.' " It is enough for us that Congress feared that a market marked at the same time by both a continuous decline in the number of small businesses and a large number of mergers would, slowly but inevitably gravitate from a market of many small competitors to one dominated by one or a few giants, and competition would thereby be destroyed. Congress passed the Celler-Kefauver Bill to prevent such a destruction of competition. Our cases since the passage of that bill have faithfully endeavored to enforce this congressional command. We adhere to them now. . . .

Reversed.

CHAPTER 48
REVIEW QUESTIONS AND PROBLEMS

1. The state of Arizona by statute under its police powers imposed maximum lengths of fourteen cars on passenger trains and seventy cars on freight trains, for the purpose of encouraging railroad safety. No other state imposes such regulations. Is the legislation constitutional?

2. South Carolina, concerned with the condition of its highways, passed legislation banning from the highways all trucks over 90 inches in width and over 20,000 lbs. gross weight. Evidence shows 85 percent of all semitrailer trucks exceed that limit. Is the statute constitutional?

3. Many states require that trucks use mudguards. The state of Illinois discovers that a curved mudguard, contoured around the rear wheel, provides an added increment of safety from thrown stones, and consequently requires their use on all trucks using Illinois highways. No other state specified the type of mudguard to be used except Arkansas, which requires the conventional "straight" mudguard. Evidence shows the added increment of safety is slight. Is the Illinois statute valid? Is the Arkansas statute valid?

4. The Department of Agriculture has set up minimum standards of ripeness based on size and weight for the marketing of avocados. A California statute was enacted that provided standards of ripeness based on

minimum oil content for the distribution and sale of avocados in California. Is the California statute preempted by the federal legislation?

5. A recreational park in Arkansas featured a swimming and boating lake, a snack bar, and a golf course. Is such a facility within the power of Congress under the commerce clause so that it is a "public accommodation" covered under the Civil Rights Act of 1964?

6. What are the limitations on the federal power to regulate business?

7. What are the limitations on the power of state government to regulate business?

8. What was the purpose of the Clayton Act?

9. What was the primary purpose of the Robinson-Patman amendment?

BOOK SEVEN

Property

The Concept of
Property

7-1. Introduction. All aspects of life are concerned with and are affected by property. One of the more powerful motivating forces in our society is the desire of people to acquire, use, and dispose of property. Property is the reason for and the subject matter of economic activity. Property is a measure of wealth and success. It is the substance of business transactions.

The right to acquire, use, and dispose of private property exists to some degree in all cultures. But the extent to which individuals have private property rights varies greatly from culture to culture and society to society, depending on the economic system and social structure involved. In our capitalistic system, we place major emphasis on private property. One of our basic civil rights has been the right to own, possess, and dispose of private property. In socialistic societies, the emphasis has been not on private property, but on public property. Today in our capitalistic society, private property rights are frequently being subordinated to the public interest, as for example, in the case of zoning laws. And in socialistic countries, individuals are now allowed to own some private property. If any common denominator exists between capitalism and socialism, it is that each system is moving toward more emphasis on the basic approach of the other. We are tending more and more toward restrictions on private property rights because of the public interest, and in socialist countries, the trend is toward more private property rights because of the need for incentives.

The concept of private property is the essential ingredient in a free enterprise economic system. Such an economic system cannot exist without a legal system which creates, protects, and enforces private property rights. As the law—both statutory and case law—has tended to limit the ownership, possession, use, and disposition of property in the public interest, our economic system has become less free enterprise in character and more regulated or socialistic—

evidence that the laws governing property are closely related to the prevailing economic philosophy.

From the standpoint of its physical characteristics, property is classified as either personal property or real property. Land and things affixed to or growing upon the land come under the heading of *real property* and as will be noted, a separate body of real property law has developed, both for historical reasons and for reasons associated with the peculiar characteristics of land. All other property is said to be *personal property,* and in general, it is subject to different treatment under the law than is real property. Personal property may be classified as either tangible or intangible, the latter referring to property rights which are invisible, such as accounts receivable.

Any definition of property depends upon the context in which it is used. It will be the purpose of the following sections to set out in detail some of the various meanings given to the term "property."

7-2. The Components of Property.   The term "property" or property itself is meaningless except as it is associated with individuals. The terms used in expressing this association are "ownership," "title," and "possession."

"Ownership" is a word signifying degrees; it is a "more or less" word. To *own* is to have. But the question is, What must one have to be an owner? Ownership denotes the *quantum* of property interest one has. An owner may have all the legal relations or interests concerning the subject matter of property, or an owner may have less than all the legal interests in a particular thing, tangible or intangible, while at the same time another may have legal interests in the same thing. Thus, a lessor has an interest in land which is limited by the interest held by the lessee. The lessor is said to hold the fee and the lessee the leasehold. Both own property and are in a position under the proper circumstances to exclude the other. The meaning of the word "owner" is dependent upon the context in which it is used.[1]

The word "title" is often used synonymously with "ownership." The word signifies the method by which ownership is acquired, whether by gift, by purchase, or by other methods. It also indicates the evidence by which the claim of ownership is established—the deed or other written instrument. It includes not only the method and the evidence, but the result. The result which obtains from the method, the evidence, and the documents used is characterized by such words as "legal title," "equitable title," "good title," "marketable title," "tax title," "fee simple title," and so forth.

The word "possession" is difficult to define precisely. It links together the concept of physical control or dominion by a person over property with his personal and mental relationship to it. It is distinguished from mere custody, since the latter is limited to physical control only, without any interest therein adverse to the true owner. Possession, however, means not only physical control or the power to have physical control but also legal sanctions therewith to enforce continued relation with the thing, or if deprived of such relation, to have the same restored.

In determining whether the legal consequence "possession" is present, the court must examine in each particular case the claimant's intent and physical relation to the thing in question. Possession may be actual; that is, physically

[1] Robinson v. Walker, page 992

held by the owner, or physically held by one over whom the owner has control, such as a servant or agent. Possession may be constructive; that is, physical control may be in one person while another has a better right. *X* finds *B's* watch, knowing it to be *B's* watch. *X* appropriates it to his own use, and sells and delivers it to *C. X* is guilty of larceny because he dispossessed *B* of the watch, although at the time *B* was not in physical possession of the watch. *B* is entitled to the return of the watch from *C.* A thief cannot pass title to stolen goods even to an innocent purchaser. A finder of lost things as against the true owner has no property right but as to all others he has a better right.

The meanings found in the word "possession" depend upon the fact situation involved and the end to be achieved. Thus, the fact situation and policy reasons resulting in possession in a finder case, abandoned property, acquisition of wild animals, trespass, crimes, attachments by sheriffs, and illegal holding under statutes are all different.

7-3. Property as Things. In early law it was difficult to understand how there could be ownership, possession, and transfer of rights, with respect to things, without possessing and transferring the thing itself. A thing could be seen, touched, possessed, and delivered; hence the *thing* was the property. Rights to the thing were embodied in the physical object, so that the handing over of the physical object was essential to endowing another with property, ownership, title, possession, and all the other attributes one could have in a thing. Things owned and possessed were of two kinds: land and chattels. Land, a fixed, immovable thing, could not be handed over or delivered. In England under the feudal system, in order to satisfy the requirement of physical delivery, land was transferred by a symbolic process called *feoffment,* by which a twig or clod taken from the land by the grantor was delivered to the grantee. This symbol is said, in the proper case, to have seised the grantee with fee simple title. This historical symbolism is reflected in our present method of conveying land. Today the transfer of land is accomplished by the execution, and delivery, of a thing—a written instrument—called a *deed.*

No difficulty was experienced in owning, possessing, and manually delivering a movable thing. The most significant movable things in early civilization were cattle. Their mobility facilitated their use as a medium of exchange. From the term "cattle" is derived the word "chattel." These two types of things, land and chattels, became known as two different kinds of property. Land became real property and chattels became personal property. Such designation arose out of the types of remedies developed to protect rights with respect to land and chattels.

One seeking a remedy against interference with the land, such as eviction or dispossession, brought an action to recover the land itself; that is, the ousted plaintiff sought to recover the thing—the *res.* The action was called an action *in rem,* or a real action. Thus, the thing protected—land—derived its name *real property.*

Since a movable thing—a chattel—could be stolen, destroyed, or transferred away, a remedy other than the recovery of the thing, or *res,* was necessary. An action against the wrongdoer for restitution by way of damages was instituted. This action was against the wrong-doing person, and was called an action *in personam,* or a personal action. Thus, the things protected—movable chattels—derived their name, *personal property.*

Land has a fixed location. Therefore, its title, ownership, method of transfer, inheritance, and succession are governed by the law of the place where it is located. The law which controls movables, however, is highly influenced by the law of the domicile of the owner of the chattels.

Land and chattels as "things" are designated as "property" not only in common parlance, but also in court opinions, legal texts, and statutes. The following examples are illustrative. "The term 'property' as commonly used denotes an external object over which the right of property is exercised." "A man's property consists of lands, buildings, automobiles, and so on." "Property is of a fixed and tangible nature, capable of being had in possession and transmitted to another, such as houses, lands and chattels." By statutes in many states, "dogs are hereby declared to be personal property."

There are certain things incapable of being included within the term "property" in this context. Such things as light, air, clouds, running water, and wild animals by reason of their nature are not subject to exclusive dominion and control and hence are not property in this sense. However, wild animals when caught and reduced to possession as physical things are included within the term "property." Although the owner of land may have no natural rights to light and air, he may acquire, by way of easement, the right to have light and air come onto his land from that of an adjacent owner. Likewise, an owner of land has the right that the air over his land be free from pollution. Property rights in running water may be acquired by use of the water or by ownership of the abutting land.

Commercial necessities and historical considerations have endowed many printed and written instruments, such as commercial paper, bills of lading, warehouse receipts, and certificates of stock, with attributes of a thing or chattel. Thus, as things, their physical delivery is often essential to serve as objective evidence of transfer of the rights which they represent.

7-4. Property as Nonphysical or Incorporeal.   The concept that only things were the subject of property and that property was more than the thing itself developed during the days of feudal land tenure in England. Out of the English feudal land system there developed many intangible and invisible inheritable rights called "incorporeal hereditaments." "These rights grew out of, touched or concerned the land, but they were not the substance of the thing itself." Among such rights were the right to use common pasture land and parks, called "the commons," and rights to annuities and rents. Such incorporeal interests are recognized in our law today. A lease granting the right to explore for oil, accompanied by a duty to pay royalties if oil is found, creates no property in a thing, but an invisible, intangible right concerning the land. Such right is property. For example, easements, leases, and various types of restrictive covenants which touch and concern land are property interests protected by the courts.

7-5. Property as Relationships.   In the preceding paragraphs land, chattels, commercial paper, bonds, negotiable instruments, and written and printed documents are considered things, called *property.*

In order to have a more complete idea of the meaning of the term "property," we shall in this section refer to things—land, chattels, commercial paper, bonds, written and printed documents, contracts, debts, and choses in action —not as property, but as the *subject matter* of property. The term "property" as here used means a part or the totality of relationships existing between persons with respect to either physical things, or with respect to the nonphysical such as contracts, debts, choses in action, patent rights, news, and pensions. The particular relationships with which we are concerned are *rights, powers, privileges,* and *immunities.*

These legal relations are defined by the Restatement of the Law of Property as follows:

"A right is a legally enforceable claim of one person against another, that the other shall do a given act or shall not do a given act." For every right there is a corresponding duty. *A*'s right concerning the ownership, possession, and use of his land, home, and chattels places *B* under a duty not to interfere with or deny *A* his rights.

"A power is an ability on the part of a person to produce a change in a given legal relation by doing or not doing a given act." For every power there is a corresponding liability. *A* gives *B,* his agent, authority to transfer his, *A*'s, land. *B* has the power to change *A*'s legal relation with respect to the land; thus *A* is under a liability that such change will be made. *Liability* here does not mean duty. One often says "liability to pay money." What is meant in this situation is duty to pay money.

"A privilege is a legal freedom on the part of one person as against another to do a given act or legal freedom not to do a given act." For every privilege there is an absence of a right. *A* has the privilege of painting his house; all others have no right or concern with his privilege.

"An immunity is a freedom on the part of one person against having a legal relation altered by a given act or omission to act on the part of another person." For every immunity on one side there is a disability on the other. *A* owes *B* money, secured by a mortgage. *A* pays *B. A* is now immune from any legal right of *B*'s to foreclose, and *B* is under a disability.

If a person has all the rights, powers, privileges, and immunities that one is capable of having with one person or with all the persons in the world with respect to or concerning land or chattels, tangible and intangible, then such aggregate of legal relations constitutes *property.*

One may, however, have property with respect to a thing or intangible situation and not have all the relationships. These relationships are continually changing. If *A* exercises a power and mortages his land to *B, A* has cut down his right relations and endowed *B* with right relations concerning the land. Again, if the state passes restrictive legislation concerning the use of *A*'s land, his legal relations have been diminished.

In order to identify the relationships termed "property" concerning things, the Restatement of the Law of Property uses the word "interest." "The word interest includes . . . varying aggregates of legal rights, powers, privileges, and immunities and distributively [means] any one of them." Thus, rights, powers, privileges, and immunities with respect to land are "interests in land," or "interest in things."

If property is to be considered with respect to things, as "legal relations," it is necessary to consider how such relationships came into existence and how they will be protected. Land and things are just items capable of being the subject of property until relations arise between people. These relations when given recognition by a government in respect to the items create property. No legal relationships or property interest can be said to exist unless some method is afforded to enforce them. This, of course, is the function of government and law; the courts and other agencies of society will protect the relations of rights, power, privileges, and immunities with which the government has endowed the person. Thus, if there is a trespass upon one's land, the trespasser can be compelled to cease trespassing by a court and in addition can be required to make restitution for damages.

It is fundamental that a person who has *property*—an enforceable legal right-duty relation—has a power of destroying his own relation and creating relations in others. Thus, he has the power to enter into contracts and transfer all his legal interests by a sale, or he can give them to someone else. He may part with some of his interests and reserve to himself those which remain. For example, he may lease his land, or he may borrow money and give a mortgage on the land as security for the mortgagee-lender. In each case he has divided his legal interests by creating legal interests in a lessee and a mortgagee and retaining legal interests in himself. When the lease expires, the interest of the lessee terminates; when the debt is paid, the interest of the mortgagee no longer exists; there is now an immunity from the interests of either the tenant or the creditor. The courts will give recognition to the interests of tenant and creditor during the period of their existence; likewise protection will be afforded to the "owner" upon their termination.

If a person has a totality of all the relationships regarding the land, he then has complete ownership or property. He may, however, from time to time, have fewer than all the relationships or interest in land. When he leases the land, grants an easement—over, above, or below—the land, or dedicates portions to the city for streets, he diminishes his legal relationships. Likewise, a person may have his relationships reduced by government through its exercise of the police power by way of zoning or its power of eminent domain or of taxation.

A person's interests in land and in things can be said to consist of a "bundle of rights"—he may have all of the elements of the bundles, or some may be vested in others. Just how few relationships one may have and still have property cannot be definitely ascertained. If a court gives a judgment in favor of the particular relationships asserted, then it may be said that a "property interest" exists. As we have seen, the term "property" connotes a multiplicity of rights, duties, powers, and immunities. The term may include all or some of the relationships. One may have or create all of these elements in another, or one may have or be endowed with a very limited number of these elements and still have a property interest. Thus, a person in possession of illegal goods as against the state may have no property; however, he may have a property interest as against third persons. Even though a statute makes ownership and possession of slot machines illegal, "there yet exists certain rights [sic: privileges] in the individual who may possess such a contraband article as against any one other than the state. The owner [sic: person in possession] at least has the privilege of destroying the machine, he also has the right to surrender it to the authorities. It is true his right to the possession of the slot machine is by law very limited; nevertheless, he has certain claims and powers not possessed by any other, which invests in him something real and tangible. . . . " There are no property rights innate in objects themselves. Such rights as there are are in certain persons as against others with respect to the particular objects in question. Since property or title is a complex bundle of rights, duties, powers, and immunities, the taking away of some or a great many of these elements does not entirely destroy the property.

The right to be free from unreasonable noise of low-flying planes and the privilege of quiet use and enjoyment of land are forms of property. The "continuing and frequent low flights over the appellant's land constituted a taking of property. . . . " Property in a thing consists not merely in its ownership and possession, but in the right of its use, enjoyment and disposal.

The change of the grade of a street which lessens the enjoyment of an easement of ingress and egress by abutting property owners is the taking of property,[2] but the placing of a dividing strip in the center of a street has been held not to be a taking of property.

Injunctive relief has been granted to restrain the chemical seeding of clouds, because such seeding dissipated and scattered the clouds, preventing rain. Such conduct is an interference with a property right, namely, the right to a possibility that it may rain.[3]

Which legal relations in the total bundle are most significant, important, and decisive cannot be given a uniform fixed determination. The relationship concept of the term "property" is used by the court as a tool to solve the particular problem before it. Whether particular relations are legally protected interests and called "property" or the "thingified" concept of property will depend upon the circumstances, the purpose and intention of the parties, and the result sought to be obtained by the court.

Thus, in construing statutes involving crimes and tort liability, the court may emphasize a "thingified" concept of property. In our technological and complex society, new relationships are continually being established and asserted which demand protection. When these new relationships are given judicial protection, they become legal interests or property. For example, in advertising and marketing, when ideas expressed in word, form, shapes, or modes of packaging acquire an economic value, the right to use and exploit such ideas becomes a property interest protected by the courts. The right to exclude others from the use of collected news items, the rebroadcasting of radio and television programs, the right to have unimpaired the rain potential of clouds over one's land, and the privilege of unhampered entrance to and from the street by an abutting landowner are illustrations of newly created property interests. The courts are frequently called upon to rule as to whether or not a given situation gives rise to property rights.[4]

7-6. Property in a Legal Environment. The foregoing discussion of the concepts of property must be considered in their proper perspective. They are

[2] In re Forsstrom et ux., page 994
[3] Southwest Weather Research v. Rounsaville, page 995
[4] Davies v. Carnation Company, page 997

simply the tools used by the courts in arriving at decisions when conflicting claims regarding land and things are brought before them. It remains true that in common parlance people think of "property" as being the thing itself rather than their relationships in connection with the thing. Thus, when a businessman states that he "owns" his business, he is conveying the notion that the building, furniture and fixtures, delivery equipment, and inventory belong to him *in toto*. He regards these *things* as his "property." It is necessary to give recognition to the "thingified concept" and to recognize that the word "property" is often used loosely—personal property, real property—without spelling out its true significance. A true understanding of the law relating to business transactions requires an understanding of what lies behind the commonly used word. It is particularly important to recognize that property encompasses much more than physical things—that contract rights and other intangibles are "property," and that more than one person may have interests in the same property.

The law is flexible and is constantly in the process of change and development as new social, economic, and business needs arise. Also, the concept of property is an expanding one and the development of new techniques in business and technological changes may result in new concepts of property as yet not conceived in the mind of man.

THE CONCEPT OF PROPERTY CASES

Robinson v. Walker
211 N.E.2d 488 (Ill.) 1965

Plaintiff, Faye Robinson, brought this suit for personal injuries allegedly resulting from an armed assault upon her by the defendant, Henry Walker. She bases her claim against the defendant on the Dram Shop Act (Ill. Rev. Stat., Ch. 43, 135 (1961), set forth below). She sought recovery against the land trustees who held title to the real estate upon which the taverns were respectively located. (A land trustee is one who is involved in a security interest in land.) One land trustee defendant, Central National Bank in Chicago, moved for summary judgment in its favor. Judgment in favor of the Bank was ordered by the trial court. Plaintiff appealed from that order.

BURMAN, J. The portion of the Dram Shop Act relevant to this appeal provides:

> Every person, who shall be injured, in person or property by any intoxicated person, shall have a right of action in his or her own name, severally or jointly, against any person or persons who shall, by selling or giving alcoholic liquor, have caused the intoxication, in whole or in part, of such person; and any person owning, renting, leasing or permitting the occupation of any building or premises, and having knowledge that alcoholic liquors are to be sold therein, . . . shall be liable, severally or jointly, with the person or persons selling or giving liquors aforesaid, . . . (Ill. Rev. Stat. ch. 43, 135 (1961)

Basing her claim against the Bank upon this language, plaintiff alleges that the Bank, as land trustee, is the "owner" of the property upon which one of the taverns is located, and that the Bank had knowledge of the sale of alcoholic liquors on the premises. Defendant contends that as a land trustee it holds "naked" title to the property, without any accompanying right to manage or to control its use; that it had disclosed to plaintiff the beneficiaries of the land trust, who are in active control of the premises; and that the Dram Shop Act, in imposing liability upon an owner, did not intend to impose liability upon a land trustee under these circumstances.

On the question of who had the right to manage and to control the use of the real estate, the Trust Agreement pertaining to that real estate, which was attached to defendant's motion for summary judgment, provides:

> The beneficiary or beneficiaries here under shall in his, her or their own right have the full management of said real estate and control of the selling, renting and handling thereof, and any beneficiary or his or her agent shall handle the rents thereof and the proceeds of any sales of said property, and said Trustee shall not be required to do anything in the management of control of said real estate.

The Trust Agreement also sets forth the names and addresses of the beneficiaries.

Appellant (Plaintiff) principally contends that the Dram Shop Act simply imposes liability upon the "owner" of the premises and makes no requirement that he have the right to manage or to control. We have not been referred to, nor have we found, any Illinois cases which are directly in point.

In cases arising under statutes other than the Dram Shop Act, the word "owner" as applied to land has been held to have no fixed meaning which can be declared to be applicable under all circumstances. The word usually signifies one who has the legal or rightful title, but this is not always the sense in which it is employed. It is not rigid in meaning, especially in ordinances and statutes, and frequently is used to denote one in control, but having less than absolute title. The meaning usually depends, in great measure, upon the context and the subject matter to which it is applied. In *Woodward Governor Company* v. *City of Loves Park* (335 Ill.App. 528), the court was required to determine whether a railroad having an easement over certain property was the "owner" of that property within the meaning of a statute relating to the disconnection of land from a city. In holding that the railroad was such an owner, the court said: " . . . there is no uniform guide as to what meaning shall be ascribed to the term 'owner' and . . . consideration must be given to the nature and purpose of the statute involved." . . .

. . . [T]he U.S. Supreme Court, in upholding the constitutionality of the Illinois Dram Shop Act as applied to the lessor of the premises, characterized the statute as, " . . . for the regulation of the traffic in intoxicating liquors, . . . with a view to repress the evil consequences which may result therefrom."

We conclude that the purposes of the Dram Shop Act would in no way be served by imposing liability upon one who, as defendant here, holds "naked" title and has no right to exercise any control over the use of the property for the sale of intoxicating liquors; and that such a title holder was not intended to be included within the provision imposing liability upon an owner. Holding a land trustee liable would not provide "discipline of traffic in liquor," for the trustee neither participates in nor has control over such traffic. . . .

The judgment is therefore affirmed.

In re Forsstrom et ux.

38 P.2d 878 (Ariz.) (1934)

LOCKWOOD, J. The question is solely one of law, and the facts may be briefly stated as follows: The main tracks of the Southern Pacific Railroad cross North Stone Avenue near an intersection of Sixth Street at the present grade of said Avenue. The authorities of the City of Tucson, believing that such grade crossing is a menace and hazard to public travel on the street determined to abolish it by the construction of an underpass or subway below the tracks. . . . (By so doing) ingress and egress to the premises of the abutting property owners will be made more difficult. . . .

We come then to the question as to whether the proposed action of the City of Tucson, insofar as it affects petitioners at all, is a ["taking of property"] within the meaning of the statute. . . .

In order that we may understand the better what is meant by a "taking" of property, we should have a clear knowledge of what property really is. The word is used at different times to express many varying ideas. Sometimes it is taken in common parlance to denote a physical object, as where one says an automobile or a horse is his property. On careful consideration, however, it is plain that "property" in the true and legal sense does not mean a physical object itself, but certain rights over the object. A piece of land in an unexplored and uninhabited region which belongs to no one does not necessarily undergo any physical change merely by reason of its later becoming the property of any person. A wild animal may be exactly the same physically before and after it is captured, but, when it is running free in the forest, no one would speak of it as property. We must therefore look beyond the physical object itself for the true definition of property. Many courts and writers have attempted to define it, using different words, but meaning in essence the same thing. One of the great writers on jurisprudence says:

"Property is entirely the creature of the law. . . . There is no form, or color, or visible trace, by which it is possible to express the relation which constitutes property. It belongs not to physics, but to metaphysics; it is altogether a creature of the mind." (Bentham: *Works* (Ed. 1843), Vol. 1, p. 308.)

> (Other authorities say) . . . Property itself, in a legal sense, is nothing more than the "exclusive right of possession, enjoying and disposing of a thing. . . . "
>
> Property, in its broader and more appropriate sense, is not alone the chattel or the land itself, but the right to freely possess, use, and alienate the same; and many things are considered property which have no tangible existence, but which are necessary to the satisfactory use and enjoyment of that which is tangible.
>
> It is used in the constitution in a comprehensive and unlimited sense, and so it must be construed. . . . It need not be any physical or tangible property which is subject to a tangible invasion. . . . The right to light and air, and access is equally property. . . .

It would follow from these definitions and explanations of the meaning of the term "property" that since it consists, not in tangible things themselves, but in certain rights in and appurtenant to them, it would logically follow that, when a person is deprived of any of these rights, he is to that extent deprived of his property, and that it is taken in the true sense although his title and possession of the physical object remains undisturbed. Any substantial interference, therefore, with rights over a physical object which destroys or lessens its value, or by which the use and enjoyment thereof by its owner is in any substantial degree abridged or destroyed, is both in law and in fact a "taking" of property. It is apparently only of recent years that the meaning of the word "taking" when used in regard to eminent domain has been properly understood by the majority of the courts, although it would seem obvious that a careful analysis of the true nature of "property" would have shown it long since. . . .

From the very nature of these rights of user and of exclusion, it is evident that they cannot be materially abridged without, *ipso facto,* taking the owner's property. If the right of indefinite user is an essential element of absolute property or complete ownership, whatever physical interference annuls this right takes "property"—although the owner may still have left to him valuable rights (in the article) of a more limited and circumscribed nature. He has not the same property that he formerly had. Then, he had an unlimited right; now, he has only a limited right. His absolute ownership has been reduced to a qualified ownership. Restricting *A*'s unlimited right of using one hundred acres of land to a limited right of using the same land, may work a far greater injury to *A* than to take from him the title in fee simple to one acre, leaving him the unrestricted right of using the remaining ninety-nine acres. Nobody doubts that the latter transaction would constitute a "taking" of property. Why not the former? . . .

> Property in land must be considered, for many purposes, not as an absolute, unrestricted dominion, but as an aggregation of qualified privileges, the limits of which are prescribed by the equality of rights, and the correlation of rights and obligations necessary for the highest enjoyment of land by the entire community of proprietors. . . .

. . . The changing of the street grade which lessens the enjoyment of the easement of ingress and egress is within the true meaning of the constitutional provision [and a "taking"] which injuriously affects the value of adjoining property [and] is "damage." The damage is to the easement of the ingress and egress.

Southwest Weather Research v. Rounsaville

320 S.W.2d 211 (Tex.) 1958

PER CURIAM. This is an appeal from an injunction issued by the Eighty-third District Court, Jeff Davis County, Texas, which said injunction commands the appellants "to refrain from seeding the clouds by artificial nucleation or otherwise and from in any other manner or way interfering with the clouds and the natural conditions of the air, sky, atmosphere and air space over plaintiffs' lands and in the area of plaintiffs' lands to in any manner, degree or way affect, control or modify the weather conditions on or about said lands. . . . "

Appellees are ranchmen residing in West Texas counties, and appellants are owners and operators of certain airplanes, and equipment generally used in what they call a "weather modification program" and those who contracted and arranged for their services.

It is not disputed that appellants did operate their airplanes at various times over portions of lands belonging to the appellees, for the purpose of and while engaged in what is commonly called "cloud seeding." Appellants do not deny having done this, and testified through the president of the company that the operation would continue unless restrained. He stated, "We seeded the clouds to attempt to suppress the hail." The controversy is really over appellants' right to seed clouds or otherwise modify weather conditions over appellees' property. . . .

We have carefully considered the voluminous record and exhibits that were admitted in evidence, and have concluded that the trial court had ample evidence on which to base his findings and with which to justify the issuance of the injunction. . . .

Appellants maintain the appellees have no right to prevent them from flying over appellees' lands; that no one owns the clouds unless it be the state, and that the trial court was without legal right to restrain appellants from pursuing a lawful occupation; also that the injunction is too broad in its terms. . . .

Appellees urge here that the owner of land also owns in connection therewith certain so-called "natural rights," and cites us the following quotation from . . . Chief Justice Nelson Phillips . . . :

> Property in a thing consists not merely in its ownership and possession, but in the unrestricted right of use, enjoyment and disposal. Anything which destroys any of these elements of property, to that extent destroys the property itself. The substantial value of property lies in its use. If the right of use be denied, the value of the property is annihilated and ownership is rendered a barren right. . . .
>
> The very essence of American constitutions is that the material rights of no man shall be subject to the mere will of another.

In Volume 34, *Marquette Law Review,* at page 275, this is said:

> Considering the property right of every man to the use and enjoyment of his land, and considering the profound effect which natural rainfall has upon the realization of this right, it would appear that the benefits of natural rainfall should come within the scope of judicial protection, and a duty should be imposed on adjoining land-owners not to interfere therewith.

In the *Stanford Law Review,* November 1948, Volume 1, in an article entitled "Who Owns the Clouds? ," the following statements occur:

> The landowner does have rights in the water in clouds; however, the basis for these rights is the common law doctrine of natural rights. Literally, the term "natural rights" is well chosen; these rights protect the landowner's use of his land in its natural condition. . . .
>
> All forms of natural precipitation should be elements of the natural condition of the land. Precipitation, like air, oxygen, sunlight, and the soil itself, is an essential to many reasonable uses of the land. The plant and animal life on the land are both ultimately dependent upon rainfall. To the extent that rain is important to the use of land, the landowner should be entitled to the natural rainfall.

In *California Law Review,* December 1957, Volume 45, No. 5, in an article, "Weather Modification," are found the following statements:

> "What are the rights of the landowner or public body to natural rainfall? It has been suggested that the right to receive rainfall is one of those natural rights which is inherent in the full use of land from the fact of its natural contact with moisture in the air. . . .
>
> "Any use of such air or space by others which is injurious to his land, or which constitutes an actual interference with his possession or his beneficial use thereof would be a trespass for which he would have remedy." (*Hinman* v. *Pacific Air Transport,* 9 Cir. 83 F.2d 755, 758.)

Appellees call our attention to various authorities that hold that although the old *ad coelum* doctrine has given way to the reality of present-day conditions, an unreasonable and improper use of the air space over the owner's land can constitute a trespass. Other cases . . . apparently hold that the landowner, while not owning or controlling the entire air space over his property, is entitled to protection against improper or unreasonable use thereof or entrance thereon. . . .

We believe that under our system of government the landowner is entitled to such precipitation as nature deigns to bestow. We believe that the landowner is entitled, therefore and thereby, to such rainfall as may come from clouds over his own property that nature in her caprice may provide. It follows, therefore, that this enjoyment of or entitlement to the benefits of nature should be protected by the courts if interfered with improperly and unlawfully.

Davies v. Carnation Company
352 F.2d 393 (1965)

The plaintiff, claiming to be a researcher in the food industry, had written an unsolicited letter to one D. D. Peebles who had developed a powdered milk product which was distributed by the Carnation Company under the name Carnation Instant Milk. In the letter she expressed interest in testing the product in her "home test kitchen." The letter was referred to the Carnation Company. The plaintiff subsequently wrote that in testing Carnation Instant Milk, she had "found a value and property therein, which is both unexpected and extremely important from the marketing and promotional aspect." She inquired as to whether she should discuss the matter with Mr. Peebles or "contact the Carnation Company directly." She concluded, "The marketing ideas we develop we assign to an interested company, in consideration of a fee or a retainer arrangement." Thereafter, the general manager of Carnation's commercial sales division advised her of his plan to visit New York City, and expressed interest in meeting with her at her convenience. This brought a written reply, in which she said:

> (a) I am ready to make written disclosure to you which if you accept or use in connection with Patent protection, or any other purpose, you would compensate me the sum of $3500. And, I am also ready to serve in a consulting capacity to your firm, or advertising agency, for an amount to be discussed. (b) If you do not use the subject of my disclosure, you will not be obligated to me.

Thereafter, a representative of Carnation's corporate department wrote a letter informing her that, because of certain considerations, Carnation had adopted a policy of not considering any suggestion or idea of this type unless the person wishing to submit the idea or suggestion first signs a release form. After receiving this letter, she replied, protesting that the nature of her work demanded an arrangement opposed to Carnation's general policy. The company replied, stating, in effect, that the policy was inflexible. Later the plaintiff wrote: "To facilitate your evaluating the project and its timeliness with respect to your competition and to determine your position, I am enclosing a complete disclosure, as I have faith and trust in the fair dealings of your company." The enclosed "disclosure" was a document containing a recommendation as to an approach by which Carnation's advertisement of its product could be improved. The only unique idea which the appellant claims to have included within her "disclosure" is that of advertising and promoting the "pouring or sprinkling" of "dry milk into warm or hot liquids, or food mixtures, during the usual cooking processes." Promptly, in a letter Carnation stated that it had "no interest in acquiring whatever rights you may have to these ideas," and pointed out, in effect, that while Carnation had not chosen to advertise the use of its products with heated liquids, the company had conducted tests and was familiar with the product's properties for such use.

Approximately eight years later, the plaintiff instituted her suit. Her complaint alleged that Carnation failed to return the report which she voluntarily forwarded on July 27, 1955, and thereby wrongfully converted property belonging to her to its own use and benefit.

The District Court dismissed the complaint and she appealed.

ELY, J. . . . The District Court was correct in its conclusion that the contents of the report revealed no substantial uniqueness or novelty to Carnation. The record reveals that Mr. Peebles, during the development of his process, tried and tested the product in warm and heated mixtures and that, as a matter of fact, the label affixed to the product before its distribution was undertaken by Carnation recommended "To hot and cold beverages, soups, etc. add PEEBLES INSTANT MILK to taste. In cooking and baking, for extra nourishment, extra richness, simply use more dry PEEBLES INSTANT MILK." A mere idea without novelty is not a property right to which one may claim exclusive ownership. (Cases cited) This most certainly is true when the one against whom the right is asserted has already entertained the idea and shared it with the general public. The fact that Carnation, at a time subsequent to its receipt of appellant's report, commenced to advertise the product for use with warm and heated liquids, as Peebles had done before, as Carnation had not done, and as appellant had recommended, did not create in appellant a property right which she had not previously enjoyed. . . .

Appellant's claim, under federal antitrust law, of a right to recover for Carnation's alleged conspiracy with others to interfere with the use of her services by defendant's competitors is baseless. Violations of the prohibitions of the antitrust laws are subject to complaint by "any person who shall be injured in his business or property" by reason of such violations. . . . The allegations, coupled with the facts and their legal effect, make it clear that there can be no support for a conclusion that if Carnation and others did conspire in the alleged manner, appellant was thereby "injured" in her "business or property."

Affirmed.

CHAPTER 49
REVIEW QUESTIONS AND PROBLEMS

1. Are trade secrets property?
2. *A* gave *B* a promissory note for $1,000 to evidence a valid debt. *C* then negligently destroyed the note. Has *B* lost a property right?
3. After serving as Navy frogmen for many years, *A* and *B* began a diving business. They had been in business twelve years when the state of Louisiana enacted legislation regulating divers. It included a provision that a diver must have five years experience under a licensed diver before he could be individually licensed. *A* and *B* do not have such experience. Do *A* and *B* have any property right which is being taken away by this law?
4. The ABC Movie Company released a film which included, among other things, a comedy-burlesque ridiculing a famous university. The school's name and symbols were used in the film. May the school obtain an injunction based on infringement of its property rights in its names or symbols?
5. *A* stores merchandise in *B*'s warehouse and receives a negotiable warehouse receipt as evidence of the bailment. What property concepts are involved in this transaction? How would these relationships be changed if *A* indorsed the warehouse receipt to *C*?
6. *A* operates a dairy farm. Fumes from a nearby smelter permeate the air and cause *A*'s pastures to become tainted with chemicals. As a result the milk produced by his cows is not marketable. Have *A*'s property rights been violated? Does he have any legal remedy?
7. A Company operates a large sawmill in Forest City. The company plans to build a paper mill at the site in order to utilize sawdust and other waste products produced by the mill. The new paper mill would be an economic advantage to Forest City but would produce vile odors. What property problems are raised by these facts?
8. *A* has operated a slaughterhouse and meat-packing plant on the outskirts of a city for many years. Over time the city has grown and now *A*'s property is within the city limits in a residential area. The noise and odors of *A*'s operation are offensive to people living in the vicinity. What conflicts of property interests do you see in this situation?

chapter 50

Personal Property

7-7. Introduction. Property rights exist in relation to both tangible and intangible things. The term "personal property" encompasses tangible objects such as goods; intangibles refers to such things as goodwill, patents, and trademarks. Intangible personal property has value just as has tangible property, and each can be transferred. The term "chattel" is used to describe personal property generally. Chattels may also be classified as *chattels real* and *chattels personal.* Chattels real describes an interest in land, such as a leasehold. Chattels personal is applied to movable personal property.

When chattel is used in connection with intangible personal property, such property is referred to as *chattels personal in action.* Chattels personal in action, or "choses in action" as they are frequently called, is used to describe those things to which one has a right to possession, but concerning which he may be required to bring some legal action in order ultimately to enjoy possession. Any contract right may be said to be a chose in action. A negotiable instrument is a common form of chose in action. Although the instrument itself may be said to be property, in reality it is simply evidence of a right to money, and it may be necessary to maintain an action to reduce the money to possession. It is noted that the negotiable instrument is movable and thus also a chattel personal.

7-8. The Distinction Between Real and Personal Property. The distinction between real and personal property is significant in three situations: (1) in determining the law applicable to a transaction; (2) in matters of inheritance; and (3) in the methods that may be used to transfer the property. The first situation refers to the principles and problems of conflict of laws that arise in connection with various types of property. As a general rule, conflict of laws principles provide that the law of the situs—the law of the state where real property is located—determines all legal questions concerning such property.

Legal issues concerning conflict of laws relating to personal property are not so easily resolved. Conflict of laws rules may refer to the law of the owner's domicile to resolve some questions, and to the law of the state with the most significant contacts with the property to resolve others. The law of the situs is also used to resolve conflicts, especially when the property involved is movable. Therefore, the description of property as real or personal has a significant impact on the determination of the body of law which is used to decide legal issues concerning the property.

The second situation in which the distinction is important is in matters of inheritance. If a person dies leaving a will, he is said to die testate. His personal property passes to the executor named in the will, to be distributed in accordance with the terms of the will, and his real property passes to the devisees named in the will.

When a person dies without leaving a will, he is said to die intestate and his property passes in conformity with the laws of "intestate succession," which are part of the probate law of every state. The laws of intestate succession frequently have different provisions for real estate than for personal property. For example, assume that *D* died leaving *W,* his widow, and *C,* a child, as his only heirs at law. A typical intestate statute might provide that the widow is entitled to all personal property but to only one-half of the real property of the deceased. In such cases, the importance of the distinction between real and personal property is obvious.

Conflict of laws problems arise in inheritance situations also. The laws of intestate succession vary from state to state. In some states, a widow might only be entitled to one-third of the real estate and one-half of the personal property. In such a case, the conflict of laws principles and the designation of each item of property as real or personal determine the interests of the heirs. Generally, according to conflict of laws principles, real property passes in accordance with the law of the situs, whereas personal property intestate succession is controlled by the domicile of the owner without regard to the physical location of the property. Therefore, real property descends to the persons designated as heirs by the law of the situs; personal property passes to the person appointed administrator by the court of the decedent's domicile. He distributes the estate of the deceased in accordance with the laws of intestacy of that state.

In connection with property passing on death, it will be recalled that the Uniform Partnership Act provides: "A partner's interest in the partnership is *personal property.*" It also provides that on death of a partner his right in *specific partnership property* vests in the surviving partners and is not a part of his estate. The estate has a general claim for the value of his interest only.

The distinction between real and personal property is also significant during the lifetime of the owner in determining the methods by which the property can be transferred. The methods of transferring personal property and real property are substantially different. Formal instruments such as deeds are required to transfer an interest in land, whereas few formalities are required in the case of personal property. A bill of sale may be used in selling personal property, but it is not generally required and does not in any event involve the technicalities of a deed. For example, a motor vehicle transfer may require the delivery of a certificate of title, but, as mentioned above, the transfer of personal property is as a rule quite simply accomplished, whereas formality is required to transfer real property.

7-9. Methods of Acquiring Title.   Title to personal property may be acquired through any of the following methods: original possession, transfer, accession, or confusion. Original possession is a method of extremely limited applicability. It may be used to obtain title over things such as wild animals and fish, for example, that are available for appropriation by individuals. Property which is in its native state and over which no one as yet has taken full and complete control belongs to the first person who reduces such property to his exclusive possession. Property once reduced to ownership, but later discarded, belongs to the first party next taking possession.

In addition to the above, it might be said that property created through mental or physical labor belongs to the creator unless he has agreed to create it for someone else, being induced to do so because of some compensation that has been agreed to by the interested parties. Such items as books, inventions, and trademarks might be included under this heading. This kind of property is usually protected by the government through means of copyrights, patents, and trademarks.

7-10. Title by Transfer.   Personal property may be transferred by sale, gift, will, or operation of law. The law relating to transfer by sale has previously been discussed in connection with Article 2 of the Uniform Commercial Code. It will be recalled that other articles of the Code specify the methods of transfer for intangibles such as negotiable instruments, accounts receivable, stock certificates, and the like. Also, since title to personal property may be encumbered as by way of an outstanding security interest, the records must be searched in order to determine the nature of the title.

There are three elements of a valid gift—intention to make the gift, delivery, and acceptance of the gift. From a legal standpoint, the element of delivery is the most significant because the law requires an actual physical change in possession of the property, with the owner's consent.

In the case of choses in action, the transfer of possession usually takes place by means of an assignment; the exception being negotiable instruments, which may be transferred either by assignment or negotiation. It will be recalled that a promise to make a gift is ordinarily not enforceable because no consideration is present to support the promise. However, an executed gift—one accomplished by delivery of the property to the donor—cannot be rescinded except in the case of a gift *causa mortis,* discussed later. The delivery can be either actual, constructive or symbolic as the situation may demand. Thus, if the property is in storage, the donor could make a delivery by giving the donee the warehouse receipt. A donor may also accomplish delivery by giving the donee something that is a token representing the latter's dominion and control. For example, a key to a strongbox given to a person with words indicating an intent to make a gift of the contents, would constitute the symbol for delivery of the gift.

It was previously noted that gifts *causa mortis* constitute an exception to the general rule on the finality of completed gifts. A gift *causa mortis* is in contemplation of death and refers to the situation in which a person who is, or who believes that he is, facing death makes a gift on the assumption that death is imminent. A person about to embark on a perilous trip or to undergo a serious operation, or one who has an apparently incurable and fatal illness might make a gift and deliver the item to the donee on the assumption that he is not long for this world. If he returns safely, the operation is successful, or the illness is miraculously cured, the donor is allowed to revoke the gift and recover the property from the donee.

A person's property is also transferred on his death. Such transfer will be to persons named in his will, or if he dies intestate, it will be to the heirs as named in the applicable law of descent and distribution (intestate statute).

The requirements of a valid will vary from state to state, but all states require that a person signing his will be of sound mind and memory and not be acting under duress or undue influence. Sound mind and memory is usually defined as the capacity to know the nature and extent of property owned, the capacity to know the natural objects of one's affection, and to make a scheme of distribution. The degree of mental capacity required in making a will is not as high as that required in entering contracts. Wills usually must be attested by two or more credible witnesses. It should be noted that with the exception of the rights of spouses—rights created by statute—testators can make whatever disposition of their property they desire. These rights of spouses generally include the right to renounce the will and take a statutory share in the estate or to elect dower. This latter subject will be discussed in the next chapter on real property. The net effect of these laws is to guarantee a spouse a minimum share of the estate.

Transfers by operation of law include such transfers as judicial sales, mortgage foreclosures, and intestate succession. In most cases of transfer of property, the transferee takes no better title than his transferor had. This is true even though the transferee believes that his transferor has a good title. Thus, an innocent purchaser from a thief obtains no title to the property purchased, and no subsequent purchaser stands in any better position. However, if the transferor of the property has a voidable title, and he sells property to an innocent purchaser, the transferee may obtain good title to the property. This topic is discussed in the Book on the Uniform Commercial Code from the standpoint of the "purchaser in the ordinary course of business" and the "good-faith purchaser for value."

7-11. Accession. *Accession* literally means "adding to." In the law of personal property, accession has two basic meanings. First of all, it refers to the right of an owner to all that his property produces. For example, the owner of a cow is also the owner of each calf born, and the owner of lumber is the owner of a table made from the lumber by another. Accession is also the legal term used to signify the acquisition of title to personal property when it is incorporated into other property or joined with other property. Problems of accession have been discussed in connection with secured transactions (Section 3-150), wherein the rights of parties with a security in the accession and in the whole are discussed, together with the right of removal of the accession in the event of default. The rights of secured parties when goods are commingled or processed are discussed in Section 3-151.

When accession occurs, the issue of who has title is frequently litigated. The general rule is that when the goods of two different owners are united together without the willful misconduct of either party, the title to the resulting product goes to the owner of the major portion of the goods. This rule is based on the principle that personal property permanently added to other property and forming a minor portion of the finished product becomes part and parcel of the larger unit; and since the title can be in only one party, it is in the owner of the major portion. The owner of the minor portion may recover damages, if his portion were wrongfully taken from him. The law of accession simply prevents the owner of the minor portion from recovering the property.

To illustrate the foregoing, assume that X owns some raw materials, and that Y inadvertently uses these materials to manufacture a product. The product belongs to X. If Y also adds some raw materials of his own, the manufactured product belongs to the party who contributed the major portion of the materials. If Y becomes the owner, X is entitled to recover his damages. If X is the owner, Y is not entitled to anything, since he used X's materials.

A similar issue arises when one party repairs goods of another without authority. In such a case, the owner is entitled to the goods as repaired irrespective of the value of the repair, unless the repairs can be severed without damaging the original goods.

The law of accession distinguishes between the rights of "innocent" and "willful" trespassers, although both are wrongful. An innocent trespasser to personal property is one who acts through mistake or conduct, less than intentionally wrongful. A willful trespasser cannot obtain title, as against the original owner, under any circumstances. As a general rule, an innocent trespasser does not acquire title by adding labor or materials, but three exceptions based on the majority ownership concept are generally recognized. First of all, if the property used by the trespasser loses its identity because of the mistake, the trespasser has title; and the original owner is limited to a suit for damages. It is difficult to apply this loss of identity rule. For example, it has been held that lumber made into a table does not lose its identity, whereas lumber incorporated into a garage does. The second exception occurs when there is great disparity in relative values, and the third occurs when a new product distinct from the raw materials is the result of the work and the innocent trespasser adds the major portion of the product.

The foregoing principles are applicable to the remedies available to one whose property is involved in an issue of accession. Under the legal principles of accession, the owner may claim the property if there is no change of title. If title does pass, the owner may bring suit for damages. If the suit is against an innocent trespasser, the owner receives the value before the additions. If the owner decides not to contest the title of a wrongful trespasser (the trespasser's title is good as against all but the original owner), the owner is entitled to recover the value of the property, as enhanced by the wrongdoer's labor and materials.

If the property involved in an issue of accession is sold to a good-faith purchaser, the rights and liabilities of the owner and the third party are the same as those of the original trespasser. A willful trespasser has no title and can convey none. The owner can get the property back without any liability to the third party. If the third party makes improvements or repairs, he has the right to remove his additions if they can be removed without damaging the original goods.[1] An innocent trespasser can convey this right to remove to a good-faith purchaser.

7-12. Confusion. Property of such a character that one unit may not be distinguished from another unit and that is usually sold by weight or measure is known as fungible property. Grain, hay, logs, wine, oil, and other similar articles afford illustrations of property of this nature. Such property, belonging to various parties, often is mixed by intention of the parties, and occasionally by accident, unintentional mistake, or by the wrongful misconduct of an owner of some of the goods. Confusion of fungible property belonging to various owners, assuming that no misconduct (confusion by consent, accident, or unintentional mistake) is involved, results in an undivided ownership of the total mass. To illustrate: Grain is stored in a public warehouse by many parties. Each owner holds an undivided interest in the total mass, his particular interest being dependent upon the amount stored by him. Should there be a partial destruction of the total mass, the loss would be divided proportionately.

Confusion of goods which results from the wrongful conduct of one of the parties causes the title to the total mass to pass to the innocent party. If the mixture is divisible, an exception exists, and the wrongdoer, if he is able to show that the resultant mass is equal in value per unit to that of the innocent party, is able to recover his share. Where the new mixture is worth no less per unit than that formerly belonging to the innocent party, the wrongdoer may claim his portion of the new mass by presenting convincing evidence of the amount added by him. If two masses are added together and the wrongdoer can only establish his proportion of one mass, he is entitled to that proportion of the combined mass.[2]

7-13. Abandoned, Lost, and Mislaid Property. Property is said to be abandoned whenever it is discarded by the true owner, who, at that time, has no intention of reclaiming it. Such property belongs to the first individual again reducing it to possession.[3]

Property is lost whenever, as a result of negligence, accident, or some other cause, it is found at some place other than that chosen by the owner. Title to lost property continues to rest with the true owner. Until the true owner has been ascertained, the finder may keep it, and his title is good as against everyone except the true owner. The rights of the finder are superior to those of the person in charge of the property upon which the lost article is found. Occasionally, state statutes provide for newspaper publicity concerning articles which have been found. Under these statutes, if the owner cannot be located, the found property reverts to the state or county if its value exceeds an established minimum.

Mislaid or misplaced property is such as is intentionally placed by the owner at a certain spot in such a manner as to indicate that he merely forgot to pick it up. In such a case the presumption is that he will later remember where he left it and return for it. The owner of the premises upon which it is found is entitled to hold such property until the true owner is located.

[1] Farm Bureau Mut. Automobile Ins. Co. v. Moseley, page 1011
[2] Troop v. St. Louis Union Trust Co., page 1012
[3] Nippon Shosen Daisha, K. K. v. United States, page 1012

7-14. Multiple Ownership.   Title to personal property may be held by two or more people. Such owners may be tenants in common or joint tenants. If the owners are tenants in common, they are entitled to equal use of the property or to their portion of the income derived from its use. In the event of the death of one of the co-owners, his share in the property passes to the executor named in the will or to the administrator of his estate.

If property is held in joint tenancy, the interest of a deceased owner automatically passes to the surviving joint owner. Such property is not subject to probate or to the debts of the deceased joint tenant. Because of these facts, husbands and wives also frequently hold personal property jointly. Joint tenancy of personal property does not arise unless a contract between the co-owners clearly states that such is the case and that the right of survivorship is to apply. Bank signature cards and stock certificates that use the term joint tenancy or "with the right of survivorship" create such a contract.

BAILMENTS OF PERSONAL PROPERTY

7-15. Definition of Bailment.   Possession of property is often temporarily surrendered by the owner. In such cases the person taking possession may perform some service pertaining to the goods, after which he returns them to the owner. Upon many occasions one person borrows or rents an article which belongs to another. A contract whereby possession of personal property is surrendered by the owner with provision for its return at a later time forms a *bailment.* The owner of the goods is known as the *bailor,* whereas the one receiving possession is called the *bailee.* From the foregoing definition it appears that three distinct requisites of a bailment exist. The three requisites are (1) retention of title by bailor; (2) possession and temporary control of the property by the bailee; (3) ultimate possession to revert to the bailor unless he orders it transferred to some designated third person. It is to be noted that a mere change in the form of the property while in the hands of the bailee does not affect the relationship. Thus, *A* floats logs downstream to *B,* to be sawed into lumber by the latter. *B* is as much a bailee of the lumber as he was of the logs.

7-16. Types of Bailment.   Bailments group naturally into three classes: bailments for the benefit of the bailor; bailments for the benefit of the bailee; and bailments for the mutual benefit of the bailor and the bailee. Typical of the first group are those cases in which the bailor leaves goods in the safekeeping of the bailee under circumstances that negative the idea of compensation. Inasmuch as the bailee is not to be paid in any manner, the bailment is for the exclusive benefit of the bailor. A bailment for the benefit of the bailee is best exemplified by a loan of some article. Thus, *A* borrows *B*'s automobile for a day. The bailment is one for the sole benefit of *A.*

The most important type of bailment is the one in which both parties are to benefit. Contracts for repair, carriage, storage, or pledge of property fall within this class. The bailor receives the benefit of some service; the bailee benefits by the receipt of certain agreed compensation; thus both parties profit as a result of the bailment.

7-17. Degree of Care Required.   Provided that proper care has been exercised by the bailee, any loss or damage to the property bailed follows title and consequently falls upon the bailor. Each type of bailment requires a different degree of care. In a bailment for the benefit of the bailor, the bailee is required to exercise only slight care, while, in one for the benefit of the bailee, extraordinary care is required.[4] A bailment for the mutual benefit of the parties demands only ordinary care on the part of the bailee. *Ordinary care* is defined as that care which the average individual usually exercises over his own property.[5]

In addition to the duty to exercise care, the bailee promises to return the property undamaged upon termination of the bailment. In an action by a bailor against a bailee based upon a breach of the contract of bailment, when the bailor proves delivery of the bailed property and the failure of the bailee to redeliver upon legal demand therefor, a prima facie case of want of due care is thereby established and the burden of going forward with the evidence shifts to the bailee to explain his failure to redeliver.[6]

The Uniform Commercial Code, Article 7—Documents of Title provides: "A warehouseman is liable for loss of or injury to the goods caused by his failure to exercise such care in regard to them as a reasonably careful man would exercise under like circumstances but unless otherwise agreed he is not liable for damages which could have been avoided by the exercise of such care." However, provision is made for the continued effective operation of any statute (state or federal) which imposes more rigid standards of responsibility for some or all failures.

Furthermore, the amount of care demanded varies with the nature and value of the article bailed. The care found to be sufficient in the case of a carpenter's tool chest would probably not be ample for a diamond ring worth $10,000. A higher standard of protection is required for valuable articles than for those less valuable.

Property leased by the bailor to the bailee must be reasonably fit for the service desired. For this reason it is the duty of the bailor to notify the bailee of all defects in the property leased, of which he might reasonably have been aware.[7] The bailor is responsible for any damage suffered by the bailee as the result of such defects, unless he notifies the bailee of them. This rule holds true even though the bailor is not aware of the defect if, by the exercise of reasonable diligence, he could have discovered it. If, on the other hand, the article is merely loaned to the bailee—a bailment for the benefit of the bailee—the bailor's duty is to notify the bailee only of known defects. A bailor who fails to give the required notice of a defect is liable to any person who might be expected to use the defective article as a result of the bailment. Employees of the bailee and members of the bailee's family may usually recover of the bailor for injuries received as a consequence of the defect.

[4] Clack-Nomah Flying Club v. Sterling Aircraft Inc., page 1013
[5] Althoff v. System Garages, Inc. page 1014
[6] David v. Lose, page 1016
[7] Perry v. Richard Chevrolet, Inc., page 1018

7-18. Exculpatory Clauses.   Bailees frequently desire to disclaim liability for damage to the property that may occur while it is in their possession. An exculpatory clause disclaiming liability for negligence is illegal if the bailee is a quasi-public institution because such contracts are against public policy. This subject was discussed in detail in the Book on Contracts in Section 2-60.

More and more bailees are being classified as quasi-public because of the inequality of bargaining power between the bailor and bailee that prevails in many situations. Not all exculpatory clauses seek to eliminate liability completely; some seek to limit the amount of damages. Contracts limiting the amount of damages are looked upon more favorably than absolute disclaimers because it is fair for both parties to know the value of the property and the risk it presents. In accordance with this theory, the Uniform Commercial Code provides that damages may be limited by a term in the warehouse receipt or storage agreement limiting the amount of liability in case of loss or damage. However, a warehouseman cannot disclaim the obligation of reasonable care by such agreement.

7-19. Rights and Duties of Bailee.   The bailment agreement governs the duties and rights of the bailee. Should he treat the property in a different manner, or use it for some purpose other than that contemplated by the contract, he becomes liable for any loss or damage to the property in the interim. This is true even though the damage can in no sense be attributed to the conduct of the bailee. To illustrate: Let us assume that *A* stores his car in *B's* public garage for the winter. *B,* because of a crowded condition, has the car temporarily moved to another garage without the consent of *A.* As the result of a tornado, the car is destroyed while at the second location. The loss falls upon *B,* as he exceeded the terms of the bailment contract. In a restricted sense, the bailee is guilty of conversion of the bailor's property during the period in which the contract terms are being violated.

The bailee has no right to deny the title of the bailor unless the bailee has yielded possession to one having paramount title. In other words, the bailee has no right to retain possession of the property merely because he is able to prove that the bailor does not have title. In order to defeat the bailor's right to possession, the bailee must show that he has turned the property over to someone having better title, or that he is holding the property under an agreement with the true owner.

COMMON CARRIERS AS BAILEES

7-20. Definition.   A common, or public, carrier is distinguished from a private carrier in that the former performs a public service for all, so that it will be liable for refusal, without excuse, to carry for all who might apply. A private carrier is one who undertakes by special arrangement to transport property without being bound to serve everyone who may request service. A private carrier may advertise and secure as much business as possible without losing the status of a private carrier.

Common carriers are licensed by public bodies such as the Interstate Commerce Commission or the commerce commissions of the various states. Their rates are uniform and a matter of public record and regulation. Rates will be further discussed in Section 7-24.

A common carrier may specialize; that is, it may restrict itself to carrying a particular type of goods, it may specialize in the means of transportation it employs, or limit its services to a specific area. Common carriers do not undertake to carry by any means, any and all property to any place. Each is limited for practical reasons, and the area served, types of goods carried, and the methods employed are all set forth in the certificate of public convenience and necessity issued by the appropriate regulatory agency governing common carriers. These certificates give common carriers a limited monopoly. In addition, they may be taxed at different rates than private carriers and they do not have freedom of contract. For example, as previously noted, their rates are regulated as is the territory served.

7-21. Care Required of the Common Carrier.

The contract for carriage of goods constitutes a mutual benefit bailment, but the care required of the carrier greatly exceeds that of the ordinary bailee. A common carrier is an absolute insurer of the safe delivery of the goods to their destination. This rule is subject to only five exceptions. Any loss or damage that results from (1) an act of God, (2) action of an alien enemy, (3) order of public authority, (4) inherent nature of the goods, or (5) misconduct of the shipper must fall upon the one possessing title. Thus, any loss that results from an accident or the willful misconduct of some third party must be borne by the carrier. For example, *A,* in order to injure a certain railway company, sets fire to several boxcars loaded with freight. Any damage to the goods falls upon the carrier. On the other hand, if lightning, an act of God, had set fire to the cars, the loss would have fallen upon the shipper.

Any damage to goods in shipment that results from the very nature of the goods, from improper crating, or from failure to protect the property must be suffered by the shipper. Thus, if a dog dies because his crate was poorly ventilated, the shipper is unable to recover from the carrier.

Goods may be damaged while in the possession of either the receiving or a connecting carrier. Damages arising while goods are being transported by a connecting carrier may be recovered by the shipper from either of the two carriers. If the shipper files a claim against the original carrier, in turn, demands restitution from the connecting carrier. The burden is on the shipper to prove that the goods were in good condition at the time and place of shipment.[8]

7-22. Contract Against Liability of Carrier.

The discussion in Section 7-18 on exculpatory clauses is applicable to carriers. Although a common carrier may not contract away its liability for goods damaged in shipment, it may limit the liability to a stated amount. A carrier may also, where lower rates are granted, relieve self from the consequences of causes or of conduct over which has no control. Such a provision in effect incorporates the five exceptions to the insurer rule stated above.

The Uniform Commercial Code provides: "A carrier who issues a bill of lading whether negotiable or non-negotiable must exercise the degree of care

---

[8] Florence Banana Corp. v. Pennsylvania Railroad, page 1018

in relation to the goods which a reasonably careful man would exercise under like circumstances." However, it must be noted that federal legislation will control interstate shipments and the Code stipulates that the section quoted "does not repeal or change any law or rule of law which imposes liability upon a common carrier for damages not caused by its negligence."

Since a carrier may limit liability to an agreed valuation, the shipper is limited in his recovery to the value asserted in the bill of lading. The rate charged for transportation will vary with the value of the property shipped. It is for this reason that the agreed valuation is binding.

7-23. Duration of the Relation.   The liability of the carrier attaches as soon as the goods are delivered to him. The receipt of the goods is usually acknowledged by a bill of lading, which sets forth the terms and conditions of shipment. The carrier becomes responsible for a carload shipment as soon as the car has been delivered to him. If the car is loaded while located upon railroad property, the carrier becomes liable at the moment the car is fully loaded.

The extreme degree of care required of the carrier may be terminated before the goods are actually delivered to the consignee. Three views prevail in this country as to when the relationship of the carrier ceases. Some states hold that the duties of the carrier end and those of a warehouseman begin as soon as the local shipment is unloaded from the car into the freight house. Others hold the carrier to strict liability until the consignee has had a reasonable time in which to inspect and remove the shipment. Still other states hold that the consignee is entitled to notice and that he has a reasonable time after notice in which to remove the goods before the liability of the carrier as a carrier is terminated. To illustrate: Let us assume that goods arrive at their destination and are unloaded in the freight house. Before the consignee has had time to take them away, the goods are destroyed by fire, although the carrier has exercised ordinary care. Under the first of these views, the loss would fall upon the shipper, as at the time of the fire the railway was no longer a carrier but a warehouseman. Under the other two views, the loss would fall on the carrier, as the extreme liability had not yet terminated, inasmuch as no time had been given for delivery.

The carload shipment is delivered as soon as it is placed on the private switch of the consignee or "spotted" at the unloading platform. Any subsequent loss, unless it results from the negligence of the carrier, must fall upon the owner of the goods.

7-24. Rates.   Rates charged by common carriers must be reasonable. Carriers engaged in interstate business are subject to the regulation of the Interstate Commerce Commission and all tariffs or rate schedules must be filed with the I.C.C. and approved. Almost all the states have commissions for the purpose of establishing rates for intrastate business. These commissions also require tariffs to be filed with them. Any rate either higher or lower than that shown in the approved tariff is illegal. Discriminatory rates by the use of rebates are also forbidden, and the giving or receiving of rebates constitutes a crime.

A carrier may insist upon the payment of the charges at the time it accepts the delivery. Since it has a lien upon the goods as security for the charges, however, it customarily waits until the goods are delivered, before collecting. The carrier usually refuses to surrender the goods unless the freight is paid, and, if the freight remains unpaid for a certain period of time, it may advertise the property for sale. Any surplus, above the charges, realized from the sale reverts to the owner of the goods.

Any undue delay on the part of the consignee in removing the goods from the warehouse or the tracks of the railway permits the carrier to add a small additional charge known as demurrage.

PERSONAL PROPERTY CASES

Farm Bureau Mut. Automobile Ins. Co. v. Moseley
90 A.2d 485 (Ill.) 1950

Plaintiff sued to recover a stolen automobile. The defendant had purchased the automobile from a used car dealer. The motor in the car had been removed and a new one had been put in its place by the thief. Defendant had added a sun visor, seat covers, and gasoline tank.

RICHARDS, J. . . . The owner of goods or chattels which have been stolen is not divested of his ownership of the property by the larcenous taking. He may follow and reclaim the stolen property wherever he finds it.

A sale by the thief, or by any person claiming under the thief, does not divest title to the property in the purchaser as against the legal owner. The fact that the sale was made in the ordinary course of business and the purchaser acted in good faith makes no difference.

The subsequent possession by the thief is a continuing wrong, and if the wrongdoer increases the value of the property by his labor upon it, or by substituting parts for those which were on it when he acquired it, or by adding new parts to it, the property in its enhanced value or changed condition, still belongs to the original owner and he may retake it with the accessions thereto.

The automobile in question having been identified as stolen property, the defendant Moseley has no title to it as against the claim of the plaintiff. . . .

The property right to the automobile being in the plaintiff, I render judgment in its favor for the automobile.

The engine which was in the automobile at the time it was stolen from Mr. Grunwell, having been removed by the thief, or someone who claimed under the thief, and another engine put in its place, the new engine became a part of the automobile and the plaintiff is entitled to retain it as his property.

It does not appear that the defendant Mosely knew that the automobile had been stolen when he purchased it, consequently there was no wilful wrongdoing by him. This being true, he is entitled to the sun visor, seat covers, and gasoline tank which he attached to the automobile while it was in his possession. The distinction between a wilful and involuntary wrongdoer is recognized by the authorities.

.   .   .

So ordered.

Troop v. St. Louis Union Trust Co.

166 N.E.2d 116 (Ill.) 1960

Plaintiff, Troop, the owner of a three-fourths working interest in an oil and gas lease and the manager of it sued the defendant, the owner of the other one-fourth to foreclose a partnership lien because the defendant had not paid his share of the operating expenses for eight years. Plaintiff also owned another lease and had commingled the oil of the two leases. Defendant counterclaimed and asserted that he was entitled to one-fourth of the total oil as commingled. The trial court held that defendant was entitled to one-fourth of the total oil from both leases, and plaintiff appeals.

SCHEINEMAN, J. . . . The doctrine of confusion of goods has been a part of English and American law for continuous centuries. It applies to any type of goods of such uniformity that, after mixing, there is no possibility of identification of the component parts. If the proportionate parts are not ascertainable, equity will declare the innocent party owner of the whole.

. . . [W]hen the commingling is proved, the burden of going forward with evidence to show the correct proportions is on the party who commingled. In the absence of such proof he bears the whole loss.

This appears to be the first case in a court of review in this state, involving the doctrine as applied to oil. We hold that oil is a type of uniform substance to which the doctrine applies. It has been so applied in other states. We cite only one of these cases, which bears some resemblance to this case. *Stone* v. *Marshall Oil Co.,* 208 Pa. 85. In that case the plaintiff owned one-fourth of the gas on one lease, which the defendant had commingled with the gas from eighteen other wells. The master applied the doctrine in question and, of the net proceeds, awarded one-fourth of the total to plaintiff. The trial court sustained exceptions, and required a computation, with the limitation that all doubts be resolved in favor of plaintiff. This rule was reversed by the court of review, which held the master was correct, that plaintiff should have his fraction of the entire amount.

We conclude that the decree properly awarded one-fourth of the commingled oil to Rust, less the expenses properly charged. . . . The decree is affirmed in all respects.

Decree affirmed.

Nippon Shosen Daisha, K.K. v. United States

288 F.Supp 55 (1964)

A vessel, the S.S. *Kokoku Maru,* collided with another ship in the Pacific Ocean and it became necessary for the crew to abandon the vessel. The cargo was phosphate rock and was insured by the Sumitomo Marine and Fire Insurance Co., Ltd. The insurance company had paid the consignee the full value of the cargo. Under a federal statutory procedure instituted by the owner of the vessel, the vessel and its cargo were sold to the highest bidder, and the federal court appointed a Trustee to represent all persons who had legal claims against the vessel. The Trustee would then make a distribution to such claimants. Sumitomo claimed that it was entitled to the proceeds of the sale allocable to the phosphate rock. The representatives of Sumitomo, according to an affidavit submitted by one Chick, had surveyed the vessel and cargo and had concluded that it would be too expensive to try to remove the cargo.

THOMAS, D. J. Court is of the opinion that Sumitomo is not entitled to the proceeds for the phosphate rock cargo because the uncontradicted evidence conclusively shows that both Sumitomo and its insured abandoned said phosphate rock cargo.

Abandonment is the intentional relinquishment of property. The letter of Chick dated July 9, 1963, with the enclosed letters of Sumitomo and of the consignees of the phosphate rock cargo, clearly evidence the intent and the act sufficient to constitute an intentional relinquishment of all right or interest in the phosphate rock cargo.

Sumitomo contends that to be legally effective an abandonment must be voluntary, and that the fact that the parties involved, including Sumitomo and its insured, were mistaken as to the value of the cargo rendered the abandonment legally ineffective.

However, the fact that the parties were mistaken as to the value of the cargo does not render the abandonment by Sumitomo and its insured any less voluntary. The affidavit of Chick, filed on behalf of Sumitomo, shows that Sumitomo and its insured made their decision to abandon the cargo only after careful consideration of information provided by those who made investigations on the scene. The fact that such information and/or their conclusion as to the value of the cargo turned out to be in error does not affect the voluntariness of the decision by Sumitomo and its insured to abandon the cargo.

Sumitomo correctly points out that one cannot abandon property to a particular person. One becomes the owner of abandoned property by subsequently appropriating it. The files and records in the case at bar at present do not reveal any appropriation of the phosphate rock cargo prior to the time when the Trustee, Arimori, acting on behalf of all legally-entitled claimants, listed the cargo in his Notice of Ship Sale. Under this view of the case, therefore, the ownership in the phosphate rock cargo passed directly to the Trustee Arimori, acting on behalf of the legally-entitled claimants. Once abandoned property has been appropriated by another, the former owner who relinquished such property cannot reclaim it. . . .

On the basis of the record presently before the Court, including the affidavits and exhibits filed on behalf of petitioner Sumitomo, the Court concludes that there is no genuine issue of fact with respect to Sumitomo's claim to the $12,467.76 in the registry of the Court representing the proceeds from the sale of the phosphate rock cargo and that the uncontradicted evidence established that Sumitomo and its insured abandoned said cargo.

Accordingly, the petition of Sumitomo for the payment from the registry of the Court of the sum of $12,467.76 is hereby denied, said order, however, is without prejudice to the rights of claimants or Shipowner in said proceeds.

Clack-Nomah Flying Club v. Sterling Aircraft, Inc.

408 P.2d 904 (Utah) 1965

The plaintiff's airplane was flown to Salt Lake City where it landed at defendant's airport. The pilot instructed the caretaker to look after the airplane and told him that it would probably be there for a day. The day in question was a gusty, windy day. About 3 p.m. a sudden heavy wind commenced to blow, the gusts of which were estimated at about 95 miles per hour. The airplane was soon turned over onto its back and destroyed, along with the other equipment.

The defendant contends that the facts merely show that there was a violent wind which caused the accident and that the plaintiff has completely failed to show any negligence which caused or contributed in causing the accident. The trial court took the view that the plaintiff had made a sufficient showing of negligence against the defendant and instructed the jury that the burden of proof was on the plaintiff to prove by a preponderance of the evidence that the defendant was guilty of negligence which proximately caused or contributed in causing the accident, and if the jury so found their verdict should be in favor of the plaintiff and the damages sustained should be determined by it. The jury rendered a verdict for the plaintiff.

WADE, J. This court has consistently held that a bailee for hire is responsible for the value of goods entrusted to him which he fails to return, reasonable wear and tear excepted, and that in such case the burden is on the bailee, defendant here, to show that he is free from negligence in the care of such goods which are placed for hire in his custody. This is the relationship of the parties which the evidence conclusively shows existed here. The plaintiff brought the airplane to defendant's old Salt Lake City airport and left it with the defendant as a bailee for hire for about a day. Under these circumstances, the defendant as the bailee had the burden of proving that the destruction of the airplane was not caused by its negligence and the plaintiff did not have the burden of proving that the defendant was guilty of negligence which proximately caused the destruction of the airplane and the other property. Thus the court's instructions to the jury covered the issue which was directly presented to the jury of whether defendant was guilty of negligence. This instruction was more favorable to the defendant airport, the bailee, than it was entitled to have. It placed the burden of proof on the plaintiff bailor instead of on the defendant bailee.

The fact that the court instructed the jury on the wrong theory of the case, as long as the instructions were more favorable to the defendant than they were entitled to, does not require a new trial.

Judgment affirmed. Costs to respondent.

Althoff v. System Garages, Inc.

371 P.2d 48 (Wash.) 1962

ROSELLINI, J. Damages resulting from the theft of the plaintiff's automobile from the defendant's parking garage, in Seattle, were sought in the instant action.

On the evening of December 19, 1959, the plaintiff left his 1958 Ford Thunderbird at the defendant's garage, where he had often parked before, and received a claim check. According to the custom of the place, he left the key in the ignition.

An intoxicated person was seen by the defendant's employee Lou Kranda at the garage at approximately 12:30 the following morning.

When the plaintiff returned to claim his automobile at approximately 2:38 A.M., it was discovered that it had been stolen. Later it was learned that it had been stolen by the intoxicated man, a sailor, who had driven it into a house in Marysville, severely wrecking it. He was killed in the accident.

This action followed and was tried to the court, which found in favor of the plaintiff. The defendant, appealing, contends that the court was not justified in finding that its employees were negligent. It is urged that the case is not distinguishable from the case of *Ramsden* v. *Grimshaw* (23 Wash.2d 864, 162 P.2d 901), which involved the theft of an automobile from a parking lot.

Speaking of the applicable rule of law, we said:

> The rule on bailment for hire in such a case as the instant one is that a prima facie case of negligence is made out when the bailee is unable to deliver the bailed article. But if the bailee shows the theft of the bailed article under circumstances that do not indicate the negligence of the bailee, the prima facie case fails and the bailor must go forward with proof that the theft resulted from negligence, that is to say from the want of due care of the bailee.

We also observed that, as applied to bailments, ordinary care means such care as ordinarily prudent men, as a class, would exercise in caring for their own property under like circumstance. Also, the usages of a particular business may be presumed to have entered into and formed a part of the contracts and understandings of persons engaged in such business and those who deal with them, and so such usages may have the effect of enlarging or qualifying the liability of a bailee the same as a special contract. . . .

The trial court in this case was justified in finding that the surveillance of the garage at night fell below the standard of reasonable care, and that, had all of the parking levels been kept under observation, the theft could have been prevented.

The defendant makes some argument that its liability should be limited to the sum of $250, because of the following words which appear on the claim check:

> Company shall not be responsible for: Cars after closing time, Loss of Use of cars; Value of or damage to car, or liability to customer, exceeding $250.00.

It is conceded by the defendant that we have adopted the general rule . . . that a professional bailee cannot contract away responsibility for his own negligence or fraud. It was so held in *Ramsden* v. *Grimshaw, supra.* But the defendant suggests that we should adopt a rule allowing a limitation of liability to a "reasonable amount." Inasmuch as there was no showing in this case that the words on the claim check were ever brought to the plaintiff's attention, and no showing that the amount to which the liability was limited was reasonable under the circumstances, we do not have before us facts which would justify a consideration of the question whether such a modification of the rule should be adopted.

The judgment is affirmed.

David v. Lose

218 N.E.2d 442 (Ohio) 1966

HERBERT, J. On February 22, 1964, the plaintiff delivered his registered Tennessee Walking mare, a show horse, to defendants' stables for breeding purposes. Plaintiff was charged a stud fee. The defendants were notified that the mare was skittish and would kick, especially if she were touched about her rear where a surgical operation had been performed on her tail.

The mare was placed in a box stall adjoining that of defendants' stallion. The walls were of solid board and measured seven feet, four inches high. Wire mesh topped the wall. The stall was the customary and conventional type, well constructed and in accepted use in the locality.

About an hour after the mare had been placed in the stall, she was taken out and led in front of the stallion's stall. When the stallion bit her on the neck, she kicked to indicate her displeasure, and she was thereupon returned to her stall.

After another 45-minute period during which the mare was quiet, the defendants' servant, Woodburn, then left his working area where he could observe the mare and engaged in other duties some distance from the barn. After about 18 minutes, he heard a noise in the barn which he thought was a kick.

Woodburn went to the barn, looked into the mare's stall and found her steaming wet and breathing hard. Her leg was broken. The stallion was standing in his stall and picking at the hay.

The mare was destroyed. The plaintiff filed an action in the Municipal Court of Canton, Ohio, against the defendants for their failure to redeliver the mare. The trial court awarded the plaintiff a judgment of $1,214 and costs. The Court of Appeals for Stark County reversed, stating in its journal "that the trial court's findings of fact are sufficient to rebut and counterbalance any presumption of negligence on the part of the defendants, and insufficient as a matter of law to establish negligence on the part of said defendants."

This court allowed plaintiff's motion to certify the record. The cause is now before this court for review.

When the plaintiff entrusted his mare to the defendants for breeding purposes and paid for this service, a bailment for hire was created. The bailee for hire is obligated by law to exercise ordinary care in the safekeeping of the bailor's property. The bailee also promises to return the property undamaged upon the termination of the bailment.

Therefore, the bailor can sue the bailee for breach of either duty, the duty of redelivery or the duty of exercising ordinary care. This was recognized in *Agricultural Ins. Co.* v. *Constantine* (1944), 144 Ohio St. 275. Paragraph two of the syllabus reads as follows:

> Where a bailor delivers property to a bailee and such bailee fails to redeliver the bailed property upon legal demand therefor, a cause of action, either *ex contractu* or *ex delicto,* accrues in favor of the bailor.

In the case at bar, the bailor's petition states a cause of action in contract for breach of the bailees' duty to return the bailed property undamaged. In order to establish a prima facie case, the bailor need prove only (1) the contract of bailment, (2) delivery of the bailed property to the bailees, and (3) failure of the bailees to redeliver the bailed property undamaged at the termination of the bailment.

In order to escape liability, the bailees must then assert and prove some affirmative defense. The bailees in their answer affirmatively plead that "they exercise that degree of prudent care necessary to safely confine and keep said mare until the acts of performance contemplated by the contract were fulfilled." The bailees thus assert that the mare was damaged through no fault of their own. In short, they assert non-negligence as an affirmative defense. The law recognizes this as a legal excuse for failure to redeliver the bailed property undamaged. However, the burden of proof on the issue of the bailees' conduct remains with the bailees throughout the trial. The law on the burden of proof on the issue of negligence in contract cases should be contrasted with that in negligence cases where the bailor, even when proceeding on the basis of *res ipsa loquitur,* has the burden of proof on the issue of negligence throughout the trial.

The rule in contract cases is stated in the fourth paragraph of the syllabus of *Agricultural Ins. Co.* v. *Constantine, supra,* as follows:

> In an action by a bailor against a bailee based upon a breach of the contract of bailment, where the bailor proves delivery of the bailed property and the failure of the bailee to redeliver upon legal demand therefor, a prima facie case of want of due care is thereby *established and the burden of going forward with the evidence shifts to the bailee to explain his failure to redeliver.*

The Court of Appeals failed to draw the distinction between the tort and contract actions available to a bailor and so confused the two that it erroneously applied the doctrine of *res ipsa loquitur* to this action in contract. Although such confusion is not without precedent, it should not be encouraged.

The Court of Appeals failed to recognize that the question is not whether the plaintiff has established negligence but whether the defendants have established a legal excuse for breach of the contract. As it was stated in 8 American Jurisprudence 2d, Bailments, Section 166: "So far as the particular duty under discussion [i.e., the bailee's duty of redelivery] is concerned, it is erroneous to say that a bailee is liable for negligence. He is liable for not delivering the subject of the bailment, but is excused if it has been lost without fault or want of care on his part."

In the case at bar, no legal excuse has been shown. The trial court's statement of facts—which is not disputed by either party—indicates that the stall was properly made, and that it was not the customary practice to station an attendant at all times to watch over the horses. No one knows how the injury to the mare occurred. Even if under the circumstances it is consistent with reasonable care for a bailee to put a mare in such a stall and leave her unguarded for a short duration, proof of those facts is not proof of a legal excuse because it is impossible to determine whether such reasonable conduct is at all relevant to how the injury occurred.

Thus, once it is known how the damage to the bailed property occurred, it is incumbent on the bailee to show that he acted reasonably in that regard. Cf. *Agricultural Ins. Co.* v. *Constantine, supra.* But where, as here, the bailee cannot show how the damage occurred, he must, in order to escape liability, affirmatively prove that he took reasonable precautions under the circumstances to prevent every possibility of damage from actually occurring.

Since the bailees failed to meet that burden and left the question of their conduct in a state of conjecture, the judgment of the trial court is affirmed, and that of the Court of Appeals is reversed.

Judgment reversed.

Perry v. Richard Chevrolet, Inc.

182 N.E.2d 297 (Mass.) 1962

WILKINS, J. The plaintiff sues in tort for personal injuries allegedly caused by the negligence of the defendant in furnishing the plaintiff an automobile in which a radiator hose clamp was defectively installed.

The subsidiary facts . . . were as follows. The plaintiff was planning on November 19, 1957, to purchase an automobile from the defendant, a dealer in motor vehicles. Pending alterations on the car he was to purchase, the defendant turned over to him a 1946 model sedan. The plaintiff was unable to start the motor because of insufficient gasoline in the tank. An employee of the defendant put gasoline in, but the motor still would not turn over. Finally, the employee started the engine, telling the plaintiff that the car was "O.K. now." The plaintiff drove the car from the defendant's premises, a distance of five or six miles, when he heard a "bang" and saw a ball of fire coming from the engine and under the dashboard. His arms and eyebrows were singed by flames. He threw himself into the street and sustained bruises. The fire department extinguished the fire. The plaintiff then noticed that the clamp used to fasten the hose running between the radiator and the engine block was off, and that alcohol was coming out of the radiator. The clamp was found at the bottom of the pan below the radiator hose. The plaintiff was using the automobile for a purpose incidental to the defendant's business. . . .

The defendant owed the duty to the plaintiff to use ordinary care in the circumstances. There is, however, nothing in the subsidiary facts to indicate that the defendant knew or should have known that the hose clamp was defective, if in fact it was defective. Certainly difficulty in starting an automobile in mid-November is no such indication. The finding of negligence in furnishing the vehicle, being based exclusively upon knowledge of or negligent failure to discover a defective hose clamp, cannot stand. On the auditor's report the cause of the accident is unexplained. It is left a matter of conjecture whether the hose clamp becoming detached was the cause of, or was caused by, the explosion.

Exceptions sustained.

Judgment for the defendant.

Florence Banana Corp. v. Pennsylvania Railroad

195 A.2d 309 (D.C.) 1963

MYERS, A. J. Florence Banana Corporation appeals from a judgment upon a directed verdict for appellee in a suit seeking the value of a carload of apples alleged to have been spoiled by negligence in transportation by the carrier.

In early January, 1960, appellant bought four carloads of apples in the state of Washington for shipment east by railroad. Inspections were made of the fruit by the U.S. Department of Agriculture on January 6, 1960, and on April 12, 1960. The apples were shipped at different times; the last carload here involved was moved on May 27, 1960. Appellant claims that the apples in this carload were unspoiled when delivered for shipment, but as a result of the negligence of the carrier in icing and checking the car enroute, they arrived here in improper condition.

The only evidence offered by appellant was the testimony of one witness, the owner of the corporate shipper, who was not present when the apples were purchased, or inspected, or shipped, and who was held by the trial judge, and properly so, incompetent to testify as to his understanding of the contents of certain official inspection reports from the Agriculture Department. Neither the inspectors nor any person who had examined or handled the apples immediately precedent to shipment on May 27, 1960, was called as a witness. The inspection reports, although denied admission at trial because "too remote in time to be material," were thereafter considered by the trial judge in passing upon the sufficiency of all evidence to make a prima facie case for appellant, and found to be of little probative value without a fair explanation of their contents.

It is conceded that the railroad as carrier of perishable goods was subject to the rule, applicable to all bailees, that if goods arrived at their destination in a damaged state, proof of their delivery to the carrier in good condition establishes a prima facie case of negligence, which must be rebutted by competent evidence from the carrier.

We are in accord with the ruling of the trial judge that the evidence, considered in the light most favorable to the appellant, was insufficient in law to prove delivery to the carrier in good condition. Absence of this essential element was fatal to appellant's claim. To submit to the jury upon this meager evidence the question of whether the apples were in good condition at time of their delivery to the shipper would have required mere conjecture or guesswork on their part in order to reach an answer.

We hold that the general testimony of the one witness, plus the inspection reports, unexplained, and the fact that appellant did not make a satisfactory showing that the fruit was delivered to the carrier in good condition (the inspection six weeks before did not suffice for that purpose), failed to establish a prima facie case warranting submission to the jury. The directed verdict was therefore proper and is
Affirmed.

CHAPTER 50
REVIEW QUESTIONS AND PROBLEMS

1. *A* and *B* separated after being married for twenty years. *B*, the wife, moves from Maryland to the District of Columbia, where she files for divorce. Would the District of Columbia court use Maryland or District

of Columbia law in determining the wife's interest in the couple's home, located in Maryland?

2. *X,* by will, left his brother *Y* "all of my tangible personal property." Would this include jewelry? Stocks and bonds? An automobile? A leasehold interest in some land?

3. Confined to a hospital bed, *A,* in anticipation of impending death, gives *B* a note saying "*B,* I hereby give you the contents of my savings account. The passbook is in the top dresser drawer." If *A* recovers, is he entitled to rescind the gift? May *A*'s heirs, if *A* dies, claim that there was no valid gift because there was no delivery?

4. *X,* manager of a clothing store, arranged to have a large portion of his inventory "stolen." *X* then sold the inventory to *Y,* who believed *X*'s representations that *X* owned the property. *Z,* owner of the store in which *X* worked, later learned of the transaction. May *Z* recover the inventory from *Y*?

5. While swimming in a pond on *X*'s farm, several boys discovered some money in a watertight jar on the bottom of the pond. *X* admits it is not his money. Who has the title to the money? Who has the right to possession?

6. While building a garage on *Y*'s property, *X,* a workman, found a wallet containing $1,000, buried under about two inches of dirt. Who has title to the $1,000? Who is entitled to possession?

7. A steamboat, owned by the XYZ Company and loaded with lead castings, sank in the Mississippi River in 1927. The XYZ Company made no effort to locate the boat. In 1961, *A* located the boat and raised it. Does the XYZ Company have any rights against *A*?

8. The XYZ Company furnished equipment to the ABC Company for the production of certain goods. *M,* the lessor of the building in which the ABC Company was located, locked up the building for nonpayment of rent by the ABC Company. Is *M* the bailee of the equipment?

9. While paying for some purchases in *Y*'s store, *X* inadvertently left his wallet containing over $1,000 on the counter. *Y* noticed it, placed it in his file cabinet, and notified *X* by phone. *X* said he would pick it up the next morning. During the night *Y*'s store was burglarized and *X*'s wallet was stolen. May *X* recover from *Y*?

10. The XYZ Motor Company loaned an automobile to *A* while *A*'s car was being repaired. *A* parked the car improperly on a busy street, and it was struck by another auto. May the XYZ Company recover from *A*?

11. *A* purchased construction equipment from the XYZ Company. However, since delivery would take over a month, the company loaned *A* some used equipment. On demand, *A* returned all but one truck, which had been destroyed. May the XYZ Company recover the value of the truck from *A*?

12. *X* shot a polar bear in Alaska and asked *Y,* a taxidermist, to mount it for him. *Y* agreed, but so improperly mounted it that *X* refused delivery and brought an action against *Y.* May *X* recover assuming improper work?

13. Upon registering at the XYZ Hotel, *A* turned his car over to *B,* the bellhop, and told him to put it on the hotel lot. *B* did so, but when *B*

went off duty, he took the car off of the lot with the permission of the lot attendant and demolished it. May *A* recover from the hotel?

14. The XYZ Company, duly licensed by the I.C.C. as a motor carrier, delivered some wood shipped by *B* to *A*. The wood was watersoaked, although there was no evidence that this resulted from the XYZ Company's negligence or fault. May *A* recover of XYZ?

15. *A* shipped some mink skins on the XYZ Airlines. The shipment was hijacked and the skins stolen. May *A* recover from the XYZ Co.?

16. *A*, an 80-year-old man, proclaimed that there were people living in the trees around his home and that they were butchering his cows. In addition to having this delusion, he was an alcoholic. Can *A* make a valid will?

17. While living in Illinois, *X* buys an automobile. *X* then moves to Florida but leaves the automobile in Illinois. If *A* sells the car to *B* in Florida, would Illinois or Florida law govern the transaction?

18. While on vacation in Wisconsin, *X*, a resident of Illinois, purchased some stock of the ABC Company. The ABC Company is a Delaware corporation. The law of which state governs the transaction?

19. *X*, the owner of an interest in a condominium apartment building, died intestate. The intestacy statute gives *Y*, his wife, one-half of all real property, and all of the personal property. What is *Y*'s interest in the condominium apartment?

20. *A* installed a replacement motor in *B*'s automobile. *C* had sold the automobile to *B*, but *B* had not paid *C* in full. In the event that *C* should reclaim the automobile from *B*—which he has a right to do under the sales contract for nonpayment of the purchase price—does *C* or *A* have a better right to the new motor?

21. *A*, who is a resident of Illinois, owns real property in Michigan and personal property that is stored in Virginia. If *A* dies without leaving a will, which state law will determine how his property passes to his heirs?

22. *A* intentionally took corn belonging to *B* and distilled it into whiskey. *B* had the sheriff seize the whiskey, but *A* contends that the whiskey belongs to him because of the great value of the whiskey over the corn. Is *A* correct?

23. *A* owns some lumber which he fraudulently mixes with lumber owned by *B*. The quality of the two piles of lumber was entirely different, but circumstances are such that the amount in each pile can no longer be determined. May *B* retain title to both amounts?

24. *A*, employed by P Hotel Company to paint certain rooms, lifted a rug and found $750 in old bills. Being told by the hotel that the owner was known, he surrendered the money to P Company. The hotel was unable to locate the owner, and *A* demands the money. Is he entitled to it?

25. A common carrier's bill of lading contains a clause relieving it of liability for all loss due to fire of any property in transit. A fire, caused by the negligence of the carrier's agent, destroyed goods in shipment belonging to *B*. Has *B* an action against the carrier?

Real Property

7-25. The Nature of Real Property. The preceding chapter dealt with personal property; the following discussion concerns land and the particular rules of law concerning real property. These rules may consider real property as "a thing" or property as "the subject matter of relationships." Whichever meaning is intended will be manifested by the purposes sought to be accomplished through the use and application of particular rules.

Real property includes not only the land but also things permanently affixed thereto including buildings, fences, trees and shrubbery, and the like. As noted previously, the Uniform Commercial Code–Article 2–Sales makes special provision for the sale of goods to be severed from the realty; and its provisions apply to contracts for the sale of timber, minerals, or the like, or a structure if they are to be severed by the seller. In other words, such transactions, together with a sale of growing crops or other things attached to realty which can be severed without material harm, fall under the heading of personal property. However, these transactions are subject to any third-party rights as disclosed by realty records. The Code also provides that a contract for sale of such items may be recorded as a document transferring an interest in land and it shall then "constitute notice to third parties of the buyers' rights under the contract for sale."

Another area in which there is an overlapping of personal and real property concepts relates to fixtures. Provisions relating to security interests in things attached to or to become attached to realty are dealt with in Secured Transactions (Book 3—see Section 3-149). However, fixture problems do arise in areas other than those involving security interests. These are discussed in the next section.

7-26. Fixtures. The Code does not contain a definition of "fixtures"—it simply provides that the rules of Article 9 do not apply and that no security interests exists in "goods incorporated into a structure in the manner of lumber, bricks, tile, cement, glass, metal work and the like. . . . " The law of the particular state determines when and whether other goods become fixtures. It therefore becomes significant to inquire into the rules generally applicable in making such a determination whether or not personal property has become so affixed to realty as to be a fixture.

There are many definitions of the term "fixtures." In a broad sense, a fixture is an article that formerly had the characteristic of personal property, but upon becoming attached, annexed, or affixed to real property becomes a part of the real property. In order to determine in a particular case whether personal property attached to realty has become part of the realty the following three tests have been developed by the courts:[1]

1. *Annexation test.* The old English law required the chattel to be "let into" or "united" to the land, or to some substance that is a part of the land. A chattel that lies upon the ground is not attached by force of gravity. The test of annexation alone is inadequate, for many things attached to the soil or buildings are not fixtures and many things not physically attached to the soil or buildings are considered fixtures. For example, articles of furniture substantially fastened but capable of easy removal are not necessarily fixtures. Physical annexation may be only for the purpose of more convenient use. On the other hand, machinery that has been annexed, but detached for repairs or other temporary reason, may still be considered a fixture although severed.

Keys, doors, windows, window shades, screens, storm windows, and the like, although readily detachable, are generally considered fixtures because they are an integral part of the building and pertain to its function. The mode and degree of attachment and whether the article can be removed without material injury to the article, the building, or land are often important considerations in determining whether the article is a fixture. Electric ranges connected to a building by a plug or vent pipe under the material-injury test are not fixtures, but the removal of wainscoting, wood siding, fireplace mantels, and water systems, including connecting pipes, would cause a material injury to the building and land.

2. *Adaptation test.* Because the annexation test alone is inadequate to determine what is a fixture, the adaptation test has been developed. Adaptation means that the article is used in promoting the purpose for which the land is used. Thus, if an article is placed upon or annexed to land to improve it, make it more valuable, and extend its use, it is a fixture. Windmills, pipes, pumps and electric motors for irrigation systems, and fruit dryers are examples of chattels that may be so adapted as to become fixtures. This test alone is not adequate because rarely is an article attached or placed upon land except to advance the purpose for which the land is to be used.

3. *Intention test.* Annexation and adaptation as tests to determine whether a chattel has become realty are only part of the more inclusive test of intention. Annexation and adaptation are evidence of an intention to make a chattel a fixture. In addition to annexation and adaptation as evidence of an intention, the following situations and circumstances are also used from which intention is deduced: (1) the kind and character of the article affixed; (2) the relation and situation of the parties making the annexation; for example, the relation of

[1] First Fed. S. & L. Assn. of Willoughby v. Smith, page 1031

landlord and tenant suggests that such items as showcases and machinery, acquired and used by the tenant, are not intended to become permanently part of the real property. Such property is called a trade fixture and is generally intended to be severed at the end of the term; (3) the structure, degree, and mode of annexation; (4) and the purpose and use for which the annexation has been made.[2] Purchasers, lienees, and mortgagees who have no notice of any security arrangement in property that becomes a fixture, are not subject to the security arrangement. The security arrangement is valid between the original parties, but the status of the property as a fixture gives priority to the person with the real property interest.

7-27. Describing Real Property.   Real property may be described by using (1) the metes and bounds system, (2) the congressional survey system, and (3) the plat system. The metes and bounds system establishes boundary lines by reference to natural or artificial monuments, that is, to fixed points, such as roads, streams, fences, trees, etc. A metes and bounds description starts with a monument, determines the angle of the line and the distance to the next monument and so forth until the tract is fully enclosed and described. Because surveyors may not always agree, the law of metes and bounds creates an order of precedence. Courses (angles) control over distances, and it is presumed that lines connect the monuments if the angle is wrong. Some metes and bounds descriptions use only courses and distances starting from a known point.

The term "congressional survey" refers to a system of describing land by using a known base line and principal meridians. The base line runs from east to west, and principal meridians run from north to south. Townships are thus located in relation to these lines. For example, a township may be described as 7 North, Range 3 East of the 3rd Principal Meridian. This township is seven townships North of the base line and three east of the 3rd principal meridian.

The townships are then divided into thirty-six sections, each section being one square mile. (There will be fractional sections due to the convergence of the meridians.) With the exception of the fractional sections, each section consists of 640 acres. Parts of the section are described by their location within it, as the drawing on page 1025 illustrates.

A plat is a recorded document dividing a tract described by metes and bounds or congressional survey into streets, blocks, and lots. The land may thereafter be described in relation to the recorded plat by simply giving the lot number, block, and subdivision name. For example, Lot 8 in Block 7 of Ben Johnson's Subdivision in the City of Emporia, Kansas, might describe real property located in that municipality.

7-28. Methods of Acquisition.   Title to real property may be acquired in several different ways: (1) by original entry, called title by occupancy; (2) by transfer through, and with the consent of, the owner; (3) by judicial sale; (4) by possession of a party under claim of title for the period of the statute of limitations, usually twenty years, called adverse possession; (5) by will; (6) by descent, under intestacy statutes; and (7) by accretion, as when a river or a lake creates new land.

[2] Dean Vincent Inc. v. Redisco, Inc., page 1032.

W1/2 NW1/4 80 acres	E1/2 NW1/4 80 acres	NE1/4 160 acres	
NW1/4 SW1/4 40 acres		N1/2 SE1/4 80 acres	
	SE1/4 SW1/4 40 acres		5 A NE1/4 of SE1/4 of SE1/4 10 acres
			20 acres

Original entry refers to a title obtained from the sovereign. Except in those portions of the United States where the original title to the land was derived from grants that were issued by the king of England and other sovereigns who took possession of the land by conquest, title to all the land in the United States was derived from the United States government. Private individuals who occupied land for the period of time prescribed by federal statute and met such other conditions as were established by law acquired title by patent from the federal government.

7-29. Transfer with the Consent of the Owner. The title to real property is most commonly transferred by the owner's executing a deed to his transferee. A deed is generally a formal instrument under seal. The deeds most generally used are warranty and quitclaim deeds. A warranty deed conveys the fee simple title to the grantee, his heirs, or assigns and is so called because of the covenants on the part of the grantor by which he warrants: (1) that, at the time of the making of the deed, he has fee simple title therein and right and power to convey the same; (2) that the property is free from all encumbrances, except those encumbrances enumerated therein,[3] (3) that his grantees, heirs, or assigns will have the quiet and peaceful enjoyment thereof and that he will defend the title to the property against all persons who may lawfully claim it. In most states the above warranties are implied from the words written in the deed.

There may be circumstances under which the grantor would not wish to make warranties with respect to the title, and under such conditions he may execute a quitclaim deed. Such a deed merely transfers all of the "right, title, and interest" of the grantor to the grantee. Whatever title the grantor has, the grantee receives, but the grantor makes no warranties. A quitclaim deed is used where the interest of the grantor is not clear, as for example, where a deed will clear a defective title.

The statutes of the various states provide the necessary formal requirements for the execution and delivery of deeds. A deed ordinarily is required to be signed, sealed, acknowledged, and delivered. A deed is not effective until it is

[3] Jones v. Grow Investment and Mortgage Company, page 1034

delivered to the grantee: that is, placed entirely out of the control of the grantor. This delivery usually occurs by the handing of the instrument to the grantee or his agents. Where property is purchased on installment contract and occasionally in other cases, the deed is placed in the hands of a third party to be delivered by him to the grantee upon the happening of some event, usually the final payment by the grantee. Such delivery to a third party is called delivery in escrow and takes control over the deed entirely out of the hands of the grantor. Only if the conditions are not satisfied is the escrow agent at liberty to return the deed to the grantor.

In order that the owner of real estate may notify all persons that he has title to the property, the statutes of the various states provide that deeds shall be recorded in the recording office of the county in which the land is located. Failure to record a deed by a new owner who has not entered into possession makes it possible for the former owner to convey and pass good title to the property to an innocent third party, although the former owner has no right to do so and would be liable to his first grantee in such a case.

7-30. Transfer by Judicial Sale.   Title to land may be acquired by a vendee at a sale conducted by a sheriff or other proper official. Such sale is one made under the jurisdiction of a court having competent authority to order the sale. In order to secure the money to pay a judgment secured by a successful plaintiff, it may be necessary to sell the property of the defendant. Such a sale is called a judicial sale. A tax sale is a public sale of land, owned by a delinquent taxpayer, for the collection of unpaid taxes. The purchaser at such sale acquires a tax title. A mortgage foreclosure sale is a proceeding in equity by which a mortgagee secures, by judicial sale, money to pay the obligation secured by the mortgage. The word "foreclosure" is also applied to the proceedings for enforcing other types of liens such as mechanic's liens, assessments against realty to pay public improvements, and other statutory liens. The character of title acquired by a purchaser at such judicial sale is determined by statute.

7-31. Title by Adverse Possession.   Title to land may be acquired under a principle known as adverse possession. Thus, a person who enters into actual possession of land and remains thereon openly and notoriously for the period of time prescribed in the statute of limitations, claiming title thereto in denial of, and adversely to, the superior title of another, will at the end of the statutory period acquire legal title. Actual knowledge by the true owner that his land is occupied adversely is not essential. However, the possession must be of such a nature as to charge a reasonably diligent legal owner with knowledge of the adverse claim. It has also been held that adverse possession will not run against a municipal corporation.

In many states, adverse possession by one with color of title who pays the real estate taxes will ripen into title in a much shorter period than is required for adverse possession without color of title. Color of title refers to a defective title but one that for the defect would be good title. For example, a mistake in a deed does not convey clear title, but does convey color of title. This use of adverse possession is very important in clearing defective titles. Errors can be ignored after the statutory period if there is adverse possession, color of title, and payment of taxes. See *Failoni* v. *Chicago and Northwestern Railway Co.,* page 1045, for a typical color of title case.

7-32. Title by Will or Descent. As previously noted, a person may make disposition of his property after death by an instrument in writing called a will. The person who carries out the provisions of the will is called an *executor.* A transfer of real property is called a devise and the beneficiary a devisee. Who may make a will, how it must be executed, who may or may not be excluded as beneficiaries, how a will may be revoked, and what rules are to be used in construing a will are controlled by state statute. These matters were briefly discussed in Section 7-10. It should be noted that a will does not interfere with the right of the owner to dispose of property during his lifetime. A will takes effect only at death and then only if it has not been revoked by the testator prior to his death.

According to the statute of descent, if a person dies without making a will his real property will pass to his heirs at law. Title passes immediately on death to the heirs, but it may be divested if the real estate is needed to pay debts of the deceased.

7-33. Title by Accretion. An accretion is the accumulation of land to the land of an owner by action of water. If land is added to that of an owner by the gradual addition of matter deposited by water, thereby extending the shore or bank, such increase is called alluvion. If a gradual increase in the land of an owner is caused by the receding of water, such increase is called reliction. If an addition to an owner's land be caused suddenly by reason of a freshet or flood, even though boundaries are changed, no change in ownership occurs. However, if such change in boundaries is slow and gradual by alluvion or reliction, the newly formed land belongs to the owner of the bed of the stream in which the new land is formed. If the opposite bank of a private stream belongs to different persons, it is a general rule that each owns the bed to the middle line of the stream. In public waters, such as navigable streams, lakes, and the sea, the title of bed of the water, in absence of special circumstances, is in the United States. Accretion to the land belongs to the riparian owner; islands created belong to the government.

7-34. Covenants and Conditions. Quite often the grantor places restrictions upon the use that may be made of the land conveyed. He may, for instance, provide that the land shall be used exclusively for residential purposes, that the style and cost of the residence meet certain specifications, that certain fences and party walls shall be maintained, that building lines shall be established, that ways and roads shall be open, and parks be established. These restrictions inserted in the deed are covenants or promises on the part of the grantee to observe them and are said to run with the land. Even though the grantee fails to include them in a subsequent deed made by him, the new owner is nevertheless subject to them. They remain indefinitely as restrictions against the use of the land. Such restrictions will not be enforced, however, if conditions have changed substantially since the inception of the covenants.[4]

Most of these covenants are inserted for the benefit of surrounding property and may be enforced by the owners of such property. This is particularly true when the owner of land which is being divided into a subdivision inserts similar restrictions in each deed or in the plat. The owner of any lot which is subject

---

[4] Paschen v. Pashkow, page 1035

to the restrictions is permitted to enforce the restrictions against the other lot owners located in the same subdivision. Occasionally a covenant is inserted for the personal benefit of the grantor, and will not run with the land. If grantee *A* as part of the consideration covenants to repair a dam on land owned by grantor *B,* such covenant will not run with the land and place a duty upon a grantee of *A.* The promise does not touch and concern the land granted from *A* to *B,* but is only a personal covenant for the benefit of *B.*

It should be noted that covenants and conditions that are designed to discriminate on the grounds of race, creed, color, or national origin are unconstitutional as a denial of equal protection of the laws. Such covenants were common at one time and many are still incorporated in restrictions that accompany plats. When challenged, such restrictions have been held to be unconstitutional; they should today be considered a nullity without a court test case.

7-35. Proving Ownership.   Ownership of real estate is a matter of public record. Every deed, mortgage, judgment, lien, or other transaction that affects the title to real estate must be made a matter of public record in the county in which the real estate is located. Deeds and other documents are usually recorded in the county's recorder's office. The records of the probate court furnish the public documents necessary to prove title by will or descent. Divorce proceedings and other judicial proceedings that affect the title to real estate are also part of the public record.

In order to establish title to real estate, it is necessary to examine all of the public records that may affect the title. Because it would be extremely difficult for an individual or his attorney to examine all of the records, businesses have been formed for the express purpose of furnishing the appropriate records for any given parcel of real estate. These companies, known as abstract companies, are usually well-established firms that have maintained tract indexes for many years which they keep current on a daily basis. Upon request, these companies prepare an abstract of record which sets forth the history of the parcel in question and all matters that may affect the title. The abstract of title is examined by an attorney who furnishes his written opinion concerning the title. The opinion will set forth any defects in the title as well as encumbrances against it. The abstract of title must be brought down to date each time the property is transferred or proof of title is required in order that the chain of title might be complete. The opinion on title will be useless unless all court proceedings, such as foreclosures, partitions, transfers by deed, and probate proceedings are shown. It should be noted that an attorney's opinion on title is just that—an opinion. If the attorney makes a mistake, for example, his opinion states that *X* has title to Blackacre, when in fact *X* does not have title to Blackacre, *X* does not have title. *X*'s only recourse would be a malpractice suit against the attorney.

Because of limited resources, many lawyers are unable to respond in damages to pay losses caused by their mistakes. Therefore the abstract of title and attorney's opinion as the means of protecting owners is in many cases not satisfactory. In addition, there may be title defects which do not appear of record and which the attorney does not cover in his title opinion. For example, an illegitimate child may be an unknown heir with an interest in property as may be a spouse in a secret marriage. In order to protect owners against such hidden claims and to offset the limited resources of most lawyers, title insurance has been developed.

Title insurance is in effect an opinion of the title company instead of the lawyer. The opinion of the title company is backed up to the extent of the face value of the title insurance policy. If the purported owner loses his property, he collects the insurance just as if it were life insurance and the insured had died. Title insurance can cover matters beyond those in a title opinion. It has the financial backing of the issuing company which is financially more secure than any law firm. Modern real estate practice uses abstracts and title policies rather than abstracts and title opinions. Title insurance companies usually maintain their own tract records thus eliminating the cost of bringing the abstract down to date.

Another method of proving ownership which is used in some localities is known as the Torrens System. This system is based on a registered title which can only be transferred upon the official registration records. The original registration of any title usually requires a judicial determination as to the current owner, and then all subsequent transfers merely involve the surrender of the registered title, much in the same way as an automobile title is transferred. The Torrens System is a much simpler system to use after a title has once been registered. However, the high cost of obtaining the original registration has prevented the Torrens System from replacing abstracts and title policies as proof of title in most areas.

ESTATES IN REAL PROPERTY

7-36. Estates in Fee Simple. A person who owns the entire estate in real property is said to be an owner in fee simple. A fee simple title is that which is usually received by the grantee of a warranty deed.

7-37. Life Estates. An owner of land may create, either by will or by deed, a life estate therein. Such a life estate may be for the life of the grantee or it may be created for the duration of the life of some other designated person. Unless the instrument that creates the life estate places limitations upon it, the interest can be sold or mortgaged like any other interest in real estate. The buyer or mortgagee takes into consideration the fact that he receives only a life estate and that it may be terminated at any time by the death of the person for whose life it was created.

The life tenant is obligated to use reasonable care to maintain the property in the condition in which it was received, ordinary wear and tear excepted. It is his duty to repair, to pay taxes, and out of the income received, to pay interest on any mortgage that may have been outstanding at the time the life estate was created. The life tenant has no right to make an unusual use of the property if such a use tends to deplete the value of the property, unless the property was so used at the time the estate was created. For instance, a life tenant would have no right to mine coal or to cut and mill timber from land in which he held only a life estate unless such operations were being conducted or contemplated at the time the life estate was created.

7-38. Remainders and Reversions.   After the termination of a life estate, the remaining estate may be given to someone else, or it may revert to the original owner or his heirs. If the estate is to be given to someone else upon the termination of a life estate, it is called an estate in remainder. If it is to revert back to the original owner, it is called a reversion. If the original owner of the estate is dead, the reversion comes back to his heirs. A remainder or a reversionary interest may be sold, mortgaged, or otherwise disposed of in the same manner as any other interest in real property.

7-39. Dower and Curtesy.   At common law, a wife is entitled, upon the death of her husband, to a life estate in one third of any real property that her husband owned at the time of his death. The common law provided that, if there was a child born alive, upon the death of the wife the husband was entitled to a life estate in the whole of the wife's property. This was known as curtesy.

Curtesy has quite generally been abolished by statute, although in some of the states the husband is given a right comparable to the wife's dower. Some of the states have also abolished dower, making some other provision for the surviving wife or husband. In those states where dower or curtesy is provided for, the husband or wife cannot defeat the other by conveying his or her property prior to his or her death. A purchaser acquires good title only if the wife and husband join in the deed, unless the statute makes some other provision. Dower and curtesy are controlled by statute.

7-40. Easements.   An easement is a right, granted by the grantor to the grantee, to use real property. For example, the grantor may convey to the grantee a right of way over his land, the right to erect a building that may shut off light or air, the right to lay drain tile under the land, or the right to extend wires over the land. If these rights of easement are reserved in the deed conveying the property, or granted by a separate deed, they pass along with the property to the next grantee and are burdens upon the land. Such easements may be made separate and distinct by contract and are binding only on the immediate parties to the agreement. If such right to use another's land is given orally, it is not an easement but a license, and the owner of the land may revoke it at any time; unless it has become irrevocable by estoppel; whereas an easement given by grant cannot be revoked or taken away, except by deed, as such a right of way is considered a right in real property. An easement, like title to property, may be acquired by prescription which is similar to adverse possession.

7-41. Tenancies—Joint Tenancy and Tenancy in Common.   Just as in the case of personal property, an estate in land may be owned by several persons. Such persons may hold the real estate, either as tenants in common or as joint tenants, according to the nature of the granting clause in the deed by which the title is transferred. A joint tenancy can be created only by a specific statement in the granting clause of the deed, which usually states that the grantees shall hold title to said premises as joint tenants with the right of survivorship, and not as tenants in common. In the absence of such clause, grantees are tenants in common.

7-42. Tenancy by Entirety and Community Property. Presumably because at common law a husband and wife were regarded as one person, a conveyance of land to a husband and wife, in absence of words to the contrary, came to be referred to as an estate in "tenancy by the entirety." To the extent that upon the death of either the survivor takes the entire estate, a tenancy by the entirety is similar to a joint tenancy. Tenancy by the entirety, however, differs from a joint tenancy in that it cannot be terminated without the consent of both parties. A joint tenancy, however, can be destroyed by either cotenant transferring his interest to a third party, thus making the transferee a tenant in common with the other owner.

Several of the southwestern and western states have what is known as community property, having inherited it in part from their French and Spanish ancestors. In these states all property acquired after marriage other than by devise, bequest, or from the proceeds of noncommunity property becomes the joint property of husband and wife. Control of the property is vested primarily in the husband, and he is authorized, in most states, to sell or to mortgage it. The proceeds of the sale or mortgage in turn become community property. Upon the death of one of the parties, title to at least half of the community property passes to the survivor. In most of the states, the disposition of the remainder may be by will or under the rules of descent.

REAL PROPERTY CASES

First Fed. S. & L. Assn. of Willoughby v. Smith
216 N.E.2d 396 (Ohio) 1965

SIMMONS, J. This cause comes on for a decision pursuant to the amended cross-petition of defendant Security Sewage Equipment Company in which it requests an order permitting it to remove sewage disposal tanks and equipment from the premises.

A hearing was held on this cross-petition and briefs submitted by the parties.

Upon consideration of same the court finds that the right of removal is dependent upon a finding by this court that the disposal tanks and equipment are personalty and did not acquire the character of fixtures following their installation. If they became fixtures in 1963 at the time the conditional sale was made by Security Sewage to the land owner, Section 1309.32, Revised Code, applied. This section provides that security interests in fixtures are invalid against any person having an interest in the real estate at the time the security interest attaches, who has not in writing consented to that interest or disclaimed an interest in the goods as fixtures. At the time the conditional sales agreement was executed on October 5, 1963, plaintiff First Federal Savings and Loan was a mortgagee of record. There is no evidence that plaintiff consented or disclaimed.

In determining whether personalty becomes a fixture so that it merges with the realty and loses its former identity three tests are considered. (1) The nature of the annexation to the realty, or the degree of the physical attachment to it.

(2) The adaptability of the item to the use or purpose of the realty to which it is attached. (3) The intention of the parties.

The court finds from the evidence that the tanks were installed in excavations and that the top of both tanks are about even with ground level and that the larger tank is set in the ground to a depth of approximately 11 feet. The court further finds that the tanks are attached by underground pipes to the sanitary sewage system of an adjacent apartment building having eight apartment suites. In the event the tanks and sewage treatment system are removed, the sewage effluent from the apartments would flow in its raw and untreated state into a gully a short distance away.

From these and other facts the court finds that the tanks and equipment are so permanently annexed to the realty, and so adapted to the performance of a necessary function which renders the apartment buildings habitable, that tests 1 and 2 stated above dictate a finding that the items are fixtures. Further, the court finds that the removal of the tanks and equipment would do injury to the realty by leaving large holes in the ground and by disrupting the sanitary piping system.

Defendant contends, however, that the intention of the parties is the chief test in determining the status of an item either as personalty or as a fixture, and that the conditional sales agreement between the defendant and the purchaser/mortgagor Smith clearly expresses the intention of both parties that title to the tanks and equipment be retained by defendant company until payment in full is received. The evidence shows a balance due of approximately $486.00 on the total purchase price of roughly $4,000.00.

It must be observed that the intention which is relevant as a test of status is an intention either that an item remain personalty or become a fixture, not an intention relative to ownership. The purchase contract involved here does reserve ownership in the defendant, but there is nothing in the contract expressing any intention of the parties that the tanks and equipment retain their identity as personalty. A conditional sales agreement is merely a method of buying an article and cannot be accepted as conclusive evidence of the intention of the parties relative to the continuing character of the article.

Further, if articles which are annexed to realty become so absorbed within it by virtue of the method and degree of annexation, and their adaptability to the use of the realty, their identity as personalty may be said to be destroyed and they become fixtures, regardless of the intention of the parties. . . .

The request of defendant Security Sewage Equipment Company for right to remove such items is denied.

Judgment accordingly.

Dean Vincent, Inc. v. Redisco, Inc.

373 P.2d 995 (Oreg.) 1962

GOODWIN, J. This is a contest for priority between secured creditors. It arises out of the building of an apartment house. The plaintiff holds a first mortgage on the real property. The defendant, Redisco, Inc., holds a conditional sales contract and a second mortgage for the price of the floor coverings and the installation charges therefor. From a decree according priority to the plaintiff's mortgage, Redisco appeals. . . .

Carpeting, like electrical ornaments, plumbing bowls, hardware, and an infinite variety of other personal property, may or may not be so annexed to the real property as to lose its identity as personal property. . . . Whether such property retains its character as personal property or loses its separate identity in the real property depends upon a combination of factors. These factors are usually spoken of as annexation, adaptation, and intention. Intention is the most important and the most difficult factor to apply. It must be objective, and not some secret plan or mental reservation. . . .

Except for the semantical influence of cases concerning "rugs," there is no reason to say that installed floor covering is any more or less movable than installed plumbing fixtures, as either may be removed by experts, properly outfitted with tools, without doing appreciable harm to the freehold. *See Roseburg Nat. Bank* v. *Camp,* 89 Or. 67, where we said:

> The old rule that all things annexed to the realty become a part of it has been much relaxed. Annexation is not the sole test for determining whether a fixture is removable or irremovable. The line between removable and irremovable fixtures is sometimes so close and difficult to ascertain that it is impossible to frame a precise, unbending and infallible rule which can be applied to all cases. Each case must depend largely upon its own special facts and peculiar circumstances. . . .

The record shows that the trial judge had our former cases in mind when he ruled upon the question below. His ruling was based upon a careful consideration of the intention of the parties as disclosed by their behavior. He also considered the manner of installation (annexation), and the actual as well as the intended adaptation and adaptability of the material installed. Insofar as his evaluation of the facts is concerned, we can find no basis for reaching a different conclusion.

It may well be true that Redisco did not intend to give up the security title it retained under its conditional sales contract. However, no vendor is likely to intend to forfeit any security. The important question is not what the vendor intended, but what an objective bystander would make of the total factual situations. . . .

The controlling intent would seem to be that of the buyer and seller concerning the function of the floor covering. Did the parties intend that the floor covering be installed in the building, there to remain during its useful life, or did they intend to put down the floor covering to be used as such only until someone might see fit to take it out and use it elsewhere?

Since it is reasonable to assume that all parties expected the financial aspects of the transaction to proceed according to plan, the principal intention of the parties, from a functional point of view, was to put the carpet down and leave it there until it wore out. If such was their intention, then the nature of the order to the factory for custom-made carpet and the cutting and fitting within the seventy units is completely consistent with the view taken by the trial court that the floor covering was intended to become a permanent part of the building.

There is no particular policy or equitable reason to favor either party in a transaction of this character. To permit the conditional seller of merchandise to go into the building and remove part of the building is no better or no worse than to wash out the security of the seller by forbidding such relief. The parties were dealing at arms' length at all times.

The first mortgage is a prior lien on the building and its fixtures. The carpet is a fixture under all the tests of annexation, adaptation, and function intention. We concur in the trial court's analysis of the factual situation, and in its application of the law of fixtures. *Affirmed.*

Jones v. Grow Investment and Mortgage Company

358 P.2d 909 (Utah) 1961

CALLISTER, J. Action to recover damages for breach of covenant against encumbrances. The trial court, sitting without a jury, awarded judgment to the plaintiffs and defendant appeals.

Defendant conveyed to plaintiffs by a statutory form of warranty deed a residential lot located in Orem, Utah County. The deed provided, in addition to the form language, that the described tract of land was "subject to deed restrictions and easements of record."

At the time of the conveyance there existed an open irrigation ditch which ran the length of the east side or rear of the lot. The ditch terminates at the southeast corner of the lot and an underground cement pipe commences at that point and runs westerly along the south of the lot. It is conceded that the ditch is a prescriptive easement and not of record. Plaintiffs attempted to fill the ditch but were prevented by the owners of the dominant estate.

Defendant makes numerous assignments of error, but, in the main, they boil down to the question as to whether the lower court erred in refusing to find that the ditch was an easement excepted from the covenant against encumbrances. It is the contention of defendant that the ditch was an open and visible easement of which the plaintiffs had notice or knowledge.

The trial judge made findings to the effect that the plaintiff, Larry L. Jones, made a personal inspection of the lot in the company of defendant's agent prior to the conveyance and saw the visible and open irrigation ditch which appeared to dead-end at the south line; that at that time the ditch appeared to be abandoned and contained tree limbs, building refuse, weeds, and trash; that the cement pipe was completely covered and not visible on a casual inspection; that Larry L. Jones made inquiry of defendant's agent and was advised that the ditch could be filled in and the yard leveled; and that the ditch was an easement by prescription and not of record. The trial judge concluded that the existence of the ditch was a breach of warranty and entered judgment in favor of the plaintiffs in the amount of $750.

There is considerable conflict among the authorities as to whether or not a visible or known easement is excepted from a covenant against encumbrances. A distinction is made in some cases between encumbrances which affect the title and those which simply affect the physical condition of the land. In the first class, it is universally held that the encumbrances are included with the covenant, regardless of the knowledge of the grantee. Those encumbrances relating to physical conditions of the property have, in many instances been treated as excluded from the covenant. Some of these cases are decided upon the theory that, whenever the actual physical conditions of the realty are apparent, and are in their nature permanent and irremediable, such conditions are within the contemplation of the parties when contracting, and are therefore not included in a general covenant against encumbrances.

There seems to be a tendency toward the proposition that certain visible public easements, such as highways and railroad rights of way, in open and notorious use at the time of the conveyance, do not breach a covenant against encumbrances. However, it still seems to be the general rule, particularly in those cases involving private rights of way, that an easement which is a burden upon the estate granted and which diminishes its value constitutes a breach of the covenant against encumbrances in the deed, regardless of whether the grantee had knowledge of its existence or that it was visible and notorious.

Ordinarily, parol evidence is inadmissible to show exceptions to express covenants in a deed or to show that a purchaser knew of the existence of an easement not referred to in the deed and took the conveyance subject to it. This rule should not be lightly disregarded for titles to real estate would be uncertain and recordation of deeds useless if their contents were to be determined by the testimony of witnesses.

Certainly, if the deed contains anything which would indicate that a known encumbrance was not intended to be within the covenant, the purchaser cannot complain that such an encumbrance was a breach of the covenant. However, with the possible exception of public easements that are apparent and in their nature permanent and irremediable, mere knowledge of the encumbrance is not sufficient to exclude it from the operation of the covenant. The intention to exclude an encumbrance should be manifested in the deed itself, for a resort to oral or other extraneous evidence would violate settled principles of law in regard to deeds.

In the instant case, the defendant's deed to plaintiffs was in the statutory form which carries with it a covenant that the premises conveyed are free from all encumbrances. The defendant saw fit to except from this covenant "deed restrictions and easements of record." Nothing is manifested in the deed that any other encumbrances were to be excluded. It would have been a simple matter for the defendant, as grantor, to exclude from the covenant the existing ditch. Under the deed, as written and delivered, a grantee could reasonably assume that the ditch was included within the encumbrance. The very purpose of the covenant is to protect a grantee against defects and to hold that one can be protected only against unknown defects would be to rob the covenant of most of its value. If from the force of the covenant it is desired to eliminate known defects, or to limit the covenant in any way, it is easy to do so. It must be concluded that the ditch was a breach of the covenant against encumbrances. ...

Affirmed.

Paschen v. Pashkow

211 N.E.2d 576 (Ill.) 1965

SULLIVAN, J. This is an appeal from a declaratory judgment in favor of the defendants entered at the close of plaintiff's case declaring that a covenant entered into in 1896 restricting Castlewood Terrace in the city of Chicago to single-family residences was binding and enforceable. Plaintiff had sought the removal of the restriction in order to construct high-rise apartments.

Castlewood subdivision was subdivided and platted in 1896.

All of the deeds to the Castlewood Terrace lots contained the following restrictions: . . .

That "no apartment or flat building or structure built, used or adapted for the separate housekeeping of more than one family shall at any time be built or maintained upon said premises."

Plaintiff acquired title to the lots in question in 1916. Between 1930 and 1935 Lincoln Park was extended from Montrose to Foster by reclaiming submerged land. Marine Drive was constructed along what was previously the water's edge. There had been fourteen high-rise buildings erected on Marine Drive between Irving Park and Foster avenue, which streets are respectively twelve blocks to the south of and five blocks to the north of Castlewood Terrace. At the southwest corner of Ainslie and Marine Drive an eight-story high-rise apartment has been erected. . . .

The record also indicates that the defendants and the owners of other lots on Castlewood Terrace have been vigilant in maintaining and enforcing the restrictive covenants. . . .

The question squarely confronting the court is whether the evidence showed such a substantial change in the character of the surrounding neighborhood as to make it impossible any longer to secure in a substantial degree the benefits sought to be realized through the performance of the building restriction.

Plaintiff properly states the law that the court will not uphold a restrictive covenant where the property and the neighborhood have, since the inception of the covenants, so changed in character or environment that the objects of the covenants are defeated or cannot be accomplished, and their enforcement would be harsh, inequitable or oppressive. . . . But each case involving restrictive covenants must be decided on its own facts. . . .

In the instant case the residential character of Castlewood Terrace has never been violated. The street is only 1200 feet long without intersections. The changes around this block caused by the construction of high-rise apartments, a motel and hospitals along Marine Drive have not affected Castlewood Terrace.

We conclude that Castlewood Terrace and the neighborhood have not so changed in character and environment that the object of the covenants are defeated or cannot be accomplished, and the restrictions are reasonable and not contrary to public policy or any positive rule of law.

Judgment affirmed.

CHAPTER 51
REVIEW QUESTIONS AND PROBLEMS

1. *X* leased a building from *Y* for the operation of a plant and retail outlet for processing and sale of meat. Under the terms of the lease, *X* could make alterations in the building. *X* ran pipelines to the street and insulated each room, in order to make each room a self-contained refrigerator. *X* also installed a new false front on the building and put in counters and showcases on the main floor. Which of the improvements could *X* remove and take with him upon termination of the lease?

2. *X* sold a home to *Y* and gave a warranty deed. Unknown to *Y*, there were valid unrecorded liens against the property. Does *Y* have any remedy against *X*?

3. While selling his home to *B*, *A* discovers that his brother, *C*, may have a claim against the land. *C*, independently wealthy, and on good terms with *A*, wishes to help *A* sell the house. What method can *A* use to clear the title?

4. *A*, the record owner of Blackacre, deeded it to *B* in May, 1958. *B* failed to record the deed until May, 1961. In June, 1961, *A* sold the timber standing on Blackacre to *C*. In April, 1961, *A* had sold Blackacre to *D*, who promptly recorded his deed in April. Does *B* have any recourse against *C* or *D*? Against *A*?

5. The XYZ Company had an easement for underground cables through *A*'s land duly recorded. *A* hired *B* to dig and prepare a foundation for a building on the property. In doing so, *B*'s tractor broke through the XYZ Company's cable. *B* was negligent. May the XYZ Company recover from *B*? Was the recording of the easement knowledge to all the world?

6. *A* and *B* owned adjoining homes. Through a surveying error in 1949, 7 feet of what *A* considers to be his lot, is in reality a part of *B*'s lot. *A* and *B* lived in their homes for twenty years, since 1949. *A* cared for the land and erected a fence and some shrubbery on the 7-foot plot. Does *A* or *B* own the 7-foot strip?

7. *A* and *B* owned Blackacre as tenants in common. They entered into an agreement to execute mutual wills leaving the property to each other and then to their son, *C*, 25 years old. *B*, the wife, died, and *A* accepted the devise under *B*'s will. Later, *A* changed his will, leaving Blackacre to *D*, a woman with whom *A* had been "friendly" for years. Upon *A*'s death, may *C* recover Blackacre?

8. When *A* purchased his home twenty years ago in the Whiteacre subdivision, he, like all other purchasers, agreed that the property was to be used "for residential purposes only." The property directly across the street from *A*'s home was in a different subdivision and had no such restrictions placed on it. Over a period of ten years, several stores and a church were erected across the street from *A*'s house. *B*, *A*'s next-door neighbor, who is subject to the restriction, wishes to build a small store on his property. May *A* obtain an injunction against *B*? Assume no zoning violation.

9. *A* sold Whiteacre to *B*, inserting the provision in the deed that "Whiteacre shall not be transferred to any Negro or colored person." *B* sells Whiteacre to *C*, a black. May *A* obtain an injunction forbidding the sale, or in the alternative, damages from *B*?

10. *X* was left Blackacre for life, and on *X*'s death, the property was to go to *Y*. When *X* took possession, Blackacre consisted of a lot and a house. When *X* inherited the property, the surrounding neighborhood was essentially residential. However, over the course of twenty years, the neighborhood became exclusively industrial, with the exception of Blackacre. *X* cannot rent the home because of noise and dust. *X* wishes

to raze the home and build a factory on the land. Can *X* do so without *Y*'s permission?

11. *A* and *B* were married in 1940. Before the marriage, *A*, the husband, had purchased Blackacre. In 1943, one child, *C*, was born. In 1948, *A* purchased Whiteacre, and sold it to *D* in 1950 for $100,000 without *B*'s consent and without *B* joining in the deed. Assuming *A* dies intestate in 1970, what would be *B*'s rights to Blackacre and Whiteacre (or the proceeds from the sale of Whiteacre) if:

   a. The state in which *A* and *B* resided retained common-law dower?

   b. The state in which *A* and *B* resided had a community property statute?

   c. The grant of Whiteacre was to *A* and *B* as joint tenants?

   d. The grant of Whiteacre was to *A* and *B* as tenants in common?

   e. The grant of Whiteacre was to *A* and *B*, at common law?

12. The owner of two adjoining buildings sold one of them to *A*. The deed provided that *A* should have the privilege of passage from the other building to the one which he purchased. Subsequently, the owner sold the remaining building to *X*. *X* tore down the building and built a new one. Does *A* have a right of passage in the new building?

13. A power company cleared a right of way across *A*'s land and suspended a power line which had been constantly maintained. No poles or towers, however, were on the property. Many years later the company replaced the old power line with a new one and part of the installation was on *A*'s land. Can *A* require the company to remove the line?

14. An outdoor advertising company, ADCO, signed an agreement with a hotel owner which granted ADCO "the exclusive right and privilege to maintain an advertising sign" on an exterior wall of the hotel. ADCO installed the sign. May the owner remove the sign during period agreed? Is the privilege conferred a license or easement?

15. *A* willed certain land to *W* for life, with the remainder to *W*'s minor children. *A* died, and sometime thereafter *W* leased the property to X Coal Company, which stripped the land of coal and destroyed it for other useful purposes. Have the children a good cause of action against the coal company?

16. Which is preferable, an abstract of title or a title insurance policy?

chapter 52

Real Estate Transactions

7-43. Introduction. Real property is involved in a variety of transactions such as contracts of sale, contracts for a deed, and leases. There are three distinct interests in land—surface rights, mineral rights and air rights. Some real estate transactions may involve only some of these rights.[1] For example, a sale or lease of surface rights only may be executed. Such a contract would not affect either the air rights or the mineral rights. Similarly, a party may sell or lease part or all mineral rights, such as the rights to oil and gas, without it affecting the surface or the air rights. However, unless the instrument transferring the property clearly separates the interests in real property, all three interests are involved.

7-44. The Real Estate Contract of Sale. Real estate contracts are subject to the same general principles of contract law as are other contracts. The sections on offer and acceptance, consideration, and competent parties in Book II on contracts noted several aspects of the law as it relates to contracts involving real estate. Your attention is also called to these sections and to the provisions of the statute of frauds relating to real estate contracts. It will be extremely helpful to review these subjects at this time.

The typical contract for sale of real estate originates with an offer from the buyer to the seller. This offer to purchase is frequently obtained by a real estate broker or agent. (The discussions on agency in Section 5-47 of Book Five should also be reviewed at this time. These sections discuss the various types of listings and the broker's authority.) In most states an offer to purchase can be prepared by a real estate broker without his being guilty of unauthorized practice of law. The offer is submitted to the seller for acceptance or rejection. If accepted, it is then taken to the buyer's or seller's attorney for preparation

[1] Failoni v. Chicago and North Western Railway Co., page 1045

1039

of the actual contract. It should be noted that after acceptance by the seller, an enforceable contract does exist, but it is desirable to have an attorney prepare the formal contract which will set forth all aspects of the transaction. For example, if there is to be a warranty of quality, it must be stated in the contract because such warranties are not implied.[2]

The typical real estate contract of sale, in addition to such obvious matters as describing the property, setting forth the price, the method of payment, and the date of possession, will contain provisions concerning the prorating of the real estate taxes, the assignment of hazard insurance, the selection of an escrow agent, and whether the proof of title will be made by furnishing an abstract or a title insurance policy. The contract will also contain provisions concerning such contingencies as default by the buyer or destruction of the premises.

An escrow provision is desirable because a deed must be delivered during the lifetime of the grantor to be effective.[3] Since it is always possible for the grantor to die between the time of executing the contract and the delivery of possession and final payment, the deed is executed concurrently with the contract and is delivered to a third person known as the escrowee or escrow agent to be delivered to the grantee upon final payment. If the seller-grantor dies, the transaction can still be consummated, his death notwithstanding. Delivery of a deed in escrow will also cut off attaching creditors of the seller and pass title clear of any claims perfected after the escrow.[4]

After the execution of the contract and deed, these documents are placed in escrow until the date for delivery of possession and final payment. During the interim period, the buyer will have his attorney either examine the abstract of title or obtain a preliminary commitment for a title insurance policy. The preliminary commitment serves as a check of the records to date to make sure that the title is clear. If the buyer obtains a loan on the premises, the lender will want to examine the title and prepare the mortgage documents. In addition, many contracts require the seller to furnish the buyer a survey of the premises, and some contracts require the seller to prepare an affidavit concerning repairs and improvements to the premises within the applicable time period for mechanic's liens. When the premises that are being sold have been constructed recently, an affidavit of the building contractor will be obtained, along with waivers of mechanic's liens by all materialmen and workers.

At the time of closing the transaction a closing statement will be prepared showing all sums due the seller and all credits due the buyer. In the event that a mortgage is being assumed it would serve as a credit to the buyer. Other credits would include abstract costs, documentary revenue stamps, if required by state law, and taxes and special assessments that are liens. The buyer will pay the net amount due to the seller or to the escrow agent for delivery to the seller, and the escrow agent will deliver the deed to the buyer for recording. At the same time the seller will deliver possession of the premises to the buyer, and the transaction will be completed.

7-45. A Contract for a Deed.   There is a special type of real estate contract that is generally referred to as a contract for a deed. Such a contract is actually

---

[2] Druid Homes, Inc. v. Cooper, page 1047
[3] Donnelly v. Robinson, page 1048
[4] Sturgill v. Industrial Painting Corp. of Nevada, page 1050

a conditional sale of real estate in which the seller retains title to the property, and the buyer makes payments for an extended period of time. The buyer's right to a deed to the property is conditioned on his making all of the payments. Such contracts are sometimes called installment land contracts and they contain the usual provisions found in other real estate contracts. The purchaser has the risk of loss during the period of the contract.[5] The escrow provision is absolutely essential in contracts for a deed because there is usually a period of several years between execution of the contract and delivery of the deed. In such cases, payments by the buyer are usually made to the escrow agent, so that at all times the escrow agent is aware of the status of the contract.

Two additional clauses in most installment land contracts are of particular significance. One of them is known as the acceleration clause; the other is known as the forfeiture clause. The acceleration clause allows the seller to declare the full amount of the contract due and payable in the event the buyer fails to make any of the payments or fails to perform any other of the contract's provisions as agreed. The default, or forfeiture, clause allows the seller, when the buyer is in default, to terminate the contract and to get the deed back from the escrow agent. The net effect of this clause is to allow the seller to keep all payments and improvements made as liquidated damages for breach of contract.

In contracts for a deed where the buyer has made substantial payments or in which he has a substantial equity, it is apparent that forfeiture of the contract might be inequitable. The principles discussed in Chapter 7 which apply to liquidated damages and forfeitures are also applicable to these contracts because courts of equity abhor forfeitures. When the buyer's equity is substantial and forfeiture would be inequitable, a court upon proper application may prohibit the forfeiture and order the sale of the property with the proceeds being distributed to the seller to the extent necessary to pay off the contract and the balance being paid to the buyer. No general rule can be stated to describe those cases in which a forfeiture will be allowed and in those in which it will not. As a part of its equitable jurisdiction, the court will examine all of the facts. If the vendee has made only a small payment, is guilty of gross laches, or has been negligent in the performance of his contract and it is not inequitable to place the vendor in his original position, forfeiture will be permitted. However, if the vendee has made only a slight default with regard to the amount and time of payment, or has largely completed his payments, and the amount of the unpaid purchase price is much less than the value of the property involved, forfeiture will be denied. Forfeiture clauses are easily waived and notice is usually required to reinstate the forfeiture provisions when default occurs without the forfeiture clause being enforced.

In recent years, the contract for a deed as a means of selling real estate has been utilized by promoters of land developments in states that have a substantial tourist business or a large number of retired persons. These land developers in such states as Florida, Colorado, and Arizona will sell real estate lots on such terms as $25 down and $25 per month for 25 years. The unpaid principal bears interest at the going rate.

[5] Briz-Ler Corporation v. Weiner, page 1051

These transactions are susceptible to several abuses. Frequently, many of the lots are not actually subdivided. There are no streets or other improvements, and many purchasers have no means of locating or possessing the property should they pay off the contract. Since many of the purchasers do not see the property prior to purchase, misrepresentation is often alleged and frequently proved. In many cases, swampland and desert have been sold for homesites. Many lots are miles from any utility service.

As a result of the above abuses, state government has attempted to regulate the sale of lots in new subdivisions. These state laws are similar to the "blue-sky" laws regulating the sale of securities. Both operate on the principle of full disclosure to purchasers and a review of promotional materials and plans by government. More and more states are enacting laws regulating subdividers in order to protect the public.

7-46. Leases.   A lease is a contract, either oral or written, express or implied, which transfers possession of real property from a landlord, or lessor, to a tenant, or lessee, for a consideration known as rent. A lease differs from a mere license, which is a privilege granted by one person to another to use land for some particular purpose. A license is not an interest in the land and is personal and not assignable.

A lease may be a tenancy for a stated period, a tenancy from period to period, a tenancy at will, or at sufferance. As its name implies, a tenancy for a stated period lasts for the specific time stated in the lease which is required to be in writing by the statute of frauds if the period exceeds one year. The lease for a stated period terminates without notice at the end of the period and is not affected by the death of either party during the period. If such a lease includes land, it is not terminated by destruction of the improvements unless the lease so provides. If the lease covers only the improvements, destruction creates impossibility of performance.

A tenancy from period to period may be created by the terms of the lease or may arise when the tenant holds over after the end of a lease for a stated period. When such a holdover occurs, the landlord may treat the tenancy as one at sufferance and evict the former tenant as a trespasser. The landlord may also elect to treat the tenant as a tenant, in which case the lease continues from period to period, with the period being identical to that of the original lease, not to exceed one year. The one-year limitation results from the language of the statute of frauds. The amount of rent is identical to that of the original lease.

Leases from year to year or from month to month can only be terminated upon the giving of proper notice. The length of the notice is prescribed by state statute.

A tenancy at will by definition has no period and can be terminated by either party at any time upon giving the prescribed statutory notice. A few states do not require notice, but if legal action is necessary to enforce the reversionary interest, a time lag will be automatically imposed.

Unless the lease provides to the contrary, a tenant has the right to remove movable fixtures that he has installed during the lease period. The right of removal terminates with the lease and unremoved fixtures become the property of the lessor.

Although the rights and duties of the parties to the lease are determined by the lease itself and by the statutes of the state in which the property is located, several general aspects of those rights and duties must be observed. First of all, the lessee is entitled to exclusive possession and control of the premises unless the lease provides to the contrary. The landlord has no right to go upon the premises except to collect rent, but is limited to his right of reversion or reobtaining possession upon termination of the lease. A landlord may also retake possession for purposes of protecting the property, if the tenant abandons the premises.

A landlord is entitled to recover from either the tenant or a third party for injuries to his reversion. In addition, in many states and by the express terms of many leases, the landlord has a lien for unpaid rent on the personal property of the tenant. This lien right is exercised in a statutory proceeding known as distress for rent. By following the prescribed procedures, the landlord is able to distrain personalty on the premises until the rent is paid. If not paid, the tenant's personal property may be sold pursuant to court order.

A tenant is estopped from denying his landlord's title and has a duty to redeliver the premises upon expiration of the lease in the same condition as received, ordinary wear and tear excepted. Unless the lease or a statute provides to the contrary, the lessee has the duty to make ordinary repairs but not to make improvements. The duty to pay rent is subject to set-offs for violations of the covenants of the lease and is released in the event of an eviction, actual or constructive. Constructive eviction occurs when the premises become untenantable due to no fault of the tenant or because some act of the landlord deprives the tenant of quiet enjoyment.[6] Failure to vacate the premises is a waiver of constructive eviction grounds, however.

Difficult legal questions arise in cases involving the landlord's and tenant's liability for injuries to persons on the premises. As a general rule, a landlord makes no warranty that the premises are safe or suitable for the intended use by the tenant, and third persons are on the premises at their own peril. A landlord does have a duty to give notice of latent defects of which he has knowledge. Some states add unknown defects of which he should have knowledge in the exercise of ordinary care to those actually known for the purpose of this notice rule.

The owner of business property, knowing that business invitees of the lessee will be constantly entering it to transact business, has an increased responsibility. The determination of the extent of this increased responsibility is a question of fact for the jury. The jury must determine whether or not the condition of the premises was so dangerous as to subject persons using them to an unreasonable risk or whether the persons owning the property had knowledge of the danger and did not exercise due care.

7-47. Condominiums.   A condominium is an individually owned apartment or town house in a multi-unit structure, such as an apartment building, or in a complex. It is a relatively new method of owning and transferring property which possesses some of the characteristics of a lease and some of a contract of sale. In addition to the individual apartment or town house, the owner has an undivided interest in the common areas of the building and land. Thus, the

[6] Gillingham v. Goldstone, page 1053

deed to a condominium covers the housing unit involved and an undivided fractional interest in the common areas. There is usually an organization to operate the common areas, make repairs, and improvements. Each owner of a unit has one vote in the management of this organization. Taxes are usually prorated on the common areas by using the fractional proportion of the undivided interests. Condominiums are of growing importance in metropolitan areas, and a determination of an owner's rights requires not only a study of the law of real property but also the law of business organizations.

7-48. The Law of Trusts.   A trust, when not modified by the words charitable, constructive, or resulting, is a fiduciary relationship with respect to property subjecting the person by whom the property is held (trustee) to equitable duties to deal with the property for the benefit of another (the beneficiary). In other words, a trust is a method of holding title in one person for the benefit of another. Since it is a fiduciary relationship, the trustee is held to the highest standards of conduct to act solely for the benefit of the beneficiary. Trusts are set up because the beneficiary may be incompetent or a spendthrift; thus, the trustee will serve as a person with capacity to contract and the ability to conserve the estate. Trusts are also used for tax planning purposes and as a method of obtaining skilled management for assets. For example, a husband may by his will put his estate in trust with the stipulation to pay the income to his wife for life and to deliver the property to their children upon her death. Such a trust would eliminate death taxes in the wife's estate and if a corporate trustee, such as a bank, were used, there would presumably be skilled investment advice and management of the estate.

All property may be placed in trust. Although trust assets usually comprise securities such as stocks and bonds, incoming producing land is a common trust asset. In the usual trust situation, the trustee manages the property and pays the net income to the trust beneficiaries. Unproductive property will not be retained, and the trustee as the owner of legal title manages the property as if it were his own.

In some states, land is also the subject matter of a special type of trust, known as the land trust. This type of trust will be discussed in the next section.

7-49. Land Trusts.   The Illinois Supreme Court recently stated, "Millions and probably billions of dollars have been and are now invested in land trusts." Several states have now authorized land trusts by statute. These trusts provide a method for placing title of record in a trustee with the actual owners' identity being unknown to the general public, but with the power to direct and control the property vested in these owners. The modern land trust statute allows the beneficiaries to retain all of the benefits of ownership such as occupying the property, leasing it, selling it, etc., but with the record title appearing in other persons. It is, in effect, a method for secret ownership.

Land trusts are created by a deed to the trustee and by a contemporaneous trust agreement. The trust agreement usually provides that the trustee may act only upon written directions of the beneficiaries. The deed to the trustee purports to give clear title to the trustee, and anyone dealing with the trustee is protected, but the trustee would have liability to the beneficiaries for any act done without a signed written direction.

There are several advantages to the land trust other than secret ownership. First of all, each beneficial interest becomes personal property, and as such is not subject to any of the restrictions such as dower rights, which are applicable to real estate. The land is not tied up in the event of an owner's death, and it would not be subject to the forced-sale proceedings, known as a partition, to which land is usually subject. The land trust is an ideal method for several people to own title together because the title is unaffected by judgments against any of them. For example, a judgment against a beneficiary or a federal tax lien against the beneficiary is not a lien against the real estate, but only against the beneficiary's intangible personal property, to wit: his interest in the trust.

Because of its secret-ownership aspect, the land trust is also valuable as a means for a corporate purchase of land; were the seller to know of the corporate buyer, the price of the land would most likely to be raised. Another advantage of this arrangement is that it enables the parties to avoid the influence of various extraneous matters such as ability to pay, for example. The land trust will undoubtedly gain importance in more and more states in the future.

REAL ESTATE TRANSACTIONS CASES

Failoni v. Chicago and North Western Railway Co.

195 N.E.2d 619 (Ill.) (1964)

DAILY, J. Chicago and North Western Railway Company, defendant, appeals from a declaratory judgment of the circuit court of Macoupin County which found that title to the mineral rights, except coal, under some 130 acres of Macoupin County land was held in fee simple by the surface owner, Catterina Failoni, the plaintiff. The jurisdiction of this court has been properly invoked since a freehold is involved.

The subject real estate consists of two separate parcels, composed of 76 acres and 54 acres, respectively. The larger tract was formerly owned by John Ottersburg and Janna Ottersburg, who in 1903 conveyed "all coal and other minerals" thereunder to B. C. Dorsey by warranty deed. By mesne conveyances of "all coal and other minerals," record title thereto became vested in defendant in 1956. In 1921 Tony Failoni, plaintiff's husband, received an administrator's deed for the Ottersburg tract which apparently made no reference to the mineral interest, and upon his death in 1956, his heirs quitclaimed the property to plaintiff.

The smaller tract was formerly owned by John McKeone, who in 1903 conveyed by warranty deed to B. C. Dorsey "all coal and other minerals" thereunder. By mesne conveyances, record title to this mineral interest also became vested in defendant in 1956. However, by deed which referred only to a prior sale of the underlying "coal," McKeone later conveyed this tract to Ernest Busse, who in turn sold it in 1939 to Tony Failoni and Catterina Failoni, as joint tenants and not as tenants in common.

It appears that for some years prior to 1942, Superior Coal Company, being then the record owner of the mineral interest, mined the coal from under the land, and during this time the coal rights were separately assessed against and taxes thereon paid by Superior Coal Company. After the coal was removed, however, no further assessment of coal rights was made. It also appears that it was the practice in Macoupin County to assess no mineral interest other than coal, and no such assessment was made at any time against the subject property even though the property was in recent years leased for the production of gas.

The plaintiff testified that she had lived on the land for the past forty years and claimed the mineral rights as well as the surface interest. She and her husband executed oil and gas leases thereon in 1923, 1940, and 1942, but at no time did anyone except Superior Coal Company ever remove, or attempt to remove, coal or minerals therefrom. Plaintiff and her family farmed the surface, however, and paid taxes assessed by government survey description.

It is admitted that record title to the surface interest and to the mineral interest is now held by plaintiff and defendant, respectively. Nevertheless, plaintiff contends that because the conveyances in her chain of title did not except the mineral interest she acquired color of title to the mineral interest which has since ripened into fee ownership under the provisions of section 7 of the Limitations Act. (Ill.Rev.Stat.1961, chap. 83, par. 7.) This is the sole question presented upon appeal.

Section 7 states: "Whenever a person having color of title, made in good faith, to vacant and unoccupied land, shall pay all taxes legally assessed thereon for seven successive years, he or she shall be deemed and adjudged to be the legal owner of said vacant and unoccupied land, to the extent and according to the purport of his or her paper title." We have construed this to mean that one claiming the benefit of this statute must prove not only that he holds vacant and unimproved land under color of title but also that he has paid taxes thereon for seven successive years and has since taken possession thereof.

It has long been recognized that the mineral estate may be severed from the surface estate by a grant specifically of the minerals, reserving the surface, or by a grant of the surface while reserving the minerals, and when this has been accomplished, both estates are subject to independent ownership and separate taxation, and both constitute "land" within the meaning of section 7.

Oil and gas, by the overwhelming weight of authority, are minerals, and when the mineral interest is severed from the surface estate, the former may also be regarded as "vacant and unoccupied land." Although deeds may in certain instances provide color of title, they do not in and of themselves operate as adverse possession, or even notice thereof where the severance of the mineral and surface estates was prior thereto. Possession of the surface does not carry possession of the minerals, nor does nonuse or abandonment of the mineral interest terminate said estate. To possess the mineral estate, one must undertake the actual removal thereof from the ground or do such other act as will apprise the community that such interest is in the exclusive use and enjoyment of the claiming party. Furthermore, payment of taxes by government survey description after severance of title between minerals and surface does not constitute payment of taxes under section 7 of the Limitations Act, regardless of whether the minerals were in fact separately assessed.

In the present case, neither plaintiff nor her predecessors in title actually removed any minerals so as to gain possession thereof, the mere executing of oil and gas leases not being sufficient for this purpose, nor did they ever pay taxes upon the separate mineral estate. In fact it appears that no minerals, except coal, were ever assessed or were intended to be assessed under the policy then in force in Macoupin County. Although plaintiff resided upon and farmed these premises, such use related only to the surface and not to the mineral interest which she now claims. Therefore, the provisions of section 7 of the Limitations Act were not complied with, and the ownership of the mineral estate rests not with the plaintiff but with defendant, the record title holder.

The judgment of the circuit court of Macoupin County is reversed and the cause remanded to that court, with directions to enter judgment for the defendant in accordance with this opinion.

Reversed and remanded, with directions.

Druid Homes, Inc. v. Cooper

131 So.2d 884 (Ala.) 1961

MERRILL, J. This appeal is from a judgment of $4,500 based upon a complaint claiming damages for the breach of a written agreement dated December 1, 1955, to purchase a house and lot wherein it was implied that the dwelling was of substantial construction and was built in a workmanlike manner. The breach complained of was that the house was not constructed in a workmanlike manner and that water drained from the bathroom facilities and emptied under the house without any drainage, and damage resulted.

During the trial, a second count was added to the complaint, claiming damages for breach of an oral agreement allegedly made on November 11, 1955, in which appellant impliedly warranted that the house was constructed in a workmanlike manner.

The complaint was not filed until October 6, 1958. This is important only to say that a written warranty for one year was given that the building was in substantial conformity with approved plans and specifications of the Administrator of Veterans Affairs. Plaintiff received his deed, this warranty and occupied the house in December, 1955, rendering any action on the written warranty unavailing after December, 1956.

The first argued assignments of error allege error in the overruling of the demurrer to the two counts of the complaint.

This presents a question of first impression in this state. The question may be posed: Is a warranty implied, as a matter of law, in a contract to purchase real estate, that the improvements located thereon were constructed in a good and workmanlike manner?

The great weight of authority does not support implied warranties in real estate transactions but requires any purported warranties to be in written contractual form. No decision has come to our attention which permitted recovery by the vendee of a house upon the theory of implied warranty.

Most of the cases on this point cite Williston on Contracts, Vol. 4, § 926 (Rev. Ed.), which states:

> The doctrine of *caveat emptor* so far as the title of personal property is concerned is very nearly abolished, but in the law of real estate it is still in full force. One who contracts to buy real estate may, indeed, refuse to complete the transaction if the vendor's title is bad, but one who accepts a deed generally has no remedy for defect of title except such as the covenants in his deed may give him. Therefore, if there are no covenants, he has no redress though he gets no title. . . . Still more

clearly there can be no warranty of quality or condition implied in the sale of real estate and ordinarily there cannot be in the lease of it.

It is generally true also that any express agreements in regard to land contained in a contract to sell it are merged in the deed if the purchaser accepts a conveyance. If, indeed, the vendor has made misrepresentations, even innocently, rescission is possible in most jurisdictions, but no remedy is generally available for any breach by the vendor of any promise contained in the contract but omitted in the deed.

In *Dennison* v. *Harden,* 29 Wash.2d 243, 186 P.2d 908, 912, the court said:

Without discussing under what circumstances implied warranties may be relied upon in the sale of personal property, we will dispose of appellant's argument on this point by saying that we have found no cases, and appellant has cited none, which recognized that there is such a thing as an implied warranty in the sale of real estate. In *Pollard* v. *Lyman,* 1 Day, Conn., 156, 2 Am.Dec. 63, certain land was found to be of no value and it was urged that there was an implied warranty of quality. The court said:

"As to the doctrine of implied warranty, that the article sold is of the ordinary quality of articles of its kind, or equal throughout to the sample seen, it applies only to articles susceptible of a standard quality, or which are sold by samples, and does not extend to lands which have no standard quality, and must depend, for their value, on a variety of circumstances, none of which are reducible to a common measure. . . . "

In the case of *Steiber* v. *Palumbo,* 219 Or. 479, 347 P.2d 978, 983, the court set out an Oregon statute disallowing any implied covenants in the sale of real estate; however, in the review of the action by purchaser for breach of implied warranty in the sale of a new house, the court gave a comprehensive review of many cases on the subject. The court concluded that "even apart from legislation such as ORS 93.140 the law refuses to imply in favor of the purchaser of an existing house warranties as to quality."

We feel that the rule of the cases cited above is sound, makes for certainty in the field of real estate law, and should prevail in this jurisdiction. Purchasers may protect themselves by express agreement embodied in their deeds, and vendors may be certain of their position as to liability for the condition of premises they have sold.

The judgment of the circuit court is reversed and one is here rendered sustaining the demurrer.

Reversed and rendered.

Donnelly v. Robinson
406 S.W.2d 595 (1966)

James Egan and Bessie Egan had a life estate in a tract of land and Melford Egan owned the remainder. An agreement between the life tenants and the remainderman provided for a fifty-fifty division of the proceeds of any sale of the property, including a sale in condemnation proceedings. On October 5, 1960, the parties executed a contract of sale and deed to the state of Missouri which provided for a sale price of $30,500. The contract and deed were placed in escrow to be held until a check in the amount of the purchase price was received from the state. The check was received November 9, 1960. James and

Bessie Egan were killed October 25, 1960, and their estates claim one-half of the proceeds. Melford Egan contends that he is entitled to all of the proceeds as the remainderman. The lower court found for the estates and the remainderman appealed.

WOLFE, J. . . . In pressing their claim for the one-half of the purchase price paid to the administrators of the life tenants' estates the appellants intervenors first assert that title had not passed to the State of Missouri at the time of James and Bessie Egan's deaths because there was no delivery of the deed to the State of Missouri. Among other cases relating to delivery the appellants cite *Klatt* v. *Wolff,* Mo., 173 S.W.2d 933, in which this court restated the established rule that a deed to be operative as a transfer of ownership of land, must be delivered to the grantee or someone for him. In *Harrison* v. *Edmonston,* Mo., 248 S.W. 586, also cited, this court restated the necessity of delivery of a deed with the intention to part with control over it, in order to pass title.

The respondents do not question these rules but they rely, as the trial court did, upon the effect of the delivery of the fully executed deed dated October 5, 1966, to the Wayne County Bank. The bank was to deliver this deed to the Missouri Highway Department upon payment of the purchase price. The purchase money was paid; the deed delivered and the respondents contend that the trial court properly held that the date of the concluded transaction related back to the date of the deed and its delivery to the bank. After so holding the court logically divided the sum paid for the property in accordance with the interests of the grantors existing at the time of the execution and delivery to the bank.

The court invoked the rule that upon final delivery by a depository of a deed deposited in escrow the instrument will be treated as relating back to, and taking effect at the time of the original deposit in escrow. This shall apply even though one of the parties to the deed dies before the second delivery. This relation back doctrine has wide and general acceptance. Its roots are ancient for as far back as the Sixteenth Century we find the Perryman's Case, 77 Eng.Rep. 181, 1. c. 183, in which it was said:

> . . . if a man delivers a writing (d) as an escrow to be his deed on certain conditions to be performed, and afterwards the obligor or obligee dies, and afterwards the condition is performed, the deed is good, for there was *traditio inchoata* in the life of the parties, *sed postea consummata existens* by the performance of the condition takes its effect by force of the first delivery, without any new delivery. . . .

The same doctrine was pronounced by this court in *Savings Trust Co. of St. Louis* v. *Skain,* 345 Mo. 46, 131 S.W.2d 566, 1. c. 570, wherein it was said:

> . . . The relation of vendor and purchaser exists as soon as a contract for the sale and purchase of land is entered into. Equity regards the purchaser as the owner and the vendor as holding the legal title in trust for him: . . . This equitable principle may be invoked in actions at law: . . . and that even though the purchaser has not been put in possession: . . .

There are also numerous cases in which the rule is applied to deeds given to one other than the grantee to be unconditionally delivered to the grantee upon the grantor's death.

Appellants concede that the "relation back doctrine" is a recognized rule in Missouri but contend that it should only be used for the protection of the buyer. They assert that upon the death of the life tenants they as remaindermen held title and the life tenants had nothing to convey. . . .

When James and Bessie Egan signed the deed with Melford and Alberta Egan all parties disposed of their interest in one deed with full agreement and knowledge of what each would receive. For them it was a completed transaction. It therefore appears that the application of the doctrine of relation back to these facts is within the intended use of the doctrine as an equitable means to effectuate the intent of the parties.

The trial court did not err in so holding and the judgment is *affirmed*.

Sturgill v. Industrial Painting Corp. of Nevada

410 P.2d 759 (Nev.) (1966)

ZENOFF, J. Owen and Thelma Rust, owners of certain real property in Clark County, entered into an escrow sale agreement wherein they agreed to sell Lot No. 6 to the Sturgills for a stated price pursuant to agreed terms.

On January 15, 1964, an escrow was opened, and on March 2, 1964, the deed to the property was deposited in the escrow. On March 12, 1964, the respondent, a judgment creditor of the sellers, levied an attachment on the property which was the subject of the sale.

Appellants asserted their third-party interest as purchasers and owners of the subject property. The attaching creditor defended, claiming that since the escrow was not closed, title to the property had not transferred from the sellers to the buyers at the time of the attachment. They based their argument on the fact that the escrow agreement contained the provisions, "close of escrow shall be on or before March 17, 1964," and "the close of escrow shall be the day on which the instruments are recorded." The escrow, in fact, did not close until April 3rd. No reason for the delay was given.

Counsel stipulated on oral argument that the down payment had been paid into escrow before the date of the attachment. It was further stipulated in the trial court that conditions one through five of the escrow agreement (including approval of the buyers to assume an existing encumbrance, transfer of a reserve account, and adjustments for taxes and insurance) were met prior to the attachment. We find that these were the only conditions relating directly to the sale and the passing of title to the property.

The trial court sustained respondent's contention. We do not agree with the ruling.

So long as the conditions of an escrow remain unperformed, the grantor's interest is subject to rights of attaching creditors. However, if title has passed to the grantee, an attaching creditor of the grantor can gain no rights in the conveyed property.

Therefore, the determinative factor in the instant case is whether at the time of attachment the legal title was in the seller or in the buyer.

The escrow had been opened, the deed executed, and the deed placed in the escrow before the attachment. All of the conditions relating to the sale were performed before the attachment, but the deed was recorded and the escrow closed subsequent to the attachment.

There is some authority for the proposition that title cannot pass until the deed is recorded when recordation is a condition in the instructions. *Lieb* v. *Webster,* 30 Wash.2d 43 (1948). In that case, the condition read: "He [the escrow agent] was to procure and record conveyance to the appellants." This condition was included among the conditions concerning other financing, policies of title insurance, and assumption of prior encumbrances.

In the instant case, the requirement of recordation was printed on the back of the agreement and merely stated that, "close of escrow shall be the day on which the instruments are recorded." Those printed instructions are not conditions of sale but rather definitions and conditions for the protection of the escrow agent.

Title passes when all conditions of sale are performed, so the closing date becomes immaterial. It seems clear to us that the phrases relating to recordation and close of escrow were merely procedural and did not impose any affirmative action on the part of the parties that could be construed as a condition to the passing of title. . . .

When the conditions of the sale had been met the escrow agent could have been compelled by either or both of the parties to the sale to deliver the deed and the purchase money regardless that the date of the close of escrow had not yet arrived, for nothing more remained to be done to effectuate the sale itself. Thus, ownership had transferred to the buyer before the attachment was levied and the seller no longer had an interest in the property that was subject to a levy of attachment.

Reversed. Judgment shall enter granting the third-party claim in accordance with its prayer for relief.

Briz-Ler Corporation v. Weiner

171 A.2d 65 (Del.) 1961

In October, 1954, plaintiff entered into a contract to purchase a four-story hotel containing a bar and liquor store together with equipment and fixtures from the defendants. Plaintiff paid $11,500 down and agreed to pay the balance of $102,500 plus interest at 6 percent in monthly installments of $865. Plaintiff also deposited sums for taxes and insurance with the escrow agent.

In December, 1957, a fire occurred on the premises causing considerable damage. At this time a substantial balance was still owing on the total purchase price. After the fire plaintiff remained in possession of the premises and operated its first floor bar and liquor store.

Plaintiff subsequently commenced negotiations with the insurance company to settle for the loss caused by the fire. Ultimately, plaintiff settled with the insurance company for a payment of $31,454.78, which sum was insufficient to meet the cost of $107,000 required to restore the entire structure in accordance with the City Building Code.

In August, 1958, a dispute arose between the parties, the defendants claiming that the plaintiff was in default. Shortly thereafter plaintiff abandoned the premises, leaving all the equipment there, and the defendants applied the entire amount of the settlement to repair the building by reducing it to one level for use as a restaurant, bar and grille, and package liquor store.

Plaintiff claims that it should be repaid all the money paid by it pursuant to the installment contract because defendants cannot now deliver what they contracted to deliver, viz., a four-story hotel structure. In the alternative, plaintiff claims that it is entitled to an equitable lien on the premises, or on the proceeds of insurance, in the full amount paid by it under the contract.

The lower court dismissed the plaintiff's complaint and plaintiff appeals.

WOLCOTT, J. . . . The basic question involved in this appeal is whether or not a loss occasioned by fire to premises under an installment contract of sale shall fall upon the seller or the purchaser. Presumably, if the loss as a matter of law falls upon the seller, then plaintiff should be entitled to relief of some nature. If, on the contrary, the loss falls upon the purchaser, the complaint was properly dismissed.

The rule followed in a majority of American jurisdictions is that an executory contract for the sale of lands requiring the seller to execute a deed conveying the legal title upon payment of the full purchase price works an equitable conversion so as to make the purchaser the equitable owner of the land and the seller the equitable owner of the purchase money. The result is that the purchaser, the equitable owner, takes the benefit of all subsequent increase in value and, at the same time, becomes subject to all losses not occasioned by the fault of the seller. . . .

The basic reason for the rule is that if a party by a contract has become in equity the owner of land and premises, they are his to all intents and purposes and, as such, any loss caused to them must be borne by him. . . .

In the case at bar the plaintiff entered into possession of the premises sold upon execution of the contract. Thereafter, it exercised all the rights ordinarily incident to ownership. We think that under any view of the rule of equitable conversion of title to real estate the fact that the purchaser has possession of the land sold and exercises sole control over it requires that any loss occasioned accidentally to the premises must fall upon him. . . .

Plaintiff argues that the destruction of the building made it impossible for the defendants to convey what they had contracted to convey, viz., the premises as they existed before the fire. There is, however, no provision in the contract providing for such event. It follows, therefore, that plaintiff wants us to hold, with a small minority of the States, that destruction of the subject matter makes inoperative the doctrine of equitable conversion. Such a view, however, is a rejection of the doctrine which we have found to be the law of this State, at least under the circumstance of admitting the purchaser into possession. It follows, therefore, that plaintiff upon the execution of the contract for the purchase of the Hotel Grande became the equitable owner of it and, as such, subject to losses occasioned other than by the fault of the defendants.

When this loss by fire occurred, the plaintiff as equitable owner became entitled under the law to two options. It could require either that the proceeds of the insurance be credited on the purchase price thus reducing its obligation, or it could require that the proceeds of the insurance be used to repair and restore the damaged premises. While it does not clearly appear that plaintiff made any election, it is clear beyond question that the entire proceeds of the insurance and more were applied by the defendants to the repair of the premises. Plaintiff therefore obtained that to which it was entitled. . . .

The judgment below is affirmed.

Gillingham v. Goldstone

197 N.Y.S.2d 237 (1959)

ARTHUR WACHTEL, J. Plaintiffs sue the defendants for return of security in the amount of $200 which had been given to the defendants at the time the parties entered into a lease on December 5th, 1958. The lease provided that the security would be forfeited if the tenant vacated "before one year." The tenants vacated on or about June 28th, 1959.

The tenants contended that there was an actual eviction on June 28th, 1959, and that the defendants breached the implied covenant of quiet enjoyment. The contention of actual eviction was not sustained. However, in the Court's opinion the preponderance of all the credible evidence supports a finding of constructive eviction. . . .

The Appellate Term, 1st Dept. has recognized that "The tenants should be protected from insult." Page J, *Manhattan Leasing Company* v. *Schleicher,* Sup., Appellate Term, 1st Dept. 1913, 142, N.Y.S. 545, at page 546. Where the landlord's conduct is "so grossly insulting and threatening in character as to seriously and substantially deprive the defendant of the beneficial enjoyment of the premises demised," and as a result, the tenant is forced to vacate the premises, there may be a constructive eviction and a breach of the covenant of quiet enjoyment (cf. Seabury, J., *Onward Construction Co.* v. *Harris, supra,* 144 N.Y.S.2d at page 318). Whether or not there are sufficient facts to support a constructive eviction is a matter to be determined upon the circumstances of each case.

Upon termination of the lease by constructive eviction, the tenant need not await the expiration date of the lease to recover the deposit. *One Hundred and Forty-Two West Fifty-Seventh Street Company* v. *Trowbridge,* Appellate Term, 1st Dept. 88 Misc. 70, 150 N.Y.S. 538.

Accordingly, judgment for the plaintiffs $200 with interest from June 28, 1959.

CHAPTER 52
REVIEW QUESTIONS AND PROBLEMS

1. *A* as seller and *B* as buyer executed a contract for the sale of a parcel of real property for $12,000. *B* paid $4,000 down, and the deed was placed in escrow pending payment of the $8,000 balance by *B* on March 12, 1963. On March 5, *A* died. *B* paid the $8,000 to the escrowee and received the deed on March 12. *A*'s heirs challenge the transaction. What result?

2. *X* executed a contract for the purchase of a commercial building from *Y.* The contract contained a provision stating that if the payments by *X* were more than thirty days overdue, *Y* could declare a default and obtain the deed back from the escrowee. After twelve years of the

twenty-year contract, X fell on hard times and made no payments for almost a year. Would a court allow Y to default the contract, cancel the deed, and reacquire possession of the property?

3. A Company leased a commercial building from B Company by an oral lease for a period of ten years. A Company went into possession. For what period was the lease enforceable?

4. X leased a house from Y. Before X took possession, Y covered a rather large hole in the floor of the attic with plaster board that was too weak to support a person's weight. X's wife, while storing goods in the attic, fell through the plasterboard and was injured. Is Y liable?

5. X, by his will, created a trust whereby $50,000 was left to the ABC Bank as trustee for X's wife and children. The bank invested the money solely in its own stock. The bank failed to pay dividends. Do X's wife and children have a remedy?

6. The ABC Bank, as a land trustee, held title to Blackacre. A trust agreement had been executed, naming X, Y, and Z as beneficiaries of the trust. W, a judgment creditor of X, seeks to have Blackacre sold at a public sale to satisfy his judgment. May he do so?

7. What are the three interests in land that may be separately transferred?

8. What is the primary reason for using an escrow agent?

9. What is an acceleration clause in a contract for a deed? What is a forfeiture clause in a contract for a deed?

10. X, the owner of an apartment building, leased an apartment to Y. During Y's absence, X inspected the property to ascertain if Y had alcoholic beverages on the premises. When X confronted Y with some empty beer bottles he had taken from the apartment, Y sued X for trespass. Is X guilty?

chapter 53

Real Property
as Security

REAL ESTATE MORTGAGES

7-50. Introduction.   A real estate mortgage is an interest in real property which is created by contract for the purpose of securing the performance of an obligation, usually the payment of money. The owner of the estate in land that is being used as security for the debt is called the *mortgagor;* the party to whom the security interest in the real estate is conveyed is called the *mortgagee.* Mortages are common transactions and are extremely important in all aspects of finance. The sections which follow will discuss some of the more important legal aspects of mortgages.

7-51. Legal Theories About Mortgages.   In the United States, three distinct legal theories relating to mortgages have developed. The first of these, known as the *title theory,* was developed at common law. At common law and in those few states following the title theory, a mortgage on land is an absolute conveyance of the title of the land by the owner to the mortgagee, upon condition that the title will revert to the mortgagor when the obligation is performed or the money is repaid. The mortgagee is granted the absolute right to the land, and he is entitled to take possession and to collect any rents and profits. If the mortgagor fails to pay the money on or before the day set, the property will never revert to him but will remain the property of the mortgagee. Notwithstanding the mortgagee's right to possession, the mortgagor is entitled to an accounting by the mortgagee at the time the obligation of the mortgagor is fulfilled. The accounting is for any income obtained from the property while in possession of the mortgagee. This right of accounting exists only in cases where the mortgagor does not default.

The second theory about mortgages is usually known as the *lien theory*, although it is sometimes called the *equitable theory*. Under this theory, a mortgage is not a conveyance of title but only a method of creating a lien on the real estate. The lien or equitable theory avoids the harshness which often results on default in title-theory states when the mortgagee is allowed to keep the real property without any obligation to the former owner. Under the lien theory, a mortgagee does not have title when the mortgagor defaults; he simply has a lien which can be foreclosed. Upon foreclosure of the lien, any proceeds of the sale in excess of the debt and the costs of sale remain the property of the mortgagor. In addition, lien-theory states grant to the mortgagor a right to redeem his property after the default and foreclosure. This right to redeem is known as the mortgagor's *equity of redemption*. The time period during which a mortgagor may redeem is usually prescribed by statute. When it is not, it is fixed by the court in the foreclosure proceedings. If a mortgagor wishes to redeem, he pays the total debt plus the costs of sale. But if the property is not redeemed within the prescribed period, it becomes the absolute property of the purchaser at the foreclosure sale.

Many states do not follow the title theory or the lien theory; they have reached a compromise between the two theories—an *intermediate theory*. By the intermediate theory, a mortgage is a conveyance of title, but the equitable theories are applied to it. Mortgages must be foreclosed and the mortgagor has an equity of redemption, even though the mortgagee has "title." The great majority of states are either lien-theory or intermediate-theory states; the title theory has little support. Therefore, in the discussion that follows, a mortgage is considered a lien on the premises.

7-52. Property Capable of Being Mortgaged.   As a general rule, both legal and equitable interests in land can be mortgaged. Property that one does not own cannot be mortgaged, but a mortgage may be so drawn as to cover property to be acquired in the future. A mortgage of such property creates no lien at the time of its execution; a court of equity, however, will recognize that the lien exists at the time the property is acquired by the mortgagor. If the mortgage is properly recorded, the lien has priority over all rights of others which arise or are created after the recording of the mortgage.

A mortgage may also be given prior to the time when the money is advanced to the mortgagor. Such a mortgage is usually called a *mortgage to secure future advances*. When the mortgagee advances the money, the mortgage is a valid lien as of the date when the mortgage was recorded.

7-53. Form of Mortgage.   The influence of the title theory is reflected in the form of mortgage in common use. It states that the property is conveyed to the mortgagee, subject to the conditions set forth in the mortgage. Such a conveyance of real property must be in writing, under seal, and executed with all the formalities of a deed. The contract between the parties with respect to the loan need not be included in the mortgage but may be set forth in a separate document. In title-theory states, a mortgage is a very formal instrument. In lien-theory states, short forms of mortgages are usually used.

7-54. Recording Mortgages.   In order that the mortgagee may give notice to third parties that he has an interest in the real estate covered by the mortgage, it is necessary that the mortgage be recorded in the recording office of the county where the real estate is situated. This recording protects the mortgagee against subsequent bona fide purchasers of the land taking the real estate free from the mortgage. The statutes of the various states specify the requirements necessary for recording mortgages.

7-55. An Absolute Conveyance May Be a Mortgage.   A deed absolute on its face may be shown by parol evidence to be a mortgage if such evidence indicates that the intention of the parties was to make the transfer security for a loan.[1] The grantor of the deed must prove by clear, precise, and positive evidence that it was the intention of the parties to use the deed for the purpose of securing a loan.

Likewise, a landowner may sell his land and give an absolute deed, with an agreement that he retain the right to repurchase for a certain price within a specified time. Parol evidence may be introduced in such a case to establish that the deed was given for the purpose of securing a loan. If the evidence is convincing, a court of equity will declare such a deed to be a mortgage. For example, a man may convey his farm worth $30,000 for a consideration of $10,000. The so-called buyer then gives the seller an option to repurchase at a figure approximating $10,000 and interest. If the evidence is clear that the parties intended to make a loan, even though the option period has expired, it is not too late for the grantor to redeem his property, because the court will treat the deed as a mortgage.

7-56. Deed of Trust in the Nature of a Mortgage.   A deed of trust, sometimes called a trust deed, may be used as a substitute for a mortgage for the purpose of securing debts. The property is conveyed by the borrower who executes the deed of trust, to a trustee to hold in trust for the benefit of the note holders. If the debt is paid at the time required by the contract, the trustee reconveys the property to the borrower, or in lien-theory states and intermediate-theory states, releases the lien. If there is a default in payment, the trustee forecloses the trust deed and applies the proceeds to the payment of the debt secured. Deeds of trust are used when the note is likely to be negotiated and when numerous notes are secured by the same property. A trust deed may also be used to secure bonds held by many different persons. For example, where it is desired to issue bonds secured by railroad or other corporate property, a trust deed may be executed to secure the entire bond issue. This method is necessary because it would be impractical to execute a separate mortgage to secure each bond. An important feature of the deed of trust is that the note secured by it can be freely negotiated separate and apart from the deed of trust. When the mortgagor pays the note, he surrenders it to the trustee under the trust deed, and the latter makes it a matter of record that the obligation has been satisfied.

7-57. Purchase-Money Mortgages.   A purchase-money mortgage is given for a part or the whole of the purchase price of land. For example, *A* wishes to purchase real estate worth $30,000. He has $10,000 in cash. Upon securing title from the vendor, *A* can complete his purchase by giving the vendor a mortgage on the real estate to secure a note for the remaining purchase price of

[1] Davis v. Stone, page 1066

$20,000. This type of mortgage is normally used in the buying and selling of real estate. It should be noted that in some jurisdictions a deficiency decree obtained upon the foreclosure of a purchase-money mortgage will not be enforced.

7-58. The Mortgagor's Obligation.   The mortgagor is usually personally liable for the mortgage debt, not by reason of the mortgage but because he makes a note, a bond, or other contract which evidences the debt secured by the mortgage. When there is more than one mortgagor, all of them need not sign the note nor be liable on the underlying obligation. In such a case, the property is given as security for the debt, but only those signing the note or incurring the obligation have personal liability.

7-59. Rights and Liabilities of the Mortgagee.   In the title-theory states, the mortgagee has legal title and theoretically the right to possess the mortgaged property during the period of the mortgage, unless the contract grants to the mortgagor the right to remain in possession. In the lien-theory states, the mortgagor is entitled to possession, unless a different arrangement is provided for in the mortgage. In both the lien- and title-theory states, the mortgagee is protected against any person who commits waste or impairs the security. Even the mortgagor may not use the property in such a manner as to reduce materially its value. Mining ore, pumping oil, or cutting timber are operations that may not be conducted unless they are provided for in the mortgage agreement, unless they are being conducted at the time the mortgage is created.

A mortgagee has a right to pay off or to redeem from any superior mortgage in order to protect his security, and he can charge the amount so paid to the mortgagor. Likewise, he may pay taxes or special assessments which are a lien on the land, defend suits which threaten the title of the mortgagor, and recover the sum so expended. The mortgagor is under a duty to protect the security, but should he fail to do so, the mortgagee has the right to make any reasonable expenditures necessary to protect the security for a debt.

Just as in the case of security agreements in personal property, a mortgage can provide for future advances to be made by the mortgagee. If the mortgagor gives a second mortgage prior to the future advances under the first, a priorities problem is presented. Generally, it is held that the first mortgage prevails unless he had actual knowledge of the second when he made the further advances.[2]

7-60. Transfer of Mortgaged Property.   The mortgagor may sell, will, or give away the mortgaged property, subject, however, to the rights of the mortgagee. A transferee from a mortgagor stands in the same position as the mortgagor and has no greater rights. Such grantee of the mortgagor's interest may redeem the land and require the mortgagee, if the latter is in possession, to account for rents and profits. A grantee of mortgaged property is not personally liable for the mortgage debt, unless he impliedly or expressly assumes and agrees to pay the mortgage. Such assumption must be established by clear and convincing evidence. A purchase "subject to" the mortgage is usually considered not to be an assumption. If the grantee assumes the mortgage, he becomes personally liable for the debt, even when the land is worth less than the mortgage.

[2] Blaustein v. Aiello, page 1067

For example, if *A* purchases real estate worth $8,000 which is subject to a mortgage of $5,000 and assumes and agrees to pay the mortgage, he pays the former owner $3,000 and assumes responsibility for the ultimate payment of the mortgage. If he merely purchases the real estate "subject to" the mortgage, he again pays the owner $3,000 but is not liable for the $5,000. The grantee may permit the land to be foreclosed without any personal liability on his part for the deficit. If he had assumed the debt, he would have been liable for any deficiency. Of course, if the grantee wants to keep the property, he must discharge the mortgage.

7-61. Liability of Mortgagor After Transfer. If the grantee of the mortgaged property assumes and agrees to pay the indebtedness, he thereby becomes the person primarily liable for the debt. As between himself and the mortgagor, by virtue of his promise to the mortgagor to pay the debt, he is the principal debtor and the mortgagor is the surety. This assumption by the grantee, however, does not relieve the mortgagor of his obligation to the mortgagee, and such mortgagor continues liable unless he is released from his indebtedness by the mortgagee. Such a release must comply with all the requirements for a novation. In those states which recognize the relationship of principal and surety between the mortgagor and his grantee, an agreement made by the mortgagee with the grantee, to extend the time of payment, will release the mortgagor from liability. If the grantee takes "subject to" the mortgage, the original debtor is not released, since suretyship is not involved directly. Many states, however, release the mortgagor of responsibility for any loss resulting from a decline in value of the mortgaged property during a period of extension.

7-62. Insurance. Both the mortgagor and the mortgagee have an insurable interest in the mortgaged property. The destruction of mortgaged property by fire gives the mortgagee no interest in the proceeds recovered under a fire insurance policy, unless the mortgage required the mortgagor to insure the property for the benefit of both parties. Since the vast majority of mortgages require insurance, insurance companies have formulated various clauses for insertion when insurance is issued on mortgaged property.

One of these clauses provides that in case of loss, payment shall first be made to the mortgagee until his debt is satisfied, any balance being paid to the insured. Such a provision is a simple loss-payable clause and gives the mortgagee no greater rights against the insurer than those possessed by the mortgagor. Thus, if property mortgaged for $7,000 is fully insured and a $9,000 loss occurs, $7,000 is payable to the mortgagee and $2,000 to the mortgagor. The amount paid to the mortgagee effectively reduces the amount owed by the mortgagor. In this manner both parties are adequately protected by a single policy.

In many states the insurer, when requested, inserts in the policy what has become known as the *standard mortgage clause*. In effect, a policy with such a clause creates two contracts, one with the mortgagor and one with the mortgagee. Consequently, if for any reason the policy is not enforceable by the mortgagor, it nevertheless is enforceable by the mortgagee to the extent of his interest. Misconduct or violation of policy terms by the mortgagor does not destroy the mortgagee's protection unless he is aware of such conduct and fails to report it to the insurance company. To terminate the policy as to the mortgagee, ten days' written notice is required. However, if at any time the insurer pays the mortgagee when under no duty to the mortgagor, the latter having violated some policy term, the mortgage debt is not reduced. To the extent payment is made to the mortgagee under these conditions, the insurer takes over that portion of the claim against the owner under the doctrine of subrogation.

7-63. Transfer of Debt.   A debt that is secured by the mortgage is a chose in action, usually evidenced by notes or bonds. If the notes or bonds are non-negotiable, the assignee of such notes or bonds takes title subject to all defenses that are available against the assignor. If, however, the notes or bonds are negotiable instruments and are transferred by negotiation, the holder takes free of personal defenses that would have been available against the transferor. The holder of the negotiable instrument secured by the mortgage has the right, upon default, to enforce the mortgage for the purpose of securing payment of the debt, as evidenced by the notes or bonds. If the mortgagee transfers the note without any formal transfer or mention of the mortgage, the transferee of the note is entitled to the benefit of the mortgage, because the security follows the debt. Since a debt secured by the mortgage is the principal and the mortgage only an incident, it would appear that an assignment of the mortgage without the debt is a nullity. Since a mortgage without a debt is difficult to comprehend, an assignment of the mortgage without the assignment of the debt accomplishes nothing. For the same reason, a debt cannot be assigned to one and the mortgage security to another. The use of a trust deed eliminates the need to transfer the mortgage with the debt. Also a note secured by a trust deed can be negotiated without the trustee's taking action.

If an assignment of the mortgage is made, the assignment should be recorded in order to give notice of the rights of the assignee to all subsequent purchasers. However, failure to record the assignment will not aid a purchaser or later mortgagee who has notice of the assignment. Actual notice should also be given to the mortgagor; otherwise, payment by the mortgagor to the mortgagee may discharge the debt secured by the mortgage.

7-64. Payment Before Default.   Payment of the mortgage debt terminates the mortgage. Upon payment by the mortgagor, a release or satisfaction is secured from the mortgagee. This release should be recorded in order to clear the title to the land; otherwise, the unreleased mortgage will remain a cloud on the title. If the mortgagee refuses to give a release, he can be compelled to do so in a court of equity by a bill to remove a cloud on the title or by other proceedings provided for by statute.

A tender of the principal by the mortgagor before the due date does not terminate the lien evidenced by the mortgage, because the mortgagee cannot be forced to lose his investment before maturity, unless the mortgage contains a clause allowing prepayment. However, a tender of principal and interest upon the due date terminates the lien, although such a tender does not discharge the debt, and the mortgagee may still enforce it personally against the mortgagor until absolute payment has taken place. Under the common-law title theory, a tender on the due date satisfies the condition and reinvests the title in the mortgagor, but a tender after the due date does not have such an effect. The condition not having been performed, a reconveyance by the mortgagee is necessary. Thus, in title-theory states, a tender at maturity reinvests the title in the mortgagor, although in lien-theory states, a tender at or after maturity terminates the lien. The mortgagor's only remedy in title-theory states is that of placing his money in court and bringing suit in equity for redemption. Such tender does, however, forestall recovery for interest and court costs.

7-65. Right to Redeem Before Foreclosure Sale. At any time after default, a mortgagor may exercise his right to redeem from the mortgage, unless this right has been barred by a period of time specified by statute. The mortgagor or any person who has an interest in the mortgaged land is entitled to redeem from the mortgage; but in order to do so, he must pay the entire mortgage debt, with interest, and all other sums, including costs, to which the mortgagee may be entitled by reason of the mortgage. If the mortgagee is in possession of the mortgaged property and refuses to consent to a redemption, the mortgagor or any party entitled to redeem may file a bill in equity for the purpose of redeeming the mortgaged property. Such person, however, must be ready and willing to pay whatever the court finds due, or tender to the court all moneys due on said mortgage.

7-66. Right to Redeem After the Foreclosure Sale. By statute in most states, any person interested in the premises, through or under the mortgagor, may, within a specified period of time from the foreclosure sale of said property, redeem the real estate so sold. To do so, he must pay to the court for the benefit of the purchaser, the sum of money, with interest and costs, for which the premises were sold. The period of time allowed for redemption varies greatly from state to state. Generally, the redeeming mortgagor is also required to pay, at the foreclosure sale, all costs incurred by the purchaser in protecting and preserving the property. In some States the redemption price includes the value of any improvements made by the purchaser.[3]

MORTGAGE FORECLOSURES

7-67. Right to Foreclose. If the mortgagor fails to perform any of his obligations as agreed, the mortgagee may declare the whole debt due and payable, and he may foreclose for the purpose of collecting the indebtedness.

7-68. Types of Foreclosure. The statutes of the various states specify the procedure by which mortgages are foreclosed. There are four types of foreclosure proceedings for the purpose of using the mortgaged property to pay the mortgage debt: (1) strict foreclosure, (2) foreclosure by suit in equity, (3) foreclosure by exercise of the power of sale, and (4) foreclosure by entry and writ of entry. Strict foreclosure is one by which the mortgagee gets the land free from the right of redemption after the date specified in the foreclosure decree; that is, the decree provides that, if the debt is not paid by a certain date, the mortgagor loses the realty and the mortgagee takes it free from the rights of junior mortgagees and lienholders. This is a harsh rule and is used only where it is clear that the mortgaged property is not worth the mortgage

[3] Ladd v. Parmer, page 1068

indebtedness, the mortgagor is insolvent, and the mortgagee accepts the property in full satisfaction of the indebtedness. Strict foreclosure is similar in effect to the forfeiture of a contract for a deed.

Foreclosure by suit in equity and by exercise of the power of sale will be discussed in the next sections. The fourth method is used in very few states. By this method, the mortgagee may foreclose by entry upon the land, after default, after publication of notice and advertisement, and in the presence of witnesses; or by the possession of the premises for a period of time. If, after a limited period, the mortgagor does not redeem, the foreclosure is said to be completed and the title to rest in the mortgagee.

7-69. Foreclosure by Suit in Equity.   The usual method of foreclosing a mortgage is a proceeding in equity, such proceeding being provided for by statute. A bill for foreclosure is filed in a court of equity; this bill sets up the mortgagee's rights, as provided for in the mortgage, and shows such breaches of the covenants in the mortgage as will give a right of foreclosure. The court will issue a certificate of sale authorizing the master in chancery or some other officer of the court to sell the land at public auction. Following the sale, he gives the purchaser a deed to the land and accounts for the funds realized as a result of the sale. To the extent that funds are available, they are used to pay court costs, the mortgage indebtedness, and inferior liens in the order of their priority. If any surplus remains, it is paid to the former owner of the property. Foreclosure by a second mortgagee is made subject to all superior liens. The buyer at the foreclosure sale takes title, and the first mortgage remains a lien on the property. All inferior liens are cut off by foreclosure except as the holders thereof have an equity in a surplus if such exists. As previously noted, the statutes in many states provide a period of time after the sale within which the mortgagor or other persons having an interest are entitled to redeem the property. Where such statutes are in force, the purchaser is not entitled to his deed until after the expiration of the period within which redemption may be made. The purchaser may request that court appoint a receiver, and order the mortgagor to pay rent during the redemption period. The purchaser is entitled to the net rent during this period.

7-70. Foreclosure by Exercise of Power of Sale.   The mortgage often provides that, upon default by the mortgagor, the mortgagee may sell the land without judicial process. This method of foreclosure can only be made in strict conformity with the terms of the mortgage. The power of sale makes the mortgagee the agent of the mortgagor to sell the land. In some states, however, a power of sale in the mortgage is expressly forbidden by statute, and foreclosures must be effected by judicial proceeding. A power of sale granted in a mortgage or a deed of trust is not revocable, since the agency is coupled with an interest; therefore, the death or insanity of the mortgagor will not revoke the power. In those states where the exercise of power is regulated by statute, the sale must be public after the prescribed notice is given. In the absence of statute or mortgage agreement, however, the sale may be private. Since a mortgagee in selling the land under a power of sale is acting as an agent for the mortgagor, he is not allowed to purchase at the sale, because an agent cannot himself purchase that which he has been given authority by his principal to sell. The purchaser at such a sale secures only such title as the mortgagor had when he made the mortgage.

When a deed of trust in which the trustee is empowered to sell the land and to apply the proceeds to the mortgage debt is given to secure the payment of a debt, the same rules apply as are set forth above.

7-71. Deficiencies. Each mortgagor who executes the note or bond secured by the mortgage is personally liable for the debt. If the property that is the security for the debt does not sell for a sum sufficient to pay the mortgage indebtedness, by statute in most states the court may enter a deficiency decree for that part of the unsatisfied debt. This decree will stand as a judgment against the mortgagor, and his other property may be levied on to satisfy such judgment. For example: *A,* the mortgagee, owns a mortgage which is security for an indebtedness of $10,000 against *B's* land. If on foreclosure and sale of the land, the sum of only $7,000 is secured, *A* may obtain a deficiency judgment against *B* for $3,000, which will be a lien against any other property that *B* may own. Such other property may then be levied on and sold to satisfy the $3,000 deficiency judgment.

In order not to impose too great a hardship on mortgagor-debtors, different schemes have been devised to limit the amount of deficiency decrees. A revaluation of the property at the time of the foreclosure is sometimes used if the property's value is less than the total debt, and this amount is deducted from the judgment. Many states have statutes applicable only to purchase-money mortgages which provide in part that when a decree is granted for the foreclosure of any mortgage given to secure payment of the balance of the purchase price of real property, the decree shall provide for the sale of the real property covered by such mortgage for the satisfaction of the decree, but the mortgagee shall not be entitled to a deficiency judgment. The elimination of deficiency decrees rests on several theories: that the mortgagee loaned his money on the security of the land and not the personal credit of the purchaser-debtor; that a mortgagee-creditor should share with the debtor the risk of declining land value; and that if the land is the limit of the security, fewer inflationary and sounder loans will be made.

7-72. Priorities. A mortgagee is a secured creditor and as such has priority over general creditors of the mortgagor. But as a rule, a judgment creditor who obtained his judgment prior to the mortgage will prevail over the mortgagee.[4] This general rule is subject to the limitations imposed by the bankruptcy laws as discussed in Chapter 34.

MECHANIC'S LIEN LAWS

7-73. Nature. Mechanic's lien laws are the result of legislation that makes possible liens upon real estate where such real estate has been improved. The purpose of such legislation is to protect the laborer and materialman in the event of insolvency of the owner or the contractor. The laws of the states vary slightly in the protection accorded and the procedure required to obtain it. For this reason, the laws of the state in which the property is located should be

---

[4] Sterlington Bank v. Terzia Lumber & Hardware, Inc., page 1069

consulted. The sections that follow relate to provisions which are generally found in the various state laws.

7-74. Persons Entitled to Lien.   Those persons are entitled to a lien, who, by either express or implied contract with the owner of real property, agree (1) to deliver material, fixtures, apparatus, machinery, forms, or form work to be used in repairing, altering, or constructing a building upon the premises; (2) to fill, sod, or do landscape work in connection with the same; (3) to act as architect, engineer, or superintendent during the construction of a building; or (4) to furnish labor for repairing, altering, or constructing a building.

Those parties who contract with the owner, whether they furnish labor or material, or agree to construct the building, are known as contractors. Thus, practically any contract between the owner and another that has for its purpose the improvement of real estate gives rise to a lien on the premises in favor of those responsible for the improvement. To illustrate: a contract to attach a permanent fixture to a building or one to beautify a lawn would create a lien in favor of the contractor.

In addition to contractors, anyone who furnishes labor, materials, or apparatus to contractors, or anyone to whom a distinct part of the contract has been sublet has a right to a lien. These parties are customarily referred to as subcontractors. Their rights differ slightly from those of contractors, and some of these differences will be considered in later sections.

In order that a lien for materials may be maintained, the material must be furnished to the contractor or subcontractor. In addition, a record of the material furnished on each job is usually required. This procedure is necessary for two reasons: First, the record is essential to accuracy in the determination of the amount of the lien, and, second, it is evidence that the contractor is not his own materialman. If the material is sold on the general credit of the contractor and no record of the deliveries is kept, title passes to the contractor, and he becomes his own materialman so that the original materialman is not entitled to the lien. The lien of a party furnishing building material arises as soon as the material is delivered to the premises. On the other hand, one who supplies equipment or machinery receives a lien only if he can show that the goods delivered have become a part of the completed structure.

7-75. Against Whom Does the Lien Arise?   Any interest in real estate may be subjected to a lien. A fee simple, a life estate, or a lease for years may have a lien against it, depending on the nature of the contract. If the owner of the fee simple contracts for the construction, or authorizes or knowingly permits the improvement to be made, the lien is good against his interest as well as against the improvement. If a lessee, without the consent or knowledge of the owner, contracts for the construction or improvement of property, the lien arises only upon the interest of the lessee. To illustrate: *A* leases a vacant lot from *B*, with the understanding that *A* is to construct a building on the premises. Any lien created will affect the interests of both *A* and *B*. If *A* had not obtained *B*'s consent to erect the building, the lien would have been created only against the interest of *A*.

The improvement of real property should not give to the lienholder a right to disturb or destroy a prior mortgage. At the same time, there is no occasion to increase the protection of the mortgagee at the expense of the lienholder.

Consequently, an existing mortgage is always given a superior lien on the value of the property in its unimproved state. In many states, however, if the improvement or its value can be segregated, the mechanic's lien will be superior on the improvement. Where separation is not feasible, a method of appraisal is usually provided for, to determine what portion of the proceeds, at time of sale, are derived from the improvement.

7-76. Formalities Required to Perpetuate Lien.   Under the law of most states the contractor's lien arises as soon as the contract is entered into. In order to protect the contractor against claims of innocent third parties who might purchase the property or obtain a mortgage thereon, the law provides that the lien must be made a matter of record within a certain time, usually three to four months after all work is completed. Failure on the part of the materialman to register his claim as required by the statute will result in the loss of the lien as against subsequent bona fide purchasers or encumbrancers. As between the owner and the contractor, however, the time limit may be extended somewhat beyond this period. During the four months' period, the lien is good against innocent third parties even though it is not recorded.

To establish their liens, the subcontractors—materialmen, laborers, and others—must, within a relatively short period of time after they have furnished the last of their materials or labor, either make the liens a matter of record or serve written notice thereof on the owner, according to the particular state statute. The period most frequently mentioned by the various states is sixty days.

7-77. Protection Accorded the Owner.   The mechanic's lien law usually states that the owner shall not be liable for more than the contract price, provided he follows certain procedure outlined in the law. The law further provides that it shall be the duty of the owner, before making any payments to the contractor, to obtain from the latter a sworn statement setting forth all the creditors and the amounts due, or to become due, to them. It is then the duty of the owner to retain sufficient funds at all times to pay the amounts indicated by the sworn statements, provided they do not exceed the contract price. In addition, if any liens have been filed by the subcontractors, it is the owner's duty to retain sufficient money to pay them. He is at liberty to pay any balance to the contractor. If the amount retained is insufficient to pay all the creditors, they share proportionately in the balance, except that many of the states prefer claims of laborers. The owner has a right to rely upon the truthfulness of the sworn statement. If the contractor misstates the facts and obtains a sum greater than that to which he is entitled, the loss falls upon the subcontractors rather than upon the owner. Under such circumstances, the subcontractors may look only to the contractor to make good their deficit. Payments made by the owner, without first obtaining a sworn statement, may not be used to defeat the claims of subcontractors, materialmen, and laborers. Before making any payment, it is the duty of the owner to require the sworn statement and to withhold the amount necessary to pay the claims indicated.

When the contractor is willing, the owner may also protect himself by stipulating in the construction contract a waiver of the contractor's lien. In most states a waiver of the lien by the contractor is also a waiver of the lien of the subcontractors, as they derive their rights through those of the contractor. Certain states require the owner to record the contract before subcontractors begin work, in order that the agreement may bar their right to a lien.

REAL PROPERTY AS SECURITY CASES

Davis v. Stone

236 F.Supp. 553 (1964)

The plaintiffs purchased properties in Washington, D.C. The purchasers assumed an existing mortgage and gave the seller a second mortgage to secure a trust note for the purchase price. The note was sold to Stone, the defendant. Thereafter, the plaintiffs were in default and in lieu of foreclosure by Stone, the plaintiffs deeded the property to him under an agreement that the property would be deeded back if the plaintiffs completed all payments due under the mortgage note. The plaintiffs defaulted in their payments again. Stone contended that he was entitled to the property under the deed. The plaintiffs claimed that the deed should be declared an equitable mortgage.

KEECH, D. J. It has been pointed out by no less authority than Chief Justice Marshall that neither the policy nor the letter of the law prohibits the sale of property with the right to repurchase reserved to the vendor. That a mortgagor may convey his equity of redemption to the mortgagee in satisfaction of a debt is also well established. . . . But courts of equity will carefully scrutinize such a transaction between mortgagor and mortgagee, to determine what was really intended. The policy of the law will not permit the conversion of a mortgage into a sale, and, because of the debtor's relative position, doubtful cases will be construed as mortgages. . . .

In these cases in which the mortgagor transfers to the mortgagee with a condition of defeasance reserved to the mortgagor, all the authorities agree that the test by which to determine whether the transaction is intended as a mortgage or as a sale is whether or not a personal debt is created or continues to exist. . . . This test applies even where the conveyance is in lieu of foreclosure. No consideration of law or public policy prevents a transfer of mortgaged property to the mortgagee in satisfaction of the debt, but the debt must be cancelled thereby. . . .

The presumption is that a deed is what it purports to be on its face and one who seeks to establish the contrary has the burden of doing so by clear and convincing evidence. But the condition of defeasance and creation or subsistence of a debt need not be on the face of the deed, but may be established by contemporaneous agreement. . . .

In the instant case, the court finds that there was no cancellation of the debt, but that the Davises continued to be indebted to Stone after delivery of the deeds.

Where evidence of the debt is retained by the grantee, the continued existence of the debt is presumed. . . . But there is no need here to resort to presumptions. Not only did the grantee retain the notes evidencing the grantor's obligations, but he continued to record Davis's payments on the second trust note itself as well as in the payment book incident to this note. . . . There was no notation on either the notes or the payment books of any cancellation or reduction of the debt on account of the transfer of the property. The only consideration on the face of the deed was ten dollars. Moreover, the intent to secure rather than cancel the existing debt, or to create a new one, is evident from the face of the agreement signed contemporaneously with the delivery of the deeds. The transfer is there limited, i.e., it is made only " . . . until all monies advanced by the party of the second part for delinquent payment on first trust, second trust on above described properties and taxes has been reimbursed, . . . It is further agreed that upon final payment of this obligation the party of the second part will reconvey the above described properties in fee simple. . . . " In conformance with this intent, plaintiffs remained in possession of the properties until they defaulted, almost a year after the transfer. . . .

The court finds that the two deeds must be construed as mortgages when read in the light of the agreement of March 20, 1959, and the actions of the parties thereto.

Judgment for plaintiffs.

Blaustein v. Aiello

190 A.2d 639 (Md.) 1963

Home Federal Savings & Loan Association (Home) entered into two construction loan agreements with Forest Knolls, Inc., a corporation engaged in building dwellings. By the terms of these agreements, Forest Knolls agreed to construct six residences upon vacant lots; in return, Home agreed to lend Forest Knolls $84,000 to be advanced in the future in accordance with schedules set forth in the agreements. These schedules provided that the final portions of the loans, amounting to $2,800 for each house, were to be made "when (the dwellings were) FULLY COMPLETED, graded and landscaped; Release of Liens for all labor and materials submitted in proper form." The agreements further provided that if the real estate were encumbered without the consent of the lender, the lender would be under no obligation to make "further payments."

In accordance with these agreements, a note and deed of trust were executed by Forest Knolls. The trust was recorded.

Thereafter a second trust note was executed and recorded. Blaustein, assignee of the second trust note brought action against Aiello, the trustee under the first trust deed to establish his priority. The lower court ruled that the first trust deed prevailed as to advances made to Forest Knolls after the execution and recordation of the second. Blaustein appealed.

PRESCOTT, J. The appellant contends: (1) that the first deed of trust was one to secure future advances; (2) that the lien of the trust under which he claims attached before the "final payments" of $2,800 each were made; (3) that the final payments were voluntary and not obligatory under the terms of the trust, as the houses had not been completed nor had releases of liens been obtained; and (4) that Home, the Holder of the first trust, had actual knowledge of the second trust at the time of the voluntary payments. From these premises, he argues that his claim is superior to that of the holder of the first trust.

For the purposes of this case, we shall assume, without deciding, that appellant's contentions (1), (2), and (3) above are correct. In *Frank M. Ewing Co.* v. *Krafft Company* (222 Md.21, 158 A.2d 654) we held, in accordance with the great weight of authority, that a voluntary advance, as distinguished from one that was obligatory, by the holder of a first trust after actual notice of the attaching of intervening liens ranks behind those liens. We were careful to point out in that case that the appellant had actual notice, i.e., such notice as actually imparts and brings home knowledge of the existence of a fact to a party to be affected thereby, or his authorized agent. There are several sound reasons for the above rule. Among these are that it would be inequitable to permit a prior lienor, with actual knowledge of subordinate liens, to diminish, voluntarily and at his whim or caprice, the security of subordinate lienors. And a contrary view would place an owner who is unable to demand advances from the holder of the first deed of trust in the unfortunate position of also being unable to borrow on his property from another by reason of the possibility that, after the giving of a later deed of trust to the latter, the holder of the prior deed of trust might make advances to the owner, which would take priority over the claim of such latter.

We hold that constructive notice by the recording of the second deed of trust was not sufficient to bring the instant case within the scope of the *Ewing* case. (We did not quite reach this specific question in *Ewing.*) . . .

In the instant case, there is not a scintilla of evidence that Home, or any authorized agent of it, had actual knowledge of the second trust when it made the final payments. Since the appellant failed to establish one of the necessary factors to place him within the ambit of our holding in *Ewing,* he cannot prevail.

Order affirmed, appellant to pay the costs.

Ladd v. Parmer

178 So.2d 829 (Ala.) 1965

PER CURIAM. This is an appeal from a final decree of the Circuit Court of Mobile County, in Equity, fixing the amount appellants (Mortgagors) should pay to redeem their real property sold to appellees at a mortgage foreclosure sale.

The trial court fixed the sum at $9,081.35, but did not in the decree break down or itemize the items composing the same. We are left to an ascertainment of the items by reading the text of the evidence. This we have done. The briefs of the parties were very helpful in this respect.

Section 727, Title 7, Code of Alabama 1940, provides for the redemption of real estate from a mortgage foreclosure sale (as here), while Section 732 of the same title lists the items and charges that must be paid in order to effect such redemption.

Our review of the evidence and an examination of the contentions of the parties rule out any dispute as to the purchase price paid at the foreclosure sale, taxes, paving and sewage assessments. The latter (paving and sewage assessments) was a lien against the real property that was foreclosed. Neither is there any quarrel with the calculation of interest on these items.

There is a dispute about the amount claimed for repairs and improvements on the property made by appellees [purchasers at foreclosure sale] during the redemptive period of two years; also an item of $6.50, for recording the foreclosure deed, is challenged.

There was substantial evidence that appellees made repairs and permanent improvements on the buildings on the foreclosed property during the redemptive period in the sum of $3,202.66. Appellees testified the value was $3,202.66. Another witness for appellees testified that such market value of the improvements and repairs was $3,950.00. The evidence being *ore tenus,* the trial court evidently accepted the figure of $3,202.66 without interest.

But included in this figure of $3,202.66 was $350.00 allowed appellee for supervising and helping in the repairs and improvements while being made; and also for time consumed, and economy effected for making purchases of materials.

We held in *Ewing* v. *First National Bank of Montgomery* (227 Ala. 46,148 So.836):

> The statute, Code 1923, 10153, does not deal with the cost, but "the value of all permanent improvements made on the land since the foreclosure sale," and, while the cost of improvements is related to the value, the reasonable value is made the basis of payment by the redemptioner.

There was evidence before the court that the value of these improvements was $3,202.66. While the cost of the improvements did include an item of $350.00 for services of appellee in supervising the work and in purchasing materials, such inclusion should not necessarily be eliminated or deducted from the value of the improvements to which the value is related. Such value is not circumscribed or limited by the cost, but only related thereto. If work, economy of purchases at a discount, and the supervision of labor by appellee contributed to the value of the improvements, then redemptioner cannot complain. The value of the improvements must be paid and not particularly the cost.

We do not think the item of $6.50 for recording the foreclosure deed is a proper charge to be paid by the redemptioner. We do not find any provision in Sec. 732, *supra,* for such charge.

The final decree of the trial court should be modified by eliminating therefrom the sum of $6.50. To this extent the decree is modified, but otherwise is affirmed.

Sterlington Bank v. Terzia Lumber & Hardware, Inc.

180 So.2d 16 (La.) 1965

The Sterlington Bank was the holder of notes and mortgages executed by Terzia Lumber and Hardware, Inc. and by the Terzias personally. Among the notes was a collateral mortgage note for $35,000 signed by F. C. Terzia, Sr., and F. C. Terzia, Jr. The bank brought foreclosure proceedings on the mortgages and another bank, the First National Bank of El Dorado, Arkansas, intervened requesting that the $35,000 mortgage be revoked as fraudulent against the Arkansas bank. That bank had obtained a judgment against the Terzias which was unsatisfied. The Arkansas bank claimed that its rights as a judgment creditor should prevail over the other bank's mortgage interest. The lower court held the foreclosure proceedings in abeyance pending a determination of this question, and decided in favor of the Arkansas bank. The Sterlington Bank appealed.

BOLIN, J. The principal ground for the revocatory actions is that the Terzias were insolvent at the time the mortgage was granted; that this circumstance was known, or should have been known, by the officers of the plaintiff bank; that the mortgage embraced all remaining property of value belonging to the Terzias; that the mortgage was not granted in the ordinary course of business but for the purpose of securing prior indebtedness for which the Terzias received no consideration, and, therefore, the mortgage was gratuitous and did not constitute security for further advances to the Terzias as mortgagors.

Answering the intervention, plaintiff asserted the $35,000 collateral note secured by the mortgage was executed and delivered in consideration of plaintiff's agreement to pay certain obligations amounting to a total principal sum of approximately $14,000 and was given in good faith in the regular course of business. Plaintiff further denied any knowledge of the interest of intervenor or the relationship existing between it and the Terzias, or any indebtedness by the latter to the Arkansas bank.

The court found that the Terzias were insolvent at the time of executing the mortgage of November 4, 1960; that officials of plaintiff bank inspected the property of the Terzias, requested an inventory and demanded the $35,000 mortgage on the individual property, all of which indicated the bank had knowledge of the insolvency of the Terzias; that the mortgage was not granted in the ordinary course of business, had no relation to the individual obligations of the Terzias who received nothing therefor. For these reasons, the plaintiff's mortgage was subordinated to intervenor's judicial mortgage.

From our study of the record we are in accord with the findings of the trial court.

Affirmed.

CHAPTER 53
REVIEW QUESTIONS AND PROBLEMS

1. *A* purchased 240 acres of land from *B* and secured the purchase price with a purchase-money mortgage to the XYZ Bank. It was later discovered that *B* did not have clear title to the land at the time of the deed from *B* to *A*. *B* took the necessary steps to clear the title and delivered another deed to *A*. Is XYZ's mortgage valid?
2. *A* sold Blackacre to *B*, being paid the full purchase price. *B* had $10,000 of the $40,000 purchase price and obtained the remainder from *C*, to whom he gave a mortgage on Blackacre. *C* failed to record his mortgage. May *B* claim that the mortgage is of no effect? If *B* sold the property to *D*, would *D* be subject to the mortgage?
3. *A* deeded a parcel of property to *B*. The deed was absolute on its face. However, an unrecorded prior contract between *A* and *B* provided that the deed of the land was intended as security for a loan which *B* had made to *A*. The contract provided that if *A* repaid the loan by May 1,

1969, *B* would reconvey the land back to *A*. *A* repaid the loan, but *B* refused to reconvey the property. May *A* use the contract to show that the deed was in reality a mortgage?

4. *X* purchased some timberland from *Y*, borrowing the purchase price by a ten-year mortgage with the Z Bank. The timber had never been cut, but the verbal understanding of all parties was that *X* was to cut it. *X* began this operation, which would take two years, and he replanted seedlings, which would take approximately forty years to mature. No express provision in the sales contract or the mortgage covered the cutting of timber. May the Z Bank enjoin further cutting?

5. *A* purchased a home and lot from *B* and secured the balance due by a thirty-year mortgage. After living in the home for eight years and making all payments due on the mortgage note, *A* sold the property to *C*, who expressly assumed the mortgage. *C* paid installments for five years and then sold the property to *D* "subject to" the mortgage. *D* paid installments for five years and then defaulted. To whom may *B* go for payment of any deficiency?

6. *A* purchased a home from *B*, secured by a mortgage held by the XYZ Bank. A total of $20,000, including all interest, was to be paid in monthly installments. After five years, *A* lost his job, became completely insolvent, and was unable to make payments for three months. The bank made a timely declaration of default and obtained a foreclosure decree according to state law. The property was sold at a judicial sale on May 1, 1965, for $8,000, though $10,000 was still due. The statute in the state gave a six month period of redemption. *A* inherited $25,000 on December 1, 1965, and wished to redeem. Could he do so? Assuming this was a contract, with no mortgage, between *A* and *B*, and *B* had declared a forfeiture, could the court order redemption?

7. *A* held a mortgage on *B*'s property. When *B* purchased the property, the land and fixtures were worth approximately $20,000, the amount of the mortgage. *B* paid approximately $2,000 before he defaulted and the mortgage was foreclosed, leaving $18,000 unpaid. At the sale, *A* offered the highest price of $4,000, leaving a deficiency of $16,000, including taxes and costs. There is evidence that the land was worth at least $15,000. Does *B* have any rights if *A* brings an action for the deficiency of $16,000?

8. A home owner *X*, executed a mortgage as security for a loan to the ABC Loan Company. The mortgage was promptly recorded. Subsequent to the recording, *X* purchased from *Y* a new furnace for the home to replace a worn-out, worthless one. *Y* delivered and installed the furnace. *X* defaulted on the loan, the ABC Company foreclosed, and a sale was held, in which *Z* purchased the property. *Y* had failed to record his lien. May he now enforce a mechanic's lien on the furnace?

9. *A* owned a commercial building which she rented to *C*. *C* wished to install plumbing fixtures in the building and contracted with *D* to do so. *C* did not obtain *A*'s express consent to the construction, but *A*'s husband, who had no interest in the property, saw it. In the event of *C*'s default, may *D* hold *A* liable on a mechanic's lien, or may he enforce it by sale of the premises?

10. Name the transaction in each of the following cases:

    a. *A* purchases a home from *B* for $20,000. He pays *B* $5,000 and gives him a mortgage to secure a promissory note for $15,000 payable in monthly installments with interest.

    b. *A* purchases a $20,000 home from *B*. He pays *B* $5,000 and obtains the rest by giving *X, Y,* and *Z* promissory notes for $5,000 each. *A* conveys the property to the RST Bank by deed, in trust for *X, Y,* and *Z*.

    c. *A* purchases a home from *B* for $20,000 and deeds the property to *C*. A private agreement between *A* and *C* shows that *C* gave *A* $20,000, and if *A* pays *C* back, *C* promises to reconvey the property to *A*.

11. *A* loaned money to *B* and gave a note secured by a mortgage. It was provided that the mortgage would also be security for future advances which *A* might make to *B*, but *A* was not obligated to make any further advances. If *A* loaned additional amounts to *B*, would the security of the mortgage extend to such amounts?

12. In April *M* gave *P* a note secured by a mortgage on his house. On October 14 *P* delivered the mortgage to the county recorder of deeds. A mechanic's lien was filed with the recorder on October 18, for materials furnished by *X* for improvement of the house over a period beginning August 31. On August 20 *Y* filed a lien for drilling an outside well that was begun on June 23. Which party has priority of lien, assuming that each was ignorant of the other? What effect would *P*'s recording of the mortgage in April have had? When did the mortgage become effective to prevent claims of other creditors becoming precedent to it?

13. *A*, desiring to borrow $15,000, gave *B* an absolute deed as security for a loan of this amount. Upon payment of the debt and interest three years later, *B* executed an agreement to reconvey the property. Is this a sale or a mortgage?

14. *A* mortgaged his hotel to *B*. The mortgage contained a provision that *A* would replace furniture in the hotel as it became necessary and that the mortgage would cover any furniture thereafter purchased. *A* purchased furniture and gave a chattel mortgage to *X*. As between *B* and *X* who has a better claim to the furniture?

15. *A* sells *B* property having a $10,000 mortgage on it in favor of *C*. *B* purchases the property "subject to" the mortgage. The property declines in value; at the maturity of the mortgage debt, it is foreclosed and sells for $8,000. May *C* recover the deficit from *B*? May he recover from *A*, assuming that *A* is the mortgagor? Would the result differ if *B* had assumed the mortgage debt?

APPENDIX
HOW TO STUDY A CASE

When reading and studying the cases which are footnoted and appear at the end of each chapter, the student should attempt to analyze the court's reasoning in terms of the discussion in this section and other sections in the Introduction. Also, he should note the relevance of the case to the particular point under discussion. The student will thereby enhance his comprehension of the cases and also improve his own reasoning powers.

In order to understand a case, it is necessary to understand how a legal issue is presented by the use of the rules of procedure called adjective law, and how this legal issue is resolved by the application of appropriate rules of substantive law.

The case of *Bloss d.b.a. Eastown Theatres* v. *Federated Publications, Inc.* appearing on page 116 is here used to illustrate the method of abstracting or "briefing" a case. Note that in this case and in many of the others in the book, the facts have already been partially digested by the authors in the paragraphs preceding the verbatim excerpts from the judge's opinion. In other cases the facts have not been set forth in this fashion, and the student must do this for himself, as the facts are often interwoven into the opinion written by the judge.

Note that the case is cited in support or illustration of a statement in the text. Here the statement is that a court may be called upon to determine whether one party can properly refuse to contract with another.

The first step in case analysis is to set forth a concise statement of the facts —the basic essential facts which gave rise to the dispute.

1. *Statement of facts:* The plaintiff, Bloss, a theater owner, submitted an advertisement for a motion picture to the defendant newspaper. The defendant refused to print it on the ground that it was not in good taste. The plaintiff contended that a newspaper must accept advertisements and brought action to recover damages for the refusal and for a decree that the advertisements must be accepted and published.

2. *Legal procedure by which the question of law is raised:* The defendant moved for a summary judgment, which was granted. The plaintiff appealed, claiming that it was error to grant this motion.

3. *Question of law:* Does a newspaper have such freedom to contract that it can reject an advertisement?

4. *Plaintiff's argument:* A newspaper is affected with a public interest and therefore does not have the freedom of contract which is enjoyed by private enterprises.

5. *Defendant's argument:* The precedent has been established by case law that the business of publishing a newspaper is a private enterprise. In the absence of legislation to the contrary, a newspaper is not legally obligated to sell advertising to all who apply for it.

6. *The opinion and decision of the court:* The court (opinion written by Judge Holbrook) answered the question of law in the affirmative and ruled that the lower court properly dismissed plaintiff's complaint. Freedom of the press is guaranteed by the First Amendment, and a newspaper's freedom to contract is essential to a free press. The common law rule is that a newspaper is strictly a private enterprise and as such is under no legal obligation to sell advertising to all who may apply for it.

Most of the cases in this book are decisions of appellate courts. Decisions of state intermediate appellate courts and supreme courts are generally reported in two sources. One of these sources is the official state reports and the other the regional reporters published by the West Publishing Company, St. Paul, Minnesota. Each regional reporter is a collection of cases decided in the appellate courts of the states in a particular region of the country.

For example, on page 121 of the text will be found the case of *Galati* v. *Potamkin Chevrolet Co.,* 181 A.2d 900. This case, which was decided on appeal in 1962, can be found in the Pennsylvania Superior Court Reports. The same case can be found in the second series of the *Atlantic Reporter,* Volume 181 on page 900. The letter "A" here means *Atlantic Reporter.* This reporter includes cases decided by the state courts in Connecticut, Delaware, District of Columbia, Maine, Maryland, New Hampshire, New Jersey, Pennsylvania, Rhode Island, and Vermont. The figure "2d" after the letter "A" indicates that the *Atlantic Reporter* is now in a second series. The first series ran to 300 and, instead of the next volume being called 301, it is designated as 1 A.2d.

In addition to the *Atlantic Reporter,* there are: the *Pacific,* cited as Pac. or P.2d; the *Southeastern,* cited as S.E. or S.E.2d; the *Southwestern,* cited as S.W. or S.W.2d; the *Southern,* cited as So. or S.2d; the *Northwestern,* cited as N.W. or N.W.2d; and the *Northeastern,* cited as N.E. or N.E.2d. In addition to these reporters there are special reporters; for example, the State of New York has a *Reporter,* the *New York Supplement,* cited N.Y.S. and N.Y.S.2d. In this *Reporter* are found trial court cases and cases decided by the intermediate appellate courts of the State of New York.

Cases decided by United States courts are found in the West's National Federal Reporter System. U. S. district court cases are found in the *Federal Supplement Reporter,* cited as F. Supp. or F.Supp.2d. United States Court of

Appeals cases are found in the *Federal Reporter,* F. or F.2d. Cases decided by the United States Supreme Court are found in the *Supreme Court Reporter,* cited S.Ct. Cases decided by the United States Supreme Court are also found in the official *U. S. Reporter* published by the U. S. Government Printing Office, cited as U.S. In addition, special United States courts and administrative boards, such as the Court of Tax Appeals, Courts of Claims, Referees in Bankruptcy, the National Labor Relations Board, and others, have their own special bound volumes for the publication of their cases.

In connection with the "briefing" of cases, there are several techniques which should be kept in mind. First, be sure to identify the parties properly. At the trial court level the complaining party is called the plaintiff and the party being sued is the defendant. At the appellate court level the party who lost at the trial and who is therefore appealing and asserting that an error was committed by the trial court, is called the *appellant.* The party who prevailed in the lower court is now called the *appellee* or *respondent.* In some, but not all of the states, the citation or title of the case in the appellate court is *appellant* v. *appellee* (respondent). This can be confusing as where the trial defendant is appealing, so that in some states the title of the case on appeal would make it appear at first glance that the defendant (appellant) is suing the plaintiff (respondent).

In briefing cases it is very helpful to use proper descriptive terms to further identify the parties and their respective roles both in the transaction which gave rise to the dispute and in the litigation. Thus, in a contract case one party can be identified as the offeror (the party who made an offer) and the other as offeree (the person to whom the offer was made). If one of the parties has performed his part of a contract, he is called an obligee, one entitled to performance by another, while the other party who has not yet performed is referred to as the obligor. In cases involving agency, one party can be described as principal, another as agent, and the party with whom the agent dealt as "the third party." Other descriptive terms will be apparent as the materials in the various books are studied.

There are some general observations that aid in understanding legal terminology. The suffixes "or" and "er" have special significance. "Or" refers to a party who is doing something or who has an obligation to another party; a mortgag*or* owes an obligation to the mortgag*ee* secured by a mortgage on the mortgagor's property; a promiss*or* makes a promise to the promiss*ee;* an oblig*or* owes an obligation to the oblig*ee;* an offer*or* is obligated by an offer made to the offer*ee* so that the latter can create a contract by accepting the offer; a pledg*or* delivers property to a pledg*ee* as security for a loan; a bail*or* entrusts property to a bail*ee;* an assign*or* transfers a right to an assign*ee.*

Sometimes the suffix "er" is used instead of "or"—for example, an indors*er* transfers a negotiable instrument to an indors*ee;* an entrust*er* places property with a trust*ee* for the former's benefit.

Glossary

Abandonment: The term applies to many situations. Abandonment of property is the giving up of the dominion and control over it with the intention to relinquish all claim to the same. Losing property is an involuntary act; abandonment is voluntary.

When used with duty, the word abandonment is synonymous with repudiation.

Abandonment of a child by its parents may be a criminal offense when such parents fail to perform their parental duty.

Abandonment in divorce law means the voluntary separation or desertion of one spouse from the other.

Abatement of a nuisance: An action to end any act detrimental to the public, such as a suit to enjoin a plant from permitting the escape of noxious vapors.

Ab initio: Latin phrase meaning, "from the beginning." A person who enters upon the land of another by permission and thereafter abuses the permission becomes a trespasser ab initio; that is, he becomes a trespasser from the time he first entered upon the land.

Acceptance*:   Under Article 3–Commercial Paper this is the drawee's signed engagement to honor a draft as presented. It must be written on the draft, and may consist of his signature alone. It becomes operative when completed by delivery or notification.

Accord and satisfaction: An agreement between two persons, one of whom has a right of action against the other, that the latter should do or give, and the former accept, something in satisfaction of the right of action different from, and usually less than, what might legally be enforced.

Account*:   Any right to payment for goods sold or leased or for services rendered which is not evidenced by an instrument or chattel paper.

Account*:   Under Article 4–Bank Deposits and Collections this means any account with a bank and includes a checking, time, interest, or savings account.

Account Debtor: The person who is obligated on an account, chattel paper, contract right, or general intangible.

*The terms followed by an asterisk are defined in the Uniform Commercial Code and therefore these terms have significance in connection with Code materials. They are often given a particular meaning as related to the Code and the definitions are therefore not necessarily in conformity with meanings outside the framework of the Code.

Accretion: The gradual and imperceptible accumulation of land by natural causes, usually next to a stream or river.

Action ex contractu: An action at law to recover damages for the breach of a duty arising out of contract. There are two types of causes of action; those arising out of contract, ex contractu, and those arising out of tort, ex delicto.

Action ex delicto: An action at law to recover damages for the breach of a duty existing by reason of a general law. An action to recover damages for an injury caused by the negligent use of an automobile is an ex delicto action. Tort or wrong is the basis of the action. See *Action ex contractu.*

Ad damnum clause: A clause in a declaration or complaint of the plaintiff that makes the demand for damages and sets out the amount.

Addendum: Something which is to be added. An addition or supplement to an agreement.

Ad hoc: Latin words meaning, "for this." An ad hoc refers to a limited or particular situation. An ad hoc decision means, for this purpose only. An ad hoc committee is one limited to a special purpose. An ad hoc attorney is one appointed to do a special task in a particular case.

Ad idem: To the same point or effect.

Adjective law: The rules of procedure used by and in courts for enforcing the duties and maintaining the rights defined by the substantive law. Adjective law primarily involves matters of evidence, procedure, and appeals. It is also called remedial law.

Adjudicate: The exercise of judicial power by hearing, trying, and determining the claims of litigants before the court.

Administrator: A person to whom letters of administration have been issued by a probate court, giving such person authority to administer, manage, and close the estate of a deceased person.

Adverse possession: To acquire, by adverse possession, the legal title to another's land, the claimant must be in continuous possession during the period prescribed in the statute. This possession must be actual, visible, known to the world, with an intention by the possessor to claim the title as owner as against the rights of the true owner. The claimant usually must pay the taxes and liens lawfully charged against the property. Cutting timber or grass from time to time on the land of another is not such adverse possession as to confer title.

Advising Bank*: A bank which gives notification of the issuance of a credit by another bank.

Affidavit: A voluntary statement of facts formally reduced to writing, sworn to, or affirmed before, some officer authorized to administer oaths. Such officer is usually a notary public.

A fortiori: Latin words meaning "by a stronger reason." The phrase is often used in judicial opinions to say that, since specific proven facts lead to a certain conclusion, there are for this reason other facts that logically follow which make stronger the argument for the conclusion.

Agency coupled with an interest: When an agent has possession or control over the property of his principal and has a right of action against interference by third parties, an agency with an interest has been created. *A,* an agent, advances freight for goods sent him by his principal. He thus has an interest in the goods.

Agent: An agent is a person authorized to act for another (a principal). The term may apply to a person in the service of another, but in the strict sense an agent is one who stands in place of his principal. *A* works for *B* as a gardener and is thus a servant; but he may be an agent. If *A* sells goods for *B,* he becomes more than a servant. He acts in the place of *B.*

Agreement*: This means the bargain of the parties in fact as found in their language or by implication from other circumstances including course of dealing or usage of trade or course of performance as provided in the Uniform Commercial Code.

Aliquot: A subdivision or portion of the whole. An aliquot part.

Alter ego: Latin words literally meaning, "the other I." In law an agent is the alter ego or other person for his principal. When members of a corporation misuse the corporate entity, the courts look behind the entity that is the alter ego of the members.

Annuity: A sum of money paid yearly to a person during his lifetime, which sum arises out of a contract by which the recipient or another had previously deposited sums in whole or in part with the grantor—the grantor to return a designated portion of the principal and interest in periodic payments upon the arrival of the beneficiary at a designated age.

Appellee: The party in a cause against whom an appeal is taken.

Appellant: The party who takes an appeal from one court or jurisdiction to another.

A priori: A generalization resting on presuppositions and not upon proven facts.

Arbitration: The submission for determination of disputed matter to private unofficial persons selected in manner provided by law or agreement.

Architect's certificate: A formal statement signed by an architect that a contractor has performed under his contract and is entitled to be paid. The construction contract provides when and how such certificates shall be issued.

Arguendo: A Latin word which means to make the case by way of argument or in an argument.

Artisan's lien: One who has expended labor upon or added to another's property is entitled to the possession of such property as security until reimbursed for the value of labor or material. *A* repairs *B*'s watch. *A* may keep the watch in his possession until paid by *B* for such repairs.

Assignee: An assign or assignee is one to whom an assignment has been made.

Assignment: An assignment is the transfer by one person to another of a right that usually arises out of a contract. Such rights are called choses in action. *A* sells and assigns his contract right to purchase *B*'s house to *C*. *A* is an assignor. *C* is an assignee. The transfer is an assignment.

Assignment*:   A transfer of the "the contract" or of "all my rights under the contract" or an assignment in similar general terms is an assignment of rights, and unless the language or the circumstances (as in an assignment for security) indicate the contrary, it is a delegation of performance of the duties of the assignor; and its acceptance by the assignee constitutes a promise by him to perform those duties. This promise is enforceable by either the assignor or the other party to the original contract.

Assignment for the benefit of creditors: *A*, a debtor, has many creditors. An assignment of his property to *X*, a third party, with directions to make distribution of his property to his creditors is called an assignment for the benefit of creditors. See *Composition of creditors.*

Assignor: An assignor is one who makes an assignment.

Assumpsit: An action at common law to recover damages for the breach of contract. Historically it was based upon an implied undertaking (the word "assumpsit" is a Latin word meaning, "undertaking") to properly perform a duty.

Attachment: A legal proceeding accompanying an action in court by which a plaintiff may acquire a lien on a defendant's property as a security for the payment of any judgment which the plaintiff may recover. It is provisional and independent of the court action, and is usually provided for by statute. *A* sues *B*. Before judgment, *A* attaches *B*'s automobile in order to make sure of the payment of any judgment that *A* may secure.

Attorney at law: A person who has been granted a license by the state giving him the privilege of practicing law.

Attorney in fact: A person acting for another under a grant of special power created by an instrument in writing. *B*, in writing, grants special power to *A* to execute and deliver for *B* a conveyance of *B*'s land to *X*.

Bad faith: The term means "actual intent" to mislead or deceive another. It does not mean misleading by an honest, inadvertent, or careless misstatement.

Bail (verb):   To set at liberty an arrested or imprisoned person upon security's being given to the state by himself or at least two other persons that will appear at the proper time and place for trial.

Bailee: A person into whose possession personal property is delivered.

Bailee*:   The person who by a warehouse receipt, bill of lading, or other document of title acknowledges possession of goods and contracts to deliver them.

Bailment: A bailment is the delivery of personal property to another for a special purpose. Such delivery is made under a contract, either expressed or implied, that upon the completion of the special purpose, the property shall be redelivered to the bailor or placed at his disposal. *A* loans *B* his truck. *A* places his watch with *B* for repair. *A* places his furniture in *B*'s warehouse. *A* places his securities in *B* Bank's safety deposit vault. In each case, *A* is a bailor and *B* is a bailee.

Bailor: One who delivers personal property into the possession of another.

Banking Day*: Under Article 4–Bank Deposits and Collections this means that part of any day on which a bank is open to the public for carrying on substantially all of its banking functions.

Bearer*: The person in possession of an instrument, document of title, or security payable to bearer or indorsed in blank.

Bearer Form*: A security is in bearer form when it runs to bearer according to its terms and not by reason of any indorsement.

Bench: A term often used to designate a court or the judges of a court. Sometimes used to name the place where the judges sit. The term "bench and bar" means the judges and attorneys of the profession.

Beneficiary: A person (not a promisee) for whose benefit a trust, an insurance policy, a will, or a contract promise is made.

Beneficiary*: A person who is entitled under a letter of credit to draw or demand payment.

Bequest: A term used in a will to designate a gift of personal property. It is used synonymously with "devise" and often is construed to include real property.

Between Merchants*: Any transaction with respect to which both parties are chargeable with the knowledge or skill of merchants.

Bid: An offering of money in exchange for property placed for sale. At an ordinary auction sale a bid is an offer to purchase. It may be withdrawn before acceptance is indicated by the fall of the hammer.

Bilateral contract: One containing mutual promises with each party being both a promisor and promisee.

Bill of Lading*: A document evidencing the receipt of goods for shipment issued by a person engaged in the business of transporting or forwarding goods, and includes an airbill. "Airbill" means a document serving for air transportation as a bill of lading does for marine or rail transportation, and includes an air consignment note or air waybill.

Bill of sale: A written evidence that the title to personal property has been transferred from one person to another. It must contain words of transfer and be more than a receipt.

Binder: A memorandum evidencing temporary insurance issued by the insurer to the insured to cover a period of time during which the insured is considering formal application for a policy. Although incomplete as to specific terms, it is understood to include the normal provisions found in regular policies of insurance.

Blue sky laws: Popular name for acts providing for the regulation and supervision of investment securities.

Bona Fide Purchaser*: A purchaser of a security for value in good faith and without notice of any adverse claim who takes delivery of a security in bearer form or of one in registered form issued to him or indorsed to him or in blank.

Bond: A promise under seal to pay money. The term is generally used to designate the promise made by a corporation, either public or private, to pay money to bearer. U.S. Government Bonds; Illinois Central Railroad Bonds.

The term also describes an obligation by which one person promises to answer for the debt or default of another—a surety bond.

Book account: A record of the debits and credits between persons evidenced by entries in a book. The record usually contains detailed statements of the transactions between the parties. It indicates rights and duties and is an assignable chose in action.

Broker: A person employed to make contracts with third persons on behalf of his principal. Such contracts involve trade, commerce, buying and selling for a fee (called brokerage or commission).

Broker*: A person engaged for all or part of his time in the business of buying and selling securities, who in the transaction concerned acts for, or buys a security from or sells a security to a customer. Nothing in this Article determines the capacity in which a person acts for purposes of any other statute or rule to which such person is subject.

Bulk Transfer*: Any transfer in bulk and not in the ordinary course of the transferor's business of a major part of the materials, supplies, merchandise or other inventory of an enterprise subject to this Article.

Burden of Establishing*:   The burden of persuading the triers of fact that the existence of the fact is more probable than its non-existence.

Buyer*:   A person who buys or contracts to buy goods.

Buyer in Ordinary Course of Business*:   A person who in good faith and without knowledge that the sale to him is in violation of the ownership rights or security interest of a third party in the goods buys in ordinary course from a person in the business of selling goods of that kind but does not include a pawnbroker. "Buying" may be for cash or by exchange of other property or on secured or unsecured credit and includes receiving goods or documents of title under a pre-existing contract for sale but does not include a transfer in bulk or as security for or in total or partial satisfaction of a money debt.

By-laws: The rules adopted by the members or the board of directors of a corporation or other organization for its government. These rules must not be contrary to the law of the land, and they affect only the rights and duties of the members of the corporation or organization. They are not applicable to third persons.

Call: An assessment upon a subscriber for partial or full payment on shares of unpaid stock of a corporation. The term may also mean the power of a corporation to make an assessment, notice of an assessment, or the time when the assessment is to be paid.

Call-in pay: Pay guaranteed by contract to workers called for work, who report and are ready, but to whom no work is made available. Sometimes used to designate pay for "featherbedding." See *Featherbedding.*

Cancellation*:   When either party puts an end to the contract for breach by the other. Its effect is the same as that of "termination" except that the cancelling party also retains any remedy for breach of the whole contract or any unperformed balance.

Capias ad respondendum: A judicial writ by which actions at law were frequently commenced, and which commands the sheriff to take the defendant and him keep safely, so that he may have his body before the court on a certain day to answer the plaintiff in the action.

Capital: The net assets of an individual enterprise, partnership, joint stock company, corporation, or business institution, including not only the original investment, but also all gains and profits realized from the continued conduct of the business.

Carrier: A natural person or a corporation who receives goods under a contract to transport for a consideration from one place to another. A railroad, a truck line, a bus line, an air line.

Cashier's check: A bill of exchange drawn by the cashier of a bank, for the bank, upon the bank. After the check is delivered or issued to the payee or holder, the drawer bank cannot put a "stop order" against itself. By delivery of the check, the drawer bank has accepted, and thus becomes the primary obligor. Note that an ordinary depositor after drawing a check, but before it is paid by the drawee bank, may countermand the same with a "stop order."

Cause of action: When one's legal rights have been invaded either by a breach of a contract or by a breach of a legal duty toward one's person or property, a cause of action has been created.

Caveat: Literally this means "let him beware." It is used generally to mean a warning.

Caveat emptor: These words express an old idea at common law—"let the buyer beware" —and mean that when goods are sold without an express warranty by the vendor as to their quality and capacity for a particular use and purpose, the buyer must take the risk of loss as to all defects in the goods. The rule of caveat emptor applies at judicial sales. The buyer takes no better title than that held by the debtor or defendant.

Caveat venditor: These words mean "let the seller beware" (in contradistinction to caveat emptor—"let the buyer beware"). Caveat venditor means that unless the seller by express language disclaims any responsibility, he shall be liable to the buyer if the goods delivered are different in kind, quality, use, and purpose from those described in the contract of sale.

Certiorari: An order issuing out of an appellate court to a lower court, at the request of an appellant directing that the record of a case pending in the lower court be transmitted to the upper court for review.

Cestui que trust: A person who is the real or beneficial owner of property held in trust. The trustee holds the legal title to the property for the benefit of the cestui que trust.

Charter: As to a private corporation, the word "charter" includes the contract between the created corporation and the state, the act creating the corporation, and the articles of association granted to the corporation by authority of the legislative act. The word is also used to define the powers and privileges granted to the corporation by the legislature. The states have enacted general laws for the purpose of the creation and organization of corporations. Formerly many corporations were created by special acts of legislatures.

As to municipal corporations, charter does not mean a contract between the legislature and the city created. A city charter is a delegation of powers by a state legislature to the governing body of the city. The term includes the creative act, the powers enumerated, and the organization authorized.

Chattel: The word "chattel" is derived from the word "cattle." It is a very broad term and includes every kind of property that is not real property. Movable properties, such as horses, automobiles, choses in action, stock certificates, bills of lading, and all "goods, wares, and merchandise," are chattels personal. Chattels real concern real property, such as a lease for years —in which case the lessee owns a chattel real. A building placed on real property by a lessee is a chattel real.

Chattel mortgage: A formal instrument used prior to the Uniform Commercial Code executed by a debtor called the mortgagor transferring an interest in a chattel to a creditor called a mortgagee, for the purpose of giving security for a debt. If the debt is not paid, the mortgagee may sell the chattel and use the proceeds to pay the debt. This proceeding is called a foreclosure.

Chattel Paper*:   A writing or writings which evidence both a monetary obligation and a security interest in or a lease of specific goods. When a transaction is evidenced both by such a security agreement or a lease and by an instrument or a series of instruments, the group of writings taken together constitutes chattel paper.

Chose in action: Words used to define the "right" one person has to recover money or property from another by a judicial proceeding. Such right arises out of contract, claims for money, debts, and rights against property. Notes, drafts, stock certificates, bills of lading, warehouse receipts, insurance policies are illustrations of choses in action. They are called tangible choses. Book accounts, simple debts, and obligations not evidenced by formal writing are called intangible choses. Choses in action are transferred by assignment.

Circumstantial evidence: If from certain facts and circumstances, according to the experience of mankind, an ordinary, intelligent person may infer that other connected facts and circumstances must necessarily exist, the latter facts and circumstances are considered proven by circumstantial evidence. Proof of fact *A* from which fact *B* may be inferred is proof of fact *B* by circumstantial evidence.

Civil action: A proceeding in a law court or a suit in equity by one person against another for the enforcement or protection of a private right or the prevention of a wrong. It includes actions on contract, ex delicto, and all suits in equity. Civil action is in contradistinction to criminal action in which the state prosecutes a person for breach of a duty.

Clearing Corporation*:   A corporation all of the capital stock of which is held by or for a national securities exchange or association registered under a statute of the United States such as the Securities Exchange Act of 1934.

Clearing House*:   Under Article 4–Bank Deposits and Collections this means any association of banks or other payors regularly clearing items.

Cloud on title: Words used to express the idea that there is some evidence of record which shows a third person has some prima facie interest in another's property.

Code: A collection or compilation of the statutes passed by the legislative body of a state. Such codes are often annotated with citations of cases decided by the State Supreme Courts. These decisions construe the statutes. Examples—Oregon Compiled Laws Annotated, United States Code Annotated.

Codicil: An addition to or a change in an executed last will and testament. It is a part of the original will and must be executed with the same formality as the original will.

Cognovit: The name of a plea by which the defendant for the purpose of avoiding a trial admits the right of the plaintiff. It is an answer to the complaint often called a "narr" in a confession of judgment action. This remedy is often used to secure judgments on promissory notes.

Co-insurer: A term in a fire insurance policy that requires the insured to bear a certain portion of the loss when he fails to carry complete coverage. For example, unless the insured carries insurance which totals 80 per cent of the value of the property, the insurer shall be liable for only that portion of the loss that the total insurance carried bears to 80 per cent of the value of the property.

Collateral: With reference to debts or other obligations, the term "collateral" means security placed with a creditor to assure the performance of the obligator. If the obligator performs, the collateral is returned by the creditor. *A* owes *B* $1,000. To secure the payment, *A* places with *B* a $500 certificate of stock in X Company. The $500 certificate is called collateral security.

Collateral*:   The property subject to a security interest, and includes accounts, contract rights and chattel paper which have been sold.

Collecting Bank*:   Under Article 4–Bank Deposits and Collections is any bank handling the item for collection except the payor bank.

Commercial Unit*:   Such a unit of goods as by commercial usage is a single whole for purposes of sale and division of which materially impairs its character or value on the market or in use. A commercial unit may be a single article (as a machine) or a set of articles (as a suite of furniture or an assortment of sizes) or a quantity (as a bale, gross, or carload) or any other unit treated in use or in the relevant market as a single whole.

Commission: The sum of money, interest, brokerage, compensation, or allowance given to a factor or broker for carrying on the business of his principal.

Commission merchant: An agent or factor employed to sell "goods, wares, and merchandise" consigned or delivered to him by his principal, for a compensation called a commission.

Common carrier: One who is engaged in the business of transporting personal property from one place to another for a compensation. Such person is bound to carry for all who tender their goods and the price for transportation. A common carrier operates a public utility and is subject to state and federal regulations.

Community property: All property acquired after marriage by husband and wife other than separate property acquired by devise, bequest, or from the proceeds of noncommunity property. Community property is a concept of property ownership by husband and wife inherited from the civil law. The husband and wife are somewhat like partners in their ownership of property acquired during marriage.

Complaint: The first paper a plaintiff files in a court in a law suit. It is called a pleading. It is a statement of the facts upon which the plaintiff rests his cause of action.

Composition of creditors: An agreement between creditors and their debtors by which they agree that the creditors will take a lesser amount in complete satisfaction of the total debt due. *A* owes *B* and *C* $500 each. *A* agrees to pay *B* and *C* $250 each in complete satisfaction of the $500 due each. *B* and *C* agree to take $250 in satisfaction. Such agreement is called a composition of creditors.

Compromise: An agreement between two or more persons, usually opposing parties in a law suit, to settle the matters of the controversy without further resort to hostile litigation. An adjustment of issues in dispute by mutual concessions before resorting to a law suit.

Condemnation proceedings: An action or proceeding in court authorized by legislation (federal or state) for the purpose of taking private property for public use. It is the exercise by the judiciary of the sovereign power of eminent domain.

Condition: A clause in a contract, either expressed or implied, that has the effect of investing or divesting the legal rights and duties of the parties to the contract. In a deed, a condition is a qualification or restriction providing for the happening or nonhappening of events that on occurrence will destroy, commence, or enlarge an estate. "*A* grants Blackacre to *B* so long as said land shall be used for church purposes." If it ceases to be used for church purposes, the title to Blackacre will revert to the grantors.

Condition precedent: A clause in a contract providing that immediate rights and duties shall vest only upon the happening of some event. Securing an architect's certificate by a contractor before he (the contractor) is entitled to payment is a condition precedent.

A condition is not a promise; hence, its breach will not give rise to a cause of action for damages. A breach of a condition is the basis for a defense. In the above illustration, if the contractor sues the owner without securing the architect's certificate, the owner has a defense.

Conditions concurrent: Conditions concurrent are conditions that are mutually dependent and must be performed at the same time by the parties to the contract. Payment of money and delivery of goods in a cash sale are conditions concurrent. Failure to perform by one party permits a cause of action upon tender by the other party. If *S* refuses to deliver goods in a cash sale, *B*, upon tender, but not delivery of the money, places *S* in default and thus may sue *S*. *B* does not part with his money without getting the goods. If *S* sued *B*, *B* would have a defense.

Condition subsequent: A clause in a contract providing for the happening of an event that divests legal rights and duties. A clause in a fire insurance policy providing that the policy shall be null and void if combustible material is stored within ten feet of the building is a condition subsequent. If a fire occurs and combustible material was within ten feet of the building, the insurance company is excused from its duty to pay for the loss.

Confession of judgment: A voluntary submission to the jurisdiction of the court by a debtor permitting judgment to be taken against him without a formal trial. Such permission often appears in promissory notes giving consent that the judgment may be taken immediately upon default. See *Cognovit.*

Confirming Bank*: A bank which engages either that it will itself honor a credit already issued by another bank or that such a credit will be honored by the issuer or a third bank.

Conforming*: Goods or conduct including any part of a performance are "conforming" or conform to the contract when they are in accordance with the obligations under contract.

Consideration: An essential element in the creation of contract obligation. A detriment to the promisee and a benefit to the promisor. One promise is consideration for another promise. This creates a bilateral contract. An act is consideration for a promise. This creates a unilateral contract. Performance of the act asked for by the promisee is a legal detriment to the promisee and a benefit to the promisor.

Consignee: A person to whom a shipper usually directs a carrier to deliver goods. Such person is generally the buyer of goods and is called a consignee on a bill of lading.

Consignee*: The person named in a bill to whom or to whose order the bill promises delivery.

Consignment: The delivery, sending, or transferring of property, "goods, wares, and merchandise" into the possession of another, usually for the purpose of sale. Consignment may be a bailment or an agency for sale.

Consignor: The person who delivers freight to a carrier for shipment and who directs the bill of lading to be executed by the carrier is called a consignor or shipper. Such person may be the consignor-consignee if the bill of lading is made to his own order.

Consignor*: The person named in a bill as the person from whom the goods have been received for shipment.

Conspicuous*: A term or clause is conspicuous when it is so written that a reasonable person against whom it is to operate ought to have noticed it. A printed heading in capitals (as: NON-NEGOTIABLE BILL OF LADING) is conspicuous. Language in the body of a form is "conspicuous" if it is in larger or other contrasting type or color. But in a telegram any stated term is "conspicuous." Whether a term or clause is "conspicuous" or not is for decision by the court.

Constitution: The Constitution of the United States constitutes the rules of organization of the United States and enumerates the powers and duties of the federal government thereby created. The constitutions of the several states prescribe the organization of each of the states and in general enumerate those powers not delegated to the federal government.

Constructive delivery: Although physical delivery of personal property has not occurred, yet by the conduct of the parties, it may be inferred that as between them possession and title has passed. *A* sells large and bulky goods to *B.* Title and possession may pass by the act and conduct of the parties.

Consumer Goods*: Goods that are used or bought for use primarily for personal, family, or household purposes.

Contract*: The total obligation which results from the parties' agreement as affected by the Code and any other applicable rules of law.

Contract Right*: Any right to payment under a contract not yet earned by performance and not evidenced by an instrument or chattel paper.

Conversion*: Under Article 3–Commercial Paper an instrument is converted when a drawee to whom it is delivered for acceptance refuses to return it on demand; or any person to whom it is delivered for payment refuses on demand either to pay or to return it; or it is paid on a forged indorsement.

Conveyance: A formal written instrument usually called a deed by which the title or other interests in land (real property) is transferred from one person to another. The word expresses also the fact that the title to real property has been transferred from one person to another.

Corporation: A collection of individuals created by statute as a legal person, vested with powers and capacity to contract, own, control, convey property, and transact business within the limits of the powers granted.

Corporation de facto: If persons have attempted in good faith to organize a corporation under a valid law (statute) and have failed in some minor particular, but have thereafter exercised corporate powers, such is a corporation de facto. Failure to have incorporators' signatures on applications for charter notarized is an illustration of noncompliance with statutory requirements.

Corporation de jure: A corporation that has been formed by complying with the mandatory requirements of the law authorizing such a corporation.

Corporeal: Physical things that are susceptible to the senses are corporeal. Automobiles, grain, fruit, and horses are corporeal and tangible and are called "chattels." The word corporeal is used in contradistinction to incorporeal or intangible. A chose in action (such as a check) is corporeal and tangible; or a chose in action may be a simple debt, incorporeal and intangible.

Costs: Costs, in litigation, are an allowance authorized by statute to a party for the expenses incurred in prosecuting or defending a law suit. The word "costs," unless specifically designated by statute or contract, does not include attorney's fees.

Counter-claims: A claim of the defendant by way of cross-action that the defendant is entitled to recover from the plaintiff. It must arise out of the same transaction set forth in the plaintiff's complaint, and be connected with the same subject matter. *S* sues *B* for the purchase price. *B* counter-claims that the goods were defective, and that he thereby suffered damages.

Course of Dealing*: This is a sequence of previous conduct between the parties to a particular transaction which is fairly to be regarded as establishing a common basis of understanding for interpreting their expressions and other conduct.

Covenant: A promise in writing under seal. It is often used as a substitute for the word contract. There are covenants (promises) in deeds, leases, mortgages, and other instruments under seal. The word is used sometimes to name promises in unsealed instruments such as insurance policies and conditional sale contracts.

Covenant (action on): The name of remedy at early common law for the breach of a promise under seal.

Cover*: After a breach by a seller the buyer may "cover" by making in good faith and without unreasonable delay any reasonable purchase of or contract to purchase goods in substitution for those due from the seller.

Credit*: ("Letter of credit") This means an engagement by a bank or other person made at the request of a customer and of a kind within the scope of Article 5–Letters of Credit that the issuer will honor drafts or other demands for payment upon compliance with the conditions specified in the credit. A credit may be either revocable or irrevocable. The engagement may be either an agreement to honor or a statement that the bank or other person is authorized to honor.

Creditor*: This includes a general creditor, a secured creditor, a lien creditor and any representative of creditors, including an assignee for the benefit of creditors, a trustee in bankruptcy, a receiver in equity and an executor or administrator of an insolvent debtor's or assignor's estate.

Creditor beneficiary: If a promisee is under a duty to a third party, and, for a consideration, secures a promise from a promisor which promise, if performed, discharges the promisee's duty to the third party, such third party is a creditor beneficiary. *A* owes *C* $100. *B,* for a consideration, promises *A* to pay *A*'s debt to *C. C* is a creditor beneficiary.

Creditor's bill: A bill filed by a judgment creditor in a court of equity to have set aside previous fraudulent conveyances, in order to find property upon which to levy execution.

Cumulative voting: A stockholder in voting for a director may cast as many votes for one candidate for given office as there are offices to be filed multiplied by the number of shares of his stock, or he may distribute this same number of votes among the other candidates as he sees fit.

Curtesy: If a child, issue of the husband, has been born alive, then upon the death of the wife, the husband will be entitled to a life estate called "curtesy" in the whole of the wife's property. Such estates are now generally abolished by statute.

Custodian Bank*: Any bank or trust company which is supervised and examined by state or federal authority having supervision over banks and which is acting as custodian for a clearing corporation.

Custody (personal property): The word custody and possession are not synonymous. Custody means in charge of, to keep and care for under the direction of the true owner, without any interest therein adverse to the true owner. A servant is in custody of his master's goods. See *Possession.*

Customer*: Under Article 4–Bank Deposits and Collections this means any person having an account with a bank or for whom a bank has agreed to collect items and includes a bank carrying an account with another bank.

Customer*: As used in Letters of Credit a customer is a buyer or other person who causes an issuer to issue a credit. The term also includes a bank which procures issuance or confirmation on behalf of that bank's customer.

Damages: A sum of money the court imposes upon a defendant as compensation for the plaintiff because the defendant has injured the plaintiff by breach of a legal duty.

d.b.a.: An abbreviation of "doing business as." A person who conducts his business under an assumed name is designated "John Doe d.b.a. Excelsior Co."

Debenture: A term used to name corporate obligations that are sold as investments. It is similar to a corporate bond. However, it is not secured by a trust deed. It is not like corporate stock.

Debt (action on): A common law remedy for the recovering of a sum certain in money.

Debtor*: The person who owes payment or other performance of the obligation secured, whether or not he owns or has rights in the collateral, and includes the seller of accounts, contract rights or chattel paper. Where the debtor and the owner of the collateral are not the same person, the term "debtor" means the owner of the collateral in any provision of the Article dealing with the collateral, the obligor in any provision dealing with the obligation, and may include both where the context so requires.

Deceit: A term to define that conduct in a business transaction by which one man, through fraudulent representations, misleads another who has a right to rely on such representations as the truth, or, who by reason of an unequal station in life, has no means of detecting such fraud.

Decision (judicial): The word "decision" may mean a final judgment of a court of last resort, a conclusion of law or facts, the opinion of the court, or the report of the court. Generally speaking, a decision means the judgment of the court as to the disposition of the case–for the plain, for the defendant, or for neither. Decision must be distinguished from opinion. An opinion of the court constitutes the reasons given for its decision or judgment. The report of the case is a printing of the opinion and decision.

Declaration: At common law, a word used to name the plaintiff's first pleading in which are set out the facts upon which the cause of action is based. The word "complaint" is used synonymously with declaration.

Declaratory judgment: A determination by a court on a question of law which simply declares the rights of the parties without ordering anything to be done.

Decree: The judgment of the chancellor (judge) in a suit in equity. Like a judgment at law, it is the determination of the rights between the parties and is in the form of an order that requires the decree to be carried out. An order that a contract be specifically enforced is a decree.

Deed: A written instrument in a special form signed, sealed, and delivered, that is used to pass the legal title of real property from one person to another. See *Conveyance.* In order that the public may know about the title to real property, deeds are recorded in the Deed Record office of the county where the land is situated.

Deed of trust: An instrument by which title to real property is conveyed to a trustee to hold as security for the holders of notes or bonds. It is like a mortgage except the security title is held by a person other than the mortgagee-creditor. Most corporate bonds are secured by a deed of trust.

De facto: Arising out of, or founded upon, fact, although merely apparent or colorable. A de facto officer is one who assumes to be an officer under some color of right, acts as an officer, but in point of law is not a real officer. See *Corporation de facto.*

Defalcation: A person occupying a trust or fiduciary relation who, by reason of his own fault, is unable to account for funds left in his hands, has committed a defalcation. The word often means to embezzle or misappropriate funds.

Defamation: The use of words that are generally understood to impute some disreputable conduct or moral delinquency about the person of whom they are spoken.

Defendant: A person who has been sued in a court of law; the person who answers the plaintiff's complaint. The word is applied to the defending party in civil actions. In criminal actions, the defending party is referred to as the accused.

Defense: The word "defense" applies to all methods of procedure used by the defendant and to all facts alleged by way of denial by the defendant in his response to the plaintiff's complaint. Demurrers, set-offs, pleas in abatement, answers, denial, confession, and avoidance are procedural means of defense.

Deficiency judgment: If, upon the foreclosure of a mortgage, the mortgaged property does not sell for a sufficient amount to pay the mortgage indebtedness, such difference is called a "deficiency" and is chargeable to the mortgagor or to any person who has purchased the property and assumed and agreed to pay the mortgage. Illus.: *M* borrows $10,000 from *B,* and as security gives a mortgage on Blackacre. At maturity *M* does not pay the debt. *B* forecloses and at a public sale Blackacre sells for $8,000. There is a deficiency of $2,000, chargeable against *M.* If *M* had sold Blackacre to *C* and *C* had assumed and agreed to pay the mortgage, he would also be liable for the deficiency.

Defraud: To deprive one of some right by deceitful means. To cheat or withhold wrongfully that which belongs to another. Conveying one's property for the purpose of avoiding payment of debts is a transfer to "hinder, delay, or defraud creditors."

Del credere agency: When an agent, factor, or broker undertakes to guarantee to his principal the payment of a debt due from a buyer of goods, such agent, factor, or broker is operating under a del credere commission or agency.

Delectus personae: A Latin phrase used to designate a chosen or selected person. Partners are chosen persons—"a copartnership cannot be compelled to receive strangers . . . " since such "association is founded on personal confidence and delectus personarum." Delectus personae is absent in joint stock companies.

Delivery: A voluntary transfer of the possession of property, actual or constructive, from one person to another with the intention that title vests in the transferee. In the law of sales, delivery contemplates the absolute giving up of control and dominion over the property by the vendor, and the assumption of the same by the vendee.

Delivery*: With respect to instruments, documents of title, chattel paper, or securities this means voluntary transfer of possession.

Delivery order*: A written order to deliver goods directed to a warehouseman, carrier, or other person who in the ordinary course of business issues warehouse receipts or bills of lading.

Demand: A request by a party entitled, under a claim of right, that a particular act be performed. In order to bind an endorser on a negotiable instrument, a demand must first be made by the holder on the primary party and such person must dishonor the instrument. Demand notes mean "due when demanded." The word "demand" is also used to mean a claim or legal obligation.

Demurrage: Demurrage is a sum, provided for in a contract of shipment, to be paid for the delay or detention of vessels or railroad cars beyond the time agreed upon for loading or unloading.

Demurrer: A procedural method used in a law suit by which the defendant admits all the facts alleged in the plaintiff's complaint, but denies that such facts state a cause of action. It raises a question of law on the facts, which must be decided by the court.

Dependent covenants (promises): In contracts, covenants are either concurrent or mutual, dependent or independent. Dependent covenants mean the performance of one promise must occur before the performance of the other promise. In a cash sale, the buyer must pay the money before the seller is under a duty to deliver the goods.

Depositary bank*: Under Article 4—Bank Deposits and Collections this means the first bank to which an item is transferred for collection even though it is also the payor bank.

Descent: The transfer of the title of property to the heirs upon the death of the ancestor; heredity; succession. If a person dies without making a will, his property will "descend" according to the Statute of Descent of the state wherein the property is located.

Destination: The "destination of goods" is the place of delivery as provided for in the shipping contract. The carrier is under a duty to deliver the goods at such a place unless ordered otherwise by the consignee.

Detinue: A common law action to recover property. It is to be distinguished from trover, which is an action to recover damages for taking property, not the recovery of the actual property.

Detriment: Legal detriment that is sufficient consideration, constitutes change of position or acts of forbearance by a promisee at the request of a promisor. See *Consideration.*

Devise: A gift, usually of real property, by a last will and testament.

Devisee: The person who receives title to real property by will.

Dictum: An expression of an idea, argument, or rule in the written opinion of a judge that has no bearing on the issues involved and that is not essential for their determination. It lacks the force of a decision in a judgment.

Directed verdict: If it is apparent to reasonable men and the court that the plaintiff by his evidence has not made out his case, the court may instruct the jury to bring in a verdict for the defendant or himself direct a verdict for the defendant. If, however, different inferences may be drawn from the evidence by reasonable men, then the court cannot direct a verdict.

Discharge: The word has many meanings. A servant or laborer upon being released from his employment is discharged. A guardian or trustee, upon termination of his trust, is discharged by the court. A debtor released from his debts is discharged in bankruptcy. A person who is released from any legal obligation is discharged.

Discovery practice: The disclosure by one party of facts, titles, documents and other things which are in his knowledge or possession and which are necessary to the party seeking the discovery as a part of a cause or action pending.

Dishonor: A negotiable instrument is dishonored when it is presented for acceptance or payment, and acceptance or payment is refused or cannot be obtained.

Dissolution: Of a corporation—The termination of a corporation at the expiration of its charter, by the Attorney General of the state under proper statutory authority, by consolidation, or by the action of the stockholders, is dissolution.

Of a partnership—The termination of a partnership by the express will of the partners at a fixed or indefinite time, or by operation of law due to the incapacity, death, or bankruptcy of one of the partners, is dissolution.

Distress for rent: The taking of personal property of a tenant in payment of rent on real estate.

Dividend: A dividend is a stockholder's pro rata share in the profits of a corporation. Dividends are declared by the board of directors of a corporation. Dividends are cash, script, property, and stock.

Document of title*: This item term includes bill of lading, dock warrant, dock receipt, warehouse receipt, or order for the delivery of goods, and also any other document which in the regular course of business or financing is treated as adequately evidencing that the person in possession of it is entitled to receive, hold and dispose of the document and the goods it covers. To be a document of title a document must purport to be issued by or addressed to a bailee and purport to cover goods in the bailee's possession which are either identified or are fungible portions of an identified mass.

Documentary draft*: Under Article 4—Bank Deposits and Collections this means any negotiable or non-negotiable draft with accompanying documents, securities or other papers to be delivered against honor of the draft.

Documentary draft*: ("Documentary demand for payment.") A draft the honor of which is conditioned upon the presentation of a document or documents. "Document" means any paper including document of title, security, invoice, certificate, notice of default, and the like.

Domicile: That place that a person intends as his fixed and permanent home and establishment and to which, if he is absent, he intends to return. A person can have but one domicile. The old one continues until the acquisition of a new one; thus, while in transit the old domicile exists. One can have more than one residence at a time, but only one domicile. The word is not synonymous with residence. See *Residence.*

Dominion: As applied to the delivery of property by one person to another, the word means the separation by the transferor or donor from all control over the possession and ownership of the property and the endowing of the transferee or donee with such control of possession and ownership. See *Gift.*

Donee beneficiary: If a promisee is under no duty to a third party, but for a consideration secures a promise from a promisor for the purpose of making a gift to a third party, such third party is a donee beneficiary. *A,* promisee for a premium paid, secures a promise from the insurance company, the promisor, to pay *A*'s wife $10,000 upon *A*'s death. *A*'s wife is a donee beneficiary.

Dormant partner: A partner who is not known to third persons, but is entitled to share in the profits and is subject to the losses. Since credit is not extended upon the strength of such partner's name, he may withdraw without notice and is not subject to debts contracted after his withdrawal.

Dower: A right for life held by a married woman in part of the lands owned by her husband, which right becomes vested upon his death.

Due care: The words express that standard of conduct which is exercised by an ordinary, reasonable, prudent person. See *Negligence.*

Due process of law: The words have a broad meaning. The constitutions of the United States and the states create and guarantee to every person the right to life, liberty, and property. These rights cannot be denied by government, except by the exercise of a fair and impartial legal procedure that is proper and appropriate. Legislation that confiscates one's property without just compensation is in the absence of due process of law. Under due process, a person accused of a crime is entitled to a trial by jury.

Duly negotiated*:   A negotiable document of title is "duly negotiated" when it is negotiated in the proper manner to a holder who purchases it in good faith without notice of any defense against or claim to it on the part of any person and for value, unless it is established that the negotiation is not in the regular course of business or financing or involves receiving the document in settlement or payment of a money obligation.

Duress (of person):   Duress means a threat of bodily injury, criminal prosecution, or imprisonment of a contracting party or his near relative to such extent that the threatened party is unable to exercise freely his will at the time of entering into or discharging a legal obligation.

Duress (of property):   The seizure by force, or the withholding of goods by one not entitled, and the demanding by such person of something as a condition for the release of the goods.

Duty (in law):   A legal obligation imposed by general law or voluntarily imposed by the creation of a binding promise. For every legal duty there is a corresponding legal right. By general law, *A* is under a legal duty not to injure *B*'s person or property. *B* has a right that *A* not injure his person or property. *X* may voluntarily create a duty in himself to *Y* by a promise to sell *Y* a horse for $100. If *Y* accepts, *X* is under a legal duty to perform his promise. See *Right.*

Earnest money: A term used to describe money that one contracting party gives to another at the time of entering into the contract in order to "bind the bargain" and which will be forfeited by the donor if he fails to carry out the contract. Generally, in real estate contracts such money is used as part payment of the purchase price.

Easement: An easement is an interest in land—a right that one person has to some profit, benefit, or use in or over the land of another. Such right is created by a deed, or it may be acquired by prescription (the continued use of another's land for a statutory period).

Ejectment: An action to recover the possession of real property. It is now generally defined by statute, and is a statutory action. See *Forcible entry and detainer.*

Ejusdem generis: Of the same class. General words taking their meaning from specific words which precede the general words. General words have the same meaning as specific words mentioned.

Eleemosynary: A word used to classify corporations and institutions engaged in public charitable work, such as a hospital or children's home owned and operated by a church.

Embezzlement: The fraudulent appropriation by one person, acting in a fiduciary capacity, of the money or property of another. See *Conversion.*

Eminent domain: The right that resides in the United States, state, county, city, school, or other public body, to take private property for public use, upon payment of just compensation. Eminent domain is to be distinguished from governmental power to take private property by limiting its use in order to eliminate nuisances. Abating a nuisance is the exercise of police power. No compensation is given for limiting the use of property under the police power.

Entirety (estate by):   Property acquired by husband and wife whereby upon the death of one, the survivor takes the whole estate. The estate is called "entirety" because the law regards the husband and wife as one. They are vested with the whole estate so that the survivor takes no new title upon death of the other but remains in possession of the whole as originally granted. Such estate must be distinguished from a joint tenancy. Neither the husband nor wife may by conveyance destroy the right of survivorship. The words in a deed, "To John Smith and Mary Smith, his wife, with the right of survivorship," and not as tenants in common, will create an estate by the entirety. For the legal effect of such estate, the state statute should be consulted. See *Joint tenants.*

Entity: The word means "in being" or "existing." The artificial person created when a corporation is organized is "in being" or "existing" for legal purposes; thus, an entity. It is separate from the stockholders. The estate of a deceased person while in administration is an entity. A partnership for many legal purposes is an entity. The marriage status is an entity.

Equipment*: Goods that are used or bought for use primarily in business (including farming or a profession) or by a debtor who is a non-profit organization or a governmental subdivision or agency or if the goods are not included in the definitions of inventory, farm products or consumer goods.

Equitable action: In Anglo-American law there have developed two types of courts and procedures for the administration of justice: law courts and equity courts. Law courts give as a remedy money damages only, whereas equity courts give the plaintiff what he bargains for. A suit for specific performance of a contract is an equitable action. In many states these two courts are now merged.

Equitable conversion: An equitable principle that, for certain purposes, permits real property to be converted into personalty. Thus real property owned by a partnership is, for the purpose of the partnership, personal property because to ascertain a partner's interest, the real property must be reduced to cash. This is an application of the equitable maxim, "equity considers that done which ought to be done."

Equitable mortgage: A written agreement to make certain property security for a debt, and upon the faith of which the parties have acted in making advances, loans, and thus creating a debt. Example: an improperly executed mortgage, one without seal where a seal is required. An absolute deed made to the mortgagee and intended for security only is an equitable mortgage.

Equity: Because the law courts in early English law did not always give an adequate remedy, an aggrieved party sought redress from the king. Since this appeal was to the king's conscience, he referred the case to his spiritual adviser, the chancellor. The chancellor decided the case according to rules of fairness, honesty, right, and natural justice. From this there developed the rules in equity. The laws of trusts, divorce, rescission of contracts for fraud, injunction, and specific performance are enforced in courts of equity.

Equity of redemption: The right a mortgagor has to redeem or get back his property after it has been forfeited for nonpayment of the debt it secured. By statute, within a certain time before final foreclosure decree, a mortgagor has the privilege, by paying the amount of the debt, interest, and costs, of redeeming his property.

Escrow: An agreement under which a grantor, promisor, or obligor places the instrument upon which he is bound with a third person called escrow holder, until the performance of a condition or the happening of an event stated in the agreement permits the escrow holder to make delivery or performance to the grantee, promisee, or obligee. *A* (grantor) places a deed to *C* (grantee) accompanied by the contract of conveyance with *B* Bank, conditioned upon *B* Bank delivering the deed to *C* (grantee) when *C* pays all moneys due under contract. The contract and deed have been placed in "escrow."

Estate: A word used to name all the property of a living, deceased, bankrupt, or insane person. It is also applied to the property of a ward. In the law of taxation, wills, and inheritance, the word has a broad meaning. Historically, the word was limited to an interest in land: i.e., estate in fee simple, estate for years, estate for life, and so forth.

Estoppel: When one ought to speak the truth, but does not, and by one's acts, representations, or silence intentionally or through negligence induces another to believe certain facts exist, and such person acts to his detriment on the belief that such facts are true, the first person is estopped to deny the truth of the facts. *B,* knowingly having kept and used defective goods delivered by *S* under a contract of sale, is estopped to deny the goods are defective. *X* holds out *Y* as his agent. *X* is estopped to deny *Y* is not his agent. Persons are estopped to deny the legal effect of written instruments such as deeds, contracts, bills and notes, court records, judgments, and the like. A man's own acts speak louder than his words.

Et al.:   Literally translated means "and other persons." Words used in pleadings and cases to indicate that persons other than those specifically named are parties to a law suit.

Et cetera–etc.:   Literally translated means "and other things" or "and so forth." When a number of things of the same class have been listed and others exist, it is customary to add the word "etc." in order to avoid full enumeration. Example: "There are many items of junk, old cars, wagons, plows, etc."

Et uxor: The words mean "and wife." Sometimes used in the name of cases. Smith v. Jones et ux.

Eviction: An action to expel a tenant from the estate of the landlord. Interfering with the tenant's right of possession or enjoyment amounts to an eviction. Eviction may be actual or constructive. Premises made uninhabitable because the landlord maintains a nuisance is constructive eviction.

Evidence: In law the word has two meanings. First, that testimony of witnesses and facts presented to the court and jury by way of writings and exhibits, which impress the minds of the court and jury, to the extent that an allegation has been proven. Testimony and evidence are not synonymous. Testimony is a broader word and includes all the witness says. Proof is distinguished from evidence in that proof is the legal consequence of evidence. Second, the rules of law, called the law of evidence, that determine what evidence shall be introduced at a trial and what shall not; also what importance shall be placed upon the evidence.

Ex contractu: See *Action ex contractu.*

Ex delicto: See *Action ex delicto.*

Ex relatione: By or on the relation or information of; used in the title of informations and special proceedings to designate the person at whose instance the state or a public officer is acting. (abbreviation: ex rel.)

Executed: As applied to contracts or other written instruments, means signed, sealed, and delivered. Effective legal obligations have thus been created. The term is also used to mean that the performances of a contract have been completed. The contract is then at an end. All is done that is to be done.

Execution: Execution of a judgment is the process by which the court through the sheriff enforces the payment of the judgment received by the successful party. The sheriff by a "writ" levies upon the unsuccessful party's property and sells it to pay the judgment creditor.

Executor (of an estate):   The person, named or appointed in a will by a testator (the one who makes the will), who by authority of the will has the power to administer the estate upon the death of the testator and to dispose of it according to the intention of the testator. The terms executor and administrator are not synonymous. An executor is appointed by the deceased to administer an estate. An administrator is appointed by the court to administer the estate of a person who dies without having made a will. See *Intestate.*

Executory (contract):   Until the performance required in a contract is completed, it is said to be executory as to that part not executed. See *Executed.*

Exemplary damages: A sum assessed by the jury in a tort action (over and above the compensatory damages) as punishment in order to make an example of the wrongdoer and to deter like conduct by others. Injuries caused by wilful, malicious, wanton, and reckless conduct will subject the wrongdoers to exemplary damages.

Exemption: The condition of a person who is free or excused from a duty imposed by some rule of law, statutory or otherwise. A workman against whom a judgment has been secured is by statute exempt from a writ of execution upon his working tools. A portion of a soldier's pay is exempt from the imposition of federal income tax.

Express warranties*:   Any affirmation of fact or promise made by the seller to the buyer which relates to the goods and becomes part of the basis of the bargain creates an express warranty that the goods shall conform to the affirmation or promise.

Any description of the goods which is made part of the basis of the bargain creates an express warranty that the goods shall conform to the description. Any sample or model which is made part of the basis of the bargain creates an express warranty that the whole of the goods shall conform to the sample or model.

Express warranty: When a seller makes some positive representation concerning the nature, quality, character, use, and purpose of goods, which induces the buyer to buy, and the seller intends the buyer to rely thereon, the seller has made an express warranty.

Factor: A factor is an agent for the sale of merchandise. He may hold possession of the goods in his own name or in the name of his principal. He is authorized to sell and to receive payment for the goods. The law concerning factors is codified in some states by legislation, and is called "Factors' Acts." See *Agent.*

Factor's lien: A lien or right that a factor has to keep the possession of goods consigned to him for the purpose of reimbursing himself for all advances previously made to the consignor.

Farm products*:   Goods that are crops or livestock or supplies used or produced in farming operations or if they are products of crops or livestock in their unmanufactured states (such as ginned cotton, wool-clip, maple syrup, milk and eggs), and if they are in the possession of a debtor engaged in raising, fattening, grazing or other farming operations. If goods are farm products they are neither equipment nor inventory.

Featherbedding: A term used in labor relations to describe the situation in which demand is made for the payment of wages for a particular service not actually rendered.

Fee simple estate: A term describing the total interest a person may have in land. Such an estate is not qualified by any other interest and passes upon the death of the owners to the heirs free from any conditions.

Felony: At common law, a felony was a criminal offense, and upon conviction the criminal forfeited his lands and goods to the crown and was subject to death. Today, by statute, the term includes all those criminal offenses that are punishable by death or imprisonment.

Feoffment: A gift of a corporeal hereditament which operates by transfer of possession and requires that the seisin be passed either by investiture or by livery of seisin.

Fidelity bond: A guaranty of personal honesty of officer furnishing indemnity against his defalcation or negligence.

Fiduciary: In general a person is a fiduciary when he occupies a position of trust or confidence in relation to another person or his property. Trustees, guardians, and executors are illustrations of persons occupying fiduciary positions.

Fieri facias: Literally means "you cause it to be made." A writ or order issued by a court directing the sheriff to levy on goods or personal property of the defendant, in order to satisfy the judgment of the plaintiff.

Financing agency*:   A bank, finance company or other person who in the ordinary course of business makes advances against goods or documents of title or who by arrangement with either the seller or the buyer intervenes in ordinary course to make or collect payment due or claimed under the contract for sale, as by purchasing or paying the seller's draft or making advances against it or by merely taking it for collection whether or not documents of title accompany the draft. "Financing agency" includes also a bank or other person who similarly intervenes between persons who are in the position of seller and buyer in respect to the goods.

Fine: A sum of money collected by a court from a person guilty of some criminal offense. The amount may be fixed by statute or left to the discretion of the court. The term "fine" is to be distinguished from "penalty," which means a sum of money exacted for the doing of or failure to perform some act. Payment of a penalty of $5 for failure to secure a license to sell tobacco is different from paying a $5 fine for committing the offense of larceny.

Firm offers*:   An offer by a merchant to buy or sell goods in a signed writing which by its terms gives assurance that it will be held open.

Floating policy: An insurance policy that covers a class of goods located in a particular place that the insured has on hand at the time the policy was issued, but which goods at the time of fire may not be the identical items that were on hand at the time the policy was issued. A fire policy covering the inventory of a grocery store is an example.

Forbearance: Giving up the right to enforce what one honestly believes to be a valid claim in return for a promise is called forbearance and is sufficient "consideration" to make binding a promise.

Forcible entry and detainer: A remedy given to a landowner to evict persons unlawfully in possession of his land. A landlord may use such remedy to evict a tenant in default.

Forfeiture: Loss of money or property by way of compensation and punishment for injury or damage to the person or property of another or to the state. One may forfeit his citizenship upon the commission of a felony. One may forfeit interest earnings for charging a usurious rate.

Forgery: Forgery is the false writing or alteration of an instrument with the fraudulent intent of deceiving and injuring another. Writing, without his consent, another's name upon a check for the purpose of securing money, is a forgery.

Franchise: A right conferred or granted by a legislative body. It is a contract right and cannot be revoked without cause. A franchise is more than a license. A license is only a privilege and may be revoked. A corporation exists by virtue of a "franchise." A corporation secures a franchise from the city council to operate a water works within the city. See *License.*

Franchise tax: A tax on the right of a corporation to do business under its corporate name.

Fraud: An intentional misrepresentation of the truth for the purpose of deceiving another person. The elements of fraud are: (1) false representation of fact, not opinion, intentionally made; (2) intent that the deceived person act thereon; (3) knowledge that such statements would naturally deceive; and (4) that the deceived person acted to his injury.

Fraudulent conveyance: A conveyance of property by a debtor for the intent and purpose of defrauding his creditors. Such conveyance is of no effect, and such property may be reached by the creditors through appropriate legal proceedings.

Freehold: An estate in fee or one for life is a "freehold." A freeholder is usually a person who has a property right in the title to real estate amounting to an estate of inheritance (in fee), or one who has title for life, or for an indeterminate period. A grant by a city to a corporation to use the sidewalks for 30 years is not a freehold. "Householder" is not synonymous with "freeholder." See *Householder.*

From and to: Generally the word "from" is a word of exclusion, and the word "to" a word of inclusion. "From May 5 to May 10," in computing time means May 5 is excluded and May 10 included; thus, the period of time is 5 days.

Funded debt: The term applies to a debt where provision is made for a method of paying off the debt and its interest at fixed periods. A funded debt of a municipality is one where provision is made for the annual raising by tax of the sum necessary to pay the interest and principal as they respectively mature.

Funding: The procedure by which the outstanding debts of a corporation are collected together and the re-issuing of new bonds or obligations for the purpose of paying the debts. Thus 10 year 3 per cent bonds may be called and paid by issuing 20 year 3 per cent bonds. This process is called funding.

Fungible*:   With respect to goods or securities this means goods or securities of which any unit is, by nature or usage of trade, the equivalent of any other like unit. Goods which are not fungible shall be deemed fungible for the purposes of this Act to the extent that under a particular agreement or document unlike units are treated as equivalents.

Fungible goods: Fungible goods are those "of which any unit is from its nature of mercantile usage treated as the equivalent of any other unit." Grain, wine, and similar items are examples.

Future goods*:   Goods which are not both existing and identified.

Futures: Contracts for the sale and delivery of commodities in the future, made with the intention that no commodity be delivered or received immediately.

Gambling: An arrangement between two or more persons to risk money or other things of value in any type of contest or game of chance wherein one of the parties wins at the expense of another.

Garnishee: A person upon whom a garnishment is served. He is a debtor of a defendant and has money or property that the plaintiff is trying to reach in order to satisfy a debt due from the defendant.

Garnishment: A proceeding by which a plaintiff seeks to reach the credits of the defendant that are in the hands of a third party, the garnishee. A garnishment is distinguished from an attachment in that by an attachment an officer of the court takes actual possession of property by virtue of his writ. In a garnishment, the property or money is left with the garnishee until final adjudication.

General agent: An agent authorized to do all the acts connected with carrying on a particular trade, business, or profession.

General intangibles*:   Any personal property (including things in action) other than goods, accounts, contract rights, chattel paper, documents and instruments.

Gift: A gift is made when a donor delivers the subject matter of the gift into the donee's hands, or places in the donee the means of obtaining possession of the subject matter, accompanied by such acts as show clearly that the donor intends to divest himself of all dominion and control over the property.

Gift causa mortis: A gift made in anticipation of death. The donor must have been in sickness and have died as expected; otherwise, no effective gift has been made. If the donor survives, the gift is revocable.

Gift inter vivos A gift inter vivos is an effective gift made during the life of the donor. By a gift inter vivos, property vests immediately in the donee at the time of delivery; whereas, a gift causa mortis is made in contemplation of death and is effective only upon the donor's death.

Good faith*: In the case of a merchant this means honesty in fact and the observance of reasonable commercial standards of fair dealing in the trade.

Good faith*: Honesty in fact in the conduct or transaction concerned.

Good title: A title free from incumbrances, such as mortgages and liens, as disclosed by a complete abstract of the title as taken from the records in the recorder's office.

Goods*: All things which are treated as movable for the purposes of a contract of storage or transportation.

Goods: This includes all things which are movable at the time the security interest attaches or which are fixtures but does not include money, documents, instruments, accounts, chattel paper, general intangibles, contract rights, and other things in action. "Goods" also include the unborn young of animals and growing crops.

Goods: All things (including specially manufactured goods) which are movable at the time of identification to the contract for sale other than the money in which the price is to be paid, investment securities and things in action. "Goods" also includes the unborn young animals and growing crops and other identified things attached to realty as described in the section on goods to be severed from realty.

Grant: A term used in deeds for the transfer of the title to real property. The words "convey," "transfer," and "grant" as operative words in a deed to pass title are equivalent. The words "grant, bargain, and sell" in a deed, in absence of statute, mean the grantor promises he has good title to transfer free from incumbrances and warrants it to be such.

Grantee: A grantee is a person to whom a grant is made; one named in a deed to receive title.

Grantor: A grantor is a person who makes a grant. The grantor executes the deed by which he divests himself of title.

Gross negligence: The lack of even slight or ordinary care.

Guarantor: One who by contract undertakes "to answer for the debt, default, and miscarriage of another." In general, a guarantor undertakes to pay if the principal debtor does not; a surety, on the other hand, joins in the contract of the principal and becomes an original party with the principal. See *Suretyship*.

Guardian: A person appointed by the court to look after the property rights and person of minors, insane, and other incompetents or legally incapacitated persons.

Guardian ad litem: A special guardian appointed for the sole purpose of carrying on litigation and preserving the interests of a ward. He exercises no control or power over property.

Habeas corpus: A writ issued to a sheriff, warden or official having custody of a person, directing the official to return the person, alleged to be unlawfully held, before a court in order to determine the legality of the imprisonment.

Hace verba: A requirement that exact words be used.

Hearsay evidence: Evidence that is learned from someone else. It does not derive its value from the credit of the witness testifying, but rests upon the veracity of another person. It is not good evidence because there is no opportunity to cross-examine the person who is the source of the testimony.

Hedging contract: A contract of purchase or sale of an equal amount of commodities in the future by which brokers, dealers, or manufacturers protect themselves against the fluctuations of the market. It is a type of insurance against changing prices. A grain dealer, to protect himself, may contract to sell for future delivery the same amount of grain he has purchased in the present market.

Heirs: Those persons upon whom the statute of descent casts the title to real property upon the death of the ancestor. See Statutes of descent for the particular state. See *Descent.*

Holder*:   A person who is in possession of a document of title or an instrument or an investment security drawn, issued or indorsed to him or to his order or to bearer or in blank.

Holding company: A corporation organized for the purpose of owning and holding the stock of other corporations. Shareholders of underlying corporations receive in exchange for their stock, upon an agreed value, the shares in the holding corporation.

Homestead: A parcel of land upon which a family dwells or resides, and which to them is home. The statute of the state or federal governments should be consulted to determine the meaning of the term as applied to debtor's exemptions, federal land grants, and so forth.

Honor*:   This means to pay or to accept and pay, or where a credit so engages to purchase or discount a draft complying with the terms of the credit.

Idem sonans: Absolute accuracy in spelling names is not required in legal documents. If a name spelled in a document is different from the correct name, it is still legally effective as sufficient name of a person, if, when pronounced, it sounds to the ear the same as the correct name. This is called the doctrine of idem sonans. For example: Smythe and Smith. Mackey and Macky.

Illegal: Conduct that is contrary to public policy and the fundamental principles of law is illegal. Such conduct includes not only violations of criminal statutes, but also the creation of agreements that are prohibited by statute and the common law.

Illusory: That which has a false appearance. If that which appears to be a promise is not a promise, it is said to be illusory. For example: "*A* promises to buy *B*'s horse, if *A* wants to," is no promise. Such equivocal statement would not justify reliance; thus, it is not a promise.

Immunity: Freedom from the legal duties and penalties imposed upon others. The "privileges and immunities" clause of the United States Constitution means no state can deny to the citizens of another state the same rights granted to its own citizens. This does not apply to office holding. See *Exemption.*

Implied: The finding of a legal right or duty by inference from facts or circumstances. See *Warranty.*

Imputed negligence: Negligence which is not directly attributable to the person himself, but which is the negligence of a person who is in privity with him and with whose fault he is chargeable.

Inalienable: The word means not capable of transfer or sale. The right to sue for a tort is inalienable. Contracts for personal service are inalienable choses in action. The word means nonassignable.

Inchoate: Incomplete situations out of which rights and duties may later arise. It also means "as yet not perfect." For example: a wife's dower is inchoate until her husband's death.

Incidental beneficiary: If the performance of a promise would indirectly benefit a person not a party to a contract, such person is an incidental beneficiary. *A* promises *B,* for a consideration, to plant a valuable nut orchard on *B*'s land. Such improvement would increase the value of the adjacent land. *C,* the owner of the adjacent land, is an incidental beneficiary. He has no remedy if *A* breaches his promise with *B.*

Incontestable: As applied to insurance, a clause in an insurance policy which states that after a certain period of time the policy may not be contested except for nonpayment of the premiums.

Incorporeal: Not manifest to the senses. The right of an owner of land to take the water of a stream for irrigation is an incorporeal hereditament.

Incumbrance: A burden on either the title to land or thing, or upon the land or thing itself. A mortgage or other lien is an incumbrance upon the title. A right of way over the land is an incumbrance upon the land and affects its physical condition.

Indebtedness: To be under a duty to another, usually for the payment of money. It is not a contract, but it may be the result of a contract.

Indemnify: Literally it means to save harmless. Thus one person agrees to protect another against loss.

Indemnity: A duty resting on one person to make good a loss or damage another has suffered. *A* contracts to build a house for *B. B* contracts with *C* for a premium to answer for any loss *B* may suffer by reason of *A*'s default. If *A* defaults and *B* suffers loss, *C* will indemnify *B.*

Indenture: A deed executed by both parties, as distinguished by a deed poll that is executed only by the grantor.

Independent contractor: The following elements are essential to establish the relation of independent contractor in contradistinction to principal and agent. An independent contractor must: (1) exercise his independent judgment as to the means used to accomplish the result; (2) be free from control or orders from any other person; (3) be responsible only under his contract for the result obtained.

Indictment: An indictment is a finding by a grand jury that it has reason to believe the accused is guilty as charged. It informs the accused of the offense with which he is charged in order that he may prepare its defense. It is a pleading in a criminal action.

Indorsement: Writing one's name upon paper for the purpose of transferring the title. When a payee of a negotiable instrument writes his name on the back of the instrument, such writing is an indorsement.

Infringement: Infringement of a patent on a machine is the manufacturing of a machine that produces the same result by the same means and operation as the patented machine. Infringement of a trademark consists in the reproduction of a registered trademark and its use upon goods in order to mislead the public to believe that the goods are the genuine, original product.

Inherit: The word is used in contradistinction to acquiring property by will. See *Descent.*

Inheritance: An inheritance denotes an estate that descends to heirs. See *Descent.*

Injunction: A writ of judicial process issued by a court of equity by which a party is required to do a particular thing or to refrain from doing a particular thing.

Injunction pendente lite: A provisional remedy granted by a court of equity before a hearing upon the merits of a suit, for the purpose of preventing the doing of any act whereby the rights in the controversy may be materially changed.

In personam: A legal proceeding, the judgment of which binds the defeated party to a personal liability.

In rem: A legal proceeding, the judgment of which binds, affects, or determines the status of property.

Insolvency proceedings*:   Any assignment for the benefit of creditors or other proceedings intended to liquidate or rehabilitate the estate of the person involved.

Insolvent: An insolvent debtor is one whose property is insufficient to pay all the debts, or out of which his debts may be collected. Within the Bankruptcy Act, "Whenever the aggregate of his property . . . shall not at a fair valuation be sufficient in amount to pay his debts."

Insolvent*:   Refers to a person who either has ceased to pay his debts in the ordinary course of business or cannot pay his debts as they become due or is insolvent within the meaning of the federal bankruptcy law.

Installment contract*:   One which requires or authorizes the delivery of goods in separate lots to be separately accepted, even though the contract contains a clause "each delivery is a separate contract" or its equivalent.

In statu quo: The conditions existing at the time of the commencement of an action, or, in case of rescission of contract, the position of the parties just prior to the creation of the contract.

Instrument*:   This means a negotiable instrument or a security or any other writing which evidences a right to the payment of money and is not itself a security agreement or lease and is of a type which is in ordinary course of business transferred by delivery with any necessary indorsement or assignment.

Instrument*:   Under Article 3–Commercial Paper this means a negotiable instrument.

Insurable interest: A person has an insurable interest in a person or property if he will be directly and financially affected by the death of the person or the loss of the property.

Insurance: By an insurance contract, one party, for an agreed premium, binds himself to another, called the insured, to pay to the insured a sum of money conditioned upon the loss of life or property of the insured.

Intent: A state of mind that exists prior to or contemporaneous with an act. A purpose or design to do or forbear to do an act. It cannot be directly proven, but is inferred from known facts.

Inter alia: Among other things.

Interim certificate: An instrument negotiable by statute in some states payable in stocks or bonds, and given prior to the issuance of the stocks or bonds in which payable.

Interlocutory decree: A decree of a court of equity that does not settle the complete issue, but settles only some intervening part, awaiting a final decree.

Intermediary bank*: Under Article 4–Bank Deposits and Collections is a bank to which an item is transferred in course of collection except the depositary or payor bank.

Interpleader: A procedure whereby a person who has an obligation, e.g. to pay money, and does not know which of two or more claimants are entitled to performance, can bring a suit that requires the contesting parties to litigate between themselves.

Inter sese: Between or among themselves.

Intestate: The intestate laws are the laws of descent or distribution of the estate of a deceased person. A person dies intestate who has not made a will.

In toto: In the whole amount. All together. As the persons were liable in toto.

Inventory*: Goods that are held by a person who holds them for sale or lease or to be furnished under contracts of service or if he has so furnished them, or if they are raw materials, work in process or materials used or consumed in a business. Inventory of a person is not to be classified as his equipment.

Irreparable damage or injury: Irreparable does not mean such injury as is beyond the possibility of repair, but it does mean that it is so constant and frequent in occurrence that no fair or reasonable redress can be had in a court of law. Thus, the plaintiff must seek a remedy in equity by way of an injunction.

Issue (in a will): The word, as applied to a will, means descendants of whatever degree.

Issue (in pleading): The purpose of pleadings in a court proceeding is to find the "issue"; that is, a point which is affirmed on one side and denied on the other.

Issue*: Under Article 3–Commercial Paper "Issue" means the first delivery of an instrument to a holder or a remitter.

Issuer*: A bank or other person issuing a letter of credit.

Issuer*: A bailee who issues a document except that in relation to an unaccepted delivery order it means the person who orders the possessor of goods to deliver. Issuer includes any person for whom an agent or employee purports to act in issuing a document if the agent or employee has real or apparent authority to issue documents, notwithstanding that the issuer received no goods or that the goods were misdescribed or that in any other respect the agent or employee violated his instructions.

Item*: Under Article 4–Bank Deposits and Collections this means any instrument for the payment of money even though it is not negotiable but does not include money.

Jeopardy: A person is in jeopardy when he is regularly charged with a crime before a court properly organized and competent to try him. If acquitted, he cannot be tried again for the same offense.

Joint adventure: When two persons enter into a single enterprise for their mutual benefit without the intention of continuous pursuit, they have entered a joint adventure. They are essentially partners.

Joint and several: Two or more persons have an obligation which binds them individually as well as jointly. The obligation can be enforced by either joint action against all of them or by separate actions against one or more.

Joint contract: If two or more persons promise upon the same consideration for the same purpose to another party, they are joint obligors to the other party to the contract and have formed a joint contract.

Joint ownership: The interest that two or more parties have in property. Such interest has no existence in the absence of the interest of the other parties. The parties together own the total interest. *A, B,* and *C* as a unit own the property. See *Joint tenants.*

Joint tenants: Two or more persons to whom is deeded land in such manner that they have "one and the same interest, accruing by one and the same conveyance, commencing at one and the same time, and held by one and the same undivided possession." Upon the death of one joint tenant, his property passes to the survivor or survivors. Some states have abolished joint tenancy; other states make joint tenants, tenants in common.

The Statute of Descent does not apply to this type of estate so long as there is a survivor. See *Entirety.*

Joint tort-feasors: When two persons commit an injury with a common intent, they are joint tort-feasors.

Joint will: A joint will is a single will of two or more persons. A mutual will is one by which each testator makes a testamentary disposition in favor of the other.

Judgment (in law): A judgment is the decision, pronouncement, or sentence rendered by a court upon an issue in which it has jurisdiction.

Judgment in personam: A judgment against a person directing the defendant to do or not to do something, is a judgment in personam. See *In personam.*

Judgment in rem: A judgment against a thing, as distinguished from a judgment against a person. See *In rem.*

Judicial sale: A judicial sale is a sale authorized by a court that has jurisdiction to grant such authority. Such sales are conducted by an officer of the court. See *Sale.*

Jurisdiction: The authority conferred upon a court by the constitution to try cases and determine causes.

Jury: A group of persons, usually twelve, sworn to declare the facts of a case as they are proved from the evidence presented to them, and, upon instructions from the court, to find a verdict in the cause before them.

Kite checks: To execute and deliver a check in payment of a debt at a time when the drawer has insufficient money in the bank, but with the intention of making a deposit to cover the shortage before the check is presented for payment.

Laches: Laches is a term used in equity to name that conduct which is neglect to assert one's rights or to do what by the law a person should have done and did not do. Such failure on the part of one to assert a right will give an equitable defense to another party.

L.S.: The letters are an abbreviation for the Latin phrase "locus sigilli," meaning "place of the seal."

Latent defect: A defect in materials not descernible by examination. Used in contradistinction to patent defect which is discernible.

Lease: A contract by which one person divests himself of possession of lands or chattels and grants such possession to another for a period of time. The relationship where land is involved is called landlord and tenant.

Leasehold: The land held by a tenant under a lease.

Legacy: Personal property disposed of by a will. Sometimes the term is synonymous with bequest. The word "devise" is used in connection with real property distributed by will. See *Bequest, Devise.*

Legal incapacity: A person who has no power to sue except by a guardian, or a person such as an infant or insane person who has the power of avoidance of contract liabilities.

Legatee: A person to whom a legacy is given by will.

Letters testamentary: The orders or authority granted by a probate court to an administrator or representative of an estate whereby such person has power to reduce to money the estate of a deceased and make proper disposition. There are two kinds of letters. "Domiciliary letters" are issued at the domicile of the testator. When property is found in places other than at the domicile of the testator, the courts of such places issue "ancillary letters." Examples: *A* lives in state *B.* At his death, he owned property in state *C.* "Ancillary letters" will be issued in state *C.*

Levy (taxes): The word as applied to taxation means to impose or assess, or to charge and collect, a sum of money against a person or property for public purposes.

Levy (writ of): The literal use refers to the seizure of the defendant's property by the sheriff to satisfy the plaintiff's judgment. The word sometimes means that a lien has been attached to land and other property of the defendant by virtue of a judgment.

Liability: In its broadest legal sense, the word means any obligation one may be under by reason of some rule of law. It includes debt, duty, and responsibility.

Libel: The malicious publication of a defamation of a person by printing, writing, signs, or pictures, for the purpose of injuring the reputation and good name of such person. "The exposing of a person to public hatred, contempt, or ridicule."

License (privilege):   A license is a mere personal privilege given by the owner to another to do designated acts upon the land of the owner. It is revocable at will, creates no estate in the land, and such licensee is not in possession. "It is a mere excuse for what otherwise would be a trespass."

License (governmental regulation):   A license is a privilege granted by a state or city upon the payment of a fee, which confers authority upon the licensee to do some act or series of acts, which otherwise would be illegal. A license is not a contract and may be revoked for cause. It is a method of governmental regulation exercised under the police power. Examples: license to keep dogs in the city, to sell commodities in the street.

Lien: A right one person, usually a creditor, has, to keep possession of or control the property of another for the purpose of satisfying a debt. There are many kinds of liens: judgment liens, attorneys' liens, innkeepers' liens, loggers' liens, vendors' liens. Consult Statute of state for type of liens. See *Judgment.*

Lien creditor*:   A creditor who has acquired a lien on the property involved by attachment, levy or the like and includes an assignee for benefit of creditors from the time of assignment, and a trustee in bankruptcy from the date of the filing of the petition or a receiver in equity from the time of appointment. Unless all the creditors represented had knowledge of the security interest, such a representative of creditors is a lien creditor without knowledge even though he personally has knowledge of the security interest.

Limitation of actions: Statutes of limitations exist for the purpose of bringing to an end old claims. Because witnesses die, memory fails, papers are lost, and the evidence becomes inadequate, stale claims are barred. Such statutes are called statutes of repose. Within a certain period of time, action on claims must be brought; otherwise, they are barred. The period varies from 6 months to 20 years.

Lineal descendant: A lineal descendant is one descended in a direct line from another person such as son, grandson, great-grandson, etc.

Liquidated: A claim is liquidated when it has been made fixed and certain by the parties concerned.

Liquidated damages: A fixed sum agreed upon between the parties to a contract, to be paid as ascertained damages by that party who breaches the contract. If the sum is excessive, the courts will declare it to be a penalty and unenforceable.

Liquidation: The process of winding up the affairs of a corporation or firm for the purpose of paying its debts and disposing of its assets. May be done voluntarily or under the orders of a court.

Lis pendens: The words mean, "pending the suit nothing should be changed." The court, having control of the property involved in the suit, issues notice "lis pendens," that persons dealing with the defendant regarding the subject matter of the suit, do so subject to final determination of the action.

Lot*:   A parcel or a single article which is the subject matter of a separate sale or delivery, whether or not it is sufficient to perform the contract.

Magistrate: A public officer, usually a judge, "Who has power to issue a warrant for the arrest of a person charged with a public offense." The word has wide application and includes justices of the peace, notaries public, recorders, and other public officers who have power to issue executive orders.

Maintenance (in law suits: The assisting of either party to a law suit by a person who has no interest therein. An officious intermeddling in a law suit.

Mala fides: Bad faith. The opposite of bona fide.

Mala in se: Acts that are "bad in themselves" and are void of any legal consequences. A contract to do immoral acts is illegal and void because mala in se. Such acts are in contradistinction to acts "mala prohibita," which means illegal because prohibited by statute.

Malice: Malice is a term to define a wrongful act done intentionally without excuse. It does not necessarily mean ill will, but it indicates a state of mind that is reckless concerning the law and the rights of others. Malice is distinguished from negligence in that in malice there is always a purpose to injure, whereas such is not true of the word "negligence."

Malicious: Possessed of a willful and purposeful intent to injure another without just cause.

Malicious prosecution: The prosecution of another at law with malice and without probable cause to believe that such legal action will be successful.

Mandamus: A writ issued by a court of law, in the name of the state, directed to some inferior court, officer, corporation, or person commanding them to do a particular thing that appertains to their office or duty.

Mandatory: As applied to statutes, a mandatory provision is one, the noncompliance with which creates no legal consequences. For example, city bonds, issued in violation of statutory requirements that are mandatory, are void.

Mandatory injunction: An injunctive order issued by a court of equity that compels affirmative action by the defendant.

Margin: A sum of money deposited by a principal, buyer, or seller, with his broker to protect the broker against any loss due to price fluctuation in buying and selling.

Marketable title: A title of such character that no apprehension as to its validity would occur to the mind of a reasonable and intelligent person. The title to goods in litigation, subject to incumbrances, in doubt as to a third party's right, or subject to lien, is not marketable.

Marshalling assets: A principle in equity for a fair distribution of a debtor's assets among his creditors. For example, when a creditor of *A*, by reason of prior right, has two funds *X* and *Y* belonging to *A* out of which he may satisfy his debt, but *B*, also a creditor of *A*, has a right to *X* fund, the first creditor will be compelled to exhaust *Y* fund before he will be permitted to participate in *X* fund.

Master in chancery: An officer appointed by the court to assist the court of equity in taking testimony, computing interest, auditing accounts, estimating damages, ascertaining liens, and doing such other tasks incidental to a suit, as the court may require. The power of a master is merely advisory and his task largely fact-finding.

Maxim: A proposition of law that because of its universal approval needs no proof or argument, and the mere statement of which gives it authority. Example: "A principal is bound by the acts of his agent, when the agent is acting within the scope of his authority."

Mechanics' lin: A mechanics' lien is created by statute to assist laborers in collecting their wages. Such lien has for its purpose to subject the land of an owner to a lien for material and labor expended in the construction of buildings, which buildings having been placed on the land become a part thereof by the law of accession.

Mens rea: The term means "guilty mind." It is an element that has to be proven to sustain a verdict of guilty for a criminal offense. It is generally presumed from the proven facts.

Merchant: A person who deals in goods of the kind or otherwise by his occupation holds himself out as having knowledge or skill peculiar to the practices or goods involved in the transaction or to whom such knowledge or skill may be attributed by his employment of an agent or broker or other intermediary who by his occupation holds himself out as having such knowledge or skill.

Merger: Two corporations are merged when one corporation continues in existence and the other loses its identity by its absorption into the first. Merger must be distinguished from consolidation, in which case both corporations are dissolved, and a new one created which takes over the assets of the dissolved corporations.

Mesne conveyance: An intermediate conveyance; one ocupying an intermediate position in a chain of title between the first grantee and the present holder.

Metes and bounds: The description of the boundaries of real property.

Midnight deadline*: Under Article 4–Bank Deposits and Collections with respect to a bank this is midnight on its next banking day following the banking day on which it receives the relevant item or notice or from which the time for taking action commences to run, whichever is later.

Ministerial duty: The performance of a prescribed duty that requires the exercise of little judgment or discretion. A sheriff performs ministerial duties.

Minutes: The record of a court or the written transactions of the members or board of directors of a corporation. Under the certificate of the clerk of a court or the secretary of a corporation, the minutes are the official evidence of court or corporate action.

Misdemeanor: A criminal offense, less than a felony, that is not punishable by death or imprisonment. Consult the local statute.

Misfeasance: The improper performance of a duty imposed by law or contract which injures another person. It is distinguished from nonfeasance which means doing nothing of an imposed duty.

Misrepresentation: The affirmative statement or affirmation of a fact that is not true; the term does not include concealment of true facts or nondisclosure or the mere expression of opinion.

Mistake of fact: The unconscious ignorance or forgetfulness of the existence or nonexistence of a fact, past or present, which is material and important to the creation of a legal obligation.

Mistake of law: An erroneous conclusion of the legal effect of known facts.

Mitigation of damages: A plaintiff is entitled to recover damages caused by the defendant's breach, but the plaintiff is also under a duty to avoid increasing or enhancing such damages. Such is called a duty to mitigate damages. If a seller fails to deliver the proper goods on time, the buyer, where possible, must buy other goods, thus mitigating damages.

Money*:   A medium of exchange authorized or adopted by a domestic or foreign government as a part of its currency.

Monopoly: The exclusive control of the supply and price of a commodity that may be acquired by a franchise or patent from the government; or, the ownership of the source of a commodity or the control of its distribution.

Moot case: A judgment in advance of a presumed controversy, the decision of which has no legal effect upon any existing controversy.

Mortgage: A conveyance or transfer of an interest in property for the purpose of creating a security for a debt. The mortgage becomes void upon payment of the debt, although the recording of a release is necessary to clear the title of the mortgaged property.

Mutual assent: In every contract each party must agree to the same thing. Each must know what the other intends; they must mutually assent or be in agreement.

Mutuality: A word used to describe the situation in every contract that it must be binding on both parties. Each party to the contract must be bound to the other party to do something by virtue of the legal duty created.

Negligence: The failure to do that which an ordinary, reasonable, prudent man would do, or the doing of some act which an ordinary, prudent man would not do. Reference must always be made to the situation, the circumstances, and the knowledge of the parties.

Negotiation*:   Under Article 3–Commercial Paper this is the transfer of an instrument in such form that the transferee becomes a holder. If the instrument is payable to order it is negotiated by delivery with any necessary indorsement; if payable to bearer it is negotiated by delivery.

Net assets: The property or effects of a firm, corporation, institution, or estate, remaining after all its obligations have been paid.

Nexus: Correction, tie, or link used in the law of taxation to establish a connection between a tax and the activity or person being taxed.

Nolle prosequi: A discharge of a particular indictment against the accused by the court upon request of the prosecuting officer. It is not an acquittal nor a pardon. The accused may be indicted again and tried for the same offense.

Nolo contendere: This plea by an accused in a criminal action is an implied confession of the offense charged. It virtually equals a plea of guilty. A judgment of conviction follows such plea.

Nominal damages: A small sum assessed as sufficient to award the case and cover the costs. In such case, no actual damages have been proven.

Non compos mentis: One who does not possess understanding sufficient to comprehend the nature, extent, and meaning of his contracts or other legal obligations.

Non obstante verdicto: A judgment given to the moving party notwithstanding the verdict already obtained. If upon re-examination, the court finds the plaintiff's pleadings demurrable, he will enter a judgment "non obstante verdicto" even though the plaintiff has a verdict.

Nonfeasance: The failure to perform a legal duty. See *Misfeasance.*

Nonresident: The citizen of another state.

Nonsuit: A judgment given against the plaintiff when he is unable to prove his case or fails to proceed with the trial after the case is at issue.

Noscitur a sociis: The meaning of a word is or may be known from the accompanying words.

Notary: A public officer authorized to administer oaths by way of affidavits and depositions; also to attest deeds and other formal papers in order that such papers may be used as evidence and be qualified for recording.

Notation Credit*: A credit which specifies that any person purchasing or paying drafts drawn or demands for payment made under it must note the amount of the draft or demand on the letter or advice of credit.

Notice*: A person has "notice" of a fact when (a) he has actual knowledge of it; or (b) he has received a notice or notification of it; or (c) from all the facts and circumstances known to him at the time in question he has reason to know that it exists.

A person "knows" or has "knowledge" of a fact when he has actual knowledge of it. "Discover" or "learn" or a word or phrase of similar import refers to knowledge rather than to reason to know.

Notifies*: A person "notifies" or "gives" a notice or notification to another by taking such steps as may be reasonably required to inform the other in ordinary course whether or not such other actually comes to know of it. A person "receives" a notice or notification when: (a) it comes to his attention; or (b) it is duly delivered at the place of business through which the contract was made or at any other place held out by him as the place for receipt of such communications.

Novation: The substitution of one obligation for another. When debtor *A* is substituted for debtor *B,* and by agreement with the creditor *C,* debtor *B* is discharged, a novation has occurred.

Nudum pactum: A naked promise—one for which no consideration has been given.

Nuisance: The word nuisance is generally applied to any continuous or continued conduct that causes annoyance, inconvenience, and damage to person or property. It usually applies to the unreasonable and wrongful use of property that produces material discomfort, hurt, and damage to the person or property of another. Example: Fumes from a factory.

Obligee: A creditor or promisee.

Obligor: A debtor or promisor.

Option: A right secured by a contract to accept or reject an offer to purchase property at a fixed price within a fixed time. It is an irrevocable offer sometimes called a "paid-for offer."

Order*: Under Article 3–Commercial Paper this means a direction to pay and must be more than an authorization or request. It must identify the person to pay with reasonable certainty. It may be addressed to one or more such persons jointly or in the alternative but not in succession.

Ordinance: An ordinance is, generally speaking, the legislative act of a municipality. A city council is a legislative body and passes ordinances that are the laws of the city.

Ordinary care: That care that a prudent man would take under the circumstances of the particular case.

Ore-tenus: By word of mouth, or orally.

Overt act: Overt means open. Overt act is any motion, gesture, conduct, or demonstration that evidences a present design to do a particular act that will lead to a desired result.

Par value: The words mean face value. The par value of stocks and bonds on the date of issuance is the principal. At a later date, the par value is the principal plus interest.

Pari delicto: The fault or blame is shared equally.

Pari materia: Latin words that mean "related to the same matter or subject." Statutes and covenants concerning the same subject matter are in pari materia, and as a general rule, for the purpose of ascertaining their meaning, are construed together.

Partition: Court proceedings brought at the request of a party in interest, that real property be taken by the court and divided among the respective owners as their interests appear. If the property is incapable of division in kind, then the property is to be sold and the money divided as each interest appears.

Party*: A person who has engaged in a transaction or made an agreement within the Uniform Commercial Code. To be distinguished from a "third party."

Patent ambiguity: An uncertainty in a written instrument that is obvious upon reading.

Payor Bank*: Under Article 4–Bank Deposits and Collections a bank by which an item is payable as drawn or accepted.

Penal bond: A bond given by an accused, or by another person in his behalf, for the payment of money if the accused fails to appear in court on a certain day.

Penalty: The term has two different meanings. In criminal law it means the punishment imposed for the commission of a crime. It is used with the word "fine." In civil law, it may mean a sum agreed upon as payable for the breach of promise. The word is sometimes used as synonymous with "forfeiture." See *Liquidated damages.*

Pendente lite: A Latin phrase which means "pending during the progress of a suit at law."

Per curiam: A decision by the full court in which no opinion is given.

Peremptory challenge: An objection, by a party to a law suit, to a person serving as a juror, for which no reason need be given.

Perjury: False swearing upon an oath properly administered in some judicial proceedings. See *Oath.*

Perpetuity: The taking of any subject matter out of the channel of commerce by limiting its capacity to be sold for a period of time longer than that of a life or lives in being and 21 years thereafter plus the period of gestation.

Per se: Literally it means "by itself." Thus a contract clause may be inherently unconscionable—unconscionable per se.

Persona ficta: The Latin phrase for a fictitious person which refers to the corporate entity or artificial legal person.

Personal property: The rights, powers, and privileges a person has in movable things such as chattels, and choses in action. Personal property is used in contradistinction to real property.

Personal representative: The administrator or executor of a deceased person. The term also means the heir, next of kin, or descendant of a deceased person. The meaning of the term must be ascertained from the context.

Personal service: The term means that the sheriff actually delivered to the defendant in person a service of process.

Plaintiff: In an action at law, the complaining party or the one who commences the action is called the plaintiff. He is the person who seeks a remedy in court.

Plea: An allegation or answer in a court proceeding.

Pleading: The process by which the parties in a lawsuit arrive at an issue.

Pledge: The deposit or placing of personal property as security for a debt or other obligation with a person called a pledgee. The pledgee has the implied power to sell the property if the debt is not paid. If the debt is paid, the right to possession returns to the pledgor.

Plenary: Fully attended or constituted; the designation of a full hearing or trial. A case may be remanded for a plenary hearing following a dismissal by the trial court.

Policy of insurance: In insurance law, the word policy means the formal document delivered by the insurance company to the insured, which evidences the rights and duties between the parties.

Polling jury: To poll the jury is to call the name of each juror and inquire what his verdict is before such is made a matter of record.

Possession: The method, recognized by law, of holding, detaining, or controlling by one's self or by another, property, either personal or real, which will exclude others from holding, detaining, or controlling such property.

Power of attorney: An instrument authorizing another to act as one's agent or attorney in fact.

Precedent: A previously-decided case that can serve as an authority to help decide a present controversy. The use of such case is called the doctrine of "stare decisis," which means to adhere to decided cases and settled principles. Literally, "to stand as decided."

Preference: The term is used most generally in bankruptcy law. Where a bankrupt makes payment of money to certain creditors enabling them to obtain a greater percentage of their debts than other creditors in the same class, and the payment is made within four months prior to the filing of a bankruptcy petition, such payment constitutes illegal and voidable preference. An intention to prefer such creditors must be shown. An insolvent person may lawfully prefer one creditor to another, if done in good faith and without intent to defraud others.

Preferred stock: Stock that entitles the holder to dividends from earnings before the owners of common stock can receive a dividend.

Premises: As applied to the occupancy of real property, the word includes a definite portion of land, the building and appurtenances thereto over which the occupant exercises control. As applied to a controversy, the word means the general statement of a proposition.

Preponderance: Preponderance of the evidence means that evidence which in the judgment of the jurors is entitled to the greatest weight, which appears to be more credible, has greater force, and overcomes not only the opposing presumptions, but also the opposing evidence.

Prerogative: Rights, powers, privileges, and immunities, which one person has that others do not possess. Ambassadors of foreign countries have certain prerogatives. A senator has the prerogative of making remarks that would be slanderous if used by an ordinary citizen.

Presenting Bank*: Under Article 4–Bank Deposits and Collections, this is any bank presenting an item exept a payor bank.

Presentment*: Under Article 3–Commercial Paper, "presentment" is a demand for acceptance or payment made upon the maker, acceptor, drawee, or other payor by or on behalf of the holder.

Presumption*: "Presumed" means that the trier of fact must find the existence of the fact presumed unless and until evidence is introduced which would support a finding of its nonexistence.

Presumption: A presumption is an assumed fact. It may serve as evidence until actual facts are introduced. In absence of actual facts, the person in whose favor a presumption exists prevails. A holder of a negotiable instrument is presumed to be a holder in due course until facts are introduced to the contrary. A disputable presumption makes a prima facie case. See local statute for a list of rebuttable and nonrebuttable presumptions.

Prima facie: The words literally mean "at first view." Thus, that which first appears seems to be true. A prima facie case is one that stands until contrary evidence is produced.

Privilege: A legal idea or concept of lesser significance than a right. An invitee has only a privilege to walk on another's land because such privilege may be revoked at will; whereas, a person who has an easement to go on another's land has a right, created by a grant which is an interest in land and cannot be revoked at will. To be exempt from jury service is a privilege.

Privity: Mutual and successive relationship to the same interest. Offeror and offeree, assignor and assignee, grantor and grantee are in privity. Privity of estate means that one takes title from another. In contract law, privity denotes parties in mutual legal relationship to each other by virtue of being promisees and promisors. At early common law, third party beneficiaries and assignees were said to be not in "privity."

Probate: The word means proof of a will by the proper court.

Proceeds*: Whatever is received when collateral or proceeds is sold, exchanged, collected or otherwise disposed of. The term also includes the account arising when the right to payment is earned under a contract right. Money, checks and the like are "cash proceeds." All other proceeds are "non-cash proceeds."

Process: In court proceeding, a process is an instrument issued by the court in the name of the state before or during the progress of the trial, under the seal of the court, directing an officer of the court to do, act, or cause some act to be done incidental to the trial.

Process of Posting*: Under Article 4–Bank Deposits and Collections, "Posting" is the usual procedure followed by a payor bank in determining to pay an item and in recording the payment including one or more of the following or other steps as determined by the bank: verification of any signature; ascertaining that sufficient funds are available; affixing a "paid" or other stamp; entering a charge or entry to a customers's account; correcting or reversing an entry or erroneous action with respect to the item.

Promise*: Under Article 3–Commercial Paper, it is an undertaking to pay and must be more than an acknowledgment of an obligation.

Properly Payable*: Under Article 4–Bank Deposits and Collections, this includes the availability of funds for payment at the time of decision to pay or dishonor.

Property: All those rights, powers, privileges, and immunities which one has concerning tangibles and intangibles. The term includes everything of value subject to ownership.

Pro tanto: "For so much." Persons are liable pro tanto or for such an amount.

Proximate cause: The cause that sets other causes in operation. The responsible cause of an injury.

Proximate damage: Damages that are direct, immediate, and the natural result of negligence or wrong, and which might reasonably have been expected.

Proxy: Authority to act for another; used by absent stockholders or members of legislative bodies to have their votes cast by others.

Public policy: There can be no strict definition for the term "public policy." Any conduct or any contract, the performance of which is against public morals or injurious to the public good, is in violation of public policy.

Punitive damages: Damages by way of punishment allowed for an injury caused by a wrong that is wilful and malicious.

Purchase*: This includes taking by sale, discount, negotiation, mortgage, pledge, lien, issue or re-issue, gift or any other voluntary transaction creating an interest in property.

Purchase Money Security Interest*: A security interest that is taken or retained by the seller of the collateral to secure all or part of its price; or taken by a person who by making advances or incurring an obligation gives value to enable the debtor to acquire rights in or the use of collateral if such value is in fact so used.

Purchaser*: A person who takes by purchase.

Quantum meruit (in pleading): An allegation that the defendant owes the plaintiff for work and labor a sum for as much as the plaintiff reasonably is entitled.

Quasi contracts: The term "quasi contracts" is used to define a situation where a legal duty arises that does not rest upon a promise, but does involve the payment of money. In order to do justice by a legal fiction, the court enforces the duty as if a promise in fact exists. Thus, if *A* gives *B* money by mistake, *A* can compel *B* to return the money by an action in quasi contract.

Quiet title: A suit brought by the owner of real property for the purpose of bringing into court any person who claims an adverse interest in the property and requiring him to either establish his claim or be barred from asserting it thereafter. It may be said that the purpose is to remove "clouds" from the title.

Quit claim: A deed that releases a right or interest in land, but which does not include any covenants of warranty. The grantor transfers only that which he has.

Quo warranto: A proceeding in court by which the state, city, county, or other governmental body tests or inquires into the legality of the claim of any person to a public office, franchise, or privilege. It is a proceeding to oust persons from public office.

Ratification: The confirmation of one's own previous act or act of another: e.g., a principal may ratify the previous unauthorized act of his agent. *B*'s agent, without authority, buys goods. *B*, by keeping the goods and receiving the benefits of the agent's act, ratifies the agency.

Ratify: To ratify means to confirm or approve.

Real property: The term means land with all its buildings, appurtenances, equitable and legal interests therein. The word is used in contradistinction to personal property which refers to moveables or chattels.

Reasonable care: The care that prudent persons would exercise under the same circumstances.

Rebuttal evidence: The evidence that is given to explain, repel, counteract, or disprove the testimony in chief given by the adverse party.

Receipt*: In the case of goods, means taking physical possession of them.

Receiver: An officer of the court appointed on behalf of all parties to the litigation to take possession of, hold, and control the property involved in the suit, for the benefit of the party who will be determined to be entitled thereto.

Recognizance: A recognizance is a contract of record or obligation made before a court by which the parties thereto obligate themselves to perform some act. It is different from a bail bond, in that a bail bond is under seal and creates a new debt. A recognizance is in the nature of a conditional judgment and acknowledges the existence of a present obligation to the state.

Recoupment: A right to deduct from the plaintiff's claim any payment or loss that the defendant has suffered by reason of the plaintiff's wrongful act. The words mean "a cutting back."

Redemption: To buy back. A debtor buys back or redeems his mortgaged property when he pays the debt.

Referee: A person to whom a cause pending in a court is referred by the court, to take testimony, hear the parties, and report thereon to the court.

Registered Form*: A security is in *registered form* when it specifies a person entitled to the security or to the rights it evidences and when its transfer may be registered upon books maintained for that purpose by or on behalf of an issuer as security so states.

Re-insurance: A contract of re-insurance is where one insurance company agrees to indemnify another insurance company in whole or in part against risks which the first company has assumed. The original contract of insurance and the re-insurance contract are distinct contracts. There is no privity between the original insured and the re-insurer.

Release: The voluntary relinquishing of a right, lien, or any other obligation. A release need not be under seal, nor does it necessarily require consideration. The words "release, remise, and discharge" are often used together to mean the same thing.

Remand: To send back a cause for the appellate court to the lower court in order that the lower court may comply with the instructions of the appellate court. Also to return a prisoner to jail.

Remedy: The word is used to signify the judicial means or court procedures by which legal and equitable rights are enforced.

Remedy*: Any remedial right to which an aggrieved party is entitled with or without resort to a tribunal.

Remise: The word means discharge or release. It is also synonymous with "quit claim."

Remitting Bank*: Under Article 4–Bank Deposits and Collections is any payor or intermediary bank remitting for an item.

Replevin: A remedy given by statute for the recovery of the possession of a chattel. Only the right to possession can be tried in such action.

Representative*: This includes an agent, an officer of a corporation or association, and a trustee, executor, or administrator of an estate, or any other person empowered to act for another.

Res: A Latin word that means "thing."

Res adjudicata: The doctrine of "res adjudicata" means that a controversy once having been decided or adjudged upon its merits is forever settled so far as the particular parties involved are concerned. Such a doctrine avoids vexatious lawsuits.

Rescission: (From rescissio) Rescission is where an act, valid in appearancee, nevertheless conceals a defect, which may make it null and void, if demanded by any of the parties.

Respondent: One who answers another's bill or pleading, particularly in an equity case. Quite similar, in many instances, to defendant in law cases.

Respondeat superior: Latin words that mean the master is liable for the acts of his agent.

Responsible bidder: The word "responsible," as used by most statutes concerning public works in the phrase "lowest responsible bidder," means that such bidder has the requisite skill, judgment, and integrity necessary to perform the contract involved, and has the financial resources and ability to carry the task to completion.

Restraining order: An order issued by a court of equity in aid of a suit to hold matters in abeyance until parties may be heard. A temporary injunction is a restraining order.

Restraint of trade: Monopolies, combinations, and contracts that impede free competition are in restraint of trade.

Retainer: The payment in advance to an attorney to cover future services and advice.

Return of a writ: A sheriff's return of a writ is an official statement written on the back of a summons or other paper that he has performed his duties in compliance with the law or a statement as to why he has not complied with the law.

Right: The phrase "legal right" is a correlative of the phrase "legal duty." One has a legal right if, upon the breach of the correlative legal duty, he can secure a remedy in a court of law.

Right of action: The words are synonymous with "cause of action": a right to enforce a claim in a court.

Rights*:   This includes remedies.

Riparian: A person is a riparian owner if his land is situated beside a stream of water, either flowing over or along the border of the land.

Robbery: The stealing or taking away from a person his money or other property either by force and violence or by putting him in fear of force and violence.

Rule (as a noun):   The regulation or direction of an administrative body is a rule. A rule of law is a general statement as to what the law is. "Every contract must be supported by consideration," is a rule of law. Rules of court are the rules for practice and procedure in a particular court.

Rule (as a verb):   The act of a court issuing an order that a defendant file a pleading is called a rule or command of the court.

Sanction: The penalty for the breach of a rule of law. Redress for civil injuries is called civil sanction; punishment for violation of criminal law is called penal sanction. The word literally means "enforcement."

Satisfaction: The term "satisfaction" in legal phraseology means the release and discharge of a legal obligation. Such satisfaction may be partial or full performance of the obligation. The word is used with accord. Accord means a promise to give a substituted performance for a contract obligation; satisfaction means the acceptance by the obligee of such performance.

Scienter: Knowledge by a defrauding party of the falsity of a representation. In a tort action of deceit, knowledge that a representation is false must be proved.

Scintilla of evidence: A very slight amount of evidence which aids in the proof of an allegation. If there is a "scintilla of evidence," the court generally presents the case to the jury.

Scrip: As applied to corporation law, "scrip" is a written certificate or evidence of a right of a person to obtain shares in a corporation.

Scrivener's error: Typographical error in reducing an agreement to writing.

Seal: A seal is to show that an instrument was executed in a formal manner. At early common law sealing legal documents was of great legal significance. A promise under seal was binding by virtue of the seal. Today under most statutes any stamp, wafer, mark, scroll, or impression made, adopted, and affixed, is adequate. The printed word "seal" or the letters "L.S." is sufficient.

Seasonably*:   An action is taken "seasonably" when it is taken at or within the time agreed or if no time is agreed at or within a reasonable time.

Secondary Party*:   Under Article 3–Commercial Paper this means a drawer or indorser.

Security: Security may be bonds, stocks, and other property placed by a debtor with a creditor, with power to sell if the debt is not paid. The plural of the term, "securities," is used broadly to mean tangible choses in action such as promissory notes, bonds, stocks, and other vendible obligations.

Security*:   An instrument which is issued in bearer form or registered form; and is of a type commonly dealt in upon securities exchanges or markets or commonly recognized in any area in which it is issued or dealt in as a medium for investment; and is either one of a class or series or by its terms is divisible into a class or series of instruments; and evidences a share, a participation or other interest in property or in an enterprise or evidences an obligation of the issuer.

Security Agreement*:   An agreement which creates or provides for a security interest.

Security Interest*:   This means an interest in personal property or fixtures which secures payment or performance of an obligation. The retention or reservation of title by a seller of goods notwithstanding shipment or delivery to the buyer is limited in effect to a reservation of a "security interest." The term also includes any interest of a buyer of accounts, chattel paper, or contract rights which is subject to Article 9. The special property interest of a buyer of goods on identification of such goods to a contract for sale is not a "security interest," but a buyer may also acquire a "security interest" by complying with Article 9. Unless a lease or consignment is intended as security, reservation of title there under is not a "security interest" but a consignment is in any event subject to the provisions on consignment sales. Whether a lease is intended as security is to be determined by the facts of each case; however, (a) the inclusion of an option to purchase does not of itself make the lease one intended for security, and (b) an agreement that upon compliance with the terms of the lease the lessee shall become or has the option to become the owner of the property for no additional consideration or for a nominal consideration does make the lease one intended for security.

Secured Party*: A lender, seller, or other person in whose favor there is a security interest, including a person to whom accounts, contract rights or chattel paper have been sold. When the holders of obligations issued under an indenture of trust, equipment trust agreement or the like are represented by a trustee or other person, the representative is the secured party.

Sell: The words "to sell" mean to negotiate or make arrangement for a sale. A sale is an executed contract. "Sell" is the name of the process in executing the contract.

Seller*: A person who sells or contracts to sell goods.

Send*: In connection with any writing or notice this means to deposit in the mail or deliver for transmission by any other usual means of communication with postage or cost of transmission provided for and properly addressed and in the case of an instrument to an address specified thereon or otherwise agreed, or if there be none to any address reasonable under the circumstances. The receipt of any writing or notice within the time at which it would have arrived if properly sent has the effect of a proper sending.

Servant: A person employed by another and subject to the direction and control of the employer in performance of his duties.

Served or service: The delivery of a writ issued out of a court to a proper officer, usually the sheriff, by which a court secures jurisdiction over the defendant. See *Process.*

Set-off: A matter of defense, called a cross-complaint, used by the defendant for the purpose of making a demamd on the plaintiff and which arises out of contract, but is independent and unconnected with the cause of action set out in the complaint. See *Counter-claims* and *Recoupment.*

Settle*: Under Article 4–Bank Deposits and Collections this means to pay in cash, by clearing house settlement, in a charge or credit or by remittance, or otherwise as instructed. A settlement may be either provisional or final.

Severable-contract: A contract, the performance of which is divisible. Two or more parts may be set over against each other. Items and prices may be apportioned to each other without relation to the full performance of all of its parts.

Several: A contract in which each promissor makes a separate promise and is separately liable thereon. There may be several promises. If the promissors make a single promise the obligation is joint. A joint and several promissory note consists of the joint promise of all and the separate promise of each. "We jointly and severally promise" is an illustration..

Share of stock: A proportional part of the rights in the management and assets of a corporation. It is a chose in action. The certificate is the evidence of the share.

Sheriff: A public officer whose authority and duties are created by legislation. His duties are to execute and administer the law.

Signed: This includes any symbol executed or adopted by a party with present intention to authenticate a writing.

Sine qua non: Literally, it means "without which not." It refers to an indispensable element.

Situs: Situs means "place, situation." The place where a thing is located. The "situs" of personal property is the domicile of the owner. The "situs" of land is the state or county where it is located.

Slander: Slander is an oral utterance that tends to injure the reputation of another. See *Libel.*

Solvent: A person is solvent when he is able to pay his debts.

Sovereignty: The word means the power of a state (organized government) to execute its laws, and its right to exercise dominion and authority over its citizens and their property subject only to constitutional limitations.

Special appearance: The appearance in court of a person through his attorney for a limited purpose only. A court does not get jurisdiction over a person by special appearance.

Special verdict: A special verdict is one in which the jury finds the facts only, leaving it to the court to apply the law and draw the conclusion as to the proper disposition of the case.

Specialty: The word "specialty" in commercial law means a promise under seal to pay money —a bond. In early law there were two kinds of specialties. "Common law specialties" were formal instruments under seal—bonds and covenants; "mercantile specialties" included bills and notes, insurance policies, and other unsealed commercial papers.

Specific performance: A remedy in personam in equity that compels such substantial performance of a contract as will do justice among the parties. A person who fails to obey a writ for specific performance may be put in jail by the equity judge for contempt of court. Such remedy applies to contracts involving real property. In absence of unique goods or peculiar circumstances, damages generally are an adequate remedy for the breach of contracts involving personal property. See Specific Performance under the Uniform Sales Act.

Stare decisis: Translated, the term means "stand by the decision." The law should adhere to decided cases. See *Precedent.*

Status quo: The existing state of affairs.

Statute: A law passed by the legislative body of a state is a statute.

Stock: The word has several meanings. When applied to "goods, wares, and merchandise," it means goods in a mercantile house that are kept for sale. As applied in corporation law, the word means the right of an owner of a share of stock to participate in the management and ownership of a corporation. See *Capital Stock.*

Stock dividend: The issue by a corporation of new shares of its own stock to its shareholders as dividends.

Stockholders: Those persons whose names appear on the books of a corporation as the owners of the shares of stock and who are entitled to participate in the management and control of the corporation.

Stock split-up: A type of readjustment of the financial plan of a corporation whereby each existing share of stock is split into such number of new shares as may be determined by the managers of the corporation.

Stock warrant: A certificate which gives to the holder thereof the right to subscribe for and purchase a given number of shares of stock in a corporation at a stated price.

Stoppage in transitu: The right of a seller of goods, which have not been paid for, upon learning of the insolvency of the buyer, to stop the goods in transit and hold the same as security for the purchase price. It is an extension of the unpaid seller's lien.

Subordinate: In the case of a mortgage or other security interest, the mortgagee may agree to make his mortgage inferior to another mortgage or interest.

Subpoena: A process issued out of a court requiring the attendance of a witness at a trial.

Subrogation: The substitution of one person in another 's place, whether as a creditor or as the possessor of any lawful right, so that the substituted person may succeed to the rights, remedies, or proceeds of the claim. It rests in equity on the theory that, where a party is compelled to pay a debt for which another is liable, such payment should vest the paying party with all the rights the creditor has against the debtor. For example: X insurance company pays Y for an injury to Y's car by reason of Z's negligent act. X insurance company will be subrogated to Y's cause of action against Z.

Subsequent Purchaser*: A person who takes a security other than by original issue.

Substantial performance: The complete performance of all the essential elements of a contract. The only permissible omissions or deviations are those which are trivial, inadvertent, and inconsequential. Such performance will not justify repudiation. Compensation for defects may be substituted for actual performance. See *Breach.*

Substantive law: A word applied to that law which regulates and controls the rights and duties of all persons in society. It is used in contradistinction to the term adjective law, which means the rules of court procedure or remedial law which prescribe the methods by which substantive law is enforced.

Succession: The word means the transfer by operation of law of all the rights and obligations of a deceased person to those who are entitled to take.

Succession tax: This tax is not a burden on property, but a tax upon the privilege of taking property, whether by will or descent.

Suit: The term refers to any type of legal proceeding for the purpose of obtaining a legal remedy; the term "suit" generally applied to "suit in equity," whereas, at law, the term is "action at law."

Summons: A writ issued by a court to the sheriff directing him to notify the defendant that the plaintiff claims to have a cause of action against the defendant and that he is required to answer. If the defendant does not answer, judgment will be taken by default.

Surety*: This term includes guarantor.

Suspends Payments*: Under Article 4–Bank Deposits and Collections with respect to a bank this means that it has been closed by order of the supervisory authorities, that a public officer has been appointed to take it over or that it ceases or refuses to make payments in the ordinary course of business.

Tacit: That which is understood from the nature of things. Those rules that are generally understood to be the law by reason of customs and mores.

Talisman: A juror summoned to fill up a panel for the trial of a particular case. Such person is not bound to serve the term.

Tangible: Tangible is a word used to describe property that is physical in character and capable of being moved. A debt is intangible, but a promissory note evidencing such debt is tangible. See *Chose in action, Chattel.*

Telegram*: This includes a message transmitted by radio, teletype, cable, any mechanical method of transmission, or the like.

Tenancy: The interest in property that a tenant acquires from a landlord by a lease is called a tenancy. It may be at will or for a term. It is an interest in land.

Tenant: The person to whom a lease is made. A lessee.

Tender: To offer money in satisfaction of a debt or obligation by producing the same and expressing to the creditor a willingness to pay. See *Legal tender.*

Tender of Delivery*: This means that the seller must put and hold conforming goods at the buyer's disposition and give the buyer any notification reasonably necessary to enable him to take delivery.

Tenement: The word has historical significance as applied to real property. In a broad sense it means an estate in land or some interest connected therewith, such as houses, rents, profits, and rights, to which a holder of the title is entitled. It is used with the word "hereditaments."

Tenure: The word is used to designate the means by which title is held to real property. For example, "tenure in fee simple," "tenure for life." It also is used to indicate the time limit of a person's right to public office. "Term" means limited time. "Tenure" means indefinite.

Term That portion of an agreement which relates to a particular matter.

Termination: This occurs when either party pursuant to a power created by agreement or law puts an end to the contract otherwise than for its breach. On "termination" all obligations which are still executory on both sides are discharged but any right based on prior breach or performance survives.

Term of court: That period of time prescribed by statute within which a court may legally hold its sessions and transact its business.

Testament: A testament is the declaration of a person's intention as to what disposition he desires to be made of his property after his death. The word is synonymous with will. The word is so used because a will is a testimonial of one's intention.

Testamentary capacity: A person is said to have testamentary capacity when he understands the nature of his business, the value of his property, knows those persons who are natural objects of his bounty, and comprehends the manner in which he has provided for the distribution of his property.

Testator: A male person who has died leaving a will. A female person is called a testatrix.

Testimony: Those statements made by a witness under oath or affirmation in a legal proceeding. See *Evidence.*

Title: This word has different meanings. It may be limited or broad in its meaning. When a person has the exclusive rights, powers, privileges, and immunities to property, real and personal, tangible and intangible, against all other persons, he may be said to have the complete title thereto. The aggregate of legal relations concerning property is the title. The term is used to describe the means by which a person exercises control and dominion over property. A trustee has a limited title. See *Possession.*

Tonnage: In marine insurance, registered tonnage means the vessel's carrying capacity as stated in the ship's papers at the date of the policy, and not the tonnage fixed by the law of the government under which the vessel is registered.

Tort: A wrongful act committed by one person against another person or his property. It is the breach of a legal duty imposed by law other than by contract. The word tort means "twisted" or "wrong." *A* assaults *B,* thus committing a tort. See *Right, Duty.*

Tortfeasor: One who commits a tort.

Total disability: In a contract of insurance, these words do not mean "absolute helplessness." Their meaning is relative, depending on the circumstances of each case, the occupation, and capabilities of the insured.

Trade fixtures: Personal property placed upon or annexed to leased land by a tenant for the purpose of carrying on a trade or business during the term of the lease. Such property is generally to be removed at the end of the term, providing it can be so removed without destruction or injury to the premises. Trade fixtures include show cases, shelving, racks, machinery, and the like.

Trade-mark: No complete definition can be given for a trade-mark. Generally it is any sign, symbol, mark, word, or arrangement of words in the form of a label adopted and used by manufacturer or distributor to designate his particular goods, and which no other person has the legal right to use. Originally, the design or trade-mark indicated origin, but today it is used more as an advertising mechanism.

Trade union: A combination of workmen usually (but not necessarily) of the same trade organized for the purpose of securing by united action the most favorable working conditions for its members.

Traditio: Delivery and transfer of possession of property by an owner.

Transfer: In its broadest sense, the word means the act by which an owner sets over or delivers his right, title, and interest in property to another person. A "bill of sale" to personal property is evidence of a transfer.

Traverse: In pleading it means a denial. In some jurisdictions a pleading which contains a denial is called a traverse.

Treason: The offense of attempting by overt acts to overthrow the government of the state to which the offender owes allegiance; or of betraying the state into the hands of a foreign power.

Treasury stock: Stock of a corporation that has been issued by the corporation for value, but that is later returned to the corporation by way of gift or purchase or otherwise. It may be returned to the trustees of a corporation for the purpose of sale.

Trespass: An injury to the person, property, or rights of another person committed by actual force and violence, or under such circumstances that the law will imply that the injury was caused by force or violence.

Trial: A proceeding by the properly authorized officials into the examination of the facts and for the purpose of determining an issue presented according to proper rules of law.

Trust: A relationship between persons by which one holds property for the use and benefit of another. The relationship is called fiduciary. Such rights are enforced in a court of equity. The person trusted is called a trustee. The person for whose benefit the property is held is called a beneficiary or "cestui que trust."

Trustee in bankruptcy: An agent of the court authorized to liquidate the assets of the bankrupt, protect them, and to bring them to the court for final distribution for the benefit of the bankrupt and all the creditors.

Trustee (generally): A person who is intrusted with the management and control of another's property and estate. A person occupying a fiduciary position. An executor, an administrator, a guardian.

Ultra vires: Literally the words mean "beyond power." The acts of a corporation are ultra vires when they are beyond the power or capacity of the corporation as granted by the state in its charter.

Unauthorized*: Refers to a signature or indorsement made without actual, implied, or apparent authority and includes a forgery.

Undertaking: A so-called informal bond without a seal is called an "undertaking."

Unfair competition: The imitation by design of the goods of another for the purpose of palming them off on the public, thus misleading the public by inducing it to buy goods made by the imitator. It includes misrepresentation and deceit; thus, such conduct is fraudulent not only as to competitors but as to the public.

Unilateral contract: A promise for an act or an act for a promise; a single enforceable promise. *A* promises *B* $10 if *B* will mow *A*'s lawn. *B* mows the lawn. *A*'s promise now binding is a unilateral contract. See *Bilateral contract.*

Usage: When conduct has been long continued and is of uniform practice, it will fall within the category of "usage." Usage is a fact, not opinion. In trade, it is a course of dealing. Customs are the rules of law that arise from usage. Customs rest on usage.

Usage of Trade*: Any practice or method of dealing having such regularity of observance in a place, vocation or trade as to justify an expectation that it will be observed with respect to the transaction in question. The existence and scope of such a usage are to be proved as facts. If it is established that such a usage is embodied in a written trade code or similar writing the interpretation of the writing is for the court.

Usurious: A contract is usurious if made for a loan of money at a rate of interest in excess of that permitted by statute.

Utter: The word means to put out or pass off. To utter a check is to offer it to another in payment of a debt. The words "utter a forged writing" mean to put such writing in circulation, knowing of the falsity of the instrument with the intent to injure another.

Vacancy: As applied to a fire insurance policy, the words "vacancy," "vacant," or "unoccupied" mean, "that if the house insured should cease to be used as a place of human habitation or for living purposes, it would then be vacant or unoccupied." The period of time is unimportant. Vacant property increases the risk of the insurer, hence violates the policy.

Valid: That which is sufficient to satisfy the requirements of the law. A valid judgment is one lawfully obtained under the proper rules of procedure and evidence.

Valuable consideration: Any consideration that will support a simple contract. A classic definition is, "valuable consideration consists of some right, interest, profit, or benefit or value accruing to the promisor, and some forbearance, detriment, loss, or responsibility given or suffered by the promisee."

Value: The term has many meanings in law. Value is any consideration sufficient to support a simple contract. Although an antecedent debt would not be value to support a simple contract, it is considered adequate to support a negotiable instrument by the Law Merchant. A "bona fide purchaser," called a "B.F.P.," gives up something of value, either money, property, or services. Value in a business sense means market value. The money equivalent of property is value.

Value*: Except as otherwise provided with respect to negotiable instruments and bank collections a person gives "value" for rights if he acquires them

(a) in return for a binding commitment to extend credit or for the extension of immediately available credit whether or not drawn upon and whether or not a charge-back is provided for in the event of difficulties in collection; or

(b) as security for or in total or partial satisfaction of a pre-existing claim; or

(c) by accepting delivery pursuant to a pre-existing contract for purchase; or

(d) generally, in return for any consideration sufficient to support a simple contract.

Valued policy: As used in fire insurance, a valued policy is one in which the sum to be paid in case of loss is fixed by the terms of the policy. No reference can be made to the real value of the property that is lost.

Vendee: A purchaser of property. The term is generally applied to the purchaser of real property. The word "buyer" is usually applied to the purchaser of chattels.

Vendor: The seller of property. The term is usually applied to the seller of real property. The word "seller" is applied to the seller of personal property.

Vendor's lien: An unpaid seller's right to hold possession of property until he has recovered the purchase price. See *Seller's lien.*

Venire: To come into court; a writ used to summon a jury. The word is used sometimes to mean jury.

Venue: The geographical area over which a court presides. Venue designates the county in which the action is tried. Change of venue means a move to another county.

Verdict: The decision of a jury, reported to the court, on matters properly submitted to it for its consideration.

Vested: The word generally applies to the title to or interests in land. The word strictly means "there is an immediate right of present enjoyment, or a present fixed right of future enjoyment." A life estate is a vested interest. Dower right of a wife, however, is not vested until the death of the husband.

Vis major: The force of nature, sometimes called "act of God," which excuses persons from liability. If the ordinary exertion of human skill and prudence cannot avoid the effect of the force of nature, then an obligor may be excused under the doctrine of impossibility of performance.

Void: That which has no legal effect. A contract that is void is a nullity and confers no rights or duties.

Voidable: That which is valid until one party, who has the power of avoidance, exercises such power. An infant has the power of avoidance of his contract. A defrauded party has the power to avoid his contract. Such contract is voidable.

Voir dire: This phrase denotes the preliminary examination of a prospective juror.

Voting Trust: A device whereby two or more persons, owning stock, with voting powers, divorce voting rights thereof from ownership, retaining to all intents and purposes the latter in themselves and transferring the former to trustees in whom voting rights of all depositors in the trust are pooled.

Voucher: A written instrument that bears witness or "vouches" for something. Generally a voucher is an instrument showing services have been performed or goods purchased, and is presented to a disbursing officer authorizing him to make payment and charge the proper account.

Wager: A relationship between persons by which they agree that a certain sum of money or thing owned by one of them will be paid or delivered to the other upon the happening of an uncertain event, which event is not within the control of the parties and rests upon chance. Consult state statutes.

Wages: Compensation or reward, usually money, paid at stated times for labor. If compensation is paid at completion of a job or task, or if compensation is earned as a profit from the labor of others, such compensation is not wages.

Waive (verb):   To "waive" at law, is to relinquish or give up intentionally a known right or to do an act which is inconsistent with the claiming of a known right.

Waiver (noun):   The intentional relinquishment or giving up of a known right. It may be done by express words or conduct which involve any acts inconsistent with an intention to claim the right. Such conduct creates an estoppel on the part of the claimant. See *Estoppel.*

Warehouseman*:   A person engaged in the business of storing goods for hire.

Warehouse Receipt*:   A receipt issued by a person engaged in the business of storing goods for hire.

Warehouse receipt: An instrument showing that the signer has in his possession certain described goods for storage, and which obligates the signer, the warehouseman, to deliver the goods to a specified person or to his order or bearer upon the return of the instrument. Consult Uniform Warehouse Receipts Act.

Warrant (noun):   An order in writing in the name of the state and signed by a magistrate directed to an officer commanding him to arrest a person.

Warrant (verb):   To guarantee, to answer for, to assure that a state of facts exists.

Warranty: An undertaking, either expressed or implied, that a certain fact regarding the subject matter of a contract is presently true or will be true. The word has particular application in the law of sales of chattels. The word relates to title and quality. The word should be distinguished from "guaranty" which means a contract or promise by one person to answer for the performance of another. See *Suretyship, Guarantor.*

Waste: Damage to the real property so that its value as security is impaired.

Watered stock: Corporate stock issued by a corporation for property at an over valuation, or stock issued for which the corporation receives nothing in payment therefor.

Wharfage: A charge against a vessel for lying at a wharf. It is used synonymously with "dockage" and "moorage."

Wholesale: The usual meaning of the word is the sale of goods in gross to retailers who, in turn, sell to consumers.

Will (testament): The formal instrument by which a person makes disposition of his property to take effect upon his death. See *Testament.*

Witness: A person who testifies under oath in a legal proceeding.

Working capital: The amount of cash necessary for the convenient and safe transaction of present business.

Writ: An instrument in writing under seal in the name of the state, issued out of a Court of Justice the commencement of, or during a legal proceeding, directed to an officer of the court commanding him to do some act, or requiring some person to do or refrain from doing some act pertinent or relative to the cause being tried.

Writing obligatory: These words refer to writings under seal.

Written or writing*: This includes printing, typewriting or any other intentional reduction to tangible form.

Zoning ordinance: An ordinance passed by a city council by virtue of the police power which regulates and prescribes the kind of buildings, residences, or businesses that shall be built and used in different parts of a city.

Index